Magic, Witchcraft, and Religion

Magic, Witchcraft, and Religion
An Anthropological Study of the Supernatural
Seventh Edition

Pamela A. Moro
Willamette University

James E. Myers
Emeritus, California State University, Chico

Arthur C. Lehmann
Late Emeritus, California State University, Chico

Boston   Burr Ridge, IL   Dubuque, IA   Madison, WI   New York   San Francisco   St. Louis
Bangkok   Bogotá   Caracas   Kuala Lumpur   Lisbon   London   Madrid   Mexico City
Milan   Montreal   New Delhi   Santiago   Seoul   Singapore   Sydney   Taipei   Toronto

Higher Education

MAGIC, WITCHCRAFT, AND RELIGION: AN ANTHROPOLOGICAL STUDY OF THE
SUPERNATURAL

ISBN: 978-0-07-340521-6
MHID: 0-07-340521-3

Vice President and Editor-in-Chief: *Emily Barrosse*
Publisher: *Phillip A. Butcher*
Senior Sponsoring Editor: *Monica Eckman*
Developmental Editor: *Kate Scheinman*
Editorial Coordinator: *Teresa C. Treacy*
Senior Marketing Manager: *Daniel M. Loch*
Managing Editor: *Jean Dal Portro*
Senior Project Manager: *Rick Hecker*
Art Director: *Jeanne Schreiber*
Art Manager: *Robin Mouat*
Senior Designer: *Preston Thomas III*
Photo Research Coordinator: *Natalia C. Peschiera*
Media Producer: *Michele Borrelli*
Production Supervisor: *Jason I. Huls*
Composition: *10/12 Sabon, by Interactive Composition Corporation*
Printing: *45# New Era Matte, R. R. Donnelley & Sons*

Library of Congress Cataloging-in-Publication Data

Magic, witchcraft, and religion : an anthropological study of the supernatural / [compiled
  by] Pamela A. Moro, James E. Myers, Arthur C. Lehmann.—7th ed.
     p. cm.
  Includes bibliographical references and index.
  ISBN: 978-0-07-340521-6 (pbk. : alk. paper)
  MHID: 0-07-340521-3 (pbk. : alk. paper)
    1. Religion. 2. Occultism. I. Myers-Moro, Pamela. II. Myers, James E. (James
Edward), 1931– III. Lehmann, Arthur C.
  BL50.M26 2008
  306.6—dc22   2006045241

To our Families and Students

In Memoriam

Arthur Lehmann, my dear friend and co-author of this book, died of lung cancer at his home in Chico, California, in September 1999. Although dreadfully weakened by his disease, Art insisted on maintaining active involvement in the fifth edition of *Magic, Witchcraft, and Religion.* Indeed, just weeks prior to his death, we worked several days at the university library, agonizing over the final selection of articles to be either added or deleted. Art would have been pleased to know that Pamela Myers Moro has become a co-author for future editions.

Throughout his long battle with cancer, Art was somehow able to keep his wonderful high spirits and *joie de vivre*. Art was revered on campus for his intellect, wit, and devotion to students and the discipline of anthropology. Blessed with a gift of blarney and love of people, he was also a favorite of the larger campus community. A short walk to the library from the anthropology building always turned into a time-consuming social trek, as Art found it necessary to hail every passing groundskeeper, maintenance person, or staff member—all of whom addressed him fondly as "Art"—and exchange bawdy jokes or the latest campus gossip.

Art's great sadness during the last months of his life was the realization that he would not be returning to Central African Republic to continue his longtime research with Pygmies.

Art is survived by his wife, Sharon, and his son, Jonathan. We all miss him terribly.

James E. Myers

Contents

10

Religion as Global Culture: Migration, Media, and Other Transnational Forces   429

Preface

The Story of This Book

This volume was initially inspired by our desire to assemble a book of readings that would captivate and engage students in undergraduate courses on the anthropology of religion. At the time of the first edition, the other available texts—though of high scholarly standards—failed to communicate the excitement of anthropology in a form accessible to undergraduate students with relatively little background in the field. In our view, the cross-cultural study of religion and the supernatural is one of the most compelling subfields of anthropology, a topic guaranteed to motivate students if presented in the right manner. The title *Magic, Witchcraft, and Religion: An Anthropological Study of the Supernatural* was selected to highlight the broad realm of religious expression addressed by anthropologists, far beyond what many students might initially think of as "religion" or "church."

Informed by our own experiences as classroom teachers, we continue to feel that the best way to teach this subject is to present a range of scholarly voices in anthology format, from both classic and contemporary authors, with ethnographic materials from North America as well as the rest of the world. The original co-editors—Arthur Lehmann and James Myers—held decades of experience teaching at a state university with students of widely varying motivations and academic backgrounds, at graduate and undergraduate levels. New co-editor Pamela Moro's teaching experience has been at liberal arts colleges, where instructors are likely to emphasize classroom discussion and the critical reading of texts.

Together we share the goal of conveying our excitement about anthropology and providing students with a solid grounding in the issues, theories, and fundamental ethnographic content of the discipline. We want to help students apply anthropological perspectives to issues that are relevant both in their own lives and in the world at large.

The Approach of the Text

As editors, our thinking about the content and scope of this book has also, of course, been shaped by our own experiences as ethnographers. Arthur held a career-long fascination with religion, medicine, and healing in Central Africa and the Caribbean, as his numerous trips to the field attested. James's research in the United States, initially with Native American communities in California and later on nonmainstream forms of body modification, led him to issues of identity, resistance, and, perhaps most simply, what it's like to be a minority in a complex, rapidly changing society. Pamela's research on music in Thailand has brought her to consider the interplay of music, ritual, festival, and the sacred worldview associated with Buddhism. Long hours watching dance processions at temples in northern Thailand, sitting with musicians at cremation services in Bangkok, and observing altars honoring the deities associated with music have inspired her consideration of religion as an integral part of human experience. Much of the thinking behind the recent editions of this book springs from these experiences as well as our observations of changes within the anthropological study of religion itself. Our inclusion of a chapter on globalization is a response to the inescapable fact of global change and its preeminent place in current anthropological scholarship. Our combined research experiences on three continents leave us profoundly aware of the significance of religious change in our world today.

The study of religion is historically significant within the discipline of anthropology. Some of the earliest questions asked by 19th-century anthropologists had to do with the development of religion and the pan-human concern with the ultimate. Throughout the 20th century, all major anthropological theorists addressed religion in one way or another. In the more recent eras of feminist, postmodern, and critical anthropology, religion and the supernatural have remained key concerns—grounds for experimental ethnographic writing and grist for new ways of thinking about culture. The study of religion has been amenable to the four-fields approach of anthropology, most evident in studies of altered states of consciousness (including the religious use of drugs), ethnomedicine, and questions about the relationship between science and religion. Inquiry into this subject brings us to many of the issues facing humanity today—such as ethnic, political, and economic conflicts expressed in terms of religion; controversies regarding religious autonomy versus state authority, in the United States and elsewhere; religion as a force for emancipation as well as a way to maintain the status quo, for local agency and globalization. In our own multicultural society, religion is one of the most salient features of difference, and, for many of us, brushing up against individuals of different faiths is one of the main ways we encounter cultural contrast on a local level. We sincerely feel that the anthropological approach to understanding religion (assisted by contributions from related fields, such as religious studies, sociology, and psychology) offers sound hope for a just and tolerant humanity.

Content and Organization

As in earlier editions of this book, in our selection of content we have chosen not to emphasize any particular ideological angle within the anthropology of religion. The multiple authors included in each chapter represent a range of interests, geographic foci, and ways of looking at each subject. Discipline-based vocabulary and style of scholarly writing varies from author to author, often reflecting the time period of each article's original publication. Our hope is that the contrasts and continuities among the various articles within each chapter will help readers begin to compare and evaluate not only content but the approaches of different anthropologists.

The book is divided into ten chapters, beginning with a broad view of anthropological ways of looking at religion and moving on to some of the core topics within the subject, such as myth, ritual, and the various types of religious specialists. Although instructors may choose to utilize articles in any order they wish, there is a loose continuity to the chapters: thinking about certain types of specialists (for example, shamans) leads us to consider the religious use of hallucinogenic drugs, which in turn takes us to religion and healing and then to the related topics of magic, divination, and witchcraft. The scope of the book widens again in the concluding chapters, as we present materials on religious change, from small-scale movements of protest to contemporary flows of culture, transcending the boundaries of nations.

Key Features

- *Chapter-Opening Essays:* These succinct, informative essays introduce the reader to the central concepts that unify each chapter.

- *Article Introductions:* Each article is prefaced with a brief introduction, drawing attention to the key themes and arguments of the work. In some cases, we have used these article introductions to make connections between selections in the volume or to recommend related scholarly works. Students may wish to use these short editorial introductions not only as preparation for reading each article but also as a review.

- *Breadth of Coverage:* As in previous editions, we have retained our commitment to integrating the analysis of religion in the West with ethnographic studies of less familiar examples. In each chapter, one or two articles deal specifically with contemporary North America.

- *Classic and Modern Selections:* Although the majority of the articles are contemporary pieces, we have also included classic readings by Mary Douglas, E. E. Evans-Pritchard, Clifford Geertz,

Horace Miner, Bronislaw Malinowski, Victor Turner, and Anthony F. C. Wallace.

Features of the Seventh Edition

• Strengthened commitment to classical anthropological literature by including works from the mid 20th century by Claude Lévi-Strauss, John Beattie, Barbara Myerhoff, Roy Rappaport, and Gerardo Reichel-Dolmatoff.

• Increased coverage of the Islamic world as studied by anthropologists. The text now includes articles devoted to the pilgrimage to Mecca by West Africans, Muslim women's dress, and female rites of passage in Egypt and Sudan.

• Articles focus on the distinction between science and religion as well as the scholarly study of religion and how it contrasts with belief. An essay by noted author Stephen Jay Gould dismisses the conflict between science and faith, arguing that the two are non-overlapping ways of understanding the world.

• A chapter on religious globalization provides insights into religion as a transnational phenomenon. This chapter includes materials on religious conflicts, religion and the state, the issues of women and religious minorities, and the impact of new technology and worldwide entertainment media.

• Chapter 3 is devoted to a lengthy treatment of ritual, a key area of anthropological inquiry.

• Chapter 7 combines the closely related topics of witchcraft, sorcery, divination, and magic and emphasizes the common theme of human attempts to control or manipulate the supernatural.

• Timely and controversial issues are addressed in new articles on religion and nationalism—including violent expressions of faith, Tibetan Buddhism under Chinese rule, witchcraft in Great Britain, and medical use of prayer.

• A list of suggested readings concludes each chapter. These lists may be of assistance to the instructor, but they are also intended to provide a foundation for students pursuing independent research on topics related to the chapter.

• A comprehensive glossary, with terms new to the present edition, as well as an extensive index of subjects, authors, and titles and a bibliography of references from the volume's articles, offer students further help.

Supplements

Visit our companion Web site at www.mhhe.com/moro7 for instructor and student resources. The student center features helpful chapter outlines and quizzes. The password-protected instructor center contains an indispensable instructor's manual and comprehensive test bank.

Acknowledgments

We would like to express our thanks to the scholars, teachers, and students who have shaped our understanding of anthropology and inspired our thinking about the anthropology of religion. We acknowledge with thanks the following reviewers, whose suggestions and comments guided our preparation of the seventh edition: Janet Bennion, Lyndon State College; Caroline B. Brettell, Southern Methodist University; Patrick D. Gaffney, University of Notre Dame; Thomas A. Green, Texas A&M University; William Leons, University of Toledo; Kathleen R. Martín, Florida International University; Lynn R. Metzger, University of Akron; and Melford S. Weiss, California State University–Sacramento. We also thank Pam's students at Willamette University for their critical evaluation of articles and their inspiring enthusiasm for anthropology. Pam owes thanks to colleagues Rebecca Dobkins, Joyce Millen, and Peter Wogan for their friendly support and bibliographic tips, as well as to Saad Moro for assistance with the hands-on aspects of manuscript preparation. We are grateful to Garrett Stephenson for his well-informed preparation of the instructional supplements. We extend a very special thank you to Sandra Booth for her cheerful and capable work on copyright permissions, including extensive correspondence with publishers. Finally, we would like to thank our families and friends for their patience and good humor throughout this project.

J.E.M.
P.A.M.

CHAPTER ONE

The Anthropological Study of Religion

Buffalo mask of the Bobo, Upper Volta.

Anthropologists have always been interested in the origins of religion, although the lack of both written records and archaeological evidence has made the subject speculative. It is reasonable to assume, however, that religion, like material culture, has a prehistory. Surely, uncertainty and change have always existed, exposing people in all ages to real and imagined threats and anxieties. The human animal alone senses a pattern behind the facts of existence and worries about life here and in the hereafter. We are born, we live, and we die. And although this is true of other animals, only humans are aware of the precariousness of life and the inevitability of death. As William Howells has observed, "Man's life is hard, very hard. And he knows it, poor soul; that is the vital thing. He knows that he is forever confronted with the Four Horsemen—death, famine, disease, and the malice of other men" (1962: 16).

Paleoanthropological evidence shows that Neanderthals buried their dead, often in a flexed position. Such deliberate burials, many feel, indicate the beginnings of religion and the conception of an afterlife. Interpretations of other items at Neanderthal sites, such as flower pollen, bear skulls, and red and black pigments, are more controversial. Such items may tell us something about the origins of religious behavior, but they may also simply be present accidentally.

In contrast, the era of *Homo sapiens sapiens* (modern humans in the biological sense) yields tremendous evidence of religious beliefs—more elaborate burials, carved figurines ("Venuses"), and magnificent cave art. And during the Neolithic period, which began about ten thousand years ago, burials indicate a deep respect for the power of the dead. It is likely that during this period, which is marked by the cultivation of crops and the domestication of animals, cycles of nature became an important feature of magic and religious beliefs. Drought, storms, and other natural perils of the farmer could have created a growing dependence on supernatural powers.

The antiquity of religion indirectly testifies to its utility; however, the usefulness of supernaturalism to contemporary societies is a clearer, more provable demonstration of its functions. The many forms of adversity facing individuals and groups require explanation and action; we are unwilling to let challenges to health, safety, and salvation go unchecked. Just

1

as adversity is universal, so, too, is the use of religion as an explanation for and solution to adversity. Although the form religion takes is as diverse as its practitioners, all religions seek to answer questions that cannot be explained in terms of objective knowledge—to permit people reasonable explanations for often unreasonable events and phenomena by demonstrating a cause-and-effect relationship between the supernatural and the human condition. This may be its most important function.

In his article "Religion: Problems of Definition and Explanation" (1966: 109–17), Melford E. Spiro has distinguished three sets of basic desires (cognitive, substantive, and expressive), each of which is satisfied by a corresponding function of religion (adjustive, adaptive, and integrative). Spiro's first and second functions are basically those of explanation and solution: the adjustive function of religion, as he defines it, is to satisfy the cognitive desires we experience as we attempt to understand what goes on around us (illness, natural phenomena); the adaptive function seeks to satisfy substantive desires (the desire for rain or for victory in war). In his third category, however, Spiro moves to different territory: the often unconscious, expressive desires made up of what Spiro calls painful drives and painful motives.

According to Spiro, painful drives are anxieties concerning infantile and primitive fears (fears of destruction or of one's own destructiveness). Painful motives are culturally forbidden—for example, types of aggressive or sexual behavior that result in feelings of shame, inadequacy, and moral anxiety. Because of the pain they create in an individual, these drives and motives are usually relegated to the unconscious, where, "in the absence of other, or of more efficient means," religion becomes the vehicle "by which, symbolically, they can be handled and expressed." Thus, in what Spiro calls the integrative function of supernaturalism, "religious belief and ritual provide the content for culturally constituted projective mechanisms by which unconscious fears and anxieties may be reduced and repressed motives may be satisfied" (1966: 115).

Over the years, scholars have taken several approaches in their attempts to understand the reasons for the existence of religious behavior. The most prominent of these approaches are psychological, sociological, and anthropological. Spiro's belief that religious behavior reduces unconscious fears typifies the psychological approach, which, briefly stated, sees religion as functioning to reduce anxiety. For example, the famous British social anthropologist Bronislaw Malinowski held that the proper use of religious rites reduced anxieties brought on by crisis. (Like all theorists who apply the psychological approach, Freud also believed that religion and ritual functioned to reduce anxieties, but, unlike others, he saw religion as a neurotic need that humans would eventually outgrow.) In contrast, the sociological viewpoint stresses the societal origins of religion. The French sociologist Emile Durkheim, for example, viewed religion as a manifestation of social solidarity and collective beliefs. According to Durkheim, members of society create religious objects, rituals, beliefs, and symbols in order to integrate their cultures. A. R. Radcliffe-Brown, a British social anthropologist, agreed with Durkheim that participation in annual religious rites functioned to increase social solidarity.

Although their functional analyses of religious behavior and phenomena do explain, in part, the universality of religion, neither the psychological nor the sociological theorists adequately provide answers to the origin of religion. Both approaches are too limited in focus, centered as they are on human emotions and social structure respectively; neither explores the wide variety of cultural expressions of religion. Because religious experience, wherever it is observed, displays such great variation of cognitive and phenomenal expression, anything less than a wide-ranging holistic approach would not allow true comparisons; as a result, generalizations about the nature of religious systems would be incomplete as well as inaccurate.

The third, the anthropological approach to the study of religion, is by its very nature holistic, combining not only sociological and psychological but historical, semantic, and evolutionary perspectives as well. Anthropologists today attempt to go beyond the observable to the analysis of symbolic forms. In order to make generalizations on pan-human religious behavior, symbology, and ideology, however, anthropologists must work from the common basis of a definition of religion. Without an acceptable and accurate definition, anthropologists would be unable to establish a common basis for comparison of religions cross-culturally.

Many definitions of religion have been generated by anthropologists. Edward B. Tylor, the father of modern anthropology, described religion as the belief in spiritual beings, what he called "animism," the most primitive form of religion. At the opposite extreme from Tylor's open-ended definition, which set no limits as to what the study of spiritual beings would embrace, are a majority of contemporary anthropologists who, like Spiro, define religion more narrowly as "an institution consisting of culturally postulated superhuman beings" (1966: 96). At first glance, Tylor's and Spiro's definitions appear similar, but Spiro's use of the term *superhuman,* unlike Tylor's *spiritual beings,* emphasizes an aura of omnipotence unknown to the living. Further, Spiro's position that religion is an institution places it in the realm of phenomena that can be empirically studied, as any other cultural institution can be. Still, similarities in Tylor's and Spiro's definitions are apparent: both show, for example, that religion is the study of the nature of the unnatural. Spirits are not of this world, nor are superhumans; indeed, both are "supernatural," which has been defined by the anthropologist Edward Norbeck "to include all that is not natural, that which is regarded as extraordinary, not of the ordinary world, mysterious or unexplainable in ordinary terms" (1961: 11).

Expanding the definition of religion beyond spiritual and superhuman beings to include the extraordinary, the mysterious, and unexplainable allows a more comprehensive view of religious behaviors among the peoples of the world and permits the anthropological investigation of phenomena such as magic, sorcery, curses, and other practices that hold meaning for both preliterate and literate societies. For this reason, this book focuses on the concept of the supernatural and incorporates a wide variety of contemporary examples of religious beliefs and practices that demonstrate the breadth of human ideology.

Through their comparative research, anthropologists have shown that religious practices and beliefs vary in part as a result of the level of social structure in a given society. In *The Birth of the Gods* (1960), Guy Swanson applied a statistical approach to support the argument that religious forms are related to social development, and in *Religion: An Anthropological View* (1966: 84–101), Anthony F. C. Wallace presented a provocative typology of religious behavior based on the concept of the cult institution—"a set of rituals all having the same general goal, all explicitly rationalized by a set of similar or related beliefs, and all supported by the same social group" (p. 75). Ranging from the simplest to the most complex, Wallace describes individualistic, shamanic, communal, and ecclesiastical cult institutions. Each succeeding or more complex level contains all components of those preceding it. The ecclesiastical, for example, contains all the elements of the less complex individualistic, shamanistic, and communal cult institutions.

According to Wallace, in the simplest, *individualistic* cult institution, each person functions as his or her own specialist without need for such intermediaries as shamans or priests. Examples occur in both modern and primitive societies (the dream cult among the Iroquois, sealing magic among the Trobriand Islanders, and various cults among the Americans). The next level, the *shamanic,* also found in cultures around the world, marks the beginning of a religious division of labor. Individual part-time practitioners are designated by experience, birth, or training to help lay clients enlist the aid of the supernatural. The *communal* cult institution is even more complex, with laypeople handling important religious rituals for people in such special categories as secret societies, kinship groups, and age groups. (Examples include the ancestor ceremonies of the Chinese and some African tribal groups, Iroquois agricultural rituals, and Australian puberty rituals.) Although specialists such as shamans, skilled speakers, and dancers may participate, the lay group assumes the primary responsibility for conducting the sacred performance; an extensive religious hierarchy is still not in evidence. It is in the fourth, *ecclesiastical* cult institution that a professional religious clergy is formally elected or appointed and the division of labor is sharply drawn, with the laypeople usually passive participants instead of active performers. Ecclesiastical cult institutions have characteristically worshipped either an Olympian pantheon of gods (as among the ancient Greeks and Romans) or a monotheistic deity (as among the Judeo-Christian and Muslim religions).

The differences between religious behavior and belief in so-called primitive and modern cultures has been of great interest to anthropologists over the years. Howells (1962: 5) observed several characteristics that he believed distinguished the major world religions from the belief systems of more primitive cultures. First, the "great faiths" are messianic, their origins stemming from such charismatic figures as Jesus, Buddha, and Muhammad. Second, they have a rigid ethical form. Third, each has a missionary, imperialistic aspect, seeing itself as the one and only religion. Finally, each displays an exclusiveness in its belief system to the degree of being intolerant of other faiths. Howells is quick to point out that he has been generalizing, reminding the reader that the varied nature and heterogeneity of native cults may make an understanding of their nature arduous, especially for anyone aware only of the differences among Christian sects (1962: 6). His concluding remark is important to an understanding of all the articles in this book; referring to the "perfect legitimacy" of native cults, he states that the

> primitive devotees are not people of another planet, but are essentially exactly like us, and are engaged with precisely the same kind of religious appetite as the civilized. And that appetite is fed and stilled by their own religions. This is very important; it is why we are taking those religions seriously. They are not toys. They are what we might be doing ourselves; and they are what most of our ancestors were indeed doing, two thousand years ago today. (1962: 7)

Tomes have been written on the universality and tenacity of religion, even when they were faced with harsh repression by governments, modernization, and economic globalization. Vernon Reynolds and Ralph Tanner maintain that

> there is more to life, it seems, than the secular state can encompass. People want religion and faith; many of them could hardly imagine life without these things. . . . Religions are also down to earth, and we believe that it is this contact with the material world that explains the continued existence of religions in all countries, why they have survived and multiplied during history, and why they are a real force in the world today. (1995: 4, 9)

The six articles in this chapter have been selected to provide a basic understanding of the anthropological approach to the study of the supernatural. Each stresses the use of the comparative method, the very anchor for anthropological thought.

In the first article, Clifford Geertz demonstrates the importance of a historical, psychological, sociological, and semantic approach to the study of religion.

Next, Marvin Harris discusses the fascinating possibility of religion among nonhuman species. In addition, he advances the notion that spiritual beings are found also in the religions of prestate societies.

In the third article, Dorothy Lee shows how religion is part and parcel of a preliterate people's total way of life. Lee tells us about preliterate societies in which ceremonies and their preparation occupy most of a year.

In the fourth selection, Stephen Jay Gould reasons that there should be no conflict between science and religion because each possesses a separate and legitimate domain of teaching authority. Gould observes that science is interested in fact and theory, whereas religion ponders moral meaning and values.

In the fifth article, Robert S. Root-Bernstein discusses the challenges of teaching evolution when a large percentage of his college students lack the scientific knowledge to evaluate evolution as a valid scientific theory.

Finally, Claude E. Stipe suggests possible explanations of why anthropologists traditionally have regarded missionaries as "the enemy."

References

Howells, William
    1962 *The Heathens: Primitive Man and His Religions.* Garden City, N.Y.: Doubleday.

Norbeck, Edward
    1961 *Religion in Primitive Society.* New York: Harper and Brothers.

Reynolds, Vernon, and Ralph Tanner
    1995 *The Social Ecology of Religion.* New York: Oxford University Press.

Spiro, Melford E.
    1966 "Religion: Problems of Definition and Explanation." In Michael Banton, ed.,
          Anthropological Approaches to the Study of Religion, pp. 85–126. London: Tavistock
          Publications Limited for the Association of Social Anthropologists of the
          Commonwealth.

Swanson, Guy
    1960 *The Birth of the Gods: The Origin of Primitive Beliefs.* Ann Arbor: University of Michigan
          Press.

Wallace, Anthony F. C.
    1966 *Religion: An Anthropological View.* New York: Random House.

1

Religion

Clifford Geertz

In his classic work "Religion as a Cultural System" (1966), Clifford Geertz argued for a broadened analysis of religion. This argument, aimed primarily at the narrowness of the British sociological approach to the study of comparative religion, was accepted by American ethnologists and reflected in their contemporary research. In the following article, Geertz pursues his goal, demonstrating the importance of his historical, psychological, sociological, and semantic approaches to the study of religion and concluding that a mature theory of religion will integrate these approaches into a conceptual system whose exact form remains to be discovered. Geertz also explores the view of scholars who regard "primitive thought" as a distinctive mode of reasoning and/or a special body of knowledge, noting that their work persists as a minor but important theme in anthropological studies of religion. The article concludes with a discussion of the highly evocative work of Claude Lévi-Strauss, the leading exponent of the French structural school of anthropology. In addition to extensive fieldwork in Java, Geertz has also conducted research in Bali and Morocco.

The anthropological study of religion has been highly sensitive to changes in the general intellectual and moral climate of the day; at the same time, it has been a powerful factor in the creation of that climate. Since the early discussion by Edward Tylor, interest in the beliefs and rituals of distant, ancient, or simpler peoples has been shaped by an awareness of contemporary issues. The questions that anthropologists have pursued among exotic religions have arisen from the workings—or the misworkings—of modern Western society, and particularly from its restless quest for self-discovery. In turn, their findings have profoundly affected the course that quest has taken and the perspective at which it has arrived.

Perhaps the chief reason for the rather special role of comparative religious studies is that issues which, when raised within the context of Western culture, led to extreme social resistance and personal turmoil could be freely and even comfortably handled in terms of bizarre, presumably primitive, and thus—also presumably—fanciful materials from long ago or far away. The study of "primitive religions" could pass as the study of superstition, supposedly unrelated to the serious religious and moral concerns of advanced civilization, at best either a sort of vague foreshadowing of them or a grotesque parody upon them. This made it possible to approach all sorts of touchy subjects, such as polytheism, value relativism, possession, and faith healing, from a frank and detached point of view. One could ask searching questions about the historicity of myth among Polynesians; when asked in relation to Christianity, these same questions were, until quite recently, deeply threatening. One could discuss the projection of erotic wishes found in the "totemic" rites of Australian aborigines, the social roots and functions of African "ancestor worship," or the protoscientific quality of Melanesian "magical thought," without

Reprinted by permission of the publisher from INTERNATIONAL ENCYCLOPEDIA OF THE SOCIAL SCIENCES, David L. Sills, Editor. Vol. 13, pp. 398–406. Copyright 1972 by Crowell Collier and Macmillan.

involving oneself in polemical debate and emotional distress. The application of the comparative method—the essence of anthropological thought—to religion permitted the growth of a resolutely scientific approach to the spiritual dimensions of human life.

Through the thin disguise of comparative method the revolutionary implications of the work of such men as Tylor, Durkheim, Robertson Smith, Freud, Malinowski, and Radcliffe-Brown soon became apparent—at first mainly to philosophers, theologians, and literary figures, but eventually to the educated public in general. The meticulous descriptions of tribal curiosities such as soul loss, shamanism, circumcision, blood sacrifice, sorcery, tree burial, garden magic, symbolic cannibalism, and animal worship have been caught up in some of the grander intellectual battles of the last hundred years—from those over evolutionism and historicism in the late nineteenth century to those over positivism and existentialism today. Psychoanalysts and phenomenologists, Marxists and Kantians, racists and egalitarians, absolutists and relativists, empiricists and rationalists, believers and skeptics have all had recourse to the record—partial, inconsistent, and shot through with simple error as it is—of the spiritual life of tribal peoples to support their positions and belabor those of their opponents. If interest in "primitive religion" among savants of all sorts has been remarkably high, consensus concerning its nature and significance has not.

At least three major intellectual developments have exercised a critical influence on the anthropological study of religion: (1) the emergence, in the latter half of the nineteenth century, of history as the sovereign science of man; (2) the positivist reaction against this sovereignty in the first decades of the twentieth century and the radical split of the social sciences into resolutely psychological approaches, on the one hand, and resolutely sociological ones, on the other; and (3) the growth, in the interwar period, of a concern with the role of ideational factors in the regulation of social life. With the first of these came an emphasis on the nature of primitive reasoning and the stages of its evolution into civilized thought. With the second came an investigation of the emotional basis of religious ritual and belief and the separate examination of the role of ritual and belief in social integration. The concern with value systems and other features of the ideational realm led to an exploration of the philosophical dimensions of religious ideas, particularly the symbolic vehicles in terms of which those ideas are expressed.

Evolutionism and Its Enemies

Like so much else in anthropology, the study of the religious notions of primitive peoples arose within the context of evolutionary theory. In the nineteenth century, to think systematically about human affairs was to think historically—to seek out survivals of the most elementary forms and to trace the steps by which these forms subsequently developed. And though, in fact, Tylor, Morgan, Frazer, and the rest drew more on the synthetic social-stage theories of such men as Comte and Hegel than on the analytic random-variation and natural-selection ideas of Darwin, the grand concept of evolution was shared by both streams of thought: namely, that the complex, heterogeneous present has arisen, more or less gradually, out of a simpler, more uniform past. The relics of this past are still to be found scattered, like Galápagos turtles, in out-of-the-way places around us. Tylor, an armchair scholar, made no "voyage of the *Beagle*." But in combing and organizing the reports of missionaries, soldiers, and explorers, he proceeded from the same general premise as did Darwin, and indeed most of the leading minds of the day. For them a comprehensive, historically oriented comparison of all forms of a phenomenon, from the most primitive to the most advanced, was the royal road to understanding the nature of the phenomenon itself.

In Tylor's view, the elementary form out of which all else developed was spirit worship—*animism*. The minimal definition of religion was "a belief in spiritual beings." The understanding of religion thus came down to an understanding of the basis upon which such a belief arose at its most primitive level. Tylor's theory was intellectualistic. Belief in spirits began as an uncritical but nonetheless rational effort to explain such puzzling empirical phenomena as death, dreams, and possession. The notion of a separable soul rendered these phenomena intelligible in terms of soul departure, soul wandering, and soul invasion. Tylor believed that the idea of a soul was used to explain more and more remote and hitherto inexplicable natural occurrences, until virtually every tree and rock was haunted by some sort of gossamer presence. The higher, more developed forms of "belief in spiritual beings," first polytheism, ultimately monotheism, were founded upon this animistic basis, the urphilosophy of all mankind, and were refined through a process of critical questioning by more advanced thinkers. For this earnest Quaker the religious history of the world was a history of progressive, even inevitable, enlightenment.

This intellectualistic, "up from darkness" strain has run through most evolutionist thought about religion. For Frazer, a nineteenth-century figure who lived for forty years into the twentieth century without finding it necessary to alter either his views or his methods, the mental progress involved was from magic to religion to science. Magic was the primordial form of human thought; it consisted in mistaking either spatiotemporal connection ("sympathetic magic," as when drinking the blood of an ox transfers its strength to the drinker) or phenomenal similarity ("imitative magic," as when the sound of drumming induces thunderheads to form) for true scientific causality. For Durkheim, evolutionary advance consisted in the emergence of specific, analytic, *profane* ideas about "cause" or "category" or "relationship" from diffuse, global, *sacred* images. These "collective representations," as he called them, of the social order and its moral force included such sacra as "mana," "totem," and "god." For Max Weber, the process was one of "rationalization": the progressive organization of religious concern into certain more precisely defined, more specifically focused, and more systematically conceived cultural forms. The level of sophistication of such theories (and, hence, their present relevance) varies very widely. But, like Tylor's, they all conceive of the evolution of religion as a process of cultural differentiation: the diffuse, all-embracing, but rather unsystematic and uncritical religious practices of primitive peoples are transformed into the more specifically focused, more regularized, less comprehensively authoritative practices of the more advanced civilizations. Weber, in whom both intellectualism and optimism were rather severely tempered by a chronic apprehensiveness, called this transformation the "disenchantment *(Entzauberung)* of the world."

On the heels of evolutionism came, of course, anti-evolutionism. This took two quite different forms. On one side there was a defense, mainly by

Roman Catholic scholars, of the so-called degradation theory. According to this theory, the original revelation of a high god to primitive peoples was later corrupted by human frailty into the idol worship of present-day tribal peoples. On the other side there was an attack, mainly by American scholars of the Boas school, upon the "armchair speculation" of evolutionary thinkers and a call for its replacement by more phenomenological approaches to the study of tribal custom.

The first of these reactions led, logically enough, to a search among the most primitive of existing peoples for traces of belief in a supreme being. The resulting dispute, protracted, often bitter, and stubbornly inconclusive as to the existence of such "primitive monotheism," turned out to be unproductive—aside from some interesting discussions by Lang (1898) concerning culture heroes and by Eliade (1949) concerning sky gods—and both the issue and the theory that gave rise to it have now receded from the center of scholarly attention. The second reaction has had a longer life and great impact on ethnographic methodology, but it too is now in partial eclipse. Its main contributions—aside from some devastating empirical demolitions of evolutionist generalization—came in the field of cultural diffusion. Leslie Spier's study of the spread of the Sun Dance through the Great Plains and A. L. Kroeber's application of the age-area approach to aboriginal religion in California are good examples of productive diffusion studies. However, apart from their importance for culture history, the contribution of such distributional studies to our understanding of religious ideas, attitudes, and practices as such has not been great, and few students now pursue these studies. The call of the Boas school for thorough field research and disciplined inductive analysis has been heeded; but its fruits, insofar as religious studies are concerned, have been reaped by others less inhibited theoretically.

Psychological Approaches

The major reaction against the intellectual tradition of the cultural evolutionists took place not within anthropology, however, but in the general context of the positivist revolt against the domination of historicist modes of thought in the social sciences. In the years before World War I the rise of the systematic psychologism of psychoanalysis and of the equally systematic sociologism of the *Année sociologique* forced evolutionist theorizing into the background, even though the leaders of both movements—Freud and Durkheim—were themselves still very strongly influenced by it. Perhaps even more relevant, it introduced a sharp split into anthropological studies of religion which has resolved into the militantly psychodynamic and the militantly social-structural approaches.

Freud's major work in this field is, of course, *Totem and Taboo*, a book anthropologists in general have had great difficulty in evaluating—as Kroeber's two reviews of it, the first facilely negative, the second, two decades later, ambivalently positive, demonstrate. The source of the difficulty has been an inability or an unwillingness to disentangle Freud's basic thesis—that religious rituals and beliefs are homologous with neurotic symptoms—from the chimerical ethnology and obsolete biology within which he insisted upon setting it. Thus, the easy demolition of what Kroeber called Freud's "just so story" concerning primal incest, parricide, and guilt within some protohuman horde ("in the beginning was the deed") was all too often mistaken for total rejection of the rather more penetrating proposition that the obsessions, dreams, and fantasies of collective life spring from the same intrapsychic sources as do those of the isolated individual.

For those who read further in Freud's writings, however—especially in "Mourning and Melancholia" and "Obsessive Acts and Religious Practices"—it became apparent that what was at issue was the applicability of theories concerning the forms and causes of individual psychopathology to the explanation of the forms and causes of public myth and group ritual. Róheim (1950) analyzed Australian circumcision rites against the background of orthodox Freudian theories of psychosexual development, especially those clustered around the Oedipal predicament. However, he explicitly avoided recourse to speculations about buried memories of primordial occurrences. Bettelheim (1954) adopted a similar, though more systematic and less orthodox, approach to initiation practices generally, seeing them as socially instituted symbolic mechanisms for the definition and stabilization of sexual identity. Kardiner (1945), taking a neo-Freudian position, sought to demonstrate that the religious institutions of tribal

peoples were projections of a "basic personality structure," formed not by the action of an unconsciously remembered historical trauma but by the more observable traumas produced by child-training practices, an approach later extended and cast into quantitative form by Whiting (Whiting and Child 1953). Erikson (1950), drawing upon developments in ego psychology which conceived the emergence of the adult personality to be a joint product of psychobiological maturation, cultural context, and historical experience, interpreted the religious notions of the Yurok and the Sioux in terms of certain basic modes of relating to the world. These relationships gradually developed during the whole course of childhood and adolescence. Others—notably Devereux (1951)—have attempted to use the autobiographical, case-history approach to determine the relations between personality dynamics and religious orientation in particular individuals; still others—notably Hallowell (1937–1954)—have employed projective tests, questionnaires, reports of dreams, or systematic interviews toward similar ends.

In all such studies, even when individual authors have dissented from many of Freud's specific views, the basic premise has been Freudian: that religious practices can be usefully interpreted as expressions of unconscious psychological forces—and this has become, amid much polemic, an established tradition of inquiry. In recent years, however, responsible work of this type has come to question the degree to which one is justified in subjecting historically created and socially institutionalized cultural forms to a system of analysis founded on the treatment of the mental illnesses of individuals. For this reason, the future of this approach depends perhaps more upon developments within psychoanalysis, now in a somewhat uncertain state, than within anthropology. So far, perhaps only Kluckhohn's pioneering *Navaho Witchcraft* (1944) has attempted to systematically relate psychological factors to social and cultural aspects of primitive religion. The great majority of psychoanalytic studies of tribal beliefs and rites remain willfully parochial.

In any case, not all psychological approaches to religion have been Freudian. Jungian influences have had a certain impact, especially on studies of myth. Campbell (1949), for example, has stressed the continuity of certain themes both cross-culturally and temporally. These themes have been interpreted as expressions of transpersonal constancies in unconscious mental functioning which are at the same time expressions of fundamental cosmic realities.

Simple emotionalist theories have also been extremely popular. There have been two main varieties of these: awe theories and confidence theories. Awe theories have been based on some usually rather vague notion of "religious thrill" experienced by human beings when brought face to face with cosmic forces. A wide range of ethnologists, from Max Müller through Lang and Marett to Lowie and Goldenweiser, have accepted such theories in one form or another. However, awe theories remain mere notations of the obvious—that religious experience is, in the nature of the case, touched with intense feelings of the grandeur of the universe in relation to the self and of the vulnerability of the self in relation to the universe. This is not explanation, but circular reasoning.

Confidence theories also begin with a notion of man's inward sense of weakness, and especially of his fears—of disease, of death, of ill fortune of all kinds—and they see religious practices as designed to quiet such fears, either by explaining them away, as in doctrines of the afterlife, or by claiming to link the individual to external sources of strength, as in prayer. The best-known confidence theory was that set forth by Malinowski. He regarded magic as enabling man to pursue uncertain but essential endeavors by assuring him of their ultimate success. Confidence, or anxiety-reduction, theories, like awe theories, clearly have empirical foundation but do not adequately explore the complex relationship between fear and religious activity. They are not rooted in any systematic conceptualization of mental functioning and so merely point to matters desperately in need of clarification, without in fact clarifying them.

Sociological Approaches

The sociological approach to the analysis of the religions of nonliterate peoples proceeded independent of, and even at variance with, the psychoanalytic approach, but it shared a concern with the same phenomenon: the peculiar "otherness," the extraordinary, momentous, "set apart" quality of sacred (or "taboo") acts and objects, as contrasted with the profane. The intense aura of high seriousness was traced by Freud to the projection of unacceptable wishes repressed from consciousness onto external objects. The dramatic ambivalence of the sacred—its paradoxical unification of the commanded and the forbidden, the pure and the polluted, the salutary and the dangerous—was a symbolic expression of the underlying ambivalence of human desires. For Durkheim, too, the extraordinary atmosphere surrounding sacred acts and objects was symbolic of a hidden reality, but a social, not a psychological one: the moral force of the human community.

Durkheim believed that the integrity of the social order was the primary requisite for human survival, and the means by which that integrity superseded individual egocentricity was the primary problem of sociological analysis. He saw Australian totemism (which he, like Freud, made the empirical focus of his work) as a mechanism to this end. For example, the collective rituals involving the emblems of the totemic beings—the so-called bull roarers—aroused the heightened emotions of mass behavior and evoked a deep sense of moral identification among the participants. The creation of social solidarity was the result of the common public veneration, by specific groups of persons, of certain carefully designated symbolic objects. These objects had no intrinsic value except as perceptible representations of the social identity of the individuals. Collective worship of consecrated bits of painted wood or stone created a moral community, a "church," upon which rested the viability of the major social units. These sanctified objects thus represented the system of rights and obligations implicit in the social order and the individual's unformulated sense of its overriding significance in his life. All sacred objects, beliefs, and acts, and the extraordinary emotions attending them, were outward expressions of inward social necessities, and, in a famous phrase, God was the "symbol of society." Few anthropologists have been able to swallow Durkheim's thesis whole, when put this baldly. But the more moderate proposition that religious rituals and beliefs both reflect and act to support the moral framework underlying social arrangements (and are in turn animated by it) has given rise to what has become perhaps the most popular form of analysis in the anthropological study of religion. Usually called "functionalism"—or sometimes, to distinguish it from certain variants deemed objectionable, "structuralism"—this approach found its champion in Radcliffe-Brown and its major development in Great Britain, though its influence has now spread very much more widely.

Radcliffe-Brown (1952) agreed with Durkheim's postulate that the main role (or "function") of religion was to celebrate and sustain the norms upon which the integration of society depends. But unlike Durkheim (and like Freud), Radcliffe-Brown was concerned with the content of sacred symbols, and particularly with the reasons why one object rather than another was absorbed into rite or woven into myth. Why here stones, there water holes, here camp circles, there personified winds?

Durkheim had held this to be an arbitrary matter, contingent upon historical accident or psychological proclivity, beyond the reach of and irrelevant to sociological analysis. Radcliffe-Brown considered, however, that man's need for a concrete expression of social solidarity was not sufficient explanation of the structure of a people's religious system. Something was needed to tie the particular objects awarded sacred status (or, in his terminology, "ritual value") to the particular social interests they presumably served and reflected. Radcliffe-Brown, resolute empiricist that he was, chose a solution Durkheim had already magisterially demolished: the utilitarian. The objects selected for religious veneration by a given people were either directly or indirectly connected to factors critical to their collective well-being. Things that had real, that is, practical, "social value" were elevated to having spiritual, or symbolic, "ritual value," thus fusing the social and the natural into one overarching order. For primitives at least (and Radcliffe-Brown attempted to establish his theory with regard to the sanctified turtles and palm leaves of the pre-agricultural Andaman Islanders and, later on, with regard to Australian totemism), there is no discontinuity, no difference even, between moral and physical, spiritual and practical relationships and processes. These people regard both men and things as parts of a single normative system. Within that system those elements which are critical to its effective functioning (or, sometimes, phenomena empirically associated with such elements, such as the Andaman cicada cycle and the shifting monsoons) are made the objects of that special sort of respect and attention which we call religious but which the people themselves regard as merely prudential.

Radcliffe-Brown focused upon the content of sacred symbols and emphasized the relation between conceptions of the moral order of existence and conceptions of its natural order. However, the claim that the sanctity of religious objects derives from their practical social importance is one of those theories which works when it works and doesn't when it doesn't. Not only has it proved impossible to find even an indirect practical significance in most of the enormous variety of things tribal peoples have regarded as sacred (certain Australian tribes worship vomit), but the view that religious concerns are mere ritualizations of real-life concerns leaves the phenomenon of sacredness itself—its aura of mystery, power, fascination—totally unexplained.

More recent structuralist studies have tended to evade both these questions and to concentrate on the role played by religion in maintaining social equilibrium. They attempt to show how given sets of religious practices (ancestor worship, animal sacrifice, witchcraft and sorcery, regeneration rites) do in fact express and reinforce the moral values underlying crucial processes (lineage segmentation, marriage, conflict adjudication, political succession) in the particular society under investigation. Arnold van Gennep's study of crisis rites was perhaps the most important forerunner of the many analyses of this type. Although valuable in their own right as ethnography and as sociology, these structural formulations have been severely limited by their rigid avoidance on the one side, of the kind of psychological considerations that could account for the peculiar emotions which permeate religious belief and practice, and, on the other, of the philosophical considerations that could render their equally peculiar content intelligible.

The Analysis of Symbolic Forms

In contrast to other approaches—evolutionary, psychological, sociological—the field of what we may loosely call "semantic studies" of religion is extremely jumbled. There is, as yet, no well-established central trend to analysis, no central figure around whom to order debate, and no readily apparent system of interconnections relating the various competing trends to one another.

Perhaps the most straightforward strategy— certainly the most disarming—is merely to *accept* the myriad expressions of the sacred in primitive societies, to consider them as actual ingressions of the divine into the world, and to trace the forms these expressions have taken across the earth and through time. The result would be a sort of natural history of revelation, whose aim would be to isolate the major classes of religious phenomena considered as authentic manifestations of the sacred—what Eliade, the chief proponent of this approach, calls hierophanies—and to trace the rise, dominance, decline, and disappearance of these classes within the changing contexts of human life. The meaning of religious activity, the burden of its content, is discovered through a meticulous, wholly inductive investigation of the natural modalities of such behavior (sun worship, water symbolism, fertility cults, renewal myths, etc.) and of the vicissitudes these modalities undergo when projected, like the Son of God himself, into the flux of history.

Metaphysical questions (here uncommonly obtrusive) aside, the weaknesses of this approach derive from the same source as its strengths: a drastic limiting of the interpretations of religion to the sort that a resolutely Baconian methodology can produce. On the one hand, this approach has led, especially in the case of a scholar as erudite and indefatigable as Eliade, to the uncovering of some highly suggestive clusterings of certain religious patterns with particular historical conditions—for example, the frequent association of sun worship, activist conceptions of divine power, cultic veneration of deified heroes, elitist doctrines of political sovereignty, and imperialist ideologies of national expansion. But, on the other hand, it has placed beyond the range of scientific analysis everything but the history and morphology of the phenomenal forms of religious expression. The study of tribal beliefs and practices is reduced to a kind of cultural paleontology whose sole aim is the reconstruction, from scattered and corrupted fragments, of the "mental universe of archaic man."

Primitive Thought

Other scholars who are interested in the meaningful content of primitive religion but who are incapable of so thoroughgoing a suspension of disbelief as Eliade, or are repelled by the cultic overtones of this somewhat mystagogic line of thought, have directed their attention instead toward logical and epistemological considerations. This has produced a long series of studies that view "primitive thought" as a distinctive mode of reasoning and/or a special body of knowledge. From Lévy-Bruhl through Lévi-Strauss, and with important contributions from members of the evolutionary, psychoanalytic, and sociological schools as well, this line of exploration has persisted as a minor theme in anthropological studies of religion. With the recent advances in linguistics, information theory, the analysis of cognition, semantic philosophy, modern logic, and certain sorts of literary investigation, the systematic study of symbolic activity bids fair to become, in a rather thoroughly revised form, the major theme for investigation. The "new key" Susanne K. Langer heard being struck in philosophy in the early 1940s—"the concern with the concept of meaning in all its forms"—has, like the historicist and positivist "keys" before it, begun to have its echo in the anthropological study of religion. Anthropologists are increasingly interested in ideational expression, increasingly concerned with the vehicles, processes, and practical applications of human conceptualization.

The development of this approach has come in two fairly distinct phases, one before and one after World War II. In the first phase there was a concern with "the mind of primitive man" and in particular with its capacity for rational thought. In a sense, this concern represented the evolutionists' interest in primitive reasoning processes detached from the historicist context. In the second phase, which is still in process, there has been a move away from, and in part a reaction against, the subjectivist emphasis of the earlier work. Ideational expression is thought of as a public activity, rather like speech, and the structure of the symbolic materials, the "language," in whose terms the activity is conducted becomes the subject of investigation.

The first, subjectivist, phase was animated by a protracted wrangle between those who used the religious beliefs and practices of tribal peoples as evidence to prove that there was a qualitative difference between the thought processes of primitives and those of civilized men and the anthropologists who considered such religious activity as evidence for the lack of any such differences. The great protagonist of the first school was the French philosopher Lévy-Bruhl whose theories of "prelogical mentality" were as controversial within anthropology as they were popular outside it. According to Lévy-Bruhl, the thought of primitives, as reflected in their religious ideas, is not governed by the immanent laws of Aristotelian logical reasoning, but by affectivity—by the vagrant flow of emotion and the dialectical principles of "mystical participation" and "mystical exclusion."

The two most effective antagonists of Lévy-Bruhl's theories concerning primitive religion were Radin and Malinowski. Radin, influenced by Boas's more general attacks on theories of "primitive mentality," sought to demonstrate that primitive religious thought reaches, on occasion, very high levels of logical articulation and philosophical sophistication and that tribal society contains, alongside the common run of unreflective doers ("men of action"), contemplative intellectuals ("men of thought") of boldness, subtlety, and originality. Malinowski attacked the problem on an even broader front. Using his ethnographic knowledge of the Trobriand Islanders, Malinowski argued that alongside their religious and magical notions (which he, too, regarded as mainly emotionally determined) the "savages" also had a rather well-developed and, as far as it went, accurate empirical knowledge of gardening, navigation, housebuilding, canoe construction, and other useful arts. He further claimed that they were absolutely clear as to the distinction between these two sorts of reasoning, between mystical-magical and empirical-pragmatic thinking, and never confused them in actual practice. Of these two arguments, the former seems to be today nearly universally accepted and was perhaps never in fact really questioned. But with respect to the latter, serious doubts have arisen concerning whether the lines between "science," "magic," and "religion" are as simple and clear-cut in the minds of tribal peoples (or any peoples) as Malinowski, never one for shaded judgments, portrayed them. Nevertheless, between them, Radin and Malinowski rather definitively demolished the notion of a radical qualitative gap between the thought processes of primitive and civilized men. Indeed, toward the end of his life even Lévy-Bruhl admitted that his arguments had been badly cast and might better have been phrased in terms of different modes of thinking common to all men. (In fact, Freud, with his contrast between primary and secondary thinking processes, had already made this distinction.)

Thus, the debate about what does or does not go on in the heads of savages exhausted itself in generalities, and recent writers have turned to a concern with the symbolic forms, the conceptual resources, in terms of which primitives (and nonprimitives) think. The major figure in this work has been Claude Lévi-Strauss, although this line of attack dates back to Durkheim and Mauss's influential 1903 essay in sociological Kantianism, *Primitive Classification*. The writings of E. E. Evans-Pritchard on Zande witchcraft, Benjamin Whorf on Hopi semantics, and Gregory Bateson on Iatmul ritual and, among nonanthropologists, works by Granet, Cassirer, and Piaget have directed attention to the study of symbolic formulation.

Symbolic Systems

Lévi-Strauss, whose rather highly wrought work is still very much in progress, is concerned with the systems of classification, the "homemade" taxonomies, employed by tribal peoples to order the objects and events of their world (see Lévi-Strauss 1958; 1962). In this, he follows in the footsteps of Durkheim and Mauss. But rather than looking, as they did, to social forms for the origins and explanations of such categorical systems, he looks to the symbolic structures in terms of which they are formulated, expressed, and applied. Myth and, in a slightly different way, rite are systems of signs that fix and organize abstract conceptual relationships in terms of concrete images and thus make speculative thought possible. They permit the construction of a "science of the concrete"—the intellectual comprehension of the sensible world in terms of sensible phenomena—which is no less rational, no less logical, no more affect-driven than the abstract science of the modern world. The objects rendered sacred are selected not because of their utilitarian qualities, nor because they are projections of repressed emotions, nor yet because they reflect the moral force of social organization ritualistically impressed upon the mind. Rather, they are selected because they permit the embodiment of general ideas in terms of the immediately perceptible realities—the turtles, trees, springs, and caves—of everyday experience; not, as Lévi-Strauss says, apropos of Radcliffe-Brown's view of totems, because they are "good to eat," but because they are "good to think."

This "goodness" exists inherently in sacred objects because they provide the raw materials for analogical reasoning. The relationships perceived among certain classes of natural objects or events can be analogized, taken as models of relationships—physical, social, psychological, or moral—obtaining between persons, groups, or other natural objects and events. Thus, for example, the natural distinctions perceived among totemic beings, their species differentiation, can serve as a conceptual framework for the comprehension, expression, and communication of social distinctions among exogamous clans—their structural differentiation. Thus, the sharp contrast between the wet and dry seasons (and the radical zoological and botanical changes associated with it) in certain regions of Australia is employed in the mythology of the native peoples. They have woven an elaborate origin myth around this natural phenomenon, one that involves a rainmaking python who drowned some incestuous sisters and their children because the women polluted his water hole with menstrual blood. This model expresses and economizes the contrasts between moral purity and impurity, maleness and femaleness, social superiority and inferiority, fertilizing agent (rain) and that which is fertilized (land), and even the distinction between "high" (initiate) and "low" (noninitiate) levels of cultural achievement.

Lévi-Strauss contends that primitive religious systems are, like all symbolic systems, fundamentally communications systems. They are carriers of information in the technical Shannon-Weaver sense, and as such, the theory of information can be applied to them with the same validity as when applied to any physical systems, mechanical or biological, in which the transfer of information plays a central regulative role. Primitives, as all men, are quintessentially multichanneled emitters and receivers of messages. It is merely in the nature of the code they employ—one resting on analogies between "natural" and "cultural" distinctions and relationships—that they differ from ourselves. Where there is a distinguishing difference, it lies in the technically specialized codes of modern abstract thought, in which semantic properties are radically and deliberately severed from physical ones. Religion, primitive or modern, can be understood only as an integrated system of thought, logically sound, epistemologically valid, and as flourishing in France as in Tahiti.

It is far too early to evaluate Lévi-Strauss's work with any assurance. It is frankly incomplete and explorative, and some parts of it (the celebration of information theory, for example) are wholly programmatic. But in focusing on symbol systems as conceptual models of social or other sorts of reality, he has clearly introduced into the anthropology of religion a line of inquiry which, having already become common in modern thought generally, can hardly fail to be productive when applied to tribal myth and ritual.

Whether his own particular formulation of this approach will prove to be the most enduring remains, however, rather more of a question. His rejection of emotional considerations and his neglect of normative or social factors in favor of an extreme intellectualism which cerebralizes religion and tends to reduce it yet again to a kind of undeveloped (or, as he puts it, "undomesticated") science are questionable. His nearly exclusive stress on those intellectual processes involved in classification, i.e., on taxonomic modes of thought (a reflex of his equally great reliance on totemic ideas as type cases of primitive beliefs), at the expense of other, perhaps more common, and certainly more powerful styles of reasoning, is also doubtful. His conception of the critical process of symbolic formulation itself remains almost entirely undeveloped—hardly more than a sort of associationism dressed up with some concepts from modern linguistics. Partly as a result of this weakness and partly as a result of a tendency to consider symbol systems as entities functioning independently of the contextual factor, many of his specific interpretations of particular myths and rites seem as strained, arbitrary, and oversystematized as those of the most undisciplined psychoanalyst.

But, for all this, Lévi-Strauss has without doubt opened a vast territory for research and begun to explore it with theoretical brilliance and profound scholarship. And he is not alone. As the recent work of such diverse students as Evans-Pritchard, R. G. Lienhardt, W. E. H. Stanner, Victor W. Turner, Germaine Dieterlen, Meyer Fortes, Edmund R. Leach, Charles O. Frake, Rodney Needham, and Susanne K. Langer demonstrates, the analysis of symbolic forms is becoming a major tradition in the study of primitive religion—in fact, of religion in general. Each of these writers has a somewhat different approach. But all seem to share the conviction that an attempt must be made to approach primitive religions for what they are: systems of ideas about the ultimate shape and substance of reality.

Whatever else religion does, it relates a view of the ultimate nature of reality to a set of ideas of how man is well advised, even obligated, to live. Religion tunes human actions to a view of the cosmic order and projects images of cosmic order onto the plane of human existence. In religious belief and practice a people's style of life, what Clyde Kluckhohn called their *design for living,* is rendered intellectually reasonable; it is shown to represent a way of life ideally adapted to the world "as it 'really' ('fundamentally,' 'ultimately') is." At the same time, the supposed basic structure of reality is rendered emotionally convincing because it is presented as an actual state of affairs uniquely accommodated to such a way of life and permitting it to flourish. Thus do received beliefs, essentially metaphysical, and established norms, essentially moral, confirm and support one another.

It is this mutual confirmation that religious symbols express and celebrate and that any scientific analysis of religion must somehow contrive to explain and clarify. In the development of such an analysis historical, psychological, sociological, and what has been called here semantic considerations are all necessary, but none is sufficient. A mature theory of religion will consist of an integration of them all into a conceptual system whose exact form remains to be discovered.

2

Why We Became Religious *and* The Evolution of the Spirit World

Marvin Harris

The following selection by anthropologist Marvin Harris originally appeared as two separate essays, one entitled "Why We Became Religious," the other "The Evolution of the Spirit World." In the first essay, Harris comments on the fascinating possibility of religion among nonhuman species. He also discusses the concept of mana *(an inherent force or power), noting that, although the concepts of superstition, luck, and charisma in Western cultures closely resemble* mana, *they are not really religious concepts. Rather, according to Harris, the basis of all religious thought is animism, the universal belief that we humans share the world with various extracorporeal, mostly invisible beings. Harris closes the first essay with some thoughts on the concept of an inner being—a soul—pointing out that in many cultures people believe a person may have more than one.*

In "The Evolution of the Spirit World," Harris advances the notion that spiritual beings found in modern religions are also found in the religions of prestate societies. Thus, he briefly examines religious thought and behavior pertaining to ancestor worship at varying levels of societal complexity, starting with band-and-village societies, the earliest of human cultures. Next, Harris notes the importance of recently deceased relatives in the religions of more complexly developed societies, such as those based on gardening and fishing. Chiefdoms represent an even higher level of development, one in which greater specialization arose, including a religious practitioner who paid special attention to the chief's ancestors. Finally, Harris observes that, with the development of early states and empires, dead ancestors assumed a place of great prominence alongside the gods.

Human social life cannot be understood apart from the deeply held beliefs and values that in the short run, at least, motivate and mobilize our transactions with each other and the world of nature. So let me . . . confront certain questions concerning our kind's religious beliefs and behavior.

First, are there any precedents for religion in nonhuman species? The answer is yes, only if one

accepts a definition of religion broad enough to include "superstitious" responses. Behavioral psychologists have long been familiar with the fact that animals can acquire responses that are falsely associated with rewards. For example, a pigeon is placed in a cage into which food pellets are dropped by a mechanical feeder at irregular intervals. If the reward is delivered by chance while the bird is scratching, it begins to scratch faster. If the reward is delivered while a bird happens to be flapping its wings, it keeps flapping them as if wing-flapping controls the feeder. Among humans, one can find analogous superstitions in the little rituals that baseball players engage in as they come up to bat, such as touching their caps, spitting, or rubbing their hands. None of this has any real connection with getting a hit, although constant repetition assures that every time batters get hits, they have performed the ritual. Some minor phobic behavior among humans also might be attributed to associations based on coincidental rather than contingent circumstances. I know a heart surgeon who tolerates only popular music piped into his operating room ever since he lost a patient while classical compositions were being played.

Superstition raises the issue of causality. Just how do the activities and objects that are connected in superstitious beliefs influence one another? A reasonable, if evasive, answer is to say that the causal activity or object has an inherent force or power to achieve the observed effects. Abstracted and generalized, this inherent force or power can provide the explanation for many extraordinary events and for success or failure in life's endeavors. In Melanesia, people call it *mana*. Fishhooks that catch big fish, tools that make intricate carvings, canoes that sail safely through storm, or warriors who kill many enemies, all have *mana* in concentrated quantities. In Western cultures, the concepts of luck and charisma closely resemble the idea of mana. A horseshoe possesses a concentrated power that brings good luck. A charismatic leader is one who is suffused with great powers of persuasion.

But are superstitions, mana, luck, and charisma religious concepts? I think not. Because, if we define religion as a belief in any indwelling forces and powers, we shall soon find it difficult to separate religion from physics. After all, gravity and electricity are also unseen forces that are associated with observable effects. While it is true that physicists know much more about gravity than about mana, they cannot claim to have a complete understanding of how gravity achieves its results. At the same time, couldn't one argue that superstitions, mana, luck, and charisma are also merely theories of causality involving physical forces and powers about which we happen to have incomplete understanding as yet?

True, more scientific testing has gone into the study of gravity than into the study of *mana*, but the degree of scientific testing to which a theory has been subjected cannot make the difference between

whether it is a religious or a scientific belief. If it did, then every untested or inadequately tested theory in science would be a religious belief (as well as every scientific theory that has been shown to be false during the time when scientists believed it to be true!). Some astronomers theorize that at the center of each galaxy there is a black hole. Shall we say that this is a religious belief because other astronomers reject such a theory or regard it as inadequately tested?

It is not the quality of belief that distinguishes religion from science. Rather, as Sir Edward Tylor was the first to propose, the basis of all that is distinctly religious in human thought is animism, the belief that humans share the world with a population of extraordinary, extracorporeal, and mostly invisible beings, ranging from souls and ghosts to saints and fairies, angels and cherubim, demons, jinni, devils, and gods.

Wherever people believe in the existence of one or more of these beings, that is where religion exists. Tylor claimed that animistic beliefs were to be found in every society, and a century of ethnological research has yet to turn up a single exception. The most problematic case is that of Buddhism, which Tylor's critics portrayed as a world religion that lacked belief in gods or souls. But ordinary believers outside of Buddhist monasteries never accepted the atheistic implications of Gautama's teachings. Mainstream Buddhism, even in the monasteries, quickly envisioned the Buddha as a supreme deity who had been successively reincarnated and who held sway over a pantheon of lower gods and demons. And it was as fully animistic creeds that the several varieties of Buddhism spread from India to Tibet, Southeast Asia, China, and Japan.

Why is animism universal? Tylor pondered the question at length. He reasoned that if a belief recurred again and again in virtually all times and places, it could not be a product of mere fantasy. Rather, it must have grounding in evidence and in experiences that were equally recurrent and universal. What were these experiences? Tylor pointed to dreams, trances, visions, shadows, reflections, and death. During dreams, the body stays in bed; yet another part of us gets up, talks to people, and travels to distant lands. Trances and drug-induced visions also bring vivid evidence of another self, distinct and separate from one's body. Shadows and mirror images reflected in still water point to the same conclusion, even in the full light of normal wakefulness. The concept of an inner being—a soul—makes sense of all this. It is the soul that wanders off when we sleep, that lies in the shadows, and that peers back at us from the surface of the pond. Most of all, the soul explains the mystery of death: a lifeless body is a body permanently deprived of its soul.

Incidentally, there is nothing in the concept of soul per se that constrains us to believe each person has only one. The ancient Egyptians had two, and so do many West African societies in which both patrilineal and matrilineal ancestors determine an individual's identity. The Jívaro of Ecuador have three souls. The first soul—the *mekas*—gives life to the body. The second soul—the *arutam*—has to be captured through a drug-induced visionary experience at a sacred waterfall. It confers bravery and immunity in battle to the possessor. The third soul—the *musiak*—forms inside the head of a dying warrior and attempts to avenge his death. The Dahomey say that women have three souls; men have four. Both sexes have an ancestor soul, a personal soul, and a mawn soul. The ancestor soul gives protection during life, the personal soul is accountable for what people do with their lives, the mawn soul is a bit of the creator god, Mawn, that supplies divine guidance. The exclusively male fourth soul guides men to positions of leadership in their households and lineages. But the record for plural souls seems to belong to the Fang of Gabon. They have seven: a sound inside the brain, a heart soul, a name soul, a life force soul, a body soul, a shadow soul, and a ghost soul.

Why do Westerners have only one soul? I cannot answer that. Perhaps the question is unanswerable. I accept the possibility that many details of religious beliefs and practices may arise from historically specific events and individual choices made only once and only in one culture and that have no discernible cost-benefit advantages or disadvantages. While a belief in souls does conform to the general principles of cultural selection, belief in one rather than two or more souls may not be comprehensible in terms of such principles. But let us not be too eager to declare any puzzling feature of human life forever beyond the pale of practical reason. For has it not been our experience that more research often leads to answers that were once thought unattainable?

The Evolution of the Spirit World

All varieties of spirit beings found in modern religions have their analogues or exact prototypes in the religions of prestate societies. Changes in animistic beliefs since Neolithic times involve matters of emphasis and elaboration. For example, band-and-village people widely believed in gods who lived on top of mountains or in the sky itself and who served as the models for later notions of supreme beings as well as other powerful sky gods. In Aboriginal Australia, the sky god created the earth and its natural features, showed humans how to hunt and make fire, gave people their social laws, and showed them how to make adults out of children by performing rites of initiation. The names of their quasi-supreme beings—Baiame, Daramulum, Nurunderi—could not be uttered by the uninitiated. Similarly, the Selk'-nam of Tierra del Fuego believed in "the one who is up there." The Yaruro of Venezuela spoke of a "great mother" who created the world. The Maidu of California believed in a great "slayer in the sky." Among the Semang of Malaysia, Kedah created everything, including the god who created the earth and humankind. The Andaman Islanders had Puluga whose house is the sky, and the Winnebago had "earthmaker."

Although prestate peoples occasionally prayed to these great spirits or even visited them during trances, the focus of animistic beliefs generally lay elsewhere. In fact, most of the early creator gods abstained from contact with human beings. Having created the universe, they withdraw from worldly affairs and let other lesser deities, animistic beings, and humans work out their own destinies. Ritually, the most important category of animistic beings was the ancestors of the band, village, and clan or other kinship groups whose members believed they were bonded by common descent.

People in band-and-village societies tend to have short memories concerning specific individuals who have died. Rather than honor the recent dead, or seek favors from them, egalitarian cultures often place a ban on the use of the dead person's name and try to banish or evade his or her ghost. Among the Washo, a native American foraging people who lived along the border of California and Nevada, souls of the dead were angry about being deprived of their bodies. They were dangerous and had to be avoided. So the Washo burned the dead person's hut, clothing, and other personal property and stealthily moved their camp to a place where they hoped the dead person's soul could not find them. The Dusun of North Borneo curse a dead person's soul and warn it to stay away from the village. Reluctantly, the soul gathers up belongings left at its grave site and sets off for the land of the dead.

But this distrust of the recent dead does not extend to the most ancient dead, not to the generality of ancestor spirits. In keeping with the ideology of descent, band-and-village people often memorialize and propitiate their communal ancestral spirits. Much of what is known as totemism is a form of diffuse ancestor worship. Taking the name of an animal such as kangaroo or beaver or a natural phenomenon such as clouds or rain in conformity with prevailing rules of descent, people express a communal obligation to the founders of their kinship group. Often this obligation includes rituals intended to nourish, protect, or assure the increase of the animal and natural totems and with it the health and well-being of their human counterparts. Aboriginal Australians, for example, believed that they were descended from animal ancestors who traveled around the country during the dream-time at the beginning of the world, leaving mementos of their journey strewn about before turning into people. Annually, the descendants of a particular totemic ancestor retraced the dream-time journey. As they walked from spot to spot, they sang, danced, and examined sacred stones, stored in secret hiding places along the path taken by the first kangaroo or the first witchetty grub. Returning to camp, they decorated themselves in the likeness of their totem and imitated its behavior. The Arunta witchetty-grub men, for instance, decorated themselves with strings, nose bones, rattails, and feathers, painted their bodies with the sacred design of the witchetty grub, and constructed a brush hut in the shape of the witchetty-grub chrysalis. They entered the hut and sang of the journey they had made. Then the head men came shuffling and gliding out, followed by all the rest, in imitation of adult witchetty grubs emerging from a chrysalis.

In most village societies an undifferentiated community of ancestral spirits keep a close watch on their descendants, ready to punish them if they commit incest or if they break the taboos against eating certain foods. Important endeavors—hunting, gardening,

pregnancy, warfare—need the blessings of a group's ancestors to be successful, and such blessings are usually obtained by holding feasts in the ancestors' honor according to the principle that a well-fed ancestor is a well-intentioned ancestor. Throughout highland New Guinea, for example, people believe that the ancestral spirits enjoy eating pork as much as living persons enjoy eating it. To please the ancestors, people slaughter whole herds of pigs before going to war or when celebrating important events in an individual's life such as marriage and death. But in keeping with a big-man redistributive level of political organization, no one claims that his or her ancestors merit special treatment.

Under conditions of increasing population, greater wealth to be inherited, and intrasocietal competition between different kin groups, people tend to pay more attention to specific and recently deceased relatives in order to validate claims to the inheritance of land and other resources. The Dobuans, South Pacific yam gardeners and fishermen of the Admiralty Islands, have what seems to be an incipient phase of a particularized ancestor religion. When the leader of a Dobuan household died, his children cleaned his skull, hung it from the rafters of their house, and provided it with food and drink. Addressing it as "Sir Ghost," they solicited protection against disease and misfortune, and through oracles, asked him for advice. If Sir Ghost did not cooperate, his heirs threatened to get rid of him. Actually, Sir Ghost could never win. The death of his children finally proved that he was no longer of any use. So when the grandchildren took charge, they threw Sir Ghost into the lagoon, substituting their own father's skull as the symbol of the household's new spiritual patron.

With the development of chiefdoms, ruling elites employed specialists whose job was to memorize the names of the chief's ancestors. To make sure that the remains of these dignitaries did not get thrown away like Sir Ghost's skull, paramount chiefs built elaborate tombs that preserved links between generations in a tangible form. Finally, with the emergence of states and empires, as the rulers' souls rose to take their places in the firmament alongside the high gods, their mummified mortal remains, surrounded by exquisite furniture, rare jewels, gold-encrusted chariots and other preciosities, were interred in gigantic crypts and pyramids that only a true god could have built.

3

Religious Perspectives in Anthropology

Dorothy Lee

At first glance, the study of the religion of non-Western cultures may appear somewhat esoteric, albeit interesting. In reality, however, religion is very much a part of everyday, practical activities in these cultures, and knowledge of a society's religion is essential for the successful introduction of social changes. In the following article, Dorothy Lee dramatically shows how religion is part and parcel of preliterate people's worldview, or Weltanschauung: the corpus of beliefs about the life and environment in which members of a society find themselves. Among preliterate societies, economic, political, and artistic behavior is permeated by religion. Lee points out that anthropologists make every attempt to understand the insiders' "emic" view of their universe, which they share with other members of their group, and demonstrates that an outsider's "etic" view is too limited a base of cultural knowledge on which to introduce innovations that do not violate the religious tenets of the society and meet with acceptance.

In primitive societies, we do not always find the worship of God or a god, nor the idea of the supernatural. Yet religion is always present in man's view of his place in the universe, in his relatedness to man and nonhuman nature, to reality and circumstance. His universe may include the divine or may itself be divine. And his patterned behavior often has a religious dimension, so that we find religion permeating daily life—agriculture and hunting, health measures, arts and crafts.

We do find societies where a Supreme Being is recognized; but this Being is frequently so far removed from mundane affairs, that it is not present in the consciousness of the people except on the specific occasions of ceremonial or prayer. But in these same societies, we find communion with the unperceiv-

able and unknowable in nature, with an ultimate reality, whether spirit, or power, or intensified being, or personal worth, which evokes humility, respect, courtesy or sometimes fear, on man's part. This relationship to the ultimate reality is so pervasive, that it may determine, for example, which hand a man will use in adjusting his loin cloth, or how much water he will drink at a time, or which way his head will point when he sleeps, or how he will butcher and utilize the carcass of a caribou. What anthropologists label "material culture," therefore, is never purely material. Often we would be at least as justified to call the operation involved religious.

All economic activities, such as hunting, gathering fuel, cultivating the land, storing food, assume a relatedness to the encompassing universe, and with many cultures, this is a religious relationship. In such cultures, men recognize a certain spiritual worth and dignity in the universe. They do not set out to control, or master, or exploit. Their ceremonials are often periods of intensified communion, even social affairs, in a broad sense, if the term may be

"Religious Perspectives in Anthropology" by Dorothy Lee from RELIGIOUS PERSPECTIVES IN COLLEGE TEACHING, Hoxie N. Fairchild (ed.), The Ronald Press Company, New York City, 1952, pp. 338–359.

extended to include the forces of the universe. They are not placating or bribing or even thanking; they are rather a formal period of concentrated, enjoyable association. In their relationships with nature, the people may see themselves as the offspring of a cherishing mother, or the guests of a generous hostess, or as members of a democratic society which proceeds on the principle of consent. So, when the Baiga in India were urged to change over to the use of an iron plow, they replied with horror that they could not tear the flesh of their mother with knives. And American Indians have hunted many animals with the consent of the generic essence of these—of which the particular animal was the carnal manifestation—only after establishing a relationship or reciprocity; with man furnishing the ceremonial, and Buffalo or Salmon or Caribou making a gift of the countless manifestations of his flesh.

The great care with which so many of the Indian groups utilized every portion of the carcass of a hunted animal, was an expression, not of economic thrift, but of courtesy and respect; in fact, an aspect of the religious relationship to the slain. The Wintu Indians of California, who lived on land so wooded that it was difficult to find clear land for putting up a group of houses, nevertheless used only dead wood for fuel, out of respect for nature. An old Wintu woman, speaking in prophetic vein, expressed this: "The White people never cared for land or deer or bear. When we Indians kill meat, we eat it all up. When we dig roots we make little holes. When we build houses, we make little holes. When we burn grass for grasshoppers, we don't ruin things. We shake down acorns and pinenuts. We don't chop down the trees. We only use dead wood. But the White people plow up the ground, pull up the trees, kill everything. The tree says, 'Don't. I am sore. Don't hurt me.' But they chop it down and cut it up. The spirit of the land hates them. They blast out trees and stir it up to its depths. They saw up the trees. That hurts them. The Indians never hurt anything, but the White people destroy all. They blast rocks and scatter them on the ground. The rock says, 'Don't! You are hurting me.' But the White people pay no attention. When the Indians use rocks, they take little round ones for their cooking. . . . How can the spirit of the earth like the White man? . . . Everywhere the White man has touched it, it is sore."

Here we find people who do not so much *seek* communion with environing nature as *find themselves* in communion with it. In many of these societies, not even mysticism is to be found, in our sense of the word. For us, mysticism presupposes a prior separation of man from nature; and communion is achieved through loss of self and subsequent merging with that which is beyond; but for many cultures, there is no such distinct separation between self and other, which must be overcome. Here, man is *in* nature already, and we cannot speak properly of man *and* nature.

Take the Kaingang, for example, who chops out a wild beehive. He explains his act to the bees, as he would to a person whom he considered his coordinate. "Bee, produce! I chopped you out to make beer of you! Yukui's wife died, and I am making beer of you so that I can cut his hair." Or he may go up to a hive and say simply, "Bee, it is I." And the Arapesh of New Guinea, going to his yam garden, will first introduce to the spirit of the land, the brother-in-law whom he has brought along to help him with the gardening. This is not achieved communication, brought about for definite ends. It implies an already present relatedness with the ultimate reality, with that which is accepted in faith, and which exists irrespective of man's cognition or perception or logic. If we were to abstract, out of this situation, merely the food getting or the operational techniques, we would be misrepresenting the reality.

The same present relatedness is to be found in some societies where the deity is more specifically defined. The Tikopia, in the Solomon Islands Protectorate, sit and eat their meals with their dead under the floor, and hand food and drink to them; the dead are all somewhat divine, progressively so as they come nearer to the original, fully divine ancestor of the clan. Whatever their degree of divinity, the Tikopia is at home with them; he is aware of their vague presence, though he requires the services of a medium whenever he wants to make this presence definite.

Firth describes an occasion when a chief, having instructed a medium to invite his dead nephew to come and chew betel with him, found himself occupied with something else when the dead arrived, and so asked the medium to tell the spirit—a minor deity—to chew betel by himself. At another time, during an important ceremonial, when this chief was receiving on his forehead the vertical stripe which was the symbol that he was now the incarnation of the highest god, he jokingly jerked his head aside, so that the stripe, the insignium of the presence of the god, went crooked. These are the acts of a man who feels accepted by his gods, and is at one with them. And, in fact, the Tikopia appear to live in a continuum which includes nature and the divine without defining bounds; where communion is present, not achieved; where merging is a matter of being, not of becoming.

In these societies, where religion is an everpresent dimension of experience, it is doubtful that religion as such is given a name; Kluckhohn reports that the Navaho have no such word, but most ethnographers never thought to inquire. Many of these cultures, however, recognized and named the spiritual ingredient or attribute, the special quality of the wonderful, the very, the beyondness, in nature. This was sometimes considered personal, sometimes not. We have from the American Indians terms such as *manitou*, or *wakan*, or *yapaitu*, often translated as power; and we have the well-known Melanesian term *mana*. But this is what they reach through faith, the other end of the relationship; the relationship itself is unnamed. Apparently, to behave and think religiously, is to behave and think. To describe a way of life in its totality is to describe a religious way of life.

When we speak of agricultural taboos and rites, therefore, we often introduce an analytical factor which violates the fact. For example, when preparing seed for planting, one of the several things a Navaho traditionally does is to mix ground "mirage stone" with the seed. And in the process of storing corn, a double-eared stalk is laid at the bottom of the storage pit. In actual life, these acts are a continuous part of a total activity.

The distinction between the religious and the secular elements may even separate an act from the manner of performance, a verb from its adverb. The direction in which a man is facing when performing a secular act, or the number of times he shakes his hand when spattering water, often have their religious implications. When the Navaho planted his corn sunwise, his act reflected a total world view, and it would be nonsense for us to separate the planting itself from the direction of the planting.

Those of us who present religion as separate from "everyday" living, reflect moreover the distinctions of a culture which will identify six days with the secular in life and only the seventh with religion. In many primitive societies, religion is rarely absent from the details of everyday living, and the ceremonials represent a formalization and intensification of an everpresent attitude. We have societies such as that of the Hopi of Arizona, where ceremonials, and the preparation for them, cover most of the year. Some years ago, Crowwing, a Hopi, kept a journal for the period of a year, putting down all events of ceremonial import. Day after day, there are entries containing some casual reference to a religious activity, or describing a ritual, or the preparation for a ceremonial. After a few weeks of such entries, we come to a sequence of four days' entries which are devoted to a description of a ball game played by two opposing groups of children and enjoyed by a large number of spectators. But, in the end, this also turns out to have been ceremonial in nature, helping the corn to grow.

Among many groups, agriculture is an expression of man's religious relatedness to the universe. As Robert Redfield and W. Lloyd Warner have written: "The agriculture of the Maya Indians of southeastern Yucatan is not simply a way of securing food. It is also a way of worshipping the gods. Before a man plants, he builds an altar in the field and prays there. He must not speak boisterously in the cornfield; it is a sort of temple. The cornfield is planted as an incident in a perpetual sacred contract between supernatural beings and men. By this agreement, the supernaturals yield part of what is theirs—the riches of the natural environment—to men. In exchange, men are pious and perform the traditional ceremonies in which offerings are made to the supernaturals. . . . The world is seen as inhabited by the supernaturals; each has his appropriate place in the woods, the sky, or the wells from which the water is drawn. The village is seen as a reflection of the quadrilateral pattern of the cosmos; the cornfield too is oriented, laid out east, west, north, and south, with reference to the supernaturals that watch over the cardinal points; and the table altars erected for the ceremonies again remind the individual of this pattern. The stories that are told at the time when men wait to perform the ceremony before the planting of the corn or that children hear as they grow up are largely stories which explain and further sanction the traditional way of life."

Art also is often so permeated with religion that sometimes, as among the Navaho, what we classify as art is actually religion. To understand the rhythm of their chants, the "plot" of their tales, the making of their sand paintings, we have to understand Navaho religion: the concept of harmony between man and the universe as basic to health and well being; the concept of continuity, the religious significance of the groups of four, the door of contact opened through the fifth repetition, the need to have no completely enclosing frame around any of their works so that continuity can be maintained and the evil inside can have an opening through which to leave.

The sand paintings are no more art than they are ritual, myth, medical practice or religious belief. They are created as an integral aspect of a ceremonial which brings into harmony with the universal order one who finds himself in discord with it; or which intensifies and ensures the continuation of a harmony which is already present. Every line and shape and color, every interrelationship of form, is the visible manifestation of myth, ritual and religious belief. The making of the painting is accompanied with a series of sacred songs sung over a sick person, or over someone who, though healed of sickness by emergency measures has yet to be brought back into the universal harmony; or in enhancing and giving emphasis to the present harmony. What we would call purely medical practices may or may not be part of all this. When the ceremonial is over, the painting is over too; it is destroyed; it has fulfilled its function.

This is true also of the art of the neighboring Hopi; where the outstanding form of art is the drama. In this we find wonderfully humorous clowning, involving careful planning and preparation, creation of magnificent masks and costumes, rehearsals, organization. Everyone comes to see and responds with uproarious hilarity. But this is not mere art. It is an important way of helping nature in her work of growing the corn. Even the laughter of the audience helps in this.

More than dramatic rehearsal and creation of costumes has gone into the preparation. The actors have prepared themselves as whole persons. They have refrained from sexual activity, and from anything involving conflict. They have had good thoughts only.

They have refrained from anger, worry and grief. Their preparations as well as their performance have had a religious dimension. Their drama is one act in the great process of the cyclical growing of corn, a divinity indispensable to man's well being, and to whose well being man is indispensable. Corn wants to grow, but cannot do so without the cooperation of the rest of nature and of man's acts and thoughts and will. And, to be happy, corn must be danced by man and participate in his ceremonials. To leave the religious dimension out of all this, and to speak of Hopi drama as merely a form of art, would be to present a fallacious picture. Art and agriculture and religion are part of the same totality for the Hopi.

In our own culture, an activity is considered to be economic when it deals with effective utilization or exploitation of resources. But this definition cannot be used when speaking of Hopi economics. To begin with, it assumes an aggressive attitude toward the environment. It describes the situation of the homesteader in Alaska, for example, who works against tremendous odds clearing land for a dairy farm, against the inexorable pressure of time, against hostile elements. By his sweat, and through ingenuity and know-how and the use of brutally effective tools, he tames nature; he subjugates the land and exploits its resources to the utmost.

The Hopi Talayesua, however, describing his work on the land, does not see himself in opposition to it. He works *with* the elements, not *against* them. He helps the corn to grow; he cooperates with the thunderstorm and the pollen and the sun. He is in harmony with the elements, not in conflict; and he does not set out to conquer an opponent. He depends on the corn, but this is part of a mutual interdependence; it is not exploitation. The corn depends on him too. It cannot grow without his help; it finds life dull and lonely without his company and his ceremonials. So it gives its body for his food gladly, and enjoys living with him in his granary. The Hopi has a personal relationship with it. He treats it with respect, and houses it with the care and courtesy accorded to an honored guest. Is this economics?

In a work on Hopi economics we are given an account of the Hopi Salt Journey, under the heading, "Secondary Economic Activities." This expedition is also described in a Hopi autobiography, and here we discover that only those men who have achieved a certain degree of experience in the Hopi way, can go on this journey, and then, only if their minds are pure and they are in a state of harmony with the universe. There is a period of religious preparation, followed by the long and perilous journey which is attended by a number of rituals along the way. Old men, lowering themselves from the overhanging ledge onto the salt deposits, tremble with fear, knowing that they may be unable to make the ascent. The occasion is solemnly religious. This is no utilization of resources, in the eyes of the Hopi who makes the journey. He goes to help the growing corn; the Salt Journey brings needed rain. Twelve adult men will spend days and court dangers to procure salt which they can buy for two dollars from the itinerant peddler. By our own economic standards, this is not an efficient use of human resources. But Hopi ends transcend our economic categories and our standards of efficiency are irrelevant to them.

In many societies, land tenure, or the transference of land, operations involved in hunting and agriculture, are often a part of a religious way of life. In our own culture, man conceives of his relationship to his physical environment, and even sometimes his human environment, as mechanistic and manipulative; in other cultures, we often find what Ruth Benedict has called the animistic attitude toward nature and man, underlying practices which are often classified miscellaneously together in ethnographics, under the heading of superstitions or taboos. The courteous speech to the bear about to be killed, the offering to the deer world before the hunter sets out, the introduction of the brother-in-law to the garden spirit, or the sacrifice to the rice field about to be sold, the refraining from intercourse, or from the eating of meat or from touching food with the hand, are expressive of such an attitude. They are the practices we find in a democratic society where there is consideration for the rights of everyone as opposed to the brutal efficiency of the dictator who feels free to exploit, considering the rights of none. They reflect the attitude of people who believe in conference and consent, not in coercion; of people who generally find personality or mana in nature and man, sometimes more, sometimes less. In this framework, taboo and superstitious act mean that man acts and refrains from acting in the name of a wider democracy which includes nature and the divine.

With such a conception of man's place in nature, what is for us land tenure, or ownership, or rights of use and disposal, is for other societies an intimate belongingness. So the Arapesh conceive of themselves as belonging to the land, in the way that flora and fauna belong to it. They cultivate the land by the grace of the immanent spirits, but they cannot dispose of it and cannot conceive of doing so.

This feeling of affinity between society and land is widespread and appears in various forms and varying degrees of intensity, and it is not found only among sedentary peoples. We have Australian tribes where the very spirit of the men is believed to reside in the land, where a bush or a rock or a peculiar formation is the present incarnation of myth, and contains security and religious value; where a social class, a structured group of relatives, will contain in addition to human beings, an animal and a feature of the landscape. Here, when a man moves away from the land of his group, he leaves the vital part of himself behind. When a magistrate put people from such societies in jail in a distant city, he had no idea of the terrifying severity of the punishment he was meting; he was cutting the tribesman off from the very source of his life and of his self, from the past, and the future which were incorporated and present in his land.

In the technology of such societies we are again dealing with material where the religious and secular are not distinct from each other. We have, for example, the description which Raymond Firth gives of the replacing of a wornout wash strake on a canoe, among the Tikopia. This operation is expertly and coherently carried out, with secular and religious acts performed without distinction in continuous succession or concurrently. A tree is cut down for the new wash strake, a libation is poured out to the deities of the canoe to announce this new timber, and a kava rite is performed to persuade the deities to step out of the canoe and on to a piece of bark cloth, where they can live undisturbed, while the canoe is being tampered with. Then comes the unlashing of the old wash strake, the expert examination of the body of the canoe in search of lurking defects, the discovery of signs indicating the work of a borer, the cutting of the body of the canoe with a swift stroke to discover whether the borer is there, accompanied by an appeal to the deities of the canoe by the expert, to witness what he is doing, and the necessity for doing it.

Now a kinsman of the original builder of the canoe, now dead and a tutelary deity, spontaneously drops his head on to the side of the canoe and wails over the wounding of the body of the canoe. The borer is discovered, in the meantime, to be still there; but only a specially consecrated adze can deal with him successfully. The adze is sent for, dedicated anew to the deity, invoked, and finally wielded with success by the expert.

All this is performed with remarkable expedition and economy of motion yet the Tikopia workers are not interested in saving time; they are concerned neither with time limits not with speed in itself. Their concern is with the dispossessed deities whose home must be made ready against their return; and the speed of their work is incidental to this religious concern. The end result is efficiency; but unlike our own efficiency, this is not rooted in the effort to utilize and exploit material and time resources to the utmost; it is rooted in that profound religious feeling which also gives rise to the time-consuming rites and the wailing procedures which, from the purely economic point of view, are wasteful and interfering.

The world view of a particular society includes that society's conception of man's own relation to the universe, human and non-human, organic and inorganic, secular and divine, to use our own dualisms. It expresses man's view of his own role in the maintenance of life, and of the forces of nature. His attitude toward responsibility and initiative is inextricable from his conception of nature as deity-controlled, man-controlled, regulated through a balanced cooperation between god and man, or perhaps maintained through some eternal homeostasis, independent of man and perhaps of any deity. The way a man acts, his feeling of guilt and achievement, and his very personality, are affected by the way he envisions his place within the universe.

For example, there are the Tiv of Southern Nigeria who as described by one of them in the thirties, people the universe with potentially hostile and harmful powers, the *akombo*. Man's function in the maintenance of his own life and the moderate well-being of the land and of his social unit, is to prevent the manifestation of *akombo* evil, through performing rites and observing taboos. So his rites render safe through preventing, through expulsion and purging. His role is negative, defending the normal course against the interference. Vis-à-vis the universe, his

acts arise out of negative motives. Thus what corresponds to a gift of first fruits to a deity in other cultures is phrased as a rite for preventing the deities from making a man's food go bad or diminish too quickly; fertility rites for a field are actually rites preventing the evil-intentioned from robbing the fields of their normal fertility.

In the writings of R. F. Barton, who studied the Ifugao of Luzon in the early part of this century, these people also appear to see deities as ready to interfere and bring evil; but their conception of man's role within the structure of the universe is a different one from that of the Tiv. In Barton's descriptive accounts, the Ifugao either accept what comes as deity-given, or act without being themselves the agents; they believe that no act can come to a conclusive end without the agency of a specific deity. They have a specific deity often for every step within an operation and for every part of the implement to be used. R. F. Barton recorded the names of 1,240 deities and believed that even so he had not exhausted the list.

The Ifugao associate a deity with every structured performance and at least a large number of their deliberate acts. They cannot go hunting, for example, without enlisting the aid of the deity of each step of the chase, to render each effective, or to nullify any lurking dangers. There is a deity for the level spot where "the hunter stands watching and listening to the dogs"; one for when the dogs "are sicced on the game"; one for when "the hunter leans on his spear transfixing the quarry"; twelve are listed as the deities of specific ways of rendering harmless to the hunter's feet the snags and fangs of snakes which he encounters. If he is to be successful in the hunt, a man does not ask the blessing of a deity. He pays all the particular deities of every specific spot and act, getting them to transitivize each act individually.

Even so, in most cases an Ifugao remains nonagentive, since the function of many of the deities is to save man from encounter, rather than to give him success in his dealing with it. For example, in the area of interpersonal relations, we have Tupya who is invoked so that, "the creditor comes for dun for what is owed, but on the way he forgets and goes about other business"; and Dulaiya, who is invoked so that "the enemies just don't think about us, so they don't attack." His tools, also, are ineffective of themselves; so that, when setting a deadfall, he invokes and bribes such deities as that for the Flat Stone of the Deadfall, the Main Posts of the Deadfall, the Fall of the Deadfall, the Trigger of the Deadfall. Most of the Ifugao economy is involved in providing sacrifices to the deities, big or little according to the magnitude of the operation and the importance of the deities. There is no warmth in the sacrifices; no expression of gratitude or appeal or belongingness. As the Ifugaos see it, the sacrifice is a bribe. With such bribes, they buy the miraculous intervention and transitivization which are essential for achievement, health, and good personal relations.

The Ifugao show no humility in the face of this ineffective role in the universe; they merely accept it as the state of things. They accept their own failures, the frequent deaths, the sudden and disastrous flaring up of tempers, as things that are bound to happen irrespective of their own desires and efforts. But they are neither passive nor helpless. They carry on great undertakings, and, even now they go on forbidden head hunts. They know when and how and whom to bribe so as to perfect their defective acts. When however, a deity states a decision, they accept it as immutable. A Catholic priest tells a story about the neighboring Iloko which illustrates this acceptance. A Christian Iloko was on his deathbed, and the priest, trying to persuade him to repent of his sin, painted to him vividly the horrors of hell; but the dying man merely answered, "If God wants me to go to hell, I am perfectly willing."

Among the Wintu Indians of California we find that man sees himself as effective but in a clearly limited way. An examination of the myths of the Wintu shows that the individual was conceived as having a limited agentive role, shaping, using, intervening, actualizing and temporalizing the given, but never creating; that man was viewed as needing skill for his operations, but that specific skill was useless without "luck" which a man received through communion and pleading with some universal power.

It is to this limited role of man, geared to the working of the universe, that I referred when I spoke earlier of Hopi drama and agriculture. Without an understanding of this role, no Hopi activity or attitude or relationship can be understood. The Hopi have developed the idea of man's limited effectiveness in their own fashion, and have elaborated it systematically in what they call the "Hopi Way." Laura Thompson says of the Hopi, "All phenomena relevant to the life of the tribe—including man, the animals, and plants, the earth, sun, moon, clouds, the ancestors, and the spirits—are believed to be interdependent. . . . In this system each individual—human and non-human—is believed to have . . . a definite role in the universal order." Traditionally, fulfillment of the law of nature—the growth of the corn, the movements of the sun—can come only with man's participation, only with man's performance of the established ceremonials. Here man was effective, but only in cooperation with the rest of the phenomena of nature.

The Indians of the Plains, such as the Crow and the Sioux, have given a somewhat different form to this conception of man's circumscribed agency. The aggressive behavior for which they have been known, their great personal autonomy, their self-assurance and assertiveness and in recent years, their great dependence and apathy, have been explained as an expression of this conception. These societies envisioned the universe as pervaded by an undifferentiated religious force on which they were dependent for success in their undertakings and in life generally. The specific formulation differed in the different tribes, but, essentially, in all it was believed that each individual and particularly each man, must tap this universal force if his undertakings were to be successful. Without this "power" a man could not achieve success in any of the valued activities, whether warfare or the hunt; and no leadership was possible without this power. This was a force enhancing and intensifying the being of the man who acted; it was not, as with the Ifugao, an effectiveness applied to specific details of activities. The individual himself prepared himself in the hardihood, self-control, skills and areas of knowledge necessary. Little boys of five or seven took pride in their ability to withstand pain, physical hardship, and the terrors of running errands alone in the night. The Sioux did not appeal for divine intervention; he did not want the enemy to forget to come. Yet neither was he fearless. He appealed for divine strength to overcome his own fears as well as the external enemy.

The relationship with the divine, in this case, is personal and intense. The Plains Indian Sioux did not, like the Hopi, inherit a specific relatedness when he was born in a specific clan. Each man, each preadolescent boy, had to achieve the relationship for himself. He had to go out into the wilderness and spend days and nights without food or drink, in the cold, among wild beasts, afraid and hungry and anxious, humbling himself and supplicating, sometimes inflicting excruciating pain upon himself, until some particular manifestation of the universal force took pity upon him and came to him to become his lifelong guardian and power. The appeals to the universal force were made sometimes in a group, through the institution of the Sun Dance. But here also they were individual in nature. The relationship with the divine was an inner experience; and when the Dakota Black Elk recounted his autobiography, he spoke mainly of these intense, personal religious experiences. Within this range of variation in form and concept and world view, we find expressed by all the same immediate relatedness to the divine.

4

Non-Overlapping Magisteria

Stephen Jay Gould

In this article, Stephen Jay Gould reasons that there should be no conflict between science and religion because each possesses a separate and legitimate magisterium (domain of teaching authority). Gould assigns the acronym NOMA (non-overlapping magesteria) to this principle, observing that science is interested in fact and theory, whereas religion ponders moral meaning and value. Or, as Gould observes, "We get the age of rocks, and religion retains the rock of ages; we study how the heavens go, and they determine how to go to heaven." However, he notes that the separation is not tidy because the magesteria of science and religion do not stand far apart; they "bump right up against each other, interdigitating in wondrously complex ways along their joint border," a phenomenon that makes the sorting of each domain extremely difficult. Much of this article is given to Gould's analysis of two widely differing papal announcements regarding the Catholic Church's position on evolution and the Catholic faith—one by Pope John Paul II (1996) and the other by Pope Pius XII (1950). Gould ends his provocative article by noting that the greatest strength of NOMA lies in "the prospect of respectful discourse" between the two domains. Gould died in 2002. He was the Alexander Agassiz Professor of Zoology and a professor of geology at Harvard University. The article was originally published in his book Leonardo's Mountain of Clams and the Diet of Worms. *Gould was the author of twenty books and hundreds of essays, reviews, and articles.*

Incongruous places often inspire anomalous stories. In early 1984, I spent several nights at the Vatican housed in a hotel built for itinerant priests. While pondering over such puzzling issues as the intended function of the bidet in each bathroom, and hungering for something more than plum jam on my breakfast rolls (why did the basket only contain hundreds of identical plum packets and not a one of, say, strawberry?), I encountered yet another among the innumerable issues of contrasting cultures that can make life so expansive and interesting. Our crowd (present in Rome to attend a meeting on nuclear winter, sponsored by the Pontifical Academy of Sciences)

From LEONARDO'S MOUNTAIN OF CLAMS AND THE DIET OF WORMS by Stephen Jay Gould, © 1998 by Turbo, Inc. Used by permission of Harmony Books, a division of Random House, Inc.

shared the hotel with a group of French and Italian Jesuit priests who were also professional scientists. One day at lunch, the priests called me over to their table to pose a problem that had been troubling them. What, they wanted to know, was going on in America with all this talk about "scientific creationism"? One of the priests asked me: "Is evolution really in some kind of trouble; and, if so, what could such trouble be? I have always been taught that no doctrinal conflict exists between evolution and Catholic faith, and the evidence for evolution seems both utterly satisfying and entirely overwhelming. Have I missed something?"

A lively pastiche of French, Italian, and English conversation then ensued for half an hour or so, but the priests all seemed reassured by my general answer—"Evolution has encountered no intellectual trouble; no new arguments have been offered. Creationism is a home-grown phenomenon of American sociocultural history—a splinter movement (unfortunately rather more of a beam these days) of Protestant fundamentalists who believe that every word of the Bible must be literally true, whatever such a claim might mean." We all left satisfied, but I certainly felt bemused by the anomaly of my role as a Jewish agnostic, trying to reassure a group of priests that evolution remained both true and entirely consistent with religious belief.

Another story in the same mold: I am often asked whether I ever encounter creationism as a live issue among my Harvard undergraduate students. I reply that only once, in thirty years of teaching, did I experience such an incident. A very sincere and serious freshman student came to my office with a question that had clearly been troubling him deeply. He said to me, "I am a devout Christian and have never had any reason to doubt evolution, an idea that seems both exciting and well documented. But my roommate, a proselytizing evangelical, has been insisting with enormous vigor that I cannot be both a real Christian and an evolutionist. So tell me, can a person believe both in God and in evolution?" Again, I gulped hard, did my intellectual duty, and reassured him that evolution was both true and entirely compatible with Christian belief—a position that I hold sincerely, but still an odd situation for a Jewish agnostic.

These two stories illustrate a cardinal point, frequently unrecognized but absolutely central to any understanding of the status and impact of the politically potent, fundamentalist doctrine known by its self-proclaimed oxymoron as "scientific creationism"—the claim that the Bible is literally true, that all organisms were created during six days of twenty-four hours, that the earth is only a few thousand years old, and that evolution must therefore be false. Creationism does not pit science against religion (as my opening stories indicate), for no such conflict exists. Creationism does not raise any unsettled intellectual issues about the nature of biology or the history of life. Creationism is a local and parochial movement, powerful only in the United States among Western nations, and prevalent only among the few sectors of American Protestantism that choose to read the Bible as an inerrant document, literally true in every jot and title.

I do not doubt that one could find an occasional nun who would prefer to teach creationism in her parochial school biology class, or an occasional rabbi who does the same in his yeshiva, but creationism based on biblical literalism makes little sense either to Catholics or Jews, for neither religion maintains any extensive tradition for reading the Bible as literal truth, other than illuminating literature based partly on metaphor and allegory (essential components of all good writing), and demanding interpretation for proper understanding. Most Protestant groups, of course, take the same position—the fundamentalist fringe notwithstanding.

The argument that I have just outlined by personal stories and general statements represents the standard attitude of all major Western religions (and of Western science) today. (I cannot, through ignorance, speak of Eastern religions, though I suspect that the same position would prevail in most cases.) The *lack of conflict* between science and religion arises from a *lack of overlap* between their respective domains of professional expertise—science in the empirical constitution of the universe, and religion in the search for proper ethical values and the spiritual meaning of our lives. The attainment of wisdom in a full life requires extensive attention to both domains—for a great book tells us both that the truth can make us free, and that we will live in optimal harmony with our fellows when we learn to do justly, love mercy, and walk humbly.

In the context of this "standard" position, I was enormously puzzled by a statement issued by Pope John Paul II on October 22, 1996, to the Pontifical Academy of Sciences, the same body that had sponsored my earlier trip to the Vatican. In this document, titled "Truth Cannot Contradict Truth," the Pope defended both the evidence for evolution and the consistency of the theory with Catholic religious doctrine. Newspapers throughout the world responded with front-page headlines, as in *The New York Times* for October 25: "Pope Bolsters Church's Support for Scientific View of Evolution."

Now I know about "slow news days," and I do allow that nothing else was strongly competing for headlines at that particular moment. Still, I couldn't help feeling immensely puzzled by all the attention paid to the Pope's statement (while being wryly pleased, of course, for we need all the good press we can get, especially from respected outside sources). The Catholic Church does not oppose evolution, and has no reason to do so. Why had the Pope issued such a statement at all? And why had the press responded with an orgy of worldwide front-page coverage?

I could only conclude at first, and wrongly as I soon learned, that journalists throughout the world must deeply misunderstand the relationship between science and religion, and must therefore be elevating a minor papal comment to unwarranted notice. Perhaps most people really do think that a war exists between science and religion, and that evolution cannot be squared with a belief in God. In such a context, a papal admission of evolution's legitimate status might be regarded as major news indeed—a sort of modern equivalent for a story that never happened, but would have made the biggest journalistic splash of 1640: Pope Urban VIII releases his most famous prisoner from house arrest and humbly apologizes: "Sorry, Signor Galileo . . . the sun, er, is central."

But I then discovered that such prominent coverage of papal satisfaction with evolution had not been an error of non-Catholic anglophone journalists. The Vatican itself had issued the statement as a major news release. And Italian newspapers had featured, if anything, even bigger headlines and longer stories. The conservative *Il Giornale,* for example, shouted from its masthead: "Pope Says We May Descend from Monkeys."

Clearly, I was out to lunch; something novel or surprising must lurk within the papal statement, but what could be causing all the fuss?—especially given the accuracy of my primary impression (as I later verified) that the Catholic Church values scientific study, views science as no threat to religion in general or Catholic doctrine in particular, and has long accepted both the legitimacy of evolution as a field of study and the potential harmony of evolutionary conclusions with Catholic faith.

As a former constituent of Tip O'Neill, I certainly know that "all politics is local"—and that the Vatican undoubtedly has its own internal reasons, quite opaque to me, for announcing papal support of evolution in a major statement. Still, I reasoned that I must be missing some important key, and I felt quite frustrated. I then remembered the primary rule of intellectual life: When puzzled, it never hurts to read the primary documents—a rather simple and self-evident principle that has, nonetheless, completely disappeared from large sectors of the American experience.

I knew that Pope Pius XII (not one of my favorite figures in twentieth-century history, to say the least) had made the primary statement in a 1950 encyclical entitled *Humani Generis.* I knew the main thrust of his message: Catholics could believe whatever science determined about the evolution of the human body, so long as they accepted that, at some time of his choosing, God had infused the soul into such a creature. I also knew that I had no problem with this argument—for, whatever my private beliefs about souls, science cannot touch such a subject and therefore cannot be threatened by any theological position on such a legitimately and intrinsically religious issue. Pope Pius XII, in other words, had properly acknowledged and respected the separate domains of science and theology. Thus, I found myself in total agreement with *Humani Generis*—but I had never read the document in full (not much of an impediment to stating an opinion these days).

I quickly got the relevant writings from, of all places, the Internet. (The Pope is prominently on line, but a luddite like me is not. So I got a cyberwise associate to dredge up the documents. I do love the fracture of stereotypes implied by finding religion so hep and a scientist so square.) Having now read in full both Pope Pius's *Humani Generis* of 1950 and Pope John Paul's proclamation of October 1996, I finally understand why the recent statement seems so new, revealing, and worthy of all those headlines. And the message could not be more welcome for evolutionists, and friends of both science and religion.

The text of *Humani Generis* focuses on the *Magisterium* (or Teaching Authority) of the Church—a word derived not from any concept of majesty or unquestionable awe, but from the different notion of teaching, for *magister* means "teacher" in Latin. We may, I think, adopt this word and concept to express the central point of this essay and the principled resolution of supposed "conflict" or "warfare" between science and religion. No such conflict should exist because each subject has a legitimate magisterium, or domain of teaching authority—and these magisteria do not overlap (the principle that I would like to designate as NOMA, or "non-overlapping magisteria"). The net of science covers the empirical realm: what is the universe made of (fact) and why does it work this way (theory). The net of religion extends over questions of moral meaning and value. These two magisteria do not overlap, nor do they encompass all inquiry (consider, for starters, the magisterium of art and the meaning of beauty). To cite the usual clichés, we get the age of rocks, and religion retains the rock of ages; we study how the heavens go, and they determine how to go to heaven.

This resolution might remain entirely neat and clean if the non-overlapping magisteria of science and religion stood far apart, separated by an extensive no-man's-land. But, in fact, the two magisteria bump right up against each other, interdigitating in wondrously complex ways along their joint border. Many of our deepest questions call upon aspects of both magisteria for different parts of a full answer—and the sorting of legitimate domains can become quite complex and difficult. To cite just two broad questions involving both evolutionary facts and moral arguments: Since evolution made us the only earthly creatures with advanced consciousness, what responsibilities are so entailed for our relations with other species? What do our genealogical ties with other organisms imply about the meaning of human life?

Pius XII's *Humani Generis* (1950), a highly traditionalist document written by a deeply conservative man, faces all the "isms" and cynicisms that rode the wake of World War II and informed the struggle to rebuild human decency from the ashes of the Holocaust. The encyclical bears the subtitle "concerning some false opinions which threaten to undermine the foundations of Catholic doctrine," and begins with a statement of embattlement:

> Disagreement and error among men on moral and religious matters have always been a cause of profound sorrow to all good men, but above all to the true and loyal sons of the Church, especially today, when we see the principles of Christian culture being attacked on all sides.

Pius lashes out, in turn, at various external enemies of the Church: pantheism, existentialism, dialectical materialism, historicism, and, of course and preeminently, communism. He then notes with sadness that some well-meaning folks within the Church have fallen into a dangerous relativism—"a theological pacifism and egalitarianism, in which all points of view become equally valid"—in order to include those who yearn for the embrace of Christian religion, but do not wish to accept the particularly Catholic magisterium.

Speaking as a conservative's conservative, Pius laments:

> Novelties of this kind have already borne their deadly fruit in almost all branches of theology. . . . Some question whether angels are personal beings, and whether matter and spirit differ essentially. . . . Some even say that the doctrine of Transubstantiation, based on an antiquated philosophic notion of substance, should be so modified that the Real Presence of Christ in the Holy Eucharist be reduced to a kind of symbolism.

Pius first mentions evolution to decry a misuse by overextension among zealous supporters of the anathematized "isms":

> Some imprudently and indiscreetly hold that evolution . . . explains the origin of all things. . . . Communists gladly subscribe to this opinion so that, when the souls of men have been deprived of every idea of a personal God, they may the more efficaciously defend and propagate their dialectical materialism.

Pius presents his major statement on evolution near the end of the encyclical, in paragraphs 35 through 37. He accepts the standard model of non-overlapping magisteria (NOMA) and begins by acknowledging that evolution lies in a difficult area where the domains press hard against each other. "It remains for Us now to speak about those questions which, although they pertain to the positive sciences, are nevertheless more or less connected with the truths of the Christian faith."

Pius then writes the well-known words that permit Catholics to entertain the evolution of the human body (a factual issue under the magisterium of science), so long as they accept the divine creation and infusion of the soul (a theological notion under the magisterium of religion).

> The Teaching Authority of the Church does not forbid that, in conformity with the present state of human sciences and sacred theology, research and discussions, on the part of men experienced in both fields, take place with regard to the doctrine of evolution, in as far as it inquires into the origin of the human body as coming from pre-existent and living matter—for the Catholic faith obliges us to hold that souls are immediately created by God.

I had, up to here, found nothing surprising in *Humani Generis,* and nothing to relieve my puzzlement about the novelty of Pope John Paul's recent statement. But I read further and realized that Pius had said more about evolution, something I had never seen quoted, and something that made John Paul's statement most interesting indeed. In short, Pius forcefully proclaimed that while evolution may be legitimate in principle, the theory, in fact, had not been proven and might well be entirely wrong. One gets the strong impression, moreover, that Pius was rooting pretty hard for a verdict of falsity.

Continuing directly from the last quotation, Pius advises us about the proper study of evolution:

> However, this must be done in such a way that the reasons for both opinions, that is, those favorable and those unfavorable to evolution, be weighed and judged with the necessary seriousness, moderation and measure. . . . Some, however, rashly transgress this liberty of discussion, when they act as if the origin of the human body from preexisting and living matter were already completely certain and proved by the facts which have been discovered up to now and by reasoning on those facts, and as if there were nothing in the sources of divine revelation which demands the greatest moderation and caution in this question.

To summarize, Pius generally accepts the NOMA principle of non-overlapping magisteria in permitting Catholics to entertain the hypothesis of evolution for the human body so long as they accept the divine infusion of the soul. But he then offers some (holy) fatherly advice to scientists about the status of evolution as a scientific concept: the idea is not yet proven, and you all need to be especially cautious because evolution raises many troubling issues right on the border of my magisterium. One may read this second theme in two rather different ways: either as a gratuitous incursion into a different magisterium, or as a helpful perspective from an intelligent and concerned outsider. As a man of goodwill, and in the interest of conciliation, I am content to embrace the latter reading.

In any case, this rarely quoted second claim (that evolution remains both unproven and a bit dangerous)—and not the familiar first argument for the NOMA principle (that Catholics may accept the evolution of the body so long as they embrace the creation of the soul)—defines the novelty and the interest of John Paul's recent statement.

John Paul begins by summarizing Pius's older encyclical of 1950, and particularly by reaffirming the NOMA principle—nothing new here, and no cause for extended publicity:

> In his encyclical "Humani Generis" (1950) my predecessor Pius XII had already stated that there was no opposition between evolution and the doctrine of the faith about man and his vocation.

To emphasize the power of NOMA, John Paul poses a potential problem and a sound resolution: How can we possibly reconcile science's claim for physical continuity in human evolution with Catholicism's insistence that the soul must enter at a moment of divine infusion?

> With man, then, we find ourselves in the presence of an ontological difference, an ontological leap, one could say. However, does not the posing of such ontological discontinuity run counter to that physical continuity which seems to be the main thread of research into evolution in the field of physics and chemistry? Consideration of the method used in the various branches of knowledge makes it possible to reconcile two points of view which would seem irreconcilable. The sciences of observation describe and measure the multiple manifestations of life with increasing precision and correlate them with the time line. The moment of transition to the spiritual cannot be the object of this kind of observation.

The novelty and news value of John Paul's statement lies, rather, in his profound revision of Pius's second and rarely quoted claim that evolution, while conceivable in principle and reconcilable with religion, can cite little persuasive evidence in support, and may well be false. John Paul states—and I can only say amen, and thanks for noticing—that the half century between Pius surveying the ruins of World War II and his own pontificate heralding the dawn of a new millennium has witnessed such a growth of data, and such a refinement of theory, that evolution can no longer be doubted by people of goodwill and keen intellect:

> Pius XII added . . . that this opinion [evolution] should not be adopted as though it were a certain, proven doctrine. . . . Today, almost half a century after the publication of the encyclical, new knowledge has led to the recognition of the theory

of evolution as more than a hypothesis. It is indeed remarkable that this theory has been progressively accepted by researchers, following a series of discoveries in various fields of knowledge. The convergence, neither sought nor fabricated, of the results of work that was conducted independently is in itself a significant argument in favor of the theory.

In conclusion, Pius had grudgingly admitted evolution as a legitimate hypothesis that he regarded as only tentatively supported and potentially (as he clearly hoped) untrue. John Paul, nearly fifty years later, reaffirms the legitimacy of evolution under the NOMA principle—no news here—but then adds that additional data and theory have placed the factuality of evolution beyond reasonable doubt. Sincere Christians must now accept evolution not merely as a plausible possibility, but also as an effectively proven fact. In other words, official Catholic opinion on evolution has moved from "say it ain't so, but we can deal with it if we have to" (Pius's grudging view of 1950) to John Paul's entirely welcoming "it has been proven true; we always celebrate nature's factuality, and we look forward to interesting discussions of theological implications." I happily endorse this turn of events as gospel—literally good news. I may represent the magisterium of science, but I welcome the support of a primary leader from the other major magisterium of our complex lives. And I recall the wisdom of King Solomon: "As cold waters to a thirsty soul, so is good news from a far country" (Proverbs 25:25).

Just as religion must bear the cross of its hard-liners, I have some scientific colleagues, including a few in prominent enough positions to wield influence by their writings, who view this rapprochement of the separate magisteria with dismay. To colleagues like me—agnostic scientists who welcome and celebrate the rapprochement, especially the Pope's latest statement—they say, "C'mon, be honest; you know that religion is addlepated, superstitious, old-fashioned BS. You're only making those welcoming noises because religion is so powerful, and we need to be diplomatic in order to buy public support for science." I do not think that many scientists hold this view, but such a position fills me with dismay—and I therefore end this essay with a personal statement about religion, as a testimony to what I regard as a virtual consensus among thoughtful scientists (who support the NOMA principle as firmly as the Pope does).

I am not, personally, a believer or a religious man in any sense of institutional commitment or practice. But I have great respect for religion, and the subject has always fascinated me, beyond almost all others (with a few exceptions, like evolution and paleontology). Much of this fascination lies in the stunning historical paradox that organized religion has fostered, throughout Western history, both the most unspeakable horrors and the most heartrending examples of human goodness in the face of personal danger. (The evil, I believe, lies in an occasional confluence of religion with secular power. The Catholic Church has sponsored its share of horrors, from Inquisitions to liquidations—but only because this institution held great secular power during so much of Western history. When my folks held such sway, more briefly and in Old Testament times, we committed similar atrocities with the same rationales.)

I believe, with all my heart, in a respectful, even loving, conconcordat between our magisteria—the NOMA concept. NOMA represents a principled position on moral and intellectual grounds, not a merely diplomatic solution. NOMA also cuts both ways. If religion can no longer dictate the nature of factual conclusions residing properly within the magisterium of science, then scientists cannot claim higher insight into moral truth from any superior knowledge of the world's empirical constitution. This mutual humility leads to important practical consequences in a world of such diverse passions.

Religion is too important for too many people to permit any dismissal or denigration of the comfort still sought by many folks from theology. I may, for example, privately suspect that papal insistence on divine infusion of the soul represents a sop to our fears, a device for maintaining a belief in human superiority within an evolutionary world offering no privileged position to any creature. But I also know that the subject of souls lies outside the magisterium of science. My world cannot prove or disprove such a notion, and the concept of souls cannot threaten or impact my domain. Moreover, while I cannot personally accept the Catholic view of souls, I surely honor the metaphorical value of such a concept both for grounding moral discussion, and for expressing what we most value about human potentiality: our decency, our care, and all the ethical and intellectual struggles that the evolution of consciousness imposed upon us.

As a moral position (and therefore not as a deduction from my knowledge of nature's factuality), I prefer the "cold bath" theory that nature can be truly "cruel" and "indifferent" in the utterly inappropriate terms of our ethical discourse—because nature does not exist for us, didn't know we were coming (we are, after all, interlopers of the latest geological moment), and doesn't give a damn about us (speaking metaphorically). I regard such a position as liberating, not depressing, because we then gain the capacity to conduct moral discourse—and nothing could be more important—in our own terms, free from the delusion that we might read moral truth passively from nature's factuality.

But I recognize that such a position frightens many people, and that a more spiritual view of nature retains broad appeal (acknowledging the factuality of evolution, but still seeking some intrinsic meaning in human terms, and from the magisterium of religion). I do appreciate, for example, the struggles of a man who wrote to *The New York Times* on November 3, 1996, to declare both his pain and his endorsement of John Paul's statement:

> Pope John Paul II's acceptance of evolution touches the doubt in my heart. The problem of pain and suffering in a world created by a God who is all

love and light is hard enough to bear, even if one is a creationist. But at least a creationist can say that the original creation, coming from the hand of God, was good, harmonious, innocent and gentle. What can one say about evolution, even a spiritual theory of evolution? Pain and suffering, mindless cruelty and terror are its means of creation. Evolution's engine is the grinding of predatory teeth upon the screaming, living flesh and bones of prey. . . . If evolution be true, my faith has rougher seas to sail.

I don't agree with this man, but we could have a terrific argument. I would push the "cold bath" theory; he would (presumably) advocate the theme of inherent spiritual meaning in nature, however opaque the signal. But we would both be enlightened and filled with better understanding of these deep and ultimately unanswerable issues. Here, I believe, lies the greatest strength and necessity of NOMA, the non-overlapping magisteria of science and religion. NOMA permits—indeed enjoins—the prospect of respectful discourse, of constant input from both magisteria toward the common goal of wisdom. If human beings can lay claim to anything special, we evolved as the only creatures that must ponder and talk. Pope John Paul II would surely point out to me that his magisterium has always recognized this uniqueness, for John's gospel begins by stating *in principio erat verbum*—in the beginning was the word.

5

Darwin's Rib

Robert S. Root-Bernstein

In this selection, Professor Robert Root-Bernstein, a 1981 MacArthur Fellowship winner, recounts the story of a student who told him that males have one fewer pair of ribs than females. Taken aback by her statement, it soon occurred to him that her comment was based on the biblical story of God creating Eve from one of Adam's ribs. He then notes the challenge of teaching evolution: a 1991 Gallup poll reported that 47 percent of respondents believed that God created humans within the last ten thousand years, and only 9 percent believed that humans evolved without God's direct intervention. At Root-Bernstein's university, only 20 percent of entering students possess enough knowledge about science to evaluate evolution as a valid scientific theory. Root-Bernstein believes just as firmly in religious freedom as he does in scientific research; he never insists that his students blindly accept scientific results. His teaching philosophy encourages students to be skeptical, as long as they apply logic and solid evidence to support their reasoning. Of course, complications still arise. As Root-Bernstein observes, nature evades every generalization humans—even scientists—try to impose on it. He concludes with the admonition "Take nothing for granted . . . that is what makes a scientist."

As all good teachers know, students will work much harder for extra-credit points than at the assigned task. I like to take advantage of this convenient trait in my introductory course on evolution. Once my students—nonscience majors at a midwestern land-grant university—understand the basic terms, I offer additional points for answering the questions I really want them to investigate. Find a dozen differences between the skeletons of a chimpanzee and a human being, I challenge them; tell me how a human female skeleton differs anatomically from a male.

The male and female skeletons I display are exemplary in their difference, and since most students should be able to guess what that difference is if they don't already know, I usually feel confident that the final answer is a giveaway. I say "usually" because

"Darwin's Rib" by Robert S. Root-Bernstein from DISCOVER, September 1995, pp. 38–41. Reprinted by permission of the author.

seven years ago, the first time I taught the course, I got a surprising answer that still crops up with alarming regularity. Five minutes into the lab period, a young woman announced that she could answer the question without even examining the human skeletons.

I waited silently for her to explain that the female pelvis is shaped slightly differently from the male's, with a larger opening for childbearing. That part was the giveaway. The real purpose of the exercise was to make her prove her conjecture with measurements—to translate the theory to practice. I also wanted her to explain why this sexual dimorphism—that is, this sexually determined physical difference—is not nearly so pronounced in nonhuman primates, such as chimpanzees.

She spoke: "Males have one fewer pair of ribs than females."

I was totally unprepared for her answer. My mandible dropped. After a moment's reflection, I realized she must be referring to the biblical story in which God creates Eve from one of Adam's ribs. My student was someone who believed in the literal truth of the Bible, and it was her religious belief, not her previous knowledge of human anatomy, that made her so sure of her answer. This was going to be a challenge.

I believe just as firmly in religious freedom as I do in the scientific search for understanding. Thus, while I adhere rigorously to teaching the best science and showing how scientists recognize it as the best, I never insist that students believe scientific results. On the contrary, I encourage them to be skeptical—as long as their skepticism is based on logic and evidence. Scientific results, in my view, should be compelling because the collected observations and experiments leave room for only one possible rational explanation. To insist that students accept my word (or the word of any scientist) about any fact would undermine the one thing that makes science different from all other belief systems. The acid test of science is the personal one of convincing yourself that you perceive what everyone else perceives, whatever reservations you may start with. The evidence should be so compelling that it convinces even the most serious skeptic—as long as that skeptic retains an open mind. Even more important, science must admit what it does not or cannot know. Questions are what drive science, not answers. A teacher who insists on blind faith might well crush some budding Darwin who sees a higher and more compelling truth about nature than the current dogma admits.

But in this instance, I was dealing with a pretty bare-bones case. The skeletons stood there as mute models of reality. Pedagogical ideals notwithstanding, I saw little hope of enlightening my young friend without attacking her religion outright.

I stalled for time. "Have you actually counted the ribs?" I asked. She admitted that she had not. "Well, since this is a science class," I admonished, "let's treat your statement as a hypothesis. Now you need to test it." So off she went to the back of the room, full of confidence that God would not let her down. The breather gave me a chance to plot out what I hoped would be an enlightened, and enlightening, approach to the crisis her assumption had precipitated.

I began by reviewing my lesson plans to see where I had gone wrong. After all, comparative anatomy lab exercises should be fairly straightforward stuff. The body of the work consists in finding and describing the usual anatomic features essential to understanding basic evolutionary theory. We look for homologies (body parts that spring from the same embryological parts but may have different functions, such as a whale's flipper, a human hand, and a bat's wing) and analogies (body parts that serve the same function but have very different developmental origins, such as the wings of birds and insects).

We go on to examine the evidence for transitional forms, using casts of the series of modifications that begins with the four-toed *Hyracotherium* and ends with the modern one-toed horse. The students generally get a few surprises while learning about divergent evolution—how living things become more and more different through geologic time. Imagine the ribs of a reptile broadening and fusing to become the bony back-plate of a tortoise. If you turn the skeleton over and look at the inside, you can even figure out how the shell evolved.

Convergent evolution is usually an eye-opener, too, since the notion that random mutations might lead to similar outcomes is anything but obvious. We study the point by examining a wonderful display of creatures that eat ants—spiny anteaters, silky anteaters, pangolins, and armadillos—each of which evolved from a different class of animals. Despite their disparate origins, they look generally similar: they all have the same long snouts; long, sticky tongues; and long, sharp claws for prying ants from their nests and eating them, and they all have little eyes and thick fur, spines, or scales to protect them from the bites of their tiny prey. Such examples of convergent evolution are among the best evidence for natural selection, because any animal that is going to eat ants, regardless of its anatomic origins, needs certain adaptations and will therefore end up looking similar to all the other animals that live in the same way.

Finally, we study vestigial traits—leftover parts that seem to serve no present function, such as the useless wings of flightless birds like ostriches and our apparently pointless appendix.

The students are required to understand these terms and be able to use their attendant principles to compare many amphibian, reptile, and mammalian skeletons, as well as a few fossil replicas. Was it really possible to learn all that and still think God created Eve from one of Adam's ribs?

"Are you sure those are male and female skeletons?" My cocksure friend was back, looking a little puzzled.

"They're the bona fide item," I answered. "Not only did they come so labeled from the company from which they were bought, but certain anatomic features that I have verified myself lead me to conclude that the labels are correct. But I'm glad you asked. Skepticism is a very useful scientific tool, and scientists do sometimes make mistakes. Not this time, though."

"Yes, but the skeletons have the same number of ribs," objected my student.

I agreed. "Why did you expect otherwise?" Best to get the argument out in the open. As I had guessed, her information came from the Bible, via Sunday school.

I had a sudden vision of whole classes being taught anatomic nonsense as truth. In my imagination, simple skeletons rose with a clamorous rattle to take on new lives as bones of contention. Wherever they appeared, dozens of Bible-toting students followed, egged on by ossified Sunday school teachers clustering around my desk to demand how I dare question Scripture. I knew my department chair would back me up, but the dean? The board of trustees? Weren't a few of them fundamentalists themselves? The problem was getting more difficult by the minute.

"But what does the Bible actually say?" I asked. Surely there had to be some way out of this mess.

"That God took a rib from Adam to create Eve."

"One rib or two?"

"One," she replied without hesitation.

"Don't forget that ribs come in pairs," I prompted her.

"Oh!" I could almost hear her mind whirring. "So men should be missing only one rib, not a pair—is that what you're saying?"

"I don't know." I shook my head. "Why should they be missing any?"

"Well, if God took a rib from Adam, wouldn't his children also be missing a rib?"

"All his children?" I countered. "Boys and girls?"

My young friend thought for a moment. "Oh, I see," she said. "Why should only males inherit the missing rib—why not females, too? That's a good question."

"I have a better one," I pressed on, a full plan of evolutionary enlightenment now formulated in my mind. "What kind of inheritance would this missing rib represent?"

In class we had discussed the differences between Lamarckian evolution by transmission of inherited somatic modifications and Mendelian inheritance through genes carried in the germ line of reproductive cells, but my student missed the point of my question. I explained. "Essentially, Lamarck maintained that anything that affects your body could affect your offspring. Lift weights regularly, and your daughter could inherit a bigger and stronger body than she would if you never stirred from the sofa. Chop off the tails of generation after generation of mice, and eventually you should end up with tailless mice. Make an antelope put its neck out for high-growing leaves, and its distant descendants will be giraffes.

"The problem is that generations of Jewish and Muslim males have been circumcised, without any effect on the presence or absence of the penile foreskin of later generations. Certain breeds of dogs have had their ears and tails cropped for hundreds of years without affecting the length or shape of the ears and tails of their offspring. In other words, Lamarck was wrong.

"In fact, if you recall from lectures, he couldn't have been right. Lamarckian types of inheritance aren't possible in higher animals. Remember: your egg cells are formed prior to birth and, mutations aside, contain essentially unalterable genetic information. Nothing you do to change your personal physiognomy, from lifting weights to having a nose job, will affect the genetic makeup of your offspring." As I reexplained these basic points, I realized that, lacking a problem to apply the information to, my student had not yet understood the important differences between Lamarck's and Mendel's theories. Information without a problem to which it can be applied is like a body without bones: a shapeless mass of muscle with nothing to work against. With Lamarck and Mendel in their fortuitous, Bible-generated problem context, I tried again.

"Look at it this way. Suppose you had an accident, and your right thumb had to be amputated. Would you expect all your children, assuming you have any, to be born lacking a right thumb?"

"Of course not," said my student. Then, after a pause, "Oh, I see. You mean that for the same reason my children would have thumbs even if I didn't, Adam's children would have the normal number of ribs even though God took one of his. Otherwise, it would be Lamarckian inheritance."

"Right!" I said. "And there is no creditable evidence to support Lamarckian inheritance. So you've actually got several problems here. First, Lamarckian inheritance doesn't work. Why should Adam's loss of a rib affect his children? Second, everyone has ribs, men and women alike. Ribs certainly aren't a sex-linked trait like excessive facial hair or a scrotum. So there's no reason I can think of that Adam's male offspring but not his female ones should be missing a rib. If the sons were missing a rib, wouldn't the daughters be missing one, too?

"Third, there is nothing in the Bible that says exactly how many ribs Adam started out with, or how many ribs we should have, is there? So you have no compelling reason to believe that in taking a rib from Adam, God left all his male offspring one short. That's an inference—and a particularly poor one since it relies on an outdated theory of evolutionary change. You don't really want to use a discarded evolutionary theory to prop up the Bible, do you?"

I was pleased to see that my ploy had worked. My student accepted this rebuff of accepted wisdom with good grace and an active intellect. Her religion was intact, but she was learning to think about her assumptions and to reason a bit more like a scientist. She was soon back at the human skeletons counting and measuring other bones. With some help, and a few broad hints ("How can you tell the difference between a man and a woman from behind, if they are the same height and have equal-length hair?"), she finally realized that the reason she wore a different cut of jeans from the men in the class was because she is built slightly differently. *Vive la différence!*

Most human females have a relatively wider pelvis than males because the human brain (even in a newborn) is too large to pass through a narrow birth canal. Thus, one of the reasons sexual dimorphism is so much more pronounced in humans than in most other primates is relative brain size. ("Don't trust me," I told her, "check it—the skeletons are there!") Bigger brains require bigger hips.

By the end of the course, five more students had reported to me that they too knew without having to look at the skeletons that women have more ribs than men. Some of them trotted off to count the ribs

and came back to report that they had verified their preconceived notion. I had to stand beside them and count the ribs two or three times before they would believe that there really are the same number in the two skeletons.

These days I'm better prepared than I was that first year. Sometimes I bring in an extra pair of skeletons or a medical textbook with X-ray photographs of the chest, so that the students can count ribs to their hearts' content. I've come to expect at least 10 percent of the students in each class to tell me that men and women differ in rib count. I have conducted surveys of nearly a thousand first-year college students who either are nonscience majors or have not yet declared a major. More than 25 percent report believing that God created the Earth within the last 10,000 years and that man was formed in God's image exactly as described in the Bible. Another 50 percent report being undecided as to whether evolution is a valid scientific theory or a hoax. Only about 20 percent enter my university having learned enough about science and the evidence for evolution to consider it a valid scientific theory.

My college classroom numbers follow fairly closely those reported in recent national polls. A 1991 Gallup poll, for example, found that 47 percent of the respondents believed that God created man within the last 10,000 years. Forty percent believed that man evolved over millions of years but that God had a direct hand in guiding that process. Only 9 percent said man evolved without God's direct intervention. In many communities, such as mine, there are ongoing, active attempts to exclude evolution from the public school curriculum. Lecturing on evolution is an interesting challenge under these circumstances.

But I always have the last laugh. I share it with my classes after they have counted ribs for themselves and know for themselves the correct answer. You see, I really do have one fewer pair of ribs than my mother.

Don't get me wrong: I'm perfectly normal. I have 12 pairs of ribs, just like almost every other human being, male or female. So, as far as we know, do my father and brother. My mother is the unusual one. She has 13 pairs of ribs.

Oh yes, and that 5,300-year-old man they found frozen in a glacier in the Alps a few years back? He's got only 11 pairs of ribs. It happens. Still, imagine what might happen if the creation "scientists" get hold of a replica of the 5,300-year-old man's skeleton and try to pawn it off as proof of the Bible. Or consider the havoc my mother might wreak if her bones find their way into some science class to be compared with a typical male skeleton.

I chuckle at the thought, but I also check my skeletons twice. You can never be too careful. For example, there's a condition known as polydactyly—literally, "many digits"—in which people have extra fingers or toes. In one town in Spain, there has been so much inbreeding that almost everyone has six or seven fingers on each hand. I don't want any of my students unexpectedly claiming that a significant difference between chimps and us is the number of fingers or toes.

On the other hand, I wouldn't say no to a seven-fingered skeleton with 13 pairs of ribs. What a wonderful extra-credit assignment that would make, and what a wonderful example of how nature evades every generalization we try to impose on it. Take nothing for granted, I counsel my students: that is what makes a scientist. But don't ignore the exceptions, either. I'll make no bones about it: anatomic differences are what drive evolution—and its teaching.

6

Anthropologists Versus Missionaries: The Influence of Presuppositions

Claude E. Stipe

In this article, Claude Stipe suggests that the general attitude of anthropologists toward missionaries has been negative, even though the discipline stresses the importance of objectivity. Stipe notes that, although there appears to be little "systematic indoctrination" that would lead to this negative attitude, it is evident that, early in the study of anthropology, students develop the attitude that missionaries are the enemy. However, he asks, if no systematic indoctrination occurs, how does one explain this basically negative attitude? Noting that the idea of an "objective observer," a long-held tenet in anthropology, is now generally regarded as a myth, Stipe points out that certain presuppositions influence the way we view situations. He then discusses in depth two presuppositions that he believes may result in the negative attitude of anthropologists toward missionaries: that preliterate cultures display an organic unity (that is, they are ideal societies and change produced in them by other cultures is harmful to them) and that religious beliefs are basically meaningless. Stipe also suggests another possible factor contributing to the negative attitude (as suggested by Salamone 1977: 409): that anthropologists and missionaries are actually similar, "both believing they have the truth, being protective of the people among whom they work, and opposing that which they define as evil."

Anthropologists in general have a negative attitude toward missionaries, especially when they conceive of missionaries as agents of culture change. Even though there seems to be little systematic indoctrination, early in their training anthropology students

Excerpts from Stipe CE, "Anthropologists Versus Missionaries: The Influence of Presuppositions" CURRENT ANTHROPOLOGY 21:2 (1980) pp. 165–179. Reprinted by permission of The University of Chicago Press.

learn that missionaries are to be regarded as "enemies." Powdermaker (1966) refers to discussions which she and fellow students at the London School of Economics had in 1925 about the necessity of keeping natives pure and undefiled by missionaries and civil servants. Missionaries were seen as enemies who wanted to change cultures. She comments that "now, with the sociological interest in social change and the knowledge of the significant roles played by missionaries and civil servants, our hostile attitude seems indeed biased."

Although the majority of anthropologists have probably come into contact with missionaries while doing field research, Salamone (1977: 408) has noted that the mention of missionaries in textbooks and ethnographies is "both brief and somewhat hidden in the text" and that "rarely is a straightforward hostile antimissionary statement found" (Salamone 1979: 54). According to Burridge (1978: 9), anthropologists and other academics who have contributed to the negative stereotype "would never dream of committing to paper as a considered opinion the things they actually said." My own survey of the literature has corroborated these statements. The term "missionary" does not appear in the index of many standard texts in cultural anthropology, and when missionaries are mentioned it is often in terms of their disapproving of certain cultural practices such as wife lending or gambling (cf. Richards 1977: 218, 335) or tending to destroy a society's culture and self-respect (cf. Ember and Ember 1977: 306). Examples of negative statements in ethnographies include the suggestions that the missionaries in question do poor translation work (Hogbin 1964), use force and cruelty (Jocano 1969), unsuspectingly carry diseases (Graburn 1969), interfere with native customs (Fortune 1963), and disapprove of dancing (Middleton 1970). Turnbull (1961) is very negative toward some Protestant missionaries who refused to pray for a non-Christian pygmy who had been gored but has high praise for a Catholic priest.

One textbook with an extended discussion of missionaries is Keesing's (1976) *Cultural Anthropology: A Contemporary Perspective,* which includes positive as well as negative aspects of missionary work. Keesing notes that anthropologists and missionaries (at least in stereotype) have been at odds with one another for decades: "The caricatured missionary is a strait-laced, repressed, and narrow-minded Bible thumper trying to get native women to cover their bosoms decently; the anthropologist is a bearded degenerate given to taking his clothes off and sampling wild rites" (p. 459). He decries the fact that Christianity was taken to Latin America and other areas as an instrument of conquest and subjugation and notes that in many regions the "wounds to peoples' self-conception and to the integrity of their cultures remain deep and unhealed" (p. 460). On the other hand, he recognizes the old and enduring tradition

of missionary scholarship and statesmanship, including, e.g., Sahagún, Lafitau, Codrington, and Schebesta as well as many present missionary ethnographers and linguists. Keesing concludes his treatment by stating (p. 462):

> Many Christian missionaries have devoted their lives in ways that have enriched the communities where they worked. Many, in immersing themselves in other languages and cultures, have produced important records of ways now vanishing. But more important, in valuing these old ways and seeing Christianization as a challenge to create syntheses of the old and new, the best missionaries have helped to enrich human lives and provide effective bridges to participation in a world community.

One ethnography with an extended negative evaluation of missionaries is Tonkinson's (1974) account of the Jigalong Mob in Australia. The situation is quite atypical, since the Apostolic Church missionaries are given no training for their work. They know nothing about linguistics, anthropology, desert survival, or the aboriginal culture (Tonkinson 1974: 119). Most devote two or more years to missionary work to fulfill what they consider to be a religious duty.

Chagnon (1974: 181–82) seems to show an antimissionary bias when commenting on a group of Yanomamö who had accepted the missionaries' teaching that tobacco, drugs, and polygyny were sin:

> They were going to stay there in that swamp and be fed and clothed by the people from God's village until their gardens began producing; they were going to learn to sing and be happy. . . . [They were] swatting incessantly at the mosquitos with which they had chosen to live, free from sin. They were a mere shadow of the people who had greeted me boisterously in their magnificent, airy and mosquito-free *shabono* deep in the jungle a few years earlier, a sovereign people, strong and confident.

It is instructive to compare this comment with his earlier report (1967: 24) from a jungle village that "everybody in the village is swatting vigorously at the voracious biting gnats, and here and there groups of people delouse each other's heads and eat the vermin." He also seems to evaluate the people's actions differently in these two publications. In the earlier (1967: 26–30) he describes their graded system of violence, which includes duels, club fights, spear fights, raids, and tricks (in which they have killed visitors). Despite their extreme aggressiveness, they show at least two qualities he admires: "they are kind and indulgent with children and can quickly forget personal angers" (p. 31). It seems valid to infer that Chagnon's negative response to the condition of the Yanomamö involved with missionaries is based on the fact of that involvement as well as on their actual condition. A comment by Keesing (1976: 459) seems appropriate here:

> Anthropologists who have battled missionaries through the years have often bolstered their position with a cultural relativism and romanticism about the "primitive" that seems increasingly anachronistic. The anthropologist who finds himself in defense of infanticide, head-hunting, or the segregation and subordination of women, and in opposition to missionization, can well be uncomfortable about the premises from which he argues.

If no systematic indoctrination takes place, how can the basically negative attitude of anthropologists toward missionaries be explained? It is now generally accepted that the concept of an "objective observer" who does not let personal values influence observations and conclusions is a myth. We realize that experiences shape attitudes and values, which in turn affect our evaluations. Presuppositions influence the way in which we look at situations. I suggest that two common presuppositions may contribute to the negative attitude of anthropologists toward missionaries: that primitive cultures are characterized by an organic unity and that religious beliefs are essentially meaningless.

The Organic-Unity Concept

Many anthropologists have a penchant for seeing the culture they are studying (especially if it is sufficiently primitive) as a "work of art whose beauty [lies] in the way in which the parts [are] counterbalanced and interrelated" (Richardson 1975: 523). According to the teleological assumption of functionalism, which is apparent in much of the ethnographic literature, the ideal society is in perfect equilibrium, and change, especially that produced by outside contacts, is harmful (Hughes 1978: 78).

Bennett (1946) has shown how the organic approach takes into account only certain facets of a culture. He contrasts Laura Thompson's "organic" approach with Esther Goldfrank's "repression" approach to Pueblo culture. Thompson sees the culture and society as "integrated to an unusual degree, all sectors being bound together by a consistent, harmonious set of values, which pervade and homogenize the categories of world view, ritual, art, social organization, economic activity, and social control" (Bennett 1946: 362–63). According to Thompson, such a culture develops an ideal personality type which fosters the virtues of gentleness, nonaggression, cooperation, modesty, and tranquility. She stresses the organic wholeness of preliterate life, contrasting it with the heterogeneity and diffuseness of modern civilization. On the other hand, Goldfrank characterizes Pueblo culture as marked by "considerable *covert* tension, suspicion, anxiety, hostility, fear, and ambition" (Bennett 1946: 363). Children are coerced subtly and sometimes brutally into behaving according to Pueblo norms. Authority is in the hands of the group and the chiefs, and the individual is suppressed and repressed. In contrasting the two positions, Bennett notes (p. 366) that "while the 'organic' approach tends to show a preference for homogeneous preliterate culture, the 'repressed' theory has a fairly clear bias in the direction of equalitarian democracy and non-neurotic 'free' behavior."

Since anthropologists have preached the integrity of each culture, change (unless it has been internally motivated) "has been seen as upsetting a delicate machine, a functioning organism, or an intricate symbolic or communication system—whichever metaphor we have used for organizing our ideas about society or culture" (Colson 1976: 267). Much has been written about the marginal person who is no longer at home in his or her own culture and is attempting to find a place of security in the larger social universe. We contrast the alienation we impute to such people with the contentment and emotional security we attribute to individuals in a closed community.

It is interesting that anthropologists for the most part have been reformers primarily with respect to other people in their *own* society. We are often uncomfortable with policies which endanger the customary ways of life of local communities, and when such communities are exposed to new, conflicting demands some of us even call those policies genocide or ethnocide. We seem to be saying that "options are bad for other people upon whom we do ethnography, but very good for ourselves, who use the teaching of social anthropology to free ourselves, and our peers, from constraining tradition" (Colson 1976: 267). As Lewis (1973: 584–85) has argued,

> The very qualities of primitive life which the anthropologist romanticizes and wants to see preserved are attributes which he finds unacceptable in his own culture. The personal freedom and self-determination he insists upon for himself he withholds from the "primitive" on the basis of cultural conditioning and the need for the accommodation of the individual within the community. He writes enthusiastically of the highly integrated life of the "primitive," of the lack of stress experienced when there is little freedom of choice and few alternatives from which to choose; yet he defends for himself the right to make his own decisions and his own choices.

A local point of view is often myopic, and anthropologists are no exception. We often do not realize that the seeming equilibrium of a tribe may have been largely created by the colonial situation. When one is concerned with a single society, it is often difficult to see how the populations of a given region are bound together in networks of trade, exchange, and the flow of ideas (Keesing 1976: 432). Although the present is a precipitate of history, attempts are often made to explain the present in terms of itself.

The organic view of cultures is due in part to the short time an anthropologist ordinarily spends in a given culture. Even though it may extend over several years, a single field trip encourages a description which emphasizes the homogeneity of a culture, the situation at a specific time being seen as the ideal condition (Colson 1976: 269). In too many cases the anthropologist does not observe a society long enough to see how the people grow dissatisfied with their condition and attempt to change it. What he/she may see as an ideal situation may be viewed by the people as an unsatisfactory compromise. As

Colson (1976: 264) notes:

> It is people who are the actors, attempting to adapt and use their institutions to attain their ends, always fiddling with the cultural inheritance and experimenting with its possibilities. They need to take thought of what they do. They lose sight of one end in pursuing another. Frequently they lose themselves in a dreadful muddle. There is no necessary feedback system that will automatically correct the state of affairs and return them to base one to start again having learned from their mistakes. And no shining model of an ideal society . . . is going to save them from their mistakes, though it may comfort them in their affliction. This is as true of those who live in African villages or the islands of the Pacific as it is of us in our cities and bureaucracies which we create and then decline to control. Ethnographers have usually presented each social group they study as a success story. We have no reason to believe this is true.

Although most people value their customary ways, they certainly are not reluctant to change when they anticipate that the changes will improve their situation. There is a sense, therefore, in which any given culture is always being tested, and this is no more true of our own than it is of others which are less complex.

O'Brien and Ploeg (1964: 291) discuss the fact that when a group of Dani met to plan for the burning of weapons, the throwing away of *jao*, and the abolition of in-law avoidances, no one questioned the desirability of these acts. "To account for this unanimity, one should realize that the motive underlying the movement—dissatisfaction with the original culture—applied with equal force to all Dani. Also, all concurred in thinking that the Europeans enjoyed a vastly superior way of life." The Dani appreciated the improvements in their standard of living which were due mainly to the cessation of warfare, availability of medical treatment, and improvement of the economic system. As Salamone (1976: 62) has noted, "Individuals will become converts to those religious systems which enable them to better adapt to their ecological niches."

Hippler (1974: 336) has argued that the introduction of Euro-American civilization to Alaskan native groups was more a blessing than a curse:

> It occurs to us that the introduction of modern medicine, freedom from the dangers and

uncertainties of the hunt, reduction in interpersonal violence and the like are positively accepted changes. The only Indians and Eskimos we know who wholly extoll the past are those too young to have experienced that untouched aboriginal culture. Mothers *do* prefer to have most of their children live; only fools wish to have unrestrained interpersonal violence. It is . . . very possible that much complaint about the "loss of one's culture" now expressed by young Eskimos and Indians is hyperbolic cant derived in part from a misreading or, unfortunately, a correct reading of some anthropological writings and the comments of local political ideologues.

Hippler concludes that the concept of the death of a culture, which is an analogy applied to an abstraction, may be less important in the scheme of individual human lives than many anthropologists make it seem.

Discussions of culture change often given the impression that indigenous peoples were passive spectators in the acculturation process and that missionization was a force which unilaterally impinged on passively recipient peoples. In actuality, there are usually "continuing interactions of Western and indigenous religious beliefs, structures, and institutional arrangements" (Tiffany 1978: 305; see also Lātūkefu 1978: 462).

From these examples, it is obvious that not all anthropologists take an idealistic view of the organic nature of a culture and therefore see culture change as necessarily bad for the indigenous peoples. However, one should not be surprised when those who do hold this position manifest a negative attitude toward missionaries who attempt to change cultures.

The Meaninglessness of Religious Beliefs

Although a missionary (Edwin Smith) was once president of the Royal Anthropological Institute, the majority of anthropologists are either atheistic or agnostic. According to Evans-Pritchard (1965, 1972), the early anthropological writers on religion (e.g., Tylor, Frazer, Malinowski, and Durkheim) had all had a relatively dreary religious upbringing which led to an animosity toward revealed religion. They were looking for a weapon which could be used with deadly effect against Christianity, for if they could explain away primitive religion as an intellectual aberration or by its social function they could discredit and explain away the higher religions as well (1965: 15). Evans-Pritchard concludes (1972: 205) that

> social anthropology has been the product of minds which, with very few exceptions, regarded all religion as outmoded superstition, suited no doubt to a pre-scientific age and historically justified, like classes in the eyes of Marxists, for a given period, but now useless, and even without ethical value, and worse than useless because it stood in the way of a rational regeneration of mankind and social progress.

The basic approach of social anthropologists to religion can be characterized by Radcliffe-Brown's (1952: 155) dictum that in studying religion "it is on the rites rather than the beliefs that we should first concentrate our attention." Gluckman (1962: 14–15) elaborated on this position by asserting that modern minds are bored with the intellectualist approach of the 19th-century anthropologists and that contemporary anthropologists demonstrate that rituals "are in fact to be understood in terms of the social relations which are involved in the rituals." Leach (1954: 15) maintained that the structure which is symbolized in ritual is "the system of socially approved 'proper' relations between individuals and groups."

Lawrence (1970) and Horton (1971) trace this view to 18th-century rationalistic philosophy. God had ceased to be personal for many people by the end of the 17th century, and by the end of the 18th century many had decided that they could do without God completely. When religion no longer provides a theory for how the world really works, man's encounter with God can easily be relegated to the "supreme archetypal social relationship" (Horton 1971: 96).

In at least some cases, anthropologists seem to have had a type of "conversion experience" away from Christianity. At the 1974 meeting of the American Anthropological Association in Mexico City I gave a paper on the role of religion in culture change, in which I demonstrated that in many instances one cannot explain the occurrence or the direction of culture change without understanding the religious *beliefs* of the people. In the same session was a paper in which the author argued that *all* differences between Protestants and Catholics in a Guatemalan village could be explained by socioeconomic and political factors. He was disturbed by my approach and explained that he had been a seminary student and that his "conversion" to anthropology involved the rejection of the position that religious beliefs were meaningful. He therefore resented being subjected (especially by another anthropologist) to the very position from which he had been converted.

The only published statement I have seen is Richardson's (1975: 519), in which he attributes to anthropology his liberation from Christian beliefs:

> My freedom from the things that nearly destroyed me (and that continue to haunt me) would come from studying them, and wrestling with them in order to expose their secret. At that point, just short of stomping on them and destroying them, for some reason my private battle stops. Today, I have no love for the Southern Baptists, but I can almost say "Billy Graham" without sneering.

This comment seems incompatible with his statement (p. 523) that cultural relativism is a "moral justification for being an anthropologist." It seems incongruous that a cultural relativist would sneer at *anyone's* religion. From an anthropological perspective, Lowie's statement that it is the responsibility of the fieldworker to understand the "true inwardness" of the beliefs and practices is more appropriate. Lowie asserts (1963: 533),

> . . . I have known anthropologists who accorded a benevolent understanding to the Hopi but denied it to Catholics, Mormons, Buddhists, or Mohammedans. This dichotomy of viewpoint strikes me as ridiculous and completely unscientific. I will study as many religions as I can, but I will judge none of them. I doubt if any other attitude is scientifically defensible.

Burridge (1978: 10) mentions an anthropologist who was in the habit of smoking on the premises of a missionary organization that had strict regulations against the use of tobacco or alcohol within its compound. In fact, he even urged some of the people living there to accept free gifts of cigarettes. One wonders if he would just as inconsiderately have offered pork chops to the caretaker of a mosque or eaten hot dogs in a Hindu temple.

I suspect that, in at least some instances, the antipathy of anthropologists toward missionaries lies in the fact that missionaries take seriously and teach other people religious beliefs which the anthropologists have personally rejected. It would be difficult for most people to maintain a positive (or even neutral) attitude toward a position they had personally rejected as being either invalid or meaningless. As Burridge (1978: 8) suggests,

> Somehow, whether the person was a physician, an agricultural expert, a technician, a schoolteacher—whatever—the fact that he or she was also a missionary seemed to neutralize the expertise being proffered. One was left with the impression that it was the rarely articulated "Christian" in the general label "missionary" that was the prime target of objection.

Conclusion

Although early anthropologists relied heavily on missionary publications and there have been many missionary ethnographers, the general attitude of anthropologists toward missionaries has been negative. It would be simplistic to suggest that this attitude is entirely due to the acceptance of one (or both) of the presuppositions I have discussed. However, the positions that cultures are organic wholes which should not be disturbed and that religious beliefs are essentially meaningless would certainly contribute to such an attitude. Another contributing factor that has been suggested (Salamone 1977: 409) is that anthropologists and missionaries are actually similar, both believing they have the truth, being protective of the people among whom they work, and opposing that which they define as evil. Burridge (1978: 5) argues that Malinowski's diaries display an animus toward missionaries which has overtones of an unresolved Oedipus problem: "Missionaries had fathered the work to which he was dedicating himself with typical missionary zeal—on the other side of the fence."

Since the involvement of some anthropologists with missionaries will no doubt continue, we should be concerned with the bases of the negative attitude which many of us manifest and be candid in dealing with it. An unwillingness to do so can result in a failure to control for bias in field research (cf. Salamone 1979: 57). This is especially important in areas such as Oceania, where an analysis of missionary endeavor is crucial to an understanding of the process of culture change.

Suggested Readings

Bowie, Fiona
    2006   *The Anthropology of Religion: An Introduction.* 2nd ed. Oxford: Blackwell.

deWaal Malefijt, Annemarie
    1968   *Religion and Culture:An Introduction to Anthropology of Religion.* New York: Macmillan.

Glazier, Stephen, D., ed.
    1999   *Anthropology of Religion: A Handbook.* Westport, Conn.: Praeger.

Klass, Morton, and Maxine Weisgrau, eds.
    1999   *Across the Boundaries of Belief: Contemporary Issues in the Anthropology of Religion.* Boulder, Colo.: Westview Press.

Lambek, Michael, ed.
    2002   *A Reader in the Anthropology of Religion.* Malden, Mass.: Blackwell.

Morris, Brian
    1987   *Anthropological Studies of Religion: An Introductory Text.* Cambridge: Cambridge University Press.

CHAPTER TWO

Myth, Symbolism, and Taboo

Indian mask of painted wood, northwest coast, North America.

Tales, legends, proverbs, riddles, adages, and myths make up what anthropologists call *folklore,* an important subject for the study of culture. Because of its sacred nature, myth is especially significant in the analysis of comparative religion. Fundamental to the definition of myths are the community's attitudes toward them. Myths are narratives that are held to be sacred and true; thus, they often are core parts of larger ideological systems (Oring 1986: 124). Myths are set outside of historical time, usually at the beginning of time up to the point of human creation, and they frequently account for how the world came to be in its present form. Many of the principal characters are divine or semi-divine; most are not human beings but animals or cultural heroes with human attributes. The place, time, and manner in which a myth is performed may be special, and even the language in which it is expressed may be out of the ordinary. Elliott Oring considers the familiar story of Adam and Eve as an example:

> For those who hold the story to be both sacred and true, the activities of this primordial couple, in concert with beguiling serpent and deity, explain fundamental aspects of world order: why the serpent is reviled, why a woman is ruled by her husband and suffers in childbirth, why man must toil to live—and most importantly—how sin entered the world and why man must die. (Ibid.)

To the anthropologist or folklorist, it is of no consequence whether the myth is objectively or scientifically true. What matters is its validity in its own cultural context. All of these characteristics distinguish myth from other forms of folk narrative, such as legend and folktale (Bascom 1965).

Beyond shaping worldview and explaining the origins of human existence, myths also serve as authoritative precedents that validate social norms. One of the founding figures of anthropology, Bronislaw Malinowski, described myth as a social "charter"—a model for behavior:

> [Myth] is a statement of primeval reality which lives in the institutions and pursuits of a community. It justifies by precedent the existing order and it supplies a retrospective pattern

of moral values, of sociological discriminations and burdens and of magical belief. . . . The function of myth is to strengthen tradition and to endow it with a greater value and prestige by tracing it back to a higher, better, more supernatural, and more effective reality of initial events. (1931: 640–41)

Some anthropologists apply a psychological approach to myth analysis and see myths as symbolic expressions of sibling rivalry, male-female tensions, and other themes. Others—structural anthropologists such as Claude Lévi-Strauss—view myths as cultural means of resolving critical binary oppositions (life-death, matrilineal-patrilineal, nature-culture) that serve as models for members of a society (Hunter and Whitten 1976: 280–81). Whether in Judeo-Christian and Muslim cultures, where myths have been transcribed to form the Torah, Bible, and Koran, or in other, less familiar cultures, these sacred narratives still serve their time-honored function for the bulk of humanity as the basis of religious belief. What is important to remember is that myths are considered to be truthful accounts of the past, whether transmitted orally in traditional societies or through the scriptural writings of the so-called great religions.

The scholarly study of myth has been important in the West since the time of the ancient Greeks. To Plato we owe the confusion over the meaning of the word *myth*, as he felt it was synonymous with *falsehood* or *lie.* Indeed, the use of *myth* to mean "fallacy" continues today, in clear contrast to the way anthropologists and other scholars of religion use the term. We can credit the anthropologists of the early twentieth century with drawing attention to how myth functions in actual societies, rather than regarding myths as texts from the past. Distinctive to the anthropological approach to myth is an emphasis upon culture-specific meanings. This perspective differs from that of popular myth theorist Joseph Campbell, whose compelling books and television appearances have inspired many in the United States. Influenced greatly by psychologist Carl Jung, Campbell's goal was to uncover common symbols and themes that lie beneath the mythic traditions of all the world's cultures. Today, the study of myth remains multidisciplinary, with important contributions continuing in the fields of anthropology, folklore, literary studies, psychology, and religion.

The study of symbolism, too, is vital to the study of religion. In fact, "the human beings who perform the rituals . . . , and those who are ostensibly a ritual's objects, are themselves representations of concepts and ideas, and therefore symbolic" (La Fontaine 1985: 13). Anthropology has been less than clear in its attempt to define the meaning of this important concept. Minimally, a symbol may be thought of as something that represents something else. The development of culture, for example, was dependent on human beings having the ability to assign symbolic meanings of words—to create and use a language. Religion is also a prime example of humanity's proclivity to attach symbolic meanings to a variety of behavior and objects. "The object of symbolism," according to Alfred North Whitehead, "is the enhancement of the importance of what is symbolized" (1927: 63).

That anthropological interest in the topic of symbolism had its start with the study of religious behavior is not surprising, especially in light of the plethora of symbols present in religious objects and ceremonies. Reflect for a moment on any religious service. Immediately on entering the building, be it a church, synagogue, or mosque, one is overwhelmed by symbolic objects—the Christian cross, the Star of David, paintings, statues, tapestries, and assorted ceremonial paraphernalia—each representing a religious principle. Fittingly, Clifford Geertz has noted that a religious system may be viewed as a "cluster of sacred symbols" (1957: 424). Unlike the well-defined symbols in mathematics and the physical sciences, these religious symbols assume many different forms and meanings: witness Turner's concept of the multivocalic nature of symbols (their capacity to have many meanings).

More than a simple reminder of some remote aspect of a religion's history, religious symbols are often considered to possess a power or force (*mana*) emanating from the spiritual world itself. The symbols provide people with an emotional and intellectual commitment to their particular belief system, telling them what is important to their society, collectively and individually, and helping them conform to the group's value system. Durkheim accounted for the universality of symbols by arguing that a society kept its value system through their use; that is, the symbols stood for the revered values. Without the symbols, the values and, by extension, the society's existence would be threatened.

Whereas symbols, like myths, prescribe thoughts and behaviors of people, taboos restrict actions. Because the term *taboo* (also known as *tabu* and *kapu*) originated in the Pacific Islands, beginning anthropology students often associate it with images of "savage" Polynesians observing mystical prohibitions. It is true that Pacific Islanders did cautiously regard these restrictions, being careful to avoid the supernatural retribution that was certain to follow violations. Taboos are not limited to the Pacific, however; every society has restrictions that limit behavior in one respect or another, usually in association with sex, food, rites of passage, sacred objects, and sacred people. The incest taboo is unique in that it is found in all societies. Although anthropologists have yet to explain adequately why the incest taboo exists everywhere, they have demonstrated that most taboos are reinforced by the threat of punishments meted out by supernatural forces.

As anthropologists have pointed out, taboos are adaptive human mechanisms: they function to counter dangers of both the phenomenal and ideational world. It is possible to theorize that the existence of fewer real or imagined dangers would result in fewer taboos, but it is equally safe to argue that all societies will continue to establish new taboos as new threats to existence or social stability arise. Certainly taboos function at an ecological level—for example, to preserve plants, animals, and resources of the sea. Taboos also function to distinguish between and control social groups, threatening violators with supernatural punishments as severe as the denial of salvation. Depending on the culture, sacred authority is often as compelling as the civil codes to which people are required to comply. Simply stated, the breaking of a sacred taboo, as opposed to a civil sanction, is a sin. The impersonal power of mana made certain objects and people in Pacific cultures taboo. Although the concept of mana does not exist in contemporary Western cultures, certain symbols and objects are similarly imbued with such an aura of power or sacredness that they, too, are considered taboo.

Using a variety of approaches to the study of myth, symbol, and taboo, the articles selected for this chapter clearly show the importance of these topics to the study of comparative religion. We begin with Leonard and McClure's exploration of myth, which introduces several ways of defining and studying myth in cross-cultural perspective. The authors consider the insights of key theorists in psychology, literary studies, and religious studies, as well as anthropology.

Leonard and McClure's overview is followed by examples of two contrasting approaches to myth within the field of anthropology. The excerpt by John Beattie illustrates the functionalist approach, with its attention to the close relationship between myth and social organization. "Harelips and Twins: The Splitting of a Myth" is an example of the structuralist approach of Claude Lévi-Strauss, one of the 20th century's most original scholars of myth.

In the fourth article, Raymond Firth discusses the power of symbolism and the contribution of anthropology to its understanding, drawing examples from his own extensive research in the Pacific.

In her examination of the concept of taboo, Mary Douglas defines and shows the significance of taboo in reducing ambiguity and injecting order into cultural systems, stressing commonalities in taboos, whether found in Polynesia or the West.

Mary Lee Daugherty's case study of snake-handling congregations in West Virginia, originally written in 1976, shows the integration of myth and symbol in religious practice. Daugherty argues that snake handling is a form of sacrament, a religious ceremony that symbolically expresses the relationship between believers and Christ.

References

Bascom, William
 1965 "The Forms of Folklore: Prose Narratives." *Journal of American Folklore* 78: 3–20.

Geertz, Clifford
 1957 "Ethos, World-View and the Analysis of Sacred Symbols." *Antioch Review* 17: 421–37.

Hunter, David E., and Phillip Whitten
 1976 *Encyclopaedia of Anthropology.* New York: Harper and Row.

La Fontaine, Joan S.
 1985 *Initiation.* Harmondsworth, England: Penguin Books.

Malinowski, Bronislaw
 1931 "Culture." In *Encyclopaedia of the Social Sciences,* Edwin R. A. Seligman, editor-in-chief, vol. 4, pp. 621–46. New York: The Macmillan Company.

Oring, Elliott
 1986 *Folk Groups and Folklore Genres: An Introduction.* Logan: Utah State University Press.

Whitehead, Alfred N.
 1927 *Symbolism.* New York: G. P. Putnam's Sons.

7

The Study of Mythology

Scott Leonard and Michael McClure

In this selection, authors Leonard and McClure help us understand the meaning and importance of myths. Myths, the authors tell us, are ancient narratives that help us understand such fundamental human questions as how the world came to be, how we came to be here, who we are, what our values should be, how we should behave or not behave, and what the consequences of such behavior are. They state that the meaning of myth has always been contested:

> *For two and a half millennia, debates over the importance and meaning of myth have been struggles over matters of truth, religious belief, politics, social custom, cultural identity, and history. The history of mythology is a tale told by idiots—but also by sages, religious fundamentalists and agnostic theologians, idealists and cynics, racists and fascists, philosophers and scholars. Myth has been understood as containing the secrets of God, as the cultural DNA responsible for a people's identity, as a means of reorganizing all human knowledge, and a justification for European and American efforts to colonize and police the world.*

In discussing the study of mythology, Leonard and McClure pay special attention to the 20th century, examining the various approaches to myth in such academic disciplines as anthropology, psychology, literary criticism, and the history of religions. They end the article with a look at the study of mythology today, suggesting that, despite intensive study over the years, we still have no single, all-encompassing explanation of myth.

Why Study Myths?

The study of myths—mythology—has a long, rich, and highly contested history of debate about exactly what myths *are*, what they *do*, and why they are worthy of systematic study. Because of the complexity of such considerations about myths, any short answer to the question "Why study myths?" will be, at best,

From PURPOSES AND DEFINITIONS, MYTH AND KNOWING: AN INTRODUCTION TO WORLD MYTHOLOGY by Scott Leonard and Michael McClure, pp. 1–31. Copyright © 2004. Reprinted by permission of The McGraw-Hill Companies.

only a starting place. Yet this very complexity is one of the reasons why such study can be so exciting. The study of myth is a field of inquiry that ranges from the earliest known history of humanity up to and including contemporary cultures and societies and even our own individual senses of self in the world.

Every part of this [inquiry] should serve more as a direction for further investigation than as a fully satisfactory explanation of settled facts. In our view, (1) the intertwined nature of the uses of myths in diverse cultures; (2) the myriad ways in which myths can be seen to embody cultural attitudes, values, and behaviors; and (3) the rich rewards awaiting questioners willing to approach myths from numerous points of view are all open-ended fields of inquiry. We see this [work] as an invitation to enter into these fields, whether briefly or as a lifelong interest. The study of myth entails discovering a way of making meaning that has been part of every human society.

What Are Myths?

Myths are ancient narratives that attempt to answer the enduring and fundamental human questions: How did the universe and the world come to be? How did we come to be here? Who are we? What are our proper, necessary, or inescapable roles as we relate to one another and to the world at large? What should our values be? How should we behave? How should we *not* behave? What are the consequences of behaving and not behaving in such ways?

Of course, any short definition, however carefully wrought, must oversimplify in order to be clear and short, so accept this definition as a starting point only. If this definition holds up under more extensive examination of myths across the world and in our own backyards, then what a promise with which to start a book, what an answer to the opening question, "Why study myths?"

Engaging thoughtfully with the myths in this book and with research projects that go far beyond what space constraints allow us to present in this book will deepen and complicate the elements of our starting definition. For example, myths are *ancient* narratives. But they are not static artifacts. They are not potsherds and weathered bone fragments. In many cases, they are living texts with which living people continue to write or narrate or perform their unique answers to basic human questions. This never-ending quality to myth is one reason we have included in this book not only ancient or "primary" versions of myths but also more contemporary tales, such as "Out of the Blue" by Paula Gunn Allen, which take up ancient myths and refashion their constituent elements in order to update answers to perennial questions and participate in ongoing cultural self-definitions.

Modern Native Americans, for example, who take up myths from their varied heritages and retell them do so in a context that includes the whole history of their people, from their ancient roots and primordial self-definitions to their contacts with European-American culture and modern self-definitions that

search for meaning in a world forever changed by that contact. Today's Irish poets, for another example, who use Celtic myths as source material and inspiration and who write in Irish, a language which came perilously close to extinction, are engaged in cultural reclamation on a number of levels, and Irish myths, ancient and modern, are an important part of that effort. Looking at examples of ancient and more contemporary uses of myths introduces their varied cultural values and behaviors to us, and, at the same time, such study helps us develop intellectual tools with which to look at and question our own ancient and contemporary mythic self-understandings. In this sense, studying myths introduces other cultures to us and, at the same time, provides us with different lenses through which to view our own.

. . .

. . . Toward the end of the 19th century, . . . early anthropology's view of myth emphasized function above all else. Interest in this functional approach to mythology led to the breakup of the largely bookish and tendentious study of literary myth. What emerged were various approaches toward myth driven by disciplinary concerns within anthropology, psychology, literary criticism, and the history of religions.

Mythology in the 20th Century

Early Anthropology

The Golden Bough The first of these disciplines, anthropology, came to view myth as primarily a living, oral, culture-preserving phenomenon. Led by such pioneers as Edward B. Tylor, Andrew Lang, Franz Boas, Sir James George Frazer, and Emile Durkheim, emphasis switched from textual comparisons and blood-and-soil interpretive theories to discovering the ways in which myths *function* in living societies. Sir James Frazer's *The Golden Bough* is the best-known and remains the most widely read example of the early versions of this anthropological work. *The Golden Bough*, which grew to 12 volumes, depicts the widely dispersed stories of dying and resurrecting gods as literary transformations of primitive, magical-religious rituals in which "sacred kings" were slaughtered in hopes of ensuring agricultural fertility. Frazer approached myth and culture from an evolutionary perspective, assuming, not unlike Vico, a progression from the "mute signs" of primitive magic (e.g., rituals believed to create desired effects) to the largely allegorical use of ritual in primitive religion (e.g., the substitutionary death of a "scapegoat") to the abstract symbolism of civilized religion (e.g., the doctrine of transubstantiation).

Frazer also assumed that myth was "primitive science," which attributed to the will of deities, people, or animals that which modern science attributes to the impersonal functioning of various physical laws and biological processes. While Frazer shared the new anthropological science's interests in myth's function in living cultures, he nevertheless did not completely break with comparative mythology's armchair approach.

The "Myth-and-Ritual" School Frazer's quasi-anthropological work had wide influence and inspired, at least in part, the also quasi-anthropological "myth-and-ritual" school. This relatively short-lived branch of mythological research was intensely functionalist in its approach, caring little for the origins of myth and looking at content only as a means of demonstrating the contention that myth is a script from which early religious rituals were performed. As Fontenrose puts it in the preface to *The Ritual Theory of Myth:* "Some . . . are finding myth everywhere, especially those who follow the banner of the 'myth-ritual' school—or perhaps I should say banners of the schools, since ritualists do not form a single school or follow a single doctrine. But most of them are agreed that all myths are derived from rituals and that they were in origin the spoken part of ritual performance" (1971, n.p.).

Modern Anthropology

Another of Frazer's admirers was Bronislaw Malinowski, whose fieldwork in the Trobriand Islands contributed much to the evolving methods of modern anthropology. In a 1925 lecture given in Frazer's honor, Malinowski lavishly praised the elder writer and then proceeded to outline what has been taken, until recently, as field anthropology's gospel:

> Studied alive, myth . . . is not symbolic, but a direct expression of its subject-matter; it is not an explanation in satisfaction of a scientific interest, but a narrative resurrection of a primeval reality, told in satisfaction of deep religious wants, moral cravings, social submissions, assertion, even practical requirements. Myth fulfills in primitive culture an indispensable function: it expresses, enhances, and codifies belief; it safeguards and enforces morality; it vouches for the efficiency of ritual and contains practical rules for the guidance of man. Myth is thus a vital ingredient of human civilization; it is not an idle tale, but a hard-worked active force; it is not an intellectual explanation or an artistic imagery, but a pragmatic charter of primitive faith and moral wisdom. (1926/1971, 79)

Malinowski's outline of anthropology's view of myth contains several crucial remarks. First, the anthropologist states emphatically that myth is not an "explanation in satisfaction of a scientific interest." This view contrasts sharply with the euhemerism of Frazer, Tylor, and the comparatists, who believed to one degree or another that myths are little more than primitive or mistaken science. Second, Malinowski saw myth as profoundly "true" in the sense that it had a visible role as "pragmatic charter of primitive faith and moral wisdom." He also saw myth as real in the sense that it could be observed by the field researcher in the form of oral performance, rituals, and ceremonies, and that it visibly influenced a living people's sociopolitical behavior. As his later fieldwork makes clear, Malinowski's views are considerably broader than those of the myth-ritualists, who would have limited myth's functionality to religious ritual only.

But we can also see from Malinowski's remarks that he did not entirely part ways with his mentor. Even though the younger man claimed to have also disputed the older's evolutionary theory of culture, it is significant that he nevertheless discusses myth's role in the "primitive faith" and in the "primitive psychology" of his research subjects. It can be argued that Malinowski and his contemporaries were not explicitly dismissive of "primitive" societies, that they were even respectful of the "face-to-face" nature of such societies when compared with more institutional and "impersonal" developed ones. Yet the effects of ethnocentric assumptions make it extremely difficult to avoid such hierarchical valuations, even if there is some question about the motives or intentions of the researchers.

Nevertheless, folkloric and anthropological methodologies profoundly influenced 20th-century mythology. For example, anthropological and folklorist approaches to myth emphasize field research and have thus underscored the importance of the real-world conditions in which myths perform their functions. As a result, those working in other disciplines have come to respect myth's functions as cultural charter and socializing agent. In addition, anthropology's correlation of myths to the material, social, political, and economic facts of living cultures helps those interested in the myths of extinct cultures to understand some of the obscure references and actions in the stories they study. Moreover, the insistence of anthropologists and folklorists on examining the function of myths in *living* societies demonstrates how ignorant the 19th century's armchair mythologists had been of what so-called primitives actually *do* understand about the physical world and the degree to which they are and are not naive about the truth-value of these narratives. In short, anthropology and folklore have encouraged all mythologists to relate their theories about myth to the lived experience of human beings.

The Rise of Psychology

About the time that Frazer and the early anthropologists were beginning to turn the focus of mythology away from questions of racial identity and to replace the comparative method of the Nature School with theories of social functionalism, psychiatric pioneers Sigmund Freud and Carl Jung had begun to investigate the relationship between myth and the unconscious. Freud and Jung believed that mythic symbols—both as they are encountered in religion and as they manifest themselves in dreams and works of the imagination—emerge from the deepest wells of the psyche. Although their conclusions about the landscape of the human mind differed, both men shared a belief that our gods and other mythic characters, as well as our dreams and works of fiction, are projections of that which the unconscious contains. For Freud, "the unconscious is the true psychical reality" (*Complete Works* 1953–1966, 612–13), but our conscious minds censor our impulses, desires, fantasies, and preconscious thoughts because they are too raw and dangerous to face unmediated. Freud saw the images that appear to us in dreams and in such imaginative works as novels and myths as tamed projections of the unconscious's ungovernable terrors. From this point of view, myths are the conscious mind's strategy for making visible and comprehensible the internal forces and conflicts that impel our actions and shape our thoughts.

Jung's view is similar to but not identical with Freud's. Jung viewed the unconscious not as the individual's personal repository "of repressed or forgotten [psychic] contents" (1959/1980, 3). Rather, he argued, "the unconscious is not individual but universal [collective]; unlike the personal psyche, it has contents and modes of behavior that are more or less the same everywhere and in all individuals" (3–4). Jung defined "the contents of the collective unconscious . . . as archetypes" (4). Just exactly what an archetype is psychologically is far too complex to discuss here, but, briefly, Jung defined them as "those psychic contents which have not yet been submitted to conscious elaboration" (5). Indeed, Jung and Freud believed that we never see the unconscious and its contents; rather, we see only projected and therefore refined images that symbolize the things it contains.

Jung and his followers argued that such mythic archetypes as the Wise Woman, the Hero, the Great Mother, the Father, the Miraculous Child, and the Shadow are aspects of every individual psyche, regardless of gender, culture, or personal history. The healthy mind, they reasoned, learns to view the contradictory impulses represented by these archetypes in a balanced pattern, or "mandala." Those with various neuroses and psychoses, however, can't balance these impulses and are overwhelmed by the unconscious's self-contradictory forces. Jung saw the universalized symbols and images that appear in myth, religion, and art as highly polished versions of the archetypes lurking in the collective unconscious. Therefore, Zeus, Yahweh, Kali, and Cybele are their respective cultures' elaborations of universally available psychic material. Jung called these elaborations "eternal images" that

> are meant to attract, to convince, to fascinate, and to overpower. [These images] are created out of the primal stuff of revelation and reflect the ever-unique experience of divinity. That is why they always give man a premonition of the divine while at the same time safeguarding him from immediate experience of it. Thanks to the labors of the human spirit over the centuries, these images have become embedded in a comprehensive system of thought that ascribes an order to the world, and are at the same time represented by . . . mighty, far-spread, and venerable institution[s like] the Church. (1959/1980, 8)

Joseph Campbell: Literary and Cultural Critic

Whereas in the 19th century what passed for literary criticism of myth was largely a matter of antiquarians, classicists, biblicists, and specialists in dead languages reading myths and theorizing the linguistic and cultural events that explained and connected them, in the 20th century literary approaches to myth grew more sophisticated. Important literary critics interested in reading myths include Robert Graves, author of *The White Goddess* and *Greek Myths*, and Northrop Frye, whose *Anatomy of Criticism* makes the case that four basic motifs corresponding to the seasons (spring–comedy, summer–romance, autumn–tragedy, and winter–satire) give shape to all literature. Many scholars wrote extensively about myth and were influential in their disciplines, but Joseph Campbell achieved a much broader popular following.

Campbell was the best-known mythologist of the 20th century if for no other reason than because he was able to present his ideas on television. His six-part series in the 1980s with Bill Moyers, *The Power of Myth,* reached a wide audience eager to hear about "universal human truths" in an age of increasing social fragmentation. At first glance it might seem odd to highlight Campbell's television success here, but in terms of general awareness of myth in America today and in terms of the argument that myth has powerful resonance even in today's modern world, Campbell's television success is precisely to the point. His first book, *The Hero with a Thousand Faces,* continues to be widely read, and, according to Ellwood, "George Lucas freely acknowledges the influence of reading . . . [it] and [Campbell's] *The Masks of God*" (1999, 127–28) on his science fiction epic, *Star Wars*. Campbell wrote voluminously throughout his life, but the ideas he lays out in *Hero* form a core that changed little during his career—even when criticism and discoveries in other fields urged the necessity to revisit them.

Campbell openly acknowledged the influence of Jung and Freud on his work. Yet he never seems quite at home with Jung's *collective* unconscious. Rather, the American mythologist always saw myth as the story of the rugged *individual* who realizes his true nature through heroic struggle. Archetypal symbols and universals there may be, Campbell seems to say, but mythology is ultimately and always the vehicle through which the individual finds a sense of identity and place in the world. Like Jung and Frazer, Campbell sought to present *the* master theory through which all myths could be understood. In his view, there was a single "monomyth" organizing all such narratives. Ellwood summarizes Campbell's *Hero with a Thousand Faces* in this way:

> The basic monomyth informs us that the mythological hero, setting out from an everyday home, is lured or is carried away or proceeds to the threshold of adventure. He defeats a shadowy presence that guards the gateway, enters a dark passageway or even death, meets many unfamiliar forces, some of which give him threatening "tests," some of which offer magical aid. At the climax of the quest he undergoes a supreme ordeal and gains his reward: sacred marriage or sexual union with the goddess of the world, reconciliation with the father, his own divinization, or a mighty gift to bring back to the world. He then undertakes the final work of return, in which, transformed, he reenters the place from whence he set out. (1999, 144)

Campbell arrived at his theory of the monomyth by synthesizing insights from psychoanalysis, methods from 19th-century comparative mythology, and analyses typical of literary and cultural criticism. He was *not* a member of the new wave of anthropology and folklore that searched myths for references to material, political, and social culture. Nor did he seem particularly interested in questions of translation, of variants, or in the possible social, religious, and ritual contexts of the myths he used. Rather, Campbell promoted what he called "living mythology," a nonsectarian spiritual path through which the individual might gain a sense of spiritual and social purpose and through which society might be returned to simplicity and moral virtue.

Claude Lévi-Strauss and Structuralism

At the other end of the spectrum from Campbell's individual-centered mythology is the work of French anthropologist Claude Lévi-Strauss, whose search for "deep structure" in myth had a profound influence on anthropologists and literary critics alike. Lévi-Strauss's search for the skeletal core of myth—and the related searches for organizing principles in literature carried out most famously by Vladimir Propp, Tzetvan Todorov, and Jonathan

Culler—came to be known as structuralism. The influence of structuralism on the mythologies of the 20th century would be difficult to overstate, and structuralism as a critical model can be applied far beyond the boundaries of mythology or literature. It is the search for the undergirding steel that holds up the buildings of all human artifacts and endeavors, including those of meaning-making through myth and literature.

As Robert Scholes discusses the application of these ideas to literature (and, in fact, to any written text), structuralism sought "to establish a model of the system of literature itself as the external reference for the individual works it considers" (1974, 10). As such, structuralism can be seen as a reaction against 19th-century comparatist and literary approaches to myth and classical literature, especially to their subjective, even idiosyncratic, interpretations of these stories. What Lévi-Strauss and others sought was an objective way of discussing literary meaning. By borrowing from linguistics such structural notions as syntax, grammar, phonemes, and morphemes, the French anthropologist attempted to develop a model that would describe how all myths worked—and do so in a way that any literature specialist could duplicate without resorting to his or her personal impressions and imagination. With its focus on discovering an unchanging core of patterned relations giving shape to narratives of all kinds, structuralism promised to put literary criticism and anthropological investigations of myth on the firm ground of empirical science.

A quick way into the issues that structuralism wanted to raise would be to look at the work of one of Lévi-Strauss's contemporaries, Vladimir Propp, who worked almost exclusively on the Russian folktale, attempting to distinguish between constant and variable elements in that genre. After studying more than a thousand stories, he concluded that the characters in fairy tales change but their functions within the plot do not. Propp argued that fairy tales have 31 functions. For examples, Propp's folktale structures begin with (1) the hero leaves home, (2) an interdiction is addressed to the hero, and (3) the interdiction is violated. The 31 total possible plot functions include (12) the hero is tested, interrogated, attacked, which prepares the way for his receiving either a magical agent or helper, (17) the hero is branded, (24) a false hero presents unfounded claims, (30) the villain is punished, and (31) the hero marries and ascends the throne (Scholes 1974, 63–64).

Lévi-Strauss, like Propp, gathered and analyzed as many versions of certain myths as he could find, hoping to penetrate their myriad surface elements and see into a basic grammar of meaning. Working among the natives of South America, Lévi-Strauss took inventory of the various references found in each myth. Ultimately, he determined that mythic structure reveals itself through a limited number of codes. For example, "among South American myths he [distinguished] a sociological, a culinary (or techno-economic), an acoustic, a cosmological, and an astronomical code" (Kirk 1970, 43). Lévi-Strauss further determined that these codes embodied polar opposites, or "binary oppositions." Thus, within the culinary code, as the title of one of his most famous books puts it, one finds the binary of the "raw and the cooked." Within the sociological code, one would find such binaries as married versus unmarried, family versus nonfamily, and *the* people versus the other.

Lévi-Strauss concluded that myths mediate the tension created by these always-present oppositions, whether individuals within a society are aware of it or not. Indeed, Lévi-Strauss discusses the codes and structures that manifest themselves in myths in much the same way that Freud and Jung discuss the unconscious. Whereas the psychologists described the unconscious as the hidden source from which individual consciousness arises, Lévi-Strauss viewed the structures of myth and language as the hidden bedrock upon which narratives are built. In fact, he sounds more like a metaphysician than a scientist when he claims that the deep structures of narrative exist—like Plato's ideal forms or St. John's *logos*—in a realm beyond and untouched by actual stories and storytellers. As Lévi-Strauss writes in *The Raw and the Cooked* (1964), "we cannot therefore grasp [in our analysis of myth] how men think, but how myths think themselves in men, and without their awareness" (1990, 20). In other words, people don't think myths into existence; mythic structures inherent in language do a people's thinking for them, expressing themselves when people use language. Ultimately, he reduced the codes and the patterned relations he discovered among South American Indian myths to a kind of algebra, a symbol system intended to express that which was always true of these stories, regardless of such surface details as plot, character, and setting.

Mircea Eliade's Time Machine

Mircea Eliade has been described as "the preeminent historian of religion of his time" (Ellwood 1999, 79), and his ideas about the essential connection between myth and religion remain influential among students of myth. As a young man Eliade invested himself in nationalist politics. Believing in the power of myth to give a downtrodden people the courage and vision necessary to stage a spiritually motivated political revolution, Eliade became involved with a proto-fascist group called the Legion of the Archangel Michael.

Recent criticism of Eliade's political associations has begun to erode his reputation as a mythologist to some extent. However, it is important to contextualize his sympathy with a political ideology that fused, in its early days, a Christian commitment to charity for the poor and outrage at injustice with a myth of a Romania that had a special destiny to fulfill. Like so many of the 19th- and early 20th-century mythologists who explored the connection between myth and *Volk*, Eliade looked to his people's Indo-European heritage for stories that would impart a spiritual authority to a people's revolution.

In his *Cosmos and History: The Myth of the Eternal Return; The Sacred and the Profane; Myths, Dreams, and Mysteries;* and *Myth and Reality,* Eliade demonstrates his own brand of structuralism. Space, time, and objects are perceived by the religious imagination, he argues, in binary terms, as either sacred or profane. Thus such objects as icons and religious utensils, such places as temples and special groves, and such times as religious festivals are designated as *sacred.* Only certain limited activities can properly be performed with or within them. The *profane,* on the contrary, are those things, places, and times available to people without special ceremony or ritual.

Another important binary in Eliade's mythology is the distinction he makes between "archaic" and modern man. In his view, archaic peoples are more attuned than modern, history-obsessed peoples to the sacred and express this understanding more clearly in their relationships to nature and in their myths. Eliade's mythology proposes yet another opposition—that which exists between cosmic time, or the time of origins, and human history. From his

perspective, moderns live in unhappy exile from the Paradise of cosmic time in which a vital connection to the sacred is natural. Myth, for Eliade, provides moderns with a vehicle through which they can periodically return to the time of origins and thus begin their lives anew. This time-machine function resembles the myth-ritualists' view that sacred narratives facilitate the putting to death of stale, profane consciousness, restoring the participants to the virgin possibilities of creation. Thus we can see that from the perspective of religious studies—at least insofar as Eliade still represents that discipline—that myth has a religious function. Like going to confession, fasting on Yom Kippur, making animal sacrifice, or doing penance, myth permits human beings, who are continually contaminated by exposure to the profane, to wipe the slate clean and make a fresh start.

Considering 20th-Century Mythology Critically

Our overview of 20th-century mythology has so far described the lenses through which myth has been studied in the past 100 years. One could easily imagine that the history of mythology presented here has been leading up to a happy ending: at last, we come to the end of the 20th century and the curtains will part to reveal state-of-the-art mythology. After millennia of deprecating myths as child's prattle and the fevered dreams of savages, after centuries of romanticizing the simplicity of our premodern past, after decades of trying to make the square peg of literature fit into the round hole of science, we have finally gotten it right. Surely we have a mythology that fairly and objectively examines the object of its study, that is methodologically but not blindly rigorous, and that duly considers history, custom, material culture, and sociopolitical and religious institutions without turning a story into a code to be cracked or a "to-do" list. But the fact is that no such mythology exists.

None of the mythologies of the past century has had it quite right—and it is instructive to see why not. Clearly, 19th-century comparative mythology was deeply flawed in its search for irrecoverable Ur-languages and highly dubious speculations about *the* German or Italian or Indian or Jewish character. The nature, ethnological, and myth-ritual schools, like Procrustes, made theoretical beds and then stretched or lopped off evidential limbs in order to achieve a perfect fit. While we owe the comparatists and their literary descendants gratitude for the thousands of myths they collected, and while we should not deny that natural environment and ritual, for example, are an important part of mythic content, we should also learn the lesson that no universal theory "explains" myth.

And we ought to ask ourselves what is to be gained from reducing all myth to a single "pattern." If we read all myths as allegories of the seasonal cycles of fertility and infertility as, for example, Frazer and Graves did, what is to be gained? Are we content to read the story of Jesus' birth, ministry, and death as one of many instantiations of the "year spirit"? Here's death and resurrection! A seasonal pattern! Is this label enough to satisfy our desire to understand mythic meanings and functions? Similarly, are we content to read all myths, as Campbell does, as yet another version of the hero's passage from home, through trial, through apotheosis, and back home again? Surely this plot line accounts for some significant events in myth, but are we content to reduce even myths of creation, fertility, and apocalypse to the story of an individual's separation, initiation, and return? What do we say after we identify, as Eliade does, the basic alienation that exists in myth between human beings and the sacred? A one-trick pony, even when the trick is pretty good, is still a one-trick pony.

But anthropology and folklore, despite the fact that they have done mythology an inestimable service by grounding it in observation-based science, are not quite the answer either. Following Malinowski, anthropologists have, to greater and lesser degrees, illuminated the relationships among myths, religion, custom, sociopolitical behaviors, and material culture. Working within this discipline, Lévi-Strauss and Propp attempted to create a completely objective typology of narrative functions through which all myths could be analyzed. To some degree, particularly in Propp's work on the morphology of the folktale, structuralism succeeded. Any student of myth can examine any number of fairy tales using Propp's model and will find that the Russian folklorist's functions are indeed present and in the described order.

Yet, for all that anthropologists and folklorists have contributed to the study of myth, their disciplined focus on the function of myths within a nexus of material, social, political, and economic phenomena has come at a considerable cost. Such concerns, as important as they are, are only partial, and they ignore the pleasures and power of narrative per se for us here and now as well as for the myth tellers and their more immediate audiences. And structuralist anthropology does not and really cannot answer one of the most important questions: So what? Once we have learned Propp's 31 elements of the folk tale, the various codes in creation myths, and the binary oppositions Lévi-Strauss claims they suggest, what do we really have? From our point of view as professors of English, anthropology's tight focus on the functionality of and within myth diverts attention away from the fundamental fact that myths are stories. We need only think of Lévi-Strauss's algebra of mythic functions or Malinowski's search for references to food, clothing, shelter, and political relationships in the myths of the Trobriand islanders to realize that something vital is lost when myth is cannibalized for its references to the "real" world. We can ask anthropologists, as we asked literary theorists, whether reducing myths to lists of material culture items or to a set of narrative functions isn't as distorting as reducing all myths to allegories of nature, the year spirit, or the hero's quest.

While anthropology and folklore focused on myth's functions and 19th- and early 20th-century literary criticism preoccupied itself largely with myth's contents, psychological approaches have contemplated those dimensions of myth and suggested a theory of psychic origins as well. Psychological approaches to myth, therefore, have been generally more holistic than others. After all, whatever else can be said about them, myths proceed from the human mind if for no other reason than the mind needs to understand "the self" in relation to the larger cosmos. For this reason, many in the latter half of the 20th century assumed that Freud's or Jung's views about myth are fundamentally sound. And the psychological approach to myth has been powerfully suggestive. Jung's archetypes, for example, offer a potent interpretation of widely distributed symbols, images, and plot lines. There's a satisfying symmetry to the notion that each individual contains and balances oppositions such as elder and child, male and female, sinner and saint. Innumerable mythic characters embody these and other human qualities. And although Freud overstates his case when he claims that myths are *nothing other* than the working out of the complex interrelationships among identity, sexuality, and family relationships, a great many myths *do* feature incest, rape, infanticide, and parricide. Myths are about relationships among the irrational, the rational, and the individual's responsibility to society, or, in Freud's terms, among the id, the ego, and the superego.

However, a principal weakness of literary, psychological, and structuralist approaches is that they are ahistorical; they don't consider the specific material and social conditions that shape myth. Indeed, most of the major mythologists of the 20th century cared little for the cultural specifics of how living myths function in the day-to-day lives of the people who told them. They cared little for cultural distinctions that might explain why one version of a myth differs from another; and, in the cases of Jung, Campbell, and Eliade, they seemed interested in myth only as far as familiarity with its presumed "core" might provide the modern individual with a return to Paradise lost—to a sense of self closely connected to the soil and fully at home in a homogeneous sociopolitical order. Thus, while the mythologies of the early- and mid-20th century demonstrated considerable genius, their lack of concern for historical and cultural context and their insistence on reading myths through analytical schema that dispensed with all but a story's most rudimentary plot structure perpetuated most of the significant shortcomings of their 18th- and 19th-century predecessors. Now, at the beginning of the 21st century, awareness of these shortcomings has bred approaches to myth that insist on the importance of context, particularly where gender, cultural norms, and the specifics of the performance events are concerned. Moreover, much like this chapter, modern scholarship has increasingly focused on mythology rather than on myth itself. We conclude with a brief survey of several of the most recent and important contributions to the study of myth and consider, even more briefly, what uses these new ideas might have for the classroom.

Mythology Today

William Doty's "Toolkit"

Doty's *Mythography* concludes with a number of appendixes for "furbishing the creative mythographer's toolkit." Among these tools are "questions to address to mythic texts." Embedded in these questions is a comprehensive methodology that urges students of myth not to choose a single approach to myth but to use as many of the questions and concerns of various mythological schools as possible. Doty's questions arise from five central concerns: (1) the social, (2) the psychological, (3) the literary, textual, and performative, (4) the structural, and (5) the political (2000, 466–67). As the term "mythographer's toolkit" implies, Doty's approach to the subject is profoundly practical. Above all he is concerned with methodology and principles of analysis, and he has distilled the concerns of many fields, including sociology, anthropology, psychology, and literary criticism into a systematic series of exploratory questions and research procedures that are well within reach of most non-specialists. The questions that Doty poses for each of the five areas of concern just mentioned are particularly congenial to the kinds of thinking, discussion, and research performed in the classroom.

Bruce Lincoln's Ideological Narratives

As suggestive as Doty's questions are, other approaches to myth have been advocated recently. Lincoln, whose *Theorizing Myth* is an important contribution to the current study of myth, would define myth and mythology as "ideology in narrative form" because, as he says, all human communication is "interested, perspectival, and partial and . . . its ideological dimensions must be acknowledged, ferreted out where necessary, and critically cross-examined" (1999, 207, 208).

Ultimately, Lincoln advocates making modern mythology the study of previous mythologies. This scholarly endeavor would revolve around "excavating the texts within which that discourse [mythology] took shape and continues to thrive . . . [explicating] their content by placing them in their proper contexts, establishing the connections among them, probing their ideological and other dimensions, explicit and subtextual" (1999, 216). How students should approach myths other than those told by scholars about myth Lincoln doesn't say—though it seems plausible that his approach would be approximately the same for myth as for mythology.

Wendy Doniger's Telescopes and Microscopes

Wendy Doniger, in her *The Implied Spider: Politics and Theology in Myth*, argues for an updated and recalibrated version of the kind of comparative mythology that the Grimm brothers and Sir James Frazer practiced. Among the ways Doniger suggests improving the comparative mythology of the 19th century is, "whenever possible . . . to note the context: who is telling the story and why"; and, she argues, that context could also include—indeed would have to include—"other myths, other related ideas, as Lévi-Strauss argued long ago" (1998, 44, 45). Doniger advocates stripping individual myths to their "naked" narrative outlines—to symbols, themes, and similarities in plot—in order to manage the amount of detail that the comparatist will have to analyze. Unlike Lévi-Strauss, Doniger wouldn't reduce myth to a level where all myths look alike. Context would still matter. Accordingly, she says, we could include in our comparison the contexts of myths. Attention to the sociopolitical and performative contexts in which myths occur would, in Doniger's method, "take account of differences between men and women as storytellers, and also between rich and poor, dominant and oppressed" (46). Doniger would also have students of myth learn how to switch back and forth between the "microscope" of a single telling to the "telescope" of the world's numerous variations on a mythological theme.

Thus Doniger's comparative mythology respects the integrity of a single myth as a unique story and, at the same time, enriches our understanding of that story through comparisons with other stories with similar plots, characters, and symbolic imagery as well as through comparisons with other mythic stories with similar contexts of telling. For one example of this last sense of comparison, we might be enriched by considering myths specifically *told by* women even as we would likely be rewarded by comparing myths with women or goddesses as central characters.

Robert Ellwood's "Real Myths"

Robert Ellwood, who, like Lincoln, was one of Eliade's students at the University of Chicago in the 1960s, suggests yet another approach in *The Politics of Myth: A Study of C. G. Jung, Mircea Eliade, and Joseph Campbell* (1999). Ellwood argues that what we call "myth" does not exist. Or, to put it more precisely, modern students of myth do not study *mythos,* in Hesiod's sense of a poet "breathing" the divinely inspired utterance. Rather, what we call myth "is

always received from an already distant past, literary (even if only oral literature), hence a step away from primal simplicity" (174). This is an important point for Ellwood and other modern mythologists because "official" myths like *The Iliad* and *Odyssey, The Theogony*—or the Bhagavad Gita or the Bible— "are inevitably reconstructions from snatches of folklore and legend, artistically put together with an eye for drama and meaning" (175). But "real" myths are, like one's own dreams, "so fresh they are not yet recognized as 'myth' or 'scripture,' [and] are fragmentary, imagistic rather than verbal, emergent, capable of forming many different stories at once" (175).

What students of myth study in mythology classes, then, are usually the *literary* product of many hands over the course of many generations. Even if a name like Homer or Hesiod gets attached to myths when they finally achieve their final form, they begin as folktales and campfire stories, as religious precepts, images, and rituals, as mystical revelations, and as entertaining fictional and speculative explorations of how the cosmos came into being and continues to operate. Over the generations, in the hands of gifted storytellers, a narrative capable of combining and artistically organizing these fragments and themes emerges. By the time a society officially authorizes a story as scripture or myth, the events it describes have slipped so far into the past that they can be believed—anything could have happened in the beginning—or disbelieved. Myth represents human truths in a variety of ways, few if any of which depend on mere plausibility of character or event. "To put it another way," as Ellwood says, "myth is really a meaning category on the part of hearers, not intrinsic in any story in its own right. Myth in this sense is itself a myth" (1999, 175).

Reading Mythology

Ellwood, like Lincoln, doesn't explicitly articulate a methodology by which students can analyze myths for themselves, but his suggestion that myths, like those contained in this book, come down to us in *literary* form suggests a well-established methodology: close reading and a consideration of how literary conventions inform and enable various levels of meaning.

Doty, when speaking of Müller's and Frazer's euhemerism, remarked that not only these two but "many other 19th-century [and 20th-century] scholars regarded myth almost exclusively as *a problem* for modern rationality" (2000, 11). Müller and Frazer, the myth-ritualists, the sociofunctionalist anthropologists, and the psychoanalysts have all attempted to "solve" the problem of the mythic irrational and to articulate in authoritative terms what myths "really" mean. Their efforts were not entirely wasted; they were simply too one-dimensional, too unable to engage with myth in a holistic sense. Our book takes the view that myths are *not* codes to be cracked or naive and mistaken perceptions that must be corrected. Rather, myths are literary truths told about the mysteries and necessities that always have and always will condition the human experience. These truths, these *mythoi*, have made sophisticated use of symbolic imagery and narrative strategy, have created unforgettable characters that continue to typify for us abstract realities such as love, bravery, wisdom, and treachery, and have enacted as compellingly as any modern novel the humor and horror, the ecstasy and anguish, and the fear and hope of the human drama.

One of the great strengths of the literary approach to myth is that one needn't dispense with the methods, concerns, and insights developed through other mythologies in order to pay appropriate attention to such features of narrative as plot, point of view, characterization, setting, symbols, and theme. Indeed, our understanding and enjoyment of myths is enhanced if, as Doty would say, we furnish our mythographer's toolkit with as many tools as possible. For example, by using such structural approaches as those developed by Campbell, Lévi-Strauss, and Propp we can sharpen our focus on such basic plotting issues as the events that constitute the rising action of the story, the precise moment at which the turning point is reached, and the events of the falling action that resolve the conflict or tension that gives the story its narrative energy. Yet, literary analysis offers students of myth more than charts and formulas because it also equips us with a conceptual vocabulary and specific language to understand and describe how the arrangement of a story's action and its setting affect our emotions and intellects. How, for example, are we affected by the opening lines that introduce the action in the Maya's *Popul Vu?*

Here follow the first words, the first eloquence:
There is not yet one person, one animal, bird, fish, crab, tree, rock, hollow, canyon, meadow, forest.

Only the sky alone is there; the face of the earth is not clear. Only the sea alone is pooled under all the sky; there is nothing whatever gathered together. It is at rest; not a single thing stirs. It is held back, kept at rest under the sky. Whatever there is that might be is simply not there: only the pooled water, only the calm sea, only it alone is pooled (see Chapter 2, page 93).

How do we feel about the difficulty the narrator seems to have expressing a state of existence that is simultaneously nothing and yet contains a primordial sea with sleeping gods shining in its depths? What questions does this paragraph raise for us? What expectations are created and what words and phrases create them? Literary analysis of such details invites us to consider the personal connections we develop to a story and encourages us to reflect upon how a gifted storyteller (or generations of gifted storytellers) can utilize and refine language to create thought-shaping, life-defining images, ideas, and feelings within their hearers and/or readers.

Similarly, consulting the methods and insights of the comparative and psychological approaches to myth can increase our sensitivity to the universality of certain character types and to a deeper appreciation of the motives, values, and actions of the various protagonists and antagonists that people the world's sacred narratives. Through close reading of myth, we can make the crucial distinction between characterization and the more ambiguous notion of character. The characterization of Heracles (Hercules in Latin), for example, utilizes certain stock phrases that emphasize his strength, resilience, and resourcefulness. While pinpointing precisely the language through which storytellers have depicted characters has rewards, it can be even more rewarding to articulate and debate the psychological makeup of this Greek hero's character. For instance, does Heracles's alienation from his divine father, with all the rejection and confusion that such a separation implies, create in him the determination necessary to accomplish his famous twelve labors? Are Heracles's many mighty deeds motivated by an obsessive need to prove his worth to a distant father whose fame and influence far outmatch his own? While these questions are clearly speculative and center upon a fictional entity, they nevertheless take us to the heart of literature's mysterious power over us. How fascinating that people, places, and things that may never have had a literal existence off the page, can nevertheless live in our minds as vividly as any of our flesh-and-blood acquaintances!

Likewise, we can borrow from early anthropology its insights and raw data about the prevalence of certain themes in myth. Preoccupations with such matters as the seasons, fertility, and disastrous consequences of intimate union between gods and mortals abound in myth and some anthropological studies supply us with a vast wealth of cases in point. We can also follow the lead of more recent anthropological study and generate lists of material culture items, social strata, customs, and technologies and our understanding of some of myth's most obscure references can be illuminated by this discipline's focus on the ritual and performance contexts as well as the socio-political functions of myth in living cultures.

Literary analysis, however, urges us also to consider how a narrative's uses of various material goods, social arrangements, and technologies work as symbols and icons. Returning to the *Popul Vu*, we notice that the creation of human beings is the culmination of four successive attempts, a creative process that is successful only after the correct material—maize—is used. While the scientist might view this reference as evidence that the Maya cultivated corn from earliest times, making similar observations about the tortilla griddles, domesticated dogs and turkeys, pots and grinding implements the story also mentions, the literary critic would likely emphasize the symbolic value of corn to the story. The gods' spoken word vibrating in the air, mud, and wood all prove inadequate materials for producing beings capable of intelligible speech and rational thought. However, the premier product of settled living and scientific observations about soil conditions, seeding, and the seasons is the perfect medium.

> And then the yellow corn and white corn were ground, and Xmucane [Grandmother of Light] did the grinding nine times. Corn was used, along with the water she rinsed her hands with, for the

creation of grease; it became human fat when it was worked by the Bearer, Begetter, Sovereign Plumed Serpent, as they are called. After that, they put it into words: the making, the modeling of our first mother-father, with yellow corn, white corn alone for the flesh, food alone for the human legs and arms, for our first fathers, the four human works. It was staples alone that made up their flesh (see Chapter 2, page 98).

When the narrator places maize at the pivotal moment in the story when the gods' at last perfect their creation, it suggests not only were human beings the pinnacle of the creation (the fourth time is the charm!) but that the Maya viewed themselves as literal children of the corn. While such archaeological evidence as carvings of corn stalks, farming implements, and the ruins of granaries and farms are sufficient to indicate that the mastery of agrarian technology supplied the nourishment and wealth necessary to build and sustain the Maya empire, those attending to the symbolic value of corn in their mythic charter know the degree to which the Maya themselves were aware of this fact.

Like an onion, a myth has many layers. Thus we urge students of myth to familiarize themselves with the methods and assumptions of each mythology and to combine them with the methods and assumptions of literary study. Euhemerism permits us to remove one layer of the myth-onion, the comparative method another, the structuralist and functionalist approaches further layers, and psychological and literary analyses still others. We should resign ourselves to the fact that, after all our efforts, we will find at the core, quite literally, no-thing, no *single* all-encompassing explanation of myth. But, those who exert the disciplined effort to peel away and examine the social, political, historical, psychological, cultural, functional, and literary layers of the myth-onion will certainly become permeated with its distinct essence. Given the fascinating subject we study, that is reward enough.

8

Nyoro Myth

John Beattie

Although numerous scholars emphasize the symbolic and structural aspects of myth, an important strand of anthropology has viewed myth instead as an explanation of the behavior and practices of present-day society. Because myth provides a sacred account of why the world is in its present form, it can authorize and underscore the legitimacy of sociopolitical arrangements. This functionalist view is associated strongly with the mid-20th-century anthropologist Bronislaw Malinowski, who considered myth to be a pragmatic set of rules, a social charter.

Malinowski's idea of myth as charter is exemplified in the following excerpt, drawn from a classic ethnography by one of Britain's best-known anthropological specialists on Africa. Beattie initially studied the Nyoro, who live in Uganda, between 1951 and 1955. Using examples of Nyoro myths, Beattie shows how the narratives—divine and indisputable—account for such features of Nyoro life as hierarchical, descent-based social categories; respect for the wisdom of the old; inheritance customs; and the legitimacy of the current king. If a ruler's credentials are based on mythological antecedents, then his power is valid. Beattie ends by warning that myth should not be taken at face value as a literal account of history but, rather, as Malinowski suggests, as a justification for present structures of authority.

What interests us most about myths is the way in which they may express attitudes and beliefs current at the present time. Mythologies always embody systems of values, judgments about what is considered good and proper by the people who have the myth. Especially, myth tends to sustain some system of authority, and the distinctions of power and status which this implies. Thus Nyoro myths tend to validate the kinds of social and political stratification which I have said are characteristic of the culture, and to support the kingship around which the traditional political system revolved. In Malinowski's phrase, Nyoro legend provides a "mythical charter" for the social and political order.

For Nyoro, human history begins with a first family, whose head is sometimes called Kintu, "the created thing." There are three children in this family, all boys. At first these are not distinguished from one another by name; all are called "Kana," which means "little child." This is of course confusing, and Kintu asks God if they may be given separate names. God agrees, and the boys are submitted to two tests. First, six things are placed on a path by which the boys will pass. These are an ox's head, a cowhide thong, a bundle of cooked millet and potatoes, a grass head-ring (for carrying loads on the head), an axe, and a knife. When the boys come upon these things, the eldest at once picks up the bundle of food and starts to eat. What he cannot eat he carries away, using the head-ring for this purpose. He also takes the axe and the knife. The second son takes the leather thong, and the youngest takes the ox's head, which is all that is left. In the next test the boys have to sit on the ground in the evening, with their legs stretched out, each holding on his lap a wooden milk-pot full of milk. They are told that they must hold their pots safely until morning. At midnight the youngest boy begins to nod, and he spills a little of his milk. He wakes up with a start, and begs his brothers for some of theirs. Each gives him a little, so that his pot is full again. Just before dawn the eldest brother suddenly spills all his milk. He, too, asks his brothers to help fill his pot from theirs, but they refuse, saying that it would take too much of their milk to fill his empty pot. In the morning their father finds the youngest son's pot full, the second son's nearly full, and the eldest's quite empty.

He gives his decision, and names the three boys. The eldest, and his descendants after him, is always to be a servant and a cultivator, and to carry loads for his younger brothers, and their descendants. For he chose the millet and potatoes, peasants' food, and he lost all the milk entrusted to him, so showing himself unfit to have anything to do with cattle. Thus he was named "Kairu," which means little Iru or peasant. The second son and his descendants would have the respected status of cattlemen. For he had chosen the leather thong for tying cattle, and he had spilt none of his milk, only providing some for his younger brother. So he was called "Kahuma," little cowherd or Huma, and ever since the cattle-herding people of this part of the inter-lacustrine region have been called Huma or Hima. But the third and youngest son would be his father's heir, for he had taken the ox's head, a sign that he would be at the head of all men, and he alone had a full bowl of milk when morning came, because of the help given him by his brothers. So he was named "Kakama," little Mukama or ruler. He and his descendants became the kings of Bunyoro, or Kitara, as the country was then called. When the three brothers had been named, their father told the two elder that they should never leave their young brother, but should stay with him and serve him always. And he told Kakama to rule wisely and well.

This myth explains and justifies the traditional division of Nyoro society into distinct social categories based on descent. At the beginning, people were undifferentiated—this is symbolized by the three boys having no separate names or identities—but this was confusing, and the only orderly solution was to grade them in three hierarchically ordered categories. It is true that in Bunyoro the distinction between Hima and Iru is of decreasing social importance, but the distinctions of status implied by the myth and especially the differential allocation of authority are still strongly marked in social life. What is validated is basically the "givenness" of differences of status and authority based on birth and, in general, the preeminence of ascribed status over personal achievement. Subordinates may find subordination less irksome, and superordinates may rule more calmly and confidently, when everyone acknowledges the difference between them and the divine origin of that difference.

Many stories, all of which point a moral, are told of the very first kings, Kakama's earliest descendants. The following is one of the best known. King Isaza came to the throne as a very young man; he was disrespectful toward the elders whom his father had left to advise him, and he drove them away from the palace, replacing them by gay youngsters with whom he used to go hunting, which was his favorite pastime. One day he killed a zebra, and he was so pleased with its gaily striped hide that he determined to dress himself in it at once. So his young companions sewed the skin on him. But as the day wore on, the hot sun dried the skin, and it quickly shrank and began to squeeze Isaza until he was nearly dead. He begged his friends for help, but they just laughed at him and did nothing. When he had driven the old men away, two had stayed nearby, and now Isaza sent to them for help. First they refused, but after a while they relented, and told Isaza's young men to throw the king into a pond. They did so, and the moisture loosened the hide so that it could be removed. Isaza was so grateful to the old men that he called them all back to the palace, gave them a feast and reinstated them. At the same time he reprimanded his young associates, telling them that they should always respect the old.

This Nyoro "cautionary tale" points the familiar moral that a person in authority neglects at his peril the advice of those older and wiser than he, and that old men are likely to be better informed than callow youths. But it also stresses another important feature of Nyoro ideas about authority—namely, that it is not inappropriate for young persons to have power. It will be remembered that in the previous myth it was the youngest son, not the eldest, who succeeded to his father's authority; in fact, succession by the youngest, or a younger, son is a characteristic feature of Nyoro inheritance. The role of the older brother is to act as guardian until the heir is old enough to assume full authority. Nyoro say that a first son should not inherit; we shall see that the Mukama may not be succeeded by his eldest son. But the Isaza myth also stresses the wisdom of the old, and the respect due to them. Age is a qualification for advisory, not executive, authority; it is right that the aged should be spared the arduousness of decision making, but right that they should guide and advise those in power. The legend of Isaza and the zebra skin is a popular one, for it expresses values important to Nyoro and which we shall meet again.

It is important also to examine the cycle of dynastic myths which merge into traditional history and link up (if the series be regarded chronologically) with the "real" history which we shall go on to consider. Nyoro believe that there have been three royal dynasties; first, the shadowy Tembuzi, of whom Kakama was the first and Isaza the last; second, the Chwezi, part-legendary hero-gods whose marvelous exploits are still spoken of; and third, the Bito, the line to which the present king belongs. We shall see that part of the significance of the myths which we now discuss lies in the way in which they link these three dynasties together into a single line of descent, so creating an unbroken chain between the present ruler and the very first king of Bunyoro.

The story is rich in descriptive detail, but here we can only give an outline account. It begins by telling how the king of the world of ghosts, called Nyamiyonga, sent a message to king Isaza (whose hunting exploit has just been recounted) asking him to enter into a blood pact with him. Isaza's councilors advised against this, so Isaza had the pact made on Nyamiyonga's behalf with his chief minister, a commoner called Bukuku. When Nyamiyonga discovered that he had been united in the blood pact with an Iru or commoner, he was angry, and he determined to get Isaza into his power. So he sent his beautiful daughter Nyamata to Isaza's court, where she so attracted the king that he married her, not knowing who she was. But he resisted all her efforts to persuade him to visit her home, for he could not bear to be parted from his cattle, which he loved more than anything else. So Nyamiyonga thought of another plan. He caused two of his most handsome cattle to be discovered near Isaza's kraal, and these were taken to the king, who soon loved them most of

all his herd. One day they disappeared, and the distracted Mukama went in search of them, leaving Bukuku to rule the kingdom in his absence. After much wandering, Isaza arrived in the country of ghosts, where he found his two cattle and also his wife Nyamata, who had gone home some time previously to bear him a child. Nyamiyonga welcomed the Nyoro king, but he had not forgiven him, and he never allowed him to return to the world of men.

In due course Nyamata's child was born and was named Isimbwa. When Isimbwa grew up he married in the world of ghosts and had a son called Kyomya, of whom we shall hear more later. Isimbwa, unlike his father, could visit the world of living men, and on a hunting expedition he came to the capital where Bukuku still reigned in Isaza's place. Bukuku was unpopular because he was a commoner and had no real right to rule, but there was no one else to do so. He had a daughter called Nyinamwiru, and at Nyinamwiru's birth diviners had told Bukuku that he would have reason to fear any child that she might bear. So he kept her in a special enclosure which could only be entered through his own well-guarded palace. When Isimbwa reached Bukuku's capital he was intrigued by this state of affairs, and after making clandestine advances to Nyinamwiru through her maid, he managed to climb into her enclosure and, unknown to Bukuku, he stayed there for three months. He then left the kingdom and was not seen again for many years.

In due course Nyinamwiru bore a son, to the consternation of Bukuku, who gave orders for the child to be drowned. So the baby was thrown in a river, but by chance its umbilical cord caught in a bush, and the child was discovered by a potter, Rubumbi, who took it home and brought it up as a member of his family. He knew that it was Nyinamwiru's child, and he told her that it was safe. Bukuku, of course, believed it to be dead. The boy grew up strong and spirited, and was constantly in trouble with Bukuku's herdsmen, for when the king's cattle were being watered he would drive them away, so that he could water Rubumbi's cattle first. This angered Bukuku, who one day came to the drinking trough himself to punish the unruly potter's son. But before Bukuku's men could carry out his orders to seize and beat him, he rushed round to the back of Bukuku's royal stool and stabbed him mortally with his spear. He then sat down on the king's stool. The herdsmen were aghast, and ran at once to tell Nyinamwiru what had happened. The story tells that she was both glad and sorry; glad because her son had taken the throne, sorry because of her father's death. So Ndahura, which is what the young man was called, came to his grandfather Isaza's throne, and he is reckoned as the first of the Chwezi kings.

There were only three—some say two—Chwezi kings; Ndahura, his half-brother Mulindwa, and his son Wamara. Many wonderful things are told of their wisdom and achievements, but during Wamara's reign things began to go badly for them. So they called their diviners and an ox was cut open so that its entrails could be examined. The diviners were astonished to find no trace of the intestines, and they did not know what to say. At that moment a stranger from north of the Nile appeared, and said that he was a diviner and would solve the riddle for them. But first he insisted (wisely, as it turned out) on making a blood pact with one of the Chwezi, so that he could be safe from their anger if his findings were unfavorable. Then he took an axe and cut open the head and hooves of the ox. At once the missing intestines fell out of these members, and as they did so a black smut from the fire settled on them, and could not be removed.

The Nilotic diviner then said that the absence of the intestines from their proper place meant that the rule of the Chwezi in Bunyoro was over. Their presence in the hoofs meant that they would wander far away; in the head, that they would, nonetheless, continue to rule over men (a reference to the possession cult, centered on the Chwezi spirits). And the black smut meant that the kingdom would be taken over by dark-skinned strangers from the north. So the Chwezi departed from Bunyoro, no one knows whither.

Meantime the diviner went back to his own country in the north, and there he met the sons of Kyomya, who was, it will be remembered, Isimbwa's son by his first wife. Kyomya had married in the country to the north of the Nile, and had settled down there. The diviner told Kyomya's sons that they should go south and take over the abandoned Nyoro kingdom of their Tembuzi grandfathers. There were four brothers altogether: Nyarwa, the eldest; the twins Rukidi Mpuga and Kato Kimera; and Kiiza, the youngest. They were the first Bito. Nyarwa (as we might expect) did not become a ruler, though some

say that he remained as adviser to his second brother Rukidi, who became the first Bito king of Bunyoro. Kato was allotted Buganda, then a dependency of the great Nyoro empire (Ganda, of course, have a rather different version of these events), and Kiiza was given a part of what is now Busoga, a country many miles to the east of present-day Bunyoro.

When the Bito first arrived in Bunyoro, they seemed strange and uncouth to the inhabitants. It is said that half of Rukidi's body was black and half white, a reference to his mixed descent. They had to be instructed in the manners appropriate to rulers; at first, they were ignorant of such important matters as cattle keeping and milk drinking. But gradually Rukidi assumed the values and manners proper to the heir of the pastoral rulers of the earlier dynasties. So began the reign of the powerful Bito dynasty, which has lasted up to the present.

This series of myths establishes a genealogical link between the three recognized dynasties of Nyoro rulers. Having noted the importance in Bunyoro of hereditarily determined status, we can see that a major function is served by the genealogical linking of the present ruling line with the wonderful Chwezi, whose exploits are still talked of throughout the region, and, through them, with the even more remote Tembuzi and so with the very beginnings of human existence. The connection enables the present ruling line to claim descent of an honor and antiquity not exceeded even by that of the pastoral Huma (who are said in some contexts to look down upon the Bito as "commoners"). The marking off of the ruling Bito from all other Nyoro contributes to their unity and exclusiveness, and so lends validity to their claims to special respect, prestige, and authority. And not only the rulers, but all Nyoro, share in the glory of their ruling line and the wonderful feats of its progenitors. The exploits and conquests of Isaza and the Chwezi rulers are known to every Nyoro. When people think of themselves, as Nyoro sometimes do (for reasons which will become plain later), as being in decline, there may be compensation in the thought of past in default of present greatness. And we may suppose that historically the genealogical link was important for the immigrant Bito, who lacked the prestige of the already existing Huma aristocracy, and needed the enhancement of status which this "genealogical charter" provided. So the main social function of Nyoro mythical history is the establishment of Bito credentials to govern, by emphasizing the distinction and antiquity of their genealogical antecedents.

According to the myth, the present Mukama is descended in an unbroken patrilineal line from the very beginning of things, and it may well be asked (as indeed it has been) why in this case there are said to have been three dynasties in Nyoro history, and not only one. But the question implies a too literal interpretation of the myth. The fact is that for Nyoro there *are* three dynasties, and whatever the truth about their real relationship to one another, if any (or even, in the case of the earlier ones, their very existence), Nyoro believe them to have been three quite different kinds of people. In other contexts the Chwezi are spoken of as a strange and wonderful people who came from far away, took over the kingdom from the Tembuzi, remained in the country for a generation or two, and then mysteriously disappeared. There is linguistic and other evidence to support the view that the Bito are of quite different racial and cultural stock from the people whose country and kingship they took over. The myth is not to be understood as an attempt to reconstruct a history that has been lost forever; it is rather to be seen as providing a genealogical charter for a structure of authority whose existence is contemporaneous with the myth itself.

Harelips and Twins: The Splitting of a Myth

Claude Lévi-Strauss

Claude Lévi-Strauss (born 1908) has been one of the most provocative and prolific anthropologists of the second half of the 20th century. He fostered a school of thought known as structuralism, which seeks to identify the underlying patterns of human thought that are common to all humans despite variations in culture. Lévi-Strauss looked especially for patterns in myth, ritual, and kinship in order to understand the unconscious structures that shape human cognition. His work often involved identifying binary oppositions—to Lévi-Strauss, a fundamental characteristic of human thought—as well as factors that mediate or resolve those oppositions. His studies of myth emphasized the cultures of South and North America.

Originally part of a radio series delivered in 1977, in this article Lévi-Strauss analyzes a related set of myths and mythological motifs that suggest an underlying similarity among twins, people with harelips, and people born feet first. Although unusually concise, this piece nonetheless encapsulates the most important features of the author's approach to myth. The analysis mixes together texts from several indigenous peoples of the Western Hemisphere. He seeks patterns or structures that, unseen at first, lie beneath the narrative sequence of events in the individual texts. In keeping with the structural study of myth, Lévi-Strauss here searches for binary pairs (in this case, human twins) as well as factors that mediate between binary oppositions. The hare, with its split lip and hence "incipient twinhood," is such an intermediary.

Because Lévi-Strauss's original works are in French, and are rich with literary allusions and double entendres, when translated into English they often prove to be challenging reading. For readers who would like a broader introduction to his work, we recommend Anthropology and Myth: Lectures 1951–1982 *(translated by Roy Willis, Oxford: Basil Blackwell, 1987). This collection of succinct summaries was originally delivered in annual lectures at his home university, Collège de France, over a period of three decades. They provide accessible introductions to all the major works published by this influential author, including his numerous volumes on myth.*

Our starting point here will be a puzzling observation recorded by a Spanish missionary in Peru,

Father P. J. de Arriaga, at the end of the sixteenth century, and published in his *Extirpacion de la Idolatria del Peru* (Lima 1621). He noted that in a certain part of Peru of his time, in times of bitter cold the priest called in all the inhabitants who were known to have been born feet first, or who had a harelip, or who were twins. They were accused of being responsible for the cold because, it was said, they had eaten salt and peppers, and they were ordered to repent and to confess their sins.

Now, that twins are correlated with atmospheric disorder is something very commonly accepted throughout the world, including Canada. It is well known that on the coast of British Columbia, among the Indians, twins were endowed with special powers to bring good weather, to dispel storms, and the like. This is not, however, the part of the problem which I wish to consider here. What strikes me is that all the mythographers—for instance, Sir James Frazer who quotes Arriaga in several instances—never asked the question why people with harelips and twins are considered to be similar in some respect. It seems to me that the crux of the problem is to find out: why harelips? why twins? and why are harelips and twins put together?

In order to solve the problem, we have, as sometimes happens, to make a jump from South America to North America, because it will be a North American myth which will give us the clue to the South American one. Many people have reproached me for this kind of procedure, claiming that myths of a given population can only be interpreted and understood in the framework of the culture of that given population. There are several things which I can say by way of an answer to that objection.

In the first place, it seems to me pretty obvious that, as was ascertained during recent years by the so-called Berkeley school, the population of the Americas before Columbus was much larger than it had been supposed to be. And since it was much larger, it is obvious that these large populations were to some extent in contact with one another, and that beliefs, practices, and customs were, if I may say so, seeping through. Any neighbouring population was always, to some extent, aware of what was going on in the other population. The second point in the case that we are considering here is that these myths do not exist isolated in Peru on the one hand and in Canada on the other, but that in between we find them over and over again. Really, they are pan-American myths, rather than scattered myths in different parts of the continent.

Now, among the Tupinambas, the ancient coastal Indians of Brazil at the time of the discovery, as also among the Indians of Peru, there was a myth concerning a woman, whom a very poor individual

succeeded in seducing in a devious way. The best known version, recorded by the French monk André Thevet in the sixteenth century, explained that the seduced woman gave birth to twins, one of them born from the legitimate husband, and the other from the seducer, who is the Trickster. The woman was going to meet the god who would be her husband, and while on her way the Trickster intervenes and makes her believe that *he* is the god; so, she conceives from the Trickster. When she later finds the legitimate husband-to-be, she conceives from him also and later gives birth to twins. And since these false twins had different fathers, they have antithetical features: one is brave, the other a coward; one is the protector of the Indians, the other of the white people; one gives goods to the Indians, while the other one, on the contrary, is responsible for a lot of unfortunate happenings.

It so happens that in North America, we find exactly the same myth, especially in the northwest of the United States and Canada. However, in comparison with South American versions, those coming from the Canadian area show two important differences. For instance, among the Kootenay, who live in the Rocky Mountains, there is only one fecundation which has as a consequence the birth of twins, who later on become, one the sun, and the other the moon. And, among some other Indians of British Columbia of the Salish linguistic stock—the Thompson Indians and the Okanagan—there are two sisters who are tricked by apparently two distinct individuals, and they give birth, each one to a son; they are not really twins because they were born from different mothers. But since they were born in exactly the same kind of circumstances, at least from a moral and a psychological point of view, they are to that extent similar to twins.

Those versions are, from the point of view of what I am trying to show, the more important. The Salish version weakens the twin character of the hero because the twins are not brothers—they are cousins; and it is only the circumstances of their births which are closely parallel—they are both born thanks to a trick. Nevertheless, the basic intention remains the same because nowhere are the two heroes really twins; they are born from distinct fathers, even in the South American version, and they have opposed characters, features which will be shown in their conduct and in the behaviour of their descendants.

So we may say that in all cases children who are said to be twins or believed to be twins, as in the Kootenay verison, will have different adventures later on which will, if I may say so, untwin them. And this division between two individuals who are at the beginning presented as twins, either real twins or equivalents to twins, is a basic characteristic of all the myths in South America or North America.

In the Salish versions of the myth, there is a very curious detail, and it is very important. You remember that in this version we have no twins whatsoever, because there are two sisters who are travelling in order to find, each one, a husband. They were told by a grandmother that they would recognize their husbands by such and such characteristics, and they are then each deluded by the Tricksters they meet on their way into believing that they are the husband whom each is supposed to marry. They spend the night with him, and each of the women will later give birth to a son.

Now, after this unfortunate night spent in the hut of the Trickster, the elder sister leaves her younger sister and goes visiting her grandmother, who is a mountain goat and also a kind of magician; for she knows in advance that her granddaughter is coming, and she sends the hare to welcome her on the road. The hare hides under a log which has fallen in the middle of the road, and when the girl lifts her leg to cross the log, the hare can have a look at her genital parts and make a very inappropriate joke. The girl is furious, and strikes him with her cane and splits his nose. This is why the animals of the leporine family now have a split nose and upper lip, which we call a harelip in people precisely on account of this anatomical peculiarity in rabbits and hares.

In other words, the elder sister starts to split the body of the animal; if this split were carried out to the end—if it did not stop at the nose but continued through the body and to the tail—she would turn an individual into twins, that is, two individuals which are exactly similar or identical because they are both a part of a whole. In this respect, it is very important to find out what conception the American Indians all over America entertained about the origin of twins. And what we find is a general belief that twins result from an internal splitting of the body fluids which will later solidify and become the child. For instance, among some North American Indians, the pregnant woman is forbidden to turn around too fast when she is lying asleep, because if she did, the body fluids would divide in two parts, and she would give birth to twins.

There is also a myth from the Kwakiutl Indians of Vancouver Island which should be mentioned here. It tells of a small girl whom everybody hates because she has a harelip. An ogress, a supernatural cannibal woman, appears and steals all the children including the small girl with the harelip. She puts them all in her basket in order to take them home to eat them. The small girl who was taken first is at the bottom of the basket and she succeeds in splitting it open with a seashell she had picked up on the beach. The basket is on the back of the ogress, and the girl is able to drop out and run away first. She drops out *feet first*.

This position of the harelipped girl is quite symmetrical to the position of the hare in the myth which I previously mentioned: crouching beneath the heroine when he hides under the log across her path, he is in respect to her exactly in the same position as if he had been born from her and delivered feet first. So we see that there is in all this mythology an actual relationship between twins on the one hand and delivery feet first or positions which are, metaphorically speaking, identical to it on the other. This obviously clears up the connection from which we started in Father Arriaga's Peruvian relations between twins, people born feet first, and people with harelips.

The fact that the harelip is conceived as an incipient twinhood can help us to solve a problem which is quite fundamental for anthropologists working especially in Canada: why have the Ojibwa Indians and other groups of the Algonkian-speaking family selected the hare as the highest deity in which they believed? Several explanations have been brought forward: the hare was an important if not essential part of their diet; the hare runs very fast, and so was an example of the talents which the Indians should have; and so on. Nothing of that is very convincing. But if my previous interpretations were right, it seems much more convincing to say: 1, among the rodent family the hare is the larger, the more conspicuous, the more important, so it can be taken as a representative of the rodent family; 2, all rodents exhibit an anatomical peculiarity which makes out of them incipient twins, because they are partly split up.

When there are twins, or even more children, in the womb of the mother, there is usually in the myth a very serious consequence because, even if there are only two, the children start to fight and compete in order to find out who will have the honour of being born first. And, one of them, the bad one, does not hesitate to find a short cut, if I may say so, in order to be born earlier; instead of following the natural road, he splits up the body of the mother to escape from it.

This, I think, is an explanation of why the fact of being born feet first is assimilated to twinhood, because it is in the case of twinhood that the competitive hurry of one child will make him destroy the mother in order to be the first one born. Both twinhood and delivery feet first are forerunners of a dangerous delivery, or I could even call it a heroic delivery, for the child will take the initiative and become a kind of hero, a murderous hero in some cases; but he completes a very important feat. This explains why, in several tribes, twins were killed as well as children born feet first.

The really important point is that in all American mythology, and I could say in mythology the world over, we have deities or supernaturals, who play the roles of intermediaries between the powers above and humanity below. They can be represented in different ways: we have, for instance, characters of the type of a Messiah; we have heavenly twins. And we can see that the place of the hare in Algonkian mythology is exactly between the Messiah—that is, the unique intermediary—and the heavenly twins. He is not twins, but he is incipient twins. He is still a complete individual, but he has a harelip, he is half way to becoming a twin.

This explains why, in this mythology, the hare as a god has an ambiguous character which has worried commentators and anthropologists: sometimes he is a very wise deity who is in charge of putting the universe in order, and sometimes he is a ridiculous clown who goes from mishap to mishap. And this also is best understood if we explain the choice of the hare by the Algonkian Indians as an individual who is between the two conditions of (a) a single deity beneficient to mankind and (b) twins, one of whom is good and the other bad. Being not yet entirely divided in two, being not yet twins, the two opposite characteristics can remain merged in one and the same person.

An Anthropologist's Reflections on Symbolic Usage

Raymond Firth

In the following selection, Raymond Firth discusses the power of symbolism and the contribution of anthropology to its understanding. Firth argues that, because anthropologists have traditionally explored the meaning and importance of symbols used by the world's cultures, they are especially prepared to help others understand the impact of symbols on behavior. Firth contends that the anthropological approach to symbolism can help us understand the problem of disjunction, *a term that he uses to describe the difference between an overt action and its real or underlying meaning. Referring to his own fieldwork in the Pacific, Firth compares disjunctions among various Tikopian religious ceremonies with disjunctions easily observable in certain Christian rituals. Firth also observes that anthropologists use their knowledge of Western religious symbolism to aid them in understanding symbolism in preliterate cultures.*

It is important to note that, although the article focuses on the relevance of anthropology to symbolism and religious symbols in particular, the material has been excerpted from a larger general work by Firth on public and private symbols, one in which he explores the power of symbolism in art, literature, philosophy, and everyday life.

Professor Raymond Firth is a scholar of international fame and is especially known for his pioneering studies in the Solomon Islands and Malaysia. His book Rank and Religion in Tikopia *is regarded as one of the outstanding works in the anthropology of comparative religion.*

Symbolization is a universal human process. But we still need to understand much more about it, especially in its comparative aspects, in different societies, different classes, different religions. Pervasive in communication, grounded in the very use of language, symbolization is part of the living stuff of societal relationships. Western literature is shot through with references which recall to us questions

Reprinted from SYMBOLS, PUBLIC AND PRIVATE, by Raymond Firth. Copyright © 1973 George Allen & Unwin Ltd. Used by permission of the publisher, Cornell University Press.

of existence and identity in symbol terms. In an essay on The Poet, Emerson wrote of the universality of the symbolic language: 'things admit of being used as symbols because nature is a symbol' (but so is culture)—'we are symbols and inhabit symbols.' In *Sartor Resartus* Carlyle held that in a symbol there is both concealment and revelation. Oriental writings show analogous views. What is it in such statements that some of us find so attractive? Is it truth or illusion about human personality? And if these are not questions for anthropologists to answer, can we at least comment meaningfully upon the forms of such statements, the conditions of their utterance, and their social effects?

In intellectual circles, symbolism in literature, art and religion has long been a subject of study; philosophers and linguists have scrutinized the concept of symbol in its more abstract significance. I show later why I think such treatment is of interest to anthropologists. But anthropologists are also concerned with the ways in which ordinary people think about symbols, behave symbolically in their daily life as members of a society, and consciously interpret what they do as having symbolic meaning.

The essence of symbolism lies in the recognition of one thing as standing for (re-presenting) another, the relation between them normally being that of concrete to abstract, particular to general. The relation is such that the symbol by itself appears capable of generating and receiving effects otherwise reserved for the object to which it refers—and such effects are often of high emotional charge.

An Anthropological Approach

I have shown the existence of a very wide range of symbolic material—things called symbols and ideas about symbols—in the current social milieu in which we all move. I have suggested too that such material can be relevant to any general anthropological study of symbols because of the problems of definition and image it raises.

But what can be a specifically anthropological contribution to the understanding of symbolism? What can an anthropologist do that has not been done already by logicians, metaphysicians, linguists, psychologists, theologians, art historians and the rest? Essentially as I see it, the anthropological approach is comparative, observationalist, functionalist, relatively neutralist. It links the occurrence and interpretations of symbolism to social structures and social events in specific conditions. Over a wide range of instances, anthropologists have observed what symbols people actually use, what they have said about these things, the situations in which the symbols emerge, and the reactions to them. Consequently, anthropologists are equipped to explain the meanings of symbols in the cultures they have studied, and to use such explanations as a means of furthering understanding of the processes of social life. Victor Turner has said of one of his studies—which have played a great part in modern developments—that it is a demonstration of the use of rite and

symbol as a key to the understanding of social structure and social process. Others have explicitly examined symbolic actions in their social contexts to clarify the understanding of phenomena of political or religious change. But I think that for many of us the prime relevance of an anthropological approach to the study of symbolism is its attempt to grapple as empirically as possible with the basic human problem of what I would call disjunction—a gap between the overt superficial statement of action and its underlying meaning. On the surface, a person is saying or doing something which our observations or inferences tell us should not be simply taken at face value—it stands for something else, of greater significance to him.

I take an illustration from my own experience in the Pacific, years ago. I remember seeing a Tikopia chief in pagan times stand up in his temple and rub the great centre post of the building with aromatic leaves drenched in coconut oil. Now, you can oil wood to preserve it or give it a polish, as decoration. And in the Pacific you can oil your body and scent it with leaves, when you decorate yourself, as for a dance. But as the chief did this rubbing he murmured: 'May your body be washed with power.' Now scrubbing a baulk of timber with a hunk of oily leaves is not a very elevated intellectual act. But think of the timber as a *body* and of the fragrant oil as a decorative medium. Think too not of a material body, but of an invisible body—not necessarily with the shape of a post, but in another context, an anthropomorphic body, of a spiritual being, believed to control crops and fish and the health of men. Think too of washing as cleansing, and cleansing as a preface to adornment, and adornment as pleasing to oneself as well as to others. So you can see this act as symbolizing the anointing of the body of a god with fragrant scents to express the status relations and emotions of worship—and to render the god more amenable to the requests of his worshippers. This may seem a very faraway symbolism. Yet think further of Christ's washing of the feet of his disciples; the anointing of Christ by Mary of Bethany; the symbolic value to Christians of the Cross, with its synonyms of the Wood, the Tree; and think also of conceptions of the Eucharist, of the Mystical Body of Christ, of the Glorified Body of the Virgin. It is not difficult to see that what we are dealing with in the Tikopia case is a set of symbolic counters which though superficially very dissimilar to the Christian ones, share some of the basic modes of symbolic conceptualization and patterning. But the symbolic arrangement is set in a social matrix of clans, chieftainship, modes of bodily decoration, even of architectural design which need intensive study for the symbolism to become fully intelligible.

The anthropological approach, fully applied, has as its objective to provide a systematic description and analysis of such a symbolic act in its verbal and non-verbal aspects; to distinguish those parts of the action held to be significant from those which are incidental; to mark the routine or standard elements as against those which are personal and idiosyncratic; to get elucidation from actor, participants and non-participants of the meanings they attach to the act; and to set all this in its general conceptual and institutional framework, and in the more specific framework of the statuses and group relationships of the people concerned. This is a demanding task. But it has been admirably done by many anthropologists—to mention here only Audrey Richards, Monica Wilson and Victor Turner. . . . Some anthropologists have also studied change in symbolic idiom—as I myself have done in the field of Tikopia religion.

The study of symbolism, especially religious symbolism, is fashionable now in social anthropology. There is a tendency to look on this study as a totally new development, but in fact, anthropological interest in symbols goes back at least 100 years, before the days of McLennan and Tylor. It is true that until recently this interest was rarely intense, systematic or sustained, and the modern interest is much more sophisticated, analytical and highly focused. I think there are several reasons for this delayed development. Firstly, as a purely professional sequence of operations, systematic studies of symbolism have had to wait until a substantial measure of progress had been made in the more formal fields of social structure, such as kinship and politics. Now that so much groundwork has been laid we can build loftier constructions of interpretation. Secondly, developments in the theory of communication and of semantics, of signs and their meanings, have focused attention on the interpretation of those elements of behaviour where the meaning of the sign has often seemed most complex and obscure. Thirdly, the growing interest in culturally-defined systems of thought, and in concepts and thought-processes

more generally, has stimulated inquiry in fields such as symbolism, where the relationships between elements seem above all to be of a conceptual kind. All this is part of the relatively straightforward operations of scholarship.

But I think two other reasons may be significant also. It is in keeping with the general temper of our time to be attracted to studies which concern themselves with the less rational aspects of human behaviour, which tend to reject or criticize a positivist approach, which make play with ideas of ambiguity, uncertainty, mystery. This is probably in part a counter to or a relief from the demands for rationality and precision of our industrial, machine-governed society. The other reason is more personal. Some anthropologists (and I think I should probably have to include myself here) find in working out their position on symbolism a means of examining and stating, perhaps resolving, some of their individual views about the nature and determinants of human social relationships and activity. Here I should say that while I am much impressed by a great deal of the modern anthropological work on symbolism, I do not share all the perspective of some of its most distinguished exponents.

It seems to me to make sense, and to be relevant in the world today, that anthropologists should try to interpret symbolical language and symbolical behaviour and relate them to the range of social forms and social values. In such study political symbols are important. But I do not think that only those issues are relevant which refer to political affairs—unless one conceives of the political, as some of my colleagues do, as involving any kind of relations between persons where power is concerned, irrespective of scale. Religious symbols are important too, but I look upon them as referring to the same order of reality as the rest, categorized by the quality of attention given to them, not by the uniqueness of the objects to which they refer. So while I include both political and religious symbols in my examination, I deliberately take in material from ordinary daily life—such as the symbolism of ways of wearing the hair, of greeting and parting, of making and of accepting gifts, of showing flags. I deliberately also try to consider private as well as public aspects of symbolic behaviour and concepts, because I think that the interrelationship between them has often been neglected, by anthropologists as well as by other students of symbolism. I think this relation between public and private, social and personal symbols is important to consider because certainly nowadays it seems that there are strong trends within society for the rejection of traditional symbols and for the discovery, even the invention, of new symbols—trends in which individual interests and decisions are brought to bear upon the recognition of communal symbolic forms.

Popular, unanalysed expressions of symbolism are of interest to anthropologists because they are part of the raw material for comparative study of processes of human thought and action. They reveal the direction and extent of peoples' involvement in social processes of various kinds, and the quality of abstraction applied to these processes. But at a more analytical level, specialized treatments of symbolism also have their anthropological importance. Much that philosophers, artists, art historians, literary critics, theologians, have written about symbolism is not immediately germane to anthropological studies.

But I think it has distinct value for anthropological purposes. Firstly, I find it a very proper satisfaction of an intellectual curiosity to know at least the outline of the arguments put forward about symbolism by specialists in other disciplines, and the range of material they cover. Secondly, some of the illustrations they give recall obliquely some of the data anthropologists deal with, and suggest possible alternative lines of treatment. Finally, some of the hypotheses they put forward about criteria for identification of symbols, the relation between public and private symbols, the relation of symbolization to expression and communication provide parallel or challenge to anthropological views. Yet they often seem to lack that social dimension which is vital to an anthropologist, and to make assertions which seem to an anthropologist to be culture-bound, or 'ethnocentric'. So I think that no systematic theoretical exploration of symbolism by anthropologists should ignore the existence of such an interest by these other disciplines.

II

Taboo

Mary Douglas

To an outside observer, a taboo or religious prohibition might seem irrational; to the believer, it simply seems right. Identifying where that sense of rightness comes from, and why it is so important, is Mary Douglas's task in the following article. Douglas's functional analysis of taboos shows that they underpin social structure everywhere. Anthropologists, studying taboos over extensive periods of time, have learned that taboo systems are not static and forever inviolate; on the contrary, they are dynamic elements of learned behavior that each generation absorbs. Taboos, as rules of behavior, are always part of a whole system and cannot be understood outside their social context. Douglas's explanation of taboos holds as much meaning for us in the understanding of ourselves as it does for our understanding of rules of conduct in the non-Western world. Whether considering the taboos surrounding a Polynesian chief's mana *or the changing sexual taboos in the Western world, it is apparent that taboo systems maintain cultural systems.*

A taboo (sometimes spelled tabu) is a ban or prohibition; the word comes from the Polynesian languages where it means a religious restriction, to break which would entail some automatic punishment. As it is used in English, taboo has little to do with religion. In essence it generally implies a rule which has no meaning, or one which cannot be explained. Captain Cook noted in his log-book that in Tahiti the women were never allowed to eat with the men, and as the men nevertheless enjoyed female company he asked the reason for this taboo. They always replied that they observed it because it was right. To the outsider the taboo is irrational, to the believer its rightness needs no explaining. Though supernatural punishments may not be expected to follow, the rules of any religion rate as taboos to outsiders. For example, the strict Jewish observance forbids the faithful to make and refuel the fire, or light lamps or put them out during the Sabbath, and it also forbids them to ask a Gentile to perform any of these acts. In his book *A Soho Address,* Chaim Lewis, the son of poor Russian Jewish immigrants in London's Soho at the beginning of this century, describes his father's quandary every winter Sabbath: he did not want to let the fire go out and he could not ask any favor outright. Somehow he had to call in a passerby and drop oblique hints until the stranger understood what service was required. Taboos always tend to land their observers in just such a ridiculous situation, whether it is a Catholic peasant of the Landes who abstains from meat on Friday, but eats teal (a bird whose fishy diet entitles it in their custom to be counted as fish), or a Maori hairdresser who after he had cut the chief's hair was not allowed to use his own hands even for feeding himself and had to be fed for a time like a baby.

In the last century, when the word gained currency in European languages, taboo was understood to arise from an inferior mentality. It was argued that primitive tribes observed countless taboos as part of their general ignorance about the physical world. These rules, which seemed so peculiar to Europeans,

"Taboo" by Mary Douglas reprinted from Richard Cavendish, ed., MAN, MYTH, AND MAGIC (London, 1979), vol. 20, pp. 2767–71, by permission of the author and BPCC/Phoebus Publishing.

were the result of false science, leading to mistaken hygiene, and faulty medicine. Essentially the taboo is a ban on touching or eating or speaking or seeing. Its breach will unleash dangers, while keeping the rules would amount to avoiding dangers and sickness. Since the native theory of taboo was concerned to keep certain classes of people and things apart lest misfortune befall, it was a theory about contagion. Our scholars of the last century contrasted this false, primitive fear of contagion with our modern knowledge of disease. Our hygiene protects from a real danger of contagion, their taboos from imaginary danger. This was a comfortably complacent distinction to draw, but hygiene does not correspond to all the rules which are called taboo. Some are as obviously part of primitive religion in the same sense as Friday abstinence and Sabbath rest. European scholars therefore took care to distinguish on the one hand between primitive taboo with a mainly secular reference, and on the other hand rules of magic which infused the practice of primitive religion. They made it even more difficult to understand the meaning of foreign taboos by importing a classification between true religion and primitive magic, and modern medicine and primitive hygiene; and a very complicated web of definitions was based on this misconception.

In the Eye of the Beholder

The difficulty in understanding primitive taboo arose from the difficulty of understanding our own taboos of hygiene and religion. The first mistake was to suppose that our idea of dirt connotes an objectively real class from which real dangers to health may issue, and whose control depends on valid rules of hygiene. It is better to start by realizing that dirt, like beauty, resides in the eye of the beholder. We must be prepared to put our own behavior under the same microscope we apply to primitive tribes. If we find that they are busy hedging off this area from that, stopping X from touching Y, preventing women from eating with men, and creating elaborate scales of edibility and inedibility among the vegetable and animal worlds, we should realize that we too are given to this ordering and classifying activity. No taboo can ever make sense by itself. A taboo is always part of a whole system of rules. It makes sense as part of a classification whose meaning is so basic to those who live by it

that no piecemeal explanation can be given. A native cannot explain the meaning of a taboo because it forms part of his own machinery of learning. The separate compartments which a taboo system constructs are the framework or instrument of understanding. To turn around and inspect that instrument may seem to be an advanced philosophic exercise, but it is necessary if we are to understand the subject.

The nineteenth-century scholars could not understand taboo because they worked within the separate compartments of their own taboo system. For them religion, magic, hygiene, and medicine were as distinct as civilized and primitive; the problem of taboo for them was only a problem about native thought. But put in that form it was insoluble. We approach it nowadays as a problem in human learning.

First, discard the idea that we have anything like a true, complete view of the world. Between what the scientists know and what we make of their knowledge there is a synthesis which is our own rough-and-ready approximation of rules about how we need to behave in the physical world. Second, discard the idea that there can ever be a final and correct world view. A gain in knowledge in one direction does not guarantee there will be no loss or distortion in another; the fullness of reality will always evade our comprehension. The reasons for this will become clear. Learning is a filtering and organizing process. Faced with the same events, two people will not necessarily register two identical patterns, and faced with a similar environment, two cultures will construe two different sets of natural constraints and regular sequences. Understanding is largely a classifying job in which the classifying human mind is much freer than it supposes itself to be. The events to be understood are unconsciously trimmed and filtered to fit the classification being used. In this sense every culture constructs its own universe. It attributes to its own world a set of powers to be harnessed and dangers to be avoided. Each primitive culture, because of its isolation, has a unique world view. Modern industrial nations, because and insofar as they share a common experience, share the same rules about the powers and dangers aroused. This is a valid difference between "Us" and "Them," their primitive taboos and ours.

For all humans, primitive or not, the universe is a system of imputed rules. Using our own distinctions, we can distinguish firstly, physical Nature, inorganic (including rocks, stars, rivers) and organic (vegetable and animal bodies, with rules governing their growth, lifespan and death); secondly, human behavior; thirdly, the interaction between these two groups; fourthly, other intelligent beings whether incorporeal like gods, devils and ghosts or mixtures of human and divine or human and animal; and lastly, the interaction between this fourth group and the rest.

The use of the word supernatural has been avoided. Even a small amount of reading in anthropology shows how very local and peculiar to our own civilization is the distinction between natural and supernatural. The same applies even to such a classification as the one just given. The fact that it is our own local classification is not important for this argument as the present object is to make clear how taboos should be understood. Taboos are rules about our behavior which restrict the human uses of things and people. Some of the taboos are said to avoid punishment or vengeance from gods, ghosts and other spirits. Some of them are supposed to produce automatically their dreaded effects. Crop failures, sickness, hunting accidents, famine, drought, epidemic (events in the physical realm), they may all result from breach of taboos.

The Seat of *Mana*

Taboos can have the effect of expressing political ideas. For example, the idea of the state as a hierarchy of which the chief is the undisputed head and his officials higher than the ordinary populace easily lends itself to taboo behavior. Gradings of power in the political body tend to be expressed as gradings of freedom to approach the physical body of the person at the top of the system. As Franz Steiner says, in *Taboo* (1956):

> In Polynesian belief the parts of the body formed a fixed hierarchy which had some analogy with the rank system of society. . . . Now the backbone was the most important part of the body, and the limbs that could be regarded as continuations of the backbone derived importance from it. Above the body was, of course, the head, and it was the seat of *mana*. When we say this, we must realize that by *"mana"* are meant both the soul aspect, the life force, and a man's ritual status. This grading of the limbs concerned people of all ranks and both sexes. It could, for example, be so important to avoid

stepping over people's heads that the very architecture was involved: the arrangements of the sleeping rooms show such an adaptation in the Marquesas. The commoner's back or head is thus not without its importance in certain contexts. But the real significance of this grading seems to have been in the possibilities it provided for cumulative effects in association with the rank system. The head of a chief was the most concentrated mana object of Polynesian society, and was hedged around with the most terrifying taboos which operated when things were to enter the head or when the head was being diminished; in other words when the chief ate or had his hair cut. . . . The hands of some great chiefs were so dangerous that they could not be put close to the head.

Since the Polynesian political systems was very competitive and chiefs had their ups and downs, great triumphs or total failures, the system of taboo was a kind of public vote of confidence and register of current distributions of power. This is important to correct our tendency to think of taboo as a rigidly fixed system of respect.

We will never understand a taboo system unless we understand the kind of interaction between the different spheres of existence which is assumed in it. Any child growing up learns the different spheres and interactions between them simultaneously. When the anthropologist arrives on the scene, he finds the system of knowledge a going concern. It is difficult for him to observe the changes being made, so he gets the wrong impression that a given set of taboos is something hard-and-fast handed down the generations.

In fact, the classifying process is always active and changing. New classifications are being pushed by some and rejected by others. No political innovation takes place without some basic reclassification. To take a currently live issue, in a stratified society, if it is taboo for lower classes or Negroes to sit down at table or to join sporting events with upper classes or whites, those who assert the rule can make it stronger if they find a basis in Nature to support the behavior they regard as right. If women in Tahiti are forbidden to eat with men, or in Europe to enter certain male occupations, some ultimate justification for the rule needs to be found. Usually it is traced back to their physical nature. Women are said to be constitutionally feeble, nervous or flighty; Negroes to smell; lower classes to be hereditarily less intelligent.

Rules of the Game

Perhaps the easiest approach is to try to imagine what social life would be like without any classification. It would be like playing a game without any rules; no one would know which way to run, who is on his side or against him. There would be no game. It is no exaggeration to describe social life as the process of building classification systems. Everyone is trying to make sense of what is happening. He is trying to make sense of his own behavior, past and present, so as to capture and hold some sense of identity. He is trying to hold other people to their promises and ensure some kind of regular future. He is explaining continually, to himself and to everyone else. In the process of explaining, classifications are developed and more and more meanings successfully added to them, as other people are persuaded to interpret events in the same way. Gradually even the points of the compass get loaded with social meanings. For example, the west room in an Irish farmer's house used to be the room where the old couple retired to, when the eldest son married and brought his wife to the farm. West meant retirement as well as sundown. In the Buddhist religion, east is the high status point; Buddha's statue is on a shelf on the east wall of the east room; the husband always sleeps to the east of his wife. So east means male and social superior. Up and down, right and left, sun and moon, hot and cold, all the physical antitheses are able to carry meanings from social life, and in a rich and steady culture there is a steady core of such agreed classifications. Anyone who is prepared to support the social system finds himself impelled to uphold the classification system which gets meaning from it. Anyone who wants to challenge the social system finds himself up against a set of manifold classifications which will have to be rethought. This is why breach of taboo arouses such strong feeling. It is not because the minor classification is threatened, but because the whole social system (in which a great investment has been made) looks like tottering, if someone can get away with challenging a taboo.

Classification involves definition; definition involves reducing ambiguity; ambiguity arises in several ways and it is wrong to think it can ever be excluded. To take the classification of animal species, they can be classified according to their obvious features, and according to the habitat they live in, and according to how they behave. This gives three ways of classifying animals which could each place the same beasts in different classes. Classed by behavior, using walking, swimming or flying as basic types, penguins would be nearer to fish; classed by bone structure and egg laying, penguins would count more clearly as birds than would flying fish, which would be birds in the other classification. Animal life is much more untidy and difficult to fit into a regular system of classification than at first appears. Human social life is even more untidy. Girls behave like boys, there are adults who refuse to grow up, every year a few are born whose physical make-up is not clearly male or female. The rules of marriage and inheritance require clear-cut categories but always there will be some cases which do not fit the regularities of the system. For human classifications are always too crude for reality. A system of taboos covers up this weakness of the classification system. It points in advance to defects and insists that no one shall give recognition to the inconvenient facts or behave in such a way as to undermine the acceptability and clarity of the system as a whole. It stops awkward questions and prevents awkward developments.

Sometimes the taboo ban appears in ways that seem a long way from their point of origin. For example, among the Lele tribe, in the Kasai district of the Congo, it was taboo to bring fishing equipment direct into the village from the streams or lakes where it had been in use. All round the village fishing traps and baskets would be hung in trees overnight. Ask the Lele why they did this and they replied that coughs and disease would enter the village if the fishing things were not left out one night. No other answer could be got from them except elaboration of the danger and how sorcerers could enter the village if this barrier were not kept up. But another kind of answer lay in the mass of other rules and regulations which separated the village and its human social life from the forest and streams and animal life. This was the basic classification at stake; one which never needed to be explained because it was too fundamental to mention.

Injecting Order into Life

The novelist William Burroughs describes the final experiences of disgust and depression of some forms of drug addiction. What he calls the "Naked Lunch" is the point where all illusions are stripped away and every thing is seen as it really is. When everyone can see what is on everyone's fork, nothing is classed as edible. Meat can be animal or human flesh, caterpillars, worms, or bugs; soup is equally urine, lentils, scotch broth, or excreta; other people are neither friends nor enemies, nor is oneself different from other people since neither has any very clear definition. Identities and classifications are merged into a seething, shapeless experience. This is the potential disorder of the mind which taboo breaks up into classes and rules and so judges some activities as right and proper and others as horrifying.

This kind of rationality is the justification for the taboos which we ourselves observe when we separate the lavatory from the living room and the bed from the kitchen, injecting order into the house. But the order is not arbitrary; it derives from social categories. When a set of social distinctions weakens, the taboos that expressed it weaken too. For this reason sex taboos used to be sacred in England but are no longer so strong. It seems ridiculous that women should not be allowed in some clubs or professions, whereas not so long ago it seemed obviously right. The same for the sense of privacy, the same for hierarchy. The less we ourselves are forced to adopt unthinking taboo attitudes to breaches of these boundaries, the easier it becomes to look dispassionately at the taboos of other societies and find plenty of meaning in them.

In some tribal societies it is thought that the shedding of blood will cause droughts and other environmental disasters. Elsewhere any contact with death is dangerously polluting, and burials are followed by elaborate washing and fumigation. In other places they fear neither homicide nor death pollution but menstrual blood is thought to be very dan-

gerous to touch. And in other places again, adultery is liable to cause illness. Some people are thickly beset with taboos so that everything they do is charged with social symbolism. Others observe only one or two rules. Those who are most taboo-minded have the most complex set of social boundaries to preserve. Hence their investment of so much energy into the control of behavior.

A taboo system upholds a cultural system and a culture is a pattern of values and norms; social life is impossible without such a pattern. This is the dilemma of individual freedom. Ideally we would like to feel free to make every choice from scratch and judge each case on its merits. Such a freedom would slow us down, for every choice would have to be consciously deliberated. On the one hand, education tries to equip a person with means for exercising private judgment, and on the other hand, the techniques of education provide a kind of mechanical decision-making, along well-oiled grooves. They teach strong reactions of anxiety about anything which threatens to go off the track. As education transmits culture, taboos and all, it is a kind of brainwashing. It only allows a certain way of seeing reality and so limits the scope for private judgment. Without the taboos, which turn basic classifications into automatic psychological reflexes, no thinking could be effective, because if every system of classification was up for revision at every moment, there would be no stability of thought. Hence there would be no scope for experience to accumulate into knowledge. Taboos bar the way for the mind to visualize reality differently. But the barriers they set up are not arbitrary, for taboos flow from social boundaries and support the social structure. This accounts for their seeming irrational to the outsider and beyond challenge to the person living in the society.

12

Serpent-Handling as Sacrament

Mary Lee Daugherty

Raised in West Virginia, author Mary Lee Daugherty was a clergywoman, theologian, and scholar who devoted herself to the study of religion in Appalachia until her death in 2004. In her films and writings about small Holiness/Pentecostal churches in the region, she maintains that the handling of snakes as a religious act reflects the social and economic challenges of the community. Here Daugherty argues that snake handling is similar to other Christian rituals, such as communion. Religious behavior that includes the handling of poisonous snakes and the drinking of such poisons as strychnine and lye has met with legal opposition in the United States. Several states specifically outlaw the handling of poisonous snakes in religious settings; West Virginia is not among them.

Other works on snake handling and Holiness churches include Thomas Burton's Serpent-Handling Believers *(University of Tennessee Press, 1993), Dennis Covington's* Salvation on Sand Mountain: Snake Handling and Redemption in Southern Apalachia *(Addison-Wesley, 1995), and the anthropological classic by Weston La Barre,* They Shall Take Up Serpents: Psychology of the Southern Snake Handling Cult *(University of Minnesota Press, 1962).*

And he [Jesus] said unto them, Go ye into all the world, and preach the gospel to every creature. He that believeth and is baptized shall be saved; but he that believeth not shall be damned. And these signs shall follow them that believe; In my name shall they cast out devils; they shall speak with new tongues; they shall take up serpents; and if they drink any deadly thing, it shall not hurt them; they shall lay hands on the sick, and they shall recover.

—Mark 16:15–18 (AV)

The serpent-handlers of West Virginia were originally simple, poor, white people who formed a group of small, independent Holiness-type churches. Serpent-handlers base their particular religious practices on the familiar passage from the "long-conclusion" of the Gospel of Mark. (They are unaware of the disputed nature of this text as the biblical scholars know it.)

The handling of serpents as a supreme act of faith reflects, as in a mirror, the danger and harshness of the environment in which most of these people have lived. The land is rugged and uncompromisingly grim. It produces little except for coal dug from the earth. Unemployment and welfare have been constant companions. The dark holes of the deep mines into which men went to work every day have maimed and killed them for years. The copperhead and rattlesnake are the most commonly found serpents in the rocky terrain. For many years mountain people have suffered terrible pain and many have died from snake bite. Small wonder that it is considered the ultimate fact of faith to reach out and take up the serpent when one is filled with the Holy Ghost. Old timers here in the mountains, before the days of modern medicine, could only explain that those who lived were somehow chosen by God's special mercy and favor.

Today serpent-handlers are experiencing, as are other West Virginians, great economic improvement. Many now live in expensive mobile homes that dot the mountain countryside. They purchase and own

"Serpent-Handling as Sacrament" by Mary Lee Daugherty from THEOLOGY TODAY, Vol. 33, No. 3, October 1976, pp. 232–243. Reprinted by permission of Theology Today.

among their possessions brand new cars and modern appliances. Many of the men now earn from twelve to eighteen thousand dollars a year, working in the revitalized mining industry. Most of the young people are now going to and graduating from high school. I know of one young man with two years of college who is very active in his church. He handles serpents and is looked upon as the one who will take over the pastor's position sometime in the future. What the effect of middle-class prosperity and higher education will be among serpent-handlers remains to be seen. It may be another generation before the effects can be adequately determined.

Knowing serpent-handlers to be biblical literalists, one might surmise that they, like other sects, have picked a certain passage of Scripture and built a whole ritual around a few cryptic verses. While this is true, I am persuaded, after years of observation, that serpent-handling holds for them the significance of a sacrament.

Tapestry paintings of the Lord's Supper hang in most of their churches. Leonardo da Vinci's *Last Supper* is the one picture I have seen over and over again in their churches and in their homes. But in West Virginia, the serpent-handlers whom I know personally do not celebrate the Lord's Supper in their worship services. It is my observation and hypothesis that the ritual of serpent-handling is their way of celebrating life, death, and resurrection. Time and again they prove to themselves that Jesus has the power to deliver them from death here and now.

Another clue to the sacramental nature of lifting up the serpents as the symbol of victory over death is to be observed at their funerals. At the request of the family of one who has died of snake bite, serpents may be handled at a funeral. Even as a Catholic priest may lift up the host at a mass for the dead, indicating belief that in the life and death of Jesus there is victory over death, so the serpent-handlers, I believe, lift up the serpent. Of course, none of this is formalized, for all is very spontaneous. But I am convinced that they celebrate their belief that "in the name of Jesus" there is power over death, and this is what the serpent-handling ritual has proved to them over and over again. This is why I believe they will not give up this ritual because it is at the center of their Christian faith, and in West Virginia, unlike all the other States, it is not illegal.

Many handlers have been bitten numerous times, but, contrary to popular belief, few have died. Their continued life, and their sometimes deformed hands, bear witness to the fact that Jesus still has power over illness and death. Even those who have not been bitten know many who have, and the living witness is ever present in the lives of their friends. If one of the members should die, it is believed that God allowed it to happen to remind the living that the risk they take is totally real. Never have I heard any one of them say that a brother or sister who died lacked faith.

The cultural isolation of these people is still very real. Few have traveled more than a few miles from home. Little more than the Bible is ever read. Television is frowned upon; movies are seldom attended. The Bible is communicated primarily through oral tradition in the church or read at home. There is little awareness of other world religions. Even contacts with Roman Catholics and Jews are rare. Most of their lives revolve around the local church where they gather for meetings two or three times a week.

When one sees the people handling serpents in their services, the Garden of Eden story immediately comes to mind. In the Genesis story, the serpent represents evil that tempts Adam and Eve and must be conquered by their descendants. But the serpent means something far different to West Virginia mountain people; it means life over death. There is never any attempt to kill the snake in Appalachian serpent-handling services. Practitioners seldom kill snakes even in the out of doors. They let them go at the end of the summer months so that they may return to their natural environment to hibernate for the winter. They catch different snakes each spring to use in their worship services. When you ask them why, they tell you quite simply that they do not want to make any of God's creatures suffer. The serpent is always handled with both love and fear in their services, but it is never harmed or killed. Handlers may be killed from bites, but they will not kill the snake. Neither do they force the handling of serpents on any who do not wish to do so.

The snake is seldom handled in private, but usually in the community of believers during a church service. Members may encourage each other to take the risk, symbolically taking on life and testing faith. Their willingness to die for their beliefs gives to their lives a vitality of faith. Handlers usually refuse medicine or hospital treatment for snake bite. But they do go to hospital for other illnesses or if surgery is needed. In the past, they usually refused welfare. They revere and care for their elderly who have usually survived numerous snake bites. Each time they handle the serpents they struggle with life once more and survive again the forces that traditionally oppressed mountain people. The poverty, the unemployment, the yawning strip mines, death in the deep mines have all been harsh, uncontrollable forces for simple people. The handling of serpents is their way of confronting and coping with their very real fears about life and the harshness of reality as experienced in the mountains in years gone by and, for many, even today.

Yet in the face of all this, they seek to live in harmony with nature, not to destroy it or any of its creatures, even the deadly serpent. It is only with the Holy Ghost, however, that they find the sustenance to survive. They live close to the earth, surrounded by woods, streams, and sky. Most live in communities of only a few hundred people or less.

The deep longing for holiness of these Appalachian people stands out in bold relief in the serpent-handling ritual of worship. The search for holiness is dramatized in their willingness to suffer terrible pain from snake bite, or even death itself, to get the feeling of God in their lives. The support of their fellow Christians is still with them. In their experience, God may not come if you don't really pray or ask only once. The person in the group who has been bitten most often and who has suffered the most pain or sickness is usually the leader. While it is the Holy Ghost who gives the power, those who have survived snake bite do get recognition and praise for their courage and their faith from the group. They have learned to cope with their anxieties by calling upon the names of Jesus and the power which he freely offers. Support is given to each member through the laying on of hands in healing ceremonies, through group prayers, and through verbal affirmations, such as: "Help her Jesus," "Bless him, Lord," "That's right, Lord." Through group support, anxiety about life is relieved. They feel ennobled as God becomes manifest in their midst.

The person of the Holy Ghost (they prefer this to Holy Spirit) enables them not only to pick up serpents, but to speak in tongues, to preach, to testify, to cure diseases, to cast out demons, and even to drink strychnine and lye, or to use fire on their skin when

the snakes are in hibernation during the winter months. In these dramatic ways, the mountain folk pursue holiness above all else. They find through their faith both meaning and encouragement. Psychological tests indicate that in many ways they are more emotionally healthy than members of mainline Protestant churches.

Having internalized my own feelings of insecurity and worthlessness for many years because I was "no count" having been born from poor white trash on one side of my family, I have in my own being a deep appreciation and understanding of the need of these people to ask God for miracles accompanied with spectacular demonstrations. Thus they are assured of their own worth, even if only to God. They have never gotten this message from the outside world. They know they have been, and many still are, the undesirable poor, the uneducated mountain folk, locked into their little pockets of poverty in a rough, hostile land. So the Holy Ghost is the great equalizer in the church meeting. One's age, sex, years of schooling are all of less value. Being filled with the Holy Ghost is the only credential one needs in this unique society.

The Holy Ghost creates a mood of openness and spontaneity in the serpent-handling service that is beautiful to behold. Even though there is not much freedom in the personal lives of these people, there is a sense of power in their church lives. Their religion does seem to heal them inwardly of aches and pains and in many instances even of major illnesses. One often sees expressions of dependence as men and women fall down before the picture of Jesus, calling aloud over and over again, "Jesus . . . Jesus . . . Jesus . . ." The simple carpenter of Nazareth is obviously a person with whom mountain people can identify. Jesus worked with his hands, and so do they; Jesus was essentially, by our standards, uneducated, and so are they; Jesus came from a small place, he lived much of his life out of doors, he went fishing, he suffered and was finally done in by the "power structure," and so have they been in the past and often are today.

As I think about the mountain women as they fall down before the picture of Jesus, I wonder what he means to them. Here is a simple man who treated women with great love and tenderness. In this sense, he is unlike some of the men they must live with. Jesus healed the bodies of women, taught them the Bible, never told jokes about their bodies, and even forgave them their sexual sins. In the mountains, adultery is usually punished with beatings. Maybe it should not surprise us that in a State where the strip miners have raped the earth that the rape of the people has also taken place, and the rape of women is often deeply felt and experienced. Things are now changing, and for this we can be grateful.

In the serpent-handlers' churches, the Bible usually remains closed on the pulpit. Since most older members cannot read very well and have usually felt shy about their meager education, they did not read the Bible aloud in public, especially if some more educated people were present. They obviously read the Bible at home, but most remember it from stories they have heard. The Bible is the final authority for everything, even the picking up of serpents and the drinking of poison. It is all literally true, but the New Testament is read more often than the Old Testament.

In former years, their churches have given these poor and powerless people the arena in which they could act out their frustrations and powerless feelings. For a short time, while in church, they could experience being powerful when filled with the Holy Ghost. Frustrated by all the things in the outside world that they could not change, frustrated by the way the powerful people of the world were running things, they could nevertheless run their own show in their own churches. So they gathered three or four times a week, in their modest church buildings, and they stayed for three to five hours for each service. On these occasions, they can feel important, loved, and powerful. They can experience God directly.

I am always struck by the healing love that emerges at the end of each service when they all seem to love each other, embrace each other, and give each other the holy kiss. They are free from restrictions and conventions to love everyone. Sometimes I have the feeling that I get a glimmer of what the Kingdom of God will be like as we kiss each other, old and young, with or without teeth, rich and poor, educated and uneducated, male and female. So I have learned much and have been loved in turn by the serpent-handlers of West Virginia. As they leave the church and go back to their daily work, all the frustrations of the real world return, but they know they can meet again tomorrow night or in a few days. So they have faith, hope, and love, but the greatest message they have given to me is their love.

There are thousands of small Holiness churches in the rural areas of West Virginia. While four-fifths of all Protestants are members of mainstream denominations, no one knows just how many attend Holiness churches. Membership records are not considered important to these people, and although I personally know of about twenty-five serpent-handling churches, there may be others, for those in one church often do not know those in another. They laugh and make jokes about churches that give you a piece of paper as you enter the door, telling you when to pray and what to sing. They find it difficult to believe that you can "order around" the worship of the Holy Ghost on a piece of paper.

Those who make up the membership of the serpent-handling churches are often former members of other Holiness churches or are former Baptists or Methodists. In the Holiness churches, the attainment of personal holiness and being filled with the Spirit is the purpose and goal of life. Members view the secular world as evil and beyond hope. Hence they do not take part in any community activities or social programs.

Fifty-four percent of all persons in the state of West Virginia still live in communities of 1,000 people or less. Freedom of worship is the heritage of the Scotch-Irish, who settled these mountains 200 years ago. In more recent times, among Holiness groups there were no trained ministers. So oral tradition, spontaneous worship, and shared leadership are important.

Holiness church members live by a very strict personal code of morality. A large sign in the church at Jolo, W. Va., indicates that dresses must be worn below the knees, arms must be covered, no lipstick or jewelry is to be worn. No smoking, drinking, or other worldly pleasures are to be indulged in by "true believers." Some women do not cut their hair, others do not even buy chewing gum or soft drinks. For years, in the mountains, people have practiced divine healing, since medical facilities are scarce. Four counties in West Virginia still do not have a doctor, nurse, clinic, dentist, or ambulance service.

In a typical serpent-handling church service, the "true believers" usually sit on the platform of the church together. They are the members who have demonstrated that they have received the Holy Ghost. This is known to them and to others because they have manifested certain physical signs in their own bodies. If they have been bitten from snakes, as many have, and have not died, they have proved that they have the Holy Ghost. And those who have been bitten many times, and survived, are the "real saints." The "true believers" also demonstrate that they have the Holy Ghost by speaking in tongues, by the jerking of their bodies, and by their various trance-like states. They may dance for long periods of time or fall on the floor without being hurt. They may drink the "salvation cocktail," a mixture of strychnine or lye and water. They may also speak in tongues or in ecstatic utterances. Usually this is an utterance between themselves and God. But sometimes members seek to interpret the language of tongues. They lay their hands upon each other to heal hurts or even serious illnesses such as cancer. They sometimes pass their hands through fire. I have witnessed this activity and no burn effects are visible, even though a hand may remain in the flame for some time. A few years ago, they picked up hot coals from the pot bellied stoves and yet were not burned. They apparently can block out pain totally, when in a trance or deep into the Spirit of God.

One woman who attended church at Scrabble Creek, W. Va., experienced, on two occasions, the stigmata as blood came out of her hands, feet, side and forehead. This was witnessed by all present in the church. When asked about this startling experience, she said that she had prayed that God would allow people to see though her body how much Jesus suffered for them by his death and resurrection.

A local church in the rural areas may be known as "Brother So and So's" or "Sister So and So's" church to those who live nearby, but the sign over the door will usually indicate that the church belongs to Jesus. Such names as "The Jesus Church," "The Jesus Only Church," "The Jesus Saves Church," and "The Lord Jesus Christ's Church" are all common names. The churches do not belong to any denomination, and they have no written doctrines or creeds. The order of the service is spontaneous and different every night. Everyone is welcome and people travel around to each other's churches, bringing with them their musical instruments, snakes, fire equipment, poison mixtures, and other gifts.

Often the service begins with singing which may last thirty to forty-five minutes. Next, they may all pray out loud together for the Holy Ghost to fall upon them during the service. Singing, testifying, and preaching by anyone who feels God's spirit may follow. Serpents then will be handled while others are singing. It is possible that serpents will be handled two or three times in one service, but usually it is only once. Serpents are only handled when they feel God's spirit within them. After dancing ecstatically, a brother or sister will open the box and pull out a serpent. Others will follow if there are other snakes available. If only one or two serpents are present, then they may be passed around from believer to believer. Sometimes a circle may be made and the snakes passed. I have only once seen them throw snakes to each other. Children are kept far away.

There is much calling on the name of Jesus while the serpents are being handled, and once the "sacrament" is over, there is a great prayer of rejoicing and often a dance of thanksgiving that no one was hurt. If someone is bitten, there is prayer for his or her healing and great care is taken. If the person becomes too ill to stay in the church, he or she may be taken home and believers will pray for the person for days, if necessary. Even if the person does not die, and usually he or she doesn't, the person is usually very sick. Vomiting of blood and swelling are very painful. Some persons in the churches have lost the use of a finger or suffered some other deformity. But in many years of serpent-handling, I believe there are only about twenty recorded deaths.

The symbolism of the serpent is found in almost all cultures and religions, everywhere, and in all ages. It suggests the ambiguity of good and evil, sickness and health, life and death, mortality and immortality, chaos and wisdom. Because the serpent lives in the ground but is often found in trees, it conveys the notion of transcendence, a creature that lives between earth and heaven. And because it sheds its skin, it seems to know the secret of eternal life.

In the Bible, the serpent is most obviously associated with the Adam and Eve temptation (Gen. 3:1–13), but we also read of the sticks that Moses and Aaron turned into snakes (Ex. 7:8–12), and of Moses' bronze serpent standard (Num. 21:6–9). The two entwined snakes in the ancient figure of the caduceus, symbolizing sickness and health, has been widely adopted as the emblem of the medical profession. And sometimes in early Christian art, the crucifixion is represented with a serpent wound around the cross or lying at the foot of the cross (cf. John 3:14). Here again good and evil, life over death, are symbolized.

In early liturgical art, John the Evangelist was often identified with a chalice from which a serpent was departing, a reference to the legend that when he was forced to drink poison, it was drained away in the snake. Among the early Gnostics, there was a group known as Ophites who were said to worship the serpent because it brought "knowledge" to Adam and Eve and so to all humanity. They were said to free a serpent from a box and that it then entwined itself around the bread and wine of the Eucharist.

But, of course, this ancient history and symbolic lore are unknown to the mountain serpent-handlers of West Virginia, and even if they were told, they probably would not be interested. Their own tradition is rooted in their literal acceptance of what they regard as Jesus' commandment at the conclusion of Mark's Gospel. The problems of biblical textual criticism, relating to the fact that these verses on which they depend are not found in the best manuscript evidence, does not bother them. Their Bible is the English King James Version, and they know through their own experience that their faith in the healing and saving power of Jesus has been tested and proven without question. In any case, their ritual is unique in church history.

What the future holds for the serpent-handlers, no one can tell. Although the young people have tended to stay in their local communities, the temptation in the past to move out and away to find work has been very great. Now many of the young people are returning home as the mining industry offers new, high-paying jobs. And a new era of relative economic prosperity is emerging as the energy problem makes coal-mining more important for the whole Appalachian area. In the meantime, serpent-handling for many mountain people remains a Jesus-commanded "sacrament" whereby physical signs communicate spiritual reality.

Suggested Readings

Babcock, Barbara, ed.
  1978   *The Reversible World: Symbolic Inversion in Art and Society*. Ithaca, N.Y.: Cornell University Press.

Douglas, Mary
  1966   *Purity and Danger: An Analysis of Concepts of Pollution and Taboo*. New York: Praeger.
  1999   *Leviticus as Literature*. Oxford: Oxford University Press.

Dundes, Alan, ed.
  1984   *Sacred Narrative: Readings in the Theory of Myth*. Berkeley: University of California Press.
  1988   *The Flood Myth*. Berkeley: University of California Press.

Georges, Robert A., ed.
  1968   *Studies on Mythology*. Homewood, Ill.: Dorsey Press.

Holden, Lynn, ed.
  2000   *Encyclopedia of Taboos*. Santa Barbara, Calif.: ABC-CLIO.

Lambek, Michael
  1992   "Taboo as Cultural Practice Among Malagasy Speakers." *Man* 27: 245–66.

Ortner, Sherry B.
  1973   "On Key Symbols." *American Anthropologist* 75: 1338–46.

Segal, Robert
  2004   *Myth: A Very Short Introduction*. Oxford: Oxford University Press.

CHAPTER THREE

Ritual

Tsham mask from Tibet.

Ritual is of crucial significance to all human societies, and since the nineteenth century it has been a major focus for anthropologists interested in the study of religion. There are numerous definitions of ritual, but nearly all emphasize repetition, formality, the reliance upon symbols, and the capacity to intensify bonds within a community. Ritual is action. Anthony Wallace highlights the elevated role of ritual when he labels it the primary phenomenon of religion: "Ritual is religion in action; it is the cutting edge of the tool. Belief, although its recitation may be part of the ritual, or a ritual in its own right, serves to explain, to rationalize, to interpret and direct the energy of the ritual performance. . . . It is ritual which accomplishes what religion sets out to do" (1966: 102). While rituals encapsulate ideas central to a culture and are often closely tied to myths, they are intended to bring about specific ends.

Through ritual, religion is able to impress on people a commitment to their system of religious beliefs. Participants in a religious ritual are able to express group solidarity and loyalty. History abounds with examples of the importance of the individual experience in religion, yet there is no denying the overwhelming effect of group participation. As William Howells has pointed out, ritual helps individuals but does so by treating them as a whole group: "They are like a tangled head of hair, and ritual is the comb" (1962: 243).

Some anthropologists believe, along with Malinowski and other early functionalists, that ritual helps allay anxiety. Through the shared performance of group dances and ceremonies, humans are able to reduce the fears that often come when life's events threaten their security and sense of well-being. Other scholars, such as A. R. Radcliffe-Brown, have taken the opposite tack, claiming that ritual may actually create rather than allay anxiety and fears.

Are all rituals religious? Early anthropological theorists assumed that all ritual was sacred in nature, most likely because they dealt with societies in which many aspects of daily life held sacred significance. More-contemporary writers have noted, however, the ritual nature of ceremonies and actions that do not clearly invoke spirits or deities yet still express the fundamental beliefs, values, and social foundations of a group. Sally F. Moore and Barbara G. Myerhoff call such actions *secular rituals*, highlighting their nonsacred status yet also drawing attention to their powerful, multifaceted meanings (1977). One example is a birthday party celebrated at a senior citizen center, as documented by Elizabeth Colson. Although the party was clearly secular, it transformed participants into a community honoring their common characteristic, age (1977).

Most introductory textbooks in anthropology divide religious ritual into rites of passage and rites of intensification. Rites of passage mark transition points in the lives of individuals—for example, birth, puberty, marriage, and death. Rites of intensification occur during a crisis for a group and are thus more important in maintaining group equilibrium and solidarity. They are typically associated with natural phenomena, such as seasonal changes or a lack of rain, but other events, such as impending warfare, could also trigger a rite of intensification. Whatever precipitates the crisis, there is need of a ritual to lessen the anxiety that is felt by the group.

Although the division of rituals into this twofold scheme is useful, it does not adequately represent the variety of ritual occurring in the world's cultures. Wallace, for example, has outlined five major categories of ritual (1966: 107–66):

1. *Technological rituals,* designed to control nature for the purpose of human exploitation, comprise three subdivisions:

  a. Divination rites, which help predict the future and gain hidden information

  b. Rites of intensification, designed to help obtain food and alcohol

  c. Protective rites, aimed at coping with the uncertainty of nature (for example, stormy seas, floods, crop disease, and bad luck)

2. *Therapy and antitherapy rituals* are designed to control human health. Curative rites exemplify therapy rituals; witchcraft and sorcery, antitherapy.

3. *Ideological rituals,* according to Wallace, are "intended to control, in a conservative way, the behavior, the mood, the sentiments and values of groups for the sake of the community as a whole." They consist of four subcategories:

  a. Rites of passage, which deal with role change and geographic movement (for example, marriages)

  b. Rites of intensification, to ensure that people adhere to values and customs (for example, Sunday church service)

  c. Taboos (ritual avoidances), courtesies (positive actions), and other arbitrary ceremonial obligations, which regulate human behavior

  d. Rites of rebellion, which provide a form of "ritualized catharsis" that contributes to order and stability by allowing people to vent their frustrations

4. *Salvation rituals* aim at repairing damaged self-esteem and other forms of impaired identity. Wallace sees three common subdivisions in this category:

  a. Possession, in which an individual's identity is altered by the presence of an alien spirit that occupies the body (exorcism is the usual treatment)

  b. Ritual encouragement of an individual to accept an alternate identity, a process similar to the ritual procedure shamans undergo upon assuming a shamanic role

  c. The mystic experience—loss of personal identity by abandoning the old self and achieving salvation by identifying with a sacred being

5. *Revitalization rituals* are aimed at what can be described as an identity crisis of an entire community. The revitalization movement may be seen as a religious movement (a ritual) that, through the help of a prophet, strives to create a better culture.

Regardless of the typological system used (and anthropologists have proposed others in addition to Wallace's), in practice the various types of ritual frequently overlap and may change over time.

It is similarly difficult to pinpoint the meaning or significance of ritual, particularly for all participants. This may vary between cultures, over time, and even between individuals in a given setting. Fiona Bowie writes (2000: 154–55):

> Reactions to ritual acts cannot be predetermined. Regular attendance at a place of worship, for instance, may reveal a wide range of possible individual responses to a liturgy, from boredom, anger, and frustration to elevation, joy, the intensity of mystical communion, and a sense of unity with fellow worshipers. The individual may inwardly assent to or dissent from the ritual process. Commentators often stress the formulaic aspect of ritual—a ritual is not simply a spontaneous event created by an individual on the spur of the moment. What, however, about the family burial of a pet rabbit? Spontaneous prayers and actions, and accumulation of symbols (a flower, a memorial, a tree planted), may dignify the committal of the deceased animal.

There is no reason to assume that the multiple experiences of ritual felt by people in the industrialized West are any less a part of ritual participation than those of people in less developed parts of the world.

Some contemporary anthropologists have found it fruitful to compare ritual to theater or drama and to interpret ritual as a kind of cultural performance. It is intriguing to consider the possible parallels between ritual and other forms of enactment, including prescribed physical movements and actions, scripted communication, the use of special costumes or props, and the demarcation of sacred space as a kind of stage. Outwardly, the similarities between ritual and theater may appear strong, but the differences become clearer if one considers the goals and internal experiences of participants. "Participants in ritual may be 'acting,' but they are not necessarily 'just pretending'" (Ibid.: 159). Taking part in a ritual can have consequences for participants. For example, some rites of passage deliver an individual into a new stage of life, with new rights, responsibilities, and privileges.

Like other aspects of culture, ritual changes over time. In the contemporary West, there are myriad examples of new and revised ritual traditions, including national commemorations intended to intensify patriotism. The African-based holiday observance Kwanzaa was invented in 1966 by Maulana Karenga, a professor of black studies. Originally intended as a substitute for the European-based customs of the Christmas season, Kwanzaa has grown in acceptance and popularity among diverse communities of Americans. Feminist and New Age movements have experimented with the creation of new forms of ritual expression, often drawing upon participants' own interpretations of non-Western religions and myths. These experiments have resulted in various self-help guides to creating one's own rituals, as well as programs such as those designed to take high school students on rites of passage modeled after the vision quests of Native North Americans. Such borrowing has been controversial, and some Native American groups have begun to protest the use of their myths and rituals by outsiders, however well intentioned. Catherine Bell writes,

> The ubiquitous dynamics of ritual appropriation are historically complex and politically charged, especially when socially or politically dominant groups appear to be mining the cultural traditions of the less powerful, taking the images they want and, by placing them in very new contexts, altering their meanings in ways that may sever these images from their own people. (1997: 240)

Whether we consider long-standing, highly formalized sacred rituals or the more inventive attempts to enact values in a ritual way, it is clear that ritual serves two functions. Ritual teaches participants—as well as anthropological observers—about the social arrangements and values of a community yet also helps construct and create those very arrangements and values.

In the six articles in this chapter, we encounter a range of rituals and possible interpretations. Building upon the seminal work of early-twentieth-century anthropologist Arnold Van Gennep, Victor W. Turner scrutinizes one phase of rites of passage as they are practiced around the world. The works of both Van Gennep and Turner have been highly influential in anthropology, and their focus upon rites of passage has undoubtedly contributed to the popularity of that phrase among the general public.

Daniel Gordon's article also scrutinizes an example of a rite of passage—female genital surgery as practiced in some countries of North Africa. Gordon emphasizes the significance of the procedures to participants themselves, including the females who advocate the surgery, and the controversial status of genital surgery within the nations where it is practiced.

Continuing in the intellectual vein of Victor Turner, Barbara G. Myerhoff's analysis of Huichol rituals explores how myth and symbolism create a sacred realm distant from everyday reality.

In the fourth article, Roy A. Rappaport takes a very different approach, emphasizing material and environmental explanations for ritual.

Elizabeth G. Harrison examines rituals carried out in Japan to memorialize dead children, including fetuses lost to miscarriage and abortion. Popular since the 1970s, these rituals have been criticized by the Japanese media and some Buddhist clergy yet are accepted by the lay public as Buddhist rituals that assist the deceased child. Harrison's study provides a strong example of how a ritual can mean different things to different people within a society and how a ritual's meaning can change over time.

In the final article, Horace Miner examines the body rituals of the Nacirema, a North American group that devotes a considerable portion of the day to ritual activity.

References

Bell, Catherine
    1997 *Ritual: Perspectives and Dimensions*. Oxford: Oxford University Press.

Bowie, Fiona
    2000 *The Anthropology of Religion: An Introduction*. Oxford: Blackwell.

Colson, Elizabeth
    1977 "The Least Common Denominator." In S. F. Moore and B. G. Myerhoff, eds., *Secular Ritual*. Assen, Netherlands: Van Gorcum, pp. 189–98.

Howells, William
    1962 *The Heathens*. Garden City, N.Y.: Doubleday.

Karenga, Maulana
    1988 *The African-American Holiday of Kwanzaa: A Celebration of Family, Community, and Culture*. Los Angeles: University of Sankore Press.

Moore, Sally F., and Barbara G. Myerhoff, eds.
    1977 *Secular Ritual*. Assen, Netherlands: Van Gorcum.

Wallace, Anthony F.C.
    1966 *Religion: An Anthropological View*. New York: Random House.

13

Betwixt and Between: The Liminal Period in *Rites de Passage*

Victor W. Turner

The following selection could not have been written were it not for the seminal writing on ritual by the French anthropologist Arnold van Gennep (1873–1957). Van Gennep is recognized by scholars as the first anthropologist to study the significance of rituals accompanying the transitional stages in a person's life—birth, puberty, marriage, and death. Ever since the publication of Les Rites de Passage *in 1909, the phrase "rites of passage" has become part and parcel of anthropological literature. Van Gennep saw in human rituals three successive but separate stages: separation, margin, and aggregation. In the following selection, Victor Turner singles out the marginal, or liminal, period for examination. The liminal stage in rites of passage is when the initiates are removed and typically secluded from the rest of society—in effect, they become invisible, or, as in the title of this article, "betwixt and between." It is Turner's belief that the neophyte at the liminal stage has nothing—no status, property rank, or kinship position. He describes this condition as one of "sacred poverty." Turner concludes his article with an invitation to researchers of ritual to concentrate their efforts on the marginal stage, believing that this is where the basic building blocks of culture are exposed and therefore open for cross-cultural comparison. Victor Turner taught at Cornell and the University of Chicago. His major field research was done in Uganda, Zambia, and Mexico.*

In this paper, I wish to consider some of the sociocultural properties of the "liminal period" in that class of rituals which Arnold van Gennep has definitively characterized as *"rites de passage."* If our basic model of society is that of a "structure of positions," we must regard the period of margin or "liminality" as an interstructural situation. I shall consider, notably

Reprinted from Victor W. Turner, "Betwixt and Between: The Liminal Period in Rites de Passages," *The Proceedings of the New American Ethnological Society (1964), Symposium on New Approaches to the Study of Religion, pp. 4–20.*

in the case of initiation rites, some of the main features of instruction among the simpler societies. I shall also take note of certain symbolic themes that concretely express indigenous concepts about the nature of "interstructural" human beings.

Rites de passage are found in all societies but tend to reach their maximal expression in small-scale, relatively stable and cyclical societies, where change is bound up with biological and meteorological rhythms and recurrences rather than with technological innovations. Such rites indicate and constitute transitions between states. By "state" I mean here "a relatively fixed or stable condition" and would include in its meaning such social constancies as legal status, profession, office or calling, rank or degree. I hold it to designate also the condition of a person as determined by his culturally recognized degree of maturation as when one speaks of "the married or single state" or the "state of infancy." The term "state" may also be applied to ecological conditions, or to the physical, mental or emotional condition in which a person or group may be found at a particular time. A man may thus be in a state of good or bad health; a society in a state of war or peace or a state of famine or of plenty. State, in short, is a more inclusive concept than status or office and refers to any type of stable or recurrent condition that is culturally recognized. One may, I suppose, also talk about "a state of transition," since J. S. Mill has, after all, written of "a state of progressive movement," but I prefer to regard transition as a process, a becoming, and in the case of *rites de passage* even a transformation—here an apt analogy would be water in process of being heated to boiling point, or a pupa changing from grub to moth. In any case, a transition has different cultural properties from those of a state, as I hope to show presently.

Van Gennep himself defined *"rites de passage"* as "rites which accompany every change of place, state, social position and age." To point up the contrast between "state" and "transition," I employ "state" to include all his other terms. Van Gennep has shown that all rites of transition are marked by three phases: separation, margin (or *limen*), and aggregation. The first phase of separation comprises symbolic behavior signifying the detachment of the individual or group either from an earlier fixed point in the social structure or a set of cultural conditions (a "state"); during the intervening liminal period, the state of the ritual subject (the "passenger") is ambiguous; he passes through a realm that has few or none of the attributes of the past or coming state; in the third phase the passage is consummated. The ritual subject, individual or corporate, is in a stable state once more and, by virtue of this, has rights and obligations of a clearly defined and "structural" type, and is expected to behave in accordance with certain customary norms and ethical standards. The most prominent type of *rites de passage* tends to accompany what Lloyd Warner (1959, 303) has called "the movement of a man through his lifetime, from a fixed placental placement within his mother's womb to his death and ultimate fixed point of his tombstone and final containment in his grave as a dead organism—punctuated by a number of critical moments of transition which all societies ritualize and publicly mark with suitable observances to impress the significance of the individual and the group on living members of the community. These are the important times of birth, puberty, marriage, and death." However, as Van Gennep, Henri Junod, and others have shown, *rites de passage* are not confined to culturally defined life-crises but may accompany any change from one state to another, as when a whole tribe goes to war, or when it attests to the passage from scarcity to plenty by performing a first-fruits or a harvest festival. *Rites de passage*, too, are not restricted, sociologically speaking, to movements between ascribed statuses. They also concern entry into a new achieved status, whether this be a political office or membership of an exclusive club or secret society. They may admit persons into membership of a religious group where such a group does not include the whole society, or qualify them for the official duties of the cult, sometimes in a graded series of rites.

Since the main problem of this study is the nature and characteristics of transition in relatively stable societies, I shall focus attention on *rites de passage* that tend to have well-developed liminal periods. On the whole, initiation rites, whether into social maturity or cult membership, best exemplify transition, since they have well-marked and protracted marginal or liminal phases. I shall pay only brief heed here to rites of separation and aggregation, since these are more closely implicated in social structure than rites of liminality. Liminality during initiation is, therefore, the primary datum of this study, though I will draw on other aspects of passage ritual where the argument demands this. I may state here, partly as an aside, that I consider the term "ritual" to be more fittingly applied to forms of religious behavior associated with social transitions, while the term "ceremony" has a closer bearing on religious behavior associated with social states, where politico-legal institutions also have greater importance. Ritual is transformative, ceremony confirmatory.

The subject of passage ritual is, in the liminal period, structurally, if not physically, "invisible." As members of society, most of us see only what we expect to see, and what we expect to see is what we are conditioned to see when we have learned the definitions and classifications of our culture. A society's secular definitions do not allow for the existence of a not-boy-not-man, which is what a novice in a male puberty rite is (if he can be said to be anything). A set of essentially religious definitions co-exist with these which do set out to define the structurally indefinable "transitional-being." The transitional-being or "liminal *persona*" is defined by a name and by a set of symbols. The same name is very frequently employed to designate those who are being initiated into very different states of life. For example, among the Ndembu of Zambia the name *mwadi* may mean various things: it may stand for "a boy novice in circumcision rites," or "a chief-designate undergoing his installation rites," or, yet again, "the first or ritual wife" who has important ritual duties in the domestic family. Our own terms "initiate" and "neophyte" have a similar breadth of reference. It would seem from this that emphasis tends to be laid on the transition itself, rather than on the particular states between which it is taking place.

The symbolism attached to and surrounding the liminal *persona* is complex and bizarre. Much of it is modeled on human biological processes, which are conceived to be what Lévi-Strauss might call "isomorphic" with structural and cultural processes. They give an outward and visible form to an inward and conceptual process. The structural "invisibility" of liminal *personae* has a twofold character. They are at once no longer classified and not yet classified. In so far as they are no longer classified, the symbols that represent them are, in many societies, drawn from the biology of death, decomposition, catabolism, and other physical processes that have a negative tinge, such as menstruation (frequently regarded as the absence or loss of a fetus). Thus, in some boys' initiations, newly circumcised boys are explicitly likened to menstruating women. Insofar as a neophyte is structurally "dead," he or she may be treated, for a long or short period, as a corpse is customarily treated in his or her society. See Stobaeus's quotation, probably from a lost work of Plutarch, "initiation and death correspond word for word and thing for thing." The neophyte may be buried, forced to lie motionless in the posture and direction of customary burial, may be stained black, or may be forced to live for a while in the company of masked and monstrous mummers representing, *inter alia*, the dead, or

worse still, the un-dead. The metaphor of dissolution is often applied to neophytes; they are allowed to go filthy and identified with the earth, the generalized matter into which every specific individual is rendered down. Particular form here becomes general matter; often their very names are taken from them and each is called solely by the generic term for "neophyte" or "initiand." (This useful neologism is employed by many modern anthropologists.)

The other aspect, that they are not yet classified, is often expressed in symbols modeled on processes of gestation and parturition. The neophytes are likened to or treated as embryos, newborn infants, or sucklings by symbolic means which vary from culture to culture. I shall return to this theme presently.

The essential feature of these symbolizations is that the neophytes are neither living nor dead from one aspect, and both living and dead from another. Their condition is one of ambiguity and paradox, a confusion of all the customary categories. Jakob Boehme, the German mystic whose obscure writings gave Hegel his celebrated dialectical "triad," liked to say that "In Yea and Nay all things consist." Liminality may perhaps be regarded as the Nay to all positive structural assertions, but as in some sense the source of them all, and, more than that, as a realm of pure possibility whence novel configurations of ideas and relations may arise. I will not pursue this point here but, after all, Plato, a speculative philosopher, if there ever was one, did acknowledge his philosophical debt to the teachings of the Eleusinian and Orphic initiations of Attica. We have no way of knowing whether primitive initiations merely conserved lore. Perhaps they also generated new thought and new custom.

Dr. Mary Douglas, of University College, London, has recently advanced (in a magnificent book *Purity and Danger* [1966]) the very interesting and illuminating view that the concept of pollution "is a reaction to protect cherished principles and categories from contradiction." She holds that, in effect, what is unclear and contradictory (from the perspective of social definition) tends to be regarded as (ritually) unclean. The unclear is the unclean: e.g., she examines the prohibitions on eating certain animals and crustaceans in Leviticus in the light of this hypothesis (these being creatures that cannot be unambiguously classified in terms of traditional criteria). From this standpoint, one would expect to find that transitional beings are particularly polluting, since they are neither one thing nor another; or may be both; or neither here nor there; or may even be nowhere (in terms of any recognized cultural topography), and are at the very least "betwixt and between" all the recognized fixed points in space-time of structural classification. In fact, in confirmation of Dr. Douglas's hypothesis, liminal *personae* nearly always and everywhere are regarded as polluting to those who have never been, so to speak, "inoculated" against them, through having been themselves initiated into the same state. I think that we may perhaps usefully discriminate here between the statics and dynamics of pollution situations. In other words, we may have to distinguish between pollution notions which concern states that have been ambiguously or contradictorily defined, and those which derive from ritualized transitions between states. In the first case, we are dealing with what has been defectively defined or ordered, in the second with what cannot be defined in static terms. We are not dealing with structural contradictions when we discuss liminality, but with the essentially unstructured (which is at once de-structured and prestructured) and often the people themselves see this in terms of bringing neophytes into close connection with deity or with superhuman power, with what is, in fact, often regarded as the unbounded, the infinite, the limitless. Since neophytes are not only structurally "invisible" (though physically visible) and ritually polluting, they are very commonly secluded, partially or completely, from the realm of culturally defined and ordered states and statuses. Often the indigenous term for the liminal period is, as among Ndembu, the locative form of a noun meaning "seclusion site" (*kunkunka, kung'ula*). The neophytes are sometimes said to "be in another place." They have physical but not social "reality," hence they have to be hidden, since it is a paradox, a scandal, to see what ought not to be there! Where they are not removed to a sacred place of concealment they are often disguised, in masks or grotesque costumes or striped with white, red, or black clay, and the like.

In societies dominantly structured by kinship institutions, sex distinctions have great structural importance. Patrilineal and matrilineal moieties and clans, rules of exogamy, and the like, rest and are built up on these distinctions. It is consistent with this to find that in liminal situations (in kinship-dominated societies) neophytes are sometimes treated or symbolically represented as being neither male nor female. Alternatively, they may be symbolically assigned characteristics of both sexes, irrespective of their biological sex. (Bruno Bettelheim [1954] has collected much illustrative material on this point from initiation rites.) They are symbolically either sexless or bisexual and may be regarded as a kind of human *prima materia*—as undifferentiated raw material. It was perhaps from the rites of the Hellenic mystery religions that Plato derived his notion expressed in his *Symposium* that the first humans were androgynes. If the liminal period is seen as an interstructural phase in social dynamics, the symbolism both of androgyny and sexlessness immediately becomes intelligible in sociological terms without the need to import psychological (and especially depth-psychological) explanations. Since sex distinctions are important components of structural status, in a structureless realm they do not apply.

A further structurally negative characteristic of transitional beings is that they *have* nothing. They have no status, property, insignia, secular clothing, rank, kinship position, nothing to demarcate them structurally from their fellows. Their condition is indeed the very prototype of sacred poverty. Rights over property, goods, and services inhere in positions in the politico-jural structure. Since they do not occupy such positions, neophytes exercise no such rights. In the words of King Lear they represent "naked unaccommodated man."

I have no time to analyze other symbolic themes that express these attributes of "structural invisibility," ambiguity and neutrality. I want now to draw attention to certain positive aspects of liminality. Already we have noted how certain liminal processes are regarded as analogous to those of gestation, parturition, and suckling. Undoing, dissolution, decomposition are accompanied by processes of growth, transformation, and the reformulation of old elements in new patterns. It is interesting to note how, by the principle of the economy (or parsimony) of symbolic reference, logically antithetical processes of death and growth may be represented by the same tokens, for example, by huts and tunnels that are at once tombs and wombs, by lunar symbolism (for the same moon waxes and wanes), by snake symbolism (for the snake appears to die, but only to shed its old skin and appear in a new one), by bear symbolism (for the bear "dies" in autumn and is "reborn" in spring), by nakedness (which is at once the mark of a newborn infant and a corpse prepared for burial), and by innumerable other symbolic formations and actions. This coincidence of opposite processes and notions in a single representation characterizes the peculiar unity of the liminal: that which is neither this nor that, and yet is both.

I have spoken of the interstructural character of the liminal. However, between neophytes and their instructors (where these exist), and in connecting neophytes with one another, there exists a set of relations that compose a "social structure" of highly specific type. It is a structure of a very simple kind: between instructors and neophytes there is often complete authority and complete submission; among neophytes there is often complete equality. Between incumbents of positions in secular politico-jural systems there exist intricate and situationally shifting networks of rights and duties proportioned to their rank, status, and corporate affiliation. There are many different kinds of privileges and obligations, many degrees of superordination and subordination. In the liminal period such distinctions and gradations tend to be eliminated. Nevertheless, it must be understood that the authority of the elders over the neophytes is not based on legal sanctions; it is in a sense the personification of the self-evident authority of tradition. The authority of the elders is absolute, because it represents the absolute, the axiomatic values of society in which are expressed the "common good" and the common interest. The essence of the complete obedience of the neophytes is to submit to the elders but only in so far as they are in charge, so to speak, of the common good and represent in their persons the total community. That the authority in question is really quintessential tradition emerges clearly in societies where initiations are not collective but individual and where there are no instructors or *gurus*. For example, Omaha boys, like other North American Indians, go alone into the wilderness to fast and pray (Hocart, 1952: 160). This solitude is liminal between boyhood and manhood. If they dream that they receive a woman's burden-strap, they feel compelled to dress and live henceforth in every way as women. Such men are known as *mixuga*. The authority of such a dream in such a situation is absolute. Alice Cummingham Fletcher tells of one Omaha who had been forced in this way

to live as a woman, but whose natural inclinations led him to rear a family and to go on the warpath. Here the *mixuga* was not an invert but a man bound by the authority of tribal beliefs and values. Among many Plains Indians, boys on their lonely Vision Quest inflicted ordeals and tests on themselves that amounted to tortures. These again were not basically self-tortures inflicted by a masochistic temperament but due to obedience to the authority of tradition in the liminal situation—a type of situation in which there is no room for secular compromise, evasion, manipulation, casuistry, and maneuver in the field of custom, rule, and norm. Here again a cultural explanation seems preferable to a psychological one. A normal man acts abnormally because he is obedient to tribal tradition, not out of disobedience to it. He does not evade but fulfills his duties as a citizen.

If complete obedience characterizes the relationship of neophyte to elder, complete equality usually characterizes the relationship of neophyte to neophyte, where the rites are collective. This comradeship must be distinguished from brotherhood or sibling relationship, since in the latter there is always the inequality of older and younger, which often achieves linguistic representation and may be maintained by legal sanctions. The liminal group is a community or comity of comrades and not a structure of hierarchically arrayed positions. This comradeship transcends distinctions of rank, age, kinship position, and, in some kinds of cultic group, even of sex. Much of the behavior recorded by ethnographers in seclusion situations falls under the principle: "Each for all, and all for each." Among the Ndembu of Zambia, for example, all food brought for novices in circumcision seclusion by their mothers is shared equally among them. No special favors are bestowed on the sons of chiefs or headmen. Any food acquired by novices in the bush is taken by the elders and apportioned among the group. Deep friendships between novices are encouraged, and they sleep around lodge fires in clusters of four or five particular comrades. However, all are supposed to be linked by special ties which persist after the rites are over, even into old age. This friendship, known as *wubwambu* (from a term meaning "breast") or *wulunda*, enables a man to claim privileges of hospitality of a far-reaching kind. I have no need here to dwell on the lifelong ties that are held to bind in close friendship those initiated into the same age-set in East African Nilo-Hamitic and Bantu societies, into the same fraternity or sorority on an American campus, or into the same class in a naval or military academy in Western Europe.

This comradeship, with its familiarity, ease and, I would add, mutual outspokenness, is once more the product of interstructural liminality, with its scarcity of jurally sanctioned relationships and its emphasis on axiomatic values expressive of the common weal. People can "be themselves," it is frequently said, when they are not acting institutionalized roles. Roles, too, carry responsibilities and in the liminal situation the main burden of responsibility is borne by the elders, leaving the neophytes free to develop interpersonal relationships as they will. They confront one another, as it were, integrally and not in compartmentalized fashion as actors of roles.

The passivity of neophytes to their instructors, their malleability, which is increased by submission to ordeal, their reduction to a uniform condition, are signs of the process whereby they are ground down to be fashioned anew and endowed with additional powers to cope with their new station in life. Dr. Richards, in her superb study of Bemba girls' puberty rites, *Chisungu*, has told us that Bemba speak of "growing a girl" when they mean initiating her (1956: 121). This term "to grow" well expresses how many peoples think of transition rites. We are inclined, as sociologists, to reify our abstractions (it is indeed a device which helps us to understand many kinds of social interconnection) and to talk about persons "moving through structural positions in a hierarchical frame" and the like. Not so the Bemba and the Shilluk of the Sudan who see the status or condition embodied or incarnate, if you like, *in* the person. To "grow" a girl into a woman is to effect an ontological transformation; it is not merely to convey an unchanging substance from one position to another by a quasi-mechanical force. Howitt saw Kuringals in Australia and I have seen Ndembu in Africa drive away grown-up men before a circumcision ceremony because they had not been initiated. Among Ndembu, men were also chased off because they had only been circumcised at the Mission Hospital and had not undergone the full bush seclusion according to the orthodox Ndembu rite. These biologically mature men had not been "made men" by the proper ritual procedures. It is the ritual and the esoteric teaching which grows girls and makes men. It is the ritual, too, which among Shilluk makes a

prince into a king, or, among Luvale, a cultivator into a hunter. The arcane knowledge or "*gnosis*" obtained in the liminal period is felt to change the inmost nature of the neophyte, impressing him, as a seal impresses wax, with the characteristics of his new state. It is not a mere acquisition of knowledge, but a change in being. His apparent passivity is revealed as an absorption of powers which will become active after his social status has been redefined in the aggregation rites.

The structural simplicity of the liminal situation in many initiations is offset by its cultural complexity. I can touch on only one aspect of this vast subject matter here and raise three problems in connection with it. This aspect is the vital one of the communication of the *sacra*, the heart of the liminal matter.

Jane Harrison has shown that in the Greek Eleusinian and Orphic mysteries this communication of the *sacra* has three main components (1903: 144–60). By and large, this threefold classification holds good for initiation rites all over the world. *Sacra* may be communicated as: (1) exhibitions, "what is shown"; (2) actions, "what is done"; and (3) instructions, "what is said."

"Exhibitions" would include evocatory instruments or sacred articles, such as relics of deities, heroes or ancestors, aboriginal *churingas*, sacred drums or other musical instruments, the contents of Amerindian medicine bundles, and the fan, cist and tympanum of Greek and Near Eastern mystery cults. In the Lesser Eleusinian Mysteries of Athens, *sacra* consisted of a bone, top, ball, tambourine, apples, mirror, fan, and woolly fleece. Other *sacra* include masks, images, figurines, and effigies; the pottery emblem *(mbusa)* of the Bemba would belong to this class. In some kinds of initiation, as for example the initiation into the shaman-diviner's profession among the Saora of Middle India, described by Verrier Elwin (1955), pictures and icons representing the journeys of the dead or the adventures of supernatural beings may be shown to the initiands. A striking feature of such sacred articles is often their formal simplicity. It is their interpretation which is complex, not their outward form.

Among the "instructions" received by neophytes may be reckoned such matters as the revelation of the real, but secularly secret, names of the deities or spirits believed to preside over the rites—a very frequent procedure in African cultic or secret associations

(Turner, 1962: 36). They are also taught the main out-lines of the theogony, cosmogony, and mythical history of their societies or cult, usually with refer-ence to the *sacra* exhibited. Great importance is at-tached to keeping secret the nature of the *sacra*, the formulas chanted and instructions given about them. These constitute the crux of liminality, for while instruction is also given in ethical and social obligations, in law and in kinship rules, and in tech-nology to fit neophytes for the duties of future office, no interdiction is placed on knowledge thus im-parted since it tends to be current among uninitiated persons also.

I want to take up three problems in considering the communication of *sacra*. The first concerns their frequent disproportion, the second their monstrous-ness, and the third their mystery.

When one examines the masks, costumes, fig-urines, and such displayed in initiation situations, one is often struck, as I have been when observing Ndembu masks in circumcision and funerary rites, by the way in which certain natural and cultural features are represented as disproportionately large or small. A head, nose, or phallus, a hoe, bow, or meal mortar are represented as huge or tiny by comparison with other features of their context which retain their nor-mal size. (For a good example of this, see "The Man Without Arms" in *Chisungu* [Richards, 1956: 211], a figurine of a lazy man with an enormous penis but no arms.) Sometimes things retain their customary shapes but are portrayed in unusual colors. What is the point of this exaggeration amounting sometimes to caricature? It seems to me that to enlarge or dimin-ish or discolor in this way is a primordial mode of ab-straction. The outstandingly exaggerated feature is made into an object of reflection. Usually it is not a univocal symbol that is thus represented but a multi-vocal one, a semantic molecule with many compo-nents. One example is the Bemba pottery emblem *Coshi wa ng'oma*, "The Nursing Mother," described by Audrey Richards in *Chisungu*. This is a clay figurine, nine inches high, of an exaggeratedly pregnant mother shown carrying four babies at the same time, one at her breast and three at her back. To this figurine is attached a riddling song:

My mother deceived me!
Coshi wa ng'oma!
So you have deceived me;
I have become pregnant again.

Bemba women interpreted this to Richards as follows:

Coshi wa ng'oma was a midwife of legendary fame and is merely addressed in this song. The girl complains because her mother told her to wean her first child too soon so that it died; or alternatively, told her that she would take the first child if her daughter had a second one. But she was tricking her and now the girl has two babies to look after. The moral stressed is the duty of refusing intercourse with the husband before the baby is weaned, i.e., at the second or third year. This is a common Bemba practice.

In the figurine the exaggerated features are the number of children carried at once by the woman and her enormously distended belly. Coupled with the song, it encourages the novice to ponder upon two relationships vital to her, those with her mother and her husband. Unless the novice observes the Bemba weaning custom, her mother's desire for grandchildren to increase her matrilineage and her husband's desire for renewed sexual intercourse will between them actually destroy and not increase her offspring. Underlying this is the deeper moral that to abide by tribal custom and not to sin against it either by excess or defect is to live satisfactorily. Even to please those one loves may be to invite calamity, if such compliance defies the immemorial wisdom of the elders embodied in the *mbusa*. This wisdom is vouched for by the mythical and archetypal midwife *Coshi wa ng'oma*.

If the exaggeration of single features is not irra-tional but thought-provoking, the same may also be said about the representation of monsters. Earlier writers—such as J. A. McCulloch (1913) in his article on "Monsters" in *Hastings Encyclopaedia of Religion and Ethics*—are inclined to regard bizarre and monstrous masks and figures, such as frequently ap-pear in the liminal period of initiations, as the prod-uct of "hallucinations, night-terrors and dreams." McCulloch goes on to argue that "as man drew little distinction (in primitive society) between himself and animals, as he thought that transformation from one to the other was possible, so he easily ran human and animal together. This in part accounts for animal-headed gods or animal-gods with human heads." My own view is the opposite one: that monsters are man-ufactured precisely to teach neophytes to distinguish clearly between the different factors of reality, as it is conceived in their culture. Here, I think, William James's so-called "law of dissociation" may help us to clarify the problem of monsters. It may be stated as follows: when *a* and *b* occurred together as parts of the same total object, without being discriminated, the occurrence of one of these, *a*, in a new combination *ax*, favors the discrimination of *a, b*, and *x* from one another. As James himself put it, "What is associated now with one thing and now with another, tends to become dissociated from either, and to grow into an object of abstract contemplation by the mind. One might call this the law of dissociation by varying concomitants." (1918: 506).

From this standpoint, much of the grotesqueness and monstrosity of liminal *sacra* may be seen to be aimed not so much at terrorizing or bemusing neophytes into submission or out of their wits as at making them vividly and rapidly aware of what may be called the "factors" of their culture. I have myself seen Ndembu and Luvale masks that combine features of both sexes, have both animal and human attributes, and unite in a single representation human characteristics with those of the natural landscape. One *ikishi* mask is partly human and partly represents a grassy plain. Elements are withdrawn from their usual settings and combined with one another in a totally unique configuration, the monster or dragon. Monsters startle neophytes into thinking about objects, persons, relationships, and features of their environment they have hitherto taken for granted.

In discussing the structural aspect of liminality, I mentioned how neophytes are withdrawn from their structural positions and consequently from the values, norms, sentiments, and techniques associated with those positions. They are also divested of their previous habits of thought, feeling, and action. During the liminal period, neophytes are alternately forced and encouraged to think about their society, their cosmos, and the powers that generate and sustain them. Liminality may be partly described as a stage of reflection. In it those ideas, sentiments, and facts that had been hitherto for the neophytes bound up in configurations and accepted unthinkingly are, as it were, resolved into their constituents. These constituents are isolated and made into objects of reflection for the neophytes by such processes as componental exaggeration and dissociation by varying concomitants. The communication of *sacra* and other

forms of esoteric instruction really involves three processes, though these should not be regarded as in series but as in parallel. The first is the reduction of culture into recognized components or factors; the second is their recombination in fantastic or monstrous patterns and shapes; and the third is their recombination in ways that make sense with regard to the new state and status that the neophytes will enter.

The second process, monster- or fantasy-making, focuses attention on the components of the masks and effigies, which are so radically ill-assorted that they stand out and can be thought about. The monstrosity of the configuration throws its elements into relief. Put a man's head on a lion's body and you think about the human head in the abstract. Perhaps it becomes for you, as a member of a given culture and with the appropriate guidance, an emblem of chieftainship; or it may be explained as representing the soul as against the body; or intellect as contrasted with brute force, or innumerable other things. There could be less encouragement to reflect on heads and headship if that same head were firmly ensconced on its familiar, its all too familiar, human body. The man-lion monster also encourages the observer to think about lions, their habits, qualities, metaphorical properties, religious significance, and so on. More important than these, the relation between man and lion, empirical and metaphorical, may be speculated upon, and new ideas developed on this topic. Liminality here breaks, as it were, the cake of custom and enfranchises speculation. That is why I earlier mentioned Plato's self-confessed debt to the Greek mysteries. Liminality is the realm of primitive hypothesis, where there is a certain freedom to juggle with the factors of existence. As in the works of Rabelais, there is a promiscuous intermingling and juxtaposing of the categories of event, experience, and knowledge, with a pedagogic intention.

But this liberty has fairly narrow limits. The neophytes return to secular society with more alert faculties perhaps and enhanced knowledge of how things work, but they have to become once more subject to custom and law. Like the Bemba girl I mentioned earlier, they are shown that ways of acting and thinking alternative to those laid down by the deities or ancestors are ultimately unworkable and may have disastrous consequences.

Moreover, in initiation, there are usually held to be certain axiomatic principles of construction, and certain basic building blocks that make up the cosmos and into whose nature no neophyte may inquire. Certain *sacra*, usually exhibited in the most arcane episodes of the liminal period, represent or may be interpreted in terms of these axiomatic principles and primordial constituents. Perhaps we may call these *sacerrima*, "most sacred things." Sometimes they are interpreted by a myth about the world-making activities of supernatural beings "at the beginning of things." Myths may be completely absent, however, as in the case of the Ndembu "mystery of the three rivers." . . . This mystery *(mpang'u)* is exhibited at circumcision and funerary cult association rites. Three trenches are dug in a consecrated site and filled respectively with white, red, and black water. These "rivers" are said to "flow from Nzambi," the High God. The instructors tell the neophytes, partly in riddling songs and partly in direct terms, what each river signifies. Each "river" is a multivocal symbol with a fan of referents ranging from life values, ethical ideas, and social norms, to grossly physiological processes and phenomena. They seem to be regarded as powers which, in varying combination, underlie or even constitute what Ndembu conceive to be reality. In no other context is the interpretation of whiteness, redness, and blackness so full; and nowhere else is such a close analogy drawn, even identity made, between these rivers and bodily fluids and emissions: whiteness = semen, milk; redness = menstrual blood, the blood of birth, blood shed by a weapon, etc.; blackness = feces, certain products of bodily decay, etc. This use of an aspect of human physiology as a model for social, cosmic, and religious ideas and processes is a variant of a widely distributed initiation theme: that the human body is a microcosm of the universe. The body may be pictured as androgynous, as male or female, or in terms of one or other of its developmental stages, as child, mature adult, and elder. On the other hand, as in the Ndembu case, certain of its properties may be abstracted. Whatever the mode of representation, the body is regarded as a sort of symbolic template for the communication of *gnosis*, mystical knowledge about the nature of things and how they came to be what they are. The cosmos may in some cases be regarded as a vast human body; in other belief systems, visible parts of the body may be taken to portray invisible faculties such as reason, passion, wisdom and so on; in others again, the different parts of the social order are arrayed in terms of a human anatomical paradigm.

Whatever the precise mode of explaining reality by the body's attributes, *sacra* which illustrates this are always regarded as absolutely sacrosanct, as ultimate mysteries. We are here in the realm of what Warner (1959: 3–4) would call "nonrational or non-logical symbols" which

> arise out of the basic individual and cultural assumptions, more often unconscious than not, from which most social action springs. They supply the solid core of mental and emotional life of each individual and group. This does not mean that they are irrational or maladaptive, or that man cannot often think in a reasonable way about them, but rather that they do not have their source in his rational processes. When they come into play, such factors as data, evidence, proof, and the facts and procedures of rational thought in action are apt to be secondary or unimportant.

The central cluster of nonlogical *sacra* is then the symbolic template of the whole system of beliefs and values in a given culture, its archetypal paradigm and ultimate measure. Neophytes shown these are often told that they are in the presence of forms established from the beginning of things. . . . I have used the metaphor of a seal or stamp in connection with the ontological character ascribed in many initiations to arcane knowledge. The term "archetype" denotes in Greek a master stamp or impress, and these *sacra*, presented with a numinous simplicity, stamp into the neophytes the basic assumptions of their culture. The neophytes are told also that they are being filled with mystical power by what they see and what they are told about it. According to the purpose of the initiation, this power confers on them capacities to undertake successfully the tasks of their new office, in this world or the next.

Thus, the communication of *sacra* both teaches the neophytes how to think with some degree of abstraction about their cultural milieu and gives them ultimate standards of reference. At the same time, it is believed to change their nature, transform them from one kind of human being into another. It intimately unites man and office. But for a variable while, there was an uncommitted man, an individual rather than a social *persona*, in a sacred community of individuals.

It is not only in the liminal period of initiations that the nakedness and vulnerability of the ritual subject receive symbolic stress. Let me quote from Hilda Kuper's description of the seclusion of the Swazi chief during the great *Incwala* ceremony. The *Incwala* is a national First-Fruits ritual, performed in the height of summer when the early crops ripen. The regiments of the Swazi nation assemble at the capital to celebrate its rites, "whereby the nation receives strength for the new year." The *Incwala* is at the same time "a play of kingship." The king's well-being is identified with that of the nation. Both require periodic ritual strengthening. Lunar symbolism is prominent in the rites, as we shall see, and the king, personifying the nation, during his seclusion represents the moon in transition between phases, neither waning nor waxing. Dr. Kuper, Professor Gluckman, and Professor Wilson have discussed the structural aspects of the *Incwala* which are clearly present in its rites of separation and aggregation. What we are about to examine are the interstructural aspects.

During his night and day of seclusion, the king, painted black, remains, says Dr. Kuper, "painted in blackness" and "in darkness"; he is unapproachable, dangerous to himself and others. He must cohabit that night with his first ritual wife (in a kind of "mystical marriage"—this ritual wife is, as it were, consecrated for such liminal situations).

> The entire population is also temporarily in a state of taboo and seclusion. Ordinary activities and behavior are suspended; sexual intercourse is prohibited, no one may sleep late the following morning, and when they get up they are not allowed to touch each other, to wash the body, to sit on mats, to poke anything into the ground, or even to scratch their hair. The children are scolded if they play and make merry. The sound of songs that has stirred the capital for nearly a month is abruptly stilled; it is the day of *bacisa* (cause to *hide*). The king remains secluded; . . . all day he sits naked on a lion skin in the ritual hut of the harem or in the sacred enclosure in the royal cattle byre. Men of his inner circle see that he breaks none of the taboos . . . on this day the identification of the people with the king is very marked. The spies (who see to it that the people respect the taboos) do not say, "You are sleeping late" or "You are scratching," but "You cause the king to sleep," "You scratch him (the king)"; etc. (Kuper, 1947: 219–220).

Other symbolic acts are performed which exemplify the "darkness" and "waxing and waning moon" themes, for example, the slaughtering of a black ox, the painting of the queen mother with a black mixture—she is compared again to a half-moon, while the king is a full moon, and both are in eclipse until the paint is washed off finally with doctored water, and the ritual subject "comes once again into lightness and normality."

In this short passage we have an embarrassment of symbolic riches. I will mention only a few themes that bear on the argument of this paper. Let us look at the king's position first. He is symbolically invisible, "black," a moon between phases. He is also under obedience to traditional rules, and "men of his inner circle" see that he keeps them. He is also "naked," divested of the trappings of his office. He remains apart from the scenes of his political action in a sanctuary or ritual hut. He is also, it would seem, identified with the earth which the people are forbidden to stab, lest the king be affected. He is "hidden." The king, in short, has been divested of all the outward attributes, the "accidents," of his kingship and is reduced to its substance, the "earth" and "darkness" from which the normal, structured order of the Swazi kingdom will be regenerated "in lightness."

In this betwixt-and-between period, in this fruitful darkness, king and people are closely identified. There is a mystical solidarity between them, which contrasts sharply with the hierarchical rank-dominated structure of ordinary Swazi life. It is only in darkness, silence, celibacy, in the absence of merriment and movement that the king and people can thus be one. For every normal action is involved in the rights and obligations of a structure that defines status and establishes social distance between men. Only in their Trappist sabbath of transition may the Swazi regenerate the social tissues torn by conflicts arising from distinctions of status and discrepant structural norms.

I end this study with an invitation to investigators of ritual to focus their attention on the phenomena and processes of mid-transition. It is these, I hold, that paradoxically expose the basic building blocks of culture just when we pass out of and before we re-enter the structural realm. In *sacerrima* and their interpretations we have categories of data that may usefully be handled by the new sophisticated techniques of cross-cultural comparison.

14

Female Circumcision in Egypt and Sudan: A Controversial Rite of Passage

Daniel Gordon

Anthropologists have known and written about female genital operations for many years, but the subject has only recently been brought to the attention of the Western public. The practice currently is a hot issue in Egypt where human rights advocates, including women's groups and many physicians, are pitted against its proponents. Also termed female genital mutilation *and (erroneously)* female circumcision, *this operation is widespread in Africa south of the Sahara; although practiced in several Islamic countries of North Africa, it is not present in 80 percent of the Muslim world.*

Blending physiological and cultural data, Daniel Gordon's research focuses on the types of genital surgery common in Egypt and Sudan and the rationales employed by members of these societies to defend the practice. Although not a ritual marking the physiological change from adolescence to adulthood, as is the case in sub-Saharan Africa, female genital surgery in Egypt and Sudan is a rite of passage that moves immature females into what Gordon calls "social puberty," giving a child the status of a woman after the operation.

Gordon's work challenges the validity of cultural relativism and accuses anthropologists of advocating female genital surgery because of their nonjudgmental position, yet he makes plain that, although these operations are deeply imbedded in the male-dominated cultures of Egypt and Sudan, which stress female constraint and the separation of male and female worlds, women themselves are the strongest proponents of genital surgery for their daughters and granddaughters. This fact demands explanation that can be found only in the intricate weave of the fabric of Egyptian and Sudanic cultures.

Despite its long history, its enduring prevalence, and the capacity of its practice to arouse emotional

"Female Circumcision and Genital Operations in Egypt and the Sudan: A Dilemma for Medical Anthropology" by Daniel Gordon from MEDICAL ANTHROPOLOGY QUARTERLY, March 1, 1991. Copyright © 1991, American Anthropological Association. Reprinted by permission.

response, the literature on female circumcision in the Arab world is surprisingly scant. . . . In the last decade, finally, with the development of feminist consciousness and the advent of an international women's health movement, there has been a growing perception that the largely descriptive approach taken in much of the existing literature is inappropriately passive in its response to the international health issue of "female genital mutilation" (Hosken 1982).

In beginning, I must make it clear that the term "female circumcision," although common throughout much of the literature, is an incorrect, euphemistic description for what is really a variety of operations which can be categorized into three main types. Literal circumcision is the least mutilating of the three procedures and is referred to as *sunna* ("duty") in Arabic, since it is thought to be commanded or at least recommended by Islam. It corresponds most closely to the operation in males, involving removal of the clitoral prepuce (foreskin) by razor, knife, or smoldering stone, depending on where and by whom it is practiced. The second form, excision or clitoridectomy, involves the cutting out of the whole clitoris as well as parts or all of the labia minora. In its varying degrees it is the most common form practiced in Egypt. In the Sudan excision is not performed, but a similar operation, referred to as "intermediate circumcision" (El Dareer 1982: 4), involves removal of the clitoris, the anterior or all of the labia minora, and slices of the labia majora. El Dareer suggests that this procedure was invented as a compromise by Sudanese midwives when British legislation forbade the most extreme operations in 1946.

Pharaonic circumcision, or *tahara farowniyya* in Arabic, is the oldest of the three operations, attributed in folk legend to the time of the ancient Pharaohs (hence the name). It is most prevalent in the Sudan and Nubian Egypt. The most radical of the operations, it is often referred to as infibulation, because of its association with the ancient Roman practice of fastening a clasp, or fibula, through the labia majora of a woman to ensure her chastity. Pharaonic circumcision involves complete removal of the clitoris, labia minora and majora, with the two sides of the wound then stitched together, leaving a small pinhole opening for the drop by drop passage of urine and menstrual blood. The operation is done in a variety of ways, depending on where it is practiced. In rural settings, a small stick is often inserted to maintain the opening, and the two sides stitched together with thorns. Adhesives such as egg, oil, or wet cigarette paper are placed over the wound to promote healing. The girl's legs are often bound together for as long as 40 days to ensure the desired tightly scarred aperture (El Dareer 1982: 1–20). In urban settings, stitching is likely to be done with catgut or silk sutures, and anesthesia and antibiotics are likely to be used.

The most extensive statistical survey of female genital operations done to date was carried out in the Sudan between 1977 and 1981 by the Faculty of Medicine at the University of Khartoum, with Dr. Asma El Dareer as chief investigator (El Dareer 1982). El Dareer's team interviewed 3,210 women and 1,545 men, representing a random sampling of households throughout Northern Sudan. In addition to El Dareer, interviewers were Sudanese social workers and medical and college students, who all received a standardized training in administration of the questionnaire. The questionnaire included demographic information on age, religion, education, occupation, income, marital status, and circumcision history (method, type, operator, healing, complications, need for treatment). Cooperative respondents were followed further with open-ended questions on their recollections of the procedure, their support or opposition, and plans for their daughters. When permitted, a physical exam was performed to corroborate type of circumcision and evidence of complications. Ninety-five percent of the sample population responded to the questionnaire, and 95% of this group proceeded to the open-ended questions. Only 12 women were willing to undergo examination, meaning that nearly all information on operation type and on sequelae was reported and could not be corroborated.

What the survey showed was that a genital operation of some sort is nearly universal. Over 98% of the women questioned were circumcised—3% with the *sunna* procedure; 12% "intermediate"; and 83%, pharaonic (El Dareer 1982: 1). The strongest predictor of operation type was level of education. Seventy-five percent of pharaonically circumcised girls were from illiterate families, while educated parents were more likely to opt for the milder forms (El Dareer 1982: 22). Over 90% of the operations in the Sudan were performed by *dayas*, or midwives, the rest by doctors, nurses, or old men and women who inherited the role (El Dareer 1982: 17).

Survey information for Egypt is not nearly so extensive, but the incidence of female genital operations is certainly much lower. Estimates range from one-third (Hosken 1978: 152) to one-half (Rugh 1984: 160) of all Egyptian women. In addition, the variety of procedures is more moderate. Except for the Nubian south, virtually no pharaonic operations are performed. A 1965 study of 651 circumcised women by two male Egyptian gynecologists reported that all circumcisions were variations of *sunna* and excision (Hansen 1972/73: 15).

That both the Egyptian and Sudanese governments recognize female genital operations as a health concern is evidenced by statutes in both countries which ban all but the most moderate forms. Sudan seems to have inherited a tradition of concern from the British Health Service, dating from the 1920s and 1930s, and now sponsors conferences and epidemiological research, such as El Dareer's, which use the language of medicine and epidemiology to oppose the practices. El Dareer, for example, is active in programs that educate rural Sudanese about the health hazards of female genital operations. In introducing the data from her survey, she explicitly states that her goal in carrying out such work is to reveal how the genital operations can best be eradicated.

Despite efforts to curb these practices, however, inadequate reporting renders the precise nature and extent of the health problem very difficult to assess. Perhaps most misleading is that few women relate the complications of circumcision to the operation, since it is generally believed to be harmless (El Dareer 1982: 28). Infections, for example, which are among the most common complications, are more likely to be attributed to the evil eye and treated by amulets, incantations, or a dip in the Nile (El Dareer 1982: 33). In addition, many women are reluctant to seek help from male physicians because of the area of the body they would have to expose on examination, and they therefore accept the painful consequences (El Dareer 1982: 28). Sufferers from the complications of the pharaonic procedure will often remain quiet because of the known illegality of the operation and the shame attached to endangering one's *daya* (El Dareer 1982: 28). El Dareer noted that of the 790 immediate complications reported to her, only 10% had been shown to medical personnel, and 85% of cases that in her opinion had later required serious medical attention went unreported (El Dareer 1982: 28). Mortality records are particularly incomplete. Primary fatalities (e.g., from hemorrhagic shock) are concealed for fear of legal repercussions, while secondary fatalities, such as death in childbirth, are not reported in a way that they can be related to the operations (Hosken 1982: 4).

Although the incidence of mortality is not known and the extent of morbidity is sketchy at best, the complications of female genital operations have been described, if not quantified, with some consistency (e.g., Dewhurst and Michelson 1964; El Dareer 1982; El Saadawi 1980; Hathout 1963; Huddleston 1944; Koso-Thomas 1987; Mustafa 1966; Worsley 1938). The most immediate of these complications include pain from lack of anesthesia, hemorrhage of major blood vessels, and fatal shock from loss of blood. Pain and the fear associated with it can lead to acute urinary retention, as can trauma to the urethra. The nearly complete sealing off of the vagina in infibulation makes chronic urinary retention a standard complaint after this operation. Inability to void urine can lead to the formation of painful stones and, particularly when preceded by the use of unsterilized equipment and dressings, makes urinary tract infections a virtual certainty. Untreated lower urinary tract infections can ascend to the bladder and kidneys (pyelonephritis) with devastating consequences, including renal failure, septicemia, and death. Pelvic inflammatory disease (infection of the uterus and fallopian tubes) is also common, excruciatingly painful, and can render a woman infertile. Local infection, often accompanied by anemia from blood loss, causes slow and incomplete healing, a condition which favors formation of excessive scar tissue, or keloid. Keloid is a particular problem in Nubian Egypt and the Sudan, as its formation is most characteristic of the healing process of blacks. By one estimation, keloids occur in about half of infibulated women in the Sudan (Worsley 1938: 687). Keloids can cause vaginal obstruction, predisposing women to urinary and menstrual blockage even in the noninfibulated. At the extreme, complete obstruction of the vagina (whether secondary to infibulation or keloids) can lead to hematocolpos, the accumulation of menstrual blood in the vagina. This condition can persist for months or even years. There are, in fact, documented cases of young women who have been put to death by their families when an abnormal swelling caused by accumulated blood was incorrectly interpreted as pregnancy out of wedlock (El Saadawi 1980: 26). Vulvar abscesses and cysts, finally, are common in operations that involve stitching (pharaonic and intermediate) and are caused by inclusion of skin into the stitched wound. These can swell to an enormous size and persist for years.

Medical sequelae, particularly of the pharaonic operations, also have a profound effect on childbirth.

Accumulated scarring favors a prolonged and painful labor, as fibrous vulvar tissue fails to dilate during contractions. Hemorrhage often results from tearing through scar tissue or through the cervix or perineum. Rupture of the vagina leads to formation of fistulae with rectum or bladder, causing lifelong incontinence, discomfort, and odor. Furthermore, in all cases of pharaonic circumcision, the woman must be disinfibulated, or cut open along the original scar, to permit passage of the baby. For its part, the child can be stillborn, brain damaged, or suffer malformations from the obstructed labor, lack of oxygen during the excessive time spent in the vaginal canal, or errant episiotomy cuts dealt by the *daya*.

While recognizing the difficulty of achieving an accurate quantification of these complications, a 1979 conference of the World Health Organization in Khartoum reported extensive experience of unanesthetized pain, hemorrhage, urinary retention, and infection in all forms of genital operation, but particularly in the pharaonic (Hosken 1982: 45). In El Dareer's survey, one-quarter of respondents reported immediate complications, with dysuria and hemorrhage the most common (each about 20% of all reported complications) (El Dareer 1982: 37).

When women in the sample were asked if they suffered from any of a list of known sequelae, 30% reported long-term consequences. Chronic urinary tract and pelvic infections were most commonly cited at about 25% each of all reported sequelae (El Dareer 1982: 28). In addition, the highest mortality rates in childbirth are reported from areas practicing circumcision (Hosken 1982: 110), although a cause and effect relationship cannot necessarily be inferred from this fact, since areas where the more radical procedures are done are also those regions with the lowest standard of living and the least adequate health care.

Evaluation of the immediate and long-term psychological impact of the operations has not been addressed, but the effects on sexual response seem fairly clear, despite the reluctance of women to discuss this topic (Rugh 1984: 110). Seventy-five percent of women in El Dareer's survey report either never experiencing sexual pleasure, or being totally indifferent to the notion (El Dareer 1982: 48). Scar tissue often makes sex painful, and with the substantial narrowing of the vaginal orifice in pharaonic circumcision, tearing and bleeding are greatly increased,

making first-time sex particularly feared (El Dareer 1982: 41). What is more, an infibulated woman usually needs to be cut open to allow intercourse. If not, full penetration can be a long and painful process taking many months (Boddy 1982: 686).

Although circumcised women do not consider many of the subsequent pains and complications they endure to be connected with their operations, one has to wonder why these operations are done in view of the immediate suffering alone. This question is intensified by the fact that on the books, at least, pharaonic circumcision in the Sudan and total clitoral excision in Egypt are forbidden, yet they continue to be practiced. Indeed, leniency of enforcement has been attributed to local riots and protests which accompanied the initial attempts to apply these laws (Hosken 1982: 105).

Several authors suggest that associations with and overtones of religious tradition make these practices more persistent than parallel customs in other cultures, such as foot binding in China, which simply disappeared when outlawed (Beck and Keddie 1980: 24). Indeed, El Dareer points out that religion and tradition are the most common reasons given by both women and men for the practice of these operations (El Dareer 1982: 67). The name *sunna*, or religious duty, which has become associated with one type of operation, implies unquestionable adherence for Muslims. When asked about these practices, people commonly respond, "We are following our religious teachings" (El Dareer 1982: 71), yet, interestingly, this same response is given even when non-*sunna* operations are being described (El Dareer 1982: 70). Thus, even to its religious defenders, the precise relationship of female genital operations to Islamic tradition, though apparently closely associated, is not so clear.

There is good evidence, in fact, that the custom is not even originally Islamic. Clitoridectomy and excision are practiced in West Africa from Mauritania to Cameroon, across central Africa to Chad, and in the East from Tanzania to Ethiopia; infibulation is customary in Mali, Somalia, Ethiopia, and Nigeria. This wide distribution of these practices in non-Islamic parts of Africa suggests that these operations are originally an African institution, adopted by Islam in its conquest of Egypt (Hansen 1972/73: 18). It should be noted in this regard that while female genital operations are practiced in several Islamic countries, they are unknown in 80% of the Islamic world, most notably Saudi Arabia, Jordan, Iran, and Iraq. Searching for precedent in Islamic texts, one finds that the operations are not mentioned anywhere in the Qur'an, although several statements from the companion *hadith*, the sayings of the Prophet, have a tradition of being interpreted as referring to female circumcision (Al Hibri 1982: 204). Even so, the traditions of *hadith* interpretation support only the most moderate of the operations. Egypt's 1959 statute banning all but partial clitoridectomy was based on a summary of religious opinion by the Ministry of Public Health. According to this source, it is unclear whether the *hadith* consider *khafd* (literally, reduction; in this context, the *sunna* operation) to be *sunna* (duty) or merely *makrama* (embellishment), but all interpretations agree that total excision is forbidden (Hosken 1982: 133).

In short, the commonly held conception among those who practice these operations, that they are dictated by religious tenets, has not been validated. Perhaps the interplay that arises between doctrine and a culturally embedded sense of what is right is more vague in Islam than some other religions, because there is no central religious authority to interpret and disseminate dogma to a largely illiterate populace. Religion and "tradition" are offered almost reflexively as an explanation for behavior patterns that are woven into the texture of society. This can be seen by the fact that many interviewees who supported the practice of female genital operations admitted to no clear or conscious rationale for doing so, or perhaps they were responding out of a deep fear of social criticism (El Dareer 1982: 78). Furthermore, many who opposed the operations still intended to subject their own daughters to them (El Dareer 1982: 82).

A window into understanding the belief patterns which undergird this sense of what is proper is offered by another popular explanation given by interviewees: cleanliness (El Dareer 1982: 73). The important role of this quality can be seen in the folk name for all the female genital operations: *tahara*, or purity. There is an extensive body of anecdotal material linking the operations to improved health, including prevention of stillbirth (Koso-Thomas 1987: 5) and relief from the generalized affliction of *el duda*, the "worm," which *dayas* sometimes claim to see jumping out when a girl is circumcised (El Dareer 1982: 13). As the name and the healing associated

with it imply, *tahara* refers to cleanliness rooted in deeper concerns.

What these concerns might be brings us to the most venerated anthropological explanation for mutilation operations—the rite of passage. In this construction, the operation serves as a marker of the movement from child to adult, in which the similarity between male and female is removed, permitting a ritual differentiation of the sexes (van Gennep 1960[1908]: 72). There is certainly support for this argument among many African tribes, where the operation takes place at puberty and is accompanied by a naming ceremony. In the Sudan and Egypt, however, female genital surgery is performed well before puberty, usually between the ages of about five to nine, and does not, therefore, correspond to actual physiological change.

The key to understanding these operations is to recognize that they serve as something of a "social puberty," powerfully signifying the young girl's future passage into sexuality. In some areas of the Sudan and Nubian Egypt, this passage is ritualized by investing the operations with the form and symbolism of a wedding. The girl is adorned with gold and henna in the style of a bride, while Qur'anic verses are chanted and a groom is exhorted to come forward (Kennedy 1970: 179). In this way, the operation becomes part of the same ceremonial complex as marriage and childbirth. The involvement with blood and genitalia foreshadows the young girl's future role as wife and mother (Kennedy 1970: 179).

Although a circumcised girl may still be a child biologically, her status becomes that of a woman after her operation. She is no longer permitted to play outside or to socialize with boys her age; in some areas even school is forbidden, as she begins the task of waiting for a husband (El Dareer 1982: 71). As a woman, she is now subject to a strict code of modesty, one of the most fundamental patterns of belief and behavior in the Arab world as a whole, involving appropriate bodily covering, character traits such as bashfulness and naiveté, and associated customs and belief relating to chastity, fidelity, separation, and seclusion (Antoun 1968: 672).

The traditional pattern of female constraint involves a separation of male and female worlds, with propriety and honor accorded women at home and men in public. If they must go out, women should be accompanied by symbols of virtuous intent: modest clothes, clear evidence of destination, the company of a child or adult relative (Rugh 1984: 186). There are separate male and female lines in stores and at bus depots, underscoring the forbidden nature of even the most superficial contact between unmarried men and women.

The reward for adherence to this code of modesty and separation is honor to the family and improved marriage prospects for the girl and her sisters. The punishment for its violation is shame (Rugh 1984: 160). An unmarried pregnant woman, for example, is considered bereft of honor and utterly alone. In certain areas it would not be unusual for her to commit suicide, or even to be murdered by her own family (El Saadawi 1980: 23).

Understanding the broader Arabic code of modesty and conceptions of female sexuality offers a clearer insight into the role of female genital operations. That the separation and seclusion of women is deeply connected to a particular orientation toward sexuality is not only intuitively plausible, but it is borne out by how early (prepubertally) these constraints are imposed and by their removal in old age. When a woman is no longer considered sexual, she is permitted to mix freely with men, often in a position of veneration and status (Antoun 1968: 677).

At the heart of the code of modesty is an ideology of female appetite, unpredictability, and lack of self-control (Antoun 1968: 678). The education of a young girl is a litany of what she is by nature likely to do but must avoid, because it is harmful, shameful, or religiously outlawed (El Saadawi 1980: 13). The ideal form of the code dictates the complete separation of the female threat to the public sphere. Absolute seclusion, however, is rarely an economically feasible option. Most Egyptians and Sudanese do not have the resources to maintain the required accoutrements of harems: extra servants, large gardens, high walls (Rugh 1984: 156). These features are more characteristic of countries, such as Saudi Arabia and Kuwait, where genital operations are not practiced. That these operations have, however, been reported as universal among nomadic Bedouin (Hosken 1982: 110) supports the contention that the genital operations, with the physical and symbolic barriers that they present, serve as a substitute for a more complete seclusion of women.

A man from the poor Bulaq community of Cairo is quoted by Rugh as saying,

In the cold countries of the north where the blood runs slowly, you do not have the need for the operation. But here in the warm countries we are more emotional and less restricted. Without this operation there is no telling what our women might do. For sure, one man would not be enough to satisfy them. (1984: 160)

It has been argued that this fear of female sexuality is a product of Arab concern with patrilineal purity (Beck and Keddie 1980: 8). Family and lineage are certainly of great importance in the Arab world, as evidenced by the slant of Islamic law and practice which, for example, do not recognize adoption (Antoun 1968: 689). Thus the genital operations can serve as a means for protecting lineage purity and, by extension, the honor of the woman's agnatic group (Beck and Keddie 1980). With extramarital sexuality at least symbolically prevented, there is a reduction of the destabilizing possibility that a given child may actually belong to another lineage. The genital scar—proudly called *nafsi*, "my own self," by the bearer (Worsley 1938: 687)—attests to the value of definite possessions for the families involved: honor for the women's family of birth and purity of patrilineage for the family of her husband (Oldfield Hayes 1975: 623). A particularly tight infibulation, in fact, is often rewarded by an increased brideprice and by gifts from the groom to the bride's family (El Dareer 1982: 41). Likewise, to call a man the son of an uncircumcised mother is one of the severest insults in the Arab world (Hansen 1972/73: 19).

A fascinating proof for the undergirding of infibulation by the issue of patrilineage is provided by Kennedy's fieldwork among the Nubians, who inhabit the Nile between Aswan, Egypt, and Dongola, Sudan. When much of their agricultural land was inundated after construction of the Aswan High Dam, their forced dependence on urban wage labor began to shift emphasis to the nuclear family, eroding the centrality of land inheritance and lineage continuity. The result has been that Nubian girls are being subjected increasingly to the milder excision operation instead of full-scale infibulation (Kennedy 1970: 186).

Despite the emphasis or the preceding arguments on a male conception of sexuality, one cannot ignore the fact that women are the strongest proponents of the operations (Oldfield Hayes 1975: 624). It is the grandmothers who make all arrangements and preparations, often without the father's consent

(Oldfield Hayes 1975: 619). An argument can be made for there being significant economic impetus to perpetuate the respected role of the *daya*, the only achieved position of prestige that is available to women. The *daya*'s work provides a substantial contribution to the village economy, particularly in areas where pharaonic circumcision is the norm (Oldfield Hayes 1975: 627). In addition to the initial infibulation, a woman often needs to be deinfibulated on her wedding night, usually at a substantial fee, since the *daya* is brought in secretly to protect the husband from the public shame of having been unable to achieve penetration (Oldfield Hayes 1975: 627). Deinfibulation and subsequent reinfibulation are done also for infections, infertility, urinary and menstrual retention, and childbirth (El Dareer 1982: 51). There is also the additional phenomenon of widows, divorcees, and married women reinfibulating to appear virginal, some of them actually going through the procedure at regular intervals (El Dareer 1982: 51).

Another argument suggests that while men view these practices in terms of chastity and honor, women understand genital operations by focusing on fertility and deemphasizing sexuality (Boddy 1982). Based on her fieldwork in the Sudan, Boddy developed a linguistic and cultural exegesis which links fertility with enclosedness—a characteristic of infibulated genitalia. The idiom of enclosure is echoed in Sudanese folk medicine, where an accumulation of demons (*djinn*) is feared at all orifices, and many remedies are based on the assumption that illness is caused by things opening or coming apart. The enclosed womb protects a woman's truest possession, her fertility, as well as the future lineage of her husband. In this way, Boddy argues, infibulation is an assertive and symbolic act, controlled by women, in which the womb becomes a social space—enclosed, guarded, and impervious.

Analyses such as this present a stumbling block to Western political agitation against female genital operations. While it may be true, as Hosken asserts, that without "the [male] preference for women who have undergone the operations, the practice would die out" (Hosken 1982: 11), hopeful assertions such as this miss the cultural point. Preferences for ritual are not so much matters of personal predilection as they are deeply embedded solutions to group concerns— in this case to issues such as sexuality, fertility, and patrilineage.

From the perspective of those who would like to see these practices completely eradicated, one of the most frustrating aspects of the current practice of female genital operations has been its peripheral incorporation into the biomedical health care system. Thus, while the World Health Organization and other medical groups assume a "passive stance" (Hosken 1982: 272) with regard to these procedures, trained medical personnel, drugs, and equipment are being disseminated and used to perform genital operations (Hosken 1982: 287). In urban Sudan there has been an official policy of using the health care system for the operations in order to reduce complications through improved surgical conditions (Hosken 1982: 47). Physicians do about 2% of the urban operations, while *dayas* with government sponsored midwifery training (a legacy of the British) do about 35% (El Dareer 1982: 15).

From a medical perspective, this development has to be seen as encouraging. Sanitation is greatly improved, and antibiotics, anesthetics, and better aseptic techniques are all more likely to be used when trained operators perform the surgery (El Dareer 1982: 16). Perhaps even more important, particularly for the future, is what seems to be a slow turning away from the more extreme operations. The most sensitive barometer of potential change is probably the opinions of those who have been subjected to operations and are now themselves the parents of young girls. The interviews conducted by El Dareer throughout the Sudan show a striking discordance between the type of operation previously performed and that currently favored. While over 80% were infibulated, only 23% of women and 16% of men actually preferred this procedure, with the majority of men opting for *sunna* instead, most women favoring intermediate, and approximately 15% of respondents preferring no operation at all (El Dareer 1982: 69). While El Dareer's survey is not exhaustive, it represents the best statistical information available, at least for the Sudan, and could well be predictive of substantial moderation of future practice.

The most significant change in these practices is likely to be rooted in the inexorable Western influences of industrialization and urbanization. Kennedy has shown how Nubian custom changed as the importance of tribal descent was replaced by the urban focus on paid labor and the nuclear family. A similar case can be made for the major urban centers of the

Sudan, where the incidence of pharaonic operations is dropping in favor of the intermediate form (El Dareer 1982: 22). In Egypt, the process of urbanization is farther along, and a majority of the middle class now abstains from genital operations altogether (Hosken 1978: 152).

These small seeds of change leave us, still, with a dilemma of cross-cultural ethics. Konner's admonition that "female circumcision is one place where we ought to draw the line" argues for the increasingly popular Western movement of opposition to an alien practice that is painful, physically disfiguring, medically treacherous, and oppressive to women. There is considerable moral force to this stance, yet it is diluted in the end by a failure to place the female genital operations within the context of anthropological thought. Hosken even asserts that the practice, in its violence and subjugation, has "nothing to do with culture" (Hosken 1982: 1). This skirts not only the issue of culturally embedded meaning for those who practice and experience female genital operations but also our own cultural assumptions.

Cultural relativism, although it is not generally considered to be so, is also a position of advocacy. The anthropological enterprise of exploring what it means to be human through consideration of alien behavior has shown how customs and rituals are not isolated practices to be chosen or discarded at will, but they form a framework of interrelated idioms, a logic of daily life through which reality is ordered and experience mediated. Numerous studies have demonstrated how an entire culture is stressed when its customs are devalued, "modernized," or eliminated by the processes of urbanization and acculturation. Hypertension, loss of respect for the elders,

fragmentation of families, increased prevalence of depression and suicide have been documented among both urbanized Zulu (Scotch 1963) and Ethiopian immigrants to Israel (Weingrod 1987), to cite two examples.

The failings of anthropology in its study of female genital operations in Egypt and the Sudan have been its inability to integrate a consideration of the medical complications of the practice into its description and a denial of its own position of moral advocacy. Because of this, the international women's rights movement has not been far off base in considering anthropologists as perpetuating a cover-up. Although this has doubtless taken place outside of conscious awareness for the most part, with no intention to mislead, a decision to describe without judging does require certain blindspots.

With a capacity perhaps unique among non-Western practices in its ability to generate emotional debate and misunderstanding, the phenomenon of female genital operations can be seen as a compelling test-case in cross-cultural ethics for medical anthropology. The challenge is to develop an explanatory model that can integrate anthropological description, public health concerns, and our own cultural sensitivities. This last point is the most likely to be ignored because of its perceived antagonism to anthropology's nonjudgmental relativism. At the limits of our ability to understand another culture's practices, however, an articulated self-awareness helps to remind us that we are ourselves looking at the world through culturally trained eyes. While relativism is a powerful descriptive tool for getting inside another culture, both the describer and his audience have cultural agendas that must be considered as well.

15

Return to Wirikuta: Ritual Reversal and Symbolic Continuity on the Peyote Hunt of the Huichol Indians

Barbara G. Myerhoff

*P*ersuasively illustrating the close integration of myth and symbolism within ritual, the following article by Barbara G. Myerhoff explores symbolic reversals and oppositions within the annual peyote hunt of the Huichol, an indigenous population of north-central Mexico. Based on fieldwork in 1965 and 1966, Myerhoff's work exemplifies the anthropological analysis of symbolism within a ritual context. A shaman leads small groups to Wirikuta, which is both an actual geographic location and a myth-based spiritual state, where everything ordinary is inverted. These reversals occur in naming, interpersonal behavior, ritual behavior, and emotional states. Through such ritual reversals, the author argues, a number of functions are served. Everyday existence is set apart from the sacred. The ordinary is turned into something extraordinary yet continuous. Peyote-seekers become supernatural deities and, in the dramatization that is ritual, act and behave within the realm of the sacred.*

Although Barbara Myerhoff's early field research took place in Mexico, later in her career she documented Jewish communities in southern California. She paid special attention to rituals in the lives of elderly Jews. Her research is highlighted in two documentary films, both of which are excellent illustrations of a skilled ethnographer at work: "Number Our Days" (1983) and "In Her Own Time" (1985), both produced by Direct Cinema Ltd.

God is day and night, winter summer, war peace, satiety hunger—all opposites, this is the meaning.

—Heraclitus

The Peyote Hunt of the Huichol Indians

Rituals of opposition and reversal constitute a critical part of a lengthy religious ceremony, the peyote hunt, practiced by the Huichol Indians of north-central Mexico.[1] In order to understand the function

1. The Huichol Indians are a quasi-tribe of about 10,000 living in dispersed communities in north-central Mexico. They are among the least acculturated Mexican Indians and

of these rituals it is necessary to adumbrate the major features and purposes of the peyote hunt. Annually, small groups of Huichols, led by a shaman-priest or *mara'akáme*, return to Wirikuta to hunt the peyote. Wirikuta is a high desert several hundred miles from the Huichols' present abode in the Sierra Madre Occidentál. Mythically and in all likelihood historically, it is their original homeland, the place once inhabited by the First People, the quasi-deified ancestors. But Wirikuta is much more than a geographical location; it is *illud tempus,* the paradisical condition that existed before the creation of the world and mankind, and the condition that will prevail at the end of time.

In Wirikuta, as in the paradise envisioned in many creation myths, all is unity, a cosmic totality without barriers of any kind, without the differentations that characterize the mundane mortal world. In Wirikuta, separations are obliterated—between sexes, between leader and led, young and old, animals and man, plants and animals, and man and the deities. The social order and the natural and supernatural realms are rejoined into their original state of seamless continuity. Wirikuta is the center of the four directions where, as the Huichol describe it, "All is unity, all is one, all is ourselves."

In Wirikuta, the three major symbols of Huichol world view are likewise fused. These are the Deer, representing the Huichols' past life as nomadic hunters; the Maize, representing their present life as sedentary agriculturalists; and peyote, signifying the private, spiritual vision of each individual. To reenter Wirikuta, the peyote pilgrims must be transformed into the First People. They assume the identity of particular deities and literally hunt the peyote which grows in Wirikuta, tracking and following it in the form of deer footprints, stalking and shooting it with bow and arrow, consuming it in a climactic ceremony of total communion. Once the peyote has been hunted, consumed, and sufficient supplies have been gathered for use in the ceremonies of the coming year, the pilgrims hastily leave and return to their homes and to their mortal condition. The entire

peyote hunt is very complex, consisting of many rituals and symbols; here I will only concentrate on one set of rituals, those which concern reversal and opposition, and the part they play in enabling the pilgrims to experience the sense of totality and cosmic unity that is their overarching religious goal.

Mythological and Ritual Aspects of Reversals

"In Wirikuta, we change the names of everything . . . everything is backwards." Ramón Medina Silva, the officiating mara'akáme, who led the Peyote Hunt of 1966 in which I participated, thus explained the reversals that obtain during the pilgrimage. "The mara'akáme tells [the pilgrims], 'Now we will change everything, all the meanings, because that is the way it must be with the *hikuritámete* [peyote pilgrims]. As it was in Ancient Times, so that all can be united.'"

The reversals to which he refers occur on four distinct levels: naming, interpersonal behavior, ritual behavior, and emotional states. The reversals in naming are very specific. Ideally, everything is its opposite and everything is newly named each year. But in fact, for many things there are often no clear opposites, and substitutions are made, chosen for reasons that are not always clear. Frequently the substitutions seem dictated by simple visual association—thus the head is a pot, the nose a penis, hair is cactus fiber. A great many of these substitutions recur each year and are standardized. Nevertheless, they are defined as opposites in this context and are treated as if they were spontaneous rather than patterned.

On the interpersonal-behavioral level, direct oppositions are more straightforward. One says yes when he or she means no. A person proffers a foot instead of a hand. Conversations are conducted with conversants standing back to back, and so forth. Behavior is also altered to correspond with the ritual identity of the participant. Thus the oldest man, transformed into a *nunutsi* or little child for the journey, is not permitted to gather firewood because "this work is too heavy and strenuous for one so young."

The deities are portrayed as the opposite of mortals in that the former have no physiological needs. Thus the pilgrims, as the First People, disguise,

---

in part their resistance to outside influence is attributable to the complex and extraordinarily rich ritual and symbolic life they lead. A detailed presentation of the peyote hunt is presented in Myerhoff 1974. The fieldwork on which the present paper was based took place in 1965 and 1966.

minimize, and forego their human physiological activities as much as possible. Sexual abstinence is practiced. Washing is forsworn. Eating, sleeping, and drinking are kept to an absolute minimum. Defecation and urination are said not to occur and are practiced covertly. All forms of social distinction and organization are minimized, and even the mara'akáme's leadership and direction are extremely oblique. The ordinary division of labor is suspended and altered in various ways. All forms of discord are strictly forbidden, and disruptive emotions such as jealousy and deceit, usually tolerated as part of the human condition, are completely proscribed for the pilgrims. No special treatment is afforded to children; no behavioral distinctions between the sexes are allowed. Even the separateness of the mara'akáme from his group is minimized, and his assistant immediately performs for him all rituals that the mara'akáme has just performed for the rest of the party.

In terms of ritual actions, reversals are quite clear. The cardinal directions, and up and down, are switched in behaviors which involve offering sacred water and food to the four corners and the center of the world. The fire is circled in a counterclockwise direction instead of clockwise as on normal ceremonial occasions. In Wirikuta, the mara'akáme's assistant sits to the latter's left instead of to his right.

Emotions as well as behaviors are altered on the basis of the pilgrims' transformation into deities. Since mortals would be jubilant, presumably, on returning to their pre-creation, mythical homeland, and grief-stricken on departing from it, the pilgrims weep as they reenter Wirikuta and are exultant on departing. This reflects the fact that they are deities leaving paradise, not mortals returning from it.

I should note also some of the attitudes and values toward the reversals that I observed. For example, there seems to be an aesthetic dimension since they regard some reversals as more satisfying than others. Humorous and ironic changes are a source of much laughter and delight. Thus the name of the wife of the mara'akáme was changed to "ugly *gringa*." The mara'akáme himself was the pope. The anthropologists' camper was a burro that drank much tequila. They also delight in compounding the reversals: "Ah what a pity that we have caught no peyote. Here we sit, sad, surrounded by baskets of flowers under a cold sun." Thus said one pilgrim after a successful day of gathering baskets full of peyote, while standing in the moonlight. Mistakes and humorous improvisations are also the source of new reversals. When in a careless moment Los Angeles was referred to as "home," everyone was very pleased and amused; from then on home was Los Angeles and even in sacred chants and prayers this reversal was maintained. Accidental reversals such as this are just as obligatory as the conventional ones and the new ones "dreamed" by the mara'akáme. Mistakes are corrected with good will but firmly, and everyone shares in the responsibility for keeping track of the changes, reminding each other repeatedly of the changes that have been instituted. The more changes the better, and each day, as more are established, more attention by all is required to keep things straight. Normal conversation and behavior become more difficult with each new day's accumulation of changes. Sunsets are ugly. No one is tired. Peyote is sweet. The pilgrimage is a failure. There is too much food to eat, and so forth.

The reversals were not instituted or removed by any formal rituals, although it is said that there are such. It became apparent that the reversals were in effect at the periphery of Wirikuta when someone sneezed. This was received by uproarious laughter, for, the nose had become a penis and a sneeze, accordingly, was an off-color joke. After the peyote hunt, the reversals were set aside gradually as the group moved away from Wirikuta. On returning home, the pilgrims regaled those who had remained behind with descriptions of the reversals and the confusions they had engendered.

The Functions and Symbolism of the Reversals

How should these ideas and actions concerning reversal and opposition be understood? In the Huichol context, they achieve several purposes simultaneously. Perhaps most familiar and straightforward is their function in transforming the mundane into the sacred by disguising the everyday features of environment, society, and behavior, and in the Durkeimian sense "setting it apart." As Ramón Medina Silva explained, "One changes everything . . . when [we] cross over there to the Peyote Country . . .

because it is a very sacred thing, it is the most sacred. It is our life, as one says. That is why nowadays one gives things other names. One changes everything. Only when they return home, then they call everything again what it is." Here the totality and scope of the reversals are important—actions, names, ritual, and everyday behaviors are altered so that participants are conscious at all times of the extraordinary nature of their undertaking. Nothing is natural, habitual, or taken for granted. The boundaries between the ordinary and the sacred are sharply defined and attention to this extraordinary state of affairs cannot lag when one has to be perpetually self-conscious and vigilant against lapses. Reversals promote the essential attitude of the sacred, the *mysterium tremendum et fascinans*.

The transformation of mortals into deities is related to this purpose. Again and again in theological, mythological, and ethnographic literature one encounters the impossibility of mortals entering a supernatural realm in their normal condition. The shaman transforms himself into a spirit in order to perform his duties as soul guide or psychopomp. This is the essence of the Symplegades motif in shamanism—the passage into the other world through the crashing gates, as Eliade (1964) points out. The "paradoxical passage" to the supernatural domain is open only to those who have been transformed from their human state into pure spirit. An apotheosis is required of those who would "cross over" and achieve the "breakthrough in planes." The peyote hunt opens Wirikuta to all proper pilgrims, but they, like the shaman, cannot enter in mortal form. To enter Wirikuta, the Huichol peyote-seekers do not merely impersonate the deities by assuming their names and garb. Ritually and symbolically, they *become* supernatural, disguising the mortal coil, abrogating human functions and forms.

This "backwardness" operates on two levels: as the deities, they are the obverse of mortals; as deities, they are going back, going backwards, and signifying this by doing everything backwards. Backwardness is found frequently in connection with supernatural states, and with the denial of humanity. Lugbara witches are inverted beings who walk on their heads (Middleton 1960). And in Genesis we find that "the inhabitants of paradise stand on their heads and walk on their hands; as do all the dead" (Graves and Patai 1966:73, citing Gen. 24:65). The

examples could be expanded indefinitely. Eliade suggests this widespread association of backwardness and the supernatural when he comments, "Consequently to do away with this state of [humanity] even if only provisionally, is equivalent to reestablishing the primordial condition of man, in other words, to banish time, to go backwards, to recover the 'paradisial' *illud tempus*" (1960:72).

A third function of these reversals is their provision of mnemonic, or aid to the imagination and memory, for conception and action. For a time the peyote pilgrims in the Huichol religion live in the supernatural. They go beyond invoking and discussing it, for Wirikuta exists in ritual as well as mythical terms. Ritual, unlike myth, requires action. Ritual is a dramatization. Pilgrims must not only imagine the unimaginable, they must behave within it. It is through its action dimension that ritual makes religious values "really real," and fuses the "lived-in" and the "dreamed-of order," as Geertz puts it. Full staging is necessary. The unfathomable—*illud tempus*, the primordial state before time—is the setting. Props, costumes, etiquette, vocabulary, emotions—all must be conceived and specified. The theme of opposition provides the details that are needed to make the drama credible and convincing; the metaphor of backwardness makes for a concretization and amplification of the ineffable. Again Eliade's writings offer an insight along these lines. He points out that the theme of *coincidentia oppositorum* is an "eschatological symbol par excellence, which denotes that Time and History have come to an end—in the lion lying down with the lamb" (1962:121). It is in the Garden of Eden that "opposites lie down together," it is there that conflicts and divisions are ultimately abolished and man's original innocence and wholeness are regained.

Separation, transformation, and concretization then are three purposes achieved by the reversals in Wirikuta. There is a fourth, perhaps the most important and common function of rituals of this nature. That is the capacity of reversals to invoke continuity through emphasis on opposition. How this operates in the Huichol case was explained in very precise terms by Ramón Medina Silva in a text he dictated about the 1966 peyote hunt five years later. He was elaborating on the beauties of Wirikuta and for the first time indicated that it was the state that would prevail at the end of time as well as that which characterized the beginning. When the world ends, the First People would return. "All will be in unity, all will be one, all will be as you have seen it there, in Wirikuta." The present world, it became clear, was but a shallow and misleading interlude, a transient period characterized by difference and separations, bracketed by an enduring condition of totality and continuity.

> When the world ends it will be like when the names of things are changed during the Peyote Hunt. All will be different, the opposite of what it is now. Now there are two eyes in the heavens, the Sun and the Moon. Then, the Moon will open his eye and become brighter. The sun will become dimmer. There will be no more difference between them. Then, no more men and no more women. No more child and no more adult. All will change places. Even the mara'akáme will no longer be separate. That is why there must always be a *nunutsi* when we go to Wirikuta. Because the old man and the tiny baby, they are the same.
>
> —Personal communication, Los Angeles, 1971

Polarity reaffirms continuity. The baby and the adult ultimately are joined, ends of a single continuum. Watts states it as follows: "What exactly is polarity? It is something much more than simple duality or opposition. For to say that opposites are polar is to say much more than that they are joined . . . , that they are the terms, ends, or extremities of a single whole. Polar opposites are therefore inseparable opposites, like the poles of the earth or of a magnet, or the ends of a stick or the faces of a coin" (1970:45).

Surely the vision of an original condition of unity, before the world and mankind began, is one of the most common themes in religions of every nature and place. Again to draw on Eliade, "Among the 'primitive' peoples, just as among the Saints and the Christian theologians, mystic ecstasy is a return to Paradise, expressed by the overcoming of Time and History . . . , and [represents] a recovery of the primordial state of Man" (1960:72).

The theme of nostalgia for lost paradise recurs so often as to be counted by some as panhuman. Theories attribute this yearning to various causes: a lingering memory of the undifferentiated state in the womb, the unfilled wish for a happy childhood, a fantasy of premortal blessedness and purity, a form of what the Jungians call uroboric incest, a fatal desire for nonbeing, and so forth (see Neumann 1954). Many theologians have viewed this vision of cosmic oneness as the essence of the mystical experience and of religious ecstasy. The particulars vary from one religion to the next but the ingredients are stable: paradise is that which existed before the beginning of time, before life and death, before light and darkness. Here animals and man lived in a state of easy companionship, speaking the same language, untroubled by thirst, hunger, pain, weariness, loneliness, struggle, or appetite. Humans knew neither discord nor distinction among themselves— they were sexless, without self-awareness, and indeed undifferentiated from the very gods. Then an irreversible and cataclysmic sundering took place and instead of wholeness there was separation, the separation that was Creation. Henceforth, the human organism was no longer indistinguishable from the cosmos. The primordial splitting left mankind as we know it now, forever haunted by remembrance of and attraction for an original condition of wholeness.

The reversals, then, express the most lamentable features of the human condition by emphasizing the loss of the paradisical state of oneness. Humans are fragmented, incomplete, and isolated from the deities; they are vulnerable and literally mortal, which is to say helpless before the ravages of pain, time, and death. At the same time, the reversals remind mankind of the primordial wholeness that will again prevail when paradise is regained. Here is the theme expressed in a cultural form familiar to most of us, the Gospel according to Thomas:

> They said to Him: Shall we then, being children enter the Kingdom? Jesus said to them: When you make the two one, and when you make the inner as the outer and the outer as the inner and the above as the below, and when you make the male and the female into a single one, so that the male will not be male and the female [not] be female, when you make eyes in the place of an eye, a hand in the place of a hand, and a foot in the place of a foot, an image in the place of an image, then shall you enter [the Kingdom].
>
> —Logia 23–35, cited in Guillaumont et al. 1959:17–19

Conclusions

The theme of reversal, in all its permutations and combinations—opposition (complementary and binary), inversion, and dualism—has always been of great interest to anthropologists, mythographers, theologians, psychologists, linguists, and artists. The subject seems inexhaustible. In anthropology alone, we continue to unravel additional layers of meaning, to discover more and more functions fulfilled by reversals in various contexts. Recent studies especially have shown how reversals can be used to make statements about the social order—to affirm it, attack it, suspend it, redefine it, oppose it, buttress it, emphasize one part of it at the cost of another, and so forth. We see a magnificently fruitful image put to diverse purposes, capable of an overwhelming range of expression. Obviously there is no question of looking for the true or correct meaning in the use of reversals. We are dealing with a symbolic referent that has new meanings in every new context and within a single context embraces multiple and contradictory meanings simultaneously. In Wirikuta, the reversals accomplish many purposes and contain a major paradox. They emphasize the difference between Wirikuta and the mundane life, and the differentiated nature of the human condition. Also they stress the nondifferentiated nature of Wirikuta. The reversals thus portray differentiation and continuity at the same time. Both are true, separation and oneness, though this is contradictory and paradoxical. But this should come as no surprise, for paradox is the very quick of ritual. In ritual, as in the Garden, opposites are made to lie down together.

Appendix: How the Names Are Changed on the Peyote Journey

Text dictated by Ramón Medina Silva, mara'akáme of San Sebastián, Mexico, to explain the reversals used on the peyote hunt.

Well, let's see now. I shall speak about how we do things when we go and seek the peyote, how we change the names of everything. How we call the things we see and do by another name for all those days. Until we return. Because all must be done as it must be done. As it was laid down in the beginning. How it was when the mara'akáme who is Tatewari[2] led all those great ones to Wirikuta. When they crossed over there, to the peyote country. Because that is a very sacred thing, it is the most sacred. It is our life, as one says. That is why nowadays one gives things other names. One changes everything. Only when they return home, then they call everything again that it is.

When everything is ready, when all the symbols which we take with us, the gourd bowls, the yarn discs, the arrows, everything has been made, when all have prayed together we set out. Then we must change everything, all the meanings. For instance: a pot which is black and round, it is called a head. It is the mara'akáme who directs everything. He is the one who listens in his dream, with his power and his knowledge. He speaks to Tatewarí, he speaks to Kauyumari.[3] Kauyumari tells him everything, how it must be. Then he says to his companions, if he is the leader of the journey to the peyote, look, this thing is this way, and this is how it must be done. He tells them, look, now we will change everything, all the meanings, because that is the way it must be with the *hikuritámete* (peyote pilgrims). As it was in ancient times, so that all can be united. As it was long ago, before the time of my grandfather, even before the time of his grandfather. So the mara'akáme has to see to everything, so that as much as possible all the words are changed. Only when one comes home, then everything can be changed back again to the way it was.

"Look," the mara'akáma says to them, "it is when you say 'good morning,' you mean 'good evening,' everything is backwards. You say 'goodbye, I am leaving you,' but you are really coming. You do not shake hands, you shake feet. You hold out your right foot to be shaken by the foot of your companion. You say 'good afternoon,' yet it is only morning."

So the mara'akáme tells them, as he has dreamed it. He dreams it differently each time. Every year they

---

2. Huichol name for the deity with whom the shaman has a special affinity, roughly translatable as Our Grandfather Fire.
3. Kauyumari is a trickster hero, quasi-deified and roughly translatable as Sacred Deer Person.

change the names of things differently because every year the mara'akáme dreams new names. Even if it is the same mara'akáme who leads the journey, he still changes the names each time differently.

And he watches who makes mistakes because there must be no error. One must use the names the mara'akáme has dreamed. Because if one makes an error it is not right. That is how it is. It is a beautiful thing because it is right. Daily, daily, the mara'akáme goes explaining everything to them so that they do not make mistakes. The mara'akáme says to a companion, "Look, why does that man over there watch us, why does he stare at us?" And then he says, "Look, what is it he has to stare at us?" "His eyes," says his companion. "No," the mara'akáme answers, "they are not his eyes, they are tomatoes." That is how he goes explaining how everything should be called.

When one makes cigarettes for the journey, one uses the dried husks of maize for the wrappings. And the tobacco, it is called the droppings of ants. Tortillas one calls bread. Beans one calls fruit from a tree. Maize is wheat. Water is tequila. Instead of saying, "Let us go and get water to drink," you say, "Ah, let us take tequila to eat." *Atole* [maize broth], that is brains. Sandals are cactus. Fingers are sticks. Hair, that is cactus fiber. The moon, that is a cold sun.

On all the trails on which we travel to the peyote country, as we see different things we make this change. That is because the peyote is very sacred, very sacred. That is why it is reversed. Therefore, when we see a dog, it is a cat, or it is a coyote. Ordinarily, when we see a dog, it is just a dog, but when we walk for the peyote it is a cat or a coyote or even something else, as the mara'akáme dreams it. When we see a burro, it is not a burro, it is a cow, or a horse. And when we see a horse, it is something else. When we see a dove or a small bird of some kind, is it a small bird? No, the mara'akáme says, it is an eagle, it is a hawk. Or a piglet, it is not a piglet, it is an armadillo. When we hunt the deer, which is very sacred, it is not a deer, on this journey. It is a lamb, or a cat. And the nets for catching deer? They are called sewing thread.

When we say come, it means go away. When we say "shh, quiet," it means to shout, and when we whistle or call to the front we are really calling to a person behind us. We speak in this direction here.

That one over there turns because he already knows how it is, how everything is reversed. To say, "Let us stay here," means to go, "let us go," and when we say "sit down," we mean, "stand up." It is also so when we have crossed over, when we are in the country of the peyote. Even the peyote is called by another name, as the mara'akáme dreamed. Then the peyote is flower or something else.

It is so with Tatewarí, with Tayaupa.[4] The mara'akáme, we call him Tatewarí. He is Tatewarí, he who leads us. But there in Wirikuta, one says something else. One calls him "the red one." And Tayaupa, he is "the shining one." So all is changed. Our companion who is old, he is called the child. Our companion who is young, he is the old one. When we want to speak of the machete, we say "hook." When one speaks of wood, one really means fish. Begging your pardon, instead of saying "to eat," we say "to defecate." And, begging your pardon, "I am going to urinate" means "I am going to drink water." When speaking of blowing one's nose, one says "give me the honey." "He is deaf" means "how well he hears." So everything is changed, everything is different or backwards.

The mara'akáme goes explaining how everything should be said, everything, many times, or his companions would forget and make errors. In the late afternoon, when all are gathered around Tatewarí, we all pray there, and the mara'akáme tells how it should be. So for instance he says, "Do not speak of this one or that one as serious. Say he is a jaguar. You see an old woman and her face is all wrinkled, coming from afar, do not say, 'Ah, there is a man,' say 'Ah, here comes a wooden image.' You say, 'Here comes the image of Santo Cristo.' Or if it is a woman coming, say 'Ah, here comes the image of Guadalupe.'"

Women, you call flowers. For the woman's skirts, you say, "bush," and for her blouse you say "palm roots." And a man's clothing, that too is changed. His clothing, you call his fur. His hat, that is a mushroom. Or it is his sandal. Begging your pardon, but what we carry down here, the testicles, they are called avocados. And the penis, that is his nose. That is how it is.

---

4. Our Father Sun.

When we come back with the peyote, the peyote which has been hunted, they make a ceremony and everything is changed back again. And those who are at home, when one returns they grab one and ask, "What is it you called things? How is it that now you call the hands hands but when you left you called them feet?" Well, it is because they have changed the names back again. And they all want to know what they called things. One tells them, and there is laughter. That is how it is. Because it must be as it was said in the beginning, in ancient times. [Adapted from Myerhoff 1974]

16

Ritual Regulation of Environmental Relations Among a New Guinea People

Roy A. Rappaport

In this article, originally published in 1967, Roy A. Rappaport takes issue with anthropologists who emphasize only the symbolic and emotional aspects of ritual. To Rappaport, ritual may have observable, measurable, practical results, even if those results are not recognizable to the participants. By expanding his focus of study to include the ecosystem of which humans are a part, the author argues that the true functions of ritual may be understood.

Rappaport documents the Tsembaga, a small, politically egalitarian population in one of the interior valleys of New Guinea. The author presents a detailed description of the Tsembaga ecosystem and subsistence methods, emphasizing the place of pigs. Tsembaga carefully control the size of their pig herds, limiting reproduction and slaughtering pigs only for ritual purposes. After considering the cycle of rituals involving pig slaughter—which relates to warfare and maintaining relationships with allies—Rappaport concludes that the size of a pig herd actually determines the timing of some rituals, especially the kaiko, *or "pig festival," which redistributes pork to a large number of people in the territory. When the cost of maintaining a large number of pigs becomes too great, social forces call for the ritual. Therefore, the timing of Tsembaga rituals is connected to the natural environment, including other humans in the region. In clear opposition to such anthropologists as Mary Douglas, Clifford Geertz, and Victor Turner, Rappaport concludes that "[r]eligious ritual may do much more than symbolize, validate, and intensify relationships."*

A key feature of Rappaport's argument is his distinction between the "operational environment," which can be observed by the anthropologist, and the "cognized environment," or the Tsembaga's perceived environment—including their reasons for rituals and beliefs about their effects. Rappaport maintains that the Tsembaga, like other peoples, do not see all the empirical effects of their rituals.

Most functional studies of religious behavior in anthropology have as an analytic goal the elucidation of events, processes, or relationships occurring within a social unit of some sort. The social unit is

"Ritual regulation of environmental relations among a New Guinea people," ETHNOLOGY 6:17–30, 1967. Reprinted by permission.

not always well defined, but in some cases it appears to be a church, that is, a group of people who entertain similar beliefs about the universe, or a congregation, a group of people who participate together in the performance of religious rituals. There have been exceptions. Thus Vayda, Leeds, and Smith (1961) and O. K. Moore (1957) have clearly perceived that the functions of religious ritual are not necessarily confined within the boundaries of a congregation or even a church. By and large, however, I believe that the following statement by Homans (1941: 172) represents fairly the dominant line of anthropological thought concerning the functions of religious ritual:

> Ritual actions do not produce a practical result on the external world—that is one of the reasons why we call them ritual. But to make this statement is not to say that ritual has no function. Its function is not related to the world external to the society but to the internal constitution of the society. It gives the members of the society confidence, it dispels their anxieties, it disciplines their social organization.

No argument will be raised here against the sociological and psychological functions imputed by Homans, and many others before him, to ritual. They seem to me to be plausible. Nevertheless, in some cases at least, ritual does produce, in Homans' terms, "a practical result on the world" external not only to the social unit composed of those who participate together in ritual performances but also to the larger unit composed of those who entertain similar beliefs concerning the universe. The material presented here will show that the ritual cycles of the Tsembaga, and of other local territorial groups of Maring speakers living in the New Guinea interior, play an important part in regulating the relationships of these groups with both the nonhuman components of their immediate environments and the human components of their less immediate environments, that is, with other similar territorial groups. To be more specific, this regulation helps to maintain the biotic communities existing within their territories, redistributes land among people and people over land, and limits the frequency of fighting. In the absence of authoritative political statuses or offices, the ritual cycle likewise provides a means for mobilizing allies when warfare may be undertaken. It also provides a mechanism for redistributing local pig surpluses in the form of pork throughout a large regional population while helping to assure the local population of a supply of pork when its members are most in need of high quality protein.

Religious ritual may be defined, for the purposes of this paper, as the prescribed performance of conventionalized acts manifestly directed toward the involvement of nonempirical or supernatural agencies in the affairs of the actors. While this definition relies upon the formal characteristics of the performances and upon the motives for undertaking them, attention will be focused upon the empirical effects of ritual performances and sequences of ritual performances. The religious rituals to be discussed are regarded as neither more nor less than part of the behavioral repertoire employed by an aggregate of organisms in adjusting to its environment.

The data upon which this paper is based were collected during fourteen months of field work among the Tsembaga, one of about twenty local groups of Maring speakers living in the Simbai and Jimi Valleys of the Bismarck Range in the Territory of New Guinea. The size of Maring local groups varies from a little over 100 to 900. The Tsembaga, who in 1963 numbered 204 persons, are located on the south wall of the Simbai Valley. The country in which they live differs from the true highlands in being lower, generally more rugged, and more heavily forested. Tsembaga territory rises, within a total surface area of 3.2 square miles, from an elevation of 2,200 feet at the Simbai river to 7,200 feet at the ridge crest. Gardens are cut in the secondary forests up to between 5,000 and 5,400 feet, above which the area remains in primary forest. Rainfall reaches 150 inches per year.

The Tsembaga have come into contact with the outside world only recently; the first government patrol to penetrate their territory arrived in 1954. They were considered uncontrolled by the Australian government until 1962, and they remain unmissionized to this day.

The 204 Tsembaga are distributed among five putatively patrilineal clans, which are, in turn, organized into more inclusive groupings on two hierarchical levels below that of the total local group. Internal political structure is highly egalitarian. There are no hereditary or elected chiefs, nor are there even "big men" who can regularly coerce or command the support of their clansmen or co-residents in economic or forceful enterprises.

It is convenient to regard the Tsembaga as a population in the ecological sense, that is, as one of the components of a system of trophic exchanges taking place within a bounded area. Tsembaga territory and the biotic community existing upon it may be conveniently viewed as an ecosystem. While it would be permissible arbitrarily to designate the Tsembaga as a population and their territory with its biota as an ecosystem, there are also nonarbitrary reasons for doing so. An ecosystem is a system of material exchanges, and the Tsembaga maintain against other human groups exclusive access to the resources within their territorial borders. Conversely, it is from this territory alone that the Tsembaga ordinarily derive all of their foodstuffs and most of the other materials they require for survival. Less anthropocentrically, it may be justified to regard Tsembaga territory with its biota as an ecosystem in view of the rather localized nature of cyclical material exchanges in tropical rainforests.

As they are involved with the nonhuman biotic community within their territory in a set of trophic exchanges, so do they participate in other material relationships with other human groups external to their territory. Genetic materials are exchanged with other groups, and certain crucial items, such as stone axes, were in the past obtained from the outside. Furthermore, in the area occupied by the Maring speakers, more than one local group is usually involved in any process, either peaceful or warlike, through which people are redistributed over land and land redistributed among people.

The concept of the ecosystem, though it provides a convenient frame for the analysis of interspecific trophic exchanges taking place within limited geographical areas, does not comfortably accommodate intraspecific exchanges taking place over wider geographic areas. Some sort of geographic population model would be more useful for the analysis of the relationship of the local ecological population to the larger regional population of which it is a part, but we lack even a set of appropriate terms for such a model. Suffice it here to note that the relations of the Tsembaga to the total of other local human populations in their vicinity are similar to the relations of local aggregates of other animals to the totality of their species occupying broader and more or less continuous regions. This larger, more inclusive aggregate may resemble what geneticists mean by the term population, that is, an aggregate of interbreeding organisms persisting through an indefinite number of generations and either living or capable of living in isolation from similar aggregates of the same species. This is the unit which survives through long periods of time while its local ecological (*sensu stricto*) subunits, the units more or less independently involved in interspecific trophic exchanges such as the Tsembaga, are ephemeral.

Since it has been asserted that the ritual cycles of the Tsembaga regulate relationships within what may be regarded as a complex system, it is necessary, before proceeding to the ritual cycle itself, to describe briefly, and where possible in quantitative terms, some aspects of the place of the Tsembaga in this system.

The Tsembaga are bush-following horticulturalists. Staples include a range of root crops, taro (*Colocasia*) and sweet potatoes being most important, yams and manioc less so. In addition, a great variety of greens are raised, some of which are rich in protein. Sugar cane and some tree crops, particularly *Pandanus conoideus*, are also important.

All gardens are mixed, many of them containing all of the major root crops and many greens. Two named garden types are, however, distinguished by the crops which predominate in them. "Taro-yam gardens" were found to produce, on the basis of daily harvest records kept on entire gardens for close to one year, about 5,300,000 calories[1] per acre during their harvesting lives of 18 to 24 months; 85 percent of their yield is harvested between 24 and 76 weeks after planting. "Sugar–sweet potato gardens" produce about 4,600,000 calories per acre during their harvesting lives, 91 percent being taken between 24 and 76 weeks after planting. I estimated that approximately 310,000 calories per acre is expended on cutting, fencing, planting, maintaining, harvesting, and walking to and from taro-yam gardens. Sugar–sweet potato gardens required an expenditure of approximately 290,000 calories per acre.[2] These energy ratios, approximately 17 :1 on taro-yam

---

1. Because the length of time in the field precluded the possibility of maintaining harvest records on single gardens from planting through abandonment, figures were based, in the case of both "taro-yam" and "sugar–sweet potato" gardens, on three separate gardens planted in successive years. Conversions from the gross weight to the caloric value of the yield were made by reference to the literature. The sources used are listed in Rappaport (1966: Appendix VIII).
2. Rough time and motion studies of each of the tasks involved in making, maintaining, harvesting, and walking to and from gardens were undertaken. Conversion to energy expenditure values was accomplished by reference to energy expenditure tables prepared by Hipsley and Kirk (1965: 43) on the basis of gas exchange measurements made during the performance of garden tasks by the Chimbu people of the New Guinea highlands.

gardens and 16:1 on sugar–sweet potato gardens, compare favorably with figures reported for swidden cultivation in other regions.[3]

Intake is high in comparison with the reported dietaries of other New Guinea populations. On the basis of daily consumption records kept for ten months on four households numbering in total sixteen persons, I estimated the average daily intake of adult males to be approximately 2,600 calories, and that of adult females to be around 2,200 calories. It may be mentioned here that the Tsembaga are small and short-statured. Adult males average 101 pounds in weight and approximately 58.5 inches in height; the corresponding averages for adult females are 85 pounds and 54.5 inches.[4]

Although 99 percent by weight of the food consumed is vegetable, the protein intake is high by New Guinea standards. The daily protein consumption of adult males from vegetable sources was estimated to be between 43 and 55 grams, of adult females 36 to 48 grams. Even with an adjustment for vegetable sources, these values are slightly in excess of the recently published WHO/FAO daily requirements (Food and Agriculture Organization of the United Nations 1964). The same is true of the younger age categories, although soft and discolored hair, a symptom of protein deficiency, was noted in a few children. The WHO/FAO protein requirements do not include a large "margin for safety" or allowance for stress; and, although no clinical assessments were undertaken, it may be suggested that the Tsembaga achieve nitrogen balance at a low level. In other words, their protein intake is probably marginal.

Measurements of all gardens made during 1962 and of some gardens made during 1963 indicate that, to support the human population, between .15 and .19 acres are put into cultivation per capita per year. Fallows range from 8 to 45 years. The area in secondary forest comprises approximately 1,000 acres, only 30 to 50 of which are in cultivation at any time. Assuming calories to be the limiting factor, and assuming an unchanging population structure, the territory could support—with no reduction in lengths of fallow and without cutting into the virgin forest from which the Tsembaga extract many important items—between 290 and 397 people if the pig population remained minimal. The size of the pig herd, however, fluctuates widely. Taking Maring pig husbandry procedures into consideration, I have estimated the human carrying capacity of the Tsembaga territory at between 270 and 320 people.

Because the timing of the ritual cycle is bound up with the demography of the pig herd, the place of the pig in Tsembaga adaptation must be examined.

First, being omnivorous, pigs keep residential areas free of garbage and human feces. Second, limited numbers of pigs rooting in secondary growth may help to hasten the development of that growth. The Tsembaga usually permit pigs to enter their gardens one and a half to two years after planting, by which time second-growth trees are well established there. The Tsembaga practice selective weeding; from the time the garden is planted, herbaceous species are removed, but tree species are allowed to remain. By the time cropping is discontinued and the pigs are let in, some of the trees in the garden are already ten to fifteen feet tall. These well-established trees are relatively impervious to damage by the pigs, which, in rooting for seeds and remaining tubers, eliminate many seeds and seedlings that, if allowed to develop, would provide some competition for the established trees. Moreover, in some Maring-speaking areas swiddens are planted twice, although this is not the case with the Tsembaga. After the first crop is almost exhausted, pigs are penned in the garden, where their rooting eliminates weeds and softens the ground, making the task of planting for a second time easier. The pigs, in other words, are used as cultivating machines.

Small numbers of pigs are easy to keep. They run free during the day and return home at night to receive their ration of garbage and substandard tubers, particularly sweet potatoes. Supplying the latter requires little extra work, for the substandard tubers are taken from the ground in the course of harvesting the daily ration for humans. Daily consumption records kept over a period of some months show

---

3. Marvin Harris, in an unpublished paper, estimates the ratio of energy return to energy input on Dyak (Borneo) rice swiddens at 10:1. His estimates of energy ratios on Tepotzlan (Meso-America) swiddens range from 13:1 on poor land to 29:1 on the best land.

4. Heights may be inaccurate. Many men wear their hair in large coiffures hardened with pandanus grease, and it was necessary in some instances to estimate the location of the top of the skull.

that the ration of tubers received by the pigs approximates in weight that consumed by adult humans, i.e., a little less than three pounds per day per pig.

If the pig herd grows large, however, the substandard tubers incidentally obtained in the course of harvesting for human needs become insufficient, and it becomes necessary to harvest especially for the pigs. In other words, people must work for the pigs and perhaps even supply them with food fit for human consumption. Thus, as Vayda, Leeds, and Smith (1961: 71) have pointed out, there can be too many pigs for a given community.

This also holds true of the sanitary and cultivating services rendered by pigs. A small number of pigs is sufficient to keep residential areas clean, to suppress superfluous seedlings in abandoned gardens, and to soften the soil in gardens scheduled for second plantings. A larger herd, on the other hand, may be troublesome; the larger the number of pigs, the greater the possibility of their invasion of producing gardens, with concomitant damage not only to crops and young secondary growth but also to the relations between the pig owners and garden owners.

All male pigs are castrated at approximately three months of age, for boars, people say, are dangerous and do not grow as large as barrows. Pregnancies, therefore, are always the result of unions of domestic sows with feral males. Fecundity is thus only a fraction of its potential. During one twelve-month period only fourteen litters resulted out of a potential 99 or more pregnancies. Farrowing generally takes place in the forest, and mortality of the young is high. Only 32 of the offspring of the above-mentioned fourteen pregnancies were alive six months after birth. This number is barely sufficient to replace the number of adult animals which would have died or been killed during most years without pig festivals.

The Tsembaga almost never kill domestic pigs outside of ritual contexts. In ordinary times, when there is no pig festival in progress, these rituals are almost always associated with misfortunes or emergencies, notably warfare, illness, injury, or death. Rules state not only the contexts in which pigs are to be ritually slaughtered, but also who may partake of the flesh of the sacrificial animals. During warfare it is only the men participating in the fighting who eat the pork. In cases of illness or injury, it is only the victim and certain near relatives, particularly his co-resident agnates and spouses, who do so.

It is reasonable to assume that misfortune and emergency are likely to induce in the organisms experiencing them a complex of physiological changes known collectively as "stress." Physiological stress reactions occur not only in organisms which are infected with disease or traumatized, but also in those experiencing rage or fear (Houssay et al. 1955: 1096), or even prolonged anxiety (National Research Council 1963: 53). One important aspect of stress is the increased catabolization of protein (Houssay et al. 1955: 451; National Research Council 1963: 49), with a net loss of nitrogen from the tissues (Houssay et al. 1955: 450). This is a serious matter for organisms with a marginal protein intake. Antibody production is low (Berg 1948: 311), healing is slow (Large and Johnston 1948: 352), and a variety of symptoms of a serious nature are likely to develop (Lund and Levenson 1948: 349; Zintel 1964: 1043). The status of a protein-depleted animal, however, may be significantly improved in a relatively short period of time by the intake of high quality protein, and high protein diets are therefore routinely prescribed for surgical patients and those suffering from infectious diseases (Burton 1959: 231; Lund and Levenson 1948: 350; Elman 1951: 85ff.; Zintel 1964: 1043ff.).

It is precisely when they are undergoing physiological stress that the Tsembaga kill and consume their pigs, and it should be noted that they limit the consumption to those likely to be experiencing stress most profoundly. The Tsembaga, of course, know nothing of physiological stress. Native theories of the etiology and treatment of disease and injury implicate various categories of spirits to whom sacrifices must be made. Nevertheless, the behavior which is appropriate in terms of native understandings is also appropriate to the actual situation confronting the actors.

We may now outline in the barest of terms the Tsembaga ritual cycle. Space does not permit a description of its ideological correlates. It must suffice to note that the Tsembaga do not necessarily perceive all of the empirical effects which the anthropologist sees to flow from their ritual behavior. Such empirical consequences as they may perceive, moreover, are not central to their rationalizations of the performances. The Tsembaga say that they perform the rituals in order to rearrange their relationships with the supernatural world. We may only reiterate here that behavior undertaken in reference to their "cognized environment"—an environment which includes as very important elements the spirits of ancestors—seems appropriate in their "operational environment," the material environment specified by the anthropologist through operations of observation, including measurement.

Since the rituals are arranged in a cycle, description may commence at any point. The operation of the cycle becomes clearest if we begin with the rituals performed during warfare. Opponents in all cases occupy adjacent territories, in almost all cases on the same valley wall. After hostilities have broken out, each side performs certain rituals which place the opposing side in the formal category of "enemy." A number of taboos prevail while hostilities continue. These include prohibitions on sexual intercourse and on the ingestion of certain things—food prepared by women, food grown on the lower portion of the territory, marsupials, eels, and while actually on the fighting ground, any liquid whatsoever.

One ritual practice associated with fighting which may have some physiological consequences deserves mention. Immediately before proceeding to the fighting ground, the warriors eat heavily salted pig fat. The ingestion of salt, coupled with the taboo on drinking, has the effect of shortening the fighting day, particularly since the Maring prefer to fight only on bright sunny days. When everyone gets unbearably thirsty, according to informants, fighting is broken off.

There may formerly have been other effects if the native salt contained sodium (the production of salt was discontinued some years previous to the field work, and no samples were obtained). The Maring diet seems to be deficient in sodium. The ingestion of large amounts of sodium just prior to fighting would have permitted the warriors to sweat normally without a lowering of blood volume and consequent weakness during the course of the fighting. The pork belly ingested with the salt would have provided them with a new burst of energy two hours or so after the commencement of the engagement. After fighting was finished for the day, lean pork was consumed, offsetting, at least to some extent, the nitrogen loss associated with the stressful fighting (personal communications from F. Dunn, W. McFarlane, and J. Sabine, 1965).

Fighting could continue sporadically for weeks. Occasionally it terminated in the rout of one of the antagonistic groups, whose survivors would take refuge with kinsmen elsewhere. In such instances, the victors would lay waste their opponents' groves and gardens, slaughter their pigs, and burn their houses. They would not, however, immediately annex the territory of the vanquished. The Maring say that they never take over the territory of an enemy for, even if it has been abandoned, the spirits of their ancestors remain to guard it against interlopers. Most fights, however, terminated in truces between the antagonists.

With the termination of hostilities a group which has not been driven off its territory performs a ritual called "planting the *rumbim*." Every man puts his hand on the ritual plant, *rumbim* (*Cordyline fruticosa* (L.), A. Chev; *C. terminalis*, Kunth), as it is planted in the ground. The ancestors are addressed, in effect, as follows:

> We thank you for helping us in the fight and permitting us to remain on our territory. We place our souls in this *rumbim* as we plant it on our ground. We ask you to care for this *rumbim*. We will kill pigs for you now, but they are few. In the future, when we have many pigs, we shall again give you pork and uproot the *rumbim* and stage a *kaiko* (pig festival). But until there are sufficient pigs to repay you the *rumbim* will remain in the ground.

This ritual is accompanied by the wholesale slaughter of pigs. Only juveniles remain alive. All adult and adolescent animals are killed, cooked, and dedicated to the ancestors. Some are consumed by the local group, but most are distributed to allies who assisted in the fight.

Some of the taboos which the group suffered during the time of fighting are abrogated by this ritual. Sexual intercourse is now permitted, liquids may be taken at any time, and food from any part of the territory may be eaten. But the group is still in debt to its allies and ancestors. People say it is still the time of the *bamp ku*, or "fighting stones," which are actual objects used in the rituals associated with warfare. Although the fighting ceases when *rumbim* is planted, the concomitant obligations, debts to allies and ancestors, remain outstanding; and the fighting stones may not be put away until these obligations are fulfilled. The time of the fighting stones is a time of debt and danger which lasts until the *rumbim* is uprooted and a pig festival (*kaiko*) is staged.

Certain taboos persist during the time of the fighting stones. Marsupials, regarded as the pigs of the ancestors of the high ground, may not be trapped until the debt to their masters has been repaid. Eels, the "pigs of the ancestors of the low ground," may neither be caught nor consumed. Prohibitions on all intercourse with the enemy come into force. One may not touch, talk to, or even look at a member of the enemy group, nor set foot on enemy ground. Even more important, a group may not attack another group while its ritual plant remains in the ground, for it has not yet fully rewarded its ancestors and allies for their assistance in the last fight. Until the debts to them have been paid, further assistance from them will not be forthcoming. A kind of "truce of god" thus prevails until the *rumbim* is uprooted and a *kaiko* completed.

To uproot the *rumbim* requires sufficient pigs. How many pigs are sufficient, and how long does it take to acquire them? The Tsembaga say that, if a place is "good," this can take as little as five years; but if a place is "bad," it may require ten years or longer. A bad place is one in which misfortunes are frequent and where, therefore, ritual demands for the killing of pigs arise frequently. A good place is one where such demands are infrequent. In a good place, the increase of the pig herd exceeds the ongoing ritual demands, and the herd grows rapidly. Sooner or later the substandard tubers incidentally obtained while harvesting become insufficient to feed the herd, and additional acreage must be put into production specifically for the pigs.

The work involved in caring for a large pig herd can be extremely burdensome. The Tsembaga herd just prior to the pig festival of 1962–63, when it numbered 169 animals, was receiving 54 percent of all the sweet potatoes and 82 percent of all the manioc harvested. These comprised 35.9 percent by weight of all root crops harvested. This figure is consistent with the difference between the amount of land under cultivation just previous to the pig festival, when the herd was at maximum size, and that immediately afterwards, when the pig herd was at minimum size. The former was 36.1 percent in excess of the latter.

I have estimated, on the basis of acreage yield and energy expenditure figures, that about 45,000 calories per year are expended in caring for one pig 120–150 pounds in size. It is upon women that most of the burden of pig keeping falls. If, from a woman's daily intake of about 2,200 calories, 950 calories are allowed for basal metabolism, a woman has only 1,250 calories a day available for all her activities, which include gardening for her family, child care, and cooking, as well as tending pigs. It is clear that no woman can feed many pigs; only a few had as many as four in their care at the commencement of the festival; and it is not surprising that agitation to uproot the *rumbim* and stage the *kaiko* starts with the wives of the owners of large numbers of pigs.

A large herd is not only burdensome as far as energy expenditure is concerned; it becomes increasingly a nuisance as it expands. The more numerous pigs become, the more frequently are gardens invaded by them. Such events result in serious disturbances of local tranquillity. The garden owner often shoots, or attempts to shoot, the offending pig; and the pig owner commonly retorts by shooting, or attempting to shoot, either the garden owner, his wife, or one of his pigs. As more and more such events occur, the settlement, nucleated when the herd was small, disperses as people try to put as much distance as possible between their pigs and other people's gardens and between their gardens and other people's pigs. Occasionally this reaches its logical conclusion, and people begin to leave the territory, taking up residence with kinsmen in other local populations.

The number of pigs sufficient to become intolerable to the Tsembaga was below the capacity of the territory to carry pigs. I have estimated that, if the size and structure of the human population remained constant at the 1962–1963 level, a pig population of 140 to 240 animals averaging 100 to 150 pounds in size could be maintained perpetually by the Tsembaga without necessarily inducing environmental degradation. Since the size of the herd fluctuates, even higher cyclical maxima could be achieved. The level of toleration, however, is likely always to be below the carrying capacity, since the destructive capacity of the pigs is dependent upon the population density of both people and pigs, rather than upon population size. The denser the human population, the fewer pigs will be required to disrupt social life. If the carrying capacity is exceeded, it is likely to be exceeded by people and not by pigs.

The *kaiko* or pig festival, which commences with the planting of stakes at the boundary and the uprooting of the *rumbim*, is thus triggered by either the additional work attendant upon feeding pigs or the destructive capacity of the pigs themselves. It may be said, then, that there are sufficient pigs to stage the *kaiko* when the relationship of pigs to people changes from one of mutualism to one of parasitism or competition.

A short time prior to the uprooting of the *rumbim*, stakes are planted at the boundary. If the enemy has continued to occupy its territory, the stakes are planted at the boundary which existed before the fight. If, on the other hand, the enemy has abandoned its territory, the victors may plant their stakes at a new boundary which encompasses areas previously occupied by the enemy. The Maring say, to be sure, that they never take land belonging to an enemy, but this land is regarded as vacant, since no *rumbim* was planted on it after the last fight. We may state here a rule of land redistribution in terms of the ritual cycle: *If one of a pair of antagonistic groups is able to uproot its* rumbim *before its opponents can plant their* rumbim, *it may occupy the latter's territory.*

Not only have the vanquished abandoned their territory; it is assumed that it has also been abandoned by their ancestors as well. The surviving members of the erstwhile enemy group have by this time resided with other groups for a number of years, and most if not all of them have already had occasion to sacrific pigs to their ancestors at their new residences. In so doing they have invited these spirits to settle at the new locations of the living, where they will in the future receive sacrifices. Ancestors of vanquished groups thus relinquish their guardianship over the territory, making it available to victorious groups. Meanwhile, the *de facto* membership of the living in the groups with which they have taken refuge is converted eventually into *de jure* membership. Sooner or later the groups with which they have taken up residence will have occasion to plant *rumbim*, and the refugees, as co-residents, will participate, thus ritually validating their connection to the new territory and the new group. A rule of population redistribution may thus be stated in terms of ritual cycles: *A man becomes a member of a territorial group by participating with it in the planting of* rumbim.

The uprooting of the *rumbim* follows shortly after the planting of stakes at the boundary. On this particular occasion the Tsembaga killed 32 pigs out of their herd of 169. Much of the pork was distributed to allies and affines outside of the local group.

The taboo on trapping marsupials was also terminated at this time. Information is lacking concerning the population dynamics of the local marsupials, but it may well be that the taboo which had prevailed since the last fight—that against taking them in traps—had conserved a fauna which might otherwise have become extinct.

The *kaiko* continues for about a year, during which period friendly groups are entertained from time to time. The guests receive presents of vegetable foods, and the hosts and male guests dance together throughout the night.

These events may be regarded as analogous to aspects of the social behavior of many nonhuman animals. First of all, they include massed epigamic, or courtship, displays (Wynne-Edwards 1962: 17). Young women are presented with samples of the eligible males of local groups with which they may not otherwise have had the opportunity to become familiar. The context, moreover, permits the young women to discriminate amongst this sample in terms of both endurance (signaled by how vigorously and how long a man dances) and wealth (signaled by the richness of a man's shell and feather finery).

More importantly, the massed dancing at these events may be regarded as epideictic display, communicating to the participants information concerning the size or density of the group (Wynne-Edwards 1962: 16). In many species such displays take place as a prelude to actions which adjust group size or density, and such is the case among the Maring. The massed dancing of the visitors at a *kaiko* entertainment communicates to the hosts, while the *rumbim* truce is still in force, information concerning the amount of support they may expect from the visitors in the bellicose enterprises that they are likely to embark upon soon after the termination of the pig festival.

Among the Maring there are no chiefs or other political authorities capable of commanding the support of a body of followers, and the decision to assist another group in warfare rests with each individual male. Allies are not recruited by appealing for help to other local groups as such. Rather, each member of the groups primarily involved in the hostilities appeals to his cognatic and affinal kinsmen in other local groups. These men, in turn, urge other of their co-residents and kinsmen to "help them fight." The channels through which invitations to dance are extended are precisely those through which appeals for military support are issued. The invitations go not from group to group, but from kinsman to kinsman, the recipients of invitations urging their co-residents to "help them dance."

Invitations to dance do more than exercise the channels through which allies are recruited; they provide a means for judging their effectiveness. Dancing and fighting are regarded as in some sense equivalent. This equivalence is expressed in the similarity of some pre-fight and pre-dance rituals, and the Maring say that those who come to dance come to fight. The size of a visiting dancing contingent is consequently taken as a measure of the size of the contingent of warriors whose assistance may be expected in the next round of warfare.

In the morning the dancing ground turns into a trading ground. The items most frequently exchanged include axes, bird plumes, shell ornaments, an occasional baby pig, and, in former times, native salt. The *kaiko* thus facilitates trade by providing a market-like setting in which large numbers of traders can assemble. It likewise facilitates the movement of two critical items, salt and axes, by creating a demand for the bird plumes which may be exchanged for them.

The *kaiko* concludes with major pig sacrifices. On this particular occasion the Tsembaga butchered 105 adult and adolescent pigs, leaving only 60 juveniles and neonates alive. The survival of an additional fifteen adolescents and adults was only temporary, for they were scheduled as imminent victims. The pork yielded by the Tsembaga slaughter was estimated to weigh between 7,000 and 8,500 pounds, of which between 4,500 and 6,000 pounds were distributed to members of other local groups in 163 separate presentations. An estimated 2,000 to 3,000 people in seventeen local groups were the beneficiaries of the redistribution. The presentations, it should be mentioned, were not confined to pork. Sixteen Tsembaga men presented bridewealth or child-wealth, consisting largely of axes and shells, to their affines at this time.

The *kaiko* terminates on the day of the pig slaughter with the public presentation of salted pig belly to allies of the last fight. Presentations are made through the window in a high ceremonial fence built specially for the occasion at one end of the dance ground. The name of each honored man is announced to the assembled multitude as he charges to the window to receive his hero's portion. The fence is then ritually

torn down, and the fighting stones are put away. The pig festival and the ritual cycle have been completed, demonstrating, it may be suggested, the ecological and economic competence of the local population. The local population would now be free, if it were not for the presence of the government, to attack its enemy again, secure in the knowledge that the assistance of allies and ancestors would be forthcoming because they have received pork and the obligations to them have been fulfilled.

Usually fighting did break out again very soon after the completion of the ritual cycle. If peace still prevailed when the ceremonial fence had rotted completely—a process said to take about three years, a little longer than the length of time required to raise a pig to maximum size—*rumbim* was planted as if there had been a fight, and all adult and adolescent pigs were killed. When the pig herd was large enough so that the *rumbim* could be uprooted, peace could be made with former enemies if they were also able to dig out their *rumbim*. To put this in formal terms: *If a pair of antagonistic groups proceeds through two ritual cycles without resumption of hostilities their enmity may be terminated.*

The relations of the Tsembaga with their environment have been analyzed as a complex system composed of two subsystems. What may be called the "local subsystem" has been derived from the relations of the Tsembaga with the nonhuman components of their immediate or territorial environment. It corresponds to the ecosystem in which the Tsembaga participate. A second subsystem, one which corresponds to the larger regional population of which the Tsembaga are one of the constituent units and which may be designated as the "regional subsystem," has been derived from the relations of the Tsembaga with neighboring local populations similar to themselves.

It has been argued that rituals, arranged in repetitive sequences, regulate relations both within each of the subsystems and within the larger complex system as a whole. The timing of the ritual cycle is largely dependent upon changes in the states of the components of the local subsystem. But the *kaiko*, which is the culmination of the ritual cycle, does more than reverse changes which have taken place within the local subsystem. Its occurrence also affects relations among the components of the regional subsystem. During its performance, obligations to other local populations are fulfilled, support for future military enterprises is rallied, and land from which enemies have earlier been driven is occupied. Its completion, furthermore, permits the local population to initiate warfare again. Conversely, warfare is terminated by rituals which preclude the reinitiation of warfare until the state of the local subsystem is again such that a *kaiko* may be staged and completed. Ritual among the Tsembaga and other Maring, in short, operates as both transducer, "translating" changes in the state of one subsystem into information which can effect changes in a second subsystem, and homeostat, maintaining a number of variables which in sum comprise the total system within ranges of viability. To repeat an earlier assertion, the operation of ritual among the Tsembaga and other Maring helps to maintain an undegraded environment, limits fighting to frequencies which do not endanger the existence of the regional population, adjusts man-land ratios, facilitates trade, distributes local surpluses of pig throughout the regional population in the form of pork, and assures people of high quality protein when they are most in need of it.

Religious rituals and the supernatural orders toward which they are directed cannot be assumed *a priori* to be mere epiphenomena. Ritual may, and doubtless frequently does, do nothing more than validate and intensify the relationships which integrate the social unit, or symbolize the relationships which bind the social unit to its environment. But the interpretation of such presumably *sapiens*-specific phenomena as religious ritual within a framework which will also accommodate the behavior of other species shows, I think, that religious ritual may do much more than symbolize, validate, and intensify relationships. Indeed, it would not be improper to refer to the Tsembaga and the other entities with which they share their territory as a "ritually regulated ecosystem," and to the Tsembaga and their human neighbors as a "ritually regulated population."

17

I Can Only Move My Feet Towards *mizuko kuyō:* Memorial Services for Dead Children in Japan

Elizabeth G. Harrison

In this article, Elizabeth G. Harrison focuses on the disjunction between the various images of the Japanese practice of mizuko kuyō (mizuko, *"water-child";* kuyō, *memorial service). Mizuko is the name given in Japan to children who have died "out of order" (before their parents). Harrison believes that these memorial services provide a formal, public, ritualized way to acknowledge the existence of these children. She writes, "The object of such services is to appeal to an appropriate deity to provide for the well-being of the dead, to transfer merit to the karmic account of the dead child so that he or she may proceed more quickly to a felicitous rebirth, and to appease the dead so that they might become a benevolent influence in the lives of their living family." Through the practice of* mizuko kuyō, *parents feel they are doing something constructive to help their* mizuko. *Harrison's article also examines the arguments of several Buddhist priests, both for and against the practice of* mizuko kuyō, *at Buddhist sites. She also describes and analyzes the attitudes of the laypeople involved in* mizuko kuyō *services. At the close of the article, Harrison suggests that the practice of* mizuko kuyō *is a silent way of making people aware of the underlying tensions in women's lives in Japan, utilizing the ritual and symbolic resources of Buddhism.*

Mizuko, literally 'water-child', is the name now given in Japan to children who have died 'out of order', that is, before their parents. This includes children who have died as a result of spontaneous or induced abortion as well as stillborn infants and those who have died from any manner of illness or accident after they were born. The Japanese practice of *mizuko kuyō*, often identified as Buddhist memorial services for these dead children, centres around the performance of some variation of a memorial service for ancestral spirits (*senzo kuyō*). As such, the *mizuko* service usually includes elements which are standard to Buddhist memorial services in Japan: the chanting of special texts and presentation of offerings by clergy and audience, manipulation of religious implements

"I Can Only Move My Feet Towards mizuko kuyō: *Memorial Services for Dead Children in Japan" by Elizabeth G. Harrison from BUDDHISM AND ABORTION by Damien Keown, pp. 93–120. Reprinted by permission of Palgrave Macmillan.*

and supervision of the audience by the clergy, and acts of purification performed by the audience.

The object of such services is to appeal to an appropriate deity to provide for the well-being of the dead, to transfer merit to the karmic account of the dead child so that he or she may proceed more quickly to a felicitous rebirth, and to appease the dead so that they might become a benevolent influence in the lives of their living family.

Visitors to Japan today can hardly miss seeing the rows of child-like figurines, as large as three or four feet or as small as two or three inches, that line pathways, shelves, and racks, both indoors and out, at temples and shrines across the country. They are visible evidence that tens of thousands of people, mostly women, have commissioned or participated in *mizuko kuyō* services for their children each year since the early 1970s. Despite the negative press which depicts them as passive dolls being manipulated by money-hungry priests, Japanese people, especially women, continue to participate, and *mizuko kuyō* has now become a routine practice at religious sites—primarily Buddhist temples—all around Japan. The connection of this practice with Buddhism is a created one, however, and until quite recently their relationship has not been an especially happy one.

Arising in the early postwar period as a reaction to the 1948 Eugenics Protection Law which made abortion legal in certain specified circumstances, *mizuko kuyō* was easily associated with Buddhism in the minds of the lay public. Historically, especially in medieval and pre-modern times, Buddhism in Japan had demonstrated a strong focus on death and the welfare of the dead. This interest was institutionalized in the early seventeenth century by the Tokugawa shogunate pronouncement that Buddhist temples would thenceforth be the site for funeral and ancestral rites for parishioners, thereby removing the locus of such formal observances from the home. The relocation was so successful that today, even though most funerals are not now done in temples, Buddhism in Japan is commonly known as 'funeral Buddhism' (*sōshiki bukkyō*), and anything having to do with death is first assumed to take place in a Buddhist context.

One interesting aspect of this Japanese Buddhist involvement in rituals associated with death is its focus on dead adults and the resulting lack of any widely recognized, formal public rites for very young children who had died. In pre-modern Japan, it was thought that a child did not become a real 'person' until some time after birth; the evidence for this lies in the many customs which distinguished a newborn baby from other 'people', such as not giving it a name and not putting its arms through sleeves for a certain number of days after birth. The pre-modern saying 'Until the age of seven, a child is of the *kami*' (*nanasai made wa kami no uchi*) suggests that a child's existence in this world remains unsettled until it reaches seven years of age. If it died before age seven, it was usually not given a proper funeral or burial in the manner of those who died at an older age; if it died before it was named, it most likely did not receive a funeral at all, and its birth would not have been registered. Such would have been the case for infants killed by infanticide, for example, as well as fetuses from pregnancies terminated by either spontaneous or induced abortion.

In the post–World War II context of the huge number of war dead and the new abortion law, when the number of reported abortions in Japan rose steadily to a peak of 1,170,143 in 1955, I would argue that children, including unborn aborted children, became recognized by some as a new type of war dead. Religious sites (most of them Buddhist) for performing memorial services for those children began to proliferate around the country in the 1970s. Several pseudo-Buddhist sites appeared as well, sites which made use of the identification of Buddhist forms with rituals for the dead to lend them legitimacy. By 1978, Buddhist priests and others who regularly performed services for *mizuko* were appearing on daytime television shows, further spreading word of the practice while the commentators sensationalized it. In 1984, when I began studying *mizuko kuyō*, it had become perhaps the most controversial practice in modern Japanese religious history: publicized by the mass media as a fad and a scam, denounced by many Buddhist clergy and some Buddhist institutions as un-Buddhist, yet nevertheless perpetuated by both clergy and lay participants all around Japan.

This paper will focus on the disjunction between the various images of the practice of *mizuko kuyō*. An overview of the images constructed in promotional literature and those presented by the media will give us a context for examining the arguments of several Buddhist priests both for and against the appropriateness of this practice at Buddhist sites. Some of these reactions were delivered publicly, in print, while others were obtained privately in taped interviews. What has tended to go unnoticed in this debate over *mizuko kuyō* are the attitudes of the lay people who participate in or request *mizuko kuyō* services. We will consider the practice as it has been constructed by lay participants and how they see it informing their lives, particularly their feelings about and relationship to their dead (aborted) children in order to demonstrate the complexity of the practice that is lost in the more public images.

Promotional and Media Images

By the mid-1980s, references to *mizuko kuyō* could be seen almost daily throughout Japan on billboards and posters, in advertisements in the public media, in newspaper and magazine articles, in publications available at religious sites and sold at bookstores, and even in comic books (*manga*). Much of this was promotional material meant to bring people to particular sites to participate in the practice as it was performed there. Many reasons were given for the need for such practice. In some cases, mothers were blamed for the death of their children, no matter how that death might have occurred, and told they must make amends through performance of *kuyō*. In others, the practice was put forth as a way for women who were grieving the loss of a child, whether before or after birth, to recover by establishing a relationship with the spirit of that child. Another approach was to promote the performance of *mizuko kuyō* as a way to help solve major, unforeseen problems occurring in a woman's life, such as the unexplained, grave illness of a living child, or a sudden, disastrous turn in the family's fortunes; in the mid-1980s such problems were often interpreted first as the result of the intervention of a forgotten *mizuko* into the family's affairs. As an extension of this, the practice was also portrayed as a way to encourage a family's *mizuko* to play the role of protector of its living family and to provide for the future of its siblings. Spiritualists went even further, often warning readers that forgotten, untended *mizuko* were angry and could be dangerous to the health and livelihood of their living relatives. In short, from the mid-1980s on, promotional literature, including television interviews, sought to establish the necessity of

the practice of *mizuko kuyō* for all dead children, although the special focus of the practice remained on dead unborn children, for they were most often forgotten.

In response to the obvious success of the new practice, the media began to publicize it in a different light, as a fad (*būmu*, lit. 'boom', implying great but short-lived popularity) and a money-making scheme. For example, a three-page photographic essay in a 1980 issue of *Shūkan Bunshun*, a popular weekly literary magazine, suggested several reasons for the 'Mizuko Jizō Boom'. According to the article, elderly women who had lost children due to the war, wives whose pregnancies had ended in miscarriage, and women who had aborted pregnancies resulting from 'free sex' were becoming religious (*busshin ga dekite*) and buying statues of Jizō to offer for their dead children. In addition, temple priests, whom the article describes as 'very good at business', were making the most of this opportunity to make money by encouraging such sales. The article ends with the statement that 'no amount of this kind of *kuyō* will help dead children rest more easily'.

A 1983 TBS television special report on the 'Mizuko Boom' echoes this presentation. After examining the amount of money represented by the rows of memorial tablets for *mizuko* at one temple, the lines of people paying entrance fees to enter another temple for *mizuko kuyō*, and the number of orders for *Mizuko Jizō* statues being received by a foundry, the show's reporter interviews a religion critic who criticizes religious establishments for using people's suffering to create a 'boom' for themselves. The studio commentator remarks later, 'If someone does *mizuko kuyō* and is helped by it, then there is a reason for doing it. But I can't help feeling that this is [primarily] a business'. Although both of the reports described above at least acknowledge that participants may obtain some benefit or help from the practice, later pieces tend to focus on the negative business and manipulative aspects alone. A 1985 article entitled 'Temples in Japan Capitalize on Abortion' in the English-language Mainichi Daily News explains that 'guilt and dark superstition still nag at many Japanese who turn to abortion. In the past decade, Buddhist temples around the country have exploited that fact to build what one Japanese magazine has called a multimillion dollar "business of terror."' The terror mentioned here is the fear of *tatari*, actual physical reprisal from forgotten and uncared-for *mizuko*, which might take the form of illness or accident, birth defects or other problems with later children, or similar changes in circumstance that would disturb the harmony of the family and thus the rhythm of a woman's life. Such media images were simply built onto an already existing critique of religion in contemporary Japan as worldly and outdated.

It was in this context that I began studying *mizuko kuyō* in 1984. At that time I found Buddhist clergy and institutions around the country struggling to define their positions with respect to the new practice in light of the negative reputation it had acquired from the media. As we shall see in the next section, those who performed *mizuko kuyō* services were searching for Buddhist justifications for doing so, while those who rejected the practice also did so for ostensibly Buddhist reasons.

Buddhist Clergy and *Mizuko Kuyō*

Perhaps the strongest reaction against *mizuko kuyō* as a Buddhist practice came from Nishi Honganji, one of the major subsects of Shin (Jōdo Shinshū or True Pure Land) Buddhism in Japan. After many years of posting messages condemning the practice on their roadside billboard in downtown Kyoto, an official sectarian study group finally published the rationale for this stance in 1988 in a small book about rebirth for women. The carefully constructed argument turns on the assertion that *mizuko kuyō* is not consistent with the original Buddhist meaning of *kuyō*: the new practice focuses on angry spirits of the dead, while originally, in the *sūtras*, *kuyō* meant to take care of the Buddha, the Dharma, and the *Sangha* with respect and offerings. The present practice is depicted as based on belief in evil spirits and the desire to appease them in order to avert disaster and bring good fortune, and for this reason it is dismissed as derived from folk customs and the intentional planning of certain individuals who sought to create a market. In Shin Buddhist terms, the practice misses the point in two ways. It defines the central problem to be the need for *kuyō* rather than the practice of abortion, which in Buddhism is seen as the taking of a life. And it draws a karmic connection between the spirits of dead children and real life problems, a belief that fourteenth-century Shin founder Shinran called

'imitation religion' (*nise no shūkyō*). Since that purported karmic connection is mistaken, *mizuko kuyō* might make the performer feel better, but it won't change the basic situation. In fact, according to this argument, the performer's real life problems will only get worse, since their true cause is not being addressed.

Most denials that *mizuko kuyō* is Buddhist have not been so well-articulated, however. As I interviewed clergy around the country in the mid- and late 1980s, I was told many times that *mizuko kuyō* was not Buddhist. The reasons given were usually very general: it is not in the *sūtras*; it's new (We've never talked about it before, have we?); it's based on *tatari*, which is not Buddhist; it was started by new religions, not Buddhist sects; it's only about making money, not about religion; it is simply a public way of condoning abortion and giving a quick moral fix. While the clergy who offered these reasons for refusing to perform the practice seemed sincere in their opposition to it, my sense was that some were as concerned with avoiding negative publicity as with the question of whether it was genuinely Buddhist or not.

On the other hand, many Buddhist clergy found *mizuko kuyō* completely within the sphere of normal and acceptable Buddhist practice. Arguments for this stance tended to be historical: it's in the *sūtras* (though no one would give a specific citation); it's just another form of ancestor worship; we've always done it, but under different names. The head priest of a Nichiren temple in Miyazu, Kyoto Prefecture, for example, explained that what is known as *mizuko kuyō* today began in medieval times as the performance of *segaki-e*, memorial services for unattended spirits of the dead wandering the lower realms of existence. Another head priest, of a Pure Land (Jōdo) temple in the city of Kyoto, claims that his temple was the birthplace of the practice of *mizuko kuyō* roughly a thousand years ago. It began with the priest Saichō's mother, according to the legend of the temple which was published as a children's story in 1982. When Saichō ascended Mt. Hiei to the northeast of Kyoto to open a monastic centre in the tenth century, his mother, unable to accompany him because she was a woman (and thus not allowed to ascend the sacred mountain), remained with her husband's family at the eastern foot of the mountain. On the death of her husband, her ties to his family were cut, and having nowhere else to go she moved to the western outskirts of Kyoto to an area controlled by her brother. There she took up residence in a Buddhist chapel built on the remains of an older temple and spent her days as a Buddhist nun, praying, taking care of the chapel and children in the area. She became recognized throughout the area for her great compassion and love of children. One day, the story continues, someone left a newborn baby on her doorstep, knowing that she would care for it. She walked far and wide to beg milk for it, and that experience opened her heart to the plight of unwanted babies and babies who had died before, during or after birth. Particularly concerned for those who had died before and during birth, she had a stone monument in the shape of the Buddhist bodhisattva Jizō erected near her chapel and performed memorial services for them, praying that Jizō protect their spirits in the other world and that they achieve a good rebirth. This concern for the welfare of dead children, articulated as it was in a Buddhist ritual vocabulary, is claimed by the author of the story and by the priest at this particular temple to be the origin of *mizuko kuyō*.

While this story would seem to solve the problem of the relationship of *mizuko kuyō* to Buddhism, I hasten to add a postscript. Not long after I made the acquaintance of this priest and heard his story, I had the opportunity to interview the author he had commissioned to write it in publishable form. I asked to see the historical sources concerning *mizuko kuyō* that he had used for the book, but he replied that there were none. The temple priest had simply told him the story and asked that he, a Buddhist priest and celebrated author of Buddhist children's stories, turn it into a children's book. As far as he could tell, this story of the origin of *mizuko kuyō* was completely made up.

The conclusions to be drawn here are perhaps not so obvious as the reader might expect. In their collection of essays entitled *The Invention of Tradition*, Hobsbawm and Ranger have demonstrated both the ordinariness and the ideological power of invented traditions; no small part of that power is the ability to re-configure the collective memory, to efface any memory of a time when the invented tradition was not common practice. In the case of *mizuko kuyō*, this was accomplished by situating the practice within the Buddhist cultural space in which matters of

death and what comes after are generally articulated in Japan. From its beginnings in the 1950s and 1960s, *mizuko kuyō* has borrowed much of its ritual vocabulary from the contemporary Buddhist repertoire, as described above. But without a more substantial link between the two, such borrowing could only lend a surface legitimacy to the new practice; simple borrowing, or adaptation, of received elements into a new form would not, in such a short span of time, engender the kind of symbolic, even ideological power and concomitant public attempts at denial that we see in *mizuko kuyō* or the kind of effacement of memory that has resulted.

In creating the story of a contemporary practice originating a thousand years ago, the head priest of the Kyoto temple has given the practice a history, and that history is demonstrably Buddhist: the mother of a great Buddhist priest living a religious life and performing rituals for the dead in a Buddhist context cannot easily be construed in other than Buddhist terms. The Nichiren priest has done the same thing, though through a different set of associations. Since medieval times in Japan, the performance of *segaki-e* services for the wandering dead has been associated with the Buddhist vision of six realms of existence and has become an unremarked part of the annual celebration, performed in a Buddhist context, of ancestral spirits that takes place during mid- and late summer in Japan. The invention of these histories, as well as the claim that the practice can be found in the *sūtras*, thus serves to make it incontrovertibly Buddhist, and as such, an observance properly performed by priests at Buddhist sites around Japan.

The invention of a Buddhist history for *mizuko kuyō* does something more, however. It situates this new concern for the welfare of dead children and for their continuing tie to their living families within the symbolic system of Japanese Buddhism. On the one hand, this means that the power of that symbolic system can be mobilized and experienced through the new practice, giving it a depth usually not found in something so new. In giving offerings both to a deity and to the dead child, in saying prayers, in chanting Buddhist texts as part of a formal service, one is not simply taking part in a newly invented practice but in a(n invented) tradition which is tied to nearly fifteen hundred years of Buddhist presence in Japan. On the other hand, by establishing the practice as old rather than new, these priests have made it a part of every-day life—not simply because it is available at more and more sites, but because it is a part of the arguably Buddhist fabric of life in Japan.

Inventing history is not the only tactic that has been used to bring the new practice of *mizuko kuyō* into the grammar of Buddhist practice in Japan, however. I have interviewed a number of local parish priests around the country who were originally strongly opposed to the practice, for many of the reasons given above, but who eventually decided to make it available to their parishioners. Their reasons for this change were similar: in the face of regular requests from temple parishioners for *mizuko* services or for a *mizuko* statue to be placed in the temple precincts as a locus for practice, they began to feel that their personal opposition to *mizuko kuyō* was leading them to avoid their duty to address the needs of their parishioners. In swallowing their misgivings and beginning to perform services for those who requested them or allowing parishioners to establish a temple site for their own *mizuko* observances, many of these priests saw themselves using a questionable practice as a means to bring lay people closer to the Buddhist path rather than as espousing or condoning the practice itself. Several described their versions of *mizuko* services not as *mizuko kuyō*, but as 'chanting the *sūtras*' (*okyō o yomu*) which, together with the homily or counselling given to the person who commissioned the service, was designed to shift the person's focus away from their dead child toward how they might lead a more Buddhist life. Even Nishi Honganji, in the same publication (cited above) in which it argues that the practice is not Buddhist and therefore should not be done, suggests that Shin priests can address followers' concerns related to *mizuko* in more generic Shin ways.

Together with the increasing repetition of *mizuko kuyō* observances at religious sites around the country since the late 1970s, these two tactics—of inventing history and of redirecting a practice toward an aim different from the one it is purported to address—have contributed in large part to the success of the invented tradition of *mizuko kuyō*. Whereas in the mid-1980s the practice was being questioned publicly in nearly every corner, today it goes largely unremarked and seems to have taken its place alongside ancestral services in the standard repertoire performed by most Buddhist clergy throughout Japan. Questions of whether it is Buddhist or not have largely disappeared, as well they should: woven into the fabric of Buddhism in Japan by the redefinition of its history and by common performance, when performed at Buddhist temples *mizuko kuyō* is now effectively a Buddhist practice.

It is important to understand that the intentionality behind these tactics becomes irrelevant once they enter the public sphere; in public such constructions easily lose their determinacy, becoming available for appropriation by anyone sharing in the cultural soup. For example, we have seen how Buddhist clergy who originally objected to performing *mizuko kuyō* began to do so in an attempt to move lay people interested in the practice away from it. While it may have helped the clergy justify to themselves their involvement in a practice they objected to, in the public view this tactic nevertheless served to spread the practice as well as to make it more identifiable with Buddhist sites. It is this public view, that is, lay people's constructions of the practice of *mizuko kuyō*, that we will turn to in the rest of the paper in order to understand how individual practitioners have appropriated public elements of the practice to make sense of their own experiences.

Lay People's *Mizuko Kuyō*

The promotional and media images of *mizuko kuyō* that we have examined above present a stereotypical image of the Japanese women who participate in the practice as passive and easily manipulated. Male participants—and there are more and more—are never mentioned. Told by money-hungry clergy and spiritualists that they must make amends to their dead children by taking part in *mizuko kuyō* services, which may mean paying substantial amounts of money, women are assumed to do so dutifully. Blamed for the death of their children, whether they were lost by abortion or otherwise, the mothers of *mizuko* are assumed to be motivated to participate in the practice by strong feelings of guilt and naive belief in the 'dark superstition' of *tatari*, which threatens that the spirits of their dead children can come back to harm them or their families. What is left out, along with recognition of men who participate in the practice, is any examination of the variety of motivations that bring people to *mizuko kuyō* and any acknowledgment of participants' actions as considered and knowing, as active attempts to deal with the strong feelings that are tied up with the loss of a child.

The Buddhist clergy we have heard from, on the other hand, appear more concerned with the doctrinal implications of the new practice than with the people who take part in it. Only in the Kyoto priest's story of Saichō's mother do we find recognition of someone trying to address her feelings for dead children, but as a historical archetype, this story, too, keeps us safely distanced from the feelings and experiences of those who find personal reason to participate in *mizuko kuyō*. As we have seen above, clergy strategy has been to establish the practice within the universalized structure of Buddhism, where it would become routine and repeatable, and thus controllable. Here, too, we find the stereotype of Japanese women as passive and unknowing, guilt-ridden and in need of the help of the professional clergy to lead them onto the proper path.

In contemporary Japanese society, the loss of a child, whether through abortion, miscarriage, or any other means, is such a personal and private experience that it is difficult for anyone outside those immediately involved to obtain personal accounts of that experience; perhaps this is one reason the media and clergy constructions of *mizuko kuyō* have gone virtually unchallenged in the public forum. Especially in the case of miscarriage, when in Japan there may be some question of the mother's responsibility for the loss, and of abortion, which always raises the issue of responsibility, few if any of those involved are willing to discuss their thoughts openly. Yet it is precisely the thoughts of lay practitioners of *mizuko kuyō* that we need in order to uncover the complexity of the practice that has been flattened in the public constructions we have examined so far.

The material in this section is based primarily on written responses to a questionnaire composed by my collaborator and myself and made available to *mizuko kuyō* participants at a wide array of religious sites in Japan during 1987. The aim of the questionnaire was not to collect statistical data, but to elicit individual statements regarding *mizuko kuyō* and respondents' personal experience of it that would help us to understand the practice from the participants' point of view. I do not present this material here with any claim of its being a more valid view than those

we have examined above, however, for we must recognize lay people's *mizuko kuyō* as the same order of construction as those others. Rather, we will use these individual glimpses to interrogate the public images and to explore the tactical uses made of them by lay practitioners.

Respondents to the questionnaire described their feelings about their loss of a child in many different ways. They found that loss regrettable (*nasakenai* and *kuyashii*), unavoidable (*yamu naku*), and the result of selfishness on their part (*watashi no mikatte*), all terms from ordinary language which they might have used about any unfortunate event in their lives for which they felt some responsibility. While some specified that they were speaking of either an abortion or a miscarriage and a few sought to distinguish a different moral responsibility in the case of abortion, others did not. Most wrote of the relief they experienced after doing *mizuko kuyō* and of their intention of continuing it as long as they live. Indeed, one of the interesting aspects of the practice as it has become formalized in Japan over the last twenty years is the lack of any distinction in the ritual itself in relation to how the children being offered *kuyō* were lost: all *mizuko* are treated the same. For the most part, participants are aware of the circumstances which led to the death of the child they are commissioning the service for, but most clergy who perform the service and offer individual counselling do not ask and say they do not want to know those circumstances. Thus although the media has continued to sensationalize the practice as aimed specifically at women who have had abortions and some Buddhist clergy have rejected it for the same reason, it is clear from participants as well as from the structure of the practice that it is construed to be appropriate for anyone who has lost a child in any manner.

It is the sense of responsibility for having done something regrettable, I think, that is simplified and stereotyped as guilt in the public image of the practice. This is not to deny that guilt is a part of what many participants feel concerning the fact that they 'have' a *mizuko*. Indeed, a number of respondents expressed this feeling of guilt quite strongly: 'As I look at it now, I am tormented by the crime of having killed an individual life'. Yet the very naturalness of this feeling is brought into question by other statements on the questionnaire. 'These children, while they had tiny lives, were consigned from darkness into darkness by the selfishness of adults when in reality they should have been growing up vigorously . . .' This common image from both the promotional and the media constructions of the practice appears verbatim in a number of responses. While it serves to define the basis for feelings of guilt (mainly in the case of abortion), it is also an effective way of eliciting those feelings.

Despite the successful deployment of this image of guilt by those interested in expanding the *mizuko kuyō* market and by elements of the media interested in sensationalizing it (which amounts to the same thing), the sense of responsibility that participants acknowledge extends beyond the single event of the loss of the child to the circumstances which brought that event about. Many respondents expressed the grief they felt at the unavoidability of aborting a child:

> We conceived a child, and as a result of talking it over with my boyfriend, I understood the difficulties in the future if I gave birth. Swallowing my tears, I aborted the child . . . (age 20)

> I got pregnant right after the birth of my first child. Since I had no way to manage and had not yet recovered from the birth, I had no choice but to abort . . . (age 57)

The source of the strong emotion in these and many other statements like them is the authors' perception that they were in a situation where there was no choice other than abortion. If there was a choice, it was earlier, when something could have been done to prevent the conception of a child:

> I had one abortion before I was married. After I married, I got pregnant right after my second child was born and had an abortion for economic reasons. I wanted to have both of those children, but in each case it was a situation in which I absolutely had to get an abortion . . . I am a nurse, and I berate myself now wondering how this could have happened. Knowing very well what to do [to prevent it], I have created two *mizuko* . . .

Yet in Japan reproductive control is in the hands of men on almost every level—sexually, as women are socialized to accept the wishes of their male partners; socially, in that women are brought up to see mothering as their main role; medically, in the overwhelmingly male control over all means of contraception (the condom is widely publicized as the most effective means of birth control, which literally puts the decision to use it in the hands of the man); legally, in the male-controlled medical and governmental worlds which legislate (both publicly and in private) the conditions for abortion. In this context, it is not difficult to understand a woman's feeling of being caught in a situation in which the only seeming solution is the often anguishing one to have an abortion. Very few of our respondents suggested that, given the chance to relive their decision to have an abortion, they would give birth to the child instead. Rather, they expressed regret that they had conceived a child in the first place, hoped never to repeat that irresponsibility again (several wrote that the experience was a call for self-reflection, *hansei*), and thought it only right that they do something for the absent child.

Miscarriage, stillbirth, and child loss by more 'natural' causes are depicted by some in a similar way:

> I lost three children by miscarriage and gave birth to one stillborn child. I have been doing *kuyō* in my own way for the stillborn child, but I felt somewhere in my heart that the three miscarriages were not my fault (*tsumi*) because they left before coming into this world. But I came to think that that wasn't so. Since each [miscarried] child came into my belly with a life that was supposed to enter into this world, after all I think they are my fault (*tsumi*), too. Now I'm simply filled with feelings of repentance for the sad thing I did [in not giving birth to them]. (age 59)

Here the sense of responsibility is more diffuse than in the case of abortion. The woman isn't sure whether to think of her miscarried children as her responsibility or not, but perhaps influenced by promotional literature or advertising for *mizuko kuyō*, she comes to think that they are no different from her stillborn child in their relationship to her. Other women who had had miscarriages stated they were always concerned to do something for the welfare of those children. In 1987 I interviewed an elderly woman who was attending the formal dedication of four small gilded *Mizuko* Jizō statues for her miscarried children at a rural Zen temple in Shiga Prefecture. Her miscarriages had come as she worked in the fields during the years after World War II. She saw the formal repertoire of *mizuko kuyō* as a way of 'doing something' for her dead children at long last—even though she had offered a cup of water for them every day at her family's home altar (*butsudan*), to her mind that informal, personal gesture was not sufficient.

Herein, I think, lies the heart of *mizuko kuyō*. It provides a formal, public, ritualized way to acknowledge the existence of a child—both its potential existence in this world as a result of its conception and its continuing existence somewhere else after death, to (re)establish a relationship with it, and to care for it wherever it may be. In this construction, although the child might be absent from this world, it nevertheless remains a child to its parents and a sibling to its living brothers and sisters. This acknowledgment of the child's existence is implicit in the way many respondents expressed their reason for doing *mizuko kuyō*: I want to apologize to it (*ayamaritai*); I feel sorry for it (*kawaisō*); I'd like to to forgive me (*yurushite moraitai*); I want it to be reborn a Buddha (*jōbutsu shite moraitai*); I'm sorry (*sumanai* and *mōshiwake nai*, both expressions commonly used as a direct form of apology as well as to describe something inexcusable); the situation calls for recompense (*tsugunai*) or amends (*wabi*) to be made.

In the Japanese religious context of which Buddhism makes up one element, those who have died are believed to be reborn into another realm after a period of time for determining which of the six Buddhist realms of existence they will proceed to next; standard funeral practice defines this period to be forty-nine days. But because young and unborn children who had died were not included in standard funeral practice historically, their movement after death is only now, with the emergence of *mizuko kuyō*, being charted.

The most ubiquitous image of their situation depicts them stranded on the barren, rocky shore of the Sai River, which serves as the boundary between the Buddhist hells and other realms of existence. There they have nothing to do but pile stones into small towers (a common practice in Japan for earning karmic merit) and bemoan their separation from their parents. When demons cross the river from the hells and begin to harass them, the bodhisattva Jizō appears as protector. It is not clear how long this displacement out of the standard route to rebirth lasts for *mizuko*, but the implication is that they are stuck in this in-between existence on the river bank. The image suggests that they are unhappy and uncomfortable, perhaps even in danger, in this place, and that they have no substantive way to help themselves. Here, once again, is an image that invites people to feel that they should do something for their *mizuko*.

Now, through the practice of *mizuko kuyō*, parents are able to do something constructive to help their *mizuko*. Attendance at or commissioning of a *mizuko* service is an opportunity for parents to accrue karmic merit on behalf of their dead children. Offerings of religious images, food, clothing and toys can be made to both the child and a deity, to bring comfort to the former and to enlist the protective aid of the latter. And money may be paid to the religious site to ensure continuing ritual care. Parents or other relatives of the *mizuko* do this with feelings of repentance (*zange*) and responsibility or guilt (*tsumi no ishiki* and *zaiakkan*) which, when coupled with the new relationship the practice enables them to establish with their absent child, has led many respondents to declare that they would not forget their absent child or children. Thus although we might view lay people's continuing participation in *mizuko kuyō* as the result of coercion or manipulation, I think we must also see that participation as an act of silent resistance and subversion which turns the practice toward their own lives and motives: we will take part in this practice, as you suggest we should, but we will do so for the sake of our dead children, whom we will not forget, for we have made them a part of our lives once again.

For many women who have lost children through abortion or other means, the practice seems to resonate deeply with their feelings of loss and of responsibility. The elderly woman with three miscarriages and a stillborn child whom we met earlier wrote:

> I went on the Saikoku pilgrimage of 33 temples. *Mizuko Jizō* was being worshipped at every one of the temples. Until then, in my heart I had never forgotten those children, and I had always felt deeply that I should do *kuyō* in some form for them. (age 59)

A twenty-five-year-old woman expressed similar feelings about her aborted child in poetic form:

> There was someone I loved I believed.
> Forgive me . . . we were too young.
> I've lost something important, seen a destiny I
>   should have known.

I can't forgive myself
What, in the end, can I do?
Lots of crying, tired, thinking
To give form to *kuyō* for that lost life
all I can do
is move my feet toward *mizuko kuyō*.

We cannot, of course, separate these women's own feelings from whatever outside influence they may have felt in an atmosphere in 1987 which encouraged women to admit their responsibility for not giving birth to and raising all their children. We can, however, acknowledge their participation in *mizuko kuyō* as a choice that made sense to them at the centre of contradictory messages from society. Socialized to believe that to be a woman is to be a mother and that as mothers they are responsible for their children's well-being, they have at the same time been socialized to accept the sexual advances of their men without real resistance and encouraged to assume responsibility for resulting pregnancies after the fact. For some, this tension between the need to mother and the need to make hard choices for the benefit of their own lives and the lives of their family is at least partially addressed by *mizuko kuyō*: it provides a way for women to mother their *mizuko* that is conceptually similar to the way they care for their living children.

In the case of a woman who has lost a child, her participation in *mizuko kuyō* acts as an acknowledgment that there was (by virtue of its conception), would have been (in that a child conceived is the seed of a child born), and still is a child, even though that child is not now present in the mundane sense of the word. Indeed, one of the most common explanations given for the failure, until now, of women to care for that absent child, wherever it may be, is its lack of a tangible form in this world; 'out of sight, out of mind' is the ruling paradigm here. To address this problem, the giving of a name (either a Buddhist 'dharma name' or, less commonly, a regular 'Keiko' or 'Tarō' name) or a form (such as Jizō or the bodhisattva Kannon) to the child is an almost universal element of *mizuko kuyō*. With this concrete artifact, the child's existence becomes visible and real.

And yet, for whom is the child's existence now made real? I think we must question the assumption that a woman's relationship with her child is based on its visible presence. While this may be the case for those around the woman-mother, whose swelling belly or newborn baby provide visual cues for our construction of her motherhood, for the woman herself the relationship begins much earlier, and without visual aid. The physiological fact of pregnancy together with the social construction of motherhood within which the woman was raised combine to place her into an imaginary (in the psychoanalytical sense) relationship with her child from the moment she knows she is pregnant, as this woman describes:

> I had a miscarriage when I was two months pregnant. I was in the hospital for a week before, but it was no use. The doctor said, 'There's no special cause for a miscarriage this early. The fetus probably wasn't strong enough'. But that fetus was my child from the day it was conceived in my body . . . So even though it was never born into this world, even though it has no form, it is still a member of my family. I did *kuyō* because that fetus's life was lost. I have the feeling that through my doing *kuyō*, that fetus will receive life sometime and give its first cry after birth somewhere . . . (age 27)

For some Japanese women, that relationship is not sustained beyond the fact of the pregnancy, and the lure of *mizuko kuyō* holds no allure at all, despite the strength of the social linking of womanhood with motherhood in Japan:

> In my case, I became very depressed emotionally [after my abortion], but it was not a simple feeling of having done something wrong (*zaiakkan*). I just felt strongly that I wanted to say, 'I'm sorry' to my child. But with the passing of time (about a week?), I recovered completely and was back on my feet. (age 40)

Indeed, it is undoubtedly the case that the majority of Japanese women who have had abortions do not participate in *mizuko kuyō*. There are no statistics available on the number of people who do *mizuko kuyō* in Japan each year, and because of the personal nature of the issue it will probably be impossible to obtain anything more than a loose estimate based on those who identify themselves at particular sites. But I believe it is safe to say that the number of living Japanese women who have lost children through abortion or other means far exceeds the admittedly large number who participate in the practice. But that does not change the fact that many women do participate and that the practice takes on a variety of meanings for them.

For some women, the practice is simply something to do because it should be done, as in these two responses from the questionnaire:

> Just before my first son's wedding, his bride came down with a high fever, and other inconvenient things happened. Because of this, I asked someone to look into the situation and was told that I had better do *mizuko kuyō*. I was surprised, but I went to [a temple] and had it done. Since then, everything has been going well.(age 62)

> Nothing in particular happened [to induce me to do *mizuko kuyō*]. I do it simply because everyone else does. Nothing bad has happened, and neither has anything good. I do it because I'm afraid I'll be talked about if I don't . . . (age 63)

It appears that the public *mizuko* rhetoric has been successful in convincing these women to take part in the practice, although their ambivalence is clear. Each does *mizuko kuyō* for her own sake, not for the sake of her absent child, and neither thinks in terms of an ongoing relationship with that child. In addition, neither sees herself becoming a better Buddhist through her participation. Then why do it? For both women, *mizuko kuyō* seems to provide a way of controlling their lives, in the face of unforeseen and unfortunate occurrences on the one hand and of social gossip on the other. The second woman almost certainly feels manipulated into performing *mizuko kuyō*; indeed, she writes later that she suspects that *mizuko kuyō* is done at temples according to 'mood' rather than from the heart. The first woman is more accepting of the practice, presumably because she feels it has helped make her situation (in this case, the situation of her son) more stable. Yet she, too, does not seem to be terribly invested in the practice. Her statement at the end of the questionnaire that 'I will continue doing *kuyō* for as long as I live' has the same unengaged ring to it as her statement that she began *kuyō* because someone told her to do it.

Many respondents wrote very differently of their involvement in *mizuko kuyō*, however. Some simply said they did *mizuko kuyō* because they could not forget, leaving the subject of their memory unspoken: there are bad feelings in my heart (*kokoro ni wadakamari ga aru*); it remains in my heart (*kokoro ni nokoru*); there's something that always pulls at my heart (*itsumo kokoro ni hikkakaru mono ga ari*). Others were more explicit:

> When my children were all grown and on their own, I was relieved, but the child I miscarried when I was young appeared before my eyes, and I wanted to do *kuyō* for it . . . (age 62)

> It was about four months after the abortion [that I first did *kuyō*]. I had really wanted to do *kuyō* as soon as I could, so now I feel somewhat relieved. Everyday I feel that I did something terrible to my child, and I've never forgotten my child once. The only thing I can do for it now is *kuyō* . . . (age 20)

> I'll continue to do *kuyō* because I'm always wondering what it would be like if that child were alive. (age 45)

These are people who cannot forget their lost children or the experience that led to their loss, and for whom *mizuko kuyō* provides the only way they can see to constructively address both the child's perceived situation and their own feelings. For these lay people the practice is a way to 'do something' for their dead children that could not be accomplished simply by remembering them informally at home. For them, the prayers, images, incense and other offerings made as part of the formalized practice become powerful through the relationship that is established between lay participant, child and deity as mediated by the Buddhist clergy and symbolic system. Many, perhaps most, participants are aware of the negative images of *mizuko kuyō* that we have reviewed above, but they do not seem to connect that criticism with their own practice; the intent of the clergy, whether it be greed or sectarian interest, is not central to the *mizuko* relationship, as one woman observes:

> Recently one hears talk of temples that do *mizuko kuyō* for purposes of making money, but setting that aside, I think the feeling that one wants to do *kuyō* is a good thing. (age 30)

What is important is that the formal practice of *mizuko kuyō* gives lay people a way to care for absent children, although it is not only parents who take part for the sake of their own children. Mothers do *kuyō* for their grown children's *mizuko*; women participate for the sake of their mothers' or sisters' or grandmothers' unmemorialized *mizuko*; individuals like the following thirty-year-old man do *kuyō* for their *mizuko* siblings:

> I've just turned thirty recently, and the other day I heard for the first time that I have siblings who did not receive life in this world and became *mizuko*. I think that if they had been born, I probably wouldn't have had my life, and in this, my thirtieth year, I did *mizuko kuyō* for them for the first time.

And most say they will continue doing *kuyō* at least once a year (on the anniversary of the death; on a Buddhist festival day) for the rest of their lives. That so many would say this demonstrates the weight of the responsibility they feel, although we cannot know whether these intentions will be carried out. Many responses shared the sense of relief (*hotto shita kimochi*) or peace of mind (*anshin shita* and *kimochi ga ochitsukimashita*) that people felt after doing *mizuko kuyō*. But others show clearly that their authors do not consider the practice to fix anything other than their own need to do something:

> I don't in the least think that everything will be forgiven by my doing *mizuko kuyō* now, but that's all there is to do. At least it's a start. (age 44)

> I don't think I'll be forgiven for what I've done, but I do think I've been able to express my prayer for the baby to 'Please be at peace' and my hope that it will 'Please be reborn soon'. (age 22)

Participants and the dead children they are remembering through *mizuko kuyō* are not the only ones to benefit from the practice, however. Many respondents wrote that they were doing *kuyō* for the sake of their living children:

> Having done *kuyō* will not take the obstruction from my heart, but I will continue in order to protect the growth of my two older sons. (age 35)

> If I left things as they were, I wondered if my child would be wandering around in that world, and I wondered if things wouldn't begin to go badly for those in this world. That's why I did *mizuko kuyō*.

> That kind of *kuyō* is for my sake and for my family's sake. I think it's necessary and very important so that life everyday will be fun and everyone will stay healthy and happy. (age 23)

These responses, and others like them, reflect several related understandings of the relationship between the world after death and this one. On the one hand,

mizuko in 'that world' may have some kind of malevolent influence on those related to them who are still living in this world. *Mizuko* may cause things to go badly in general (several respondents wrote that they had led very unlucky lives), or they may cause specific problems such as illness for specific individuals. A particular target for such interventions from 'that world' are the living siblings of *mizuko*. These children receive the constant attention of their parents and relatives, while *mizuko* have tended to be left out of the circle of family attention. This is the belief in *tatari*, reprisal from the spirit world, that spiritualists teach, the media hawks, and Buddhist clergy deplore. Several respondents gave very specific examples of ways in which they saw their *mizuko* asking for attention by intruding on their lives. In this context, the practice of *mizuko kuyō* becomes a redressive action by means of which practitioners can placate their *mizuko* and thereby alleviate the problems they have caused.

The quotations above suggest another construction of this relationship, however. If *mizuko* are taken to be members of the family, then they may be expected to take part in the family in a useful way, just as any living child would. From their vantage point in 'that world', they can influence the lives of their family for the better, becoming, in effect, private protective deities, and several respondents wrote of *mizuko kuyō* as a way to enlist the protective services of their *mizuko* in assuring the health and success of other family members. In particular, the practice offers mothers new aid in raising their living children, and thus it becomes multivalent: it helps women mother all their children, both living and dead.

It should be clear from our treatment of lay people's constructions of *mizuko kuyō* above that this new Japanese practice is much more complex than either the promotional and media or the Buddhist clergy images allow. For the women we have heard, *mizuko kuyō* serves several functions. It provides a formalized public mechanism for acknowledging the existence of a child that may never have been formally recognized and for establishing a continuing relationship with that child in 'that world' after death. The *mizuko*, in effect, is reclaimed as part of the family and as such is given much the same kind of attention that those other absent members of the family, the ancestors, are given in Japan. This reclamation of absent children in turn helps some women reclaim their place as mothers and provides a means for them to both care for and mourn the absence of their children—an absence which, although seen to be unavoidable in many cases (miscarriage, accident or abortion under social or family pressure, for example), was not necessarily a felicitous event for the woman involved.

Constructed in this way, the practice of *mizuko kuyō* becomes a silent way of bringing to the foreground of public awareness some of the underlying tensions in women's lives in Japan: the loneliness of being held responsible for almost single-handedly producing and raising children properly; the frustration of being in the middle of a sexual politics in which their sexuality is held ransom to the needs of their men and the state; the anguish of losing a child and of having few, if any, public ways of dealing with that loss. Integral as they are to the fabric of Japanese women's lives, such issues remain largely unspeakable as personal issues in Japan today despite (or perhaps because of) the beginnings of some academic discussion by Japanese feminists in recent years. Indeed, I would suggest that it is the unspeakable nature of these issues which lies behind the flattened, over-simplified images of the practice that we have seen coming from media and clergy. To give credence to the lay constructions we have explored above would be to open a space for discourse; instead, we have loud, dismissive public images constructed almost with the force of Freudian denial.

I think we must see *mizuko kuyō* as a way for women to speak on those issues—not in so many words, but physically, to act out their personal sense of loss and responsibility and frustration from where they are, without threat of disruption to their lives. Buddhism provides the means for doing this, a powerful symbolic system, a rich repertoire of ritual, both of which are mediated by a cadre of experts, and a space (the physical space of its sites around Japan; the conceptual space opened by its symbols and ritual) in which to speak safely yet with effect.

18

Body Ritual Among the Nacirema

Horace Miner

This article is a classic of anthropological literature. In it, Horace Miner gives readers a thorough and exciting ethnographic account of the myriad of taboos and ceremonial behaviors that permeate the everyday activities of the members of a magic-ridden society. Focusing on secret rituals that are believed to prevent disease while beautifying the body, Miner demonstrates the importance of ceremonial specialists, such as the "holy-mouth-men" and the "listeners," in directing even the most routine aspects of daily life among the Nacirema. Miner finds it difficult to understand how the Nacirema have managed to exist so long under the burdens that they have imposed on themselves.

The anthropologist has become so familiar with the diversity of ways in which different peoples behave in similar situations that he is not apt to be surprised by even the most exotic customs. In fact, if all of the logically possible combinations of behavior have not been found somewhere in the world, he is apt to suspect that they must be present in some yet undescribed tribe. This point has, in fact, been expressed with respect to clan organization by Murdock (1949: 71). In this light, the magical beliefs and practices of the Nacirema present such unusual aspects that it seems desirable to describe them as an example of the extremes to which human behavior can go.

Professor Linton first brought the ritual of the Nacirema to the attention of anthropologists twenty years ago (1936: 326), but the culture of this people is still very poorly understood. They are a North American group living in the territory between the Canadian Cree, the Yaqui and Tarahumare of Mexico, and the Carib and Arawak of the Antilles.

Reprinted by permission of the American Anthropological Association from AMERICAN ANTHROPOLOGIST, vol. 58 (1956), pp. 503–507. Not for further reproduction.

Little is known of their origin, though tradition states that they came from the east. According to Nacirema mythology, their nation was originated by a culture hero, Notgnishaw, who is otherwise known for two great feasts of strength—the throwing of a piece of wampum across the river Pa-To-Mac and the chopping down of the cherry tree in which the Spirit of Truth resided.

Nacirema culture is characterized by a highly developed market economy which has evolved in a rich natural habitat. While much of the people's time is devoted to economic pursuits, a large part of the fruits of these labors and a considerable portion of the day are spent in ritual activity. The focus of this activity is the human body, the appearance and health of which loom as a dominant concern in the ethos of the people. While such a concern is certainly not unusual, its ceremonial aspects and associated philosophy are unique.

The fundamental belief underlying the whole system appears to be that the human body is ugly and that its natural tendency is to debility and disease. Incarcerated in such a body, man's only hope is to avert these characteristics through the use of the powerful influences of ritual and ceremony. Every household has one or more shrines devoted to this purpose. The more powerful individuals in the society have several shrines in their houses and, in fact, the opulence of a house is often referred to in terms of the number of such ritual centers it possesses. Most houses are of wattle and daub construction, but the shrine rooms of the more wealthy are walled with stone. Poorer families imitate the rich by applying pottery plaques to their shrine walls.

While each family has at least one such shrine, the rituals associated with it are not family ceremonies but are private and secret. The rites are normally only discussed with children, and then only during the period when they are being initiated into these mysteries. I was able, however, to establish sufficient rapport with the natives to examine these shrines and to have the rituals described to me.

The focal point of the shrine is a box or chest which is built into the wall. In this chest are kept the many charms and magical potions without which no native believes he could live. These preparations are secured from a variety of specialized practitioners. The most powerful of these are the medicine men, whose assistance must be rewarded with substantial gifts. However, the medicine men do not provide the curative potions for their clients, but decide what the ingredients should be and then write them down in an ancient and secret language. This writing is understood only by the medicine men and by the herbalists who, for another gift, provide the required charm.

The charm is not disposed of after it has served its purpose, but is placed in the charm-box of the household shrine. As these magical materials are specific for certain ills, and the real or imagined maladies of the people are many, the charm-box is usually full to overflowing. The magical packets are so numerous that people forget what their purposes were and fear to use them again. While the natives are very vague on this point, we can only assume that the idea in retaining all the old magical materials is that their presence in the charm-box, before which the body rituals are conducted, will in some way protect the worshipper.

Beneath the charm-box is a small font. Each day every member of the family, in succession, enters the shrine room, bows his head before the charm-box, mingles different sorts of holy water in the font, and proceeds with a brief rite of ablution. The holy waters are secured from the Water Temple of the community, where the priests conduct elaborate ceremonies to make the liquid ritually pure.

In the hierarchy of magical practitioners, and below the medicine men in prestige, are specialists whose designation is best translated "holy-mouth-men." The Nacirema have an almost pathological horror and fascination with the mouth, the condition of which is believed to have supernatural influence on all social relationships. Were it not for the rituals of the mouth, they believe that their teeth would fall out, their gums bleed, their jaws shrink, their friends desert them, and their lovers reject them. (They also believe that a strong relationship exists between oral and moral characteristics. For example, there is a ritual ablution of the mouth for children which is supposed to improve their moral fiber.)

The daily body ritual performed by everyone includes a mouth-rite. Despite the fact that these people are so punctilious about care of the mouth, this rite involves a practice which strikes the uninitiated stranger as revolting. It was reported to me that the ritual consists of inserting a small bundle of hog hairs into the mouth, along with certain magical powders, and then moving the bundle in a highly formalized series of gestures.

In addition to the private mouth-rite, the people seek out a holy-mouth-man once or twice a year. These practitioners have an impressive set of paraphernalia, consisting of a variety of augers, awls, probes, and prods. The use of these objects in the exorcism of the evils of the mouth involves almost unbelievable ritual torture of the client. The holy-mouth-man opens the client's mouth and, using the above-mentioned tools, enlarges any holes which decay may have created in the teeth. Magical materials are put into these holes. If there are no naturally occurring holes in the teeth, large sections of one or more teeth are gouged out so that the supernatural substance can be applied. In the client's view, the purpose of these ministrations is to arrest decay and to draw friends. The extremely sacred and traditional character of the rite is evident in the fact that the natives return to the holy-mouth-men year after year, despite the fact that their teeth continue to decay.

It is to be hoped that, when a thorough study of the Nacirema is made, there will be a careful inquiry into the personality structure of these people. One has but to watch the gleam in the eye of a holy-mouth-man, as he jabs an awl into an exposed nerve, to suspect that a certain amount of sadism is involved. If this can be established, a very interesting pattern emerges, for most of the population shows definite masochistic tendencies. It was to these that Professor Linton referred in discussing a distinctive part of the daily body ritual which is performed only by men. This part of the rite involves scraping and lacerating the surface of the face with a sharp instrument. Special women's rites are performed only four times during each lunar month, but what they lack in frequency is made up in barbarity. As part of this ceremony, women bake their heads in small ovens for about an hour. The theoretically interesting point is that what seems to be a preponderantly masochistic people have developed sadistic specialists.

The medicine men have an imposing temple, or *latipso*, in every community of any size. The more elaborate ceremonies required to treat very sick patients can only be performed at this temple. These ceremonies involve not only the thaumaturge but a permanent group of vestal maidens who move sedately about the temple chambers in distinctive costume and headdress.

The *latipso* ceremonies are so harsh that it is phenomenal that a fair proportion of the really sick natives who enter the temple ever recover. Small children whose indoctrination is still incomplete have been known to resist attempts to take them to the temple because "that is where you go to die." Despite this fact, sick adults are not only willing but eager to undergo the protracted ritual purification, if they can afford to do so. No matter how ill the supplicant or how grave the emergency, the guardians of many temples will not admit a client if he cannot give a rich gift to the custodian. Even after one has gained admission and survived the ceremonies, the guardians will not permit the neophyte to leave until he makes still another gift.

The supplicant entering the temple is first stripped of all his or her clothes. In every-day life the Nacirema avoids exposure of his body and its natural functions. Bathing and excretory acts are performed only in the secrecy of the household shrine, where they are ritualized as part of the body-rites. Psychological shock results from the fact that body secrecy is suddenly lost upon entry into the *latipso*. A man, whose own wife has never seen him in an

excretory act, suddenly finds himself naked and assisted by a vestal maiden while he performs his natural functions into a sacred vessel. This sort of ceremonial treatment is necessitated by the fact that the excreta are used by a diviner to ascertain the course and nature of the client's sickness. Female clients, on the other hand, find their naked bodies are subjected to the scrutiny, manipulation, and prodding of the medicine men.

Few supplicants in the temples are well enough to do anything but lie on their hard beds. The daily ceremonies, like the rites of the holy-mouth-men, involve discomfort and torture. With ritual precision, the vestals awaken their miserable charges each dawn and roll them about on their beds of pain while performing ablutions, in the formal movements of which the maidens are highly trained. At other times they insert magic wands in the supplicant's mouth or force him to eat substances which are supposed to be healing. From time to time the medicine men come to their clients and jab magically treated needles into their flesh. The fact that these temple ceremonies may not cure, and may even kill the neophyte, in no way decreases the people's faith in the medicine men.

There remains one other kind of practitioner, known as a "listener." This witch-doctor has the power to exorcise the devils that lodge in the heads of people who have been bewitched. The Nacirema believe that parents bewitch their own children. Mothers are particularly suspected of putting a curse on children while teaching them the secret body rituals. The counter-magic of the witch-doctor is unusual in its lack of ritual. The patient simply tells the "listener" all his troubles and fears, beginning with the earliest difficulties he can remember. The memory displayed by the Nacirema in these exorcism sessions is truly remarkable. It is not uncommon for the patient to bemoan the rejection he felt upon being weaned as a babe, and a few individuals even see their troubles going back to the traumatic effects of their own birth.

In conclusion, mention must be made of certain practices which have their base in native esthetics but which depend upon the pervasive aversion to the natural body and its functions. There are ritual fasts to make fat people thin and ceremonial feasts to make thin people fat. Still other rites are used to make women's breasts large if they are small, and smaller if they are large. General dissatisfaction with breast shape is symbolized in the fact that the ideal form is virtually outside the range of human variation. A few women afflicted with almost inhuman hyper-mammary development are so idolized that they make a handsome living by simply going from village to village and permitting the natives to stare at them for a fee.

Reference has already been made to the fact that excretory functions are ritualized, routinized, and relegated to secrecy. Natural reproductive functions are similarly distorted. Intercourse is taboo as a topic and scheduled as an act. Efforts are made to avoid pregnancy by the use of magical materials or by limiting intercourse to certain phases of the moon. Conception is actually very infrequent. When pregnant, women dress so as to hide their condition. Parturition takes place in secret, without friends or relatives to assist, and the majority of women do not nurse their infants.

Our review of the ritual life of the Nacirema has certainly shown them to be a magic-ridden people. It is hard to understand how they have managed to exist so long under the burdens which they have imposed upon themselves. But even such exotic customs as these take on real meaning when they are viewed with the insight provided by Malinowski when he wrote (1948: 70):

> Looking from far and above, from our high places of safety in the developed civilization, it is easy to see all the crudity and irrelevance of magic. But without its power and guidance early man could not have mastered his practical difficulties as he has done, nor could man have advanced to the higher stages of civilization.

Suggested Readings

Beattie, John
  1970   "On Understanding Ritual." In Bryan R. Wilson, ed. *Rationality*. Oxford: Blackwell.

Bell, Catherine
  1997   *Ritual: Perspectives and Dimensions*. New York: Oxford University Press.

Moore, Sally Falk, and Barbara, Myerhoff, eds.
  1977   *Secular Ritual*. Assen, Netherlands: Van Gorcum.

Turner, Victor
  1967   *The Forest of Symbols: Aspects of Ndembu Ritual*. Ithaca, N.Y.: Cornell University Press.

CHAPTER FOUR

Shamans, Priests, and Prophets

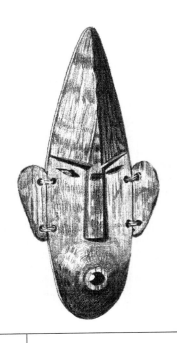

Where and how do religious leaders get their power? What is the distinction between a shaman and a priest, or a prophet and a priest? How do sorcerers, diviners, and magicians differ? This chapter introduces the topic of religious specialists.

Any member of society may approach the supernatural on an individual basis; for example, a person may kneel to the ground, all alone, and recite a prayer for help from the spiritual world. But the religions of the world, whether small, animistic cults or the "great faiths," also have intermediaries: religious people who, acting as part-time or full-time specialists, intervene on behalf of an individual client or an entire community. Paul Radin (1937: 107) argued that the development of religion can be traced to the social roles undertaken by each of these "priest-thinkers"—at once, a philosopher of religion, a theologian of beliefs, a person who is the recognized master of worship.

If all religions appear to have specialists, anthropologists have also found that some societies place more emphasis on these religious experts than others do. Robert Textor has noted, for example, that the societies that are more likely to have religious specialists tend to produce food rather than collect it, use money as a medium of exchange, and display different social classes and a complex political system (1967). In other words, the more complex the society, the greater is the likelihood of having religious intermediaries.

Early anthropologists were drawn to the view of unilineal evolution: how institutions progressed from savagery to barbarism, finally achieving a civilized state. As societies advance, all institutions become more complex and specialized. In this classic work *Primitive Culture* (1871), E. B. Tylor posited an early definition of religion that prompted his colleagues to concern themselves with religious specialization. Describing religion as the belief in spiritual beings, what he called "animism," Tylor implied that a society's degree of religious specialization was directly related to its position on the evolutionary scale. Unilineal evolutionary theory was pockmarked with faulty premises, of course: although cultures do evolve, they do not necessarily follow a prescribed series of stages. What is important to note here, however, is that Tylor and his contemporaries began to look carefully at religious specialization and categories of religious phenomena. J. G. Frazer, in *The Golden Bough* (1890), distinguished between magic and religion and described the role of specialists. And Herbert Spencer's approach, in the *Principles of Sociology* (1896), that religious stages could be comprehended only if the functions of religion and the interrelationships of religion with other institutions were known, demanded that religious specialization be studied in terms of its functions in society—an approach that anthropologists still adhere to today. Anthropological data have shown the importance of shamans, priests, prophets, and other specialists to the maintenance of economic, political, social, and educational institutions of their societies.

The anthropological literature devoted to religious specialists is extensive; much work remains, however, to define and distinguish adequately between the actual functions they perform for members of their societies. Because of limitations on the application of biomedical (Western) therapy in the Third World, traditional doctors play a crucial role in healing (Hepburn 1988: 68). Shamans, for example, have duties and religious obligations that differ from society to society, although their basic duty of curing through the use of the supernatural is accepted by anthropologists. J. M. Atkinson's review article, "Shamanisms Today" (1992), demonstrates the continuing importance of shamanic practices in the contemporary non-Western world. The same kinds of differences exist in the tasks performed by prophets, priests, sorcerers, and others designated as "intermediaries" with the supernatural. Without a clear understanding of these distinctions, systematic cross-cultural comparisons would be impossible.

In addition to the definitional problem associated with specialists, anthropologists must also determine whether to place the tasks performed by these experts under the rubric of "the religious" or to create other categories for such activities. Is the performance of magic, witchcraft, and sorcery "religious" behavior, or are these examples of nonreligious, indeed antireligious acts? If those who practice these acts are outside the religious realm, then what, if any, connection do they have with the sacred? The real question becomes, What is religion? In Western culture, witchcraft, magic, and sorcery are assigned to the occult and are considered outside of and, ordinarily, counter to religion. In the non-Western world, however, specialists who take part in these kinds of activities are often considered to be important parts of the total religious belief system. It is a common view in Africa south of the Sahara that people are often designated witches by God, and that sorcerers and magicians receive their power from the spirit world—that is, from supernatural agencies controlled by God. In these terms, is drawing upon supernatural aid from shamans, priests, or prophets more "religious" than turning to magicians, sorcerers, and other specialists who also call upon supernatural agents but for different ends? In light of these questions, anthropologists have found it necessary to consider all specialists whose power emanates from supernatural agents to be in the realm of the religious, although some specialists serve, whereas others harm society through their actions.

Because not all societies contain identical religious specialists, determining why certain specialists exist and others do not is important to our understanding of the structure of a society and its supernatural world, as well as of the causal forces behind good and bad fortune. In societies where witches do not exist, for example, it is frequently malicious ghosts or ancestors who are believed to bring misfortune and illness. In such cases, elders may play an important role as diviners, in contrast to the diviner specialists that exist in other groups. Such data not only aid our understanding of supernatural causation and specialization but also demonstrate the connection between the social structure of the living—the position of the elder in society—and that of the ancestor or ghost in the afterworld.

The difficulty in making distinctions among non-Western specialists may be further realized by considering the position of the religious layleader in the United States. Although not a specialist in the traditional sense, this individual is nevertheless more involved and usually more knowledgeable than the typical church member. Is the layleader significantly different from one of the more traditional part-time specialists? The problem of the degree of participation comes to mind—part-time versus full-time—accompanied by the complicating factor of training—formal versus on-the-job learning. Making distinctions such as these is an important part of analytic accounts of religious functionaries.

The five excellent articles that follow tell us much about the religious specialist. Victor W. Turner's lead-off essay provides a broad-spectrum account of the various specialists who appear in ethnographic descriptions of religions around the world.

William Howells discusses the positive functions offered by Siberian shamans to the societies they serve. Shamanistic leadership, the result of psychological and physiological aid given their followers, is also based on their control of malevolent powers that can be dangerous to the people.

Reflecting on research in Peru, Michael Fobes Brown rejects romanticized views of shamanism, reminding readers of the anxiety and violence that may accompany the phenomenon.

The fourth article, by Gerardo Reichel-Dolmatoff, provides a detailed account of priesthood among the Kogi of Colombia. The author focuses on the lengthy and elaborate training young men must undergo to become priests.

Michael Barkun concludes the chapter with an in-depth look into the minds of the Branch Davidians and their prophetic leader, David Koresh, as well as the FBI and ATF authorities and the tragic clash at Waco, Texas.

References

Atkinson, J. M.
    1992 "Shamanisms Today." *Annual Reviews in Anthropology* 21: 307–30.

Frazer, J. G.
    1890 *The Golden Bough.* London: MacMillan.

Hepburn, Sharon J.
    1988 "Western Minds, Foreign Bodies." *Medical Anthropology Quarterly* 2 (New Series): 59–74.

Radin, Paul
    1937 *Primitive Religion: Its Nature and Origin.* New York: Dover.

Spencer, H.
    1896 *Principles of Sociology.* New York: D. Appleton.

Textor, Robert
    1967 *A Cross-Cultural Summary.* New Haven, Conn.: HRAF Press.

Tylor, E. B.
    1871 *Primitive Culture: Researches into the Development of Mythology, Philosophy, Religion, Language, Art and Custom.* London: J. Murray.

19

Religious Specialists

Victor W. Turner

Noted for his contributions to the study of symbolism and the structure of rituals, Victor W. Turner here introduces the basic terms for different types of religious specialists, as conventionally used by anthropologists. Turner focuses upon the most commonly used terms such as shaman, priest, and prophet, but includes other, less prominent but often equally important religious specialists as well—diviners, seers, mediums, witches, sorcerers, and magicians—and discusses how each type of specialist is likely to appear in societies with particular levels of social complexity and political specialization. While these terms appear throughout the anthropological literature with a fair degree of consistency, in some cases (for example, the term "shaman"), anthropologists disagree about how widely or narrowly the term should be applied. Turner's overview lays the groundwork for the articles to follow, which deal specifically with shamans, priests, and prophets.

A religious specialist is one who devotes himself to a particular branch of religion or, viewed organizationally, of a religious system. "Religion" is a multivocal term whose range of meanings varies in different social and historical contexts. Nevertheless, most definitions of religion refer to the recognition of a transhuman controlling power that may be either personal or impersonal. A religious specialist has a culturally defined status relevant to this recognition. In societies or contexts where such power is regarded as impersonal, anthropologists customarily describe it as *magic,* and those who manipulate the power are magicians. Wherever power is personalized, as deity, gods, spirits, daemons, genii, ancestral shades, ghosts, or the like, anthropologists speak of *religion.* In reality, religious systems contain both magical and religious beliefs and procedures: in many of them the impersonal transhuman (or mystical, or non-empirical, or supernatural) power is considered to be a devolution of personal power, as in

the case of the mystical efficacy of rites established *in illo tempore* by a deity or divinized ancestor.

Priest and Prophet

Scholars have tended to distinguish between two polarities of religious specialization. Max Weber, for example, although well aware of numerous historical instances of their overlap and interpenetration, contrasts the roles of priest and prophet. He begins by making a preliminary distinction between priest and magician. A priest, he writes, is always associated with "the functioning of a regularly organized and permanent enterprise concerned with influencing the gods—in contrast with the individual and occasional efforts of magicians." Accordingly, the crucial feature of priesthood is that it represents the "specialization of a particular group of persons in the continuous operation of a cultic enterprise, permanently associated with particular norms, places and times, and related to specific social groups." In Weber's view, the prophet is distinguished from the priest by "personal call." The priest's claim to religious authority derives from his service in a sacred tradition; the authority of the prophet is founded on revelation and personal "charisma." This latter term has been variously defined by Weber (in some contexts it seems almost to represent the *Führerprinzip*), but it may broadly be held to designate extraordinary powers. These include, according to Weber, "the capacity to achieve the ecstatic states which are viewed, in accordance with primitive experience, as the preconditions for producing certain effects in meteorology, healing, divination and telepathy." But charisma may be either ascribed or achieved. It may be an inherent faculty ("primary charisma") or it may be "produced artificially in an object or person through some extraordinary means." Charisma may thus be "merited" by fastings, austerities, or other ordeals. Even in such cases, Weber asserts, there must be some dormant capacity in the persons or objects, some "germ" of extraordinary power, already vested in them. The prophet, then, is a "purely individual bearer of charisma," rather than the representative of a sacred tradition. He produces discontinuity in that cultic enterprise which it is the priest's major role to keep "in continuous operation." Weber's prophet feels that he has a "mission" by virtue of which he "proclaims religious doctrine or divine commandment." Weber refuses to distinguish sharply between a "renewer of religion" who preaches "an older revelation, actual or supposititious" and a "founder of religion" who claims to bring completely new "deliverances," for, he says, "the two types merge into one another." In Weber's view, the charisma of a prophet appears to contain, in addition to ecstatic and visionary components, a rational component, for he proclaims "a systematic and distinctively religious ethic based upon a consistent and stable doctrine which purports to be a revelation" [(1922)].

Weber's distinction between priest and prophet has its main relevance in an analytical frame of reference constructed to consider the relationship between religion as "a force for dynamic social change" and religion as "a reinforcement of the stability of societies" (Parsons 1963). It has been found effective by such anthropologists as Evans-Pritchard ([1956] 1962) and Worsley (1957a; 1957b) who are dealing directly with social transitions and "the prophetic break," or what Parsons calls "the primary decision point [between] a direction which makes for a source of evolutionary change in the . . . established or traditional order, and a direction which tends either to reinforce the established order

or at least not to change it drastically" (1963; p. xxix in 1964 edition).

Priest and Shaman

Anthropologists who are less concerned than Weber with the genesis of religions and with internal developments in complex societies or their impact on the "primitive" world are inclined to contrast priest not with prophet but with shaman or spirit medium and to examine the relationship between these statuses as part of the normal working of the religious system in the simpler societies. In their excellently representative *Reader in Comparative Religion* (1958), the editors W. A. Lessa and E. Z. Vogt devote a whole section to this distinction.

Often, where there is a priest the shaman is absent, and vice versa, although both these roles may be found in the same religion, as among the Plains Indians. According to Lowie (1954), a Plains Indian shaman is a ritual practitioner whose status is acquired through a personal communication from a supernatural being, whereas a priest does not necessarily have a face-to-face relationship with the spirit world but must have competence in conducting ritual. Lessa and Vogt ([1958] 1965: 410) expand these differences: a shaman's powers come by "divine stroke," a priest's power is inherited or is derived from the body of codified and standardized ritual knowledge that he learns from older priests and later transmits to successors. They find that shamanism tends to predominate in food-gathering cultures, where the shaman most frequently performs a curing rite for the benefit of one or more patients and within the context of an extended family group. Shamanistic rites are "non-calendrical," or contingent upon occasions of mishap and illness. The priest and priestly cult organization are characteristically found in the more structurally elaborated food-producing—usually agricultural—societies, where the more common ceremonial is a public rite performed for the benefit of a whole village or community. Such rites are often calendrical, or performed at critical points in the ecological cycle.

Shaman and Medium

Raymond Firth (1964a: 638) regards shamanism as itself "that particular form of spirit mediumship in which a specialist (the *shaman*) normally himself a medium, is deemed to exercise developed techniques of control over spirits, sometimes including mastery of spirits believed to be possessing another medium." This definition, like that of Howells (1948), stresses the *control* exercised over spirits. Howells describes the shaman as "bullyragging" gods or spirits and emphasizes his intellectual qualities as a leader. This element of mastery makes the shaman a distinctive type of spirit medium, one who is believed to be "possessed by a spirit (or closely controlled by a spirit) [and who] can serve as a means of communication between other human beings and the spirit world" (Firth 1964b: 689). The spirit medium per se need not exert mastery; he is rather the vessel or vehicle of the transhuman entity.

Thus, although we sometimes find the two functions of priest and shaman combined in the same individual (Piddington 1950), mediums, shamans, and prophets clearly constitute subtypes of a single type of religious functionary. The priest communicates with transhuman entities through ritual that involves cultural objects and activities. The medium, shaman, and prophet communicate in a person-to-person manner: they are in what Buber (1936) would describe as an I-thou relationship with the deities or spirits. The priest, on the other hand, is in what may be called an I-it relationship with the transhuman. Between the priest and the deity intervenes the institution. Priests may therefore be classified as institutional functionaries in the religious domain, while medium, shaman, and prophet may be regarded as subtypes of inspirational functionaries. This distinction is reflected in characteristically different modes of operation. The priest presides over a rite; the shaman or medium conducts a seance. Symbolic forms associated with these occasions differ correlatively: the symbols of a rite are sensorily perceptible to a congregation and have permanence in that they are culturally transmissible, while those of a seance are mostly in the mind of the entranced functionary as elements of his visions or fantasies and are often generated by and limited to the unique occasion. The inspirational functionary may describe what he has clairvoyantly perceived (or "been shown" as he might put it), but the institutional functionary manipulates symbolic objects with prescribed gestures in full view of this congregation.

Sociocultural Correlates

Since the priest is an actor in a culturally "scripted" drama, it is but rarely that priests become innovators, or "dramatists." If they do assume this role it is mainly as legislative reformers—by altering the details of liturgical procedure—that they do so. If a priest becomes a radical innovator in religion, he is likely to become a prophet to his followers and a heretic to his former superiors. From the priestly viewpoint it is the office, role, and script that are sacred and "charismatic" and not the incumbent of priestly office. The priest is concerned with the conservation and maintenance of a deposit of beliefs and practices handed down as a sacred trust from the founders of the social or religious system. Since its symbols at the semantic level tend to condense the critical values, norms, and principles of the total cultural system into a few sensorily perceptible representations, the sanctification of these symbols is tantamount to a preservative of the entire culture. What the priest is and does keeps cultural change and individual deviation within narrow limits. But the energy and time of the inspirational functionary is less bound up with the maintenance of the total cultural system. His practice has more of an ad hoc flavor; he is more sensitive and responsive than the priest to the private and personal, to the mutable and idiosyncratic. This type of functionary thrives in loosely structured food-gathering cultures, where he deals individually with specific occasions of trouble, or during periods of social turbulence and change, when societal consensus about values is sharply declining and numerically significant classes of persons and social groups are becoming alienated from the orthodox social order. The shaman subtype is completely a part of the cultural system of the food-gatherers; the prophet may well stand outside the cultural system during such a period of decomposition and propose new doctrines, ethics, and even economic values.

The shaman is not a radical or a reformer, since the society he services is traditionally flexible and mobile; the prophet is an innovator and reformer, for he confronts a tightly structured order that is moribund and points the way to religious forms that will either provide an intensified cognitive dynamic for sociocultural change or codify the new moral, ideational, and social structures that have been inarticulately developing.

There are of course significant differences in the scale of the societies in which shaman and prophet operate. The shaman enacts his roles in small-scale, multifunctional communities whose religious life incorporates beliefs in a multitude of deities, daemons, nature spirits, or ancestral shades—societies that Durkheim might have described as possessing mechanical solidarity, low moral density, and segmental organization. The prophet tends to come into his own when the division of labor is critically replacing "mechanical" by "organic" solidarity, when class antagonisms are sharpened, or when small-scale societies are decisively invaded by the powerful personnel, ideas, techniques, and cultural apparatus (including military skills and armaments) of large-scale societies. The shaman deals in a personal and specific way with spirits and lesser deities; the prophet enters into dialogue, on behalf of his whole community, with the Supreme Being or with the major deities of a traditional pantheon, whose tutelary scope embraces large numbers of persons and groups, transcending and transecting their traditional divisions and animosities. Alternatively he communicates with the generalized ancestors or *genii loci*, conceived to be a single anonymous and homogeneous collectivity rather than a structure of known and named shades, each representing a specific segment of society. Whereas the shaman's function is associated with looseness of structure in small-scale societies, the prophet's is linked with loosening of structure in large-scale societies or with incompatibilities of scale in culture-contact situations.

Divination and Religious Specialists

In its strict etymological sense the term "divination" denotes inquiry about future events or matters, hidden or obscure, directed to a deity who, it is believed, will reply through significant tokens. It usually refers to the process of obtaining knowledge of secret or future things by mechanical means or manipulative techniques—a process which may or may not include invoking the aid of non-empirical (transhuman) persons or powers but does not include the empirical methods of science.

In the analysis of preliterate societies divination often is concerned with the immediate problems and interests of individuals and subgroups and but

seldom with the destinies of tribes and nations. It is this specificity and narrowness of reference that primarily distinguishes divination from prophecy. Nadel (1954: 64) has called the kind of guidance it offers "mechanical and of a case-to-case kind." The diviner "can discover and disentangle some of the hidden influences which are at work always and everywhere. . . . He cannot uncover any more embracing design. . . . Yet within the limits set to it divination has a part to play, providing some of the certainty and guidance required for provident action." Thus, although its range and scope are more circumscribed than those of prophecy, divination is believed to reveal what is hidden and in many cases to forecast events, auspicious and inauspicious.

Divination further refers to the analysis of past events, especially untoward events; this analysis often includes the detection and ascription of guilt with regard to their perpetrators, real or alleged. Where such untoward events are attributed to sorcerers and witches the diviner has great freedom of judgment in detecting and determining guilt. Diviners are frequently consulted by victims' relatives and show intuitive and deductive virtuosity in discovering quarrels and grudges in their clients' kin groups and local communities. Social anthropologists find important clues to areas and sources of social strain and to the character and strength of supportive social norms and values in the diviners' diagnoses.

There is evidence that mediums, shamans, and priests in various cultures have practiced divination. The medium and shaman often divine without mechanical means but with the assistance of a tutelary spirit. In the work of Lessa and Vogt there is a translation of a vivid first-person account by a Zulu informant of a diviner's seance. This mediumistic female diviner

dramatically utilizes some standard procedures of her art—ventriloquism, prior knowledge of the clients, the overhearing of the client's unguarded conversation, and shrewd common sense—to enable her spirits to provide the clients with advice. In this example, . . . a boy is suffering from a convulsive ailment. The spirits discover that an ancestral spirit is spitefully causing the boy's illness: the spirits decree that the location of the family's village must be moved; a goat must be sacrificed to the ancestor and the goat's bile poured over the boy; the boy must drink *Itongo* medicine.

The treatment thus ranges from physical to social actions—from propitiation of wrathful ancestors to prescription of a medicinal potion (Lessa & Vogt [1958] 1965: 340).

Similar accounts of shamanistic divinatory seances have been recorded by anthropologists working among North and South American Indians, Eskimos, and Siberian tribes, in many parts of Africa, and among Afro-Americans.

Divination was a function of members of the priesthood in many of the complex religious systems of Polynesia, west Africa, and ancient Mexico; in the religions of Israel, Greece, Etruria, and Rome; in Babylonia, India, China, Japan, and among the Celts. According to Wach,

> The Etruscans made these practices so much a part of their culture that the discipline has been named after them (*disciplina Etrusca* or *auguralis*). Different phenomena and objects were used as media to ascertain the desires of the gods (regular and irregular celestial events, lightning, fire, and earthquakes, the shape or utterances of animals, flights of birds, movements of serpents, barking of dogs, forms of liver or entrails). Both in Etruria and Rome a numerous and well-organized hierarchy of functionaries existed for practice of the sacred arts (1958, p. 111 in 1961 edition).

Indeed, diffused through the Roman world, many of these techniques passed into medieval and modern culture.

Diviner and Doctor

Callaway's account (1868–1870) of the combined divinatory and curative seance in Zululand emphasizes the close relationship believed to hold in many preliterate societies between the functions of divination and therapy. Sometimes, as in the case cited, the diviner and "doctor" are the same person, but more often the roles are specialized and performed by different individuals. Modern therapy is taking increasingly into account the psychosomatic character of many maladies and the importance of sociological factors in their etiology. In most preliterate societies bodily symptoms are regarded as signs that the soul or life principle of the patient is under attack or has been abstracted by spiritual forces or beings. Furthermore, it is widely held that these attacks are motivated by animosities provoked by breaches of cultural, mainly religious, prescriptions and/or breaches of social norms regarded as binding on members of kin groups or local communities. Thus, to acquire a comprehensive understanding of why and how a patient was afflicted with certain symptoms by a spirit or witch, primitives seek out a diviner who will disclose the secret antagonisms in social relations or the perhaps unconscious neglect of ritual rules (always a threat to the cultural order) that incited mystical retribution or malice. The diviner is a "diagnostician" who refers his clients to his colleague, the doctor or "therapist." The doctor in question has both shamanistic and priestly attributes. The division of labor which in more complex societies segregates and institutionalizes the functions of priest and medical man has hardly begun to make its influence felt. The diviner-doctor dichotomy does not depend, as does the priest-shaman dichotomy, upon contrasting roles in regard to the transhuman realm but upon different phases in a social process which involves *total* human phenomena—integral personalities, many psychosomatic complexes, multiple social relationships, and multiform communities.

Modes of Religious Specialization

As the scale and complexity of society increase and the division of labor develops, so too does the degree of religious specialization. This process accompanies a contraction in the domain of religion in social life. As Durkheim stated with typical creative exaggeration in his *Division of Labor in Society* ([1893] 1960: 169): "Originally [religion] pervades everything; everything social is religious; the two words are synonymous. Then, little by little, political, economic, scientific functions free themselves from the religious function, constitute themselves a part and take on a more and more acknowledged temporal character."

Simple Societies

In the simplest societies every adult has some religious functions and the elders have most; as their capacity to hunt or garden wanes, their priestlike role comes into ever greater prominence. Women tend to receive more recognition and scope as religious functionaries than in more developed societies. There is some tendency toward religious specialization in such societies, based on a variety of attributes, such as knowledge of herbalistic lore, skill in leechcraft, the capacity to enter a state of trance or dissociation, and sometimes physical handicap that compels a man or woman to find an alternative means of support to subsistence activities. (I have met several diviners in central Africa with maimed hands or amputated limbs.) But such specialization can hardly be defined, in the majority of cases, as more than part-time or even spare-time specialization. Michael Gelfand's description of the Shona *nganga,* variously translated in the ethnographic literature as "medicine man," "doctor," or "witch doctor," exemplifies the sociocultural situation of similar practitioners in very many preliterate societies (1964). The Shona *nganga* is at once a herbalist, a medium, and also a diviner who, possessed by a spirit of a dead relative, diagnoses both the cause of illness and of death. Yet, reports Gelfand,

> when he is not engaged in his medical practice he leads exactly the same life as the other men of his village. He cultivates his land, looks after his cattle, repairs his huts, makes blankets or other equipment needed by his family. And the same applies to a woman *nganga,* who busies herself with the tasks expected of every Shona woman. . . . The amount the *nganga* does in his village depends, of course, on the demands of his patients, but on the average he has a fair amount of spare time. . . . A fair guess would be [that there is a *nganga*] to every 800 to 1,000 persons. . . . The *nganga* is given no special status in his village, his chances of being appointed headman are the same as anyone else's (1964: 22–23).

Complex Societies

To bring out best the effects of increase in scale and the division of labor it is necessary to examine religious systems at the opposite end of the gradient of complexity. Religion no longer pervades all social domains; it is limited to its own domain. Furthermore, it has acquired a contractual and associational character; people may choose both the form and extent of their religious participation or may opt out of any affiliation. On the other hand, within each religious group a considerable amount of specialization has taken place. Much of this has been on the organizational level. Processes of bureaucratization, involving rationality in decision making, relative

impersonality in social relations, routinization of tasks, and a hierarchy of authority and function, have produced a large number of types, grades, and ranks of religious specialists in all the major religious systems.

For example, the Catholic clerical hierarchy may be considered as (1) the hierarchy of order, whose powers are exercised in worship and in the administration of the sacraments, and (2) as the hierarchy of jurisdiction, whose power is over the members of the church. Within the hierarchy of jurisdiction alone we find such manifold statuses as pope and bishop (which are held to be of divine institution); cardinal, patriarch, exarch, and primate (whose powers are derived by delegation expressed or implied from the holy see); metropolitan and archbishop (who derive their powers from their patriarch, exarch, or primate); archdeacon, vicar general, vicar forane, rural dean, pastor, and rector (who derive their powers from their diocesan bishop).

In addition to the clerical hierarchy there are in the Catholic church numerous institutes of the religious, that is, societies of men and women approved by ecclesiastical superiors, in which the members in conformity with the special laws of their association take vows, perpetual or temporary, and by this means aspire to religious perfection. This is defined as "the heroic exercise of the virtue of supernatural charity" and is pursued by voluntary maintenance of the vows of poverty, chastity, and obedience, by ascetical practices, through charitable works, such as care of the poor, sick, aged, and mentally handicapped, and by contemplative techniques, such as prayer. Within each religious institution or congregation there is a marked division of function and gradation of office.

Thus there are many differences of religious status, rank, and function in a developed religious system such as the Catholic church. Differences in charismata are also recognized in such terms as "contemplative," "ascetic," "mystic," "preacher," "teacher," "administrator." These gifts may appear in any of the major divisions of the church: among clergy or laity, among hermits, monks, or friars, among female as well as male religious. Certain of these charismata are institutionalized and constitute the devotional pattern particular to certain religious institutions: thus there are "contemplative orders," "friars preachers," and the like.

Medium-Scale Societies

Other developed religions, churches, sects, cults, and religious movements exhibit degrees of bureaucratic organization and specialization of role and function. Between the situational specialization of religious activities found in small-scale societies and the full-time and manifold specialization in large-scale societies falls a wide variety of intermediate types. A characteristic religious dichotomy is found in many of the larger, politically centralized societies of west and east Africa, Asia, Polynesia, and pre-Columbian Central and South America. National and tribal gods are worshiped in the larger towns, and minor deities, daemons, and ancestral shades are venerated in the villages. At the village level we find once more the multifunctional religious practitioner. But where there are national gods there are usually national priests, their official servants, and worship tends to take place in temples or at fixed and elaborate shrines. Parrinder writes:

> In the cults of the West African gods [for example, in Dahomey, Yoruba, and Ashanti] there are priests who are highly trained to do their work. These priests are often set aside from birth, or they may be called to the service of the god by being possessed by his spirit. They will then retire from their families and public life, and submit to the training of an older priest. The training normally lasts several years, during which time the novice has to apply himself to learn all the secrets of consulting and serving the god. The training of a priest is an arduous matter. . . . [He] has to observe chastity and strict taboos of food and actions. He frequently has to sleep on a hard floor, have insufficient food, and learn to bear hardship. He is regarded as married to the god, though later he may take a wife. Like an Indian devotee, he seeks by self-discipline to train himself to hear the voice of his god. He learns the ritual and dances appropriate to the cult, receives instruction in the laws and taboos of the god, and gains some knowledge of magical medicines (1954: 100–101).

In these west African cults of deities there is a formal division of function between priests and mediums. In general, priests control mediums and carefully regulate their experience of possession. This situation is one solution to the perennial problem posed for priesthoods by what Ronald Knox (1950) has termed "enthusiasm," that is, the notion that one can become possessed by or identified with a god or God and that one's consequent acts and words are divinely inspired, even if they transgress religious or secular laws. In Dahomey, for example (Herskovits 1938), there are communal training centers, called cult houses or "convents," for mediums and assistants to priests. Here the novices are secluded for considerable periods of time. Part of their training involves the attempt to induce the return of the initial spirit possession that marked their calling. They learn later to produce coherent messages in a state of trance. During this period they are under the surveillance of priests. The Catholic church has similarly brought under its control as members of contemplative orders mystics and visionaries who claim "experimental knowledge of God's presence."

Religious and Political Specialization

In many primitive societies an intimate connection exists between religion and politics. If by politics we denote those behavioral processes of resolution of conflict between the common good and the interests of groups by the use of or struggle for power, then religion in such societies is pragmatically connected with the maintenance of those values and norms expressing the common good and preventing the undue exercise of power. In centralized political systems that have kings and chiefs, these dignitaries themselves have priestly functions; in many parts of Africa, for example, they take charge of observances which safeguard many of the basic needs of existence, such as rainmaking, sowing, and harvest rites, rituals to promote the fertility of men, domestic and wild animals, and so on. On the other hand, even where this is the case, there are frequently other specialized religious functionaries whose duties are bound up with the office of kingship. An illustration of this occurs among the Bemba of Zambia, where the *Bakabilo*

> are in charge of ceremonies at the sacred relic shrines and take possession of the *babenye* when the chief dies. They alone can purify the chief from the defilement of sex intercourse so that he is able to enter his relic shrine and perform the necessary rites there. They are in complete charge of the accession ceremonies of the paramount and the bigger territorial chiefs, and some of their number are described as *bafingo*, or hereditary buriers of the chief. Besides this, each individual *mukabilo* has his

own small ritual duty or privilege, such as lighting the sacred fire, or forging the blade of the hoe that is to dig the foundations of the new capital (Richards 1940, p. 109 in 1955 edition).

The *Bakabilo* constitute a council that exerts a check on the paramount's power, since the members are hereditary officials and cannot be removed at will. They are immune to the paramount's anger and can block the implementation of decisions that they consider to be detrimental to the interests of the Bemba people by refusing to perform the ritual functions that are necessary to the exercise of his office. A priesthood of this type thus forms a constituent part of the interior structure of the government of a primitive state.

In stateless societies in Africa and elsewhere, incumbents of certain ritual positions have similar functions in the maintenance of order and the resolution of conflict. The "leopard-skin chief" or "priest of the earth" (as this specialist has been variously called) among the Nuer of the Nilotic Sudan is a person whose ritual relationship with the earth gives him power to bless or curse, to cleanse a killer from the pollution of bloodshed, and, most important, to perform the rites of reconciliation between persons who are ready to terminate a blood feud. A similar role is performed by the "masters of the fishing spear" among the Dinka and the *tendaanas*, or earth priests, among the Tallensi and their congeners in the northern territories of Ghana. Similar religious functionaries are found in many other regions of Africa. They serve to reduce, if not to resolve, conflict within the society. As against sectional and factional interests they posit the commonweal. In these contexts, moreover, the commonweal is regarded as part of the cosmic order; breach, therefore, is mystically punished. The religious specialists are accorded the function of restoring the right relation that should obtain between society, the cosmos, and the deities or ancestral shades.

20

The Shaman: A Siberian Spiritualist

William Howells

In this classic work, William Howells demonstrates the many positive functions of Arctic shamans in their roles as mediums and diviners, clearly differentiating their character from the evil nature of witches. Like witches, however, shamans have "familiars"—animal souls that give them their powers. Through their familiars, for example, shamans might travel into all three realms of nature (upper, middle, and lower) to recapture the lost souls of villagers enticed into the lower realm of darkness and evil by a demon. At the same time, the power of animal souls allows the shamans to do witchlike harm, and this, along with their ability to cure and keep the balance between the spirits of the upper and lower realms of nature, inspires awe in the villagers' minds. The shamans foster this awe through their artful use of prestidigitation and ventriloquism, justifying their trickery because it enables them to help their followers in the cause of good and to perpetuate their religion.

Although shamanism is both dangerous and burdensome, in Siberia as many women as men become shamans, and each sex often takes on the behavior of its opposite. Members of society may disapprove of this behavior but don't voice their disapproval due to fear of shamanic retribution. It is the shaman's power, expressed in dramatic performance, that provides the psychological benefits for the society by reducing tensions in both individuals and groups and thereby returning emotional balance.

Howells's view of the functions of shamanism anticipated the current view of medical anthropologists who have positively reappraised the role of the traditional healer.

Witches are all evil, and hide themselves from common men; they are "secret, black and midnight hags"; fell creatures, they hypocritically put on the mien of ordinary folk, the better to stalk and strike their prey unknown. But there are other men and women with extraordinary powers of their own, who have no need to skulk, because their purposes are good, and who are given public recognition and respect. The type specimen of such people is known under the Tungus word *shaman*, and the shaman is a figure of importance among the aboriginal people of Siberia and the Eskimos, among most of the American Indians, and to a lesser extent among various other primitive tribes elsewhere in the world. He has been sometimes called a witch doctor, especially with reference to Africa.

A shaman is a medium and a diviner, but his powers do not stop there. He differs from men in general, and resembles a witch, because he can shift gears and move in the plane of the supernatural. He can go at will to the other world, and he can see and treat with souls or spirits, meeting them on their own ground. And that is his business. He differs from a witch, who exists solely in the heads of the victimized, in that he is an actual person, who not only conducts his profession publicly, making the people think that he goes on brave errands among ghosts and goblins, but in many if not most cases really believes he has the powers he claims. This, of course, would be something difficult to get the truth of. Nonetheless he acts as though he can and does do the things which are traditionally his to do, and the public believes and acclaims him. That is the important thing.

His duties are to ride herd on the souls of the departed and to discover the general disposition of other important spirits, according as it is swayed by the behavior of human beings. He may do only a little of this; among some people there is a shaman in every family, who simply makes contact with the spirits from time to time to flatter them and assure himself of their serene humor, as we look at a barometer. Elsewhere he may do it as his trade: general divining, diagnosis of sickness, and ghost chasing. And he may be the most important person of the village, as well as the center of religion; this position he has in easternmost Siberia and among the Eskimos. With such people communities are small and religion is otherwise crude, and the people look to the shaman to take care of their relations with the supernatural both public and private. While he thus acts for them much as does a medicine man or a diviner, he is no magician. He does not endeavor to find the formula to the supernatural, working it as though it were made up of wires and joints, while remaining on the outside; instead, he boldly enters it himself and meets its inhabitants man to man. Nor is he a priest, who leads the people in supplication and represents them before their gods. He may work in their behalf, but he does not represent them; he is acting on his own hook, and through skill and power, not through supplication.

The stronghold of the shaman is among the reindeer herders and fishers of northeast Asia: the Yakuts and the Tungus, two widespread groups of tribes, and others living around the western shore of the Bering Sea: the Chuckchis, the Koryaks, the Gilyaks, and the Kamchadals of Kamchatka. Some of these live nomadically in felt tents and others in wooden villages, and in the long arctic nights of their bleak environment the comfort and entertainment that the shaman gives them is very well received. Typically it is believed that there are three realms of nature: an upper one, of light and of good spirits; a middle one, which is the world of men and of the spirits of the earth; and a lower one, for darkness and evil spirits. Men of the usual sort can move about the middle realm, and have some dealings with its spirits, but only a shaman can go above or below. A shaman also has the power of summoning spirits to come to him. Thus he can speak directly to spirits and ask what they want, which is his form of divining. Not only this, but a shaman deals with sickness in various ways through these same powers. If you have a disease spirit inside you, he can detect it and he knows how to send it off, perhaps by having a personal contest with it. Or you may have lost your soul—this explanation of illness turns up almost everywhere in the world—and the shaman gets it back. It has probably been enticed against its will by a stronger demon, and taken to the lower regions, and only the shaman can go after it, see it, identify it, and return it.

Both in Asia and America shamans, like witches, are generally believed to have familiar spirits, or animal souls, which are the things that give them their peculiar qualities and powers. A Yakut shaman has two or three (Casanowicz 1924; Czaplicka 1914). One, called *emekhet*, is the shaman's own guardian angel, which is not only a sort of impersonal power like mana but also a definite spirit, usually that of a shaman already dead. This spirit hovers around its protégé, guiding and protecting him all the time, and comes at once when he calls for it, and gives him the advice he needs. Another spirit, the *yekyua*, has more character but is less accommodating. This one is an external soul, which belongs both to the shaman and to a living wild animal, which may be a stallion, a wolf, a dog, an eagle, a hairy bull, or some mythical creature, like a dragon. The yekyua is unruly and malevolent; it is dangerous and enables the shaman to do harm, rather like a witch, so that the people are in awe of him, but at the same time it has no consideration for the shaman himself and gives him continual trouble and anxiety, because his own fortunes are bound up with it. It is independent and lives far away, rather than upon the immediate tribal scene, and only another shaman can see it anyway.

"Once a year, when the snow melts and the earth is black, the yekyua arise from their hiding places and begin to wander" (Czaplicka 1914). When two of them meet, and fight, the human shamans to whom they are linked undergo the evil effects and feel badly. If such an animal dies or is killed, its shaman dies as well, so that a shaman whose yekyua is a bear or a bull can congratulate himself that his life expectancy is good. Of this phantasmal zoo the least desirable soul partners to have are carnivorous animals, especially dogs, because the shaman must keep them appeased, and if they go hungry they are not above taking advantage of their connection with the poor shaman to gnaw at his vitals to stay their appetites. When a person takes to shamanizing, the other shamans round about can tell whether a new yekyua has made its appearance far away, which will cause them to recognize the new shaman and accept him into the profession.

Siberian shamans all dress the part, as do so many shamans and medicine men of North America. The northeastern Asiatics wear clothing which is made of skin and tailored. A shaman has a cap and a mask, but it is his coat which distinguishes him like a collar turned around. It is a tunic made of hide—goat, elk, etc.—and usually comes down to his knees in front and to the ground behind, and is decorated to the point of being a textbook of shamanistic lore. On the front may be sewed metal plates which protect him from the blows of hostile spirits which he is always encountering. One of these plates represents his emekhet, and usually two others suggest a feminine appearance, since shamans have a hermaphroditic character, as we shall see. All over the tunic are embroidered or appliquéd the figures of real and mythical animals, to represent those he must face on his travels in spirit realms, and from the back there hang numerous strips of skin falling clear to the ground, with small stuffed animals attached to some of them, all this alleged to be for attracting to the shaman any spiritual waifs of the vicinity, who might like to join his retinue. The whole getup would remind you of the unusual headdresses and paraphernalia in which medicine men are turned out among Indians of the Plains and Canada.

Siberian shamans have a tambourine drum whenever they are working, and this is true of Eskimo shamans as well. It is a round or oval drum, covered like a tambourine on one side only, and decorated with the same kind of symbolism as the coat. It is held by a crosspiece or strips of hide in the frame, and is beaten to accompany all the invocations of spirits.

When a shaman goes into action the result is not a rite but a séance, which is full of drama and which the people enjoy immensely. A typical performance is a summoning of spirits, and is carried out in the dark (for the same reasons as among ourselves—i.e., to hide the shenanigans), in a house, a tent, or an Eskimo igloo. The people all gather, and the shaman says what he is going to do, after which he puts out the lamps and the fire, being sure that there is little or no light. Then he begins to sing. There may be a wait, and he beats his tambourine drum first of all, an immediate dramatic effect. The song starts softly. The sense of the song is of no consequence as far as the listeners are concerned; it is often incomprehensible, and may have no words at all. Jochelson knew a Tungus shaman who sang his songs in Koryak (1908). He explained that his spirits were Koryak and said that he could not understand Koryak himself. Jochelson found this last suspicious statement to be quite true; the shaman had memorized the songs subconsciously when he had first heard them.

As the singing goes on, other sounds begin to make themselves heard, supposedly made by animal spirits and said to be remarkably good imitations. The shaman may announce to the audience that the spirits are approaching, but he is apt to be too absorbed or entranced himself to bother. Soon voices of all kinds are heard in the house, in the corners and up near the roof. The house now seems to have a number of independent spirits in it, all moving around, speaking in different voices, and all the time the drum is sounding, changing its tempo and its volume; the people are excited, and some of them who are old hands help the shaman out by making responses and shouting encouragement, and the shaman himself is usually possessed by a spirit or spirits, who are singing and beating the drum for him. The confusion of noises goes on increasing in intensity, with animal sounds and foreign tongues as well as understandable communications (among the

Chuckchis, the wolf, the fox, and the raven can speak human language), until it finally dies down; the spirits give some message of farewell, the drumming ceases, and the lights are lit. Often the shaman will be seen lying exhausted or in a faint, and on coming to he will assert that he cannot say what has been happening.

This is all a combination of expert showmanship and management and of autohypnosis, so that while the shaman knows perfectly well he is faking much of the performance he may at the same time work himself into a trance in which he does things he believes are beyond his merely human powers. He warns his audience strictly to keep their places and not try to touch the spirits, who would be angered and assault the offender, and perhaps even kill the shaman. When the show starts, the shaman produces his voices by moving around in the dark and by expert ventriloquism, getting the audience on his side and rapidly changing the nature and the force of the spirit sounds he is making. He may allow the impression that some of the visiting spirits are possessing him and speaking through his mouth and beating on his drum, but he may hide the fact that he is using his own mouth at all.

A shaman does not perform only in the dark. He carries out some of his business in full view, especially when it is a matter of his going to the spirit world himself, rather than summoning the spirits to this world. The idea seems to be that he is in two places at once; i.e., his soul is traveling in spiritdom while he himself is going through the same actions before his watchers. He does a furious dramatic dance, rushing about, advancing and retreating, approaching the spirits, fighting them or wheedling them, all in a seeming trance. He may foam at the mouth and be so wild that he must be held for safety in leather thongs by some of the onlookers. After vivid adventures in the other realms, portrayed in his dance, he will accomplish his purpose, which may be to capture a wandering soul or to get some needed information from his spectral hosts. Then he becomes his normal self again and gives an account of what he has done.

After a death it is a regular thing for a Mongolian shaman to be called in to "purify" the *yurt* (felt hut) of the deceased's family, by getting rid of the soul of the dead, which of course cannot be allowed to hang around indefinitely. The mourners assemble late in the day, and at dusk the shaman himself comes, already drumming in the distance. He enters the yurt, still drumming, lowering the sound until it is only a murmur. Then he begins to converse with the soul of the newly departed, which pitifully implores to be allowed to stay in the yurt, because it cannot bear to leave the children or the scenes of its mortal days. The shaman, faithful to his trust, steels himself and pays no attention to this heartrending appeal. He goes for the soul and corners it by means of the power in his drum, until he can catch it between the drum itself and the drum stick. Then he starts off with it to the underworld, all in play acting. Here at the entrance he meets the souls of other dead members of the same family, to whom he announces the arrival of the new soul. They answer that they do not want it and refuse it admission. To multiply the difficulties, the homesick soul, which is slippery, generally makes its escape from the shaman as the two of them are on the way down, and comes rushing back to the yurt, with the shaman after it; he catches it all over again. It is lucky the people have a shaman! Back at the gate of the lower world he makes himself affable to the older souls and gives them vodka to drink, and in one way or another he manages to smuggle the new one in.

Europeans who have seen Siberian shamans perform say that it is tremendous and exciting melodrama for them, and it must therefore have still more of an impact on the natives, whose belief and interest are greater. Aside from ventriloquism and histrionics, shamans use other tricks to heighten their effects, and even give small magic shows to maintain the awe of the populace. They are masters of prestidigitation, especially considering that they must work with little apparatus—no trap doors or piano wire. In their séances they can make it appear that there are spirits in several parts of the yurt at once, mischievously throwing things around. Many stick knives into themselves and draw them out again, making the wound heal immediately (all faked, of course). Or they will have themselves trussed up, like Houdini, and call on their spirits, who will set them free. Bogoras saw a Chuckchi woman shaman take a rock between her hands and, without changing it in any way, produce a pile of smaller stones from it, and to defy the skeptics she wore nothing above her waist (Bogoras 1904–09). She repeated the trick at Bogoras's request, but he could not find out what she did.

The shamans know, of course, that their tricks are impositions, but at the same time everyone who has studied them agrees that they really believe in their power to deal with spirits. Here is a point, about the end justifying the means, which is germane to this and to all conscious augmenting of religious illusion.* The shaman's main purpose is an honest one and he believes in it, and does not consider it incongruous if his powers give him the right to hoodwink his followers in minor technical matters. If shamanism were a conspiracy or a purposeful fraud, it would attract only the clever and the unscrupulous, interested in their own aggrandizement, and the public would shortly see the snare, being no bigger fools than we are. But shamanism is an institution, and the things that keep the public from rejecting it are religious characteristics: shamanism does something to help them, and the shamans themselves are inside the system and believe in it too. A sick shaman will call in a superior shaman to cure him. Actually, shamans are among the most intelligent and earnest

---

* Shaw has the following to say about it, through two characters in *Saint Joan:*

THE ARCHBISHOP: A miracle, my friend, is an event which creates faith. That is the purpose and nature of miracles. They may seem very wonderful to the people who witness them, and very simple to those who perform them. That does not matter; if they confirm or create faith they are true miracles.

LA TRÉMOUILLE: Even when they are frauds, do you mean?

THE ARCHBISHOP: Frauds deceive. An event which creates faith does not deceive; therefore it is not a fraud, but a miracle.

Elsewhere the archbishop says: "Miracles are not frauds because they are often—I do not say always—very simple and innocent contrivances by which the priest fortifies the faith of his flock. When this girl picks out the Dauphin from among his courtiers, it will not be a miracle for me, because I shall know how it has been done, and my faith will not be increased. But as for the others, if they feel the thrill of the supernatural, and forget their sinful clay in a sudden sense of the glory of God, it will be a miracle and a blessed one. And you will find that the girl herself will be more affected than anyone else. She will forget how she really picked him out. . . ."

people of the community, and their position is one of leadership.

Evans-Pritchard has the same thing to say about Zande witch doctors, who do shamanizing of a less distinct type. They divine for the people, usually dancing in a group. A question will be asked one of them, and he will "dance" to it, very vigorously, working himself into a transport or half frenzy, throwing himself on the ground and perhaps gashing himself. In this state he begins to make an answer to the question, at first tentatively and in a faraway voice, but then more certainly and finally in loud and arrogant tones, although the terms of the answer remain a little obscure, with no names mentioned, and probably phrased in such a way that only the questioner can gather up the meaning. They do not claim to be guided by spirits, and they could be accused of making any answer they chose. It is unlikely, however, that they do such a thing consciously; actually they possess a knowledge of the village and its people, and of the background of any question asked them, so that they have a good basis for judgment, and they juggle all these elements loosely in their heads until, under the stimulation of their abandoned physical activity, they feel struck by an inspiration, an effect which they would not experience without the dancing. These witch doctors also cure by sucking intrusive magical objects out of their patients, if that is the cause of illness, and at their shindigs the doctors who are not busy dancing to a question will stage contests of shooting the same kind of thing—bones or beetles—into one another, or into the spectators, if they are unruly, and then removing them again. This is generally known by the Azande to be nothing but sleight of hand, good as it is, and the doctors will admit it, saying that their success is really due to their medicines; the people are also often skeptical of them to the point of laughing outright at them, because a doctor may fail completely when tested by so simple a question as what is hidden in a pot. Nonetheless Evans-Pritchard feels that these doctors, who do not occupy as responsible a position as the Asiatic shamans, are basically honest; and also that they are usually above the average mentally. In spite of their higher intelligence, and their awareness of their own trickery, they believe in their magic and their powers as much as anyone else, and the people, laugh as they may, always go to them when taken sick.

In Asia and North America some tribes think that shaman spirits run in the family, and that a boy or young man will sooner or later be seized by such a legacy. This is the usual thing on the Northwest Coast of America, so that normally only the descendants of shamans became shamans. However, a man with none of them in the family tree may nevertheless become one by going to the bier of a newly dead shaman, which in the northern region was set out in a hut on a point of land, and there he will sit and bite the dead man's little finger all night long. This will offend the departed soul, who will react by sending a small spirit to torment the offender, and the latter, if he is courageous and has his wits about him, may capture the spirit for his own ends, and so become a shaman.

The most general belief as to recruitment is simply that a spirit appears, to anyone at all, and insists on the person's becoming a shaman, which is tantamount to accepting the spirit as an internal boarder, whether it is wanted or not. Being a shaman is considered dangerous and burdensome, because you are committed to it and have to observe certain tabus, and so people generally try to avoid it. If you play on a drum, or show yourself in any way receptive, you are laying yourself open, and anyone not wishing to become a shaman will be careful to do no such thing. Usually the spirits pick out young men. In Siberia there are as many women shamans as men, and they are by no means subservient to their male colleagues. In this area also, there is something of an assimilation of male and female shamans; the former, as I said, wear some marks suggestive of femininity, and may braid their hair, and vice versa, female shamans acting somewhat like men. They may go so far as to marry someone of their own sex, a woman getting a wife to keep house for her. This is considered strange, as you might think, and it is not approved of by right-thinking people, but right-thinking people do not like to antagonize shamans and so they keep their mouths shut. Actually, shamans are not thought of as bisexual so much as sexless.

This is one significant thing about the temperamental nature of individuals who become shamans. Another is the reason often given as to why they do so deliberately. A Siberian will say that he became ill, and that in desperation over being melancholy, or on the verge of dying, he began to solicit a spirit and prepare for a shaman's career, whereupon he got well; he now has a bull by the tail, however, and must continue to shamanize or fall ill again. He has to undergo a long training, under the tutelage of an older shaman, and during this period he is subject to mental suffering and sickness; but once he is a practicing shaman he regains his balance, and no shamans suffer from insanity. Europeans report that they can distinguish a shaman by his expression, which is nervous and bright compared to that of ordinary people. Furthermore, the Buriats allege that a future shaman can be told while he is still a child, by certain signs: he is meditative and likes to be alone, and he has mysterious dreams, and sometimes fits, in which he faints.

It is clear from these clues that shamanism is a calling for a certain psychological type: those who are less stable and more excitable than the average, but who have at the same time intelligence, ability, and what is vulgarly called "drive." They are familiar to us, perhaps most so in what we think of as the artistic temperament; they fail of the balance and solidity and self-confidence, not to say aggressiveness, that are necessary in a business executive, or a politician, but their mental powers and their quickness demand expression, goaded by their dissatisfaction at being somewhat maladjusted socially. We are given to calling them introverted, and think them somewhat difficult. They find the expression they need mainly in the arts. Now of course I do not mean that every artist must have bats in his belfry, but only that there is some relation between one variety of human temperament and the insistence of artistic expression. There are plenty of placid and well-adjusted artists; nevertheless, we often say that artists are temperamental people, actually meaning that it is temperamental people who become artists. So it is with shamans, who have in their profession a socially useful exhibitionist release, and a device by which they can discipline their own nervous tendencies by orienting them according to a defined pattern. We have a somewhat stereotyped parallel in people who soothe their nerves by playing the piano; and Conan Doyle made Sherlock Holmes (who was such a bad case that he was addicted to the needle) play the violin.

Some of the native diviners of South Africa, of either sex, are much the same as shamans, being recognized as people of a special type (Hoernle 1937). They enter into this life because of an illness, or hallucinations, or spirit possession; and since the novitiate involves months of solitude, training, and medical treatment by an older diviner, few go into it voluntarily, and most will try to resist it as long as possible. When they come out of this phase they are believed to have second sight and spirit connections, and have developed a peculiar faraway look. As elsewhere, the profession automatically picks out people of a high-strung temperament and appears to give them social satisfaction and psychiatric help.

Shamanism is the more adapted to Siberian and North American native cultures because hysterical tendencies seem to be common among the peoples of the Arctic, giving rise to the term "Arctic hysteria" (Czaplicka 1914; Jochelson 1926). Hysterical seizures, cramps, and trances are the simpler expressions of it. Eskimos will suddenly run wild, tearing off their clothes and rushing out, plunging into a snowbank and sometimes freezing before they can be caught. In Siberia, victims fall into a state, generally on being startled, in which they lose command of themselves and cannot help repeating the words and actions of others. Jokers used to tease known sufferers by tricking them in this way into throwing their belongings into the water, and a Russian colonel was once faced with a troop of natives who had gone hysterical in a body, and were helplessly roaring his orders back at him, and his curses too. A native boy, who knew two older men were both subject to this failing, managed to get them each repeating the other, which they kept up until they both collapsed. I do not know what the basis for this is—i.e., whether it is culturally suggested, like running amok among the Malays—but it is not as merry for the people concerned as it sounds, and is a disturber of the normal social welfare of a group. The contribution of shamanism is not only that it exhausts the special tensions of the shaman himself, and makes him a figure of consequence rather than a slightly psychopathic social liability, but also that it drains off the potential hysteria of the whole community, through the excitement and the drama of the shaman's performances.

Shamans seem to flourish, as might be expected, mainly among people whose religion is not highly organized and whose social structure is also simple and loosely knit. Something that can be called

shamanizing often exists in other cultures and cults, but when it does, it is apt to be subservient to some higher political or religious authority. A true shaman is a lone wolf, following his own dictates, and so a well-developed cult, with important gods in it, cannot tolerate any such freebooting approach to the supernatural, and is bound to restrict this kind of activity, and to deprecate the importance to shamans, mediums, and their like. Two generally similar examples will show this. I have already described the *kaula* of the Polynesians, the prophet who was temporarily occupied by a god, and who then spoke with the voice of the god, often going into violent frenzies while possessed. These prophets also held séances of an entirely shamanistic kind, conducted in a dark house, with ventriloquism, sleight of hand, and all the other appurtenances of shamans as I have described them. Handy (1927) refers to a well-known story about a Maori priest whom a missionary was assiduously trying to convert: he stopped the missionary in his tracks by holding up a sprig of dry brown leaves and causing it to turn green before the good man's eyes. The report does not say whether the missionary saw the light and became a Maori. At any rate, the public business of the Polynesian prophets was limited to divining—the primary overt, if not actual, office of all shamans—and in their public appearances at Tahitian feasts they were kept under the thumb of the priests proper, who received the word of the gods in the indistinct mutterings and shouts of the kaula, and then interpreted it themselves and divulged it to the people.

A good parallel to this exists in female functionaries, called *woyei* (singular *woyo*) by the Gã of West Africa, and common to many tribes of the same region (Field 1937). It is an area of polytheistic cults, in which worshipers are free to choose their favorite god, with each god having his own temple, manned by a priest. Such a god enters and possesses certain women, who will therefore be officially appointed to his temple; and their duty is to dance and become possessed at any ceremony, and while possessed to speak for the god. They show various typical signs of possession, and dance in a semi-abandoned manner. If a practicing woyo becomes possessed while no ceremony is going on, a dance is organized at once in order to maintain the possession and get the message which the god is transmitting. Such a woman generally has her first seizure at a dance, having an apparently genuine fit, and acting bewildered and abstracted, talking incoherently. This is a sign that the god has chosen her, and she must leave home and go into training. Eventually she becomes able to deliver the words of her god with more coherence. Sometimes one has been found to talk in languages of other tribes, which she once knew but can no longer speak in her ordinary conscious state. On completing her training she resumes her normal life, and may be appointed to a temple, serving under the priest at ceremonies, and becoming possessed; or else she may practice freelance, as she sees fit.

I have not seen any comments of the same sort on Polynesian kaulas, but Miss Field states that Gã women who become woyei are, like shamans, individuals of a more nervous and less stable temperament than the average, and that the satisfactions of office, together with the license to throw a periodic fit of prophylactic hysterics, actually result in their living more serene, well-balanced, and happier everyday lives than perfectly "normal" women.

If you follow native philosophy, shamanism can be made to look something like witchcraft, as I said earlier. And it also resembles witchcraft, as we have seen, in the psychological benefits it bestows. Both of them relieve certain kinds of tensions in individuals, such as can be harmful to the social climate, and both of them do it dramatically, which means artistically, which in turn means in a manner calculated to give emotional satisfaction. Shamanism should be the more successful, because witchcraft is more of a fantasy and brings its own difficulties, while shamanism is a real emotional exercise, with practically no drawbacks. It allows some of the people to let off steam by indulging in uninhibited antics, while it allows the others to enjoy these antics and at the same time to make use of some of the shaman's real gifts.

21

Dark Side of the Shaman

Michael Fobes Brown

Spiritual seekers in the United States have long turned to non-Western and indigenous cultures for inspiration, often adopting practices they perceive as superior or more natural than their Western biomedical and religious counterparts. Shamanism has been particularly attractive to some Americans in recent decades, including those in the therapeutic professions and self-improvement movement. Anthropologist Michael Fobes Brown, who spent two years with the Aguaruna of northeastern Peru, offers a contrasting point of view. His research yielded first-hand knowledge of the complexity of Aguaruna shamanism and its accompanying beliefs, including sorcery intended to cause harm. Individuals identified as sorcerers face execution, and shamans in turn are at risk for sorcery accusations or vengeance from a sorcerer's family. To Brown, shamanism and sorcery function well for the Aguaruna, providing rituals of community support, ethnomedical treatment, and rules and punishments in a society without a police force or written laws. However, Brown strongly dismisses the romantic attitude of U.S. enthusiasts who strip shamanism of its original cultural context and who seek an easily acquired set of techniques for personal development.

For another discussion of the distinction between Western neo-shamanism and shamanism as traditionally studied by anthropologists, see Fiona Bowie, The Anthropology of Religion: An Introduction *(Malden, Mass.: Blackwell, 2006, pp. 191–95).*

Santa Fe, New Mexico, is a stronghold of that eclectic mix of mysticism and folk medicine called "New Age" thought. The community bulletin board of the public library, just around the corner from the plaza and the venerable Palace of the Governors, serves as a central bazaar for spiritual guides advertising instruction in alternative healing methods. Many of these workshops—for example, classes in holistic massage and rebirthing—have their philosophical roots in the experiments of the 1960s. Others resist easy classification: What, I've wondered, is Etheric Body Healing and Light Body Work, designed to "resonate the light forces within our being"? For thirty-five dollars an hour, another expert offers consultations in "defense and removal of psychic attack." Most of the classes, however, teach the healing arts of non-Western or tribal peoples. Of particular interest to the New Agers of Santa Fe is the tradition known as shamanism.

Shamans, who are found in societies all over the world, are believed to communicate directly with spirits to heal people struck down by illness. Anthropologists are fond of reminding their students that shamanism, not prostitution, is the world's oldest profession. When, in my role as curious ethnographer, I've asked Santa Feans about their interest in this exotic form of healing, they have expressed their admiration for the beauty of the shamanistic tradition, the ability of shamans to "get in touch with their inner healing powers," and the superiority of spiritual treatments over the impersonal medical practice of our own society. Fifteen years ago, I would have sympathized with these romantic ideas. Two years of fieldwork in an Amazonian society, however, taught me that there is peril in the shaman's craft.

A man I shall call Yankush is a prominent shaman among the Aguaruna, a native people who make their home in the tropical forest of northeastern Peru. Once feared headhunters, the Aguaruna now direct their considerable energies to cultivating cash crops and protecting their lands from encroachment by settlers fleeing the poverty of Peru's highland and coastal regions.

Yankush is a vigorous, middle-aged man known for his nimble wit and ready laugh. Like every other able-bodied man in his village, Yankush works hard to feed his family by hunting, fishing, and helping his wife cultivate their fields. But when his kinfolk or friends fall ill, he takes on the role of *iwishín*—shaman—diagnosing the cause of the affliction and then, if possible, removing the source of the ailment from the patient's body.

In common with most peoples who preserve a lively shamanistic heritage, the Aguaruna believe that life-threatening illness is caused by sorcerers. Sorcerers are ordinary people who, driven by spite or envy, secretly introduce spirit darts into the bodies of their victims. If the dart isn't soon removed by a shaman, the victim dies. Often the shaman describes the dart as a piece of bone, a tiny thorn, a spider, or a blade of grass.

The Aguaruna do not regard sorcery as a quaint and colorful bit of traditional lore. It is attempted homicide, plain and simple. That the evidence of sorcery can only be seen by a shaman does not diminish the ordinary person's belief in the reality of the sorcerer's work, any more than our inability to see viruses with the naked eye leads us to question their existence. The Aguaruna insist that sorcerers, when discovered, must be executed for the good of society.

Shaman and sorcerer might seem locked in a simple struggle of good against evil, order against chaos, but things are not so straightforward. Shamans and sorcerers gain their power from the same source, both receiving spirit darts from a trusted instructor. Because the darts attempt to return to their original owner, apprentice shamans and sorcerers must induce them to remain in their bodies

by purifying themselves. They spend months in jungle isolation, fasting and practicing sexual abstinence. By wrestling with the terrifying apparitions that come to plague their dreams, they steel themselves for a life of spiritual struggle.

There the paths of sorcerer and shaman divide. The sorcerer works in secret, using spirit darts to inflict suffering on his enemies. The shaman operates in the public eye and uses his own spirit darts to thwart the sorcerer's schemes of pain and untimely death. (I say "he" because to my knowledge all Aguaruna shamans are men. Occasionally, however, a woman is accused of sorcery.) Yet because shamans possess spirit darts, and with them the power to kill, the boundary between sorcerer and shaman is sometimes indistinct.

The ambiguities of the shaman's role were brought home to me during a healing session I attended in Yankush's house. The patients were two women: Yamanuanch, who complained of pains in her stomach and throat, and Chapaik, who suffered discomfort in her back and lower abdomen. Their illnesses did not seem life threatening, but they were persistent enough to raise fears that sorcery was at the root of the women's misery.

As darkness fell upon us, the patients and their kin waited for Yankush to enter into a trance induced by a bitter, hallucinogenic concoction he had taken just before sunset (it is made from a vine known as *ayahuasca*). While the visitors exchanged gossip and small talk, Yankush sat facing the wall of his house, whistling healing songs and waving a bundle of leaves that served as a fan and soft rattle. Abruptly, he told the two women to lie on banana leaves that had been spread on the floor, so that he could use his visionary powers to search their bodies for tiny points of light, the telltale signature of the sorcerer's darts. As Yankush's intoxication increased, his meditative singing gave way to violent retching. Gaining control of himself, he sucked noisily on the patients' bodies in an effort to remove the darts.

Family members of the patients shouted words of concern and support. "Others know you are curing. They can hurt you, be careful!" one of the spectators warned, referring to the sorcerers whose work the shaman hoped to undo. Torn by anxiety, Chapaik's husband addressed those present: "Who has done this bewitching? If my wife dies, I could kill any man out of anger!" In their cries of encouragement to

Yankush, the participants expressed their high regard for the difficult work of the shaman, who at this point in the proceedings was frequently doubled over with nausea caused by the drug he had taken.

Suddenly there was a marked change of atmosphere. A woman named Chimi called out excitedly, "If there are any darts there when she gets back home, they may say that Yankush put them there. So take them all out!" Chimi's statement was an unusually blunt rendering of an ambivalence implicit in all relations between Aguaruna shamans and their clients. Because shamans control spirit darts, people fear that a shaman may be tempted to use the cover of healing as an opportunity to bewitch his own clients for personal reasons. The clients therefore remind the shaman that they expect results—and if such results are not forthcoming, the shaman himself may be suspected of, and punished for, sorcery.

Yankush is such a skilled healer that this threat scarcely caused him to miss a step. He sucked noisily on Yamanuanch's neck to cure her sore throat and, after singing about the sorcery darts lodged in her body, announced she would recover. For good measure, he recommended injections of a commercial antibiotic. Yankush also took pains to emphasize the intensity of his intoxication. Willingness to endure the rigors of a large dose of *ayhausca* is a sign of his good faith as a healer. "Don't say I wasn't intoxicated enough," he reminded the participants.

As Yankush intensified his singing and rhythmic fanning of the leaf-bundle, he began to have visions of events taking place in distant villages. Suddenly he cried out, "In Achu they killed a person. A sorcerer was killed." "Who could it be?" the other participants asked one another, but before they could reflect on this too long, Yankush had moved on to other matters. "I'm concentrating to throw out sickness, like a tireless jaguar," he sang, referring to Chapaik, who complained of abdominal pains. "With my help she will become like the tapir, which doesn't know how to refuse any kind of food."

After two hours of arduous work, Yankush steered the healing session to its conclusion by reassuring the patients that they were well on their way to recovery. "In her body the sickness will end," he sang. "It's all right. She won't die. It's nothing," he added, returning to a normal speaking voice. Before departing, the patients and their kin discussed the particulars of Yankush's dietary recommendations and made

plans for a final healing session to take place at a later date. As the sleepy participants left Yankush's house for their beds in other parts of the village, they expressed their contentment with the results of his efforts.

During the year I lived near Yankush, he conducted healing sessions like this one about twice a month. Eventually, I realized that his active practice was only partly a matter of choice. To allay suspicions and demonstrate his good faith as a healer, he felt compelled to take some cases he might otherwise have declined. Even so, when I traveled to other villages, people sometimes asked me how I could live in a community where a "sorcerer" practiced on a regular basis.

When a respected elder died suddenly of unknown causes in 1976, Yankush came under extraordinary pressure to identify the sorcerer responsible. From the images of his *ayahuasca* vision he drew the name of a young man from a distant region who happened to be visiting a nearby village. The man was put to death in a matter of days. Because Yankush was widely known to have fingered the sorcerer, he became the likely victim of a reprisal raid by members of the murdered man's family. Yankush's willingness to accept this risk in order to protect his community from future acts of sorcery was a source of his social prestige, but it was also a burden. I rarely saw him leave his house without a loaded shotgun.

In calling attention to the violent undercurrents of shamanism, my intention is not to disparage the healing traditions of the Aguaruna or of any other tribal people. I have no doubt that the cathartic drama I witnessed in Yankush's house made the two patients feel better. Medical anthropologists agree that rituals calling forth expressions of community support and concern for sick people often lead to a marked improvement in their sense of well-being. Shamans also serve their communities by administering herbal medications and other remedies and even, as in Yankush's case, helping to integrate traditional healing arts with the use of modern pharmaceuticals. At the same time, however, they help sustain a belief in sorcery that exacts a high price in anxiety and, from time to time, in human life.

In their attempts to understand this negative current, anthropologists have studied how shamanism and accusations of sorcery define local patterns of power and control. Belief in sorcery, for example, may provide a system of rules and punishments in societies that lack a police force, written laws, and a formal judicial system. It helps people assign a cause to their misfortunes. And it sustains religions that link human beings with the spirit world and with the tropical forest itself.

What I find unsettling, rather, is that New Age America seeks to embrace shamanism without any appreciation of its context. For my Santa Fe acquaintances, tribal lore is a supermarket from which they choose some tidbits while spurning others. They program computers or pursue other careers by day so that by night they can wrestle with spirit-jaguars and search for their power spots. Yankush's lifetime of discipline is reduced to a set of techniques for personal development, stripped of links to a specific landscape and cultural tradition.

New Age enthusiasts are right to admire the shamanistic tradition, but while advancing it as an alternative to our own healing practices, they brush aside its stark truths. For throughout the world, shamans see themselves as warriors in a struggle against the shadows of the human heart. Shamanism affirms life but also spawns violence and death. The beauty of shamanism is matched by its power—and like all forms of power found in society, it inspires its share of discontent.

22

Training for the Priesthood Among the Kogi of Colombia

Gerardo Reichel-Dolmatoff

Gerardo Reichel-Dolmatoff's writings on the Kogi, published during the 1950s through 1970s, document one of the most fascinating examples of religious specialists to be found anywhere in anthropology. The Kogi are an indigenous people of Colombia, who sought refuge in the mountains to escape the brutality of Spanish conquerors. Relatively untouched by other cultures until recent times, and despite the hardship of their highland natural environment, they developed a worldview with what the author calls "profound spiritual satisfactions," supported by a highly formalized priesthood.

This article begins with an overview of the Kogi environment, subsistence methods, and social organization, as well as their elaborate cosmology, which includes a Mother-Goddess and distinctive, culturally specific ethical values. Reichel-Dolmatoff's chief concern here, however, is with the training of the mámas, *men whose priestly functions require years of training and are carried out in solemn rituals. If selected to be trained as a* máma, *a young boy is separated from his family, segregated from females, kept indoors during the day, and fed a special diet. The author stresses how the training of the young* máma, *which normally takes eighteen years, shapes his later behavior as an adult priest. The priest's responsibilities include officiating at ceremonial centers and listening to the confession of misdeeds.*

The Kogi claim to be elder brothers of humanity and to possess the only true religion. They are, therefore, deeply concerned for the education of future priests, who will maintain not only Kogi society but the entire world. Reichel-Dolmatoff warns us, however, not to think of the Kogi as noble savages living in harmony with nature but as people who have developed a spiritual means of accepting harsh reality and misfortune.

The Kogi of the Sierra Nevada de Santa Marta in northeastern Colombia are a small tribe of some 6,000 Chibcha-speaking Indians, descendants of the ancient Tairona who, at the time of the Spanish

Source: Gerardo Reichel-Dolmatoff, "Training for the priesthood among the Kogi of Columbia," in ENCULTURATION IN LATIN AMERICA; AN ANTHOLOGY, edited by Johannes Wilbert (Los Angeles: UCLA Latin American Center Publications, 1976), 265–288. Reproduced with permission of The Regents of the University of California.

conquest, had reached a relatively high development among the aboriginal peoples of Colombia. The Sierra Nevada, with its barren, highly dissected slopes, steep and roadless, presents a difficult terrain for Creole settlement and, owing to the harshness and poor soils of their habitat, the Kogi have been able to preserve, to a quite remarkable degree, their traditional way of life.

The present tribal territory lies at an altitude of between 1,500 and 2,000 meters, where the Indians occupy several small villages of about ten to several dozen round huts, each of about 3 to 4 meters in diameter and built of wattle and daub covered with a conical thatched roof. Each house is inhabited by one nuclear family composed of four or five people who sleep, cook, and eat in this narrow, dark space that they share with their dogs and with most of their material belongings. The huts of a village cluster around a larger, well-built house, also round in its ground plan, but provided with a wall of densely plaited canes; this is the ceremonial house, the temple, access to which is restricted to the men, and where women and children are not allowed to enter. Kogi villages are not permanently occupied; most Indians live in isolated homesteads dispersed over the mountain slopes, and the villages are hardly more than convenient gathering places where the inhabitants of a valley or of a certain restricted area can come together occasionally to exchange news, discuss community matters, discharge themselves of some minor ritual obligations, or trade with the visiting Creole peasants. When staying in the village, the men usually spend the night in the ceremonial house where they talk, sing, or simply listen to the conversation of the older men. As traditional patterns of family life demand that men and women live in not too close an association and collaborate in rigidly prescribed ways in the daily task of making a living, most Kogi families, when staying in their fields, occupy two neighboring huts, one inhabited by the man while the other hut serves as a kitchen and storeroom, and is occupied by his wife and children.

The economic basis of Kogi culture consists of small garden plots where sweet manioc, maize, plantains, cucurbits, beans, and some fruit trees are grown. A few domestic animals such as chicken, pigs, or, rarely, some cattle, are kept only to be sold or exchanged to the Creoles for bush knives, iron pots, and salt. Some Kogi make cakes of raw sugar for trading. Because of the lack of adequate soils, the food resources of one altitudinal level are often insufficient, and many families own several small gardens and temporary shelters at different altitudes, moving between the cold highlands and the temperate valleys in a dreary continuous quest for some harvestable food. Although the starchy tubers provide a fairly permanent food supply, protein sources are few, and a chronic state of malnutrition seems to be the rule. Slash-and-burn agriculture is heavy

work, and the harsh, mountainous environment makes transportation a laborious task. Much agricultural work is done by women and children who collaborate with the men in clearing and burning the fields.

The objects of material culture are coarse and simple, and generally are quite devoid of ornamentation. Some heavy wooden benches, a pair of old string hammocks, smoke-blackened cooking vessels and gourd containers, and a few baskets and carrying bags are about all an average family owns. It is evident then that, to the casual observer, Kogi culture gives the impression of deject poverty, and the disheveled and sullen countenance of the Indian adds to this image of misery and neglect. Indeed, if judged by their external appearance and their austere and withdrawn manner, one would easily come to the conclusion that by all standards of cultural evolution these Indians are a sorry lot.

But nothing could be more misleading than appearances. Behind the drab façade of penury, the Kogi lead a rich spiritual life in which the ancient traditions are being kept alive and furnish the individual and his society with guiding values that not only make bearable the arduous conditions of physical survival, but make them appear almost unimportant if measured against the profound spiritual satisfactions offered by religion. After days and weeks of hunger and work, of ill health and the dreary round of daily tasks, one will suddenly be taken into the presence of a scene, maybe a dance, a song, or some private ritual action that, quite unexpectedly, offers a momentary glimpse into the depths of a very ancient, very elaborate culture. And stronger still becomes this impression in the presence of a priest or an elder who, when speaking of these spiritual dimensions, reveals before his listeners this coherent system of beliefs which is the Kogi world view.

Traditional Kogi religion is closely related to Kogi ideas about the structure and functioning of the Universe, and Kogi cosmology is, in essence, a model for survival in that it molds individual behavior into a plan of actions or avoidances that are oriented toward the maintenance of a viable equilibrium between Man's demands and Nature's resources. In this manner the individual and society at large must both carry the burden of great responsibilities which, in the Kogi view, extend not only to their own society but to the whole of mankind.

The central personification of Kogi religion is the Mother-Goddess. It was she who, in the beginning of time, created the cosmic egg, encompassed between the seven points of reference: North, South, East, West, Zenith, Nadir, and Center, and stratified into nine horizontal layers, the nine 'worlds,' the fifth and middlemost of which is ours. They embody the nine daughters of the Goddess, each one conceived as a certain type of agricultural land, ranging from pale, barren sand to the black and fertile soil that nourishes mankind. The seven points of reference within which the Cosmos is contained are associated or identified with innumerable mythical beings, animals, plants, minerals, colors, winds, and many highly abstract concepts, some of them arranged into a scale of values, while others are of a more ambivalent nature. The four cardinal directions are under the control of four mythical culture heroes who are also the ancestors of the four primary segments of Kogi society, all four of them Sons of the Mother-Goddess and, similarly, they are associated with certain pairs of animals that exemplify the basic marriage rules. The organizing concept of social structure consists of a system of patrilines and matrilines in which descent is reckoned from father to son and from mother to daughter, and a relationship of complementary opposites is modeled after the relationship between certain animal species. The North is associated with the marsupial and his spouse the armadillo; the South with the puma and his spouse the deer; the East with the jaguar and his spouse the peccary; and the West with the eagle and his spouse the snake. In other words, the ancestral couples form antagonistic pairs in which the "male" animal (marsupial, puma, jaguar, eagle) feeds on the "female" animal (armadillo, deer, peccary, snake) and marriage rules prescribe that the members of a certain patriline must marry women whose matriline is associated with an animal that is the natural prey of the man's animal. The equivalence of food and sex is very characteristic of Kogi thought and is essential for an understanding of religious symbolism in myth and ritual. Moreover, each patriline or matriline has many magical attributes and privileges that together with their respective mythical origins, genealogies, and precise ceremonial functions, form a very elaborate body of rules and relationships.

The macrocosmic structure repeats itself in innumerable aspects of Kogi culture. Each mountain peak of the Sierra Nevada is seen as a "world," a house, an abode, peopled by spirit-beings and enclosed within a fixed set of points of reference: a top, a center, a door. All ceremonial houses contain four circular, stepped, wooden shelves on the inside of their conical roofs, representing the different cosmic layers, and it is thought that this structure is repeated *in reverse* underground, the house being thus an exact reproduction of the Universe, up to the point where its center becomes the "center of the world." Moreover, the cosmic egg is conceived as a divine uterus, the womb of the Mother-Goddess, and so, in a descending scale, our earth is conceived as a uterus, the Sierra Nevada is a uterus, and so is every mountain, house, cave, carrying bag, and, indeed, every tomb. The land is conceived as a huge female body that nourishes and protects, and each topographic feature of it corresponds to an inclusive category of anatomical detail of this vast mother-image. The large roof apexes of the major ceremonial houses, constructed in the shape of an open, upturned umbrella, represent the sexual organ of the Mother-Goddess and offerings are deposited there representing a concept of fertilization.

The Kogi conceive the world in terms of a dualistic scheme that expresses itself on many different levels. On the level of the individual as a biological being, it is the human body that provides the model for one set of opposed but complementary principles, manifest in the apparent bilateral symmetry of the body and the distinction between male and female organisms. On the level of society, the existence of groups of opposed but complementary segments is postulated, based on the mythical precedency and controlled by the principles of exogamy. The villages themselves are often divided into two parts and a divisory line, invisible but known to all, separates the village into two sections. The ceremonial houses are imagined as being bisected into a "right side" and a "left side," by a line running diametrically between the two doors that are located at opposite points of the circular building, and each half of the structure has its own central post, one male and another female. On a cosmic level, the same principle divides the Universe into two sides, the division being marked by the tropical sun, which, going overhead, separates the world into a right and a left half. The dualistic elaborations of this type are innumerable: male/female, man/woman, right/left, heat/cold, light/dark, above/below, and the like, and they are furthermore associated with certain categories of animals, plants, and minerals; with colors, winds, diseases, and, of course, with the principles of Good and Evil. Many of these dualistic manifestations have the character of symbolic antagonists that share a common essence; just as the tribal deities who, in one divine being, combine benefic and malevolent aspects, thus man carries within himself this vital polarity of Good and Evil.

Apart from the Mother-Goddess, the principal divine personifications are her four sons and, next to them, a large number of spirit-owners, the masters of the different aspects of Nature, the rulers over rituals, and the beings that govern certain actions. That all these supernatural beings are the appointed guardians of certain aspects of human conduct—cultural or biological—has many ethical implications that provide the basis for the concept of sin. When the divine beings established the world order, however, they made provision for individual interpretation and thus confirmed a person's autonomy of moral choice. Life is a mixture of good and evil and, as the Kogi point out very frequently, there can be no morality without immorality. According to Kogi ethics one's life should be dedicated entirely to the acquisition of knowledge, a term by which are meant the myths and traditions, the songs and spells, and all the rules that regulate ritual. This body of esoteric knowledge is called by the Kogi the "Law of the Mother." Every object, action, or intention has a spirit-owner who jealously guards what is his own, his privilege, but who is willing to share it with mankind if compensated by an adequate offering. The concept of offerings, then, is closely connected with divinatory practices because it is necessary to determine the exact nature of the offerings that will most please a certain spirit-being. These details—some of them esoteric trivia but nonetheless functional units of a complex whole—can only be learned in the course of many years. Closely related to this body of knowledge, Kogi learning includes a wide range of information on phenomena that might be classified as belonging to tribal history, geography, and ecology, animal and plant categorization, and a fair knowledge of anatomy and physiology.

But all this knowledge has a single purpose: to find a balance between Good and Evil and to reach old age in a state of wisdom and tolerance. The

process of establishing this balance is called *yulúka*, an expression that might be translated as "to be in agreement with" or "to be in harmony with." One should be careful, however, not to see in this concept a kind of romantic *Naturphilosophie*, of noble savages living in harmony with nature, but take it for what it is—a harsh sense of reality paired, at times, with a rather cynical outlook on human affairs. The concept of yulúka does not stand for blissful tranquillity, but means grudging acceptance of misfortune, be it sickness or hunger, the treachery of one's closest of kin, or the undeserved ill will of one's neighbor. A Kogi, when faced with hardships or high emotional tensions will rarely dramatize his situation, but will rather try to establish an "agreement" by a process of rationalization.

Another philosophical concept of importance is called *aluna*. There are many possible translations ranging from "spiritual" to "libidinous," and from "powerful" to "traditional" or "imaginary." Sometimes the word is used to designate the human soul. An approximate general translation would be "otherworldly," a term that would imply supernatural power with vision and strength, but otherwise the meaning of this concept has to be illustrated by examples, to convey its significance to the outsider. For example, to say that the world was created "in *aluna*" means that it was designed by a spiritual effort. The deities and the tribal ancestors exist in aluna, that is, in the Otherworld, and in an incorporeal state. Similarly, it is possible to deposit an offering in aluna at a certain spot, without really visiting that place. A man might sin in aluna, by harboring evil intentions. And to go further still: to the Kogi, concrete reality quite often is only appearance, a semblance that has only symbolic value, while the true essence of things exists only in aluna. According to the Kogi, one must therefore develop the spiritual faculty to see behind these appearances and to recognize the aluna of the Universe.

The divine personifications of the Kogi pantheon are not only continuously demanding offerings from men but, being guardians of the moral order, also watch any interaction between mortals, and punish the breaking of the rules that govern interpersonal relations. The Kogi put great emphasis on collaboration, the sharing of food, and the observance of respectful behavior toward elders and other persons of authority. Unfilial conduct, the refusal to work for one's father-in-law, or aggressive behavior of any kind are not only social sins, but are transgressions of the divine rules, and for this the offender is bound to incur the displeasure of the divine beings. Among the worst offenses are violations of certain sexual restrictions. Kogi attitudes toward sex are dominated by deep anxieties concerned with the constant fear of pollution, and prolonged sexual abstinence is demanded of all men who are engaged in any ritual activity. The great sin is incest, and the observation of the rules of exogamy is a frequent topic of conversations and admonitions in the ceremonial house.

Kogi culture contains many elements of sexual repression, and there is a marked antifeminist tendency. The men consider the acquisition of esoteric knowledge to be the only valid objective in life and claim that women are the prime obstacle on the way of achieving this goal. Although a Kogi husband is expected to be a dutiful provider and should produce sufficient food to keep his family in good health, it is also stated that a man should never work for material gain and should not make efforts to acquire more property than he needs in order to feed and house his family. All his energies should be spent on learning, on taking part in ritual, and on acquiring the necessary knowledge of procedure and moral precepts to contribute to the maintenance of the ordained world order. Now women have very few ritual functions and, except when quite old, show but little interest in metaphysical matters. To them the balance of the Universe is of small concern; they eat, they sleep, they chat and idle; in other words, to a Kogi man they personify all the elements of indulgence, of disruption, and of irresponsibility. "They are like cockroaches," the Kogi grumble, "always near the cooking place, and eating all the time!" Besides, Kogi women are not squeamish about sex and, being oblivious to the delicate details of ritual purity, appear to their men as eternal temptresses bent upon destroying the social order and, with it, the religious concepts that are so closely connected with it.

The Kogi are a deeply religious people and they are guided in their faith by a highly formalized priesthood. Although all villages have a headman who nominally represents civil authority, the true power of decision in personal and community matters is concentrated in the hands of the native priests, called *mámas*. These men, most of whom have a profound knowledge of tribal custom, are not simple curers or shamanistic practitioners, but fulfill priestly functions, taught during years of training and exercised in solemn rituals. The *mámas* are sun-priests who, high up in the mountains behind the villages, officiate in ceremonial centers where people gather at certain times of the year, and each ceremonial house in a village is under the charge of one or two priests who direct and supervise the nightlong meetings of the men when they gather in the settlement. The influence of this priesthood extends to every aspect of family and village life and completely overshadows the few attributes of the headmen.

To begin with, all people must periodically visit a priest for confession—in private or in public—of all their actions and intentions. An important mechanism of control is introduced here by the idea that sickness is, in the last analysis, the consequence of a state of sinfulness incurred by not living according to the "Law of the Mother." A man will therefore scrutinize his conscience in every detail and will try to be absolutely honest about his actions and intentions, to avoid falling ill or to cure an existing sickness. Confession takes place at night in the ceremonial house, the *máma* reclining in his hammock while the confessant sits next to him on a low bench. The other men must observe silence or, at least, converse in subdued voices, while between the priest and the confessant unfolds a slow, halting dialogue in which the *máma* formulates several searching questions about the confessant's family life, social relations, food intake, ritual obligations, dreams, and many other aspects of his daily life. People are supposed to confess not only the actual fault they have committed, but also their evil intentions, their sexual or aggressive fantasies, anything that might come to their minds under the questioning of the priest. The nagging fear of sickness, the hypochondriacal observation and discussion of the most insignificant symptoms, will make people completely unburden themselves. There can be no doubt that confession is a psychotherapeutic institution of the first order, within the general system of Kogi religion.

To act as a confessor to people as metaphysically preoccupied as the Kogi puts high demands upon a *máma*'s intelligence and empathy; his role is never that of a passive listener but he must be an accomplished conversationalist, able to direct the confessant's discourse into channels that allow him to probe deeply into the troubled mind of his confidant.

But confession in the ceremonial house is not the only occasion when an individual can relieve himself of his intimate doubts and conflicts. At any time, any man, woman, or child can approach a máma and ask him for advice. It is natural then that a máma obtains, in this manner, much information on individual attitudes and community affairs which allows him to exercise control over many aspects of local sociopolitical development. I know of no case, however, where a máma would have taken advantage of this knowledge for his own ends. The mámas constitute a truly moralizing force and, as such, occupy a highly respected position.

Kogi priests are the products of a long and arduous training, under the strict guidance of one or several old and experienced mámas. In former times it was the custom that, as soon as a male child was born, the máma would consult in a trance the Mother-Goddess, to ascertain whether or not the newborn babe was to be a future priest. It is also said that a máma might dream the name of a certain family and thus would know that their newborn male child would become a priest. Immediately the máma would then "give notice" to the newborn during a visit to his family, and it is pointed out that, in those times, the parents would have felt greatly honored by the knowledge that their son would eventually become a priest. From several traditions it would appear that certain families or, rather, patrilines, may have had hereditary preeminence in priesthood, and even today priests belonging to a high-ranking exogamic group are likely to be more respected than others.

Ideally, a future priest should receive a special education since birth; the child would immediately be separated from his mother and given into the care of the máma's wife, or any other woman of childbearing age whom the máma might order to join his household as a wet nurse. But occasionally the mother herself would be allowed to keep the child, with the condition that he be weaned before reaching the age of three months. From then on the child would have to be fed a mash of ripe bananas and cooking plantains, and soon afterwards would have to be turned over to the máma's family. If, for some reason, a family refused to give up the child, the civil authorities might have to interfere and take the child away by force. It was always the custom that the

family should pay the máma for the education of the boy, by sending periodically some food to his house, or by working in his fields.

These ideal conditions, it might be said, probably never existed; under normal circumstances—and this refers also to the present situation—the training begins at about two or three years of age, but certainly not later than the fifth year, and then continues through childhood, adolescence, and young adulthood, until the novice, aged now perhaps twenty or twenty-two, has acquired his new status as máma by fulfilling all necessary requirements. The full training period should be eighteen years, divided into two cycles of nine years each, the novice reaching puberty by the end of the first cycle.

There exist about three or four places in the Sierra Nevada where young people are being trained for the priesthood. In each place, two, or at most, three boys of slightly different ages live in an isolated valley, far from the next village, where they are taken into the care of their master's family. The geographical setting may vary but, in most cases, the small settlement, consisting of a ceremonial house and two or three huts, is located at a spot that figures prominently in myth and tradition. It may be the place where a certain lineage had its origin, or where a culture hero accomplished a difficult task; or perhaps it is the spot where one of the many spirit-owners of Nature has his abode. In any case, the close association of a "school" with a place having certain religious-historical traditions is of importance because at such a spot there exists the likelihood of ready communication with the supernatural sphere; it is a "door," a threshold, a point of convergence, besides being a place that is sacred and lies under the protection of benevolent spirit-beings.

The institution of priestly training has a long and sacred tradition among the Kogi. Several lengthy myths tell of how the four sons of the Mother-Goddess created Mount Doanankuívi, at the headwaters of the Tucurinca River and, inside the mountain, built the first ceremonial house where novices were to be trained for the priesthood. The first legendary máma to teach such a group of disciples was Búnalyue, and once they had acquired the status of priests, they settled in the nearby valley of Mukuánauiaishi which, thereafter, became the center for the training of novices from all over the Sierra Nevada. According to several myths, it was

Búnkuasé, one of the sons of the Mother-Goddess, who established the rules according to which a future máma was to be chosen and educated. Búnkuasé, "the shining one," is the personification of the highest moral principles in Kogi ethics and is thus taken to be the patron and spiritual guardian of the priesthood. It is, however, characteristic of Kogi culture that there should exist several other traditions according to which it is Kashindúkua, the morally ambivalent jaguar-priest, who is the tutelary divine personification. Kashindúkua, also a son of the Mother-Goddess, had been destined by her to be a great curer of human ills, a thaumaturge able to extract sickness from the patient's body as if it were a concrete, tangible substance. But occasionally, and much to his brother's grief, he misused his powers and then did great harm to people. Kashindúkua came to personify sexual license and, above all, incest but, as an ancient priest-king, curer, and protector of all ceremonial houses, he continues to occupy a very important place in the Kogi pantheon.

A novice, training for the priesthood, is designated by the term *kuívi* (abstinent). This concept refers not only to temperance in food and drink, but also to sex, sleep, and any form of overindulgence. This attitude of ascetic self-denial is said to have been the prime virtue of the ancient mámas of mythical times. But, as always, the Kogi introduce an element of ambivalence, of man's difficult choice of action, and also tell of outstanding sages and miracle workers who, at the same time, were great sinners.

At the level of cultural development attained by the Kogi, the teacher position is well recognized and there is full agreement that all priests must undergo a long process of organized directed training, in the course of which the novice's education is functionally specialized. The ideal image of the great teacher and master, the ancient sage, is often elaborated in myths and tales, and in their context the máma is generally represented as a just but authoritarian father figure. In the great quest for knowledge and divine illumination, the teacher never demands from his pupils more than he himself is willing to give; he suffers patiently with them and is a model of self-control and wisdom. In other tales, the opposite is shown, the vicious hypocrite who stuffs himself with food while his disciples are fasting, or the lecherous old man who seduces nubile girls while publicly preaching chastity. These images of the saint and the sinner—patterned after those of the hero and the villain, in another type of tale—are always present in Kogi thought and, in many aspects, are statements of the importance society attributes to the role of the priesthood. Some of these tales are really quite simplistic in that they tend to measure a máma's stature merely in terms of his cunning, his reconciliatory abilities, rote memory, or miracle-working capacity, but other tales contain examples of true psychological insight, high moral principles, and readiness for self-sacrifice. The image of the teacher is thus well defined—though somewhat stereotyped—in Kogi culture and is also referred to in situations that lie quite outside the sphere of priestly training and that are connected—to give some examples—to the acquisition of skills, the tracing of genealogical ties, or the interpretation of natural phenomena. On the one hand, then, it is plain that not all mámas are thought to be adequate teachers and to be trusted with the education of a small child. On the other hand, not all mámas will accept disciples; some live in abject poverty, others are in ill health, and others still feel disinclined to carry the responsibilities that teaching entails. Old age is not of the essence if it is not accompanied by an alert mind and a manifestly "pure" behavior, and quite often a fairly young máma has great renown because of his high moral status, while older men are held in less esteem.

The novices should spend most of their waking hours inside the ceremonial house. In former times they used to live in a small enclosure (*hubi*) within the ceremonial structure, but at present they sleep in one of the neighboring huts. This hut, which is similar to the ceremonial house but smaller, has an elaborate roof apex and the walls of plaited canes have two doors at opposite points of the circumference, while the hut of the máma's family lacks the apex and has only one door. All during their long training the novices must lead an entirely nocturnal life and are strictly forbidden to leave the house in daylight. Sleeping during the day on low cots of canes placed against the walls, the novices rise after sunset and, as soon as darkness has set in, are allowed to take their first meal in the kitchen annex or outside the máma's house. A second meal is taken around midnight and a light third meal shortly before sunrise. Even during the night, the novices are not supposed to go outside except in the company of a máma and then only for a short walk. The principal interdictions, repeated most emphatically over and over again, refer to the sun and to women; a novice should be educated, after weaning, only by men and among men, and should never see a girl or a woman who is sexually active; and throughout his training period, he should never see the sun nor be exposed to his rays. "The sun is a máma," the Kogi say; "And this máma might cause harm to the child." When there is a moon, a novice should cover his head with a specially woven basketry tray (giíshi) when leaving the house at night.

During their training period the novices are supervised and strictly controlled by one or two attendant wardens (hánkua-kúkui), adult men who have joined the máma's household, generally after having spent some years as novices under his guidance. These wardens are mainly in charge of discipline, but may occasionally participate to some degree in the educational process, according to the máma's orders.

Apart from the little group of people who constitute the settlement—the máma and his family, the wardens, and some aged relatives of either—the novices should avoid any contact with other people; in fact, they should never even be *seen* by an outsider. The manifest danger of pollution consists in the presence of people who are in contact with women; should such a person see a novice or should he speak to him, the latter would immediately lose the spiritual power he has accumulated in the course of his apprenticeship. It is supposed, then, that the community consists only of "pure" people, that is, of persons who abstain from any sexual activity and who also observe very strict dietary rules.

As in many primitive educational systems, the observance of dietary restrictions is a very important point in priestly training. In general, a novice should soon learn to eat sparingly and, after puberty has been reached, should be able to go occasionally without food for several days. He should eat very little meat, but rather fowl such as curassow, and should avoid all foodstuffs that are of non-Indian origin such as bananas, sugar cane, onions, or citrus fruits. He should never, under any circumstances, consume salt, nor should he use any condiments such as peppers. A novice, it may be added here, should not touch his food with his left hand because this is the "female" hand and is polluted. During the first nine years the prescribed diet consists mainly of some small river catfish and freshwater shrimp, certain yellow-green grasshoppers of nocturnal habits, land snails collected in the highlands, large black túbi beetles, and certain white mushrooms. Vitamin D appears to be sufficient to compensate for the lack of sunlight during these years. Three or four different classes of maize can also be eaten, as well as some sweet manioc, pumpkins, and certain beans. Some mámas insist that all food consumed by the novices should be predominantly of a white color: white beans, white potatoes, white manioc, white shrimps, white land snails, and so forth. Only after puberty are they allowed to eat, however sparingly, the meat of game animals such as peccary, agouti, and armadillo. These animals, it is said, "have great knowledge, and by eating their flesh the novices will partake in their wisdom." In preparing their daily food, only a clay pot made by the máma himself should be used and all food should be boiled, but never fried nor smoked. Shoe-shaped vessels (or, rather, breast-shaped ones) are used especially for the preparation of a ritual diet based on beans.

The boys are dressed in a white cotton cloth woven by the máma or, later on, by themselves, which is wrapped around the body, covering it from under the armpits to the ankles, and held in place by a wide woven belt. For adornment they wear bracelets, armlets, necklaces, and ear ornaments, all of ancient Tairona origin and made of gold, gilded copper, and semiprecious stones. There is emphasis on cleanliness and at night the boys go to bathe in the nearby mountain stream.

In former times, that is, perhaps until three or four generations ago, it was the custom to educate also some female children who, eventually, were to become the wives of the priests. The girls were chosen by divination and then were brought up by the wife of a máma. Aided by other old women, the girls were taught many ancient traditions primarily referring to the dangers of pollution. They were trained to prepare certain "pure" foods, to collect aromatic and medical herbs, and to assist in the preparation of minor rituals. At present, the education of girls under the guidance of a máma's wife is institutionalized in some parts, but the aim is not so much to prepare spouses for future priests than to educate certain intelligent girls "in the manner of the ancients" and send them back to their families after a few years of schooling, so they can teach the women-folk of their respective villages the traditions and precepts they have learned in the máma's household, and be thus living examples of moral conduct.

But I must return now to the boy who has been taken into a strange family and who is now undergoing a crucial period of adaptation.

The novice is exposed to the varied influences of a setting that differs notably from that of his own family. Although the child will find in the máma's household a certain well-accustomed set of familial behavioral patterns, he is made aware that he now lives in a context of nonkin. This is of special relevance where the novice was educated for the first three or four years by his own family and has thus acquired a certain cultural perspective that, in his new environment, is likely to differ from the demands made by the máma's kin. Between teacher and pupil, however, there generally develops a fairly close emotional tie; the novice addresses the máma with the term *hátei* (father), and he, in turn, refers to his disciples as his "children," or "sons." Only after the novice has reached puberty does the apprentice-master relationship usually acquire a more formal tone.

During the first two years of life, Kogi children are prodded and continuously encouraged to accelerate their sensory-motor development: creeping, walking, speaking. But in later years they are physically and vocally rather quiet. A Kogi mother does not encourage response and activity, but rather tries to soothe her child and to keep him silent and unobtrusive. Very strict sphincter training is instituted, and by the age of ten or twelve months the boy is expected to exercise complete control during the daytime hours. Play activity is discouraged by all adults and, indeed, to be accused of "playing" is a very serious reproach. There are practically no children's games in Kogi culture and for this reason a teacher's complaints refer rather to lack of attention or to overindulgence in eating or sleeping, than to any boisterous, playful, or aggressive attitudes.

Although older children are sometimes scolded for intellectual failures, the Kogi punish or reward children rather for behavioral matters. Punishment is often physical; a máma punishes an inattentive novice by depriving him of food or sleep, and quite often beats him sharply over the head with the thin hardwood rod he uses to extract lime from his gourd-container when he is chewing coca. For more serious misbehavior, children may be ordered to kneel on a handful of cotton seeds or on some small pieces of a broken pottery vessel. A very painful punishment consists in kneeling motionless with horizontally outstretched arms while carrying a heavy stone in each hand.

In practically all ceremonial houses one can see a large vertical loom leaning against the wall, with a half-finished piece of cloth upon it. The weaving of the coarse cotton cloth the Kogi use for the garments of both sexes is a male activity and has a certain ritual connotation. But to weave can also become a punishment. An inattentive novice—or a grown-up who has disregarded the moral order—can be made to weave for hours, sitting naked in the chill night and frantically working the loom, while behind him stands the máma who prods him with his lime rod, sometimes beating him over the ears and saying: "I shall yet make you respect the cloth you are wearing!"

Life in the ceremonial house is characterized by the regularized scheduling of all activities and thus expresses quite clearly a distinct learning theory. We must, first of all, look at the general outline of the aims of education. In doing so, it is necessary to use categories of formal knowledge in the way they are defined in *our* culture, a division that would make no sense to a Kogi, but which is useful here to give an order to the entire field of priestly instruction. The main fields of a máma's learning and competence are, thus, the following:

1. Cosmogony, cosmology, mythology

2. Mythical social origins, social structure, and organization

3. Natural history: geography, geology, meteorology, botany, zoology, astronomy, biology

4. Linguistics: ceremonial language, rhetoric

5. Sensory deprivations; abstinence from food, sleep, and sex

6. Ritual; dancing and singing

7. Curing of diseases

8. Interpretation of signs and symbols, dreams, animal behavior

9. Sensitivity to auditory, visual, and other hallucinations

The methods by which these aims of priestly education are pursued are many and depend to a high degree upon the recognition of a sequence of stages in the child's mental and physical development. During the early years of training, at about five or six years of age, the child is literally hand-reared, in that he is in very frequent physical contact with or, at least, proximity to, his teacher. While sitting on a low bench, the máma places both hands upon the hips of the boy who stands before him and rhythmically pushes and bends the child's body to the tune of his songs or recitals, or while marking the pace with a gourd-rattle. During this period, the Kogi say, the child "first learns to dance and only later learns to walk."

During the first two years of training, the teaching of dances is accompanied only by the humming of songs and by the sound of the rattle; only later on are the children taught to sing. During these practices the children always wear heavy wooden masks topped with feather crowns and are adorned with all the heavy ornaments mentioned above. The peculiar smell of the ancient mask, the pressure of its weight, and the overall restriction of body movements caused by the stiff ceremonial attire and the hands of the teacher produce a lasting impact on the child, and even decades later, people who have passed through this experience refer to it with a mixture of horror and pride. For hours on end, night after night, and illuminated only by torches and low-burning fires, the children are thus taught the dance steps, the cosmological recitals, and the tales relating to the principal personifications and events of the Creation story. Many of the songs and recitations are phrased in the ancient ceremonial language which is comprehensible only to an experienced máma, but which has to be learned by the novices by sheer memorization. During these early years, myths, songs, and dances become closely linked into a rigid structure that alone—at least, at that time—guarantees the correct form of presentation.

One of the main institutionalized teaching concepts consists in iterative behavior. This is emphasized especially during the first half of the curriculum, when the novices are made to repeat the myths, songs, or spells until they have memorized not only the text and the precise intonation, but also the body movements and minor gestures that accompany the performance. Rhythmic elements are important and the learning of songs and recitals is always combined with dancing or, at least, with swaying motions of the body. This is not a mere mechanistic approach to the learning process and does not represent a neurally based stimulus-response pattern, but the child is simultaneously provided with a large number of interpretative details that make him grasp the context and meaning of the texts.

Between the end of the first nine-year cycle of education and the onset of the second cycle, the novice reaches puberty. It is well recognized by the Kogi that during this period significant personality changes occur, and for this reason allowance is made for the eventual interruption of the training process or, as a matter of fact, for its termination. Having reached puberty, a boy who fails to display a truly promising attitude toward priesthood, demonstrated, above all, by his repressive attitude toward sexuality, is allowed to return to his family. At no time is such a boy forced to stay on, even if he should wish to do so; if his master believes that the youth does not have the calling to become a máma, he will insist on his returning to his people. But these cases seem to be the exception rather than the rule; more often puberty is reached as a normal transition, and a few years later, at the age of fourteen or fifteen years, the boy is initiated by the máma and receives from him the lime container and the little rod—a female and a male symbol—together with the permission to chew from now on the coca leaves the youth forthwith toasts in a special vessel.

Ideally, a Kogi priest should divest himself of all sensuality and should practice sexual abstinence, but this prohibition is contradicted in part by the rule that all nubile girls must be deflowered by the máma who, alone, has the power to neutralize the grave perils of pollution that according to the Kogi are inherent in this act. Similar considerations demand that, at puberty, a boy should be sexually initiated by the máma's wife or, in some cases, by an old woman specially designated by the máma. During the puberty ritual of a novice, the master's wife thus initiates the youth, an experience frought with great anxiety and which is often referred to in later years as a highly traumatic event.

During the second cycle, the teachings of the master concentrate upon divinatory practices, the preparation of offerings, the acquisition of power objects, and the rituals of the life cycle. During this period, education tends to become extremely formal because now it is much more closely associated with ritual and ceremony. The youth is taught many divinatory techniques, beginning with simple yes-or-no alternatives, and going on to deep meditation accompanied by exercises of muscular relaxation, controlled breathing, and the "listening" to sudden signs or voices from within. Power objects are acquired slowly over the years and consist of all kinds of "permits" (sewá) granted by the spirit-owners of Nature. Most of these permits consist of small archaeological necklace beads of stone, of different minerals, shapes, colors, and textures, that are given to the novice as soon as he has mastered the corresponding knowledge. At that age, a novice will need, for example, a permit to chew coca, to eat certain kinds of meat, to perform certain rituals, or to sing certain songs. During this period the novices are also taught the complex details of organization of the great yearly ceremonies that take place in the ceremonial centers, higher up in the mountains.

The novices have ample opportunity to watch their master perform ritual actions, a process during which a considerable body of knowledge is transmitted to them. The seasons of the year are paced with special ritual markings: equinoxes and solstices, planting and harvesting, the stages of the individual life cycle. Now that they themselves begin to perform minor rituals, the recurrent statements contained in the texts, together with the identical behavioral sequences, become linked into a body of highly patterned experiential units. The repetition of the formulas, "This is what happened! Thus spoke our forefathers! This is what the ancient said!" insists upon the rightness, the correctness of the actions and contents that constitute ritual.

During the education of a novice there is no skill training to speak of. Kogi material culture, it has been said already, is limited to an inventory of a few largely undifferentiated, coarse utilitarian objects, and the basic skills of weaving or pottery making—both male activities—are soon mastered by any child. There is hardly any specialization in the manufacture of implements and a máma is not expected to have any manual or artistic abilities. He is not a master-craftsman; as a matter of fact, he should avoid working with his hands because of the ever-present danger of pollution.

Language training, however, is a very different matter. In the first place, since early childhood the

novice learns a very large denotative vocabulary. The Kogi are fully aware that any intellectual activity depends upon linguistic competence and that only a very detailed knowledge of the language will permit the precise naming of things, ideas, and events, as a fundamental step in establishing categories and values. In part, linguistic tutoring is concerned with correctness of speech, and children are discouraged from using expressions that are too readily associated with their particular age group. As most of the linguistic input comes from a máma, the novices soon demonstrate a very characteristic verbal behavior consisting of well-pronounced, rather short, sentences, with a rich vocabulary, and delivered in an even but very emphatic voice.

While in normal child-training techniques care is taken to transmit a set of simple behavioral rules that tend to advance the child's socialization process, in training for the priesthood socialization is not a desirable goal. An average child is taught to collaborate with certain categories of people and is expected to lend a helping hand, to share food, to be of service to others. Emphasis is placed on participation in communal labor projects such as road building, the construction of houses or bridges, or on attendance at meetings in which matters of community interest are being discussed. But priestly education does not concern itself with these social functions of the individual. On the contrary, it is evident that a máma is quite intentionally trained *not* to become a group member, but to stand apart, aloof and superior. To the Kogi, the image of the spiritual leader is that of a man whose ascetic hauteur makes him almost unapproachable. A máma should not be too readily accessible, but should keep away from the discussion of public affairs and the petty details of local power politics, because only by complete detachment and by the conscious elimination of all emotional considerations can he become a true leader of his people.

This aloofness, this standing alone, is, in part, the consequence of the narrow physical and social environment in which the novices spend their long formative years of schooling. They *are* socialized, of course, but they are socialized in a context of a very small and very select group of people associated into a unit that is not at all representative of the larger society. It is a fact that the novice learns very little about the practical aspects of the society of which he is eventually becoming a priest. Life in the ceremonial house or in the small group of the máma's family does not give the novices enough social contacts to enable them to obtain a clear picture of the wider society. It is a fact that, during the years of a priest's training period, he hardly becomes acquainted with the practical aspects of land tenure and land use, of seed selection and soil qualities, or of the ways in which gossip, prestige, envy, and the wiles of women are likely to affect society. A novice brought up quite apart from society forms an image of the wider scene, which, at best, is highly idealized, and at worst, is an exaggeration of its evils and dangers.

In Kogi culture, sickness and death are thought to be the direct consequences of sin, and sin is interpreted mainly in terms of sex. Even in those relationships that are culturally approved, that is, in marriage between partners belonging to complementary exogamic units, the Kogi always see an element of pollution, of contamination, because most men are periodically engaged in some ritual demanding purity, abstinence, fasting, attendance at nightly sessions in the ceremonial house, or prolonged travel to some sacred site. Kogi women are often, therefore, quite critical of male religious activities, being in turn accused by their husbands of exercising a "weakening" influence upon their minds, which are bent upon the delicate task of preserving the balance of the Universe. Kogi priests live in a world of myth, of heroic deeds and miraculous events of times past, in which the female characters appear cast in the role of evil temptresses. To a young priest who, after years of seclusion, finally returns to village life and community affairs, women constitute the main danger to cultural survival and are a direct threat to the moral order. Therefore, it again takes several years before the máma learns about life in society and acquires a practical understanding of the daily problems of life.

Moral education is, of course, at the core of a priest's training. Since childhood, a common method of transmitting a set of simple moral values consists in the telling and retelling of the "counsels," cautionary tales of varying length that contain a condensed social message. These tales are a mixture of myth, familial story, and recital, and often refer to specific interpersonal relations within the family setting: husband and wife, elder brother and younger brother, son-in-law and father-in-law, and so on. Other tales might refer to some famous máma of the

past, to culture heroes and their exploits, or to animals that behave like humans. The stories are recited during the nightly sessions when a group of men has gathered or they are told to an individual who has come for advice. In all these stories, what is condemned is overindulgence in food, sleep, and sex; physical aggressiveness is proscribed; theft, disrespectful behavior, and cruelty to children and animals are disapproved of, and inquisitiveness by word or deed is severely censured, especially in women and children. Those qualities that receive praise are economic collaboration, the sharing of food, the willingness to lend household utensils, respectful attitudes towards one's elders, and active participation in ritual. The behavioral message is quite clear and there are no ambivalent solutions: the culprits are punished and the virtuous are rewarded. These counsels, then, do not explain the workings of the Universe and are not overburdened with esoteric trivia, but refer to matters of daily concern, to commonplace events and to average situations. They form a body of entertaining, moralizing stories that can be embroidered or condensed to fit the situation. It may be mentioned here that it is characteristic of the highly impersonal quality of social relations among the Kogi that friendship is not a desirable institution. It is too close, too emotional a relationship, and social rules quite definitely are against it.

It is evident that the counsels constitute a very simplistic level of moral teaching. These stories are useful in propagating some elementary rules among the common people; they are easy to remember and their anecdotal qualities and stereotyped characters have become household words. Everyone knows the story of Sekuishbúchi's wife or how Máma Shehá forfeited his beautiful dress. But it is also obvious that there is another, deeper level where the moral issues are far more complex.

According to the Kogi, our world exists and survives because it is animated by solar energy. This energy manifests itself by the yearly round of seasons that coincides with the position of the sun on the horizon at the time of the solstices and equinoxes. It is the máma's task to "turn back the sun" when he advances too far and threatens to "burn the world," or to "drown it with rain," and only by thus controlling the sun's movements with offerings, prayers, and dances can the principles of fertility be conserved. This control of the mámas, however, depends on the power and range of their esoteric knowledge and this knowledge, in turn, depends upon the purity of their minds. Only the pure, the morally untainted, can acquire the divine wisdom to control the course of the sun and, with it, the change of the seasons and the times for planting and harvesting. It is for this reason that the Kogi, both priests and laymen, are deeply concerned about the education of future generations of novices and about their requirements of purity. Their survival as well as that of all mankind depends on the moral stature of Kogi priests, now and in the future; and it is only natural, then, that the correct training of novices should be of profound concerns to all.

The Kogi claim to be the "elder brothers" of mankind and, as they believe they are the possessors of the only true religion, they feel responsible for the moral conduct of all men. There is great interest in foreign cultures, in the strange ways of other peoples, and the Kogi readily ask their divine beings to grant protection to the wayward "younger brothers" of other nations. The training of more novices is, therefore, a necessity not only for Kogi society, but also for the maintenance of the wider moral order.

From the preceding pages it would, perhaps, appear that, during all these years of priestly education, most knowledge is acquired by rote memory or by the endless repetition of certain actions meant to transmit a set of socioemotional messages that are not always fully understood by the novice, but have to be dealt with nevertheless. But it would be a mistake to think that training for the priesthood consists only, or mainly, of these repetitious, empty elements of a formalized ritual. The true goals of education are quite different and the iterative behavior described above is only a very small part of the working behavior of the novices.

First of all, the aim of priestly education is to discover and awaken those hidden faculties of the mind that, at a given moment, enable the novice to establish contact with the divine sphere. The mámas know that a controlled set or sequence of sensory privations eventually produces altered states of consciousness enabling the novice to perceive a wide range of visual, auditory, or haptic hallucinations. The novice sees images and hears voices that explain and extol the essence of being, the true sources of Nature, together with the manner of solving a great variety of common human conflict situations. In this way, he is able to receive instructions about offerings to be made, about collective ceremonies to be organized, or sickness to be cured. He acquires the faculty of seeing behind the exterior appearances of things and perceiving their true nature. The concept of aluna, translated here as "inner reality," tells him that the mountains are houses, that animals are people, that roots are snakes, and he learns that this manipulation of symbols and signs is not a simple matter of one-to-one translation, but that there exist different levels of interpretation and complex chains of associations. The Kogi say: "There are two ways of looking at things; you may, when seeing a snake, say: 'This is a snake,' but you may also say: 'This is a rope I am seeing, or a root, an arrow, a winding trail.'" Now, from the knowledge of these chains of associations that represent, in essence, equivalences, he acquires a sense of balance, and when he has achieved this balance he is ready to become a priest. He then will practice the concept of yulúka, of being in agreement, in harmony, with the unavoidable, with himself, and with his environment, and he will teach this knowledge to others, to those who are still torn by the doubts of polarity.

The entire teaching process is aimed at this slow, gradual building up to the sublime moment of the self-disclosure of god to man, of the moment when Sintána or Búnkuasé or one of their avatars reveals himself in a flash of light and says: "Do this! Go there!" Education, at this stage, is a technique of progressive illumination. The divine personification appears bathed in a heavenly light and, from then on teaches the novice at night. From out of the dark recesses of the house comes a voice and the novice listens to it and follows its instructions. A máma said: "These novices hear everything and know everything but they don't know who is teaching them."

To induce these visionary states the Kogi use certain hallucinogenic drugs the exact nature of which is still uncertain. Two kinds of mushrooms, one of them a bluish puffball, are consumed only by the mámas, and a strong psychotropic effect is attributed to several plants, among them to the chestnutlike fruits of a large tree (Meteniusa edulis). But hallucinatory states can, of course, be produced endogenously by sensory privations and other practices; most trancelike states during which the mámas officiate at certain rituals are produced, in all probability, by a combination of ingested drugs and strenuous body exercise. The Kogi say: "Because the mámas were educated in darkness, they have the gift of visions and of knowing all things, no matter how far away they might be. They even visit the Land of the Dead."

In the second place, an important aspect of priestly education consists of training the novice to work alone. Although a Kogi priest has many social functions, his true self can find expression only in the solitary meditation he practices in his hut when he is alone. In order to evaluate people or events, he must be alone; he may discuss occasionally some difficult matter with others, but to arrive at a decision, he must be quite alone. This ability to stand alone and still act on behalf of others is a highly valued behavioral category among the Kogi, and children, although they often learn by participation, are trained already at an early age to master their fears and doubts and to act alone. A máma's novice might be sent alone, at night, to accomplish a dangerous task, perhaps a visit to a spot where an evil spirit is said to dwell, or a place that is taken to be polluted by disease. A máma takes pride in climbing—alone—a steep rock, or in crossing a dangerous cleft, and he readily faces any situation that, in the eyes of others, might entail the danger of supernatural apparitions of a malevolent type.

But what really counts is his moral and intellectual integrity, his resolution when faced with a choice of alternative actions. The adequate evaluation of his followers' attitudes and needs requires a sense of tolerance and a depth of understanding of human nature, which can only be attained by a mind that is conscious of having received divine guidance.

The final test comes when the master asks the novice to escape from the tightly closed and watched ceremonial house. The novice, in his trance, roams freely, visiting faraway valleys, penetrating into mountains, or diving into lakes. And when telling then of the wanderings of his soul, the others will say: "You have learned to see through the mountains and through the hearts of men. Truly, you are a máma now!"

The education of a máma is, essentially, a model for the education of all men. Of course, not everyone can or should become a máma, but all men should follow a máma's example of frugality, moderation, and simple goodness. There are no evil mámas, no witch doctors or practitioners of aggressive magic; they only exist in myths and tales of imagination, as threatening examples of what *could be*. On the contrary, Kogi priests are men of high moral stature and acute intellectual ability, measured by any standards, who are deeply concerned about the ills that afflict mankind and who, in their way, do their utmost to alleviate the burdens all men have to carry. But they are also quite realistic in their outlook. An old máma once said to me: "You are asking me what is life; life is food, a woman—then, a house, a field—then, god."

Reflecting back on what was said at the beginning of this essay where I tried to trace an outline of Kogi culture, it is clear that priestly education constitutes a very coherent system that, as a model of conduct, obeys certain powerful adaptive needs.

Kogi culture is characterized by a marked lack of specificity in object relations. To a Kogi, people can exist only as categories, such as women, children, in-laws, but not as individuals among whom close emotional bonds might be established. The early weaning of the child is only the beginning of a series of mechanisms by which all affective attachments with others are severed. Sphincter training, accomplished at about ten months, reinforces this independence of affective rewards. A child's crying is never interpreted as an expression of loneliness and the need for affection, and a baby is always cared for by several mother-substitutes such as older siblings, aunts, or most any woman who might be willing to take charge of the child for a while. During the first two years of life, all sensory-motor development is optimized while, at the same time, all emotional bonds are inhibited. It is probable that the highly impersonal quality of all social relations among adults is owing in a large measure to these early child-training patterns.

That novices chosen for the priesthood must be exposed to a máma's teaching *before* they reach five years of age plainly refers to the observation that, at that precise stage of development, their cognitive functioning is beginning and that mental images of external events are being formed. If educated within the social context of their families, the child would develop a normative cognitive system, which has to be avoided because the cognitive system of a priest must be very specific and wholly different from that of an average member of society.

As has been said, there are no children's games, that is, there is no rehearsal for future adult behavior. Nothing is left to fantasy, can be solved in fantasy;

everything is stark reality and has to be faced as such. And as the child grows up into an adolescent, these precepts are continuously restated and reinforced. The youth must eradicate all emotional attitudes, because nothing must bias his judgment—neither sex, hunger, fear, nor friendship. A man once said categorically: "One never marries the woman one loves!" Moreover, most cultural mechanisms in Kogi behavior are accommodative. The individual has to adapt himself to the reality that surrounds him and cannot pretend to change the world, not even momentarily—not even in his fantasies. The concept of yulúka, too, becomes an accommodative tool because it represents an undifferentiated state of absolute unconsciousness.

To exercise spiritual leadership over his society, the priest must be completely detached from its daily give-and-take, and it is evident that separation, isolation, and emotional detachment are among the most important guiding principles of priestly education. This "otherness" of the Kogi priest is expressed in his training in many ways: from his nocturnal habits, which make him "see the world in a different light," to his isolation from society, which makes of him a lonely observer, devoid of all affection.

The Spartan touch in Kogi culture must be understood in its wider historical perspective. During almost one hundred years, from the time of the discovery of the mainland to the early years of the seventeenth century, the Indian population of the Sierra Nevada de Santa Marta was exposed to the worst aspects of the Spanish conquest. After long battles and persecutions, the chieftains and priests were drawn and quartered, the villages were destroyed, and the maize fields were burned by the invading troops. In few other parts of the Spanish Main did the Conquest take a more violent and destructive form than in the lands surrounding Santa Marta and in the foothills of the neighboring mountains. During the colonial period, the Indians lived in relative peace and isolation and were able to recuperate and reorganize higher up in the mountains. But modern times brought with them new pressures and new forms of violence. Political propaganda, misdirected missionary zeal, the greed of the Creole peasants, the ignorance of the authorities, and the irresponsible stupidity of foreign hippies have made of the Sierra Nevada a Calvary of tragic proportions on which one of the most highly developed aboriginal cultures of South America is being destroyed. So far the Kogi have withstood the onslaught, thanks mainly to the stature of their priests, but it is with a feeling of despair that one foresees the future of their lonely stand.

23

Reflections After Waco: Millennialists and the State

Michael Barkun

No question existed in the minds of the Branch Davidians that the predictions of their charismatic prophet, David Koresh, were correct; the apocalypse engineered by God and the millennia it promised were at hand. Their conscious attempt to change their culture under the direction of their messiah-like leader fit well the model of revitalization movements set out by Wallace (see Chapter 9). As Michael Barkun makes clear, parties in the Waco, Texas, tragedy accurately fulfilled the millennialists' prophecy of the battle between good and evil.

More than simply recounting the events at Waco, Barkun analyzes the characteristics of millenarianism and charismatic leadership and demonstrates that neither the Bureau of Alcohol, Tobacco, and Firearms (ATF) nor the Federal Bureau of Investigation (FBI) understood or took seriously the millenarian beliefs of the Branch Davidians. Falling victim to the "cult concept," the ATF and FBI perceived the activity of Koresh and his followers not as the manifestation of a religion but as that of a psychopathology to be dealt with as they would deal with hijackers or hostage takers. The direct assaults on the compound at Waco were, as Barkun points out, fulfillment of the millenarian-ists' prophecy. It is important to recall Reverend Jim Jones and the tragedy at Jonestown, Guyana, in November 1978 to put in proper perspective the reaction of the Branch Davidians to federal author-ity. But it appears that these types of movements may not be exclusively American. The reader is re-minded of the mass immolations of fifty-two members of the Order of the Solar Temple in Quebec and Switzerland in 1994 and the murder-suicide ritual that took the lives of sixteen more members of the group in a woods near Grenoble, France, the day before Christmas, 1995, in what appears at this point to be a ritual timed for the winter solstice. At this writing, little is known of the Order of the Solar Temple or its deceased leader, Luc Jouret.

Barkun ends his article with two questions. First, will U.S. federal authorities come to understand the worldview of millennialists, particularly those who follow the "posttribulationist" approaches of some survivalists, and change their agencies' strategies of force? Second, and more important in the long run, will the First Amendment's guarantee of the free exercise of religion be shared equally by all groups in the future?

Not since Jonestown has the public been gripped by the conjunction of religion, violence and communal living as they have by the events at the Branch Davidians' compound. All that actually took place near Waco remains unknown or contested. Nonethe-less, the information is sufficient to allow at least a preliminary examination of three questions: Why did it happen? Why didn't it happen earlier? Will it happen again?

As a *New York Times* editorialist put it, "The Koresh affair has been mishandled from beginning to end." The government's lapses, errors and misjudgments can be grouped into two main categories: issues of law-enforcement procedure and technique, with which I do not propose to deal; and larger issues of strategy and approach, which I will address.

The single most damaging mistake on the part of federal officials was their failure to take the Branch Davidians' religious beliefs seriously. Instead, David Koresh and his followers were viewed as being in the grip of delusions that prevented them from grasping reality. As bizarre and misguided as their beliefs might have seemed, it was necessary to grasp the role these beliefs played in their lives; these beliefs were the basis of *their* reality. The Branch Davidians clearly possessed an encompassing worldview to which they attached ultimate significance. That they did so carried three implications. First, they could entertain no other set of beliefs. Indeed, all other views of the world, including those held by government negotiators, could only be regarded as erroneous. The lengthy and fruitless conversations between the two sides were, in effect, an interchange between different cultures—they talked past one another.

Second, since these beliefs were the basis of the Branch Davidians' sense of personal identity and meaning, they were nonnegotiable. The conventional conception of negotiation as agreement about some exchange or compromise between the parties was meaningless in this context. How could anything of ultimate significance be surrendered to an adversary steeped in evil and error? Finally, such a belief system implies a link between ideas and actions. It requires that we take seriously—as apparently the authorities did not—the fact that actions might be based on something other than obvious self-interest.

Conventional negotiation assumes that the parties think in terms of costs and benefits and will calculate an outcome that minimizes the former and maximizes the latter. In Waco, however, the government faced a group seemingly impervious to appeals based upon interests, even where the interests involved were their own life and liberty. Instead, they showed a willingness to take ideas to their logical end-points, with whatever sacrifice that might entail.

The Branch Davidians did indeed operate with a structure of beliefs whose authoritative interpreter was David Koresh. However absurd the system might seem to us, it does no good to dismiss it. Ideas that may appear absurd, erroneous or morally repugnant in the eyes of outsiders continue to drive believers' actions. Indeed, outsiders' rejection may lead some believers to hold their views all the more tenaciously as the group defines itself as an island of enlightenment in a sea of error. Rejection validates their sense of mission and their belief that they alone have access to true knowledge of God's will.

These dynamics assumed particular force in the case of the Branch Davidians because their belief system was so clearly millenarian. They anticipated, as historian Norman Cohn would put it, total, immediate, collective, imminent, terrestrial salvation. Such commitments are even less subject than others to compromise, since the logic of the system insists that transcendent forces are moving inexorably toward the fulfillment of history.

Federal authorities were clearly unfamiliar and uncomfortable with religion's ability to drive human behavior to the point of sacrificing all other loyalties. Consequently, officials reacted by trying to assimilate the Waco situation to more familiar and less threatening stereotypes, treating the Branch Davidians as they would hijackers and hostage-takers. This tactic accorded with the very human inclination to screen out disturbing events by pretending they are simply variations of what we already know. Further, to pretend that the novel is really familiar is itself reassuring, especially when the familiar has already provided opportunities for law-enforcement officials to demonstrate their control and mastery. The FBI has an admirable record of dealing effectively with hijackers and hostage-takers; therefore, acting as if Waco were such a case encouraged the belief that here too traditional techniques would work.

The perpetuation of such stereotypes at Waco, as well as the failure to fully approach the religious dimension of the situation, resulted in large measure from the "cult" concept. Both the authorities and the media referred endlessly to the Branch Davidians as a "cult" and Koresh as a "cult leader." The term "cult" is virtually meaningless. It tells us far more about those who use it than about those to whom it is applied. It has become little more than a label slapped on religious groups regarded as too exotic, marginal or dangerous.

As soon as a group achieves respectability by numbers or longevity, the label drops away. Thus books on "cults" published in the 1940s routinely applied the term to Christian Scientists, Jehovah's Witnesses, Mormons and Seventh-Day Adventists, none of whom are referred to in comparable terms today. "Cult" has become so clearly pejorative that to dub a group a "cult" is to associate it with irrationality and authoritarianism. Its leaders practice "mind control," its members have been "brainwashed" and its beliefs are "delusions." To be called a "cult" is to be linked not to religion but to psychopathology.

In the Waco case, the "cult" concept had two dangerous effects. First, because the word supplies a label, not an explanation, it hindered efforts to understand the movement from the participants' perspectives. The very act of classification itself seems to make further investigation unnecessary. To compound the problem, in this instance the classification imposed upon the group resulted from a negative evaluation by what appear to have been basically hostile observers. Second, since the proliferation of new religious groups in the 1960s, a network of so-called "cult experts" has arisen, drawn from the ranks of the academy, apostates from such religious groups, and members' relatives who have become estranged from their kin because of the "cult" affiliations. Like many other law-enforcement agencies, the FBI has relied heavily on this questionable and highly partisan expertise—with tragic consequences. It was tempting to do so since the hostility of those in the "anti-cult" movement mirrored the authorities' own anger and frustration.

These cascading misunderstandings resulted in violence because they produced erroneous views of the role force plays in dealing with armed millenarians. In such confrontations, dramatic demonstrations of force by the authorities provoke instead of intimidate. It is important to understand that millenarians possess a "script"—a conception of the sequence of events that must play out at the end of history. The vast majority of contemporary millenarians are satisfied to leave the details of this script in God's hands. Confrontation can occur, however, because groups often conceive of the script in terms of a climactic struggle between forces of good and evil.

How religious prophecy is interpreted is inseparable from how a person or a group connects events with the millenarian narrative. Because these believers' script emphasizes battle and resistance, it requires two players: the millenarians as God's instruments or representatives, and a failed but still resisting temporal order. By using massive force the Bureau of Alcohol, Tobacco, and Firearms on February 28, and the FBI on April 19, unwittingly conformed to Koresh's millenarian script. He wanted and needed their opposition, which they obligingly provided in the form of the initial assault, the nationally publicized siege, and the final tank and gas attack. When viewed from a millenarian perspective, these actions, intended as pressure, were the fulfillment of prophecy.

The government's actions almost certainly increased the resolve of those in the compound, subdued the doubters and raised Koresh's stature by in effect validating his predictions. Attempts after the February 28 assault to "increase the pressure" through such tactics as floodlights and sound bombardment now seem as pathetic as they were counterproductive. They reflect the flawed premise that the Branch Davidians were more interested in calculating costs and benefits than in taking deeply held beliefs to their logical conclusions. Since the government's own actions seemed to support Koresh's teachings, followers had little incentive to question them.

The final conflagration is even now the subject of dispute between the FBI, which insists that the blazes were set, and survivors who maintain that a tank overturned a lantern. In any case, even if the FBI's account proves correct, "suicide" seems an inadequate label for the group's fiery demise. Unlike Jonestown, where community members took their own lives in an isolated setting, the Waco deaths occurred in the midst of a violent confrontation. If the fires were indeed set, they may have been seen as a further working through of the script's implications. It would not have been the first time that vastly outnumbered millenarians engaged in self-destructive behavior in the conviction that God's will required it.

In 1525, during the German Peasants' Revolt, Thomas Münzer led his forces into a battle so hopeless that five thousand of his troops perished, compared to six fatalities among their opponents.

Just as the authorities in Waco failed to understand the connections between religion and violence, so they failed to grasp the nature of charismatic leadership. Charisma, in its classic sociological sense, transcends law and custom. When a Dallas reporter asked Koresh whether he thought he was above the law, he responded: "I *am* the law." Given such self-perception, charismatic figures can be maddeningly erratic; they feel no obligation to remain consistent with pre-existing rules. Koresh's swings of mood and attitude seemed to have been a major factor in the FBI's growing frustration, yet they were wholly consistent with a charismatic style.

Nevertheless, charismatic leaders do confront limits. One is the body of doctrine to which he or she is committed. This limit is often overcome by the charismatic interpreter's ingenuity combined with the texts' ambiguity (Koresh, like so many millennialists, was drawn to the vivid yet famously obscure language of the Book of Revelation).

The other and more significant limit is imposed by the charismatic leader's need to validate his claim to leadership by his performance. Charismatic leadership is less a matter of inherent talents than it is a complex relational and situational matter between leader and followers. Since much depends on followers' granting that a leader possesses extraordinary gifts, the leader's claim is usually subject to repeated testing. A leader acknowledged at one time may be rejected at another. Here too the Waco incident provided an opportunity for the authorities inadvertently to meet millennialist needs. The protracted discussions with Koresh and his ability to tie down government resources gave the impression of a single individual toying with a powerful state. While to the outer world Koresh may have seemed besieged, to those in the community he may well have provided ample evidence of his power by immobilizing a veritable army of law-enforcement personnel and dominating the media.

Given the government's flawed approach, what ought to have been done? Clearly, we will never know what might have resulted from another strategy. Nonetheless, taking note of two principles might have led to a very different and less violent outcome. First, the government benefited more than

Koresh from the passage of time. However ample the Branch Davidians' material stockpiles, these supplies were finite and diminishing. While their resolve was extraordinary, we do not know how it might have been tested by privation, boredom and the eventual movement of public and official attention to other matters. Further, the longer the time that elapsed, the greater the possibility that Koresh in his doctrinal maneuvering might have constructed a theological rationalization that would have permitted surrender. Messianic figures, even those cut from seemingly fanatic cloth, have occasionally exhibited unpredictable moments of prudential calculation and submission (one thinks, for example, of the sudden conversion to Islam of the seventeenth century Jewish false messiah Sabbatai Zevi). Time was a commodity the government could afford, more so than Koresh, particularly since a significant proportion of the community's members were almost certainly innocent of directly violating the law.

As important as patience, however, would have been the government's willingness to use restraint in both the application and the appearance of force. The ATF raid, with its miscalculations and loss of life, immediately converted a difficult situation into one fraught with danger. Yet further bloodshed might have been averted had authorities been willing both to wait and to avoid a dramatic show of force. Federal forces should have been rapidly drawn down to the lowest level necessary to prevent individuals from leaving the compound undetected. Those forces that remained should have been as inconspicuous as possible. The combination of a barely visible federal presence, together with a willingness to wait, would have accomplished two things: it would have avoided government actions that confirmed apocalyptic prophecies, and it would have deprived Koresh of his opportunity to validate his charismatic authority through the marathon negotiations that played as well-rehearsed millenarian theater. While there is no guarantee that these measures would have succeeded (events within the compound might still have forced the issue), they held a far better chance of succeeding than the confrontational tactics that were employed.

The events in Waco were not the first time in recent years that a confrontation between a communal group and government forces has ended in violence. Several years ago the Philadelphia police accidentally burned down an entire city block in their attempt to evict the MOVE sect from an urban commune. In 1985 surrender narrowly averted a bloody confrontation at Zarephath-Horeb, the heavily armed Christian Identity community in Missouri organized by the Covenant, Sword and Arm of the Lord. In August 1992 a federal raid on the Idaho mountaintop cabin of a Christian Identity family resulted in an eleven-day armed standoff and the deaths of a U.S. marshal and two family members. In this case, too, the aim was the arrest of an alleged violator of firearms law, Randy Weaver, whose eventual trial, ironically, took place even as the FBI prepared its final assault on the Branch Davidians. In retrospect, the Weaver affair was Waco in microcosm—one from which, apparently, the ATF learned little.

These cases, which should have been seen to signal new forms of religion-state conflict, were untypical of the relationships with government enjoyed by earlier communal societies. While a few such groups, notably the Mormons, were objects of intense violence, most were able to arrive at some way of living with the established order. Many, like the Shakers, were pacifists who had a principled opposition to violence. Some, like the German pietist sects, were primarily interested in preserving their cultural and religious distinctiveness; they only wanted to be left alone. Still others, such as the Oneida perfectionists, saw themselves as models of an ideal social order—exemplars who might tempt the larger society to reform. In all cases, an implied social contract operated in which toleration was granted in exchange for the community's restraint in testing the limits of societal acceptance. When external pressure mounted (as it did in response to the Oneida Community's practice of "complex marriage"), communitarians almost always backed down. They did so not because they lacked religious commitment, but because these communities placed such a high value on maintaining their separate identities and on convincing fellow citizens that their novel social arrangements had merit.

The Branch Davidians clearly were not similarly motivated, and it is no defense of the government's policy to acknowledge that Koresh and his followers would have sorely tested the patience of any state. Now that the events of Waco are over, can we say that the problem itself has disappeared? Are armed millenarians in America likely to be again drawn or provoked into violent conflict with the established order? The answer, unfortunately, is probably yes. For this reason Waco's lessons are more than merely historically interesting.

The universe of American communal groups is densely populated—they certainly number in the thousands—and it includes an enormous variety of ideological and religious persuasions. Some religious communities are millenarian, and of these some grow out of a "posttribulationist" theology. They believe, that is, that Armageddon and the Second Coming will be preceded by seven years of turmoil (the Tribulation), but they part company with the dominant strain of contemporary Protestant millennialism in the position they assign to the saved. The dominant millenarian current (dispensational premillennialism) assumes that a Rapture will lift the saved off the earth to join Christ before the tribulation begins, a position widely promulgated by such televangelists as Jerry Falwell. Posttribulationists, on the other hand, do not foresee such a rescue and insist that Christians must endure the tribulation's rigors, which include the reign of the Antichrist. Their emphasis upon chaos and persecution sometimes leads them toward a "survivalist" lifestyle—retreat into defendable, self-sufficient rural settlements where they can, they believe, wait out the coming upheavals.

Of all the posttribulationists, those most likely to ignite future Wacos are affiliated with the Christian Identity movement. These groups, on the outermost fringes of American religion, believe that white "Aryans" are the direct descendants of the tribes of Israel, while Jews are children of Satan. Not surprisingly, Identity has become highly influential in the white supremacist right. While its numbers are small (probably between 20,000 and 50,000), its penchant for survivalism and its hostility toward Jews and nonwhites renders the Christian Identity movement a likely candidate for future violent conflict with the state.

When millenarians retreat into communal settlements they create a complex tension between withdrawal and engagement. Many communal societies in the nineteenth century saw themselves as showcases for social experimentation—what historian Arthur Bestor has called "patent office models of society." But posttribulationist, survivalist groups are defensive communities designed to keep at bay a world they despise and fear. They often deny the legitimacy of government and other institutions. For some, the reign of Antichrist has already begun. To white supremacists, the state is ZOG—The Zionist Occupation Government. For them, no social contract can exist between themselves and the enemy—the state. Their sense of besiegement and their links to paramilitary subcultures virtually guarantee that, no matter how committed they may be to lives of isolation, they will inevitably run afoul of the law. The flash-point could involve firearms regulations, the tax system, or the treatment of children.

These and similar groups will receive a subtle but powerful cultural boost as we move toward the year 2000. Even secularists seem drawn, however irrationally, toward the symbolism of the millennial number. The decimal system invests such dates with a presumptive importance. We unthinkingly assume they are watersheds in time, points that divide historical epochs. If even irreligious persons pause in expectation before such a date, is it surprising that millennialists do so? As we move closer to the year 2000, therefore, millenarian date-setting and expectations of transformation will increase.

If this prognosis is valid, what should government policy be toward millennial groups? As I have suggested, government must take religious beliefs seriously. It must seek to understand the groups that hold these beliefs, rather than lumping the more marginal among them in a residual category of "cults." As Waco has shown, violence is a product of interaction and therefore may be partially controlled by the state. The state may not be able to change a group's doctrinal propensities, but it can control its own reactions, and in doing so may exert significant leverage over the outcome. The overt behavior of some millenarian groups will undoubtedly force state action, but the potential for violence can be mitigated if law-enforcement personnel avoid dramatic presentations of force. If, on the other hand, they naively become co-participants in millenarians' end-time scripts, future Wacos will be not merely probable; they will be inevitable. The government's inability to learn from episodes such as the Weaver affair in Idaho provides little cause for short-term optimism. The lesson the ATF apparently took from that event was that if substantial force produced loss of life, then in the next case even more force must be used. Waco was the result.

Admittedly, to ask the government to be more sensitive to religious beliefs in such cases is to raise problems as well as to solve them. It raises the possibility of significant new constitutional questions connected with the First Amendment's guarantee of the free exercise of religion. If the state is not to consign all new and unusual religious groups to the realm of outcast "cults," how is it to differentiate among them? Should the state monitor doctrine to distinguish those religious organizations that require particularly close observation? News reports suggest that Islamic groups may already be the subjects of such surveillance—a chilling and disturbing prospect. Who decides that a group is dangerous? By what criteria? If beliefs can lead to actions, if those actions violate the law, how should order and security be balanced against religious freedom? Can belief be taken into account without fatally compromising free exercise?

These are difficult questions for which American political practice and constitutional adjudication provide little guidance. They need to be addressed, and soon. In an era of religious ferment and millennial excitation, the problems posed by the Branch Davidians can only multiply.

Suggested Readings

Fuller, C. J.
  1984   *Servants of the Goddess: The Priests of a South Indian Temple.* Cambridge: Cambridge University Press.

Johnson, Douglas, H.
  1994   *Nuer Prophets: A History of Prophecy from the Upper Nile in the Nineteenth and Twentieth Centuries.* Oxford: Clarendon Press; New York: Oxford University Press.

Kehoe, Alice Beck
   2000   *Shamans and Religion: An Anthropological Exploration in Critical Thinking.* Prospect Heights, Ill.: Waveland Press.

Kendall, Laurel
   1985   *Shamans, Housewives, and Other Restless Spirits: Women in Korean Ritual Life.* Honolulu: University of Hawaii Press.

Leavitt, John, ed.
   1997   *Poetry and Prophecy: The Anthropology of Inspiration.* Ann Arbor: University of Michigan Press.

Lewis, I. M.
   1971   *Ecstatic Religion: An Anthropological Study of Spirit Possession and Shamanism.* Harmondsworth, UK: Penguin. (Rev. ed. 1978.)

Spiro, Melford E.
   1971   *Buddhism and Society: A Great Tradition and Its Burmese Vicissitudes.* Berkeley: University of California Press.

Vitebsky, Piers
   1995   *The Shaman.* Boston: Little, Brown.

Walter, Mariko Namba, and Eva Jane Neumann Fridman
   2004   *Shamanism: An Encyclopedia of World Beliefs, Practices, and Culture,* vols. I and II. Santa Barbara, Calif.: ABC-CLIO.

CHAPTER FIVE

The Religious Use of Drugs

Zapotec mask representing life and death, from Oaxaca, Mexico.

Because the people of the world have such a myriad of uses for and attitudes toward what we call "drugs," it is impossible to define the term to the satisfaction of all. In the West, for example, chemical substances are prescribed to alleviate disease, but they are also used, often illegally, to provide "kicks" for the user; in many non-Western societies, religious specialists utilize these materials as a vehicle for entry into the realm of the supernatural. Perhaps Marston Bates has most correctly defined the term as "almost all materials taken for other than nutritional reasons" (1971: 113). Using this definition, one can count an extraordinary number of substances as falling into the category of drugs.

Every culture, whatever the level of technological accomplishment, has an inventory of drugs and a medical system. The use of drugs is so ancient that Weston La Barre has posited the theory that shamanism itself developed from the use of hallucinogens (1972). The aim of this chapter is to describe the religious functions of drugs. This purpose almost totally eliminates the role of drugs in the West, where they are either medicinal or recreational. At varying periods in Western history, most recently in the social ferment of the 1960s, drug usage was proclaimed by some people to have religious overtones, but few fool themselves today by believing that drugs provide the taker with a religious experience. Hedonism and escapism leading to addiction are the most prominent characteristics of Western drug use and pose immense problems for governments that recognize the changing values that have encouraged the availability of illicit drugs. Certainly anthropologists have found the pleasure and escape motivation for drug use in non-Western societies as well, but the interrelationship of drugs and religion is dominant in traditional societies, where specialists, such as shamans, utilize plant and animal substances to contact the spirit world.

In an attempt to better understand the role of drugs in shamanic healing, some anthropologists have ingested hallucinogens themselves. In his book *The Way of the Shaman* (1980), Michael Harner, for example, recounts his use of *ayahuasca* while among the Conibo Indians of Peru, and, in *Yanomamo: The Fierce People* (1977), Napoleon Chagnon described his use of *ebene* snuff while carrying out fieldwork in Venezuela.

Cross-cultural comparison demonstrates not only that drugs are perceived differently but also that they may actually have different effects on the users from one society to the next (despite having an identical chemical makeup). Indeed, physiological and psychological reactions to drugs vary among individuals in the same society, a phenomenon that is often explained in terms of supernatural intervention.

Because most of us know little of the scientific properties of drugs, it is worthwhile to categorize them as to their effects on users. Lewis Lewin, the famous German toxicologist, whose drug classification is still basically sound and continues to be used by pharmacologists, offered the following categories (after Lewin as quoted by Bates 1971: 115–16):

I. *Euphoria:* sedatives which reduce mental activity and induce mental and physical comfort, such as morphine, cocaine and the like.

II. *Phantastica:* hallucinogens, bringing on visions and illusions which vary greatly in chemical composition, but may be followed by unconsciousness or other symptoms of altered brain states. This group includes: mescal buttons, hashish and its source, marijuana.

III. *Inebriantia:* drugs which produce an initial phase of cerebral excitation followed by a state of depression which sometimes leads to unconsciousness. Chloroform, alcohol, ether, and others are members of this group.

IV. *Hypnotica:* sedatives or sleep producers such as chloral, sulphonol and some recent synthetic barbiturates.

V. *Excitania:* mental stimulants today referred to as analeptics. Coffee, tea, betel, and tobacco; that is, all plants containing caffeine, nicotine and the like.

Today we would add a sixth category to these—the tranquilizers, sometimes termed *ataraxics*. In reality, none are new drugs; rather, they are relatively newly discovered.

Interestingly, none of the first five categories, indeed, even the sixth (ataraxics), was unknown to so-called primitive people. Although the history of the use of these drugs is so ancient as to make attempts at tracing their origins academic exercises, not until the development of synthetics, prompted by the shortages of natural products during World War II, did we learn that hunting and gathering societies knew of and used the same basic chemical substances of medicines as modern technological cultures. For their knowledge of the chemical properties of the plants and animals in their environments, modern people's debt to "primitive people" is great.

The focus of drug use in traditionally based non-Western cultures is on the religious specialist, particularly the shaman, whose duty it is to control the spirit world for the benefit of the members of his society. Of all the categories of drugs, it is the hallucinogens, Lewin's "phantastica," that command our attention, for it is these psychotropic plant and animal substances that provide the shamans with their visions of the supernatural realm. What one society considers to be real or unreal is not always shared by another society. Michael Harner's article in this chapter demonstrates, for example, that the Jívaro of the Ecuadorian Amazon consider reality to be what is found in the hallucinogenic state that results from drinking a tea made from the Banisteriopsis vine; the nonhallucinogenic, ordinary state is considered to be an illusion. Indeed, some drugs not considered hallucinogens in Western pharmacology do cause a visionary state; such is the case of the Warao shamans' use of tobacco (Wilbert 1972). The point is that, whether we agree or not with the folk categories of drugs in other societies, the mainspring of shamanistic power is centered on drugs that produce visual hallucinations as well as hallucinations of the other senses.

The shamanistic use of a variety of hallucinogenic drugs for trance inducement has not in itself guaranteed that a shaman's patient would recover, or that an enemy would suffer. To this end, many other, nonhallucinogenic drugs and practices have also been used, some of which involved effective chemical properties or constituted successful non-drug techniques, such as the sucking-out of evil forces. Even substances having only inert chemicals were often effective in the hands of the shaman. Surely, other reasons must be offered for those successes. The illnesses of non-Western traditional societies have sometimes been described as being due to imbalances or disruptions of the patients' social environment. Physical and mental illnesses are difficult to separate, particularly in groups where belief systems are shared by a high percentage of the population. The treatment offered by shamans is relatively standard and almost always considered correct by patients, as well as by their families and friends, who are often present for the curing process and ceremony. The anxiety of the patient, on the one hand, and the confidence of the shaman, on the other, work to develop a level of suggestibility that literally sets the stage for effective treatment. Shamans, with their secret formulas, chants, and personal contact and control over spirit helpers—knowledge and power the patient does not possess—appear omnipotent and inordinately powerful. The encouragement and support of family and friends in a familiar environment both contribute to the eventual cure. Westerners have learned much from shamanistic treatment, for it treats the physical and the psychological, both of which are irrevocably intertwined with the supernatural causes of illness.

The first three articles in this chapter were chosen because each one focuses on a different aspect of drug use in traditional societies.

In the first selection, Thomas J. Csordas introduces the reader to Mike Kiyaani, a Navajo leader of peyote rites. Kiyaani recounts his first introduction to peyote.

Furst and Coe's "Ritual Enemas" is an ethnohistorical reconstruction of Maya drug usage through an analysis of their pottery.

In "The Sound of Rushing Water," Michael Harner offers an insight into Jívaro reality, a state that can be achieved only through consumption of the hallucinogenic drink, *natema.*

Finally, in the fourth article, Robert S. de Ropp discusses the dynamic and disruptive history of psychedelic cults of the Flower Children movement of the 1960s in the United States.

References

Bates, Marston
  1971 *Gluttons and Libertines: Human Problems of Being Natural.* New York: Vintage Books.

Chagnon, Napoleon
  1977 *Yanomamo: The Fierce People.* 2nd ed. New York: Holt, Rinehart and Winston.

Harner, Michael
  1980 *The Way of the Shaman.* New York: Harper and Row.

La Barre, Weston
  1972 "Hallucinogens and the Shamanistic Origins of Religion." In Peter T. Furst, ed., *Flesh of the Gods: The Ritual Use of Hallucinogens,* pp. 261–78. New York: Praeger.

Wilbert, Johannes
  1972 "Tobacco and Shamanistic Ecstasy Among the Warao Indians of Venezuela." In Peter T. Furst, ed., *Flesh of the Gods: The Ritual Use of Hallucinogens,* pp. 55–83. New York: Praeger.

24

On the Peyote Road

Mike Kiyaani and Thomas J. Csordas

The peyote religion—or "Peyote Way," as it is known by its members—is followed by some 250,000 American Indians. Peyote (the name is derived from the Aztec word peyotl*) was used by Indians in central and northern Mexico in pre-Columbian years, its use spreading north to the Indians in the United States and Canada around 1890. Since 1918, peyotists have been organized as the Native American Church, and, despite recurring legal issues (peyote contains the hallucinogenic agent mescaline and thus is classified as a controlled substance), it has become an important religious movement among North American Indians. Although there are tribal and community differences in the ceremonies and beliefs of Native American Church members, the practice of peyotism is decidedly similar across groups. The leader of a peyote rite is known as a road man because he leads the group along the peyote road to a life of dignity and respect for nature and for other people. In this brief selection, Thomas J. Csordas introduces the reader to one such road man, Mike Kiyaani. Kiyaani, a Navajo who first used peyote in the late 1940s, served in World War II as a marine "code talker." (Due to its complexity, the Navajo language proved to be an ideal way to communicate secret information.) Kiyaani recounts his first introduction to peyote and how it changed his life, then briefly describes a peyote ceremony and how ingestion of the peyote buttons affects the individual. Kiyaani ends the selection by expressing his worry about white people becoming involved with peyote, observing that Native Americans use the herb with more sincerity.*

Most Americans know peyote only as a cactus containing an illegal psychotropic substance, but to some 250,000 American Indian adherents of the peyote religion, it is a sacrament and a spirit. To live according to its inspiration is to follow the peyote road of personal dignity and respect for nature and for other people. Those recognized as having the ability to lead others along this path are known as "road men." Mike Kiyaani, who underwent his own long apprenticeship, is such a road man. Now seventy-seven, Kiyaani is a Navajo who first used peyote in the late 1940s, after returning to his native Arizona

"On the Peyote Road" by Mike Kiyanni and Thomas Csordas reprinted from NATURAL HISTORY, March 1997, pp. 48–50; copyright © Natural History Magazine, Inc., 1997.

as an honored veteran of military service. He had served in an elite Marine unit, along with other Navajos who used their complex native language to communicate sensitive information—a code that defied penetration.

The peyote religion, formally institutionalized as the Native American Church, was introduced to the Navajos in the 1930s by members of several Plains Indian tribes. Its practices and spirituality differ from those of the traditional Navajo religion, although both are fundamentally concerned with healing. Traditional Navajo medicine men—Kiyaani's own father was one—lead ceremonies known as chants. Lasting as long as nine consecutive nights, chants involve prayers in the form of songs, specific acts by the healer and patient, and the creation of potent visual symbols such as sand paintings. A peyote ceremony, in contrast, is a prayer meeting during which peyote is eaten by participants under the leadership of a road man. Combining singing, drumming, and prayers, the ceremony typically lasts one night, from dusk to dawn.

Assembled in a tepee or hogan, the participants focus their prayers on an altar or fire place. In the style learned by Mike Kiyaani, the centerpiece of the fire place is a crescent of heaped-up earth on which rests a special cactus button known as the chief peyote. The road man cherishes his chief peyote and may pass it down through several generations. Kiyaani concentrates on his chief peyote and the fire place to facilitate his dialogue with nature. He says that whereas white people talk directly to God, the humble prefer going through the intermediary of nature—the air and the sunshine, which are God's creations. Kiyaani is not a shaman who takes spirit flights to other worlds but a healer who prays through the elements of nature in which, for him, God already resides.

Mike Kiyaani's mentor was Truman Dailey, an Oto Indian who instructed him not to imitate Plains Indian ways but to take the medicine home and adapt its use to the Navajo culture and way of life. For Dailey, the elements of the altar represent parts of the eagle, which is sacred to his clan. Kiyaani stresses the Navajo understanding of corn as a symbol of growth and life. He performs the traditional corn pollen blessing, sprinkling some grains to make a path that corresponds to the peyote road. He also uses a song learned from his father that metaphorically connects the prayer meeting to the growth of the life-giving corn plant.

Navajo adherents of the peyote religion once faced opposition from their own tribal government, which decreed the religion illegal in 1940 and did not move for tolerance until 1966. Only in 1994 did the federal government adopt a law that guarantees the right of American Indians to practice the peyote religion. Mike Kiyaani remains deeply concerned that, against the background of a long struggle for freedom of religion, the use of peyote be protected for its importance in healing, spirituality, and identity. He has traveled widely to describe his work to audiences of health care professionals, and on the reservation his reputation as a road man keeps him in great demand by Navajos who travel considerable distances to seek his assistance.—T.J.C.

I'm a Navajo veteran—World War II, Navajo Code Talker, wounded in action. My clan is Salt Clan. I got my name from Kiyaani; that's my grandfather's clan. When I came back from the war, I was a sick man. There was something wrong with my mind, something wrong all over my body. No pain, but I felt kind of lousy. My father had died in 1944, and I guess that's what got into me. One man I got acquainted with took me to Oklahoma. I met this man Truman Dailey there, and he noticed my condition. He said, "You take this peyote," and gave me a twenty-five-pound flour sack filled with Mexican dry peyote. I took that back home.

During that time I was way up there where nobody lives, herding sheep, and I used peyote. Just a little bit during the day, every day. It seemed like it went all through my system. Then one particular day I felt like eating, and I had fifty buttons. In about another hour and a half, I ate another fifty buttons—maybe four times, fifty buttons. At midnight everything started coming. My life seemed to be coming to an end. That's the way the medicine showed me, but I still kept on eating until morning. Everything began coming out different. There was a lot of sagebrush out there, and everything was too beautiful. But every time I looked to the peyote, it wasn't pleasant to look at.

Then toward noon I looked for that peyote, and now I saw it was real pure, real white. It kind of talked to me, "Your body is like that, your body is pure. Now you don't need treatment, you're a well man. You wanted to get well, now you're well." I understood it to be that way. At that time I sure cried. I was all right then. After that I was pretty much on the go most of the time performing ceremonies for sick people. I kind of experimented with the peyote eating, how it works, how it can heal.

At the start of the ceremony, I don't know what's ailing the patient, but when you take some peyote into your system, the peyote affects you, and then you kind of know. A lot of people just say, "I'm sick," that's all. They don't know exactly what's bothering them. But peyote does wonderful things. My patient eats peyote. He has peyote in his system. Peyote is in my system, too. He's talking; then I kind of know. I kind of see things, what's wrong in that way. It's the peyote that shows me things. It's my patient talking his mind—the way he talks, the way he expresses himself. It might be his action in there that's kind of unusual; that tells me. But I don't watch him directly, I keep my eyes on the fire all the time.

I say, "You come to me, and I want you to help yourself; whatever it is that's bothering your mind, whatever it is you think that's bothering your health, get your mind off of it. You get on to this medicine, this fire place, this singing that you hear, the prayers that you are hearing in here, which are all for you. The people sitting here, they're talking for you. They're singing for you. Everybody wants you to get well. Whatever's bothering you—maybe it's an evil, maybe it's that lightning struck near you, maybe something else. Get your mind off of it." He might have a hard time [from nausea] through the peyote effect, but that's going to help him. That's the time he's going to figure out what's wrong, why he's sick.

I go outside for a special ceremony at midnight. I get my bone whistle out. Some medicine men take their flashlight out there or maybe take somebody with them out there. I don't do those things. I'd rather be in the dark, praying by myself. A lot of Navajos, while they're out there, they see something, visualize something. I don't look for those things. But I might be hearing that the patient's mind is bothered by witchcraft or maybe some lightning struck that might be affecting his body, his mind.

Peyote. You eat it and it goes through your body, your blood veins, your flesh, your bone, your brain, and we talk to this peyote. And this peyote goes through all the patient's blood veins, goes to his brain, brain vessel; it seems like we talk to the peyote like that. Talking with nature; that's all it is. Whatever you do, peyote knows it, nature knows it. Whatever is wrong inside here, nature knows it. The Almighty knows it, so there's no way you can get away from this peyote, from this Almighty, from nature. If at some place you get off the road, then you notice it. Then you come back and pray. You go back to the Almighty, back to peyote. You get back on the road.

The spirit peyote came up among the Navajo people on a very hard road. But peyote found its way here, and so you see it has some kind of power. It found its way into the Navajo people, into the Navajo hogan, into the heart. Where the heart is, this peyote goes in there. So I want this thing to go on, this peyote religion, peyote worship. It's something for Indians who are humble. Just like in the Bible—it says the meek shall inherit the earth.

Now I'm worried the white man is going to go for it. That's what they usually do. That's what we don't want to happen. I don't think it's for the white people. This natural herb peyote is used by Native Americans with more sincerity. Indian people are more serious in their mind, in their heart, in the way they worship. Just let the Indians have it, let the Indians use it the way they want it, just natural. Our identity is there.

25

Ritual Enemas

Peter T. Furst and Michael D. Coe

As we have seen in earlier articles, many of the world's cultures contain religious specialists and laypeople who routinely undergo, for ritual purposes, an altering of their normal state of consciousness. Although this state can be obtained by non-drug-related methods, it is not uncommon to find ethnographic accounts of drugs being used to enhance and quicken an altered state of consciousness. This article is about the religious use of various psychoactive substances among the Mayan Indians of central Mexico. The authors note that, although hallucinogenic mushrooms, morning glories, and other psychedelic plants were known and used by the Maya, yet another substance seems to have been employed—intoxicating enemas. This phenomenon quite clearly appears in Maya art as early as the first millennium A.D.; it is curious that it has not been described in the literature over the years. Ritual enemas were well known in South America, where rubber tree sap was used for bulbed syringes. Furst and Coe reason that a rectal infusion of intoxicants could result in a more quickly and more radically changed state of consciousness, with fewer negative side effects.

When the Spaniards conquered Mexico in the sixteenth century, they were at once fascinated and repelled by the Indians' widespread use not only of alcoholic beverages but also of numerous hallucinogenic plants.

From the Spaniards' point of view, however, both served the same purpose—to conjure up visions of demons and devils and to take imbibers from their daily life to supernatural realms.

Distillation was unknown in the New World before the conquest, but Mesoamerican Indians were making, as they still do, a variety of intoxicating ritual drinks, principally by fermenting cactus fruit; agave, or century plant, sap; or maize kernels. Among the Maya, the ritual beverage was balche, made from fermented honey mixed with a bark extract from the balche tree, *Lonchocarpus longistylus*. These concoctions were all taken orally.

But according to a Spanish writer known only as the Anonymous Conqueror, the Huastec people of northern Veracruz and southern Tamaulipas had pulque (fermented agave sap) "squirted into their breech," meaning that they used intoxicating enemas. There are indications that the Aztecs, as well as several other Mesoamerican groups, also followed this practice.

Mesoamerican Indians generally used liquor only on sacred occasions, when, according to such sixteenth-century observers as Bishop Diego de Landa of Yucatán, the Indians often drank themselves into states approaching oblivion. Similarly, the use of many botanical hallucinogens, first described by Fray Bernardino de Sahagún and his contemporaries, was strictly limited to occasions when direct communication with the otherworld was required. Today, the best known of these is peyote, *Lophophora williamsii*, a small, spineless cactus native to the north-central desert of Mexico and southern Texas. The plant now serves as sacrament for 225,000 adherents of the Native American Church and also plays an important role in the religious life of the

Huichol Indians of western Mexico. Before the conquest, peyote was widely traded throughout Mexico, where the Aztec priests numbered it among their important magical and medicinal plants.

At the time of the conquest the seeds of the white-flowered morning glory *Turbina corymbosa* were a widely used hallucinogen. In 1960, Albert Hofmann, the Swiss discoverer of LSD (a synthetic hallucinogenic drug), isolated the active alkaloids in this morning glory species and a related species, the purple- or blue-flowered *Ipomoea violacea,* and found them to be lysergic acid derivatives closely resembling LSD-25. The latter species is often referred to as "heavenly blue" in the United States.

Mushrooms also played an important role in preconquest Mesoamerican Indian life. Certain species, most of them now known to belong to the genus *Psilocybe,* were perhaps the most extraordinary natural hallucinogens in use in Mexico. The Aztecs called them *teonanácatl,* or "God's flesh." Psychedelic fungi were widely employed in Mexico when the Spaniards came, and their use in divination and supernatural curing survives to this day in central Mexico, as well as in the state of Oaxaca (*see* "Drugs, Chants, and Magic Mushrooms," *Natural History,* December 1975). The Indians even used tobacco to induce ecstatic trance states, which the Spanish only saw as diabolic communication.

While Spanish writers of the sixteenth and seventeenth centuries left us relatively detailed accounts of the use of hallucinogens in central Mexico, there is little mention of this intriguing aspect of native religion among the Maya, who lived farther to the south. The silence is the more puzzling because we have circumstantial evidence of a very early cult of sacred mushrooms in the Maya highlands of Guatemala and the adjacent lowlands, in the form of more than 250 mushroom effigies made of carved stone, many dating to the first millennium B.C.

The Maya were an integral part of Mesoamerican civilization and shared many of its basic assumptions about the nature of the universe and the relationship of humans to the natural and supernatural environment. Like the central Mexicans, they divided the cosmos into upperworlds and underworlds with their respective gods, believed in the cyclical destruction and regeneration of the earth and its inhabitants, and followed the 260-day ritual calendar.

In view of these many similarities, as the Maya scholar J. Eric Thompson has written, it was hard to believe that the Maya did not use intoxicating plants. Thompson searched the pages of sacred traditional books of the Yucatec Maya, set down in the European alphabet in the colonial period, for hints of ecstatic visionary trances through which the priests made their prophecies. In the *Books of Chilam Balam* (jaguar-priest) of Tizimín and Maní, he found mention of trancelike states but no hint whatever of any hallucinogenic plants. He also discovered scattered scenes in Maya relief sculpture that suggested visionary experiences characteristic of hallucinogenic ritual.

This is slim evidence, however, compared with the data from central Mexico, and some Maya scholars are not convinced that the Maya practiced the kinds of ecstatic shamanistic rituals or vision quests with botanical hallucinogens that played so pervasive a role in central Mexico, or among the Zapotecs, Mixtecs, Mazatecs, and other peoples of Oaxaca.

The silence of Spanish colonial writers on the subject of hallucinogenic plants or rituals among the Maya accords well with the view, once widely held among scholars, that the Maya were quite unlike their Mexican contemporaries in temperament, being less preoccupied with warfare and the Dionysian excesses than with the contemplative interpretation of the heavens and the passage of time. But the discovery at Bonampak, Chiapas, of mural paintings that depict, among other events, a fierce battle among Maya warriors, indicate that this traditional view is very wide of the mark.

As specialists have more closely examined Maya art and iconography in recent years, they have accumulated increasing evidence that among the classic Maya, ecstatic ritual was important. One suggestion for this is that some of the major Mexican hallucinogens—among them the morning glories and the hallucinogenic mushroom *Stropharia cubensis*—occur in the Maya country. These and other psychedelic plants were undoubtedly known to the Maya.

Had Maya specialists looked more closely at the earliest dictionaries of the Quiché and Cakchiquel languages, compiled in the first centuries after the conquest of highland Guatemala, they would have discovered mention of several varieties of mushrooms with hallucinogenic properties. One is called *xibalbaj okox (xibalba* means "underworld," or "land of the dead," and *okox,* "mushroom"), said by the sixteenth-century compiler to give those who eat it visions of hell. If the association of this species with the Maya underworld left any doubt of its psychedelic nature, it is dispelled by a later reference to the same species in Fray Tomas Coto's dictionary of the Cakchiquel language. According to him, *xibalbaj okox* was also called *k'aizalah okox*, which translates as the "mushroom that makes one lose one's judgment." Still another fungus, *k'ekc'un*, had inebriating characteristics, and another, *muxan okox*, apparently brought on insanity or caused one to "fall into a swoon."

We have recently come across a wholly unexpected use of psychoactive substances among the Maya—the ritual use of intoxicating enemas, unmistakably depicted in classic Maya art of the first millennium A.D., but not mentioned either in the colonial or the modern literature. This practice is well documented among the inhabitants of South American tropical forests as well as among the Inca and their contemporaries in the Andes, where archeologists have discovered enema syringes.

Sixteenth-century sources describe the Incas as regularly intoxicating themselves with infusions of *willka,* now known to be the potent hallucinogenic seeds of the acacialike *Anadenanthera colubrina* tree. Lowland Indians also used tobacco enemas.

South American Indians were the first people known to use native rubber tree sap for bulbed enema syringes. While medical enemas had a long history in the Old World, having been used by ancient Sumerians and Egyptians, as well as by Hindus, Arabs, Chinese, Greeks, and Romans, the rubber bulb syringe was unknown in Europe until two centuries after the discovery of the New World.

The native Amerindian enema was distinguished from its Old World counterpart in that its primary purpose was to introduce medicines and intoxicants into the body, while the Old World enema was employed principally to clear the bowels. During the seventeenth and eighteenth centuries, the enema as a relief for constipation, real or imagined, became a craze in Europe—so much so, that Louis XIV had more than 2,000 enemas administered to him during his reign, sometimes even receiving court functionaries and foreign dignitaries during the procedure.

The wide dissemination of the intoxicating enema in South America suggests the discovery by Indians that the rectal administration of intoxicants could radically alter one's state of consciousness more rapidly, and with fewer undesirable side effects, such as nausea, than oral administration. The physiological reason is simple: Substances injected into the rectum enter the colon, the last segment of the large intestine; the principal function of the large intestine is the reabsorption of liquids into the system and the storage of wastes until they can be evacuated. The absorbed liquid immediately enters the bloodstream, which carries it to the brain. An intoxicant or hallucinogen injected rectally closely resembles an intravenous injection in the rapidity of its effects.

The first evidence that not only the Huastecs, whose language is related to the Maya languages, but also the classic Maya knew of and employed the intoxicating enema came to light this past year through the examination of a painted vase in a private collection in New York. This polychrome jar, with a high, vertical neck and flaring rim, was probably painted in the heavily forested Petén district of northern Guatemala during the classic Maya phase, which dated from the third century A.D. to the first decades of the seventh century. Seven male-female pairs, the women easily distinguished by their robes and long hair, are depicted in two horizontal rows. That one woman is fondling a child suggests a familial setting. The activity being portrayed would have brought blushes to the cheeks of the traditional Maya specialist, for while one man is inserting a syringe into his rectum, this delicate task is being carried out for another male by his consort. One male also has a bulbed enema syringe tucked into his belt.

Nine vases, identical in shape to the actual vessel, are painted between the couples, and painted dots at the mouth of each represents a foaming, fermented liquid that is probably balche, the common alcoholic drink among the Maya at the time of the conquest. We must conclude that the people on the vase are taking intoxicating enemas, a practice previously unrecorded for this culture.

An understanding of the scenes depicted on the Maya vase was only the first link in a chain of iconographic discovery of the Mesoamerican enema phenomenon. Suddenly, several previously enigmatic scenes and objects in classic Maya art had new meaning. A small clay figurine from a burial excavated in 1964 by Mexican archeologists on the island of Jaina, in the Gulf of Campeche, depicts a male in squatting position, his hand reaching back to his rectum. For a long time Maya experts were puzzled because the figure's position seemed to represent defecation. But would the Maya have interred such a scene as an offering to their dead?

A small hole in the anus suggested that a piece was missing—that some small object previously inserted there had either become lost during excavation or had been made of some perishable material, long since decayed. The discovery of the enema vase from the Petén district seems to have solved the riddle. The little Maya was probably not defecating but was in the act of giving himself an enema.

The gods themselves were also depicted as indulging in the enema ritual. One Maya vase has the figures of thirty-one underworld deities painted on it. A naturalistically designed enema syringe dangles from the paw of one of the principal figures. Maya experts did not recognize the significance of the object until they had examined the enema vase in New York. As another example, a polychrome bowl from Yucatán, now in the National Museum of Anthropology in Mexico City, shows a naked being with a pointed head injecting himself with liquid.

The ritual importance of the intoxicating enema is highlighted by the involvement in the rite of one of the greatest underworld deities, an old lord associated with earth, water, and agricultural fertility. The Maya may have believed that this god—now identified by Mayanists only by the letter N, but very likely the same deity as the ancient Yucatecan god Pauhatun—consisted of four parts, each part living in the underworld and supporting the four corners of the earth.

The quadripartite god is depicted on a fine vase in a private collection in Chicago. Each of the four parts has a characteristically chapfallen face. Four young and fetching consorts are apparently preparing each of the god's representations for the enema rite. Enema pots with syringes on top are in front of two of the consorts. The female consorts may well represent the important Mother Goddess of the Maya, known as Ixchel, as several figurine examples of the god N embracing this goddess have been found.

The same association of the god N, females and enemas is depicted on another pottery vase, with a consort shown standing behind each god representation and untying his loincloth. Again, the same enema pots are in front of the consorts. So often are the pottery forms and syringes encountered together that we must conclude that they were commonly used in the enema rite.

The explicit depiction of enema rituals on Maya vases has led us to take a new look at a hitherto puzzling type of clay figurine from central Veracruz, which also dates from the classic Maya period. Some archeologists have interpreted these curious sculptures as representing human sacrifice. They are usually of males whose facial expressions suggest pleasure or ecstatic trance, not death. Their legs are raised, either draped over a high pillow or some other type of support of else slightly spread, with the feet up in the air. The posture—and the enraptured look—suggest the intoxicating enema. The reclining position also conforms to the Anonymous Conqueror's description of the method of enema intoxication among the Huastecs.

The hallucinogenic or intoxicating enema has apparently not disappeared altogether from Middle America. While conducting linguistic research in the Sierra Madre Occidental in western Mexico some years ago, ethnographer Tim Knab was shown a peyote apparatus reportedly used by an elderly woman curer. The bulb was made from a deer's bladder and the tube from the hollow femur of a small deer. The curer prepared peyote by grinding it to a fine pulp and diluting it with water. Instead of taking the peyote by mouth, as for example, the Huichols normally do, either whole or ground (see "An Indian Journey to Life's Source," Natural History, April 1973), she injected it rectally, experiencing its effects almost at once while avoiding its bitter and acrid taste and the nausea that even some experienced Indian peyoteros continue to feel as they chew the sacred plant.

We do not know what materials the ancient Maya used for their syringes. The deer was sacred to the Maya, as it still is to Indians in western Mexico. Still, to make the transition from contemporary western Mexico to the Maya requires an enormous jump in time and space. Fish bladders and the bones of birds, which are prominent in Maya art, might have served for the syringe, as might rubber from the latex tree, which is native to the Maya region. More important than the precise technology, however, is the discovery that, no less than the simpler folk of the South American tropical rain forests, the creators of the most flamboyant and intellectually advanced native civilization in the New World hit upon the enema as a technique of intoxication or ecstasy—a practical means of ritually altering or transforming the ordinary state of consciousness.

26

The Sound of Rushing Water

Michael Harner

Native peoples of the Amazon region, as in the case of forest dwellers everywhere, have a tremendous depth of understanding of the chemical properties of plants indigenous to their habitats. Extracts of plants are prepared as medicines that are used both in the Western pharmacological sense and in the supernatural sense. Preparations take a variety of forms and range from ebene, *the snuff used by the Yanomamo of Brazil and Venezuela, to the hallucinogenic drink* natema, *used by the Jívaro of Ecuador. Both contain hallucinogenic properties, provide the taker entry into the spirit world, and offer powers otherwise unattainable without ingestion of potent alkaloid compounds. However, elsewhere, as among the Warao of South America, nonhallucinogenic drugs, such as tobacco, are consumed by shamans to achieve a similar ecstatic state, which, as in the case of* ebene *and* natema, *provides visions of spirit helpers and other agents of the supernatural world (Wilbert 1972). Comparisons such as these give anthropologists insight into the importance of shared belief systems and suggestibility. Describing the use of the* Banisteriopsis *vine by Jívaro shamans, Michael Harner draws on his field data to illustrate the use of the hallucinogenic drink* natema. *Called by a variety of names in other Amazonian societies, this drug gives extraordinary powers to cure or bewitch, and shamans specialize in either one or the other.*

He had drunk, and now he softly sang. Gradually, faint lines and forms began to appear in the darkness, and the shrill music of the *tsentsak,* the spirit helpers, arose around him. The power of the drink fed them. He called, and they came. First, *pangi,* the anaconda, coiled about his head, transmuted into a crown of gold. Then *wampang,* the giant butterfly, hovered above his shoulder and sang to him with its wings. Snakes, spiders, birds, and bats danced in the air above him. On his arms appeared a thousand eyes as his demon helpers emerged to search the night for enemies.

The sound of rushing water filled his ears, and listening to its roar, he knew he possessed the power of *tsungi,* the first shaman. Now he could see. Now he could find the truth. He stared at the stomach of the sick man. Slowly, it became transparent like a shallow mountain stream, and he saw within it, coiling and uncoiling, *makanchi,* the poisonous serpent, who had been sent by the enemy shaman. The real cause of the illness had been found.

The Jívaro Indians of the Ecuadorian Amazon believe that witchcraft is the cause of the vast majority of illnesses and non-violent deaths. The normal waking life, for the Jívaro, is simply "a lie," or illusion, while the true forces that determine daily events are supernatural and can only be seen and manipulated with the aid of hallucinogenic drugs. A reality view of this kind creates a particularly strong demand for specialists who can cross over into the supernatural world at will to deal with the forces that influence and even determine the events of the waking life.

These specialists, called "shamans" by anthropologists, are recognized by the Jívaro as being of two types: bewitching shamans or curing shamans. Both kinds take a hallucinogenic drink, whose Jívaro name is *natema,* in order to enter the supernatural world. This brew, commonly called *yagé,* or *yajé,* in Colombia, *ayahuasca* (Inca "vine of the dead") in Ecuador and Peru, and *caapi* in Brazil, is prepared from segments of a species of the vine *Banisteriopsis,* a genus belonging to the Malpighiaceae. The Jívaro boil it with the leaves of a similar vine, which probably is also a species of *Banisteriopsis,* to produce a tea that contains the powerful hallucinogenic alkaloids harmaline, harmine, d-tetrahydroharmine, and quite possibly dimethyltryptamine (DMT). These compounds have chemical structures and effects similar, but not identical, to LSD, mescaline of the peyote cactus, and psilocybin of the psychotropic Mexican mushroom.

When I first undertook research among the Jívaro in 1956–57, I did not fully appreciate the psychological impact of the *Banisteriopsis* drink upon the native view of reality, but in 1961 I had occasion to drink the hallucinogen in the course of field work with another Upper Amazon Basin tribe. For several hours after drinking the brew, I found myself, although awake, in a world literally beyond my wildest dreams. I met bird-headed people, as well as dragon-like creatures who explained that they were the true gods of this world. I enlisted the services of other spirit helpers in attempting to fly through the far reaches of the Galaxy. Transported into a trance where the supernatural seemed natural, I realized that anthropologists, including myself, had profoundly underestimated the importance of the drug in affecting native ideology. Therefore, in 1964 I returned to the Jívaro to give particular attention to the drug's use by the Jívaro shaman.

The use of the hallucinogenic *natema* drink among the Jívaro makes it possible for almost anyone to achieve the trance state essential for the practice of shamanism. Given the presence of the drug and the felt need to contact the "real," or supernatural, world, it is not surprising that approximately one out of every four Jívaro men is a shaman. Any adult, male or female, who desires to become such a practitioner, simply presents a gift to an already practicing shaman, who administers the *Banisteriopsis* drink and gives some of his own supernatural power—in the form of spirit helpers, or *tsentsak*—to the apprentice. These spirit helpers, or "darts," are the main supernatural forces believed to cause illness and death

in daily life. To the non-shaman they are normally invisible, and even shamans can perceive them only under the influence of *natema.*

Shamans send these spirit helpers into the victims' bodies to make them ill or to kill them. At other times, they may suck spirits sent by enemy shamans from the bodies of tribesmen suffering from witchcraft-induced illness. The spirit helpers also form shields that protect their shaman masters from attacks. The following account presents the ideology of Jívaro witchcraft from the point of view of the Indians themselves.

To give the novice some *tsentsak,* the practicing shaman regurgitates what appears to be—to those who have taken *natema*—a brilliant substance in which the spirit helpers are contained. He cuts part of it off with a machete and gives it to the novice to swallow. The recipient experiences pain upon taking it into his stomach and stays on his bed for ten days, repeatedly drinking *natema.* The Jívaro believe they can keep magical darts in their stomachs indefinitely and regurgitate them at will. The shaman donating the *tsentsak* periodically blows and rubs all over the body of the novice, apparently to increase the power of the transfer.

The novice must remain inactive and not engage in sexual intercourse for at least three months. If he fails in self-discipline, as some do, he will not become a successful shaman. At the end of the first month, a *tsentsak* emerges from his mouth. With this magical dart at his disposal, the new shaman experiences a tremendous desire to bewitch. If he casts his *tsentsak* to fulfill this desire, he will become a bewitching shaman. If, on the other hand, the novice can control his impulse and reswallow the first *tsentsak,* he will become a curing shaman.

If the shaman who gave the *tsentsak* to the new man was primarily a bewitcher, rather than a curer, the novice likewise will tend to become a bewitcher. This is because a bewitcher's magical darts have such a desire to kill that their new owner will be strongly inclined to adopt their attitude. One informant said that the urge to kill felt by bewitching shamans came to them with a strength and frequency similar to that of hunger.

Only if the novice shaman is able to abstain from sexual intercourse for five months, will he have the power to kill a man (if he is a bewitcher) or cure a victim (if he is a curer). A full year's abstinence is considered necessary to become a really effective be-witcher or curer.

During the period of sexual abstinence, the new shaman collects all kinds of insects, plants, and other objects, which he now has the power to convert into *tsentsak*. Almost any object, including living insects and worms, can become a *tsentsak* if it is small enough to be swallowed by a shaman. Different types of *tsentsak* are used to cause different kinds and degrees of illness. The greater the variety of these objects that a shaman has in his body, the greater is his ability.

According to Jívaro concepts, each *tsentsak* has a natural and supernatural aspect. The magical dart's natural aspect is that of an ordinary material object as seen without drinking the drug *natema*. But the supernatural and "true" aspect of the *tsentsak* is revealed to the shaman by taking *natema*. When he does this, the magical darts appear in new forms as demons and with new names. In their supernatural aspects, the *tsentsak* are not simply objects but spirit helpers in various forms, such as giant butterflies, jaguars, or monkeys, who actively assist the shaman in his tasks.

Bewitching is carried out against a specific, known individual and thus is almost always done to neighbors or, at the most, fellow tribesmen. Normally, as is the case with intratribal assassination, bewitching is done to avenge a particular offense committed against one's family or friends. Both bewitching and individual assassination contrast with the large-scale headhunting raids for which the Jívaro have become famous, and which were conducted against entire neighborhoods of enemy tribes.

To bewitch, the shaman takes *natema* and secretly approaches the house of his victim. Just out of sight in the forest, he drinks green tobacco juice, enabling him to regurgitate a *tsentsak*, which he throws at his victim as he comes out of his house. If the *tsentsak* is strong enough and is thrown with sufficient force, it will pass all the way through the victim's body causing death within a period of a few days to several weeks. More often, however, the magical dart simply lodges in the victim's body. If the shaman, in his hiding place, fails to see the intended victim, he may instead bewitch any member of the intended victim's family who appears, usually a wife or child. When the shaman's mission is accomplished, he returns secretly to his own home.

One of the distinguishing characteristics of the bewitching process among the Jívaro is that, as far as I could learn, the victim is given no specific indication that someone is bewitching him. The bewitcher does not want his victim to be aware that he is being supernaturally attacked, lest he take protective measures by immediately procuring the services of a curing shaman. Nonetheless, shamans and laymen alike with whom I talked noted that illness invariably follows the bewitchment although the degree of the illness can vary considerably.

A special kind of spirit helper, called a *pasuk*, can aid the bewitching shaman by remaining near the victim in the guise of an insect or animal of the forest after the bewitcher has left. This spirit helper has his own objects to shoot into the victim should a curing shaman succeed in sucking out the *tsentsak* sent earlier by the bewitcher who is the owner of the *pasuk*.

In addition, the bewitcher can enlist the aid of a *wakani* ("soul," or "spirit") bird. Shamans have the power to call these birds and use them as spirit helpers in bewitching victims. The shaman blows on the *wakani* birds and then sends them to the house of the victim to fly around and around the man, frightening him. This is believed to cause fever and insanity, with death resulting shortly thereafter.

After he returns home from bewitching, the shaman may send a *wakani* bird to perch near the house of the victim. Then if a curing shaman sucks out the intruding object, the bewitching shaman sends the *wakani* bird more *tsentsak* to throw from its beak into the victim. By continually resupplying the *wakani* bird with new *tsentsak*, the sorcerer makes it impossible for the curer to rid his patient permanently of the magical darts.

While the *wakani* birds are supernatural servants available to anyone who wishes to use them, the *pasuk*, chief among the spirit helpers, serves only a single shaman. Likewise a shaman possesses only one *pasuk*. The *pasuk*, being specialized for the service of bewitching, has a protective shield to guard it from counterattack by the curing shaman. The curing shaman, under the influence of *natema*, sees the *pasuk* of the bewitcher in human form and size, but "covered with iron except for its eyes." The curing shaman can kill this *pasuk* only by shooting a *tsentsak* into its eyes, the sole vulnerable area in the *pasuk*'s armor. To the person who has not taken the hallucinogenic drink, the *pasuk* usually appears to be simply a tarantula.

Shamans also may kill or injure a person by using magical darts, *anamuk,* to create supernatural animals that attack a victim. If a shaman has a small, pointed armadillo bone *tsentsak,* he can shoot this into a river while the victim is crossing it on a balsa raft or in a canoe. Under the water, this bone manifests itself in its supernatural aspect as an anaconda, which rises up and overturns the craft, causing the victim to drown. The shaman can similarly use a tooth from a killed snake as a *tsentsak,* creating a poisonous serpent to bite his victim. In more or less the same manner, shamans can create jaguars and pumas to kill their victims.

About five years after receiving his *tsentsak,* a bewitching shaman undergoes a test to see if he still retains enough *tsentsak* power to continue to kill successfully. This test involves bewitching a tree. The shaman, under the influence of *natema,* attempts to throw a *tsentsak* through the tree at the point where its two main branches join. If his strength and aim are adequate, the tree appears to split the moment the *tsentsak* is sent into it. The splitting, however, is invisible to an observer who is not under the influence of the hallucinogen. If the shaman fails, he knows that he is incapable of killing a human victim. This means that, as soon as possible, he must go to a strong shaman and purchase a new supply of *tsentsak.* Until he has the goods with which to pay for this new supply, he is in constant danger, in his proved weakened condition, of being seriously bewitched by other shamans. Therefore, each day, he drinks large quantities of *natema,* tobacco juice, and the extract of yet another drug, *pirípirí.* He also rests on his bed at home to conserve his strength, but tries to conceal his weakened condition from his enemies. When he purchases a new supply of *tsentsak,* he can safely cut down on his consumption of these other substances.

The degree of illness produced in a witchcraft victim is a function of both the force with which the *tsentsak* is shot into the body, and also of the character of the magical dart itself. If a *tsentsak* is shot all the way through the body of a victim, then "there is nothing for a curing shaman to suck out," and the patient dies. If the magical dart lodges within the body, however, it is theoretically possible to cure the victim by sucking. But in actual practice, the sucking is not always considered successful.

The work of the curing shaman is complementary to that of a bewitcher. When a curing shaman is called in to treat a patient, his first task is to see if the illness is due to witchcraft. The usual diagnosis and treatment begin with the curing shaman drinking *natema,* tobacco juice, and pirípirí in the late afternoon and early evening. These drugs permit him to see into the body of the patient as though it were glass. If the illness is due to sorcery, the curing shaman will see the intruding object within the patient's body clearly enough to determine whether or not he can cure the sickness.

A shaman sucks magical darts from a patient's body only at night, and in a dark area of the house, for it is only in the dark that he can perceive the drug-induced visions that are the supernatural reality. With the setting of the sun, he alerts his *tsentsak* by whistling the tune of the curing song; after about a quarter of an hour, he starts singing. When he is ready to suck, the shaman regurgitates two *tsentsak* into the sides of his throat and mouth. These must be identical to the one he has seen in the patient's body. He holds one of these in the front of the mouth and the other in the rear. They are expected to catch the supernatural aspect of the magical dart that the shaman sucks out of the patient's body. The *tsentsak* nearest the shaman's lips is supposed to incorporate the sucked-out *tsentsak* essence within itself. If, however, this supernatural essence should get past it, the second magical dart in the mouth blocks the throat so that the intruder cannot enter the interior of the shaman's body. If the curer's two *tsentsak* were to fail to catch the supernatural essence of the *tsentsak,* it would pass down into the shaman's stomach and kill him. Trapped thus within the mouth, this essence is shortly caught by, and incorporated into, the material substance of one of the curing shaman's *tsentsak.* He then "vomits" out this object and displays it to the patient and his family saying, "Now I have sucked it out. Here it is."

The non-shamans think that the material object itself is what has been sucked out, and the shaman does not disillusion them. At the same time, he is not lying, because he knows that the only important thing about a *tsentsak* is its supernatural aspect, or essence, which he sincerely believes he has removed from the patient's body. To explain to the layman that he already had these objects in his mouth would serve no fruitful purpose and would prevent him from displaying such an object as proof that he had effected the cure. Without incontrovertible evidence, he would not be able to convince the patient and his family that he had effected the cure and must be paid.

The ability of the shaman to suck depends largely upon the quantity and strength of his own *tsentsak*, of which he may have hundreds. His magical darts assume their supernatural aspect of spirit helpers when he is under the influence of *natema*, and he sees them as a variety of zoomorphic forms hovering over him, perching on his shoulders, and sticking out of his skin. He sees them helping to suck the patient's body. He must drink tobacco juice every few hours to "keep them fed" so that they will not leave him.

The curing shaman must also deal with any *pasuk* that may be in the patient's vicinity for the purpose of casting more darts. He drinks additional amounts of *natema* in order to see them and engages in *tsentsak* duels with them if they are present. While the *pasuk* is enclosed in iron armor, the shaman himself has his own armor composed of his many *tsentsak*. As long as he is under the influence of *netema*, these magical darts cover his body as a protective shield, and are on the lookout for any enemy *tsentsak* headed toward their master. When these *tsentsak* see such a missile coming, they immediately close up together at the point where the enemy dart is attempting to penetrate, and thereby repel it.

If the curer finds *tsentsak* entering the body of his patient after he has killed *pasuk*, he suspects the presence of a *wakani* bird. The shaman drinks *maikua* (*Datura*), an hallucinogen even more powerful than *natema*, as well as tobacco juice, and silently sneaks into the forest to hunt and kill the bird with *tsentsak*. When he succeeds, the curer returns to the patient's home, blows all over the house to get rid of the "atmosphere" created by the numerous *tsentsak* sent by the bird, and completes his sucking of the patient. Even after all the *tsentsak* are extracted, the shaman may remain another night at the house to suck out any "dirtiness" (*pahuri*) still inside. In the cures which I have witnessed, this sucking is a most noisy process, accompanied by deep, but dry, vomiting.

After sucking out a *tsentsak*, the shaman puts it into a little container. He does not swallow it because it is not his own magical dart and would therefore

kill him. Later, he throws the *tsentsak* into the air, and it flies back to the shaman who sent it originally into the patient. *Tsentsak* also fly back to a shaman at the death of a former apprentice who had originally received them from him. Besides receiving "old" magical darts unexpectedly in this manner, the shaman may have *tsentsak* thrown at him by a bewitcher. Accordingly, shamans constantly drink tobacco juice at all hours of the day and night. Although the tobacco juice is not truly hallucinogenic, it produces a narcotized state, which is believed necessary to keep one's *tsentsak* ready to repel any other magical darts. A shaman does not even dare go for a walk without taking along the green tobacco leaves with which he prepares the juice that keeps his spirit helpers alert. Less frequently, but regularly, he must drink *natema* for the same purpose and to keep in touch with the supernatural reality.

While curing under the influence of *natema*, the curing shaman "sees" the shaman who bewitched his patient. Generally, he can recognize the person, unless it is a shaman who lives far away or in another tribe. The patient's family knows this, and demands to be told the identity of the bewitcher, particularly if the sick person dies. At one curing session I attended, the shaman could not identify the person he had seen in his vision. The brother of the dead man then accused the shaman himself of being responsible. Under such pressure, there is a strong tendency for the curing shaman to attribute each case to a particular bewitcher.

Shamans gradually become weak and must purchase *tsentsak* again and again. Curers tend to become weak in power, especially after curing a patient bewitched by a shaman who has recently received a new supply of magical darts. Thus, the most powerful shamans are those who can repeatedly purchase new supplies of *tsentsak* from other shamans.

Shamans can take back *tsentsak* from others to whom they have previously given them. To accomplish this, the shaman drinks *natema*, and, using his *tsentsak*, creates a "bridge" in the form of a rainbow between himself and the other shaman. Then he shoots a *tsentsak* along this rainbow. This strikes the ground beside the other shaman with an explosion and flash likened to a lightning bolt. The purpose of this is to surprise the other shaman so that he temporarily forgets to maintain his guard over his magical darts, thus permitting the other shaman to suck them back along the rainbow. A shaman who has had his *tsentsak* taken away in this manner will discover that "nothing happens" when he drinks *natema*. The sudden loss of his *tsentsak* will tend to make him ill, but ordinarily the illness is not fatal unless a bewitcher shoots a magical dart into him while he is in this weakened condition. If he has not become disillusioned by his experience, he can again purchase *tsentsak* from some other shaman and resume his calling. Fortunately for anthropology some of these men have chosen to give up shamanism and therefore can be persuaded to reveal their knowledge, no longer having a vested interest in the profession. This divulgence, however, does not serve as a significant threat to practitioners, for words alone can never adequately convey the realities of shamanism. These can only be approached with the aid of *natema*, the chemical door to the invisible world of the Jívaro shaman.

27

Psychedelic Drugs and Religious Experience

Robert S. de Ropp

To members of the older generation, the mere mention of psychedelic drugs immediately brings to mind the Flower Children movement of the 1960s; Timothy Leary's famous line "turn on, tune in, drop out"; and the Vietnam War. Here, Robert S. de Ropp blends a crystal-clear picture of the dynamic and disruptive history of psychedelic cults of the period with both the theo-philosophical dissection of the cause and nature of religious experience and the socio-legal ramifications of drug use in the West. Going far beyond Leary's so-called seven basic spiritual questions, which were actually scientific questions concerned with knowing rather than with being, de Ropp calls up the views of the apostle Paul, William James, Aldous Huxley, and others in order to differentiate religious experience from the varieties of psychedelic experience. To de Ropp, all evidence, with minor exception, shatters the theory that psychedelics allow the drug taker to attain a permanently higher level of being. In fact, the author argues, the effects achieved through the use of psychedelic drugs to gain religious experience may be acquired in a number of less destructive ways, such as meditation, hypnosis, or yoga postures.

The cult that developed in the United States among the "Flower Children" of the 1960s had some features that distinguished it from the older cults of peyote and *teo-nanacatyl*. First, the drugs used were mainly synthetic; second, the founders of the cult were white Americans—physicians and psychologists—whose interests in the phenomena observed were scientific as well as religious.

The spiritual forefather of the movement was William James, whose studies of the effects of anesthetics on consciousness are described in *The Varieties of Religious Experience* (1902). It was James who declared that both nitrous oxide and ether, when sufficiently diluted with air, "stimulate the mystical consciousness in an extraordinary degree." It was James who made the statement, so often quoted by the high priests of the psychedelic cult, that "our normal waking consciousness, rational consciousness as we call it, is but one special type of consciousness, whilst all about it, parted from it by the filmiest of screens, there lie potential forms of consciousness entirely different."

James concluded that no account of the universe in its totality could be final if it disregarded those other forms of consciousness. He thought that drugs could open a region but that they failed to provide a map of it. Anesthetics, including alcohol, could lead

From ENCYCLOPEDIA OF RELIGION, by Robert S. de Ropp, 16, Thomson Gale, © 1987, Thomson Gale. Reprinted by permission of the Gale Group.

the explorer into that region, but the insights they offered might not be trustworthy. Nitrous oxide, for instance, might seem to reveal "depth after depth of truth to the inhaler," but the truth tended to fade at the moment of awakening. Alcohol, lifeblood of the cult of Dionysus, was the great exciter of the "yes function" in man and brought its votaries "from the chill periphery of things to the radiant core." James found it part of the mystery and tragedy of life that "whiffs and gleams of something we recognize as excellent should be vouchsafed only in the opening phases of what in its totality, is so degrading a poisoning."

The spiritual descendants of William James did not have much faith in either nitrous oxide or alcohol. For the most part they worked with synthetic psychedelics such as psilocybin, mescaline, and LSD. Their approaches ranged from manic enthusiasm (coupled with the feverish urge to proselytize) to cool scientific detachment. The did not limit themselves to investigating responses that could be defined as religious. The drugs were supposed to exert therapeutic effects quite apart from the religious emotions they aroused, and in various experiments psychedelics were given to prison inmates, neurotics, psychotics, and alcoholics, as well as to those who were dying of cancer. Indeed, it seemed for a while that the psychedelics might be a modern version of the universal panacea.

Timothy Leary was the leader of the more aggressive segment of the psychedelic cult. Witty, charming, and erudite, he possessed an extraordinary capacity to inflame the paranoid tendencies of those solid citizens who collectively constituted "the establishment." His own conversion to the psychedelic religion, a result of his having eaten seven sacred mushrooms, left him with an irresistible urge to proselytize. His new religion, summarized in the three commandments "turn on, tune in, drop out," was firmly linked to the use of psychedelics.

Psychedelics and Religious Experience

There was no doubt in Leary's mind that the effects the psychedelics produced were true religious experiences. To support his opinion he quoted the results obtained by Walter Pahnke, in an experiment described in the press as "the miracle of Marsh Chapel." This experiment involved twenty theology students who had never taken psychedelic drugs and ten guides with considerable psychedelic experience. The students were divided into five groups of four, with two guides assigned to each group. After attending the Good Friday service in the chapel two students in each group and one of the guides received thirty milligrams of psilocybin. The others received a placebo containing nicotinic acid, which produces a tingling sensation but no psychedelic effect. Neither guides nor students knew who had received the psychedelic and who the placebo. Nine subjects who had received psilocybin reported having had what they considered to be religious experiences. Only one of those receiving the placebo made such a claim.

Leary, of course, had gathered much experimental material of his own. In the early 1960s, until he was forced to resign from Harvard, he and Richard Alpert had given psychedelics to a variety of people including psychologists, priests, students, and criminals. Their results indicated that when the setting was supportive but not spiritual, between 40 and 75 percent of psychedelic subjects reported intense, life-changing religious experiences; when the set and setting were supportive and spiritual, from 40 to 90 percent of the experiences were revelatory and mystico-religious.

Leary's attempts to organize a religion around the use of LSD or psilocybin took various external forms: the International Federation for Internal Freedom (IFIF), 1963; the Castalia Foundation, 1963–1966; and the League for Spiritual Discovery, 1966. The aim of this work was to provide conditions in which the state of *ecstasis*, or the expansion of consciousness, could be experienced. In an article entitled "Rationale of the Mexican Psychedelic Training Center," Leary, Alpert, and Ralph Metzner (in Bloom et al., 1964) described the psychedelic experience as a means of attaining *ecstasis* provided the set and the setting were appropriate.

Set and setting were important. In fact they could make the difference between an uplifting religious experience and a terrifying descent into a personal inferno. The authors also stressed the importance of preparation. The psychedelic experience, they said, was a tool, like a telescope or microscope, that could bring other space-time dimensions into focus. People had to be trained to use the tool, after which they would use it not once but whenever a situation arose that called for the examination of other dimensions of reality. The Mexican program was the first to provide a series of guided psychedelic sessions for prepared volunteer subjects. Subjects were encouraged to plan their own sessions. They might, at a certain time, arrange to listen to a particular reading, view an object that would open up a line of association, or hear a certain piece of music.

Special use was made by Leary's group of the Tibetan *Book of the Dead,* which was regarded not only as a guide for the dying but also as an aid to the living. It was "a manual for recognizing and utilizing altered states of consciousness and applying the ecstatic experience in the postsession life." To make the book more relevant to their subjects' psychedelic sessions Leary and company retranslated it from the scholarly style of W. Y. Evans-Wentz into "psychedelic English."

Leary confronted the problem of what constitutes a real religious experience and solved it to his own satisfaction: "The religious experience is the ecstatic, incontrovertibly certain, subjective discovery of answers to seven basic spiritual questions." All issues that did not involve the seven basic questions belonged, in Leary's opinion, to secular games. Liturgical practices, rituals, dogmas, and theological speculations could be, and too often were, completely divorced from spiritual experience.

The "seven basic spiritual questions" listed by Leary were the Power Question, the Life Question, the Human Being Question, the Awareness Question, the Ego Question, the Emotional Question, and the Escape Question. The list covered the entire field of scientific inquiry, from atomic physics to the highest levels of psychology. If science and religion addressed themselves to the same basic questions then what, Leary asked, was the distinction between the two disciplines? He answered by saying that science concerned itself with the measurement of energy processes and sequences of energy transformations; it answered the basic questions using objective, observed, public data. Religion, however, involved a systematic attempt to answer the same questions subjectively, in terms of direct personal experience.

It is interesting to compare Leary's definition of the religious experience with that given earlier by William James. James devoted two chapters in *The Varieties of Religious Experience* to that condition of being he called "saintliness." It was, he declared, "the collective name for the ripe fruits of religion." A group of spiritual emotions in the saintly character formed the habitual center of personal energy. Saintliness was the same in all the religions, and its features could easily be described. They involved

1. a feeling of being in a wider life than that of the world's selfish little interests and a direct conviction of the existence of an ideal power

2. a sense of the friendly continuity of this power with our life and a willing self-surrender to its control

3. a feeling of elation and freedom resulting from the escape from confining selfhood

4. a shifting of the center of emotions toward loving and harmonious affections; a move toward yes and away from no

These characteristics may strike an objective observer as being closer to the essence of religion than Leary's "seven basic spiritual questions," which are really scientific (concerned with knowing) rather than religious (concerned with being). The aim of the religious life is to raise the level of being of its practitioner. Expansion of consciousness is one of the signs of a raised level of being. Indifference to possessions, a capacity for impartial, objective love, indifference to physical discomfort, and a complete freedom from fear of death are other fruits of this raised level. Furthermore, the saintly character does not fluctuate. Its possessor is not saintly today and demonic tomorrow. There is a stability in such a character, an inner consistency, a permanent set of values. There is also an awareness of the presence of the power that some religions call God, and such awareness is a source of repose and confidence.

Of all the fruits of the religious life, the capacity for objective love, for compassion, is the most highly esteemed. The apostle Paul defined this all important emotion in a well-known passage: "Though I speak with the tongues of men and angels, and have not charity, I am become as sounding brass, or a tinkling cymbal" (*1 Cor.* 13:1). What would Paul have said about Leary's seven basic spiritual questions? "Though I . . . understand all mysteries, and all knowledge: and though I have all faith, so that I could remove mountains, and have not charity, I am nothing." Nor is Paul alone in extolling charity as the choicest fruit of the spiritual life. The concept of the *bodhisattva*, who regards with compassion all sentient beings, puts the same emphasis on charity as we see in Christian teachings.

In light of such considerations, it would seem reasonable to ask not whether psychedelic drugs help those who take them to answer Leary's seven questions, but whether they enable the drug taker to attain a permanently higher level of being according to the criteria listed by James. The most that can be said for the psychedelic experience is that sometimes it helps.

R. E. L. Masters and Jean Houston, in their book *The Varieties of Psychedelic Experience*, described the range of subjects' reactions to LSD. They were less naive and dogmatic than Leary and were careful to distinguish what they called "nature mysticism" from real religious experience. The important question was whether, as a result of the insights obtained during the psychedelic experience, the subject really underwent a change equivalent to a religious conversion. One of their subjects, a highly intelligent but devil-obsessed psychologist, did show behavioral changes of a positive character, which suggested that a permanent transformation had occurred. Many other subjects found the experience useful in that it revealed to them unsuspected heights and depths in themselves. On the whole, however, the psychedelic experience did not transport the subjects to a permanently higher level of awareness.

Richard Alpert, who worked closely with Leary at Harvard and later in Mexico and at Millbrook, New York, was also compelled finally to admit that the psychedelic experience led nowhere. He had certainly tried everything: LSD, psilocybin, mescaline, hashish. He had even, on one occasion, locked himself and five other people in a building for three weeks and taken 400 micrograms of LSD every four hours, a total of 2,400 micrograms a day. (One hundred micrograms is enough to produce a strong reaction in anyone unaccustomed to the drug.) "We were very high," said Alpert, describing the experience. But they walked out of the house at the end of three weeks, and within a few days severe depression set

in, which was hardly surprising. The orgy of drug taking had left the participants so drained that it was surprising that they could function at all.

Alpert later went to India and found his guru in the foothills of the Himalayas. The guru amazed him by swallowing 915 micrograms of Alpert's "White Lightning," a special batch of high-quality LSD. That much LSD, taken by one unaccustomed to the drug, would constitute an enormous overdose, but the guru showed no reaction whatever. "All day long I'm there, and every now and then he twinkles at me and nothing—nothing happens! That was his answer to my question."

That demonstration of the power of mind over matter was enough for Alpert. He finally stopped trying to obtain results with psychedelics and took up a serious study of yoga. He returned to America transformed into Baba Ram Dass and wrote a book called *Remember: Be Here Now,* a very lively and honest account of his researches. In a section entitled "Psychedelics as an *Upaya*" (the Sanskrit term *upa-ya* is generally translated as "skillful means") he conceded that psychedelics might help a person break out of an imprisoning model of reality created by his own mind. But no matter how high a person soared on the wings provided by such drugs, he would always come down, and coming down could bring despair.

How the Psychedelics Work

The psychedelic drugs, which range from simple chemical compounds to highly complex ones, have no single feature in common. The "anaesthetic revelation" so thoroughly explored by William James could be produced by substances as simple as nitrous oxide or ether. Details of molecular composition strongly affect psychedelic action, however. For example, cannabinol, a major component of the hemp resin, appears to produce no effect on the human psyche, but the closely related Δ-9–tetrahydrocannabinol is highly active. Lysergic acid diethylamide is the most powerful psychedelic presently known, but a very small change in the structure of this molecule is sufficient to render it inactive.

Aldous Huxley, whose experiences with mescaline I described earlier, was inclined to attribute the action of this drug to its effect on brain enzymes. Enzymes, he declared, regulate the supply of glucose to the brain cells. Mescaline inhibits the production of these enzymes and thus lowers the amount of glucose available to an organ that is in constant need of sugar. Slowed by its lack of sugar, the brain ceases to function effectively as a reducing valve, making it possible for the possessor of that brain to make contact with Mind at Large, a concept Huxley had borrowed from the Cambridge philosopher C. D. Broad.

Broad's theory suggested that the function of the brain and nervous system is eliminative rather than productive. Each person, said Broad, is capable at each moment of remembering all that has ever happened to him and of perceiving everything that is happening everywhere in the universe. The brain acts as a reducing valve to protect us from being overwhelmed and confused by a mass of useless and irrelevant knowledge. In consequence, although each of us is potentially Mind at Large, what we actually perceive is a mere fraction of what we could perceive. The brain's reducing valve cuts down to a mere trickle the profusion of Mind at Large, leaving the individual free to concentrate on the problem of how to stay alive on the surface of the planet.

Aldous Huxley suggested that in some people a kind of bypass circumvents the reducing valve or that temporary bypasses may be developed as a result of spiritual exercises, through hypnosis, or from the use of drugs. Through these bypasses human beings make contact with certain elements of Mind at Large outside of the carefully selected material that our individual minds regard as a complete picture of reality.

This theory is beyond the reach of science, for it postulates the existence of an entity (Mind at Large) that no physical instrument we possess can detect. But the assertion that mescaline acts by reducing the capacity of the brain to utilize glucose is not likely to be correct. More effective ways of reducing the glucose supply to the brain are known and were formerly employed in the treatment of schizophrenia. The chief of these methods is insulin shock treatment, which certainly cuts down the brain's sugar supply, resulting in convulsions and loss of consciousness by the patient. If Huxley's theory were correct, the schizophrenics who received this treatment should have experienced, before losing consciousness, the sort of effects that are produced by mescaline. There is no evidence that they did so.

To discover how the psychedelics work it would seem that we must postulate something other than oxygen starvation or glucose starvation of the brain. Oxygen starvation does produce strange effects on the brain, as is evident from the experiences of people who have been clinically dead but were later revived. (Their stories have been chronicled by such noted researchers as Elisabeth Kübler-Ross.) It seems probable that such experiences form the basis of the various visions described in the Tibetan *Book of the Dead*. It is also possible that yogins who have mastered *prāṇāyāma*, which allows them to reduce their oxygen intake, can experience after-death states without actually dying. It would be too simple, however, to assume that all the psychedelics operate by reducing the brain's oxygen consumption. The fact is that we really do not know how these substances produce their effects.

Legal, Social, and Spiritual Questions

The abuse of drugs is so widespread in the United States that calm discussion of the religious aspect of certain drug experiences is next to impossible. The general public hysteria regarding drugs reaches a climax when the subject under discussion is the effect of drugs on the young. Young people, the argument goes, are innocent and must be protected. Laws are therefore passed making it a criminal offense to possess even such a relatively harmless weed as *Cannabis sativa*.

But it is exactly the young who are most likely to seek the psychedelic experience. There are several reasons for this. The young are often rebellious and attracted by forbidden fruit; they are enormously curious and want to explore all aspects of the world; finally, they often have religious impulses that are not satisfied by the standard forms of religion. These religious impulses arise from a deeply rooted craving to experience altered states of consciousness, a craving that becomes particularly powerful during adolescence. The modern teenager—rebellious, confused, and often defiant of authority—may feel particularly fascinated by drugs that offer, or seem to offer, new and strange experiences.

Some thinkers have imagined a society in which supervised psychedelic experience is provided those members, young and not so young, who seek to expand their awareness, but neither our own nor any other industrialized society has yet institutionalized such a practice. It was precisely this idea of the "guided trip" that underlay Leary's ill-starred efforts to found a new religion based on the psychedelic revelation. Given the hostility to drugs that prevails in American official circles, his attempts were bound to fail. He made that failure all the more inevitable by openly defying "the establishment" and taking every opportunity to provoke its wrath. Even two very cautious physicians, John W. Aiken and Louisa Aiken, were unable to win official permission to use peyote in their Church of the New Awakening. They argued that if Indian members of the Native American Church could legally use peyote for religious purposes, members of other races should enjoy the same right. But this logic was not accepted by the authorities.

Prohibition, however, has not prevented the use of psychedelics any more than it prevented the use of alcohol. The results of prohibitory legislation have been to ensure that those who do obtain these drugs pay outrageous prices, are often sold adulterated materials, and, because of lack of guidance and prevailing paranoia, often have bad trips. As long as alcohol and tobacco can be obtained legally, laws prohibiting the possession of substances such as marijuana and peyote will remain unenforceable.

The question that both legal and social prohibitions fail to confront is why some people want to use, or feel they need to use, psychedelic substances. To ask this question is to be open to the understanding that the problems lie not with drugs but with people. These problems are the result of a growing sense of futility that has affected our society. More and more occupations are taken over by automatic machinery and computerized robots. More and more people confront the fact that they will probably never find employment in a society dominated by automation. Under these circumstances, it is not surprising that millions experience what Paul Tillich in *The Courage to Be* called "the abyss of meaningless." To escape from that experience, they may stupefy themselves with alcohol, blunt their sensibilities with barbiturates or heroin, or attempt to get high with the aid of psychedelics.

Those who have experimented with psychedelic drugs and had what they consider to be authentic religious experiences are likely to fall into two groups. In the first are people who understand that the drugs act by using up certain vital energies of the body and that those energies must be replaced. For this reason, they will use drugs rarely and only under special conditions. They will also seek other, less destructive, ways of getting the same results, such as meditation or yoga postures. Sooner or later members of this group will probably abandon the use of psychedelics altogether.

In the second group are those who make the drug experience the center of their spiritual lives, failing to realize that using the drug is robbing them of strength and damaging their health. People in this group inevitably find themselves in trouble not because they have broken man-made laws but because they have broken the laws governing their own spiritual development. Inevitably, the psychedelic used becomes less and less effective and larger doses must be taken. Finally, the drug ceases to have any effect. But the drug user's reliance on his drug may have so weakened his will by that time that serious spiritual efforts become virtually impossible.

This is the main objection to the overuse of psychedelic drugs: they weaken the will, they substitute a dream world for the real world and a dream of religious experience for the real thing. But only personal experience with these drugs can bring this truth home to their votaries.

Suggested Readings

Furst, Peter T.
  1976   *Hallucinogens and Culture.* Novato, Calif.: Chandler and Sharp.

Myerhoff, Barbara G.
  1974   *The Peyote Hunt: The Sacred Journey of the Huichol Indians.* Ithaca, N.Y.: Cornell University Press.

Schultes, Richard Evans, and Albert Hofmann
    1979   *Plants of the Gods: Origins of Hallucinogenic Use.* New York: Alfred van der Marck Editions.

Tart, Charles T., ed.
    1969   *Altered States of Consciousness: A Book of Readings.* New York: John Wiley.

Wilbert, Johannes
    1987   *Tobacco and Shamanism in South America.* New Haven and London: Yale University Press.

Zinberg, Norman E., ed.
    1977   *Alternate States of Consciousness.* New York: Free Press.

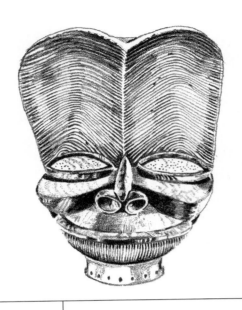

Bacham dance mask from Cameroun.

CHAPTER SIX

Ethnomedicine: Religion and Healing

If a single pervasive thought were to be singled out in this chapter, it would be the importance of culture in determining the etiology and treatment of disease and mental disorders. Just as humans have always suffered from disease, so, too, have we always responded to it, seeking ways to reduce its debilitating nature or, we hope, to banish it completely. All human societies have belief systems and practices that people turn to in order to identify disease and effect a cure. The integration of the study of these systems of beliefs and practices into the study of non-Western societies has created medical anthropology, the most recent addition to the discipline of anthropology (see Hahn 1995; Lindenbaum and Lock 1993; Mascie-Taylor 1993; Nichter 1992).

Explanations and cures of illnesses may be either natural or supernatural (a naturalistic response would not involve supernatural aid). As P. Stanley Yoder has clearly pointed out, one of the medical anthropologist's most important tasks is to distinguish between different types of causation and to understand the relationship between them, especially because "different types of causal explanations may be involved at different points during the process of diagnosis and treatment, or may characteristically demand differing treatments" (1982: 15). Moreover, because the range and variability of medical beliefs and practices among the peoples of the world are immense, there will be no easy explanation or simple generalization regarding causation and treatment of diseases. But always it will be possible to see the close relationship between medicine and religion, a cultural bonding that occurs in nonliterate, nonindustrialized cultures as well as in modern, technological cultures.

The importance of our understanding of ethnomedical systems is made clear by the fact that a great percentage of the non-Western world's population reside in areas that are little exposed to Western medical treatment. Primary among the concerns of such international groups as the World Health Organization is the role that improved health care can play in the socioeconomic development of Third World countries. The lack of implementation of modern medical care in these areas of the world is caused by a lack of both available funds and information. Partly in response to the dearth of funding, some health planners have proposed that the most effective way to expand modern primary care would be for

212

Western-trained practitioners to collaborate with traditional practitioners (Bichmann 1979: 175); however, lack of information is the greatest barrier to assessing the feasibility of such proposals in relation to national health goals and planning (Good 1977: 705). Because little substantive information concerning indigenous health care systems is available for non-Western countries, the identification and use of agents of change, such as local curers, to improve the quality of life in rural areas is extremely difficult.

It is noteworthy to point out also that intercultural contact seems to have caused an increase in both physical and psychological Western-based diseases among non-Western populations; the frustrations of not being able to cure these modern illnesses are liable to increase the use of traditional methods of healing. Other problems of contact also exist. Western-trained medical practitioners find little in traditional systems of health care they consider effective in either the physical or the mental realm. On the other hand, modern medical treatment is often rejected by those in the culture. For example, in rural contemporary Kenya, modern medical technology is not changing the pervasive "ancestor spirit-sorcery theory" of disease causation that has traditionally been used to account for all major misfortunes (Kramer and Thomas 1982: 169): as late as 1969 there was still no indication among the rural Kamba of Kenya that modern medicine had made prominent inroads at the level of prevention, either in effecting behavioral change or in modifying etiological beliefs, despite their long exposure to Western techniques.

Determining why the ill choose to accept or reject a system of treatment not only would define whom the people in the culture perceive as the proper healer but also would delineate their etiology of disease and their perception of appropriate treatment. What applied anthropologists are attempting to determine are the advantages and disadvantages of each of the health care systems—traditional and modern—in the eyes of the patients, as well as the nature of the knowledge healers and their clients draw upon in the process of selecting treatment. Unfortunately, previous research in traditional medical systems has essentially ignored the studied people's own explanations of these criteria, criteria that ordinarily include both natural and supernatural explanations.

Knowledge of the naturalistic treatments and ethnopharmacological systems of non-Western societies is also important, for much of the pharmacopoeia administered by traditional healers does work. (Societies everywhere possess naturalistic explanations and treatments. Cures derived from hundreds of wild plants were used by the North American Indians, for example, and techniques for the treatment of headaches and stomachaches, the setting of broken bones, bloodletting, lancing, cauterization, and other naturalistic skills are well known to the nonliterate world.) However, as the effectiveness of the traditional healer is dependent upon more than the use of proper chemical treatment, diagnosis is made not only at the empirical level but at the psychological and social levels as well. In speaking of Africa, for example, Wolfgang Bichmann notes that illness does not mean so much an individual event but a disturbance of social relations (1979: 177), and M. F. Lofchie points out that "African medical research has much to contribute to Western medicine: its wholism, emphasis on treatment of the entire family as well as the 'ill' person, and its encyclopedic lore of information about the curative properties of items available in nature—all of these principles are now working their way into Western medical vocabulary" (1982: vii).

For years it was widely believed that only "civilized" people were subject to mental illness, whereas the preliterates of the world led a blissful life free of neuroses and psychoses. It did not take anthropology long to prove that Rousseau's Noble Savage was just as susceptible to the major disorders of the mind as was the individual coping with life in the so-called civilized societies of the world. Anthropologists have sought answers to such important questions as whether mental illness rates differ cross-culturally; whether styles and types of illnesses vary; and whether it is more difficult to adjust to life in industrialized societies than in others. Anthropologists and others have shown, moreover, that traditional healers are particularly effective in the treatment of mental illness, and that their approaches to curing are beneficial to physical diseases as well. Not only are traditional healers' services readily available to the ill, for example, but their system of care is also nondisruptive to those in the culture, and the patient has the support of family members who are nearby or in actual attendance during the treatment. Beyond these advantages, and in contrast with the Western world, Third World countries frequently are much more accepting of those having mental illnesses. Sufferers of these disorders are often stigmatized in the West, and many attempt to hide their medical history.

A seven-year multicultural pilot study of severe mental illness by the World Health Organization reported in the magazine *Science '80* showed that relatively fast and complete recoveries from major psychoses are achieved in developing countries, such as Nigeria and India. In the United States and other Western countries, however, almost one-half of those who suffer psychotic breakdowns never recover. For example, whereas 58 percent of the Nigerians and 51 percent of the Indians studied had a single psychotic episode and were judged cured after treatment, the cure rate in the industrialized countries ranged from only 6 percent in Denmark to a high of 27 percent in China ("World Psychosis" 1980: 7). Certainly non-Western healing techniques are effective in the treatment of the mentally ill; however, the treatment of physiological diseases cannot match that of the West. The fact that many non-Western pharmaceuticals may be effective in one society and not in another demonstrates the important relationship of beliefs and cures—in particular, the interaction of the healer and the supernatural.

Throughout the world it is possible to place supernaturally caused illnesses into five categories: (1) sorcery, (2) breach of taboo, (3) intrusion of a disease object, (4) intrusion of a disease-causing spirit, and (5) loss of soul (Clements 1932: 252). It is important to note that these categories may not be recognized by certain societies. Indeed, it is a difficult task to determine the frequency and incidence of illnesses, especially mental illnesses, in non-Western, nonindustrialized countries. Native peoples may avoid seeking medical help from a modern health facility, for example, or, if they do seek treatment, there may be a question of accurate recordkeeping.

Anthropologists have correctly noted that the types of cures sought are based not only on the cause but also on the severity of the illness in terms of level of pain and difficulty of curing. Treatment based on cause and severity varies greatly; some non-Western groups maintain that most diseases are of natural origin, whereas others blame the supernatural realm for the misfortunes.

It is apparent that anthropologists must understand the integration of ethnomedical systems with the other areas of culture if they are successfully to conduct comparative studies. Ethnomedical systems are deeply ingrained in the structure of societies, functioning in ways that create a positive atmosphere for health care. No longer can we view non-biomedical medical methods as inferior; indeed, Western society owes much to traditional medicine, not the least of which is the support given to the patient by the family and the community.

The readings in this chapter, for the most part, deal with supernaturally caused diseases and mental illnesses and their etiology and treatment. Arthur C. Lehmann opens the chapter with an analysis of ethnomedicine among the Aka hunters and Ngando farmers. He stresses disease categories, disease etiology, treatment, and the role traditional healers *(ngangas)* play in interethnic contacts.

The second article, Robert Bergman's "A School for Medicine Men," helps us see the similarities and dissimilarities between Navajo medicine men and Western-trained psychiatrists. Bergman also discusses the establishment of a school for Navajo medicine men.

In the next article, William Wedenoja focuses on the role of women as curers in the Balm yards of Jamaica; he keys especially on the relationship between the Balm healers and their patients.

In the fourth article, L. A. Rebhun discusses anger and illness in northeast Brazil, where women use the term *swallowing frogs* to mean suppressing anger, hatred, or irritation and withstanding unfair treatment silently.

In the final selection, Edward C. Halperin, MD, examines the efficacy of prayers for the restoration of health. He also reviews the philosophical basis and pitfalls of clinical trials of intercessory prayer.

References

Bichmann, Wolfgang
  1979 "Primary Health Care and Traditional Medicine—Considering the Background of Changing Health Care Concepts in Africa." *Social Science and Medicine* 13B: 175–82.

Clements, Forrest E.
  1932 "Primitive Concepts of Disease." University of California *Publications in American Archaeology and Ethnology* 32 (2): 252.

Good, Charles M.
  1977 "Traditional Medicine: An Agenda for Medical Geography." *Social Science and Medicine* 11: 705–13.

Hahn, Robert A.
  1995 *Sickness and Healing: An Anthropological Perspective*. New Haven, Conn.: Yale University Press.

Kramer, Joyce, and Anthony Thomas
  1982 "The Modes of Maintaining Health in Ukambani, Kenya." In P. S. Yoder, ed., *African Health and Healing Systems: Proceedings of a Symposium*, pp. 159–98. Los Angeles: Crossroads Press, University of California.

Lindenbaum, Shirley, and Margaret Lock, eds.
  1993 *Knowledge, Power, and Practice: The Anthropology of Medicine and Everyday Life*. Berkeley: University of California Press.

Lofchie, M. F.
  1982 "Foreword." In P. Stanley Yoder, ed., *African Health and Healing Systems: Proceedings of a Symposium*, pp. vii–ix. Los Angeles: Crossroads Press, University of California.

Mascie-Taylor, C. G. N., ed.
  1993 *The Anthropology of Disease*. New York: Oxford University Press.

Nichter, Mark, ed.
  1992 *Anthropological Approaches to the Study of Ethnomedicine*. Philadelphia: Gordon and Breach.

"World Psychosis." *Science '80* 1 (6): 7.

Yoder, P. Stanley
  1982 "Issues in the Study of Ethnomedical Systems in Africa." In P. Stanley Yoder, ed., *African Health and Healing Systems: Proceedings of a Symposium*, pp. 1–20. Los Angeles: Crossroads Press, University of California.

28

Eyes of the *Ngangas:* Ethnomedicine and Power in Central African Republic

Arthur C. Lehmann

People of the Third World have a variety of therapies available for combating diseases but, because of cost, availability, and cultural bias, most rely on ethnomedical, or traditional, treatment rather than "biomedical," or Western, therapies. Dr. Lehmann's field research focuses on the importance of ngangas (traditional healers) as a source of primary health care for both the Aka Pygmy hunters and their horticultural neighbors, the Ngando of Central African Republic. Tracing the basis and locus of the ngangas' *mystical diagnostic and healing powers, he shows that they are particularly effective with treatments for mental illness and, to an unknown extent, with herbal treatment of physical illnesses. The powers of the Aka* ngangas, *however, are also used to reduce the tensions between themselves and their patrons and to punish those Ngando who have caused the hunters harm. Lehmann points out the necessity of recognizing and treating the social as well as the biological aspects of illness and appeals to health care planners to establish counterpart systems that mobilize popular and biomedical specialists to improve primary health care in the Third World.*

Ethnomedicine (also referred to as folk, traditional, or popular medicine) is the term used to describe the primary health care system of indigenous people whose medical expertise lies outside "biomedicine," the "modern" medicine of Western societies. Biomedicine does exist in the Third World, but it is unavailable to the masses of inhabitants for a number of reasons. Conversely, although popular medicine has largely been supplanted by biomedicine in the Western world, it still exists and is revived from time to time by waves of dissatisfaction with modern medicine and with the high cost of health care, by the health food movement, and by a variety of other reasons. The point is, all countries have pluralistic systems of health care, but for many members of society the

combat against the diseases that have plagued mankind is restricted to the arena of popular medicine.

This is particularly true in the developing nations, such as those of the sub-Saharan regions of Africa, where over 80 percent of the population live in rural areas with a dearth of modern medical help (Bichmann 1979; Green 1980). Between 1984 and the present, I have made six field trips to one such rural area (the most recent in 1994) to study the primary health care practices of Aka Pygmy hunter-gatherers and their horticultural neighbors, the Ngando of Central African Republic (C.A.R.).

The Aka and the Ngando

Several groups of the Pygmies live in a broad strip of forested territory stretching east and west across the center of Equatorial Africa. The two largest societies

This selection was written especially for this volume.

are the Mbuti of the Inturi Forest of Zaire and the Aka, who live in the Southern Rainforest that extends from the Lobaye River in Central African Republic into the People's Republic of the Congo and into Cameroun (Cavalli-Sforza 1971). Like the Mbuti, the Aka are long-time residents of their region. It is on the edge of the Southern Rainforest in and near the village of Bagandu that the Aka Pygmies and the Ngando come into the most frequent contact. The proximity, particularly during the dry season from December to April, allows for comparisons of health care systems that would be difficult otherwise, for the Aka move deep into the forest and are relatively inaccessible for a good portion of the year.

Since Turnbull described the symbiotic relationship between Mbuti Pygmies and villagers in Zaire (1965), questions remain as to why Pygmy hunters continue their association with their sedentary neighbors. Bahuchet's work shows that the relationship between the Aka and the Ngando of C.A.R. is one of voluntary mutual dependence in which both groups benefit; indeed, the Aka consider the villagers responsible for their well-being (1985: 549). Aka provide the Ngando with labor, meat, and forest materials while the Ngando pay the Aka with plantation foods, clothes, salt, cigarettes, axes and knives, alcohol, and infrequently, money.

This mutual dependence extends to the health care practices of both societies. Ngando patrons take seriously ill Aka to the dispensary for treatment; Aka consider this service a form of payment that may be withheld by the villagers as a type of punishment. On the other hand, Aka *ngangas* (traditional healers) are called upon to diagnose and treat Ngando illnesses. The powers believed to be held by the *ngangas* are impressive, and few, particularly rural residents question these powers or the roles they play in everyday life in Central African Republic.

Eyes of the *Ngangas*

The people believe that the *ngangas* intervene on their behalf with the supernatural world to combat malevolent forces and also use herbal expertise to protect them from the myriad of tropical diseases. Elisabeth Motte (1980) has recorded an extensive list of medicines extracted by the *ngangas* from the environment to counter both natural and supernatural illnesses; 80 percent are derived from plants and the remaining 20 percent from animals and minerals.

Both Aka and Ngando *ngangas* acquire their power to diagnose and cure through an extensive apprenticeship ordinarily served under the direction of their fathers, who are practicing healers themselves. This system of inheritance is based on primogeniture, although other than first sons may be chosen to become *ngangas*. Although Ngando *ngangas* may be either male or female, the vast majority are males; all Aka *ngangas* are males. In the absence of the father or if a younger son has the calling to become a healer, he may study under an *nganga* outside the immediate family.

During my six trips to the field, *ngangas* permitted me to question them on their training and initiation into the craft; it became apparent that important consistencies existed. First, almost all male *ngangas* are first sons. Second, fathers expect first sons to become *ngangas*; as they said, "It is natural." Third, the apprenticeship continues from boyhood until the son is himself a *nganga,* at which time he trains his own son. Fourth, every *nganga* expresses firm belief in the powers of his teacher to cure and, it follows, in his own as well. As is the case with healers around the world, despite the trickery sometimes deemed necessary to convince clients of the effectiveness of the cure, the *ngangas* are convinced that their healing techniques will work unless interrupted by stronger powers. Fifth, every *nganga* interviewed maintained strongly that other *ngangas* who were either envious or have a destructive spirit can destroy or weaken the power of a healer, causing him to fail. Sixth, and last, the origin and locus of the *ngangas'* power is believed to be in their eyes.

Over and over I was told that during the final stages of initiation the master *nganga* had vaccinated the initiate's eyes and placed "medicine" in the wound, thus giving the new *nganga* power to divine and effectively treat illnesses. At first I interpreted the term *vaccination* to mean simply the placement of "medicine" in the eyes, but I was wrong. Using a double-edged razor blade and sometimes a needle, the master *nganga* may cut his apprentice's lower eyelids, the exterior corners of the eyes, or below the eyes (although making marks below the eyes is now considered "antique," I was told); he concludes the ceremony by placing magical medicine in the cuts. At this moment, the student is no longer an apprentice; he has achieved the status of an *nganga* and the ability to diagnose illnesses with the newly acquired power of his eyes.

Not until my last field trip in 1994 did I witness a master *nganga* actually cut the whites of his apprentice's eyes. At the end of an hour-long interview with an *nganga,* which focused on my eliciting his concept of disease etiology in treatment of illness, I casually posed the question I had asked other *ngangas* many times before: "Do you vaccinate your apprentice's eyes?" The *nganga* beckoned his apprentice seated nearby, and, to my amazement, the apprentice immediately placed his head on the master's lap. I quickly retrieved my camcorder which I had just put away! The master removed a razor blade from a match box, spread the student's eyelids apart, deftly made five cuts on the whites of each eye, and squeezed the juice of a leaf (the "medicine") into the wounds. This astounding procedure performed on perhaps the most sensitive of all human parts took less than a total of three minutes and did not appear to cause the apprentice any degree of pain, albeit his eyes were red and his tears profuse.

During the career of an *nganga,* his eyes will be vaccinated many times, thus, it is believed, rejuvenating the power of the eyes to correctly diagnose illness and ensure proper therapy. It is clear that the multiple powers of *ngangas* to cure and to protect members of their band from both physical and mental illnesses as well as from a variety of types of supernatural attacks reside in their eyes.

It follows that the actual divinatory act involves a variety of techniques, particular to each *nganga*, that allows him to use his powers to "see" the cause of the illness and determine its treatment. Some burn a clear, rocklike amber resin called *paka* found deep in the rain forest, staring into the flames to learn the mystery of illness and the appropriate therapy. Some stare into the rays of the sun during diagnosis or gaze into small mirrors to unlock the secret powers of the ancestors in curing. Others concentrate on plates filled with water or large, brilliant chunks of glass. The most common but certainly the most incongruous method of acquiring a vision by both Aka and Ngando *ngangas* today is staring into a light bulb. These are simply stuck into the ground in front of the *nganga* or, as is the case among many village healers, the light bulb is floated in a glass of water during consultation. The appearance of a light bulb surfacing from an Aka *nganga's* healing paraphernalia in the middle of a rain forest is, to say the least, unique. Western methods of divining—of knowing

the unknown—were not, and to some degree are not now, significantly different from the techniques of the *ngangas*. Our ways of "seeing," involving gazing at and "reading" tea leaves, crystal balls, cards, palms, and stars, are still considered appropriate techniques by many.

Therapy Choices and Therapy Managers

A wide variety of therapies coexist in contemporary Africa, and the situation in the village of Bagandu is no exception. The major sources of treatment are Aka *ngangas*, Ngando *ngangas*, kinship therapy (family councils called to resolve illness-causing conflicts between kin), home remedies, Islamic healers (marabouts), and the local nurse at the government dispensary, who is called "doctor" by villagers and hunters alike. In addition, faith healers, herbalists, and local specialists (referred to as "fetishers") all attempt, in varying degrees, to treat mental or physical illness in Bagundu. Intermittently Westerners, such as missionaries, personnel from the U.S. Agency for International Development, and anthropologists also treat physical ailments. Bagandu is a large village of approximately 3,400 inhabitants; however, most communities are much smaller and have little access to modern treatment. And, as Cavalli-Sforza has noted,

> If the chances of receiving Western medical help for Africans living in remote villages are very limited, those of Pygmies are practically nonexistent. They are even further removed from hospitals. African health agents usually do not treat Pygmies. Medical help comes exceptionally and almost always from rare visiting foreigners. (Cavalli-Sforza 1986: 421)

Residents of Bagandu are fortunate in having both a government dispensary and a pharmacy run by the Catholic church, but prescriptions are extremely costly relative to income, and ready cash is scarce. A more pressing problem is the availability of drugs. Frequently the "doctor" has only enough to treat the simplest ailments such as headaches and small cuts; he must refer thirty to forty patients daily to the Catholic pharmacy, which has more drugs than the dispensary but still is often unable to fill prescriptions for the most frequently prescribed drugs such as penicillin, medicine to counteract parasites, and antibiotic salves. Although the doctor does the best he can under these conditions, patients must often resort only to popular medical treatment—in spite of the fact that family members, the therapy managers, have assessed the illness as one best treated by biomedicine. In spite, too, of the regular unavailability of medicine, the doctor's diagnosis and advice is still sought out—"although many people will consent to go to the dispensary only after having exhausted the resources of traditional medicine" (Motte 1980: 311).

Popular, ethnomedical treatment is administered by kin, *ngangas* (among both the Aka and Ngando villagers), other specialists noted for treatment of specific maladies, and Islamic marabouts, who are recent immigrants from Chad. According to both Aka and Ngando informants, the heaviest burden for health care falls to these ethnomedical systems. Ngando commonly utilize home, kin remedies for minor illnesses, but almost 100 percent indicated that for more serious illnesses they consulted either the doctor or *ngangas* (Aka, Ngando, or both); to a lesser extent they visited specialists. The choice of treatment, made by the family therapy managers, rests not only on the cause and severity of the illness, but also on the availability of therapists expert in the disease or problem, their cost, and their proximity to the patient. Rarely do the residents of Bagandu seek the aid of the marabouts, for example, in part because of the relatively high cost of consultation. Clearly, both popular and biomedical explanations for illness play important roles in the maintenance of health among Bagandu villagers, although popular medicine is the most important therapy resource available. Popular medicine is especially vital for the Aka hunters, whose relative isolation and inferior status (in the eyes of the Ngando) have resulted in less opportunity for biomedical treatment. Yet even they seek out modern medicine for illnesses.

Whatever the system of treatment chosen, it is important to understand that "the management of illness and therapy by a set of close kin is a central aspect of the medical scene in central Africa. . . . The therapy managing group . . . exercises a brokerage function between the sufferer and the specialist" (Janzen 1978: 4). It is the kingroup that determines which therapy is to be used.

Explanations of Illness

The choice of therapy in Bagandu is determined by etiology and severity, as in the West. Unlike Western medicine, however, African ethnomedicine is not restricted to an etiology of only natural causation. Both the Aka and the Ngando spend a great deal of time, energy, and money (or other forms of payments) treating illnesses perceived as being the result of social and cultural imbalances, often described in supernatural terms. Aka and Ngando nosology has accommodated biomedicine without difficulty, but traditional etiology has not become less important to the members of these societies. Frequent supernatural explanations of illness by Aka and Ngando informants inevitably led me to the investigation of witchcraft, curses, spells, or the intervention of ancestors and nameless spirits, all of which were viewed as being responsible for poor health and misfortune. The Aka maintain, for example, that the fourth leading cause of death in Bagandu is witchcraft (diarrhea is the principal cause; measles, second, and convulsions, third [Hewlett 1986: 56]). During my research, it became apparent that a dual model of disease explanation exists among the Aka and Ngando: first, a naturalistic model that fits its Western biomedical counterpart well, and second, a supernaturalistic explanation.

Interviews with village and Pygmy *ngangas* indicated that their medical systems are not significantly different. Indeed, both groups agree that their respective categories of illness etiology are identical. Further, the categories are not mutually exclusive: an illness may be viewed as being natural, but it may be exacerbated by supernatural forces such as witchcraft and spells. Likewise, this phenomenon can be reversed: an illness episode may be caused by supernatural agents but progress into a form that is treatable through biomedical techniques. For example, my relatively educated and ambitious young field assistant, a villager, was cut on the lower leg by a piece of stone while working on a new addition to his house. The wound, eventually becoming infected, caused swelling throughout the leg and groin. As was the case in some of his children's illnesses, the explanation for the wound was witchcraft. It was clear to him that the witch was a neighbor who envied his possessions and his employment by a foreigner. Although the original cut was caused by a supernatural agent, the resulting infection fitted the biomedical model. Treatment by a single injection of penicillin quickly brought the infection under control, although my assistant believed that had the witch been stronger the medicine would not have worked. Here is a case in which, "in addition to the patient's physical signs and social relationships," the passage of time is also crucial to "the unfolding of therapeutic action" (Feierman 1985: 77). As the character of an illness changes with time as the illness runs its course, the therapy manager's decisions may change, because the perceived etiology can shift as a result of a variety of signs, such as a slow-healing wound or open conflict in the patient's social group (Janzen 1978: 9).

Studies on disease etiologies among select African societies (Bibeau 1979; Janzen 1978; Warren 1974) reported that most illnesses had natural causes, and this finding holds for the Ngando villagers as well. At first glance, these data would seem to reduce the importance of ngangas and of popular medicine generally, but it is necessary to recognize that ngangas treat both natural and supernatural illnesses utilizing both medical and mystical techniques. The question posed by Feierman, "Is popular medicine effective?" (1985: 5), is vital to the evaluation of ngangas as healers. Surely some traditional medicines used by these cures must in many cases work, and work regularly enough to earn the sustained support of the general public.

Illnesses of God and Illnesses of Man

Both the Ngando and Aka explanations for natural illnesses lack clarity. Some ngangas refer to them as "illnesses of God"; others simply identify them as "natural"; and still others frequently use both classifications, regularly assigning each label to specific ailments. Hewlett maintains that the Aka sometimes labeled unknown maladies as illnesses of God (1986: personal communication). On the other hand, the Bakongo of neighboring Zaire defined illnesses of God as those "generally, mild conditions which respond readily to therapy when no particular disturbance exists in the immediate social relationships of the sufferer. . . . The notion of 'god' does not imply divine intervention or retribution but simply that the cause is an affliction in the order of things unrelated to human intentions" (Janzen 1978: 9).

Both Janzen's and Hewlett's data are accurate, but my field data show as well that the explanations of natural illnesses among the Ngando and Aka not only refer to normal mild diseases and sometimes unknown ones but also to specific illnesses named by the ngangas and the residents of Bagandu. The confusion surrounding these mixed explanations of disease causation is an important topic for future ethnosemantic or other techniques of emic inquiry by ethnographers.

Residents of Bagandu and both Aka and Ngando ngangas categorized sickness caused by witchcraft, magic, curses, spells, and spirits as "illnesses of man." This is the second major disease category. Witchcraft, for example, while not the main cause of death, is the most frequently named cause of illness in Bagandu. Informants in Bagandu cite the frequency of witchcraft accusations as proof of their viewpoint. Antisocial or troublesome neighbors are frequently accused of being witches and are jailed if the charge is proven. Maladies of all sorts, such as sterility among females, are also commonly attributed to the innate and malevolent power of witches. These types of explanations are not unusual in rural Africa. What is surprising are reports of new illnesses in the village caused by witches.

All Ngando informants claimed, furthermore, that the problem of witchcraft has not diminished over time; on the contrary, it has increased. The thinking is logical: because witchcraft is believed to be inherited, any increase in population is seen also as an inevitable increase in the number of witches in the village. Population figures in the region of the Southern Rainforest have increased somewhat in the past few decades despite epidemics such as measles; accordingly, the incidence of maladies attributed to witches has increased. One informant from Bagandu strongly insisted that witches are not only more numerous but also much more powerful today than before. Offiong (1983) reported a marked increase of witchcraft in Nigeria and adjacent states in West Africa, caused not by inflation of population but by the social strain precipitated by the frustration accompanying lack of achievement after the departure of colonial powers.

Insanity is not a major problem among the Ngando. When it does occur, it is believed to be caused by witchcraft, clan or social problems, evil spirits, and breaking taboos. Faith healers, marabouts, and ngangas are seen as effective in the treatment of mental illness due to witchcraft or other causes. The role of faith healers is particularly important in the lives of members of the Prophetical Christian Church in Bagandu. They have strong faith in the healing sessions and maintain that the therapy successfully treats the victims of spirits' attacks. Informants also claim the therapy lasts a long time.

The curse is a common method of venting anger in Bagandu, used by both male and female witches. Informants stated that women use curses more than men and that the subjects of their attacks are often males. The curses of witches are counted as being extremely dangerous in the intended victim. One villager accused the elderly of using the curse as a weapon most frequently. Spell-casting is also common in the area, and males often use spells as a method of seduction.

Most, if not all, residents of Bagandu use charms, portable "fetishes," and various types of magical objects placed in and around their houses for protection. Some of these objects are counter-magical: they simultaneously protect the intended victim and turn the danger away from the victim to the attackers. Counter-magic is not always immediate; results may take years to appear. Charms, fetishes, and other forms of protection are purchased from *ngangas,* marabouts, and other specialists such as herbalists. For example, the Aka and Ngando alike believe that wearing a mole's tooth on a bracelet is the most powerful protection from attacks by witches.

To a lesser extent, spirits are also believed to cause illness. It is problematic whether or not this source of illness deserves a separate category of disease causation. Bahuchet thinks not; rather, he holds that spirit-caused illnesses should be labeled illnesses of God (1986: personal communication). It is interesting to note that in addition to charms and other items put to use in Bagandu, residents supplicate ancestors for aid in times of difficulty. If the ancestors do not respond, and if the victim of the misfortune practices Christianity, he or she will seek the aid of God. Non-Christians and Christians alike commonly ask diviners the cause of their problem, after which they seek the aid of the proper specialist. Revenge for real or imagined attacks on oneself or on loved ones is common. One method is to point a claw of a mole at the wrongdoer. Ngando informants maintain the victim dies soon after. Simple possession of a claw, if discovered, means jail for the owner.

My initial survey of Aka and Ngando *ngangas* in 1984 brought out other origins of illness. Two *ngangas* in Bagandu specifically cited the devil, rather than unnamed evil spirits, as a cause for disease. The higher exposure of villagers to Christianity may account for this attribution: seven denominations are currently represented in the churches of Bagandu. Urban *ngangas* questioned in Bangui, the capital, stressed the use of poison as a cause of illness and death. Although poisonings do not figure prominently as a cause of death among the Aka and Ngando, it is common belief that *ngangas* and others do use poison.

Finally, while not a cause for illness, informants maintained that envious *ngangas* have the power to retard or halt the progress of a cure administered by another. All *ngangas* interviewed in 1984 and 1985 confirmed not only that they have the power to interrupt the healing process of a patient but also that they frequently invoke it. Interestingly, *ngangas* share this awesome power with witches, who are also believed by members of both societies to be able to spoil the "medicine" of healers. This kind of perception of the *ngangas'* power accounts, in part, for their dual character: primarily beneficial to the public, they can also be dangerous.

While the numerical differences in the frequency of physiologically and psychologically rooted illnesses in Bagandu are unknown, Ngando respondents in a small sample were able to list a number of supernaturally caused illnesses that are treatable by *ngangas,* but only a few naturally caused ones. Among the naturalistic illnesses were illnesses of the spleen; *katungba,* deformation of the back; and *Kongo,* "illness of the rainbow." According to Hewlett (1986: 53), *Kongo* causes paralysis of the legs (and sometimes of the arms) and death after the victim steps on a dangerous mushroom growing on a damp spot in the forest where a rainbow-colored snake has rested. Had the Ngando sample been more exhaustive, it is probable that the list of natural diseases would have been greater, although perhaps not as high as the twenty natural illnesses the *ngangas* said they could treat successfully. That impressive list includes malaria, hernia, diarrhea, stomach illness, pregnancy problems, dysentery, influenza, abscesses, general fatigue, traumas (snake bite, miscellaneous wounds, and poisoning), and general and specific bodily pain (spleen, liver, ribs, head, and uterus).

Powers of the *Ngangas*

The powers of the *ngangas* are not limited to controlling and defeating supernatural or natural diseases alone. In the village of Bagandu and in the adjacent Southern Rainforest where the Ngando and Aka hunters come into frequent contact, tensions exist due to the patron-client relationship, which by its very economic nature is negative. These tensions are magnified by ethnic animosity. Without the Akas' mystical power, their economic and social inferiority would result in an even more difficult relationship with the Ngando. Here the powers of the Pygmy *ngangas* play an important part in leveling, to bearable limits, the overshadowing dominance of the Ngando, and it is here that the *ngangas* demonstrate their leadership outside the realm of health care. Each Aka has some form of supernatural protection provided by the *nganga* of his camp to use while in the village. Still, the need exists for the extraordinary powers of the *nganga* himself for those moments of high tension when Aka are confronted by what they consider the most menacing segments of the village population: the police, the mayor, and adolescent males, all of whom, as perceived by the Aka, are dangerous to their personal safety while in the village.

In the summer of 1986, I began to study the attitudes of village patrons toward their Aka clients and, conversely, the attitudes of the so-called wayward servants (Turnbull's term for the Mbuti Pygmy of Zaire, 1965) toward the villagers. Participant observation and selective interviews of patrons, on the one hand, and of hunters, on the other, disclosed other important tangents of power of the Aka in general and of their *ngangas* in particular. First, the Aka often have visible sources of power such as scarification, cords worn on the wrist and neck, and bracelets strung with powerful charms for protection against village witches. These protective devices are provided the Aka by their *ngangas*. Second, and more powerful still, are the hidden powers of the Aka in general, bolstered by the specific powers of the *ngangas*. Although the villagers believe the hunters' power is strongest in the forest, and therefore weaker in the village setting, Aka power commands the respect of the farmers. Third, the villagers acknowledge the Aka expertise in the art of producing a variety of deadly poisons, such as *sepi*, which may be used to punish farmers capable of the most

serious crimes against the Pygmies. The obvious functions of these means of protection and retribution, taken from the standpoint of the Aka, are positive. Clearly these powers reduce the tension of the Aka while in the village, but they also control behavior of villagers toward the hunters to some undefinable degree.

Villagers interpret the variety of punishments which the Aka are capable of meting out to wrongdoers as originating in their control of mystical or magical powers. Interestingly, even poisonings are viewed in this way by villagers because of the difficulty of proving that poison rather than mystical power caused illness or death. Although the use of poison is rare, it is used and the threat remains. Georges Guille-Escuret, a French ethnohistorian working in Bagandu in 1985, reported to me that prior to my arrival in the field that year three members of the same household had died on the same day. The head of the family had been accused of repeated thefts of game from the traps and from the camp of an Aka hunter. When confronted with the evidence—a shirt the villager had left at the scene of the thefts—the family rejected the demands of the hunter for compensation for the stolen meat. Soon thereafter, the thief, his wife, and his mother died on the same day. Villagers, who knew of the accusations of theft, interpreted the deaths as the result of poisoning or the mystical powers of the hunter.

Stories of Aka revenge are not uncommon, nor are the Akas' accusations of wrongdoing leveled against the villagers. To the Ngando farmers, the powers of the Aka *ngangas* include the ability to cause death through the use of fetishes, to cause illness to the culprit's eyes, and to direct lightning to strike the perpetrator. These and other impressive powers to punish are seen as real threats to villagers—but the power of the *ngangas* to cure is even more impressive.

Attempts in my research to delineate the strengths and weaknesses of the *ngangas* and other health care specialists discovered a number of qualities/characteristics widely held to be associated with each. First, each specialist is known for specific medical abilities; that is, Aka and Ngando *ngangas* recognize the therapeutic expertise of others in a variety of cures. A *nganga* from Bangui maintained that Aka *ngangas* were generally superior to the village healers in curing. This view is shared by a number of villagers interviewed, who maintained that the power of Aka *ngangas* is greater than that of their own specialists.

The Aka strongly agree with this view, and in a sense the Aka are more propertied in the realm of curing than are the villagers. There is no question that the Aka are better hunters. Despite the Ngandos' greater political and economic power in the area and the social superiority inherent in their patron status, the Ngando need the Aka. All these elements help balance the relationship between the two societies, although the supernatural and curative powers of Aka *ngangas* have not previously been considered to be ingredients in the so-called symbiotic relationship between Pygmy hunters and their horticultural neighbors.

Second, *ngangas* noted for their ability to cure particular illnesses are often called upon for treatment by other *ngangas* who have contracted the disease. Third, with one exception, all the *ngangas* interviewed agree that European drugs, particularly those contained in hypodermic syringes and in pills, are effective in the treatment of natural diseases. One dissenting informant from the capital disdained biomedicine altogether because, as he said, "White men don't believe in us." Fourth, of the fourteen Aka and Ngando *ngangas* interviewed in 1985, only five felt that it was possible for a *nganga* to work successfully with the local doctor (male nurse) who directed the dispensary in Bagandu. All five of these *ngangas* said that if such cooperation did come about, their special contribution would be the treatment of patients having illnesses of man, including mental illness resulting from witchcraft, from magical and spiritual attacks, and from breaking taboos. None of the *ngangas* interviewed had been summoned to work in concert with the doctor. Fifth, as a group, the *ngangas* held that biomedical practitioners are unable to successfully treat mental illnesses and other illnesses resulting from attacks of supernatural agents. In this the general population of the village agree. This is a vitally important reason for the sustained confidence in popular therapy in the region—a confidence that is further strengthened by the belief that the *ngangas* can treat natural illnesses as well. Sixth, the village doctor recognized that the *ngangas* and marabouts do have more success in the treatment of mental illnesses than he does. Although the doctor confided that he has called in a village *nganga* for consultation in a case of witchcraft, he also disclosed that on

frequent occasions he had to remedy the treatment administered by popular specialists for natural diseases. It is important to recognize that unlike biomedical specialists in the capital, the local doctor does appreciate the talents of traditional therapists who successfully practice ethnopsychiatry.

All respondents to this survey recognized the value of biomedicine in the community, and little variation in the types of cures the doctor could effect was brought out. No doubts were raised regarding the necessity of both biomedicine and popular therapy to the proper maintenance of public health. The spheres of influence and expertise of both types of practitioners, while generally agreed on by participants of the Ngando survey, did show some variation, but these were no more serious than our own estimates of the abilities of our physicians in the West. In short, all informants utilized both systems of therapy when necessary and if possible.

The continuation of supernatural explanations of illness by both the Ngando and the Aka results in part from tradition, in combination with their lack of knowledge of scientific disease etiology, and in part because of the hidden positive functions of such explanations. Accusations of witchcraft and the use of curses and malevolent magic function to express the anxiety, frustrations, and social disruptions in these societies. These are traditional explanations of disease, with more than a single focus, for they focus upon both the physical illness and its sociological cause. "Witchcraft (and by extension other supernatural explanations for illness and disaster) provides an indispensable component in many philosophies of misfortune. It is the friend rather than the foe of mortality" (Lewis 1986: 16). Beyond this rationale, reliance upon practitioners of popular medicine assures the patient that medicine is available for treatment in the absence of Western drugs.

The Role of Ethnomedicine

Among the Aka and Ngando and elsewhere, systems of popular medicine have sustained African societies for centuries. The evolution of popular medicine has guaranteed its good fit to the cultures that have produced it; even as disruptive an element of the system as witchcraft can claim manifest and latent functions that contribute to social control and the promotion of proper behavior.

Unlike Western drug therapies, no quantifiable measure exists for the effectiveness of popular medicine. Good evidence from World Health Organization studies can be brought forth, however, to illustrate the relatively high percentage of success of psychotherapeutic treatment through ethnomedicine in the Third World compared to that achieved in the West. The results of my research in Bagandu also demonstrate the strong preference of villagers for popular medicine in cases involving mental illness and supernaturally caused mental problems. At the same time, the doctor is the preferred source of therapy for the many types of natural disease, while *ngangas* and other specialists still have the confidence of the public in treating other maladies, referred to as illnesses of man and some illnesses of God. Whatever the perceived etiology by kingroup therapy managers, both popular and biomedical therapists treat natural illnesses. It is in this realm of treatment that it is most important to ask, "What parts of popular medicine work?" rather than, "Does popular medicine work?" Because evidence has shown that psychotherapy is more successful in the hands of traditional curers, it is therefore most important to question the effectiveness of popular therapy in handling natural illnesses. Currently, the effectiveness of traditional drugs used for natural diseases is unknown; however, the continued support of popular therapists by both rural and urban Africans indicates a strength in the system. The effectiveness of the *ngangas* may be both psychological and pharmaceutical, and if the ecological niche does provide drugs that do cure natural illnesses, it is vital that these be determined and manufactured commercially in their countries of origin. If we can assume that some traditional drugs are effective, governments must utilize the expertise of healers in identifying these.

It is unrealistic to attempt to train popular therapists in all aspects of biomedicine, just as it is unrealistic to train biomedical specialists in the supernatural treatments applied by popular practitioners. However, neither type of therapist, nor the public, will benefit from the expertise of the other if they remain apart. The task is to make both more effective by incorporating the best of each into a counterpart system that focuses on a basic training of healers in biomedicine. This combination must certainly be a more logical and economic choice than attempting to supply biomedical specialists to every community in Central African Republic, a task too formidable for any country north or south of the Sahara. The significance of this proposal is magnified by the massive numbers for whom biomedicine is unavailable, those who must rely only upon ethnomedicine.

Even if available to all, biomedicine alone is not the final answer to disease control in the Third World. Hepburn succinctly presents strong arguments against total reliance upon the biomedical approach:

> Biomedicine is widely believed to be effective in the cure of sickness. A corollary of this is the belief that if adequate facilities could be provided in the Third World and "native" irrationalities and cultural obstacles could be overcome, the health problems of the people would largely be eliminated. However, this belief is not true, because the effectiveness of biomedicine is limited in three ways. First, many conditions within the accepted defining properties of biomedicine (i.e., physical diseases) cannot be treated effectively. Second, by concentrating on the purely physical, biomedicine simply cannot treat the social aspects of sickness (i.e., illness). Third, cures can only be achieved under favorable environmental and political conditions: if these are not present, biomedicine will be ineffective (1988: 68).

The problems facing societies in Africa are not new. These same issues faced Westerners in the past, and our partial solutions, under unbelievably better conditions, took immense time and effort to achieve. If primary health care in the non-Western world is to improve, the evolutionary process must be quickened by the utilization of existing popular medical systems as a counterpart of biomedicine, by the expansion of biomedical systems, and by the cooperation of international funding agencies with African policymakers, who themselves must erase their antagonism toward ethnomedicine.

29

A School for Medicine Men

Robert Bergman

The anthropological study of mental illness demonstrates that the types and frequency of mental disorders vary from one culture to another, as do the diagnosis and treatment of the illness. In this article, Robert Bergman discusses a training school for Navajo medicine men founded by the Navajo themselves at Rough Rock, Arizona, a community on the Navajo reservation. As a non-Indian psychiatrist working for the Indian Health Service, the author volunteered his professional services to the fledgling school. Working side by side with the Navajo medicine men, or "singers," as they are called, Bergman analyzed the nature of Navajo curative ceremonies and their effects on patients. The clash of folk medicine and scientific biomedicine has received considerable attention by anthropologists, and reports of fear and grief felt by non-Western patients undergoing modern medical treatment are common. If indigenous patients and their curers are ignorant of the procedures and philosophies underlying biomedicine, so, too, are those trained in biomedicine ignorant of folk medicine and its accomplishments.

This paper is an account of how a Navajo community set up its own medical school and how a non-Indian psychiatrist became involved in it. In order to understand what happened one must have some acquaintance with the nature of Navajo medicine. This subject has received an enormous amount of attention from anthropologists and other behavioral scientists. I will make no attempt here to review the extensive anthropologic literature except to recommend the great works of Haile (1950), Reichard (1938), and Kluckhohn and associates (1940, 1956, 1967 [see "References" in the Bibliography]). The psychiatric literature is less extensive. It includes the early article of Pfister (1932), which seems to me to be remarkably insightful and sound in spite of having been based on very little and quite secondhand evidence. The Leightons in 1941 described Navajo

Reprinted from the AMERICAN JOURNAL OF PSYCHIATRY, vol. 130, no. 6 (1973), pp. 663–66, by permission of the author and the American Psychiatric Association. Copyright 1973 the American Psychiatric Association.

ceremonials beautifully and explained many of their beneficial elements. Sandner (1970) reported his work with Navajo medicine men to the APA three years ago. Almost everyone agrees that the ceremonies work.

Background

Navajo practitioners generally fall into three categories. The herbalists know a variety of medicinal plants, which are used primarily for symptomatic relief. The diagnosticians are shamans who work by inspiration. By one of several techniques, such as hand trembling, crystal gazing, or star gazing, they divine the nature and cause of an illness and make an appropriate referral to a member of the third and highest status group, the singers. The singers (I will use the terms "ceremonialist," "medicine man," and "singer" synonymously) do the only truly curative work, and it is a school to train them that I will be discussing.

Navajo nosology classes diseases by etiology; identical illnesses often have similar symptoms, but they need not. Note that psychiatric nosology is similar, e.g., depression is often characterized by insomnia, but sometimes the reverse can be true. A seriously oversimplified statement of Navajo etiology is that disease is caused by a disharmony with the universe, including the universe of other men. A singer restores this harmony by performing a ceremony proper to the case. Little or no reliance is placed on herbs or other medicines and, as is the case with psychiatry (at least from the psychoanalytic viewpoint), this absence of organic measures confers high status.

No one seems to know precisely how many ceremonies there are, but there are many. Important ones last five or nine nights and are difficult and elaborate to a degree approached among us physicians, I think, only by open heart surgery. The proper performance of a major sing requires the presence of the entire extended family and many other connections of the patient. The immediate family must feed all of these people for days. Many of the people present have important roles in the performance, such as chanting, public speaking, dancing in costume, leading group discussions, and many other prescribed activities of a more or less ritualized nature. For the singer himself the performance requires the letter-perfect performance of 50 to 100 hours of ritual chant (something approaching the recitation of the New Testament from memory), the production of several beautiful and ornate sand paintings, the recitation of the myth connected with the ceremony, and the management of a very large and difficult group process.

Non-Navajo explanations of why all this effort helps anyone tend to be rather offensive to the medicine men themselves, and *their* explanations, if they should feel like giving any, tend to be unsatisfying to us since they are based on the supernatural. The difference may not be as great as it appears, however. Traditional Navajos talk frequently in symbols: "We are glad you came from Washington to talk with us. There are many mountains between here and Washington," which translates as, "Communication with the federal government is difficult. We are glad you are making an effort to improve it." They also reject the notion that they are using figures of speech. They do not attach as much significance to the distinctions among different levels of reality as we do, and like some poets, they reject as stupid and destructive any attempt to translate their words into ordinary language. Though it seems to me that their myths and chants are symbols of human social-psychological forces and events, they would regard such a statement as silly and missing the point. Nevertheless, I will make a slight attempt in that direction.

The Rituals

For the past six years, I have been practicing psychiatry among the Navajo people. I have often referred patients to medicine men (who in turn occasionally refer patients to me). I have also often consulted medicine men, and patients have often told me about the medicine men's traditional cures and their feelings about these cures. It seems to me, although my knowledge of the sings is very limited, that the ceremony performed is almost always symbolically appropriate to the case. Pathologically prolonged grief reactions, for example, are almost always treated with a ceremony that removes the influence of the dead from the living and turns the patient's attention back toward life. "Treatment of a dream by a dream," Pfister called it.

It seems to me that the singers and we psychiatrists are the converse of one another with regard to our attitude toward ritual. To them ritual is the main focus: What is unvaryingly their practice from one case to another is at the center of their thought. Informal interaction with the patient and his family is considered important in an informal sort of way. This kind of interaction is not what is taught explicitly but only what is taught by the by. Our ritual, which I would argue is fairly elaborate, is not taught as the central part of psychiatry; rather, the more varying interaction is taught explicitly to psychiatry residents—ritual being taught by the by. In any event the singers do manage an intricate family interaction that, I think, has several important effects: (1) the patient is assured that his family cares for him by the tremendous effort being made; (2) the prolonged and intense contact makes it inevitable that conflicts are revealed and, if things are handled skillfully, resolved; and (3) a time of moratorium and turning point are established.

At the time I first heard of the medicine-man school in 1967, I was already quite convinced of the value of Navajo medicine. Aside from the cases I had seen, I was greatly influenced by my contact with a singer named Thomas Largewhiskers. Mr. Largewhiskers, who is now 100 years old, agreed to be my consultant and to teach me a little of what he knew. I first looked him up after seeing a formerly psychotic patient who attributed her remarkable and well-documented improvement to him. At the time of our first meeting I tried to explain what I do and said that I wanted to learn from him. He replied, "I don't know what you learned from books, but the most important thing I learned from my grandfathers was that there is a part of the mind that we don't really know about and that it is that part that is most important in whether we become sick or remain well." When he told me some of his life story it impressed me that he had become interested in being a singer when, as a young man, he had had an accident and the singer who took care of him explained that it had been unconsciously determined.

Mr. Largewhiskers and many other extremely old men are still practicing very actively. There is a growing demand for their services—growing because the population is increasing and their belief in traditional medicine is continuing. The trouble is that younger people are not becoming singers. The reasons behind the lack of students are largely economic. To learn to perform even one short ceremony takes at least a year of full-time effort. To learn a major ceremony takes much longer, and many medicine men know several. Since the end of the old herding economy, almost no one can afford to give up earning a living for such a long time. At the time of starting the school for medicine men Yazzie Begay, one of its founders, said "I have been acquainted with several medicine men who have recently died. They were not able to teach the ceremonies which they knew to their grandchildren or to anyone else. Today their sacred instruments and paraphernalia are sitting unused."

The School

The school is at Rough Rock, Ariz., a community near the center of the Navajo Reservation. It is part of the Rough Rock Demonstration School, the first community-controlled Indian school. The Demonstration School was started in 1965, when the Bureau of Indian Affairs (BIA) gave the buildings and equipment to a nonprofit corporation of Navajo leaders called Dine, Inc. Dine helped the Rough Rock chapter of the tribe set up and elect its own board of education

(no one on the original board could speak English and all were ceremonialists) and then contracted with the board to operate an elementary boarding school. BIA contributed funds that would have been equal to the budget of such a school if they had been operating it; funds also came from the Office of Economic Opportunity (OEO) and other sources. Soon after the school began operations in 1966, the people became convinced that their ideas really were taken seriously in its daily workings, and several local people suggested setting up the medicine-man school to the board. It was pointed out at a board meeting that white people have medical schools and give students scholarships to attend them and that what was needed most on the reservation were new medicine men. Therefore they felt Rough Rock should set up a school for singers and provide scholarships.

The idea was taken up enthusiastically by the board, and the details were worked out over the course of the next year. It was decided to alter the traditional method of teaching and learning sings as little as possible. (The old way is by apprenticeship and takes place in the teacher's home.) It was also decided that each medicine man would teach two apprentices of his own selection; that is, application for admission to the school would be made by trios consisting of a medicine man and two trainees. The school board would select among them on the basis of the medicine man's reputation, the trainees' apparent ability, and the importance of and threat of extinction to the ceremony that was proposed to be taught. The medicine men were to be paid a very modest salary and the trainees considerably less for their subsistence.

Obtaining Funds

Ever since the Demonstration School started, I had been going there once a month or more to consult with the guidance counselor and teachers. At one time the school administration, at the direction of the board, was preparing a project proposal in an attempt to obtain funds; I was asked to attend a meeting about the project, and here my support for the proposal was enlisted. This was the first of several project discussions in which I took part, and ultimately the board kindly included me in the proposal. It was decided that I should meet regularly with the trainees to discuss non-Navajo medicine, particularly psychiatry. I strongly suspect that my in-clusion was a move to make the project look more reasonable to funding agencies.

I flatter myself that from time to time my col-leagues in the school and the trainees have been glad to have me around, but I am sure that I have gained much more from this than they have. Before the pro-ject could materialize, however, we had to obtain funds.

The first proposal was made to OEO, which turned it down. The second proposal went to the Training and Special Projects Branch of the National Institute of Mental Health (NIMH). This one was accepted, although not, I suspect, without some trepidation. At the time of the site visit by NIMH it became apparent how many mountains there really were between Rough Rock and Bethesda, Md. First of all, the weather became very bad and the site visi-tors felt they were stranded in Albuquerque, which is 250 miles away from Rough Rock. Luckily the school board was able to go to Albuquerque, so we had a meeting. Two incidents seemed to me to epito-mize the meeting. The first was a question from the visitors: "How can a project that supports the contin-uance of superstition promote mental health?" The reaction of the ceremonialist school board members was more restrained than I had expected. They an-swered at length, and I added my endorsement. The visitors seemed satisfied. Later one of them, in leaf-ing through the documents, said, "The project direc-tor is to be full-time, and the salary listed here is $5000. Can that possibly be right?" When that ques-tion had been translated, Mr. John Dick, the director in question, who was a medicine man a former school board member, asked anxiously, "Is it too much?" I am very grateful that the project was funded, and I know that the board is also appreciative.

The Training Program

The work began in September 1969 and is still con-tinuing. There are six medicine men and 12 trainees. Most of the original trainees are still in the program. One of the faculty members died during the first year and was replaced. The ceremonies being taught so far have been one and two nights in length, and almost all of the trainees have completed learning them. Soon they will be performing them for the first time. They will then go on to major ceremonies. Although the lessons (excluding the ones I teach) are conducted at various homes scattered over consider-able territory in which there are no paved roads, Mr. Dick as director maintains close supervision. He travels to each home and watches over the teaching and its results. As the trainees have progressed, he and other medicine men have tested them. My only criticism has been that Mr. Dick's supervision seems rather harsh at times. He has demanded continuous effort and has been very hard on some people whom he surprised when he thought they should be work-ing and they weren't. Still, apart from minor profes-sional jealousy, the group's morale seems high. The program has been well accepted, and there clearly will be a demand for the services of the graduates. Other communities are trying to start similar schools. Recently one of the medicine men had one of his students perform a sing over him.

My sessions are a full day every two weeks. Be-fore I started holding them I met with the medicine men to describe what I intended to do and to ask their permission. To my great pleasure they not only agreed to my plans but said they would like to at-tend along with the trainees. Attendance has varied from time to time, but usually most of the trainees are present as well as three to five of the medicine men. During the first year I talked about somatic medicine, attempting to cover elements of anatomy, physiology, pathology, diagnosis, and treatment. I discovered that the entire group, including the trainees, had considerable knowledge of anatomy and some of physiology. The sessions were lively. The medicine men and the trainees enjoyed trying out stethoscopes, otoscopes, ophthalmoscopes, and blood-pressure cuffs. Microscope slides of blood smears and pathology specimens were also very popular. In return I was learning more about cere-monial practice, although not as much as I was to learn the next year when we began discussing psychology.

One of the high points of the first year was a visit that the group made to the Gallup Indian Medical Center. It was characteristic, I thought, that the two things the medicine men most enjoyed seeing at the hospital were an operation and a particularly good view of a sacred mountain peak from the windows of the psychiatric ward. They also had criticisms and suggestions. They were horrified by the pediatric ward because the children were so lonely. They kept asking, "Where are the parents?" They urged that better provision be made for parents to stay with their children. They also suggested that we build two hogans at the hospital for ceremonial purposes. They remarked that they all had performed brief ceremonies in the hospital but that they could do more in a real hogan. They said that the medical staff could see the patients during the sing and could go back and forth if necessary. Their suggestion still has not been followed, but I hope that it will be soon.

During the second year I began discussing psychiatry, and in this area there has been more of a two-sided interchange. We have spent much time on European and Navajo notions of the unconscious, a subject in which difficulties in translation have been great. Navajo metapsychology still largely eludes me, but it is clear that the medicine men know about the dynamic interpretation of errors and dreams and were pleased to discover that all of us followed the same custom with regard to them. We all, it turned out, spend our first waking moments in the morning contemplating and interpreting our dreams. One of the medicine men gave an example. He had dreamt about an automobile accident and said that that kind of a dream meant something serious was going on within him and that in order to prevent some disaster from happening to him, it was important to perform a chant about it.

There has been a good deal of case presentation on both sides, particularly, for some reason not clear to me, regarding returned Viet Nam veterans. My feeling of trust and closeness to this group ultimately became such that I presented my own case, describing some things that had led me to enter my analysis and something of the analysis itself. When I finished this rather long account, one of the singers asked me the name of my analyst and where he is now. When I told him, he said, "You were very lucky to find a man who could do so much for you. He must be a very intelligent person."

Another high point for me was demonstrating hypnosis. The group ordinarily looks half asleep—as seems to be the custom with medicine men in meetings. This was unnerving at first, until I found out from their questions and comments that they had been paying very close attention. When hypnosis was demonstrated, however, they were obviously wide awake, although at times I wondered if they were breathing. Working with a carefully prepared subject (I was unwilling to face failure before this audience), I demonstrated a number of depth tests, somnambulism, age regression, positive and negative hallucinations, and some posthypnotic suggestions. When I was done, one of the faculty members said, "I'm 82 years old, and I've seen white people all my life, but this is the first time that one of them has ever surprised me. I'm not surprised to see something like this happen because we do things like this, but I am surprised that a white man should know anything so worthwhile." They also pointed out the resemblance of hypnosis to hand trembling, a diagnostic procedure in which the shaman goes into a trance and his hand moves automatically and indicates the answers to important questions. After we had discussed the similarity, they asked that my subject, a young Navajo woman, diagnose something. I objected, saying that neither she nor I knew how to do this and that it was too serious a matter to play with. They insisted that we try, however, and finally we decided that a weather prediction was not too dangerous to attempt. They were particularly interested in the weather at that time because we were in the midst of an especially severe drought, and someone in the community had predicted that it would continue for another year. When my subject was in a deep trance, I instructed her to visualize the weather for the next six months. She predicted light rain within the week, followed by a dry spell of several months and finally by a good rainy season in late summer. I make no claim other than the truthful reporting of facts: She was precisely correct.

My involvement in this project has, of course, been extremely interesting to me. It is hard, however, to assess the effects of the project on the medicine men and on me. The medicine men say that they know better when and how to refer patients to the white doctors, and I think they feel more kindly toward us. In turn, I feel better able to understand my Navajo patients and know better when to refer them to medicine men. I have adopted some Navajo styles of thought, I think. I use hypnosis more than I used to. And one of my Navajo colleagues in the Indian Health Service Mental Health Program claims that I try to act like a medicine man all the time.

30

Mothering and the Practice of "Balm" in Jamaica

William Wedenoja

William Wedenoja has conducted field research in Jamaica since 1972, specializing in, among other interests, Afro-Jamaican religious cultism and folk healing. In this article, he centers on the gender of healers, a subject rarely treated in anthropological literature. In particular, Wedenoja aims his research at women who practice Balm, an Afro-American folk healing tradition in Jamaica that, he maintains, brings about maternal transference, encourages patients' dependency and regression, and appears to be a ritualized extension of mothering. Traditional therapy in Jamaica can be complex at first glance, but the author makes a clear distinction among Balm healers, obeah men (sorcerers), and scientists (who provide their clients good luck charms) and demonstrates the relationship of these specialists to Myalist healing cults, Revivalism, and Pentecostalism.

Wedenoja explains the incompatibility of so-called biomedical (modern) practitioners with the majority of Jamaicans whose disease etiology is not restricted to Western explanations of illness but includes ghosts (duppies), attacks by obeah men, fallen angels, demons, ancestor spirits, and the devil himself. The charismatic Mother Jones typifies Balm healers in Jamaica, and Wedenoja's description of her shows the importance of her strength and powers in primarily combating spiritual afflictions. The characterization of Mother Jones and others who practice Balm goes far in explaining why the author feels the feminine powers of women are vital to successful curing. Wedenoja's discussion of diagnostic divination ("concentration") is reminiscent of Lehmann's article, "Eyes of the Ngangas," in this chapter and suggests that healing, in all its forms, represents the strongest remnants of African culture in Jamaica.

. . .

Jamaican peasants show great concern for illness. It is a very common topic of discussion and a source of constant anxiety. There is, however, little understanding of the scientific theory of disease. Illnesses are blamed on drafts and exposure to cold temperature or imbalances of blood or bile in the body (M. F.

Mitchell 1980: 28). They are also, perhaps more often, attributed to spiritual causes.

According to one Balm healer, the majority of illnesses are "chastisements" from God for "disobedience" to His ways. However, another said that "most sickness coming from nigromancy," which refers to Obeah (sorcery), and this is the most common belief. In the behavioral or perceived environment of Jamaican peasants, there are four types of malevolent spirits that can cause suffering: *duppies* (ghosts), fallen angels, demons, and the devil. In addition, ancestor spirits may punish their

Reprinted from Carol Shepherd McClain, ed., WOMEN AS HEALERS, CROSS-CULTURAL PERSPECTIVES (New Brunswick and London, 1989), pp. 76–97, by permission.

descendants. Jamaican peasants also worry that neighbors and relatives will turn, in envy or spite, to an *obeahman* (sorcerer), who has the supernatural power to manipulate spirits and use them to do harm.

The first resort in cases of illness is, of course, self-medication. Though Jamaica has a lengthy and extensive tradition of folk cures, it is dying out and rapidly being replaced by over-the-counter drugs. If an illness persists for several days, help may be sought from a private doctor or a government medical clinic, but there is widespread dissatisfaction with them. A sophisticated comparison of ninety-seven patients of healers and doctors in Jamaica by Long (1973: 217–32) showed that Balm healers are better liked, spend significantly more time with patients, and give more satisfying diagnoses than doctors.

The expense of a doctor's examination and prescription drugs is a serious drain on the financial resources of the average Jamaican, and seeing a doctor often involves significant travel and a long wait at the office. The greatest problem with the doctor-patient relationship, however, is communication, which is inhibited by cultural and class differences.

Doctors and patients normally come from separate subcultures of Jamaican society; they use different terms to describe symptoms and label diseases and they hold different beliefs about etiology and treatment. Consequently, a doctor may find it difficult to elicit diagnostically meaningful symptoms from a patient, and a patient may not understand a doctor's diagnosis or the purpose of prescribed medication. In addition, a patient may regard diagnostic inquiry as a sign of incompetence, because it is the custom of Balm healers to divine an illness before speaking with a patient. These factors undermine a patient's faith in a doctor and his expectation of successful treatment.

. . .

In general, rural Jamaicans are dissatisfied with the treatment they receive from doctors and have little faith in their effectiveness. Moreover, they believe doctors are incapable of dealing with illnesses of a "spiritual" nature. Therefore, many turn to religion and folk healers for relief.

A patient may consult an obeahman or a "scientist," but these magical practitioners are not generally viewed as healers. Obeahmen are widely feared for their power to curse others and control ghosts.

People turn to scientists principally for good-luck charms like rings and bracelets, which are used to avoid accidents or to bring success.

Balm, which has been practiced for over one hundred years in Jamaica, is closely associated with an indigenous religious cult called Revival. Although Jamaicans regard Revivalism as a Christian faith, it is actually a syncretic, Afro-Christian religion that relies heavily on the intervention of spirits, often through dreams and "trance" states. Revival cults are descended from Myalist healing cults, which emerged in the late eighteenth century to counter Obeah (Wedenoja 1988). Many Revivalist ceremonies and practices are concerned with the prevention or alleviation of illness and misfortune, and about half of all Revival cults offer treatment for outsiders as well as members. Some Revivalists operate *balmyards* devoted entirely to the practice of healing. These healing centers employ Revivalist beliefs and practices but are not Revival cult centers.

. . .

Healing in Balmyards and Revival Cults

Jamaican peasant culture makes a distinction between the sacred and the profane, referred to indigenously as the "spiritual" and the "temporal." Revivalism is commonly called "the spiritual work" and Balm is often called "spiritual science," because they deal with spirits, treat spiritual afflictions, and rely on trance states. Although God is held to be the source of their healing power, the power is delivered to them through angels by means of the Holy Spirit. In contrast, Obeah is called "temporal science" because it can be learned and is not a gift. Moreover, Revivalists and balmists routinely rely on visions, dreams, precognition, glossolalia, and ceremonial possession trance, whereas the obeahman depends on magic and does not use altered states of consciousness.

The Balm healer is essentially a shaman, a person who has received—generally during a severe illness—a spiritual "calling to heal the nation" and the "spiritual gifts" of divination and healing. The balmist's power to heal is based on spirit mediumship; she works with angel familiars who advise her in diagnosis and treatment.

. . .

Patients are called out of a healing service, one at a time, to a shed where they are bathed in water that herbs have been boiled in. This bath is normally accompanied by the recitation of psalms. After being bathed, the patient is led to a private room for a consultation with the healer.

In order to diagnose an affliction, a Balm healer will perform a spiritual divination or "reading," which psychologically is an institutionalized form of empathy. There are several ways to read a patient, but in all cases symptoms are never elicited from the patient prior to a reading. The balmist must demonstrate her gift of healing by telling the patient what his or her problems are. One of the more common methods of divination is called "concentration": typically, the healer will gaze intently at a silver coin or a plant leaf in a glass of water until a "message" from an angel is received in her mind. Other forms of reading include interpreting the movement of the flame of a candle, reading a patient's tongue, card cutting, passing hands over the body of a patient, interpretation of dreams, and palm reading. Very powerful healers may be able to read patients simply by looking at them.

Balm healers deal with every conceivable form of human suffering except serious wounds and broken bones, but the most common complaint is pain in any part of the body. Another frequent problem is a vague syndrome called "bad feeling," which is generally characterized by sudden onset, "feeling out of self," losing self-control, feeling weak and fearful, profuse sweating, and fainting. Other popular problems include weakness, indigestion, headaches, and a feeling of "heaviness" or "beating" in the head. Every healer sees some cases of paralysis, blindness, crippled limbs, deafness, and dumbness. Mental disorders are almost always blamed on spirits, and they are frequently treated by healers. Patients also complain of problems in living such as excessive worry or "fretting," difficulties in raising children, and conflicts with family members, boyfriends, girlfriends, or spouses. Many patients believe that neighbors or relatives are trying to "kill" them—that is, using sorcery on them. Some are filled with hate and want to harm others supernaturally.

. . .

Balm healers specialize in spiritual afflictions. Although they usually provide or prescribe herbal remedies and common drugs, they also use rituals and magical items to counteract spiritual forces. Balmists routinely tell their patients to burn candles or frankincense and myrrh, recite prayers, and read psalms. They often anoint patients with lavender oil and perfumes or tell them to fast to "build up the spirit." Sometimes they will open and close a pair of scissors over the head of a patient to "cut"—that is, to exorcise—a spirit or use a padlock to "lock" a spirit.

A belief that conversion to Christianity and the living of a Christian life will protect one from Obeah and ghosts has been prevalent in Jamaica since the eighteenth century. Revivalism had its origin in antisorcery movements, and many of its ceremonies involve ritual combat with ghosts. . . .

Portrait of a Balm Healer

Ethnographic fieldwork is a fortuitous enterprise. By chance rather than by design, the hamlet I chose to live in had a very successful Revival cult led by a popular healer, who made me her "godson" on my first visit with her. During the following year and a half we spent a great deal of time together, and I came to know her as well as I have ever known anyone.

The Reverend Martha Jones, generally called "Mother" Jones (these are pseudonyms), is a stocky sixty-four-year-old black woman who stands about five feet five inches tall and weighs about 140 pounds. She lives with about thirty followers and children in a large house next to her church, which she founded in 1950.

Mother Jones was born in the community where she now lives, and spent her first twelve years there. Her father, who died in 1953, made his living as a painter and was also a leader in the local Missionary Alliance church, where she was baptized. She describes him as a quiet, strict, stern, sober, and hardworking man, who was close to her. Her mother, who died in 1937, was a housewife who gave birth to ten children, four of whom are still living. She too was quiet, strict, and home-loving.

Mother Jones was sickly throughout childhood and worried constantly about getting ill or hurt. She contracted malaria and typhoid fever, and lost her hair. Because she was their youngest child and so sickly, her parents were very protective, even keep-ing her from school, and gave her a great deal of attention.

At the age of twelve Mother Jones went to Kingston to live with an older sister, and she worked there as a maid for eighteen years. She married a black American sailor when she was twenty-two but never had any children. In her late twenties she had a number of "spiritual experiences"—epileptiform states and visions—and went to a Balm woman who told her she had a "spiritual gift."

Mother Jones moved to Washington, D.C., when she was thirty to work as a parlormaid for the British ambassador, but she became "crippled" during her first year there and received a vision telling her to re-turn to Jamaica and start a healing ministry. After an-other year in Kingston, she and her husband moved to her home town and started a "work." Her hus-band, however, left in the following year, and she has not seen or heard from him since.

Mother Jones was ordained in the National Baptist church in 1960 and appointed "overseer" for four or five churches in the area. They eventually broke away, and she changed her membership to an-other American sect. Over the past twenty-five years, every moment of her life has been devoted to her church and healing. She once remarked to me, "my task is not an easy one, my time is not my own. I couldn't tell the day when I am able to rest my head on the pillow." Every Monday she holds a healing service and sees from ten to thirty patients. Through-out the week other patients come individually to her. And her church holds a variety of services and classes almost every day or night of the week.

The people in her community have great respect for Mother Jones, and she has many devoted fol-lowers throughout the island and among Jamaican communities in England, Canada, and the United States. No one doubts her integrity and devotion. Everyone refers to her as "Mother" and relates to her as a mother. She shows concern not only for her patients and followers but for the entire commu-nity and society as well. She likes children and they are attracted to her. About twenty children live with her: some are ill or handicapped and others have been left with her for discipline or because their mothers are unable to care adequately for them.

Mother Jones says that people come to her for healing when a doctor fails to find anything wrong with them and they think it must be a spiritual, not a physical, problem. She sends her patients to a doctor if she thinks they need one and, for her protection, usually insists that they see a doctor before coming under her care; otherwise she could be liable for prosecution. She does not normally treat someone who is on medication, because "you can't mix the spiritual and the temporal."

Mother Jones tells her patients that "the Lord will help them and they will be healed just through faith, if they believe." But, she laments, "Some people want more. . . . They want something to take way with them. . . . They seem to think it is someone's bad intents. . . . They don't believe prayer and God will be able to keep them. . . . They feel they have to pay a lot of money . . . and get some superstitious some-thing, or they are unsatisfied." Unlike some Jamaican healers, who blame many problems on Obeah and duppies and provide "guards" (protective amulets), Mother Jones often rebukes these patients by telling them "their thoughts are not right."

Mother Jones told me she wanted to be a preacher rather than a healer, but healing was the gift she re-ceived through the Holy Spirit. Although she says that spiritual healing is not a gift one can learn or teach, she does have pamphlets on gospel healing and an ancient book on anatomy, and she listens to radio talk shows on health problems.

One of Mother Jones's "spiritual gifts" is an abil-ity to feel a patient's pain while she is "in the spirit." She also uses "concentration" to "read" a patient by staring at a glass of water with a leaf in it and asking the patient to drop a silver coin in "as a love offer-ing" to an angel. Like most Balm healers, she does not ask patients to describe their symptoms, because she is supposed to be able to "read" them. But after giving a rather general diagnosis, she will question the patient and discuss the problem in detail before prescribing treatment.

All of the patients at a Monday healing service re-ceive a glass of consecrated water and an herbal bath before seeing Mother Jones. In her private consulta-tions with patients she often assigns them specific chapters of Scripture to read and gives them a "heal-ing prayer" to wear next to the place of their illness. The latter is a sheet of "spirit writing," a propitiation to God written in cabalistic script while in a state of trance. She gives her patients "bush medicine" or herbs, prescriptions for vitamins and over-the-counter drugs, and offers advice on living. But she attributes her healing ability largely to her gift for spiritually absorbing a patient's suffering into her own body: "If you take their condition, you draw it off, the people goes free." She constantly complains about the suffering she bears for others, and says her gift might kill her if she entered a hospital.

A Healer's Personality

. . .

Mother Jones's roles as religious leader and healer appear to meet most of her personality needs well. They give her autonomy and dominance over others and gain her love, affection, and admiration. As a surrogate mother for many people, she can identify with her own mother, which gives her a strong sense of identity and relieves her of guilt. Healing provides her with a defense mechanism, undoing, which disguises her hostility toward others. It offers opportunities to criticize others and impose her strong sense of morality on those she dislikes. It is also, by means of projection, a way to satisfy her own need for nurturance. Mother Jones's ritual roles provide frequent and sanctioned outlets for her dissociative tendencies in the form of visions, trance, and ceremonial possession states. And her entire life is governed by such a narrow range of role expectations that she is seldom threatened and finds predictability and security in them. This restrictiveness is, however, something of a problem too: Mother Jones is always, in a sense, "on stage" and performing roles, which limits her personality and makes her lonely.

In order to have a successful balmyard or Revival cult, healing or leadership roles must be gratifying to patients and followers as well as to the healer or leader. I found several individuals who had a strong desire to become healers or leaders and had tried many times to establish a Balm practice or Revival cult, but had always failed to attract a clientele or devotees. They were not lacking in spiritual knowledge, but they did not meet the psychological needs of others. Given the renown and large following of Mother Jones, it is apparent that she not only meets her own needs but satisfies those of her patients and followers as well.

Mother Jones's characteristic optimism is encouraging to patients and raises their expectations for relief. Her sensitivity to the affective needs of others—that is, her warmth and concern—evokes feelings of love and security in her patients and allows her to establish rapport with a patient quickly. The psychological tests also show her to be a very creative and intuitive person, someone who thinks in a holistic manner and can easily make convincing interpretations of a case on the basis of a few clues.

Scheff (1975, 1979) has emphasized both the need for emotional arousal in therapy and the importance of group support if therapeutic change is to persist, and these elements are amply present in Mother Jones's practice. Her healing services employ drums and tambourines, singing and dancing, histrionic preaching, and ecstatic behavior, all of which is emotionally rousing. She holds periodic "Patient Tables," which are lengthy and ecstatic ceremonies, to honor former patients. And her patients often become involved in the regular cycle of ceremonies of her church, at which members are expected to "testify" often to their salvation or personal rebirth; normally, this involves declarations of the important influence of Mother Jones on their lives. The changes she instigates in her patients are then reinforced by her presence and by the support of other followers.

Women and Balm

. . .

This association of women with healing is not restricted to Balm and Revivalism. The medical system relies heavily on nurses and midwives, too. In rural areas, babies are delivered by government midwives, traditional nanas, or resident nurses at community clinics. The day-to-day operation of a rural hospital is managed almost entirely by the Matron and her nurses, with doctors serving mainly as surgeons and consultants. Obeahmen and scientists are, however, to my knowledge always men.

This sexual division of labor may be due, in part, to considerations of wealth and prestige. The practice of Obeah or Science is reputedly very remunerative and a source of great influence. But the practice of Balm, though it may bring one honor and respect, usually offers little in the way of income or formal prestige and power. As in most societies, men monopolize public positions of wealth and power and leave the less lucrative positions to women.

The association of men with sorcery and women with healing may also be based on cultural stereotypes about the sexes. In interviews and TAT responses, men are generally depicted as violent, troublesome, unreliable, untrustworthy, sexually aggressive, deceitful, and exploitative. Obeahmen are feared because they work in secret, with malicious ghosts (duppies), and cause harm or misfortune. Women, in contrast, are portrayed as peaceful, benevolent, nurturing, caring, responsible, and trustworthy. Correspondingly, Balm and Revivalism are benign institutions; their purpose is to counteract Obeah and malicious ghosts or provide protection from them. Thus we have a simple semiotic equation of Obeah with men, aggression, harm, and evil, on the one hand, and Balm and Revivalism with women, protection, helping, and good, on the other.

Mothering and Balm

. . .

The relationship between Balm healers and patients is a ritualized version of the mother-child relationship, and this is openly recognized in Jamaican culture. Healers are referred to as "mothers" and they are expected to play a maternal role. They are idealized as supermothers and adopted as surrogate mothers. Moreover, healers often refer to patients as their "children."

Familial idioms are used extensively in Revivalism, and they are not merely metaphors. Cultists behave according to the familial roles associated with their positions. The social organization of Revival cults strongly reflects the mother-centered pattern of the family in Jamaica, and one of the attractions of Revival cults is that they are fictive family groups.

The "Mother" is usually the central figure in a cult, and everything revolves around her. The "Armor Bearer," Mother Jones's "right hand," is in charge of the day-to-day activities of the cult, a role resembling that of the eldest daughter in a large family. Other women are referred to as "sisters." Some of the younger sisters, who are known as the "workers," serve the Armor Bearer much as younger daughters work under the eldest daughter in a family.

In general, women have instrumental roles that involve a great deal of work but little recognition, whereas men are given expressive roles that have prestige but little responsibility. The "Father" or "Daddy" is sometimes the dominant but more often a removed but respected figure. Many of the men are deacons, and they seem to play the role of uncles. The pastor of Mother Jones's church, who was raised by Mother Jones, is a handsome and charming young public health inspector. His official duties are to preach sermons and perform weddings and funerals, but he also fills the familial role, common in Jamaican families, of a favorite son who is admired by all. Other men are referred to as "brothers." Mother Jones always called me "my son," and her followers referred to me as "Brother Bill."

Mother Jones is a mother not just to her patients and followers but to the entire community. She is its moral standard and conscience and, more generally, a symbol of the love, affection, and devotion of mothers. There is a great respect for mothers in Jamaica, and the mother-child tie is the strongest bond in the society. Children are often reluctant to leave home and mother when they reach adulthood, and the most traumatic event in the life cycle is the death of one's mother. Mothers have almost total responsibility for their children; the role of fathers is largely limited to punishment for severe offenses. In addition, mothers delegate many domestic tasks and child-care responsibilities to their daughters, while sons are free to roam and play. The needs of rural children are therefore met largely by women.

The cultural patterning of the healer-patient relationship on the mother-child bond encourages maternal transference, regression, and the development of a dependency relationship. This can give the Balm healer a great deal of influence over her patients, because it makes them more receptive and suggestible. Moreover, the mother-child bond probably has some effect on all other relationships, because it is usually the first and most influential relationship in life. Maternal transference can thus provide the healer with an opportunity to make some rather fundamental changes in the personality and behavior of her patients.

Maternal dependency can be very supportive for patients. The healer, as a surrogate mother, consoles them, looks after them, and takes control when things go wrong. She gives them attention, affection, nurturance, encouragement, and offers them direction and purpose. Through attachment to her, they can regain a childlike sense of protection and security.

Western therapists would regard the dependency aspect of the healer-patient relationship in Balm as a problem, but it is not seen as one in Jamaica. Jamaicans are very sociable and they do not place much value on independence and self-reliance. Dependency is not condemned or discouraged.

. . .

Illness and Emotional Needs

. . .

Jamaican Balm exemplifies what I believe to be a basic principle of psychological anthropology, that every culture produces a unique set of personality needs and conflicts and develops institutionalized means for their satisfaction or resolution. Balm is not simply a traditional medical system but also, and perhaps more importantly, a source of psychological support. The psychological processes involved in Balm are not just techniques that facilitate healing but ends in themselves. Patients come to healers not only to be cured of illnesses but to gratify affective needs as well.

One of the dominant concerns of Jamaicans is "love." Many older people remarked to me that Jamaicans were once very "loving," but they are too "selfish" today. The plague of violence that Kingston has experienced over the past two decades is generally blamed on lack of love. Church sermons often dwell on social disorder, and Christian love is put forward as the salvation of society. "Peace and love" and the need for brotherly love and unity are central themes in popular music and in the ideology of the messianic cult of Rastafarianism. Mother Jones is of the opinion that most illnesses are due to "stress" in general and "lack of love" in particular. She says Jamaicans are not close, they fear each other, and they cannot give love to others. So she offers them her love, and tries to teach them to love others, to "make them whole."

What Jamaicans mean by "love" is closeness, caring, and concern for others—unity, sharing, and cooperation. Family ties are strong, and they want community relations to be close and friendly as well. Although there has probably been some erosion of *gemeinschaft* and a weakening of kin ties over the past few decades, I cannot agree with Mother Jones that Jamaicans are unloving. They are at least as "loving" as Americans, but they have a much stronger need for affiliation and place a higher value on interpersonal relations (Jones and Zoppel 1979; Phillips 1973). "Love" is a cultural focus, part of the Jamaican ethos, and one of the principal functions of Balm and Revivalism is to gratify that need.

Women and Healing

As Spiro (1978: xvi–xvii) has noted, "The practitioner of anthropology as 'science,' placing the local setting in a theoretical context, is concerned with the local as a variant of—and therefore a means for understanding—the universal." According to my analysis, the relationship between healers and patients in Balm is modeled on the mother-child relationship, a very strong bond in Jamaican society, and the mothering behavior of maternal figures such as Mother Jones provides emotional support for distressed and demoralized individuals. To what extent can this interpretation be generalized to other cultures?

A pioneering article by Carl Rogers (1957) identified congruence (genuineness and personality integration), unconditional positive regard (warm acceptance and nonpossessive caring), and accurate empathy as personal qualities that a healer must communicate to a patient if psychotherapeutic change is to take place. Additional research has indicated that effective healers are also intelligent, responsible, creative, sincere, energetic, warm, tolerant, respectful, supportive, self-confident, keenly attentive, benign, concerned, reassuring, firm, persuasive, encouraging, credible, sensitive, gentle, and trustworthy (J. D. Frank 1974; Lambert, Shapiro, and Bergin 1986). It should be noted, however, that these conclusions are based on research on American psychotherapists and thus the characteristics may not be universal.

Many of the personal qualities noted above seem to apply to women more than men. Women are said to be more empathic and have more positive feelings about being close to others, to be more cooperative and altruistic, to share more, to be more accommodative and interested in social relationships, to be more vocal, personal, and superior at nonverbal communication (G. Mitchell 1981), "more sensitive to social cues and to the needs of others" (Draper, quoted in Quinn 1977: 198), and more nurturant or kind and supportive to others (Martin and Voorhies 1975). In a study of kibbutz children, Spiro (1979: 93) found that girls showed more "integrative behavior"—aid, assistance, sharing and cooperation—than boys, and regularly consoled victims of aggression.

These claims about universal differences in adult male and female "styles" of behavior have apparently not been put to the test of a systematic cross-cultural study. However, there are excellent data on children aged three through eleven from the Six Cultures Study (Whiting and Whiting 1975), which found that girls are more intimate-dependent (touch and seek help) and nurturant (offer help and support) and that boys are more aggressive (assault, insult, horseplay) and dominant-dependent (seek dominance and attention).

Characteristics associated with women seem to be closely related to their role as mothers. Although this may reflect an innate predisposition to bond with and nurture infants (Rossi 1977), it can also be adequately explained by socialization practices. Women have the main responsibility for child care in every society, and they are prepared for that role in childhood. A well-known cross-cultural survey on sex differences in socialization concluded that there is "a widespread pattern of greater pressure toward nurturance, obedience, and responsibility in girls, and toward self-reliance and achievement striving in boys" (Barry, Bacon, and Child 1957: 332).

There is a close correspondence between the personal qualities of effective healers and women, and it seems to be due to strong similarities between the roles of healing and mothering. According to Kakar (1982: 59), many psychotherapists claim that "the 'feminine' powers of nurturance, warmth, concern, intuitive understanding, and relatedness . . . are essential in every healing encounter and for the success of the healing process."

If "feminine powers" are essential for healing, then women should, on average, be more effective at it than men. In fact, a review of research on the sex of psychotherapists concluded that "there appear to be some demonstrable trends, under certain circumstances, toward greater patient satisfaction or benefit from psychotherapy with female therapists and no studies showing such trends with male therapists" (Mogul 1982: 1–3).

It might also be reasonable to expect that the majority of healers in the world are, as in Jamaica, women. However, a cross-cultural survey of seventy-three societies by Whyte (1978) found that male shamans were more numerous or powerful in

54 percent; female shamans were more numerous or powerful in only 10 percent. This finding does not necessarily disprove the hypothesis that women generally make better healers. Personal qualities are only one factor in recruitment to a healing role and social, political, and economic factors can be important too. Given what we know about sexual inequality, it would not be surprising to find that women occupy healing roles when these roles are low in prestige or income, while men come to monopolize them when healing is high in prestige or income. It would be worthwhile to conduct a more extensive cross-cultural survey on the sex of healers in a study that would broaden the subject from shamans to include other types of healers and would attempt to identify social conditions associated with a preponderance of male or female healers.

Although "feminine powers" such as nurturance, warmth, and concern may, as Kakar suggests, be necessary for effective healing, they are probably not sufficient. Healers also seem to be firm and often domineering. For example, Raymond Prince (personal communication) notes that Nigerian healers, who are almost all male, are "abrupt, authoritarian, and sometimes punitive in their relations with patients, particularly psychotic ones."

It is probably more accurate to say that the personal qualities of effective healers are androgynous. Mother Jones is not only warm, empathic, caring, sensitive, and supportive with her patients but also firm, assertive, and domineering. Male shamans often dress in female clothing and assume female roles (Halifax 1979:24). I noticed that the husky voice of a Jamaican male healer changed to a high pitch when he entered a trance to treat his patients, and he became warmer and more empathic as well. Torrey (1972:103) described a male healer in Ethiopia as having a fatherly relationship with his patients and an "underlying warmth . . . partly masked by an authoritarian manner."

The personal qualities of an effective healer may vary with the degree of involvement of men and women in child care in a society. However, the maternal element of healing is probably more constant than the paternal element, because women are always heavily involved in child care and there is much greater variation in the involvement of men. The emphasis on mothering in Balm is a reflection of the strong degree of maternal dependency in

Jamaican society, which is encouraged by a high rate of father-absence and a general lack of involvement of men in child rearing. In addition, the androgynous character of Jamaican healers seems to be due to the fact that Jamaican mothers often have to play maternal and paternal roles in child care and family life.

Healing relationship may also vary with, and reflect, the style of parenting in a society. Jamaican mothers tend to be very domineering, restrictive, nagging, scolding, punitive, directive, and even dictatorial with their children. I observed a popular Balm healer who matched this description when I was asked to drive two patients to a balmyard. She was very abrasive and publicly scolded her patients, and I was quite surprised to hear my companions extolling her on our journey home. When I asked them if they would like her for a mother, they enthusiastically replied that she would be splendid.

31

Swallowing Frogs: Anger and Illness in Northeast Brazil

L. A. Rebhun

In northeast Brazil, women use the term swallowing frogs *to mean suppressing anger, hatred, or irritation, and withstanding unfair treatment silently. In connection with "swallowing frogs," women in L. A. Rebhun's field research also complained of such folk illnesses as* nervos *("nerves"),* susto *(shock sickness), blood-boiling bruises,* mao olhado *(evil eye), and* peito aberto *(open chest). All of these illnesses are discussed by Rebhun in this selection, each of which she argues is as much an emotional syndrome as a folk medical syndrome and should be seen as an embodiment of distress in which physical symptoms and psychological experiences are identical. Thus, physical, social, and personal aspects of a situation all serve as evidence about whose bad behavior is making the individual sick. Rebhun also suggests that, through the women's use of emotional folk medical vocabulary, combined with culturally recognized behavioral symptoms, these folk medical syndromes can serve as powerful tactics for controlling and manipulating others.*

Coração do pobre não bate, apanha.
The hearts of the poor do not beat, they are beaten.

—Brazilian proverb

In Latin American folk medicine, emotion is recognized as a powerful force that can cause sickness. In addition, certain emotions, especially strong or unpleasant ones, can become sicknesses in themselves. In Northeast Brazil, both men and women suffer from emotion syndromes and the effects of suppressing strong sentiment, but the spectrum of allowed emotion is different for men and for women, as are the moral connotations of particular emotions; men and women also have different permitted means of expressing particular sentiments. While conducting

"Swallowing Frogs: Anger and Illness in Northeast Brazil" by L. A. Rebhun from MEDICAL ANTHROPOLOGY QUARTERLY, December 1, 1994. Copyright © 1994, American Anthropological Association. Reprinted by permission. [Endnotes and some references have been omitted for the present volume.]

fieldwork in Northeast Brazil, I often heard women say that they had to "swallow frogs" (*engolir sapos*) in particular situations. They used the term to mean both suppressing anger, hatred, or irritation, and putting up with unfair treatment silently.

In connection with "swallowing frogs," women also frequently complained of folk illnesses like *nervos* ("nerves"), *susto* (shock sickness), blood-boiling bruises, *mal olhado* (evil eye), and *peito aberto* (open chest). These syndromes constitute an interrelated group of emotion-based ailments, generally typical of women, which form part of sociomoral discourse on the proprieties of social interaction.

They may also be seen as symptoms of the pain of bridging gaps between cultural expectation and personal experience in emotion, a process neither easy nor simple. Often, several similar folk medical complaints are interrelated, as in the Northeast Brazilian versions of "nerves," susto, evil eye (cf. Scheper-Hughes 1992: 173) and peito aberto. A patient may be diagnosed with any or all of these, and the diagnosis reflects more opinion about the patient's personality and personal situation than the details of her symptoms. All of these complaints have in common strong sentiments such as anxiety, shock, envy, hatred, and anger, which are both common and disturbing in women who are generally expected to be self-sacrificing, loving, and generous. Diagnosis of one or more of these ailments reflects opinions on the appropriateness of a woman's experience of negative emotions.

These ailments are as much emotional as folk medical. As Finkler has shown, the idea that these kinds of syndromes are body metaphors for psychological distress is too Cartesian; they are better seen as embodiments of distress in which body symptom and psychological experience are one and the same (1989: 82). The physical and psychological also combine in social aspects of folk medical diagnosis. To say that one is suffering from "nerves," for example, is to describe both a set of symptoms and a psychosocial situation.

Individuals use emotional folk medical vocabulary as one aspect of self-presentation. Speakers combine behavioral symptoms (trembling, limping, and so forth), gossip about social situations, and such emotional indicators as facial expression, other body language, and voice inflection with folk medical vocabulary to create evidence for moral interpretations of their situations. Physical, social, and personal experiential aspects of their situation all combine as evidence for the truths of their moral assertions about whose bad behavior is making them sick. Because of embedded moral discourses, emotional folk medical syndromes can become powerful tactics in the struggle to control and manipulate friends, neighbors, and family members.

Emotion and Folk Illness

Over the last two decades, cross-cultural research has revealed how deeply culture and emotion are interwoven, how sentiments are shaped by the very disparate vocabularies of different languages, how cultural expectations shape emotional expression in particular circumstances, how intellect and emotion are indistinguishable in many cultural settings, and how medical and emotional concepts are intertwined in the folk medicine of many cultures.

Some folk medical vocabularies incorporate folk theories of emotion, as in the Andean *pena* in which

suffering, seen as inevitable, is believed to slowly turn the heart into stone, causing chest pains, sadness, erratic thinking, and, in extreme cases, rage attacks (Toussignant 1984: 387). Others express sociomoral concepts as when evil eye is attributed to the emotions of envy, jealousy, and anger, thought to be wicked and therefore destructive. Emotional folk medical complaints may also reflect ethnicity or group membership, constitute tactics in attempts at social manipulation, or embody distress not otherwise expressable. Such complaints may constitute what happens when people are not able to live up to the emotional expectations of their cultures, or when emotional expectations are contradictory, convoluted, or in flux.

"Nerves," susto, evil-eye sickness, and analogues of open chest have been described in other Latin American settings, often as separate syndromes, each with its own etiology and symptoms. They have been called culture-bound or culturally mediated syndromes and seen either as embodied expressions of psychosocial distress or as local variations of universal human psychiatric diseases.

Variations of such syndromes as evil eye and "nerves" can be found throughout the Mediterranean, North Africa, Latin America, and parts of Great Britain, as well as in some areas of North America. The great variety in diverse forms of such syndromes as evil eye, for example, has led some to posit that it is not one but rather several different syndromes while others insist that it constitutes a related cluster of variations on the same themes. In either case, both evil eye and "nerves" are complex, multivocal, multimeaning syndromes, so that different interpretations and significances may attach to them in dissimilar cultural settings or even in distinct circumstances within one cultural setting.

Field Site and Methods

From December 1988 to December 1990, I conducted research on emotion, family relations, and folk ailments in the context of Brazil's shifting economy. I worked in the Northeast Brazilian city of Caruaru, Pernambuco (population 200,000), and neighboring villages, using a combination of methods in my research, including both direct and participant observation, survey of archival sources and prior research on the region, interviews with local politicians and other officials about the legal framework of marriage, domestic violence, and child custody, and 120 interviews with local residents.

Because I was interested in extended networks of kin, friends, and neighbors, I used a snowball sampling method that has been shown to be effective in studies of small populations (Bernard 1994: 97–98). Interviews addressed demographic issues (age, marital status, birthplace, and so forth) and the meanings of words comprising emotional vocabulary, including what is called *sentimento* (sentiment) in local parlance as well as words used to describe body states considered part of sentiment. In addition, I asked informants to tell me their life stories and to comment on things that had happened to them and those they knew, for thematic analysis. I also interviewed religious healers and their patients about emotion-related folk medical complaints.

Brazil's Northeast is its most impoverished region, characterized by monetary instability, extremes of social inequality, low life expectancy, and very high infant mortality (IGBE/UNICEF 1986; Nations and Amaral 1991: 208). The past 30 years have seen the largest rural-to-urban migration in Brazil's history: one in five Brazilians migrated to cities between 1960 and 1970 (Perlman 1976: 5), and by 1980 55 percent of the Northeast's population was urban (de Araujo 1987: 167). Caruaru is the first urban stop for many former rural residents. Economic disarray has intensified reliance on social networks of friends and relatives. The region's population, struggling with new economic patterns in the midst of abject poverty, endemic disease, and an unstable economy, is deeply dependent on relatives and friends for the goods, services, and connections they need to survive. However, unable to trust old solidarities in the face of new, urban opportunities, they are frequently wracked by anger, resentment, and envy, all of which find expression in folk medical complaints.

Despite its relatively large population, Caruaru is organized like a series of villages pushed together. Residents know their immediate neighbors very well, and city blocks are often inhabited by single extended families. But few people have friends living more than a few blocks away, and many neighborhoods are inhabited by members of no more than two or three large extended families. Often, these families also have members in any of several small towns within about an hour's commute by bus of Caruaru. Economic and social ties to these out-of-town relatives are often stronger than ties to fellow Caruaruenses from different neighborhoods.

The Northeast is a semiarid region, subject to periodic droughts but lacking the reservoirs, irrigation, and piping technologies that would make it fully habitable. To the poor, life is a *luta* or struggle in which people survive through a combination of astute manipulation of opportunity and the capacity to endure suffering.

In Caruaru, economic opportunities include work in its famous markets, blue jeans factories, and the burgeoning tourist trade, centered on the sale of little clay figurines. My informants were drawn largely from the lower working class, including housewives, market vendors, blue jeans pieceworkers, factory workers, bakers, seamstresses, maids, baby-sitters, and laundresses as well as their auto mechanic, artisan, and factory-worker male companions. In addition, I interviewed a number of local school teachers and some farmers and field workers from the rural zone. They ranged in age from 14 to 78, with most in their 30s and 40s. Most were at least nominally Catholic, although about a third were Seventh-Day Adventist or other Protestant.

Power, Interpretation, and Vocabulary in Emotional Folk Ailments

Both the study of folk medical systems and that of emotion cross-culturally have been influenced by Foucault's emancipation of the concept of power from strict confinement in the political sphere to something immanent in all social bonds, ascending from the micropolitics of interpersonal relations, through local institutions, to national and international establishments (Foucault 1986: 229–235). As the interpretive nature of both medical diagnoses and emotional labeling has become clearer, so has the power struggle underlying interpretation. Lutz's point that emotion is a "cultural and interpersonal process of naming, justifying, and persuading by people in relationship to each other" (1988: 5) is equally valid for folk medical diagnoses.

Especially with emotion-related folk syndromes, the questions of whether, when, and how to be sick are important elements of social stratagems. As

Crandon asserts in a study of susto in Bolivia, the folk-illness label constitutes a social judgment about the situation of the sufferer. Crandon suggests that researchers ask not "what is susto," but rather "why is susto diagnosed in any particular case," since the same constellation of symptoms can also be diagnosed as indicating any of several other folk syndromes (Crandon 1983: 154). The same question can be asked of "nerves," peito aberto, and evil eye. What do these diagnoses mean, how are they interrelated, and how do they fit into the micropolitics of power in families and local communities?

One of the ways these diagnoses fit the micropolitics of family power is in their gendered nature. Men and women become angry at different things, and express their anger differently. In addition, the moral connotations of angry behavior are different for men and for women. A man, for example, may drink himself to unconsciousness or beat his wife and children regularly with little serious social consequence from his point of view, while women are more likely to express despair through folk medical syndromes. While both men and women see poor people as suffering strugglers, the religious veneration of suffering as a key social value is greater for women than for men. Women's suffering is both a consequence of their powerlessness vis-à-vis men and an image used to manipulate men through guilt (Rebhun 1993). While both men and women see themselves as oppressed by the opposite sex, there is also general agreement that women suffer more because of men than men do because of women.

Swallowing Frogs: The Cultural Context of Anger

The folk syndromes of "nerves," evil eye, peito aberto, and susto are interrelated through their relation to strong emotions, especially anger. Despite an infectious public joyousness and open sensuality, Northeast Brazilians tend to display a profound distrust of particular strong emotions, especially envy, anger, and certain forms of grief, which are seen as socially disruptive because of their very intensity (Nations and Rebhun 1988; Scheper-Hughes 1992). At the same time, people encounter many reasons to feel these, from the anguish of frequent bereavement, to the frustrating humiliations of trying to get basic services from an uncaring government bureaucracy, to the injustices of poverty, to the many betrayals perpetrated by those who are supposed to love one another.

My informants spoke of evil eye, "nerves," peito aberto, and susto as the result of their own and others' anger (raiva, cólera), hatred (ódio), fear (medo), envy (inveja), and worry (preocupação). Sadness (tristeza), grief (pena), and depression (depressão, abatimento) also figured into the experience of these ailments. Commonly, it was not the expression but rather the suppression of these emotions that was seen as causing sickness.

The word my informants most frequently used to refer to anger was raiva, from the Latin rabia, meaning madness. Raiva also refers to the disease rabies. Brazilian dictionaries tend to define raiva by using the word ódio (from the Latin odi, "I hate"), although bilingual dictionaries give "raiva" as "anger," and "ódio" as "hatred." The Brazilian Dicionário Aurélio lists as its second definition of raiva (after the disease) "the violent sentiment of hatred [sentimento violento de ódio]." Unlike the English, where anger, anxiety, and strangulation are etymologically associated, in Brazilian Portuguese, anger, hatred, violence, and the disease of mad dogs are associated.

Emotions have associated scenarios; that is, any given sentiment is bounded by beliefs about what situations properly inspire it, how it ought to be expressed or not expressed, and what the consequences of its experience should be, both for the individual and for the group. In Brazilian Portuguese, anger is violent, powerful, and associated with a dangerous disease. Its associated scenarios include furious action, attacks, fighting, and the possibility of death. It is no wonder that so many Northeast Brazilian women find it a particularly frightening, dangerous emotion to experience and to inspire in others.

Emotion also constitutes a moral idiom, it is a moral reaction to a particular perception of events. The moral statements implied through emotions are complex for several reasons. For one, they depend on shared understandings of the presumptions underlying them, and these understandings may not be as similar as people assume.

In Northeast Brazil, disagreements about who has wronged whom are common. Through gossip and argument, the legitimacy of the participants' emotions and their response to those emotions as well as the facts of any given case are analyzed and reanalyzed by the social group (cf. Crandon 1983, who describes a similar process in Bolivia). By communicating sentiment either in words or symptoms, people make moral arguments for their point of view on each others' behavior. Emotion-related folk ailments become statements in the ongoing struggle to control one another's behavior through moral suasion. Because the facts of any given case may be ambiguous and because the implications of any given emotion are also ambiguous, multiple interpretations may attach to any given case (cf. White 1990: 51). Emotional life becomes a series of battles over interpretation and consequences of moral behavior.

This process is particularly acute in the cases of anger, hatred, and envy in Northeast Brazil. Averill (1982), in a discussion of emotion in the United States, posits that the emotions of anger, envy, and jealousy vary neither in their experience nor in their expression but rather in the nature of the perceived moral wrong that inspires them: anger is a reaction to a perceived injustice to oneself or one's group, jealousy regards one's loss to another as unjust, and envy sees the good fortune of another as an unacceptable threat to one's own situation. All three involve resentment of the power or the primacy of another over self (1982: 11). This analysis can also be applied to Northeast Brazil, where anger, jealousy, and envy are incompatible with the female obligation to be compassionate and selfless.

The Heat of Anger: Blood-Boiling Bruises

My informants did not see emotions as concepts but rather as a kind of energy that is physically present, taking up space inside their bodies, leaping the divide between bodies, and acting according to the same physical properties as water (cf. Solomon 1984). Anger was described as being like steam, rising from the boiling of its heat and hurting with its pressure unless expressed. Women described their unexpressed anger as suffocating, unrelieved pressure.

Women often showed me small bruises on their thighs and arms, which they attributed to the force of their blood boiling in their veins with anger. *Preto* (black) is used as a synonym for rage as in the phrase *fiquei preto* ("I was furious [black]"). Bruises may occur in conjunction with sick headaches, in which

pounding, shooting pains in the forehead and neck combine with nausea and dizziness.

> It feels like someone tied a rope around my head and stayed twisting it and tightening it, and I go vomiting and dying of anger, and I have to go lie down or I'll faint.

Despite the presence of hot, suffocating rage, women often described themselves as unable to express their strong emotions openly.

> Once my husband said to me, "Tonight I'm going to take you out." So I went, got my nails done, my hair done, new dress, put makeup on, and I waited, waited, waited. He did not come home that night. I was so angry, my stomach hurt with anger [raiva], I had bruises on my thighs, you know, my blood boiling, vomiting with hatred [ódio]. But I never said anything to him, undressed, went to bed. The next day, it was like it never happened. I never mentioned it, he never mentioned it. . . . I don't know why. I never forgot it, my stomach hurt for days. But I never said anything.

One reason for silence is fear of open conflict, especially given anger's violent associations.

> I want to say everything that I feel, you know, that I suffer, but I don't say in order to not cause problems. Understand, I'm like this, my daughter, I suffer in my nerves because I keep things inside of me. I can't express, I don't want to bother anyone, and I can't say what I want to say.

The unexpressed emotion does not go away; instead, it stays as a suffocating, sickening presence inside the body.

> When I am angry at a person, I stay with a suffocation imprisoned inside of me. . . . I stay shut up. I continue vibrating.

There are a number of reasons for this inability to express anger. In some cases, the woman is afraid that her emotion will overpower her self-control, leading her to actions she will later regret.

> I am a very aggressive person, when I am angry, I really lose control. I'm afraid of myself sometimes.

In other cases, the anger is diverted onto easier targets, especially children. The woman feels such an accumulation of outrage that small irritations like childish pranks become too much to tolerate and she explodes in violence.

Ave Maria! Too nervous! Ave Maria! I swear a lot, fight too much with my kids, I want to beat them, to kill them in that moment, but then afterwards I cry, I repent, I see in myself that it isn't a normal thing, you know? That I am very nervous. Whatever little thing, it's enough if I tidy the house and then my little girl drops something on the floor, Ave Maria! I'm ready to die. The children have a damned fear of me because I'm, My Virgin Mary! Explosive. It's anger.

Women may also be constrained by economic dependence and fear, especially women in physically and emotionally abusive relationships. For example, one informant I shall call Rejanne was unable to escape an abusive boyfriend for ten years. Married at age 12, at 13 she had been kicked out by her husband because of rumors of infidelity, and none of her small-town neighbors would take her in or give her work. Desperate to avoid being forced into taking up residence as a prostitute at a local bordello, she went to live with a man who offered her a home in return for sex and housework. He brought her far away to São Paulo and kept her locked in their apartment, beating her if he suspected her of talking to anyone other than himself. Socially isolated, economically dependent, physically and emotionally battered, young and alone in her desperation, she was terrified to leave him and unable to assert herself within their relationship.

I always had to swallow frogs, you know, because I was totally dependent on him. . . . Even when I knew I was right and he was unjust, I had to swallow it, I had to obey. I had to apologize, I had to humble myself and submit, and even thank him for mistreating me, in fear of my life.

Only when he brought her back to her hometown after ten years away was she able to escape him with the help of her parents, who had forgiven her youthful escapades in the intervening years.

Rejanne's story, while dramatic, was not unusual. Domestic violence is common, and legal penalties are few for abusive husbands. While some women leave men who beat them, resist, or fight back, many feel trapped by fear, family pressure, economic dependence, and/or fear of scandal.

Despite attempts to diminish the importance of anger, women feel strongly. Like bereaved mothers of infants who consciously suppress their grief

(Nations and Rebhun 1988: 162), angry women use specific techniques to calm themselves when they are angry, like slow breathing, clenching their teeth to avoid speech, drinking herbal teas, taking tranquilizers, lying down, praying, or leaving the area until they feel composed.

When I have a problem with anger, I only get better if I leave and walk because if I stay in the house I will get even angrier . . . if not we will come to blows, so I prefer to leave a little bit. I get a cigarette and go into the world, disappearing.

For others, "swallowing frogs" is so habitual that they do it without thinking. Infuriating events simply leave them speechless.

My neighbor arrived saying [my husband] was betraying me with another woman. I was all shut up, I shut up, my daughter, I didn't have any voice, I said nothing, I don't like to fight, I don't like to quarrel, to exchange words, I only like peace, I like unity in my house, understand. . . . I do everything to have peace inside my house, but it is a torment for a mother to rule over [dominar] all these people, to have lots of kids and not to have problems with arguments. . . . We get angry at something and our nerves get tired, isn't it just like that?

Anger is seen as a force or energy that can enter people's bodies, causing harm. It is especially dangerous to the weakest.

Did you see Dona Maria passing by here with that crippled daughter of hers? Because when she was seven months' pregnant, her mother-in-law made her so angry, she fainted with anger boiling inside her, and it burst the baby's head so she was born like that, can't walk, can't talk, all stiff. A pregnant woman can't get angry, shouldn't even be in a place where other people are angry.

Infants are often seen as suffering the effects of other people's anger, either directly in the form of blows struck in anger, or because some adult quarrel spilled over and hit them with the force of adult emotion. A fetus is vulnerable to any shock, anger, or stress its mother may feel while pregnant, and infants and small children are vulnerable to an atmosphere of resentment, or anger, envy, or hatred directed at their adult relatives. Depending on the strength of the emotion, it can kill or physically harm a baby, or, as it does with adults, it can leave the baby with a nervous temperament.

The Rezadeira

Although folk diagnoses are not specifically part of Catholic doctrine, they are most likely to be diagnosed by folk Catholic faith healers, called *rezadeiras* if female and *rezadores* if male. Folk Catholic faith healers use prayers, rituals, advice, herbs, and pharmaceuticals in their treatments of common ailments. The folk medical systems used by popular and religious practitioners do not make Western biomedicine's sharp distinction between diseases of the body or mind and other types of misfortunes. These healers are as likely to be consulted for a run of bad luck as for a physical complaint.

Of rural origin, rezadeiras now flourish in cities where crowding and poor sanitation increase sickness. Whereas rural Catholic healers are as likely to be men as women, in cities, most are women and the majority of their patients are also women. Rezadeiras treat patients with prayers mixed with rhymes specific to particular ailments.

Some ailments, such as fallen fontanelle, are unique to infants, whereas others, such as peito aberto, are typical of adults. Even when adults and infants are diagnosed as having the same syndrome, the symptoms are different. Such labels as evil eye or susto refer to irritability, frequent crying, or physical symptoms like diarrhea in infants; in adults they describe embodied emotional distress (see also Crandon 1983: 159–60).

"Nerves": Daily Anxiety

Illnesses called "nerves" have been described throughout Europe and the Americas (Low 1989). Like many other aspects of European and New World folk medicine, they can be traced back to ancient Greek medicine. Both Hippocrates and Galen posited the existence of physical structures in the body that translated the desires of the mind into the actions of the body. They called these "nerves" (Davis and Whitten 1988). In Northeast Brazilian folk medicine, the nerves are seen as little strings that control the muscles and transmit tension. They can get worn out by too much use in the form of worry and tension or by the accumulation of shocks. When that happens, the person becomes *nervoso*, or nervous, a permanent state.

The nervoso person frequently experiences headaches, trembling, dizziness, fatigue, belly aches, and sometimes partial paralysis, tingling of the extremities, and appetite disturbances. But the hallmark of the condition of nervoso is the inability to tolerate or control stressful emotions. Through constant exposure to the shocks of painful emotion, the "nerves" sufferer has become too sensitive to life's emotional hardships. Nervosa women described themselves as "uncontrolled" (*descontrolada*), prone to attacks of rage or bouts of crying (Rebhun 1993: 138–40).

Nervos is perhaps more an idiom of daily life than a medical complaint per se.

> It gets me in the nerves, this difficult life, that I bear it, bear it, bear it, bear it, but also I don't have patience, it gives me that hatred [ódio] inside of me, it stays that, that [thing] locked inside. I stay with too much anger.

Both men and women can be nervoso (Duarte 1986), but the symptoms of the condition have different connotations. To the extent that *nervosismo* (nervousness) is a state of victimization, a constant vulnerability in which the person has lost her ability to withstand emotional shocks, it is feminine. However, some of the behaviors associated with a nervoso individual, irritability, bouts of rage, and violent outbursts, are considered normal in men but unacceptable in women (cf. Dunk 1989: 38), whereas fits of uncontrollable crying or moments of intense, paralyzing terror are more acceptable as feminine symptoms. Nervosismo is not only more typical of women, but because women's emotional repertoire is less constrained than men's, they can adapt it to a wider range of situations and plumb it for a greater number of meanings than can men.

Nervosismo is a chronic state, often described as either an innate or an acquired personality trait. It is related to evil eye and susto because either of those can cause it and because, along with them, it forms part of a discourse on anger. The presence of too much anger inside the body frazzles the nerves, leaving them unable to stand even mild negative emotions.

Open Chest: Sickness and Emotional Vulnerability

Anger can either be the person's own suppressed rage, or it can be other people's anger that enters a body not properly closed. This state of dangerous emotional openness is called peito aberto (open chest). It is said to be caused by carrying too much weight, which makes the heart expand, opening the chest, and allowing evil influences to enter. Rezadeiras diagnose open chest by measuring a string twice against the patient's forearm and then looping it around the chest. If the measured length does not close securely around the chest (and it never does), a diagnosis of open chest is made. It is treated by tying the string around the chest, praying while making the sign of the cross over the chest, and pushing inward on the chest and breasts. Then the string is measured again and again looped over the chest. This time, it fits, and the rezadeira declares the chest properly closed.

I have argued elsewhere (Rebhun 1994) that the "weight" (peso) in open chest is a metaphor: the emotional weight of unshed tears, unspoken fury, unexpressed hatred. Women speak of these sentiments as taking up space inside their bodies, pressing against the inside of the face, the chest, or the belly, and having to be restrained with a physical effort. When the emotional weight becomes too heavy to carry, it bursts out, leaving openings where it left the body. Other people's anger and envy can enter these openings in the form of evil eye.

The expansion of the chest in peito aberto is related to the idea that a woman's heart is large and grows each time she comes to care about another person. When the "weight" of caring for and worrying about others becomes too great, the woman's heart expands too much and pushes her chest open. The condition of being open is generally seen as associated with women, because their genitals are seen as physically open in form and because their hearts are thought emotionally open. Openness has a specifically sexual connotation; the word fechada (closed) can be used to mean "virgin." Defloration, pregnancy, childbirth, and the accumulated weight of emotional troubles open women's bodies even more, while men remain with closed bodies and emotionally closed hearts that evil influences cannot enter as easily (cf. Robben 1988: 115).

Peito aberto is tied to evil eye because it is through evil eye that anger and envy enter the opened body. Rezadeiras' treatments for evil eye usually start with peito aberto, in an effort to close the body, and then proceed to remove any existing evil eye. Relief is thought to be immediate but temporary because the situations that give rise to peito aberto and evil eye are recurrent.

Evil Eye: The Sickness of Others' Anger

References to evil eye and attempts to deflect it are ubiquitous in Northeast Brazil. People often follow compliments with "but I don't give evil eye" or write the phrase "o seu olho gordo é cego p'ra mim [your evil eye is blind to me]" on truck bumpers or the walls of stores, restaurants, and booths in the marketplace. In addition, people ward off evil eye with amulets such as figas and tiny glass eyes (often blue), as well as small figures of Buddha, placed in corners or on windowsills with their backs to any potential watchers and with a small plate of coins or water nearby.

Evil eye is designated by a number of words in Brazilian Portuguese including olhado (gaze), olho gordo (fat eye), and olho grande (big eye). Mau olhado (bad gaze) is the most common of these terms. The Northeastern Brazilian evil-eye belief is similar to the belief that some people can cause harm by gazing while experiencing envy or anger found in northern Africa, the Mediterranean, and nonindigenous Latin America (Dundes 1980; Roberts 1976). In Northeast Brazil, as in these areas, the belief occurs in two forms that are not clearly distinguished; in one, evil eye is deliberately used by the evil hearted to cause harm; in the other it is inadvertent. Evil-eye beliefs have been explained as a consequence of the notion that one person's gain is another's loss (Dundes 1980; Foster 1965, 1972), part of the psychodynamics of patronage (Garrison and Arensberg 1976), and fear of loss of vital fluids (Dundes 1980).

Many Northeast Brazilian customs forestall any possible envy and therefore prevent evil eye. For example, guests are typically offered water, coffee, and food upon entering homes, at least in part so that their hunger will not lead to envy of the household's food. Evil eye beliefs also show up in responses to compliments and in any other situations that may involve envy or anger. The standard response to a compliment is to offer the object of admiration to the admirer, who is honor bound to refuse it. Infants are believed especially vulnerable to evil eye, partly because they are weak, and partly because they are so highly desired, inviting envy by the childless (cf. Dundes 1980). Babies are kept indoors as much as possible, and when carried outside, they are carefully hidden from view with elaborate clothing. The whole baby bundle is then shaded from the glare of the sun and the view of passersby under a shawl for transport outside the home.

Mothers also pin amulets to babies' clothing as a protection against evil eye (cf. Cosminsky 1967: 167). Anyone who admires the baby will be jokingly importuned to adopt it. In addition, childless women who enter homes may be told to take one or more of the children. This forces them to explicitly deny any desire for or envy of the children, deflecting any evil eye they might have cast.

Rezadeiras treat evil eye with Catholic prayers mixed with charms specific to the ailment. As one healer explained, to treat evil eye:

> I pray the Lord's Prayer, the Apostle's Creed, the Hail Mary, the Hail Holy Queen, then for olhado I pray like this: "with two you were put on," it's the two eyes, isn't it? "With three I take you off," [that is] with the powers of the three people of the Holy Trinity. Pray three times and the olhado heals.

Evil eye can cause infertility and bad luck, make cattle stop giving milk, or cause dishes to break, crops to fail, plants to die, and house walls to crack. It is also said to cause a number of physical complaints.

Like other folk illnesses, evil-eye sickness affects infants differently from adults (cf. Crandon 1983). In infants, evil eye is said to cause recurrent problems such as frequent ear infection, fever, or nagging cough, and also diarrhea and symptoms of dehydration. It can lead to death. In older children and adults, evil eye can cause any wound to delay healing, any recurrent or persistent symptom, diarrhea, or fever. It can also cause dry, frizzy hair, split ends, and hair loss. Evil eye also describes illness related to family tensions, as in the case of Nezinha, described below.

Nezinha: A Case of Evil Eye

One thirty-five-year-old woman from Caruaru I shall call Nezinha sought treatment from rezadeira Dona Maria for insomnia, headache, body aches,

and general distress. After praying a general blessing in her front room where five or six other women gossiped about their symptoms while awaiting treatment, Dona Maria invited Nezinha and me to share a Coca-Cola in the kitchen. This provided the opportunity for a more private consultation during which the healer questioned her patient at length about her personal situation while providing me with explanatory asides. Nezinha said that she had run away with a boyfriend at a young age. During the eight years she lived with him, she had three children. When her marriage broke up, she moved to her parents' house. Because of difficulties in the early years of her parents' marriage, Nezinha (the firstborn) had been raised by her grandmother. This was the first time she had lived for any length of time at her parents' house. At the time she moved back, her brother had been planning to marry his longtime fiancée and to live with her in the second story of the house, but the addition of Nezinha, her three children, her maid, and the maid's children to the household destroyed that plan. The wedding was put off indefinitely, and the household reluctantly set about absorbing the new members.

The maid and her young daughter earned their keep with household labor, but Nezinha was unable to find work until her brother's fiancée got her a job at the fiancée's place of work. The job was enormously important to Nezinha's self-esteem and her desire for independence. She longed to earn enough to establish her own household. The fiancée wanted to help Nezinha because she could marry only if Nezinha were out of the household.

Old resentments caused tension between Nezinha and her mother: her parents had never gotten along well; her brother resented her presence; and she suspected that the maid was having an affair with her father as she had years earlier with Nezinha's husband. Nezinha stated that all of these tensions had frazzled her nerves, leaving her permanently nervosa, with trembling and heart palpitations. Then something else happened that drove her over the edge.

> It happens that my brother had an affair with a friend of mine. So my mother liked it a lot, because she doesn't like his fiancée and she hoped he would leave her. So she told the fiancée about the affair in hopes they would break up. But he left my friend. So then my mother was angry at me about something and said to the fiancée that I was the one

who arranged everything for the affair, who introduced them, you know, but I didn't, it's a lie. So the fiancée had a fight with my brother. So now my brother is angry at me, thinking that I told his fiancée, but I didn't tell her; my mother did. The fiancée hates me because she believes my mother's untrue story. My friend is angry with me because she's angry with my brother and the whole family, and she also thinks I told, but I didn't. My mother is mad at me because, because, well because she's always mad at me! I didn't do anything! Everybody is mad at me. Whenever there's tension in the house the kids start fussing and hanging on me and I hate that and then I yell at them and I feel bad. And I am here without being able to sleep, with a headache, constantly sick.

The rezadeira diagnosed evil eye and open chest. She performed the requisite blessings and sold Nezinha a candle, telling her to place her anger at her mother in the candle, scratch her mother's name on its side, and burn it in the cathedral. In addition, she prescribed an herbal tea to be taken before bedtime and told Nezinha to invite the fiancée to go to a movie and ask her advice on how to treat headaches. She further advised that Nezinha should take the children to play on a ferris wheel set up for a forthcoming town festival to distract them from the family tension and work on trying to stay out of her mother's way. Dona Maria explained to us that Nezinha's friends and relatives do not mean to make her sick, and she had to help them help her get better. With the protection of the prayer to "close" her body to evil influences and the removal of her own anger to be burned up by the candle, they could not hurt her.

The herbal tea (chamomile) was to help her feel calm enough to sleep. By asking the fiancée's advice, Nezinha would communicate her friendship and also let the fiancée know that she was suffering from the situation. The fiancée would be obligated to help Nezinha in order to avoid feeling guilty, and helping her would restore the two women's friendship on which Nezinha's job depended. Dona Maria continued her interpretation of Nezinha's situation:

> Some people think that evil eye is a supernatural thing, but it isn't. It's that no one likes it when others are angry or jealous. And we always sense the feelings of others in the same way that we can see and hear. So we stay nervous, thinking of what could happen. Everyone is afraid to be abandoned or attacked. So the fear, the anger, and the anxiety combine, and the person stays sick. So you have to protect with the powers of God, calm, and also improve the situation for the person to get better.

Dona Maria's explanation of evil eye was not unusual. Although a few rezadeiras described evil eye as a supernatural force, most described it in naturalistic terms, as a kind of "energy" or, like Dona Maria, as a consequence of emotional interactions. Several rezadeiras described evil eye as a "superstition of the people," explaining that it is really a kind of tension caused by the awareness of other people's anger and envy. In choosing to diagnose evil eye, Dona Maria was making a statement about Nezinha's personal situation.

Susto: Fear and Violence

Variants of folk ailments called susto (fright sickness) or *espanto* (the sickness of fright from seeing a ghost) have been widely described in Latin America and among U.S. Latinos (Clark 1978; Crandon 1983; Foster and Anderson 1978; Gillen 1948; Madsen 1964; Rubel 1964; Toussignant 1979). There are four major theoretical explanations for susto beliefs. They have been interpreted as forms of depression, anxiety, or hysteria. Alternatively, they have been seen as socially defined sick roles, which afflicted individuals use to deal with stress by eliciting community attention, moral support, and temporary respite from obligations.

Susto has been described as a cultural label for physiological syndromes such as hypoglycemia (Bolton 1981) and certain kinds of diarrhea in infants (Crandon 1983; Nations 1982). Crandon, in a study of Bolivian villagers, posits that when the label susto is applied to adults, it constitutes a communal statement about the situation of the patient. She sees the diagnosis of susto as a claim of vulnerability, deprivation, and disenfranchisement (1983: 161–64). A similar interpretation can be made in Northeast Brazil, where susto can cause the sufferer to become nervoso, losing the ability to withstand emotional or physical strain calmly.

Susto also carries implications of mistreatment in Northeast Brazil. Although descriptions of susto from other areas have emphasized the role of ghost encounters and soul loss, my informants used it to refer primarily to three kinds of shock: the trauma of a sudden death; the anguish of discovering sexual betrayal; and the impact of violent blows. In some cases, two or more of these types of shock are viewed as causing susto.

> When my mother died, I was in the 22nd day of confinement after the birth of a child. I fainted . . . because I can't under any circumstances have a fright. And after that I kept on getting nervos . . . and then I suffered a terrible grief with my husband because he was with another woman. I was one day away from giving birth, wanting to give him a son, and he was with this woman. So I was very disgusted with this. So the two sustos together gave me this problem with my nerves. Sometimes I have a great anger that I can't avenge, it's like I'm crying with anger, it's locked inside of me. I get revolted, disgusted, any little thing happens and I can't stand it any more, I get hurt. It's nervos, is what it is.

The term susto also came up frequently in interviews when I asked about the cause of the death of a child. Saying a child died of susto was often a reference either to the child having been killed violently or to a miscarriage attributed to a strong blow to the belly of a pregnant woman.

> My mother had six children, three died and three stayed [with us]. They died because of susto, because my father, he beat my mother, so the cause of the deaths of my siblings was my father and the susto he gave. . . . I remember that my mother was pregnant with a baby that her name was going to be Taxa. My mother was preparing the bottle for my little sister Paxa, so Papa came up behind her and kicked her in the back so that her belly hit the stove, and the hot gruel fell on top of her belly. Later that day she started to hemorrhage and lost the baby, because of the susto.

Some women described their own nervosismo as due to the susto from beatings that also killed their unborn children. For example, one 34-year-old woman had lost 6 of her 13 pregnancies after beatings by her husband. Paula described each of these miscarriages as having been due to susto.

> They died of susto. It was like, I lost my second child because of susto. Oxente! Because my husband really passed the limits with me, grabbed me by my feet and swung me upside down, he hit my head over there on the chairs, and I was all—I hit my head there on the corner of the wardrobe, and I was dizzy. . . . I was in agony, he was drunk you know. . . . And I was pregnant, and then he knocked me down and he gave me a punch in the

belly, so I started to lose the baby, so I picked up my daughter, you know she was 8 months old, and I went running to Papa's house.

But like Rejanne, Paula was not on good terms with her family. Her father was furious about what he considered to be her husband's disgraceful behavior. Her husband had convinced Paula's father to let her marry him despite his reputation as a drunk, by declaring himself cured and proving it by remaining sober over the course of a year of engagement. But the night before the wedding he went out drinking with his friends.

> So when it was getting to be about 5 o'clock, the steer was arriving [a reference to the marriage cart], I received notice that he was sick at his mother's house. So we went to find him with my father, and so when we arrived he didn't know anybody, even his bride he didn't recognize, and the stink of rum on him! . . . He seemed to be possessed by a demon [endemoniado]. . . . I was afraid to approach him. And because of this my father was disgusted with him, that his eldest daughter was getting married and the groom would behave this way on the day of the wedding! He said it was an insult to his honor, a disgrace to his daughter. But I married him anyway, because I loved him.

Her father's rage was so great that he disowned Paula, saying that if she wanted to marry a disgraceful man like that, she would have to bear the consequences. While fleeing the beating in panic, she remembered her father's words and fearful of being turned away, doubled over in pain, she stopped along the way.

> And then in the middle of the road, I was squatting and hemorrhaging, I met my mother-in-law . . . and she said, "A fight between husband and wife you resolve at home" and she brought me crying and miscarrying back. So I lost that baby because of the susto, and the other ones later, and it got me in my nerves, that I just lived trembling all the time.

Paula did not think it was possible to leave her husband because she had nowhere to go and no one to help her raise her seven children. She also stated that although she did not love her husband anymore, she had pity (pena) for him, and she hoped that someday he would stop drinking. Believing that he was basically a good man, she regarded his drinking as a kind of demonic possession rather than an aspect of his character, as her father did.

She had suffered from nervos for many years until she had a profound religious experience while speaking with a Jehovah's Witness missionary who came to her door. She stated that the personal relationship she now felt with Jesus had enabled her to replace anger with loving compassion and thereby to bear her burdens without sickness. During the year and a half that I knew her, she did not report any symptoms of "nerves."

Folk Ailments and the Suppression of Anger

Emotion is a supremely social phenomenon. It is the idiom in which social bonds are negotiated and maintained, the substance of which social tactics are made. As a personal experience, emotion is rooted in the body and suffuses the psyche; as a social experience, emotion responds to interpretations of the actions of others and moral connotations of social situations. As a moral statement, it has a uniquely evocative potency, making it ideal for social manipulation. It frequently finds expression in the form of folk medical syndromes.

In Northeast Brazil, nervos, peito aberto, evil eye, and susto together form a discourse on the sickening power of anger. Although each of these syndromes has similar symptoms, they connote different things about the sufferer. Susto is a state of emotional vulnerability caused by one or more shocking events. It can lead to nervos, or the frazzling of a person's ability to remain calm through repeated worry, grief, anger, and sadness. Peito aberto occurs when a woman's heart expands to encompass all those for whom she feels compassion and, combined with the seething of her own suppressed anger, pushes open her chest, allowing negative influences to enter. Evil eye is caused by the envy and anger of others, victimizing the sufferer.

The folk models of these syndromes allow individuals to use them as claims about themselves and the actions and motives of those they blame for their condition (cf. Migliore 1983: 8). Susto and nervos are statements about the impossibility of withstanding stress, shocks, and violence. Peito aberto is a comment on the challenges of opening one's heart to love while protecting oneself from hurt. Evil eye is a condemnation of those who are supposed to love but instead envy. Through these folk illnesses, Northeast Brazilian women and men discuss their traumas, weaknesses, and victimization, and negotiate social relations.

32

Should Academic Medical Centers Conduct Clinical Trials of the Efficacy of Intercessory Prayer?

Edward C. Halperin, MD

A close relationship between religion and healing is not confined to cultures outside of the urbanized West, as shown by the following article by a professor of radiation oncology and pediatrics at Duke University Medical Center. Dr. Halperin reports on Americans' rising interest in the use of prayer to solve medical problems. The author focuses on intercessory prayer—prayers that request aid for others. Though the effectiveness of intercessory prayer has begun to be addressed in scientific settings, Halperin raises the possibility that clinical trials on prayer are inappropriate. He presents a series of arguments for and against the testing of prayer's efficacy, suggesting that prayer is a form of human behavior not amenable to the scientific method. These arguments might well be considered in light of Stephen Jay Gould's article on the relationship between science and religion in Chapter 1.

In April 2006, popular media and news sources publicized the results of the very sort of study Halperin discusses. Researchers studied more than 1,800 cardiac bypass patients at six U.S. hospitals, some of whom received intercessory prayer. The study concluded that intercessory prayer had no effect on complication-free recovery in the patients, and in fact patients who had been told that they received prayer (whether or not they actually did) had a higher incidence of complications. The study was published in American Heart Journal, *volume 151, issue 4, pp. 934–42.*

A recent article in *Time* described a clinical trial conducted in the cardiology unit of a Veterans Administration Medical Center. Patients undergoing invasive procedures were randomized into two groups. Some patients were prayed for by Buddhist Monks in Nepal, at a Roman Catholic Carmelite Convent near Baltimore, at an interdenominational Christian prayer center in Missouri, by Jews at the Western Wall in Jerusalem, and by supplicants at several other sites. The remaining patients served as controls. The study was designed to determine "whether prayer by strangers might influence the medical outcomes of 30 patients" in the cardiac catheterization laboratory. The magazine report indicated that "the outcomes of those prayed over were 50% to 100% better than those of a control group." The primary investigator felt these results were "sufficient . . . to be intriguing." A larger-scale study is planned.

Edward C. Halperin, "Should Academic Medical Centers Conduct Clinical Trials of the Efficacy of Intercessory Prayer?" Academic Medicine, vol. 76, no. 8, August 2001, pp. 791–97. Reprinted by permission of Lippincott Williams & Walkins.

Upon reading the above, the reader might ask whether clinical trials of the efficacy of intercessory prayer fall within the realm of scientific medicine or are an attempt to use the methods of science to answer a theological question. This essay is my attempt to confront that question, which underlies the question stated in the essay's title. To do so, I define the concept of intercessory prayer . . . contrast it with other forms of prayer, and review the literature concerning clinical trials of the efficacy of intercessory prayer. The arguments for and against conducting such trials are described so that the reader may consider their relative merits. Last, I discuss the potential power of faith in healing, review the philosophical basis and pitfalls of clinical trials of intercessory prayer, and reflect on the place of these trials in academic medicine.

Clinical Studies of Intercessory Prayer

The work described in *Time* is one of many studies of intercessory prayer published in the medical literature. The point of the brief survey that follows is not to engage in a detailed critique of the methods and results of these studies. I wish, rather, to give the reader a sense of the literature. In this way we can subsequently turn our attention to the question reflected in the title of this essay: Is the academic medical center the appropriate forum for the study of intercessory prayer?

Sir Francis Galton (1822–1911), explorer, anthropologist, student of human intelligence, and eugenicist, conducted one of the first studies of intercessory prayer.

> It is asserted by some that men possess the faculty of obtaining results over which they have little or no direct personal control, by means of devout and earnest prayer, while others doubt the truth of this assertion. The question regards a matter of fact, that has to be determined by observation and not by authority; and it is one that appears to be a very suitable topic for statistical inquiry . . . Are prayers answered or are they not? . . . Do sick persons who pray, or are prayed for, recover on the average more rapidly than others?

Galton considered that, of all classes of English society, the groups most prayed for were the Royal Family and the clergy's children. If prayer is effective, he reasoned, these people should live longer than other persons exposed to similar health risks. Galton, therefore, compared the average lifespans of kings with those of lords and the lifespans of children of clergy with those of children of other professional men. He found, contrary to the hypothesis, that much-prayed-for persons had slightly shorter lives than did those with whom he compared them. Galton also assessed the frequency with which ships carrying missionaries experienced disaster at sea compared with the frequency of this event with other ships. He found that missionaries sank slightly more often and with greater loss of life.

Moving to the present, in 1965, Joyce and Whelldon reported a small double-blind study of 11 pairs of adult outpatients with physiologic and rheumatic diseases. They assigned one patient in each pair to receive intercessory prayers and the other not to receive prayers, as a control. Over a 15-month interval the patients were evaluated using psychiatric and physical measures. In seven pairs of patients the prayed-for individual did better, in five the control did better.

In 1969 in a study of children with leukemia reported by Collipp, ten were prayed for in a Protestant church and eight not. After 15 months of prayer, seven of the ten prayed-for children were alive compared with two of the eight control children. Byrd of the University of California at San Francisco reported on 393 patients entered into a prospective double-blind randomized trial conducted in 1982–83 and reported in 1988. All patients were admitted to the coronary care unit at San Francisco General Hospital. Half were assigned to be prayed for by "born again" Christians and half not. Of the 29 variables studied (such as days in the coronary care unit, days in the hospital, number of discharge medications, development of congestive heart failure, need for antibiotics), there was no difference between the two groups in 23. For six variables the results favored the prayed-for group. By combining the data into a good-, intermediate-, or bad-outcome composite score, the study is reported to favor prayer ($p < .01$).

In 1992, O'Laoire took 496 volunteers, attracted by advertisements in San Francisco Bay Area newspapers, and assigned half to a prayed-for group and half to a control group. Several psychological metrics were used to assess anxiety, self-esteem, mood, and depression. The 1997 report of the study indicated that there was no difference in outcomes between the two groups.

In a 1997 report, Walker et al., from the University of New Mexico, randomized 40 patients admitted for therapy for alcoholism so that 22 were the recipients of distant prayer by volunteers (who reported "more than five years of regular intercessory prayer experience") and 18 were in the control group. No difference was found between prayer intervention and nonintervention with respect to the patients' alcohol consumption over time.

In 1998, Sicher et al. reported a randomized double-blind trial of the effect of distant healing in a population with advanced AIDS. Forty pairs of patients were randomized to prayer by "healers from Christian, Jewish, Buddhist, Native American, and shamanic traditions as well as graduates of secular schools of bioenergetic and meditative healing." At six months a review of the medical records showed no difference in the CD4 counts of the prayed-for group versus those in the control group. The prayed-for patients, however, were stated to have significantly fewer AIDS-defining illnesses and less severe illness, and to require fewer doctor visits and hospitalizations, as well as showing improved mood compared with the controls.

In 1999 Harris et al. reported a trial involving 1,019 patients admitted to a coronary care unit. The 990 analyzed cases were randomized to receive distant intercessory prayer by Christian intercessors or to be in a control group. The institutional review board at the Mid-America Heart Institute granted permission to conduct the trial without the individual patients' giving informed consent to participate. This decision was based on the basis of the absence of risk in the study and the possibility that obtaining consent might increase anxiety in some patients. Thirty-seven outcome measures were studied (such as need for interventional cardiac procedure, antibiotics, temporary pacemaker placement, and two global outcome scores). There was no significant difference in outcomes ($p > .05$) for 36 of the 37 measures and one of the two global outcome scores. Because there was a benefit in what the authors view as the more important global outcome score, the trial is reported as being positive, favoring the prayer group. The trial has been extensively critiqued on statistical design, technique of randomization, lack

of validation of global outcome scoring system, and interpretation.

Arguments in Favor of and Against AMCs' Conducting Studies of Prayer's Efficacy

One can mount several arguments in favor of and several against the conduct of clinical trials concerning the efficacy of intercessory prayer. I consider these in turn, leaving the reader to judge how persuasive they are individually or in the aggregate.

In Favor

(1) *The academic medical center should seek new knowledge concerning therapeutics, irrespective of the source of the original hypotheses.*

Academic medical centers exist for the purpose of the generation, conservation, and dissemination of new knowledge concerning the causes, prevention, and treatment of human disease. There is a long history of treatment of human disease's being faith-based. While faith-based treatment has been supplanted, in many circles, by reliance on scientific medicine, it is frequently relied upon by patients and some physicians. Academic medical centers should rigorously investigate such a widely used treatment modality. Interest in alternative or complementary medicine is growing rapidly in the United States. Prayer "therapy" may fall into this category.

An obvious corollary to this line of argument is that it might open the door to the testing of other hypotheses that may be less palatable, to some academicians, than investigations of prayer. If one accepts, for example, the premise that alleged forms of therapeutics are worthy of study if they are of interest to a significant portion of the public, this might lead to agreement to test an infinite dilution of a bacterial extract in water (what some would call a homeopathic therapy and others might call distilled water) for the treatment of pneumococcal pneumonia.

(2) *Medical research has an obligation to respond to the demands of the body politic in selecting topics for research.*

Academic medical centers are well accustomed to seeking research grants. It is, in fact, a large part of their raison d'être. These research grants derive from taxpayer dollars funneled through federal agencies and philanthropy. If the public demands new therapies for AIDS, breast cancer, or mental illness, then their elected officials will pressure federal agencies to set up mechanisms to fund research in these areas. Similarly, if the public has a strong interest in the value of prayer as medical therapy, it is appropriate for grant-funding agencies to promote such research and for academic medical centers, which have a fiduciary obligation to the society that ultimately supports them, to perform such research.

(3) *Clinical trials of intercessory prayer take no position on the existence of God.*

A clinical trial of the efficacy of prayer is designed to test whether or not prayer influences the clinical course of the patients in the study. The trial is not designed to prove or disprove the existence of a God who answers prayer. If the trial shows that the prayed-for patients have a better outcome than do those in the control group, then a second-generation trial might look at the mechanism of action of the observed outcome. The investigator, however, is not taking a position with respect to the existence or non-existence of God by studying, initially, whether prayer influences clinical outcomes.

One way of framing this argument is to assert that studies of intercessory prayer are designed to explore a phenomenon and not a mechanism. If "prayer works," that is if a clinical trial of prayer is positive, one may then consider natural or supernatural explanations. Are the effects of prayer attributable to currently unknown physical forces associated with intercessory prayer and received by patients? Are the effects of prayer related to a supernatural cause, i.e., a God who responds to prayer? Clearly one must do clinical trials of prayer first and show they are positive before addressing the mechanism of action. Physicians administered aspirin and digitalis before fully understanding their pharmacology and biochemistry, used radiation therapy before understanding DNA damage and clonogenic death, and did oophorectomies for breast cancer before understanding hormone receptors. It is clear that medicine is comfortable basing therapies on observational studies, with mechanistic explanations following decades or centuries later.

Not in Favor

(1) *It is impossible to design a controlled trial of the efficacy of intercessory prayer.*

A clinical study of intercessory prayer must face the problem of identifying statistically similar groups of subjects for the treatment and control arms of the study. Even if one found wholly comparable groups of patients based upon type and stage of disease, it would be impossible to find equivalent groups based upon faith or "worthiness" to be healed by prayer. It is also difficult to imagine how one would find equivalent groups of intercessors and prayers.

The end-point of the trial must also be specified. Death is an unequivocal end-point. Measuring end-points such as number of days in the intensive care unit, the need for cardiac catheterization, or administration of antibiotics is somewhat more subjective. Some investigators try to solve this problem by using "outcome scores." Such scoring systems need to be generally agreed upon, validated, and reproducible. Finally, the laws of statistical reasoning caution us that if we measure enough outcome measures for two groups of patients, some measures will show a statistically significant difference, by chance, when no real difference exists.

Intercessory prayer experiments might be associated with a dose–response relationship. How "much" prayer works? How is prayer measured? Is it measured by the time, by the degree of fervency of the prayer, and/or by the degree of sincerity or faith of the prayer? Does the faith tradition (e.g., Buddhism, Christianity, etc.) of the intercessor matter? Unless we have some concept of dose, we cannot study the effect of prayer as therapy.

Establishing a true control group of persons for whom there is no prayer may be impossible. Patients and their friends and family will certainly pray for recovery. Enemies may pray for the reverse. If an investigator believes that prayer matters, how does one account for the "unintentional doses" of such possible unplanned-for interventions? If a patient who is participating in a study of the effects of prayer asks a hospital chaplain to pray with or for him or her, will the patient be dropped from the study?

(2) *An academic medical center conducting a clinical trial of intercessory prayer is offensive to religion.*

Studies of intercessory prayer are evaluating one particular type of prayer—a request for a specific action. In attempting a study of the probability of miraculous divine intervention, academic medical centers are, in fact, trying to prove the existence of a God who answers prayers. People of faith generally do not demand that God perform healing and they do not give God a timetable to perform the task. For example, the injunction against man's asking God to perform on demand is found in both the Old Testament and the New Testament. "You shall not test the Lord thy God, as you tested him in Massah" (Deuteronomy 6:16); and "Jesus said to him. It is written again. Thou shalt not test the Lord thy God" (Matthew 4:7). This principle of faith is also described when God addresses man in the Book of Job: "Where wast thou when I laid the foundations of the earth? Declare, if thou has understanding . . . Shall he that contendeth with the Almighty instruct *him*? He that reproveth God, let him answer it" (Job 38:2–40:2).

K. S. Thompson describes an attempt at a "scientific" proof of the existence of God as an effort

> to create a situation in which God must show himself or herself and perform a miracle— something that gods in general do only very rarely. Even more rarely do they perform on demand. If God or gods feel the need to give us a sign, he or she or they tend to choose the time, place, and form; not us. Simply put, I am sure that such tests are hideously arrogant at best and certainly blasphemous.

Intercessory prayers for the good health of others raise philosophical and theological problems. Will God, who is all-knowing, all-powerful, and all-good (by definition for the good of His people), turn away from His intended purpose because of a human's expressing his or her desires? One would have difficulty accepting the concept of a God who preferentially heals people who, in a clinical trial, are selected to be prayed for by strangers rather than healing those randomly assigned to receive no prayer. God should not be conceived of as so capricious.

(3) *Clinical trials of the efficacy of prayer are attempts to prove the existence of God.*

It is true that some effective drugs were discovered serendipitously. Some forms of therapy were employed for years before there was any sound scientific explanation for their efficacy. "If prayer works," continues the argument, "then it doesn't matter if we cannot derive the explanation for its mechanism of action." This is the so-called "black box" argument—if something works clinically, it does not matter if we can explain why or how.

Remote intercessory prayer, if it works, could be explained only by the intervention of God in the physical world by a supernatural mechanism or by telekinesis. Neither mechanism can or will be demonstrable by a credible replicable scientific experiment. A clinical trial of the efficacy of prayer is an attempt to prove the existence of God. To claim that these studies are exploring only a phenomenon and not a mechanism is a ruse.

Experimental therapeutics should be based on pathophysiology and a likely mechanism of the proposed therapy's action. Physicians should not expend effort in the pursuit of irrational treatments. In a world of scarce resources, we should select subjects for clinical research on the basis of evidence-based hypotheses. Political pressure or public infatuations should not hold sway.

(4) *The methods of scientific medicine are inapplicable to theology.*

Theology concerns itself with truths derived by deductive reasoning: An apparently rational universe exists. What are its origins? Whence arose its first cause? A higher power or higher being directs the world and our actions. Who or what is it? Is it appropriate to worship it? The theologian reasons back from what currently is to what caused it.

Scientific knowledge is different. Science acquires information by feel and touch. The physician is required to see, handle, weigh, and measure phenomena. After extensive categorization of information, physician-scientists seek to identify truths generated by artful arrangement of the data. The theologian is interested in explaining why things are as they are based on logical deductions from the truths acquired through revelation. The physician-scientist, on the other hand, attempts to discover how things are by observing and measuring them.

Medicine has the possibility of continual acquisition of knowledge and a change in its dominant paradigms. New understandings of biology lead to new hypotheses, new experiments, new therapeutic targets, and new clinical practices. Theology, on the other hand, is concerned with fundamental truths. While some religions accept changes over time in certain aspects of their practices and rituals because they believe in "progressive revelation," the fundamental underpinnings are generally thought of as immutable.

Theology and scientific medicine, therefore, intellectually operate in different spheres. Attempting to use an established truth of molecular biology to explain the truths endorsed by the faithful as their theology, or vice versa, seems analogous to asking the astrophysicist to use his or her special expertise to lecture on 16th-century Spanish art history.

The distinction between theology and science was summarized by Cardinal Newman over 150 years ago:

> Theology begins, as its name denotes, not with sensible facts, phenomenon or results, not with nature at all, but with the Author of nature—with the one invisible approachable basis and source of all things. It begins at the other end of knowledge and is occupied not with finite but with the infinite. It enfolds and epitomizes what He Himself has told of Himself, of His nature, His attributes, His will, and His acts . . . physical science is experimental, theology traditional; physical science is the richer, theology the more exact; physics is the bolder, theology the shorter; physics progressive, theology in comparison, stationary; theology is loyal to the past, physics has visions of the future.

Weighing the Arguments About Faith and Healing

Sir William Osler clearly understood the power of faith to contribute to healing. Osler, however, saw faith as a general concept involving faith in authority. Osler realized that patients may be aided by faith in the power and knowledge of the physician as well as in God or the saints. In an essay, "The Faith That Heals," Osler wrote

> As Galen says, confidence and hope do more than physick—'he cures most in whom most are confident' . . . Faith in the Gods or in the Saints cures one, faith in little pills another, suggestion a third, faith in a plain common doctor a fourth . . . The cures in the temples of Aesculapius, the miracles of the Saints, the remarkable cures of those noble men, the Jesuit missionaries, in this country, the modern miracles at Lourdes and at St. Anne de Beaupré in Quebec, and the wonder-workings of our latter day saints are often genuine and must be considered in discussing the foundations of therapeutics. We physicians use the same power every day. If a poor lass, paralyzed apparently, helpless, bed-ridden for years, comes to me having worn out in mind, body and estate a devoted family, if she in a few weeks or less by faith in me, and faith alone, takes up her bed and walks, the Saints of old could not have done more.

There is clearly a human desire to fill a void science cannot. The problem is well described by Normal Levitt.

> The rift between the scientific world view and the common need for some assurance that human existence is not a pointless accident ensures that, well into the future, a substantial portion of the population will contrive ideological and psychological defenses against science. Large numbers of people, perhaps amounting to a majority in even the most scientifically advanced societies, will remain alienated from science, though that condition will often be covert and inarticulate, embodied in quiet reservations rather than public manifestos . . . in the presumptions and prejudices that undergird our social structure, science is something of a foreign body, consequently it draws antibodies to itself.

As Osler recognized, physicians must not denigrate the importance of spirituality or faith in the healing process or the inadequacies of science for some patients. Not all of healing is explicable by medicinal therapeutics. Healing is a complex process that involves the medications we physicians prescribe, the surgery we perform, and the diagnostic x-rays we order. Healing also requires human interaction, faith, and a family support structure. There are facets of healing that are complementary to scientific medicine and deserve to be integrated with it. There can be little objection to the use of harmless complementary forms of healing with scientific medicine so long as these forms are used in addition to scientific medicine and not in lieu of it.

Scientific understanding does not necessarily contradict religion—depending upon one's understanding of God and sacred texts. Sir Francis Bacon, for example, felt that by separating "the absurd mixture of matters divine and human," what science would allow us to do is "to render unto faith the things that are faith's." Recourse to prayer during illness is not an indication that the patient or family lacks confidence in traditional medical therapy. In many religious traditions, confidence in the healing power of God is not intended to usurp or negate the essential functions of physicians and medical science.

The community of scholars of the academic medical center must understand the limits of both science and religion. There are various ways to seek truth that cannot, by their nature, overrule each other. The academic medical center should be devoted to the generation, conservation, and dissemination of knowledge and should utilize intellectual tools suitable for the purpose. Physicians should have an informed appreciation of theology as it affects their patients, their own lives, and both the physicians' and the patients' understanding of their place in the world.

The debate over clinical trials of intercessory prayer raises questions concerning the exploration of the universe of faith utilizing the scientific method. Medical academicians must engage in a serious weighing of the arguments for and against such trials.

Suggested Readings

Crapanzano, Vincent
    1973   *The Hamadha: A Study in Moroccan Ethnopsychiatry.* Berkeley: University of California Press.

Csordas, Thomas J.
    1994   *The Sacred Self: A Cultural Phenomenology of Charismatic Healing.* Berkeley: University of California Press.

Danforth, Loring M.
    1989   *Firewalking and Religious Healing: The Anatenaria of Greece and the American Firewalking Movement.* Princeton, N.J.: Princeton University Press.

Nichter, Mark, ed.
    1992   *Anthropological Approaches to the Study of Ethnomedicine.* Yverdon, Switzerland and Langhorne, PA: Gordon and Breach Science Publishers.

Roseman, Marina
    1991   *Healing Sounds from the Malaysian Rainforest: Temiar Music and Medicine.* Berkeley: University of California Press.

Sargent, Carolyn F., and Thomas M. Johnson, eds.
    1996   *Medical Anthropology: Contemporary Theory and Method.* Westport, Conn.: Praeger.

Devil mask from the Tyrol.

CHAPTER SEVEN

Witchcraft, Sorcery, Divination, and Magic

All societies recognize the frailness of the human condition; wherever pain, illness, injury, and unjustness exist, so do culturally prescribed explanations. In many parts of the world, where opportunities for formal education are limited to a small elite, although their economic and political power may be considerable, explanations of phenomena are still rooted deeply in traditional interpretations passed from generation to generation by word of mouth. In rural Africa, for example, where 70 to 90 percent of the population is not covered by public health services (Shehu 1975: 29), mental and physical illness are often accounted for in terms of a formidable array of supernatural sources, including witchcraft, sorcery, magic, curses, spirits, or a combination of these. Whether explanations for illness are "scientific" or "mystical," all societies must have explanations for crises. Mental and physical illness cannot be permitted to go unchecked. Witchcraft, sorcery, divination, and magic are ways of dealing with the supernatural, explaining the unexplainable, attempting to control or manipulate what otherwise cannot be controlled.

In many parts of the world, a vast number of daily crises are attributed to witchcraft, particularly in sub-Saharan Africa, where the highest level of belief in witchcraft exists today. Here witchcraft explanations are logical—indeed, some say indispensable. In short, witchcraft is an integral part of traditional African belief systems, as are sorcery and magic, and it is considered by many anthropologists to be essential to African religions.

Lucy Mair, a British social anthropologist and a leading authority on African witchcraft, points out that the belief in witchcraft is universal. Around the world, greed and sexual motifs are commonly associated with witches, as is the "nightmare" witch that prowls at night and is distinguished from the everyday witch by nocturnal habits (1969: 36–37). Women are more often labeled witches than men, and societies frequently associate particular types of personalities with individuals who they feel have the highest probability of becoming witches. According to Mair (1969: 43), many of the qualities associated with being a poor neighbor, such as unsociability, isolation, stinginess, unfriendliness, and moroseness, are the same qualities ascribed to the everyday witch. Nothing compares in terms of sheer evil,

258

however, to the nightmare witch, whose hatred of the most basic tenets of human decency earns it a special place of infamy.

Witches, wherever they exist, are the antithesis of proper behavior. Their antisocial acts, moreover, are uncontrollable. A final commonality of witch beliefs is that their powers are innate, unlike those of the sorcerer, whose powers are learned; the witch inherits the power for evil or is given the power by God.

To the beginning student in anthropology, witchcraft surely must appear to affect a society negatively; a careful analysis of belief systems demonstrates more positive than negative functions, however. In his analysis of the functions of witchcraft among the Navaho, Clyde Kluckhohn evaluated the belief more positively than negatively in terms of economic and social control and the psychological states of a group (1967; Kluckhohn and Leighton 1962). Beliefs in witchcraft level economic differences, for example. Among the Navaho, the rich are believed to have gained their wealth by secret supernatural techniques. The only way to quell this kind of rumor is through generosity, which may take the form of redistribution of wealth among relatives and friends (Kluckhohn and Leighton 1962: 247). Kluckhohn demonstrated that witchcraft beliefs help reinforce social values. For example, the belief that uncared-for elderly will turn into witches demands that the Navaho treat the aged with proper care. The worry that the death of a close relative may cast suspicion of witchcraft on survivors also reinforces their social values regarding obligations to kin. Ironically, because leaders are thought to be witches, people were hesitant to be disobedient for fear of supernatural retribution (1967: 113).

Kluckhohn maintained that at the psychological level witchcraft was an outlet for hostility because frustrated individuals used witches as scapegoats. Anxiety and neglect could also be accommodated through commonly held witchcraft beliefs, for people showing symptoms of witchcraft-caused illnesses would reaffirm their importance to kin and the group at the public curing ceremonies (1967: 83–84).

The terms *witchcraft* and *sorcery* are often used interchangeably to mean any kind of evil magic; however, E. E. Evans-Pritchard's (1937) analysis of Azande witchcraft and sorcery resulted in a distinction between the two terms that is accepted by most anthropologists today. Generally speaking, a sorcerer intentionally seeks to bring about harm. Sorcerers have learned how to cast spells and use certain formulas and objects to inflict evil. The sorcerer's methods are real, not psychic like those of the witch. Sorcery is conscious and an acquired skill, whereas witchcraft is unconscious and innate. Contrary to witchcraft, sorcery is not always antisocial or illegitimate and occurs with a higher frequency than does witchcraft.

Interestingly, some scholars believe that witchcraft does not, in truth, exist despite the strong beliefs of those in the culture. Witchcraft, they argue, exists only in the minds of the people, whereas sorcery is proven by the presence of paraphernalia, medicines, and the identification of sorcerer specialists in the community. The point is, however, that witchcraft serves so many functions it is hard to believe its importance can be whittled away by the difficulties involved in trying to prove its existence or in distinguishing it from sorcery. Everywhere there is social conflict: People become angry, get insulted, or perhaps become jealous of someone's success; it is during such uncomfortable times that witches may be found at fault and sorcerers may be called upon for help.

When someone in North American culture thinks of witches and witchcraft, the usual association is with early modern European witchcraft and the Salem trials in New England in 1692. However, these European-based witch beliefs, including the Salem case, were quite different from those of the preliterate societies in which witchcraft occurs, where it functions as an everyday, socially acceptable way of managing tension, explaining the otherwise unexplainable, leveling disparities in wealth and status, and resolving social conflict. In contrast, early modern European witchcraft was a response to the strains of a time of profound change, marked by immense political and religious conflict. Although witch beliefs had been a feature of European culture since the Dark Ages, the Church managed to keep the situation under control until the turmoil of the sixteenth and seventeenth centuries, when the practice of labeling Church heretics as witches became popular and the witchhunt craze occurred. Naturally, the Salem witch-hunt of 1692 is of the greatest interest to Americans, but Salem's 200 arrests and 19 executions pale in comparison with the approximately 500,000 people who were executed in Europe during the fifteenth, sixteenth, and seventeenth centuries after having been convicted of witchcraft. At the end of this period, the witchcraze was coming to an end. "Cartesian and scientific thought had no room for witchcraft; ecclesiastical and civil authorities agreed that witch prosecutions had got out of hand; and European society was settling down to two centuries (1700–1900) of relative peace and prosperity" (Russell 1987: 196).

Ethnographic reports on witchcraft and sorcery dominate the literature, but other forces of evil are also responsible for much unjust suffering. One such power, but certainly not the only one, is the evil eye—widely known in the Middle East, parts of Europe, Central America, and Africa, areas characterized by Islamic and Judeo-Christian as well as so-called indigenous religious traditions. The evil eye was believed to be a voluntary power brought about by the malicious nature of the possessor, on the one hand, or an involuntary but still dangerous, uncontrolled power on the other. Strangers, dwarfs, old women, certain types of animals, menstruating women, and people with one eye have been often viewed as being particularly dangerous. Children and farm animals, the most precious of one's possessions, were thought most vulnerable to the evil eye, which could cause various disasters to occur immediately or in the future, particularly by asserting control over the victim. A variety of protective measures have been prescribed to ward off the evil eye. Glass evil eyes and variously shaped metal amulets, for example, are sold to tourists and residents alike in modern Greece. Plants, certain avoidance actions, colors, and magical words and gestures have also at different times and places been felt to be effective against the evil eye.

In addition to the evil eye, anguish can be created by malicious ghosts, spirit possession, attacks by enemy shamans, curses of the envious, and the spells of evil magicians and other specialists who have learned how to manipulate power to harm others. Each of these causes harms and creates fear in a community and as such is an index of social strain; however, each may also function positively by allowing individuals to blame supernatural agencies rather than kin and neighbors for illness or misfortunes that befall them.

Demons, spirits, ancestors, and gods all exist as realities in the human mind and possess the power to harm and harass the living. Good and evil are counterbalanced in every society through a variety of rituals and other forms of protection, yet this balance is inevitably broken by human weaknesses and transgressions that invite the evil nature of supernatural agents. The malicious acts of these agents inflict pain and anguish on the innocent as well as on those deserving of punishment. Although all supernaturals can possess an individual and cause an unending variety of harm, the most commonly known agent of possession is the demon. Demons may aid their human consorts from time to time, but generally they are seen as being responsible for diseases, injuries, or a myriad of major and minor personal and group disasters. More powerful than mere humans, they are also generally believed to be less powerful than gods and ancestral spirits (Collins 1978: 195).

Possession by demons is ordinarily considered dangerous, but this is not always the case. For the Aymara Indians of Bolivia, for example, possession results in serious consequences for the victims and their community, whereas among the Haitians it is actively sought at voodoo ceremonies in order to obtain the supernatural knowledge of the spirits. The acceptance or the actual seeking out of beneficent spirits and situating them in a medium where they can be called on when needed is termed "adorcism" by L. DeHeusch (1971). I. M. Lewis distinguishes between "central possession cults" and "peripheral possession cults." In the former, spirits, such as ancestors, most commonly possess men and sustain the moral order of society. In the latter, women and others having lesser status are possessed by malevolent spirits; possession of this type is often considered an illness and damages the social fabric of the group (1989). Haitians, however, conceive of both good and evil spirits, and all fear possession by the latter. "Possession, then, is a broad term referring to an integration of spirit and matter, force or power and corporeal reality, in a cosmos where the boundaries between an individual and her environment are acknowledged to be permeable, flexibly drawn, or at least negotiable" (Boddy 1994: 407).

The functions of possession commonly go unnoticed, overshadowed by the dramatic expressive actions of the possessed and those in attendance. Stanley and Ruth Freed (1964: 71) showed that spirit possession in a north Indian village functioned primarily to relieve the individual's intropsychic tensions while giving the victim the attention and sympathy of relatives and friends. The possession itself and its overt demonstration were only a vehicle for these functions. Even rules designed to avoid demons, such as the *jinns* of Islamic countries, can promote individual self-discipline and propriety in behavior, both as William Howells has pointed out, desirable qualities (1962: 202). The prohibitions promoted to avoid *jinns* do direct behavior toward socially approved goals, but, despite these positive functions, demons cause suffering and pain to members of both Western and non-Western societies and every society is forced to cope with their devious nature.

Exorcism—the driving away of evil spirits, such as demons, by chanting, praying, commanding, or other ritual means—occurs throughout the world and is invoked when an evil spirit has caused illness by entering a person's body. (A belief in exorcism assumes a related belief in the power of ritual to move an evil spirit from one place to another.) Although the idea that foreign objects can enter the body and cause illness has been widespread, it was especially prevalent among American Indians, where curers, shamans, and sometimes a specialist known as a "sucking doctor" had the ability to remove these materials by such techniques as rubbing and kneading the patient's body, gesturing over the diseased area, and directly sucking out the evil object. Shamans, because of the "trick" aspect of their rituals, are especially well versed in the intricacies of exorcism as a means of removal of disease-causing objects. Typically, a sleight-of-hand maneuver is used to show the patient that the harmful substance has been removed.

Howells (1962: 92–94) has described several techniques used around the world for exorcising evil spirits and diseases: using sweat-baths, cathartics, or emetics to flush out the offending spirits; trephining; manipulating and massaging the body; scraping or sponging the illness off the body; reciting magical spells, coaxing, or singing songs to lure the spirit away; tempting the spirit to evacuate the body by laying out a sumptuous meal for it; keeping the patient uncomfortable, sometimes by administering beatings, so the spirit will be discontented with the body and want to depart; building a fire under the patient to make it uncomfortably warm for the spirit; placing foul-smelling, overripe fruit near the patient; and scandalizing the demon by having the patient's naked wife jump over the patient.

Until the recent popularity of movies, television shows, and novels about possession by demons, the American public was largely unaware that exorcism has been practiced throughout the history of Western religions. Somewhat alarming to many Americans was the realization that the Catholic Church continued to approve exorcisms in twentieth-century America. The following seventeenth-century conjuration was recited by priests in order to exorcise evil spirits from troubled houses. The words may be different, as are the names for the supernatural beings referred to, but the intent of the conjuration is identical to incantations uttered by religious specialists in preliterate societies during exorcism rites for similar purposes:

> I adjure thee, O serpent of old, by the Judge of the living and the dead; by the Creator of the world who hath power to cast into hell, that thou depart forthwith from this house. He that commands thee, accursed demon, is He that commanded the winds and the sea and the storm. He that commands thee, is He that ordered thee to be hurled down from the height of heaven into the lower parts of the earth. He that commands thee is He that bade thee depart from Him. Hearken, then, Satan, and fear. Get thee gone, vanquished and cowed, when thou art bidden in the name of our Lord Jesus Christ who will come to judge the living and the dead and all the world by fire. Amen. (Crehan 1970: 873)

William James saw religion as the belief in an unseen order. If one important aspect of religion is helping believers come to know that unknown, it follows that divination is important to religion. *Divination* means learning about the future or about things that may be hidden. Although the word itself may be traced to *divinity,* which indicates its relationship to gods, the practice of divination belongs as much to magic as it does to religion proper. From the earliest times, human beings have wanted to know about such climatic changes as drought and heavy rainfall. Without scientific information to help predict natural events, early humans looked for "signs" in the flight of birds, the entrails of small animals, or perhaps the positions of coals in a fire or pebbles in a stream. To this day, the methods of divination in the world's cultures are far too varied and numerous to mention here.

Until recently, controversy has surrounded the definition of magic and religion by anthropologists. Only in the last few years have they come close to agreement that the dichotomy is a false one or that, if a dichotomy does exist, its ramifications are not significant to the study of the practitioners of each. Both magic and religion deal directly with the supernatural, and our understanding of the cultural applications of each provides deeper insights into the worldview of the people practicing them.

Magic is usually divided into types, depending on the techniques involved. For example, Sir James Frazer distinguished "imitative magic," in which the magician believes that the desired result can be achieved by imitation, from "contagious magic," in which materials or substances once in contact with the intended victim are used in the magical attack. Other scholars would include "sympathetic magic," a form of magic in which items associated with or symbolic of the intended victim are used to identify and carry out the spell. Obviously, sympathetic magic contains elements of both imitative and contagious magic.

These forms of magic, still in use today, have been important methods of reducing anxiety regarding problems that exceeded the ability of people to understand and control them, especially because of a lack of technological expertise. Divination, special formulas and incantations, spells and curses—all are considered magical, and all can be used for good or evil. Because these activities are learned, they should be differentiated from witchcraft, which is considered innate and, most believe, uncontrollable.

It is logical to assume that non-Western reliance on explanations of events in terms of magic, sorcery, and witchcraft is a natural outcome of a lack of scientific training. But it is equally important to note that Westerners also rely on religious beliefs, with faith playing a strong role in determining actions and behaviors in our daily lives. Our ethnocentrism still blinds us to the similarities between ourselves and our fellow humans throughout the world. The great questions concerning the human condition are asked by all peoples, and despite the disparate levels of technology our sameness is demonstrated by the universality of religion.

In the lead article of this chapter, James L. Brain employs a cross-cultural approach to witchcraft, emphasizing the near-universal image of woman as witch, and presents his theory that the mobility of nomadic societies, such as hunter-gatherers, accounts for the absence of witchcraft among those groups and its presence among the hunter's sedentary horticultural neighbors.

In the second article, Naomi M. McPherson investigates sorcery and concepts of deviance among the Kabana of Papua New Guinea. She shows the Kabana to be quite unusual in that, unlike most other groups, they do not always consider the practice of sorcery to be evil, and they believe that under certain conditions it can function positively in their society.

The third article is by T. M. Luhrmann; it describes typical contemporary witches and their rituals. Luhrmann's work is based on research with middle-class, urban witches in England in the 1980s.

In the fourth selection, E. E. Evans-Pritchard describes the Azande poison oracle *benge* and the beliefs surrounding its usage.

The Bronislaw Malinowski article is a classic work identifying circumstances in which magic is used, and it is based on the author's research in the Trobriand Islands of Melanesia. Rejecting the once-popular idea that primitive peoples are incapable of rational thought, Malinowski argues that Melanesians make use of an experience-based understanding of the world in a manner much like science, and they rely on magic only in situations of uncertainty.

In the last article, George Gmelch cleverly applies Malinowski's ideas on magic to baseball.

References

Boddy, Janice
   1994 "Spirit Possession Revisited: Beyond Instrumentality." *Annual Reviews in Anthropology* 23: 407–34.

Collins, John J.
   1978 *Primitive Religion*. Totowa, N.J.: Littlefield, Adams.

Crehan, J. H.
   1970 "Exorcism." In Richard Cavendish, ed., *Man, Myth and Magic*, vol. 7, pp. 869–73. London: BPCC/Phoebus.

DeHeusch, L.
   1971 *Why Marry Her? Society and Symbolic Structures*. Translated by J. Lloyd. Cambridge: Cambridge University Press.

Evans-Pritchard, E. E.
   1937 *Witchcraft, Oracles and Magic Among the Azande*. Oxford: Clarendon Press.

Freed, Stanley A., and Ruth S. Freed
   1964 "Spirit Possession as Illness in a North Indian Village." *Ethnology* 3: 152–71.

Howells, William
   1962 *The Heathens*. Garden City, N.Y.: Doubleday.

Kluckhohn, Clyde
  1967 *Navaho Witchcraft.* Boston: Beacon Press (first published, 1944).

Kluckhohn, Clyde, and Dorothea Leighton
  1962 *The Navaho.* Cambridge, Mass.: Harvard University Press (first published 1946).

Lewis, I. M.
  1989 *Ecstatic Religion: A Study of Spirit Possession and Shamanism.* 2nd ed. London: Routledge.

Mair, Lucy
  1969 *Witchcraft.* New York: McGraw-Hill.

Russell, Jeffrey Burton
  1987 "Witchcraft." In Mircea Eliade, ed., *The Encyclopedia of Religion,* pp. 415–23. New York: Macmillan.

Shehu, U.
  1975 *Health Care in Rural Areas.* AFRO Technical Papers, no. 10.

33

An Anthropological Perspective
on the Witchcraze

James L. Brain

At first glance, it would appear impossible that an anthropological investigation of the European witchcraze, so far removed from contemporary America, could shed light on current attitudes toward gender. In this article, however, James L. Brain demonstrates that the idea of the witch is closely related to the subversion of male authority, a reversal of patriarchal authority that Saint Paul asserted was divinely ordered. The denigration of women in European thought can, in part, be traced to Aristotle, who saw women's souls and bodies as being inferior. Weaknesses such as these, it was thought, predisposed women to be witches. Close on the heels of this came the idea of ritual pollution of men by women, female emissions being further evidence of women's inferiority.

The image of women as witches is widespread, but it was not until witchcraft was linked to the devil that it was considered heresy, a crime punishable by death. It is not difficult to link these historical attitudes toward women with the present. In fact, Brain maintains that "the witchcraze ended, but misogyny and gynophobia are still alive and well at the end of the twentieth century."

In addition to the issue of gender and witchcraft, Brain addresses the question of why witches are believed to exist in some societies and not others. Here the author's "mobility theory," based on the nomadic lifestyle of hunter-gatherers, offers a provocative explanation for the absence of witchcraft among these peoples but its presence among sedentary horticultural societies.

Our understanding of historical attitudes toward gender may be illuminated by a comparative cross-cultural approach to witchcraft. Two issues are especially important: the reason for the near universality of the image of woman as witch, and the idea that geographic and spatial mobility may be an important and overlooked factor in the absence of witchcraft accusations and in the decline of their frequency.

Reprinted from Jean R. Brink, Allison P. Coudert, and Maryanne C. Horowitz, eds., THE POLITICS OF GENDER IN EARLY MODERN EUROPE (Kirksville, Mo.: Sixteenth Century Journal Publishers, Inc., 1989), pp. 15–27. By permission of the publisher. The article's citations, originally numbered footnotes, have been interpolated into the text in this volume for consistency of presentation.

The Image of the Witch

Anthropological and historical evidence shows that the specific details of beliefs about witches and their behavior will vary according to the concerns of a particular society. There are, however, two universal constants about witch beliefs that cut across cultures: witches represent people's deepest fears about themselves and society, and they represent a reversal of all that is considered normal behavior in a particular society. This has been documented for small-scale societies (Wilson 1951; Mair 1969), but the situation in Europe needs to be examined. Norman Cohn discusses the European witchcraze in terms of "collective fantasies," "obsessive fears," and "unacknowledged desires" in the minds of sixteenth- and seventeenth-century men and women (Cohn 1975: 258–63). Margaret Murray and, to a certain extent, Carlo Ginzburg locate the origins of European witchcraft beliefs in pre-Christian religions (Ginzburg 1983; Murray 1931/1970).

It would be unfortunate if we were to revive Murray's hypothesis. The beliefs about witches can be explained without reference to pre-Christian religions, if we assume that witch-like behavior is a simple reversal of normal and socially accepted behavior. In Catholic Europe, the Church demanded attendance at mass in the daytime on Sundays; the predominant color there was white. By reversing this, one can easily predict that witches will celebrate their own sabbath at night, and that black will be the predominant color in their community or congregation—hence the term "black mass." Reversal also predicts that whatever ritual or service is performed will be a reversal of the Christian mass—the recitation of prayers backwards, the reversed cross, and worship of some form of Antichrist. The Church demanded acceptance of the doctrine of the Trinity, in which subliminally one can perceive that Mary is made pregnant by her own son in the shape of the Holy Ghost; the reversal of this doctrine makes profane incest an attribute of witches. If there was a sacred act of ritual cannibalism in Holy Communion, then witches could be expected to take part in some blasphemous form of cannibalism. The belief in Jesus' conquest of death and decay manifested itself in the idea that the bodies of saints do not decay at death; in witch beliefs, this finds its reversal in the belief in vampires that do not decay. If heterosexuality is the extolled norm, then homosexuality will be seen as witch-like, and if chastity is the ultimate condition of holiness then obviously one should expect witches to engage in sexual orgies.

This point can be carried even further: if patriarchal authority is divinely ordained, as Saint Paul insisted, then any attempt by women to subvert or to assume that authority can be seen as an illicit reversal and hence as witch-like behavior. The first example of the subversion of divine authority, of course, is attributed to Eve in her disobedience. Both Protestants and Catholics were concerned with issues of authority and women. Martin de Castañega's treatise on superstition and witchcraft (1529) answers the question of why women are more prone to be witches than men thus: "The first reason is because

Christ forbade them to administer the sacraments and therefore the devil gives them the authority to do it with his execrations" (Darst 1979: 298–322). Here we see not only the reversal of normal, i.e., God-given authority, but also the idea of the administration of blasphemous, heretical sacraments. Additional reversals occur in his explanations of how and why witches, like angels and Christ, can fly; how and why they, like Christ can walk on water; and how and why they, like Christ and the devil, can become invisible or change their shape (Darst 1979: 306). In the pattern of inheritance D. H. Darst records another reversal. Instead of passing on inheritance from father to son, witches inherit their discipleship to the devil from mother to daughter, from aunt to niece, or from grandmother to granddaughter.

To the issue of authority, feminist anthropological scholarship offers very cogent insights (Rosaldo 1974: 1–42). Authority is always legitimate; power may be, but often is not. Where women are denied authority, they inevitably seek their ends by the manipulation of the power they possess: by denying sex, food or nurture; by failing to perform household tasks, by outright disobedience, or by passive resistance in the form of sulking, scolding, and gossiping. All of these possibilities subvert legitimate male authority and can, therefore, be seen as evidence of witchcraft. One can conceive of a sliding scale: the less authority—or responsibility—women possess, the more manipulation of power will occur, and vice versa. Thus we can confidently expect to find the paradox that women are often extremely powerful in societies in which they are denied any authority; in these social organizations they develop strategies to attain their ends outside the legitimate parameters of authority.

This paradigm has great relevance to women in Renaissance Europe in terms of the generation of misogyny. As Lamphere demonstrates, the image of women in patrilineal and patrilocal societies is invariably negative: women are believed to be deceitful, untrustworthy and manipulative (Lamphere 1974: 97–112). This negative image is a direct result of marriage practices: the men are all related by blood; the women, because of rules of clan exogamy, are all strangers both to the men and to each other. In a large extended family, the men will have the solidarity of kinship; the women will lack any solidarity. In such societies the only possible way for a woman to achieve her goals is for her to manipulate those who possess legitimate authority—her husband and her sons. Lamphere contrasts this inevitably negative image of women with the very positive image enjoyed by Navajo women. In that matrilineal society marriage is often matrilocal, so that it is the husband who moves to his wife's family. Here he is the one surrounded by strangers and must depend on his wife to negotiate concessions for him. Under these circumstances women are viewed as competent managers and good negotiators. This shows that the locality of marriage is crucial in determining the image of women. While it is true that in northern European societies bilateral descent was the norm, most marriages probably have demanded that women move to join their husbands. If manipulation of power is the only available route a woman can follow to achieve her ends then inevitably her image will be that of a manipulative bitch—as the *Malleus Maleficarum* makes abundantly clear.

There is little doubt that a contributing factor to the denigration of women in European thought was the legacy of Aristotle by way, particularly, of Augustine. "Conceiving of the soul as possessing nutritive, sensitive or appetitive and reasonable faculties, Aristotle saw women's souls as deficient in all three aspects, but especially in the faculty of reason" (Robertson n.d.). Acceptance of this idea leads inexorably to the dicta of the *Malleus* about the predisposition of women to be witches because of their manifold weaknesses (Question 4) (Kramer and Sprenger 1971).

Not only was the woman's soul seen as inferior; her body was too. "In Aristotelian and Galenic terms, woman is less fully developed than man. Because of lack of heat in germination, her sexual organs have remained internal, she is incomplete, colder and moister in dominant humors. She has less body heat and thus less courage, liberality, moral strength" (Robertson n.d.). That these ideas may appear absurd to us has to be tempered by their legacy and persistence in more recent times. Darwin believed that women were less evolved than men because of their childlike skins and softness (Dykstra 1986: 167–73), and the Freudian doctrine of penis-envy surely owes something to them.

The denigration of the body leads into another area germane to the witch stereotype and one that has been much explored by anthropology. The question of ritual pollution is used widely to "prove" that women are inferior, and doubtless has much to do with latter-day disputes about the ordination of women. All bodily emissions are considered polluting or, in our modem idiom, disgusting. Among others, Mary Douglas seeks an explanation for this attitude (Douglas 1966). In her opinion, all such substances are considered threatening because they are liminal, because they have "traversed the boundary of the body" and are thus of the body but yet not of the body, and thus do not fit our standard categories. While I do not dispute this point, I have argued elsewhere that what makes these substances so deeply threatening is that they remind us of death (Brain 1977b: 371–84). It is no coincidence that they are often sought for and used in magic intended to bring about the death of the victim. Of course, both men and women produce polluting emissions, but only women menstruate, give birth messily, and lactate. Customarily women take care of small babies who, like animals, are uncontrolled in their excretions, and the association with babies makes women additionally polluting. The issue of pollution throws additional light on why midwives were disproportionately often accused of witchcraft. Because they assisted at birth, they inevitably became contaminated with polluting substances. It should also be recalled that midwives traditionally laid out the dead and were contaminated by death, the ultimate pollutant.

Women's very physiology therefore makes them appear more polluted and polluting than men. Even in regard to the sexual act itself, a man can more easily be cleansed since his genitals are external and can be readily washed. A woman cannot be so readily cleansed, since her own polluting bodily fluids have been augmented by the deposition of the man's semen. Pollution alone would not make a witch, yet the *Malleus* makes clear that pollution is a primary aspect of sexuality. Sexuality is allied to temptation, and the Devil is the great tempter. Nowhere is this more powerfully demonstrated than through the medium of lust for women—"though the devil tempted Eve to sin, yet Eve seduced Adam" (*Malleus*: Part 1, Question 6).

Although the *Malleus* is obsessive in its misogyny and loathing of sex, it seems to deal only indirectly with one sexual matter—the nature of semen. Literary references of the Shakespearian period show that this was a subject that exercised men's minds. In some ways, this belief is still widely held as part of folk beliefs even today in the United States. The basic assumption of this belief is that marrow and semen are the same substance; the skull is the largest bone in the body and the brain is its marrow. Therefore any emission of semen depletes a man's life force and intelligence. "As the main storehouse of bone marrow, the brain is the source of semen, via the spinal cord. The supply is limited. . . . Loss of manhood, power, and ultimate life itself results from the 'spending' of the life force, which is a finite capital" (La Barre 1984: 130). Francis Bacon wrote in 1626 that "The skull has Braines, as a kind of Marrow, within it"; and even Leonardo da Vinci apparently believed in a duct connecting the brain to the penis via the spinal cord (La Barre 1984: 115–18). Understanding the belief that semen and marrow were one and the same gives point to the many references in literature to the danger of expending a man's marrow. If we grasp this unfounded fear, we can well understand yet another aspect of the witch image: that of the succubus and its terrifyingly debilitating potential.

Claude Lévi-Strauss suggested that the primary pair of oppositions is that of nature versus culture (Leach 1970: 35). Sherry B. Ortner claims that universally women are perceived as being, if not *part of* nature, at least as *closer to* nature than men, who are perceived as the generators of culture (Ortner 1974: 67–87). This position has been challenged (McCormack and Strathern 1980), but it is convincing. It generates the following sets of oppositions (always unequal in value):

Nature—Culture
Women—Men
Darkness—Light
Left—Right
Disorder—Order
Death—Life

It is significant that in many languages the word for left is synonymous with female and right with male (Brain 1977a: 180–92). One should note that "right" as in side or hand and "right" as in correct or "the right to" are not merely homonymous. The same is true of "droit" or "recht." Perceptually, witches are always believed to do and to be everything that is the reverse of normal and right. Similarly, all the

other characteristics in the left column are applicable to the witch stereotype.

The link between women and nature suggested by Ortner was hardly an unfamiliar one in Renaissance Europe. Bacon in particular took the view that the mission of science was the subjugation of nature. Moreover, he participated in the "rhetoric that conjoins the domination of nature with the insistent image of nature as female" (Fox-Keller 1983: 116).

That the image of witch as woman (or vice versa) is extremely widespread in the world is beyond doubt. Elsewhere in the world, and in Europe before the association of witchcraft with heresy, witchcraft was considered bad but of minor importance. During the witchcraze a new doctrine emerged that linked witchcraft with devil worship and hence with heresy. This change in doctrine made the image of woman as witch lethal to women. The change did not occur in a vacuum, and there are many powerful reasons why the witchcraze occurred. The witchcraze ended, but misogyny and gynophobia are still alive and well at the end of the twentieth century.

Mobility as a Factor in the Nonexistence or Decline of Witchcraft Beliefs

Examining non-Western small-scale societies, one discovers a rather startling fact. Societies with the simplest technologies of all—hunter-gatherers such as the San of the Kalahari, the Mbuti pygmies of the Ituri Forest, and the Hadza of northwest Tanzania—are quite unconcerned about witchcraft and do not think that it occurs in their societies (Marshall 1962: 221–52; Turnbull 1968: 132–37; Woodburn 1968: 49–55). They do, however, impute it to their sedentary agricultural neighbors (Turnbull 1961: 228; Woodburn 1982a: 431–51; Lee 1976: 127–29). When they themselves are forced into a sedentary way of life, "witchcraft fears are rampant" (Woodburn 1982b: 187–210). Why fears of witchcraft are unimportant to such peoples is described by several authors. Of the San peoples, L. Marshall writes, "the composition of a band is fluid—marriage takes individuals from one band to another, and whole families move from one band to another; bands split and disband completely" (Marshall 1976: 180). Similarly, Richard Lee notes that "hunters have a great deal of latitude to vote with their feet, to walk out of an un-pleasant situation" (Lee 1972: 182). In J. Woodburn's description of conflict resolution in these societies lies the key to the absence of witchcraft beliefs. When conflict arises, people move, giving an ecological reason. Thus, "they solve disputes simply by refusing to acknowledge them" (Woodburn 1968: 156; 1979: 244–60).

It is significant that all these African hunter-gatherers possess negligible property and practice bilateral descent. The situation is very different in societies that practice unilineal descent. In his essay, Meyer Fortes suggests that unilineal descent is characteristic of societies in which property rights are acknowledged (Fortes 1953: 17–41). Such societies invariably subscribe to a belief in sorcery or witchcraft or both. Unlike their African counterparts, Australian hunter-gatherers practice unilineal descent. They claim ownership over totemic sites and believe in evil magic, as evidenced by accounts of "bone-pointing" (Thomas 1906; Spencer and Gillen 1904: 462–63; Spencer and Gillen 1899/1938: 533; Elkin 1938: 203–05; Meggitt 1962: 139, 176). All the accounts emphasize, however, that only men are involved; that the practice is thought to be rare. It is also believed that "the professional worker of magic is always to be found in another tribe" (Elkin 1938: 203). Woodburn suggests that the crucial factor that differentiates African from Australian hunter-gatherers is "the relatively tight control which men exercise over women" among the Australians (Woodburn 1979: 258). This point has relevance to the European witch-craze. It is also important that Woodburn describes the African hunter-gatherers as having an "immediate return system" of economics, whereas the Australians, more like sedentary peoples, have "delayed return systems" (Woodburn 1982a: 258). A comparable people, the Ona (or Selk'nam) of Tierra del Fuego, are a hunting-gathering people. Anne Chapman describes them as inegalitarian, oppressive to women (unlike the African hunter-gatherers). They put an "emphasis on patrilineality, and patrilocality [and] the preeminence of territoriality" (Chapman 1984: 63). Like the Australians, they change campsites frequently; like them they believe in sorcerers; like them they claim that sorcerers belong to another tribe (Bridges 1949: 213, 373).

If we turn to the nomadic pastoral peoples, we should, according to my hypothesis, find a situation similar to that found among the Australians and the Ona/Selk'nam, since all pastoralists practice patrilineal descent, and own property, but move fairly frequently. This proves to be the case. There is no mention of witchcraft among the Fulani (Peuls) of the Sahel region of West Africa (Stenning 1959, 1965), while among the pastoral Somali "magic, witchcraft and sorcery play a small part" (Lewis 1965). The same is true of the Turkana and Dodos of Northern Kenya (Gulliver and Gulliver 1953: 86), and the Karamojong of Northern Uganda (Dyson-Hudson 1966: 40), where "in theory, witches are never found in one's own settlement but always in a different group from one's own" (Gulliver and Gulliver 1953: 49). The closely related Jie, their neighbors, have adopted a partially sedentary mode of existence. They diagnose witchcraft as the cause for a sequence of misfortunes, and their "normal procedure [then] is to move to a new homestead to avoid the evil influence" (Gulliver 1955: 104). Similarly, the nomadic pastoral Maasai of Kenya and Tanzania believe that one can learn the techniques of sorcery, but "they have no conventional category of supernatural 'witches' . . . and they often make fun of their Bantu neighbors who they know do possess such beliefs" (Jacobs 1985). Their linguistically and ethnically similar sedentary neighbors, the Arusha (il Arusa), on the other hand, are very concerned about witchcraft (Gulliver 1963: 21). The same holds true for the closely related agricultural Nandi and Kipsigis in Kenya (Peristiany 1939: 94–95; Langley 1979: 10, 62), and for the related Lango and Teso of Uganda (Driberg 1923: 241ff; Lawrence 1957: 182; Gulliver and Gulliver 1953: 26). The ethnically different, click-speaking Sandawe, not far away, who were probably formerly hunter-gatherers, now practice agriculture. Predictably, G. W. B. Huntingford says of them that "witchcraft is prevalent and illness and death are attributed either to it or to the anger of ancestral spirits" (Huntingford 1953: 137–38).

The ethnographic data show that in societies with total mobility and little attachment to property and with consequently little development of hierarchy and authority, there are no fears about witchcraft. Where there is considerable mobility but some attachment to property—often expressed by the presence of unilineal descent—we can expect to find a belief that witchcraft exists. The assumption is, however, that it is located in some other group and can easily be avoided by the move of a homestead. As dwellings are temporary huts in a thorn corral or something similar, this is not considered a particularly serious matter. When we turn to the sedentary peoples of the non-industrial world, however, we can expect always to find beliefs in witchcraft. The details of the beliefs may vary, but, as I have already mentioned, there is a remarkable consistency about aspects of the beliefs.

At the same time, it is manifest that particular forms of social organization or socio-political situations can generate more or less acute fears of witchcraft. Siegfried Frederick Nadel shows convincingly that two peoples that are almost identical ethnically, linguistically, and culturally can demonstrate radically different attitudes to witchcraft (Nadel 1952: 18–29). One society was rife with fears and accusations; the other had none. The only difference between the two societies is that the former has three age grades; the latter six. To move into the next higher grade, men had to forego the privileges of the age group they were relinquishing. Where there are six grades this presents no problem; where there are only three, suspicions and accusations proliferate between the young men and those in the middle grade—who are understandably reluctant to assume the mantle of old age and to eschew sexual activity and other privileges. Comparably, J. C. Mitchell shows that even in the circumstances of a modern tobacco estate in Zimbabwe (then Rhodesia), relatively well-educated permanent staff members constantly suspected their colleagues of evil magic directed against them (Mitchell 1965: 196). Uneducated casual laborers on the same estate who in their home areas might well have been anxious about witchcraft were quite unconcerned during their temporary sojourn on the estate. The more highly educated workers were in constant contact with one another and were always in competition for the favors of the white management.

. . . That virtually everywhere people believed in witchcraft from time immemorial until the eighteenth century is well established (Trevor-Roper 1969: 91). Why, then, was there the enormous surge of accusations during the Renaissance period? And why did the craze draw to a close? As Thomas notes of the decline in belief and the acceptance of a more rational viewpoint, "the ultimate origins of this faith in unaided human capacity remain mysterious."

Thomas accepts that "the decline of magic coincided with a marked improvement in the extent to which the environment became amenable to control" (Thomas 1971: 650, 663). Better food supplies and conditions of health, the cessation of plague (Midelfort 1972: 194), better communications and banking services, insurance, better fire-fighting—all these factors undoubtedly contributed to a greater sense of security. While it is true that the human impulse to seek scapegoats remains with us in the twentieth century, we have, in the main, abandoned the idea of personal malice as a cause for misfortune. In contemporary small-scale societies this personal view of misfortune persists, as numerous anthropological studies show.

It is quite clear to anyone who has worked in countries where there is still a general belief in witchcraft that education alone, even at university level, does not destroy the belief. It is quite easy to graft a theory of witchcraft onto a scientific theory of causation such as the germ theory (Offiong 1985: 107–24), and thus to assume that even a microorganism can attack one person rather than another because some person used evil magic. Moreover, most rational scientific observers would admit that psychological factors are important in reducing immunity. The reality of psychosomatic afflictions, however, is rather different from imputing each misfortune to the malevolence of one's kin or neighbors. If we look at the history of Europe it is only too evident that education per se was not the major reason for the waning of the craze; indeed, as Joseph Klaits notes, "the educated were in the forefront of the witch hunts" (Klaits 1985: 1–2). The rebirth of ideas after the medieval period should, one would think, have signalled the end of belief, yet Trevor-Roper observes, "There can be no doubt that the witch-craze grew, and grew terribly, after the Renaissance" (Trevor-Roper 1969: 91).

The skeptics who had the courage to challenge the prevailing orthodoxy about witches did not dispute the existence of witchcraft. Not to believe in witches was often seen as tantamount to being an atheist, as Sir Thomas Browne pointed out (Browne 1964: 29). What Weyer and Scot in the sixteenth century objected to was the injustice of accusing the wrong people. Bekker in the seventeenth century based his challenge on a fundamentalist piece of theology: if the devil on his fall from heaven was locked up in hell, how then could he be involved with witches here on earth (Trevor-Roper 1969: 174).

Precisely what caused the change from the relatively benign attitude toward witches in the Middle Ages to the hysterical attitude characteristic of the *Malleus Maleficarum* (Midelfort 1972: 193–94) is the subject of an ongoing debate. Cross-cultural study may contribute to our understanding of what caused the end of the witchcraze. One reason may be the only conceivable aspect that our social organization shares with that of the African hunter-gatherers: our mobility.

Humanity is by its nature a mass of contradictions. Impulses for conformity war with those for individualism. Tension develops and somehow has to be resolved. Where it is possible physically to remove oneself from those with whom one is in conflict, the tension disappears. Where this is not possible and where it is socially unacceptable to admit to tension arising from feelings of hate toward close kin, spouses, affines or neighbors, the human imagination seems to build up a whole edifice of fantasy about witches based on childish fears and imaginings. This holds especially true for societies where childrearing practices are harsh. While the details of beliefs may vary according to cultural prescription, the broad outlines are remarkably similar worldwide. They retain their fascination even in our skeptical, secular world, as Bruno Bettelheim has reminded us (Bettelheim 1977).

It is Thomas's contention that the surge in witchcraft accusations in the late sixteenth and early seventeenth centuries was not generated by any fundamental change in folk beliefs, but by a change in the structure of society. He speaks of the "increasingly individualistic forms of behavior which accompanied the economic changes" (Thomas 1971: 561). Cross-culturally one might draw a parallel with present-day Africa, where scholars have universally reported the widespread belief that the practice of evil magic has proliferated (Middleton and Winter 1963: 25). In Europe the change was from a feudal society with its well-understood certitudes about class and status; in Africa from a tribal form of social organization in which status was largely ascribed to the emerging societies, in which status can be achieved through education, wage employment, cash-cropping, entrepreneurial, political and religious activities; class divisions have begun to appear and become institutionalized (Gluckman 1965).

During the sixteenth and seventeenth centuries there was enormous social, political, economic, and religious ferment in Europe. This led initially to feelings of deep insecurity in all these arenas of human activity, exacerbated by the Copernican revolution; it also led to unrivaled opportunities for the acquisition of wealth, power, and social status. All this activity generated great divisions in society, as well as powerful emotions such as envy, jealousy, hostility, self-questioning, and guilt. This is entirely consistent with the large number of witchcraft accusations in the Tudor and early Stuart periods. A similar phenomenon—though not on quite so lethal a scale—is taking place in Africa today. . . .

34

Sorcery and Concepts of Deviance Among the Kabana, West New Britain

Naomi M. McPherson

Most beginning students of comparative religion picture sorcerers as practitioners of evil with few, if any, positive functions in their societies. Contrary to this general view, Naomi McPherson's data demonstrate that, depending on the circumstances that initiate the attack, sorcery may or may not be considered by the Kabana as a criminal act. She writes (Anthropologica, vol. 33, no. 1–2, 1991, p. 127):

> *For the Kabana of New Britain, deviant behavior is essentially the advancement of self-interest untempered by self-regulation such that the individual infringes on the ability of others to pursue their own self-interest. Social labeling is applied to deviant behaviors, but no permanent stigma attaches to individuals. Reactions to deviance include shame, gossip and ridicule, proceedings before the village magistrate, and sorcery. The performance of sorcery, a major cause of death, is a complex and ambiguous event, insofar as a sorcerer's threat may both inhibit deviance and mediate conflict, but the actual enactment of the threat is itself a deviant act. In cases where a victim's illness is attributed to sorcery, a moot may be held to discern the motives of sorcery and identify the sorcerer. In a particular case, which is examined at length here, failure clearly to identify the sorcerer was followed by the victim's death.*

Deaths resulting from sorcery are always classified as "bad deaths" by the Kabana.

In the study of what we now recognize as "deviance" in Pacific societies, the work of Malinowski is central. Vincent considers his treatment of sorcery, in particular, to be "pathbreaking." In the Trobriands, sorcery was *both* a criminal practice and a method of administering justice. Which it was in any particular case depended on who was practising it on whom and when he was doing it. On the one hand, sorcery was

> the main criminal agency (Malinowski 1926: 85); on the other, the Trobriand chief used sorcery to punish offenders. . . . Thus he concluded that where there was no *formal* code or administration of justice, it was very difficult to draw a line between the "quasi-legal" and the "quasi-criminal." (Vincent 1990: 165–66)

The line was usually drawn in some public arena.

"Sorcery and Concepts of Deviance Among the Kabana, West New Britain" reprinted with permission from ANTHROPOLOGICA, Vol. 33, No. 1–2, 1991, pp. 127–43.

In this early view, sorcery may be either deviance per se, or it may be the *control* of deviance. This treatment is compatible with the labelling theory of deviance that has developed since Malinowski wrote, especially in its focus on reactions to deviance rather than deviance itself. Indeed, the earliest statement of labelling theory by Becker (1963: 10–11) included a lengthy citation of one of Malinowski's cases from *Crime and Custom in Savage Society* (Malinowski 1967). Becker used this quote to differentiate between the relatively common commission of an act and the rare adjudication of the same act as *deviant by virtue of the reaction to it.*

In this paper, a similar analysis is applied to the Kabana of West New Britain, Papua New Guinea. Labelling theory is used to call attention to the multiple levels of political negotiation that go into a decision about whether an act of sorcery is—or is not—deviant. In the process, the analysis leads us to an examination of the organizational complexity of labelling. In order to provide context for the analysis, I begin with a discussion of Kabana morality and then move to a discussion of lower, "pre-sorcery" levels of social control among the Kabana, and, finally, I examine Kabana notions of sorcery as a social sanction. With this background established, the paper then moves to an extended analysis of a particular case of alleged sorcery and the political negotiation that took place, when villagers tried to decide whether the sorcery was deviance or had been used as a means to *control* deviance. The case is a provocative and rich one, because the outcome of the negotiation was indeterminate. The line between sorcery as deviance and sorcery as control of deviance could not be drawn, and the case entered Kabana history as backdrop for some dispute that would arise later.

Kabana Morality

Among the Kabana of West New Britain, Papua New Guinea, the framework of ideal social values and morals is grounded in concepts of human nature and the obligations inherent in the structure of human relations. It is this ethic of morality which provides a guide for individual action, and against which actions are judged. In this non-literate society, where the locus of individual experience is social, relations among individuals and groups do not exist in the abstract but always and only in connection with some-

one or something else. Given the extensive and overlapping network of Kabana social relations, there is an equally extensive range of behaviour that can be perceived as deviant to some degree and can elicit varying degrees of response from a particular audience. What constitutes deviant behaviour thus depends on whether relevant others perceive a certain act as a threat to the basic tenets of Kabana social life, that is, to the moral obligations which structure human relations.

Offended persons may select from a hierarchy of responses of increasing complexity to restore and restructure their interpersonal relations. Ultimately, social conformity derives from a fundamental principle of reciprocal self-interest which is based upon two related concepts: self-regulation and self-help. Self-regulation entails that all individuals are deemed to be in control of their own existence and, therefore, are accountable to, and responsible for, others. Self-help is the principle whereby individuals who perceive their rights to have been infringed upon may rightfully take retaliatory action against those who have infringed upon them (cf. Lawrence 1984: 161). The interrelated concepts of self-help and self-regulation are, in turn, based on the Kabana belief in personal autonomy, that is, that all individuals have the freedom to empower their existence as a basic human right. For the Kabana, deviant behaviour is essentially the advancement of self-interest untempered by self-regulation such that the individual infringes on the ability of others to pursue their own self-interest.

The Kabana label behaviour but not individuals as deviant, and the imposition of negative sanctions in no way implies an intent to permanently discriminate against or stigmatize an offender. The aim of any sanction is to provide the culprit with the opportunity for expiation thereby limiting the consequences of the transgression to that single event. There is no intentional discrimination against, and no stigma applied to, offenders, for to stigmatize persons is to set aside and mark them permanently as incorrigibly different, thus denying them the opportunity to redress the imbalance in social relations caused by their offenses. By not allowing a person to rectify wrongful behaviour, others arbitrarily rescind that individual's personal autonomy, integrity and right to self-help, thus effectively reducing the individual to a non-social (and, therefore, non-human) being. To label an individual permanently as deviant is to place him or her outside the pale of human relations as a social pariah. Ultimately, such action is tantamount to a death sentence, because in societies of this nature, no one can exist outside the context of social relations. The only options left to the stigmatized individual would be exile or suicide (cf. Counts and Counts 1984; Lawrence 1984: 132).

Most reactions to deviance occur at the level of personal relations, though they may involve whole families. On occasion, however, reactions to deviance can be escalated to levels that involve multiple families within villages, and may even include whole villages. Sorcery events also involve their own levels of organization and styles of political negotiation.

After briefly delineating the range of responses to lower levels of deviance, I focus on a traditional village "court" proceeding which was convened in reaction to a particular sorcery event. Sorcery is the most pervasive and powerful regulatory device that the Kabana have for dealing with deviant behaviour. The practice of sorcery is not unambiguously right or wrong. As a negative sanction, sorcery is a legitimate form of social control, both an expected and accepted consequence of a breach of morality. Since sorcery is always potentially lethal, however, any act of sorcery, regardless of the circumstances, can be construed as a deviant act and thus be subject to negative social sanctions itself. The case history presented here demonstrates how the community reacted to the ambiguous nature of sorcery, when they attempted to determine whether or not one woman's imminent death by sorcery was a legitimate form of social control or a case of homicide, which, in turn, would require control.

Lower Levels of Social Control

All Kabana relationships are face-to-face relations and everyone is known to, and knows about, everyone else. Anonymity is impossible and no behaviour, albeit good, bad or indifferent, goes undiscovered. For the most part, a perceived breach of the ideal of reciprocal self-interest is couched in terms of positive criticism. Someone who ignores the rules of reciprocity is advised or reminded of the potentially negative consequences that could be experienced as a result of the impropriety. For example, a youth who avoids

assisting his kin in cutting and hauling trees to make a garden fence may be criticized for his laziness and warned that when he needs the aid of these same kin in some venture of his own, such as the amassing of his bride-wealth, help may not be forthcoming. Continued failure to observe proper behaviour reduces a person's chances for success in other desired achievements, and, since it is in their own best interests to do so, most people adjust their behaviour in response to the pressure exerted on them to conform.

The Kabana do not equate simple non-conformity with deviance. Idiosyncratic personality types are marked, for example, by teasing or nicknaming. They may become the butt of jokes, be lampooned, criticized or otherwise disparaged, but there is no stigma imposed on them. When a person is recognized as having social or physical disabilities, others compensate for the idiosyncratic personality by lowering their expectations. Acknowledging individual differences defines the attributes of individuals who comprise a relationship, but the relationship itself remains unaffected, operating according to the level of expectations of all involved. Within the framework of lowered expectations, the idiosyncratic personality is recognized but not stigmatized in the sense of being negatively stereotyped or marginalized.

Shaming, gossip and ridicule are extremely effective means of sanctioning deviant behaviour. The power of shame as an overt negative sanction derives from the discomfort of "an intrusion of one's private self into public awareness and the reciprocal invasion of the self by public scrutiny" (Jorgensen 1983–84: 123). Shaming and gossip expose the inadequacies of the individual and exert pressure on the target to behave according to commonly held values and to repair the imbalance in social relations. The balance between public and private, self and other, is restored through a process of negotiations and settled when the culprit presents a gift of wealth to those who have gossiped about or shamed the victim. The gift of wealth both relieves the culprit of the sense of shame and obliges the recipients to curtail their slander or risk censure themselves for perpetuating a situation that has been resolved satisfactorily.

At a higher level of response, theft, physical violence and adultery often result in the perpetrator being brought before the village magistrate by the injured party. More often than not, in communities of this type, "the culprit is condemned on the basis of ideal social values even by those who have been guilty of the same offense in the past" (Lawrence 1984: 132). Again, since the Kabana label only behaviour, not individuals, as deviant, any sanction imposed by the public court allows the culprit the opportunity for expiation and limits the consequences of the transgression to a single event. Once reparation is made, usually in the form of a compensation payment, the incident is forgiven, although rarely forgotten, and the culprit resumes his or her usual place in the community. There is no intentional discrimination against, and no permanent stigma applied to, the offender.

For the Kabana, observation of the moral obligations that structure and organize normal relations can be, ultimately, a life-and-death matter. Persons who survive to an extreme old age are by definition those persons who have lived a morally correct life. Death from old age is a good death (cf. Counts and Counts 1976–77), a death which is the result of, and performs closure on, a socially correct and moral life span. The Kabana observe, however, that human nature being what it is, very few people survive to the culturally defined life span that culminates in a good death. With few exceptions, most people die a bad death as victims of sorcery (see Scaletta 1985).

Sorcery as Social Sanction and as Deviance

Sorcery can be defined as a form of esoteric knowledge bestowing personal power which the adept can use willfully to realize desired ends. While not everyone could or would acquire the knowledge and skill to become a sorcerer, all have access to sorcery as a mode of self-help by purchasing the services of a known sorcerer. Awareness of the fact that others can choose to exercise their right to self-help through sorcery serves to define sorcery as the primary deterrent to deviant behaviour. Victims of sorcery are assumed to be persons who have violated social mores and values thereby infringing on the rights of others. Because sorcery is notoriously difficult to control once unleashed, both the decision to sorcerize and the execution of that decision should result from corporate deliberation and follow certain other procedural rules. The injured party should discuss any intention to instigate redressive action in the form of sorcery with his or her kin. If one's kin are not in

agreement with such measures, the whole matter is dropped or deferred. If there is sufficient agreement to warrant action, however, usually because others have complaints against the intended victim or because the offence is such that sorcery is the only appropriate form of punishment, then the services of a sorcerer are solicited. Sorcery is a male prerogative acquired through apprenticeship and arranged in the *lum*, "men's house." Once the sorcerer has been approached and all the details have been worked out, the sorcerer and his clients exchange equal lengths of the most highly valued category of shell-money, *bula misi*. This exchange of wealth "buys" both the sorcerer's services and the silence and complicity of those employing him. Since the men's house is a semi-public domain, there is no question that the business of soliciting a sorcerer has been witnessed by other men in or near the building, and the whole episode becomes a topic for discreet gossip, a public secret, and moves into a wider area of involvement.

The sorcerer's role may also be construed as that of a mediator hired to resolve a conflict between two parties. Acting on behalf of his client, the sorcerer leaves a "calling card" (Zelenietz 1981: 105) which alerts the recipient that some action on his or her part has offended another party, thus jeopardizing their relationship. The calling cards of Kabana sorcerers can take a number of forms: a large basket, of the type only sorcerers carry, lodged in the rafters of the victim's house; a gutted frog pinioned on the footpath the victim travels to the gardens; a bundle of croton leaves tied in a particular way and placed conspicuously where the victim will find it, and so on.

Kabana sorcerers also send calling cards in the form of ensorcelled stones that they throw onto or into the victim's house. The stone called *pamododonga* carries a form of sorcery that causes the victim to become ill for an indefinite period or time. It is generally assumed that, during the illness, victims will examine their consciences, review their actions and deduce for themselves the nature of their transgressions. They can then take steps to rectify the situation by approaching those with whom they are in conflict and trying to negotiate a resolution to the difficulty. If a resolution is reached, they pay the sorcerer to rescind his spell. If they are unable to identify the locus of conflict, the sorcerer might approach them, inform them why they have been ill, remove the spell and restore health. It is more common, however, because sorcery is a non-confrontational social act, for spells to be removed as stealthily as they were applied. Then, a second stone, *angual*, is thrown on the victim's house. Sorcery of this type puts transgressors on notice that they should discover the source of the conflict and repair the rift in their relationships, before they develop into open confrontation.

Although sorcery is an expected negative sanction for breach of expected behaviour, the actual implementation of sorcery as a form of self-help is, in itself, a deviant act. Evidence of sorcery indicates that someone has succeeded in a private act of collusion. When sorcery is suspected, "the contradiction between autonomy and control is flagrantly exposed and every villager is witness to his or her own vulnerability" (Weiner 1976: 223). Sorcery takes away from the victim all that the Kabana define as human rights: the right to self-help, personal autonomy and control over one's existence. To be a victim of sorcery is to be threatened with death, for one's "personal autonomy has collapsed" (Weiner 1976: 219). It is for this reason that death by sorcery is a bad death. It is a bad death not just because of the manner in which it occurred, but also because of the manner in which it was incurred. Death by sorcery entails a negative judgment upon the behaviour of the victim by relevant others, but does not allow the culprit to amend the situation in his or her own best interests. Personal autonomy is negated and the target becomes a victim of the power that others wield in pursuit of their own self-interest. Death by sorcery is a moral issue, and those who practise it are themselves subject to public disapprobation: "Individual power, the cause of all death, demands the display of group power" (Weiner 1976: 226).

A Case of Sorcery

Jean had been seriously ill for three months. During this time, attempts to cure her had proved fruitless. Treatments at the local hospital and by local healers, and the attempts of a sorcerer-curer to heal her by extracting foreign substances from her body were all ineffective. From the beginning of her illness, Jean was convinced that she had been sorcerized, a conviction reinforced when all attempts to cure her

failed. Only the sorcerer who inflicts the spell has the correct formula for rescinding it and restoring the victim to health. As her illness progressed, Jean became more and more incapacitated. She became a non-participant in the myriad conceptual and social minutiae that make life worth living. As an invalid, her social interactions were essentially passive. She was dependent on others to care for her, and she resented being powerless, the victim of someone's ill-will. There was no question in anyone's mind, least of all Jean's, that she was dying. Her family refused, however, to open the magic bundle containing her vital essence, *tautau*, and kept it in contact with her body to prevent her death. The final indignity, from Jean's perspective, was that she was denied the right to take control of the situation and end her own life. (See Scaletta 1985 for a detailed discussion of these events.)

Given that illness or death caused by sorcery are the result of specifically inflicted punishment for a breach of socially expected behaviour on the part of the victim (or her family), Jean's condition created a climate of heightened awareness of a variety of social relations. Relations between Jean and other individuals, between her family and other family groups, between her hamlet and the other three hamlets in the village, and between her village as a unit and other villages, particularly the two villages where the majority of her cognatic kin lived, were all minutely scrutinized. There was constant re-evaluation and discussion of past events, interpersonal and intergroup interactions, in order to determine why, and by whom, she was sorcerized. Jean's personal crisis as an individual escalated to the level of an intervillage social crisis.

Jean added to the escalating tensions by making specific charges of sorcery against three men in the village. She accused Ken, her deceased husband's brother. His motive, she said, was revenge: Ken and his kin group were avenging the death of their brother by attacking his wife. The second man she accused was Lari. She had no specific reason for accusing him, except that he had renown as a powerful sorcerer, and was, at the time, under suspicion by everybody in the area as the individual responsible for the current drought. She argued that if Lari would create hardship in the whole area in his efforts to destroy a rival, then it was reasonable that he should attack her for no motive other than that it was in the nature of his disposition to do so. The third man she accused was Tomi, her sister's husband. Tomi was obsessively jealous of his wife and resented the time she spent in Jean's company. By eliminating her, Jean reasoned, Tomi was eliminating a major competitor for his wife's affection.

In all these accusations, Jean portrayed herself as an innocent victim. At no time did she name anyone who may have had reason to resort to sorcery in retaliation for some misdeed on her part. In proclaiming her innocence, she was implying that sorcery was being practised arbitrarily and, therefore, that everyone was vulnerable unless it could be stopped. Jean's steady decline, the general unease generated by the active presence of sorcery in their midst, the increasing strain between her cognatic and affinal kin and the intervillage tensions arising from Jean's accusations coalesced one morning with the arrival of a delegation of Jean's male kin from her natal village. They came both to express their anger that someone was "killing" their sister and to demand that a meeting be convened to "break the talk," to expose and punish the sorcerer.

Breaking the Talk

To "break the talk" means to cut through the multitude of conjecture and gossip about why a person has been sorcerized and by whom. When the "talk is broken," it is exposed to public scrutiny so that its veracity can be analyzed and a logical sequence of events leading up to the illness or death can be reconstructed. When the nature of the victim's offence has been determined, thereby identifying those who had reason to sorcerize her, witnesses can either refute or confirm the charges of culpability. The meeting to "break the talk" also provides a forum where persons who are associated with the illness or death, because of past disputes with the victim, can proclaim their innocence and clear their names, thereby avoiding the possibility that they might be sorcerized by the victim's avenging kin group. Ideally, this procedure culminates in a solid case of circumstantial evidence identifying the protagonists in the conflict, and leaves no doubt as to who caused the victim to become ill or to die. Any doubt as to the identity of the sorcerer is dispelled when those who witnessed the meeting between the sorcerer and the persons who employed him produce the length of

shell-money they were given to "buy" their silence. Ultimately, the "talk is broken" when the silence surrounding the act of collusion is broken, thus publicly exposing those who participated in the decision to sorcerize.

A meeting to "break the talk" is a highly charged public confrontation and represents the most complex level of the adjudication of deviance in Kabana culture. At such meetings in the past, it is said, the end came with a fight and the killing of the exposed sorcerer. The sorcerer's death was considered compensation for the death of the victim, and obviated (in theory, if not always in practice) the need for retributive sorcery by balancing the losses on both sides of the conflict. The death of the sorcerer was a public statement to those who sought control over others that homicidal sorcery was an amoral act so heinous that death was the only appropriate social response.

On the day of the meeting, all the adult males from the four concerned villages convened in the plaza in front of the "men's house." There were no women (except myself) or children visibly present. It was dangerous for them to be there. The meeting lasted for five hours, during which the discussion ranged widely. Several young men professed their lack of knowledge of sorcery, and called on their senior male relatives to attest to the fact that they had not instructed them in the ways and means of sorcery. Another man acknowledged that he had disputed with Jean and her sister over the ownership of certain sago palms, but said they had settled the problem, and that the altercation could not, therefore, be construed as a motive for sorcery on his part. Much of the meeting proceeded in this manner, the underlying premise being that unchallenged, public denials of guilt or involvement are sufficient to prove innocence. The most important contributions came from the three men specifically accused by Jean, and from Jean's brother.

The three accused took the opportunity to refute Jean's charges against them. Tomi, Jean's sister's husband, stated that he did not and could not know sorcery because he was associated with women (a consequence of his jealous obsession with his wife). This was common knowledge, he went on, for did not everyone refer to him as "first woman"? Sorcery is the business of men, and a man who spends his time with women would not have occasion to learn the art. Even if he did, his powers would be diminished by his contact with females, who are "different" (Tok Pisin: *narapela kain*) from men. It was true, he admitted, that he had tried to purchase rain magic (a form of sorcery) from an old man in another village, but he had been refused. Tomi had given valid reasons why he could not know sorcery, and why, even if he did have some skill as a sorcerer, this skill would be minimal. He had admitted to being in the company of a sorcerer, given reasons for being there and revealed the outcome of the meeting, thus forestalling any misconstruction of his behaviour by others who might have witnessed the meeting. No one challenged what he had to say.

Ken, Jean's husband's brother, also denied her accusations against him. He pointed out that when she first became ill, she had come to him on her own initiative and asked him to use his skills to cure her. He had assumed she was suffering from the effects of "bad blood," a problem peculiar to post-menopausal women. He had prepared the appropriate cure, which proved ineffective. Because of this and her worsening condition, she became fearful and accused him of sorcerizing rather than curing her. He also noted that she, and perhaps other members of her family, thought he might have attacked her in revenge for the death of his brother, Jean's husband. He denied the credibility of such speculations on the grounds that he was a member of the Catholic Church which forbade the practice of sorcery. He further denied the fact of sorcery, saying that sickness and death were not caused by human actors, but by God, as divine punishment for sins committed. Jean was dying, he concluded, because God was punishing her as a sinner.

The third man accused by Jean was Lari. As the person considered responsible for the drought and a self-acknowledged sorcerer, Lari defended himself on both counts. He argued that no one could claim they had actually seen him practising weather magic. Even though he had all the paraphernalia, which he then produced for all to see, without eyewitnesses, all the talk about him was nothing but air, insubstantial and without truth value. Did people think, he demanded, that he or a member of his family would be so "insane" (Kabana: *mangamanga*) as to attack this woman and run the risk of retaliation from her kin? They must look to the woman herself, he admonished, for the origin of her problem. From the time of their ancestors, he continued, there were

two reasons why females were attacked by sorcery. They were sorcerized for being foul-tempered, malicious gossips, and for repulsing the sexual advances of males, or conversely, for engaging in illicit love affairs. (The seeming paradox of this situation is more apparent than real, but a detailed discussion is beyond the scope of the task at hand.)

Lari's point here was to prompt people to examine Jean's behaviour rather than continuing to look for wrongdoing on the part of others. He was, in effect, both denying the validity of the scenario that Jean had created in which she played the role of innocent victim, and situating the whole episode within the accepted explanatory framework—people are sorcerized for breach of social norms. It then came out that during the weeks of Jean's illness, there had been a great deal of discussion about her reputation for maligning others, particularly two senior women who were highly respected. There was also talk of her affair with a married man who was also a person of some renown. It was further reported that she had accepted a proposal of marriage, and the shell money that accompanied it, from a man in the Kove district. She had later reneged on her promise to marry him, claiming that she wanted to remain a widow and live near her children, but had failed to return the shell money. The rejected man thus had motive—the loss of his shell money, not the broken promise—and the wherewithal to attack her, the Kove being notorious sorcerers. All agreed that any one of the foregoing was a likely origin of her illness and, if so, that (1) she had gotten only what she deserved, and (2) that, if the sorcery originated with the Kove man, her chances of recovery were slim because no one knew either the Kove techniques, or, consequently, the specific counter spell to effect a cure.

Discussion turned to the possibility that Jean was part of a long-standing vendetta to eliminate all the members of her family. In the past five years, sorcery had claimed the lives of Jean's father, her 20-year-old son, a classificatory son and her eldest son's wife. Everyone knew that her father had died of *mosi* "privately owned designs." Without permission or payment, he had used the traditional totemic designs of another kin group on a set of spirit masks of his own group. Death by sorcery was the expected and accepted response to such a serious crime; hence, there had been no "talk" or retaliation, and the incident was closed. Perhaps, however, the issue was not closed, and Jean was the most recent casualty of the offended group's unrequited anger for her father's transgression against them.

These observations focussed attention on indigenous ancestral laws, and Lari began a forceful harangue about the loss of traditional customs. In the past, he began, this meeting would have taken place inside the men's house, not in the open plaza. Now the men's house stood abandoned, and young men no longer gathered there to learn from their elders. Now men slept, not in the men's house, but with their wives and children in the women's houses. Even the practice of sorcery was no longer done according to tradition. In the time of their grandfathers, sorcery was always undertaken by two or three men with the sanction of their kin group. With these several people involved, it was possible to "break the talk," discover who worked the sorcery and why, and thus permit resolution of the situation. This was no longer possible because sorcery was being practised on an individual basis, making it impossible to expose and control the practice of sorcery.

Jean's elder brother Karl, located at the outer perimeter of the assembly, had stood quietly throughout the foregoing, awaiting his opportunity to speak. When he had everyone's attention, he began by reprimanding people for listening to Jean's accusations. The ravings of a sick person should not be given credibility. Such talk is *mangamanga*, "hysterical," and based on fear. He went on to point out that those who brought up his father's death by sorcery were wrong to revive this incident, for it implied that he, or a member of his family, had avenged their father's death and that Jean's illness was retaliation for that second death. When their father died, he and his brothers had "put on the grass skirt" worn by women. Metaphorically, he was arguing that they had become like women, and thus did not know or engage in sorcery. The death of their father had nothing to do with his sister's dying, and such talk must cease, he emphasized, so that old animosities were not revived. He reiterated that they must look to Jean's own behaviour as the cause of her dying, and, having nicely set the mood, he went on to elaborate what, in his opinion, that behaviour might have been.

Some years before, Jean and her husband had contracted a marriage between one of their sons and the daughter of Rio and Sandra, a couple who have considerable prestige in the area. During a ceremonial feast at another village, Jean's son had an affair with another woman. The young people were discovered, and, when confronted with the options of either paying fines to "buy their shame," or with getting married, the two said they wished to be married. With this public declaration of intent, they were married *de facto,* and the betrothal previously arranged by the young man's parents was nullified.

When the jilted girl's parents heard this, they were furious and confronted Jean and her husband. While venting her anger, the girl's mother assumed the stylistic stance associated with throwing spears during battle, and called down the name of her personal protective spirit upon Jean's head, an effective and sometimes deadly curse. She berated Jean for breaking the marriage contract, thereby shaming both her and her daughter. Jean claimed she had nothing to do with the situation, and had heard of her son's behaviour and marriage only after the fact.

Two days after this confrontation, Jean sat on some wood shavings on her verandah, and, several days later, her legs became swollen. It was assumed that Jean had been sorcerized by the offended parents through the medium of wood shavings. She was treated by a curer familiar with that type of sorcery, and the condition was removed. It now appeared that the sorcery had not been neutralized, but had lain dormant in her body these past years, and was only now manifesting itself as her current illness.

Karl's speech was extremely effective. He had discredited Jean's accusations against others as the ravings of a sick and frightened person, thus soothing the anxieties of the accused; he had denied that her illness was a continuation of the conflict that resulted in their father's death, thus avoiding the possibility of old animosities resurfacing, and he had described a specific breach of moral obligation—the breaking of a marriage contract. At the same time, he had left it an open question whether or not Jean was responsible for the breach. (Everybody knew that nowadays children made up their own minds about whom they would or would not marry.) His suggestion that specific, known events and individuals might be responsible for Jean's illness helped defuse the tensions that had built up around people's fears that sorcery was being practised arbitrarily. The individuals implicated had been away from the village for the past year, living in urban centres, and so were not on hand to give their interpretation or to defend themselves. No one else present hurried to defend them either, possibly because one of them was already considered responsible for other recent, and unresolved, sorcery related incidents. At the conclusion of his speech, the meeting was brought to a close. Karl had provided an acceptable explanatory framework for Jean's condition, thus redressing the "threat of disorderliness" that a motiveless death implies (Zelenietz 1981: 9). The consensus was, however, that the meeting had not been totally satisfactory. They had been unable to "break the talk" and prove conclusively the validity of the reconstruction. No one had come forth to bear witness against the sorcerer whose behaviour threatened Jean's life and the moral infrastructure of social order. Because the situation was not totally resolved, there was little hope that Jean could be cured.

Three weeks later, Jean died. When the funeral rites and period of mourning were finished, life in the village reverted to the status quo ante; the crisis created by Jean's dying and death might never have occurred. When I inquired of my informants what steps, if any, would be taken to avenge her death or punish the sorcerer, I was advised that we ought not to discuss such matters. Others might hear of our talk, assume we are plotting vengeance and take steps to protect themselves by striking first; we could be sorcerized. Circumstances surrounding her death are not forgotten. The entire experience will be woven into the fabric of ongoing personal and social relations where it will affect people's motives and behaviour in the future.

Conclusion

This analysis of sorcery and deviant behaviour in Kabana society shows that the generic processes noted in labelling theory can be applied to the cross-cultural study of deviance, even in a society in which deviants are not specifically "labelled." Certain kinds of behaviour, under certain conditions, are reacted to as deviant in Kabana society, and there are rules about what constitutes a socially acceptable response to deviant behaviour. The Kabana data show that, regardless of the level of community involvement, the reaction to deviant behaviour does not result in the typing of individuals as permanently

deviant, or in the differentiation of people into groups defined as "normals" and "deviants." Given the egalitarian ideology and lack of stratification in Kabana society, the creation of a class of deviants is unlikely, and, in Kabana terms, philosophically untenable. Rather, deviance is a highly negotiated, highly complex phenomenon which occurs in an interpersonal network. Sorcery is an interesting case in point. While it is inherently neither deviant nor a normative sanction for the social control of deviance, it may be negotiated as *either* according to the specifics of any particular case. It may begin with individual relations and end there; it may rise to the familial level and end there or escalate to even more complex levels before it is publicly mooted. In the moot, sorcery may be judged to be a device for the legitimate control of deviance, deviance in and of itself, or the problem of what it is may prove to be insoluble. *Whatever* the outcome, the case remains in the cultural memory of the groups involved and forms part of relevant knowledge that will be brought to bear in subsequent cases of sorcery or other trouble.

Afterword

The events described above took place in early 1983. When I returned to the village in 1985, one of the first pieces of news that I was given was that Ken, Jean's husband's brother, had been ill for some months and was currently at the local health clinic for medical treatment. The public explanation for his illness was that he "had no blood" (acute anaemia, possibly leukaemia?); the *very* private explanation was that he had been sorcerized. In response to my queries about who had sorcerized him and why, people referred to the case of Jean and her accusations against her brother-in-law. I was also advised not to pursue this matter with "certain other people," lest those people infer that my inquiries were informed by the (malicious) speculation of the people who spent time with me, thus placing them at risk. It was clear that Ken's lingering illness was linked to Jean's death by sorcery, but people preferred not to make this connection a matter of public record or public moot. The feeling was that, if ignored, the attacks and counter-attacks of sorcery would cease, and order and well-being would prevail. I respected these views and did not pursue the matter further. Ken died in 1986 after a prolonged and painful dying process.

35

The Goat and the Gazelle: Witchcraft

T. M. Luhrmann

The following material is an excerpt from the author's book-length study of contemporary witches in England, based on fieldwork in London beginning in 1983. Luhrmann traces the modern revival of witchcraft to the influential writings of Gerald Gardner in the 1940s. However, from the point of view of present-day participants, nature-centered, or earth-centered, witchcraft is the most ancient of all religions, honoring goddess figures as personifications of nature. Its rituals relate to seasons and the natural world and are based on participants' reconstructions of pagan, or pre-Christian, religious practices. The author describes typical contemporary witches and their motivations for involvement, as well as their covens, including the one into which Luhrmann herself was initiated. She describes witches' rituals as typically involving chanting; the reading of texts; the use of magical circles, altars, and candles; and the symbolic offering of fruits.

Luhrmann's ethnography raises questions central to the anthropological consideration of magic, be it in England, Africa, or elsewhere (Luhrmann 1989: 7–8): Why do people find magic persuasive? How is it that some people, more than others, come to accept or "believe in" what is irrational and unacceptable to others? The witches documented by Luhrmann are ordinary people, well educated and usually middle-class, not mentally ill or in economic desperation (ibid.). The author documents the process by which emotional patterns and intellectual strategies change as participants come to accept the reality of magic. Such processes are at work, Luhrmann argues, in any circumstances in which specialized knowledge is acquired. What she discovers about contemporary witches holds intriguing parallels for us all, as we acquire the knowledge necessary to carry out our jobs or other roles in adult life.

. . .

Full moon, November 1984. In a witches' coven in northeast London, members have gathered from as far away as Bath, Leicester and Scotland to attend the meeting at the full moon. We drink tea until

Reprinted by permission of the publisher from PERSUASIONS OF THE WITCH'S CRAFT: RITUAL MAGIC IN CONTEMPORARY ENGLAND by T. M. Luhrmann, pp. 42–54, Cambridge, Mass.: Harvard University Press, Copyright © 1989 by T. M. Luhrmann.

nine—in London, most rituals follow tea—and then change and go into the other room. The sitting room has been transformed. The furniture has been removed, and a twelve foot chalk circle drawn on the carpet. It will be brushed out in the morning. Four candlesticks stake out the corners of the room, casting shadows from the stag's antlers on the wall. The antlers sit next to a sheaf of wheat, subtle sexual symbolism. In spring and summer there are flowers everywhere. The altar in the centre of the circle is a chest which seems ancient. On top an equally ancient box holds incense in different drawers. On it, flowers and herbs surround a carved wooden Pan; a Minoan goddess figure sits on the altar itself amid a litter of ritual knives and tools.

The high priestess begins by drawing the magic circle in the air above the chalk, which she does with piety, saying 'let this be a boundary between the world of gods and that of men'. This imaginary circle is then treated as real throughout the evening. To leave the circle you slash it in the air and redraw it when you return. The chalk circle is always drawn with the ritual knife; the cakes, wine and the dancing always move in a clockwise direction. These rules are part of what makes it a witches' circle and they are scrupulously observed. On this evening a coven member wanted us to 'do' something for a friend's sick baby. Someone made a model of the baby and put it on the altar, at the Minoan goddess' feet. We held hands in a circle around the altar and then began to run, chanting a set phrase. When the circle was running at its peak the high priestess suddenly stopped. Everyone shut their eyes, raised their hands, and visualized the prearranged image: in this case it was Mary, the woman who wanted the spell, the 'link' between us and the unknown child. We could have 'worked' without the model baby, but it served as a 'focus' for the concentration. Witches of folklore made clay and waxen effigies over which they uttered imprecations—so we made effigies and kept a packet of plasticene in the altar for the purpose. By springtime, Mary reported, the child had recovered, and she thanked us for the help.

. . .

Modern witchcraft was essentially created in the forties—at least in its current form—by a civil servant, Gerald Gardner, who was probably inspired by Margaret Murray's historical account of witchcraft as an organized pre-Christian fertility religion branded devil-worship by the demonologists, and more generally by the rise of interest in anthropology and folklore. Gardner had met Aleister Crowley, knew of the Golden Dawn, and may have been a Freemason. (Indeed his rituals show Crowleyan and Masonic influence.) In the early fifties, Gardner published fictitious ethnographies of supposedly contemporaneous witches who practised the ancient, secret rites of their agrarian ancestors and worshipped the earth goddess and her consort in ceremonies beneath the full moon. He claimed to have

been initiated into one of these groups, hidden from watchful authorities since the 'burning times'. In his eyes, witchcraft was an ancient magico-religious cult, secretly practised, peculiarly suited to the Celtic race. Witches had ancient knowledge and powers, handed down through the generations. And unlike the rest of an alienated society, they were happy and content. This paragraph gives the flavour of his romanticism:

> Instead of the great sabbats with perhaps a thousand or more attendents [the coven] became a small meeting in private houses, probably a dozen or so according to the size of the room. The numbers being few, they were no longer able to gain power, to rise to the hyperaesthetic state by means of hundreds of wild dancers shrieking wildly, and they had to use other secret methods to induce this state. This came easily to the descendants of the heath, but not to the people of non-Celtic race. Some knowledge and power had survived, as many of the families had intermarried, and in time their powers grew, and in out of the way places the cult survived. The fact that they were happy gave them a reason to struggle on. It is from these people that the surviving witch families probably descend. They know that their fathers and grandfathers belonged, and had spoken to them of meetings about the time of Waterloo, when it was an old cult, thought to exist from all time. Though the persecution had died down from want of fuel, they realized that their only chance to be left alone was to remain unknown and this is as true today as it was five hundred years ago.[1]

The invention of tradition is an intriguing topic: why is it that history should grant such authority, even in so rational an age? Witches speak of a secretive tradition, hidden for centuries from the Church's fierce eye, passed down in families until the present generation. There is no reason that such claims could not be true, but there is very little evidence to support them. The most sympathetic scholarship that speaks of an organized, pre-Christian witchcraft has very shaky foundations—although there is more recently work that suggests that there were at least shared fantasies about membership in witch-related societies. But those accused of witchcraft in early modern Europe were very likely innocent of any practice.

---

1. Gardner (1954: 46).

Witches have ambivalent attitudes towards their history, as a later chapter details. They share, however, a common vision of their past, differing only on whether this past is myth or legend. Many of them say that the truth of the vision is unimportant: it is the vision itself, with its evocative pull, that matters. The basic account—given by someone who describes it as a myth—is this:

> Witchcraft is a religion that dates back to paleolithic times, to the worship of the god of the hunt and the goddess of fertility. One can see remnants of it in cave paintings and in the figurines of goddesses that are many thousands of years old. This early religion was universal. The names changed from place to place but the basic deities were the same.
>
> When Christianity came to Europe, its inroads were slow. Kings and nobles were converted first, but many folk continued to worship in both religions. Dwellers in rural areas, the 'Pagans' and 'Heathens', kept to the old ways. Churches were built on the sacred sites of the old religion. The names of the festivals were changed but the dates were kept. The old rites continued in folk festivals, and for many centuries Christian policy was one of slow cooptation.
>
> During the times of persecution the Church took the god of the Old Religion and—as is the habit with conquerors—turned him into the Christian devil. The Old Religion was forced underground, its only records set forth, in distorted form, by its enemies. Small families kept the religion alive and in 1951, after the Witchcraft Laws in England were repealed, it began to surface again.[2]

It is indeed an evocative tale, with secrecy and martyrdom and hidden powers, and whether or not witches describe it as actual history they are moved by its affect.

Witchcraft is meant to be a revival, or re-emergence, of an ancient nature-religion, the most ancient of religions, in which the earth was worshipped as a woman under different names and guises throughout the inhabited world. She was Astarte, Inanna, Isis, Cerridwen—names that ring echoes in archaeological texts. She was the Great Goddess whose rites Frazer and Neumann—and Apuleius—recorded in rich detail. Witches are people who read their books and try to create, for themselves, the tone

and feeling of an early humanity, worshipping a nature they understand as vital, powerful and mysterious. They visit the stone circles and pre-Christian sites, and become amateur scholars of the pagan traditions behind the Easter egg and the Yule log.

Above all, witches try to 'connect' with the world around them. Witchcraft, they say, is about the tactile, intuitive understanding of the turn of the seasons, the song of the birds; it is the awareness of all things as holy, and that, as is said, there is no part of us that is not of the gods.[3] One witch suggests a simple exercise to begin to glimpse the nature of the practice:

> Perhaps the best way to begin to understand the power behind the simple word *witch* is to enter the circle . . . Do it, perhaps, on a full moon, in a park or in the clearing of a wood. You don't need any of the tools you will read about in books on the Craft. You need no special clothes, or lack of them. Perhaps you might make up a chant, a string of names of gods and goddesses who were loved or familiar to you from childhood myths, a simple string of names for earth and moon and stars, easily repeatable like a mantra.
>
> And perhaps, as you say those familiar names and feel the earth and the air, the moon appears a bit closer, and perhaps the wind rustling the leaves suddenly seems in rhythm with your own breathing. Or perhaps the chant seems louder and all the other sounds far away. Or perhaps the woods seem strangely noisy. Or unspeakably still. And perhaps the clear line that separates you from bird and tree and small lizards seems to melt. Whatever else, your relationship to the world of living nature changes. The Witch is the change of definitions and relationships.[4]

The Goddess, the personification of nature, is witchcraft's central concept. Each witch has an individual understanding of the Goddess, which changes considerably over time. However, simply to orient the reader I will summarize the accounts which I have heard and have read in the literature. The Goddess is multi-faceted, ever-changing—nature and nature's transformations. She is Artemis, virgin huntress, the crescent moon and the morning's freshness; Selene,

2. Adler (1986: 45–46).

3. This is a phrase taken from Crowley's Gnostic Mass (Crowley 1929: 345–61). It sometimes appears in witchcraft rituals or in writings about the practice.
4. Adler (1986: 43–44).

Aphrodite and Demeter, in the full bloom of the earth's fertility; Hecate and axe-bearing Cerridwen, the crone who destroys, the dying forests which make room for new growth. The constant theme of the Goddess is cyclicity and transformation: the spinning Fates, the weaving spider, Aphrodite who each year arises virgin from the sea, Isis who swells and floods and diminishes as the Nile. Every face of the Goddess is a different goddess, and yet also the same, in a different aspect, and there are different goddesses for different years and seasons of one's life.

The Goddess is very different from the Judaeo-Christian god. She is in the world, of the world, the very being of the world. 'People often ask me whether I *believe* in the Goddess. I reply, "Do you believe in rocks?"'[5] Yet she is also an entity, a metaphor for nature to whom one can talk. 'I relate to the Goddess, every day, in one way or another. I have a little chitchat with Mommy.'[6] Witches have talked to me about the 'duality' of their religious understanding, that on the one hand the Goddess merely personifies the natural world in myth and imagery, and that on the other hand the Goddess is there as someone to guide you, punish you, reward you, someone who becomes the central figure in your private universe. I suspect that for practitioners there is a natural slippage from metaphor to extant being, that it is difficult—particularly in a Judaeo-Christian society—genuinely to treat a deity-figure as only a metaphor, regardless of how the religion is rationalized. The figure becomes a deity, who cares for you.

Gardner began initiating people into groups called 'covens' which were run by women called 'high priestesses'. Covens bred other covens; people wandered into the bookstore, bought his books and then others, and created their own covens. By now there are many types of witchcraft: Gardnerian, Alexandrian, feminist, 'traditional' and so forth, named for their founders or their political ideals. Feminist covens usually only initiate women and they usually think of themselves as involved with a particularly female type of spirituality. Groups stemming from Gardner are called 'Gardnerian'. Alexandrian witchcraft derives from Alex Sanders' more ceremonial version of Gardnerian witchcraft.

Sanders was a charismatic man who deliberately attracted the attention of the gutterpress and became a public figure in the late sixties. Some of those who read the sensationalistic exposés and watched the television interviews were drawn to witchcraft, and Sanders initiated hundreds of applicants, sometimes on the evening they applied. Traditional witches supposedly carry on the age-old traditions of their families: whether by chance or otherwise, I met none who could substantiate their claim to an inherited ritual practice.

Covens vary widely in their style and custom, but there is a common core of practice. They meet on (or near) days dictated by the sky: the solstices and equinoxes and the 'quarter days' between them, most of them fire-festivals in the Frazerian past: Beltane (1 May), Lammas (1 August), Halloween (31 October), Candlemas (2 February). These are the days to perform seasonal rituals, in which witches celebrate the passage of the longest days and the summer's harvest. Covens also meet on the full moons—most witches are quite aware of the moon's phases—on which they perform spells, rituals with a specific intention, to cure Jane's cold or to get Richard a job. Seasonal ritual meetings are called 'sabbats', the full moon meetings, 'esbats'.[7] Membership usually ranges between three and thirteen members, and members think of themselves—or ideally think of themselves—as 'family'. In my experience, it usually took about a year of casual acquaintance before someone would be initiated. The process took so long because people felt it important that a group should be socially very comfortable with each other, and—crucially—that one could trust all members of the group. As a result, covens tended to be somewhat socially homogeneous. In the more 'traditional' covens, there are three 'degrees'. First degree initiates are novices, and in their initiation they were anointed 'witch' and shown the witches' weapons. Second degree initiates usually take their new status after a year. The initiation gives them the authority to start their own coven. It consists in 'meeting' death—the initiate acts the part of

---

5. Starhawk (1979: 77).
6. Witch, Z. Budapest, quoted in Adler (1986: 105).

7. The terms are probably drawn from Margaret Murray, although *esbat* appears in a sixteenth-century French manuscript (Le Roy Ladurie 1987: 7). *Sabbat* is a standard demonologist's term.

death if he is male; if she is female, she meets death and accepts him. The intended lesson of the ritual is that the willingness to lose the self gives one control over it, and over the transformations of life and death. Third degree initiation is not taken for years. It is essentially a rite of mystical sexuality, though it is sometimes 'symbolic' rather than 'actual'. It is always performed in privacy, with only the two initiates present. Behind the initiation lies the idea that one becomes the Goddess or God in one of their most powerful manifestations, the two dynamic elements of the duality that creates the world.

Witchcraft is a secretive otherworld, and more than other magical practices it is rich in symbolic, special items. Initiates have dark-handled knives they call 'athames', which are the principal tools and symbols of their powers: they have special cups and platters and incense burners, sometimes even special whips to 'purify' each other before the rite begins. There is always an altar, usually strewn with herbs and incense, with a statue of the Goddess, and there are always candles at the four directions, for in all magical practice the four directions (east, south, west, north) represent the four ancient elements (air, fire, water, earth) which in turn represent different sorts of 'energies' (thought; will power; emotion; material stability). Then, another symbol of the secrecy and violation of convention, most covens work in the nude. This is ostensibly a sign of freedom, but probably stems from the evocative association of witchcraft and sexuality, and a utopian vision of a paradisial past. There are no orgies, little eroticism, and in fact little behaviour that would be different if clothes were being worn. That witches dance around in the nude probably is part of the attractive fantasy that draws outsiders into the practice, but the fantasy is a piece with the paganism and not the source of salacious sexuality. Or at least, that seemed to be the case with the five covens I met.

I was initiated into the oldest of these witches' groups, a coven which has remained intact for more than forty years. It was once Gardner's own coven, the coven in which he participated, and three of the current members were initiated under his care. It pleases the anthropologist's heart that there are traces of ancestor worship: the pentacle, the magical platter which holds the communion 'mooncakes', was Gardner's own, and we used his goddess statue in the circle.

The coven had thirteen members while I was there. Four of them (three men and one woman) had been initiated over twenty-five years ago and were in their fifties: an ex-Cambridge computer consultant, who flew around the world lecturing to computer professionals; a computer software analyst, high priest for the last twenty years; a teacher; an ex-Oxford university lecturer. The high priestess was initiated twenty years ago and was a professional psychologist. Another woman, in her forties, had been initiated some ten years previously. She joined the group when her own coven disbanded; another man in his fifties also came from that coven. He was an electronic engineer in the music industry. By the time I had been in the group several months, Helga and Eliot's coven had disbanded (this was the coven associated with the Glittering Sword) and Helga at any rate preferred to think of herself as a Nordic Volva rather than as a Celtic witch. So she abandoned witchcraft altogether, though she became deeply engaged in the other magical practice, and Eliot and another member of his coven, the young Austrian who was also in the Glittering Sword, joined the group. The rest of the younger generation included a woman in her thirties who was a professional artist but spent most of her time then raising a young child. Another member was a middle-level manager of a large business. He was in his late thirties and was my 'psychic twin': we were both initiated into the group on the same night. Another man, thirtyish, managed a large housing estate. The computer consultant and the teacher had been married twenty-five years, the high priest and high priestess had lived together for twenty. Four other members had partners who did not belong to the group, but two of them belonged to other magical groups. Three members of the group were married to or closely related to university lecturers—but this was an unusually intellectual group.

This coven, then, had a wide age range and was primarily composed of middle-class intellectuals, many of whose lovers were not members of the group. This was not particularly standard: another coven with whom this group had contact had nine members, all of whom were within ten years of age, and it included three married couples and three single individuals. A Cambridge coven had a similarly great age span, and as wide a range of professions. But one in Clapham was entirely upper working class, and its members were within about fifteen years of age. For the meetings, the group relied upon a standard ritual text. Gardner (with the help of Doreen Valiente, now an elder stateswoman in what is called the 'Craft') had created a handbook of ritual practice called the 'Book of Shadows', which had supposedly been copied by each initiate through the ages. ('Beltane special objects: jug of wine, earthenware chalice, wreaths of ivy . . . High priestess in east, high priest at altar with jug of wine and earthenware chalice . . .') The group performed these rites as written, year in and year out: they were fully aware that Gardner had written them (with help) but felt that as the original coven, they had a responsibility to tradition. In fact, some of them had been re-written by the high priest, because Gardner's versions were so simple: he felt, however, that he should treat them as Gardner's, and never mentioned the authorship.

The seasonal rituals were remarkable because in them, the priestess is meant to incarnate the Goddess. This is done through a ritual commonly known as 'drawing down the moon'. The high priestess' ritual partner is called the 'high priest', and he stands opposite her in the circle and invokes her as the Goddess; and as Goddess, she delivers what is known as the 'Charge', the closest parallel to a liturgy within the Craft. Gardner's Book of Shadows has been published and annotated by two witches, and it includes this text.

The high priest: *Listen to the words of the great Mother; she who of old was called among men Artemis, Astarte, Athene, Dione, Melusine, Aphrodite, Cerridwen, Dana, Arianhod, Isis, Bride, and by many other names.*

The high priestess: *Whenever ye have need of anything, once in the month, and better it be when the moon is full, then shall ye assemble in some secret place and adore the spirit of me, who am Queen of all witches. There shall ye assemble, ye who are fain to learn all sorcery, yet who have not won its deepest secrets; to these will I teach things that are yet unknown. And ye shall be free from slavery; and as a sign that ye be really free, ye shall be naked in your rites; and ye shall dance, sing, feast make music and love, all in my praise. For mine is the ecstacy of the spirit, and mine is also joy on earth; for my law is love unto all beings. Keep pure your highest ideal; strive ever towards it; let naught stop you or turn you aside. For mine is the secret door which opens up the Land of Youth, and mine is the cup of the wine of life, and the*

Cauldron of Cerridwen, which is the Holy Grail of immortality. I am the gracious Goddess, who gives the gift of joy unto the heart of man. Upon earth, I give the knowledge of the spirit eternal; and beyond death, I give peace, and freedom, and reunion with those who have gone before. Nor do I demand sacrifice; for behold, I am the mother of all living, and my love is poured out upon the earth.

The high priest: *Hear ye the words of the Star Goddess; she in the dust of whose feet are the hosts of heaven, and whose body encircles the universe.*

The high priestess: *I who am the beauty of the green earth, and the white Moon among the stars, and the mystery of the waters, and the desire of the heart of man, call unto thy soul. Arise and come unto me. For I am the soul of nature, who gives life to the universe. From me all things proceed, and unto me all things must return; and before my face, beloved of Gods and men, let thine innermost divine self be enfolded in the rapture of the infinite. Let me worship be with the heart that rejoiceth; for behold all acts of love and pleasure are my rituals. And therefore let there be beauty and strength, power and compassion, honour and humility, mirth and reverence within you. And thou who thinkest to seek for me, know that seeking and yearning shall avail thee not unless thou knowest the mystery; that if that which thou seekest thou findest not within thee, thou wilt never find it without thee. For behold, I have been with thee from the beginning; and I am that which is attained at the end of desire.*[8]

The nature-imagery, the romantic poetry, the freedom—this is the style of language commonly heard within these ritual circles. The point of this speech is that every woman can be Goddess. Every man, too, can be god. In some Gardnerian rituals—like Halloween—the high priestess invokes the stag god in her priest, and he gives similar speeches.

When the coven I joined performed spells, no ritual form was prescribed because no spell was identical to any other. The idea behind the spell was that a coven could raise energy by calling on their members' own power, and that this energy could be concentrated within the magical circle, as a 'cone of power', and directed towards its source by collective imagination. The first step in a spell was always to chant or meditate in order to change the state of

---

8. Farrar and Farrar (1981: 42–43).

consciousness and so have access to one's own power, and then to focus the imagination on some real or imagined visual representation of the power's goal. The most common technique was to run in a circle, hands held, all eyes on the central altar candle, chanting what was supposedly an old Basque witches' chant:

Eko, eko, azarak
Eko, eko, zamilak
Eko, eko, Cernunnos
Eko, eko, Aradia[9]

Then, the circle running at its peak, the group suddenly stopped, held its linked hands high, shut its eyes and concentrated on a pre-arranged image.

Sometimes we prefixed the evening with a longer chant, the 'Witches' Rune':

Darksome night and shining moon
East, then South, then West, then North;
Hearken to the Witches' Rune—
Here we come to call ye forth!
Earth and water, air and fire,
Wand and pentacle and sword,
Work ye unto our desire,
Hearken ye unto our word!
Cords and censer, scourge and knife,
Powers of the witch's blade—
Waken all ye unto life,
Come ye as the charm is made!
Queen of Heaven, Queen of Hell,
Horned hunter of the night—
Lend your power unto the spell,
And work our will by magic rite!
By all the power of land and sea,
By all the might of moon and sun—
As we do will, so mote it be;
Chant the spell, and be it done![10]

The tone of the poem captures much about witchcraft; the special 'weapons' with special powers, the earthly power and goddess power used within the spell, the dependence of the spell upon the witches' will.

Most of the coven meetings I attended in England—in all I saw the rituals of some six Gardnerian-inspired groups—were similar in style. However, there were also feminist covens, a type of witchcraft relatively rare in England but quite important in the

States. Witchcraft appeals to feminists for a number of reasons. Witches are meant to worship a female deity rather than a male patriarch, and to worship her as she was worshipped by all people before the monotheistic religions held sway: as the moon, the earth, the sheaf of wheat. Members of feminist covens talk about witchcraft and its understanding of cyclic transformation, of birth, growth and decay, as a 'woman's spirituality', and the only spirituality in which women are proud to menstruate, to make love, and to give birth. These women (and sometimes also men) are often also compelled by the desire to reclaim the word 'witch', which they see as the male's fearful rejection of a woman too beautiful, too sexual, or past the years of fertility. The witches of European witch-craze fantasies were either beautiful young temptresses or hags.

Feminist covens emphasize creativity and collectivity, values commonly found in that political perspective, and their rituals are often quite different from those in Gardnerian groups. Perhaps I could offer an example, although in this example the women did not explicitly describe themselves as 'witches' but as participating in 'women's mysteries'.

On Halloween 1983 I joined a group of some fifteen women on top of a barrow in Kent. One of the women had been delegated to draw up a rough outline of the ritual, and before we left for the barrow she held a meeting in which she announced that she had 'cobbled together something from Starhawk and Z Budapest [two feminist witchcraft manual authors]'. (Someone shouted, 'don't put yourself down'.) She explained the structure of the rite as it stood and then asked for suggestions. Someone had brought a pot of red ochre and patchouli oil which she wanted to use, and someone else suggested that we use it to purify each other. Then it was suggested that we 'do' the elements first, and people volunteered for each directional quarter. The person who had chosen earth asked if the hostess had any maize flour which she could use. We talked about the purpose of the rite. The meeting was like many other feminist organization meetings: long on equality, emotional honesty and earthiness, short on speed.

When we arrived on the barrow some hours later, we walked round in a circle. Four women invoked the elements, at the different directions, with their own spontaneously chosen words. It was an impressive midnight: leafless trees stark against a dark sky,

---

9. Farrar and Farrar (1984: 17).
10. Farrar (1981: 20).

some wind, an empty countryside with a bull in the nearby field. Then one woman took the pot of red ochre and drew a circle on the cheek of the woman to her left, saying, 'may this protect you on Halloween night', and the pot passed around the circle. Then the woman who had drafted the ritual read an invocation to Hecate more or less taken from Starhawk, copied out in a looseleaf binder with a pentacle laminated on the front:

> This is the night when the veil that divides the worlds is thin. It is the New Year in the time of the year's death, when the harvest is gathered and the fields lie fallow. The gates of life and death are opened; the dead walk, and to the living is revealed the Mystery: that every ending is but a new beginning. We meet in time out of time, everywhere and nowhere, here and there, to greet the Death which is also Life, and the triple Goddess who is the cycle of rebirth.

Someone lit a fire in a dustbin lid (the cauldron was too heavy to carry from London) and each of us then invited the women that we knew, living or dead, to be present. We then chanted, the chant also taken from Starhawk, in which we passed around incense and each person said, 'x lives, x passes, x dies'—x being anger, failure, blindness, and so forth. The chorus was: 'it is the cold of the night, it is the dark'. Then someone held up a pomegranate (this was found in both Starhawk and Z Budapest) and said, 'behold, I show you the fruit of life'. She stabbed it and said, 'which is death' and passed it around the circle, and each woman put a seed in the mouth of the woman to her left, saying, 'taste of the seeds of death'. Then that woman held up an apple—'I show you the fruit of death and lo'—here she sliced it sideways, to show the five pointed star at its centre—'it contains the five pointed star of life'. The apple was passed around the circle, each woman feeding her neighbour as before and saying, 'taste of the fruit of life'. Then we passed a chalice of wine and some bread, saying 'may you never be hungry', pulled out masks and sparklers, and danced around and over the fire. Many of these actions required unrehearsed, unpremeditated participation from all members present, unlike the Gardnerian coven, where those not doing the ritual simply watch until they are called to worship or to take communion (members often take turns in performing the rituals, though). There was also the sense that the group had written some

of the ritual together, and that some of the ritual was spontaneous.

There are also 'solo' witches, individuals who call themselves witches even though they have never been initiated and have no formal tie to a coven. I met a number of these women (they were always women). One had an organization she called 'Spook Enterprises' and sold candles shaped like cats and like Isis. Another called herself a witch but had never been initiated, although she was well-established in the pagan world. Another, the speaker at the 1983 Quest conference, gave talks on 'village witchcraft': on inquiry, it appeared that she had been born in Kent, and was an ex-Girtonian.[11]

Mick, the woman of this sort whom I knew best, owned a Jacobean cottage where she lived alone on the edge of the Fens, the desolate drained farmland outside Cambridge. She managed a chicken farm. She told me that she discovered her powers at the age of ten, when she 'cursed' her math teacher and he promptly broke his leg in two places. It was clear that witchcraft was integral to her sense of self, and she took it seriously, albeit with theatre. She called her cottage 'Broomstick Cottage', kept ten cats and had a cast iron cauldron near the fire place. In the corner of the cottage she had a small statue of Pan on an altar, alongside a ritual knife stained with her own blood. Many of the villagers knew her and in Cambridge I heard of the 'Fen witch' from at least four different sources. Once, when I was sitting in her garden (her Elizabethan herb garden), two little boys cycled past. One shouted to the other, 'that's where the witch lives!' Mick got 'collected' for her personality, she told me: people seem to think it exotic to have a witch to supper. And this may have been one of the reasons she cherished her claims. She was a very funny, sociable woman, always the centre of a party, but a bit lonely, I think, and a bit romantic: witchcraft served a different function for her than fervent Christianity might have done, but like all religions, the witchcraft reduced the loneliness, lent charm to the bleak landscape, and gave her a social role.

There is a certain feel to witchcraft, a humour and an enthusiasm, often missing in other groups. Witchcraft combines the ideal and the mundane. It blends

---

11. Girton is the oldest women's college at Cambridge.

spiritual intensity and romanticism with the lovable, paunchy flaws of the flesh. Fantasies of elfin unicorns side comfortably with bawdy Pans. The high priest of the coven I joined described this as 'the goat and the gazelle': 'all witches have a little of each'. Part of this is the practice itself. People can look slightly ridiculous standing around naked in someone's living room. One needs a sense of humour in order to tolerate the practice, as well as enough

romanticism to take it seriously. And witches are perhaps the only magicians who incorporate humour into their practice. Their central invocation, the declamation of the priestess-turned-goddess, calls for 'mirth and reverence'. Laughter often rings within the circle, though rarely in the rites. One high priestess spontaneously explained to me that 'being alive is really rather funny. Wicca [another name for witchcraft] is the only religion that captures this'.

36

Consulting the Poison Oracle Among the Azande

E. E. Evans-Pritchard

If one important aspect of religion is helping believers come to know the unknown, it follows that divination is important to religion. Divination *means learning about the future or about things that may be hidden. Although the word itself can be traced to* divinity, *which indicates its relationship to gods, the practice of divination belongs as much to magic as it does to religion proper. In this selection, E. E. Evans-Pritchard describes the Zande poison oracle* benge, *a substance related to strychnine, and the myriad sociocultural beliefs surrounding its usage. Anthropological literature has long confirmed the great importance of divination to the Azande; it is a practice that cuts across every aspect of their culture. Azande diviners frequently divine with rubbing boards and termite sticks, but for the most important decisions they consult* benge *by "reading" its effect on chickens. Control over the poison oracle by older men assures them power over young men and all women. More importantly, control of* benge *in all legal cases provides Zande princes with enormous power. Indeed, the entire legal system of the Zande rests with divination-based decisions.*

E. E. Evans-Pritchard (1902–1973) was one of the most outstanding ethnographers of Africa in the first half of the 20th century, and his writings on the Azande and the Nuer are classics in anthropology. His work epitomized the British structural functional approach, which emphasized synchronic analyses and the study of social organization.

The usual place for a consultation is on the edge of cultivations far removed from homesteads. Any place in the bush screened by high grasses and brushwood is suitable. Or they may choose the corner of a clearing at the edge of the bush where crops will later be sown, since this is not so damp as in the bush itself. The object in going so far is to ensure secrecy, to avoid pollution by people who have not observed the taboos, and to escape witchcraft, which is less likely to corrupt the oracle in the bush than in a homestead.

Excerpted from Part III, Chapter 3: "Consulting the Poison Oracle," pp. 281–312 from WITCHCRAFT, ORACLES AND MAGIC AMONG THE AZANDE (1963) by E. E. Evans Pritchard. Reprinted by permission of Oxford University Press.

Oracle poison is useless unless a man possesses fowls upon which to test it, for the oracle speaks through fowls. In every Zande household there is a fowl house, and fowls are kept mainly with the object of subjecting them to oracular tests. As a rule they are only killed for food (and then only cocks or old hens) when an important visitor comes to the homestead, perhaps a prince's son or perhaps a father-in-law. Eggs are not eaten but are left to hens to hatch out. Generally a Zande, unless he is a wealthy man, will not possess more than half a dozen grown fowls at the most, and many people possess none at all or perhaps a single hen which someone has given to them.

Small chickens, only two or three days old, may be used for the poison oracle, but Azande prefer them older. However, one sees fowls of all sizes at oracle consultations, from tiny chickens to half-grown cockerels and pullets. When it is possible to tell the sex of fowls Azande use only cockerels, unless they have none and a consultation is necessary at once. The hens are spared for breeding purposes. Generally a man tells one of his younger sons to catch the fowls the night before a séance. Otherwise they catch them when the door of the fowl house is opened shortly after sunrise, but it is better to catch them and put them in a basket at night when they are roosting.

Old men say that fully grown birds ought not to be used in oracle consultations because they are too susceptible to the poison and have a habit of dying straight away before the poison has had time to consider the matter placed before it or even to hear a full statement of the problem. On the other hand a chicken remains for a long time under the influence of the poison before it recovers or expires, so that the oracle has time to hear all the relevant details concerning the problem placed before it and to give a well-considered judgment.

Any male may take part in the proceedings. However, the oracle is costly, and the questions put to it concern adult occupations. Therefore boys are only present when they operate the oracle. Normally these are boys who are observing taboos of mourning for the death of a relative. Adults also consider that it would be very unwise to allow any boys other than these to come near their poison because boys cannot be relied upon to observe the taboos on meats and vegetables.

An unmarried man will seldom be present at a séance. If he has any problems his father or uncle can act on his behalf. Moreover, only a married householder is wealthy enough to possess fowls and to acquire poison and has the experience to conduct a séance properly. Senior men also say that youths are generally engaged in some illicit love affair and would probably pollute the poison if they came near it. It is particularly the province of married men with households of their own to consult the poison oracle and no occupation gives them greater pleasure. It is not merely that they are able to solve their personal problems; but also they are dealing with matters of public importance, witchcraft, sorcery, and adultery, in which their names will be associated as witnesses of the oracle's decisions. A middle-aged Zande is happy when he has some poison and a few fowls

and the company of one or two trusted friends of his own age, and he can sit down to a long séance to discover all about the infidelities of his wives, his health and the health of his children, his marriage plans, his hunting and agricultural prospects, the advisability of changing his homestead, and so forth.

Poor men who do not possess poison or fowls but who are compelled for one reason or another to consult the oracle will persuade a kinsman, blood-brother, relative-in-law, or prince's deputy to consult it on their behalf. This is one of the main duties of social relationships.

Control over the poison oracle by the older men gives them great power over their juniors and it is one of the main sources of their prestige. It is possible for the older men to place the names of the youths before the poison oracle and on its declarations to bring accusations of adultery against them. Moreover, a man who is not able to afford poison is not a fully independent householder, since he is unable to initiate any important undertaking and is dependent on the good will of others to inform him about everything that concerns his health and welfare. In their dealings with youths older men are backed always by the authority of the oracle on any question that concerns their juniors, who have no means of directly consulting it themselves.

Women are debarred not only from operating the poison oracle but from having anything to do with it. They are not expected even to speak of it, and a man who mentions the oracle in the presence of women uses some circumlocutory expression. When a man is going to consult the poison oracle he says to his wife that he is going to look at his cultivations or makes a similar excuse. She understands well enough what he is going to do but says nothing.

The poison oracle is a male prerogative and is one of the principal mechanisms of male control and an expression of sex antagonism. For men say that women are capable of any deceit to defy a husband and please a lover, but men at least have the advantage that their oracle poison will reveal secret embraces. If it were not for the oracle it would be of little use to pay bridewealth, for the most jealous watch will not prevent a woman from committing adultery if she has a mind to do so. And what woman has not? The only thing which women fear is the poison oracle; for if they can escape the eyes of men they cannot escape the eyes of the oracle. Hence it is said that women hate the oracle, and that if a woman finds some of the poison in the bush she will destroy its power by urinating on it. I once asked a Zande why he so carefully collected the leaves used in operating the oracle and threw them some distance away from the bush, and he replied that it was to prevent women from finding them and polluting them, for if they pollute the leaves then the poison which has been removed to its hiding place will lose its power.

Occasionally very old women of good social position have been known to operate the poison oracle, or at least to consult it. A well-known character of the present day, the mother of Prince Ngere, consults the poison oracle, but such persons are rare exceptions and are always august persons.

When we consider to what extent social life is regulated by the poison oracle we shall at once appreciate how great an advantage men have over women in their ability to use it, and how being cut off from the main means of establishing contact with the mystical forces that so deeply affect human welfare degrades woman's position in Zande society. I have little hesitation in affirming that the customary exclusion of women from any dealings with the poison oracle is the most evident symptom of their inferior social position and means of maintaining it.

Great experience is necessary to conduct a séance in the correct manner and to know how to interpret the findings of the oracle. One must know how many doses of poison to administer, whether the oracle is working properly, in what order to take the questions, whether to put them in a positive or negative form, how long a fowl is to be held between the toes or in the hand while a question is being put to the oracle, when it ought to be jerked to stir up the poison, and when it is time to throw it on the ground for final inspection. One must know how to observe not only whether the fowl lives or dies, but also the exact manner in which the poison affects it, for while it is under the influence of the oracle its every movement is significant to the experienced eye. Also one must know the phraseology of address in order to put the questions clearly to the oracle without error or ambiguity, and this is no easy task when a single question may be asked in a harangue lasting as long as five or ten minutes.

Everyone knows what happens at a consultation of the poison oracle. Even women are aware of the procedure. But not every man is proficient in the art, though most adults can prepare and question the oracle if necessary. Those who as boys have often prepared the poison for their fathers and uncles, and who are members of families which frequent the court and constantly consult the oracle, are the most competent. When I have asked boys whether they can prepare the poison and administer it to fowls they have often replied that they are ignorant of the art. Some men are very expert at questioning the oracle, and those who wish to consult it like to be accompanied by such a man.

Any man who is invited by the owner of the oracle poison may attend the séance, but he will be expected to keep clear of the oracle if he has had relations with his wife or eaten any of the prohibited foods within the last few days. It is imperative that the man who actually prepares the poison shall have observed these taboos, and for this reason the owner of the poison, referred to in this account as the owner, generally asks a boy or man who is under taboos of mourning to operate the oracle, since there can be no doubt that he has kept the taboos, because they are the same for mourning as for oracles. Such a man is always employed when as in a case of sudden sickness, it is necessary to consult the oracle without warning so that there is no time for a man to prepare himself by observation of taboos. I shall refer to the man or boy who actually prepares the poison and administers it to fowls as the "operator." When I speak of the "questioner" I refer to the man who sits opposite to the oracle and addresses it and calls upon it for judgments. As he sits a few feet from the oracle he ought also to have observed all the taboos. It is possible for a man to be owner, operator, and questioner at the same time by conducting the consultation of the oracle by himself, but this rarely, if ever, occurs. Usually there is no difficulty in obtaining the services of an operator, since a man knows which of his neighbors are observing the taboos associated with death and vengeance. One of his companions who has not eaten tabooed food or had sexual relations with women for a day or two before the consultation acts as questioner. If a man is unclean he can address the oracle from a distance. It is better to take these precautions because contact of an unclean person with the oracle is certain to destroy its potency, and even the close proximity of an unclean person may have this result.

The owner does not pay the operator and questioner for their services. The questioner is almost invariably either the owner himself or one of his friends who also wishes to put questions to the oracle and has brought fowls with him for the purpose. It is usual to reward the operator, if he is an adult, by giving him a fowl during the séance so that he can place one of his own problems before the oracle. Since he is generally a man who wears a girdle of mourning and vengeance he will often ask the oracle when the vengeance magic is going to strike its victim.

To guard against pollution a man generally hides his poison in the thatched roof of a hut, on the inner side, if possible, in a hut which women do not use, but this is not essential, for a woman does not know that there is poison hidden in the roof and is unlikely to come into contact with it. The owner of the poison must have kept the taboos if he wishes to take it down from the roof himself, and if he is unclean he will bring the man or boy who is to operate the oracle into the hut and indicate to him at a distance where the poison is hidden in the thatch. So good a hiding place is the thatched roof of a hut for a small packet of poison that it is often difficult for its owner himself to find it. No one may smoke hemp in a hut which lodges oracle poison. However, there is always a danger of pollution and of witchcraft if the poison is kept in a homestead, and some men prefer to hide it in a hole in a tree in the bush, or even to build a small shelter and to lay it on the ground beneath. This shelter is far removed from human dwellings, and were a man to come across it in the bush he would not disturb it lest it cover some kind of lethal medicine. It is very improbable that witchcraft will discover oracle poison hidden in the bush. I have never seen oracle poison under a shelter in the bush, but I was told that it is frequently housed in this manner.

Oracle poison when not in use is kept wrapped in leaves, and at the end of a séance used poison is placed in a separate leaf-wrapping from unused poison. The poison may be used two or three times and sometimes fresh poison is added to it to make it more potent. When its action shows that it has lost its strength they throw it away.

Special care is taken to protect a prince's oracle poison from witchcraft and pollution because a prince's oracles reveal matters of tribal importance, judge criminal and civil cases, and determine whether vengeance has been exacted for death. A prince has two or three official operators who supervise his poison oracle. These men must be thoroughly reliable since the fate of their master and the purity of law are in their hands. If they break a taboo the whole legal system may become corrupted and the innocent be judged guilty and the guilty be judged innocent. Moreover, a prince is at frequent pains to discover witchcraft or sorcery among his wives and retainers which might do him an injury, so that his life is endangered if the oracle is not working properly.

. . .

Control of the poison oracle in all legal cases gave the princes enormous power. No death or adultery could be legally avenged without a verdict from their oracles, so that the court was the sole medium of legal action and the king or his representative the sole source of law. Although the procedure was a mystical one it was carried out in the king's name and he was vested with judicial authority as completely as if a more common-sense system of justice had obtained.

Azande are very secretive about oracle séances and wish no one to be present when they are inquiring about private matters unless he is a trusted friend. They do not tell any one except trusted friends that they are going to consult the oracle, and they say nothing about the consultation on their return. It frequently happens when a man is about to set out from his homestead to the place of the oracle that he is visited by someone whom he does not wish to acquaint with his business. He does not tell the unwelcome visitor that he must hurry off to consult the oracle, but uses any pretext to get rid of him, and prefers to abandon the consultation rather than confess his intentions.

After this short introduction I will describe the manner in which poison is administered to fowls. The operator goes ahead of the rest of the party in order to prepare for the test. He takes with him a small gourdful of water. He clears a space by treading down the grasses. Afterwards he scrapes a hole in the earth into which he places a large leaf as a basin for the oracle poison. From *bingba* grass he fashions a small brush to administer the poison, and from leaves he makes a filter to pour the liquid poison into the beaks of the fowls; and from other leaves he makes a cup to transfer water from the gourd to the poison when it needs to be moistened. Finally, he tears off some branches of nearby shrubs and extracts their bast to be used as cord for attaching to the legs of fowls which have survived the test so that they can be easily retrieved from the grass when the business of the day is finished. The operator does not moisten the poison till the rest of the party arrive.

There may be only one man or there may be several who have questions to put to the oracle. Each brings his fowls with him in an open-wove basket. As it has been agreed beforehand where the oracle consultation is to take place they know where to foregather. As each person arrives he hands over his basket of fowls to the operator who places it on the ground near him. A man who is used to acting as questioner sits opposite to it, a few feet away if he has observed the taboos, but several yards away if he has not observed them. Other men who have not kept the taboos remain at a greater distance.

When every one is seated they discuss in low tones whose fowl they will take first and how the question shall be framed. Meanwhile the operator pours some water from the gourd at his side into his leaf cup and from the cup on to the poison, which then effervesces. He mixes the poison and water with his finger tips into a paste of the right consistency and, when instructed by the questioner, takes one of the fowls and draws down its wings over its legs and pins them between and under his toes. He is seated with the fowl facing him. He takes his grass brush, twirls it round in the poison, and folds it in the leaf filter. He holds open the beak of the fowl and tips the end of the filter into it and squeezes the filter so that the liquid runs out of the paste into the throat of the fowl. He bobs the head of the fowl up and down to compel it to swallow the poison.

At this point the questioner, having previously been instructed by the owner of the fowl on the facts which he is to put before the oracle, commences to address the poison inside the fowl. He continues to address it for about a couple of minutes, when a second dose of poison is usually administered. If it is a very small chicken two doses will suffice, but a larger fowl will receive three doses, and I have known a fowl to receive a fourth dose, but never more than four. The questioner does not cease his address to the oracle, but puts his questions again and again in different forms, though always with the same refrain, "If such is the case, poison oracle kill the fowl," or "If such is the case, poison oracle spare the fowl." From time to time he interrupts his flow of oratory to give a technical order to the operator. He may tell him to give the fowl another dose of poison or to jerk it between his toes by raising and lowering his foot (this stirs up the poison inside the fowl). When the last dose of poison has been administered and he has further addressed it, he tells the operator to raise the fowl. The operator takes it in his hand and, holding its legs between his fingers so that it faces him, gives it an occasional jerk backwards and forwards. The questioner redoubles his oratory as though the verdict depended upon his forensic efforts, and if the fowl is not already dead he then, after a further bout of oratory, tells the operator to put it on the ground. He continues to address the poison inside the fowl while they watch its movements on the ground.

The poison affects fowls in many ways. Occasionally it kills them immediately after the first dose, while they are still on the ground. This seldom happens, for normally a fowl is not seriously affected till it is removed from the ground and jerked backwards and forwards in the hand. Then, if it is going to die, it goes through spasmodic stretchings of the body and closing of the wings and vomits. After several such spasms it vomits and expires in a final seizure. Some fowls appear quite unaffected by the poison, and when, after being jerked backwards and forwards for a while, they are flung to the ground peck around unconcernedly. Those fowls which are unaffected by the poison generally excrete as soon as they are put to earth. Some fowls appear little affected by the poison till put to earth, when they suddenly collapse and die.

One generally knows what the verdict is going to be after the fowl has been held in the hand for a couple of minutes. If it appears certain to recover the operator ties bast to its leg and throws it to the ground. If it appears certain to die he does not trouble to tie bast to its leg, but lays it on the earth to die. Often when a fowl has died they draw its corpse in a semicircle round the poison to show it to the poison. They then cut off a wing to use as evidence and cover the body with grass. Those fowls which survive are taken home and let loose. A fowl is never used twice on the same day.

· · ·

The main duty of the questioner is to see that the oracle fully understands the question put to it and is acquainted with all facts relevant to the problem it is asked to solve. They address it with all the care for detail that one observes in court cases before a prince. This means beginning a long way back and noting over a considerable period of time every detail which might elucidate the case, linking up facts into a consistent picture of events, and the marshalling of arguments, as Azande can so brilliantly do, into a logical and closely knit web of sequences and interrelations of facts and inference. Also the questioner is careful to mention to the oracle again and again the name of the man who is consulting it, and he points him out to the oracle with his out-stretched arm. He mentions also the name of his father, perhaps the name of his clan, and the name of the place where he resides, and he gives similar details of other people mentioned in the address.

An address consists usually of alternate directions. The first sentences outline the question in terms demanding an affirmative answer and end with the command, "Poison oracle kill the fowl." The next sentences outline the question in terms demanding a negative answer and end with the command, "Poison oracle spare the fowl." The consulter then takes up the question again in terms asking an affirmative answer; and so on. If a bystander considers that a relevant point has been left out he interrupts the questioner, who then makes this point.

The questioner has a switch in his hand, and while questioning the oracle beats the ground, as he sits cross-legged, in front of it. He continues to beat the ground till the end of his address. Often he will gesticulate as he makes his points, in the same manner as a man making a case in court. He sometimes plucks grass and shows it to the poison and, after explaining that there is something he does not wish it to consider, throws it behind him. Thus he tells the oracle that he does not wish it to consider the question of witchcraft but only of sorcery. Witchcraft is *wingi,* something irrelevant, and he casts it behind him.

. . .

While the fowl is undergoing its ordeal men are attentive to their behavior. A man must tighten and spread out his bark-cloth loin-covering lest he expose his genitals, as when he is sitting in the presence of a prince or parent-in-law. Men speak in a low voice as they do in the presence of superiors. Indeed, all conversation is avoided unless it directly concerns the procedure of consultation. If anyone desires to leave before the proceedings are finished he takes a leaf and spits on it and places it where he has been sitting. I have seen a man who rose for a few moments only to catch a fowl which had escaped from its basket place a blade of grass on the stone upon which he had been sitting. Spears must be laid on the ground and not planted upright in the presence of the poison oracle. Azande are very serious during a séance, for they are asking questions of vital importance to their lives and happiness.

37

Rational Mastery by Man of His Surroundings

Bronislaw Malinowski

Rare is the anthropology course that sometime during the semester is not directed to the thought and writings of Bronislaw Malinowski (1884–1942). This world-famous Polish anthropologist was trained in mathematics but shifted his interests to anthropology after reading Sir James Frazer's The Golden Bough. *Malinowski's fieldwork in the Trobriand Islands of Melanesia influenced the direction of anthropology as an academic discipline. He is recognized as the founder of functionalism, an anthropological approach to the study of culture that believes each institution in a society fulfills a definite function in the maintenance of human needs. His major works include* Crime and Customs in Savage Society *(1926),* The Sexual Life of Savages *(1929), and* Coral Gardens and Their Magic *(1935). Malinowski was professor of anthropology at the University of London from 1927 until his death in 1942.*

In this classic article, originally published in 1925, Malinowski asks two important questions: Do preliterate people have any rational mastery of their surroundings and can primitive knowledge be regarded as a beginning or rudimentary type of science, or is it merely a crude hodgepodge devoid of logic and accuracy? Although the author's use of the word savage *is considered a pejorative by anthropologists today, in Malinowski's time it was commonplace.*

The problem of primitive knowledge has been singularly neglected by anthropology. Studies on savage psychology were exclusively confined to early religion, magic, and mythology. Only recently the work of several English, German, and French writers, notably the daring and brilliant speculations of Professor Lévy-Bruhl, gave an impetus to the student's interest in what the savage does in his more sober moods. The results were startling indeed: Professor Lévy-Bruhl tells us, to put it in a nutshell, that primitive man has no sober moods at all, that he is hopelessly and com-

pletely immersed in a mystical frame of mind. Incapable of dispassionate and consistent observation, devoid of the power of abstraction, hampered by "a decided aversion towards reasoning," he is unable to draw any benefit from experience, to construct or comprehend even the most elementary laws of nature. "For minds thus orientated there is no fact purely physical." Nor can there exist for them any clear idea of substance and attribute, cause and effect, identity and contradiction. Their outlook is that of confused superstition, "prelogical," made of mystic "participations" and "exclusions." I have here summarized a body of opinion, of which the brilliant French sociologist is the most decided and the most competent spokesman, but which numbers besides, many anthropologists and philosophers of renown.

Reprinted from MAGIC, SCIENCE AND RELIGION (New York: Doubleday, 1955), pp. 25–35, by permission of the Society for Promoting Christian Knowledge.

But there are dissenting voices. When a scholar and anthropologist of the measure of Professor J. L. Myres entitles an article in *Notes and Queries* "Natural Science," and when we read there that the savage's "knowledge based on observation is distinct and accurate," we must surely pause before accepting primitive man's irrationality as a dogma. Another highly competent writer, Dr. A. A. Goldenweiser, speaking about primitive "discoveries, inventions and improvements"—which could hardly be attributed to any preempirical or prelogical mind—affirms that "it would be unwise to ascribe to the primitive mechanic merely a passive part in the origination of inventions. Many a happy thought must have crossed his mind, nor was he wholly unfamiliar with the thrill that comes from an idea effective in action." Here we see the savage endowed with an attitude of mind wholly akin to that of a modern man of science!

To bridge over the wide gap between the two extreme opinions current on the subject of primitive man's reason, it will be best to resolve the problem into two questions.

First, has the savage any rational outlook, any rational mastery of his surroundings, or is he, as M. Lévy-Bruhl and his school maintain, entirely "mystical"? The answer will be that every primitive community is in possession of a considerable store of knowledge, based on experience and fashioned by reason.

The second question then opens: Can this primitive knowledge be regarded as a rudimentary form of science or is it, on the contrary, radically different, a crude body of practical and technical abilities, rules of thumb and rules of art having no theoretical value? This second question, epistemological rather than belonging to the study of man, will be barely touched upon at the end of this section and a tentative answer only will be given.

In dealing with the first question, we shall have to examine the "profane" side of life, the arts, crafts and economic pursuits, and we shall attempt to disentangle in it a type of behavior, clearly marked off from magic and religion, based on empirical knowledge and on the confidence in logic. We shall try to find whether the lines of such behavior are defined by traditional rules, known, perhaps even discussed sometimes, and tested. We shall have to inquire whether the sociological setting of the rational and empirical behavior differs from that of ritual and cult. Above all we shall ask, do the natives distinguish the two domains and keep them apart, or is the field of knowledge constantly swamped by superstition, ritualism, magic or religion?

Since in the matter under discussion there is an appalling lack of relevant and reliable observations, I shall have largely to draw upon my own material, most unpublished, collected during a few years' field work among the Melanesian and Papuo-Melanesian tribes of Eastern New Guinea and the surrounding archipelagoes. As the Melanesians are reputed, however, to be specially magic-ridden, they will furnish an acid test of the existence of empirical and rational knowledge among savages living in the age of polished stone.

These natives, and I am speaking mainly of the Melanesians who inhabit the coral atolls to the N.E. of the main island, the Trobriand Archipelago and the adjoining groups, are expert fishermen, industrious manufacturers and traders, but they rely mainly on gardening for their subsistence. With the most rudimentary implements, a pointed digging-stick and a small axe, they are able to raise crops sufficient to maintain a dense population and even yielding a surplus, which in olden days was allowed to rot unconsumed, and which at present is exported to feed plantation hands. The success in their agriculture depends—besides the excellent natural conditions with which they are favored—upon their extensive knowledge of the classes of the soil, of the various cultivated plants, of the mutual adaptation of these two factors, and, last not least, upon their knowledge of the importance of accurate and hard work. They have to select the soil and the seedlings, they have appropriately to fix the times for clearing and burning the scrub, for planting and weeding, for training the vines of the yam plants. In all this they are guided by a clear knowledge of weather and seasons, plants and pests, soil and tubers, and by a conviction that this knowledge is true and reliable, that it can be counted upon and must be scrupulously obeyed.

Yet mixed with all their activities there is to be found magic, a series of rites performed every year over the gardens in rigorous sequence and order. Since the leadership in garden work is in the hands of the magician, and since ritual and practical work are intimately associated, a superficial observer might be led to assume that the mystic and the rational behavior are mixed up, that their effects are not distinguished by the natives and not distinguishable in scientific analysis. Is this so really?

Magic is undoubtedly regarded by the natives as absolutely indispensable to the welfare of the gardens. What would happen without it no one can exactly tell, for no native garden has ever been made without its ritual, in spite of some thirty years of European rule and missionary influence and well over a century's contact with white traders. But certainly various kinds of disaster, blight, unseasonable droughts, rains, bush-pigs and locusts would destroy the unhallowed garden made without magic.

Does this mean, however, that the natives attribute all the good results to magic? Certainly not. If you were to suggest to a native that he should make his garden mainly by magic and scamp his work, he would simply smile on your simplicity. He knows as well as you do that there are natural conditions and causes, and by his observations he knows also that he is able to control these natural forces by mental and physical effort. His knowledge is limited, no doubt, but as far as it goes it is sound and proof against mysticism. If the fences are broken down, if the seed is destroyed or has been dried or washed away, he will have recourse not to magic, but to work, guided by knowledge and reason. His experience has taught him also, on the other hand, that in spite of all his forethought and beyond all his efforts there are agencies and forces which one year bestow unwonted and unearned benefits of fertility, making everything run smooth and well, rain and sun appear at the right moment, noxious insects remain in abeyance, the harvest yields a superabundant crop; and another year again the same agencies bring ill luck and bad chance, pursue him from beginning till end and thwart all his most strenuous efforts and his best-founded knowledge. To control these influences and these only he employs magic.

Thus there is a clear-cut division: there is first the well-known set of conditions, the natural course of growth, as well as the ordinary pests and dangers to be warded off by fencing and weeding. On the other hand there is the domain of the unaccountable and adverse influences, as well as the great unearned increment of fortunate coincidence. The first conditions are coped with by knowledge and work, the second by magic.

This line of division can also be traced in the social setting of work and ritual respectively. Though the garden magician is, as a rule, also the leader in practical activities, these two functions are kept strictly apart. Every magical ceremony has its distinctive name, its appropriate time and its place in the scheme of work, and it stands out of the ordinary course of activities completely. Some of them are ceremonial and have to be attended by the whole community, all are public in that it is known when they are going to happen and anyone can attend them. They are performed on selected plots within the gardens and on a special corner of this plot. Work is always tabooed on such occasions, sometimes only while the ceremony lasts, sometimes for a day or two. In his lay character the leader and magician directs the work, fixes the dates for starting, harangues and exhorts slack or careless gardeners. But the two roles never overlap or interfere: they are always clear, and any native will inform you without hesitation whether the man acts as magician or as leader in garden work.

What has been said about gardens can be paralleled from any one of the many other activities in which work and magic run side by side without ever mixing. Thus in canoe building empirical knowledge of material, of technology, and of certain principles of stability and hydrodynamics, function in company and close association with magic, each yet uncontaminated by the other.

For example, they understand perfectly well that the wider the span of the outrigger the greater the stability yet the smaller the resistance against strain. They can clearly explain why they have to give this span a certain traditional width, measured in fractions of the length of the dugout. They can also explain, in rudimentary but clearly mechanical terms, how they have to behave in a sudden gale, why the outrigger must be always on the weather side, why the one type of canoe can and the other cannot beat. They have, in fact, a whole system of principles of sailing, embodied in a complex and rich terminology, traditionally handed on and obeyed as rationally and consistently as is modern science by modern sailors. How could they sail otherwise under eminently dangerous conditions in their frail primitive craft?

But even with all their systematic knowledge, methodically applied, they are still at the mercy of powerful and incalculable tides, sudden gales during the monsoon season and unknown reefs. And here comes in their magic, performed over the canoe during its construction, carried out at the beginning and in the course of expeditions and resorted to in moments of real danger. If the modern seaman, entrenched in science and reason, provided with all sorts of safety appliances, sailing on steel-built steamers, if even he has a singular tendency to superstition—which does not rob him of his knowledge or reason, nor make him altogether prelogical—can we wonder that his savage colleague, under much more precarious conditions, holds fast to the safety and comfort of magic?

An interesting and crucial test is provided by fishing in the Trobriand Islands and its magic. While in the villages on the inner lagoon fishing is done in an easy and absolutely reliable manner by the method of poisoning, yielding abundant results without danger and uncertainty, there are on the shores of the open sea dangerous modes of fishing and also certain types in which the yield greatly varies according to whether shoals of fish appear beforehand or not. It is most significant that in the lagoon fishing, where man can rely completely upon his knowledge and skill, magic does not exist, while in the open-sea fishing, full of danger and uncertainty, there is extensive magical ritual to secure safety and good results.

Again, in warfare the natives know that strength, courage, and agility play a decisive part. Yet here also they practice magic to master the elements of chance and luck.

Nowhere is the duality of natural and supernatural causes divided by a line so thin and intricate, yet, if carefully followed up, so well marked, decisive, and instructive, as in the two most fateful forces of human destiny: health and death. Health to the Melanesians is a natural state of affairs and, unless tampered with, the human body will remain in perfect order. But the natives know perfectly well that there are natural means which can affect health and even destroy the body. Poisons, wounds, burns, falls are known to cause disablement or death in a natural way. And this is not a matter of private opinion of this or that individual, but it is laid down in traditional lore and even in belief, for there are considered to be different ways to the nether world for those who died by sorcery and those who met "natural" death. Again, it is recognized that cold, heat,

overstrain, too much sun, overeating can all cause minor ailments, which are treated by natural remedies such as massage, steaming, warming at a fire and certain potions. Old age is known to lead to bodily decay and the explanation is given by the natives that very old people grow weak, their esophagus closes up, and therefore they must die.

But besides these natural causes there is the enormous domain of sorcery and by far the most cases of illness and death are ascribed to this. The line of distinction between sorcery and the other causes is clear in theory and in most cases of practice, but it must be realized that it is subject to what could be called the personal perspective. That is, the more closely a case has to do with the person who considers it, the less will it be "natural," the more "magical." Thus a very old man, whose pending death will be considered natural by the other members of the community, will be afraid only of sorcery and never think of his natural fate. A fairly sick person will diagnose sorcery in his own case, while all the others might speak of too much betel nut or overeating or some other indulgence.

But who of us really believes that his own bodily infirmities and the approaching death is a purely natural occurrence, just an insignificant event in the infinite chain of causes? To the most rational civilized men health, disease, the threat of death, float in a hazy emotional mist, which seems to become denser and more impenetrable as the fateful forms approach. It is indeed astonishing that "savages" can achieve such a sober, dispassionate outlook in these matters as they actually do.

Thus in his relation to nature and destiny, whether he tries to exploit the first or to dodge the second, primitive man recognized both the natural and the supernatural forces and agencies, and he tries to use them both for his benefit. Whenever he has been taught by experience that effort guided by knowledge is of some avail, he never spares the one or ignores the other. He knows that a plant cannot grow by magic alone, or a canoe sail or float without being properly constructed and managed, or a fight be won without skill and daring. He never relies on magic alone, while, on the contrary, he sometimes dispenses with it completely, as in fire-making and in a number of crafts and pursuits. But he clings to it, whenever he has to recognize the impotence of his knowledge and of his rational technique.

I have given my reasons why in this argument I had to rely principally on the material collected in the classical land of magic, Melanesia. But the facts discussed are so fundamental, the conclusions drawn of such a general nature, that it will be easy to check them on any modern detailed ethnographic record. Comparing agricultural work and magic, the building of canoes, the art of healing by magic and by natural remedies, the ideas about the causes of death in other regions, the universal validity of what has been established here could easily be proved. Only, since no observations have methodically been made with reference to the problem of primitive knowledge, the data from other writers could be gleaned only piecemeal and their testimony though clear would be indirect.

I have chosen to face the question of primitive man's rational knowledge directly: watching him at his principal occupations, seeing him pass from work to magic and back again, entering into his mind, listening to his opinions. The whole problem might have been approached through the avenue of language, but this would have led us too far into questions of logic, semasiology, and theory of primitive languages. Words which serve to express general ideas such as *existence, substance,* and *attribute, cause* and *effect,* the *fundamental* and the *secondary;* words and expressions used in complicated pursuits like sailing, construction, measuring and checking; numerals and quantitative descriptions, correct and detailed classifications of natural phenomena, plants and animals—all this would lead us exactly to the same conclusion: that primitive man can observe and think, and that he possesses, embodied in his language, systems of methodical though rudimentary knowledge.

Similar conclusions could be drawn from an examination of those mental schemes and physical contrivances which could be described as diagrams or formulas. Methods of indicating the main points of the compass, arrangements of stars into constellations, co-ordination of these with the seasons, naming of moons in the year, of quarters in the moon—all these accomplishments are known to the simplest savages. Also they are all able to draw diagrammatic maps in the sand or dust, indicate arrangements by placing small stones, shells, or sticks on the ground, plan expeditions or raids on such rudimentary charts. By co-ordinating space and time they are able to arrange big tribal gatherings and to combine vast tribal movements over extensive areas. The use of leaves, notched sticks, and similar aids to memory is well known and seems to be almost universal. All such "diagrams" are means of reducing a complex and unwieldly bit of reality to a simple and handy form. They give man a relatively easy mental control over it. As such are they not—in a very rudimentary form no doubt—fundamentally akin to developed scientific formulas and "models," which are also simple and handy paraphrases of a complex or abstract reality, giving the civilized physicist mental control over it?

This brings us to the second question: Can we regard primitive knowledge, which, as we found, is both empirical and rational, as a rudimentary stage of science, or is it not at all related to it? If by science be understood a body of rules and conceptions, based on experience and derived from it by logical inference, embodied in material achievements and in a fixed form of tradition and carried on by some sort of social organization—then there is no doubt that even the lowest savage communities have the beginning of science, however rudimentary.

Most epistemologists would not, however, be satisfied with such a "minimum definition" of science, for it might apply to the rules of an art or craft as well. They would maintain that the rules of science must be laid down explicitly, open to control by experiment and critique by reason. They must not only be rules of practical behavior, but theoretical laws of knowledge. Even accepting this stricture, however, there is hardly any doubt that many of the principles of savage knowledge are scientific in this sense. The native shipwright knows not only practically of buoyancy, leverage, equilibrium, he has to obey these laws not only on water, but while making the canoe he must have the principles in his mind. He instructs his helpers in them. He gives them the traditional rules, and in a crude and simple manner, using his hands, pieces of wood, and a limited technical vocabulary, he explains some general laws of hydrodynamics and equilibrium. Science is not detached from the craft, that is certainly true, it is only a means to an end, it is crude, rudimentary, and inchoate, but with all that it is the matrix from which the higher developments must have sprung.

If we applied another criterion yet, that of the really scientific attitude, the disinterested search for knowledge and for the understanding of causes and reasons, the answer would certainly not be in a direct negative. There is, of course, no widespread thirst for knowledge in a savage community, new things such as European topics bore them frankly and their whole interest is largely encompassed by the traditional world of their culture. But within this there is both the antiquarian mind passionately interested in myths, stories, details of customs, pedigrees, and ancient happenings, and there is also to be found the naturalist, patient and painstaking in his observations, capable of generalization and of connecting long chains of events in the life of animals, and in the marine world or in the jungle. It is

enough to realize how much European naturalists have often learned from their savage colleagues to appreciate this interest found in the native for nature. There is finally among the primitives, as every field worker well knows, the sociologist, the ideal informant, capable with marvelous accuracy and insight to give the *raison d'être,* the function and the organization of many a simpler institution in his tribe.

Science, of course, does not exist in any uncivilized community as a driving power, criticizing, renewing, constructing. Science is never consciously made. But on this criterion, neither is there law, nor religion, nor government among savages.

38

Baseball Magic

George Gmelch

In the preceding article, Malinowski observed that in the Trobriand Islands magic did not occur when the natives fished in the safe lagoons but when they ventured out into the open seas: then the danger and uncertainty caused them to perform extensive magical rituals. In the following article, anthropologist George Gmelch demonstrates that America's favorite pastime is an excellent place to put the test to Malinowski's hypothesis about magic. Anyone who has watched baseball, either at a ballpark or in front of a television set, is aware of some of the more obvious rituals performed by the players, but Gmelch, drawing upon his previous experience as a professional baseball player, provides an insider's view of the rituals, taboos, and fetishes involved in the sport. (The following is a 1999 revision of Gmelch's original article.)

On each pitching day for the first three months of a winning season, Dennis Grossini, a pitcher on a Detroit Tiger farm team, arose from bed at exactly 10:00 A.M. At 1:00 P.M. he went to the nearest restaurant for two glasses of iced tea and a tunafish sandwich. Although the afternoon was free, he changed into the sweatshirt and supporter he wore during his last winning game, and one hour before the game he chewed a wad of Beech-Nut chewing tobacco. After each pitch during the game he touched the letters on his uniform and straightened his cap after each ball. Before the start of each inning he replaced the pitcher's rosin bag next to the spot where it was the inning before. And after every inning in which he gave up a run, he washed his hands.

When asked which part of the ritual was most important, he said, "You can't really tell what's most important so it all becomes important. I'd be afraid to change anything. As long as I'm winning, I do everything the same."

Trobriand Islanders, according to anthropologist Bronislaw Malinowski, felt the same way about their fishing magic. Among the Trobrianders, fishing took two forms: in the *inner lagoon* where fish were plentiful and there was little danger, and on the *open sea* where fishing was dangerous and yields varied widely. Malinowski found that magic was not used in lagoon fishing, where men could rely solely on their knowledge and skill. But when fishing on the open sea, Trobrianders used a great deal of magical ritual to ensure safety and increase their catch.

Baseball, America's national pastime, is an arena in which players behave remarkably like Malinowski's Trobriand fishermen. To professional ballplayers, baseball is more than just a game. It is an occupation. Since their livelihoods depend on how well they perform, many use magic to try to control the chance that is built into baseball. There are three essential activities of the game—pitching, hitting, and fielding. In the first two, chance can play a surprisingly important role. The pitcher is the player least able to control the outcome of his own efforts. He may feel great and have good stuff warming up in the bullpen and then get into the game and not have it. He may make a bad pitch and see the batter miss it for a strike out or see it hit hard but right into the hands of a fielder for an out. His best pitch may be blooped for a base hit. He may limit the opposing team to just a few hits yet lose the game, or

Revised from the original article that appeared in TRANSACTION, vol. 8, no. 8 (1971), pp. 39–41, 54. Reprinted by permission of the author.

he may give up a dozen hits but still win. And the good and bad luck don't always average out over the course of a season. Some pitchers end the season with poor won-lost records but good earned run averages, and vice versa. For instance, this past season (1998) Andy Benes gave up over one run per game more than his teammate Omar Daal but had a better won-lost record. Benes went 14–13, while Daal was only 8–12. Both pitched for the same team—the Arizona Diamondbacks—which meant they had the same fielders behind them. Regardless of how well a pitcher performs, on every outing he depends not only on his own skill, but also on the proficiency of his teammates, the ineptitude of the opposition, and luck.

Hitting, which Hall of Famer Ted Williams called the single most difficult task in the world of sports, is also full of risk and uncertainty. Unless it's a home run, no matter how well the batter hits the ball, fate determines whether it will go into a waiting glove, whistle past a fielder's diving stab, or find a gap in the outfield. The uncertainty is compounded by the low success rate of hitting: the average hitter gets only one hit in every four trips to the plate, while the very best hitters average only one hit every three trips. Fielding, as we will return to later, is the one part of baseball where chance does not play much of a role.

How does the risk and uncertainty in pitching and hitting affect players? What do they do to introduce some control over the outcomes of their performance? These are questions that I first became interested in many years ago as both a ballplayer and an anthropology student. I'd devoted much of my youth to baseball and played professionally as first baseman in the Detroit Tiger organization in the 1960s. It was shortly after the end of one baseball season that I took an anthropology course called "Magic, Religion, and Witchcraft." As my professor described the magic practiced by a tribe in Papua New Guinea, it occurred to me that what these so-called primitive people did wasn't all that different from what my teammates and I had done to give ourselves luck and confidence in baseball.

The most common way players attempt to reduce chance and their feelings of uncertainty is to develop and follow a daily routine. By routine I mean a course of action that is regularly followed. Florida Marlins coach Rich Donnelly talked about the routines of his ballplayers:

> They're like trained animals. They come out here [to the ballpark] and everything has to be the same, they don't like anything that knocks them off their routine. Just look at the dugout and you'll see every guy sitting in the same spot every night. It's amazing, everybody in the same spot. And don't you dare take someone's seat. If a guy comes up from the minors and sits here, they'll say, 'Hey, Jim sits here, find another seat.' You watch the pitcher warm up and he'll do the same thing every time. And when you go on the road its the same way. You got a routine and you adhere to it and you don't want anybody knocking you off it.

Routines are comforting; they bring order into a world in which players have little control. And sometimes practical elements in routines produce tangible benefits, such as helping the player to concentrate. But a lot of what players do often goes beyond mere routine and is what anthropologists define as *ritual*—prescribed behaviors in which there is no empirical connection between the means (e.g., tapping home plate three times) and the desired end (e.g., getting a base hit). Because there is no real connection between the two, rituals are not rational. Similar to rituals are the nonrational beliefs that form the basis of taboos and fetishes which players also use to reduce chance and bring luck to their side. But first let's look closer at the ballplayers' rituals.

Rituals

Most rituals are personal, that is, they're performed as individuals rather than as a team or group. Most are done in an unemotional manner, in much the same way as players apply pine tar to their bats to improve the grip or dab eye black on their upper cheeks to reduce the sun's glare. Baseball rituals are infinitely varied. A ballplayer may ritualize any activity—eating, dressing, driving to the ballpark—that he considers important or somehow linked to good performance. For example, White Sox pitcher Jason Bere listens to the same song on his Walkman on the days he is to pitch. Tampa's Wade Boggs eats chicken before every game (that's 162 meals of chicken per year), and he has been doing that for twelve years. Jim Leyritz eats turkey, and Dennis Grossini tunafish. Infielder Julio Gotay always played with a cheese sandwich in his back pocket (he had a big appetite, so there might also have been a measure of practicality here). San Francisco Giants pitcher Ron Bryant added a new stick of bubble gum to the collection in his bulging back pocket after each game he won. Jim Ohms put another penny in the pouch of his supporter after each win. Clanging against the hard plastic genital cup, the pennies made an audible sound as he ran the bases toward the end of a winning season.

Many hitters go through a series of preparatory rituals before stepping into the batter's box. These include tugging on their caps, touching their uniform letters or medallions, crossing themselves, tapping or bouncing the bat on the plate, or swinging the weighted warm-up bat a prescribed number of times. Red Sox shortstop Nomar Garciaparra tightens his batting gloves and pounds the toes of his shoes into the earth several times before each pitch. Mike Hargrove, former Cleveland Indian first baseman, had a dozen elements in his batting ritual, from grabbing his belt to pushing his helmet down tight. And after each pitch he would step out of the batter's box and repeat the entire sequence, believing that his batting ritual helped him regain his concentration. His ritual sequence was so time-consuming that he was known as the "human rain delay."

Latin Americans draw upon rituals from their Catholic religion. Some make the sign of the cross or bless themselves before every at bat, and a few like the Rangers' Pudge Rodriguez do so before every pitch. Some, like Juan Gonzalez, wear very visible religious medallions around their neck, while others wear them discretely inside their undershirts.

One ritual associated with hitting is tagging a base when leaving and returning to the dugout between innings. Some players don't "feel right" unless they tag a specific base on each trip between the dugout and the field. Dave Jaeger added some complexity to his ritual by tagging third base on his way to the dugout only after the third, sixth, and ninth innings. Baseball fans observe a lot of ritual behavior—such as tagging bases, pitchers tugging their caps or touching the rosin bag after each bad pitch, smoothing the dirt on the mound before each new batter or inning—never realizing the importance of these actions to the player. One ritual that many fans do recognize, and one that is a favorite of TV cameramen, is the "rally cap"—players in the dugout folding their caps and wearing them bill up in hopes of sparking a rally.

Most rituals grow out of exceptionally good performances. When a player does well, he seldom attributes his success to skill alone. He knows that his skills were essentially the same the night before. What was different about today that explains his three hits? He decides to repeat what he did today in an attempt to bring more good luck. And so he attributes his success, in part, to a food he ate, not having shaved, or just about any behavior out of the ordinary. By repeating that behavior, he seeks to gain control over his performance. Outfielder John White explained how one of his rituals started:

> I was jogging out to centerfield after the National Anthem when I picked up a scrap of paper. I got some good hits that night, and I guess I decided that the paper had something to do with it. The next night I picked up a gum wrapper and had another good night at the plate. . . . I've been picking up paper every night since.

One of Mike Saccocia's rituals concerned food. "I got three hits one night after eating at Long John Silver's. After that when we'd pull into town, my first question would be, 'Do you have a Long John Silver's?'" Like most players, White and Sacciocia abandoned their rituals and looked for new ones when they stopped hitting.

Because starting pitchers play once every four days, they perform their rituals less frequently than do hitters. But their rituals are just as important to them, perhaps more so. A starting pitcher cannot make up for a poor performance the following day like other players can. And having to wait three days to redeem oneself can be miserable. Moreover, the team's performance depends more on the pitcher than on any other player. Considering the pressures to do well, it is not surprising that pitchers' rituals are often more complex than those of hitters. Mike Griffin begins his ritual a full day before he pitches by washing his hair. The next day, although he does not consider himself superstitious, he eats bacon for lunch. When Griffin dresses for the game he puts on his clothes in the same order, making certain he puts the slightly longer of his two stirrup socks on his right leg. "I just wouldn't feel right mentally if I did it the other way around," he explains. He always wears the same shirt under his uniform on the day he pitches. During the game he takes off his cap after each pitch, and between innings he sits in the same place on the dugout bench. He, too, believes his rituals provide a sense of order that reduces his anxiety about pitching.

Some pitchers involve their wives or girlfriends in their rituals. One wife reported that her husband insisted that she wash her hair each day he was to pitch. In her memoirs, Danielle Torrez reported that one "rule" she learned as a baseball wife was "to support your husband's superstitions, whether you believe in them or not. I joined the player's wives who ate ice cream in the sixth inning or tacos in the fifth, or who attended games in a pink sweater, a tan scarf, or a floppy hat" (Torrez 1983).

When in a slump, most players make a deliberate effort to change their rituals and routines in an attempt to shake off their bad luck. One player tried taking different routes to the ballpark; several players reported trying different combinations of tagging and not tagging particular bases in an attempt to find a successful combination. I knew one manager who would rattle the bat bin when his players weren't hitting, as if the bats were in a stupor and could be aroused by a good shaking. Similarly, I have seen hitters rub their hands along the handles of the bats protruding from the bin in hopes of picking up some power or luck from bats that are getting hits for their owners. Some players switch from wearing their contact lenses to glasses. In his book, Brett Mandel described how his Pioneer League team, the Ogden Raptors, tried to break a losing streak by using a new formation for their pre-game stretching (Mandel 1997).

Taboo

Taboos are the opposite of rituals. The word *taboo* comes from a Polynesian term meaning prohibition. Breaking a taboo, players believe, leads to undesirable consequences or bad luck. Most players observe at least a few taboos, such as never stepping on the foul lines. One teammate of mine would never watch a movie on a game day, despite the fact that we played nearly every day from April to September. Another teammate refused to read anything before a game because he believed it weakened his batting eye.

Many taboos take place off the field, out of public view. On the day a pitcher is scheduled to start, he is likely to avoid activities he believes will sap his strength and detract from his effectiveness. Some pitchers avoid eating certain foods; others will not shave on the day of a game and won't shave as long as they are winning. Early one season Oakland's Dave Stewart had six consecutive victories and a beard by the time he lost. Ex-St. Louis Cardinal Al Hrabosky took this taboo to extremes. Samson-like, he refused to cut his hair or beard during the entire season, which was part of the basis for his nickname the "Mad Hungarian."

Taboos usually grow out of exceptionally poor performances, which players, in search of a reason, attribute to a particular behavior. During my first season of pro ball, I ate pancakes before a game in which I struck out four times. A few weeks later I had another terrible game, again after eating pancakes. The result was a pancake taboo: I never again ate pancakes during the season. White Sox pitcher Jason Bere has a taboo that makes more sense in dietary terms: After eating a meatball sandwich and not pitching well, he swore them off for good.

While most taboos are idiosyncratic, there are a few that all ballplayers hold and that do not develop out of individual experience or misfortune. These form part of the culture of baseball; some are learned as early as Little League. Mentioning a no-hitter while one is in progress is a well-known example. It is believed that if a pitcher hears the words *no-hitter*, the spell accounting for this hard-to-achieve feat will be broken and the no-hitter lost. This taboo is also observed by many sports broadcasters, who use various linguistic subterfuges to inform their listeners that the pitcher has not given up a hit, never saying "no-hitter."

Fetishes

Fetishes are material objects believed to embody "supernatural" power (i.e., luck) that can aid or protect the owner. Such charms are standard equipment for some ballplayers. These include a wide assortment of objects from coins, chains, and crucifixes to a favorite baseball hat. In the words of Jim Snyder, "When you are going good you take notice of what you are doing. I still use my glove from college. It's kind of beat up but it's got 40 wins in it, so I still use it. I use my professional glove in practice and my college glove in games." The fetishized object may be a new possession or something a player found that happens to coincide with the start of a streak and that he holds responsible for his good fortune. While playing in the Pacific Coast League, Alan Foster forgot his baseball shoes on a road trip and borrowed a pair from a teammate. That night he pitched a no-hitter, which he attributed to the shoes. Afterwards he bought them from his teammate and they became a fetish. Expo farmhand Mark LaRosa's rock has a very different origin and use:

> I found it on the field in Elmira after I had gotten bombed [pitched poorly]. It's unusual, perfectly round, and it caught my attention. I keep it to remind me of how important it is to concentrate. When I am going well I look at the rock and remember to keep my focus. It reminds me of what can happen when I lose my concentration.

For one season Marge Schott, owner of the Cincinnati Reds, insisted that her field manager rub her St. Bernard "Schotzie" for good luck before each game. When the Reds were on the road, Schott would sometimes send a bag of the dog's hair to the field manager's hotel room.

During World War II American soldiers used fetishes in much the same way. Social psychologist Samuel Stouffer and his colleagues found that in the face of great danger and uncertainty, soldiers developed magical practices, particularly the use of protective amulets and good luck charms (crosses, Bibles, rabbits' feet, medals) and jealously guarded articles of clothing they associated with past experiences of escape from danger (Stouffer 1965). Stouffer also found that pre-battle preparations were carried out in fixed "ritual" order, much as ballplayers and certain other athletes prepare for a game.

Uniform numbers have special significance for some players who request their lucky number. Since the choice is usually limited, they try to at least get a uniform that contains their lucky number, such as 14, 24, 34, or 44 for the player whose lucky number is 4. Oddly enough, there is no consensus about the effect of wearing number 13. Some players will not wear it, others will, and a few request it. Number preferences emerge in different ways. A young player may request the number of a former star, hoping that—through what anthropologists call *imitative* magic—it will bring him the same success. Or he may request a number he associates with good luck. Vida Blue changed his uniform number from 35 to 14, the

number he wore as a high school quarterback. When 14 did not produce better pitching performance, he switched back to 35. Larry Walker has a fixation with the number 3. Besides wearing 33, he takes three practice swings before stepping into the batter's box and sets his alarm for three minutes past the hour (Thrift and Shapiro 1990). Fans in ballparks all across America rise from their seats for the seventh inning stretch before the home club comes to bat because the number 7 is "lucky."

Clothing, both the choice and the order in which they are put on, combine elements of both ritual and fetish. Some players put on their uniform in a ritualized order. Expos farmhand Jim Austin always puts on his left sleeve, left pants leg, and left shoe before the right. Most players, however, single out one or two lucky articles or quirks of dress. After hitting two home runs in a game, for example, infielder Jim Davenport discovered that he had missed a buttonhole while dressing for the game. For the remainder of his career he left the same button undone. For Brian Hunter the focus is shoes, "I have a pair of high tops and a pair of low tops. Whichever shoes don't get a hit that game, I switch to the other pair." At the time of our interview, he was struggling at the plate and switching shoes almost every day. For Birmingham Baron pitcher Bo Kennedy the arrangement of the different pairs of baseball shoes in his locker is critical:

> I tell the clubbies [clubhouse boys] when you hang stuff in my locker don't touch my shoes. If you bump them move them back. I want the Pony's in front, the turfs to the right, and I want them nice and neat with each pair touching each other. . . . Everyone on the team knows not to mess with my shoes.

During streaks—hitting or winning—players may wear the same clothes day after day. Once I changed sweatshirts midway through the game for seven consecutive nights to keep a hitting streak going. Clothing rituals, however, can become impractical. Catcher Matt Allen was wearing a long-sleeve turtleneck on a cool evening in the New York-Penn League when he had a three-hit game. "I kept wearing the shirt and had a good week," he explained. "Then the weather got hot as hell, 85 degrees and muggy, but I would not take that shirt off. I wore it for another ten days—catching—and people thought I was crazy." Also taking a ritual to the extreme, Leo Durocher, managing the Brooklyn Dodgers to a pennant in 1941, is said to have spent three and a half weeks in the same gray slacks, blue coat, and knitted blue tie. During a 16-game winning streak, the 1954 New York Giants wore the same clothes in each game and refused to let them be cleaned for fear that their good fortune might be washed away with the dirt.

Losing often produces the opposite effect. Several Oakland A's players, for example, went out and bought new street clothes in an attempt to break a 14-game losing streak. When I recently joined the Birmingham Barons for a road trip, outfielder Scott Tedder was in a slump. He changed batting gloves daily and had already gone through a dozen pairs trying to find one that would change his luck and get him some hits.

Baseball's superstitions, like most everything else, change over time. Many of the rituals and beliefs of early baseball are no longer observed. In the 1920s and 1930s sportswriters reported that a player who tripped en route to the field would often retrace his steps and carefully walk over the stumbling block for "insurance." A century ago players spent time on and off the field intently looking for items that would bring them luck. To find a hairpin on the street, for example, assured a batter of hitting safely in that day's game. Today few women wear hairpins—a good reason the belief has died out. To catch sight of a white horse or a wagon-load of barrels were also good omens. In 1904 the manager of the New York Giants, John McGraw, hired a driver and a team of white horses to drive past the Polo Grounds around the time his players were arriving at the ballpark. He knew that if his players saw white horses, they'd have more confidence and that could only help them during the game. Belief in the power of white horses survived in a few backwaters until the 1960s. A gray-haired manager of a team I played for in Quebec would drive around the countryside before important games and during the play-offs looking for a white horse. When he was successful, he'd announce it to everyone in the clubhouse before the game.

One belief that appears to have died out recently is a taboo about crossed bats. Some of my Latino teammates in the 1960s took it seriously. I can still recall one Dominican player becoming agitated when another player tossed a bat from the batting cage and it landed on top of his bat. He believed that the top bat might steal hits from the lower one. In his view, bats contained a finite number of hits, a sort of baseball "image of limited good." It was once commonly believed that once the hits in a bat were used up, no amount of good hitting would produce any more. Hall of Famer Honus Wagner believed each bat contained only one hundred hits. Regardless of the quality of the bat, he would discard it after its hundredth hit. This belief would have little relevance today, in the era of light bats with thin handles—so thin that the typical modern bat is lucky to survive a dozen hits without being broken. Other superstitions about bats do survive, however. Hitters on the Class A Asheville Tourists would not let pitchers touch or swing their bats, not even to warm up. The poor-hitting pitchers were said to pollute or weaken the bats.

Uncertainty and Magic

The best evidence that players turn to rituals, taboos, and fetishes to control chance and uncertainty is found in their uneven application. They are associated mainly with pitching and hitting—the activities with the highest degree of chance—and not fielding. I met only one player who had any ritual in connection with fielding, and he was an error-prone shortstop. Unlike hitting and pitching, a fielder has almost complete control over the outcome of his performance. Once a ball has been hit in his direction, no one can intervene and ruin his chances of catching it for an out (except in the unlikely event of two fielders colliding). Compared with the pitcher or the hitter, the fielder has little to worry about. He knows that in better than 9.7 times out of 10 he will execute his task flawlessly. With odds like that there is little need for ritual. Clearly, the ritual behavior of American ballplayers is not unlike that of the Trobriand Islanders studied by Malinowski many years ago (1948). In professional baseball, fielding is the equivalent of the inner lagoon while hitting and pitching are like the open sea.

While Malinowski helps us understand how ballplayers and other people respond to chance and uncertainty, behavioral psychologist B. F. Skinner sheds light on why personal rituals get established in the first place (Skinner 1938, 1953). With a few grains of seed Skinner could get pigeons to do anything he wanted. He merely waited for the desired behavior (e.g., pecking) and then rewarded it with some food. Skinner then decided to see what would happen if pigeons were rewarded with food pellets regularly, every fifteen seconds, regardless of what they did. He found that the birds associate the arrival of the food with a particular action, such as tucking their head under a wing or walking in clockwise circles. About ten seconds after the arrival of the last pellet, a bird would begin doing whatever it associated with getting the food and keep doing it until the next pellet arrived. In short, the pigeons behaved as if their actions made the food appear. They learned to associate particular behaviors with the reward of being given seed.

Ballplayers also associate a reward—successful performance—with prior behavior. If a player touches his crucifix and then gets a hit, he may decide the gesture was responsible for his good fortune and touch his crucifix the next time he comes to the plate. If he gets another hit, the chances are good that he will touch his crucifix each time he bats. Unlike pigeons, however, most ballplayers are quicker to change their rituals once they no longer seem to work. Skinner found that once a pigeon associated one of its actions with the arrival of food or water, only sporadic rewards were needed to keep the ritual going. One pigeon, apparently believing that hopping from side to side caused pellets to fall into its feeding cup, hopped ten thousand times without a single pellet appearing before finally giving up. But, then, hasn't Wade Boggs continued to eat chicken, through slumps and good times, before every game for the past dozen years? Obviously the rituals and superstitions of baseball do not make a pitch travel faster or a batted ball locate gaps between the fielders, nor do Trobriand rituals calm the seas or bring fish. What both do, however, is give their practitioners a sense of control, and with that, confidence. And we all know how important that is.

Suggested Readings

Bowen, Elenore Smith [Laura Bohannan]
1964   *Return to Laughter.* Garden City, N.Y.: Doubleday.

Colby, Benjamin N., and Lore M. Colby
1981   *The Daykeeper: The Life and Discourse of an Ixil Diviner.* Cambridge, Mass.: Harvard University Press.

Douglas, Mary, ed.
1970   *Witchcraft Confessions and Accusations.* London: Tavistock.

Kapferer, Bruce
1997   *The Feast of the Sorcerer: Practices of Consciousness and Power.* Chicago: University of Chicago Press.

Orion, Loretta
1995   *Never Again the Burning Times: Paganism Revived.* Prospect Heights, Ill.: Waveland Press.

Peek, Philip, ed.
1991   *African Divination Systems: Ways of Knowing.* Bloomington: Indiana University Press.

CHAPTER EIGHT

Ghosts, Souls, and Ancestors: Power of the Dead

Ivory pendant mask from Benin, Nigeria.

Religions universally promise believers that there is life after death. Although the worship of ancestors is not universal, a belief in the immortality of the dead occurs in all cultures. There is variation among cultures in the degree of interaction between the living and the dead, however, as well as in the intensity and concern a people may have for the deceased. Eskimos are never free of anxieties about ghosts, whereas Pueblo Indians are seldom bothered by them; the Plains Indians of North America constructed elaborate ghost beliefs, whereas the Siriono of South America, although believing in ghosts, paid little attention to them.

Perhaps humans have some basic need that causes us to believe in ghosts and to worship ancestors: to seek verification that, although the mortal body may die, the soul survives after death. The nineteenth-century sociologist Herbert Spencer speculated that the beginnings of religion were in ancestor worship—the need for the living to continue an emotional relationship with their dead relatives. A major problem with Spencer's argument is that many societies at the hunting-and-gathering level do not practice ancestor worship. The Arunta of Australia, for example, worshipped their totemic plants and animals, but not their human ancestors. This objection to Spencer's belief notwithstanding, ancestor worship does remind the living of a vital continuing link between the living and the dead. "Ritually, the most important category of animistic beings was the ancestors of the band, village, and clan or other kinship groups whose members believed they were bonded by common descent" (Harris 1989: 399).

One writer has pointed out that two major attitudes are widely held about the dead: that they either have left the society or remain as active members (Malefijt 1968: 156–59). In societies that separate the dead from the living social group, any possibility of the dead returning is regarded as undesirable because they could disrupt the social order and the daily routine of life. In such cultures, Annemarie de Waal Malefijt believes, the dead are likely to be greatly feared, and an elaborate belief system—a cult of the dead—is constructed and practiced in order to separate them from the living. The primary function of cults of the dead is to aid the survivors in overcoming the grief they may feel about the dead. Such cults are not found in societies where the dead are seen as active members of the group; instead, funeral ceremonies are undertaken with the hope the deceased will return to society in their new status. These beliefs, according to Malefijt, result in the development of ancestor cults instead of cults of the dead. S. C. Humphreys's *Comparative Perspectives on Death* (1981) sets out the great variety of belief concerning the fate of the dead, as does M. Bloch and J. Parry's work *Death and the Regeneration of Life* (1982).

Ancestor cults and the ritual that surrounds them may also be seen as an elaboration of cults of the dead. The Bantu of Africa, for example, outline distinct ancestral deities for each lineage and clan. All of these ancestral gods are gods to their living relatives, but not to individuals who belong to other kinship organizations. Further elaboration of Bantu ancestor worship may be seen in Bantu beliefs about the supernatural beings believed to head their royal clans. Gods of such royal clans are worshipped by the entire kingdom, not just the royal clan itself.

The study of ancestor worship conducted by American and British anthropologists has emphasized the connection between the identity and behavioral characteristics of the dead, on one hand, and the distribution and nature of their authority in both domestic and political domains of the society, on the other (Bradbury 1966: 127). Although the belief in ghosts of ancestors is universal, the functions ancestors play vary greatly among societies. It is also clear that variations in ancestor worship are directly related to social structure and that this relationship is not based on mere common religious interests alone: rather, the structure of the kin group and the relationships of those within it serve as the model of ancestor worship (Bradbury 1966: 128). Among the Sisala of Ghana, for example, only a select number of Sisala elders, based on their particular status and power within the group, can effectively communicate with the ghosts of ancestors (Mendonsa 1976: 63–64). In many other parts of the non-Western world, non-elder ritual specialists, such as heads of households, are responsible for contacting the ancestors. A cross-cultural study of fifty societies found that, where important decisions are made by the kin group, ancestor worship is a high probability (Swanson 1964: 97–108).

Many, but certainly not all, non-Western societies believe ancestors play a strong and positive role in the security and prosperity of their group, and anthropological data offer many of these kinds of examples. It is important, however, to recognize that ancestors are but one of several categories of spirits whose actions directly affect society. John S. Mbiti's study of East and Central Africa shows that the status of spirits may change through time. Ancestor spirits, the "living dead," are those whose memory still exists in the minds of their kin and who are primarily beneficial to the surviving relatives. When the living dead are forgotten in the memory of their group and dropped from the genealogy as a result of the passing of time (four or five generations), they are believed to be transformed into "nameless spirits," non-ancestors, characterized as malicious vehicles for misfortune of all kinds (1970). In keeping with Mbiti's model, the Lugbara of Uganda recognize two types of dead. The first group, simply called "ancestors," comprises nameless, all deceased relatives; these are secondary in importance to the recently deceased, called "ancestor spirits" or "ghosts," who can be invoked by the living to cause misfortune to befall those whose acts threaten the solidarity of the kin group (Middleton 1971: 488).

Clearly spirits, ghosts, and ancestors are often given unique statuses in the afterlife and are viewed as having different functions and effects on the living. In many respects, the relationship of fear and responsibility of elders toward ancestors is mirrored by the son-father relationship among the living. The ancestral world in many cases is an extension or a model of the real world. The supernatural status of the ancestors exhibits major differences, for, although one can argue to a point with an elder, no one questions the wisdom and authority of an ancestor.

The power of the dead is an important aspect of religion and social control. If, for example, a Lugbara man threatens the solidarity of the clan or lineage in any of a number of ways, the elder may invoke ghosts to punish the troublemaker (Middleton 1971: 488–92). Without doubt this veneration of the ancestors and the fear of their power help control many societies. Interestingly, ancestor worship also contributes to the conservative nature of those cultures where it is practiced. Typically, dead ancestors do not smile on any kind of change in the cultures of their living relatives. Because ghosts are capable of severely punishing an earthly mortal desirous of change, the force for conformity is strong.

Not all societies assign power to ancestors. In many cultures, North America included, a high god (monotheism) or gods (polytheism) exert authority over the living, punishing those who violate religious tenets, rules that often are duplicated in civil law and serve as the bases of appropriate social behavior. In these groups, ancestor cults and worship of the deceased are not found, although the spiritual nature of ancestors and belief in the afterlife persevere.

Among people where the deceased are believed to take an active role in society, the living are understandably concerned with the welfare of ancestors. Customs are established to assure the comfort of the dead in their life after death. Most commonly, rituals carried out at funerals, burials, and in some cases reburial or cremation, ensure that loved ones arrive safely at what the living believe is the proper abode of the dead. The care taken in preparing the deceased for the afterlife is an important reinforcement of the society's customs and an expression of unity among its members. Participation helps ensure that the same care can be expected to be given at the time of one's own death. Beyond this motivation, however, the power to rain down misfortunes is a major reason for carefully following customs surrounding the preparation, interment, and propitiation of the dead. No one wants to be subjected to supernatural punishment by vengeful and angry ghosts.

To most people in Western culture the word *ghost* brings forth an image of a disembodied spirit of a dead person swooping through dark halls, hovering frighteningly over a grave, or perhaps roaming aimlessly through damp woods. Typically, the ghost is observed wearing white sheets—an image that undoubtedly arises from the shroud or winding sheet used to wrap the corpse for its placement in the grave. There is a wide variety of shapes available to would-be ghosts, however. Some are transparent; some are lifelike apparitions of their former selves; others appear with horribly gaunt, empty faces, devoid of eyes and lips. Not all ghosts take a human or even vaguely human shape: horses frequently appear in phantom form, as do dogs and large birds, and ghost lore is full of accounts of ghost trains, stagecoaches, and, of course, such phantom ships as the Flying Dutchman.

Very few cultures do not support the idea of a separate spirit world—a land of the dead. It is to this other world that souls will travel and, once there, will rest in eternal peace. At some point in history, however, the notion arose that not all souls deserve an easy trip to a blissful spiritual world. Murderers, miscreants, and evil people, for example, might become ghosts doomed to wander the earthly world. Inadequate funerals also might give rise to restless ghosts, thus explaining the attention paid by cultures everywhere to meticulously preparing and dressing the corpse for burial and to placing gifts, food, and weapons in the grave or at the gravesite to enhance the spirit's journey to the place of eternal rest.

In the first article of this chapter, William E. Mitchell discusses the granting of the first gun permits to a New Guinea group and the resulting formation of a cult. Mitchell shows how the cult's belief in vengeful spirits helps them understand why they are sometimes unsuccessful at hunting.

In the second selection, Paul Barber vividly illustrates the fear with which eighteenth-century Europeans regarded vampires.

Karen McCarthy Brown examines the practice of Vodou in Haiti, pointing out that, despite the distorted popular version we see all too frequently in the mass media, it is a legitimate religious practice of 80 to 90 percent of Haitians.

In the fourth selection, Peter A. Metcalf compares American and Berawan funeral rites. As Metcalf learned to see Berawan funerary customs as natural, American treatment of the dead began to seem exotic.

In the fifth article, Stanley Brandes describes the cross-cultural complexities arising from the death of an immigrant Guatemalan living in the United States and the individual's subsequent cremation. Brandes notes that the cremation was an unthinkable end for a deceased person in the individual's home village in Guatemala.

In the final selection, Haney, Leimer, and Lowery discuss spontaneous memorials and memorialization, the phenomenon whereby mourners leave at the site of a death a collection of mementoes, such as flowers, flags, and teddy bears.

References

Bloch, M., and J. Parry, eds.
　　1982　*Death and Regeneration of Life.* Cambridge: Cambridge University Press.

Bradbury, R. E.
　　1966　"Fathers, Elders, and Ghosts in Edo Religion." In Michael Banton, ed., *Anthropological Approaches to the Supernatural,* pp. 127–53. London: Tavistock.

Harris, Marvin
　　1989　*Our Kind.* New York: Harper and Row.

Humphreys, S. C.
　　1981　*Comparative Perspectives on Death.* New York: Academic Press.

Malefijt, Annemarie de Waal
　　1968　*Religion and Culture: An Introduction to Anthropology of Religion.* New York: Macmillan.

Mbiti, John S.
　　1970　*African Religions and Philosophies.* Garden City, N.Y.: Doubleday.

Mendonsa, Eugene L.
　　1976　"Elders, Office-Holders and Ancestors Among the Sisala of Northern Ghana." *Africa* 46: 57–64.

Middleton, John
　　1971　"The Cult of the Dead: Ancestors and Ghosts." In William A. Lessa and Evon Z. Vogt, eds., *Reader in Comparative Religion: An Anthropological Approach,* 3rd ed., pp. 488–92. New York: Harper and Row.

Swanson, Guy A.
　　1964　*The Birth of the Gods.* Ann Arbor: University of Michigan Press.

39

A New Weapon Stirs Up Old Ghosts

William E. Mitchell

In the following article, William E. Mitchell describes the Wape shotgun cult, a belief and behavioral system that sprang up in New Guinea after the introduction of guns to the area in the late 1940s and early 1950s. Mitchell tells how Wape villagers pool their money to collectively purchase a shotgun and then select a candidate from within their ranks to take the firearm test administered by officials. If the applicant is successful, a permit is issued, and the individual must agree to shoot game for his village. Of special interest for this chapter is the role of ancestral ghosts in the system. Among the Wape, the dead are believed not only to protect the living from harm but also to supply them with meat and punish anyone who may have wronged them. Thus, a dead male relative becomes an invaluable aide to the hunter. The author shows how the cult's belief in vengeful spirits helps them understand why they sometimes experience unsuccessful hunting.

When, in 1947, the Franciscan friars went to live among the nearly 10,000 Wape people of New Guinea, the principal native weapons were bone daggers and the bow and arrow. Even then, game was scarce in the heavily populated mountains where the Wape live, and the killing of a wild pig or a cassowary, New Guinea's major game animals, was an important village event. The Wape live in the western part of the Sepik River Basin. Their small villages lie along the narrow ridges of the Torricelli Mountains, above the sago palm swamps where women process palm pith, the Wape staff of life.

Today the Wape hunter's principal weapon is still the bow and arrow and game is even scarcer. This is partially the result of a new addition to the hunter's armory—the prosaic shotgun—which has had a profound moral impact on Wape village life.

The first guns were brought into this area in the late 1940s and early 1950s by missionaries, traders, and Australian government officials. Although natives were not permitted to own guns, they could use them if employed by a white man to shoot game for his table. This was a very prestigious job.

In 1960, government regulations were changed to permit natives to purchase singleshot shotguns. At first only a few Wape men, living in villages close to the government station and helpful to government officials, were granted gun permits. Eventually more permits were issued, but today, in hopes of preserving the remaining game, one permit is issued for every 100 people.

Within ten years of the granting of the first gun permits, a belief and behavioral system had evolved around the shotgun. It was based on traditional Wape hunting lore but had distinctive elaborations stemming from native perceptions of the teachings of government officials and missionaries. For descriptive purposes I call this system of formalized beliefs and ritual the "Wape shotgun cult." It is one of several Wape ceremonial cults, but the only one originating after contact with Europeans. Although the specific practices of the shotgun cult vary from village to village, the underlying beliefs are the same.

In creating the shotgun cult the Wape faced the challenge of adapting an introduced implement to their culture. Unlike steel axes and knives, which replaced stone adzes and bamboo knives, the shotgun has never replaced the bow and arrow. The shotgun is a scarce and expensive machine. This, together with the European sanctions imposed upon its introduction, places it in a unique position, both symbolically and behaviorally, among the Wape.

The cult is a conservative institution. It breaks no new cognitive ground by challenging established Wape concepts. Instead it merges traditional hunting concepts with European moral teachings to create a coherent system. The cult upholds traditional beliefs, accepts European authority, and most important, provides an explanation for unsuccessful hunting.

In 1970, my family and I arrived in Lumi, a small mountain settlement, which is the government's subdistrict headquarters in the middle of Wapeland. For the next year and a half, we lived in the village of Taute, near Lumi. There my wife and I studied Wape culture.

Taute, which has a population of 220, is reached by narrow foot trails, root strewn and muddy, passing through the dense, damp forest. The low houses— made of sago palm stems and roofed with sago thatch—are scattered about in the sandy plaza and among the coconut palms and breadfruit trees along the ridge. Towering poinsettias, red and pink hibiscus, and multicolored shrubs contrast with the encircling forest's greens and browns. A few small latrines perch on the steep slopes, concessions to Western concepts of hygiene. In the morning, flocks of screeching cockatoos glide below the ridge through the rising mists. When the breadfruit trees are bearing, giant fruit bats flop across the sky at dusk.

Since the mid-1950s the Franciscan friars have maintained, off and on, a religious school in Taute. There, Wape boys are instructed by a native catechist in Catholicism, simple arithmetic, and Melanesian Pidgin. A priest from Lumi visits the village several times a year, and the villagers, Catholic and heathen alike, are proud of their affiliation with the Franciscans and staunchly loyal to them. But their Catholicism is nominal and superficial—a scant and brittle frosting that does not mask their own religious beliefs, which dominate everyday life.

The ethos of Wape society is oriented around sacred curing rituals. Whereas some Sepik cultures aggressively center their ceremonial life around headhunting and the raising of sturdy and brave children, the Wape defensively center theirs in the ritual appeasement of malevolent ghosts and forest demons, who they believe cause sickness. Most men belong to one of the demon-curing cults where, once initiated as priests, they are responsible for producing the often elaborate curing ceremonies for exorcising the demon from the afflicted.

The little money that exists among the Wape is earned primarily by the men, who work as two-year contract laborers on the coastal and island copra plantations. Because of the lack of money to buy canned meats, the scarcity of game, and the paucity of fish in the mountain streams, the protein intake of the Wape is exceedingly low. The most common meal is sago dumplings and boiled leaves. Malnutrition is common among youngsters, and physical development is generally retarded. According to studies by Dr. Lyn Wark, a medical missionary who has worked widely among the Wape, the average birth weight of the Wape baby is the lowest recorded in the world. Correspondingly, secondary sex characteristics are delayed. For example, the mean age for the onset of menses is over eighteen years.

Before contact with Westerners, Wape men were naked and the women wore short string skirts. Today most men wear shorts and the women wear skirts purchased from Lumi's four small stores. To appear in a semblance of European dress, however meager or worn, is a matter of pride and modesty to both sexes. "Savages" do not wear clothes, but white men and those who have been enlightened by white men do. In this sense, the Wape's Western-style dress represents an identification with the politically and materially powerful white man. The identification is with power; it is an ego-enhancing maneuver that permits the Wape to live with dignity, even though they are subservient to Western rule and influence. The tendency of the Wape to identify with, and incorporate, the alien when it serves to preserve their culture will help us to understand how they have woven diverse cultural strands into the creation of the shotgun cult.

From the first day I arrived in Taute, the men repeatedly made two urgent requests of me. One was to open a store in the village, saving them the difficult walk into Lumi; the other was to buy a shotgun to help them kill game. This was the least, they seemed to indicate, a fair-minded and, in Wape terms, obviously rich neighbor should do. One of the hardest things the anthropologists in the field must learn is to say "no" to deserving people. To be stingy is almost to be un-American, but we had come halfway around the world to learn about the Wape way of life, not to introduce stores and shotguns that would alter the established trading and hunting patterns.

After several months the people of the major Taute hamlets, Kafiere, where we lived, and Mifu, a ten-minute walk away, each decided to buy a group-owned shotgun. The investment was a sizable forty-two Australian dollars; forty dollars for the gun, and two dollars for the gun permit. Each hamlet made a volunteer collection from its members and I, as a fellow villager, contributed to both guns. A week later the villagers purchased the guns from one of the Lumi stores, and I began to learn about the shotgun's ritual and moral importance to the Wape. The villagers were already familiar with the significance of the shotgun for they had purchased one several years before. The cult ended, however, when the gun broke.

The shotgun, like Melanesian Pidgin, is associated by the Wape with Europeans and modernity. Not surprisingly, Pidgin is favored for shotgun parlance. The licensed gunman is not only called *sutboi* ("shootboy") but also *laman* ("law man"), the latter a term that connotes his official tie to European law and government as perceived by the villagers.

When a candidate for a gun permit appears before the government official in Lumi, he is examined orally on the use of firearms, then given an unloaded shotgun and tested on his handling knowledge. Under the direct and questioning gaze of the examining official, candidates sometimes become flustered. One inadvertently aimed the gun first toward the wife of the assistant district commissioner and then toward a group of observers. His examination ended ignominiously on the spot.

If the candidate passes the test and the examining official approves of his character, he is then lectured on the use of the gun: only the candidate can fire it,

he must willingly shoot game for his fellow villagers, and the gun must be used exclusively for hunting. He is strongly warned that if any of these rules are broken or if there is trouble in the village, he will lose the gun and the permit and will be imprisoned.

The candidate's friends and the inevitable audience are present for the lecture. Here, as in many spheres of native life, the official's power is absolute, and the Wape know this from long experience. Guns have been confiscated or destroyed without reimbursement and gunmen have been jailed.

The official's charge to the candidate is willingly accepted. Henceforth, he will never leave the village without carrying his gun. He is now a *laman*, and he has the gun and permit, printed entirely in English, to prove it.

The government official's strong sanctions against village quarrels are motivated by his fear that the gun might be used in a dispute among villagers. The sanctions are further upheld by the missionaries' and catechists' sermons against quarreling and wrongdoing as they attempt to teach the Christian doctrine of brotherly love. The message the villagers receive is this: To keep the white man's gun, they must follow the white man's rules. This the Wape do, not in servile submission, but with some pride because the presence of the gun and the public focus on morality mark the village as progressive and modern. The licensed gunman, therefore, is not only the guardian of the gun but of village morality as well.

Rain or shine, he is expected to go into the forest without compensation to hunt for his fellow villagers, who give him cartridges with some personal identifying mark upon them. After a gunman makes a kill, the owner of the cartridge receives the game and distributes it according to his economic obligations to others. But the gunman, like the bow and arrow hunter, is forbidden to eat from the kill; to do so would jeopardize further successful hunting.

In the hamlet of Kafiere, the clan that had contributed the most money toward the gun and on whose lands the most game was to be found appointed Auwe as gunman. But Auwe's wife, Naiasu, was initially against his selection. Her previous husband, Semer, now dead several years, had been Kafiere's first *sutboi* and she argued that the heavy hunting responsibilities of a *sutboi* took too much time, forcing him to neglect his own gardening and hunting obligations.

When Auwe first requested a gun permit he was turned away. The villagers believed that the ghost of Naiasu's dead husband, Semer, had followed Auwe to Lumi and influenced the examining official against him. Semer's ghost was acting to fulfill Naiasu's wish that her young son, now Auwe's stepson, would have a stepfather who was always available. This was the first of many stories I was to hear about the relationship between ghosts and the gun. When Auwe returned to Lumi for a second try, he passed the examination and was given the official permit.

The hamlet now had its own gun and hunting could begin in earnest. The first step was an annunciation feast called, in Pidgin, a *kapti* ("cup of tea"). Its purpose was to inform the villagers' dead ancestors about the new gun. This was important because ancestral ghosts roam the forest land of their lineage, protecting it from intruders and driving game to their hunting descendants. The hunter's most important hunting aide is his dead male relatives, to whom he prays for game upon entering his hunting lands. The dead remain active in the affairs of the living by protecting them from harm, providing them with meat, and punishing those who have wronged them.

The small sacrificial feast was held in front of Auwe's house. Placing the upright gun on a makeshift table in the midst of the food, Auwe rubbed it with sacred ginger. One of Auwe's elderly clansmen, standing and facing his land, called out to his ancestors by name and told them about the new gun. He implored them to send wild pigs and cassowaries to Auwe.

Several men spoke of the new morality that was to accompany hunting with a gun. The villagers should not argue or quarrel among themselves; problems must be settled quietly and without bitterness; malicious gossip and stealing were forbidden. If these rules were not obeyed, Auwe would not find game.

In traditional Wape culture there is no feast analogous to the *kapti*. Indeed, there are no general community-wide feasts. The *kapti* is apparently modeled on a European social gathering.

For the remainder of my stay in Taute, I followed closely the fortunes of the Taute guns and of guns in nearby villages as well. All seemed to be faced with the same two problems: game was rarely seen; and when seen, was rarely killed. Considering that a cartridge belongs to a villager, not the gunman, how was this economic loss handled? This presented a most intriguing and novel problem for there were no analogs to this type of predicament within the traditional culture. By Wape standards, the pecuniary implications of such a loss, although but a few Australian shillings, could not graciously be ignored by the loser. At the very least the loss had to be explained even if the money for the cartridges could not be retrieved.

Now I understood the concern about the ancestral ghosts. If the hunter shot and missed, the owner of the fired shells was being punished by being denied meat. Either he or a close family member had quarreled or wronged another person whose ghost-relative was securing revenge by causing the hunter to miss. This, then, was the functional meaning of the proscription against quarreling. By avoiding disputes, the villagers were trying to prevent the intervention of ancestral ghosts in human affairs. In a peaceful village without quarrels, the gunman could hunt undisturbed by vengeful ghosts chasing away game or misrouting costly shells.

Although a number of factors in European culture have influenced the shotgun cult, the cult's basic premise of a positive correlation between quarreling and bad hunting is derived directly from traditional Wape culture. In bow and arrow hunting, an individual who feels he was not given his fair share of a hunter's kill may punish the hunter by gossiping about him or quarreling openly with him. The aggrieved person's ancestral ghosts revenge the slight by chasing the game away from the offending hunter or misdirecting his arrows. But this is a private affair between the hunter and the angered person; their quarrel has no influence upon the hunting of others. And it is rare for an issue other than distribution of game to cause a ghost to hinder a bowman's success. The hunter's prowess is restored only when the angered person performs a brief supplication rite over the hunter.

This, then, is the conceptual basis for the tie between quarreling and bad hunting. Originally relevant only to bow and arrow hunting, it was then broadened to accommodate the government's pronouncements about the shotgun and keeping the village peace. And it applies perfectly to the special circumstances of shotgun hunting. Because the shotgun is community owned and many villagers buy cartridges for it, the villagers are identified with both the gun and the gunman. As a proxy hunter for the villagers, the gunman is potentially subject to the ghostly sanctions resulting from their collective wrongs. Thus gun hunting, unlike bow and arrow hunting, is a community affair and the community-wide taboo against quarrels and personal transgressions is the only effective way to prevent spiteful ghosts from wrecking the hunt.

No village, however, even if populated by people as disciplined and well behaved as the Wape, can constantly live in the state of pious peace considered necessary for continuous good gun hunting. When the hunting is poor, the gunman must discover the quarrels and wrongs within the village. After having identified the individuals whose ancestral ghosts are sabotaging the hunting, the gunman must also see to it that they implore the ghosts to stop. Embarrassed by the public disclosure, they will quickly comply.

The common method for detecting points of friction within the village is to bring the villagers together for a special meeting. The gunman will then document in detail his misfortunes and call on the villagers to find out what is ruining the hunting. If confessions of wrongdoing are not forthcoming, questioning accusations result. The meeting, beginning in Pidgin, moves into Wape as the discussion becomes more complex and voluble. It may last up to three hours; but even if there is no resolution, it always ends amiably—at least on the surface. For it is important to create no new antagonisms.

The other technique for locating the source of the hunting problem is to call in a professional clairvoyant. As the villagers must pay for his services, he is usually consulted only after a series of unsuccessful meetings. Clairvoyants have replaced the shamans, who were outlawed by the government and the mission because they practiced sorcery and ritual murders. The Wape do not consider a clairvoyant a sorcerer; he is a man with second sight who is experienced in discovering and treating the hidden causes of intractable problems. As such, shotguns are among his best patients.

Mewau, a clairvoyant from a neighboring village, held a "shotgun clinic" in Taute to examine the Mifu and Kafiere guns. For about an hour he examined the two guns and questioned the villagers. Then he declared the reasons for their misfortune.

Kapul, a dead Mifu shaman, was preventing the Mifu gun from killing game because a close relative of the gunman had allegedly stolen valuables from Kapul's daughter. Because of the family ties between the gunman and the thief, Kapul's ghost was punishing the gunman.

The Kafiere gun, Mewau declared, was not able to find game because a widow in the village felt that her dead husband's clan had not previously distributed game to her in a fair way. By interfering with the Kafiere gun, her husband's ghost was punishing his clan for the neglect of his family.

Once the source of trouble is named, there are several possible types of remedial ritual depending upon the seriousness of the situation. For example, the circumstances surrounding the naming of the husband's ghost were considered serious, and a *kapti* was held to placate him. Another, simpler ritual involves the preparation of taro soup, which the gunman consumes. But the simplest, commonest remedial rite is the supplication ritual without sacrificial food offerings, a ritual in which I became involved.

Mifu's gunman had shot a pig with one of his own cartridges but did not give me the small portion due me as a part owner of the gun. Partly as a test to see if my ancestors counted for anything in Taute and partly because I did not want to let this calculated slight go unchallenged, I, in typical Wape fashion, said nothing to the gunman but gossiped discreetly about his selfishness. The gunman continued to hunt but had no further success. When his bad luck persisted, a meeting was called to find out the reason. The gunman asked me if I was angry because I had not been given my portion of the pig. When I acknowledged my anger, he handed the shotgun to me and I dutifully spoke out to my ancestors to stop turning the game away from the gun.

But the gunman still had no success in the hunt, and the villagers decided there were other wrongs as well. The search for the offending ghosts continued. Eventually the villagers became so discouraged with the Mifu gun that they stopped giving cartridges to the gunman. The consensus was that a major undetected wrong existed in the hamlet, and until it was uncovered and the guilty ghost called off, hunting with the gun was senseless and extravagant. Thus the propriety of a remedial rite is established if there is success on the next hunt. The system is completely empirical: if no game is seen or if seen, is not killed, then the search for the wrong must continue.

Wape people are generally even tempered, and their villages, in contrast to many in New Guinea, strike the newcomer as almost serene. But the social impact of the guns at this time was pervasive, and life in Taute literally revolved around the guns and their hunting fortunes. Whereas the villagers previously had kept to their own affairs, they now became embroiled in meeting after meeting, seeking out transgressions, quarrels, and wrongdoing. As the gunman continued to have bad luck, his efforts to discover the cause became more zealous. A certain amount of polarization resulted: the gunman accused the villagers, the men accused the women, and the adults accused the young people of hiding their wrongs. And a few who had lost many cartridges wondered if the *sutboi* was keeping the game for himself. But no one ever suggested that he was an inexperienced shotgun hunter. The gunman was generally considered to be blameless; in fact, the more game he missed, the more self-righteous he became and the more miscreant the villagers.

Six months of poor hunting had gone by; the villagers felt that the only recourse left to them was to bring a bush demon named *mani* into the village from the jungle for a festival. The *mani*'s small stone heart is kept enshrined in a rustic altar in a corner of Kafiere's ceremonial house and after a kill the animal's blood is smeared upon it. The *mani* will reward the village with further kills only if he is fed with blood. *Mani* is the only spirit, other than ghosts, who can cause both good and bad hunting depending upon the way he is treated. Soon after the shotgun arrived in Taute, the gunman and some other men left their homes to sleep in the men's ceremonial house to keep *mani*'s stone heart warm. They thought *mani*, in appreciation, would send game to the gunman.

When little game was killed, the villagers decided on the hunting festival. In a special house outside of the village, men constructed the great conical mask that depicts *mani*. For several weeks they worked to cover the mask's frame with the spathes of sago palm fronds painted with designs traditional to *mani*. Finally, a priest of the *mani* cult, wearing a 20-foot-high mask festooned with feathers and leaves, pranced into the village to the thunderous beat of wooden drums.

For the next week and a half men from other villages who wished us well came and joined in the all-night singing of the *mani* song cycle. In the morning, if the weather was clear, *mani* led the bow and arrow hunters and the gunman to the edge of the village and sent them on their way to hunting success. But in spite of the careful attentions the villagers directed toward *mani*, he rewarded them with only one wild pig. The villagers became openly discouraged, then annoyed. Finally the hunters, disgusted and weary from numerous long futile hunts, and other men, their shoulders sore and bloody from constantly carrying the heavy mask around the plaza, decided that *mani* was simply taking advantage of them; all of their hard work was for nothing. Disgusted, they decided to send *mani* back to his home in the forest.

One late afternoon the *mani* appeared in the plaza but he did not prance. He walked slowly around the plaza, stopping at each house to throw ashes over himself with his single bark cloth arm. The villagers said he was in mourning because he had to leave by dusk and would miss the company of men. Silently the people watched the once gay and graceful *mani* lumber out of the village. The men and boys followed him into the forest. Then the gunman split open the mask, to insure the spirit's exit and eventual return to his forest home, and hurled it over the edge of the cliff into the bush below.

A few months after the *mani* hunting festival, the shotgun cult as I had known it in Taute ceased to function. All but one of the able young men of the hamlet of Kafiere went off to work on a coastal plantation for two years. With no young men, the ceremonial activities of the hunting and curing cults were suspended and the fault-finding meetings halted until their return. The drama and excitement of the previous months had vanished with the men.

40

The Real Vampire

Paul Barber

Tales of the undead in eighteenth-century Europe were preeminent in establishing the folklore of the vampire, a figure whose bloodlust struck stark terror into the hearts of believers of that day. Images of evil of such magnitude die hard. Bram Stoker's novel introduced the horrors of vampiric attack to the rest of the world through the character of Count Dracula, later immortalized on the American screen in the 1930s by Bela Lugosi. However, to many eighteenth-century Europeans, vampires were not fictional; they were real and accounted for deaths due to contagion in a world that had no theory of communicable disease. Paul Barber's forensic evidence provides a physiological basis for the belief that the dead could return from the grave, for Europeans then believed that any corpse having what they considered an abnormal or peculiar condition was most certainly a vampire. But the sociological explanations for the existence of vampires and the techniques for protecting themselves from them are equally provocative. One protective measure was the act of consuming the blood of a vampire, thereby invoking the elementary concept of similia similiis curantur *(similar things are cured by similar things), a rationale commonly found in folklore.*

Personal characteristics attributed to those with the potential to become vampires are amazing, like the characteristics of those accused of witchcraft today—for example, in Africa. Like the witches of Africa, vampires of Europe had the ability to leave the body and attack their victims unseen and, like witches, vampires were responsible for a wide variety of everyday, rather pedestrian misfortunes. Clearly, the human propensity to create monstrous mental images, such as vampires, responsible for misfortunes of such an extreme caliber as death, was and is common and functions as an explanation of the unexplainable. The negative effects on society, however, of the dysfunctional aspects of fear and accusation resulting from these mystical types of explanations cannot be discounted.

I saw the Count lying within the box upon the earth, some of which the rude falling from the cart had scattered over him. He was deathly pale, just like a waxen image, and the red eyes glared with the horrible vindictive look which I knew too well. . . .

The eyes saw the sinking sun, and the look of hate in them turned to triumph.

But, on the instant, came the sweep and flash of Jonathan's great knife. I shrieked as I saw it shear through the throat; whilst at the same moment Mr. Morris's bowie knife plunged into the heart.

It was like a miracle; but before our very eyes, and almost in the drawing of a breath, the whole body crumbled into dust and passed from our sight.

—Bram Stoker, *Dracula*

If a typical vampire of folklore were to come to your house this Halloween, you might open the door to encounter a plump Slavic fellow with long finger-nails and a stubbly beard, his mouth and left eye open, his face ruddy and swollen. He would wear informal attire—a linen shroud—and he would look for all the world like a disheveled peasant.

If you did not recognize him, it would be because you expected to see—as would most people today—a tall, elegant gentleman in a black cloak. But that would be the vampire of fiction—the count, the villain of Bram Stoker's novel and countless modern movies, based more or less on Vlad Tepes, a figure in Romanian history who was a prince, not a count; ruled in Walachia, not Transylvania; and was never viewed by the local populace as a vampire. Nor would he be recognized as one, bearing so little resemblance to the original Slavic revenant (one who returns from the dead)—the one actually called *upir* or *vampir*. But in folklore, the undead are seemingly everywhere in the world, in a variety of disparate cultures. They are people who, having died before their time, are believed to return to life to bring death to their friends and neighbors.

We know the European version of the vampire best and have a number of eyewitness accounts telling of the "killing" of bodies believed to be vampires. When we read these reports carefully and compare their findings with what is now known about forensic pathology, we can see why people believed that corpses came to life and returned to wreak havoc on the local population.

Europeans of the early 1700s showed a great deal of interest in the subject of the vampire. According to the *Oxford English Dictionary*, the word itself entered the English language in 1734, at a time when many books were being written on the subject, especially in Germany.

One reason for all the excitement was the Treaty of Passarowitz (1718), by which parts of Serbia and Walachia were turned over to Austria. The occupying forces, which remained there until 1739, began to notice, and file reports on, a peculiar local practice: exhuming bodies and "killing" them. Literate outsiders began to attend such exhumations. The vampire craze was an early "media event," in which educated Europeans became aware of practices that were by no means of recent origin.

In the early 1730s, a group of Austrian medical officers were sent to the Serbian village of Medvegia to investigate some very strange accounts. A number of people in the village had died recently, and the villagers blamed the deaths on vampires. The first of these vampires, they said, had been a man named Arnold Paole, who had died some years before (by falling off a hay wagon) and had come back to haunt the living.

To the villagers, Paole's vampirism was clear: When they dug up his corpse, "they found that he was quite complete and undecayed, and that fresh blood had flowed from his eyes, nose, mouth, and ears; that the shirt, the covering, and the coffin were completely bloody; that the old nails on his hands and feet, along with the skin, had fallen off, and that new ones had grown; and since they saw from this that he was a true vampire, they drove a stake through his heart, according to their custom, whereby he gave an audible groan and bled copiously."

This new offensive by the vampires—the one that drew the medical officers to Medvegia—included an attack on a woman named Stanacka, who "lay down to sleep fifteen days ago, fresh and healthy, but at midnight she started up out of her sleep with a terrible cry, fearful and trembling, and complained that she had been throttled by the son of a Haiduk by the name of Milloe, who had died nine weeks earlier, whereupon she had experienced a great pain in the chest and became worse hour by hour, until finally she died on the third day."

In their report, *Visum et Repertum* (Seen and Discovered), the officers told not only what they had heard from the villagers but also, in admirable clinical detail, what they themselves had seen when they exhumed and dissected the bodies of the supposed victims of the vampire. Of one corpse, the authors observed, "After the opening of the body there was found in the *cavitate pectoris* a quantity of fresh extravascular blood. The *vasa* [vessels] of the *arteriae* and *venae*, like the *ventriculis cordis*, were not, as is usual, filled with coagulated blood, and the whole *viscera*, that is, the *pulmo* [lung], *hepar* [liver], *stomachus, lien* [spleen], *et intestina* were quite fresh as they would be in a healthy person." But while baffled by the events, the medical officers did not venture opinions as to their meaning.

Modern scholars generally disregard such accounts—and we have many of them—because they invariably contain "facts" that are not believable, such as the claim that the dead Arnold Paole, exhumed forty days after his burial, groaned when a stake was driven into him. If that is untrue—and it surely seems self-evident that it must be untrue—then the rest of the account seems suspect.

Yet these stories invariably contain detail that could only be known by someone who had exhumed a decomposing body. The flaking away of the skin described in the account of Arnold Paole is a phenomenon that forensic pathologists refer to as "skin slippage." Also, pathologists say that it is no surprise that Paole's "nails had fallen away," for that too is a normal event. (The Egyptians knew this and dealt with it either by tying the nails onto the mummified corpse or by attaching them with little golden thimbles.) The reference to "new nails" is presumably the interpretation of the glossy nail bed underneath the old nails.

Such observations are inconvenient if the vampire lore is considered as something made up out of whole cloth. But since the exhumations actually took place, then the question must be, how did our sources come to the conclusions they came to? That issue is obscured by two centuries of fictional vampires, who are much better known than the folkloric variety. A few distinctions are in order.

The folklore of the vampire comes from peasant cultures across most of Europe. As it happens, the best evidence of actual exhumations is from Eastern Europe, where the Eastern Orthodox church showed a greater tolerance for pagan traditions than the Catholic church in Western Europe.

The fictional vampire, owing to the massive influence of Bram Stoker's *Dracula*, moved away from its humble origin. (Imagine Count Dracula—in formal evening wear—undergoing his first death by falling off a hay wagon.)

Most fiction shows only one means of achieving the state of vampirism: people become vampires by being bitten by one. Typically, the vampire looms over the victim dramatically, then bites into the neck to suck blood. When vampires and revenants in European folklore suck blood—and many do not—they bite their victims somewhere on the thorax. Among the Kashubes, a Slavic people of northern Europe, vampires chose the area of the left breast; among the Russians, they left a small wound in the area of the heart; and in Danzing (now Gdansk), they bit the victim's nipples.

People commonly believed that those who were different, unpopular, or great sinners returned from the dead. Accounts from Russia tell of people who were unearthed merely because while alive they were alcoholics. A more universal category is the suicide. Partly because of their potential for returning from the dead or for drawing their nearest and dearest into the grave after them, suicides were refused burial in churchyards.

One author lists the categories of revenants by disposition as "the godless [people of different faiths are included], evildoers, suicides, sorcerers, witches, and werewolves; among the Bulgarians the group is expanded by robbers, highwaymen, arsonists, prostitutes, deceitful and treacherous barmaids and other dishonorable people."

A very common belief, reported not only from Eastern Europe but also from China, holds that a person may become a revenant when an animal jumps over him. In Romania there is a belief that a bat can transform a corpse into a vampire by flying over it. This circumstance deserves remark if only because of its rarity, for as important as bats are in the fiction of vampires, they are generally unimportant in the folklore. Bats came into vampire fiction by a circuitous route: the vampire bat of Central and South America was named after the vampire of folklore, because it sucks (or rather laps up) blood after biting its victim. The bat was then assimilated into the fiction: the modern (fictional) vampire is apt to transform himself into a bat and fly off to seek his victims.

Potential revenants could often be identified at birth, usually by some defect, as when (among the Poles of Upper Silesia and the Kashubes) a child was born with teeth or a split lower lip or features viewed as somehow bestial—for example, hair or a taillike extension of the spine. A child born with a red caul, or amniotic membrane, covering its head was regarded as a potential vampire.

The color red is related to the undead. Decomposing corpses often acquire a ruddy color, and this was generally taken for evidence of vampirism. Thus, the folkloric vampire is never pale, as one would expect of a corpse; his face is commonly described as florid or of a healthy color or dark, and this may be attributed to his habit of drinking blood. (The Serbians, referring to a redfaced, hard-drinking man, assert that he is "blood red as a vampire.")

In various parts of Europe, vampires, or revenants, were held responsible for any number of untoward events. They tipped over Gypsy caravans in Serbia, made loud noises on the frozen sod roofs of houses in Iceland (supposedly by beating their heels against them), caused epidemics, cast spells on crops, brought on rain and hail, and made cows go dry. All these activities attributed to vampires do occur: storms and scourges come and go, crops don't always thrive, cows do go dry. Indeed, the vampire's crimes are persistently "real-life" events. The issue often is not whether an event occurred but why it was attributed to the machinations of the vampire, an often invisible villain.

Bodies continue to be active long after death, but we moderns distinguish between two types of activity: that which we bring about by our will (in life) and that which is caused by other entities, such as microorganisms (in death). Because we regard only the former as "our" activity, the body's posthumous movements, changes in dimension, or the like are not real for us, since we do not will them. For the most part, however, our ancestors made no such distinction. To them, if after death the body changed in color, moved, bled, and so on (as it does), then it continued to experience a kind of life. Our view of death has made it difficult for us to understand earlier views, which are often quite pragmatic.

Much of what a corpse "does" results from misunderstood processes of decomposition. Only in detective novels does this process proceed at a predictable rate. So when a body that had seemingly failed to decompose came to the attention of the populace, theories explaining the apparent anomaly were likely to spring into being. (Note that when a saint's body failed to decompose it was a miracle, but when the body of an unpopular person failed to decompose it was because he was a vampire.) But while those who exhumed the bodies of suspected vampires invariably noted what they believed was the lack of decomposition, they almost always presented evidence that the body really was decomposing. In the literature, I have so far found only two instances of exhumations that failed to yield a "vampire." (With so many options, the body almost certainly will do something unexpected, hence scary, such as showing blood at the lips.) Our natural bias, then as now, is for the dramatic and the exotic, so that an exhumation that did not yield a vampire could be expected to be an early dropout from the folklore and hence the literature.

But however mythical the vampire was, the corpses that were taken for vampires were very real. And many of the mysteries of vampire lore clear up when we examine the legal and medical evidence surrounding these exhumations. "Not without astonishment," says an observer at the exhumation of a Serbian vampire in 1725, "I saw some fresh blood in his mouth, which, according to the common observation, he had sucked from the people killed by him." Similarly, in *Visum et Repertum*, we are told that the people exhuming one body were surprised by a "plumpness" they asserted had come to the corpse in the grave. Our sources deduced a cause-and-effect relationship from these two observations. The vampire was larger than he was because he was full to bursting with the fresh blood of his victims.

The observations are clinically accurate: as a corpse decomposes, it normally bloats (from the gases given off by decomposition), while the pressure from the bloating causes blood from the lungs to emerge at the mouth. The blood is real, it just didn't come from "victims" of the deceased.

But how was it that Arnold Paole, exhumed forty days after his death, groaned when his exhumers drove a stake into him? The peasants of Medvegia assumed that if the corpse groaned, it must still be alive. But a corpse does emit sounds, even when it is only moved, let alone if a stake were driven into it. This is because the compression of the chest cavity forces air past the glottis, causing a sound similar in quality and origin to the groan or cry of a living person. Pathologists shown such accounts point out that a corpse that did not emit such sounds when a stake was driven into it would be unusual.

To vampire killers who are digging up a corpse, anything unexpected is taken for evidence of vampirism. Calmet, an eighteenth-century French ecclesiastic, described people digging up corpses "to see if they can find any of the usual marks which leads them to conjecture that they are the parties who molest the living, as the mobility and suppleness of the limbs, the fluidity of the blood, and the flesh remaining uncorrupted." A vampire, in other words, is a corpse that lacks rigor mortis, has fluid blood, and has not decomposed. As it happens, these distinctions do not narrow the field very much: Rigor mortis is a temporary condition, liquid blood is not at all unusual in a corpse (hence the "copious bleeding" mentioned in the account of Arnold Paole), and burial slows down decomposition drastically (by a factor of eight, according to a standard textbook on forensic pathology). This being the case, exhumations often yielded a corpse that nicely fit the local model of what a vampire was.

None of this explains yet another phenomenon of the vampire lore—the attack itself. To get to his victim, the vampire is often said to emerge at night from a tiny hole in the grave, in a form that is invisible to most people (sorcerers have made a good living tracking down and killing such vampires). The modern reader may reject out of hand the hypothesis that a dead man, visible or not, crawled out of his grave and attacked the young woman Stanacka as related in *Visum et Repertum.* Yet in other respects, these accounts have been quite accurate.

Note the sequence of events: Stanacka is asleep, the attack takes place, and she wakes up. Since Stanacka was asleep during the attack, we can only conclude that we are looking at a culturally conditioned interpretation of a nightmare—a real event with a fanciful interpretation.

The vampire does have two forms: one of them the body in the grave; the other—and this is the mobile one—the image, or "double," which here appears as a dream. While we interpret this as an event that takes place within the mind of the dreamer, in nonliterate cultures the dream is more commonly viewed as either an invasion by the spirits of whatever is dreamed about (and these can include the dead) or evidence that the dreamer's soul is taking a nocturnal journey.

In many cultures, the soul is only rather casually attached to its body, as is demonstrated by its habit of leaving the body entirely during sleep or unconsciousness or death. The changes that occur during such conditions—the lack of responsiveness, the cessation or slowing of breathing and pulse—are attributed to the soul's departure. When the soul is identified with the image of the body, it may make periodic forays into the minds of others when they dream. The image is the essence of the person, and its presence in the mind of another is evidence that body and soul are separated. Thus, one reason that the dead are believed to live on is that their image can appear in people's dreams and memories even after death. For this reason some cultures consider it unwise to awaken someone suddenly: he may be dreaming, and his soul may not have a chance to

return before he awakens, in which case he will die. In European folklore, the dream was viewed as a visit from the person dreamed about. (The vampire is not the only personification of the dream: the Slavic *mora* is a living being whose soul goes out of the body at night, leaving it as if dead. The *mora* first puts men to sleep, and then frightens them with dreams, chokes them, and sucks their blood. Etymologically, *mora* is cognate with the *mare* of nightmare, with German *Mahr*, and with the second syllable of the French *cauchemar.*)

When Stanacka claimed she was attacked by Milloe, she was neither lying nor even making an especially startling accusation. Her subsequent death (probably from some form of epidemic disease; others in the village were dying too) was sufficient proof to her friends and relatives that she had in fact been attacked by a dead man, just as she had said.

This is why our sources tell us seemingly contradictory facts about the vampire. His body does not have to leave the grave to attack the living, yet the evidence of the attack—the blood he has sucked from his victims—is to be seen on the body. At one and the same time he can be both in the grave in his physical form and out of it in his spirit form. Like the fictional vampire, the vampire of folklore must remain in his grave part of the time—during the day— but with few exceptions, folkloric vampires do not travel far from their home towns.

And while the fictional vampire disintegrates once staked, the folkloric vampire can prove much more troublesome. One account tells that "in order to free themselves from this plague, the people dug the body up, drove a consecrated nail into its head and a stake through its heart. Nonetheless, that did not help: the murdered man came back each night." In many of these cases, vampires were cremated as well as staked.

In Eastern Europe the fear of being killed by a vampire was quite real, and the people devised ways to protect themselves from attacks. One of the sources of protection was the blood of the supposed vampire, which was baked in bread, painted on the potential victim, or even mixed with brandy and drunk. (According to *Visum et Repertum,* Arnold Paole had once smeared himself with the blood of a vampire—that is, a corpse—for protection.) The rationale behind this is a common one in folklore, expressed in the saying "similia similiis curantur" (similar things are cured by similar things). Even so, it is a bit of a shock to find that our best evidence suggests that it was the human beings who drank the blood of the "vampires," and not the other way around.

Perhaps foremost among the reasons for the urgency with which vampires were sought—and found—was sheer terror. To understand its intensity we need only recall the realities that faced our informants. Around them people were dying in clusters, by agencies that they did not understand. As they were well aware, death could be extremely contagious: if a neighbor died, they might be next. They were afraid of nothing less than death itself. For among many cultures it was death that was thought to be passed around, not viruses and bacteria. Contagion was meaningful and deliberate, and its patterns were based on values and vendettas, not on genetic predisposition or the domestic accommodations of the plague-spreading rat fleas. Death came from the dead who, through jealousy, anger, or longing, sought to bring the living into their realm. And to prevent this, the living attempted to neutralize or propitiate the dead until the dead became powerless—not only when they stopped entering dreams but also when their bodies stopped changing and were reduced to inert bones. This whole phenomenon is hard for us to understand because although death is as inescapable today as it was then, we no longer personify its causes.

In recent history, the closest parallel to this situation may be seen in the AIDS epidemic, which has caused a great deal of fear, even panic, among people who, for the time being at least, know little about the nature of the disease. In California, for instance, there was an attempt to pass a law requiring the quarantine of AIDS victims. Doubtless the fear will die down if we gain control over the disease—but what would it be like to live in a civilization in which all diseases were just as mysterious? Presumably one would learn—as was done in Europe in past centuries—to shun the dead as potential bearers of death.

41

Vodou

Karen McCarthy Brown

It is likely that no other topic in this book is as misunderstood as the religious practices of Haiti known as Vodou. Sensationalized popular culture and travelers' accounts have been merciless in delivering to the public a highly distorted picture of Haitian religious life. In this article, Karen McCarthy Brown explains that Vodou, often misspelled as Voodoo, is an African-based religion that serves several categories of spiritual beings through elaborate ceremonies and a loosely organized priesthood of both men and women. The country's dominant Roman Catholicism co-exists with Vodou, and a majority of Haitians comfortably follow both religions. Several prominent Haitian political leaders of the 20th century have been known for their strong involvement with Vodou, and as Brown explains here, Vodou plays a vital role in the large Haitian immigrant communities of North America.

Haiti, Vodou, and other examples of African-based culture in the Americas have received lively attention from anthropologists. Exemplary ethnographic works include E. Wade Davis's account of secret Vodou societies, The Serpent and the Rainbow *(1985), and Karen McCarthy Brown's own study of an individual healer-priestess in New York,* Mama Lola: A Vodou Priestess in Brooklyn *(1991, 2001).*

Vodou is a sometimes misleading, but nevertheless common, name for the religious practices of the majority of Haitians. Outsiders have given the name Vodou to the complex web of traditional religious practices followed in Haiti. Only recently, and still to a limited extent, have Haitians come to use the term as others do. Haitians prefer a verb to identify their religion: they speak of "serving the spirits."

A mountainous, poverty-stricken, largely agricultural country of approximately eight million people, Haiti has a land area of 10,700 square miles and occupies the western third of the island of Hispaniola, which it shares with the Dominican Republic.

This is where Caribbean Vodou began, but Haiti is not the only place Vodou in practiced. Vodou is also a central part of everyday life in Haitian diaspora communities in New Orleans and Santiago, Cuba, both products of the upheaval caused by the Haitian Revolution (1791–1804). More recent political and economic struggles in Haiti have also led to Vodou communities in New York City, Miami, Montreal, and Paris.

In Haiti, *vodou* originally referred to one ritual style among many in their syncretic religious system, the style most closely connected to Dahomey and the Fon language. The word *vodou* is derived from the Fon *vodun*, which means "god" or "spirit." *Hoodoo* is a related term from the same Fon word, yet, in the United States, it is almost always used as a derogatory term that focuses on black magic spells and charms.

Sensationalized novels and films, as well as spurious travelers' accounts, have painted a negative picture of Haitian religion. Vodou has been depicted as primitive and ignorant. Vodou rituals have been

From ENCYCLOPEDIA OF RELIGION 2nd edition, by Karen McCarthy Brown, Thomson Gale © 2005, Thomson Gale. Reprinted by permission of The Gale Group.

described as arenas for uncontrolled orgiastic behavior, and even cannibalism. The same writers stir up fear of Vodou and suggest that if whites get too close to a Vodou ceremony terrible things could happen. These distortions are attributable to the fear that the Haitian slave revolution sparked in whites. Haiti achieved independence in 1804, and thus became the first black republic in the Western Hemisphere at a time when the colonial economy was still heavily dependent on slave labor.

In Vodou there are three (not always clearly distinguished) categories of spiritual beings: *lemò, lemistè,* and *lemarasa* (respectively, "the dead," "the mysteries," and "the sacred twins"). While certain Vodou prayers, songs, and invocations preserve fragments of West African languages, Haitian Creole is the primary language of Vodou. Creole is the first and only language of more than one half the population of Haiti. It has a grammatical structure familiar to speakers of West African languages and an eighteenth-century French vocabulary mixed with a smattering of English words and expressions.

Although individuals and families regularly serve the Vodou spirits without recourse to religious professionals, throughout most of Haiti there is a loosely organized priesthood open to both men and women. The male priest is known as an *oungan* and the female priest is a *manbo.* There is a wide spectrum of Vodou ritualizing. There are individual acts of piety, such as lighting candles to petition particular spirits, and elaborate feasts, sometimes lasting days and including the sacrifice of several animals as part of the meals offered to the spirits. Energetic singing, dancing, and polyrhythmic drumming accompany the larger rituals. In the countryside, rituals often take place outdoors, on family land set aside for the spirits, and there is often a small cult house on that land where the family's altars are kept. Urban Vodou rituals tend to take place in an *ounfò* ("temple"). Urban altars, dense with sacrificial food and drink, sacred stones, and chromolithographs of the Catholic saints and other images, are maintained in *jèvo* ("altar rooms") off the central dancing and ritualizing space of the temple, the *peristyl.* In the cities, those who serve the spirits also tend to keep more modest altars in their own homes.

The goal of Vodou drumming, singing, and dancing is to *chofè,* to "heat up," the situation sufficiently to bring on possession by the spirits. As a particular spirit is summoned, a devotee enters a trance and becomes that spirit's *chwal* ("horse"), thus providing the means for direct communication between human beings and the spirits. The spirit is said to ride the *chwal.* Using the person's body and voice, the spirit sings, dances, and eats with the people and also deals out advice and chastisement. The people in turn offer the spirit a wide variety of gifts and acts of obeisance, the goal being to placate the spirit and ensure his or her continuing protection.

There are marked differences in Vodou as it is practiced throughout Haiti, but the single most important distinction is that between urban and rural Vodou. Haitian society is primarily agricultural, and the manner in which peasants serve the spirits is determined by questions of land tenure and ancestral inheritance. Urban Vodou is not tied to specific plots of land, but the family connection persists in another form. Urban temple communities become substitutes for the extended families of the countryside. The priests are called "papa" and "mama"; the initiates, who are called "children of the house" or "little leaves" refer to one another as "brother" and "sister." In general, urban Vodou is more institutionalized and often more elaborate in its rituals than its rural counterpart.

African Influence

Haiti's slave population was built up in the eighteenth century, a period in which Haiti supplied a large percentage of the sugar consumed in Western Europe. Vodou was born on sugar, sisal, cotton and coffee plantations out of the interaction among slaves who brought with them a variety of African religious traditions, but due to inadequate records, little is known about this formative period in Vodou's history. It has been argued by Haitian scholars such as Michel-Rolph Trouillot that the religion did not coalesce until after the revolution, but others suggest it had an effective presence, particularly in northern Haiti, during the latter part of the eighteenth century. James G. Leyburn in *The Haitian People* (1941) and Carolyn Fick in *The Making of Haiti* (1990) argue that Vodou played a key role in the organization of the slave revolt.

Among the African ethnic groups brought to Haiti as slave laborers, the most influential in shaping Haitian culture, including Vodou, were the Fon,

Mahi, and Nago from old Dahomey (the present Republic of Benin), those who came to be known as the Yoruba (Nigeria), and Kongo peoples (Angola, and the Democratic Republic of the Congo). Many of the names of Vodou spirits are easily traceable to their African counterparts; however, the spirits have undergone change in the context of Haiti's social and economic history. For example, Ogun among the Yoruba is a spirit of ironsmithing and other activities associated with metal, such as hunting, warfare, and modern technology. Neither hunting nor modern technology plays much of a role in the lives of Haitians. Haiti, however, does have a long and complex military history. Thus, the Haitian spirit Ogou is first and foremost a soldier whose rituals, iconography, and possession-performance explore both the constructive and destructive uses of military power, as well as its analogues with human relations—anger, self-assertion, and willfulness.

Africa itself is a powerful concept in Vodou. Haitians speak of Ginen ("Guinea") both as their ancestral home, the Guinea coast of West Africa, and as the watery subterranean home of the Vodou spirits. Calling a spirit *franginen*, ("fully and completely African") is a way of indicating that the spirit is good, ancient, and proper. The manner in which an individual or a group serves the spirits may also be called *franginen*, with similar connotations of approval and propriety.

Roman Catholic Influence

For the most part, the slaveholders were Catholics and baptism for slaves was mandatory by French law. Many have argued that slaves used a veneer of Catholicism to hide their traditional religious practices from the authorities. While Catholicism may well have functioned in this utilitarian way for slaves on plantations, it is also true that the religions of West Africa from which Vodou was derived, already had a tradition of borrowing the deities of neighbors and enemies alike. Whatever Catholicism represented in the slave world, it was most likely also used as a means to expand Vodou's ritual vocabulary and iconography, thus helping captive laborers function in a nominally Catholic world. In 1804, immediately after Haiti declared its liberation, the Catholic Church withdrew all of its clergy from the new republic. Yet Catholicism survived in Haiti

for fifty years without contact with Rome and it did so through the imitative ritualizing of a Vodou figure known as *prêtsavan* ("bush priest") as well as the competitive market for healing charms and talismans that was kept going by defrocked Catholic priests and the self-appointed "clergy" who ended up in Haiti in the early nineteenth century.

Catholicism has had the greatest influence on the traditional religion of Haiti at the level of rite and image rather than theology. This influence works in two ways. First, those who serve the spirits call themselves Catholic, attend Mass, and undergo baptism and first communion. Because these Catholic rituals at times function as integral parts of larger Vodou rites, they can be even directed to participate by their Vodou spirits. Second, Catholic prayers, rites, images, and saints' names are integrated into the common ritualizing of Vodou temples. The prêtsavan is an active figure in Vodou. He achieves his title by knowing the proper, that is the Latin or French, form of Catholic prayers.

Over the years, a system of parallels has been developed between the Vodou spirits and the Catholic saints. For example, Dambala, the ancient and venerable snake deity of the Fon people, is venerated in Haiti both as Dambala and as St. Patrick, who is pictured in the popular chromolithograph with snakes clustered around his feet. In addition, the Catholic liturgical calendar dominates in much Vodou ritualizing. Thus the Vodou spirit Ogou is honored in Haiti and in the Haitian diaspora on July 25, the feast day of his Catholic counterpart.

Bondye, "the good God" is identified with the Christian God, and is said to be the highest, indeed the only, god. The spirits are said to have been angels in Lucifer's army whom God sent out of heaven and down to Ginen. Although the Vodou spirits may exhibit capricious behavior, they are not evil. Rather, they are seen as intermediaries between the people and the high god, a role identical to the one played by the so-called lesser deities in the religions of the Yoruba and Fon. Bondye is remote and unknowable. Although evoked daily in ordinary speech (almost all plans are made with the disclaimer *si dye vle* ("if God wills"), Bondye's intervention is not sought for help with life's problems. That is the work of the spirits.

Both the Catholic Church in Haiti and the government of Haiti have participated energetically in the persecution of those who serve the Vodou spirits. The last "antisuperstition campaign" was in the 1940s, but clerical and upperclass disdain for the religion has persisted much longer. In the twentieth century, Catholic clergy routinely preached against serving the spirits, and those who served them remarked, "That is the way priests talk." Many Catholic holy days have a Vodou dimension that church officials routinely manage to ignore.

For years Catholicism was the only religion in Haiti with official approval. Thus, the degree to which Vodou has been attacked, oppressed, tolerated, or even encouraged through the years has been largely a function of local politics. Presidents Dumarsais Estime (1946–1950) and Francois Duvalier (1957–1971) stand out from other Haitian heads of state because of their sympathy with Vodou. Jean-Bertrand Aristide, who was first elected president in 1990, was also a supporter of Vodou; in fact he changed the balance of religious power. On April 5, 2003, President Aristide fully recognized and fully empowered Vodou as a Haitian religion that could legally exercise its influence throughout Haiti according to the constitution and the laws of the republic.

Vodou Spirits

The Vodou spirits are known by various names: *lwa,* a common name with an uncertain origin; *sen,* "saints"; *mistè,* "mysteries"; *envizib,* "invisibles"; and more rarely, *zanj,* "angels." At some point in the development of Vodou the spirits were sorted into *nanchon,* "nations." The nanchon at an early point in their development appear to have functioned primarily as ethnic slave categories. The majority of the nation names are easily traceable to places in Africa: Rada, Ibo, Nago, Kongo. Later, however, these so-called nations became religious categories, diverse ritual styles of drumming, dancing, and honoring the Vodou spirits.

The Rada spirits (named after the Dahomean principality Allada, once a busy slave depot) comprise a collection of ancient, sweet-tempered, wise, and usually patient *lwa.* Then there are the fiery and powerful Petwo spirits. The origin of the name "Petwo" is contested, but the strong Kongo influence is not. The home of the Ogou, also hot spirits, is the Nago *nanchon,* a Dahomean name for Ketu Yoruba. Most big feasts end with the playful Gede, inveterate rule breakers, who insist they are a *fami* ("family"),

not a *nanchon.* In rural Vodou, a person may inherit responsibilities to one or more of these *nanchon* through maternal or paternal kin. Familial connections to the land, where the *lwa* are said to reside in trees, springs, and wells, may determine which particular spirits are served. In urban Vodou, there are a few important spirit *nanchon* that make their appearance, according to seniority and importance, in most major rituals. In Port-au-Prince, two *nanchon,* the Rada and the Petwo, have emerged as dominant largely by absorbing other *nanchon.* Rada and Petwo spirits contrast sharply. The Rada are *dous,* "sweet," and the Petwo, *cho,* "hot." When an individual, family, or temple is described as ritualizing in a mode that is *Rada net* ("straight Rada"), a great deal is being said about how that person or group functions socially as well as ritualistically. Each spirit has drum rhythms, dances, and food preferences that relate to its identifying characteristics. For example, Danbala, the gentle Rada snake spirit, is said to love *orja,* thick sugary almond syrup. His devotees perform a graceful spine-rippling dance called *yanvalu.* By contrast, the Petwo rhythm played for rum-drinking spirits is energetic and pounding, and the accompanying dance is characterized by fast, strong body movements.

The Vodou View of Person

In Vodou teachings the human being is composed of various parts: the body, that is, the gross physical dimension of the person who perishes after death, in addition to two to four souls, of which the most widely acknowledged are the *gwo bonanj,* and *ti bonanj. The gwo bonanj* ("big guardian angel") is roughly equivalent to consciousness or personality. When a person dies the *gwo bonanj* lingers, and immediately after death it must be protected because it is most vulnerable to capture and misuse by sorcerers. During possession, it is the *gwo bonanj* who is displaced by the spirit and sent to wander away from the body, as it does routinely during sleep. The *ti bonanj* ("little guardian angel") may be thought of as the spiritual energy reserve of a living person and, at times, as the ghost of a dead person.

Each person has one special *lwa* who is their *mèt-tet,* "master of the head." (The top of the head and the back of the neck are places where spirits may enter and leave.) The *mèt-tet* is the most important *lwa* served by a particular person and it reflects that person's personality to some degree. A Haitian whose family serves the spirits may inherit spiritual responsibilities to a deceased family member's *mèt-tet*. That is a big responsibility, but there are also things that can be gained. If the *mèt-tet* is conscientiously fed and honored, good luck and protection from both ancestor and *lwa* will be gained. In addition to the so-called masters of the head, most people who serve the spirits have a small number of other *lwa* with whom similar reciprocity has been established.

Unlike Catholic saints who are usually known through formulaic hagiography, Vodou *lwa* have richly developed histories, personalities, needs, desires, character strengths, and flaws, and even taste in food and drink. Because the *lwa* are fully developed characters and interact so intimately with *vivan-yo*, "the living," the practice of Vodou also functions as a system for categorizing and analyzing human behavior, in the individual and in the group. One of the characteristics of virtually all Caribbean African-based religions is the great amount of care given to analyzing social behavior and dealing with the results of that behavior.

Vodou and the Dead

Cemeteries are major ritual centers in both urban and rural Haiti. The first male buried in any cemetery is known as Bawon Samidi. Bawon's wife (or sister) is Gran Brijit, the first woman buried in the cemetery. Most cemeteries have a cross for Bawon either in the center of the cemetery or near its gate. Lakwa Bawon ("Bawon's Cross") marks the site's ritual center. Lighted candles and food offerings are left at the base of this cross. People stand with their hands on the cross praying aloud. Rituals for healing, love, or luck performed in rural cult houses or urban temples are not considered complete until physical remnants of the "work" are deposited at crossroads or at Bawon's Cross, which is itself a kind of crossroads marking the intersection of the land of the living and the land of the dead.

Haitians who serve the *lwa* usually make a clear distinction between the dead and the spirits. Yet a few of the ancestors, particularly if they were exceptional people when alive, actually evolve into spirits or *lwa*. Jean-Jacques Dessalines, Toussaint L'Ouverture, and John Kennedy have all been reported making cameo appearances through possession in Vodou ceremonies. The group of spirits, known as the Gede,

have Bawon as their leader and are spirits of the dead as might be expected, but they are not ancestral spirits. Instead, they stand in for the entire community of human beings now deceased and in this context, Gede's crude comic performances make some sense. They are designed to bring the naughty to their knees and convince them that in the end, human beings all face the same fate. The Gede are inclusive, with no limits, and therefore almost any image will work on a Gede altar. Statues of the Buddha, Lao Tzu, King Kong, St. Gerard, and Elvis Presley have all been sighted on Vodou altars. In and around Port-au-Prince, the capital of Haiti and its largest city, the Gede are the object of elaborate ritualizing in the cemeteries and Vodou temples during the season of the Feast of All Souls, Halloween.

The Gede are not only spirits of death but also boosters of human sexuality, protectors of children, and irrepressible social satirists. Dances for Gede tend to be boisterous affairs, and new Gede spirits appear every year. The satirical, and often explicitly sexual, humor of the Gede levels social pretense. The Gede use humor to deal with new social roles and to challenge alienating social structures. Through possession-performance, they not only appear as auto mechanics and doctors, they also critique government bureaucrats, military figures, and Protestant missionaries.

Vodou Ceremonies

In some parts of rural Haiti, the ideal Vodou ceremony is one that serves the spirits as simply as possible because simplicity is said to reflect discrete but strong spiritual power, the African way of doing things (Larose, 1977). In practice, rural ritualizing tends to follow the fortunes of extended families. Bad times are often attributed to the displeasure of family spirits. When it is no longer possible to satisfy the spirits with small conciliatory offerings, the family will hold a large drumming and dancing feast that includes animal sacrifice. Urban Vodou, by contrast, has a more routine ritualizing calendar, and events tend to be larger and more elaborate. Ceremonies in honor of major spirits take place annually on or around the feast days of their Catholic counterparts and usually include sacrifice of an appropriate animal—most frequently a chicken, a goat, or a cow.

In both rural and urban settings, a rich variety of ceremonies meet specific individual and community needs: For example, healing rites, dedications of new temples and new ritual regalia, and spirit marriages in which a devotee is wed to a spirit usually of the opposite sex and must pledge sexual restraint one night each week, when he or she receives that spirit in dreams. There is also a cycle of initiation rituals that has both public segments and segments reserved for initiates. The latter include the *kanzo* rituals, which mark the first stage of initiation into Vodou, and those in which the adept takes the *ason*, the beaded gourd rattle symbolizing Vodou priesthood. Certain rituals performed during the initiation cycle, such as the *bule zen* ("burning the pots") and the *chirè ayzan* ("shredding the palm leaf") may also be used in other ritual contexts. Death rituals include the *desounen*, in which the soul is removed from the corpse and sent under the waters of Ginen, which is followed by the *wète mò nan dlo* ("bringing the dead from the waters"), a ritual that can occur only after a person has been dead for one year and one day. Herbal good-luck baths are routinely administered during the Christmas and New Year season. Elizabeth McAlister's 2002 book on Rara has convinced scholars, in the habit of dismissing Rara as an entertaining aspect of Carnival, of the deeply religious character of these irreverent parades that pour from the Vodou temples into the cemeteries and streets during the Catholic Lent.

Annual pilgrimages draw thousands of urban and rural followers of Vodou. The focal point of these Catholic-Vodou events is often a church situated near some striking feature of the natural landscape that is sacred to the *lwa*. The two largest pilgrimages are one held for Ezili Danto (Our Lady of Mount Carmel) in mid-July in the small town of Saut d'Eau, named for its spectacular waterfall, and one held for Ogou (St. James the Elder) in the latter part of July in the northern town of Plain du Nord, where a shallow, muddy pool adjacent to the Catholic church is dedicated to Ogou.

Vodou and Magic

Serge Larose (1977) has demonstrated that magic is not only a stereotypic label that outsiders have applied to Vodou, but also a differential term internal to the religion. Thus an in-group among the followers of Vodou identifies its own ritualizing as "African" while labeling the work of the out-group

as *maji* ("magic"). Generally speaking, this perspective provides a helpful way to grasp the concept of magic within Vodou. There are, however, those individuals who, in search of power and wealth, self-consciously identify themselves with traditions of what Haitians would call "the work of the left hand." This includes people who deal in *pwen achte* ("purchased power points"), which means spirits or powers that have been bought rather than inherited, and people who deal in *zonbi*. A *zonbi* may be either the disembodied soul of a dead person whose powers are captured and used for magical purposes, or a soulless body that has been raised from the grave to do drone labor in the fields. Also included in the category of the left hand are secret societies known by such names as Champwel, Zobop, Bizango, and Zanglando. In urban settings in the late twentieth century secret societies began to operate as if they were a branch of the Mafia, but their deep history is quite different: They once represented religiously enforced rural law and order. The secret societies were groups of elders who used their power not for personal gains but to enforce social sanctions. For example, Wade Davis (1985) says that *zonbi* laborers were created by secret society tribunals who voted to use *zonbi* powder against a sociopath in their community.

The "work of the left hand" should not be confused with more ordinary Vodou ritualizing that can have a magical flavor, such as divination, herbal healing, and the manufacture of *wanga*, charms for love, luck, or health, or for the protection of the home, land, or person. Much of the work of Vodou priests is at the level of individual client-practitioner interactions. Theirs is a healing system that treats problems of love, health, family, and work. Unless a problem is understood as coming from God, in which case the Vodou priest can do nothing, the priest will treat it as one caused by a spirit or by a disruption in human relationships, including relations with the dead. Generally speaking, Vodou cures come about through ritual adjustment of relational systems.

Vodou in the Haitian Diaspora

Drought and soil erosion, poverty, high urban unemployment, and political oppression have led to massive emigrations from Haiti in the last half-century. Vodou has gone along with the Haitians who, in search of a better life, have come to major urban centers of North America. In New York, Miami, and Montreal, the cities with the greatest concentrations of Haitian immigrants, Vodou ceremonies are carried on in storefronts, rented rooms, high-rise apartments, and basement storage areas. North American rituals are often somewhat truncated versions of their Haitian counterparts. There may be no drums, and the only animals sacrificed may be chickens.

However it is possible to consult a manbo or oungan in immigrant communities with ease, and the full repertoire of rituals can be followed there, in one form or another. Even the pilgrimages are duplicated. On 16 July, rather than going to the mountain town of Saut d'Eau to honor Ezili Danto, New York Vodou practitioners take the subway to the Italian-American Church of Our Lady of Mount Carmel in East Harlem.

42

Death Be Not Strange

Peter A. Metcalf

*I*n this article, Peter A. Metcalf compares American and Berawan funeral and mortuary rites and shows why Western practices so shocked the Berawan. To the Berawan, we trap the deceased in a suspended condition between life and death, producing evil, not beneficent spirits. "For the Berawan, America is a land carpeted with potential zombies." Metcalf's fieldwork not only explains the fate of the Berawan dead and demonstrates their beliefs to be as coherent and reasonable as any but also draws attention to the exotic nature of American funerary practices. His comparison reminds us that our level of ethnocentrism both leads us to view the beliefs of others as illogical and sometimes reprehensible and causes us to ignore our own death rituals and practices.

The popular view of anthropology is that it is concerned with faraway places, strange peoples, and odd customs. This notion was neatly captured by a nineteenth-century wit who described the field as "the pursuit of the exotic by the eccentric." In recent decades many anthropologists have tried to shake this image. They see the exotic as dangerously close to the sensational and, therefore, a threat to the respectability of a serious academic discipline. They argue that anthropology has solid theoretical bases, and that some anthropologists routinely work in cities right here in America. And they are right. Nevertheless, anthropologists are as much involved with the exotic as ever, and I think that this concern actually works to scholarship's advantage.

This continuing involvement is a result of the characteristic *modus operandi* of anthropologists. First, we seek out the exotic, in the sense of something originating in another country or something "strikingly or excitingly different," as my *Webster's* puts it. Second, we try to fit this alien item—culture trait, custom, piece of behavior—into its social and cultural context, thereby reducing it to a logical, sensible,

even necessary element. Having done that, we feel that we can understand why people do or say or think something instead of being divorced from them by what they say, think, or do.

Sir James Frazer, whose classic study of primitive religions, *The Golden Bough*, was first published in 1890, provides an excellent example of the eccentric in pursuit of the exotic. For him, the process of reducing the mysterious to the commonplace was the very hallmark of scientific progress. Like many anthropologists of his time, Frazer assumed that some societies were superior and others inferior, and that anthropology's main task was to describe how the latter had evolved into the former. To Frazer, Europe's technological achievements were proof of social, intellectual, and moral superiority. The dominance of the West represented the triumph of science, which in Frazer's evolutionary schema, superseded even the most rational of world religions. Science's clear light was to shine far and wide, driving superstition, the supernatural, and even God himself back into shadows and dimly lit corners.

But Frazer might have found a second aspect of the anthropological *modus operandi* less to his taste. In the course of making sense of someone else's behavior or ideas, we frequently begin to observe our own customs from a new angle. Indeed, this reflexive objectivity is often acclaimed as one of the great

"Death Be Not Strange" by Peter A. Metcalf reprinted from *NATURAL HISTORY*, June–July 1978, pp. 6–12; copyright © *Natural History Magazine, Inc., 1978.*

advantages of our methods and cited as a major justification for the long, expensive physical and psychic journeys that we make, seeking out societies far removed from our own cultural traditions. Less often remarked upon, however, is that the exotic possesses its own reflexive quality. As we learn to think of other people's ways as natural, we simultaneously begin to see our own as strange. In this sense, anthropologists import the exotic, and that, I suppose, puts us on the side of the angels.

An incident that occurred about four years ago during my field work in north-central Borneo brought home to me the depth and subtlety of anthropologists' involvement with the exotic. I was working with the Berawan, a small tribe comprising four communities, each made up of several hundred people living in a massive wooden longhouse. The four longhouses stand beside the great rivers that are the only routes into the interior of Borneo. Berawan communities live on fish and on rice planted in clearings cut anew in the rain forest each year. In the late nineteenth century, which was a stormy period of tribal warfare, each longhouse was a fortress as well as a home, and the Berawan look back with pride on the military traditions of that era.

Among the things that interested me about the Berawan were their funeral rites, which involve what anthropologists call "secondary burial," although the Berawan do not usually bury the dead at all. Full rites consist of four stages: the first and third involve ritual preparation of the corpse; the second and fourth make up steps in storage of the remains. The first stage, lasting two to ten days, consists of rites performed immediately after death. During the second stage, the bereaved family stores the corpse in the longhouse or on a simple platform in the graveyard. This storage lasts at least eight months and sometimes for several years if the close kin cannot immediately afford to complete the expensive final stages. Third, if the corpse has been in the graveyard, the family brings it back to the longhouse, where it is kept for six to ten days, while the family lavishly entertains guests who have been summoned from far and wide. Finally, the remains are removed to a final resting place, an impressively proportioned mausoleum.

Within this four-part plan, details of the corpse's treatment vary considerably. During the first storage stage, the family may place the corpse in a large

earthenware jar or in a massive coffin hewn from a single tree trunk. For secondary storage, the family may use a valuable glazed jar or the coffin left over from the first stage. During the third-stage rites, the family may take out the bones of the deceased and clean them. As the corpse decomposes, its secretions may be collected in a special vessel. Some neighbors of the Berawan reportedly consume liquids of decomposition mixed with rice—a variety of endocannibalism.

For anthropologists, this intimate interaction with the corpse is certainly exotic. For Americans not professionally trained in the niceties of cultural relativism, Berawan burial is no doubt disgusting: keeping corpses around the house, shuttling them between the graveyard and the longhouse, storing them above ground instead of burying them, manipulating the bones, and, to Western eyes, paying macabre attention to the process of decay itself. My Berawan informants were aware that some phases of their ritual bothered Europeans. They soon learned, moreover, that I had a lot of questions about their funerals. One of the pleasures of working in Borneo is that people soon begin to cross-examine their interviewer. They are as curious about the stranger as he or she is about them. So before long, they began to quiz me about the death ways of my country.

On one memorable occasion, during a lull in ritual activity, I responded to one of these questions by outlining American embalming practices—the treatment of the corpse with preservative fluids and its display in an open coffin. I was well into my story, concentrating on finding the right words to describe this unfamiliar topic, when I became aware that a sudden silence had fallen over my audience. They asked a number of hesitant questions just to be sure that they had understood me correctly and drew away from me in disgust when they found that they had. So shocked were they that I had to backtrack rapidly and change my story. The topic was never broached again.

At the time, I did not understand why American embalming practices had so unnerved the Berawan. Now, having thought about the meaning of Berawan death rituals, I think that I do understand.

The death rituals of central Borneo early attracted the interest of explorers and ethnologists. In 1907, Robert Hertz, a young student of French sociologist Emile Durkheim, wrote an essay about these rites that has become a classic. Never having set foot in Borneo, Hertz relied on the accounts of travelers. Had he not been killed during the First World War, he might well have undertaken firsthand research himself. Nevertheless, his analysis is still routinely cited in discussions and comparisons of funeral customs. Yet, oddly, Hertz's central thesis has received very little attention. Hertz hypothesized that peoples who practice secondary burial have certain beliefs about the afterlife, namely, that the fate of the body provides a model for the fate of the soul.

Since Hertz did not know of the Berawan, they provided me with an appropriate test case for his hypothesis. I collected data on everything related to Berawan death rites: the people involved, mourning practices, related rituals, myths and beliefs, and so on. I also pressed my informants for interpretations of rituals. All the material I accumulated revealed a consistent set of ideas very similar to those described by Hertz. The Berawan believe that after death the soul is divorced from the body and cannot reanimate the already decaying corpse. However, the soul cannot enter the land of the dead because it is not yet a perfect spirit. To become one of the truly dead, it must undergo a metamorphosis. As the body rots away to leave dry bones, so the soul is transformed slowly into spirit form. As the corpse is formless and repulsive until putrefaction is completed, so the soul is homeless. It lurks miserably on the fringes of human habitation and, in its discomfort, may affect the living with illness. The third stage of the mortuary sequence, which Hertz called the "great feast," marks the end of this miserable period. The soul finally passes to the land of the dead, and the mortal remains of the deceased join those of its ancestors in the tomb.

But before this happy conclusion is reached, the hovering soul is feared because it may cause more death. Even more dread surrounds the body itself, caused not by the process of rotting, for that releases the soul of the deceased from the bonds of the flesh, but by the possibility that some malignant spirit of nonhuman origin will succeed in reanimating the corpse. Should this occur, the result will be a monster of nightmarish mien, invulnerable to the weapons of men, since it is already dead.

I once witnessed an incident that dramatically demonstrated how real is the Berawan fear of reanimated corpses. Toward sunset, a group of mourners and guests were chatting casually beside a coffin that was being displayed on the longhouse veranda in preparation for primary storage. Suddenly there was a tapping sound, apparently from inside the coffin. The noise could have come from the house timbers, contracting in the cool of the evening, but the people present saw a different explanation. After a moment of shock, the women fled, carrying their children. Some panic-stricken men grabbed up what weapons were handy, while others tied up the coffin lid with yet more bands of rattan. Calm was not restored until later in the evening when a shaman investigated and declared that nothing was amiss.

We can now see why American mortuary practices so shock the Berawan. By delaying the decomposition of corpses, we commit a most unnatural act. First, we seem to be trying to trap our nearest and dearest in the unhappiest condition possible, neither alive nor in the radiant land of the dead. Second, and even more perverse and terrifying, we keep an army of undecomposed corpses, each and every one subject to reanimation by a host of evil spirits. For the Berawan, America is a land carpeted with potential zombies.

After a couple of years of field work, and an application of the ideas of Hertz and others, I can offer a relatively full account of Berawan death ways: what they express about Berawan notions of life and death; how they are manipulated by influential men in their struggles for power; how they relate to their sense of identity, art forms, and oral history. Meanwhile, I have also explored the literature on American death ways—and have found it wanting. For the most part, it is restricted to consideration of psychological variables—how people react to death, either the possibility of their own or that of close relatives and friends. None of these studies begins to explain why American funerals are the way they are; why they differ from British funerals, for instance.

Jessica Mitford, author of *The American Way of Death*, tried to explain the form that American funerals take by arguing that they are a product of the death industry's political power. But Mitford's theory does not explain the tacit support that Americans give to this institution, why successive immigrant groups have adopted it, or why reform movements have failed.

I have tried to relate American practices to popular ideas about the nature of a fulfilling life and a proper death. Despite these intellectual efforts, I am left with a prickly sense of estrangement. For, in fact, I had spared my Berawan friends the more gruesome details of embalming: replacement of the blood with perfumed formaldehyde and other chemicals; removal of the soft organs of the chest and abdomen via a long hollow needle attached to a vacuum pump; injection of inert materials. I did not mention the American undertaker's elaborate restorative techniques: the stitching up of mutilated corpses, plumping out of emaciated corpses with extra injections of waxes, or careful cosmetic care of hands and face. Nor did I tell the Berawan about the padded coffins, grave clothes ranging in style from business suits to negligees, and other funeral paraphernalia. Had I explained all this, their shock might have been transformed into curiosity, and they might have reversed our roles of social scientist and informant.

In the meantime, something of their reaction has rubbed off on me. I have reduced the celebrated mortuary rites of remote and mysterious Borneo to a kind of workaday straightforwardness, only to be struck by the exotic character of an institution in our very midst.

43

The Cremated Catholic: The Ends of a Deceased Guatemalan

Stanley Brandes

In this selection, Stanley Brandes describes the cross-cultural complexities arising from the accidental death of an immigrant Guatemalan living in the San Francisco Bay Area. The deceased, given the pseudonym "Axel Flores" by Brandes, could be buried in the Bay Area, cremated with the ashes disposed locally, or cremated with the ashes shipped to Guatemala. The most expensive option was to send the corpse back home for burial. Axel's father in Guatemala immediately rejected cremation, believing it was necessary to have his son's recognizable presence at the wake. A disintegrated body was unthinkable. The father insisted that his son's corpse be returned home and given the traditional ceremonies of his native village and those sanctioned by the Catholic Church. The story quickly became further complicated when Axel's sister, living in San Francisco, discovered not only that the San Mateo county coroner had confused her brother's body with that of another recently deceased man but also that the body had been sent to a funeral home and cremated. Because of his knowledge of Latino cultures, Professor Brandes was hired as a researcher and consultant by the lawyer representing Axel's family. Brandes discusses the ensuing legal suit by Axel's family against San Mateo County and the funeral home, observing that the complex legal proceedings demonstrate the globalization of liability claims and the monetary value of a mishandled corpse. As part of his research on the case, Brandes visited Axel's village in Guatemala and learned why the family so strongly resented cremation, noting especially the family's concern over the deceased's destiny in the afterlife and their own status within the village. Further complications discussed by Brandes involve the differing beliefs about cremation held by Roman Catholic teachings, the Guatemalan Catholic clergy, and village parishioners.

Stories about the commodification of dead bodies are generally sad and this one is no exception. The body in question belongs to a 31-year-old Latino

Stanley Brandes, "The Cremated Catholic: The Ends of a Deceased Guatemalan," BODY AND SOCIETY, vol. 7 (2–3), 2001, pp. 111–20. Reprinted by permission of Sage Publications, Incorporated.

migrant to the San Francisco Bay Area. On the night of 11 December 1994, in the city of Brisbane and for still unclear motives, the man strolled onto a busy highway, where he was hit by a car and instantly killed. His body was brought to the San Mateo County Morgue and was identified as that of Axel Flores, my pseudonym for this Guatemalan, who had come to the USA, among other reasons, to escape from dangers presented him by the civil war then raging in his native land. At the time of his death, Axel had already established a police record in northern California, a circumstance which facilitated his ready identification through fingerprints.

Axel's sister, residing in San Francisco, was immediately notified of the accident. She consulted with her parish priest, who reviewed her options and informed her that cremation was the least expensive choice. She then telephoned her father in Nahualtenango—the name I give to the small village near the southwest coast of Guatemala, where most of Axel's family still resides—to explain the alternatives to him and find out how he wanted her to dispose of the body. Axel could be buried in the San Francisco Bay Area, cremated with the remains shipped to Guatemala for burial, or cremated and the ashes disposed of locally. By far the most expensive alternative was to send Axel's corpse to Nahualtenango for burial.

When presented these alternatives, Axel's father immediately rejected cremation as utterly unthinkable. Despite the enormous cost, he insisted that the corpse should be returned to Nahualtenango intact so that his son could undergo the proper mortuary ceremonies—that is, ceremonies traditional to Nahualtenango and those commonly believed to be sanctioned by the Church. In order to follow through on this decision, Axel's father mortgaged his simple house and borrowed money at high interest from a moneylender in order to secure the necessary funds on short notice. Back in San Francisco, Axel's sister arranged to collect the body from the morgue and ship it to Guatemala. When she arrived to identify the body, however, she was presented first with one, then another cadaver, neither of which was Axel's. Investigation revealed that the County Coroner had confused Axel's body with that of another recently deceased man. (The Coroner's office explained feebly that both men were heavy and dark-skinned.) Axel's body, released to a funeral parlor several days earlier under the incorrect name, was accidentally cremated before the error could be detected. A thoroughly irreversible mistake had occurred. This case precipitated a legal suit by Axel's family against both San Mateo County and the funeral parlor. The funeral parlor settled with the family out of court. The complaint against San Mateo County, however, remains unresolved because the US embassy has refused to issue visas to the deceased's family to

travel to California for deposition. Until Axel's aggrieved relatives can make their depositions, the case can come to no final resolution.

The lawsuit of Axel's family against a funeral parlor and a California county morgue demonstrates globalization of liability claims as well as the potential monetary value of a mishandled corpse. US lawyers representing the family have asked for a total of $300,000 from the two defendant agencies. The plaintiffs' mediation brief states that:

> Under California law, a decedent's family and heirs have sole authority over the disposition of the remains following a death. Plaintiffs' authority in this regard was violated through a chain of errors, oversight and insufficient safeguards. . . . Beyond a doubt, the law holds that persons situated such as plaintiffs have standing to assert a claim for damages due to the mishandling of a corpse. Quesada v. Oak Hill Improvement Co. (1989) . . . establishes that individuals, entities and businesses engaged in the practice of handling a decedent's remains owe a duty to persons such as plaintiffs, and can be held liable for the negligent mishandling of a decedent's remains.

The monetary claims of Axel's family are, nonetheless, somewhat unusual. As the plaintiffs' mediation brief itself explains, 'We are presented with a situation that is relatively rare in our practice—a case where the sole damages are for emotional distress.'

The plaintiffs, Axel's father and siblings, claim that his accidental cremation has caused undue hardship and suffering. They harbor two interrelated concerns: first, Axel's destiny in the afterlife, and, second, their own status within Nahualtenango. Consider first Axel's presumed destiny. In Guatemala, say family members, the very idea of cremation is repulsive. 'It's the way you treat a dog', states Axel's older brother, Genaro. Moreover, it is 'a sin', says one of Axel's sisters; it is sinful not only for those who carried out the deed, but also for Axel himself, despite his innocence in the matter. There is no doubt in the minds of Axel's entire family that he will be barred forever from heaven. '*Está sufriendo el alma*'—'His soul is suffering', they claim. In the body's cremated state, the soul can never find release. Cremation itself is sufficient to prevent salvation.

The family adheres strongly to this belief, even though it controverts Roman Catholic teachings. In fact, since the Second Vatican Council in the mid-1960s, cremation has been permitted. It is also fair to say, however, that it has never been encouraged. The extreme infrequency of cremation in Latin America perhaps explains why clergy themselves are uncertain about its legitimacy. When Axel's family approached their parish priest with the confidential news that he had been cremated, the priest was stymied and forced to display his ignorance of Church policy. Catholic law requires that a *misa del cuerpo presente*—a Mass of the Present Body—be celebrated the day after a person dies. But, in the absence of the intact body, could the Mass of the Present Body be recited? The family had held a wake in Axel's father's home. However, it was a highly unconventional wake, taking place several weeks after death had occurred and in the absence of a corpse. Unwilling to risk making a decision contrary to Church teachings, the parish priest decided against celebrating the Mass of the Present Body. Subsequently, however, he did celebrate two additional customary Masses: one commemorating 40 days after death, the other commemorating the first anniversary of the death.

As a researcher on this legal case, I consulted with the two parish priests of Santo Tomás in nearby Chichicastenango, who agreed that, despite the concerns of Axel's family, cremation would not automatically bar the deceased from entering heaven. One of them replied matter-of-factly, 'How can we ever know who will enter heaven and who not?' Nor had the priests heard of a single instance of cremation in all of Guatemala, despite the incontrovertible presence of crematoriums. In fact, crematoriums, a recent introduction into the country, advertise on Guatemalan television and radio. To promote business, they use the airwaves to combat popular claims that the Catholic Church opposes cremation.

Padre Alberto, the older of the two Chichicastenango priests, vigorously denounced these commercials as false advertising. At the beginning of our interview, he steadfastly maintained that the Church always has and still does oppose cremation. Only after being challenged by Padre Rodolfo, his younger, more learned colleague, did he waver. 'As far as I know', said Padre Alberto, 'the Church neither opposes nor approves of cremation. It has never said anything about the matter.' Padre Roberto is well informed about Church policy; as we sit here today he is in Rome, probably being groomed for a

high-level Church post. Even he, however, is beset by uncertainty. For example, he was wrong about his estimation of when cremation became legal. 'Surely it came in with the present Pope', he said. Nor can he define authoritatively proper mortuary proceedings in a case like Axel's. He would only speculate that, when cremation occurs, the Mass of the Present Body should be celebrated prior to actual incineration.

If this interview indicates the general state of affairs in provincial Guatemala, is it any wonder that Axel's family flatly rejects cremation? In 1997—exactly 34 years after the Vatican legitimized cremation—the Guatemalan clergy still shows utter unfamiliarity with how the cremated body should be treated. This circumstance clearly undermines the time-honored anthropological distinction between religious orthodoxy and popular belief (Badone, 1990). A 'two-tiered' approach to religion (Brown, 1981), in which the unreflective beliefs of the superstitious but devout masses are distinguished from the religious teachings of an erudite clergy, is entirely inapplicable to the case. With regard to cremation, the Guatemalan clergy seem as ignorant about procedure as do their poorly educated parishioners.

But, according to Axel's family, his destiny in the afterlife depends upon more than adherence to proper ritual. The very disintegration of his body, that his body has lost its wholeness, is equally threatening. During my brief visit to Nahualtenango, Axel's brother Genaro reiterated numerous times the statement from the Creed, which is recited in every Mass: '*Se levantarán los muertos*', 'The dead shall rise again.' Genaro shrugs his shoulders and throws out his arms in despair as he asks, 'How can Axel be resurrected if there is no body?' Genaro is not alone in his desperation. The anxiety provoked by the material discontinuity of the body is a familiar theme in Roman Catholic tradition, a tradition in which venerated body parts—foreskins and fingernails and strands of hair—nonetheless populate churches throughout Christendom.

Practically from the time of Saint Augustine, says Caroline Walker Bynum, 'Scholastic theologians worried not about whether body was crucial to human nature, but about how part related to whole—that is, how bits could and would be reintegrated after scattering and decay' (Bynum, 1992: 253–54). In the 2nd and 3rd centuries, Christians fretted over the power of God to reinstate the divided body so that it could be properly resurrected (Bynum, 1992: 267–68). Although educated writers expressed confidence that the maimed bodies of saints would achieve salvation, 'Ordinary believers . . . often went to extraordinary lengths to collect and reassemble the dismembered pieces of the martyrs for burial' (Bynum, 1992: 268). By the Middle Ages, states Bynum (1992: 272), 'So highly charged was bodily partition that torturers were forbidden to effect it; they were permitted to squeeze and twist and stretch in excruciating ways, but not to sever or divide.' Bodily fragmentation was so horrifying that theologians opposed cremation and physicans 'tried to preserve corpses forever from crumbling and putrefaction' (1992: 280). 'Drawing and quartering, or burning (that is reduction to the smallest possible particles: ashes), were punishments reserved for treason, witchcraft and heresy' (1992: 276). Remarkably, these concerns endure to the present day. They are what inform contemporary Guatemalan mortuary beliefs and are the cause of Axel's family unremitting suffering.

But the family is tormented about more than Axel's fate. Concerned about their social status within Nahualtenango, they have struggled to keep Axel's shameful cremation a secret. Even I was implicated in this ultimately futile effort. While watching a soccer match one Sunday morning, Axel's brother introduced me to the village pharmacist, his closest friend and confidant in Nahualtenango. When the pharmacist asked why I had come so far, I almost confessed my true mission: to gather information on behalf of the lawyer representing Axel's family. Stopping short in my reply, I simply stated that I knew Axel's sister in California and she suggested that on my visit to Guatemala I stop at Nahualtenango personally to convey her greetings. By hiding my real motive, I was attempting to protect the family reputation. Only later did I discover that the pharmacist also knows about the cremation and was disguising his knowledge. A former neighbor and close friend of the family is informed too, and has been sworn to secrecy. One can only guess the extent to which the community at large is aware of what happened to their native son, Axel, during his self-imposed California exile. In recounting the reaction of the community to Axel's death, Genaro claims that everyone asked the family, 'And the body? Where is the body? When will it arrive?' The family had recourse to only one excuse: they could not afford the expense of bringing Axel home. To make such an admission, in the context of Nahualtenango, is itself shameful. And yet the family saw no alternative. The cremated remains might have been transported easily and inexpensively to Guatemala for burial. But this is an option that neither the family nor the community would find even minimally acceptable. A disintegrated body, in their view, is not only unworthy of Christian burial, it is unidentifiable. 'How would we know that those ashes are Axel's?', the family asked. Their skepticism is entirely understandable. After all, if rich, powerful Californians could be so careless as to cremate the wrong corpse, there is little hope that they can properly sort human ashes.

To understand why cremation is an unacceptable alternative to the people of Nahualtenango, more than religious conviction and social status must be taken into account. After all, the family admits, with some reluctance but unmistakable certainty, that even without cremation, Axel might never have entered heaven. He had lived in an unmarried state with several women, two of whom gave birth to his children. This circumstance is sufficient to have compromised his destiny. The real crime of the San Mateo County Morgue is to have deprived his surviving relatives of his bodily presence. His recognizable presence was needed at the wake, during which villagers would have gathered at his home to help the family mourn the loss. His recognizable presence was needed for the Mass of the Present Body and for the burial that would have followed. His recognizable presence was even more urgently necessary for his mother, ailing at home in Nahualtenango in an advanced state of cancerous decay. When she died, only a few months after Axel, her quick demise was attributed to the fact that she never got to view Axel's corpse, rather than to her son's passing. For those who have survived the loss of mother and son, the greatest agony of all is Axel's absence from the village cemetery. Without his bodily presence, there is no way of relieving one's grief by visiting his grave and praying for his eternal soul. In Nahualtenango, visits to deceased relatives are normal on three occasions: 40 days after the death, a year after the death, and annually during All Souls and All Saints days, on 1 and 2 November. It is primarily in order to celebrate these occasions, to be near his son, that Axel's father was willing to go to such financial sacrifice to return the body to its proper resting place.

It is 20 July 1997, two and a half years after Axel's death. I walk with Axel's father, with his common-law son, with his siblings and their respective families from one end of the village to the other until we arrive at the Nahualtenango cemetery. As we enter holy ground, Axel's brother stops short, looks at me with penetrating eyes, and says, '*Esta es nuestra última morada. Aquí es donde venimos a parar todos [los del pueblo]. Esten donde esten, aquí vienen a parar*'—'This is our final abode. Here is where all of us from the village come to rest. Wherever we may be, here we come to rest.' Indeed, the cemetery has the aspect of a miniature village, filled with hundreds of small houses decorated with miniature towers and gables. The graves stretch out in long, evenly spaced, parallel rows, a virtual replica of the grid plan town of the living residents of Nahualtenango. The graves themselves are brightly colored crypts, painted in the vivid purples, yellows, blues, oranges and maroons of the village houses themselves. The deceased lie, not below ground, but in cement sepulchers, many of them piled on top of one another, resting adjacent to one another, like so many cramped living quarters, in the fashion of pueblo houses. Nahualtenango tombs are reminiscent of small apartment buildings, where deceased members of a family congregate in eternal companionship. They bear nothing of the somber quality of most graves in Europe and the USA.

Axel's brother walks me to his mother's lonely grave, a low-lying concrete structure painted sky blue. Poking up out of each corner are tall steel construction poles, evidence that yet another crypt is meant to lie on top of this one. 'Axel would have been here', says the brother, pointing to his mother's tomb. 'She's dead', he says, 'but at least she is here. We can come to visit her.' His following statement is disarming: '*Esta panteón es alegría*'—'This cemetery is happiness.'

At that moment, Robert Hertz's (1960) classic insights assumed immediate significance. Death does not occur when the heart stops beating; rather, the deceased retains a presence among the living for years after the actual physical demise. In Nahualtenango, the intact corpse is an enduring presence, a being that enjoys its own happy home in holy ground, forever accompanied by loving relatives,

both dead and alive. Cremation, the drastic fragmentation of the body into its most minimal parts, deprives both the deceased and the survivors of everlasting companionship. The dead body which retains its wholeness remains connected to others, integrated within society. Societal integrity depends upon the integrity of the cadaver. It is the cremated body that is doomed forever to exist alone and that provokes a tragic separation from the survivors. This irremediable loneliness constitutes the true agony of Axel and his family. It is the reason why, years after his death, there seems no sign of solace, nor is solace likely soon to come.

There is no doubt that Axel's death has exacted a steep emotional price from his family. And yet, it produced an immediate economic impact as well. Axel fathered a son by a woman from whom he is separated and whom he never legally married. With neither parent able to care for the child, Axel placed the boy in his father's care. The father, himself recently widowed, received regular payments from Axel, which he used to sustain both the boy and himself. These payments terminated abruptly upon Axel's death, thereby leaving the father with the responsibility of caring for his grandson but without adequate means to do so. 'The situation doesn't allow me to support the son', says Axel's father gravely. Not only did Axel's father suddenly cease to receive remittances from abroad, in order to adhere to his community's religious guidelines, he was also forced to sacrifice his limited assets in order to bring Axel's body home. On the day we first met, he stated to me:

> When this terrible news [of Axel's death] arrived, I was filled with pain [from his wife's mortal illness]. . . . Well, there was no longer any money, señor. I mortgaged my house, because I desperately wanted to bring him home. . . . I had to put myself in debt, míster, I had to put myself in debt in order to wait for my son's arrival. I had to find the way to borrow money, Axel's mother was gravely ill.

To add to these financial problems, Axel's father became gravely ill. The cause for this illness is no doubt complex. It is safe to say, however, that the stress of his wife and son's almost simultaneous deaths must have aggravated his already poor state of health. At least he is convinced that Axel's death has had an adverse effect. As proof of his frailty, within minutes of meeting me he pulled out a large bag of medicine and counted the items one by one: 22 cardboard boxes, glass bottles and plastic containers in all. 'This medicine costs a lot of money as well', he said.

Axel's death therefore exacted a high price from his Guatemalan relatives. The cremated corpse would cause eternal suffering for Axel's soul, forever unable to find heavenly peace. It would produce shame beyond anyone's imagining for Axel's family, unable to explain to the community of Nahualte-nango the corpse's mysterious disappearance. Also, knowledge of the cremation was held responsible for hastening the mother's departure from this world. But Axel's cremated body, precisely because it received treatment contrary to the family's wishes, might justify the kind of monetary compensation that instantaneously would confer fabulous wealth upon any member of the family, in local terms. Indeed, the family might reasonably expect financial compensation. In recent years, in the San Francisco Bay Area alone, at least 62 people have won between $10,000 and $250,000 in lawsuits involving the careless mixing of ashes in local crematoriums (Anonymous, 1996; Holding, 1996). According to a newspaper report:

> The plaintiffs claimed that Pleasant Hill [Cemetery Inc.] had caused them severe emotional distress by cremating their relatives' bodies with those of others, dumping remains in existing graves and failing to return all the ashes. They also accused the cemetery of trying to hide its mistakes. (Holding, 1996: A12)

In one case alone—*Hansell v. Pleasant Hill Cemetery*—plaintiffs' attorney Kevin McInerney was reported to seek more than $2.5 million in fees. 'You do these cases, and you hope to make a lot of money', stated McInerney, whose earnings in class action suits against crematoriums already amount to $25 million (Fried, 1998). In further cases, disclosure was made in 1997 of a small aircraft company in northern California which failed to honor hundreds of contracts with deceased clients and their relatives to scatter ashes over sea and countryside. According to one report, two hikers in Amador County, California accidentally stumbled across the unidentified bones of some 5,000 people.

> Turned out the bones were part of the cremated remains that a pilot named B.J. Elkin was supposed to scatter over the Sierra and elsewhere. But instead of doing the job he was paid to do, he had merely dumped the remains onto his property. (Elias, 1997)

The resulting lawsuit involved dozens of crematoriums and mortuaries in settlements exceeding $32 million. According to reporter Paul Elias, this case 'exposed a new and lucrative area for plaintiffs' lawyers to mine' (1997). It seems that burnt bodies are big business in California.

The California lawsuits against mortuary parlors and crematoriums revolve mainly around the disposal of remains. In all these instances, cremation was at least the families' preferred way to treat their relatives' corpses. In Axel's case, however, the family issued an explicit order not to cremate. The accidental cremation undoubtedly has caused terrible suffering for Axel's family—even, depending on one's religious beliefs, to Axel's soul. And yet the cremated body, abomination though it might be in terms of religious beliefs and community standing, might more than compensate the father for the loss of meagre remittances which the son provided while alive. The cremated body also has potential financial value to the rest of his relatives in Nahualtenango, who have suffered the social and emotional consequences of what they believe to be a sacrilegious treatment of his corpse.

Though Axel's cremated body might well leave his soul beyond heavenly salvation, it has become in some sense the hope for earthly salvation for his family. At first (and still) a sinful aberration, a horrific deviation from sacred norms, Axel's ashes have suddenly attained extravagant monetary value. In the hands of the US legal system, they have been converted into a commodity, a chip on the bargaining table, the hope for financial security for his family—and a source of income for lawyers and anthropologist alike.

44

Spontaneous Memorialization: Violent Death and Emerging Mourning Ritual

C. Allen Haney, Christina Leimer, and Juliann Lowery

In this article, the authors introduce and define the concepts of spontaneous memorialization and resulting spontaneous memorials. They also describe the features of this emerging American mourning ritual, reasoning that death rituals are important in contemporary United States but that they are changing in response to the needs of a changing society. The authors believe that spontaneous memorialization is a public response to the unanticipated—to deaths of people who die violently but who do not fit into the categories of those we expect to die, deaths of people who were engaging in routine activities that normally would have been considered safe, and deaths of people with whom the participants in the ritual have a common identification. Haney, Leimer, and Lowery view spontaneous memorials as the collection of mementoes that mourners leave at the site of the death or perhaps some other site associated with the deceased. These mementoes usually consist of such symbolic items as flowers, crosses, flags, teddy bears, and personal notes. The authors discuss seven characteristics of spontaneous memorialization. They point out that spontaneous memorialization does not replace traditional funeral rites, and they see the phenomenon as a more immediate, almost urgent response.

Introduction

In the last fifty years, the United States has invested heavily in controlling death. We have eradicated many previously fatal diseases and control others with medical technology. Infant mortality rates have

plunged while adult life expectancy has surged. We have developed automobile air bags, emergency response systems, warning devices, and safety standards for nearly everything that could put our lives at risk. Even our risk of dying in war has been reduced by strategies such as airstrikes rather than deployment of ground troops. We have gained such control over death that we now expect to die only of old age or as a result of our choosing a risky lifestyle. The issue of quantity of life, once the only consideration, now competes with and is often overshadowed by quality of life issues: how we are to die and who will make the decision.

C. Allen Haney, Christina Leimer, and Juliann Lowery, "Spontaneous Memorialization: Violent Death and Emerging Mourning Ritual," in OMEGA—Journal of Death and Dying, vol. 35 (2), pp. 159–71 (1997), Baywood Publishing Company, Inc.

In this cultural milieu of heavy investment in sustaining human life, and the confidence born of success in doing so, the growing recognition that people who are not old and who are not engaging in risky behavior are dying suddenly, unexpectedly, violently, and sometimes en masse results in tremendous personal insecurity and cultural uncertainty. When children are kidnapped from their bedrooms and murdered, when diners are massacred in a restaurant in mid-afternoon, when a federal building where people are attending to routine, daily business explodes, when a shopkeeper is murdered by robbers over little more than pocket change, the deaths seem senseless, meaningless, and deeply personal even to individuals not directly involved in the events. Such violent deaths complicate the mourning process for survivors, heighten insecurity among people who can identify with the victim, the victim's family or the circumstances of the death, erode cultural values, and threaten the continued existence of society.

Under these circumstances, we might expect that rituals would become highly salient, since they are often evoked in times of crisis to provide structure and meaning, restore disrupted human relationships, and assure the continuation of the group. However, other arguments suggest that the contemporary United States may not be conducive to the use of rituals of any kind. One such argument states that, as reason prevails, rituals will be obsolete, therefore rational, highly technological, secular societies, which arguably describes the contemporary United States, do not need rituals. A second argument contends that contemporary Americans are so individuated that community and collective behavior, which rituals traditionally require, is all but nonexistent in the United States. These arguments, combined with the longstanding ambivalence toward ritual in American culture, and the deemphasis and abandonment of many traditional forms of ritual over the last three decades, suggest that ritual may not be necessary or even possible, despite the ramifications of these deaths.

In this article, we introduce the concepts of spontaneous memorialization and the resulting spontaneous memorials, delineate the characteristics of this emerging American mourning ritual and use it to illustrate our contention that death ritual is important in the contemporary United States but that it is changing form in response to the needs of a changing society.

Spontaneous Memorialization as Emerging Ritual

"Ritual is the symbolic use of bodily movement and gesture in social situation to express and articulate meaning." Used to structure society, initiate people into a community, provide guidelines for human behavior, instill meaning in life and mark transitions, rituals connect emotion and reason through physical action. It is believed that rituals begin as spontaneous responses to a given situation, fulfilling needs which people may not even be able to verbalize. This is why rituals are so critical in crisis situations where the question of meaning is initially raised in emotional rather than rational form. When effective responses to crises become ritualized, their very familiarity brings about a feeling of comfort and empowerment. But, when ritual no longer captures the emotion on which it was based, or when the experience around which it is focused changes so that it calls up a different emotion, rituals lose their usefulness and can feel empty, constraining, boring and superficial. In a world where change is rapid and technology spawns unprecedented experiences, it can be expected then that many rituals which originated in response to experiences in a slower, more homogeneous world will become obsolete. When they do, people will abandon them, alter them if possible, or continue to participate if forced. One response to the inadequacy of contemporary U.S. death rituals is the emergence of spontaneous memorialization.

Spontaneous memorialization is a public response to the unanticipated, violent deaths of people who do not fit into the categories of those we expect to die, who may be engaging in routine activities in which there is a reasonable expectation of safety, and with whom the participants in the ritual share some common identification. This process does not replace traditional funerary rites. Instead, it emerges as an adjunct ritual which extends the opportunity for mourning to individuals not conventionally included in traditional rites and calls attention to the social and cultural threat raised by these deaths.

Spontaneous memorials are the collection of mementoes which mourners bring to and leave at the site of the death, or some other site associated with the deceased. Usually consisting of symbolic items such as flowers, crosses, flags, teddy bears, and notes, these shrines are the focal point of the ritual.

Spontaneous memorialization is characterized by the following:

1. Spontaneous memorialization is a private individualized act of mourning which is open for public display. Not formally organized, at least at its inception, mourners make individual decisions as to whether memorialization is appropriate and whether to participate. They also determine the form and extent of their own participation. The public component of this ritual involves making a pilgrimage to the site of the death, or a site associated with the deceased, where mourners place mementoes which are left there in public view.

2. Spontaneous memorialization often occurs at the site of the death, or some site which is associated with the deceased, rather than at a prescribed place of mourning such as a church, funeral home, or cemetery. This site may continue to be the focus of ritual offerings or visits even after official markers have been placed elsewhere.

3. No one is automatically included in or excluded from spontaneous memorialization. People who participate in this ritual are often not included in the culturally prescribed group of mourners, i.e., relatives, friends, and associates. By participating in this ritual, individuals, who may not even have known the deceased, define themselves as mourners, thus creating a role for themselves which allows them to express their feelings occasioned by the death. Therefore, spontaneous memorialization extends the boundaries of who is allowed or expected to participate in the mourning process.

4. Spontaneous memorials are shrines composed of an eclectic combination of traditional religious, secular, and highly personalized ritual objects. This differs from most traditional death rituals in which the ritual objects are primarily religious symbols and are not specifically tailored to the deceased or the circumstances of the death. This

mixture of mementoes can result in the juxtaposition of seemingly unrelated, and even contradictory objects such as crosses and teddy bears, bibles, and beer cans.

5. Mementoes left at the site are often personally meaningful to the mourner and illustrate the meaning of the event for him or her rather than, or in addition to, reflecting the identity of the deceased or an abstract religious ideology. These ritual offerings also may relate to public issues and concerns exemplified by the death, such as notes which reflect the mourner's desire for more effective law enforcement or regret at the loss of human potential inherent particularly in the deaths of young people. Additionally, these ritual objects may reflect emotions, such as anger or vulnerability, which may be felt but typically are not displayed in traditional American death rituals.

6. Spontaneous memorialization is not constrained by culturally-based norms which prescribe the amount of time alloted for ritual action nor the appropriate amount of time for bereavement. Unlike traditional funeral rites, which occur at set times and continue for a set duration, spontaneous memorialization ebbs and flows as individual mourners make their pilgrimages and contribute their offerings either immediately after the death, or during the weeks or months that follow. Reminiscent of traditional cemetery patterns, individual mourners may visit the site once or return again and again, either alone or accompanied by others.

7. While these rituals do commemorate the deceased, they extend the focus beyond the victim and the private mourning of friends and family to the social and cultural implications of their death. These violent deaths not only threaten our personal sense of security, they alter the existing social order and negate cultural values which bind us together. For example, random violence may prompt individuals to buy guns, businesses to hire security guards or police forces to form special units, but violence also calls into question cultural values such as our ability to control death and our belief that we are a culture that values human life. Spontaneous memorialization provides a method for grieving such personal, social and cultural losses.

Examples and Interpretations of Spontaneous Memorials

The most widely observable spontaneous memorials are those which emerge after extensive news media coverage of acts of violence such as the drowning of the two Smith boys by their mother in Union, South Carolina, the abduction and murder of Polly Klaas in California, the ATF-Branch Davidian shootout in Waco, Texas, and the bombing of the Alfred P. Murrah Federal Building in Oklahoma City, Oklahoma. In many instances, spontaneous memorials occur locally as well, even though the deaths may not have received widespread media coverage.

One such death which received only local media attention in Houston illustrates most of the characteristics of spontaneous memorialization. After the owner of a family-run quick shop in Houston's Heights district was murdered in a robbery, bouquets of carnations, asters, and roses appeared on the sidewalk at the entrance to the store. A stack of flyers announced a memorial service and the establishment of a memorial fund for the family. Through notes taped to the store window, neighbors and patrons expressed their identification with this man, their anger, guilt, sorrow, and desire for revenge.

An anonymous, handwritten note said: "Mr. Habib spent 12 hours a day, 7 days a week working in this store just trying to eke out a living for his family. His wife and three children would have preferred that he be home. Now he can't. He is dead." On a torn, yellow legal page, an eleven-year-old boy recounted his friendship with the man who gave him candy even though he didn't have money. Another referred to the numerous times Habib Amirali Kabani had painted over the graffiti on his store's walls and wished that he had helped Kabani paint those walls. Others expressed anger at the teenage killers, the killers' parents, and the police.

Clearly, spontaneous memorialization does not replace traditional funeral rites. Instead, it is a more immediate, almost urgent, response in terms of its occurrence soon after the discovery of the death and its physical proximity to the place of death. Often formalized initiatives and memorials, such as the fund to assist Kabani's family, spring from spontaneous memorials.

Through spontaneous memorialization, participants can express emotions not typically addressed in traditional rituals but which are often part of bereavement, such as anger, revenge, and guilt. The social dimension of spontaneous memorials is also evident in the notes left at Kabani's store. They express feelings which imbue deaths such as Kabani's with meaning beyond the loss of an individual life, to the meaning of the death for the state of American society, and for the fate of our culture. These deaths are viewed as emblematic of the threat that the systems designed to protect us are unable to do so, and that we can no longer assume that fundamental social values are shared. While spontaneous memorials are a forum in which this collective fear and grief can be expressed, they also attempt to reduce this anxiety and reaffirm threatened cultural values by demonstrating that outrage at an injustice and compassionate caring remain potent social forces.

In spontaneous memorialization, objects which exist at the scene of the death become focal points for the expression of grief. This is evident in the case of Susan Smith. At a boat launch in Union, South Carolina, Smith released the parking brake on her automobile and allowed it to roll into the lake with her two young sons strapped in by their seat belts. Flowers, crosses, teddy bears, stuffed animals, candles, flags, and notes filled the area, many affixed to the large, wooden sign which displays the rules for using the boat launch. In order to keep the visitors and the impromptu shrine from restricting public access to the lake, a stone commemorative marker inscribed with the boys' pictures and names were erected near the boat launch.

In the use of such common, secular objects as the wooden sign at the pier as ritual objects, spontaneous memorializations differ from traditional rituals, in which the ritual objects used are commonly understood to be sacred and are used only for sacred purposes. Spontaneous memorialization disavows the traditional separation of the sacred and the profane, mixes them together and, in the process, makes sacred that which previously contained only a secular meaning.

Although most spontaneous memorials dissipate within days or weeks, in some cases, mourners continue to visit and bring mementoes to the death site even if formal markers have been placed elsewhere.

One of the best known cases is that of Polly Klaas. Twelve-year-old Polly Klaas was abducted from a slumber party in her hometown of Petaluma, California on October 1, 1993. After weeks of community fundraisers and police and citizen searches for the girl, a suspect in policy custody led authorities to Polly's body in a wooded area fifty miles from town. A nationally-televised memorial service was held for Polly, the Polly Klaas Foundation was established to disburse donated funds, the Polly Hannah Klaas Performing Arts Center was dedicated and Marc Klaas, Polly's father, formed the Marc Klaas Foundation to search for missing children and advocate tougher crime control measures for children's safety. In spite of all these formalized responses to her death, a makeshift marker still exists at the site where Polly's body was found and people still visit bringing flowers and toys.

The Polly Klaas case illustrates the importance of the site in spontaneous memorialization. Spontaneous memorializations usually occur at the place of death, the site where the body was found, or at a location which is linked in some way to the victim. While some individuals have a morbid attraction to any site of death, most participants in spontaneous memorialization visit the site seeking to comprehend the seemingly incomprehensible or to find closure by confronting some physical reality of the death. It is as if a site that previously had no special meaning takes on a sacred quality once human blood has been spilled there, a quality which formal memorials cannot replace. Also, for mourners who are not closely enough associated with the victim to be permitted participation in conventional funeral rites, those who Doka would refer to as disenfranchised, visiting the site enables them to express the identification they feel with the victim or the circumstances of the death through the forging of a tangible link, i.e., having made a pilgrimage to the site of death.

Spontaneous memorials often occur at the sites of mass deaths, especially where some of the victims may be unidentifiable or even unrecoverable as was the case in the bombing of the federal building in Oklahoma City in 1995. This disaster, in a single instant, killed 167 people, several of whom were children, and reduced a symbol of American society to rubble. Even before the nationally-televised memorial service attended by the U.S. President, other government dignitaries, and famous religious leaders, flowers, ribbons, balloons, crosses, rosaries, wreaths, stuffed animals, dolls, baby shoes, toys, banners, notes, and American flags piled up outside the police barricade.

This incident differs from those previously cited both in the scale and traumatic nature of the deaths and in the magnitude of the cultural values brought into question. According to Rando, mass deaths, and deaths resulting in disfigured or unrecoverable bodies, complicate the mourning process, extending it and often requiring additional measures to aid survivors in obtaining closure. The need to engage in mourning cut across a large cross-section of the city's population so there were many ways in which people could identify with the victims of the Oklahoma City bombing. Employees died while on the job, children died in their day care center, and ordinary citizens died while seeking government services. The victims were males and females of varying ages, races, and socioeconomic statuses.

In addition to the complications associated with mass death, the Oklahoma bombing violated fundamental American cultural values. One of the first responses to this incident was disbelief that an event of this nature could occur in the United States, especially in Oklahoma City. In the mass media, the city was commonly described as having many of the characteristics attributed to small towns. It was considered a close-knit community in which people shared common values and performed everyday tasks in a climate of safety. The bombing suggested that a small town milieu could no longer be considered a guarantor of personal safety, a threat that was particularly poignant given that U.S. citizens, rather than foreign nationals, were accused of the crime. In a situation where such basic human needs are threatened, spontaneous memorials help minimize the threat by reaffirming that values which promote personal safety and justice are shared by a majority of the community.

In some cases, the cultural ramifications of a death are so pronounced that the victim can take on legendary, even mythical, status. This was the case in Texas with the 1995 murder of the Tejano singer Selena, whose rising popularity was pushing her toward mainstream stardom. Mexican Americans felt that Selena represented the values of their culture; overcoming obstacles through virtue and character, family and community-orientation, loyalty and trust.

As such, her death at the hands of a friend was viewed as an attack on Mexican-American culture. Spontaneous memorials for Selena sprang up at many sites in several cities, including at her San Antonio boutique, her Corpus Christi home, and the motel where she was shot. These shrines included her photo, flowers, balloons, posters, and several notes. People stood quietly and read the notes and just milled around. "They wanted to see, to touch, to connect somehow."

A unique characteristic in the mourning of Selena's death was the mobile spontaneous memorials created by some mourners. In Houston, San Antonio, and other cities and towns in the Southwest, many Mexican Americans painted or shoe-polished Selena's name or short messages on their cars. "We love you Selena," and "Selena Our Angel," "Selena Lives On," and "Missing You Selena" were common sentiments scrawled on windshields and doors. These mobile memorials are reminiscent of the cultural custom common throughout Central and South America of using one's car as a rolling billboard or placard for holidays, religious, or political occasions, and to indicate neighborhood solidarity. Though this custom is not generally used in conjunction with death, it was adapted as a device for expressing the personal and cultural effects of the death of Selena.

Some spontaneous memorializations may be limited to a particular segment of the population, as in the case of Selena, because the victim was primarily known and valued within that group. Spontaneous memorials carry the value of the individual into the larger society or affirm that value in the face of the broader society's indifference. In other cases, the decedent may be differentially valued by the subgroup and the rest of society. When Huey Newton, the founder of the Black Panther Party, was shot and killed in 1989 in the streets of the neighborhood where he began his career as a political activist, a significant portion of the U.S. population felt relieved. Although defined as a threat by White America due to his violent and criminal past and his advocacy of armed violence in pursuit of his social policy objectives, Newton was considered a folk hero in his own territory among those he attempted to mobilize for civil rights. From an article that appeared in the *Los Angeles Times*, and an un-captioned photograph which appeared in the *San Francisco Chronicle*, Lule describes how, on the

sidewalk where Newton died, flowers and notes were placed, banners were draped on a nearby fence, and candles and incense were burned. The memorialization countered what the subgroup considered a misperception of the victim while reaffirming their own values and identification with the victim.

In some spontaneous memorials, victims and perpetrators are indistinguishable, at least to someone outside of the neighborhood. All of those who died from violence there, whether children, subway riders, store clerks, the elderly robbed for their social security checks, street people, gang members, even a police officer and the officer's killer are mourned as victims caught in the web of urban poverty and decay. In the Crown Heights section of Brooklyn, Bedford-Stuyvesant, the South Bronx and Harlem, mourners paint the names of these dead on buildings or transit way walls and leave tokens and mementoes at the sites. Many mourners make repeat visits but there is also a steady flow of new mourners since new names continue to be added to the walls. The commingling of names of victims and perpetrators suggests the sociological difficulty in making a clear distinction between aggressor and victim since, in high crime neighborhoods, turning to crime may be perceived as another form of victimization by an indifferent society. Though other structures may be defaced, these walls are revered and protected, representing something so precious that they cannot be violated. They are a living symbol of the individual and collective cost of violence, the loss of human potential, of security, of community, of control, and of respect for the dignity of human life.

Although the cases previously cited involved intentional violence, spontaneous memorials may also spring up around accidental deaths. Rasa Gustaitus recounted her response to an auto accident that occurred one night in her urban neighborhood and which killed a ninety-one-year-old man, two other adults, and two children. The following morning, no sign revealed the fact that human lives had ended there for the city cleanup crew had done their job well. "I felt a need to call out to my neighbors, to gather everyone in a circle around this place of violent death." Instead, she cut flowers from her garden and walked toward the intersection. Joined by a neighbor, they found that someone had already placed a bouquet of asters at the corner. By afternoon, a small teddy bear had been tied to the stop sign pole with yellow police block-ade tape. In the evening, a votive candle burned, then a row of candles. Then, in the moonlight, a woman dressed in a black skirt and black shawl stood, hands folded, among the burning candles and mounds of flowers. "In another country, an-other culture, there would be an acknowledgment. Everything would stop for awhile . . . We have no common rituals here to help us."

Discussion and Conclusion

According to Moller, human societies respond to death in ways that are consistent "with the values and structures that shape the society as a whole." In the contemporary United States where ritual, cere-mony, and community have given way to bureau-cracy and medical control, and social accounting tab-ulates and calculates every aspect of existence, it is easy to believe that death, certainly our own death, cannot occur in a capricious and arbitrary manner. Even if we cannot prevent death, we feel relatively assured that we can at least predict it and influence the events that surround it.

Bureaucratization and medicalization have also made death "culturally invisible." Most people die in hospitals or nursing homes, away from home, family and friends, under the auspices of profession-als whose technological expertise gives them prior-ity over the family in managing the person's death. Corpses are taken to a morgue or funeral home, rather than prepared at home by family or commu-nity members as in the past, and the funeral services are held in a church or funeral home chapel, most likely among a group of family and friends rather than in the midst of the larger community.

Since most death in America is controllable and invisible, grieving logically follows the same norms. Corporations and agencies, whether implicitly or explicitly, establish rules governing how long one's absence from work is excusable due to death in the family. Some kinship ties to the deceased earn more leave time than others. Grieving is given formal recognition by and large only for family members. Coworkers and friends may discharge their social obligation to attend the funeral but are generally not expected to display signs of mourning nor is mourning permitted to impair behavior for any extended period of time. Psychiatric care may be

recommended for those who fail to contain their grieving within these restrictions. Older traditions such as wearing mourning garb or proceeding through lengthy and carefully proscribed stages of mourning are no longer tolerated. Death and griev-ing have become private problems to be handled in a controlled, yet private fashion.

As these processes have occurred, death rituals have been pared down, privatized and dissociated from their collective functions. When death was re-moved from the home, public ritual and formal mourning rites become less extensive or were aban-doned. The death of an individual no longer de-manded rituals that announced to the collective that a death had occurred because the continuity of soci-ety was not noticeably altered by deaths which had been anticipated and isolated from society. In essence, ritual became more limited in terms of ex-pected participation, length of mourning and extent of personal involvement as death became a pre-dictable event occurring at the end of a long life in the remote, professionalized atmosphere of a hospi-tal. In such a climate, any effort to alter the pro-scribed ritual, for example, extending the mourning or expressing personal responses beyond those cus-tomary in a eulogy, would appear as problematic in that they would be perceived as a failure to acknowl-edge the essential "rightness" of such a death.

Although limited private rituals may reflect the meanings ascribed to death for the collectivity, they may be less adequate in conveying the significance of death to individuals and the immediate survivors. By underscoring the relatively small impact of death on larger social units, they imply that individual life is also of less value. According to Simon, Haney and Buenteo, one possible trend emerging to counter this isolation and sanitization of death may be attempts to balance collective needs with the needs of the in-dividuals involved. If the formalism of more tradi-tional rituals is perceived as failing to capture the distinct meaning of an individual life or the extent of loss felt by survivors, those survivors may be more likely to alter and customize standard ritual practices to inject personal meanings. In the process, death may take on a "collage of meanings and opportunities," which could result in new social patterns.

The need to invent new social patterns becomes highly salient in the case of violent, public deaths where individual deaths are horrific, unexpected, and inextricably bound up in collective concerns. Against the climate of controlled death, violent deaths stand out in stark relief, making the experience much more traumatic by negating the perception of control and containment. The more remote, sanitized experience of death which we typically encounter ill prepares us to encounter evidence of the realities of death in daily life. We do not expect to see bombed sites or mangled bodies in the United States, but violent deaths, which cannot be confined behind institutional walls, force us to confront death. Thus, they represent a threat to all members of the community, not just immediate family members, especially when the deaths occur while people are performing routine, everyday functions as happened in Oklahoma City. Such an event carries a message that death can occur arbitrarily and unfairly, themes which are notably absent from the prevailing myth of controlled death, and suggests severe limits to our cultural promise of safety and control. Some of the deaths resulting in spontaneous memorialization contradict not only the message of death controlled but other cultural myths and values which comprise our assumptive world. For example, the Smith case confronts our ideas surrounding childhood as a safe life stage protected by caring adults and safeguarded by social agencies. The Oklahoma City bombing shatters the safety we expect to take for granted in performing routine, daily tasks, and calls into question the extent to which we still share common beliefs and values, e.g., that political opposition should follow democratic principles and that human life should be respected.

In a society undergoing rapid change, whose institutions appear gridlocked and unable to provide immediate responses, a state some might call a "breakdown of hierarchy" people take it upon themselves to act. Depending on individuals' subjectively interpreted experience with such a societal crisis, their emergent "ritual action" can bond them to a society or subgroup's values or lead them to demand new action and new social values.

The cross-cultural pervasiveness of spontaneous memorialization shows not only the existence of shared needs but, in some cases, an insistence upon recognition of values held by subgroups and a demand for reinterpretation of the individual or event by the broader culture. In these ways, spontaneous memorialization can become a political act, perhaps made more effective by its status as a mourning ritual demanding respect and attention.

According to Driver, ritual is as universal and as essential to the human condition as is language. If rituals have been deemphasized and abandoned over the last three decades, then it is likely due to the inadequacy and obsolescence of traditional rituals rather than to Americans' lack of need for ritual. Spontaneous memorialization suggests instead the effort to reinvest ritual with new meaning by moving ritual into the public sphere, by acknowledging the fears and losses felt by the members of the larger community, by reinserting the importance of the individual through emphasizing both individual qualities of the deceased and individual needs of the survivors, by enlarging the definition of those impacted by a death to include previously excluded groups, and by acknowledging the social issues implied in violent deaths through allowing the grieving to be done in public without institutional guidance. In this manner, spontaneous memorialization reflects features of a society undergoing massive change and may also be exhibiting some of the characteristics of the new social order.

Suggested Readings

Ahern, Emily M.
   1973   *The Cult of the Dead in a Chinese Village.* Stanford, Calif.: Stanford University Press.

Danforth, Loring M.
   1982   *The Death Rituals of Rural Greece.* Princeton, N.J.: Princeton University Press.

Huntington, Richard, and Peter Metcalf
    1979   *Celebrations of Death: The Anthropology of Mortuary Ritual.* Cambridge: Cambridge University Press.

Kopytoff, Igor
    1971   "Ancestors and Elders in Africa." *Africa* 43 (2): 129–42.

Meyer, Richard E.
    1992   *Cemeteries and Gravemarkers: Voices of American Culture.* Logan: Utah State University Press.

Santino, Jack, ed.
    1994   *Halloween and Other Festivals of Death and Life.* Knoxville: University of Tennessee Press.

Vitebsky, Piers
    1993   *Dialogues with the Dead: The Discussion of Mortality Among the Sora of Eastern India.* Cambridge: Cambridge University Press.

CHAPTER NINE

Old and New Religions: The Changing Spiritual Landscape

Anthropologists agree that all cultures experience continuous change. However, in the past, anthropology often emphasized cultural stasis among non-Western peoples and addressed change only as acculturation—the process by which populations adjust to life under a dominant power, usually colonial and Western. By the late 20th century, however, anthropologists had increasingly acknowledged cultural change as a continuous and universal process. Such change has accelerated and intensified on a global scale since the dawn of the industrial era, due to expanding economic structures, rapid innovations in technology, worldwide movements of populations, and new ways of relating to the natural environment. The end of the colonial era, around the mid 20th century for many countries, marked shifts in patterns of power as formerly colonized people gained political, though frequently not economic, independence. For the anthropologist interested in religion, these often interconnected social, economic, and environmental changes yield a wealth of fascinating subjects. This chapter includes articles addressing religious change and stability primarily within the confines of specific societies or communities.

Religion both shapes and is affected by larger changes, in a number of ways. As the articles here illustrate, in some cases religious practices are profoundly altered by radical, top-down transformations in politics, or the domination of one society by another (for example, in response to intrusive control by the state or under the persuasive influence of missionaries). In other cases, religion is a conservative force, such as when communities strive to maintain a lifestyle based on the past, validated by religious beliefs, or seek to reestablish a perceived golden age from the culture's past. Michael Lambek (2002) notes this contradictory pull of religious changes, commenting that, while the state and other powerful institutions may attempt to shape religion for their own ends, individuals and communities may use religion as a way to exercise power and control in their own lives; this may occur through intensified religious commitment—perhaps fundamentalism—or through various forms of ethical engagement, such as the human rights movement or environmentalism (p. 511).

Protective mask from the Sepik River region, New Guinea.

One of the most dramatic examples of how a social group might actively attempt to transform its life through religious means is what, in a classic anthropological contribution, Anthony F. C. Wallace termed a revitalization movement: "a deliberate, organized, conscious effort by members of society to construct a more satisfying culture by rapid acceptance of a pattern of multiple innovations" (1956: 265). Wallace (1956) outlined several major types of revitalization movements that are clearly religious in nature and can coexist within a given society at any time. Key to the idea of revitalization movements is that they challenge what participants perceive as unacceptable conditions, such as poverty, disease, oppression, or, most commonly, the disruptive impact of a dominant, power-holding group. In Wallace's view, revitalization movements intially spring up around the inspiration of charismatic leaders but, under the right conditions, may become established, routinized religions.

Wallace's categories and definitions have been broadly accepted. Nativistic movements are characterized by a strong emphasis on the elimination of alien persons, customs, values, and material from the "mazeway," which Wallace defined as the mental image an individual has of the society and its culture, as well as of his or her own body and its behavior regularities, in order to act in ways to reduce stress at all levels of the system. Revivalistic movements emphasize the readoption of customs, values, and even aspects of nature in the mazeway of previous generations. Cargo cults emphasize the importation of alien values, customs and material into the mazeway, these being expected to arrive, metaphorically, as a ship's cargo. Vitalistic movements also emphasize the importation of alien elements into the mazeway, although not via a cargo mechanism. Millenarian movements emphasize changes in the mazeway through an apocalyptic world transformation engineered by the supernatural. Messianic movements emphasize the actual participation of a divine savior in human flesh in bringing about desired changes in the mazeway (1956: 267). (This categorization of revitalization movements, however, is only one of many schemes used by ethnographers, and, as John Collins has noted, "Any such scheme, basically, is merely a device to initiate thought and comparison" [1978: 137]).

The religious nature of revitalization in the non-Western world, particularly in Melanesia, is made clear not only by the expectation of a messiah and the millennium in some of the movements but also by the very structure of movement phenomena, in which prophets play an indispensable role. I. C. Jarvie maintains that the religious character of these movements can be explained by the fact that traditional institutions are not able to adopt and respond to social changes, and that the only new organizational system offered these societies by European colonialists is Christianity. Melanesians, for example, have learned more about organization from religion than from any other foreign institution, and it is logical for them to mold revitalization movements in religious form in order to accommodate, indeed combat, the impact of European society (1970: 412–13).

Revitalization in the broad sense of bringing new vigor and happiness to society is certainly not restricted to traditional groups or to the religious realm. Edward Sapir (1924), for example, spoke of cultures "genuine" and "spurious": in the former, individuals felt well integrated into their culture, and in the latter they experienced alienation from the mainstream of society. Examples of attempts to change Western cultures abound. Political and economic conditions have frequently moved modern prophets to seek power to change, sometimes radically, the institutional structure and goals of society.

Throughout the readings in this chapter, reference is frequently made to *churches, cults,* and *sects.* These terms have been used by scholars as well as the lay public to describe particular types of religious organizations, particularly in the context of Christianity. Typically, the word *church* is applied to the larger community's view of the acceptable type of religious organization, whereas the term *sect* is used to refer to a protest group. Sects represent dissent from the established or mainstream form of a religion, and they generally involve smaller numbers of people. The word *cult* is not as clearly defined as *sect* and *church* and appears to refer to a more casual, loosely organized group. Cults seem to have a fluctuating membership whose allegiance can be shared with other religious organizations. Of the three, *cult* has taken on such a perjorative character that the term is almost useless (Barkun 1994: 43). What is a church to one person may be viewed as a sect or cult by outsiders.

During the last few decades, there has been an immense growth in the number of religious groups in the United States; many of these groups have received substantial attention in the media. The Children of God, the Hare Krishna movement, the followers of Bhagwan Shree Rajneesh, and the Reverend Sun Myung Moon's Unification Church are a few examples of groups that have attracted thousands of adherents who apparently were disenchanted with more traditional religious options. Even within Christianity—the dominant religion of North America—countless organizations have arisen independently or splintered off from more established denominations, ranging from neighborhood storefront churches to such large, public relations– and media-savvy organizations as Vineyard Christian Fellowships and Promisekeepers. World history is replete with examples of new religious groups springing to life as people who are spiritually, politically, or economically dissatisfied seek alternatives to traditional religious organizations.

What is the appeal of these movements? What social forces underlie the development and rapid growth of religious movements? Many sociological and psychological analyses have attempted to answer these important questions (see especially Glock and Stark 1965; Eister 1972; Talmon 1969; Zaretsky and Leone 1974). Briefly, these studies draw a picture of people who have become attracted to new movements because of such lures as love, security, acceptance, and improved personal status.

Charles Y. Glock (1964) has listed five types of deprivation that may result in the establishment of a new sect or that may lead individuals to join one: (1) *economic deprivation*, which is suffered by people who make less money, have fewer material goods, and are financially beholden to others; (2) *organismic deprivation*, which applies to those who may exhibit physical, mental, and nutritional problems; (3) *ethical deprivation*, which grows out of a perceived discrepancy between the real and the ideal; (4) *psychic deprivation*, which can result in the search for meaning and new values (and which is related to the search for closure and simplicity); and (5) *social deprivation*, which results from a society's valuation of some individuals and their attributes over others. Established religions have tremendous staying power, and "it is certainly premature to conclude that religions as forces in the world and as forces in individual lives are a thing of the past" (Reynolds and Tanner 1994: 44). This is not to say that the so-called great faiths (such as Islam, Christianity, and Judaism) do not lose followers; they do. "It seems to be mainly in the northwest of Europe, in Scandinavia, and in parts of the United States that religion remains in the doldrums" (Reynolds and Tanner 1994: 44).

The first article in this chapter describes a religion under strong state control. Mervyn C. Goldstein documents life today in a Tibetan Buddhist monastery, where Chinese governmental policies have radically altered traditional religious practice. Goldstein stresses the ways in which Tibetan monks have actively carved out ways to revive their monastic traditions in this new context.

Taking a historical perspective that spans 1,000 years, James Steel Thayer shows how periodic pilgrimages to Mecca have shaped Islam as practiced by Muslims in West Africa.

In the third article, Anthony F. C. Wallace builds on his earlier analysis of revitalization movements, here emphasizing five distinct stages of such movements and some of the psychological aspects of participation.

The next two articles provide intriguing examples of revitalization movements. Alice Beck Kehoe discusses a short-lived movement that drew together Native Americans and others during a time of profound hardship. Peter M. Worsley describes a form of revitalization movement found in the Pacific region. Such cults blossomed in response to the rapid intrusion of foreign military installations during World War II.

Just as revitalization movements can be interpreted as responses to oppression and deprivation, more established religious movements can also be forms of protest. Focusing on three men in Kingston, Jamaica, William F. Lewis brings to life some of the beliefs and practices of Rastafari, a faith that voices dissent against the status quo, including racial inequality.

In "Adoring the Father," William Jankowiak and Emilie Allen write about a small community in the western United States whose residents model their lives on what they feel are the original Mormon practices of the 19th century, including polygamy.

In the final article, John Whitmore draws attention to the religious aspects of narratives about UFO abductions. Whitmore's work helps us ponder how rapid changes in technology lead humans to reimagine their place in the universe and their relationship to the unfamiliar—quests that frequently take religious form.

References

Barkun, Michael
　　1994 "Reflections After Waco: Millennialists and the State." In James R. Lewis, ed., *From the Ashes: Making Sense of Waco,* pp. 41–49. Lanham, Md.: Rowman and Littlefield.

Collins, John J.
　　1978 *Primitive Religion.* Totowa, N.J.: Rowman and Littlefield.

Eister, Allen
　　1972 "An Outline of a Structural Theory of Cults." *Journal for the Scientific Study of Religion* 11: 319–33.

Glock, Charles Y.
　　1964 "The Role of Deprivation in the Origin and Evolution of Religious Groups." In R. Lee and M. E. Marty, eds., *Religion and Social Conflict.* New York: Oxford University Press.

Glock, Charles, Y., and Rodney Stark
　　1965 *Religion and Society in Tension.* Chicago: Rand McNally.

Jarvie, I. C.
　　1970 "Cargo Cults." In Richard Cavendish, ed., *Man, Myth and Magic,* pp. 409–12. New York: Marshall Cavendish.

Lambek, Michael, ed.
　　2002 *A Reader in the Anthropology of Religion.* Boston: Blackwell.

Reynolds, Vernon, and Ralph Tanner
　　1994 *The Social Ecology of Religion.* New York: Oxford University Press.

Sapir, E.
　　1924 "Culture, Genuine and Spurious." *American Journal of Sociology* 29: 401–29.

Talmon, Yonina
　　1969 "Pursuit of the Millennium: The Relation Between Religious and Social Change." In Norman Birnbaum and Gertrude Lenzer, eds., *Sociology and Religion: A Book of Readings.* Englewood Cliffs, N.J.: Prentice Hall.

Wallace, A. F. C.
　　1956 "Revitalization Movements." *American Anthropologist* 58: 264–81.

Zaretsky, Irving S., and Mark P. Leone, eds.
　　1974 *Religious Movements in Contemporary America.* Princeton, N.J.: Princeton University Press.

45

The Revival of Monastic Life in Drepung Monastery

Melvyn C. Goldstein

In this article, abridged from a lengthier work, Melvyn C. Goldstein documents changes in the lives and experiences of Tibetan Buddhist monks since 1950, when China took control of Tibet. Prior to the Chinese occupation, monasteries were a central part of Tibetan culture, with perhaps 10 to 15 percent of the male population serving as monks. The largest monasteries were essentially towns with important cultural, economic, and political functions, and they were lifelong homes to males who became monks as children. After describing traditional Tibetan monasticism, Professor Goldstein traces the effects of Chinese control by examining a series of policy changes and subsequent accommodations at Drepung, which was the largest monastery in Tibet before the imposition of communist rule. The number of monks at the Drepung monastery plummeted from 10,000 in 1959 to 306 in 1976. Beginning in the late 1970s, however, liberalization in China allowed a revival of monastic activities. Drepung has faced the challenge of reinterpreting traditional practices under continuing state supervision and new economic conditions, and with a smaller community of monks.

Since the 1980s, the struggle over the political status of Tibet and its relationship to China—often referred to as the Tibet Question—has provoked international attention. The head of state of Tibet's government in exile, His Holiness the Dalai Lama, is an active leader whose tours and speeches have gained the attention of many in the United States and Europe. In Lhasa, the capital of the traditional Tibetan state, monks and nuns have led a campaign of political dissidence since 1987. The place of Buddhism in Tibet and China raises significant issues regarding the interplay of religion, human rights, and the state.

Melvyn C. Goldstein is one of very few anthropologists to have carried out extensive research in the Tibetan region of China. He has authored more than eighty books and articles on Tibetan history, society, and language. He is the John Reynolds Harkness Professor, and directs the Center for Research on Tibet, at Case Western Reserve University.

Religion in Tibet played a role that went beyond its universal functions as an explanation of suffering and a template for salvation. Tibetans saw religion as a symbol of their country's identity and of the superiority of their civilization.

At the heart of Tibetan Buddhism in the traditional society was the monastery and the institution of the monk. Monasteries were (ideally) collectivities of individuals who had renounced attachments to materialism and family and had made a commitment to devote their lives to the pursuit of Buddhist

From Melvyn C. Goldstein and Matthew Kapstein, eds., *BUDDHISM IN CONTEMPORARY TIBET*, pp. 15–52. Copyright © 1998 by the University of California Press. Reprinted by permission of the publisher. Endnotes have been omitted.

teachings, including a vow of celibacy. Their presence was both the concrete manifestation and the validation of Tibetans' belief in their society's religiosity. In this chapter I examine the revival of Drepung, Tibet's largest monastery in the precommunist period.

Tibetan monasticism shared many features with its Buddhist counterparts in South, Southeast, and East Asia but also differed in several important ways. First, the overwhelming majority of monks were placed in monasteries by their parents as young children, generally between the ages of six and twelve. They were chosen without particular regard to their inclination or personality and were expected to remain celibate monks for their entire lives. Tibetans articulate a straightforward rationale for a system of child enrollment: it is better to enroll candidates at a young age before they have had much exposure to secular life (in particular, to girls).

Second, monasticism in Tibet was pursued with an implicit ideology of "mass monasticism" in that it enrolled as many monks as sought entrance and expelled very few. Size rather than quality became the objective measure of the success of monasticism (and Buddhism) in Tibet, and there were a staggering number of monks. In 1951, at the time of the Lhasa uprising, there were approximately 2,500 monasteries and 115,000 monks in Tibet proper, comprising roughly 10 to 15 percent of Tibet's male population. The magnitude of this can be appreciated by comparing it with Thailand, another prominent Buddhist society, where only 1 to 2 percent of the total number of males were monks. Monasticism in Tibet, therefore, was not the otherworldly domain of a minute elite but a mass phenomenon.

There were many reasons why parents sent their sons to become monks in traditional Tibet. For many, it was a deep religious belief that this bestowed a great privilege on the child and brought good merit and esteem to the parents. For others, it was a culturally valued way to reduce the number of mouths to feed while also ensuring that the child would avoid the hardships of village life. Parents sometimes also committed a son to monkhood to fulfill a solemn promise to a deity to dedicate a sick boy to a religious life if the deity spared the boy. Occasionally, an older monk asked a brother or a sister to send a son to the monastery to live with him, and in yet other cases, recruitment was simply the result of a corvée tax obligation (grwa-khral) that some monasteries were entitled to collect from their subjects.

Parents occasionally broached the topic with the child before making him a monk but usually simply told him of their decision. In theory the monastery asked the young candidates whether they wanted to join, but in reality this was pro forma. For example, if a new child monk ran away from the monastery, he was inevitably returned by his parents and welcomed by the monastic administration. There was no thought of dismissing him on the grounds that he obviously did not want to be a monk. Tibetans feel that young boys cannot comprehend the value of being a monk and that it is up to their elders to see to it that they have the right opportunities.

In addition to the high prestige of being a monk, the emphasis on mass monasticism can be seen in the manner in which monasteries made it easy for monks to find a niche within the monastic community by allowing all sorts of personalities to coexist. The monastery did not place severe restrictions on comportment, nor did it require rigorous educational or spiritual achievement. New monks had no exams to pass in order to remain in the monastery, and monks who had no interest in studying or meditating were as welcome as the dedicated scholar monks. Even illiterate monks were accommodated and could remain part of the monastic community. In fact, rather than diligently weed out young monks who seemed temperamentally unsuited for a rigorous life of prayer, study, and meditation, the Tibetan monastic system allowed all sorts of deviance to exist, including a type of "punk monk" (ldab-ldob) who fought, engaged in sports competition, and was notorious for stealing young boys for use as homosexual partners. Monks were expelled only if they committed murder or major theft or engaged in heterosexual intercourse.

The lofty status of monasteries was reflected in their position as semiautonomous units within the Tibetan state. Drepung, for example, had the right to judge and discipline its monks for all crimes except murder and treason and to own land and peasants. The three great monastic seats around Lhasa, Drepung, Ganden, and Sera, moreover, exercised an almost vetolike power over major government policy. They believed that the political and economic system in Tibet existed to further Buddhism and that they, not the government, could best judge what was in religion's short- and long-term interests. Thus, although they were not involved in the day-to-day ruling process, when the monastic leadership felt strongly on some issue, their views could not easily be ignored by the Dalai Lama's government. The 20,000 monks resident in Drepung and its two sister monastic seats dwarfed numerically the small military contingent maintained by the government in Lhasa and represented a genuine physical threat that on occasion has been used. For example, in 1947 Sera Monastery's Che College rebelled against the Regent, and in 1912–13 Drepung's Loseling College together with (Lhasa's) Tengyeling Monastery supported the Chinese Amban against the Dalai Lama. Drepung and its two sister monastic seats also had an important political role by virtue of the presence of their abbots (and former abbots) in Tibet's National Assembly where they had an often-pivotal say on major issues.

The power and influence of monasteries like Drepung also extended to the economic sphere. Economic support for monasteries in the "old society" was extensive, and many owned large tracts of productive land in the form of estates that had been obtained from the state and individual donors. Between 37 and 50 percent of the arable land in Tibet, in fact, was held by monasteries and incarnate lamas. By contrast, only 25 percent of the land was in the hands of the lay aristocracy and about the same was held by the government. The state also provided generous subsidies to select monasteries, funding religious rites such as the annual Great Prayer Festival in Lhasa and the daily morning prayer chanting assemblies in the three monastic seats.

Monasteries and monks, therefore, were integral to Tibetan Buddhism and to Tibetan's perception of the glory of their civilization and state. And as a result of the ideology of mass monasticism, Tibet contained thousands of monasteries and monks. These monasteries, however, varied considerably in size and scope. Some held only five or ten village monks; others contained thousands of monks from all over Tibet as well as Mongolia and India. The focus of this [article], Drepung, exemplifies the latter category.

Drepung in Traditional Tibetan Society: Overview

The largest monastic institution in traditional Tibet was Drepung. Founded in 1416 by Jamyang Chöje and located about five miles west of Lhasa, it was a virtual town housing about ten thousand monks at the time of the Chinese invasion in 1950–51. It epitomized the institutionalization of mass monasticism in Tibet and was at that time the world's largest monastery.

Drepung was organized in a manner that resembled the segmentary structure of classic British universities like Oxford in that the overall entity, the monastery, was a combination of semiautonomous subunits known as *tratsang*. These are conventionally called "colleges" in the English literature, although there were no schools (with teaching faculties) in the Western sense. In 1959 Drepung consisted of four functioning colleges: Loseling, Gomang, Deyang, and Ngagba. Each was a mini-monastery with thousands of monks, an administrative structure headed by an abbot, and its own rules and traditions. Each was a corporate entity in the sense that it had an identity (a name), owned property and wealth, and had its own internal organization and leadership. The monks came and went over the decades, but the entity and its property endured. A monk's loyalties, in fact, were primarily rooted in his college.

The highest official of a college was the abbot. He held his office for a term of six years and could be renewed for another six-year term. He was appointed by the ruler (the Dalai Lama or in his minority, the regent) from a list containing six or seven ranked nominees submitted by the college in question. The ruler had the final authority over the appointment and could select someone not on the list, although this was rarely done. Nevertheless, power to choose the administrative leadership of colleges was one of the main ways that the Tibetan government maintained control over powerful and potentially unruly monasteries like Drepung. Under the abbot, various officials such as the *gegö* (disciplinary officer) and *nyerba* (economic manager) oversaw specific aspects of monastic life. Also, an "assembly" of the more senior monks periodically met to discuss collegewide issues.

Large monastic colleges were normally subdivided into smaller, named residential units known as *khamtsen*, or residence halls as I shall refer to them. These units, similar to the colleges in terms of administrative structure, consisted of one or more buildings divided into apartments (*shag*) where the monks lived. Residence halls had a strong regional flavor since each khamtsen held rights to recruit monks from a specific geographic area or areas. Because great monasteries like Drepung recruited monks from all over the Tibetan cultural world as well as from non-Tibetan areas such as Mongolia, this system helped to facilitate the initial period of acculturation by situating a new monk in a residence together with others who spoke his dialect or language.

Drepung as a whole functioned as an alliance of colleges. There was no single abbot at the helm. Instead, monasterywide issues were decided by a council made up sometimes by the abbots of the different colleges and sometimes by the current and the former abbots. The monastery as a whole also owned property, and there were several important monasterywide monk stewards whose responsibility was to manage these. There were also monasterywide disciplinary officers.

At the level of the individual monk, Drepung's ten thousand members were divided into two broad categories—those who studied a formal curriculum of Buddhist theology and philosophy and those who did not. The former, known as *pechawa*, or bookish ones, were a small minority, amounting to only about 10 percent of the total monk population. These "scholar monks," as I shall refer to them, pursued a fixed curriculum that involved approximately fifteen classes or levels ('dzin-grwa), each of which took a year to complete (Anon. 1986). This curriculum emphasized learning Buddhist theology by means of extensive formal debating. Like much else in Drepung Monastery, the theological study program was conducted at the college rather than the monastic level. Three of Drepung's four colleges offered such a curriculum (Gomang, Loseling, and Deyang); the other, Ngagba, taught tantric rituals. The scholar monks in Gomang, Loseling, and Deyang met three times a day to practice debating in their respective college's outdoor walled park called a *chöra*, or dharma grove. The curriculum in each college used a slightly different set of texts, although in the end they all covered the same material. Monks pursuing this trajectory started in the lowest class and worked their way up until they were awarded one of several titles or degrees of *geshe* by their college's abbot. The title of geshe was sought by both monks and incarnate lamas of the Dalai Lama's Gelugpa sect, including the Dalai Lama himself. Monks came to Drepung from all over the Tibetan Buddhist world to see if they could master the difficult curriculum and obtain the degree of geshe. The intellectual greatness

of the Gelugpa sect's monastic tradition was measured by the brilliance of these scholar monks.

The overwhelming majority of common monks—the *tramang* or *tragyü*—however, did not pursue this arduous course and were not involved in formal study. Many could not read much more than one or two prayer books, and some, in fact, were functionally illiterate, having memorized only a few basic prayers. These monks had some intermittent monastic work obligations in their early years but otherwise were free to do what they liked. However, because Drepung did not provide its monks with either meals via a communal kitchen or payments in kind and money sufficient to satisfy their needs, they had to spend a considerable amount of time in income-producing activities. Some monks, therefore, practiced trades like tailoring and medicine, some worked as servants for other monks, some engaged in trade, and still others left the monastery at peak agricultural times to work for farmers.

The reason for the monastery's financial shortfall was not a lack of resources. Drepung, for example, owned 151 agricultural estates and 540 pastoral areas, each of which had a population of hereditarily bound peasant families who worked the monastery's (or college's) land without wages as a corvée obligation. Drepung also was heavily involved in money- and grain lending and had huge capital funds with thousands of loans outstanding at any given time. The monastery's inability to fund its monks, therefore, derived primarily from its decisions on how to utilize its income vis-à-vis its monks. On the one hand, Drepung allocated a substantial portion of monastic income to rituals and prayer chanting assemblies rather than to monks' salaries; on the other, it did not attempt to restrict the number of monks to the income it had available. Rather, it allowed all to join. Despite a traditional government-set ceiling of 7,700 monks, monasteries like Drepung made no attempt to determine how many monks they could realistically support and then admit only that many. How monks financed their monastic status was, by and large, their own problem.

The monks most affected by the insufficient funding were those who had made a commitment to study Buddhist theology full-time, that is, the scholar monks. They were sorely disadvantaged since they had no time to engage in trade or other income-producing activities because of their heavy academic burdens. Consequently, they typically were forced to lead extremely frugal lives unless they were able to find wealthy patrons to supplement their income or were themselves wealthy, as in the case of the incarnate lamas. Tales abound in Drepung of famous scholar monks so poor that they had to eat the staple food—*tsamba* (parched barley flour)—with water rather than tea, or worse, who had to eat the leftover dough from ritual offerings (*torma*).

Consequently, in the traditional society monasteries like Drepung (and Sera and Ganden) were full of monks who spent a large part of their time engaged in moneymaking activities. Periodically, some monastic leaders sought to reform this situation and return the monastery to a more otherworldly orientation, but this was not the dominant point of view. The karma-grounded ideology of Tibetan Buddhism saw the enforcement of morality and values as an individual rather than an institutional responsibility. Individuals, monks or otherwise, were responsible for their actions. Depending on the morality of their behavior, actors reaped quantities of "merit" or "demerit," which in the end interacted to determine the nature of their future rebirths. Monks, by virtue of their commitment to monastic life, especially their forsaking of the binding "this-world" attachment to sex and family life, had elevated themselves to a higher moral-spiritual plane than laymen, and the need of many to engage in secular work to secure subsistence was viewed as secondary in comparison to the extraordinary merit-producing behavioral commitment they had made. Thus it was only in the most serious cases such as heterosexual intercourse that the monastery as an institution felt the need to enforce morality and eliminate those who lapsed.

Consequently, at the time Mao Zedong incorporated Tibet into the new Chinese state in 1951, the ideology and practice of mass monasticism were in full play in Drepung.

Incorporation into the People's Republic of China

During the first phase of the new Sino-Tibetan relationship—the years from 1951 until the abortive Tibetan uprising of 1959—China's strategy in political Tibet, today's Tibet Autonomous Region (TAR), focused on gradually winning over the majority of the Tibetan elite rather than on immediately trying to implement socialist reforms.

Instructions sent by the Central Committee of the Chinese Communist Party (CCP) to the Chinese leaders in Lhasa in mid-1952 regarding the Three Monastic Seats convey the gist of this gradualist policy:

> The united front work of the three main monasteries is like other united front work in Tibet. The emphasis should be on the upper hierarchy. We should try to win any of those close to the top of the hierarchy, provided that they are not stubborn running dogs of imperialists, or even bigger bandits and spies. Therefore, you should try patiently to win support among those upper level lamas whom you referred to as those full of hatred to the Hans and to our government. *Our present policy is not to organize people at the bottom level to isolate those at the top.* We should try to work on the top, get their support, and achieve the purpose of building harmony between the masses and us.

The arrival of the Chinese communists in Tibet, therefore, did not change monastic life or the monastery's ownership of estates and peasants/serfs during the initial period. The abortive uprising in 1959 ended Beijing's gradualist policy in Tibet, changing overnight all facets of monastic life in Drepung. Beijing now moved to destroy the political, economic, and ideological dominance of the estate-holding elite, including the monasteries.

The overwhelming majority of Drepung monks were not active participants in the Lhasa uprising, although certainly all had great faith in and support for the Dalai Lama. However, a number of monks from Drepung had defended the Dalai Lama's summer palace and fought in Lhasa. Because of that, Drepung was classified as a rebellious monastery and had all its estates and granaries confiscated without compensation. Similarly, all the loans it had made which were still outstanding were canceled. Chinese accounts state that Drepung at this time had 140,000 tons of grain and 10 million yuan in cash (equal then to U.S. $5 million) outstanding in such loans. The flow of income to Drepung (in kind and cash) totally ceased.

Monastic life and monastic administrative structure were also fundamentally altered. In the initial months following the uprising, a group of officials called a work team (*las-don ru-khag*) was sent from

Lhasa to take charge of the monastery. They ended up staying continuously in the monastery until the onset of the Cultural Revolution in 1966. These officials immediately terminated the power and authority of the traditional leadership and appointed a new administrative committee selected from among the poorer and "progressive" monks in a manner analogous to what was done in the rest of China years earlier. The new administration was called the Democratic Management Committee (*dmangs-gtso bdag-gnyer u-yon lhan-khang*, henceforth DMC). It has continued to the present.

One of the main initial tasks of the work team (and the new DMC) was determining how monks should be grouped into the various class categories used by the state. Monks involved in the uprising and virtually all the monastery administrators/leaders were classified as "exploiters" and imprisoned or sent to labor camps. The rest of the monks were given several months of "education" in the new socialist ideology, including the need to engage in productive labor. At this time all the monks, and especially the young ones, were encouraged to leave the monastery—to return to their home areas or to join nonmonk work units. The number of monks in Drepung decreased sharply, and by the end of 1959 there were only about four thousand remaining. A Drepung monk described this period: "At first, at this time there was [political] education all day. We were taught things we never heard before like the 'three antis' and the 'two exemptions' and the 'three great mountains.' . . . [How we got food] depended on the wealth of the monks. The poor monks ate together using the food the monastery had amassed in its storerooms, while the better off monks ate in their apartments using their own food supplies. I was among the latter." After a few months of this political reeducation and reorganization, the remaining monks began to engage in manual labor projects, initially as "volunteers" and then as part of work units. Another monk recalled,

> At first we ate the monastery's food in our own residence halls, but then after many monks were sent off and the total number of monks became much less, the remaining monks gathered together in Loseling College where we ate food together. After about 5–6 months, the monastery's food stores ran out. However, by then we were all engaged in productive labor so we got food through that work.

> At this time only the old monks were [regularly] left in the monastery. All the younger monks were out working on projects. How often we returned to the monastery varied; some returned once a week, some daily. These jobs weren't permanent postings.

> After communal dining at Loseling broke up, we divided into smaller production units that worked and ate together; for example, there was a sewing unit, a masonry unit, a construction unit, a carpentry unit and a firewood collecting unit. Later some of these were again divided into two units. Each unit, therefore, had its own livelihood [i.e., was organized as a collective] and ate together. The tsamba was divided among the monks, and the butter was kept jointly and used to make tea for all. The monks ate their tsamba separately and took tea together. The older monks who couldn't work and wouldn't go home were organized as an "old people's unit" (gensogang) and lived off subsidies from the government.

In 1965, six years after the uprising, one foreign visitor to Drepung reported that only 715 of the 10,000 monks present in Drepung in 1959 remained. The physical shell of Drepung stood and those monks who remained had vows and prayed in their rooms when not working, but the defining institutional religious activities—joint prayer chanting sessions and the dharma grove theology curriculum—had ended. The monastery ceased to function as an institution where religious study, debate, and ritual were practiced. But the worst was still to come.

The third, and most devastating, period for Drepung began with the onset of the Cultural Revolution in 1966. It brought an end to the religion practiced by individual laypersons and monks alike. Drepung remained "open" in the sense that monks continued to live there, but the monks were no longer allowed to wear their robes or maintain private altars in their rooms, and all religious acts were now prohibited. At the same time, political struggle sessions attacked religious beliefs and practices as well as former leaders. Lay and monk Tibetans were encouraged and pressured to ridicule and deride religious laws and gods as well as despoil sacred sites. And although Drepung was fortunate in that most of its building were not destroyed during this period (as were so many other Tibetan monasteries), it was no longer a monastery: those who remained were simply former monks living and working in what used to be a monastery. By the end of the Cultural Revolution in 1976, the number of monks in Drepung had decreased to only 306, and a number of these were married.

The fourth, or current, period began with the liberalizing decisions made in Beijing in 1978 at the Eleventh Party Plenum. In Lhasa the new policy quickly resulted in the reemergence of "individual" religion, that is, the religious practices performed by individuals. At the same time, a number of temples and shrine rooms were reopened so the public could make religious visits and offerings to deities as in the past. Tibetans responded enthusiastically to the new opportunities and began a host of traditional practices such as circumambulating holy sites. By 1980–81 the shrine rooms in Drepung Monastery were receiving religious visitors from Central Tibet as well as from the ethnic Tibetan areas in Qinghai, Gansu, and Sichuan provinces daily. However, the revival of monasticism per se did not progress as rapidly as did that of individual religion. . . .

When Drepung's DMC finally decided in 1981 that the time was right to revive monastic life in an active sense, they also understood that this would be neither easy nor straightforward. It would need the agreement of the government of the TAR. Many officials in Tibet were hostile to this, believing that Tibetan monasteries were an anachronism, that they were unnecessary or even worse, a threat to socialism and the domination of the Communist party. Nothing should be done, they felt, to allow monasteries and lamas to once again function as unifying institutions for the Tibetan masses since this would inevitably give new hope to those most reactionary and hostile to Beijing and foster nationalistic, pro-independence dissidence.

Moreover, the laws governing religious freedom included a number of important limitations to which a "new" Drepung would have to conform. For example, the 1982 Chinese constitution's definition of religious freedom specifies, "In our country, citizens may believe in religion or disbelieve, but politically they have one thing in common, that is, they are all patriotic and support socialism. . . . The State protects legitimate religious activities, but no one may use religion to carry out counter-revolutionary activities or activities that disrupt public order, harm the health of citizens, or obstruct the educational system of the State . . . [and] no religious affairs may be controlled by any foreign power." And there were other important caveats. Because religious freedom was part of the more basic freedom to believe or *not to believe*, the state sought to create a level playing field by prohibiting religious education and recruitment of individuals into the priesthood who were under the age of eighteen.

Religious freedom in China, therefore, was predicated on religious practitioners and organizations accepting the principle of the unity of the nation, eschewing any activities that foster separatism, remaining completely free from foreign control, and not engaging in activities the government deemed "exploitive." However, whether Tibetan monasteries would actually abide by these rules was uncertain and, given the history of the monks' opposition to communism and their likely sympathy with the exiled Dalai Lama, entailed a considerable risk.

Despite such dangers, China's new policy toward Tibet compelled it to permit the process of revival to begin. In 1978–79 Beijing had set out to improve conditions in Tibet and if possible induce the Dalai Lama to return from exile. In particular, it sought to reverse the cultural assimilationist policies of the Cultural Revolution period. . . .

The new Chinese policy made a revival of monastic life feasible but, as mentioned above, did not eliminate the need for the monastery's leaders (the DMC) to proceed carefully. Drepung's DMC, as they contemplated how to transform the new Chinese policy into practice, had to make difficult decisions regarding what functioning as a monastery meant in the context of the ideology and values of both the old and the new society. They had to prioritize and structure the revival so as to restore an institution that would both be accepted by Tibetans as authentic and at the same time fall within the purview of China's definition of religious freedom, that is, would avoid precipitating a government crackdown and renewed suppression. Drepung's leaders focused initially on two essential aspects of the monastic way of life: collective prayer assemblies and the recruitment and education of new monks.

Unlike tightly structured Christian monasteries, Drepung traditionally had no activities that required the participation of all monks. Whether a monk spent his time praying or studying or sitting in the sun was his own decision. In Tibetan Buddhism, as indicated earlier, individuals were responsible for their own religious behavior and, via karmic cause and effect, reaped rewards or punishments in their next life based on their decisions in this one. Nevertheless, there were large-scale joint activities that symbolized the monastery as a collectivity. The most important of these were the meetings at which large numbers of monks assembled to chant prayers for the benefit of all sentient beings. Collective chanting sessions lasted several hours, including a break during which the monks were served tea (and sometimes food). These prayer assembly meetings also had direct economic importance traditionally because they were the time when patrons distributed alms to the assembled monks.

In 1980–81, the DMC sought and received permission from the Lhasa Religious Affairs Bureau to begin to hold these prayer chanting sessions on a regular basis. One old monk recalled the first assembly meeting in 1982:

> When we got permission, we immediately tried to get the stoves in the monastic kitchen back in shape so we could have the first prayer chanting assembly on the 30th of the fifth lunar month. However, we couldn't manage this so we had to be satisfied with a "dry" assembly [i.e., a prayer assembly at which tea was not served]. We kept on working and quickly got the kitchen operating again so on the festival that commemorates the first sermon of the Buddha on the 4th of the sixth lunar month (Trugpa tsheshi), we held our first full prayer assembly with tea. On that day the DMC sponsored [financed] the tea and gave each of us a small torma religious offering made from tsamba.

From then on, Drepung held prayer chanting assemblies regularly, at first three times a month and then five times a month. In addition, special sessions were held on holidays such as the Great Prayer Festival of the first lunar month.

While this was going on, Drepung sought and received permission to revive a second critical monastic activity—enrolling new (young) monks. It is not surprising, given the energetic revival of individual religion in 1979–81, that there was a revival of interest among some parents, their motives involving the old mix of economic and religious reasons but also a strong new religionationalistic belief that Tibetan religion, the basis of the greatness of the Tibetan nationality, should be revived to its former greatness. Demographically, this was not problematic since the Chinese government's "one-child policy" had not been implemented in Tibet and rural Tibetans had large families.

Parents seeking to make a son a monk went about this in accordance with the customs of the old society; they sought an older monk (usually a relative or family friend) to serve as the boy's sponsor-guardian (*kegya gegen*) and take the boy in to live with him. Since a foundation of traditional Tibetan monasticism was that monkhood should be available to as many people as possible, it was difficult for older monks to refuse such requests, especially since parents assured them they would provide all the food and clothes their boys needed. Consequently, by 1981 a number of the older monks in Drepung had young boys living in their monastic apartments. These boys took monastic vows. But they were monks without a monastery, for although they were living in Drepung, they were not officially accepted in its monastic rolls.

In the old society, when a guardian monk took a young ward to the abbot of his college, he was invariably admitted and immediately became a "legal" monk in the monastery. In the new society, the situation was different. The DMC, like the college's abbot in the old society, had the authority to select applicants, but now this decision was not final. It had to seek approval from the government, which was reluctant to permit the reemergence of monasteries housing many thousands of monks and thus did not readily give such approval. While the government wanted to try to meet the religious aspirations of Tibetans by permitting Drepung and other formerly great monasteries to reopen, it did not want them to become too large or powerful. Consequently, the young boys who went to live with guardian monks in Drepung did not immediately obtain official status and thus were not eligible to participate in prayer assemblies or to receive alms from patrons. Only official monks could partake of these. They were, therefore, novice monks living in Drepung waiting to be formally admitted.

In 1982 the government gave approval to officially enroll the first such monks and fifteen to twenty of those who were already in residence were entered into the monastic roll. This occurred at the same time that Drepung received permission to begin regular prayer chanting sessions. The "new" Drepung, therefore, emerged at this time.

These successes raised the question of what sort of rules should be established for the new monks. Should all monks be forced either to work for the monastery or to study religious theology, or should monks be permitted to work or not work according to their own wishes? And should monks be allowed to engage in private business as in the old society, or must they only work for the monastery? Basic to such questions was the underlying issue of whether the focus of the monastery should be quantity or quality. Was it better for Drepung to try to maximize the number of monks even if most of these would primarily be engaged in manual labor or business, or should Drepung support fewer monks, most of whom would be engaged in the rigorous study of Buddhist theology?

In the traditional society, the answer to this question was clearly quantity. The ideology of mass monasticism dominated. In the new society, Drepung, as I shall show below, had difficulty supporting even a small number of monks financially, and the new political and social climate opposed allowing monasteries to fill up with monks who neither studied nor worked, or worse, became private businessmen as was typical of pre-1959 Tibet. The issue of shifting the monastic emphasis from quantity to quality, however, was not merely a response to the values of the new society or financial constraints. It also had deep roots in the old society and . . . it was a contentious issue.

. . .

Drepung and Political Dissidence

Like much else in contemporary Tibet, it is difficult to divorce the revival of Buddhism and monasticism from the struggle over the political status of Tibet vis-à-vis China, that is, from what is often referred to as the Tibet Question. This nationalistic conflict is being played out in two major arenas. Abroad, there is the vocal and active independence movement led by the Dalai Lama and his exile government. In Tibet, the center of Tibetan political consciousness is Lhasa (and its environs), the capital of the traditional Tibetan state. There, monks and nuns launched a very visible campaign of active political dissidence beginning in 1987. From Drepung alone, ninety-two monks were arrested for participating in ten antigovernment political demonstrations between 1987 and 1993.

However, at the time the Chinese government liberalized its policy on religion in 1978–80, resolution of the Tibet conflict seemed promising. Beijing had invited the Dalai Lama to send fact-finding delegations to visit Tibet, and the exiles had begun discussions with China aimed at reaching a mutually acceptable solution to the Tibet Question. But this was not to be. The talks stalemated when the gap between the Chinese position emphasizing enhanced cultural autonomy and the exiles' position emphasizing real political autonomy could not be bridged. By the mid-1980s, therefore, the momentum for reconciliation had collapsed and both sides unilaterally pursued policies aimed at improving their position relative to the other.

For the Dalai Lama and his government-in-exile, this meant launching a new political offensive that sought to persuade the United States and Europe to use their economic and political leverage to force concessions from Beijing. At the same time, they sought to counter China's policies aimed at winning over Tibetans within Tibet by conveying to Tibetans there not only that the Dalai Lama was actively working on their behalf in the West but also that his endeavors were successful—that he represented a realistic hope for securing Western assistance to settle the Tibet Question in Tibet's favor.

The key innovation in this strategy was having the Dalai Lama himself carry the exile's political message to the United States and Europe. Prior to this, the Dalai Lama traveled as a religious leader and did not make overtly political speeches. In 1987 there were several important breakthroughs. In June the U.S. House of Representatives adopted a bill that condemned human rights abuses in Tibet, instructed the president to express sympathy for Tibet, and urged China to establish a constructive dialogue with the Dalai Lama. Then, in September, the Dalai Lama made a major visit to the United States during which he presented his first political speech to the Congressional Human Rights Caucus (on 21 September). It was a carefully crafted talk arguing that Tibet had been independent when China invaded it. Specifically, he said, "though Tibetans lost their freedom, under international law Tibet today is still an independent state under illegal occupation." The speech also raised serious human rights charges, referring twice to a "holocaust" inflicted by the Chinese on the Tibetan people.

The Dalai Lama's activities in the United States were widely known and eagerly followed in Lhasa where Tibetans regularly listen to the Chinese-language broadcasts of the Voice of America and the BBC. The Chinese government's media also covered this trip on radio and television, making vitriolic attacks on his visit and views. Among Tibetans in Lhasa the visit was widely taken as confirmation that the tide of history was shifting in Tibet's favor and that the Dalai Lama was on the verge of achieving victory.

At this juncture, a group of about twenty Drepung monks staged an overt political demonstration in Lhasa—the first political demonstration of its type. They did not demonstrate to protest any particular problem Drepung was facing at the time but rather to show Beijing and the West that Tibetans in Tibet support the Dalai Lama and independence. On the morning of 27 September, while the Dalai Lama was still in the United States, they met in Lhasa's central marketplace, the Bargor, unfurled signs that included a handmade Tibetan national flag, and walked around the circular "Bargor" road three times. When nothing happened to them, they marched about a mile down one of the main east-west streets and continued their protest in front of the headquarters of the Tibet Autonomous Region government. At this point they were detained by security forces. Their arrest made news throughout the Western world.

A few days later, on the morning of 1 October, a group of monks from several other monasteries in the area staged a demonstration to show support for the Dalai Lama and the previous monk demonstrators and to demand the latter's release from jail. Police quickly took them into custody in the Bargor and allegedly started beating them. A crowd of Tibetans demanded the release of these monks, and before long this escalated into a full-scale riot. In the end, a number of vehicles and buildings were burned, and anywhere from six to twenty Tibetans were killed when police (including ethnic Tibetan police) fired at the rioters.

Over the next year and a half scores of monk- and nun-led demonstrations occurred, three more of which ended in bloody riots. Martial law was finally declared in 1989 and was not lifted until 1990. In the eight years since then, monk and nun demonstrations have continued, although tight security measures have prevented them from turning into riots. The political atmosphere is volatile, however, and the danger that some monk- or nun-led incident or protest will precipitate a new riot remains ever-present.

These events rocked Drepung, creating a serious crisis that threatens its viability and future. One of the key negative consequences of the political activism was its inadvertent decimation of Drepung's nascent theological study program. Not only were many of the young monk demonstrators part of the dharma grove program, but the most gifted of Drepung's young scholar monks were involved, arrested, and thus lost to the monastery. Still other young monks have fled to India to join the Dalai Lama and the exile community. For a time, Drepung's dharma grove actually ceased to be used.

The political conflict also negatively affected the government's attitude toward Drepung and other similarly involved monasteries. The risk Beijing took in allowing a monastic revival in Tibet has turned out poorly as monks have become, as many hardliners in China predicted at the outset of the liberalization, leaders in the nationalistic opposition to Chinese rule in Tibet. Although the principle of religious freedom continued to be espoused, with, of course, the inherent caveats mentioned earlier, and although the government claims it does not hold the monastery responsible for the political protests of individual monks, in reality the government's attitude toward Drepung hardened demonstrably. Monastic requests from Drepung's DMC on a range of issues, such as assistance in renovating the main prayer assembly hall, payments for teachers, and, critically, permission to increase the number of monks, were denied or approved only on a limited basis. At the same time, the government instituted much closer security scrutiny and supervision over Drepung. Moreover, with regard to Tibet in general, these dissident activities have led Beijing to implement a more hard-line policy that minimizes the importance of meeting Tibetans' cultural and religious expectations and maximizes Tibet's economic and political integration with the rest of China.

Equally significant is the negative effect the political activism has had on the morale and purpose of the monks themselves. As the monastery's revitalization gained momentum in the early 1980s there was hope among the older monks that a serious monastic community could be restored, despite Tibet's presence as part of communist China. There was even hope that regular contact with the Drepung Monastery in exile (in India) would ultimately be possible and that lamas from India could participate in Drepung's revival. The initial focus of their attention, therefore, was on how to operationalize a high-quality revitalization—i.e., how to structure finances, education, recruitment, discipline, and so forth—not politics or nationalism. The major escalation of political activity in the mid-1980s challenged this orientation by thrusting nationalistic and political issues onto center stage where they competed head to head with solely religious interests.

Traditionally a monk's primary loyalty was to his monastery/college and Buddhism rather than the state and nation, and great monasteries like Drepung (or even colleges within them) were not reluctant to oppose the Tibetan government. As mentioned earlier, Tengyeling Monastery and Drepung's Loseling College gave support to the Manchu/Chinese Ambans and troops in Lhasa after the fall of the Manchu dynasty in 1911–12.

The Chinese invasion and incorporation of Tibet into the People's Republic of China in 1951 changed this in important ways. It created a heightened sense of national identity and political purpose among Tibetans, including the monks. Tibetans, whether rich or poor, monk or layman, Easterner or Westerner, now more than ever before defined their identity primarily in terms of political nationalism, as Tibetan vis-à-vis the Han Chinese. Defending the religious interests of one's monastery (and religion in general) now was projected to a larger arena where defending Tibet as a nation-state was seen as synonymous with defending and preserving Buddhism against an atheistic enemy. Such feelings intensified after the abortive Tibetan uprising of 1959 when the Chinese government devastated Tibet's proud monastic tradition. Communism and the Chinese state became a hated enemy for all monks.

But history does not stand still, and China's dramatic shift in policy in 1978 ushered in a new chapter in the relations between Tibetan Buddhism and the Chinese state. In Drepung this revival process started in the early 1980s and had begun to gain momentum by the middle of the decade when political issues exploded on the scene. Once some Drepung monks began political dissidence in 1987, all monks

were forced to reassess whether their primary loyalty was to Buddhism and their monastery as in the past or to their nationality and the Dalai Lama. The question facing monks, in essence, was whether the restoration of monasticism and the study of Buddhist theology took precedence over the political struggle to wrest Tibet from Chinese control, and in particular, to support the Dalai Lama.

Every Drepung monk believes in the sanctity of the Dalai Lama and wants him to return to Tibet, and virtually all support his efforts to secure Tibetan independence. Nevertheless, some monks believe these efforts are not only unrealistic but also harmful to the monastery and the revival of religion. The DMC, for example, has repeatedly tried to persuade the monks that Drepung's interests are best served by focusing their efforts on religious study and eschewing political activism. Some senior monks have similarly tried to persuade their young wards to reject political activism because of the personal and monastic dangers. However, by and large, such efforts were not successful. Most Drepung monks believed that the Dalai Lama was moving to free Tibet with U.S. assistance, and there was a broad consensus that this was a time for monks—who have no wives and children to worry about—to sacrifice themselves for the good of the Dalai Lama, religion, and Tibet. The intense distrust of the motives of the atheistic communist state toward Buddhism and the caveats and constraints Drepung operates under made it easy for some monks to conclude that Buddhism cannot flourish in China despite the new liberalism. Accepting the risks entailed in openly demonstrating against the Chinese state, therefore, for some monks became not only a nationalistic-political activity but also, by extrapolation, a religious one. Moreover, for the young monk activists, the traditional notion of acceptable political action to defend religion was infused with new meanings from the West in the form of the incorporation of notions of universal human rights. Such new constructs, however, were not shared by all monks, some of whom, as mentioned above, value the efflorescence of Buddhism in Tibet above abstract universal values such as democracy and human rights, neither of which, of course, existed in the traditional society.

In any case, Beijing has chosen not to close the monastery, and monastic life goes on with the leaders of Drepung trying to make the best of the situation, despite deep-seated frustration at their inability to control the events in which they are mired.

. . .

Conclusion

The central place of monks and monasteries in Tibetan society made it inevitable that the new era of religious freedom in China would produce powerful pressures to revive Tibet's monastic tradition. The freedom to practice religion as individuals was clearly not enough for Tibetans, and local communities throughout Tibet have rebuilt or repaired traditional monasteries, usually without government financial help. In Lhasa the desire to restore famous monastic centers like Drepung to their former greatness was especially strong. By representing the sophistication of Tibetan culture, monasteries like Drepung bolstered Tibetans' cultural identity and fostered ethnic pride vis-à-vis that of the politically dominant Chinese. And so, as the changes implicit in China's new rules became understood and believed in Drepung, a slow monastic revival commenced. The first major step in this process occurred in 1982 when new youths were admitted and regular collective prayer chanting assemblies started.

The five years following those events were characterized by a period of "institutional revival." The DMC and senior monks set out to operationalize a new monastic community and culture, making difficult decisions about how to finance, educate, and discipline the new monks. Through a delicate, and not entirely conscious, process of adaptation, traditional values, customs, and beliefs were restored, in some cases intact and in other cases with modifications and innovations. The result was an emergent monastic social matrix that was sociopolitically compatible with the realities of the current socialist society yet culturally authentic. From a baseline of zero religion at the end of the Cultural Revolution in 1976, Drepung was able to revive a practicing monastic community with new young monks, regular prayer chanting sessions, and a large theological study program.

This process of institutional reconstruction changed dramatically in the fall of 1987 when open political demonstrations by monks ushered in a new era—the period of "religiopolitical confrontation." Monks (and nuns) suddenly leaped to the forefront of active political opposition and received worldwide attention and plaudits. The monastic revival had become politicized, at least in the regions in and around Lhasa.

This new religious militancy challenged all monks and nuns, confronting them with an emotionally powerful alternative to quietly (apolitically) working within China to rebuild their monastic tradition; that is, it presented them the emotionally compelling alternative of participating in the nationalistic struggle to free Tibet from Chinese rule. Feelings of anger and hatred toward the Communist party and the Chinese, of course, were present before the first demonstration, but after it, Drepung's monks consciously had to choose between conflicting loyalties—Buddhism or the Tibetan nation—or, as some who chose the latter course did, to eliminate the cognitive dissonance by trying to redefine the interests of Buddhism as being best served by political activism.

All of this placed Beijing in a very difficult situation. Although it is still committed to a policy of religious freedom in Tibet (so long as its political caveats are adhered to) and does not officially hold Drepung responsible for the acts of individual monks, it is also committed to stop monks from continuing to fan the flames of political dissidence. Since intensified "political education" in Drepung has heretofore not succeeded in stopping activism, how Beijing will move to ensure this without simply closing down the monastery is not at all clear. It is reasonable to assume that the government's tolerance of monasteries like Drepung will decrease in the coming years if monastic leaders do not work out some way to stop the political protests of the monks.

This scenario is understood by Drepung's leaders and is creating an underlying atmosphere of frustration and depression. Despite the laudatory objective gains in reviving their monastic community, most of Drepung's leaders are disheartened about the future. Cut off from fellow monks and lamas in India, under scrutiny from a government they consider hostile (or at best unfriendly), unable to convince current monks to eschew political militancy (or prevent them from doing so), they find themselves embroiled in constant political tension and conflict they cannot control. And some, undoubtedly, have doubts whether they should be trying to control this. Their successes, no matter how impressive, are always just a demonstration away from disaster. There is a gnawing fear, moreover, that the continued involvement of monks in demonstrations is setting the stage for the worst of all outcomes—that the Tibet Question will not be settled in Tibet's favor and the monastery will be destroyed.

The revival of Drepung Monastery seventeen years after liberalization, therefore, has been somewhat mixed. On one level, the progress has been impressive; yet on another, the gains seem very unstable. At the heart of this contradiction, like so much else in contemporary Tibet, is the Tibet Question.

The older monks love their monastery and want to see it thrive again as a great center of Tibetan religion. Most laypersons feel the same. Consequently, despite their pessimism and apprehension, the monastery's leaders will certainly continue to work to adapt the basic elements of the monastic way of life to whatever obstacles the unpredictable national and international sociopolitical environments throw in its way. But, whatever happens, Drepung's leaders are unlikely to be able to return to the more placid times of the period of institutional revival unless some major breakthrough in the struggle over the Tibet Question occurs. With the monks, especially the younger monks, torn between nationalistic and religious ideals and loyalties, the future of Drepung is uncertain and unpredictable. Only time will tell whether Drepung will move into a third, more positive phase of revival in which it regains most of its former greatness, or whether monk-led confrontations will escalate and the state will decide to crack down harshly on the monastery and reverse most of the gains of the past decade and a half. The leaders of Drepung, therefore, find themselves trapped between two forces they cannot control, and while they hope that Drepung can weather the storm, they are far from optimistic.

Epilogue

The political fears mentioned above materialized in the summer of 1996 when Beijing launched a major new "patriotism education" campaign aimed at enhancing its control over the most visible source of opposition—the monasteries. As part of its general "get tough" policy in Tibet, this campaign sought not merely to educate monks on the "proper," apolitical, role of religion in China, but more important, to

demonstrate to monks that if they did not adhere to these rules they could not remain in the monastery. The campaign sought to take steps to reduce the danger that monasteries like Drepung would continue to function as breeding grounds for political opposition. The vehicle for enforcement was what is known in China as a "work team," that is, a group of officials pulled together from various government offices and sent to carry out a political campaign. In Drepung's case, more than a hundred officials arrived there in summer 1996 and remained in residence until roughly the end of that year.

The ideological brief of the work team is illustrated by a document handed out to the monks of Drepung's sister monastery, Sera, at the start of the parallel campaign there:

> The time has arrived for patriotic education to take place in Sera monastery by means of Comprehensive Propaganda Education [*gcig sdud kyis dril bsgrags slab gso*]. The purpose of carrying out this education session is to implement the Party's policy on religion totally and correctly, to stress the management of religious affairs according to law, and to initiate efforts for the harmonious coexistence between the religious and socialist societies. It is also aimed at creating the thought of patriotism and implanting in the masses of the monks the view of the government, the political view and the legal view. The campaign is also for the purpose of educating [monks] to oppose completely any activities aimed at splitting the motherland.

Work teams had been sent to Drepung on a number of occasions in the past so the presence of this one in Drepung itself was not exceptional. However, the task of the 1996 work team differed from previous ones in that its brief included vetting each monk with respect to his political views and his future acceptability as a monk.

The work team sent to Drepung interviewed monks and led sessions on topics such as Chinese law, Tibetan history, patriotism, and the government's view that the Dalai Lama and his Western supporters were playing a negative role in trying to split Tibet from China. All monks were required to study political education materials that spelled out these views, attend classes that went over the official positions, and convey their attitudes about these issues verbally and in writing.

In keeping with the strident rhetoric of the new hard-line policy in Tibet, the work team directly attacked the Dalai Lama, removing his photographs from the monastery's chapels and temples (and other public venues) while asserting that the monks must denounce the Dalai Lama as a duplicitous "splittist." The harsh personal attacks on the Dalai Lama, however, assaulted Tibetan ethnic and religious sensibilities and precipitated a major test of wills in Drepung (and in many other monasteries).

Faced with the necessity of attacking the Dalai Lama by name and agreeing to historical views and "facts" they considered untrue, many monks dug in their heels and, in a variety of ways, refused to participate in what was commonly perceived as a throwback to the mass political campaigns of the 1960s and 1970s, even if this stance meant having to leave the monastery. A few monks expressed their protest by openly challenging the veracity of the work team's facts at public sessions. Four such monks, it is said, ultimately were sent to reform-though-labor camps when they repeatedly refused to recant. A larger number of Drepung monks—about sixty—adopted a less confrontational method to protest. They chose to leave the monastery on their own accord rather than accept the campaign's demands. Some of these quietly fled to India, producing the first reports of the campaign abroad. One very old monk, it is said, became so distraught by the thought of either leaving the monastery or denouncing the Dalai Lama that he committed suicide.

Most monks, however, were willing to accept—at least on the surface—the basic ideological "points" of the campaign to remain in the monastery, but they drew a line with regard to the demand that they comment negatively about the Dalai Lama's political persona. A meeting of work team members with Drepung's elderly monks illustrates the depth of this opposition. At this meeting, three or four monks rose and said emotionally, tears in their eyes, that as simple monks they knew nothing of the Dalai Lama's politics but only his religious stature, and this they could not oppose. Consequently, if the work team insisted that they speak against the Dalai Lama, they would have to leave Drepung and go begging in the streets of Lhasa. Comments like this coming from monks who were basically nonpolitical and had lived most of their lives in the monastery had a powerful impact on the work team's thinking, leading to

a reconsideration of the campaign's anti–Dalai Lama component. The campaign had sought to cleanse the monastery of politically unreliable monks and convince the rest that it was in their and their monastery's best interests to dissociate themselves from political dissidence, not purge Drepung of virtually all senior monks. Consequently, it was decided that trying to force monks to criticize the Dalai Lama directly would be counterproductive, and this was removed from the list of "conditions" the monks had to accept publicly, leaving only the following items: to cherish the nation and cherish religion; to oppose separatism/splittism; to accept the correct ideology of the Chinese Communist party; to respect the motherland's unity; to work to continue the socialist system and to obey the orders of one's superior officials. Monks who "passed" the political education program by stating their acceptance of these conditions were reaffirmed as official Drepung monks and issued a new registration document (in the form of a red handbook with their name, photo, birthdate, etc.).

Although it is easy to dismiss the rhetorical "parroting" the Socialist Education campaign generated as a kind of political charade that changed no one's views, the 1996 campaign was not limited to rhetoric. It also initiated a number of real structural changes. One such "reform" was the addition of a new criterion for official membership as a Drepung monk—proper age. As mentioned earlier, the laws of the People's Republic of China prohibited the recruitment of monks and priests under the age of eighteen. Religious freedom in Chinese law meant the freedom to believe or not to believe, and the party from early on felt it was important to prevent young children from being indoctrinated into a religious life before they had the maturity to make an informed judgment. Nevertheless, exceptions were made, most notably in Tibet where the great emphasis Tibetans placed on child recruitment was tacitly respected by not enforcing the minimum age rule. The 1996 campaign reversed that policy, the government announcing that Tibetan monks must now be at least eighteen. And it implemented this standard, albeit with a few concessions, the most important of which were that for the duration of the campaign the minimum age for the monks already present in Drepung would be reduced to fifteen, and even younger monks were admitted in a few hardship cases involving those who were orphans with no home to return to or child monks whose coresident guardian monk was so old or infirm that he depended on the young monk. In the future, however, the government decreed that new monks would have to be at least eighteen years of age.

The work team also eliminated the hundreds of unofficial monks who had been residing in Drepung at the start of the campaign "waiting" to be admitted officially. These youths, frustrated and angry at the government's refusal to allow them to become official Drepung monks, were clearly a fertile breeding ground for political dissent. They were eliminated in two ways. The underage monks (numbering between 80 and 100) were sent home with no political prejudice or stigma attached to this expulsion. They were told to enter secular schools and reapply for admission if they wished when they reached the age of eighteen. The remainder of the older "waiting" monks (numbering more than 160) were officially admitted into the monastery, increasing Drepung's size by about 30 percent to 706 official monks. This number constituted Drepung's new official maximum size, although the number of resident monks was actually higher since about eighty unofficial "visiting" monks from outside the TAR continued to live and study in Drepung as in the past. To prevent the reemergence of a new cohort of "waiting" monks, older monks were warned not to allow nonofficial monks to live with them regardless of their age.

Equally significant were changes made in the administration of Drepung. The government tightened its supervision over the monks by replacing the monk-staffed Democratic Management Committee with a new committee called the "Management Committee" (do dam u yon lhan khang), which included secular cadres who lived in the monastery along with monks. The presence of these lay cadres in the monastery has given the government important firsthand control over the monastery's day-to-day operational decisions. Some changes were also made in monk administrative personnel; the former monk head of the Democratic Management Committee, for example, was replaced with another monk, as was the former disciplinary official, the gegö.

The 1996 campaign also brought about a series of lesser changes in the life of Drepung. A number of the major monastic economic enterprises were converted to the "responsibility" system, the monks working for these having to guarantee the monastery a fixed annual "lease fee." For example, the monastery's store has to guarantee to pay 90,000¥ a year to the monastery, and the restaurant, 80,000¥. Anything these enterprises earn above this key can keep, but it is interesting to note that the monks operating these have pledged that they will only take a salary equal to the salary of other working monks (regardless of how much profit they generate) since as monks they have no desire to become rich.

From another direction, Drepung's income suffered a severe blow in 1997 when its most revered spiritual leader, Gen Lamrim, died. Overnight the monks lost the several hundred thousand yuan that his biannual public religious teachings generated, as well as his spiritual leadership. The increases in income from implementing the "responsibility" system will not make up for this loss.

Changes were also made in Drepung's school for younger monks. In 1996 the curriculum was expanded to include Chinese and English, and the school was established as a full six-year primary school. In July 1997 the school enrolled 178 monks. The content of the dharma grove educational program was not altered, but a formal ceiling was set at 230 full-time monks (i.e., 33% of the total number of Drepung monks). These scholar monks continued to receive salaries to support themselves while they studied; the advanced scholar monks receive 7¥ per day, the middle level 5¥ per day, and the newer ones (those admitted in 1996) 2.5¥ per day. Monks from outside the TAR were still permitted to study in the dharma grove, although they did not receive salaries from the monastery.

The 1996 monastery rectification campaign reflects the government's new hard-line strategy in Tibet, one characteristic of which is less conciliation toward ethnic culture, as well as its frustration with the monks' hostility and political activism. However, although the campaign was launched with a torrent of tough rhetoric and initially seemed likely to marginalize monasteries like Drepung, in the end its results were somewhat equivocal. Rather than drastically scale back the number of monks, the government again offered up its standard religious compromise—if you concentrate on religion and eschew political dissidence, we will permit you to stay as monks and allow monasticism to develop—and it actually allowed Drepung to increase by more than 30 percent despite the fact that the monks would not denounce the Dalai Lama. However, the campaign also revealed clearly to the monks that the government will no longer tolerate monasteries like Drepung functioning as centers of political and nationalistic opposition and that this was more than empty rhetoric—it was now ready to intervene and forcibly alter elements of monastic life to prevent this.

The future of monasteries like Drepung, therefore, more than ever depends on the monks' acceptance of the government's separation of religion and political dissidence, that is, the government's demand that monks devote themselves to their religion and eschew all antigovernment political activity. So while Drepung can continue to try to train a new generation of scholar monks, the government has made it clear that it will not tolerate the monastery being used as a breeding ground for political dissidence and, of course, that resistance is futile and counterproductive.

Drepung's future, therefore, remains uncertain and precarious since it is impossible to predict how its monks will respond to future vagaries of the Tibet Question, in particular, to events outside of China. The Chinese government's attempt to persuade (and/or intimidate) Drepung's monks to delink religion from nationalistic politics reached a new plateau of intensity in 1996 but did not truly resolve the fundamental conflict of many at Drepung between their political aspirations and their religious loyalties.

46

Pilgrimage and Its Influence on West African Islam

James Steel Thayer

Travel to sacred places has been a key feature of many religions, and it serves a variety of functions. In many ways akin to ritual, pilgrimage is spiritually fulfilling to individuals but also can unite participants, renew and solidify their beliefs, and—as Thayer shows—bring pilgrims into contact with new ideas from far away, with profound effects. One of the most significant examples of pilgrimage is the hajj, *the journey to Mecca that is required of every Muslim at least once in his or her life. Until recently, the* hajj *required long and difficult travel, yet the pilgrimage has been an important way of disseminating Islamic learning.*

In this article, anthropologist James Steel Thayer takes a historical perspective to show how Muslims in West Africa have been affected by participation in the hajj *over the past 1,000 years. Because during certain historical periods West Africa was isolated from the Middle East, the region was often cut off from Islam as it was practiced closer to its origins and its most holy sites. Thayer argues that the pilgrimage allowed periodic renewal and reform in West African approaches to Islam, as pilgrims took back ideas from the Maghrib (North Africa), Egypt, and the Hijaz (the region of Saudi Arabia where the cities of Mecca and Medina are located). Today, more people than ever are able to take part in the pilgrimage, with stays of perhaps just a couple of weeks in Saudi Arabia. To Thayer, this suggests a changing function for the pilgrimage, with more emphasis on the fulfillment of individual religious obligations and a lessening of the pedagogical functions, which have been taken up instead by educational institutions.*

Note that, in this article, "the Sudan" refers to the region of sub-Saharan West Africa, not the modern Republic of Sudan.

Islam is a religion that encourages and even requires certain forms of wandering or travel. The best known is the *hajj*, the pilgrimage to Mecca that takes place every year and is required of every Muslim

once in his life if he is financially and physically capable of it.

The Islamic pilgrimage is a religious practice central to Islam but has its origin in pre-Islamic Arabia. The city of Mecca and its environs (especially the plain of 'Arafat) had served as the sites of shrines and pilgrimage long before the lifetime of Muhammad the Prophet (c. A.D. 570–632). During the traditional month of pilgrimage in pre-Islamic times, many different tribal groups came from all over the Arabian peninsula to participate in religious rituals in the western part of the peninsula (called the Hijaz). This assemblage was possible only if these warlike and often feuding tribes could come and go in peace, so the month of pilgrimage (along with the months preceding and following it) was a month of peace. Warring, feuding, and violence were proscribed during this time, and no weapons could be carried in the pilgrimage territory. In addition to the religious activities of the Hijaz, large fairs were associated with the pilgrimages, and merchants from all over the peninsula assembled to sell their wares to the pilgrims in Mecca.

The pilgrimage was continued in an altered state under the leadership of Muhammad. Muhammad himself, after the submission of Mecca to his rule and to the religion of Islam (A.D. 628), purified the Meccan shrines of their pagan elements and consecrated the sites to Allah, the one true God of Islam. Many of the ancient customs were banned, and other pre-Islamic rituals and peregrinations were given new Islamic interpretations. For example, the *Ka'ba* was now interpreted as the structure built by Abraham. The Prophet led the pilgrimage several times, thus publicly instituting and validating the rituals of the Islamic pilgrimage for all time. The genius of the institution of the *hajj* can be seen not only in the fact that it occurs at a specific time every year but also in the fact that the ritual actions of the pilgrims, from the donning of the pilgrim robes to the final circumambulations of the *Ka'ba*, are carefully laid down and specified from the life of the founder himself. This exactness provides a rich sense of historical continuity and a concrete expression of the unity of Muslims the world over.

The *hajj* is one of the so-called five pillars of Islam (the others being the confession of faith, fasting during the month of Ramadan, prayer, and alms-giving). The *hajj,* because of the personal sacrifice and traditional difficulty involved in making the journey, has always been regarded as an honor and the high point in the life of any Muslim who succeeds in this venture. Any Muslim who has made the *hajj* has the right to bear the title *hajji* (pilgrim). In many parts of the Muslim world, the departure to, and return from, the pilgrimage are marked by special services and celebrations by the pilgrim's family and community.

One aspect of the importance of the *hajj* is reflected in the numbers of people who participate.

Before the modern era of widespread air travel, the numbers of pilgrims were usually in the tens of thousands. Besides the arduous and often lengthy journey to Mecca, epidemics among the pilgrims often reduced their number and discouraged others from undertaking the *hajj.* Today, however, with better conditions and organization, over a million Muslims travel every year to Saudi Arabia to participate in the annual pilgrimage.

The spiritual and intellectual impact of the *hajj* is realized in different ways. Through participation in the pilgrimage rituals, the pilgrim increases his piety or devotion to God and his fidelity to the teachings and practices of Islam. Further, by coming into contact with Muslims from all over the world, his sense of participation in, and belonging to, the *'ummah* (community of the faithful) is increased and strengthened. In some cases the pilgrim may be fired with zeal to preach Islam in his native country, which might be noted for the imperfection of the practice of Islam or the half-hearted commitment of the believers.

The thesis of this chapter deals with the impact of the *hajj* for the Muslims who made the pilgrimage to Mecca from West Africa. Islam was brought to West Africa by means of the Arab and Berber traders who came south across the Sahara Desert from North Africa. The new religion became the cult of the royal and noble classes, and from the twelfth century onward there are records of Muslims (both rich nobles and their Muslim *'ulama,* scholars) making the pilgrimage to Mecca. Except for these pilgrims, there was almost no contact between the great centers of Islam in Egypt, Arabia, and the Middle East with the territories of the Western Sudan, separated as they were by that sea of sand, the Sahara Desert, a desert approximately the size of the continental United States. These pilgrims served throughout history as the vehicles for communicating the ethos and teachings of the Arabian and North African theological, spiritual, and reform movements. Because of their prestige as pilgrims and their strong relationship to the secular powers, these pilgrims were in a position to institute religious reforms in West African societies on their return from the *hajj.* With the loss of political cohesion in the savannah area after 1591, the relationship of the pilgrim to the general society was altered. The function of pilgrims was altered once again during the era of the *jihads*[1] (1700–1885) and the colonial era. A further, significant change in the role of the pilgrim has occurred during the modern, post-colonial era. In other words, the pilgrimage and the pilgrim have served different functions for West African Islam over time, and this chapter investigates these different functions and the reasons for them.

Because of the time depth involved, this chapter is necessarily historical in nature. To many people it still comes as something of a surprise to learn that the history of many peoples in sub-Saharan Africa can be traced to the tenth or eleventh centuries. Arab historians took a lively interest in West Africa, and the writings of al-Bakri, ibn Battuta, and others provide a rich and informative narrative. In time, some African Muslims became fluent in Arabic, and their writings, such as those of the schools at Timbuktu or of the *jihadist* Uthman dan Fodio, provide insights into the nature of Islam throughout the centuries. My own field research among the Susu people of Sierra Leone and Guinea focused on problems of religion and social organization, but the recent increase in the number of people making the pilgrimage to Mecca drew my attention to the whole subject of the pilgrimage, particularly to its forms and influence in West Africa.

The interest in pilgrimage as a theoretical problem has been increasing in recent times. Victor Turner (1979) and others (Geertz 1968; Eickelman and Piscatori 1990) have greatly expanded our understanding of pilgrimage, particularly with regard to its symbolic dimensions and the ways in which its rituals and symbols affect and transform the pilgrim. While fully appreciating the contributions of writers like Turner, I have a somewhat different emphasis. In researching this chapter, I saw clearly that, beyond whatever effects the pilgrimage may have had on individuals, it had far-reaching consequences for the Muslim societies of West Africa. Inasmuch as

pilgrims came into prolonged contact with Arabic society in Egypt and Arabia, they were influenced sufficiently by developments in Arabian Islamic society, thought, or spirituality that many of them sought to reform West African Islam to make it conform more closely to the Arabian model. The pilgrimage, then, served primarily a didactic or reformative function within the context of West African Islam, and the reader is invited to compare and contrast the evidence and conclusions of this chapter with other ethnographic or historical examples of pilgrimage, either within Islam or within other religious traditions.

West Africa, unlike North Africa or East Africa, is isolated from the Middle East. There was an unbroken line of conquest that united Arabia with North Africa, from Egypt to Morocco and up into Spain. Even with initial difficulties from the fickle Berbers and political differences with the indigenous peoples (Cooley 1972: Chapters 1, 2), Islam took root among these people as Christianity, apparently, naver did. More significantly, there was a slow "arabization" of the peoples and cultures of North Africa. Not only did many of the native peoples adopt Arabic as their native language (including the Moors—who speak the Hassani dialect of Arabic—as far west and south as Mauritania), but some Arab tribes contributed to this cultural transformation by actual immigration into North Africa and the Sahara—Arab tribes migrated as far south as southern Chad,[2] and parts of Algeria, Tunis, Libya, Morocco, and the northern part of the present-day Republic of the Sudan have substantial populations of Arabs.

In East Africa, the situation was slightly different. Because of the existence of Christian Nubian kingdoms until the fourteenth century, the expansion of Islam southward (overland) from Egypt was blocked (Trimingham 1964: 37). The Arabs, however, had a navy and a sizable merchant marine fleet, and exploration, trade, and settlement soon began to take place from Somalia all the way south to Tanzania and Madagascar. For various reasons, Islam did not spread inland but remained the religion of the coastal peoples. Arab and Persian traders plied their

---

1. *Jihad,* derived from the Arabic word meaning to strive for, means, in its religious context, to strive or struggle for the cause of God and Islam. Although *jihad* can be interpreted in moral, political, or economic terms, it has most frequently been understood as a military campaign waged to defend the borders of the *dar al-Islam* or to propagate Islam among unbelievers who refuse to accept it.

2. These were the Shuwa Arabs of the southern Chad–northern Nigeria region.

trade up and down the coast. Occasionally traders would settle and marry native women and live the rest of their lives in one of these trading ports (this hybrid race along the coast was called in the local dialect *Swahili*, coastal dwellers), but they were in no sense cut off from Arabia and Persia. Ships traveled to and fro constantly, and even when these Afro-Arab settlements coalesced into city-states in the eighteenth and nineteenth centuries, just as often as not they requested their rulers to come from Arabia or Persia (Trimingham 1964: 52).

In any study of the spread of Islam, the influence of traders as missionaries of Islam is crucial, from the earliest days up to the present. Any number of well-known authors (Trimingham 1962 and 1964; Kaba 1974; Levtzion 1980) have pointed out the influence that Muslim traders have had in the spread of Islam throughout West Africa, principally through the influence they exerted on (and often through alliances subsequently formed with) the local ruling houses. With regard to this chapter, it is clear that pilgrimage would hardly have been possible without the routes and caravans of traders. My contention, however, is that, during much of the history of Islam in West Africa, the pilgrims themselves, by virtue of their royal or religious status, transmitted from Egypt and Arabia much of the thought, spirituality, or spirit of reform that they learned during their travels or their stay in the Middle East. While traders may have been the carriers of popular Islam, these pilgrims—kings or nobles or religious savants—were often those who were strongly impressed by the example or reforms of Islam in its "pure" form, that is, as found among Muslims in the Holy Places. Further, because of the pilgrims' high social status, they were able to bring about changes in Islamic belief and practice in their homelands in ways that traders never could.

The history of Islam in West Africa is entirely different from that in other parts of Africa because of the great sea of sand that separates North Africa from the Sudan.[3] The Sahara is one of the world's largest and most awesome deserts. Even with pack animals like camels, well-adapted to the climate, it has been estimated that the trip from northern Nigeria to the nearest seaport on the Mediterranean took from seventy to ninety days (Boahen 1963: 356), and this estimate assumes that there were no calamities such as sickness among the animals or humans. There has always been a high mortality rate among those who travel the Sahara. For Africans, the great fluctuations in temperature between the heat of the day and the cold of the night often brought on fever or cough. Also, the unpredictable and fierce sandstorms of the Sahara have literally buried caravans. Besides these dangers, many people and even whole caravans perished because well-known water holes and oases dried up periodically and unpredictably (Boahen 1963: 354–55).

In spite of these hazards and hardships, trade between North Africa and West Africa has been going on at least since 1000 B.C. (Boahen 1963: 350–51). With the introduction of the camel into the region around the beginning of the Christian era, trade to and from North Africa increased steadily, reaching its height from the eleventh to the sixteenth centuries (Boahen 1963: 349–50). Gold, ivory, slaves, salt, dyes, and kola nuts were taken from the Sudan. Indeed, by the fourteenth century ibn Khaldun reports that in one caravan 12,000 camels went forth from Cairo and were bound for the kingdom of Mali in West Africa (Trimingham 1962: 72).

In the latter part of the seventh century of the Christian era, the Arab Muslims had brought all of the Maghrib under their domination. Within a short time Arab and Berber Muslims also took over the caravan trade from the Maghrib to the Sudan. Because the traders were few in number, they did not effect much in the way of islamization of the Sudanese. In 1076, however, the Muslim Almoravids of Morocco subdued the kingdom of Ghana (not to be confused with the present state of Ghana, but rather a kingdom in the Senegal-Mauritania region). Two things are noteworthy of this conquest. The first is that when the Almoravids arrived in the capital of Ghana, they found that Islam was already present there as the religion of the traders (Trimingham 1962: 27–28, also 31, 53). In fact, reserved for the Muslims was a quarter of the city, complete with mosque, *madrasa* (school), and *imams* (prayer leaders). The

---

3. The word *Sudan* in this sense is not to be understood as the modern Republic of the Sudan but rather to the area south of the Sahara and, unless otherwise noted, to the area north of the tropical forest zone. Primarily, in this chapter the word will be used to mean sub-Saharan West Africa.

second fact is that the royal family of Ghana, along with some of the nobles, accepted Islam at the time of the conquest. In Ghana and in succeeding empires members of the ruling class came to embrace Islam as their own religion (although, in their official capacity, they often had to perform other non-Islamic rites, such as rites of veneration for the royal ancestors), but Islam did not become the religion of the masses. Specialists were trained who ran the schools and observed the Islamic rituals, but besides this "clerical" class and the nobility, Islam did not make much of an impact on the religious beliefs or practices of the masses (Works 1976: 6).

This elitist character of West African Islam continued into the following centuries, and the pattern of Islamic allegiance and practice was followed by the empire of Mali, which succeeded Ghana as the principal power of West Africa in the thirteenth and fourteenth centuries. J. Spencer Trimingham quotes ibn Khaldun, who writes, "The first of their Mali kings to join Islam was Baramandana who made the pilgrimage, an example followed by his successors" (1962: 62). The most famous Malian ruler to make the pilgrimage was Mansa Musa, who went to Mecca in 1324 with a retinue of 6,000 slaves, servants, and followers. According to historical sources and contemporary accounts, he was fabulously rich, carrying with him so much gold that when his party arrived in Cairo, they created a fiscal crisis by flooding the market and thus devaluing the price of gold throughout the city. The Egyptian merchants were quick to seize the advantage, however, and inflated their prices so that the Africans spent more than even they could afford. Mansa Musa and his retinue ran up large debts, and on the return trip they were accompanied by a good number of merchants who went with them to collect on the king's debts from him back in Mali. On his return trip Mansa Musa also brought with him Arab poets and adventurers (Trimingham 1962: 65). In addition, this pilgrimage apparently involved serious discussions for Mansa Musa, for he learned in Cairo that Islam does not allow the taking of free Muslim women as concubines. His pilgrimage took almost three years to complete, and it is noteworthy that Arabs were interested enough in this remote area of the Islamic world that a good number of writers

and adventurers accompanied Mansa Musa back to his kingdom. Besides Baramandana and Mansa Musa, two other emperors of Mali made the *hajj*—Mansa Ule (reigned c. 1260–1270) and Sakura (reigned c. 1290–1300). The latter was murdered on his return from Arabia.

The early period of Islam in West Africa culminated with the rise of the Songhay Empire (1493–1591). As in Mali, one of the emperors, Askiya Muhammad, made a pilgrimage well-known to Arab chroniclers. The founder of the Songhay Askiya dynasty (*askiya* is a title), Muhammad Ture ibn Abu Bakr, went to Mecca accompanied by a large number of important people from the administrative and scholarly "classes" of his empire, gave 1,000 gold dinars as alms in the holy city, and built a hostel for African pilgrims (Trimingham 1962: 98). It might be mentioned that he was not the only West African monarch to build hostels for his countrymen on pilgrimage. One monarch of the kingdom of Kanem-Bornu (in the northern Nigeria–southern Chad region) built, as early as 1242, a Maliki *madrasa*-hotel in Cairo for the comfort and instruction of Kanembu pilgrims (Trimingham 1962: 115).

There is every indication that these pilgrims, although a mere trickle of the population of West Africa, came into contact with important and influential Muslims in Arabia and Egypt. Muhammad Ture ibn Abu Bakr, mentioned above, is said to have met and talked with prominent reformers in Mecca such as Abd al-Rahman al-Suyuti and al-Majhili; this latter savant initiated one pilgrim, 'Umar ibn al'Bakka'i of the Kunta tribe, who was to become, in Trimingham's words, "the propagator of Qadiriyya in the Sahel" (Trimingham 1962: 98n).[4] He himself is said to have met with the caliph and to have been installed as caliph(?) (*'amil? wakil?*) of Songhay by the sharif of Mecca, but this story is highly suspect (al-Naqar 1972: 21–25). On the basis of his conversations with the jurist al-Siyuti, he instituted reforms regarding slaving within the empire after he returned to West Africa. Indeed, Sufism spread rapidly into the Sudanic region because of the pilgrims and the traders who came from the Maghrib. Many Sufis,

---

4. Qadiriyya is one of the largest of the Sufi brotherhoods (*tariqa*) in Africa.

in the pre-Wahhabi period,[5] chose to settle in Mecca or Medina, and they undoubtedly came into contact with many West African pilgrims. "The mystics have spiritualized the *hajj*, and spoken of the importance of the 'inner pilgrimage,' but most of them have performed this duty not only once, but many times. Some of them lived for a certain period in the sacred environment, so that Mecca was always a center where scholars from every part of the Islamic world would meet" (Schimmel n.d.: 155). It must be remembered that the people who went on the *hajj* in this early period were nobility and royalty, but the religious class that served them as scholars and *imams* also accompanied them on the pilgrimage, and this latter group was particularly sensitive to the intellectual and spiritual currents flowing through the Islamic world, and these people, with their royal patrons, were most often the agents of religious revivalistic or reform movement in their native lands (Levtzion 1979: 84). Many of the early royal pilgrims were among the most enthusiastic reformers. In 1048, Yahya b. Ibrahim recruited the Maliki scholar Abdullahi b. Yasin to instruct his people in the true religion. His rigorous instruction was not well received by Yahya b. Ibrahim's people, the Juddala, but the point here is that reform was prompted and facilitated by the combined forces of pilgrim kings and scholars (Levtzion 1979: 91).

Besides the religious activity in central West Africa (i.e., the empires of Ghana, Mali, and Songhay), the areas of Kanem-Bornu, territories loosely bordering what is now Lake Chad, were very active Muslim centers. The earliest recorded pilgrimage is that of *Mai* (a royal title) Dunama b. Umme, who between 1098 and 1150 made the pilgrimage two times and died while making his third. Over the next four centuries over twenty kings or *mai* made the pilgrimage from Kanem-Bornu to Arabia. One of the kings of Kanem-Bornu, Idris ibn Ali, did a great deal to further Islam in his kingdom and not only built a pilgrim hostel in Mecca for his countrymen but also instituted *shari'a* and *shari'a* courts in his native land. His learning was not entirely spiritual and theological, however, for we learn that on his pilgrimage to Mecca, c. 1575, he "discovered the value of firearms. He imported Turkish musketeers. Another innovation was his employment of Arab camelry" (Trimingham 1962: 122). My point here is to show that the Maghrib and the Hijaz were the focal points in the dissemination of different kinds of innovations and reforms from the Islamic heartland and that the pilgrims from the western Sudan were the agents of their dissemination. In fact, they were probably the only carriers of such ideas to the Western Sudan (although we must not overlook the influence of traders) and were, because of their high status or relation to royalty, the very agents capable of implementing change in West Africa.[6]

In 1591 Morocco sacked the capital of the Songhay empire and brought it to an end. In retrospect, this event marks the end of the first, early period of Islam and the beginning of what I shall call the middle period of Islam in West Africa, a period of decline and stagnation. To recapitulate the main features of the early period, Islam in the Sudan was characterized by its isolation from other centers of the Islamic world because of geographical factors, by its non-Arabic character, and by its confinement to the ruling elite and a clerical class. In spite of these factors, the royal and clerical pilgrims to Mecca

5. The Wahhabi movement was founded in Arabia by Muhammad ibn Abdul Wahhab (1703–1787). This is a reform movement, puritanical in the sense that it attempted to remove all innovations after the third century of Islam from Muslim belief and practice. The movement was extremely anti-Sufi, and Wahhab's polemics were aimed at the cult of the saints and all that that implied (mentioning the name of a saint in prayer, asking the saint to intercede on behalf of the suppliant, making vows to the saint in return for favors, and making pilgrimages to the tombs of saints). Wahhabism became the reigning orthodoxy on the Arabian peninsula (under the patronage of the royal house of Sa'ud), and Sufi shrines were destroyed and their practices outlawed (cf. *Shorter Encyclopedia of Islam*, 1953: 618).

6. An observer might well point out that historical records focus on the powerful and wealthy, not on the common people. While it certainly is true that historiography is traditionally elitist in its focus. I do not feel that the emphasis is misplaced in the study of West African Islam. The aristocratic class was the Muslim population during much of this period (witness the mass conversions that occurred only after the *jihads*). Also, because of the expense involved, it would be highly unlikely that commoners could afford to make the pilgrimage to Mecca, unless as a servant or companion to a noble patron.

established hostels in the Maghrib and the Hijaz and met many Muslim religious leaders whose ideas and reforms they took back with them and instituted among Muslims in their homelands.

What caused the decline of Islam in the ensuing era? Several factors can be noted, each of which had some effect. A. Adu Boahen (1963: 350) points out that political conditions in the Sudan deteriorated after the fall of Songhay. The Sudanic region was rent asunder by wars, and no central power came forward to assert itself in the midst of this chaos. With the region in a continual state of flux and unrest, the trade routes that had connected the Sudan with the Maghrib were disrupted. After all, much of the glory of the empires of Ghana, Mali, and Songhay had had its basis in the fact that these empires all served as the centers of trade routes. The empires not only were the beneficiaries of these trade routes but provided security for the caravans against bandits and opposing armies. Now there was no central authority capable of providing such security, and the trade routes dwindled and the caravans were greatly reduced in number. This last fact bears directly on pilgrimage, for many nobles and clerics accompanied trade caravans through the Sahara, not only because the traders knew the route and the oases but also because there was safety in numbers against thieves or marauders. Besides these advantages, the existence of a caravan meant that the pilgrim was spared the cost of raising a retinue to serve as his personal guard. Also, Boahen points out that the loose federation of tribes generally known as the Bambara, who had always resisted islamization and were generally hostile to Islamic kingdoms, now held sway over much of the Sudan, with no Islamic power to counteract their aggression (Boahen 1963: 350–51).

Another reason for the decline of the caravan trade was the increase of the coastal trade. The Portuguese had first appeared along the coast toward the middle of the fifteenth century, and by the sixteenth century, English, Portuguese, Spanish, Dutch, and French ships were dropping anchor off the coast and negotiating with local Africans for gold, ivory, indigo, and, most importantly, slaves. Trade that had formerly gone inland to the great trading centers in the Sudan now turned away from the savannah regions and headed, instead, to the coast. It might be added, parenthetically, that the American Indian indirectly participated in a population explo-

sion in West Africa, for many of the traders introduced New World foodstuffs into the tropical forest areas of West Africa and made those areas much more attractive for permanent settlement. Among other things, yams, maize, sweet potatoes, mangoes, beans, cassava, pineapples, tomatoes, and new forms of peppers were introduced here, creating a plentiful food supply and enticing savannah peoples to this tropical region. All of the above reasons contributed to the general decline of Islam in West Africa.

It must not be thought, however, that Islam died out at this time. To the contrary, it continued to exist, but it lacked the political base necessary for expansion, and its ties with the Islamic fatherland in Egypt and Arabia grew more and more tenuous as fewer and fewer pilgrims made the pilgrimage because of the dangers involved, to say nothing of the time and expense.

J. S. Birks makes the point that Muslim savants of this period also concocted theological formulations that denigrated the *hajj* and sometimes even claimed that it was not one of the five pillars of the faith (Birks 1978: 10). Too much, however, can be made of this theological polemic against the necessity of the *hajj*—after all, few people could read such works, and the traditional Muslim reverence for the *hajj* had certainly taken hold among the Muslims in West Africa, particularly under the influence of the Maliki school of Muslim law, which states unequivocally that it is the duty of all Muslims in good health and of proper age to make the pilgrimage to Mecca.

Furthermore, as M. Hiskett makes clear, there were centers of Islamic learning and piety that did continue in this age. Indeed, his article relating to the state of learning among the Fulani before the era of the *jihads* shows that, while the quantity of Arabic scholarship may have been small, the quality of the works of these Muslim Fulani savants was often of a high caliber. The schools continued to exist, even expand—it was the political basis of the Islamic societies that had disappeared. Other aspects of the religion continued as before. Hiskett makes the point that wandering, learned men contributed, even in this age, to the propagation of Islam and that their peregrinations were directly linked to the *hajj*: "The teaching of religious sciences was in the hands of a number of famous scholars. Sometimes these teachers were peripatetic; at other times they taught in the mosques and the schools. The peripatetic system was bound up with the pilgrimage, for the teacher passed up and down the country on his way to and from the East; and with him went his students" (1957: 573–74).

The era of the *jihads*, which started around the end of the eighteenth century, marks a significant change in the nature and form of Islam in West Africa and can be said to initiate the modern period of Islam in West Africa. There is every reason to believe that the *jihadist* reformers, both those from Futa Toro (in northern Senegal) and those from the Hausa states (in northern Nigeria), were influenced either directly or indirectly by the pilgrimage to Mecca. One of the *jihadist* leaders, a well-known reformer and Sufi, was Al-Haji 'Umar ibn Said (known more popularly as Al-Haji 'Umar Tal), who had made the pilgrimage to Mecca (1827–1830) and in Mecca or Egypt was initiated into the Tijaniyya order of Sufism. In fact, much of his subsequent activity in the western Sudan has been ascribed to his desire to overcome the influence of the Qadiriyya brotherhood (Trimingham 1962: 181); however, another famous *jihadist*, Uthman dan Fodio, had as his teacher Al-Haji Jibril ibn 'Umar, a well-known pilgrim and reformer who had spent many years in the Middle East (Levtzion 1980: 84). Other *jihadist* pilgrims deserve mention. Muhammad al-Min al Kanimi, ruler of Bornu from 1808 to 1837, made the pilgrimage before becoming ruler and later was a leader, with Uthman dan Fodio, of the *jihads* in this eastern section of West Africa. A later figure, named Muhammad al-Amin al-Sarakole, a ruler in Senegal, also made the pilgrimage and was a follower of Al-Haji 'Umar Tal and a member of the Tijaniyya. He led a short-lived *jihad* in 1885 but was defeated and killed in 1887.

The *jihads* were widespread from 1780 to 1890 throughout the entire Sudan. Although the focus in this chapter is on the western Sudan, it must not be forgotten that the Mahdist movement in the eastern Sudan (in what is today the Republic of the Sudan) in the 1880s was also an example of a *jihad*, so one can rightly say that all of the Sudan experienced this form of religious and political upheaval.

The causes of the *jihad* are difficult to determine. Hiskett seems to give primacy to religious revivalism inspired, in part, by the ferment that was moving the whole Islamic world. The eighteenth and nineteenth centuries were the time of the Sufi revival, and the founding of the influential Sanusi brotherhood

had repercussions all through the Sudan. Also, the *tariqa* (Sufi orders) known as Rashidiyya and Amirghaniyya were formed at this time under the influence of the general "neo-Sufi revival" (Rahman 1966: 206–7) and had great influence in North and Sudanic Africa. Further, the Wahhabi movement, founded in the eighteenth century, began at this time to exert influence beyond Arabia, especially via the pilgrims (Kaba 1974: 48).[7] There may certainly have been other factors that contributed to the rise of the *jihads*. Hiskett, although he favors the more religiously oriented explanations, does concede that the *jihadic* conflicts did often pit different classes and occupations on opposite sides of the conflict. For example, Al-Haji 'Umar Tal's movement attracted many escaped slaves who flocked to his cause, and the Tijaniyya brotherhood in West Africa (which Al-Haji 'Umar Tal espoused) became allied with the poorer classes in open opposition to the more aristocratic Qadiriyya brotherhood. Finally, many of the *jihads* involved different classes in opposition throughout these wars: nomads versus peasants, slaves versus enslavers, commoners versus aristocrats, and provincials versus urban intellectuals (Hiskett 1977: 166–67). Thus, under the influence of a pilgrim reformer like Al-Haji 'Umar Tal, the *jihad* was not simply a method for spreading Islam or the Tijaniyya brotherhood but the means for the most rapid and far-reaching reordering of society and social life in general that West Africa had ever before witnessed.

The consequences of the *jihads* were enormous. Not only were ruling families, classes, and states upset over the western Sudan, but Islam was enjoined on the native population as it had never been before. For the first time since it was introduced into West Africa in the tenth century, Islam was not simply the cult of the noble or clerical classes but now became, through the medium of the *jihad*, a mass religion. Islam was purified of many pagan elements that had been heretofore permitted, particularly in the Futa Toro, Futa Jallon, and Kanem-Bornu-Hausa regions, and millions of the indigenous peoples were

---

7. Also, G. S. Rentz (1969: 283) writes, "In Africa the great *jihads* of the nineteenth century, led by Uthman dan Fodio, Al-Haji 'Umar Tal, and others, were marked by striking similarities to their Arabian counterparts [i.e., the Wahhabis]."

converted to Islam. Islamic institutions and schools, the Arabic language, and the daily practice of the religion spread to almost all parts of the western Sudan.

As pointed out above, in the period prior to the time of the *jihads* the number of people going on pilgrimage had declined, a fact attributable both to the decline of Islam itself and to the decline of the caravan trade, a decline justified by new revisionist tendencies in West African Muslim theology that denigrated the *hajj*. With the revival and spread of Islam through the medium of the *jihads*, however, the institution of the *hajj* was slow to assert or reestablish itself.

The question of why the pilgrimage to Mecca did not also revive in popularity along with the revival of Islam is a difficult one. To begin with, travel conditions throughout the region were still unsettled and precarious. Not only was the western Sudan in chaos because of the *jihads* that periodically swept over large areas, but North Africa itself was experiencing a great deal of trouble and interference from European powers. At the beginning of the nineteenth century, Europeans began occupying areas along the coast of Africa, usually under the pretext of pacifying the Barbary pirates or of protecting their commercial interests. From Egypt to Morocco, Christian Europeans were making their economic and political presence felt in a way that proved most unsettling to the traditional economic and political patterns of the area. Given the rise of trade along the African coast and the turbulence in the northern countries along the Maghrib, caravan trade almost ceased to exist. Route after route closed because of the impossibility of making a profit and because of the danger involved in such expeditions. This abandonment of the caravan routes further discouraged would-be pilgrims from making the dangerous and arduous journey.

There was also a theological reason, which, like the theological reasoning of the pre-*jihadic* era, provided even normally pious Muslims with a perfectly acceptable excuse for not going on the *hajj*, namely, that waging the *jihad* was more efficacious in God's eyes than the *hajj*. Birks makes the following comment: "The *jihad* did not oust the view of abstention from pilgrimage prevailing in West Africa and, in fact, devalued the *hajj* still further: the deed of the Holy War gave heavenly rewards equal to, if not

greater than, those accruing from a visit to the Holy Places" (1978: 11). As Lansine Kaba (1974: 47) points out, there had long been an equivalence in West African Muslim thought between the *hajj* and the *jihad*, whereby it was reckoned that the sufferings and privations of the *hajj* were equivalent to the *jihad*, a striving in the way or cause of Allah.

The pilgrimage, however, certainly did not cease altogether at this time. In fact, in comparison with the pre-*jihadic* period, the number of pilgrims increased somewhat. As the desert routes closed, more and more pilgrims made the trek across the savannah from west to east and went from the area of northern Nigeria eastward to the Red Sea through southern Chad and through the northern part of what is now the country of Sudan. Birks makes the point that those who went on the pilgrimage were not the kings or nobility of yesteryear but were, rather, "religious extremists" (1978: 11). What Birks means by this phrase in unclear, but what is clear is that the *jihads* did not stop the movement of pilgrims to Mecca. The *jihadists* did not promote or encourage the use of the traditional trans-Saharan routes of pilgrimage, and because of the incorporation of many peoples as practicing Muslims, the *jihads* did have the effect of altering the types of pilgrims who now went to Mecca.

As in times past, the movement of pilgrims, even during this difficult period, facilitated the dissemination of Islamic learning from the Hijaz to West Africa. Ivor Wilks notes that in the eighteenth and early nineteenth centuries the number of pilgrims from the eastern Guinea–northern Ivory Coast increased considerably and that the Dyula towns (i.e., of the Muslim people he was studying) were prosperous enough to support many teachers "[whose] passage to and from the Hijaz would create an intellectual climate within which learning could flourish" (1978: 176). As mentioned above, some of the *jihadists* themselves, notably Al-Haji 'Umar Tal in 1827, went on the pilgrimage and returned from that experience profoundly affected by what they had seen and heard in the Holy Places.

One work from this period has recently been translated from Arabic and narrates the pilgrimage of a Moor from Mauritania who set off for the Hijaz in 1838, the middle of the *jihadic* era. The work, which has the charming title of *The Pilgrimage of Ahmed, Son of the Little Bird of Paradise*, is a journal of the pilgrim's progress through North Africa and Arabia. Being a Moor, Ahmed spoke the Hassani dialect of Arabic and thus had an immense advantage over many of his Sudanese fellow Muslims who did not speak Arabic as their mother tongue. He was both a pious and a learned man (and apparently quite rich, because on his return from Arabia he founded and endowed a *zawiya* in Fez). On his way to Arabia he passed through Fez (where he swore allegiance to Mawlay 'Abd al-Rahman, a Moroccan *shaykh* and a *sharif*, d. 1859) and Marakesh and went by sea from Morocco to Egypt. His journey was interrupted repeatedly by the French, who by now controlled the area and placed travelers in quarantine as a matter of course to control cholera and other diseases; the fact that the French thought that diseases were caused and controlled through natural means rather than through the power of God alone, noted Ahmed rather sourly, just proves that they are *kaffar* (pagan). He entered Alexandria, where he visited shrines and local *shaykhs*. After the fast during Ramadan he proceeded to Cairo, where he again visited the shrines of dead saints and talked with the scholars, *qadi*, and *mufti* in that city. Having made the pilgrimage, he made his way homeward through many of the same towns, and also visited Tripoli, Tunis "the verdant" (he skipped Algiers "because it was in the hands of the Christians"), and Gibraltar, before returning to Morocco. He was well received everywhere, even by the Christian authorities in Gibraltar, and stayed for long periods of time with each of his hosts, various *shaykhs* and *muftis*. Since he was a scholar, many of his hosts gave him books (he returned with over 400 books, all acquired on his travels, either as gifts or by purchase—and in the days before many Arabic books were produced by movable type). In all, the pilgrimage took just about six years. My point here is that Ahmed's account was probably fairly typical for many pilgrims at that time and a typical pattern of pilgrimage experienced by Africans for centuries. Not only did he deepen his faith, but he came into close and intimate contact with these cognoscenti of the Islamic world, a familiarity with them and their works that he would otherwise never have had in his out-of-the-way homeland in Mauritania. Through the pilgrimage and the contacts he made throughout North Africa and the Middle East, his intellectual and spiritual world was greatly expanded, and although the journal ends with his return to his homeland, we may assume that his tribal group and his students became the immediate beneficiaries of this *'ilm* (knowledge).

But all of West Africa was in a great state of flux. Not only were the *jihads* raging through the area at this time (the first half of the nineteenth century), but European powers were establishing permanent colonial bases where, before, there had been only trading posts or coastal enclaves. By the extension of their influence or through military means, the European powers slowly encroached on the African continent throughout the second half of the nineteenth century. Although the whole of West Africa was not pacified from the colonial point of view until almost the beginning of the Great War, by the 1880s the Europeans were confident enough of their general hegemony and respective spheres of influence that an amicable agreement could be reached at the Conference of Berlin in 1884 concerning the partition of the continent.

With regard to Islam, colonialism had several immediate and far-reaching consequences. First of all, it stopped the *jihads*. Samori, Al-Haji 'Umar Tal, and their followers were all discouraged from continuing the *jihads*, and their empires were dismantled. In a sense, then, the natural evolution of Islamic history in this area was halted. With the imposition of the colonial Pax, however, Islam spread more rapidly than ever, far faster than it had even under the impetus of the *jihads*. Muslim traders and clerics in the colonized areas had access to territories and peoples that were once closed or off-limits to them. Movement across West Africa was freer than ever, particularly into the forest zone along the coast, and as Muslims came to settle there, they made converts in greater and greater numbers. Another reason for the increase of Islam may also be laid to the fact that Muslims no longer came among "pagan" peoples as *jihadists* or as slave traders but as missionaries and as fellow Africans. People like the Bambara, who had resisted Islam for centuries, now converted rapidly in great numbers. Lastly, Africans may have felt drawn to Islam at this time as a covert protest against European domination—Islam offered literacy, a historical tradition, and a world religion that could confound European notions of African "primitiveness" and that served as a rebuke to the hordes of white missionaries swarming throughout the colonies of West Africa.

The *hajj* continued to draw increasing numbers to Mecca, albeit along slightly different routes. The colonial era witnessed the complete demise of the trans-Saharan caravan trade. The coastal cities were now the trading centers (as well as serving as the capital cities for colonial administration), and all commerce went south and west toward the coast. Birks points out that more and more desert routes were closed so that by 1911 the route from Mauritania to Fez was closed due to lack of traders (1978: 13) (along which pilgrims like Ahmed and many others had gone to Mecca, via Fez, where they could venerate the tomb of al-Tijani, founder of the Tijaniyya brotherhood). The French were so alarmed at the decrease in caravan trade (and the imminent pauperization of the Bedouins) that they forbade the transport of salt by lorries; that is, they insisted that it be transported by camel to the coastal cities. Pilgrims, then, were left with no alternative but to cross the continent from west to east along the savannah and proceed on to the Hijaz by crossing the Red Sea in boats. The British, trying to ingratiate themselves with the Muslim population under their control, sponsored pilgrimages for the members of the Muslim nobility.

All in all, the colonial powers left Islam to itself during this period. While the French were in some ways hostile to Islam (they expected that the more advanced natives would adopt Catholicism as a matter of course), the British were quite supportive of Islam, permitted *shari'a* courts in northern Nigeria to continue to rule on matters pertaining to family law in cases involving Muslims, and forbade Christian missionaries from establishing mission stations in these Muslim territories. Among Africans, the colonial presence brought about a situation in which it became a title of distinction to be called a Muslim, and many formerly oppressed classes in African society realized a new status by becoming Muslim. Elliott Skinner writing at the end of the colonial era, notes: "Today there are obvious rewards for those Mossi who embrace Islam; besides such tangible ones as getting wives and children, there are intangible ones of upward social mobility and greater prestige. It is important to note that most liberated slaves and serfs are now Moslems. Formerly these non-Mossi had low status, but today those who have been to Mecca bear such proud titles as Hadji" (1958: 1108).

With the withdrawal of the colonial powers and the coming of independence, African peoples and states entered a new era. The consequences for Islam were no less momentous than they had been during the three previous eras. Although it is still too early to discern all the forms and features of Islam in post-independence Africa, it is possible to say that the new states are very conscious of Islam and of the Muslim populations within their borders, although, no matter how strong Islam may be, it does not prevent states from trying to manipulate Islamic institutions and peoples in such ways as to promote the interests of the secular powers. In other words, many of the new African states attempt to pacify and please their Muslim subjects and to manipulate them through good and even favored treatment in much the same way that the colonial powers before them had used Islam and Muslims to their advantage. Among other things, many states encourage the Muslim majorities within their borders. Not only does this action bring a certain stability to the government, but it encourages an inter-ethnic solidarity among disparate peoples within one nation-state. Even radical socialists, such as Ahmed Sekou Toure, president of Guinea, committed their countries to a brand of socialism that they consider to be compatible with, or supportive of, a vision of Islamic socialism or an Islamic society.

One concrete way in which states show their support of Islam and their Islamic populations is to support pilgrimage flights to Mecca. Guinea, Nigeria, and Senegal all subsidize air travel to and from Jidda for those who wish to go during the month of pilgrimage. One result of this policy has been that many thousands can go to Mecca who in the past would have lacked the means or the stamina to make this demanding trip. In 1978, 135,326 pilgrims made the pilgrimage from black (non-Arab) Africa, of whom all but 47 arrived by air. From Senegal, 4,825 pilgrims went to Mecca, all but 7 of whom went by air. From Mauritania, 1,084 went on the *hajj*, and all but 8 went by air (Kingdom of Saudi Arabia, *Statistical Yearbook* 1978).

Besides the fact that many more people now go on the pilgrimage, I believe that air travel on these subsidized flights has even more profound consequences for Islam in West Africa. These trips to and from Jidda encompass a time span between two and four weeks (depending on the day the pilgrim departs from his homeland and the day that he is put aboard the plane for the return trip after the pilgrimage). The pilgrim disembarks in Jidda and, after processing by the Saudi government, is shuttled to Mecca to begin the pilgrimage, after which he is brought back to Jidda to be taken home. Without too much thought, one can see how different this type of pilgrimage is from one made by Ahmed over 150 years ago. Not only does this pilgrimage not take six years, but the intimate contacts that Ahmed made with scholars, *shaykhs, mufti,* and *qadi* in the Hijaz and North Africa are entirely absent. In days gone by, pilgrims lingered in the Holy Places and often made lesser pilgrimages to Medina and Jerusalem, besides living in the Holy Places and meeting their fellow Muslims from all over the world. Ahmed relates that, after the pilgrimage itself, he visited the graves of 'Aisha and Khadijah, wives of the Prophet, besides visiting Medina "the illumined" and praying in the Mosque of the Prophet. Such lesser pilgrimages in the Hijaz made a profound impression upon him, as did all the shrines of saints (as well as living teachers) he visited in Cairo, Alexandria, Tunis, and Fez. In short, what was once a pious peregrination through the sacred places of Islam has now been reduced to a shuttle flight from a West African entrepot to Jidda with just enough time to perform the pilgrimage rites before being shunted onto a return flight to West Africa.

As we have seen throughout this chapter, the pilgrimage to Mecca has provided Muslims in West Africa with contact with the heartland of Islam for 1,000 years, and the great revival and reform movements of the Islamic world were brought back and incorporated into West African Islam through the medium of pilgrims. In short, the function of the pilgrimage was pedagogical as well as pious, and this pedagogical aspect or function is the one that has been lost under the present circumstances. In the eighteenth century the influence of the Wahhabi movement had been felt by many of the pilgrims who had lingered in the Hijaz and had been influenced or instructed by the Wahhabi *'ulama*; in turn, they had gone back to West Africa with a burning desire to reform Islam. Today, however, such influences and pedagogy would be lost on pilgrims who do not remain in Arabia long enough to perfect their spoken Arabic and who must subdue their educational and pious interests to the exigencies of airline schedules.

The centers of Islam, however, have not relinquished their self-imposed duty to foster and propagate Islam. To the contrary. But it is no longer the pilgrimage or the pilgrim who is the focus or medium of propaganda. No longer do pilgrims return to the western Sudan with a newfound familiarity with Islamic trends or thought that they gleaned from Saudi Arabia, nor do pilgrims inspire the reform movements in the Western Sudan as they once did. The pedagogical function of the pilgrimage has ceased to exist among the pilgrims from West Africa (and from many other parts of the world).

Instead, as Tareq Ismael and others have pointed out, in the post-colonial period various Islamic countries have taken upon themselves the duty of propagating Islam south of the Sahara by different means. The leader in this field was Egypt, and its effort was initiated after Nasser's coup. Shortly after Nasser became president of Egypt, he, along with King Saud of Arabia and Ghulan Muhammed of Pakistan, established Egypt's leadership in Muslim affairs in Africa (Ismael 1971: 147–48). More specifically, the educational institutions of Egypt were used to promote Islamic religion and Arabic culture south of the Sahara. In the law of the Reorganization of Al-Azhar University, one of the oldest in the Islamic world, it states that Al-Azhar "carries the burden of Islamic missions to all nations and works to expose the truth of Islam" (Ismael 1971: 149). The rector of that university, Sheik Hassan Ma'amun, declared that "the most prominent role of Al-Azhar is the international call to Islam, its propagation of the Holy Koran, the Arabic language and religious jurisprudence among people who do not speak the language of the Holy Book" (Ismael 1971: 151). Under the direction of Nasser, Egypt greatly increased its commitment to educating students at Al-Azhar and at secular universities. In 1952–1953, the last year of the old regime, 15,000 Egyptian pounds were expended for scholarships for foreign students. By 1963–1964, this sum had risen to 375,000 Egyptian pounds (Ismael 1971: 151). Saudi Arabia also expanded its number of foreign students, and although the records of Libya are not open to the public, I would guess that Colonel Qadaffi's expenditure for foreign students to study Islam in Libya far exceeds Saudi Arabia's and Egypt's earlier contributions.

Besides encouraging students to come to Egypt to study, Al-Azhar established in 1963 Islamic Arab missions throughout Africa. These were complexes consisting of grammar and secondary schools, a mosque, and a small infirmary run by qualified *'ulama* from Al-Azhar. In other words, Egypt under Nasser undertook an ambitious program of missionary activity throughout sub-Saharan Africa. In interviews I conducted with various leaders of the Sierra Leone Muslim Brotherhood, it was reported to me that during the sixties several hundred Egyptian teachers came to teach in the Brotherhood schools throughout Sierra Leone (note that this Muslim Brotherhood has no relation to the militant Egyptian organization but is, rather, an educational and missionary society founded by Sierra Leone. At the present time there are about a dozen Egyptian teachers still in Sierra Leone.[8]

Thus, while the convenience of modern transportation has effectively ruined the pilgrimage as a vehicle for teaching pilgrims about the nature of Islam in the Middle East, this function has been taken over, with the help of oil money and an increased consciousness of the *dar al-Islam,* by the countries of Saudi Arabia, Egypt, and Libya. Because of the need to limit the scope of this chapter, I have not even mentioned the educational activities of such movements as the Ahmadiyyah movement,[9] but they are of increasing importance in their role of informing Islamic consciousness in West Africa, Asia, and the Caribbean. For almost 1,000 years the pilgrim transmitted currents of Islamic teaching, spiritual life, legal interpretation, and reform from Egypt and Arabia back to West Africa. What was once the function of pilgrims returning from the *hajj*—to teach, to institute reforms, to spread Islam throughout West Africa—has now been taken over by foreign Muslim missionaries or by African Muslim students who have returned from their formal studies in Egypt, Arabia, or North Africa.

In conclusion, I think that it is now clear that the *hajj* has served different functions in the life of West African Muslims. Its primary function, which occupied the place of paramount importance until the

modern era, was the diffusion or dissemination of Islam from its intellectual and spiritual capitals in North Africa and the Middle East back to West Africa. Because the pilgrimage was, in effect, a migration of an elite, they were capable of reorganizing their society and religious practices so that they conformed to what they had learned or seen on pilgrimage. For much of the history of West Africa, the pilgrimage was the medium by which these African Muslim elites (both clerical and aristocratic) were informed of movements and developments in the *dar al-Islam,* and they, in turn, were the media for the dissemination of such ideas throughout West Africa.

It is significant that the post-colonial era has greatly changed the nature and function of the Islamic pilgrimage for West Africa. No longer is the *hajj* restricted to aristocrats and their cleric escorts. Masses of West Africans are flown to and from Jidda and spend only the month of pilgrimage in Arabia. Clearly, the mode of transportation and the almost unseemly haste with which the Saudi government processes the pilgrims in, through, and out of the country have also radically changed the experience and importance of pilgrimage for West African Islam. What was once the great source of education and inspiration for Islam in the western Sudan has been replaced by the education of Muslim students in North Africa and Near Eastern countries. I would predict that these young students will be the agents of the dissemination of Islamic thought and practice as the pilgrims once were in West Africa.

In general, the *hajj* in the context of West African Islam can be seen as a vehicle for the diffusion of religious and cultural concepts and practices. Thus, while the pilgrimage always served a religious end for those who participated in it, because of the knowledge, books, Sufi initiation, or whatever else they acquired in the Holy Places, the pilgrims themselves served as the conduit through which these were spread throughout West Africa. Thus, the emphasis in this chapter has been on the pedagogical function of pilgrimage in the spread of religion and culture. One crucial factor in this study of pilgrimage is the participation of elites. West African Islamic elites made the pilgrimage to Mecca for a variety of reasons, most of them probably rooted in their Muslim piety, but the pilgrimage itself greatly enhanced their status and prestige. In addition, as

8. This information is from my research in Sierra Leone, 1979–1980.
9. A good discussion of the Ahmadiyyah movement in West Africa can be found in H. J. Fisher, *Ahmadiyyah: A Study in Contemporary Islam on the West African Coast.*

mentioned before, because of their aristocratic status, whatever may have inspired them in the Hijaz might be instituted in their homelands. The migration of elites via pilgrimage can be seen in historical perspective as the thread that has tied together the Islamic world north and south of the Sahara. Without it West African Islam would have had a very different history and character.

Finally, I would like to suggest that the discussion of the *hajj* presented in this chapter may be of some interest in the wider context of the anthropology of pilgrimage. Perhaps the most interesting point in that light might refer to the functions that the *hajj* has played over time. Although it served originally as the means for the diffusion of Islamic religion and culture, it now serves different, more individual functions. Yet the *hajj* continues, its popularity unabated. The institution has persevered regardless of the function it has served or serves, collectively or individually. To be sure, the attraction of the *hajj* may ultimately lie beyond any social benefits that accrue to the participants. It may rest instead in the fundamental religious sensibility of the pilgrims, who sing as they approach the Sacred Mosque at the start of the *hajj*: "I am here, O God, I am here; at Thy command, I am here."

47

Revitalization Movements

Anthony F. C. Wallace

Wallace's article shows how people use religious principles to cope with a cultural crisis that has prevented them from achieving a more satisfying culture. Revitalization movements have been witnessed frequently in diverse geographic regions, and each displays variation of expression that may be explained by the culturally specific conditions under which they are formed. As a social process, they have the goal of reconstituting a way of life that has been destroyed for one reason or another. Wallace helps us understand the phenomenon of revitalization by describing five overlapping but distinct stages. A revitalization movement, unlike cultural evolution and historical change, is a relatively abrupt culture change that frequently completes itself in the span of a few years.

During the middle decades of the 20th century, Wallace was one of the most prominent anthropologists working in the areas of cognition and psychology. He was particularly interested in the psychological effects of acculturation and rapid technological change. These interests are clearly apparent in the present article when he discusses "mazeway resynthesis" and "hysterical conversion," concepts that highlight the psychological aspects of abrupt social change. Wallace (b. 1923) has been a prolific author. His most acclaimed book is Rockdale: The Growth of an American Village in the Industrial Revolution *(New York: Knopf, 1978).*

During periods of stable moving equilibrium, the sociocultural system is subject to mild but measurable oscillations in degree of organization. From time to time, however, most societies undergo more violent fluctuations in this regard. Such fluctuation is of peculiar importance in culture change because it often culminates in relatively sudden change in cultural *Gestalt*. We refer, here, to revitalization movements, which we define as deliberate and organized attempts by some members of a society to construct a more satisfying culture by rapid acceptance of a pattern of multiple innovations (Wallace 1956b; Mead 1956).

The severe disorganization of a sociocultural system may be caused by the impact of any one or combination of a variety of forces that push the system

Reprinted from Anthony F. C. Wallace, CULTURE AND PERSONALITY, 2nd ed. (New York: Random House, 1970), pp. 188–99, by permission of the publisher and the author.

beyond the limits of equilibrium. Some of these forces are climatic or faunal changes, which destroy the economic basis of its existence; epidemic disease, which grossly alters the population structure; wars, which exhaust the society's resources of manpower or result in defeat or invasion; internal conflict among interest groups, which results in extreme disadvantage for at least one group; and, very commonly, a position of perceived subordination and inferiority with respect to an adjacent society. The latter, by the use of more or less coercion (or even no coercion at all, as in situations where the mere example set by the dominant society raises too-high levels of aspiration), brings about uncoordinated cultural changes. Under conditions of disorganization, the system, from the standpoint of at least some of its members, is unable to make possible the reliable satisfaction of certain values that are held to be essential to continued well-being and self-respect. The mazeway of a culturally disillusioned person, accordingly, is an image of a world that is unpredictable, or barren in its simplicity, or both, and is apt to contain severe identity conflict. His mood (depending on the precise nature of the disorganization) will be one of panic-stricken anxiety, shame, guilt, depression, or apathy.

An example of the kind of disorganization to which we refer is given by the two thousand or so Seneca Indians of New York at the close of the eighteenth century. Among these people, a supreme value attached to the conception of the absolutely free and autonomous individual, unconstrained by and indifferent to his own and alien others' pain and hardship. This individual was capable of free indulgence of emotional impulses but, in crisis, freely subordinated his own wishes to the needs of his community. Among the men, especially, this ego-ideal was central in personality organization. Men defined the roles of hunting, of warfare, and of statesmanship as the conditions of achievement of this value; thus the stereotypes of "the good hunter," "the brave warrior," and "the forest statesman" were the images of masculine success. But the forty-three years from 1754, when the French and Indian War began, to 1797, when the Seneca sold their last hunting grounds and became largely confined to tiny, isolated reservations, brought with them changes in their situation that made achievement of these ideals virtually impossible. The good hunter could no longer hunt: the game was scarce, and it was almost suicidally dangerous to stray far from the reservation among the numerous hostile white men. The brave warrior could no longer fight, being undersupplied, abandoned by his allies, and his women and children threatened by growing military might of the United States. The forest statesman was an object of contempt, and this disillusionment was perhaps more shattering than the rest. The Iroquois chiefs, for nearly a century, had been able to play off British and French, then Americans and British, against one another, extorting supplies and guarantees of territorial immunity from both sides. They had maintained an extensive system of alliances and hegemonies among surrounding tribal groups. Suddenly they were shorn of their power. White men no longer spoke of the League of the Iroquois with respect; their western Indian dependents and allies regarded them as cowards for having made peace with the Americans.

The initial Seneca response to the progress of sociocultural disorganization was quasipathological: many became drunkards; the fear of witches increased; squabbling factions were unable to achieve a common policy. But a revitalization movement developed in 1799, based on the religious revelations reported by one of the disillusioned forest statesmen, one Handsome Lake, who preached a code of patterned religious and cultural reform. The drinking of whiskey was proscribed; witchcraft was to be stamped out; various outmoded rituals and prevalent sins were to be abandoned. In addition, various syncretic cultural reforms, amounting to a reorientation of the socioeconomic system, were to be undertaken, including the adoption of agriculture (hitherto a feminine calling) by the men, and the focusing of kinship responsibilities within the nuclear family (rather than in the clan and lineage). The general acceptance of Handsome Lake's Code, within a few years, wrought seemingly miraculous changes. A group of sober, devout, partly literate, and technologically up-to-date farming communities suddenly replaced the demoralized slums in the wilderness (Wallace 1970).

Such dramatic transformations are, as a matter of historical fact, very common in human history, and probably have been the medium of as much culture change as the slower equilibrium processes. Furthermore, because they compress into such a short space of time such extensive changes in pattern, they are somewhat easier to record than the quiet serial changes during periods of equilibrium. In general, revitalization processes share a common process structure that can be conceptualized as a pattern of temporally overlapping, but functionally distinct, stages:

I. *Steady State.* This is a period of moving equilibrium of the kind discussed in the preceding section. Culture change occurs during the steady state, but is of the relatively slow and chainlike kind. Stress levels vary among interest groups, and there is some oscillation in organization level, but disorganization and stress remain within limits tolerable to most individuals. Occasional incidents of intolerable stress may stimulate a limited "correction" of the system, but some incidence of individual ill-health and criminality are accepted as a price society must pay.

II. *The Period of Increased Individual Stress.* The sociocultural system is being "pushed" progressively out of equilibrium by the forces described earlier: climatic and biotic change, epidemic disease, war and conquest, social subordination, acculturation, internally generated decay, and so forth. Increasingly large numbers of individuals are placed under what is to them intolerable stress by the failure of the system to accommodate the satisfaction of their needs. Anomie and disillusionment become widespread, as the culture is perceived to be disorganized and inadequate; crime and illness increase sharply in frequency as individualistic asocial responses. But the situation is still generally defined as one of fluctuation within the steady state.

III. *The Period of Cultural Distortion.* Some members of the society attempt, piecemeal and ineffectively, to restore personal equilibrium by adopting socially dysfunctional expedients. Alcoholism, venality in public officials, the "black market," breaches of sexual and kinship mores, hoarding, gambling for gain, "scapegoating," and similar behaviors that, in the preceding period, were still defined as individual deviances, in effect become institutionalized efforts to circumvent the evil effects of "the system." Interest groups, losing confidence in the advantages of maintaining mutually acceptable interrelationships, may resort to violence in order to coerce others into unilaterally advantageous behavior. Because of the malcoordination of cultural changes during this period, they are rarely able to reduce the impact of the forces that have pushed the society out of equilibrium, and in fact lead to a continuous decline in organization.

IV. *The Period of Revitalization.* Once severe cultural distortion has occurred, the society can with difficulty return to steady state without the institution of a revitalization process. Without revitalization, indeed, the society is apt to disintegrate as a system: the population will either die off, splinter into autonomous groups, or be absorbed into another, more stable, society. Revitalization depends on the successful completion of the following functions:

1. Formulation of a code. An individual, or a group of individuals, constructs a new, utopian image of sociocultural organization. This model is a blueprint of an ideal society or "goal culture." Contrasted with the goal culture is the existing culture, which is presented as inadequate or evil in certain respects. Connecting the existing culture and the goal culture is a transfer culture: a system of operations that, if faithfully carried out, will transform the existing culture into the goal culture. Failure to institute the transfer operations will, according to the code, result in either the perpetuation of the existing misery or the ultimate destruction of the society (if not of the whole world). Not infrequently in primitive societies the code, or the core of it, is formulated by one individual in the course of a hallucinatory revelation; such prophetic experiences are apt to launch religiously oriented movements, since the source of the revelation is apt to be regarded as a supernatural being. Nonhallucinatory formulations usually are found in politically oriented movements. In either case, the formulation of the code constitutes a reformulation of the author's own mazeway and often brings to him a renewed confidence in the future and a remission of the complaints he experienced before. It may be suggested that such mazeway resynthesis processes are merely extreme forms of the reorganizing dream processes that seem to be associated with REM (rapid-eye-movement) sleep, which are necessary to normal health.

2. Communication. The formulators of the code preach the code to other people in an evangelistic spirit. The aim of the communication is to make converts. The code is offered as the means of spiritual salvation for the individual and of cultural salvation for the society. Promises of benefit to the target population need not be immediate or materialistic, for the basis of the code's appeal is the attractiveness of identification with a more highly organized system, with all that this implies in the way of self-respect. Indeed, in view of the extensiveness of the changes in values often implicit in such codes, appeal to currently held values would often be pointless. Religious codes offer spiritual salvation, identification with God, elect status; political codes offer honor, fame, the respect of society for sacrifices made in its interest. But refusal to accept the code is usually defined as placing the listener in immediate spiritual, as well as material, peril with respect to his existing values. In small societies, the target population may be the entire community; but in more complex societies, the message may be aimed only at certain

groups deemed eligible for participation in the transfer and goal cultures.

3. Organization. The code attracts converts. The motivations that are satisfied by conversion, and the psychodynamics of the conversion experience itself, are likely to be highly diverse, ranging from the mazeway resynthesis characteristic of the prophet, and the hysterical conviction of the "true believer," to the calculating expediency of the opportunist. As the group of converts expands, it differentiates into two parts: a set of disciples and a set of mass followers. The disciples increasingly become the executive organization, responsible for administering the evangelistic program, protecting the formulator, combatting heresy, and so on. In this role, the disciples increasingly become full-time specialists in the work of the movement. The tri-cornered relationship between the formulators, the disciples, and the mass followers is given an authoritarian structure, even without the formalities of older organizations, by the charismatic quality of the formulator's image. The formulator is regarded as a man to whom, from a supernatural being or from some other source of wisdom unavailable to the mass, a superior knowledge and authority has been vouchsafed that justifies his claim to unquestioned belief and obedience from his followers.

In the modern world, with the advantages of rapid transportation and ready communication, the simple charismatic model of cult organization is not always adequate to describe many social and religious movements. In such programs as Pentecostalism, Black Power, and the New Left, there is typically a considerable number of local or special issue groups loosely joined in what Luther Gerlach has called an "acephalous, segmentary, reticulate organization" (1968). Each segment may be, in effect, a separate revitalization organization of the simple kind described above; the individual groups differ in details of code, in emotional style, in appeal to different social classes; and, since the movement as a whole has no single leader, it is relatively immune to repression, the collapse of one or several segments in no way invalidating the whole. This type of movement organization is singularly well adapted to predatory expansion; but it may eventually full under the domination of one cult or party (as was the case, for instance, in Germany when the SS took over the fragmented Nazi party, which in turn was heir to a large number of nationalist groups, and as is the case when a Communist party apparatus assumes control of a revolutionary popular front).

4. Adaptation. Because the movement is a revolutionary organization (however benevolent and humane the ultimate values to which it subscribes), it threatens the interests of any group that obtains advantage, or believes it obtains advantage, from maintaining or only moderately reforming the status quo. Furthermore, the code is never complete; new inadequacies are constantly being found in the existing culture, and new inconsistencies, predicative failures, and ambiguities discovered in the code itself (some of the latter being pointed out by the opposition). The response of the code formulators and disciples is to rework the code, and, if necessary, to defend the movement by political and diplomatic maneuver, and, ultimately, by force. The general tendency is for codes to harden gradually, and for the tone of the movement to become increasingly nativistic and hostile both toward nonparticipating fellow members of society, who will ultimately be defined as "traitors," and toward "national enemies."

True revolutions, as distinguished from mere coups d'état, which change personnel without changing the structure, require that the revitalization movement of which they are the instrument add to its code a morality sanctioning subversion or even violence. The leadership must also be sophisticated in its knowledge of how to mobilize an increasingly large part of the population to their side, and of how to interfere with the mobilization of the population by the establishment. The student of such processes can do no better than to turn to the works of contemporary practitioners such as Che Guevara and Mao Tse Tung for authoritative explications and examples of the revolutionary aspect of revitalization.

5. Cultural transformation. If the movement is able to capture both the adherence of a substantial proportion of a local population and, in complex societies, of the functionally crucial apparatus (such as power and communications networks, water supply, transport systems, and military establishment), the transfer culture and, in some cases, the goal culture itself, can be put into operation. The revitalization, if successful, will be attended by the drastic decline of the quasi-pathological individual symptoms of anomie and by the disappearance of the cultural distortions. For such a revitalization to be

accomplished, however, the movement must be able to maintain its boundaries from outside invasion, must be able to obtain internal social conformity without destructive coercion, and must have a successful economic system.

6. Routinization. If the preceding functions are satisfactorily completed, the functional reasons for the movement's existence as an innovative force disappear. The transfer culture, if not the goal culture, is operating of necessity with the participation of a large proportion of the community. Although the movement's leaders may resist the realization of the fact, the movement's function shifts from the role of innovation to the role of maintenance. If the movement was heavily religious in orientation, its legacy is a cult or church that preserves and reworks the code, and maintains, through ritual and myth, the public awareness of the history and values that brought forth the new culture. If the movement was primarily political, its organization is routinized into various stable decision-making and morale-and-order-maintaining functions (such as administrative offices, police, and military bodies). Charisma can, to a degree, be routinized, but its intensity diminishes as its functional necessity becomes, with increasing obviousness, outmoded.

V. *The New Steady State.* With the routinization of the movement, a new steady state may be said to exist. Steady-state processes of culture change continue; many of them are in areas where the movement has made further change likely. In particular, changes in the value structure of the culture may lay the basis for long-continuing changes (such as the train of economic and technological consequences of the dissemination of the Protestant ethic after the Protestant Reformation). Thus in addition to the changes that the movement accomplishes during its active phase, it may control the direction of the subsequent equilibrium processes by shifting the values that define the cultural focus. The record of the movement itself, over time, gradually is subject to distortion, and eventually is enshrined in myths and rituals which elevate the events that occurred, and persons who acted, into quasi- or literally divine status.

Two psychological mechanisms seem to be of peculiar importance in the revitalization process:

mazeway resynthesis (Wallace 1956a) and hysterical conversion. The resynthesis is most dramatically exemplified in the career of the prophet who formulates a new religious code during a hallucinatory trance. Typically, such persons, after suffering increasing depreciation of self-esteem as the result of their inadequacy to achieve the culturally ideal standards, reach a point of either physical or drug-induced exhaustion, during which a resynthesis of values and beliefs occurs. The resynthesis is, like other innovations, a recombination of preexisting configurations; the uniqueness of this particular process is the suddenness of conviction, the trance-like state of the subject, and the emotionally central nature of the subject matter. There is some reason to suspect that such dramatic resyntheses depend on a special biochemical milieu, accompanying the "stage of exhaustion" of the stress (in Selye's sense) syndrome, or on a similar milieu induced by drugs. But comparable resyntheses are, of course, sometimes accomplished more slowly, without the catalytic aid of extreme stress or drugs. This kind of resynthesis produces, apparently, a permanent alteration of mazeway: the new stable cognitive configuration, is, as it were, constructed out of the materials of earlier configurations, which, once rearranged, cannot readily reassemble into the older forms.

The hysterical conversion is more typical of the mass follower who is repeatedly subjected to suggestion by a charismatic leader and an excited crowd. The convert of this type may, during conversion display various dissociative behaviors (rage, speaking in tongues, rolling on the ground, weeping, and so on). After conversion, his overt behavior may be in complete conformity with the code to which he has been exposed. But his behavior has changed not because of a radical resynthesis, but because of the adoption under suggestion of an additional social personality which temporarily replaces, but does not destroy, the earlier. He remains, in a sense, a case of multiple personality and is liable, if removed from reinforcing symbols, to lapse into an earlier social personality. The participant in the lynch mob or in the camp meeting revival is a familiar example of this type of convert. But persons can be maintained in this state of hysterical conversion for months or years, if the "trance" is continuously maintained by the symbolic environment (flags, statues, portraits, songs, and so on) and continuous suggestions (speeches, rallies, and so on). The most familiar contemporary example is the German under Hitler who participated in the Nazi genocide program, but reverted to *Gemütlichkeit* when the war ended. The difference between the resynthesized person and the converted one does not lie in the nature of the codes to which they subscribe (they may be the same), but in the blandness and readiness of the hysterical convert to revert, as compared to the almost paranoid intensity and stability of the resynthesized prophet. A successful movement, by virtue of its ability to maintain suggestion continuously for years, is able to hold the hysterical convert indefinitely, or even to work a real resynthesis by repeatedly forcing him, after hysterical conversion, to reexamine his older values and beliefs and to work through to valid resynthesis, sometimes under considerable stress. The Chinese Communists, for instance, apparently have become disillusioned by hysterical conversions and have used various techniques, some coercive and some not, but all commonly lumped together as "brain-washing" in Western literature, to induce valid resynthesis. The aim of these communist techniques, like those of the established religions, is, literally, to produce a "new man."

It is impossible to exaggerate the importance of these two psychological processes for culture change, for they make possible the rapid substitution of a new cultural *Gestalt* for an old, and thus the rapid cultural transformation of whole populations. Without this mechanism, the cultural transformation of the 600,000,000 people of China by the Communists could not have occurred; nor the Communist-led revitalization and expansion of the USSR; nor the American Revolution; nor the Protestant Reformation; nor the rise and spread of Christianity, Mohammedanism, and Buddhism. In the written historical record, revitalization movements begin with Ikhnaton's ultimately disastrous attempt to establish a new, monotheistic religion in Egypt; they are found, continent by continent, in the history of all human societies, occurring with frequency proportional to the pressures to which the society is subjected. For small tribal societies, in chronically extreme situations, movements may develop every ten or fifteen years; in stable complex cultures, the rate of a societywide movement may be one every two or three hundred years.

In view of the frequency and geographical diversity of revitalization movements it can be expected that their content will be extremely varied, corresponding to the diversity of situational contexts and cultural backgrounds in which they develop. Major culture areas are, over extended periods of time, associated with particular types: New Guinea and Melanesia, during the latter part of the nineteenth and the twentieth centuries, have been the home of the well-known "cargo cults." The most prominent feature of these cults is the expectation that the ancestors soon will arrive in a steamship, bearing a cargo of the white man's goods, and will lead a nativistic revolution culminating in the ejection of European masters. The Indians of the eastern half of South America for centuries after the conquest set off on migrations for the *terre sans mal* where a utopian way of life, free of Spaniards and Portuguese, would be found; North American Indians of the eighteenth and nineteenth centuries were prone to revivalistic movements such as the Ghost Dance, whose adherents believed that appropriate ritual and the abandonment of the sins of the white man would bring a return of the golden age before contact; South Africa has been the home of the hundreds of small, enthusiastic, separatist churches that have broken free of the missionary organizations. As might be expected, a congruence evidently exists between the cultural *Anlage* and the content of movement, which, together with processes of direct and stimulus diffusion, accounts for the tendency for movements to fall into areal types (Burridge 1960).

48

The Ghost Dance Religion

Alice Beck Kehoe

During the late 1860s, a Northern Paiute Indian named Wodziwob ("white hair") experienced several visions telling him to create the Ghost Dance religion. By following Wodziwob's vision-revealed instructions, the Indians would hasten the day when white people would disappear, dead Indians would live again, and the old Indian way of life would return. The movement experienced early success and quickly expanded from the Great Basin area into California and Oregon but eventually faltered. In 1889, years after Wodziwob's religion had died, a second and more extensive Ghost Dance movement began, this time led by another Paiute Indian, Jack Wilson, or, in the Paiute language, Wovoka ("the woodcutter"). In this selection, Alice Beck Kehoe describes Wovoka's early life with David Wilson, an Anglo rancher, and his family, as well as his preaching as a young adult and his 1889 vision that resulted in his becoming a prophet. Kehoe believes that the Ghost Dance religion was a complete religion and that its basic message, though aimed primarily at Indians, was applicable to all people of goodwill. Wovoka's gospel was especially appealing to the Indians, who in 1889 were suffering from persecution by the whites, epidemics, loss of their economic resources and lands, and continuing attempts to eradicate their customs and beliefs. The Ghost Dance religion spread to the tribes of the Northwest, eventually reaching the plains from Oklahoma to Canada. The religion came to a violent end for the Sioux in late December 1890, with the killing of 370 Indians at Wounded Knee.

New Year's Day, 1892. Nevada.

A wagon jounces over a maze of cattle trails crisscrossing a snowy valley floor. In the wagon, James Mooney, from the Smithsonian Institution in faraway Washington, D.C., is looking for the Indian messiah, Wovoka, blamed for riling up the Sioux, nearly three hundred of whom now lie buried by Wounded Knee Creek in South Dakota. The men in the wagon see a man with a gun over his shoulder walking in the distance.

"I believe that's Jack now!" exclaims one of Mooney's guides. "Jack Wilson," he calls to the messiah, whose Paiute name is Wovoka. Mooney's other guide, Charley Sheep, Wovoka's uncle, shouts to his nephew in the Paiute language. The hunter comes over to the wagon.

"I saw that he was a young man," Mooney recorded, "a dark full-blood, compactly built, and taller than the Paiute generally, being nearly 6 feet in height. He was well dressed in white man's clothes, with the broad-brimmed white felt hat common in the west, secured on his head by means of a beaded ribbon under the chin. . . . He wore a good pair of boots. His hair was cut off square on a line below the base of the ears, after the manner of his tribe. His countenance was open and expressive of firmness and decision" (Mooney [1896] 1973: 768–69).

That evening, James Mooney formally interviewed Jack Wilson in his home, a circular lodge ten feet in diameter, built of bundles of tule reeds tied to a pole frame. In the middle of the lodge, a bright fire of sagebrush stalks sent sparks flying out of the wide smoke hole. Several other Paiutes were with Jack, his wife, baby, and little son when Mooney arrived with a guide and an interpreter. Mooney noticed that although all the Paiutes dressed in "white man's" clothes, they preferred to live in traditional wicki-ups. Only Paiute baskets furnished Jack Wilson's home; no beds, no storage trunks, no pots or pans, nothing of alien manufacture except the hunting gun and knife lay in the wickiup, though the family could have bought the invaders' goods. Jack had steady employment as a ranch laborer, and from his wages he could have constructed a cabin and lived in it, sitting on chairs and eating bread and beef from metal utensils. Instead, Jack and Mary, his wife, wanted to follow the ways of their people as well as they could in a valley overrun with Euro-American settlement. The couple hunted, fished, and gathered pine nuts and other seeds and wild plants. They practiced their Paiute religion rather than the Pres-byterian Christianity Jack's employer insisted on teaching them. Mooney was forced to bring a Euro-American settler, Edward Dyer, to interpret for him because Jack would speak only his native Paiute, though he had some familiarity with English. This was Mason Valley, in the heart of Paiute territory, and for Jack and Mary it was still Paiute.

Jack Wilson told Mooney that he had been born four years before the well-remembered battle be-tween Paiutes and American invaders at Pyramid Lake. The battle had been touched off by miners seiz-ing two Paiute women. The men of the Paiute com-munity managed to rescue the two women. No harm was done to the miners, but they claimed they were victims of an "Indian outrage," raised a large party of their fellows, and set off to massacre the Paiutes. Expecting trouble, the Paiute men ambushed the mob of miners at a narrow pass, and although armed mostly with only bows and arrows, killed nearly fifty of the mob, routing the rest and saving the fam-ilies in the Indian camp. Jack Wilson's father, Tavibo, was a leader of the Paiute community at that time. He was recognized as spiritually blessed—gifted and trained to communicate with invisible powers. By means of this gift, carefully cultivated, Tavibo was said to be able to control the weather.

Tavibo left the community when his son Wovoka was in his early teens, and the boy was taken on by David Wilson, a Euro-American rancher with sons of his own close in age to the Paiute youth. Though employed as a ranch hand, Wovoka was strongly en-couraged to join the Wilson family in daily prayers and Bible reading, and Jack, as he came to be called, became good friends with the Wilson boys. Through these years with the Wilsons, Jack's loyalty to, and pride in, his own Paiute people never wavered. When he was about twenty, he married a Paiute woman who shared his commitment to the Paiute way of life. With his wages from the ranch, Jack and Mary bought the hunting gun and ammunition, good-quality "white man's" clothes, and ornaments suited to their dignity as a respected younger couple in the Mason Valley community.

As a young adult, Jack Wilson began to develop a reputation as a weather doctor like his father. Paiute believe that a young person lacks the maturity and inner strength to function as a spiritual agent, but Jack was showing the self-discipline, sound judg-ment, and concern for others that marked Indians gifted as doctors in the native tradition. Jack led the circle dances through which Paiute opened them-selves to spiritual influence. Moving always along the path of the sun—clockwise to the left—men, women, and children joined hands in a symbol of the community's living through the circle of the days. As they danced they listened to Jack Wilson's songs celebrating the Almighty and Its wondrous manifes-tations: the mountains, the clouds, snow, stars, trees, antelope. Between dances, the people sat at Jack's feet, listening to him preach faith in universal love.

The climax of Jack's personal growth came dur-ing a dramatic total eclipse of the sun on January 1, 1889. He was lying in his wickiup very ill with a fever. Paiute around him saw the sky darkening al-though it was midday. Some monstrous force was overcoming the sun! People shot off guns at the ap-parition, they yelled, some wailed as at a death. Jack Wilson felt himself losing consciousness. It seemed to him he was taken up to heaven and brought be-fore God. God gave him a message to the people of earth, a gospel of peace and right living. Then he and the sun regained their normal life.

Jack Wilson was now a prophet. Tall, handsome, with a commanding presence, Jack already was re-spected for his weather control power. (The unusual snow blanketing Mason Valley when James Mooney visited was said to be Jack's doing.) Confidence in his God-given mission further enhanced Jack

Wilson's reputation. Indians came from other districts to hear him, and even Mormon settlers in Nevada joined his audiences. To carry out his mission, Jack Wilson went to the regional Indian agency at Pyramid Lake and asked one of the employees to prepare and mail a letter to the President of the United States, explaining the Paiute doctor's holy mission and suggesting that if the United States government would send him a small regular salary, he would convey God's message to all the people of Nevada and, into the bargain, make it rain whenever they wished. The agency employee never sent the letter. It was agency policy to "silently ignore" Indians' efforts toward "notoriety." The agent would not even deign to meet the prophet.

Jack Wilson did not need the support of officials. His deep sincerity and utter conviction of his mission quickly persuaded every open-minded hearer of its importance. Indians came on pilgrimages to Mason Valley, some out of curiosity, others seeking guidance and healing in that time of afflictions besetting their peoples. Mormons came too, debating whether Jack Wilson was the fulfillment of a prophecy of their founder, Joseph Smith, Jr., that the Messiah would appear in human form in 1890. Jack Wilson himself consistently explained that he was *a* messiah *like* Jesus but not the Christ of the Christians. Both Indians and Euro-Americans tended to ignore Jack's protestations and to identify him as "the Christ." Word spread that the Son of God was preaching in western Nevada.

Throughout 1889 and 1890, railroads carried delegates from a number of Indian nations east of the Rockies to investigate the messiah in Mason Valley. Visitors found ceremonial grounds maintained beside the Paiute settlements, flat cleared areas with low willow-frame shelters around the open dancing space. Paiutes gathered periodically to dance and pray for four days and nights, ending on the fifth morning shaking their blankets and shawls to symbolize driving out evil. In Mason Valley itself, Jack Wilson would attend the dances, repeating his holy message and, from time to time, trembling and passing into a trance to confirm the revelations. Delegates from other reservations were sent back home with tokens of Jack Wilson's holy power: bricks of ground red ocher dug from Mount Grant south of Mason Valley, the Mount Sinai of Northern Paiute religion; the strikingly marked feathers of the magpie;

pine nuts, the "daily bread" of the Paiutes; and robes of woven strips of rabbit fur, the Paiutes' traditional covering. James Mooney's respectful interest in the prophet's teachings earned him the privilege of carrying such tokens to his friends on the Cheyenne and Arapaho reservations east of the mountains.

Jack Wilson told Mooney that when "the sun died" that winter day in 1889 and, dying with it, he was taken up to heaven,

> he saw God, with all the people who had died long ago engaged in their oldtime sports and occupations, all happy and forever young. It was a pleasant land and full of game. After showing him all, God told him he must go back and tell his people they must be good and love one another, have no quarreling, and live in peace with the whites; that they must work, and not lie or steal; that they must put away all the old practices that savored of war; that if they faithfully obeyed his instructions they would at last be reunited with their friends in this other world, where there would be no more death or sickness or old age. He was then given the dance which he was commanded to bring back to his people. By performing this dance at intervals, for five consecutive days each time, they would secure this happiness to themselves and hasten the event. Finally God gave him control over the elements so that he could make it rain or snow or be dry at will, and appointed him his deputy to take charge of affairs in the west, while "Governor Harrison" [President of the United States at the time] would attend to matters in the east, and he, God, would look after the world above. He then returned to earth and began to preach as he was directed, convincing the people by exercising the wonderful powers that had been given him. (Mooney [1896] 1973: 771–72)

Before Mooney's visit, Jack Wilson had repeated his gospel, in August 1891, to a literate young Arapaho man who had journeyed with other Arapaho and Cheyenne to discover the truth about this fabled messiah. Jack instructed his visitors, according to the Arapaho's notes:

> When you get home you make dance, and will give you the same. . . . He likes you folk, you give him good, many things, he heart been sitting feel good. After you get home, will give good cloud, and give you chance to make you feel good. and he give you good spirit. and he give you all a good paint. . . .

Grandfather said when he die never no cry. no hurt anybody. no fight, good behave always, it will give you satisfaction, this young man, he is a good Father and mother, dont tell no white man. Jueses [Jesus?] was on ground, he just like cloud. Everybody is alive agin, I dont know when they will [be] here, may be this fall or in spring.

Everybody never get sick, be young again,— (if young fellow no sick any more,) work for white men never trouble with him until you leave, when it shake the earth dont be afraid no harm any body.

You make dance for six weeks night, and put you foot [food?] in dance to eat for every body and wash in the water. that is all to tell, I am in to you. and you will received a good words from him some time, Dont tell lie. (Mooney [1896] 1973:780–81)

Seeing the red ocher paint, the magpie feathers, the pine nuts, and the rabbit skin robes from the messiah, his Arapaho friends shared this message with James Mooney. Jack Wilson himself had trusted this white man. Thanks to this Arapaho document, we know that Jack Wilson himself obeyed his injunction, "Dont tell lie": he had confided to the Smithsonian anthropologist the same gospel he brought to his Indian disciples.

"A clean, honest life" is the core of Jack Wilson's guidance, summed up seventy years later by a Dakota Sioux who had grown up in the Ghost Dance religion. The circling dance of the congregations following Jack Wilson's gospel symbolized the ingathering of all people in the embrace of Our Father, God, and in his earthly deputy Jack Wilson. As the people move in harmony in the dance around the path of the sun, leftward, so they must live and work in harmony. Jack Wilson was convinced that if every Indian would dance this belief, the great expression of faith and love would sweep evil from the earth, renewing its goodness in every form, from youth and health to abundant food.

This was a complete religion. It had a transcendental origin in the prophet's visit to God, and a continuing power rooted in the eternal Father. Its message of earthly renewal was universalistic, although Jack Wilson felt it was useless to preach it to those Euro-Americans who were heedlessly persecuting the Indian peoples. That Jack shared his gospel with those non-Indians who came to him as pilgrims demonstrates that it was basically applicable to all people of goodwill. The gospel outlined personal behavior and provided the means to unite individuals into congregations to help one another. Its principal ceremony, the circling dance, pleased and satisfied the senses of the participants, and through the trances easily induced during the long ritual, it offered opportunities to experience profound emotional catharsis. Men and women, persons of all ages and capabilities, were welcomed into a faith of hope for the future, consolation and assistance in the present, and honor to the Indians who had passed into the afterlife. It was a marvelous message for people suffering, as the Indians of the West were in 1889, terrible epidemics; loss of their lands, their economic resources, and their political autonomy; malnourishment and wretched housing; and a campaign of cultural genocide aimed at eradicating their languages, their customs, and their beliefs.

Jack Wilson's religion was immediately taken up by his own people, the Northern Paiute, by other Paiute groups, by the Utes, the Shoshoni, and the Washo in western Nevada. It was carried westward across the Sierra Nevada and espoused by many of the Indians of California. To the south, the religion was accepted by the western Arizona Mohave, Cohonino, and Pai, but not by most other peoples of the American Southwest. East of the Rockies, the religion spread through the Shoshoni and Arapaho in Wyoming to other Arapaho, Cheyenne, Assiniboin, Gros Ventre (Atsina), Mandan, Arikara, Pawnee, Caddo, Kichai, Wichita, Kiowa, Kiowa-Apache, Comanche, Delaware (living by this time in Oklahoma), Oto, and the western Sioux, especially the Teton bands. The mechanism by which this religion spread was usually a person visiting another tribe, observing the new ceremonial dance and becoming inspired by its gospel, and returning home to urge relatives and friends to try the new faith. Leaders of these evangelists' communities would often appoint respected persons to travel to Nevada to investigate this claim of a new messiah. The delegates frequently returned as converts, testifying to the truth of the faith and firing the enthusiasm of their communities. Those who remained skeptics did not always succeed in defusing the flame of faith in others.

Never an organized church, Jack Wilson's religion thus spread by independent converts from California through Oklahoma. Not all the communities who took it up continued to practice it, when months or years passed without the hoped-for earth renewal. Much of Jack Wilson's religion has persisted, however, and has been incorporated into the regular religious life of Indian groups, especially on Oklahoma reservations. To merge into a complex of beliefs and - rituals rather than be an exclusive religion was entirely in accordance with Jack Wilson's respect for traditional Indian religions, which he saw reinforced, not supplanted, by his revelations. Though the Sioux generally dropped the Ghost Dance religion after their military defeats following their initial acceptance of the ritual, older people among the Sioux could be heard occasionally singing Ghost Dance songs in the 1930s. The last real congregation of adherents to Jack Wilson's gospel continued to worship together into the 1960s, and at least one who survived into the 1980s never abandoned the faith. There were sporadic attempts to revive the Ghost Dance religion in the 1970s, though these failed to kindle the enthusiasm met by the original proselytizers.

"Ghost Dance" is the name usually applied to Jack Wilson's religion, because the prophet foresaw the resurrection of the recently dead with the hoped-for renewal of the earth. Paiute themselves simply called their practice of the faith "dance in a circle," Shoshoni called it "everybody dragging" (speaking of people pulling others along as they circled), Comanche called it "the Father's Dance," Kiowa, "dance with clasped hands," and Caddo, "prayer of all to the Father" or "my [Father's] children's dance." The Sioux and Arapaho did use the term "spirit [ghost] dance," and the English name seems to have come from translation of the Sioux. The last active congregation, however, referred to their religion as the New Tidings, stressing its parallel to Jesus' gospel.

To his last days in 1932, Jack Wilson served as Father to believers. He counseled them, in person and by letters, and he gave them holy red ocher paint, symbolizing life, packed into rinsed-out tomato cans (the red labels indicated the contents). With his followers, he was saddened that not enough Indians danced the new faith to create the surge of spiritual power that could have renewed the earth, but resurrection was only a hope. The heart of his religion was his creed, the knowledge that a "clean, honest life" is the only good life.

49

Cargo Cults

Peter M. Worsley

A cargo cult, one of the several varieties of revitalization movements, is an intentional effort on the part of the members of society to create a more satisfying culture. Characteristic of revitalization movements in Melanesia, but not restricted to that area, cargo cults bring scattered groups together into a wider religious and political unity. These movements are the result of widespread dissatisfaction, oppression, insecurity, and the hope for fulfillment of prophecies of good times and abundance soon to come. Exposure to the cultures and material goods of the Western world, combinations of native myth with Christian teachings of the coming of a messiah, and belief in the white man's magic—all contributed to the New Guinean's faith that the "cargo" would soon arrive, bringing with it the end of the present order and the beginning of a blissful paradise.

Peter M. Worsley's article depicts a movement that often was so organized and persistent as to bring government work to a halt. Cargo cult movements still occur in Melanesia, where they are often intermixed with other types of revitalization movements.

Patrols of the Australian government venturing into the "uncontrolled" central highlands of New Guinea in 1946 found the primitive people there swept up in a wave of religious excitement. Prophecy was being fulfilled: The arrival of the Whites was the sign that the end of the world was at hand. The natives proceeded to butcher all of their pigs—animals that were not only a principal source of subsistence but also symbols of social status and ritual preeminence in their culture. They killed these valued animals in expression of the belief that after three days of darkness "Great Pigs" would appear from the sky. Food, firewood, and other necessities had to be stockpiled to see the people through to the arrival of the Great Pigs. Mock wireless antennae of bamboo and rope had been erected to receive in advance the news of the millennium. Many believed that with the great event they would exchange their black skins for white ones.

This bizarre episode is by no means the single event of its kind in the murky history of the collision of European civilization with the indigenous cultures of the southwest Pacific. For more than one hundred years traders and missionaries have been reporting similar disturbances among the peoples of Melanesia, the group of Negro-inhabited islands (including New Guinea, Fiji, the Solomons, and the New Hebrides) lying between Australia and the open Pacific Ocean. Though their technologies were based largely upon stone and wood, these peoples had highly developed cultures, as measured by the standards of maritime and agricultural ingenuity, the complexity of their varied social organizations, and the elaboration of religious belief and ritual. They were nonetheless ill prepared for the shock of the encounter with the Whites, a people so radically different from themselves and so infinitely more powerful. The sudden transition from the society of the ceremonial stone ax to the society of sailing ships and now of airplanes has not been easy to make.

After four centuries of Western expansion, the densely populated central highlands of New Guinea remain one of the few regions where the people still carry on their primitive existence in complete independence of the world outside. Yet as the agents of the Australian Government penetrate into ever more remote mountain valleys, they find these backwaters of antiquity already deeply disturbed by contact with the ideas and artifacts of European civilization. For "cargo"—Pidgin English for trade goods—has long flowed along the indigenous channels of communication from the seacoast into the wilderness. With it has traveled the frightening knowledge of the white man's magical power. No small element in the white man's magic is the hopeful message sent abroad by his missionaries: the news that a Messiah will come and that the present order of Creation will end.

The people of the central highlands of New Guinea are only the latest to be gripped in the recurrent religious frenzy of the "cargo cults." However variously embellished with details from native myth the Christian belief, these cults all advance the same central theme: the world is about to end in a terrible cataclysm. Thereafter God, the ancestors, or some local culture hero will appear and inaugurate a blissful paradise on earth. Death, old age, illness, and evil will be unknown. The riches of the white man will accrue to the Melanesians.

Although the news of such a movement in one area has doubtless often inspired similar movements in other areas, the evidence indicates that these cults have arisen independently in many places as parallel responses to the same enormous social stress and strain. Among the movements best known to students of Melanesia are the "Taro Cult" of New Guinea, the "Vailala Madness" of Papua, the "Naked Cult" of Espiritu Santo, the "John Frum Movement" of the New Hebrides, and the "Tuka Cult" of the Fiji Islands.

At times the cults have been so well organized and fanatically persistent that they have brought the work of government to a standstill. The outbreaks have often taken the authorities completely by surprise and have confronted them with mass opposition of an alarming kind. In the 1930's, for example, villagers in the vicinity of Wewak, New Guinea, were stirred by a succession of "Black King" movements. The prophets announced that the Europeans would soon leave the island, abandoning their property to the natives, and urged their followers to cease

paying taxes, since the government station was about to disappear into the sea in a great earthquake. To the tiny community of Whites in charge of the region, such talk was dangerous. The authorities jailed four of the prophets and exiled three others. In yet another movement, that sprang up in declared opposition to the local Christian mission, the cult leader took Satan as his god.

Troops on both sides in World War II found their arrival in Melanesia heralded as a sign of the Apocalypse. The G.I.'s who landed in the New Hebrides, moving up for the bloody fighting on Guadalcanal, found the natives furiously at work preparing airfields, roads and docks for the magic ships and planes that they believed were coming from "Rusefel" (Roosevelt), the friendly king of America.

The Japanese also encountered millenarian visionaries during their southward march to Guadalcanal. Indeed, one of the strangest minor military actions of World War II occurred in Dutch New Guinea, when Japanese forces had to be turned against the local Papuan inhabitants of the Geelvink Bay region. The Japanese had at first been received with great joy, not because their "Greater East Asia Co-Prosperity Sphere" propaganda had made any great impact upon the Papuans, but because the natives regarded them as harbingers of the new world that was dawning, the flight of the Dutch having already given the first sign. Mansren, creator of the islands and their peoples, would now return, bringing with him the ancestral dead. All this had been known, the cult leaders declared, to the crafty Dutch, who had torn out the first page of the Bible where these truths were inscribed. When Mansren returned, the existing world order would be entirely overturned. White men would turn black like Papuans, Papuans would become Whites; root crops would grow in trees, and coconuts and fruits would grow like tubers. Some of the islanders now began to draw together into large "towns"; others took Biblical names such as "Jericho" and "Galilee" for their villages. Soon they adopted military uniforms and began drilling. The Japanese, by now highly unpopular, tried to disarm and disperse the Papuans; resistance inevitably developed. The climax of this tragedy came when several canoe-loads of fanatics sailed out to attack Japanese warships, believing themselves to be invulnerable by virtue of the holy water with which they had sprinkled themselves.

But the bullets of the Japanese did not turn to water, and the attackers were mowed down by machine-gun fire.

Behind this incident lay a long history. As long ago as 1857 missionaries in the Geelvink Bay region had made note of the story of Mansren. It is typical of many Melanesian myths that became confounded with Christian doctrine to form the ideological basis of the movements. The legend tells how long ago there lived an old man named Manamakeri ("he who itches"), whose body was covered with sores. Manamakeri was extremely fond of palm wine, and used to climb a huge tree every day to tap the liquid from the flowers. He soon found that someone was getting there before him and removing the liquid. Eventually he trapped the thief, who turned out to be none other than the Morning Star. In return for his freedom, the Star gave the old man a wand that would produce as much fish as he liked, a magic tree and a magic staff. If he drew in the sand and stamped his foot, the drawing would become real. Manamakeri, aged as he was, now magically impregnated a young maiden; the child of this union was a miracle-child who spoke as soon as he was born. But the maiden's parents were horrified, and banished her, the child, and the old man. The trio sailed off in a canoe created by Mansren ("The Lord"), as the old man now became known. On this journey Mansren rejuvenated himself by stepping into a fire and flaking off his scaly skin, which changed into valuables. He then sailed around Geelvink Bay, creating islands where he stopped, and peopling them with the ancestors of the present-day Papuans.

The Mansren myth is plainly a creation myth full of symbolic ideas relating to fertility and rebirth. Comparative evidence—especially the shedding of his scaly skin—confirms the suspicion that the old man is, in fact, the Snake in another guise. Psychoanalytic writers argue that the snake occupies such a prominent part in mythology the world over because it stands for the penis, another fertility symbol. This may be so, but its symbolic significance is surely more complex than this. It is the "rebirth" of the hero, whether Mansren or the Snake, that exercises such universal fascination over men's minds.

The nineteenth-century missionaries thought that the Mansren story would make the introduction of Christianity easier, since the concept of "resurrection,"

not to mention that of the "virgin birth" and the "second coming," was already there. By 1867, however, the first cult organized around the Mansren legend was reported.

Though such myths were widespread in Melanesia, and may have sparked occasional movements even in the pre-White era, they took on a new significance in the late nineteenth century, once the European powers had finished parceling out the Melanesian region among themselves. In many coastal areas the long history of "blackbirding"—the seizure of islanders for work on the plantations of Australia and Fiji—had built up a reservoir of hostility to Europeans. In other areas, however, the arrival of the Whites was accepted, even welcomed, for it meant access to bully beef and cigarettes, shirts and paraffin lamps, whisky and bicycles. It also meant access to the knowledge behind these material goods, for the Europeans brought missions and schools as well as cargo.

Practically the only teaching the natives received about European life came from the missions, which emphasized the central significance of religion in European society. The Melanesians already believed that man's activities—whether gardening, sailing canoes, or bearing children—needed magical assistance. Ritual without human effort was not enough. But neither was human effort on its own. This outlook was reinforced by mission teaching.

The initial enthusiasm for European rule, however, was speedily dispelled. The rapid growth of the plantation economy removed the bulk of the able-bodied men from the villages, leaving women, children, and old men to carry on as best they could. The splendid vision of the equality of all Christians began to seem a pious deception in face of the realities of the color bar, the multiplicity of rival Christian missions and the open irreligion of many Whites.

For a long time the natives accepted the European mission as the means by which the "cargo" would eventually be made available to them. But they found that acceptance of Christianity did not bring the cargo any nearer. They grew disillusioned. The story now began to be put about that it was not the Whites who made the cargo, but the dead ancestors. To people completely ignorant of factory production, this made good sense. White men did not work; they merely wrote secret signs on scraps of paper, for which they were given shiploads of goods. On the other hand, the Melanesians labored week after week for pitiful wages. Plainly the goods must be made for Melanesians somewhere, perhaps in the Land of the Dead. The Whites, who possessed the secret of the cargo, were intercepting it and keeping it from the hands of the islanders, to whom it was really consigned. In the Madang district of New Guinea, after some forty years' experience of the missions, the natives went in a body one day with a petition demanding that the cargo secret should now be revealed to them, for they had been very patient.

So strong is this belief in the existence of a "secret" that the cargo cults generally contain some ritual in imitation of the mysterious European customs which are held to be the clue to the white man's extraordinary power over goods and men. The believers sit around tables with bottles of flowers in front of them, dressed in European clothes, waiting for the cargo ship or airplane to materialize; other cultists feature magic pieces of paper and cabalistic writing. Many of them deliberately turn their backs on the past by destroying secret ritual objects, or exposing them to the gaze of uninitiated youths and women, for whom formerly even a glimpse of the sacred objects would have meant the severest penalties, even death. The belief that they were the chosen people is further reinforced by their reading of the Bible, for the lives and customs of the people in the Old Testament resemble their own lives rather than those of the Europeans. In the New Testament they find the Apocalypse, with its prophecies of destruction and resurrection, particularly attractive.

Missions that stress the imminence of the Second Coming, like those of the Seventh Day Adventists, are often accused of stimulating millenarian cults among the islanders. In reality, however, the Melanesians themselves rework the doctrines the missionaries teach them, selecting from the Bible what they themselves find particularly congenial in it. Such movements have occurred in areas where missions of quite different types have been dominant, from Roman Catholic to Seventh Day Adventist. The reasons for the emergence of these cults, of course, lie far deeper in the life-experience of the people.

The economy of most of the islands is very backward. Native agriculture produces little for the world market, and even the European plantations

and mines export only a few primary products and raw materials: copra, rubber, gold. Melanesians are quite unable to understand why copra, for example, fetches thirty pounds sterling per ton one month and but five pounds a few months later. With no notion of the workings of world-commodity markets, the natives see only the sudden closing of plantations, reduced wages and unemployment, and are inclined to attribute their insecurity to the whim or evil in the nature of individual planters.

Such shocks have not been confined to the economic order. Governments, too, have come and gone, especially during the two world wars: German, Dutch, British, and French administrations melted overnight. Then came the Japanese, only to be ousted in turn largely by the previously unknown Americans. And among these Americans the Melanesians saw Negroes like themselves, living lives of luxury on equal terms with white G.I.'s. The sight of these Negroes seemed like a fulfillment of the old prophecies to many cargo cult leaders. Nor must we forget the sheer scale of this invasion. Around a million U.S. troops passed through the Admiralty Islands, completely swamping the inhabitants. It was a world of meaningless and chaotic changes, in which anything was possible. New ideas were imported and given local twists. Thus in the Loyalty Islands people expected the French Communist Party to bring the millennium. There is no real evidence, however, of any Communist influence in these movements, despite the rather hysterical belief among Solomon Island planters that the name of the local "Masinga Rule" movement was derived from the word "Marxian"! In reality the name comes from a Solomon Island tongue, and means "brotherhood."

Europeans who have witnessed outbreaks inspired by the cargo cults are usually at a loss to understand what they behold. The islanders throw away their money, break their most sacred taboos, abandon their gardens, and destroy their precious livestock; they indulge in sexual license, or, alternatively, rigidly separate men from women in huge communal establishments. Sometimes they spend days sitting gazing at the horizon for a glimpse of the long-awaited ship or airplane; sometimes they dance, pray and sing in mass congregations, becoming possessed and "speaking with tongues."

Observers have not hesitated to use such words as "madness," "mania," and "irrationality" to characterize the cults. But the cults reflect quite logical and rational attempts to make sense out of a social order that appears senseless and chaotic. Given the ignorance of the Melanesians about the wider European society, its economic organization and its highly developed technology, their reactions form a consistent and understandable pattern. They wrap up all their yearning and hope in an amalgam that combines the best counsel they can find in Christianity and their native belief. If the world is soon to end, gardening or fishing is unnecessary; everything will be provided. If the Melanesians are to be part of a much wider order, the taboos that prescribe their social conduct must now be lifted or broken in a newly prescribed way.

Of course the cargo never comes. The cults nonetheless live on. If the millennium does not arrive on schedule, then perhaps there is some failure in the magic, some error in the ritual. New breakaway groups organize around "purer" faith and ritual. The cult rarely disappears, so long as the social situation which brings it into being persists.

At this point it should be observed that cults of this general kind are not peculiar to Melanesia. Men who feel themselves oppressed and deceived have always been ready to pour their hopes and fears, their aspirations and frustrations, into dreams of a millennium to come or of a golden age to return. All parts of the world have had their counterparts of the cargo cults, from the American Indian Ghost Dance to the Communist-millenarist "reign of the saints" in Münster during the Reformation, from medieval European apocalyptic cults to African "witch-finding" movements and Chinese Buddhist heresies. In some situations men have been content to wait and pray; in others they have sought to hasten the day by using their strong right arms to do the Lord's work. And always the cults serve to bring together scattered groups, notably the peasants and urban plebeians of agrarian societies and the peoples of "stateless" societies where the cult unites separate (and often hostile) villages, clans, and tribes into a wider religio-political unity.

Once the people begin to develop secular political organizations, however, the sects tend to lose their importance as vehicles of protest. They begin to relegate the Second Coming to the distant future or to the next world. In Melanesia ordinary political bodies, trade unions and native councils are becoming the normal media through which the islanders express their aspirations. In recent years continued economic prosperity and political stability have taken some of the edge off their despair. It now seems unlikely that any major movement along cargo-cult lines will recur in areas where the transition to secular politics has been made, even if the insecurity of prewar times returned. I would predict that the embryonic nationalism represented by cargo cults is likely in future to take forms familiar in the history of other countries that have moved from subsistence agriculture to participation in the world economy.

50

Urban Rastas in Kingston, Jamaica

William F. Lewis

William F. Lewis's anthropological research and publications focused largely on religion and social movements, most recently with Rastafari culture. In this selection Professor Lewis describes in rich ethnographic detail the personalities and attributes of Nigel, Lion, and David, three urban Rastas living in Kingston, Jamaica. As Lewis describes his interviews with the three Rastas, the reader learns about Rastafarian beliefs, rituals, symbols, diet, and language, as well as other aspects of the people he refers to as "Soul Rebels."

Many Americans think of the Rastafarians as members of a deviant subculture, knowing only the reggae music of the Rastafarian song-prophet Bob Marley, or the Rasta "dreadlocks," or perhaps the Rastafarian reputation as prodigious ganja smokers. The Rastafarian movement began in Jamaica in the early 1930s. Rastas believe that Haile Ras Tafari Selassi I of Ethiopia is their black Messiah—the King of Kings and Lord of Lords—and that black true believers will some day dismiss their white oppressors and be repatriated to Ethiopia, their spiritual homeland. Although the largest number of Rastas live in Jamaica, there are also followers in the United States, England, Canada, Ethiopia, and other parts of the world.

Nigel

On a sultry day in downtown Kingston a weary walker might come upon Nigel lounging on his front steps, shirtless, with a towel draped around his shoulders as he carefully dries himself after one of his periodic splash baths. That is how I first met him. A careless observer might take Nigel to be mad, a stigma with which Jamaican society labels the solitary life free from the cares of family and the demands of social responsibility. However, Nigel is affable, courteous and willing to share his wisdom with sympathetic listeners. I was one of them.

Nigel's conversations with passers-by can become serious communications. He interprets such a happy occasion as the result of a mutual consciousness that compels people to reason with him. True communication is never mere serendipity. Once a male stranger (Nigel seldom if ever converses seriously with a female) demonstrates that his interests are compatible with Nigel's, his scrutiny and suspicion change to a more relaxed and intimate tone. Then Nigel asks the visitor to remove his shoes, unburden himself of his baggage, and empty his pockets of money, tobacco, and combs, things Nigel finds polluting. He requires all to relieve themselves of these demonic influences before any can enter his mansion. I complied.

Nigel's mansion turns out to be the building that housed his formerly prosperous clothing boutique which catered to the sartorial demands of the

Jamaican elite. The quarters are large, two stories high, with spacious rooms that are now bereft of furniture and decoration. Nigel's mansion is but a vestige of the glamour and prestige he enjoyed as one of the wealthiest tailors in Jamaica. The yellow clippings that hang willy-nilly from the flaking walls of the main room bear silent witness to Nigel's renunciation of both his business and family. The Jamaican media once celebrated him as a promising designer of clothes for both the wealthy and the celebrated. That was before his commitment to the principles of Rastafari.

Nigel explains his conversion to Rastafari as an odyssey, a passage that began shortly after his appendectomy operation. Then modern drugs and treatments were of no avail in restoring his energy, vitality and spirit. However, an encounter with a Rasta turned into meetings of mutual communication and disclosure. On the Rasta's advice, Nigel drank large amounts of ganja tea and smoked equally large amounts of marijuana. He recovered his health. From then on, he affiliated himself with the ways of Rastafari, and he too hallowed the herb as the healing of nations. Furthermore, he attributes the restoration and continuance of his health to his dedication to the Rasta principles of love, meditation, reasoning and *ital* (natural) foods of which marijuana is a part.

Nigel found peace when he embraced Rastafari. His fashion industry and family were the weapons he created to wage warfare on people. Thus, he divested himself of his career and married life.

Shortly after his conversion in 1981, Nigel began to send funds to Rastas in the rural interior. At that time, Jamaican businesses were recouping their losses suffered under the democratic socialism of the Manley government which had threatened their profits. Nigel recalls how the bank officials thought that he was donating funds to a subversive group in the interior. A popular rumor at the time was that Manley's allies had contingents ready in the country who would help Cuban communists infiltrate Jamaica. Nigel was under great suspicion. The bank refused to handle any of his transactions. The government harassed him on charges of tax evasion. His wife tried to commit him to a mental institution. Nigel muses: "Because I was becoming aware of my own identity, I had to go through this

suffering. That's in the past, the price I paid. Now I am free."

Now Nigel is neither an entrepreneur nor an artist but an ascetic. He refuses to touch money, and only the free will offerings of others sustain him. His meatless diet consists only of fruits, vegetables and an occasional fish. He abhors the eating of animal meat because dead flesh will only cause sickness for the person who consumes it. Nor will he accept any fruit or vegetable whose natural appearance has been altered by any cutting, mashing or peeling. Nigel seems lanky and anorexic. However, his appearance belies his vigor and vitality which are evident in his darting about and enthusiastically engaging the visitor in philosophical discussion about the affairs of the world, the way to health and the meaning of sexuality.

An aroma of ganja smoke clings to Nigel's long, unkempt and natural dreads. This slovenliness too is deceptive because Nigel is particularly fastidious about the cleanliness of his body and he meticulously monitors its functions. This leads him to administer frequent purgatives to himself lest the accumulation of toxins within cause harm for the whole body. His frequent cleansings and purgations of the body as well as the avoidance of contact with any decaying matter, especially a dead body, are normative in Nigel's life. Were these norms violated, his spiritual and physical health would be imperiled.

Without his regimen, Nigel would be unable to find the strength to weave his philosophical reflections through his writings, his conversations and solitary moments of meditation. Esoteric writings and volumes are scattered throughout his quarters. He has amassed stacks of newspaper clippings and sundry writings whose relationship to the philosophy of Rastafari at first glance appears obscure. Nevertheless, Nigel can explain every metaphor and symbol in his literary collection and connect them to what he believes are the truths of Rastafari. Included in his assemblage of works are titles such as: "Dread Locks Judgement," "Anthropology: Races of Man," "Radical Vegetarianism," "Rasta Voice Magazine," "Economy and Business," "Women as Sex Object," and "Pan African Digest." His own essays range from glosses on Joseph Owens' *Dread* and Dennis Forsythe's *Healing of Nations* to highly idealistic writing on a new economic order. Among these pieces is correspondence from previous English and American visitors to Nigel's mansion.

Nigel's own writings have an intense and highly involuted style which gives them an arcane quality, a form somewhat reminiscent of James Joyce's stream of consciousness. Tolerance and patience are demanded of the reader who wishes to decipher Nigel's turn of phrase and novel transformation of words. Indeed, the uninitiated reader might wonder if the police are not correct in simply shrugging him off as a Rasta who has had too much ganja. His prose is obscure and agonistic, but, nevertheless, he can elicit sense from every syllable, word and line. Nigel's deftness in turning his twisted writings into an articulate message makes him a shaman and mythmaker of sorts, for his vocalizations about the revelation he bears have the rhythm, cadence and timbre of a person standing outside of the self.

. . .

The Upper Room

Nigel's "Upper Room" is on the second level of the building with two large windows opening to a view of eastern Kingston and allowing the cool breezes from the sea to circulate through the room. It is furnished with a few mats, a raggedy sleeping cot over to the side, a square table on which the herb is blessed, and shelves along the wall on which lie chillum pipes of various lengths. The chillum pipes are stored for other Rastas who might visit and join Nigel for reasoning. In his Upper Room Nigel undergoes his most intense experience with ganja and elaborates ecstatically on Rastafari. In accord with what he believes to be Rastas' tradition, he excludes women from these sessions.

When the brethren have gathered in the Upper Room, Nigel raises his arms toward the East in a grand gesture and blesses the herb with vocalizations resembling glossolalia. "Amharic," he says as an aside, "the Ethiopian language." The blessings are spontaneous and ecstatic, but on listening closely I detected a word that sounded like *mirrikat*, the Amharic word for blessing. Later Nigel mentioned that he learned some Amharic at the Ethiopian Orthodox Church in Kingston.

After the chillum is filled, and the herb is burning, Nigel is the first to draw deeply from the pipe. His chest expands as smoke fills his lungs. He exhales billows of smoke through his nostrils and mouth, and the whiffs frame his lionlike face with tendrils of plumes that seep through his long locks and beard. Through the clouds of smoke, Nigel stares at all in the room with a fierce look, regal, but cutting and penetrating. His demeanor demands a response.

"The conquering Lion of Judah shall break every chain," I acclaim.

Nigel seems pleased with this affirmation of his link with the Emperor Haile Selassie, the Lion of Judah.

Another's turn comes to partake of the chalice, and Nigel passes the pipe with a most respectful gesture. Kneeling before the next brother with his own head bowed low to the floor, his outstretched arms offer him the chillum. The brother accepts, draws from it, and proclaims, "Jah Rastafari."

The chillum moves from participant to participant, brother to brother, each honoring the other with gestures of deference but never permitting their flesh to meet. Bodily contact is assiduously avoided. Soon the participants assume unusual bodily postures. The effect is startling. Nigel takes the lead in displaying great physical agility and dexterity by twisting his body into yogalike positions. All the brethren follow suit. They throw their bodies into lionlike leaps. Nevertheless, their bodily deportments are undertaken with great concentration and awareness, for not once did their acrobatic feats threaten to harm anyone in the room.

"What is love?" asks one of the brothers.

"Love is where there are no starving people. As long as there are hungry people, hatred is in power. Caring and supporting . . ."

Their dance continues, and perhaps ten minutes passes.

"Sex is a performance, a duty."

"Women are for pickneys (babies)."

Another interval, and more of their dancing.

"Burn Babylon." Some begin chanting the familiar lyric.

"Why the police brutality and why youths beaten by Babylon? They steal because they are hungry and want to fill their bellies. No crime in taking food because you are hungry."

"Africa for the blacks, Europe for the whites, Jamaica for the Arawaks."

. . .

David and Lion

Tourists and Jamaicans alike must cross an unsteady, wooden pier in order to board the ferry that takes passengers from Kingston Harbor to the legendary Port Royal across the bay. Once celebrated as a haunt for pirates and a playground for debauchery, Port Royal now rests quietly on the bay, chastised forever, it seems, by the raging earthquake it suffered in the late seventeenth century. That cataclysm hurled much of the port into the Caribbean.

Near the ramp leading to the pier lazes David, a Rasta brother. He is attending his concession stand which is simply a large crate hoisted on a dolly for maneuverability. From the cart, David sells Red Stripe beer, D & G sodas, as well as Benson cigarettes by ones and twos, and, of course, raw sugar cane and coconut, the most popular items. A sampling from his assortment of refreshments often comes as welcome relief for the overheated traveler after the half-hour trip across the bay.

David and Lion live together in a hovel about twenty yards from their stand. The shack rests precariously on the side of the pier, supported in part by the hanging branches of a huge tree on which part of it also leans. The roof and sidings are constructed of huge pieces of cardboard and plastic sheeting. Nearby, a slipshod folding chair, unworthy of any task, clings to the pier's edge and marks out an area that serves as a reception space for guests. The sound of the rushing water against the piles, the squeaking of the rats, and the dust from the parched earth fill the place David and Lion call home with a romantic irony. They sit between two worlds, perhaps a sign of their liminality. From one viewpoint, Port Royal's outlines loom across the bay standing witness to wanton living long ago. From another angle stands the symbol of law and order, a police station, to which the Rastas pay no heed.

Lion and David eat *ital* food, a healthy low-salt, low-fat and low-cholesterol diet, that consists mainly of vegetables, plantains and the occasional red snapper, caught off the pier. At a clearing away from their hut, they prepare the food on an aluminum can cover some twenty-four inches in diameter. The fare is seasoned with hot pepper and served on tin plates. Sometimes a rat might boldly rush a dish at what appears to be an opportune moment in an effort to wrest a morsel from a distracted diner. The Rastas, however, are generous and share their food with any of their guests, human and animal alike.

When business is slow at their stand, Lion, David and other brethren hustle on the streets of Kingston, selling anything from boxed donuts to belts and tams (knitted headgear which they themselves have crafted). They are talkative entrepreneurs and quick to prevail upon a prospective customer, especially a white tourist, to purchase one of their handiworks or products.

Reasoning

Toward late afternoon on a hot July day, two brethren arrive at the pier and exchange greetings with David. David assures the visiting brethren that I, the white guest sitting near the hut, have respect and love for Rastafari. Lion emerges from below the rafters of the pier where he was resting and lends support to David's assurances that their white visitor is trustworthy.

When the group is ready, David places the Bible on the ground and marks off a few pages from which he will draw his inspiration. The spliffs are lit with a short grace: "Give thanks." At that moment, however, some youths happen on the scene, probably drawn by the whiff of ganja smoke overcoming the salty sea breezes. They ask for some herb. Lion rebukes the boys and says: "This is high reasoning, boys, and not play." They run off. The Rastas return to the matter at hand.

David mulls over the scriptural passage about the Nazarites and the proscription on the cutting of hair. "Love is the foundation of Rastafari. The covenant is the hair, the locks. This is Godly."

As a group of commuters disembarks from the ferry and hurries by the group, scarcely giving them a glance, Lion comments: "Jamaican people cannot see the truth. They have eyes, hands, feet, but don't use them properly for justice and love. They are blinded."

Rashi holds his spliff and remarks pensively: "Rastas are clever, living for truth. The weed is important. It is healing."

After reflecting a bit on the wisdom in the herb, the Rastas turn to excoriating the success of reggae musicians, a discussion that enlivens the group. Few endearing words are spent on reggae musicians who, the Rastas believe, preach the philosophy of

Rastafari, give interviews to magazines, enrich themselves, but filter none of their profits into the creation of a stronger culture for the rest of the brethren.

"Look how they draw up around Nesta's place on New Hope, clean and shining. Burn reggae."

All agree.

Soon the brethren fall into a quiet, meditative mood. A few reflect in low voices on the similarity between the churches and reggae. This prompts David to take up a verse from the scriptures and freely elaborate on it. The verse is: "Let the dead bury the dead."

"The churches in Jamaica bury only dead people, and take people's money to build bigger church buildings, instead of providing work and industry for people. The Rasta never dies but has life eternal, as Christ promised. God cannot lie. To have life eternal one must follow the Rasta culture in the Bible. Rasta is a new name. It is the new Jerusalem that Isaiah promised in the prophecy."

David's words excite the group, and they all affirm the equality of people. They denounce the hypocrisy of organized religion, reggae and the government for manipulating the Bible and authority. The more their anger with society increases, so much the more does the spontaneity of the gathering quicken.

David takes the spliff from a Rasta reclining next to him. Holding it, he prays that the chalice be not a source of condemnation but a guardian of life eternal. He inhales deeply, holds the smoke within, and for almost a minute after exhalation he gazes intently on me, the white visitor sitting across from him. Then:

"Rasta is not the color of the skin. Blacks hate their fellow man, just like white man hates. Even some Rastas have words on their lips but not in their hearts."

As darkness draws closer, and fewer people queue up for the ferry, the Rastas become more vociferous.

"Living is for the Rastas. Moses and the prophets are not dead, but reign in Zion, a Kingdom that is better than the one here. I have life. I will never die but go to Zion with Ras Tafari Selassie I" [pronounced as "aye"].

Interspersed among their exultations of Selassie are monotone chantings expressing a yearning for repatriation to a land of freedom from which they have been exiled.

"Africa yes! But not the Africa of today because it is just as corrupt as Jamaica."

Silence. The spliffs are lit again, passed around and blessed. The mood changes. The brethren become serious and playful, ecstatic and earthly. Lion leads this flow of sensuousness. He rolls on the ground, smiles, laughs lightly while singing an improvisation on liberty, freedom and repatriation. He kisses the roots of a nearby tree and exclaims: "Jah Rastafari."

The others participate in his display with their own paeans on liberation and freedom. Soon they too tumble over the ground, enjoying themselves immensely, and encouraging me to "ride the vibes and feel freedom."

At dusk, bright lights illumine the decks of a British warship that had docked in the harbor earlier in the day. The sharp relief of the ship in the distance prompts Lion to remark:

"War is against Rastafari. Rastas do what is right for life and live forever. Jamaican people love war too much. I don't know why."

David pursues the thought further. "I-n-I is never listened to. We are rejected. They have no culture. They steal, kill and shoot."

Lion snuggles closer to the roots of the tree which are bulging from the parched earth. He seems to caress them.

"I-n-I Rastafari are the love in the world. We are very peaceful, loving and don't eat poisonous things, no salt, no liver, no dead animals."

Rashi adds: "We want wholeness, fullness of justice, fullness of love."

When asked to identify the source of his power, Rashi responds:

"I-n-I is the bible in the heart. The true bible is yet to be written. I-n-I moves beyond the bible. It is a word that we must move beyond. I-n-I live naturally in the fullness of divinity, don't have to go to school. Truth is in the heart. I-n-I have to learn our flesh and blood. Then everybody gets food, shelter. This is the truth."

Popes and priests irritate them. "Burn the pope. Burn the pope man. The Church is a vampire with their cars and living in the hills [an area where the elite reside]. The pope is a vampire, wants our blood. Selassie I is the head. The pope is the devil."

The light fades. More silence. The bay water slaps against the pilings. A rat tears across the planks and startles me. I jump. Lion, however, admonishes me with a reminder that the rat is only a creature.

"The barber shop is the mark of the beast. Comb and razor conquer. The wealth of Jah is with locks, in fullness of his company."

All nod in agreement. I mention that my understanding is increasing.

"Be careful with words, brother," Lion says, "overstand not understand. I people are forward people not backward."

Another interjects: "It is a brand new way of life. The language of I-n-I is forward. I-n-I people will pay no more. For five hundred years, they built Babylon on us, but they will do it no more."

. . .

51

Adoring the Father: Religion and Charisma in an American Polygamous Community

William Jankowiak and Emilie Allen

Based on fieldwork in a small town in the western United States, the following article seeks to explain the relationship between the emotional dynamics of polygamous family life and the male-centered theology of a Mormon offshoot movement. Mainstream Mormonism, represented by the Church of Jesus Christ of Latter-Day Saints, has banned plural marriages since 1890 and today excommunicates individuals who practice plural marriage. However, a small minority of practitioners, many of whom live in isolated rural communities, maintain that the polygynous marriage of one man to many women is an expression of God's will and practice what the present authors call Fundamentalist Mormonism. Polygamy is illegal in the United States, but the U.S. government has tacitly adopted a "live and let live" attitude toward the community documented here, and the U.S. Supreme Court has ruled that children cannot be taken away from parents living polygamously.

Most anthropological studies of polygamy focus on the structure of marriage and household; Jankowiak and Allen instead take a psychological perspective. They explore the emotional experience of individuals in polygamous households, documenting how emotion, memory, and theology generate cultural symbols—in this case, that of the revered father.

The example of polygamous non-orthodox Mormons illustrates the ability of religious communities to redefine themselves in response to changing social and political conditions. Among 19th-century Mormons, 10 to 20 percent of the families were polygamous; more than 30 percent of the families in pseudonymous "Angel Park" are polygamous. It is one of five polygamous communities in the western United States, Canada, and northern Mexico.

"A father's ghost is the one we can never shake."

—A son's comment in Ibsen's *The Ghost*

William Jankowiak and Emilie Allen, "Adoring the Father: Religion and Charisma in an American Polygamous Community" in ANTHROPOLOGY AND THEOLOGY: GODS, ICONS, AND GOD-TALK edited by Walter Randolph Adams and Frank A. Salamone. Lanham, MD: University Press of America, pp. 293–316 © 2000. Reprinted by permission.

Introduction

There are few modern cultures where religious meaning is derived entirely from its theological tenets and where religious dogma is forcefully applied uniformly. Most cultures find themselves adjusting to other psychological needs, cultural values, and social and personal interests. Religious meanings, like all cultural meanings, invariably reflect the interplay between official creed and other structural and psychocultural factors. This interplay accounts, in large measure, for the institutionalization of father adoration, or reverence, in the Fundamentalist Mormon cosmology.

In this chapter we will explore the origins, persistence and meaning of a social and familial institution we will call father adoration or father reverence. It is our contention that father adoration is a psychocultural configuration that arises from four separate, yet intertwined, components: (1) a theology that endows men with a supernatural essence that commands the regeneration of a religious organization primarily, but not exclusively, through copious reproduction; (2) a closed-corporate, theological community that confers its greatest esteem on men in leadership positions as members of the church's priesthood council or on men who are independently wealthy; (3) a polygamous family system organized around a husband/father, who is the primary focal point—at least at the symbolic level—and, who unites the often competing female-centered natal family units; and (4) an American cultural ethos that values emotional familial involvement over a detached, albeit respectful, role performance. Together, these forces introduce new factors into the fundamentalist cosmology which, over time, become incorporated as a new, albeit sacred, aspect of the community's world-view. Within this world-view, fathers are the most valued social category.

We intend to explore how these components not only foster the formation of father adoration; but, also account, in large part, for the variation found within that formation. Specifically, we will examine father adoration as it manifests itself most powerfully: a fondly-remembered, deeply troubling, and socially salient experience of adulthood. The institution of father adoration is a product of numerous factors that are, in themselves, suggestive; but, when they cohere, as they do in Angel Park, they form a seminal family form. The data presented in this chapter were collected between 1993 and 1995, during a seventeen month study of a Fundamentalist Mormon polygamous community we will call Angel Park.

Angel Park: The Religious Community

Angel Park is a sectarian religious community that forms one of five polygamous communities found in the western United States, Canada and Northern Mexico. Each of these communities is separately governed and maintains only nominal, if any, contact with one another. The population of Angel Park, located in the western United States, is approximately 9,000, including 687 families ranging greatly in size from four to six-eight family members, accounting, in all, for less than one tenth of the 21,000 to 50,000 Americans (depending on which source one uses) who follow a polygamous lifestyle (Quin 1991; Kilbride 1994).

On the whole, Angel Park is a town which from first appearances looks like a rather quaint and ordinary community. Like other small American rural communities, all of its main roads (seven in all) are paved, whereas its side streets are not. It has one grocery store, a health food store, a post office, a police station, a volunteer fire department, two elementary schools, two junior high schools, one high school, three private home schools, and one religious school (first through twelfth grade), one dentist (who is non-Mormon), two gas stations, a small motel, several auto shops, a milk plant, a large mortgage company, three restaurants (two for locals; the other more upscale for tourists on their way through the Southwest), and a petting zoo. The houses and mobile trailers range in size from 32,000 square feet to around 1,100 square feet, with many in various stages of completion or renovation. Because of its location, Angel Park's economy cannot support all of its residents. Most men work in the construction industry while other men and women work in a variety of other kind of jobs (e.g., accountants, janitors, masseuses, caretakers, teachers, nurses, mechanics, and long-distance truck drivers) *outside* the community.

Given the uniqueness of the community's family system, it is easy to overlook the commonalities that Fundamentalist Mormons share with mainstream American culture. Forged out of the nineteenth century American frontier experience, Fundamentalist Mormonism embraces many American middle class values: basic frugality of means, emphasis on controlling one's destiny, a striving of upward mobility and a belief in personal autonomy.

Although many residents of Angel Park feel certain that aspects of the mainstream culture are immoral—e.g., cigarettes, drugs (but not alcohol or caffeine consumption), MTV, R-rated movies, and so forth—most residents occasionally participate in the American consumption ethic even while simultaneously voicing their disapproval of that ethic. Several polygynous families have even appeared on various talk shows to defend their religiously based lifestyle from stereotypical and shallow attacks. Thus, contemporary fundamentalists are not like the Amish, who sweepingly disapprove of, and strive to withdraw from, contemporary American culture. For the fundamentalist, life is to be enjoyed and that enjoyment includes many of its sensual pleasures (coffee-drinking, alcohol consumption, and eating at all-you-can-eat buffets). Common dinner topics range from religious issues, the merits of secular philosophy, the entertainment value of Jurassic Park to President Clinton's seemingly uneasy marriage and its reflection of changes in American culture, and what herbs are best for preventing sickness.

Angel Park is not isolationist by choice or inclination. Fundamentalist Mormons never rejected American society as much as they feared provoking its wrath. As a middle-aged man puts it, "We follow the law of the land except when it contradicts God's law of plural marriage." Nonetheless, for most of its 80-year existence, the community has repeatedly encountered social harassment and political persecution. Whatever physical and psychological withdrawal fundamentalism has made has been for its own self-preservation.

From 1882 on, federal and state governments sought to disenfranchise the Mormons in Utah. As a result, many polygynists went into hiding, fleeing into remote areas of Utah, Idaho, Arizona and into Mexico. By 1897, almost 200 Mormons were sent to prison for practicing polygyny (Bohannan 1985: 81). However, despite the arrests and the often vocal opposition from Americans outside the community, several church leaders—including some of the founders of the Angel Park community—came to believe that the 1890 Manifesto which declared that polygamy was a sin and, thus, prohibited to any devout Mormon as invalid, and against God's will. During the 1930s, small groups of "true" or "fundamentalist" Mormons rejected the 1890 Manifesto and sought to establish new intentional communities which would provide encouragement, support, and protection for those who wanted to practice their religion in its entirety, which meant the formation of a polygamous family system.

Thus began an ongoing antagonistic and sometimes bitter conflict between Mormon Fundamentalists, the mainstream Mormon church, and state and federal government. From the 1930s until the 1950s, Angel Park was the site of numerous governmental raids, the last and largest taking place in 1953, which resulted in the arrest of 39 men and 86 women and their 263 children. The children were placed in foster homes for up to two years (Van Wagoner 1991; Bradley 1993: 110). An unintended consequence of the raids was to

Strengthen everyone's conviction and dedication to maintain their lifestyle. Outside pressure had in effect turned everyone into a community of believers" (Bradley 1993: 110).

Since the late 1960s there has emerged a greater tolerance, albeit a reluctant one, between the State and the polygamous community. Although the State remains adamant in its insistence that polygamy is illegal, it has tacitly adopted a "live and let live" attitude toward Angel Park.

Given contemporary American mainstream culture's tolerance toward cohabitation, alternative child rearing practices, and other related social experiments in family living, the polygamist community is culturally and politically tolerated—a position that has been reinforced by the 1987 Supreme Court ruling which found that children could not be taken from their mother solely on the basis of living in a polygamous household. The Court ruled that documentation of child abuse and not unorthodox family form was the primary basis for police intervention (Quin 1991). Today, some community members are openly proud that, after decades of persecution, their religiously inspired way of life has finally received legal protection.

Angel Park is an intentional community where practitioners live, or expect to live, in a plural family. Unlike nineteenth century Mormonism, where an estimated 10 to 20 percent of the families were polygamous (Foster 1991), more than 30 percent of the families are polygamous. Often, individuals who do not plan to create a plural family leave the community. This practice ensures that the community is constantly replenishing itself with those who are committed to living "the principle" (i.e., plural marriage). Recent disagreements within the community have resulted, however, in Angel Park splitting into two rival religious communities or wards (e.g., first and second ward). With the exception of different notions of political succession within the church organization, both wards are, by and large, remarkably similar in their cultural and theological orientation. In this and every other way,

Angel Park has remained, throughout its history, both demographically and culturally, a male-centered theologically governed, family oriented religious community.

Mormon Theology—Christianity and Honoring Thy Father

Mormonism, or the Church of Jesus Christ of Latter Day Saints (LDS), emerged out of the American frontier experience which shaped, and continues to shape, its interpretation of Christian doctrines. Its theology is grounded in the teachings of three books: *The Bible, The Book of Mormon,* and *The Doctrine and Covenants.* The latter two books are prescribed as holy scripture, the words of God revealed directly to Joseph Smith (Musser 1944).

These revelations and doctrines contributed to the formation and growth of a distinctly new kind of American religious canon. Although Mormonism is derived from a Judeo-Christian cultural heritage, it is not a typical Christian denomination. Rather, as Jan Shipps (1985) points out, its reinterpretation of many of Christianity's most basic axioms produced a strikingly novel synthesis which, she insists, generated a new American religion.

With the exception of plural marriage, there are several non-negotiable tenets forming the core of Mormon theology. One such tenet holds that God is a polygamous man who loves all his children, but confers on men and not on women, an elevated spiritual essence which insures that "righteous" living men will obtain a higher spiritual standing. Women's standing, on the other hand, is determined by their performance in the highly valued complimentary roles of wife and mother. Men, on the other hand, occupy leadership positions in their families, on the church council, as well as having the potential, in the next life, to become a godhead with dominion over all their descendants. Within this cosmological framework the father is charged with the duty to constantly expand his kingdom by entering into the institution of plural marriage (Musser 1944).

A second tenet holds that an individual's celestial rank is determined by the performance in this life of virtuous deeds. It is important to point out that a man's celestial rank is not determined by the number of wives he has or the number of children he reproduces. It is determined, primarily, by a person's ability to live righteously, correctly, according to God's will, with the highest virtue reserved to those who enter into a plural family. In contrast, women achieve salvation primarily by becoming a sister-wife (i.e., a co-wife) in a celestial, or plural, family. Because the family unit extends beyond the grave into an eternal world, whereby the marriage contract "seals" a man and woman together "for time and eternity" in the Heavenly Kingdom, it is in a woman's "best interest to advance her husband's interest, which means that she should bear a large number of children" (Bohannan 1985: 81), while also striving to uphold her husband's behavior, especially in front of his children.

Accordingly, Fundamentalist Mormons, more than those of the contemporary mainstream, hold that a central purpose of this life is to prepare for the coming of the Celestial Kingdom, a belief that supports the Fundamentalist's conviction that they are God's chosen people born to live "the fullness of the Gospel" and, thus, create God's ideal—the polygamous family (Baur 1988). This conviction lies at the heart of Angel Park's communitarian impulse to create a socially-unified and spiritually-harmonious united order. Significantly, the creation of this new order depends upon the contribution of the fathers.

Honoring of Fathers and Competing with Fathers

Social standing in every American town is organized around race, wealth, religious membership, and ethical conduct. This is certainly true in Angel Park, a small town which is governed by a religious elite who is "called by God," in a rank order of succession, to the office of the Brethren, or the priesthood council. It constitutes, as such, a sacred charter dedicated to creating a social environment conducive to supporting the polygamous family system.

To achieve this ideal, Angel Park was formally incorporated into a religious trust in order to provide social and economic assistance to its members. The ideal was to create a supportive environment which would enable one to transcend his or her more base human nature and become, in the process, a more tolerant and loving person, and, thus, spiritually worthy to enter into the kingdom of God. Within this religiously-inspired framework, men, as fathers, occupy an important place. Not only are they the religious specialist in their family, the final arbiter of all spiritual and ethical conflicts, but also the high priests of the entire community.

The history of any group is often shaped through the stories it tells itself. None are as powerful as the historical testimonials that people tell one another in gatherings of public remembrance. In Angel Park, these testimonials invariably focus on their father's heroic deeds and accomplishments which ultimately advanced or improved the community. These testimonials, devotional in tune and presentation, honor the deceased father's memory through the selection of hagiographic accounts that ritualistically praise the fathers' actions, while, at the same time, overlook their shortcomings.

The hagiographies are remarkably alike in their content. They typically tell a story of a just and honorable man whose steadfastness to his religious convictions, often in the face of personal financial loss and hardship, demonstrate his commitment to cherished community ideals or participation in important community activities. These activities included the building of some structures, often a drainage ditch, the operation of a much needed saw mill, the creation of a mortgage company which would employ residents, make large contributions to the community's legal defense, or strive to uphold the United Order.

The public testimonials are customarily received as wonderful tales of loving devotion. The devotional tone can be heard in a mid-twenties woman's remembrance of the role her deceased father played in her life. Delivered during a church service, she stressed how "my father always explained the importance and meaning of the Gospel to his family." "Although," she added, "he was strict and diligent in his work, he was also a concerned and loving parent who always worked with his children so they never got in trouble." She concluded by saying how she loved to "see him in the morning pour milk into his coffee; and; that even today every time she makes coffee the smell reminds me of his wonderful presence." This palpable visionary presence of the father is not uncommon.

The love of the father is found, too, in the remarks of a woman in her mid-thirties, who recalled that, as a young girl, she would go on walks with her father who never failed to explain the importance of the living God's law (i.e., polygamy). She declared, with an emotional timbre in her voice, that through "his kindness and love, I am a better person." A teenaged, unmarried woman whose father had passed away when she was eight years old, remembered her father as a sensitive man who "I appreciated for his kindness and commitment to the family." She added that "he will always be an inspiration to me."

Father adoration is often expressed outside of church. A man in his forties said at his family's Sunday dinner, where the entire family eats together, to his wives and children, that his father always stressed the importance of eating, at the very least, one meal a week together as a family. "Dad always said," he added (with tears in his eyes), "the family that eats together stays together." He dwelled on his father's enlightenment and how he, too, as a father, wanted to continue what was, for him, a memorable family tradition.

The honoring of the father as either an important founder of the community or the founder of a family line is reinforced by Angel Park's private school requirement that every graduating senior must write a report about either his or her family history or the history of a significant community founder. In this context, a community founder is defined as anyone who made a significant contribution to Angel Park's growth and development. Such a man is regarded as a kind of father to the whole community; and, in a way, everyone's father. Significantly, women, as mothers or wives, are seldom the subject of these student essays. Nor are they ever commemorated during church services. Hagiographies, in Angel Park, are reserved only for fathers.

These examples do not mean that mothers are less loved or regarded as unimportant in Angel Park. Adults are quick to acknowledge their mother's contribution (discussed below). Appreciation of the mother is more private, though not necessarily less emotionally intense. In the public arena, however, Fundamentalists prefer to speak entirely in the idiom of father adoration and seldom in terms of mother adoration. Typically, after the father has "passed to the other side," he is commemorated by the placement of his photo in a prominent place in the family living room. A deceased mother's photo, however, is usually smaller or, if it is the same size, is placed under his, or inconspicuously, on an adjacent wall. The placement of the photos of the deceased constitute the highest form of remembrance and the declaration of filial affection. In this sense, there is a restricted form of ancestor reverence in Angel Park, with almost exclusive focus on one's father.

Familism: Competing with a Father's Reputation

Although Fundamentalist Mormon theology and church leadership actively discourage familial ranking (i.e., the ranking of families into a hierarchy of relative social worth), it nevertheless flourishes in Angel Park. Its social repercussions encourage a kind of clannishness whereby individuals seek to advance their own reputation; and, indirectly, their family's status through economic achievement and superior moral performance. Although an individual's actions are felt to be either an aspect of family inheritance or something unique to one's own personality, status competition often involves the advancing, or smearing, of a father's reputation. It is not surprising that children but not necessarily adults, often believe their relative social standing depends upon advancing or criticizing one another's accomplishments. There is nothing novel in this pan-human propensity. What is illustrative is the fact that gentle and not so gentle "digs" are couched in a father-centered discourse, which often is nothing more than an exercise in status leveling or status assertion. Such inter-family competition takes place in a variety of settings: 'song duels' between children of rival families, general peer group teasing, and public criticism and ridicule of another's behavior.

One popular form, the song duel, takes place only between children and never, as in the case of the Eskimo song duel, between adults. As an example, an eight-year-old girl encounters two seven-year-old half-sisters from rival religious factions, and immediately sings: "Your family is too simple, just too simple . . . " The seven-year-olds just as quickly repeat the song fragment by substituting the eight-year old's family name in place of their own. Claims and counter-claims are flung backward for the peer group.

Teasing always involves mockery in the name of one's father, another child's supposed family-centered personality traits that the family, and its figurehead, the father are implicated in the defect can be seen in the interaction of children playing a game of playground basketball. When one boy repeatedly

kicked the ball, some children ridiculed his physical clumsiness as "typical of all the Jacksons." In a reversal of father adoration, the Jackson's father is belittled, for he is the source of the clumsiness. Father mockery is inevitable in a community where his adoration is crucial. If the father is mocked, he can also be praised. Positive attributes are seen as a trait typical of a certain family. For example, when a particularly gifted musician performed at her school reception, she was warmly applauded with many in attendance noting in appreciation that "all the Boyds are gifted musicians, just like their father." When one wants to raise up in awe or mock, the image of the father is invoked as an indication of strong feelings either way.

Unlike children's status competitions, which take place in semi-public arena and are directed at a specific person, adults prefer to voice their negative evaluations in private settings amongst family members and close friends. These evaluations invariably take the form of teasing put-downs such as the so-and-so "family puts on airs" or "they think they are so special," in order to uphold, on the hone hand, a community ethos of fellowship while, also defending, if not advancing one's own family reputation. There is, thus, in Angel Park, a kind of balance of power involving mockery of fathers and adoration of them as a way of preserving the historical continuity of status. Mockery is one way of keeping certain fathers in their place within the local social hierarchy.

Adult family rivalry often involves the embellishment of one's father's accomplishments through the manipulation of historical facts. Before the religious split in the community, a man who arrived in the community during the 1960s instructed his children, who performed in a school play about the history of the community, a scene that glorified his communal contributions (many of which never happened), while neglecting to mention other men who played a more pivotal historical role. Immediately after the performance, other family members returned home and retold to one another the special exploits of their father in building up Angel Park. Of course, status competition or the manipulation of local history occur in communities and cultures all across America; but, in Angel Park these are invariably expressed in the name of honoring or dishonoring someone's father.

Not every embellished historical account is made to advance a father's accomplishments. Some accounts are invoked to defend what the family considers to be slanderous charges made against their father and, indirectly, themselves. A family's low status can be altered with pervasive historical revisionism. In the 1930s, for example, one man was charged by police for sexual indecency. Fifty years later, his middle-aged daughter habitually explains to anyone who will listen how her father was framed and thus was never sexually immoral. In this way, adults try to maximize their father's memory in order to advance or maintain their position in a social hierarchy that is only partially shaped by principles derived from its fundamentalist theology. In essence, because father adoration is so strong and pervasive a phenomenon in Angel Park, the historically-based status of one's family has a long and durable shelf-life.

The Charismatic Father: Imaging the Polygamous Family

The polygamous family's social organization is derived, in part, from theological axioms which uphold men as the religious specialist and authority in the family; and, in part, from the social dynamics of polygamous family life which make men, as husbands and fathers, the pivotal axis by which wives and children organize attention and internalize family identity. From an organizational perspective, intense and persistent familial attention is on the father as the ultimate adjudicator of family affairs. For children of a plural marriage, the notion of familism and thus belongingness stems from an image of the all-powerful father who is the biological, social and religious pater to his children. In a very practical way, the plural family is held together as much by an image of sharing a common bond as it is with actual memories of interacting with one's father (who embodies the common bond at its highest). It is a bond that needs the active involvement, participation, and affirmation of fathers, co-wives, and mothers.

American psychologists have long noted that, for American children of both sexes, the mother is "the most important figure" (Sered 1994: 57). Because families tend to be organized, in the daily give and take of life, around the mother, there is a general tendency, especially among White American middle-class families, toward developing greater emotional

ties between mothers and children than between fathers and children. Sered (1994) points out that matrifocal units often arise within patrilineal social organizations. In Angel Park, this American tendency toward matrifocality is undermined by the cultural emphasis on the spiritual and administrative authority of the father, while giving equal attention to the husband-wife and mother-child relationship.

Unlike other polygamous societies, Mormon polygamous couples expect to develop strong intense emotional relationships with each other. Such strong husband-wife relationships may undermine a woman's ability to challenge her husband's authority. It is the desire for romantic intimacy that intensifies a woman's identification with the role of wife/lover in addition to that of mother—an orientation that stands in sharp contrast to the mainstream matrifocal ideal where the image of motherhood holds the greater emotional and cultural salience. In Angel Park, a woman's primary emotional and psychological identity often swings between that of wife and mother. This split dampens the pull toward de facto matrifocal units. In a sense, a woman's role is to balance and humanize the desires of marginal intimacy with the needs of her children. To lean too far in either direction would undermine the whole delicately [woven] structure in the polygamous family life.

Because co-wives are often in competition for their husband's attention, they contribute to the idealization process by focusing their children's attention on their father. They are focused on him for attention; so, in a turn, should their children. He becomes the symbolic link between himself, the family, and the community. As mothers, co-wives instruct their children to love and cherish their father and strive to fulfill his expectations. This effort, along with the child's own desire to bond with his father, enhances the father's stature and esteem.

Zablocki (1980) reminds us that charismatic leaders have to constantly prove that they are worthy of the special grace extended to them. He adds (1980: 326) that "tangible failures in the external domain have a way of increasing, rather than decreasing, [a father's] charismatic legacy." Left to themselves, the ideological dreams and day-to-day organizational realities soon go separate ways (Zablocki 1980: 326). The community of Angel Park recognizes the tendency to fragment and strives to achieve consensus by stressing obedience to higher ideals, as does any close-knit culture or religious group. In the case of polygamists, scriptural authority enhances a father's authority by conferring the priesthood on men alone. A priest can withhold blessings; and, thus, delay a son from going before the priesthood council to request a wife. At the family level, the father's authority is reinforced whenever he leads the family in Sunday school service (usually conducted in his home), participates in arranging the marriage of the children, leads the family in its daily prayers, and reveals his religious dreams to his wives and children.

The experience of visions and dreams are the most vivid evidence of a person's ability to interact with the spirit world. By imparting such religious visions and their meaning to his children and wives, a father's authority is unmistakably affirmed. It is understood that personal visions are of profound religious significance and must betaken very seriously. To this end, polygamists seek to understand God's will through the aid of visions and dreams. Prayers, visionary dreams, and one's own inner promptings are evaluated in an attempt to understand God's will processes; not unlike the approach taken by American Puritans to spiritual values and conflicts. The validity of dreams as a vehicle of truth are so strong in the Fundamentalist religion that they are often the critical guide in making important decisions.

A middle-aged man, for example, told his family about an angel who instructed him that his oldest son would live the fullness of the Gospel (i.e., would stay in the community and form a plural family). In another dream, a father told of his son's ability to support the family and sustain the family unity. Still another father reminded his wives of a vision he had when he was a young man, which signaled that he would life a short life, but very fulfilling. This dream affirmed his religious righteousness and the need to follow his instructions, cherishing his time with them. Such dreams circulate within the family and, at times into the community, serving to uphold the father's authority (directly supported by God) and to make him not only a moral force, but a charismatic presence within the family.

In every moral community there is identification of the self with the leader. If "identification is the process of developing bonds to an object and altering one's actions because of these attachments" (Ross 1993: 58), then the peculiar inter-dynamics of

the American Mormon polygamous family likewise contribute to transforming the father from an important, albeit respected parent, into an all-powerful charismatic figure whose memory is privately cherished and socially adored. Since the father is given God's will, he is the voice of spiritual idealism, he must be heeded. In doing so, he imposes the conditions for transcendence which is derived, in part, from social organization and, in part, from emotional identification with father, the man. This image may or may not be at odds with a son or daughter's actual experience and thus remembrance of their father. Even when it is, however, the power of father adoration is so strong that it can erase the discrepancies.

Love, Ambivalence and Hostility: Resolving the Father

The internal dynamics of polygamous family life contributes to the production of charismatic awe felt towards the father. It is an adoration that will continue throughout most people's lives. It is, however, an adoration tempered by the actual quality of the childhood and teenage relationship with the father. For those whose father passed away when they were children, there is only an unqualified adoration for the father. However, for those who had long-term interaction with their father, their memories are less clouded with idealization and based on fantasy and more grounded in actual reality. The reality forces or compels many sons and daughters to assimilate the cultural ideal to their own more personal encounter which may be less than perfect. Before exploring the darker side of father-child interaction, we want to look at the children's perspective, especially those whose father died when they were too young to have many meaningful or memorable interactions.

A common theme, a consistent lament, in Angel Park is the yearning of children for a closer relationship with their deceased father. A fourteen year-old boy, for example, whose father had passed away six years earlier, when asked about the importance of a father, said that

> A father is so important for a boy. He will give you guidance, leadership and direction. I regret I didn't have a closer relationship with my Dad before he passed to the other side.

The intensity of such idealism is revealed in the following event. An eleven year-old girl was walking up a mountain path when she spontaneously exclaimed, "I remember going up here with Dad. It was so wonderful." She turns to her mother and asks, "Mom, did I go up here with Dad?" The mom nods, and the girl says, "Yes! I remember it was so often."

Another example of how yearnings for close intimacy contribute to generating an idealized posture toward one's father can be seen in a twenty-five year-old woman's efforts to come to terms with her biological father who abandoned her mother and left the community when she was a toddler only to return when she was a teenager. She refused to accept her step-father as her father, but rather maintained a detached and resentful posture toward him. Toward her biological father, however, she maintained a positive, albeit fantasy grounded, relationship. Although now in her late twenties and with seven children, she calls her biological father twice a week "just to talk about things with the man I adore." One's ego identification is based, in part, on recognizing one's biological roots and, in part, on rendering homage, regardless of biology, to whoever is the patriarchal family head. In this instance, however, she refused to accept her step-father and preferred to dwell on an idealized image of her biological father who would some day return and be worthy of her love.

The above idealizations are as much about fantasy as they are about reality. As psychological projections, they are a familiar theme in mainstream American society. What is unusual about these accounts from Angel Park is the tendency to recall only enjoyable or blissful childhood experience involving one's father.

Although Fundamentalist Mormons want nothing more than to honor and admire their fathers, often as not, despite their best efforts, it is a qualified honor. It is, nonetheless, the depth and persistence of the desire to do so that indicates the hold of father adoration as an institution. Because the father's actual involvement with his family ranges from intimate involvement to outright indifference, it is not surprising that there is a deep underlying ambivalence toward one's father; who, as a valued social symbol, is the focal point of family organization and identity. In effect, the father is the key metaphor that links the church and self together into a unified cultural system.

There are two often competing images of the father in Angel Park. The cherished and revered public image (discussed above) is often modified, in private conversation, by a more guarded and obviously ambivalent attitude which ranges from clear fondness to smoldering resentment and outright rejection. Given the community's social dynamics and the core tenets of its religious creed, most are uncomfortable in acknowledging their ambivalence, and prefer instead to praise their deceased father's memory. However, the actual reality of their father-child interactions, as often as not, gets into the way.

The quality of one's feelings toward one's father depends on the degree of the father's involvement in his child's life. If the father passed away when his children were young, as we have shown above, there is a tendency to internalize their father as a revered and valued symbol. Here the idealization is personal in tone and substance. It is a fantasy but it is still valued. For those who maintained a long-term interaction with a father who was an active parent, but emotionally aloof, the idealization process is seldom complete.

We found that if the father had a warm relationship with his children there is no contradiction between the father's public image and the child's actual remembrance (as an adult) of their interaction. However, if the father-child relationship was grounded in what a child believed was an abusive relationship, then that adult daughter or son's attitude could veer from absolute adoration to smoldering resentment. If one felt anger toward one's father and still lived in the community of Angel Park, that anger would be reconciled with that the cultural ideal of the father as the central person. The reconciliation often takes place in three ways: absolute adoration, guarded adoration, and rejection. Guarded adoration, by far the most common attitude toward the father, is characterized by maintaining a clear distinction between the accomplishments of the father, the cultural and family symbol, and the qualities of the father as a man. For example, sons of a prominent family repeatedly praised their father's accomplishments and what he had meant to them. But, in private, they acknowledged their lack of real closeness and the emotional gap it left in their lives.

Significantly, brothers, more than sisters, admitted a fear of their father and, even, at times, a deep resentment. One brother recalled that he admired deeply his father, but often wondered if he loved him. He noted that, personally, he had no difficulty in distinguishing between his father as a cultural symbol from his actions as a man. Such an ability to compartmentalize is not shared by most of his nineteen other brothers who feared the consequences and were anxious of the implications of a failure to completely honor their father's memory. The brother further observed that

> My brothers are afraid that if they acknowledge the more personal aspects of his [father] character they might hate him. They do not want to look or acknowledge that he was also a man. They can only handle him as my honored father. They think they have to adore him in every way or not at all.

For them, there could never be guarded adoration, only an absolute one.

An example of guarded adoration can be heard in one middle-aged woman's reminiscence that she "wasn't close to my dad. The only reason I want to write my father's life history is to do it before someone else does and then read it at our church service." For her, it is celebrating the father's public image and publicly proclaiming that hold the greater interest.

Another attitude is total rejection. When a son or daughter rejects, especially in conversation, his or her father, it usually means that they no longer participate in the community's social life. By rejecting the father as a critical cultural symbol, the individual effectively severs his ties to the wider cultural and religious order. He or she can now leave the community, which they invariably do. Rejection of the father entails a kind of self-exile from Angel Park—so deep is the necessity of father adoration that when rejections occur, the child will often bitterly curse his or her father.

It is important to point out that in every polygamous culture there is a shortage of women. Angel Park is no different. Most sons must leave the community to search for a wife who, more often than not, refuses to convert to the religion and move back to the community. In these instances, the son leaves the community to find a wife and not because of a strained relationship with his parents, living or dead; whereas rejection of the father usually means

rejecting the religion; rejecting the religion or its community does not necessarily mean it will result in the rejection of the father.

The various attitudes toward the father hide a deep-seated ambivalence and emotional vitality which can fuel his idealization as bearer of family pride and identity. We believe that ambivalent anger toward the father actually contributes to the institutionalization of father adoration in Angel Park primarily by rechanneling the guilt that accompanies the rejection. The characteristic ambivalence does not satisfactorily reconcile the father-son relationship; and, as such, constitutes an emotional reservoir for the unresolved emotions that shape the style in which father adoration is manifested in ceremonial and ordinary life in Angel Park.

In contrast, mothers are seen as an emotional constant: warm, nurturing and intimate. They embody strength and continuity and are seldom perceived to be a force to contend with. Seldom feared or rejected, they are the emotional, but not symbolic, glue that holds the polygamous family together. More importantly, there is not the difficulty and sometimes troubling expectations and pressure of adoration or reverence. It is not a culturally proscribed response. The bifurcation of the father into two parts, the symbol and the man, is one means that men and women in Angel Park use to manage what is, for many, a ghost they can never shake.

Conclusion

The emergence of father adoration arises, in part, from theological centrality of the father in the Fundamentalist Mormon religious system as well as from the peculiar social dynamics of the polygamous family household. It is the social dynamics, and not just an endemic form of child-rearing practice that generates this phenomenon.

We have sought to explore the interplay between the psychocultural dynamics of the polygamous family and its male-centered theology and how its transforms the father into a revered cultural, if not personal, symbol. Although fundamentalist theology discourages familial ranking, the dynamics of living in a close-corporate community, especially one organized around a patriarchal theology, encourages the development of an intense sense of familism that is crystallized in the adoration of the father.

It is the transformation of the father, but not the mother, into a venerable, powerful, and loving memory that distinguishes the contemporary Fundamentalist Mormon community from the mainstream Mormon church as well as from the numerous Christian denominations. In periodically gathering together in the name of the father, the family and the community celebrate their cultural heritage as well as renew their dedication to the creation and maintenance of what it believes to be the Heavenly Father's ideal family unit—the polygamous family.

52

Religious Dimensions of the UFO Abductee Experience

John Whitmore

Although rarely discussed in terms of religion, UFO abduction—or the belief that one has been abducted by unidentified aliens—holds fascinating parallels with religious experiences, as argued in the following article by John Whitmore. The stories told by abductees fit the typical patterns of many religious narratives worldwide, including visions, initiations, encounters with godlike leaders, and the receipt of profound messages intended to benefit humanity. Like other religious experiences, the idea of contact with aliens suggests an encounter with the nonhuman Other. In modern tales of supernatural abduction, however, the encountered Other is not a deity, spirit, or demon but a being with extremely advanced technology. Whitmore bases his study on primary source materials about UFO abduction, such as popular books and magazines, and notes that participants themselves often interpret their experiences in religious terms. Without directly attacking the credibility or authenticity of UFO narratives, Whitmore gently suggests that UFO beliefs stem from the same psychological and cultural sources as more traditional religious beliefs. He ends with a plea for scholars of religion to pay attention to this significant theme in popular culture.

Stories of UFO abduction have been reported more frequently in the United States than in other countries, and they became increasingly prominent in the last decades of the 20th century. These narratives prompt us to consider the relationship between emergent forms of religious experiences, concepts of Otherness, and the effects of changing technology on humans' view of their place in the universe.

In recent times, the subject of UFO abductions has gained immense popularity, both with the public and with a small group of scholars and writers who have turned their attention to the UFO phenomenon. The number of people who claim to have been abducted by occupants of UFOs has been rising almost exponentially since the early 1970s when the subject was first granted acceptance by the media and the

Reprinted by permission from THE GODS HAVE LANDED: NEW RELIGIONS FROM OTHER WORLDS, edited by James R. Lewis, the State University of New York Press. © 1995 State University of New York. All rights reserved.

ufological community. With the publication in 1987 of Whitley Strieber's *Communion,* interest in abductions and abductees exploded. Strieber's account, written with skill by an accomplished author, presented the bizarre details of UFO abduction in an accessible way, spurring the book to the top of the *New York Times* bestseller list. In the wake of this success, talk shows on radio and television fed the public interest in the abduction phenomenon with a steady diet of reports of individuals who believed that they, too, had been abducted.

Contemporaneous with the rise in popularity of Strieber's book was the work of UFO researchers who were dedicated to examining abductions. Individuals like Bud Hopkins, whose own book *Intruders* (1987) made it to the bestseller list, came to dominate the field of ufology. Hopkins and those who share his methodology believe that UFO abductions are a widespread phenomenon that are not always remembered by the victims. Hypnosis is considered a powerful and reliable tool for retrieving these memories, which Hopkins and others argue reveal a specific pattern of action on the part of UFO occupants. In contradistinction to Strieber, who considers his own experiences to be mainly inexplicable, hypnosis-using researchers tend to have clearly defined theories about the nature and purpose of the abduction phenomenon. These theories have come to dominate the field of ufology. A quick examination of UFO books published in the last eight years reveals that books on abductions have outnumbered books on all other subjects related to UFOs combined, by a substantial margin. Popular magazines devoted to UFOs have become almost exclusively concerned with abductions in recent years.

The popularity of abductions has led to a proliferation of first-person accounts, both remembered consciously and retrieved through hypnosis, which are accessible to the researcher. These primary sources reveal a wealth of bizarre detail which is not wholly amenable to the neat theories of many ufologists. A careful examination of abduction narratives indicates that the patterns alleged to have been discovered by abduction investigators often have religious overtones or similarities with more traditional types of religious experience. In addition, the abduction experience is often given a religious meaning by the percipient, and these interpretations are habitually overlooked or ignored by the UFO investigator. The purpose of this chapter will be to examine the abduction phenomenon from the standpoint of religious studies, concentrating on the primary sources with careful attention to religious interpretations of the events that form the pattern of abduction experience.

Sketching the general characteristics of the phenomenon is the first step in such an analysis. In coming to grips with the claims of abductees and researchers, the practice of hypnosis must first be considered. The use of hypnosis to investigate UFO abductions dates back to one of the earliest instances of the phenomenon, the story of Betty and Barney Hill in 1963 (Fuller 1966). In the overwhelming majority of cases available for research, the memory of the abduction event was obtained or clarified through hypnosis. Typically, the abductee consciously recalls little or nothing about the experience. Certain telltale signs, such as unaccounted for spans of time, uneasy feelings associated with UFOs, or the sense of a presence in the bedroom before falling asleep, serve to clue the vigilant researcher into the possibility that an abduction has occurred (Hopkins 1987). Hypnosis is then generally used to explore the abduction experience.

While the reliance on hypnosis is heavy among abduction researchers, most seem to be aware of the difficulties inherent in the process. Hypnosis apparently allows access to a subconscious level of an individual's psyche, allowing him or her to recall repressed memories of actual events, but also making it possible to derive "memories" of things which have never happened (Klass 1988). Hypnotism greatly increases a subject's suggestibility, infusing him or her with a desire to please the questioner and making the subject very susceptible to leading questions (Jacobs 1992). Although they recognize these limitations, researchers, with few exceptions (Vallee 1988), contend that when used competently hypnosis is an accurate tool for uncovering factual details of the abduction event. It would be premature, however, to dismiss the possibility that many, if not all, abduction memories are confabulations of the subconscious, guided by the preconceptions of the hypnotist. Noted UFO debunker Philip Klass favors this view, and rather plausibly dismembers some better known cases by applying this theory. Scott Rogo (1990) also argues for a more psychological view of UFO abductions and his work applies psychoanalytical principles to abduction experiences, showing how such experiences could easily be products of the anxieties of participants.

The nature of accounts obtained through hypnosis is important for understanding the religious characteristics of the abduction phenomenon. As Jung (1958) has argued, specifically in relation to UFOs, the subconscious is a storehouse of religious ideas and symbols. Such symbols can become exteriorized through anxiety or stress. Thus, the religious imagery and interpretation brought out by hypnosis could be confabulations of the subject's subconscious and perhaps worked into a UFO narrative in an effort to please the hypnotist. In his research, Jung noted that certain complexes of religious symbols appeared time and time again in widely separated subjects. The prevalence of similar patterns in part gave rise to his theory of a collective unconscious, a fund of ideas and imagery shared by all people. This theory may also help to explain the similar patterns, filled with religious overtones, which abduction researchers claim to find among their subjects.

The applicability of a Jungian form of analysis to UFO abductions is further strengthened by the markedly dreamlike character of the experience. Dreams are the most common arena in which religious symbolism is encountered. One of the signs noted by abduction researchers as indicative of an abduction event is the prevalence of dreams containing UFOs or alien-related imagery. In many of the cases in which the abduction is at least partially recalled prior to the use of hypnosis, it is recalled as a dream rather than as an objective event. For example, Kathy Davis, the main subject of Bud Hopkins's bestseller *Intruders,* consistently believes that her experiences were a series of dreams about UFO abductions. In his investigation, Hopkins hypnotically examines the alleged abduction events by directing her towards these dreams and asking her to recount their details. Hopkins explains that Davis remembers these events as dreams in order to shield her psyche from the unsettling implications of their reality. Unless one is strongly committed to a theory of extraterrestrial genetic engineers, as is Hopkins, it is difficult to dismiss Kathy Davis's contention that the events were in fact dreams.

An examination of the available primary accounts of abductions also reinforces the dreamlike character of the phenomenon. Often the abductee reports being outside her body during certain stages of the event, or views herself in the third person throughout. Abductees report very common dream imagery during the course of their ordeals, such as floating or flying, falling endlessly, or appearing naked in a public place. Time and space appear disjointed in a nonsensical, dreamlike way. Day instantly becomes night, the inside of a room or craft appears far larger than its exterior dimensions would allow, and events which subjectively seem to have taken hours are found to have taken minutes, or vice versa. Massive structures or huge gatherings of people are reported in places familiar to the abductee, places where they could not possibly have been (Fiore

1989). The phantasmagoric texture of a reported abduction is arguably its prime characteristic, and, much like dreams of a more prosaic kind, the abduction contains patterns and images of religious significance.

The patterns alleged to exist in tales of UFO abductions are, upon first glance, quite convincing. The presence of so many intricate details concerning the appearance of the aliens, the procedures undergone, and the messages imparted to the victim seem to argue strongly against the hypothesis that abductees are simply lying. Researchers such as Hopkins and David Jacobs (1992) contend that these patterns only begin to make sense if the abductions themselves are objective events perpetrated by extraterrestrials with scientific motives. However, such researchers tend to ignore the religious connotations of these patterns and details.

Abductions often begin with the perception of light: extremely bright light that causes the percipient to become paralyzed, blinded, or generally disoriented. Sometimes the light renders the abductee unconscious. This intense light is usually identified as the light of a flying saucer or extraterrestrial vehicle. The religious symbolism inherent here is quite obvious. The appearance of a brilliant light is often said to herald an encounter with the divine Other. Paralysis, blindness, and disorientation are associated with this light. The experience of Saul on the road to Damascus, Muhammad on the Night of Power, or Arjuna in the *Mahabharata* are well-known examples of divine encounters which conform to the model. Bright lights and their attendant effects are stock harbingers of the numinous experience.

Alternately, the experience begins in the nighttime, at the abductee's home, right before falling asleep. The abductee sees one or more beings approaching her bedside, often after passing through walls or closed windows. The abductee usually feels paralyzed at this point, and often loses consciousness. The bedside visitors then take the abductee into their craft, once again passing through walls and taking their victim with them. Visions of beings or faces over the bed before one falls asleep is among the most common of all hallucinations, occurring in the distinctive mental state that lies between waking and sleeping. The visions of abductees have analogies to the experiences of religious ecstatics and saints, who report seeing angels, demons, or revered religious figures coming to them in the night (Evans 1985). Often, these figures lead the mystic on a journey to view heaven or hell, or counsel him in religious matters. Strieber (1988) reports being transported by his visitors to strange, unearthly realms, as do Davis (Hopkins 1987) and Andreasson (Fowler 1990).

After the light, the abductee encounters the aliens. The alien is, as the name suggests, the personification of the Other, utterly nonhuman. Although descriptions vary somewhat, the alien is described as having a large forehead, denoting superhuman intelligence; dressed in shining garments without seams or fasteners; with unblinking, penetrating eyes. The alien often floats or flies, and speaks to the abductee without moving its lips. This complex of attributes is standard for many types of supernatural beings, from angels as described in Christian medieval texts (Vallee 1988) to the devas encountered by Nala in the *Mahabharata*. The alien's appearance marks it as not of this world, and the technology which surrounds it, spacecraft and high tech machinery, shows it to be superior to humanity.

In their encounters with this superhuman Other, abductees report being floated upwards into a waiting craft. Oftentimes, they pass through walls or other obstacles and feel disembodied, as if their soul only were being taken to the UFO (Hopkins 1987; Fowler 1989). Aboard the ship, abductees report frightening details. They are poked, prodded, and molested, most often in a sexual manner. They are subjected to painful medical procedures by groups of aliens, and are even dismembered, body parts severed and organs removed, only to be reassembled (Hopkins 1987; Fiore 1991). After the physical ordeal, they are subjected to some sort of spiritual examination. An alien, generally taller or more authoritative than his fellows, probes their souls. Abductees often report feeling that their memories are being examined or their souls scrutinized, perhaps for some spiritual flaw. After this, abductees are given messages in their minds which they take back with them when they return to normal life. Often these messages concern the purpose of the alien's visit—to interbreed with humanity in order to produce a new hybrid race. Abductees are told that they themselves, or humanity as a whole, are somehow creations of the aliens. The messages can be eschatological in character, forecasting a coming catastrophe or the dawning of a new age.

This scenario has many exact parallels to traditional accounts of shamanistic initiations. Shamanism, an archaic religious complex centered around ecstatic visionary experiences, is widespread among primordial peoples across the globe. The psychological factors inherent in shamanism have been discussed (Silverman 1967) and the broad stages which characterize shamanistic initiation have been outlined (Halifax 1982), in ways that reveal striking similarities with the patterns of UFO abductions. Shamanistic initiations begin with the individual being pulled into the world of the Other, experiencing an isolation from society. They involve brutal physical and mental ordeals, often centering around dismemberment and torture. After being judged worthy by his tormentors, the shaman's nature and mystical ancestry are revealed to him, much as the abductee is given knowledge of her descent. The shaman is often given eschatological knowledge, and returns to society as a healer and religious authority chosen by the spiritual realm. Inexplicable healings and feelings of having been chose are also reported by UFO abductees. Both types of experience are extremely frightening, personality-altering encounters with the Other, perceived at least at first as the Jungian Shadow, mysterious and threatening to the conscious self. Both leave definite, permanent imprints on the psyche of the percipient.

The most important part of the procedures undergone by the abductee, at least in terms of the amount of time spent on it by abduction researchers, is the genital examination. Abductees, both male and female, report having their reproductive systems scrutinized by the aliens, either by hand or with sophisticated-looking instruments. Quantities of sperm and ova are obtained in a process often involving some type of sexual stimulation. In one very early abduction case, a Brazilian farmer actually had intercourse with an attractive female alien (Vallee 1989). Such direct means of obtaining genetic material are sometimes reported, but most often the abductee is aroused in some inexplicable mental way, and often brought by this shadowy means to orgasm (Hopkins 1987; Jacobs 1992). Abductees' minds are filled with erotic images, exciting them against their will. Female abductees are often vaginally penetrated at some point during their experience, and male abductees also tend to report anal penetration by some uncomfortable instrument (Strieber 1988).

The presence of this overt sexual imagery may at first glance offer no insight into the religious significance of the abduction phenomenon. However, as Jung has noted (1958), sexual imagery is often found to be associated with the encounter with the Other. Sexuality is a powerful component of the individual psyche, and one of the primary arenas for the day-to-day confrontation with otherness is the individual's dialogue with the opposite sex. The sexual symbolism often associated with religious experience is in this view an underscoring of the otherness which typifies the encounter with the numinous.

Some abductees report the healing of some ailment as a result of their abduction. The medical processes undergone are in these cases directed at correcting some chronic condition. Abductees claim that other humans aboard the UFO with them also undergo healings, and the aliens explain that these healings have a spiritual component as well as a physical effect. In one case, an abductee viewed a group of people who the aliens said was to be sent down to disadvantaged areas of Earth in order to engage in healing missions (Fiore 1989). The healing powers of God or superhuman beings have long been a subject of religious belief, and to find aliens involved in miraculous, if technological, healings is perhaps not surprising. The connection with shamanistic initiation, in which the shaman returns from his trip as a healer, has already been noted.

At some point in their experience, many abductees report meeting a leader of the aliens. This leader, who is usually physically distinguishable from his fellow aliens, spurs a strong reaction in the minds of the abductees. The alien often reassures the abductee, mysteriously removing any pain felt during the exam (Fiore 1989). Some abductees seem to feel that the alien leader is extremely "good," and bond to him in a warm, emotional way. The abductee implicitly trusts the leader, and feels as if she has known him all her life. Often, the abductee simply feels love for the alien (Jacobs 1992). The feelings may even be sexual, once again emphasizing the otherness of the encounter. Such feelings of goodness, trust, and deep love, linked in abduction cases to the alien leader, are in more traditional types of religious experience often predicated of the divine. The leader of the aliens is the ruler of the numinous realm of the Other into which the abductee is drawn, and is as

such a personification of Otherness, in a manner analogous to God.

A more detailed examination of the messages received by abductees from UFO occupants reveals a wealth of religious details. The content of these communications is often extremely difficult for the abductee to recall, even under hypnosis, and requires great effort on the part of both the hypnotist and the abductee to uncover. Often, the abductee only remembers that she was given some sort of message, and is told by the aliens that she will be unable to remember the content until a later date, "when the world is ready to accept it" (Fiore 1992). These messages can be divided into four distinct classes, each with a specifically religious connotation.

The first type of message is the moral injunction. The aliens tell the abductee that humankind has been behaving very badly, and that if they don't mend their ways, the planet will suffer some sort of chastisement. Sometimes the moral message is quite practical; if the nations of the earth do not stop their constant bickering and experimentation with nuclear weapons, they will assuredly destroy themselves (Fiore 1989). Others are more metaphysical, proclaiming that humans must adopt a more loving attitude towards their fellows and their planet if they are to survive. Sometimes the aliens themselves claim that they will take an active role in the moral sphere, and are ready to destroy humanity if we do not spiritually mature or if we pose a threat to other worlds. These types of messages bear strong resemblances to the prophetic utterances of the UFO contactees of the '50s and '60s. The theme that humankind's moral activity is the interest of some superhuman being is of course a stock theme of Christianity and most other religions, although in this case the judgment is meted out to man not by Jesus Christ but by a powerful alien race.

Other messages are more strictly apocalyptic in character, forecasting a horrible catastrophe on a worldwide scale that will bring about the end of history. Some form of drastic ecological collapse is currently the most popular scenario, ozone depletion or the corruption of the world's oceans being particularly favored (Strieber 1989). The human race however will survive, either by being transplanted to some safe planet to live in paradisiacal comfort, or through becoming one with the aliens through their process of hybridization. The union of man and alien, sharing in the technological power and moral strength of the latter, raised by this union to a superlative degree and redeemed from the perils of earthly existence, is the aliens' final goal according to these abduction narratives (Fowler 1990).

The theme of being chosen also forms an important part of the messages received by abductees. They are told that they are special or important to the aliens and that their experiences are part of some larger plan (Jacobs 1992). They are sometimes charged with conveying the aliens' message to the people of earth, or informed that the aliens have chosen to reveal themselves to humanity through them (Fiore 1989). They are often told that they will know when the time is right to reveal their election and the aliens' gospel.

Other messages claim to reveal the identity and purpose of the aliens. The aliens have come from a distant planet and are busy on earth performing some type of genetic experimentation (Hopkins 1987; Jacobs 1992). Abductees are basically breeding stock for these aliens, supplying them with the eggs and sperm needed for their hybridization mission. The aliens claim to be responsible for the genetic development of man from his primal ancestor (Fowler 1990). That is, they are the creators of humanity; they made us and have guided our evolutionary development and have even intervened in history. The aliens are returning in such great numbers now in preparation for the aforementioned catastrophe. In this scenario, the aliens perform many of the traditional functions of God. They create humanity, guide it through history, and eventually offer a form of salvation, all through a nearly omnipotent technology that replaces the miraculous will of God for modern humankind.

The content of these messages underscores a phenomenon that is encountered time and time again in an analysis of the UFO phenomenon—the projection of traditional religious themes onto a technological science fiction framework. The parallels of these messages to doctrines of the Christian religion are particularly striking. In the moralizing messages, we get the sense that time is running out, that humans must reform or face judgment by the aliens who are superior not merely technologically but also, apparently, ethically. This is the message of the Old Testament prophet, warning of the calamities God will visit upon His people unless they mend their ways.

Apocalyptic messages invoke images of Armageddon and mass catastrophe from which a faithful remnant will be preserved. Abductees are informed that they are chosen to play a special part in a suprahuman plan, and they must evangelize among the nonelect, spreading an alien gospel. The aliens' messages about themselves and the role they play in the development of human culture reveal history to be the unfolding of that plan, in order to produce a new, superior hybrid being—the next step in human evolution. The aliens take the place of a God of salvation history working for humanity's redemption. The goal of history, according to abduction narratives, is not the union of God and man in Christ; rather, it is the union of humanity and alien towards which the UFO godlings strive. The barely disguised grafting of these theological elements of America's most popular religion onto the bizarre phenomenon of UFO abductions argues strongly for that phenomenon's essentially religious nature.

The psychological profiles of UFO abductees reveal differences from those of nonabductees, differences which can be said to indicate the effect of some type of religious experience. Psychologist Kenneth Ring's recent study (1992) finds abductees reporting changes in their mentalities after their encounters. Abductees tend to become more spiritual in outlook, to see in the universe the workings of some supernatural force. Their religious views are more syncretic, finding in all religions some form of spiritual truth. Many abductees report paranormal talents gained as a result of their experience. The ability to cause electromagnetic disturbances, to travel out of body, or to read minds is often claimed. This pattern of personality change is quite similar to that found among people who report near-death experiences, another phenomenon with heavy religious overtones. These experiences, however subjective they may be, have powerful and long-lasting effects upon the psyche of the individual, prompting permanent changes in worldview and lifestyle. In this respect, UFO abductions are like the paranormal events connected with conversion experiences in Puritan New England or modern charismatic Pentacostals: intrusions of another world associated with adoption of a spiritual creed.

Considered in a broad and general sense, the very idea of UFO abductions is an intensely religious concept. Humans of all times and places have held some belief in beings of another order of intelligence—not gods, but sentient creatures different from humanity. This expression of the idea of the Other has traditionally fallen under the supervision of religion, which conceived of these beings spiritually and attributed their great powers to subtleness of nature or superior magical knowledge. The Other still takes this form in modern abduction tales, now a physical extraterrestrial possessing advanced technology rather than a djinn composed of fire. The aliens still retain magical powers—the ability to pass through walls, to fly, to speak with telepathy. As the demons and fairies of previous cultures, they kidnap humans and snatch babies for some inscrutable purpose (Vallee 1969).

To interpret the phenomenon of UFO abductions within a scholarly framework is a difficult task, considering the scope and detail that the phenomenon manifests. Even abductees have severe problems making sense out of their experiences, and tend to turn to researchers/hypnotists who hold highly imaginative views of what is happening for advice and guidance. On one level, abductions are simply uninterpretable. A dreamlike confusion seems to be the hallmark of these reports, and the statements of abductees, although somewhat consistent in terms of overall patterns, is at times widely contradictory. The experiences of many abductees after the abduction event (or between abductions in an ongoing case) are so bizarre as to seem nonsensical. What is one to make of an abductee's report that sinister government agents, with fake identification and license plates, came to harass her about her experiences (Keel 1988)? Or of Kathy Davis's claim that unmarked black helicopters buzzed her house after UFO sightings (Hopkins 1987)? It is tempting to dismiss the entire subject of UFO abductions, and interpret them simply as the rantings of paranoids, yet to do this would be to ignore the significance they have for the study of religion.

The abductees themselves often tend to explain their experiences in terms of religion. Although some abductees strongly reject the idea that their terrifying encounters could have any spiritual significance, many interpret the aliens a priori as supernatural beings. The specific reasons for this will be postulated in the conclusion. At this point, it is interesting to note that the cases which are the most extensively documented and least manhandled by hypnotist-researchers show the most religious details and the greatest degree of personal consciousness on the part of the abductee that her experience was religious in character.

An excellent example is that of Betty Andreasson, whose ongoing abduction experiences have been the subject of three books (Fowler 1980, 1982, 1990). Andreasson herself, a devout Christian, believes that her abductors, as frightening as they are to her, are angels, servants of God. These aliens show an interest in the Bible and baptize her at the beginning of her encounters. They teach her spiritual lessons concerning the nature of the soul and resurrection, and take her out of her body to cavort with them as beings of light. She reports what can only be called a mystical experience, in which the aliens introduce her to a being called the One, with whom she experiences ecstatic union. Andreasson feels that the aliens, the Watchers as she calls them, guide mankind at the command of God, the One.

Whitley Strieber, the most famous of the abductees, also believes his experiences to have been primarily religious in character. Although raised a Catholic, Strieber no longer adheres to any organized religion, and his encounters lack the specifically Christian references of Betty Andreasson's. The "visitor experience," as he terms the abduction phenomenon, is concerned with the evolution of human consciousness, and the science used by the visitors is a "technology of the soul" aimed at heightening man's awareness of his spiritual dimension. He compares the aliens to demons, cosmic predators whose task it is to jolt humanity's spiritual capabilities by subjecting individuals to shock and pain. Upon attaining a sufficiently high state of consciousness, Strieber speculates, humanity may become a fit companion for God. Strieber believes that mystic experience is central to the solution of the UFO mystery, and adopts this attitude in his own investigations, encouraging people with similarly religious abduction experiences to speak out against the prevailing genetic experimentation theories of Hopkins and others (Conroy 1989).

The interpretation of abduction stories by UFO researchers also reveals undercurrents of religion. Many writers from outside the field of religious studies have noted the similarities between modern abduction accounts and the folklore of earlier years concerning fairies and "little people" (Bullard 1987). The belief in diminutive nonhuman beings has always been present in some form in Western culture, and as late as the last century Evans-Wentz (1966) was able to chronicle the details of a living belief in fairies in Scotland and Ireland. Fairies, like UFO occupants, enjoyed abducting humans and causing their victims to experience temporal distortions, periods of "missing time" resembling those that modern UFO experts say are reliable signs of an abduction. Fairies, it was believed, could not properly reproduce and needed the help of humans to sustain their species. Encounters with them were often erotic experiences for the humans involved, and sometimes led to a continuing series of contacts resembling the repeat abductions seen in modern stories. Fairies, however inexplicable their activities, had a firm place in the theology of their time: they were fallen angelic beings, condemned to spend history as exiles from heaven.

Throughout the Middle Ages, both scholars and lay people accepted a belief in incubi and succubi, sexually ravenous demons that invaded bedrooms to molest innocent Christians. These diabolical entities were only one of the folkloric cousins of modern alien abductors found in the medieval period. Medieval chronicles report sightings of flying ships captained by the strange denizens of Magonia (Vallee 1969), who often carried off humans to their land beyond the clouds. In even earlier times the legends of the Norsemen bear witness to belief in a race of dwarves who abducted human beings for the purpose of reproduction.

The existence of a diminutive species of creatures who fly through the air and steal humans for sexual purposes is a belief by no means confined to Western culture. Vallee (1989) notes similar folklore among Native Americans of Mexico and South America. Wherever the idea is found, the beings are always assigned a place in the religious framework of the culture and their existence and purpose is granted a religious significance. The persistent linkage of folklore and religion on this issue is suggestive in terms of the modern attempt to interpret UFO abductions. As will be argued in the conclusion, humanity appears to have no choice but to evaluate its confrontations with the Other in terms of some religious experience. To ignore this connection when interpreting abductions may well be impossible, and at any rate is not conducive to a complete understanding of the phenomenon.

Further strengthening the argument for the essentially religious nature of UFO abductions are the interpretive efforts of abduction researchers who, while not intending to raise issues of religion, still construct "theologies of abduction" when attempting to explain these phenomenon. Some, like Michael Persinger (1989), adopt what could be termed a reductionist position in regards to UFOs and abductions which can be equally well applied to religion. Persinger argues that abductions, as well as near-death experiences and mystical experiences, are the results of naturally occurring electrical charges affecting the temporal lobe of the brain. Such temporal lobe disturbances produce the hallucinations, disorientation, and heightened sense of meaning that are characteristic both of abductions and of religious experiences. Thus, in Persinger's view, religion and abductions are much the same thing: products of discombobulated brains.

Other researchers adopt interpretive schemes which border on the fantastic. Keel (1988) and Vallee (1988) argue that UFOs and abductions are encroachments upon our world by another reality, a distinct dimension of otherness harboring classes of beings of which humanity is not normally aware. Abductions and other paranormal events are the mechanism by which the intelligences of this alternate reality control humanity, manipulating our beliefs and opinions in a rather sinister fashion. The deities and demons which fill religions are based upon these intelligences, and abductions are simply the latest device being used by extradimensional beings to influence human development. The theory that our world is subject to control by alternate realities is used to explain everything from Bigfoot to appearances of the Blessed Virgin Mary.

By far the most popular scenario for interpreting the abduction experience is the theory that extraterrestrial biologists are using humans for genetic experiments. This is the stance adopted by the majority of UFO books and magazines towards the abduction phenomenon. Most of the well-known hypnotist-researchers, like Hopkins, are strongly committed to this view, and, due to the uncertainties of hypnosis discussed earlier, it is difficult to determine if the theory is derived from the subject matter, or if the extraterrestrial theory influences the hypnotic recall of the abductee. As noted, the idea that aliens were responsible for the creation and evolution of humanity in the manner described by abductees carries with it religious connotations.

An inseparable corollary to the notion that aliens are abroad kidnapping humans is the theory that the government is fully aware of this but conceals it from the public. Some argue that the United States and other world powers have cut a Faustian deal with the aliens, ignoring the extraterrestrial attacks on citizens in exchange for advanced technology (Hall 1988). Such a scenario pits a small group of the Elect who are knowledgeable about the aliens' existence and motives against government conspirators who have sold out the human race to diabolical alien monsters. Other conspiracy theorists believe that our planet is a pawn in a battle between two advanced alien species, one benevolent and concerned with human welfare, and the other evil and heartless with a desire to enslave humankind (Hamilton 1991). Abductions are carried out by both sides, with the beneficent aliens spiritually educating people so that they may resist the sinister extraterrestrials who abduct in order to torture and control. The government would appear to be on the wrong side of this Manichean war of Light and Darkness, and those who know must expose the conspiracy so that all people may come to the aid of the good extraterrestrials.

Searching for some methodological underpinnings for a conclusive analysis of the abduction phenomenon has been a difficult task. The scope and strangeness of abduction accounts strongly resist any attempt to pigeonhole the phenomenon neatly, but the one consistent thread that can be traced in the complex tapestry of abductions is the theme of religion. Any theoretical exercise aimed at interpreting abductions must take religion into account. Throughout this discussion, Jungian categories have been useful in coming to grips with the dynamics that seem to be at work in these stories. These categories allow the inherent bizarreness and incomprehensibility that are characteristic of abduction narratives to be preserved in the discussion, while also using religion as a rallying point for understanding the patterns that emerge from the confusing details. Since recollections of abductions are dreamlike and uncovered through a process of hypnosis in which the individual's subconscious can play a major part, Jung's psychological categories

seem tailor-made for an analysis of the phenomenon. The concept of the Other has been especially valuable for this investigation.

Whatever else UFO abductions may be, they are an encounter with the Other. Every detail of an abduction story emphasizes the idea of otherness. Abductees are subjected to an otherness of space, taken aboard an extraterrestrial spacecraft and even at times pulled out of their bodies, isolating them from any sense of the familiar. They experience an Otherness of time, which does not seem to flow at the same rate or with the same laws as in day-to-day existence. They are surrounded by Other beings, aliens with visages and powers which are simply not human. The aliens are physically Other, with their short statures, enormous eyes, and oversized heads. They are sexually Other, arousing the abductee and sparking feelings of love. They are spiritually Other, superintelligent and either morally superior or clinically amoral. The abduction experience is a very condensation of the strange and unfamiliar.

As encounters with the Other, UFO abductions are essentially religious. Humanity seems to innately separate the prosaic from the unfamiliar, and the sacred from the profane. Things which do not fit into the definitions of the familiar humanity tends to sacralize. The sacred, the numinous, is that which is "wholly other," completely beyond the pale of human experience as normally considered. Abduction by aliens certainly falls into that category, and this is perhaps the reason for the tendency of abductees to interpret their experiences within some sort of religious framework. Researchers who devise interpretive scenarios tend to encounter religion whether they mean to or not, and even resort to theologizing about alternate realities and the final goal of human history. The otherness of the abduction phenomenon makes religion impossible to escape, and no understanding of the phenomenon can be complete without a consciousness of its religious nature.

Abduction narratives seem to emerge, at least in part, from the subconscious of the abductee. Thus, the stories often contain images drawn from popular culture as well as archetypal symbols drawn from the abductee's psyche. The myth of the flying saucer and its alien occupants has been an important part of Western culture in the years since World War II, and the image of the UFO has been used in literature and cinema to represent everything from the threat of communist invasion to the hope of a united world. The pervasiveness of UFOs in the popular consciousness has increased in recent years along with the number of abduction accounts. More interest in the phenomenon seemed to breed more accounts, which in turn increase the topic's popularity. Abduction accounts seem to absorb whatever details or issues are being discussed in the ufological community, leading to the interesting observation that abduction researchers tend to find whatever they are currently looking for within abduction accounts to support the theory of the day. The increased suggestibility characteristic of the hypnotic state makes it virtually impossible for researchers to hide their biases, and details of previous accounts are repeated by other abductees who pick them up from the hypnotist, from the media, or from UFO literature. The popular concerns of the day are invariably reflected in the abduction narrative, with worries about the environment replacing the fear of nuclear war as facets of the abduction account now that East–West tensions have eased. The ability of abductees to incorporate cultural symbols and concerns into their tales, coupled with the inherently religious nature of abductions as encounters with the Other, goes a long way towards explaining the religious themes discovered in the analysis of the patterns of abduction narratives.

An excellent example of this is the way in which abduction narratives incorporate characteristically American themes. UFO abductions seem to be primarily an American phenomenon; although several important cases have been reported outside the U.S., some argue that abductions are mainly confined to this country. Certainly, no other nation displays such an incredible interest in abduction stories. One reason for this could be the similarities of abductions stories to one of America's favorite literary themes, the captivity tale. Heavily influenced by theological motifs of early Protestant New England, emphasizing imprisonment and bondage, captivity narratives base themselves upon the capture of Americans by culturally distinct, physically different, alien Others: Native Americans, Barbary pirates, or the communist Vietnamese of a modern Rambo movie (Lewis 1989). The captives, usually women, are menaced by their alien captors, and such stories often concentrate on the details of their torture or rape. Anyone familiar with current tales of UFO abductions, especially

as related in popular magazines, can recognize the connection. Here the Other is truly alien, nonhuman and extraterrestrial, whose actions are threatening but inexplicable. The abductees, 80 percent of whom are women, are tortured and sexually violated by bizarre medical experiments, the prurient details of which are discussed on afternoon talk shows. In standard captivity narratives victims are often rescued by a morally perfect hero who destroys the victim's tormentors; in abduction tales the hero is the researcher hypnotist, who alone knows the chilling agenda behind the victim's capture. In captivity narratives American moral virtue is favorably distinguished from the savage excesses, sexual and otherwise, of the captors. The aliens of abduction narratives, coldly clinical and amorally utilitarian, treat their victims more like mere objects of scientific study, perhaps revealing a concern, often expressed in science fiction, that our modern society is becoming increasingly detached from human values.

The phenomenon of UFO abductions is a gold mine for scholars of religion. My brief examination of abductions in a search for patterns has revealed that these encounters can look quite similar to other more traditional forms of religious experience. Similar to dreams and called forth by the use of hypnosis, abductions manifest subconscious imagery which is often religious in nature. The general pattern of the abduction experience manifests congruencies with numinous encounters, and with archaic shamanistic symbolism. The consequences of the event for the abductee are the same as with other forms of subjective paranormal religious experiences. Even the interpretive scenarios developed by abduction researchers, which ignore the religious character of the abductee's experiences, are themselves rife with religious significance. Finally, the abductee's own interpretations of the phenomenon show a propensity, or even a need, to understand the religious significance of the phenomenon. As an important theme in popular culture, abductions deserve to be investigated by trained scholars, employing a number of methodologies, in order to determine the significance they have for the study of religion. It would be a great shame to leave such a topic, so rich with potential for increasing the understanding of popular religious concepts, in the hands of amateur hypnotists and believers in spaceships and government conspiracies.

Suggested Readings

Brown, Michael F.
    1997   *The Channeling Zone: American Spirituality in an Anxious Age.* Cambridge, Mass.: Harvard University Press.

Goldberg, Harvey E.
    1987   *Judaism Viewed from Within and from Without: Anthropological Studies.* Albany: State University of New York Press.

La Barre, Weston
    1970   *The Ghost Dance: Origins of Religion.* Garden City, N.Y.: Doubleday.

Mardin, S.
    1989   *Religion and Social Change in Modern Turkey: The Case of Bediuzzaman Said Nursi.* Albany: State University of New York Press.

Marty, Martin E., and R. Scott Appleby
    1991–95   *The Fundamentalism Project.* 5 vols. Chicago: University of Chicago Press.

Thrupp, Sylvia, ed.
    1970   *Millenial Dreams in Action: Studies in Revolutionary Religious Movements.* New York: Schocken Books.

Volkman, Toby Alice
    1985   *Feasts of Honor: Ritual and Change in the Toraja Highlands.* Urbana: University of Illinois Press.

Goat mask of a modern witch high priestess.

CHAPTER TEN

Religion as Global Culture: Migration, Media, and Other Transnational Forces

Throughout much of the history of anthropology, anthropologists tended to view cultures as discrete and homogeneous units—as groups of people who are pretty much alike and live in communities that are bounded in some identifiable way. Many anthropologists emphasized contrasts between the West and elsewhere and presented non-Western cultures in static terms, either overlooking the changes that occur over time in all societies or viewing change as a one-way process, with Western powers imposing unidirectional change on passive, less developed communities. By the last decades of the 20th century, however, anthropologists had begun to pay more attention to complex and multidirectional interconnections between societies. Localized religious change was the main theme of Chapter 9. Our concluding chapter considers how religion shapes and is shaped by cultural phenomena on a global scale, spreading beyond the boundaries of particular human groups.

Examination of how societies affect one another, and how different groups within a society affect one another, has led anthropologists to a number of new areas of inquiry, many of which have profound significance for the study of religion and the supernatural. Like other aspects of culture, religion has come to be seen in relation to politics, the state, international economic structures, and the media. These have all been areas of intense recent interest for anthropology. With the discipline's traditional emphasis on cultural relativism, it has been natural for anthropologists to also take a strong interest in systems of power and inequality, including race and gender. Historical perspectives have been particularly important in such analyses; for example, areas of focus have included the relationship between religion and colonialism in Africa, the effects of missionaries on Native Americans and in the Pacific, and the ways in which women have resisted control by traditional modes of religious authority.

One of the most influential contemporary anthropologists to grapple with the reformulation of culture in a global context is Arjun Appadurai of Yale University. He has coined a set of five terms to describe the dimensions through which cultural materials flow around the world (Appadurai 1996: 33–37). By utilizing the suffix *-scape* rather than a more common term, Appadurai highlights what he calls the disjunctures among these five flows, all of which transcend boundaries of culture, society, and nation. The five "scapes" are building blocks that shape our imagined worlds, or the ways individuals and groups conceive of themselves and think about their place in the world—who they are and how they want to be.

1. *Ethnoscapes* are the moving groups of people in our world, such as tourists, immigrants, refugees, exiles, and guest workers. These humans move around, carrying goals, values, and ideas about themselves and others.

2. *Technoscapes* are the patterns by which all kinds of technology, high and low, move at high speeds across the world.

3. *Financescapes* refers to the distribution of capital and such nation-transcending phenomena as currency markets, stock exchanges, and commodity speculations.

4. *Mediascapes* are the images and the media themselves that disseminate information globally, such as newspapers, magazines, television, and electronic information sources. These profoundly influence how we perceive our lives and imagine the lives of people who live elsewhere.

5. *Ideoscapes* are frequently shaped by state ideologies. On all continents, components of many globally dispersed ideoscapes derived from the Enlightenment worldview and include such notions as *freedom, rights,* and *democracy.*

The point is that our modern-day cultures, or perhaps even past cultures, cannot be thought of as bounded, isomorphic entities, coherent in themselves. The relationships among Appadurai's five scapes are unpredictable, rapidly changing, and highly dependent on particular circumstances and contexts.

Such ways of thinking about culture and global interconnections offer a number of new avenues for understanding religion. A key question concerns the degree to which religion is a force for conformity and homogenization, especially in a global context. Is religion part of the McDonaldization of the world? In a recent book on religion and globalization, Hopkins et al. write:

> If religion is one of the most fundamental means of organizing human life, then the seeds of globalization may lie within religion itself. We cannot talk about globalization without talking about religion, and we cannot talk about religion without considering how it might have laid the foundations for globalization's inception and launching. Does religion prepare the ground, both culturally and socially, for globalization?… Might a dialectical tension exist between religion and globalization, a codependence and codetermination, manifesting in different modes of religious revitalization? Religion, in various contexts, may serve as an agent of homogenization or an agent of heterogenization. (2001: 4)

The term *globalization* itself is provocative and has swept through both scholarly and popular discussions to become one of the major concepts guiding our understanding of social processes. In its narrowest sense, *globalization* refers to the worldwide movement of finance capital but, in its more common, broader sense, it refers to the international spread of ideas, materials, technology, labor, and even people. Responses to globalization run the gamut from positive to negative. As examples of the negative impacts of globalization, one might point to deforestation; the spread of infectious diseases, such as HIV, ebola, and SARS; the extinction of local languages; and the exploitation of labor in the sweatshops of multinational manufacturers. On the other hand, globalization offers opportunities for the expansion of human rights and democracy; the growth of nongovernmental organizations (NGOs) to protect the environment; the emancipation of women; and the territory-less exchange of ideas on the Internet (Hopkins et al. 2001: 3). In terms of religion, processes of globalization at work for centuries have spread Christianity, Islam, and Buddhism far beyond their geographic points of origin, and today's information technologies allow anyone who uses the Web or watches TV to cruise the "spiritual marketplace," to use a term coined by journalist Donald Lattin (quoted in Batstone 2001: 228).

There are close connections among globalization (however one defines it), the spread of capitalism, and the consumer culture that goes along with capitalism. Because anthropologists are interested in how groups of people resist structures of power, many have turned their attention to religion as a form of anti-systemic protest (Robbins 1999). Some feel that the only groups around the world that actually seek to overthrow or replace the culture of capitalism are religious groups, including Liberation Theology Catholics in Latin America, Islamic fundamentalists in Arab and Southeast Asian countries, and some Protestant fundamentalists in the United States. The so-called fundamentalist movements that are offshoots of major world religions (especially Protestant Christianity and Islam) are markedly different in scope and organization from the smaller religious protest movements examined in Chapter 9, such as the Ghost Dance movement and cargo cults. However, contradictions abound. In the upcoming articles, Brouwer et al.'s account of religion in Korea argues that American-style capitalism is influential in the spread of evangelical Christianity, while Mark Juergensmeyer's survey of religious nationalist movements around the world highlights examples that are decidedly anti-capitalism and anti-globalization.

An ethnographic study by Simon Coleman (2000) exemplifies the anthropological approach to studying religion in relation to globalization and documents the interplay of people, technology, finance, media, and ideology noted by Appadurai. During the 1990s, Coleman studied conservative Protestant Christians in Uppsala, Sweden, and found that the spread of charismatic Christianity across national borders reveals much about how the global and the local shape one another. By talking with Swedish charismatic Christians, attending their worship services, and observing their use of television, video, and Internet technologies, Coleman came to understand how participants strike a complex balance between their immediate community, their national identity, and a sense of global belonging.

In the selections that follow, we have chosen to highlight only a small number of topics related to religion, globalization, and the spread of culture across national boundaries. We begin with an example of the movement of people, and its potential for increased understanding as well as intolerance. Homa Hoodfar's work on Muslim women's clothing addresses the historical effects of confrontational contact between Western and Middle Eastern peoples and includes a discussion of Muslim communities in North America. Hoodfar dispels the notion that modest Islamic women's dress is "traditional" and unchanging or is a sign of oppression. Given this background of misunderstanding, how will the participation of Muslims in Canadian universities and communities shape life in the 21st century?

The second article documents the spread of religion beyond national borders. Brouwer, Gifford, and Rose discuss evangelical Christianity in South Korea, reflecting on Korean history to explain why contemporary South Koreans are drawn in huge numbers to American-style evangelicalism.

Mark Juergensmeyer's article turns our attention to one of the more disturbing implications of globalized religious phenomena: the rise of violent activist movements advocating what he calls religious nationalism. Juergensmeyer's work includes examples that readers will frequently find mentioned in the news.

Clearly, the increasingly rapid spread of religious ideas on a transnational level is possible because of contemporary changes in technology. O'Leary's article considers the connection between communications technology and religious change, discussing the print revolution of the 1500s, as well as religion and the Internet today. His main example is the use of the Internet by neo-pagans.

The issue of how popular and entertainment-oriented media represent religion is significant, with rich potential for comparison across cultures. How are religious institutions depicted in the soap operas of Latin America? How are spiritual resources drawn on in the supernatural TV dramas of South and Southeast Asia? What happens when commercial entertainment is shaped strongly by a few capital-rich industry centers, such as the United States, Japan, and India? Our concluding article takes a look at U.S. religion as depicted in the television show *The Simpsons*. What have the world's millions of viewers of *The Simpsons* learned from that show about religion in America?

References

Appadurai, Arjun
   1996 *Modernity at Large: Cultural Dimensions of Globalization.* Minneapolis: University of Minnesota Press.

Batstone, David
   2001 "Dancing to a Different Beat: Emerging Spiritualities in the Network Society." In Dwight N. Hopkins et al., *Religions/Globalizations: Theories and Cases,* pp. 226–42. Durham, N.C.: Duke University Press.

Coleman, Simon
   2000 *The Globalisation of Charismatic Christianity: Spreading the Gospel of Prosperity.* Cambridge: Cambridge University Press.

Hopkins, Dwight N., Lois Ann Lorentzen, Eduardo Mendieta, and David Batstone, eds.
   2001 *Religions/Globalizations: Theories and Cases.* Durham, N.C.: Duke University Press.

Robbins, Richard H.
   1999 *Global Problems and the Culture of Capitalism.* Boston: Allyn & Bacon.

53

The Veil in Their Minds and on Our Heads: Veiling Practices and Muslim Women

Homa Hoodfar

Anyone who has read a newspaper or magazine from the Western press in recent years is likely to recognize that their depictions of Islam and Muslim societies prominently feature women's dress. In many news photographs, women's head coverings signify the status of women or the modernity of a culture. Immigration, the global spread of faiths, and the international political and economic conflicts of recent years have made Muslim communities increasingly visible in North America and Europe. Western tradition has long equated the veil with oppression or ignorance, so Muslim women frequently bear the brunt of misunderstanding and intolerance, especially from well-intentioned non-Muslims who are concerned about women's rights. A goal of anthropology, however, is to look within cultures to discover meaning and significance, rather than to assume that the observer already knows what something means or to impose facile judgments.

Homa Hoodfar, a Canadian anthropologist of Iranian descent, here shows the malleability and complexity of veiling by paying careful attention to the experiences of Muslim women, arguing that many Western images of the veil are inaccurate and romanticized. To illustrate how Islamic women's dress has varied in response to changing social conditions, the author focuses on women's dress in Iran between the 1930s and the 1980s, including anecdotes from her own family. Finally, Hoodfar discusses her fieldwork among Muslim communities in Canada, highlighting difficulties faced by women who wear modest dress. Hoodfar argues that misconceptions about Muslim women are a form of racism that prevents Muslims and others from joining together to fight injustice.

The scholarly literature on women and Islam, including the role of dress, is voluminous. Interested students might wish to read In Search of Islamic Feminism *by Elizabeth Fernea (Doubleday, 1998) and* Beyond the Veil: Male-Female Dynamics in a Modern Muslim Society *by Fatima Mernissi (Saqi Books, rev. ed. 2003).*

Muslim women, and particularly Middle Eastern and North African women, for the past two centuries have been one of the most enduring subjects of discussion in the Western media. I can also assert without hesitation that the issue of the veil and the oppression of Muslim women has been the most frequent topic of conversation and discussion I have been engaged in, often reluctantly, during some twenty years of my life in the Western world (mostly in the UK and Canada). Whenever I meet a person of white/European descent, I regularly find that as soon as he or she ascertains that I am Muslim/Middle Eastern/Iranian, the veil very quickly emerges as the prominent topic of conversation. This scenario occurs everywhere: in trains, at the grocery store, at the launderette, on the university campus, at parties. The range of knowledge of these eager conversants varies: some honestly confess total ignorance of Islam and Islamic culture or Middle Eastern societies; others base their claims and opinions on their experiences in colonial armies in the Middle East, or on their travels through the Middle East to India during the 1960s; still others cite as reference films or novels. What I find remarkable is that, despite their admitted ignorance on the subject, almost all people I have met are, with considerable confidence, adamant that women have a particularly tough time in Muslim cultures. Occasionally Western non-Muslim women will tell me they are thankful that they were not born in a Muslim culture. Sometimes they go so far as to say that they are happy that I am living in their society rather than my own, since obviously my ways are more like theirs, and since now, having been exposed to Western ways, I could never return to the harem!

For years I went through much pain and frustration, trying to convey that many assumptions about Muslim women were false and based on the racism and biases of the colonial powers, yet without defending or denying the patriarchal barriers that Muslim women (like women in many other countries, including Western societies) face. I took pains to give examples of how Western biases against non-Western cultures abound. In research, for example, social scientists often fail to compare like with like. The situation of poor illiterate peasant women of the South is implicitly or explicitly compared with the experiences of educated upper-middle-class women of Western societies. Failing to adequately contextualize non-Western societies, many researchers simply assume that what is good for Western middle-class women should be good for all other women. It is frustrating that, in the majority of cases, while my conversants listen to me, they do not hear, and at the end of the conversation they reiterate their earlier views as if our discussion were irrelevant. In more recent years, they treat me as an Islamic apologist, which silences me in new ways that often preclude argument.

I had assumed that my experiences were unique and were the result of my moving in milieux that had little contact with or knowledge about Muslim communities and cultures. However, through my recent research on the integration of Muslim women in educational institutions and the labor market in Canada, which has brought me into contact with many young Muslim women, I have come to realize that these reactions on the part of the dominant group are much more prevalent than I had thought. Moreover, the Muslim community, and in particular veiled women, suffer the psychological and socioeconomic consequences of these views. This situation has created a high level of anger and frustration in response to the deliberate racism toward Muslims in Canada and the unwillingness, despite ample examples, to let go of old colonial images of passive Muslim women. The assumption that *veil* equals *ignorance* and *oppression* means that young Muslim women have to invest a considerable amount of energy to establish themselves as thinking, rational, literate students/individuals, both in their classrooms and outside.

In this essay, I draw on historical sources, my research data on young Muslim women in Canada, as well as my own experience as a nonveiled Muslim woman of Iranian descent. I argue that the veil, which since the nineteenth century has symbolized for the West the inferiority of Muslim cultures, remains a powerful symbol both for the West and for Muslim societies. While for Westerners its meaning has been static and unchanging, in Muslim cultures the veil's functions and social significance have varied tremendously, particularly during times of rapid social change. Veiling is a lived experience full of contradictions and multiple meanings. While it has clearly been a mechanism in the service of patriarchy, a means of regulating and controlling women's lives, women have used the same social institution to free themselves from the bonds of patriarchy. Muslim women, like all other women, are social actors, employing, reforming, and changing existing social institutions, often creatively, to their own ends. The static colonial image of the oppressed veiled Muslim woman thus often contrasts sharply with the lived experience of veiling. To deny this is also to deny Muslim women their agency.

The continuation of misconceptions and misinterpretations about the veil and veiled women has several consequences, not just for Muslim women but also for occidental women. The mostly man-made images of oriental Muslim women continue to be a mechanism by which Western dominant cultures recreate and perpetuate beliefs about their superiority. The persistence of colonial and racist responses to their societies has meant that Muslim communities and societies must continually struggle to protect their cultural and political identities, a situation that makes it harder for many Muslim women, who share the frustration of their community and society, to question the merits and uses of the veil within their own communities. Moreover, the negative images of Muslim women are continually presented as a reminder to European and North American women of their relative good fortune and as an implied warning to curb their "excessive" demands for social and legal equality. Yet all too often Western feminists uncritically participate in the dominant androcentric approaches to other cultures and fail to see how such participation is ultimately in the service of patriarchy. Significantly, Western feminists' failure to critically interrogate colonial, racist, and androcentric constructs of women of non-Western cultures forces Muslim women to choose between fighting sexism or racism. As Muslim feminists have often asked, must racism be used to fight sexism?

To illustrate the persistence of the social and ideological construction of the veil in colonial practices and discourses and its contrast to the lived experience of veiling, I first briefly review a history of the veil and its representation in the West. Then, by examining some of the consequences of both compulsory de-veiling and re-veiling in Iran, I demonstrate the costs to Iranian women of generalized and unsubstantiated assumptions that the veil is inherently oppressive and hence that its removal is automatically liberating. I then discuss some of my findings on the representation of the veil and its usage in the context of Canadian society and its consequences for young Muslim women in their communities and in their interaction with other women, particularly feminists. I point out how the androcentric images and stereotypes of occidental and oriental women inhibit women's learning about and from each other

and weakens our challenge to both patriarchy and Western imperialism.

The Origins of the Veil

The practice of veiling and seclusion of women is pre-Islamic and originates in non-Arab Middle Eastern and Mediterranean societies. The first reference to veiling is in an Assyrian legal text that dates from the thirteenth century B.C., which restricted the practice to respectable women and forbade prostitutes from veiling. Historically, veiling, especially when accompanied by seclusion, was a sign of status and was practiced by the elite in the ancient Greco-Roman, pre-Islamic Iranian, and Byzantine empires. Muslims adopted the veil and seclusion from conquered peoples, and today it is widely recognized, by Muslims and non-Muslims, as an Islamic phenomenon that is presumably sanctioned by the Qur'an. Contrary to this belief, veiling is nowhere specifically recommended or even discussed in the Qur'an. At the heart of the Qur'anic position on the question of the veil is the interpretation of two verses (Surah al-Nur, verses 30–31) that recommend women to cover their bosoms and jewelry; this has come to mean that women should cover themselves. Another verse recommends to the wives of the Prophet to wrap their cloak tightly around their bodies, so as to be recognized and not be bothered or molested in public (Surah al-Ahzab, verse 59). Modern commentators have rationalized that since the behavior of the wives of the Prophet is to be emulated, then all women should adopt this form of dress. In any case, it was not until the reign of the Safavids (1501–1722) in Iran and the Ottoman Empire (1357–1924), which extended to most of the area that today is known as the Middle East and North Africa, that the veil emerged as a widespread symbol of status among the Muslim ruling class and urban elite. Significantly, it is only since the nineteenth century, after the veil was promoted by the colonials as a prominent symbol of Muslim societies, that Muslims have justified it in the name of Islam, and not by reference to cultural practices.

Although the boundaries of veiling and seclusion have been blurred in many debates, and particularly in Western writing, the two phenomena are separate, and their consequences for Muslim women are vastly different. Seclusion, or what is sometimes known as *purdah,* is the idea that women should be protected, especially from males who are not relatives; thus they are often kept at home where their contact with the public is minimized. Seclusion may or may not be combined with the veiling that covers the whole body.

It has been argued that seclusion developed among Mediterranean and Middle Eastern societies because they prefer endogamous marriages; consequently they tend to develop social institutions that lend themselves to more control of young people, particularly women. The argument is made even more strongly for Muslim women because they inherit wealth and remain in control of their wealth after marriage. Although a daughter's inherited share is equal to half that of a son, it is also established, by religion, that a father does not have the power to disinherit his daughters. It is an irony of history that the more economic rights women have had, the more their sexuality has been subject to control through the development of complex social institutions. Nonetheless, outside the well-to-do social elites, seclusion was rarely practiced to any considerable degree, since women's economic as well as reproductive labor was essential for the survival of their households. In reality, the majority of social classes, particularly in rural settings, practiced segregation and sexual division of labor rather than seclusion. The exertion of these controls often created an obstacle but did not erase Muslim women's control of their wealth (if they had any), which they managed.

However, as the socioeconomic conditions changed and factory production and trade became the major sources of wealth and capital, elite women lost ground to their male counterparts. The ideology of seclusion prevented their easy access to the rapidly changing market and to information, thus limiting their economic possibilities. Consequently their socioeconomic position vis-à-vis their husbands deteriorated. Moreover, the informal social institutions, class alliances, and kin networks that had protected women to some extent were breaking down very rapidly. In the twentieth century, this context is an important, though often neglected, reason for women of the upper classes in the Middle East to become more radically involved in the women's movement. In Egypt, where the socioeconomic changes were most rapid, the women's movement developed into an organized and effective political force that other political groups could not afford to ignore. As for women in other social groups, the "modern" and "traditional" ideologies of domesticity often excluded women from better-paying jobs in the public sector, particularly if this involved traveling outside their neighborhoods and being in contact with unrelated males. Moreover, the early modern governments that sponsored the training of many citizens in fields such as commercial and international law, engineering, and commerce, following the European model, closed these options to women until a much later date, thereby reproducing and occasionally intensifying the gap already existing between men's and women's economic opportunities.

The veil refers to the clothing that covers and conceals the body from head to ankle, with the exception of the face, hands, and feet. Incidentally, this is also a very accurate description of the traditional male clothing of much of the Arab world, although in different historical periods authorities have tried, with varying degrees of success, to make the clothing more gender specific. The most drastic difference between male and female clothing worn among the Arab urban elite was created with the Westernization and colonization of Muslim societies in the Middle East and North Africa. Men, particularly, began to emulate European ways of dress much sooner and on a larger scale than women did.

Although in Western literature the veil and veiling are often presented as a unified and static practice that has not changed for more than a thousand years, the veil has been varied and subject to changing fashion throughout past and present history. Moreover, like other articles of clothing, the veil may be worn for multiple reasons. It may be worn to beautify the wearer, much as Western women wear makeup; to demonstrate respect for conventional values, or to hide the wearer's identity. In recent times, the most frequent type of veiling in most cities is a long, loosely fitted dress of any color combination, worn with a scarf wrapped (in various fashions) on the head so as to cover all the hair. Nonetheless, the imaginary veil that comes to the minds of most Westerners is an awkward black cloak that covers the whole body, including the face, and is designed to prevent women's mobility. Throughout history, however, apart from the elite, women's labor was necessary to the functioning of the household and the economy, and so they wore clothing that would not hamper their movement. Even a casual survey of clothing among most rural and urban areas in the Middle East and other Muslim cultures would indicate that these women's costumes, though all are considered Islamic, cover the body to different degrees. The tendency of Western scholars and the colonial powers to present a unidimensional Islam and a seamless society of Muslims has prevented them from exploring the socioeconomic significance of the existing variations that were readily available, sometimes in their own drawings and paintings. Similarly, scholarly study of Islamic beliefs and culture focused on Islamic texts and use of Islamic dialogues, while overlooking the variations in the way Islam was practiced in different Islamic cultures and by different classes.

Although clothing fulfills a basic need of human beings in most climates, it is also a significant social institution through which important ideological and nonverbal communication takes place. Clothing, in most aspects, is designed to indicate not only gender and stage of life cycle, but also to identify social group and geographic area. Moreover, in the Middle East, veiling has been intertwined with Islamic ethics, making it an even more complex institution. According to Muslims, women should cover their hair and body when they are in the presence of adult men who are not close relatives; thus when women put on or take off their veil, they are defining who may or may not be considered kin. Furthermore, since veiling defines sexuality, by observing or neglecting the veil, women may define who is a man and who is not. For instance, high-status women may not observe the veil in the presence of low-status men.

In the popular urban culture of Iran, in situations of conflict between men and women who are outside the family group, a very effective threat that women have is to drop their veil and thus indicate that they do not consider the contester to be a man. This is an irrevocable insult and causes men to be wary of getting into arguments with women. Similarly, by threatening to drop the veil and put on male clothing, women have at times manipulated men to comply with their wishes. One such example can be drawn from the Tobacco Movement of the late nineteenth century in Iran. In a meeting on devising resistance strategies against the tobacco monopoly and concessions given to Britain by the Iranian government, men expressed reluctance to engage in radical political action. Observing the men's hesitation, women nationalists who were participating in the meeting (from the women's section of the mosque) raised their voices and threatened that if the men failed to protect their country for the women and children, then the women had no alternative but to drop their veil and go to war themselves. Thus, the men were obliged to consider more radical forms of action.

The Making of the Veil in Their Minds

It was in the late eighteenth and early nineteenth century that the West's overwhelming preoccupation with the veil in Muslim cultures emerged. Travel accounts and observations from commentators prior to this time show little interest in Muslim women or the veil. The sexual segregation among all sects (Muslims, Christians, and Jews) in Mediterranean and Middle Eastern cultures was established knowledge and prior to the nineteenth century rarely attracted much attention from European travelers. Some pre-nineteenth-century accounts did report on oriental and Muslim women's lack of morality and shamelessness based on their revealing clothes and their free mobility. Others observed and commented on the extent of women's power within the domestic domain, an aspect totally overlooked in the latter part of the nineteenth century.

The representation of the Muslim orient by the Christian occident went through a fundamental change as the Ottoman Empire's power diminished and the Muslim orient fell deeper and deeper under European domination. The appearance and circulation of the earliest version of *A Thousand and One Nights* in the West coincided with the Turkish defeat. By the nineteenth century the focus of representation of the Muslim orient had changed from the male barbarian, constructed over centuries during the Crusades, to the "uncivilized" ignorant male whose masculinity relies on the mistreatment of women, primarily as sex slaves. In this manner images of Muslim women were used as a major building block for the construction of the orient's new imagery, an imagery that has been intrinsically linked to the hegemony of Western imperialism, particularly that of France and Britain.

Scholars of Muslim societies, including feminists, have recently begun to trace the entrenchment of the Western image of the oppressed Muslim woman. This informal knowledge about Muslim women seeped into numerous travel books and occasionally into historical and anthropological accounts of the region. In a century and a half, 1800 to 1950, an estimated sixty thousand books were published in the West on the Arab orient alone. The primary mission of these writings was to depict the colonized Arabs/Muslims as inferior/backward and urgently in need of progress offered to them by the colonial superiors. It is in this political context that the veil and the Muslim harem, as the world of women, emerged as a source of fascination, fantasy, and frustration for Western writers. Harems were supposed to be places where Muslim men imprisoned their wives, who had nothing to do except beautify themselves and cater to their husbands' huge sexual appetite. It is ironic that the word *harem,* which etymologically derives from a root that connotes *sacred* and *shrine,* has come to represent such a negative notion in the Western world. Women are invariably depicted as prisoners, frequently half-naked and unveiled and at times sitting at windows with bars, with little hope of ever being free. How these mostly male writers, painters, and photographers have found access to these presumably closed women's quarters/prisons is a question that has been raised only recently.

Western representations of the harem were inspired not only by the fantasies of *A Thousand and One Nights,* but also by the colonizers' mission of subjugation of the colonized, to the exclusion of the reality of the harems and the way women experienced them. Of little interest to Western readers was the fact that during the nineteenth century in most Middle Eastern societies over 85 percent of the population lived in rural areas, where women worked on the land and in the homes, with lives very different from the well-to-do urban elites (who, in any case, were a very small minority). When Western commentators of the nineteenth century came across a situation that contradicted their stereotype of the power structure in Muslim households, they simply dismissed it as exceptional.

It is important to bear in mind that the transformation in the representation of Muslim women during the nineteenth century did not occur in isolation

from other changes taking place in the imperial land, as Mabro has pointed out. During the same period, the ideology of femininity and what later came to be known as the Victorian morality was developing in Britain, and variations on this theme were coming into existence in other areas of the Western world. Yet Western writers zealously described the oppression of Turkish and Muslim women, with little regard for the fact that many of these criticisms applied equally to their own society. Both Muslim oriental and Christian occidental women were thought to be in need of male protection and intellectually and biologically destined for the domestic domain. Moreover, in both the orient and occident women were expected to obey and honor their husbands. In his book *Sketches of Persia,* Sir John Malcolm reports a dialogue between himself and Meerza Aboo Talib in which he compares the unfavorable position of Persian women relative to European women. Aboo Talib makes the point that "we consider that loving and obeying their husbands, giving proper attention to their children, and their domestic duties, are the best occupations for females." Malcolm then replies that this made the women slaves to their husbands' pleasure and housework. That is, of course, quite correct, but, as Mabro has pointed out, Aboo Talib's comment on Persian women was an equally correct description of women's duty in most European societies, including Britain, at the time.

Neither did Western women traveler-writers draw parallels between the oppression of women in their own society and that of women in the orient. For instance, European women of the nineteenth century were hardly freer than their oriental counterparts in terms of mobility and traveling, a situation of which many European female expatriates repeatedly complained. Mobile Shaman, in her book *Through Algeria,* lamented that women were not able to travel unless accompanied by men. Western women travelers often wrote about the boredom of oriental women's lives. It often escaped them that in many cases it was precisely the boredom and the limitation of domestic life that had been the major motivating force behind many Western women's travels to the orient, an option no doubt open only to very few. Similarly, while Western writers of the nineteenth century wrote about the troubled situation of women in polygamous marriages and the double standard applied to men and women, they totally ignored the plight of "mistresses" in their own societies and the vast number of illegitimate children, who not only had no right to economic support but as "bastards" were also condemned to carry the stigma of the sin of their father for the rest of their life. Clearly, societies in the Muslim orient and the Christian occident both practiced a double standard as it applied to men and women. Both systems of patriarchy were developed to cater to men's whims and to perpetuate their privileges. But the social institutions and ethos of the orient and occident that have developed in order to ensure male prerogatives were/are different. The Western world embraced a monogamous ideology, overlooking the bleak life of a huge group of women and their illegitimate children. In the orient, at the cost of legitimization of polygynous marriages and institutionalizing the double standard, women and their children received at least a limited degree of protection and social legitimacy. Although the occident demonstrated little interest in the oriental images of the European world, numerous nineteenth-century documents indicate that oriental writers were conscious of the contradiction between the presentation of a civilized façade and the hideous and cruel reality of the Western world for many women and children.

Women in Qajar Iran were astonished by the clothing of Western women and the discomfort that women must feel in the heavy, tight garments; they felt that Western societies were unkind to their women by attempting to change the shape of their bodies, forcing them into horrendous corsets. A scenario quoted in Mabro has aptly captured the way oriental and occidental women viewed each other: "When Lady Mary Montague was pressed by the women in a Turkish bath to take off her clothes and join them, she undid her blouse to show them her corset. This led them to believe that she was imprisoned in a machine which could only be opened by her husband. Both groups of women could see each other as prisoners and of course they were right."

As the domination by Europe over the orient increased, it shattered Islamic societies' self-confidence as peoples and civilizations. Many, in their attempt to restore their nations' lost glory and independence, sought to Westernize their society by emulating Western ways and customs, including the clothing. The modernizers' call for women's formal education

was often linked with unveiling, as though the veil per se would prevent women from studying or intellectual activities. The reformers proposed a combination of unveiling and education in one package, which at least partly stemmed from their belief that the veil had become in the West a symbol of their society's "backwardness." In many Muslim societies, particularly among urban elites, patriarchal rulers had often enforced (and in some cases still do) the veil to curtail women's mobility and independence. The reformers' criticisms were mostly directed at the seclusion in the name of the veil, for clearly, seclusion and public education were incompatible. Nonetheless, given the connections between the veil and Islamic ethics in Muslim cultures, the reformers and modernizers made a strategic mistake in combining unveiling with formal education. Conservative forces, particularly some of the religious authorities, seized the opportunity to legitimize their opposition to the proposed changes in the name of religion and galvanized public resistance. Though education is recommended by Islam equally for males and female, in fact the public is largely opposed to unveiling.

Despite much opposition from religious and conservative forces, many elite reformists in the Middle East (both males and females) pressed for de-veiling. In Egypt, where feminist and women's organizations had emerged as important political forces vocally criticizing colonial power, it was the women activists who initiated and publicly removed the veil during a demonstration in Cairo in 1923. Egypt thus became the first Islamic country to de-veil without state intervention, a situation that provoked heated debates in Egypt and the rest of the Arab and Muslim world. Recent assessment of de-veiling has dismissed the importance of this historical event on the grounds that veiling only affected upper-class women. But, as I have argued elsewhere, "although Egyptian women of low-income classes never veiled their faces and wore more dresses which did not prevent movement, they nevertheless regarded the upper-class veil as an ideal. It was not ideology which prevented them from taking 'the veil,' rather it was the lack of economic possibilities." The de-veiling movement among upper-class Egyptian women questioned not only the ideology of the veil but also the seclusion of women in the name of the veil and Islam.

In other countries, such as Iran and Turkey, it was left to the state to outlaw the veil. Although the rhetoric of de-veiling was to liberate women so they could contribute to build a new modern nation, in reality women and their interests counted little. Rather, they had become the battlefield and the booty of the harsh and sometimes bloody struggle between the secularists and modernists on one side, and the religious authorities on the other. The modernist states, eager to alienate and defeat the religious authorities, who historically had shared the state's power and who generally opposed the trend toward secularization, outlawed the veil and enlisted the police forces to compel deveiling without considering the consequences of this action for women, particularly those outside the elite and middle classes of large urban centers. Ataturk (1923–38), who represented the secularist, nationalist movement in Turkey, outlawed the veil and in fact all traditional clothing including the fez; the Turks were to wear European-style clothing in a march toward modernity. Iran followed suit and introduced clothing reform, albeit a milder version, but the stress was put on de-veiling. Feminists and women activists in Iran were less organized than their counterparts in Egypt and Turkey. Debates on women's issues and the necessity of education were primarily championed by men and placed in the context of the modernization of Iran to regain its lost glory. In these discussions, women were primarily viewed as the mothers of the nation, who had to be educated in order to bring up educated and intelligent children, particularly sons. The veil was often singled out as the primary obstacle to women's education.

The Veil on Our Heads: Iran, a Case Study

De-veiling, particularly without any other legal and socioeconomic adjustments, can at best be a dubious measure of women's "liberation" and freedom of movement, and it can have many short- and long-term consequences. To illustrate this point, here I review the experiences of my own grandmother and her friends during the de-veiling movement in the 1930s, and then compare this with some of the trends that have developed with the introduction and strict enforcement of compulsory veiling under the current Islamic Republic of Iran.

In 1936, the shah's father, as part of his plan to modernize Iran, decided to outlaw the veil. The government passed a law that made it illegal for women to be in the street wearing the veil (or, as Iranians refer to it, the *chador*, which literally means *tent* and consists of a long cape-type clothing that covers from head to ankle but normally does not cover the face) or any other kind of head covering except a European hat. The police had strict orders to pull off and tear up any scarf or *chador* worn in public. This had grievous consequences for the majority of women, who were socialized to see the veil and veiling as legitimate and the only acceptable way of dressing. Nonetheless, it is important to note the impact of the compulsory de-veiling for rural and urban women, younger and older women, as well as women of different classes. As the state had little presence in the countryside and since most rural women dressed in their traditional clothing, the law had only a limited impact in the countryside. The women who were urban modern elites welcomed the change and took advantage of some of the educational and employment opportunities that the modern state offered them. Women of the more conservative and religious social groups experienced some inconvenience in the early years of compulsory de-veiling, but they had the means to employ others to run their outdoor errands. However, it was the urban lower middle classes and low-income social groups who bore the brunt of the problem. It is an example of these social groups that I present here.

Contrary to the assumptions and images prevalent in the West, women generally were not kept in harems. Most women of modest means who lived in urban households often did the shopping and established neighborly and community networks, which, in the absence of any economic and social support by the state, were a vital means of support during hard times. Many young unmarried women, including some of my aunts, went to carpet weaving workshops, an equivalent activity in many ways to attending school. Attending these workshops gave the young women legitimate reason to move about the city and socialize with women outside their circle of kin and immediate neighbors. Learning to weave carpets in this traditional urban culture was, however, fundamentally different from the crocheting and embroidery engaged in by Victorian ladies: carpet weaving was a readily marketable skill which enabled them to earn some independent income, however small, should they have need.

The introduction of the de-veiling law came at a time of rapid social change created by a national economy in turmoil. In search of employment, thousands of men, especially those with no assets or capital, had migrated to Tehran and other large cities, often leaving their families behind in the care of their wives or mothers, since among the poor, nuclear families were the prevalent form of household. Those men who did not migrate had to spend longer hours at their jobs, usually away from home, while leaving more household responsibilities to their wife. My grandmother, a mother of seven children, lived in Hamedan, an ancient city in the central part of Iran. By the time of de-veiling, her husband, whose modest income was insufficient to cover the day-to-day expenses of his family, had migrated to Tehran in the hope of finding a better job, and she carried sole responsibility for the public and private affairs of her household. According to her, this was by no means an exceptional situation but was in fact common for many women. Evidently this commonality encouraged closer ties between the women, who went about their affairs together and spent much time in each other's company.

Because the women would not go out in public without a head covering, the de-veiling law and its harsh enforcement compelled them to stay home and beg favors from their male relatives and friends' husbands and sons for the performance of the public tasks they normally carried out themselves. My grandmother bitterly recounted her first memory of the day a policeman chased her to take off her scarf, which she had put on as a compromise to the *chador*. She ran as the policeman ordered her to stop; he followed her, and as she approached the gate of her house he pulled off her scarf. She thought the policeman had deliberately allowed her to reach her home decently, because policemen had mothers and sisters who faced the same problem: neither they nor their male kin wanted them to go out "naked." For many women it was such an embarrassing situation that they just stayed home. Many independent women became dependent on men, while those who did not have a male present in the household suffered most because they had to beg favors from their neighbors. "How could we go out with nothing on?"

my grandmother asked us every time she talked about her experiences. Young women of modest income stopped going to the carpet weaving workshops. Households with sufficient means would sometimes set up a carpet frame at home if their daughters were skilled enough to weave without supervision. Gradually, however, the carpet traders started to provide the wool, the loom, and other necessary raw materials to the households with lesser means and, knowing that women had no other option, paid them even smaller wages than when they went to the workshops. Moreover, this meant that women lost the option of socializing with those outside their immediate kin and neighbors, thus young women were subject to stricter control by their family. Worse yet, male relatives began to assume the role of selling completed carpets or dealing with the male carpet traders, which meant women lost control over their wages, however small they were.

Apart from the economic impact, de-veiling had a very negative impact on the public, social, and leisure activities of urban women of modest means. For instance, historically, among urban Shi'ites, women frequently attended the mosque for prayer, other religious ceremonies, or simply for some peace and quiet or socializing with other women. They would periodically organize and pay a collective visit to the various shrines across town. The legitimacy of this social institution was so strong that even the strictest husbands and fathers would not oppose women's participation in these visits, although they might ask an older woman to accompany the younger ones. My grandmother, and women of her milieu, regretfully talked about how they missed being able to organize these visits for a long time, almost until World War II broke out. She often asserted that men raised few objections to these limitations, and said, "Why would they, since men always want to keep their women at home?"

One of the most pleasant and widespread female social institutions was the weekly visit to the public bath, of which there were only a few in the town. Consequently, the public bath was a vehicle for socialization outside the kin and neighbor network. Women would go at sunrise and return at noon, spending much time sharing news, complaining about misfortune, asking advice for dealing with business, family, and health problems, as well as finding suitors for their marriageable sons, daughters, kin, and neighbors. At midday, they would often have drinks and sweets. Such a ritualized bath was especially sanctioned within Muslim religious practices, which require men and women to bathe after sexual intercourse; bathing is also essential for women after menstruation before they resume the daily prayers. A long absence from the public bath would alarm the neighbors of a possible lapse in the religious practices of the absentee. Therefore they had to develop a strategy that would allow them to attend to their weekly ablutions without offending modesty by "going naked" in the street, as the de-veiling law would require them to do.

The strategies they developed varied from bribing the police officers to disappear from their route, to the less favored option of warming up enough water to bathe and rinse at home. Due to the cold climate in Hamedan, and the limited heating facilities available, this option was not practical during the many cold winter months. One neighbor had heard of women getting into big bags and then being carried to the public bath. So, women of the neighborhood organized to make some bags out of canvas. The women who were visiting the public bath would get into the bags, and their husbands, sons, or brothers would carry them in the bags over their shoulder, or in a donkey- or horse-driven cart to the public bath, where the attendant, advised in advance, would come and collect them. At lunch time the women would climb back in the bags and the men would return to carry them home.

Although this strategy demonstrates how far people will go to defy imposed and senseless worldviews and gender roles envisaged by the state, it is also clear that in the process women have lost much of their traditional independence for the extremely dubious goal of wearing European outfits. One can effectively argue that such outfits, in the existing social context, contributed to the exclusion of women of popular classes and pushed them toward seclusion, rather than laying the ground for their liberation. The de-veiling law caused many moderate families to resist allowing their daughters to attend school because of the social implication of not wearing a scarf in public. Furthermore, as illustrated above, women became even more dependent on men since they now had to ask for men's collaboration in order to perform activities they had previously performed

independently. This gave men a degree of control over women they had never before possessed. It also reinforced the idea that households without adult men were odd and abnormal. Moreover, not all men collaborated. As my grandmother observed, many men used this opportunity to deny their wives the weekly money with which women would pay their public bath fare and the occasional treat to consume with women friends. Yet other men used the opportunity to gain complete control over their household shopping, denying women any say in financial matters.

Wearing the *chador* remained illegal, although the government eventually relaxed the enforcement of the de-veiling law. In the official state ideology, the veil remained a symbol of backwardness, despite the fact that the majority of women, particularly those from low and moderate income groups and the women of the traditional middle classes in the urban centers, continued to observe various degrees of *hijab* (covering). The government, through its discriminatory policies, effectively denied veiled women access to employment in the government sector, which is the single most important national employer, particularly of women. The practice of excluding veiled women hit them particularly hard as they had few other options for employment. Historically, the traditional bazaar sector rarely employed female workers, and while the modern private sector employed some blue-collar workers who wore the traditional *chador*, rarely did they extend this policy to white-collar jobs. A blunt indication of this discrimination was clear in the policies covering the use of social facilities such as clubs for civil servants provided by most government agencies or even private hotels and some restaurants, which denied service to women who observed the *hijab*.

This undemocratic exclusion was a major source of veiled women's frustration. To demonstrate but a small aspect of the problem for women who observed the *hijab*, I give two examples from among my own acquaintances. In 1975 my father was paid a visit by an old family friend and her daughter to seek his advice. The family was deeply religious but very open-minded, and the mother was determined that her daughters should finish their schooling and seek employment before they marry. She argued that there is no contradiction between being a good

Muslim and being educated and employed with an independent income of one's own. After much argument, the father agreed that if the oldest daughter, who had graduated from high school, could find a job in the government sector, he would not object to her working. Since, as a veiled woman, she had little chance of even obtaining an application, she asked an unveiled friend to go to the Ministry of Finance and fill out the application form. With the help of neighbors, the mother managed to arrange an interview for her. The dilemma was that, should she appear at the interview with *chador* or scarf on her head, she would never get the job and all their efforts would be wasted. It was finally agreed that she would wear a wig and a very modest dress and leave for the interview from a relative's house so that the neighbors would not see her. After a great deal of trouble, she finally was offered a position and convinced her father not to object to her wearing a scarf while at work. Thus she would leave her house wearing the *chador* and remove it, leaving just a scarf on her hair, before she arrived at work. To her colleagues, she explained that because she lived in a very traditional neighborhood, it would shame her family if she left the house without a *chador*.

A similar example can be drawn from the experience of a veiled woman I met at university in Iran. She came from a religious family with very modest means. She had struggled against a marriage arranged by her family, and managed to come to university always wearing her *chador*. She graduated with outstanding results from the Department of Economics and taught herself a good functional knowledge of English. She hoped, with her qualifications, to find a good job and help her family, who had accommodated her nontraditional views. To satisfy the modesty required by her own and her family's Islamic beliefs, and the need to be mobile and work, she designed for herself some loosely cut, but very smart, long dresses that included a hood or a scarf. But her attempt to find a job was fruitless, though she was often congratulated on her abilities. Knowing that she was losing her optimism, I asked her to come and apply for an opening at the Irano-Swedish company where I worked temporarily as assistant to the personnel manager. When she visited the office, the secretary refused to give her an application form until I intervened. Later, my boss

inquired about her and called me to his office. To my amazement, he said that it did not matter what her qualifications were, the company would never employ a veiled woman. I asked why, since the company had Armenians, Jews, Baha'is, and Muslims, including some very observant male Muslims, we could not also employ a practicing female Muslim, especially since we needed her skills. He dismissed this point, saying it was not the same thing; he then told the secretary not to give application forms to veiled women, as it would be a waste of paper. My friend, who had become quite disappointed, found a primary teaching job at an Islamic school at only an eighth of my salary, though we had similar credentials.

A few years prior to the Iranian revolution, a tendency toward questioning the relevance of Eurocentric gender roles as the model for Iranian society gained much ground among university students. During the early stages of the revolution this was manifested in street demonstrations, where many women, a considerable number of whom belonged to the nonveiled middle classes, put on the veil and symbolically rejected the state-sponsored gender ideology. Then, in 1980, after the downfall of the shah and the establishment of the Islamic Republic, the Islamic regime introduced compulsory veiling, using police and paramilitary police to enforce the new rule. Despite the popularity of the regime, it faced stiff resistance from women (including some veiled women) on the grounds that such a law compromised their democratic rights. The resistance led to some modification and a delay in the imposition of compulsory veiling. After more than a decade of compulsory veiling, however, the regime still is facing resistance and defiance on the part of women, despite its liberal use of public flogging, imprisonment, and monetary fines as measures of enforcement of the veil. The fact is that both rejection of the shah's Eurocentric vision and the resistance to the compulsory veil represents women's active resistance to the imposed gender role envisaged for women by the state.

The Islamic regime has no more interest in the fate of women per se than did the shah's modernist state. Women paid heavily, and their democratic rights and individual freedom once again were challenged. The Islamic regime, partly in celebration of its victory over the modernist state of the shah and partly as a means for realizing its vision of "Islamic" Iran, not only introduced a strict dress code for women but also revoked many half-hearted reforms in the Iranian Personal Law, which had provided women with a limited measure of protection in their marriage. The annulment meant wider legal recognition of temporary marriage, polygyny, and men's right to divorce at will. Return to the *shariah* (Muslim law) also meant women were prevented from becoming judges. The new gender vision was also used to exclude women from some fields of study in the universities. These new, unexpected changes created such hardship, insecurity, and disillusionment for many women, regardless of whether they had religious or secular tendencies, that they became politically active to try to improve their lot. However, strategies that women with religious and Islamic tendencies have adopted are very different from those of secular women's groups.

The impact of compulsory veiling has been varied. There is no doubt that many educated middle-class women, who were actually or potentially active in the labor market, either left their jobs (and a considerable number left the country) voluntarily or were excluded by the regime's policies. However, these women were replaced by women of other social groups and not by men. Labor market statistics indicate that, contrary to the general expectation of scholars, the general public, and the Islamic state itself, the rate of female employment in the formal sector has continued to increase in the 1980s even during the economic slump and increased general unemployment. Similarly, the participation of women in all levels of education, from adult literacy to university level, has continued to increase.

Significantly, whether women believe and adhere to the veiling ideology or not, they have remained active in the political arena, working from within and outside the state to improve the socioeconomic position of women. Iranian women's achievements in changing and redefining the state vision of women's rights in "Islam" in just over one and a half decades have been considerable. For instance, the present family protection law, which Muslim women activists lobbied for and Ayatollah Khomeini signed in 1987, offers women more actual protection than had been afforded by the shah's Family Code, introduced in 1969, since it entitles the wife to

half the wealth accumulated during the marriage. More recently, the Iranian parliament approved a law that entitles women to wages for housework, forcing the husbands to pay the entire sum in the event of divorce.

Although, as in most other societies, the situation of Iranian women is far from ideal or even reasonable, nonetheless the lack of interest or acknowledgment of Muslim women activists' achievements on the part of scholars and feminist activists from Europe and North America is remarkable. Such disregard, in a context where the "excesses" of the Islamic regime toward women continue to make headlines and Muslim women and religious revivalism in the Muslim world continue to be matters of wide interest, is an indicator of the persistence of orientalist and colonial attitudes toward Muslim cultures. Whenever unfolding events confirm Western stereotypes about Muslim women, researchers and journalists rush to spread the news of Muslim women's oppression. For instance, upon the announcement of compulsory veiling, Kate Millett, whose celebrated work *Sexual Politics* indicates her lack of commitment to and understanding of issues of race, ethnicity, and class (although she made use of Marxist writings on development of gender hierarchy), went to Iran supposedly in support of her Iranian sisters. In 1982 she published a book, *Going to Iran,* about her experiences there. Given the atmosphere of anti-imperialism and anger toward the American government's covert and overt policies in Iran and the Middle East, her widely publicized trip to Iran was effectively used to associate those who were organizing resistance to the compulsory veil with imperialist and pro-colonial elements. In this way her unwise and unwanted support and presence helped to weaken Iranian women's resistance. According to her book, Millett's intention in going to Iran, which is presented as a moment of great personal sacrifice, was not to understand why Iranian women for the first time had participated in such massive numbers in a revolution whose scale was unprecedented, nor was it to listen and find out what the majority of Iranian women wanted as women from this revolution. Rather, according to her own account, it was to lecture to her Iranian sisters on feminism and women's rights, as though her political ideas, life expectations, and experiences were universally applicable. This is symptomatic of ethnocentrism (if we don't call it racism) and the lingering, implicit or explicit assumption that the only way to "liberation" is to follow Western women's models and strategies for change; consequently, the views of third world women, and particularly Muslim women, are entirely ignored.

Veiled Women in the Western Context

The veiling and re-veiling movement in European and North American societies has to be understood in the context not only of continuing colonial images but also of thriving new forms of overt and covert chauvinism and racism against Islam and Muslims, particularly in these post–cold war times. Often, un-critical participation of feminists/activists from the core cultures of Western Europe and North America in these oppressive practices has created a particu-larly awkward relationship between them and feminists/activists from Muslim minorities both in the West and elsewhere. This context has important implications for Muslim women, who, like all other women of visible minorities, experience racism in all areas of their public life and interaction with the wider society, including with feminists and feminist institutions. Muslim women, faced with this un-pleasant reality, feel they have to choose between fighting racism and fighting sexism. Their strategies have to take account of at least three interdependent and important dimensions: first, racism; second, how to accommodate and adapt their own cultural values and social institutions to those of the core and dominant cultures that are themselves changing very rapidly; and finally, how to devise ways of (for-mally and informally) resisting and challenging pa-triarchy within both their own community and that of the wider society without weakening their strug-gle against racism. In my ongoing research on young Muslim women in Montreal, I was impressed by how the persistence of the images of oppressed and victimized Muslim women, particularly veiled women, creates barriers for them, the majority of whom were brought up in Canada and feel a part of Canadian society. Consequently, many now do not even try to establish rapport with non-Muslim Québecoise and Anglo women. A college student, angered by my comment that "when all is said and done, women in Canada share many obstacles and must learn to share experiences and develop, if

not common, at least complementary strategies," explained to me:

> it is a waste of time and emotion. They [white Canadian women] neither want to understand nor can feel like a friend towards a Muslim. Whenever I try to point out their mistaken ideas, for instance by saying that Islam has given women the right to control their wealth, they act as if I am making these up just to make Islam look good, but if I complain about some of the practices of Muslim cultures in the name of Islam they are more than ready to jump on the bandwagon and lecture about the treatment of women in Islam. I wouldn't mind if at least they would bother to read about it and support their claims with some documentation or references. They are so sure of themselves and the superiority of their God that they don't think they need to be sure of their information! I cannot stand them any more.

Another veiled woman explained the reasons for her frustration in the following manner:

> I wouldn't mind if only the young students who know nothing except what they watch on television demonstrated negative attitudes to Islam, but sometimes our teachers are worse. For instance, I have always been a very good student, but always when I have a new teacher and I talk or participate in the class discussion the teachers invariably make comments about how they did not expect me to be intelligent and articulate. That I am unlike Muslim women. . . . What they really mean is that I do not fit their stereotype of a veiled woman, since they could hardly know more Muslim women than I do and I cannot say there is a distinctive model that Muslim women all fit into. Muslim women come from varieties of cultures, races, and histor-ical backgrounds. They would consider me unso-phisticated and criticize me if I told them that they did not act like a Canadian woman, because Canada, though small in terms of population, is socially and culturally very diverse.

Some Western feminists have such strong opin-ions about the veil that they are often incapable of seeing the women who wear them, much less their reasons for doing so. Writing in the student news-paper, one McGill student said that she could not de-cide whether it is harder to cope with the sexism and patriarchy of the Muslim community, or to tolerate the patronizing and often unkind behavior of white feminists. She then reported that her feminist house-mate had asked her to leave the house and look for other accommodations because she couldn't stand the sight of the veil and because she was concerned about what her feminist friends would think of her living with a veiled woman, totally disregarding the fact that, though veiled, she was nonetheless an activist and a feminist.

The stereotypes of Muslim women are so deep-rooted and strong that even those who are very conscious and critical of not only blatant racism but of its more subtle manifestations in everyday life do not successfully avoid them. To the Western feminist eye, the image of the veiled woman obscures all else. One of my colleagues and I were discussing a veiled student who is a very active and articulate feminist. I made a comment about how intelligent and imaginative she was. While he admiringly agreed with me, he added (and I quote from my notes): "She is a bundle of contradictions. She first came to see me with her scarf tightly wrapped around her head . . . and appeared to me so lost that I wondered whether she would be capable of tackling the heavy course she had taken with me. . . . She, with her feminist ideas, and critical views on orientalism, and love of learning, never failed to amaze me every time she expressed her views. She does not at all act like a veiled woman." As a "bundle of contradictions" only because she wears the veil, consisting of a neat scarf, while otherwise dressed like most other students, she has to overcome significant credibility barriers. The fact that, at the age of nineteen, without language proficiency or contacts in Montreal, she came to Canada to start her university studies at McGill has not encouraged her associates to question their own assumption about "veiled women." Neither has anyone wondered why Muslim women, if by virtue of their religion they are so oppressed and deprived of basic rights, are permitted by their religious parents to travel and live alone in the Western world.

I had thought that part of the problem was that the veil has become such an important symbol of women's oppression that most people have difficulty reducing it to simply an article of clothing. However, I discovered that the reality is much more complicated than the veil's being simply a visible marker. For instance, a Québecoise who had converted to Islam and observed the veil for the past four years said she had no evidence that wearing the veil was a hindrance to a woman's professional and educational achievements in Canada. In support of her claim she told me of her recent experience at work:

> When I was interviewed for my last job, in passing I said that I was a Muslim and since I wear the veil I thought they made note of it.... I was offered the job and I was working for almost nine months before I realized nobody seemed to be aware that I was a Muslim. One day, when I was complaining about the heat, one of my colleagues suggested that I take off my scarf. To which I answered that as a practicing Muslim I did not want to do that. At first he did not believe me, and when I insisted and asked him and others who had joined our conversation if they had seen me at all without the scarf, they replied, no, but that they had thought I was following a fashion!

She then added that while she is very religious and believes that religion should be an important and central aspect of any society, the reality is that Canada is a secular society and that for the most part people care little about what religious beliefs one has.

While her claim was confirmed to varying degrees by a number of other white Canadian veiled women, converts to Islam, my own experience, and that of other nonwhite, non-Anglo/French Canadian veiled women is markedly different. Here is a recent experience. Last year, my visit to a hairdresser ended in disastrously short hair. I was not accustomed to such short hair and for a couple of weeks I wore a scarf loosely on my head. While lecturing in my classes I observed much fidgeting and whispered discussions but could not determine the reason. Finally, after two weeks, a student approached me to ask if I had taken up the veil. Quite surprised, I said no and asked what caused her to ask such a question. She said it was because I was wearing a scarf; since I was always saying positive things about Islam they thought I had joined "them." "Them?" I asked. She said, "Yes, the veiled women." Perplexed, I realized that what I discuss in lectures is not evaluated on the merits of my argument and evidence alone, but also on the basis of the listener's assumption about my culture and background. My colorful scarf, however loosely and decoratively worn, appears to my students as the veil, while the more complete veil of a practicing but culturally and biologically "white" Muslim who had worn the veil every day to work is seen as fashion! The main conclusion that I draw from these incidents is that the veil by itself is not so significant, after all; rather, it is who wears the veil that matters. The veil of the visible minorities is used to confirm the outsider and marginal status of the wearer. Such incidents have made me realize why many young Muslim women are so angry and have decided against intermingling with Anglo/Québecoise women. After all, if I, as a professor in a position of authority in the classroom, cannot escape the reminder of being the "other," how could the young Muslim students escape it?

Many Muslim women who are outraged by the continuous construction of Islam as a lesser religion and the portrait of Muslims as "less developed" and "uncivilized" feel a strong need for the Muslim community to assert its presence as part of the fabric of Canadian society. Since the veil, in Canadian society, is the most significant visible symbol of Muslim identity, many Muslim women have taken up the veil not only from personal conviction but to assert the identity and existence of a confident Muslim community and to demand fuller social and political recognition.

In the context of Western societies, the veil can also play a very important role of mediation and adaptation, an aspect that, at least partly due to colonial images of the veil, has been totally overlooked by Western feminists. The veil allows Muslim women to participate in public life and the wider community without compromising their own cultural and religious values. Young Canadian Muslim women, particularly those who are first-generation immigrants to Canada, have sometimes seen the wearing of the veil as affording them an opportunity to separate Islam from some of their own culture's patriarchal values and cultural practices that have been enforced and legitimated in the name of religion. Aware of the social and economic consequences of wearing the veil in the Western world, taking it up is viewed by many Muslims as an important symbol of signifying a woman's commitment to her faith. Thus many veiled women are allowed far more liberty in questioning the Islamic foundation of many patriarchal customs perpetuated in the name of Islam. For instance, several veiled women in my sample had successfully resisted arranged marriages by establishing that Islam had given Muslim women the right to choose their own partners. In the process, not only did they secure their

parents' and their communities' respect, but they also created an awareness and a model of resistance for other young women of their community.

Wearing the veil has helped many Muslim women in their effort to defuse their parents' and communities' resistance against young women going away to university, particularly when they had to leave home and live on their own in a different town. Some of the veiled women had argued successfully that Islam requires parents not to discriminate against their children and educate both male and female children equally; hence, if their brothers could go and live on their own to go to university, they should be given the same opportunities. The women in the study attributed much of their success to their wearing of the veil, since it indicated to their parents that these young women were not about to lose their cultural values and become "white Canadian"; rather, they were adopting essential and positive aspects of their Canadian and host society to blend with their own cultural values of origin.

Many Muslim women have become conscious of carrying a much larger burden of establishing their community's identity and moral values than their male counterparts, the great majority of whom wear Western clothes entirely and do not stand out as members of their community. Yet frequently, when Muslim women criticize some of the cultural practices of their own community and the double standards often legitimized in the name of Islam, they are accused by other elements in their community of behaving like Canadians and not like Muslims. Many women eager to challenge their family's and community's attitude toward women have found that wearing the veil often means they are given a voice to articulate their views and be heard in a way that nonveiled Muslims are not. Their critics cannot easily dismiss them as lost to the faith. However, in wearing the veil they often find that they are silenced and disarmed by the equally negative images of Muslim and Middle Eastern women held by white Anglo/Québecoise women, images that restrict the lives of both groups of women.

Conclusion

In this paper I have tried to demonstrate how the persistence of colonial images of Muslim women, with their ethnocentric and racist biases, has formed a major obstacle to understanding the social significance of the veil from the point of view of the women who live it. By reviewing the state-sponsored de-veiling movement in the 1930s in Iran and its consequences for women of low-income urban strata, and the reemergence of veiling during the anti-shah movement as an indication of rejection of state Eurocentric gender ideology, I argued that veiling is a complex, dynamic, and changing cultural practice, invested with different and contradictory meanings for veiled and nonveiled women as well as men. Moreover, by looking at the reintroduction of compulsory veiling in the Islamic Republic of Iran under Khomeini and the voluntary veiling of Muslim women in Canada, I argued that while veiling has been used and enforced by the state and by men as means of regulating and controlling women's lives, women have used the same institution to loosen the bonds of patriarchy imposed on them.

Both de-veiling, as organized by the Egyptian feminist movement in the 1920s, and the current resistance to compulsory veiling in Iran are indications of defiance of patriarchy. But veiling, viewed as a lived experience, can also be a site of resistance, as in the case of the anti-shah movement in Iran. Similarly, many Muslim women in Canada used the veil and reference to Islam to resist cultural practices such as arranged marriages or to continue their education away from home without alienating their parents and communities. Many veiled Muslim women employ the veil as an instrument of mediation between Muslim minority cultures and host cultures. Paradoxically, Western responses to Muslim women, filtered through an orientalist and colonialist frame, effectively *limit* Muslim women's creative resistance to the regulation of their bodies and their lives.

The assumption that veiling is solely a static practice symbolizing the oppressive nature of patriarchy in Muslim societies has prevented social scientists and Western feminists from examining Muslim women's own accounts of their lives, hence perpetuating the racist stereotypes that are ultimately in the service of patriarchy in both societies. On the one hand, these mostly man-made images of the oriental Muslim women are used to tame women's demand for equality in the Western world by subtly reminding them how much better off they are than their Muslim counterparts. On the other hand, these oriental and negative stereotypes are mechanisms by which Western-dominant culture re-creates and perpetuates beliefs about its superiority and dominance. White North American feminists, by adopting a racist construction of the veil and taking part in daily racist incidents, force Muslim women to choose between fighting racism and fighting sexism. The question is, why should we be forced to choose?

54

South Korea: Modernization with a Vengeance, Evangelization with the Modern Edge

Steve Brouwer, Paul Gifford, and Susan D. Rose

A prominent feature of religion in the late 20th century was the increasing spread of the major faiths, including fundamentalist movements, beyond boundaries of nations. Authors Brouwer, Gifford, and Rose document the growth of U.S.-inspired Christian fundamentalism in South Korea and, in the book from which the present article is drawn, other nations worldwide. A key piece of the authors' argument is that evangelical movements that spread the message of American-style economics and anti-communism have been particularly successful. The authors describe two charismatic evangelists from South Korea, both of whom have attracted global followings. Paul Yonggi Cho is a Pentecostalist who uses the techniques of American televangelists and others to recruit large numbers of converts, within Korea and abroad. The Reverend Sun Myung Moon and the Unification Church have cultivated their own version of Christianity, reaching a far smaller number of converts but amassing vast amounts of wealth and power internationally. Brouwer, Gifford, and Rose connect the post-1950 rise of Korean Christianity to social changes within the country, especially the growth of a capitalist economy, the rise of an affluent middle class, and an increase in political opposition movements.

The evangelical Christianity of Korea illustrates the multidirectional flow of cultural changes in the contemporary world. Though Christianity was introduced to Korea by the West, Paul Yonggi Cho's organization has sent missionaries to the United States, Germany, and Japan; has set up seminaries abroad; and has spread its message over broadcast media.

An art collector will naturally be drawn to Florence, a mountain climber to the Himalayas.

"South Korea: Modernization with a Vengeance, Evangelization with the Modern Edge" by Steve Brouwer, Paul Gifford, and Susan D. Rose in EXPORTING THE AMERICAN GOSPEL: GLOBAL CHRISTIAN FUNDAMENTALISM, pp. 105–130. Reproduced by permission of Routledge/Taylor & Francis Group, LLC.

In much the same way a social scientist interested in modernization will have his attention fixed on East Asia.

—Peter L. Berger

If one visits with Protestants in Central America, Africa, South America, or the Philippines, the dominant influence of the U.S. church and parachurch groups and their particular kind of conservative evangelicalism is obvious. In spite of this, believers in many regions of the world are often most excited by an evangelist who is neither an American nor a fellow countryman, but a Korean. They talk of Paul Yonggi Cho, the neo-Pentecostal leader who purposefully chose a first name that signifies that he is following in the shoes of the universal evangelizer of the first century of Christianity.

Another strong Korean presence has for at least fifteen years spent millions of dollars to bring scholars, journalists, and religious leaders by the thousands to educational conferences in Japan, Europe, the United States, and Korea. This sponsor—under auspices of the New Ecumenical Research Association, the International Religious Foundation, the Parliament of World Religions, International Christians for Unity and Social Action, the World Media Conferences, the Washington Institute for Values in Public Policy, and a host of other organizations—has invited intellectuals and writers from around the world to look at the globalization of religions, communications, and social relations. The sponsor is the Korean-based Holy Spirit Association for the Unification of World Christianity, better known as The Unification Church of Reverend Sun Myung Moon.

Koreans have become prominent in endeavors that twenty or thirty years ago would have been controlled by evangelical representatives of the United States. Yonggi Cho has become the foremost practitioner of Pentecostalism and church growth evangelism; the Reverend Moon has availed himself of the resources and opportunities to start transforming the conservative American civil religion into a global anticommunist civil religion. Those attracted by instrumentalist conspiracy theories might make a facile correlation: South Korea, sitting on the front lines of the Cold War, has been occupied by the United States military forces for almost fifty years and has been required to perform certain tasks dictated by conservative U.S. religious/political ideology. Such a superficial dismissal of religious belief would fail to give credit to the character of Korean Christianity, and it would also miss the depth of the historical transformation of Korea during this century. South Korea (and North Korea, too, but in different ways) has undergone a one-hundred-year period of modernization—culturally, economically, and politically—that has been as complete, and

maybe as ruthless, as anywhere on earth. South Korea, a completely industrialized country, borders on First World status; it is much closer to the development levels of the West and Japan than to the Third World status of many other areas where the new fundamentalist Christianity is growing most rapidly.

Japanese Domination, Korean Authoritarianism

In 1884, just as Japan was about to take over the destiny of Korea, the first Protestant missionary, the American Dr. Allen, arrived to be the physician of the Korean royal family. Only three years later the monarchs were forced by the competing interests of Japanese, Chinese, Russian, and Western nations to dismantle the laws and structures that supported their totally intact, ancient feudal society. Korea had been socially and productively backward, dominated by a small Yangban or landlord class that lived off the labor and goods produced by an impoverished peasantry and an auxiliary slave system. As Japan won out over its rivals and established a subservient colony, Korea began a steady transition from the poor, completely agricultural, and feudal institutions of the old Yi dynasty to the prosperous, modern, capitalist, urbanized, and bureaucratized society of the present day. During most of this hundred-year period, the Korean people were forced to live under political conditions as repressive and authoritarian as those imposed by the old feudal regime, though different sectors of society have mounted strong rebellions and resistance at various times.

The Japanese imperialistic control of Korea, begun in 1895 and turned into formal colonial ownership from 1910 to 1945, was as harsh as any fascist regime imposed in Europe; the exploitation of Korean farmers, miners, workers and women was totally directed toward feeding the Japanese and their war machine. After Japan was defeated in World War II, the authoritarian government that grew up in South Korea under American supervision from 1945 to 1987 (giving up any pretense of democracy in 1960) was not as grim; it allowed for economic expansion under Korean ownership, although at the price of severe repression of the Korean laboring classes and dissenting political groups.

The South Korean people, having already been subjected to the brutal work ethic of the Japanese occupation, were prepared (dare we say modernized?) in spirit to adapt to the regimen that would produce great industrial growth from the 1960s through the 1980s. The economic miracle that has transformed the country and dazzled economists worldwide has come at a stiff price: at the end of the 1980s the South Koreans worked the longest workweek in the industrialized world. Their average workweek was fifty-five hours in 1987. At this point they had outstripped their erstwhile developmental rivals, Singapore and Taiwan, the two other "Asian tigers" who also achieved spectacular industrial growth by applying highly authoritarian discipline; by 1987 those two countries had backslid a bit, requiring only forty-seven and forty-eight hours per week, respectively, from the average worker. South Korea's rate of industrial accidents, the highest in the world for many years, has even jumped dramatically in recent years, by about 33 percent between 1986 and 1990.

Consequently, South Korea has grown and modernized itself significantly by imposing draconian measures upon the majority of Koreans and by leaving many workers in a state of relative deprivation. The Korea National Bank wrote that in 1991:

> 88 percent of the GNP comes from unearned income . . . the worst obstacle to the healthy development of the Korean economy is the concentration of economic wealth in several big companies and the monopolistic possession of these properties and management by individual families.

The level of political repression required to usher in modern capitalism was severe and steady, but did not usually degenerate into "apocalyptic" destruction of the kind employed in such Central American countries as Guatemala, where terroristic military regimes had neither prospects nor ability for creating economic growth or a modern state. (Although one should not forget that apocalyptic events immediately preceded Korean development: the Korean War, 1950–53, which left one million civilians dead and two-thirds of the nation's industrial capacity destroyed.) An exception in recent years was the military terror imposed in the Kwangju massacre in May 1980, when the Korean Army attacked the civilian population of the city of Kwangju and killed as many as two thousand people. More generally the

Korean state employed steadier intimidation through large networks of spies, police, and enforcers employed by the Army, the Korean CIA, the municipal and national governments, and the large employers.

The Korean government encouraged a highly "planned economy" and worked closely with the giant companies, called "chaebol," to make their manufacturing production for export the centerpiece of Korean industrial production. These chaebol, usually under single-family ownership, have been allowed to expand horizontally into unnumerable industries with the approval of the state: as of 1990 the four biggest chaebols—Hyundai, Samsung, Lucky Kumsung, Saewoo—had achieved total sales that were equal to 60 percent of the gross national product.

The fact that the chaebol system has made a few families very rich has been perceived as something akin to robbery: "Many working-class people think of rich people as 'thieves.' A certain wealthy district in Seoul is called Thieves Village." Korean political scientist Hang Yul Rhee asserts that most Koreans are much more egalitarian-minded than North Americans, and that U.S.-style income inequality is a prescription for political havoc in Korea.

Popular outrage finally plunged South Korea into political turmoil. In 1987, fed by general resentment that Korean prosperity had not trickled down to the majority, the Korean people rebelled and forced an opening for both political democracy and free labor unions. Growing democratic, labor, and student movements combined forces in the "Grand Labor Struggles" of the summer of that year, which initiated a wave of seven thousand labor strikes that would last from 1987 to 1990.

Although new unions succeeded in establishing themselves in many companies and made some gains in wage bargaining, the force unleashed against them was fierce. Not only did police and Army units help to suppress working people, but many companies hired their own private squads, called Kusadae, to intimidate employees. Long, staged battles took place in the Hyundai and Daewoo chaebols. In 1987, fifteen thousand troops and police attacked workers barricaded within the Hyundai shipbuilding yards—"by helicopter, land, and sea"; the following year the same battle was fought again, this time with nineteen thousand government troops. Some multinational firms such as the ICC Corporation, a Japanese-owned company that is one of the largest shoemakers in the world (twenty thousand workers), employed the Kusadae in the customary Korean fashion. Thugs hired off the street, management personnel, and some male workers armed themselves with clubs and iron bars and attacked about one thousand low-paid female workers who were conducting a sit-down strike. Among other foreign employers who used Kusadae to terrorize young women employees was a subsidiary of the U.S. Tandy Corporation (Radio Shack products). In both cases many victims were beaten, sexually abused, and later fired by the companies.

The democratic movement and the violence it evoked from the corporate sector and the state were disruptive enough to force the military dictator, Chun, out of power in favor of the more conciliatory Roh Tae Woo, another Army general chosen in the semi-democratic election of 1988. Roh, in turn, was replaced by a democratically elected civilian, Kim Young Sam, in December 1992. Kim Young Sam, until the previous year, had been an important leader of the democratic political opposition; his thirty-year career of defying the authoritarian state was made possible by his ability to operate safely within the structures of the Protestant churches of South Korea. Kim Dae Jung, the other perennial opposition figure, had survived over the same period of time through his ties to the Catholic Church.

Although politically and theologically liberal Protestants and Catholics make up a small percentage of Korean Christians, the major churches—particularly the National Council of Churches in Korea, the liberal Presbyterian Church in the Republic of Korea, and the Catholic Church—have offered a haven for the oppressed and an outspoken voice when others were silenced. This narrow political refuge gave voice to students who otherwise would have been tracked down by the very large and efficient state security forces; to labor activists who otherwise would have been beaten or jailed or thrown out of their jobs; and to teachers and journalists who might likely have joined tens of thousands of others from their professions in Armed Forces' sponsored re-education camps. This egalitarian, democratic, left-leaning element in Christianity is found most clearly in "minjung," or people's theology, the Korean version of liberation theology that finds support from both Protestants and Catholics.

Catholic theology, on its original entry into feudal Korean society via Jesuits and others in the eighteenth century, was seen as particularly subversive to the complex, extremely inegalitarian "yangban" structure. Carter J. Eckert and other historians have argued that "it is clear what attracted Koreans to Catholicism was above all its creed of equality, its tenet that the whole of humankind are alike the children of God. . . . It must have been a moving experience for . . . commoners to . . . worship Him on a basis of equality with the yangban." "Catholicism was in itself a grave and growing indictment of yangban society," hence the severe "Persecution of 1801" and "Persecution of 1839" were meant to eradicate Catholics and Catholicism in Korea.

Anti-democratic rule has evoked spirited and very constant resistance in South Korea, and one portion of the large Christian presence in the country has done a great deal to keep the democratic spirit alive. Surprisingly, perhaps, this progressive tendency has not grown rapidly with the successes of the democracy movement in recent years. The large majority of Korean Christians, in particular within the dominant and quickly growing Protestant branch, are very conservative and either opposed to or uninterested in political opposition. They are generally characterized as right-wing and fundamentalist by their more liberal brethren. Song Kon-ho, a Christian and former editor of a large Korean newspaper, describes them this way:

> Conservative churches, however, still boast nearly ninety-five per cent of the Christian followers and continue to expand their influence at a rapid pace through the Pentecostal movement, as for example, the Full Gospel Church. These churches invariably lack any social or political concern.

A Tradition of Religious Opposition

Lest we think that Christianity is the only faith that has found an oppositional role to the ways in which modernization, Japanization, Westernization, and capital formation have been achieved in South Korea, it is worth noting that Koreans have experimented with various new religious influences. They have sought an antidote to their distress in divine solace, restitution, legitimation, and deliverance. Throughout the past century, Koreans have repeatedly resisted and rebelled against their subordination in religious terms, beginning with the Tonghak Peasant Rebellion of 1894.

The Tonghak movement was based on a new syncretic religion—Tonghak means "Eastern learning"—that drew on elements of Taoism, Buddhism, Confucianism, and even some parts of Catholicism (even though the last influence was emblematic of the evil "Western Learning" that supposedly accompanied imperialism). Tonghak taught that Mankind is God and all people are equal. Its adherents probably would have overthrown the Korean monarchy if both China and Japan had not sent troops in to quell the peasant armies.

Tonghak not only helped inspire later rebellions, but also a whole stream of new Korean religions that have thrived in the twentieth century. For many people, as their social structure was being made over for "the economic miracle" by Western and Japanese influences, the new religions offered a way to save Korean values, keep faith in the face of extreme adversity, and wait for the transformation of Korea into the "promised land." One study done in 1971 estimated that these religious sects numbered about two hundred and forty, variously associated with the traditions of shamanism, Chungsan, Taoism, Buddhism, Christianity, "Eastern Learning," and Confucianism. Most of these sects were syncretic, drawing on other religious traditions, and so held some beliefs in common: (1) that the chosen people were the Koreans; (2) that they were awaiting the imminent advent of a perfect world; (3) that they would found a universalistic faith that other nations could also accept; (4) that they would be led by a Savior or leader with special powers who would bring them together; (5) that this would occur at the proper apocalyptic moment; (6) that in the meantime, believers should accept the shamanistic magic of the leader as the appropriate way to drive off evil influences and gain worldly success.

These new religions have attracted about ten percent of the South Korean population and constitute one of the two expanding sectors in religious life, the other being Protestant Christianity, which now represents more than 25 percent of all South Koreans. The tendencies listed above describe not only the new religions, but also the beliefs of the Protestant fundamentalists and Pentecostals.

Up until World War II, the numbers of Protestants, led by Presbyterians, grew modestly but represented less than 2 percent of the population. In the early part of the century, however, the influence of Protestants exceeded their numbers because many middle-class believers, most of them educated in Presbyterian and Methodist schools, were able to pursue careers in education, medicine, and other emerging professions (sometimes even studying in the United States). The mission-run hospitals, schools, and universities were often the best in the country and gained a reputation for Christian service to the poor. Protestants had the opportunity to modernize Korea in a way that would counteract Japanese influence and promote democratic reforms.

Some Korean writers contend that the Protestant churches might have grown larger in the early 1900s if they had not imitated the quietistic performance of the Americans who controlled the direction of the Korean denominations. (Presbyterians, followed by Methodists, completely dominated early Korean evangelization.) The U.S. missionaries chose not to offend the Japanese rulers (and perhaps bring on their own expulsion), during nationalistic revolts of 1907–1911 and the March 1st Movement that began in 1919. This was more than a tactical decision, for the most important missionary figures deplored the political activities of some of their new converts. The Presbyterian influence derived directly from the fundamentalist side of the church and the new conservative theology emanating from Princeton; it taught a dispensational faith that cautioned waiting for the coming of Christ rather than political rebellion.

Many young Korean Christians felt torn between different Biblical interpretations of their fate. One convert, An Ch'angho, in keeping with his American teachers, saw his nation's suffering and sinfulness in acquiescent terms: "Christ told the Jews that it was because they were full of evil deeds and devoid of all goodness that God took the rights from them and handed them over to others, and this surely applies to Korea today." Other new Christians found national hope in millenarian beliefs; Yang Yusan, a Korean evangelist who moved to San Francisco in 1907, wrote to a Korean Nationalist newspaper "not to forget that Christianity is expected to rescue Korea from Japan just as the Israelites were delivered from the Egyptians."

It is within this ambivalent context that the entry of Protestantism into Korea must be understood. On the one hand, it was appealing as a creed supporting nationalism and the possibility of a more benign kind of modernization, particularly since it had no connection to the Japanese modernizers who were so efficiently crushing and reordering the traditional Korean social structure. The faith grew very quickly between 1887 and 1907 and emboldened young Christian patriots to join other nationalists, including the Choundo-gyo (Heavenly Way) descendants of the Tonghak movement, in opposing Japanese imperialism.

Missionaries, on the other hand, attributed their rapid early growth to the giant nationwide revival of 1907, "an outpouring of the Holy Spirit." David Kwang-sun Suh explains that the orientation of the Americans put a fundamentalistic stamp on Korean religion that has lasted until the present day. "The revival meetings . . . set the tone of Korean Protestantism: emotional, conservative, Pentecostal, individualistic, and other-worldly."

The revivals initially did recruit more believers, but they also stressed fundamentalist and dispensationalist avoidance of the sinful world. Since the revivals were intentionally inaugurated by the missionaries to counteract specific nationalist uprisings, including the Righteous Armies of 1907–11 and the March 1st Movement of 1919, many Koreans wondered whether the Americans had conspired with the colonizers or were just avoiding the overlords' wrath. Later, in 1938, many Korean pastors humiliated themselves (or humbled themselves, depending on one's point of view), by agreeing to engage in Shinto ceremonies imposed by the militaristic Pan-Japanese regime.

When Americans appeared again in Korea as liberators in 1945, their religion did not appear as passive as it once had. Syngman Rhee, a Christian nationalist in exile, returned to head the government, and U.S. missionaries and Korean pastors alike resumed preaching their conservative message, but they added very direct nationalist sentiments, inextricably mixed with anti-communism, that had been missing before the war. The Protestant churches began growing rapidly: six hundred thousand members in 1950, 1.14 million in 1960, 2.2 million in 1970. Then, in the next decade the faith exploded more than tripling in numbers as it added five million new adherents. As in many parts of the world, Pentecostalism spearheaded the remarkable increase.

With the Pentecostal dimension added, and the nationalist longing no longer denied, fundamentalist Protestantism in Korea now had a great deal in common with the new Korean religions. The powerful spiritual connection that is evidenced in the miracle cure of the Pentecostal and charismatic revival meeting is also central to the shamanistic tradition in Korea. According to a study on new religious movements, "Most new religions in Korea accomplish their missionary work by way of faith healing."

The healing miracle involves more than just applying "good" hands and personal magical powers upon "bad" bodily sickness; it requires the good spirit—in Pentecostalism, the one and only Holy Spirit—to drive out the demons or evil spirits that are causing the affliction. In the Korean new religions, the healer follows the shamanist tradition of allowing oneself to be possessed by the good spirit: "most universal in shamanism is the relation between its believers and shamans through the latter's personal experience and exorcist rites called *kut*. A shaman is regarded as a professional officiant of exorcism who can display his special function of experiencing a state of self-effacing ecstasy."

The Korean Pentecostal pastor is just such a powerful officiant. Through the processes of speaking in tongues, prophecy, and other gifts of the Spirit, he allows his body, given up to ecstatic experience, to be the conduit of the Holy Ghost's overwhelming power. Such shamanistic power, added to the other considerable attributes of the Christian faith, allows the Pentecostal to emulate and possibly outperform the spirit power evoked in the other new religions: for example, "Ch'oe Che-u's 'ardor to get in touch with spirits' the 'incantation of the divine general' of Nuryang Ch'ondo-gyo: the 'spell to chase the devils away' of the Pongnam-gyo; and the 'art of moving spirits and attaining a godly spirit' of the Ch'on'gyo-do."

The new religions have also emphasized a Korean-centered world, at least in the future, where the Korean example would inspire other nations of Asia and the rest of the globe toward a faith of universal understanding. The spirit and destiny of the nation are tied into the sense of religious triumphalism. The Chongdo-gyo religion, which has headquarters on Mount Kyeryong (the concept of a prayer mountain is important to many, including Korean Pentecostals in Yoido Full Gospel Church), teaches that "Korean will become an international language and the Korean people the messiah for all the peoples of the world." Another sect, the Ch'onji Taean-gyo, has an understanding that "Korea is the land of the Five Elements and the center of the world." In the Segye Ilka Konghoe religion, preachers assert that the Koreans are "the newly chosen people." T'ongil-gyo prophesies that "Korea is the country which will witness the advent of Christ."

The last mentioned, T'ongil-gyo, is the Korean name for the Unification Church. Reverend Moon's assertion that the Second Coming will take place in Korea may seem extreme by Christian standards of the West (especially if Moon himself is taken to be a Messiah figure; at times he has depicted his own role as more akin to a second John the Baptist); however, his belief in Korea's role as a leading evangelizing nation is shared by a good many more orthodox Protestants.

Lee Daniel Soonjung has traced the history of the National Evangelization Movement, which has "challenged the church to accept God's special commission of the Han-race (Korean people)." The Protestant pastor who led the movement, Shin Hyun Gyoon, was as adamant as the non-Christian new religions about the central role of his people: "We are the priesthood nation to all the world . . . the role of the Western church is at an end." Shin's enthusiasm for Korea's special role was not only acceptable in mainstream denominations but was encouraged by Korean President Park during the 1960s and 1970s. Naturally, Shin provided Biblical justification for injecting this strong nationalism into the faith, and emphasized the nation's direct connection to Israel:

> God chooses his people from the Semitic line. We Koreans are in the line of Shem, the first-born of Noah, a nation from the East, a single-race people, and a small and weak nation. Korea is a nation divinely chosen for tomorrow.

The sense of great national mission is shared by a great many South Korean Protestants; it has been encouraged as well by post–World War II governments in order to generate patriotic, anti-communist fervor and include the masses, otherwise disenfranchised, in the mission of building up the Korean economy. Park, president from 1961 to 1979, is credited both with backing the leader of the Korean Campus Crusade for Christ, Billy Kim, and injecting evangelical crusades into the ranks of the South Korean Army. A

U.S. missionary who collects data on Christian conversions estimates that 50 percent of the Army are evangelical believers.

Since they had been associating with U.S. post-war missionaries who carried the Christian/nationalist germ themselves, South Koreans understandably felt a touch of Manifest Destiny coursing through their veins. This kind of religious nationalism might be competitive, or it might end up being complementary to the U.S. Christian purpose. The most far-reaching applications of Christian nationalism/anti-communism, as transformed into an international anti-communism, were engineered through the complex religious/business apparatuses constructed by Sun Young Moon.

Religious Modernization: The Leading Edge, Cho and Moon

Even though the new Christian fundamentalism usually has deep roots in the United States, it can develop specific characteristics within different national contexts. Sometimes very large churches have emerged with strong indigenous attributes, charismatic leadership, and nationalistic ambitions, especially during the 1960s and 1970s: for example, Brasil para Cristo, and the Iglesia in Kristo in the Philippines. In Korea, new developments go further, suggesting that religious structures and beliefs can be made over by religious entrepreneurs and reintroduced to the world market in forms that are even more effective than the original American exports.

In Korea, as in many parts of the world, Protestantism has fragmented more rapidly than has its American counterpart, although along the same lines: the older denominational system is stagnant; new independent church entities have emerged. Fragmentation can occur within existing old denominations as well as through the development of new sects; Presbyterians in Korea had splintered into forty-one groups and churches by 1981. (They were not of equal size, however, and the two largest sub-denominations still claimed the loyalty of most Presbyterians.)

Now that a Pentecostal revival seems to be sweeping many parts of the Earth, the fresh appeal of Christianity is often linked to the tiny "templos," chapels, and tents that seem to pop up overnight for every would-be pastor who has heard the call. The egalitarian impact and the individual spiritual empowerment of such an accessible faith, unimpeded by hierarchy, is not to be denied; those who have documented the Pentecostal trend find much of its strength in its very fragmentation and atomization. On the other hand the very newest Pentecostal and charismatic churches are involved in something different, a reaggregation and reorganization of Christian believers into new, large-scale forms. This is even occurring in the poorest countries, as well as in the more developed nations. In the United States, where traditional denominations remain large and institutionally influential, the entrepreneurship of the evangelical broadcasters reflects the larger reality of evangelical success: conservative, fundamentalist, and Pentecostal church members now outnumber the so-called "mainline" stalwarts of the National Council of Churches.

We should not be surprised by the reaggregation within this fundamentalist/Pentecostal mix, especially as the lives of believers become more settled and they find a big organization appealing for its identification with success and spiritual power. If this is the modernizing trend, then within Korea we find the most modern developments in the form of highly organized megachurches and parachurches that are led by strong entrepreneurial pastors with entourages of subpastors and elders. David Martin has identified the Korean Protestant scene as "a spiritual enterprise culture" that requires "in the top echelon, a kind of international manager 'of the spirit.'"

The concentrated ownership and hierarchical control of the Korean chaebol, so effective for an export-oriented, state-controlled manufacturing economy, is mirrored in church and parachurch structures, particularly the Yoido Full Gospel Church of Paul Yonggi Cho and the Unification Church of Sun Myung Moon. Cho and Moon are impressive entrepreneurs; in addition to their spiritual leadership qualifications, they have strong technical backgrounds: Cho with degrees in technology and law, Moon in electrical engineering. One is the church builder par excellence; the other the creator of the most impressive worldwide parachurch, a quasicorporate entity that can raise and dispose of billions of dollars in many parts of the globe.

These men have their parallels in the United States, most notably in the field of evangelical broadcasting. Jeffrey K. Hadden and Anson Shupe, in

documenting the ascendency of Robertson, Falwell, Swaggart (and many lesser figures) stress their businesslike approach to the task: "Many broadcasters pastor churches, but they have independently incorporated their broadcast ministries as autonomous *parachurch* structures, answerable only to boards they have hand selected." Moreover, the televangelists have successfully identified their market "[the] niche within the broader context of the free-enterprise system. Evangelicals have a product to sell. The product is Jesus Christ and his gift of salvation to those who will accept." Hadden thinks the new evangelical and charismatic forces have simply outmaneuvered the more out-moded church structures:

> Denominational bureaucracies are cumbersome structures for the creation of new initiatives. . . . The mainline Protestant and Catholic traditions simply don't have the organizational structure or fiscal resources to successfully compete with evangelical broadcasters. The entrepreneurial model, free from the constraints of church bureaucracy, is simply a more efficient means for developing a television ministry.

Protestant behavior in the late twentieth century seems to turn Weber on his head: rather than religious asceticism allowing for the development of capitalist behaviors (presumably inculcated in a society over a century or two), we now have capitalist behaviors adopted in order to accelerate the efficacy of religious faith (with results expected within a decade or less). There is no better place to see this phenomenon at work than in South Korea.

Paul Yonggi Cho

In 1952, the Pentecostal churches in South Korea barely existed; eight congregations with five hundred members between them met to form the Assemblies of God. Six years later, Yong Gi Cho, a twenty-two-year-old pastor trained by the Assemblies, launched a tent church outside Seoul with a membership of five people. In 1961, Cho acted as interpreter for Samuel J. Todd, an American Assembly of God healer who was staging a revival tour in Korea; Todd's example inspired Cho to use revivalist techniques and display divine healing powers in order to enlarge his own church. The revival center established for Todd's tour became Cho's

Yoido Full Gospel Central Church in 1962. Because Pentecostalism established itself rather late in Korea, Cho's presence has been instrumental in promoting the "third wave" association between the church growth movement and the Pentecostal boom.

Furthermore, because the late start of Pentecostalism was more or less simultaneous with postwar Korean economic success, the "spirit-filled" faith was not a church of the poor, as Pentecostal churches often were in their early years in the United States and Latin America. Cho's church was not associated with material deprivation or the denial of worldly goods. Therefore, it was possible for Cho to build a gigantic Assembly of God Church on his own terms, having a heterogeneous membership that had a strong middle-class component: by 1974, only twelve years after founding the Yoido Church, a new ten thousand-seat auditorium was built, the church hosted the Tenth World Pentecostal Conference, and the Full Gospel Prayer Mountain retreat was established. By 1994 Cho was admired worldwide for his success because he had built the largest church in the world, with eight hundred thousand members. For those who doubt the possibility of "real" church membership accommodating hundreds of thousands, a description of how worship services were held in August 1986, when the Yoido Church recorded an exact membership of 513,601, indicates that three hundred fifty thousand could be seated each Sunday:

> The main sanctuary of YFGC seats 25,000 members and is surrounded by 15 auxiliary chapels connected by closed-circuit television. A total of 50,000 members and participants can worship simultaneously together in one of the seven services on Sunday.

The "economic miracle" achieved by the growth of the Korean chaebols has its parallel in the organizational and demographic miracle achieved in the religious "chaebol" of Paul Yonggi Cho; obviously such achievement is revered by all Protestant pastors who aspire to multiplying their flocks. Less obvious is the way in which Cho had a vision of the "cell principle" in 1976 and began to systematize the growth theories of Fuller Theology missiologist Donald McGavran and other Western evangelists. Cho writes that he followed McGavran's advice: "Men and women do like to become Christians without crossing barriers." His strategy was to divide up his church into homogeneous cells made up of five to ten families. By homogeneous, he usually means common orientations or occupations (racial homogeneity being almost complete in Korea)—businessmen, schoolteachers, housewives—and gives this example:

> Mr. Chun the banker is in charge of the cell meeting, his cell will be comprised mainly of financial people. Their one hour cell meeting might take place in a local restaurant and look very much like a business lunch. . . . They might spend some time praying for their specific needs. . . . They will discuss one potential convert. Perhaps it is another financial person who has a problem.

However, says Cho, he used the "homogenous principle" for developing the cell system, not for the entire church: "We do not differentiate between rich and poor, high and low, or well-educated and uneducated." The cell system allows Cho's Yoido Full Gospel Church to evangelize *Our Kind of People* (the title of a church growth book by McGavran's successor at Fuller Theological Seminary, Peter Wagner), and then strictly organize these cells into a giant structure of more heterogeneous elements. As of 1990, when the church had six hundred fifty thousand members, there was the following hierarchy: 48,009 gome cell leaders, 48,009 assistant home cell leaders, 6,740 section leaders, 402 subdistrict leaders, 24 district leaders, 11 regional chapel leaders, a director of pastoral care department, and Dr. Paul Yonggi Cho himself.

Of the above, about seven hundred people were salaried pastors whose activities were planned on elaborate maps and charts in the main church:

> In fact, it looks like a military strategy room. This is a war we are fighting. The enemy is the Devil. The battlefield is the hearts of lost humanity. The objective is to get as many souls saved as possible before Jesus comes.

As the quote indicates, Cho holds to a dispensationalist interpretation of history and awaits the return of the Savior. Like present-day American fundamentalists and their predecessors, the conservative missionaries who founded the Presbyterian Church in Korea, he believes in Biblical inerrancy. Cho also celebrates the power of the Holy Spirit to heal disease and drive out evil demons, and he encourages his followers to use the same Spirit to derive success and prosperity in this world. The emphasis on the Holy Spirit not only is at the heart of Pentecostal faith, but it also echoes strong tendencies within the new Korean religions mentioned earlier and the shamanistic tradition that orients Koreans toward this-worldly application of their devotions.

Cho sees his organization Church Growth International as being part of the work of the Holy Spirit, "who opened my eyes to see the reality of the cell system as God's plan to cause growth of a new era of superchurches." Jae Bum Lee, a Korean pastor who attended Cho's Full Gospel Bible School and then completed a doctoral program at the Fuller Theology School, has written about the effect of Yoido Full Gospel Church on other Korean churches. He points out that superchurches are a Korean phenomenon. This holds true in the historic Protestant denominations: the largest Presbyterian, Methodist, Holiness, and Baptist churches in the world are all in Korea, with sixty thousand, thirty thousand, six thousand, and forty thousand members respectively. Of these four, only the Young Nak Presbyterian Church is not Pentecostal, although it does rely heavily on a cell system and intensive prayer meetings similar to the Yoido Church. The other three churches have those two characteristics and share distinct Pentecostal features including baptism in the Holy Spirit, healing miracles, and the exorcism of demons. The pastor of the world's largest Methodist church, Ho Moon Lee of the Soong Eui Church in Inchon, is a disciple of Cho who closely studied the workings of the Yoido Church.

The Sung Rak Baptist Church led by Ki Dong Kim began with only seven members in 1969 and was associated with the Southern Baptist Mission in Korea. Its growth to forty thousand members in eighteen years made it the fastest growing super church in the world but also marked its departure from the Southern Baptist denomination in 1987. The Southern Baptists, based in the United States, could not tolerate the strong emphasis on Pentecostal practice; the speaking in tongues and healings performed in prayer meetings, and the overwhelming emphasis on exorcism, were contrary to acceptable "old-style" Baptist fundamentalistism. Kim "believes that everyone who is a Christian can cast out demons and perform signs and wonders," and has written three

books based on Biblical methods of eradicating evil spirits (aptly named *Demonology I, II, and III*).

If Kim's preoccupation with evil and sin may seem quite compatible with North American Baptist theology (his favorite piece of scripture is "The reason the Son of God appeared was to destroy the devil's work"), his methods of dealing with them are not: his rites of direct attack through "power evangelism," as advocated by Cho and many other neo-Pentecostals and charismatics, indicate that independent Baptists in Korea and many other lands may be taking a different route than the comparatively staid approach of independent Baptists in the United States (the theology and decidedly non-Pentecostal practice of Jerry Falwell's giant, independent Thomas Road Baptist Church, for instance, are more or less identical to the Southern Baptist norm).

Paul Yonggi Cho has helped generate the movement of charismatic practice into the non-Pentecostal churches because he believes there is new intervention of the Holy Spirit on Earth. His goal is to make the Korean church and other Protestant churches around the globe "dynamically equivalent to the New Testament Church," so that Christians may reasonably expect the Second Coming of Christ and the Kingdom of God. On behalf of racially and ethnically diverse Christians around the globe, Cho hopes to accomplish what the apostle Paul did for the Gentiles in the first century A.D.; that is, to demonstrate that Christian power, through its use of Pentecostal and charismatic powers, is superior to all the lesser demons, diseases, false gods, and shamanistic exercises that people have heretofore feared and worshiped. It would not be inappropriate if he were to describe himself, not in self-praise but rather in the sense of his mission, with the words Paul used in Romans 15:18–19:

> I will not venture to speak of anything except what Christ has accomplished through me in leading the Gentiles to obey God by what I've said and done— by the power of signs and miracles, through the power of the Spirit.

This conception of the purpose of "power evangelism" is not unique to Cho for much of it was developed and popularized at Fuller Theological Seminary in California by John Wimber—"The explanation of the gospel" is accompanied by "a demonstration of God's power." Many Koreans and many of Cho's protegés study at Fuller's School of World Mission, where there are two professors of Korean studies and one of East Asian studies. Fuller has facilitated the inclusion of charismatic and Pentecostal theological perspectives into mainstream American evangelical training and is credited by Protestant scholar George Marsden as being both the least doctrinaire and the most accomplished in scholarship of all theology schools that follow in the conservative tradition.

Yoido Full Gospel Church has a highly developed program of world mission itself; it may seem ironic that Cho's evangelism is being aimed back at its source and concentrates on the United States, where over half of its five hundred missionaries were sent as of 1992. Next in numbers are missions to two other rich, but much less successfully evangelized countries, Japan and Germany. To facilitate its missions, the church has founded its own Full Gospel Seminaries in Kobe (Japan), Los Angeles, Berlin, and New York. The church is also expanding its broadcasting activities thoughout the world; the highest concentration of its foreign television programming is in Japan, where it has special plans for converting ten million Japanese souls.

Skeptics might suggest that a church that gives primacy to a gospel of success and prosperity is simply following its instincts and heading, like Willie Sutton the bank robber, "where the money is." This may be true in the same measure that U.S. charismatic churches, catering to the middle classes, are found disproportionately in prosperous suburban areas and shopping malls. On the other hand, Cho and his followers in Korea and elsewhere are consciously targeting cities because this is "where the people are" in a rapidly urbanizing world. South Korea's urbanization has been as rapid as any in the world—75 percent of the people lived in rural areas in the 1940s, and an estimated 80 percent will be urban by the year 2000. In addition there are almost one million Korean-Americans in the United States—most of them Christian, urbanized, and middle class—who can serve as a potential base for building megachurches and launching evangelization efforts in other countries.

Cho's Full Gospel Church is not so different from many megachurch and parachurch efforts launched by American televangelists and neo-Pentecostal revivalists. The entrepreneurial experiments of a charismatic authority figure take form in a businesslike and profitable sort of evangelism that finds many customers, people in need of that particular type of religion. There is a vertically integrated church bureaucracy with clear lines of authority to the top and the possibility of horizontal expansion into other lucrative or challenging fields: publishing, Bible colleges, old-age homes, overseas evangelizing.

In Korea, however, the modernization of Protestantism is more recent and less encumbered by past structures and the rubble of past doctrinal battles; and thus the possibility for unimpeded, innovative growth has presented itself to Pastor Cho, much as a few industrial families in Korea have been free to create giant chaebols that dominate manufacturing and distribution at home and abroad. Cho's religious chaebol features the clear-cut pyramidal structure of neighborhood leaders, subpastors, and pastors under his authority, but with sufficient lateral openness through the "cell system" that they do not necessarily threaten bureaucratic stagnation at a certain size; in fact, expansion in the religious market seems to promise an almost unlimited growth of adherents. Certainly as this chaebol gets larger and increases its revenues and its core of skilled and dedicated practitioners, it is all the more capable of funding and staffing new efforts at home and abroad. At this point no one knows if a church like Yoido Full Gospel can be institutionalized to the point of surviving Cho's demise (or can survive in the patriarchal, family-owned form common to both chaebol corporations and some American evangelical parachurch operations), but it certainly is inspiring many young evangelists around the world to mimic Cho's mixture of Pentecostalism, prosperity theology, and "church growth" structure.

In terms of pastoral business authority, Cho's accomplishments look very striking indeed, for he has taken a Pentecostal church of the kind that are forever splitting into more and more egalitarian little "sect" temples, and transformed it into a centralized church that is as large as many established religious denominations. His Yoido Church deals in mass production, formulating and marketing a neat, standardized product, thoroughly American and Korean and internationally acceptable. Its beliefs, practices, and much of its structure can be immediately transplanted and replicated in one hundred cities on five continents.

In this sense, Cho is an able religious engineer/industrialist who has gathered together straightforward fundamentalist components, eliminated the quirkier elements that cause too much denominational friction, and thrown out extraneous old production habits and standardized the new ones. He has come up with a more appealing and more effective way to be religious—a better way, to quote Hadden, "to sell Jesus."

The Reverend Moon

The Holy Spirit Association for the Unification of World Christianity was founded by a young man whose family converted to Presbyterianism when he was ten years old. Six years later, on Easter Sunday 1936, he met Christ as he walked through the hills near his village in Northern Korea. "You are the son I have been seeking, the one who can begin my eternal history," said Jesus.

In the years that followed, Sun Myung Moon had other direct communications with Jesus and God, as well as with Buddha and Moses, which led him to found the Unification Church in South Korea on May 1, 1954. Like other Korean leaders of new religions, he claimed that God had chosen him to play a semi-messianic role in the restoration of earthly paradise, "to restore the Kingdom of Heaven on earth," which he sees emanating from Korea: "All aspects of culture and civilization must bear fruit in this nation."

American evangelical writer Richard Quebedeaux has called the Unification Church "a Korean form of Christianity." However, the point here is not to establish the legitimacy of the Unification Church, which is tiny in membership, either as a world religion in its own right or as an accepted adjunct of conservative evangelicalism. Instead, let it be noted that an organization that calls itself "The Holy Spirit Association for the Unification of World Christianity" considers itself to be Christian. What is significant in relationship to Korea, and to the ways in which "modernization" and "modern" religious influence are intertwined in a larger global framework, is how the Unification Church has used its anti-communist supranationalism to exert worldwide influence. If Cho has modernized Pentecostalism and given energy and organizational direction to the "supershamanistic" aspect of

Christianity (a first century "miracle religion" revitalized for the millennium 2000), then Reverend Moon has been very clever and businesslike in building a transnational religious and business web in which "supranationalism" is the most important element. Something larger than pure nationalism (or even simple empire-building) is at work, as Moon uses religion to conflate the goals of U.S. and South Korean anti-communism (attaching Korean destiny to U.S. manifest destiny rather than simply imitating it):

> America's existence was according to God's providence. God needed to build one powerful Christian nation on earth for his future work. Korea has replaced Israel as the land of the Messiah.

Moon's peculiar genius has been to recognize that he could graft his Unification theology onto the universalizing trends exemplified by the growing hegemony (and possibly, global agenda) of the United States: anti-communism, free enterprise, and Christianity. He, perhaps more than any other religious leader, has demonstrated how effectively a religious organization can operate as an entrepreneurial business enterprise with political objectives; and how, in spite of small membership, the Unification Church can accumulate vast amounts of wealth and power in strategic areas of the globe.

Moon's operations are in a different league than the reasonably large-scale broadcasting/evangelizing business of American Christian entrepreneur Pat Robertson, which generated over $200 million in sales in 1987. In Moon's more varied, much larger and murkier portfolio, the profits alone, not sales, were likely to exceed that amount, if ever one could find a way to account for them. One scholar who has often written sympathetically about the church alludes to this mystery:

> One might, indeed, view Unification-related businesses, were they to be regarded as a single entity, as comprising a not inconsiderable multinational corporation. No one outside the movement has been able to work out precisely where all the money in the so-called "Moon Empire" comes from or goes to.

Just to get an idea of the size and reach of this empire, consider just a few figures related to money raised in the 1980s: $20 million per year income within the United States; about $122 million annually from Japan, 90 percent of which was exported to other countries (including $800 million to the U.S. over a nine-year period); nearly $10 million in direct yearly profits from Korean industries, including Tong'il Industries, the armaments producer. By 1990, the church was credited with owning ten banks in Uruguay; other fresh funds were flowing to China, where the People's Republic had approved $250 million investment in a new automobile factory. Recent U.S. investments have included shared ownership of the Nostalgia Network on nationwide cable television and an interest-free $50.5 million loan that gained the church financial control of the bankrupt University of Bridgeport in Connecticut. As of 1993, one investigator estimated "that the movement controls over $10 billion worth of business assets worldwide."

The Unification Church's justification for its preoccupation with building up its wealth sounds remarkably similar to prosperity theology; an excerpt from a training manual tries to correct misinformed Christians:

> Christians think the Messiah must be poor and miserable. He did not come for this. Messiah must be the richest. Only he is qualified to have dominion over things. Otherwise, neither God nor Messiah can be happy.

But unlike the charismatic "faith" churches, the Unification Church is not preoccupied with channeling prosperity back to individual members; quite the contrary. Individualism is discouraged and unselfish service to the "Family," to the church under "Father" Moon, is paramount. Profits are plowed back into the "family" businesses.

In addition to investing in profit-making enterprises, the Unification Church spends large sums on political and journalistic activities. Since 1982 the church has continuously sustained multimillion-dollar annual losses at its influential right-wing newspaper, *The Washington Times*. The paper was Ronald Reagan's main source of journalistic information during his presidency; it also served as the front organization for the Nicaraguan Freedom Fund, a nonprofit charity that raised $14 million for the Contra War when Congress denied the Reagan administration that amount of money in 1985. The Church has also produced other ultra-conservative

newspapers that steadily lose money, including the *New York Tribune, Noticias del Mundo* (New York), *Ultimas Noticias* (Uruguay), *Middle East Times* (Crete), and *World Daily News* (Japan).

Such activities, in which religious motivation is combined with the political will to counter leftist influences around the globe, are certainly not limited to the Unification Church. The fight against satanic communism has long been fertile soil for American evangelists who want to raise money, prove their patriotic mettle, or simply perform their Christian/American duties on the world stage. For example, Jimmy Swaggart's and Pat Robertson's efforts on behalf of the Nicaraguan Contras and the right-wing governments in Guatemala and El Salvador were substantial in the 1980s. And Robertson's Christian Broadcasting Network gives him the ability to interpret the news as he sees fit. However, his activities, and those of other American preachers, pale alongside Moon's ambitious range of networking apparatuses, which begin with very explicit, confrontational political organizations and end with seemingly non-ideological intellectual/scholarly associations.

On the political side, the Unification Church has spawned dozens of organizations. The most prominent, CAUSA, has chapters and affiliates in many countires. CAUSA has mustered considerable right-wing cohesion within Central America, backed the legislative ambitions of a whole slate of conservative politicians in Brazil (fifty seven candidates in the 1986 elections), supported rebel activities against the leftist government of Angola, enlisted the vice president of the Philippines and his wife as spokespeople, actively assisted Low Intensity Conflict indoctrination in a number of countries, and otherwise been a very influential component of the World Anti-Communist League. Concentrating mostly on geopolitical struggle, CAUSA only occasionally touches theological matters, referring to "Godism" as an antidote to Marxism.

CAUSA spends little time on evangelizing, being content to fight communism and socialism and other revolutionary movements in concert with whatever religious beliefs are held by its right-wing associates in any particular country. Within the church, however, leaders and theologians have emphasized that Godism is part and parcel of Unificationism, and it necessitates a global authoritarian theocracy ruled by the True Father, Reverend Moon. Godism is by nature undemocratic, wrote Chun Hwan Kwak in a church missionary magazine:

> Godism, however, has not been the majority idea. God's teaching has not been the majority teaching. Therefore through democratic elections, people have not selected God's will, goodness, True Parents, or the messiah. Our goal and purpose is to follow Godism.

For more amplification of Church doctrine and its ultimate societal implications, one can look to church theoreticians who are removed from direct political activities; one leading thinker, San Hun Lee, laid out the ultimate social and theological goals of the movement in his 1985 book, *The End of Communism:*

> [the goal is] the eradication of Communism and the final synthesis of all sciences and philosophies under Unification Thought as the basis of a new world order.

Within the United States, the Unification Church pursued an interesting course of influence building among the new Christian right, where it convinced a number of important political and religious operatives that its theology is substantially Christian (or at least not threatening) and that its money is acceptable (or, at least, that one can accept the money without endorsing the theology). Until the late 1980s, when their funding from U.S. sources began to wane, many new right leaders had stayed clear of Moon's organizations (not all did; Terry Dolan's National Conservative Action coalition collected $750,000 in 1984).

By 1987, however, "conservative strategist and fund-raising genius" Richard Viguerie faced impending bankruptcy and was bailed out by Moon's top U.S. aide, Bo Hi Pak, in order to start the American Freedom Coalition, which promoted the direct alliance of the conservative Christian lobby, Christian Voice, with Moon organizations. Even evangelicals who had previously taken offence at Unification theology were won over: Ron Godwin, a former vice president of Jerry Falwell's Moral Majority, had attacked another American fundamentalist leader in 1984 for taking "Moon money," condemning him for accepting "support from a church whose founder believes he's divine." In 1986, Godwin joined *The Washington Times* as senior vice president and began acting as an "emissary to conservative Christian leaders."

In the case of influencing the Christian Right, Moon and his deputies have great amounts of money to spend, but they do not usually demand public recognition or support for their theology, nor do they necessarily demand control over the message or the messenger, especially in the religious/cultural realm. For the Unification Church it can be a victory simply that their money is accepted. Howard Ruff, founder of influential conservative PAC "Free the Eagle," commented on the phenomena in 1987: "It's a brilliant plan to gain influence, prestige, and power, because Moon doesn't have to convert you to succeed."

The Unification Church and its organizations have sought influence in the realm of journalistic, cultural, and academic circles that deal with politics and economics by sponsoring meetings and junkets. Journalists have been treated to group excursions to global hotspots or gathered for large, broadly based World Media Conferences. The church also supports academic conferences and scholarship; when the subject is economics or politics the personnel are generally conservative, free-market anti-communists who favor American geopolitical aims. The papers are often presented by retired American senior military and diplomatic officers, or by stalwart Asian members of the Professors for World Peace Academy. (PWPA is the organization through which the Unification Church purchased the University of Bridgeport in Connecticut in 1993; the organization represents several thousand scholars.) These contributions are published in a "PWPA Book" series through the church-owned Paragon House Publishers in New York City. Recent titles from the late 1980s, for instance, were: *Taiwan in a Time of Transition* (which, among other things, tries to explain and justify the transition form "hard" authoritarianism to "soft" authoritarianism); *Chinese Economic Policy; Political Change in South Korea;* and *The Strategic Triangle: China, the U.S., and the Soviet Union.*

Also working in the political realm is The Washington Institute for Values in Public Policy, funded with about $1.5 million per year for conferences and publications. The orientation of the institute is also toward conservative, anti-communist scholarship but offers more sophisticated treatment and allows for some dissenting viewpoints. For example, the institute's own press published *The Politics of Latin American Liberation Theology* in 1988;

though most contributors were vigorous opponents of this left-leaning religious tendency, some offered more measured critiques emphasizing that the strength of liberation theology had been exaggerated, and one scholar who supported liberation theology was allowed.

As Moon's search for legitimacy reaches into the cultural and theological realm, the sponsored discourse gets decidedly more liberal. Among the myriad church-funded organizations that are explicitly religious—such as the International Religious Foundation, the Religious Youth Service, Youth Seminar on World Religions, the Parliament for World Religions—the New ERA, or New Ecumenical Research Association, stands out. New ERA is dedicated to open scholarship and academic commentary on new religions, religious globalization, and the interpenetration of theological ideas that might "unify" world religions.

"New ERA Books" report the contributions that have been presented at various academic conferences sponsored by the church. Many volumes have been edited by very well-known scholars in the world of sociology and religion: *Religion and the Global Order,* edited by Roland Robertson and William R. Garrett, appeared in 1991; other volumes edited by Rodney Stark, Anton Shupe, Jeffrey Hadden, Bryan Wilson, and Joseph Fichter have appeared over the past ten years. Most of these books deal briefly with the Unification Church's point of view (one or two papers), but not always: a New ERA title called *World Religions and Global Ethics* (1989), seemingly a natural place to hear from a syncretist Christian viewpoint originating in the East, had no commentary on Unificationism.

These scholarly activities proceed even though a millenarian Biblical worldview is certainly present in Unification teaching; the church has partaken heavily of the anti-communist Manicheanism that has featured post–World War II American fundamentalism:

> At the consummation of human history, both the heavenly side and the satanic side have come to operate on the world-wide level. Thus, the two worlds of democracy and Communism co-exist. But after the third world struggle the two worlds will be united. Seen from God's dispensation, the Third World War will inevitably take place. However, there are two ways for that war to be

fought. First, the satanic world could be subjugated by a wholly internal fight through ideology. God does not desire judgment or destruction (Ezekial 33:14–16) but salvation. Thus he desires Satan to submit ideologically, and with the least amount of external sacrifice. If this fails, the satanic side will inevitably attack the heavenly side. The heavenly side must then defeat the satanic side by force.

It is interesting to note how some conservative U.S. scholars, like Richard Rubenstein of the Washington Policy Institute, have translated the unification millenarian belief into a much more subtle explanation of benign "globalization" in religion and and societal relationships:

> As the growth of the Roman Empire rendered obsolete many of the earlier small communities based upon tribal and kinship bonds, so too the rise of Asia and the world marketplace calls for a new and more broadly based moral community than has previously existed. The rise of the Holy Spirit Association for the Unification of World Christianity and the teachings of Sun Myung Moon can be seen as an important response to that need.

Such evaluations seldom deal with some important questions, such as how the structure of the Unification Church transcends common expectations of the religious "marketplace," even as practiced by televangelists and the religious right in the United States. The Unification Church has constructed a "chaebol" apparatus that is more business than religion, that merges authoritarian political objectives so completely with authoritarian business practices that no one can ultimately disentangle the spiritual, financial, and anti-communist connections that date back to the founding of the church in the 1950s.

Almost from the very beginning of the Unification Church, Reverend Moon recruited powerful lieutenants and formed invaluable liaisons in the world of politics and covert operations. In 1957, Bo Hi Pak—a Korean Army colonel, Korean CIA agent and assistant military attaché in Washington—joined the church and started directing many of its activities in the United States. This initiated a long and fruitful interaction between the church, militant ultraright groups around the world, and various government intelligence agents within Korea.

In the same year Moon founded a branch of the church in Japan, called Genri Undo, which ever since has performed three important support functions: it was the conduit for huge amounts of cash coming from Japan to Korea; it supported the Japanese branch of the World Anti-Communist League; and it provided close contact with ultra-right Japanese business leaders. Critics of the Unification Church in Korea are able to document a long history of direct involvement in harassment and intimidation, including violent attacks against its political opponents as well as against the wage laborers employed in its businesses.

When the Tongil Industry Co., Ltd. (the largest manufacturing company owned by the Unification Church in South Korea) was beset by labor difficulties in 1987, it unleashed its own force: more than five hundred Kusadae attacked laborers as they staged a sit-in and inflicted many injuries on the workers. (Tongil is a weapons manufacturer and is named after T'ong-il-gyo, the short name for the Unification Church in Korean.)

A different kind of gathering was met by similar violence on October 18, 1987, when "250 Moonie thugs" attacked speakers and beat priests at the Sekwong Church because they were holding a seminar on the Unification Church that was expected to be critical. The Unification Church's use of violence is not only understandable within the Korean context, but also within the context of the Reverend Moon's view of the shortcomings of contemporary political societies. In 1983, he said:

> The more democratic a society is, the more serious the collapse of its traditional value system appears to be. This shows that democracy is failing to provide solutions to the problems facing our societies and the world.

Korean Derivatives and the New Fundamentalism

On one level the Unification Church is tiny and does not appear very threatening to anyone: there probably were never more than two hundred thousand members worldwide, and the U.S. membership never came close to its goal of reaching thirty thousand faithful. In fact, many observers believe the number of adherents within the United States has declined substantially. When Reverend Moon was imprisoned for tax evasion in the United States, he won considerable support from both conservative and liberal church groups who were concerned about threats to religious freedom (and possibly to the freedom of other "nonprofit" religious entrepreneurs, no matter what their persuasion, to raise money); however, this should not be construed as proof of his power.

However, the remarkable wealth, influence, and breadth of activities of the Unification Church demand attention. As Eileen V. Barker has put it:

> Reverend Moon's most telling achievement lies not in the changes he has wrought in the lives of Unificationists . . . it lies, rather, in the networks that he and his followers have organized throughout those structures and cultures that lie beyond the boundaries of the Unification Church.

The possibilities open to this new derivative of Christianity suggest that church structure, church businesses and concerns, and church belief systems may be greatly altered by the effect of new American fundamentalism taking root in other parts of the world. The new fundamentalism not only is free to grow or metamorphasize outside of U.S. borders, but it can also return to the United States in its new form.

In the case of Reverend Moon's religion, the Biblical inerrancy that we usually associate with Christian fundamentalists is somewhat lacking (although dispensational interpretations are still important), and there is more interest in intellectual exchange with other Christian traditions and other world religions than is shown by most of the religious right in the U.S. Within this church that operates like a giant chaebol, closely controlled by its "family" owners, it is difficult to ascertain which of the many tentacles and interests, spiritual and material, are most important. What is most striking in terms of fundamentalist Americanism is the degree to which American civil religion, in particular twentieth-century anti-communism as a central belief and driving force, has been grasped by Moon and embodied in the beliefs and activities of the church. By the nature of Korea's special place on the battle line of the Cold War, the church has been able to develop the eschatological confrontation between God and Satan into a global struggle between U.S./Korean Christian righteousness (and Manifest Destiny) and global communism. This is a special version of the fundamentalist connection to civil religion noted by Robertson and Chirico in respect to globalization and religious resurgence:

> the rise of the new fundamentalist Right can be seen as an attempt on the part of adherents to a particular world-view to establish their position as the civil religion of America (and American civil religion as the civil religion of the world).

Not only has Moon seized upon this aspect of civil religion and made it global, or "unificationist," instead of merely American, but he has also managed to directly insert himself in the middle of the right-wing American theologization of politics and then provide some real "unification," at least through his substantial organizational and funding apparatus. Perhaps the instrumental services that he renders through his parachurch apparatus are more important than his church itself. By coming from the outside, from Korea, Moon entered the American scene with an agenda that was so acceptable to those of the Christian right that they overcame their theological doubts and disregarded the foreign elements of unification thought. The acceptance of

Moon not only proves the strength of his funding largesse but more importantly, indicates the primacy of anti-communism as a central binding value of the new fundamentalism.

In terms of Moon's elaborate and secretive relationships with authoritarian governments and political influences, it is not particularly clear who was using whom most effectively. The extremely powerful head of the Korean CIA, Kim Jong Pil, probably saw the Reverend Moon as his pawn; he thought that "the Unification Church should be organized satisfactorily to be utilized as a political tool whenever he and KCIA needed it." On the other hand, Moon's calculation was that if he was "serving the government, the government would be serving him."

It is clear that Moon's authoritarian religion fits in rather nicely with the authoritarian goals of the state, and vice versa. The Unification Church features a psychological authority structure based on a father figure, dictatorial control exercised through the closely held ownership of assets, and precisely designated roles of good and evil. Such a structure seems ideally suited to helping merge fundamentalist belief and repressive political action in the late twentieth century.

55

The Global Rise of Religious Nationalism

Mark Juergensmeyer

As we see every day in the news, a disturbing aspect of the globalization of religion is the violent conflicts, worldwide, that are rooted in religion or expressed in religious terms. To author Mark Juergensmeyer, such conflicts are expressions of religious nationalism, an ideology that combines traditional religious beliefs in divine law and authority with the modern notion of the nation-state. Frequently associated with quests for ethnic autonomy, religious nationalism draws on a religion as a repository of powerful symbols, ready to be tapped and put into action, as politics come to be seen in religious terms. Citing examples from across the globe, Juergensmeyer identifies patterns common to all such movements, discerning surprising similarities in such cases as the Oklahoma City bombing in 1995 and the Iranian revolution of 1979.

The present article was originally published shortly before the World Trade Center tragedy of September 11, 2001. Readers may wish to consult Juergensmeyer's books on this topic, including Terror in the Mind of God: The Global Rise of Religious Violence *(University of California Press, 2000).*

If it can be said that the modernist ideology of the post-Enlightenment West effectively separated religion from public life, then what has happened in recent years—since the watershed Islamic revolution in Iran in 1979—is religion's revenge. After years of waiting in history's wings, religion has renewed its claim to be an ideology of public order in a dramatic fashion: violently. From Algeria to Idaho, a legion of religious activists have expressed a hatred of secular governments that exudes an almost transcendent passion, and they dream of revolutionary changes that will establish a godly social order in the rubble of what the citizens of most secular societies regard as modern, egalitarian democracies.

Their enemies seem to most of us to be both benign and banal: modern secular leaders such as Indira Gandhi and Yitzhak Rabin and such symbols of prosperity and authority as international airlines and the World Trade Center. The logic of their ideological religious view is, although difficult to comprehend, profound, for it contains a fundamental critique of the world's post-Enlightenment secular culture and politics. In many cases, especially in areas of the world where modernization is a synonym for Westernization, movements of religious nationalism have served as liberation struggles against what their supporters perceive to be alien ideologies and foreign powers.

"Palestine is not completely free," a leader of Hamas's policy wing told me, "until it is an Islamic state." The Hamas activist voiced this opinion only a few months before the January 1996 elections, an event that not only brought Yasir Arafat triumphantly into power but also fulfilled the Palestinian dream of an independent nation. Yet it was not the kind of nation that the Islamic activist and his Hamas colleagues had hoped for. For that reason, they refused to run candidates for public office and urged their followers to boycott the polls. They threatened that the movement would continue to carry out "political actions," as the Hamas leader called them—terrorist attacks such as the series of suicide bombings conducted by a militant faction that rocked Jerusalem, Tel Aviv, and elsewhere in Israel in February and March 1996, threatening to destroy the peace process and Arafat's fragile alliance.

On the Israeli side of the border, Jewish activists have also attacked the secular leadership of their nation, and again a virulent mixture of religion and politics has led to bloodshed. Yigal Amir, who is accused of assassinating Israel's prime minister Yitzhak Rabin in Tel Aviv on 4 November 1995, claimed that he had religious reasons for his actions, saying that "everything I did, I did for the glory of God." Amir has adamantly rejected attempts by his lawyers to assert that he was not guilty by reason of insanity. "I am at peace," he explained, insisting that he was "totally normal." His murder of Rabin, Amir argued, was deliberate and even praiseworthy under a certain reading of religious law that allows for a defense against those who would destroy the Jewish nation.

A few weeks before the assassination, a conversation with Jewish activists near Hebron indicated that they shared many of Amir's views. They were still grieving over the killing of Dr. Baruch Goldstein by an angry Muslim crowd in February 1995, after he murdered thirty-five Muslims as they were saying their prayers in the mosque at the Cave of the Patriarchs, revered as the burial place of Abraham, Isaac, and Jacob. Goldstein's grave has now been made into a shrine. The militant Jews at the site explained that acts such as Dr. Goldstein's were necessary not only to protect the land but also to defend the very notion of a Jewish nation—one that for reasons of redemption and history had to be established on biblical terrain. Religious duty required them to become involved politically and even militarily. "Jews," one of them said, "have to learn to worship in a national way."

This potentially explosive mixture of nationalism and religion is an ingredient even in incidents that might appear initially to be isolated terrorist incidents: the bombing of the federal building in Oklahoma City on 19 April 1995, for instance, or the 20 March 1995 nerve gas attack on a Tokyo subway station. In the Oklahoma City case, the Christian militia movements with which Timothy McVeigh and Terry Nichols have been associated have accepted a certain conspiratorial view of American politics: the nation is not free, they reason, because of a vast international conspiracy involving Jews and Freemasons. They believe that the nation needs to be liberated through an armed struggle that will establish America as an independent and Christian nation.

Strangely, the same conspiracy was articulated by members of Aum Shinrikyo (On Supreme Truth), the eclectic Buddhist-Hindu religious movement in Japan that has been accused of unleashing canisters of nerve gas in a Tokyo subway station, killing twelve people and injuring thousands. A young man who had been public affairs officer for the main Tokyo headquarters of the movement at the time said that the first thing that came to his mind when he heard about the attack was that the "weird time had come": the Third World War was about to begin. He had been taught by his spiritual master, Shoko Asahara, that Armageddon was imminent. He had also been taught that the Japanese government, in collusion with America and an international network of Freemasons and Jews, had triggered the January 1995 Kobe earthquake and then planned the nerve gas attack. He was surprised when Asahara himself was implicated in the plot—after all, the spiritual leader had portrayed himself as the protector of Japanese society and had begun to create an alternative government that would control the country after Armageddon had ended.

In all these cases, the alleged perpetrators possessed worldviews that justified the brutality of such terrorist acts: they perceived a need to defend their faiths and held a heady expectation that what they did would lead to radically new social and political orders. The events they staged were therefore religious as much as they were political and provide examples of religious involvement and political change that might seem, at first glance, to be curiously out of step with the twentieth century.

But these religious rebels against modernity are becoming increasingly vocal. Their small but potent groups of violent activists represent growing masses of supporters, and they exemplify currents of thinking that have risen to counter the prevailing modernism—the ideology of individualism and skepticism that in the past three centuries has emerged from post-Enlightenment Europe and spread throughout the world. For that reason, and because of the rising tide of violence associated with movements of religious nationalism in the Middle East, South Asia, and elsewhere, it is important to try to understand what religious nationalists want: why they hate secular governments with such a virulent passion, how they expect to effect their virtually revolutionary changes, and what sort of social and political order they dream of establishing in their own vision of a coming world order.

The Ideological Dimensions of Religious Nationalism

Some forms of religious nationalism are largely ethnic—that is, linked to people and land. The struggle of the Irish—both Protestant and Catholic—to claim political authority over the land in which they live is a paradigmatic example. The attempts of Muslims in Chechnya to assert their independence from the rule of Russia, and other Muslims in Tajikistan to assert a cultural element to Tajikistan's resurgent nationalism, are examples that have emerged in the wake of the collapse of the former Soviet Union. In what used to be Yugoslavia, several groups of ethnic religious nationalists are pitted against one another: Orthodox Serbs, Catholic Croats, and Muslim Bosnians and Kosovars. In South Asia, the independence movements of Sri Lankan Tamil Hindus, Kashmiri Muslims, and to some extent the Khalistan supporters in the Punjab are also movements of ethnic religious nationalism. In these cases, religion provides the identity that makes a community cohere and links it with a particular place.

Ideological religious nationalism is attached to ideas and beliefs. In using the term "ideology," I mean a framework of values and moral positions. In the case of religious nationalism, the ideology combines traditional religious beliefs in divine law and religious authority with the modern notion of the nation-state. If the ethnic religious nationalism *politicizes* religion by employing religious identities for political ends, an ideological form of religious nationalism does the opposite: it *religionizes* politics. It puts political issues and struggles within a sacred context. Compatibility with religious goals becomes the criterion for an acceptable political platform.

The Islamic revolution in Iran, for instance, was a classic example of ideological religious nationalism that turned ordinary politics upside down. Instead of a nonreligious political order providing space for religious activities—which in the West we regard as the "normal" arrangement—in Iran, a religious authority set the context for politics. In fact, the constitution of the Islamic Republic of Iran provides for a "just ruler," a cleric such as the Ayatollah Khomeini, who will be the ultimate arbiter in legislating the moral basis of politics. For that reason, the Iranian experience was a genuine revolution, an extraordinary change from the modern Westernized nation that the Shah prior to the Ayatollah had imagined for Iran. Because ideological religious nationalism embraces religious ideas as the basis for politics, national aspirations become fused with religious quests for purity and redemption, and religious law replaces secular law as the pillar of governmental authority. Although the enemy of ethnic religious nationalists is a rival ethnicity—usually the dominant group that has been controlling them—ideological religious nationalists do not need to look beyond their own ethnic community to find an ideological foe: they often loathe their own kind. As Yigal Amir dramatically illustrated when he shot Yitzhak Rabin, religious nationalists may target as enemies the secular leaders of their own nations. For that reason, tensions have been growing in nominally Muslim countries such as Saudi Arabia, Pakistan, and Turkey, where militant Islamic revolutionaries have identified their own moderate Muslim leaders as obstacles to progress. In the United States, it appears that this passionate hatred of secular government led to incidents such as Ruby Ridge and the bombing of the federal building in Oklahoma City. In India, a widespread disdain for secular politics has propelled the Bharatiya Janata Party (BJP) into becoming the largest movement for religious nationalism in the world. Buddhist movements in Sri Lanka, Mongolia, and Tibet have characterized their secular political opponents as being not just immoral and unprincipled but also enemies of dhammic (righteous) social order.

Some religious nationalists see their own secular leaders as part of a wider, virtually global conspiracy—

one controlled by vast political and economic networks sponsored by European and American powers. For that reason, they may hate not only the politicians in their home countries but also these leaders' political and economic allies in lands far beyond their own national boundaries. Islamic militants associated with Egypt's radical Gamaa i-Islamiya (Islamic Group), for example, have attacked not only Egyptian politicians—killing President Anwar Sadat and attempting to kill his successor, Hosni Mubarak—but also foreigners.

The Gamaa i-Islamiya literally moved its war against secular powers abroad when its leader, Sheik Omar Abdul Rahman, moved to New Jersey and became involved in a bombing attack on the World Trade Center on 26 February 1993 that killed six and injured a thousand more. The trial that convicted him in January 1996 of conspiracy in the attack also implicated him in an elaborate plot to blow up a variety of sites in the New York City area, including the United Nations buildings and the Lincoln Tunnel. Algerian Muslim activists have brought their war against secular Algerian leaders to Paris, where they have been implicated in a series of subway bombings in 1995. Hassan Turabi in Sudan has been accused of orchestrating Islamic rebellions in a variety of countries, linking Islamic activists in common cause against what is seen as the great satanic power of the secular West. In some cases, this conspiratorial vision has taken bizarre twists, as in the view shared by both the Japanese Aum Shinrikyo and certain American Christian militia movements that Jews and Freemasons are collaborating to control the world.

Often religious nationalism is "ethno-ideological," in that it is both ethnic and ideological in character. Such religious nationalists have double sets of enemies: their ethnic rivals and the secular leaders of their own people. Their efforts at delegitimization are "split" between secular and religious foes. The Hamas movement in Palestine is a prime example. While waging a war of independence against Israel, they are simultaneously sparring with Yasir Arafat; often the attacks leveled at Israelis are also intended to wound the credibility of Arafat's fledgling Palestinian Authority. It is not a coincidence that the Hamas suicide bombings aimed at Israelis increased in the months immediately before and after the January 1996 elections—a poll that Hamas wished to

discredit. The leaders of the movement believed, as their founder Sheik Ahmed Yassin said in a conversation several years ago, that "the only true Palestinian state is an Islamic state." This means that the movement must simultaneously war against both Israeli leaders such as Rabin and Peres and secular Palestinian leaders such as Arafat.

Like the militant Muslims in Hamas, the Sikh separatists that flourished in Northern India until 1993 were both ethnic and ideological and, like their Palestinian counterparts, also had a double set of enemies. In the Sikh case, the Khalistani side of the movement aimed at creating a separate nation of Sikhs and tried to purge the rural Punjab of Hindus. But there was also a more ideologically religious side to the movement, the one led by Sant Jarnail Singh Bhindranwale, which aimed at establishing the Sikh religious tradition as authoritative in both secular and political spheres and targeted moderate Sikh leaders and secular politicians as foes. Followers of this wing succeeded in assassinating several important secular politicians including Prime Minister Indira Gandhi in 1984. A spectacular explosion that killed Punjab's chief minister, Beant Singh, on 31 August 1995, shows that some aspects of the movement are still potent threats to civil order.

Other movements of religious nationalism—even ones that appear to be primarily ethnic—may also have, at some level, an ideological component. This is so because religion, the repository of traditions of symbols and beliefs, stands ready to be tapped by those who wish to develop a new framework of ideas about social order. In the case of the former Yugoslavia, for example, the anger of Serbs—frequently described in the media as the residue of ancient ethnic rivalries—is also fueled by an imaginative religious myth. The Serb leaders are Orthodox Christians who see themselves as surrogate Christ figures in a contemporary political understanding of the Passion narrative. A drama and an epic poem have been invented to retell the New Testament's account of Christ's death in a way that portrays historical Serbian leaders as Christ figures, and Muslims in both Bosnia and Kosovo as Judases. This mythologized dehumanization of the Muslims allows them to be regarded as a subhuman species, one that in the Serbian imagination deserves the genocidal attacks of "ethnic cleansing" that killed so many in the darkest hours of the Kosovo conflict and the Bosnian civil war. As these cases show, there is often a fine line between ethnic and ideological forms of religious nationalism.

In general, ethnic religious nationalism is easier for modern Americans and Europeans to understand, even though it may be just as violent as ideological nationalism. The London terrorist bombings by the Irish Republican Army after the cease-fire broke down in February 1996, and the Sri Lankan Tamils' suicide attacks that demolished downtown Colombo in January 1996, are examples. Yet these acts of violence are understandable because they are aimed at a society that the terrorists regard as exerting direct military or political control over them. The violence of ideological religious movements is focused on those who are ideologically different—secularists—and whose control over them may be cultural and economic, and therefore less obvious. But their impact on the changing shape of global politics is perhaps even more profound.

The Logic of Ideological Religious Nationalism

Since the mid-1980s, I have been following movements of ideological religious nationalism in various parts of the world with the hope of discerning common patterns or themes within them. Although each movement is shaped by its own historical and social context, there are some common elements due in part to the massive economic and political changes of this moment in history, an experience that has been shared by many around the world. What follows, then, is an attempt to identify the stages in development of ideological religious nationalism that has resulted from this common experience, beginning with the disaffection over the dominance of modern Western culture and what is perceived to be its political ally, secular nationalism.

Despair over Secular Nationalism

The shifts in economic and political power that have occurred following the breakup of the Soviet Union and the sudden rise and fall of Japanese and other Asian economies in the past fifteen years have had significant social repercussions. The public sense of insecurity that has come in the wake of these changes is felt not only in the societies of those

nations that are economically devastated by the changes—especially countries in the former Soviet Union—but also in economically stronger areas as well. The United States, for example, has seen a remarkable degree of disaffection with its political leaders and witnessed the rise of rightwing religious movements that feed on the public's perception of the immorality of government. At the extreme end of this religious rejection are the militant Christian militias and cults such as Waco's Branch Davidian sect. Similar movements have emerged in Japan, which is also experiencing disillusion about its national purpose and destiny. As in America, the critique and sectarian experiments with its alternatives often take religious forms, including new religious movements such as Soka Gakkai, Agon-shu, and the now infamous Aum Shinrikyo.

The global shifts that have led to a crisis of national purpose in developed countries have, in a somewhat different way, affected developing nations as well. Leaders such as India's Jawaharlal Nehru, Egypt's Gamal Abdel Nasser, and Iran's Riza Shah Pahlavi had once been pledged to creating versions of America—or a kind of cross between America and the Soviet Union—at home. But a new generation of leaders is emerging in countries that were formerly European colonies, and they no longer believe in the Westernized vision of Nehru, Nasser, or the Shah. Rather, they are eager to complete the process of decolonization. They want to assert the legitimacy of their countries' own traditional values in the public sphere, and to build a "postcolonial" national identity based on indigenous culture. This eagerness is made all the more keen when confronted with the media assault of Western music, videos, and films that satellite television now beams around the world, and which threaten to obliterate local and traditional forms of cultural expression.

The result of this disaffection with the culture of the modern West has been what I have called a "loss of faith" in the ideological form of that culture, secular nationalism. Although a few years ago it would have been a startling notion, the idea has now become virtually commonplace that nationalism as we know it in the modern West is in crisis, in large part because it is seen as a cultural construction closely linked with what Jürgen Habermas has called "the project of modernity." Increasingly we live in a multicultural, postmodern world where a variety of views of nationhood are in competition, and the very concept of nationalism has become a matter of lively debate among scholars. It has become even more important—a matter of political life and death—to leaders of nations that are still struggling to establish a sense of national identity, and for whom religious answers to these questions of definition have extraordinary popular appeal.

Seeing Politics in a Religious Way

The second step in the development of ideological religious nationalism is the perception that the problem with politics is, at some level, religious. This means "religionizing" politics, as I described it earlier in this essay, in two ways: by showing that political difficulties have a religious cause, and that religious goals have a political solution. If one looks at politics from a religious perspective, it may appear that secular nationalism has failed because it is, in a sense, religiously inadequate. As one of the leaders of the Iranian revolution put it, secular nationalism is "a kind of religion." He went on to explain that it was not only a religion but one peculiar to the West, a point that was echoed by one of the leaders of the Muslim Brotherhood in Egypt. Behind this charge is a certain vision of social reality, one that involves a series of concentric circles. The smallest are families and clans; then come ethnic groups and nations; the largest, and implicitly most important, are religions, in the sense of global civilizations.

Among these are to be found Islam, Buddhism, and what some who hold this view call "Christendom" or "Western civilization" or "Westernism." Particular nations such as Germany, France, and the United States, in this conceptualization, stand as subsets of Christendom/Western civilization; similarly, Egypt, Iran, Pakistan, and other nations are subsets of Islamic civilization. From this vantage point, it is both a theological and a political error to suggest that Egypt or Iran should be thrust into a Western frame of reference. In this view of the world, they are intrinsically part of Islamic, not Western, civilization, and it is an act of imperialism to think of them in any other way. Those who hold this view would solve the problem of secular nationalism by replacing what they regard as an inappropriate religion, "Westernism," with Islam or some other religion related to the local population.

At the same time that religion is solving political problems, politics can help to solve religious ones. In the view of Messianic Zionists such as Dr. Baruch Goldstein and his mentor, Rabbi Meir Kahane, for example, the redemption of the world cannot take place until the Messiah comes, and the Messiah cannot return until the biblical lands—including the West Bank—are restored to Jewish control. "Miracles don't just happen," Kahane said in a conversation in Jerusalem a year before he was assassinated in New York City by Muslims associated with Sheik Omar Abdul Rahman's New Jersey mosque. Referring to the return of the Messiah, which he felt could only come after Jews had created the right political conditions, Kahane said, "Miracles are made."

Some Messianic Jews think that the correct conditions for the return of the Messiah include the reconstruction of the Jerusalem temple described in the Bible on its original site—now occupied by the Muslim shrine, the Dome of the Rock. Some of these activists have been implicated in plots to blow up the shrine in order to hasten the coming of the Kingdom. One who served time in prison for his part in such a plot said that the rebuilding of the temple was a "national obligation" for the sake of redemption, a political position for which Israel should make "no compromise."

Religious activists who embrace traditions such as Millenarian Christianity and Shiite Islam, which have a strong sense of the historical fulfillment of prophecy, look toward a religious apocalypse that will usher in a new age. The leader of Aum Shinrikyo, borrowing Christian ideas from the sixteenth-century French astrologer Nostradamus (Michel de Nostredame), predicted the coming of Armageddon in 1999 in the form of World War III, after which the survivors—mostly members of his own movement—would create a new society in the year 2014, led by Aum-trained "saints." Activists in other religious traditions may see a righteous society being established in a less dramatic manner, but even Sunni Muslims, Hindus, and Buddhists have articulated a hope for a political fulfillment of their notions of religious society. They believe that "dharmic society can be established on earth," as one activist

Buddhist monk in Sri Lanka put it, by creating a religious state.

Identifying the Enemy

Perceiving politics in a religious way leads to the next step, identifying who or what religious power is at fault when things go wrong. In a religionized view of politics, the root of social and political problems is portrayed in religious terms. An opposition religious group—perhaps a minority group such as the Tamils in Sri Lanka, or the Coptic Christians in Egypt—is sometimes targeted as the corrupting influence in public life. Or the foe of religion may be seen as irreligion—a force opposed to religion altogether. The secular state could fit either of those categories, depending on whether one sees it as the outcome of a "religious" tradition—"Westernism"—or as the handmaiden of those who are opposed to religion in any form. A great many religious activists regard anyone who attempts to curb the influence of religion—for example, by promoting a civil society shaped by secular values—to be opposed to religion. Hence anyone who encourages secularism is, in a sense, a religious foe.

The most extreme form of this way of thinking is satanization. Some members of the Christian militia in the United States refuse to pay taxes in part because they feel that the government is controlled by an evil foreign power. During the early days of the Gulf War in 1991, the Hamas movement issued a communiqué stating that the United States "commands all the forces hostile to Islam and the Muslims" and singled out George Bush, who, it claimed, was not only "the leader of the forces of evil" but also "the chief of the false gods." As this communiqué indicates, this line of reasoning often leads down a slippery slope, for once secular institutions and authorities begin to loom larger than life and take on a satanic luster, the conclusion rushes on that secular enemies are more than mortal foes: they are mythic entities and satanic forces.

Even in 1997, Iranian politicians, without a trace of hyperbole, could describe America as the "Great Satan." This rhetoric first surfaced in Iran during the early stages of the Islamic revolution when both the Shah and President Carter were referred to as Yazid (in this context an "agent of satan"). "All the problems of Iran," the Ayatollah Khomeini elaborated, are "the work of America." By this he meant not only

political and economic problems but also cultural and intellectual ones, fostered by "the preachers they planted in the religious teaching institutions, the agents they employed in the universities, government educational institutions, and publishing houses, and the Orientalists who work in the service of the imperialist states." The vastness and power of such a conspiratorial network could only be explained by its supernatural force.

The Inevitable Confrontation

Once the enemy of religion has been identified, the fourth step follows naturally: the idea of cosmic war. There are parallels in many religious movements to the idea of the coming Armageddon that was feared by both Christian militia members in the United States and members of the Aum Supreme Truth in Japan. Rabbi Meir Kahane, for instance, spoke of God's vengeance against the Gentiles, which began with the humiliation of the pharaoh in the exodus from Egypt more than three thousand years ago and continues in the present with the humiliation of Arab forces that resulted in the creation of Israel, and would come to a head in what Kahane expected would be a great struggle against Arabs and other corrupting forces in Israel in the near future. "When the Jews are at war," Kahane said, "God's name is great." Another Israeli activist explained that "God always fights against His enemies," and that militants such as himself "are the instruments of this fight."

Elsewhere I have argued that the language of warfare—fighting and dying for a cause—is appropriate and endemic to the realm of religion. Although it may seem strange that images of destruction often accompany a commitment to realizing a more harmonious form of existence, there is a certain logic at work that makes this conjunction natural. In my view, religion is the language of ultimate order and for that reason provides those who use it with some way of envisioning disorder, especially the ultimate disorder of life: death. Most believers are convinced that death and disorder on an ultimate scale can be encompassed and domesticated. Ordinarily, religion does this through images projected in myth, symbol, ritual, and legend. The cross in Christianity is not, in the eyes of the faithful, an execution device but a symbol of redemption; similarly, the sword that is a central symbol of both Islam and Sikhism is proudly worn by the most pious members of those faiths not as weapons of death but as symbols of divine power.

Thus violent images are given religious meaning and domesticized. These violent images are usually symbols—such as the cross, or historic battles, or mythical confrontations—but occasionally the image of symbolic violence is not a picture or a play but a real act of violence. The sacrifice of animals and, of course, human sacrifice are examples from ancient traditions. Today conceptual violence can be identified with real acts of political violence, such as firebombings and political assassinations.

These religious acts of political violence, although terribly destructive, are sanitized by virtue of the fact that they are religiously symbolic. They are stripped of their horror by being invested with religious meaning. Those who commit such acts justify and therefore exonerate them because they are part of a religious template that is even larger than myth and history: they are elements of a ritual scenario that makes it possible for people involved in it to experience the drama of cosmic war.

For that reason, it is necessary for the activists who support such acts of terrorism to believe that a confrontation exists, even when it does not appear to, and even when the other side does not seem to provoke it. When one visits Gaza, one can feel a tremendous sense of anticipation among many pro-Hamas activists that the real battle for freedom is yet to come, coupled with a deep disappointment over the superficial freedom resulting from the peace efforts of Yasir Arafat. It was as if the peace that Arafat was entering into had been purchased too cheaply: it had not come as the result of an extraordinary denouement. They expected—perhaps even wanted—that eschatological moment of confrontation: some great war that would usher in the beginning of their new age. The suicide attacks carried out by young and remarkably committed Palestinians in the months before and after the January 1996 elections were in some sense attempts to deny the very normalcy that elections imply. It is as if they wanted to precipitate a confrontation where none had existed, or rather—in their mythologized view of the world—to bring to public attention the fact that an extraordinary war, albeit an invisible one, was raging all around them. Their acts would bring this cosmic confrontation to light.

The Future of Religious Nationalism

In a strange way, the point of all this terrorism and violence is peace. Or rather, it is a view of a peaceful world that will come into being when the cosmic war is over, and when the vision of righteous order held by militant religious nationalists triumphs. The leader of the policy wing of the Palestinian Hamas movement told me that the bombings in Jerusalem, Tel Aviv, and elsewhere would ultimately "lead to peace." The leader of Japan's Aum Shinrikyo—convicted for his alleged masterminding of the subway nerve gas attack—prophesied that after a colossal global conflict around the year 2000 involving nerve gas and nuclear weapons, a thousand years of peace would be ushered in, led by the coming of a new messiah who would establish a "paradise on earth."

What is common to these and virtually all other "terrorists"—as those of us who experience their shocking violent actions usually regard them—is their self-conception as peacemakers. They are soldiers in a war leading to peace. What they do not agree on, however, is the kind of peaceful world they want to bring about. This difference in political goals is caused not only by a difference in religious backgrounds but by an uncertainty about what form of politics is most appropriate to a religiously defined nation.

Yet the prognosis for peace in a world increasingly filled with religious nationalists is guarded. Ideological religious nationalism is a strident and difficult force in contemporary world affairs. As I have described in this essay, it follows a process that begins with a disaffection with secular nationalism, then moves to perceiving politics in a religious way, identifying mortal enemies as satanic foes, and envisioning the world as caught up in a cosmic confrontation, one that will ultimately lead to a peaceful world order constructed by religious nations. The result of this process is a form of global order radically different from secular versions of globalization, a difference so severe that it could usher in a new cold war, an ideological confrontation on virtually a global scale.

This process of religionizing politics, however, is still mercifully rare. Most forms of religion do not lead to religious nationalism. The reasons why the process begins and is nurtured are to be found in the social and historical contexts in which it emerges. That is to say that the religionizing process I have described is largely a response to social and political crises. This is certainly the case with the phenomenal growth of religious nationalism in recent years. The common geopolitical crisis experienced throughout the world explains why there have been so many movements of religious nationalism in such disparate religions and places within the last ten years.

In the present period of social turbulence and political confusion—which the collapse of the Soviet Union and the decline of American economic power have created around the world—it was inevitable that new panaceas would emerge that involved religion, sometimes perceived as the only stable rudder in a swirl of economic and political indirection. Moreover, as nations rejected the Soviet and American models of nationhood, they turned to their own past, and to their own cultural resources.

Politicized religious movements are the responses of those who feel desperate and desolate in the current geopolitical crisis. The problem that they experience is not with God but with politics, and with their profound perceptions that the moral and ideological pillars of social order have collapsed. Until there is a surer sense of the moral legitimacy of secular nationalism, religious visions of moral order will continue to appear as attractive solutions, and religious activists will continue to attempt to impose these solutions in violent ways, seeing themselves as soldiers in a cosmic drama of political redemption. Can these religious nationalists succeed? Certainly for a time. They may terrify political leaders, shake regimes to their foundations, and even gain the reigns of power in unstable states such as Iran. But it remains to be seen whether nations can long endure with only the intangible benefits that religious solutions provide.

56

Cyberspace as Sacred Space: Communicating Religion on Computer Networks

Stephen D. O'Leary

Do an online Web search for information on any aspect of religion or the supernatural, and one will be struck immediately by the great volume of available cyber-material. Few realms can compete with the spiritual in terms of popularity on the Web. The following article by Stephen D. O'Leary was originally published in 1996, already a long time ago in the rapidly changing era of computer networks and electronic information access. However, O'Leary's work addresses the larger question of how religion is transformed by new developments in technology, and it prompts us to consider further the potential of the World Wide Web to shape religious beliefs and practices.

O'Leary draws on the theoretical works of Walter J. Ong, an influential scholar of the relationship between communication technology and culture. Summarizing one of Ong's most important examples—the Reformation period of Christianity and how it was shaped by the beginnings of print and widespread literacy—O'Leary argues that a similar transformation in religious life is occurring now. To illustrate these changes, the author ends with an examination of online neo-pagan rituals.

No observer of the contemporary communication scene can fail to have noticed the phenomenally rapid growth of the Internet, which has expanded in a few years from an elite core of academic and scientific experts to a global network with millions of users, as well as the development of a number of private network services gatewayed to the global Internet, including Compuserve, America OnLine, Prodigy, and others. Those who have learned to navigate through the vast reaches of cyberspace, mastering the elementary technology of Usenet newsreading, Web browsers, and Listservs, find on the Net an astonishing variety of conversations taking place daily, a tropical greenhouse of discourse communities in bloom, a laboratory of extended conversations and social experiments organized around every conceivable topic or interest on matters scientific, philosophical, political, and social, from Aesthetics to Zoology.

The increasing coverage in the print media of the exploding use of computer networks as a social phenomenon, such as the column on "Cyburbia" in the *Los Angeles Times* and the regular pages now devoted to "Netwatching" in *Time* magazine, provide further evidence that we are witnessing the growth of a new form of sociability. Computer networks have been hailed as sites for the revival of democratic public culture, and a best-selling book has celebrated the utopian possibilities afforded by *The*

"Cyberspace as Sacred Space: Communicating Religion on Computer Networks" by Stephen D. O'Leary from JOURNAL OF THE AMERICAN ACADEMY OF RELIGION, Vol. 54(4) 1996, pp. 781–808. Reprinted by permission of Oxford University Press.

Virtual Community (Rheingold). If the Internet is truly forming a culture, or a complex of cultures, that both reflects and differs from the larger technological and political culture in which it is housed, it should not surprise anyone that as more people come to spend more and more of their time online, they have begun to devise ways to fulfill the religious needs and identities that form such an important part of the fabric of our society. It would indeed be an anomaly if a cultural force of this magnitude were not to find expression in the newly developing world of computer networks.

Readers of this journal hardly need to be persuaded that religion is a powerful force in human culture. However, they may not be accustomed to seeing manifestations of this force on their computer screens; and it may take some convincing to establish the credibility of the thesis that our conceptions of spirituality and of community are undergoing profound and permanent transformations in the era of computer-mediated communication. No less an authority than Pope John Paul II has recognized the crucial importance of this topic. In a 1990 address titled "The Church Must Learn to Cope with Computer Culture," the pontiff noted the revolutionary impact of contemporary developments in communication: "[O]ne no longer thinks or speaks of social communications as mere instruments or technologies. Rather they are now seen as part of a still unfolding culture whose full implications are as yet imperfectly understood and whose potentialities remain for the moment only partially exploited." These implications and potentialities are the focus of this essay. While the pope appears to celebrate the technological revolution declaring that "With the advent of computer telecommunications and what are known as computer participation systems, the Church is offered further means for fulfilling her mission," my purpose is to qualify the optimism of technology advocates by exploring potentially troubling questions about the future of religious institutions in an era of computer-mediated communication.

Recent popular and scholarly literature has noted that computer linkages presently provide new forums and new tools for the public advocacy of faith and for participation in public acts of ritual communication that constitute new, virtual congregations (see Kellner; O'Leary and Brasher). This paper seeks not to provide a comprehensive map of religious landscapes in cyberspace, nor an in-depth analysis of the communicative practices of any particular religious community, but only to speculate on the transformation of religious beliefs and practices as these are mediated by new technologies. The examples and texts offered here may or may not be typical of current trends in cyber-religion; they were chosen because they raise significant issues about the status of religion on computer networks and, more generally, about the evolution of religion in what some choose to call a "postmodern" age. My intention is to raise these questions rather than to answer them; but in so doing, I will provide qualified support for the claim that something revolutionary is taking place, while peering "through a glass darkly" to see how religious institutions and practices may be affected by the transformation of our communications media.

The theoretical framework for this inquiry is drawn from the work of Walter J. Ong. No one studying the impact on religion of the evolution of communication technologies can afford to ignore the provocative insights of this seminal thinker, who, in a series of brilliant books, has developed an evolutionary theory of culture that focuses attention on the modes of consciousness and forms of communality enabled and promoted by communication technologies and practices, from oral speech to written discourse to printing, radio, television, and computer-mediated communication. While it is the last of these developments that is my primary focus here, I believe that a full understanding of religion in the era of the electronic word is best accomplished by attending to historical contexts and comparisons. Hence, my study of contemporary religious discourses will begin with an excursus into historical narrative. After a brief exposition of an Ongian view of communication and culture, I turn to an extended discussion of one of Ong's primary examples of how religious practices may be transformed by a revolution in communication—the Reformation. By investigating the links between changing concepts of the nature and functions of word and symbol in Christian liturgy and the advent of print culture, I hope to demonstrate that contemporary electronic culture can be expected to effect a similar transformation of religious beliefs and practices. The essay closes with an examination of some unusual religious texts that illustrate this transformation, a series of neopagan rituals conducted online in the electronic "conference rooms" of the Compuserve network.

An Ongian Framework for the Study of Religious Communication

The most succinct theoretical exposition of Ong's evolutionary theory of communication and culture is found in his *Orality and Literacy*. In less than two hundred pages this book traces the development of communication technology through a series of stages from preliteracy, or in his terms, "primary orality," through the eras of chirographic writing, printing, and electronic media ("secondary orality") and offers a provocative analysis of the cultural impacts of technological change. Ong's thesis is that each of the forms of communication utilizes a different complex of the senses and that the particular complex peculiar to the material practices of communication in each culture—the "sensorium"—has profound impact on the formation of individual and cultural identity. For example, sound will play a larger role in the life world of a preliterate culture relying on oral speech for all communication than it does for people whose communication is dominated by print media. It is therefore not surprising that we find speech figuring prominently in the myths and religious practices of primarily oral cultures, which often attach magical significance to the spoken word, or that, lacking the concept of the written record, such cultures rely on expanded powers of memory to preserve their mythic heritage and a record of past events. As chirographic literacy spread through Western culture, sight and textuality were privileged over sound and speech, and the composition of sacred books transformed ancient oral narratives by fixing them into a text that could be consulted and interpreted in a way that was not possible before the invention of writing. According to Ong, "writing restructures consciousness" (1982: 78) by divorcing the production of a communicative act from its reception. This made it possible to address audiences remote in time and space, and turned communication from a public act requiring the presence of others into a private, solipsistic activity of writing and reading. As Ong puts it, writing "makes possible increasingly articulate introspectivity, opening the psyche as never before not only to the external objective world distinct from itself but also to the interior self

against whom the objective world is set" (1982: 105). The religious implications of this insight are profound; for, if we accept Ong's argument that writing generated a new, interior awareness of the self and a subsequent alienation of this self from the external world, then we may see religions that offer solutions to this alienation as, to some degree, an after-effect of the psychological changes wrought by literacy.

Since literacy skills were slow to spread in the millennia between the introduction of writing and the invention of the printing press, recitation and memorization still retained a significant role, and the written word could not completely divorce itself from its social contexts or from sounds and images. The communication practices of Western culture in this stage can thus be characterized as a hybrid of different forms which might differ according to the social position of participants. However, the invention of printing privileged sight still more, accelerating the alienation of the word from its aural basis, and narrowing the sensorium by focusing on the abstract symbols of typography as the predominant carriers of information and meaning. The consequences of these developments were immense. Among the phenomena that Ong links to the dominance of printing technology are the standardization of vernacular grammars and the subsequent move away from Latin as the lingua franca of Western culture and the rise of science, since printing enabled the replicability and wide dissemination of "exactly worded descriptions of carefully observed complex objects and processes" (1982: 127). The impact on religion was no less fundamental. In the chirographic culture of manuscript writing the Bible could be controlled by clerics, who preserved the roots of the Word in speech by mediating the sacred writings in public recitations connected with ritual; but the wide distribution of vernacular printed Bibles effectively ended the interpetive monopoly of the institutional church and enabled the reformers to circumvent ecclesiastical authority by proclaiming *sola scriptura* as the ultimate touchstone for authoritative claims. Ultimately, the culture of print gave birth to the unique sensibility of modernism, which bore fruits both in science and in the development of literary genres such as the novel.

The dominance of electronic media in the twentieth century brings us to the present stage of cultural evolution in Ong's scheme, that of "secondary orality." In this stage the sensorium expands again to include first sound and voice (with the advent of radio), and then image and gesture (with film and television). Though print culture is based in the primary sense of sight, its emphasis on typography devalues icons and images in favor of the printed word. The visual emphasis of print is fundamentally different from that of television and film; as any contemporary college instructor will testify, it is extremely difficult to train students saturated in modern visual media to accept the discourse conventions and abstractions of print literacy. Film and television restore the prominence of the visual sense in its full glory and create a much richer feast for the senses than printed text; few of today's students will willingly give up this feast and return to the restricted sensorium of typographic culture. Some critics, such as Jacques Ellul (1985), view the devaluation of the printed and spoken word in favor of the image with alarm, seeing in it a temptation toward the idolatry of consumer culture. Whether we celebrate the revitalization of image and icon (Taylor and Saarinen) or are nostalgic for the old days of print literacy, there can be little doubt that this development will have profound consequences for religious belief and practice.

The term "secondary orality" refers to the fact that in the new electronic media the divorce between word and image begun by print culture is reversed, so that the total sensorium again includes sight and sound, voice, image, and music. This stage "has striking resemblance to the old [primary oral cultures] in its participatory mystique, its fostering of a communal sense, its concentration on the present moment, and even its use of formulas"; it differs from the old in that it "generates a sense for groups immeasurably larger than those of primary oral culture—McLuhan's 'global village'" (Ong 1982: 136). Modern electronic media change our senses of time and of community by again enabling speech to be shared in the immediacy of real time; but they also retain the self-awareness of print culture, since in most cases media messages, whether political speeches or entertainment, still originate with an act of writing. If, as McLuhan has it television created the global village, this medium was still a one-way channel from the broadcaster to the audience. In computer networks the global village has found its public square (the analogy to London's Hyde Park may be apt), whereby media users are transformed

from vegetative "couch potatoes" to active participants in dialogues performed before potentially vast publics, linked not by geography but by technology and interests alone. With this new medium, aspects of orality and literacy are combined into a new, hybrid form of communication that, in the words of one networker, "is both talking and writing yet isn't completely either one. It's talking by writing. It's writing because you type it on a keyboard and people read it. But because of the ephemeral nature of luminescent letters on a screen, and because it has such a quick—sometimes instant—turnaround, it's more like talking" (Coate).

I will presently address the implications for religious discourse of this newest shift in communication technology. At this stage of the inquiry however, some caveats are in order. Any short summary of a theory of this complexity will inevitably diminish its impact, and I do not pretend to do Ong's work justice here. Readers who wish further elaboration and defence of these ideas, and a much more nuanced interpretation of the history of religious communication in particular, are invited to explore Ong's work for themselves, especially *The Presence of the Word*. In anticipation of possible objections, it is worth noting that the evolutionary model of culture that Ong proposes is neither deterministic nor strictly linear. While the thesis that technology—and especially communication technology—restructures consciousness and thus the whole of human culture is amply supported in Ong's work, he never proposes a simplistic cause-and-effect mechanism by which this is accomplished but rather views technology as both a cause and an effect of the transformation of the human spirit. Further, humans do not abandon earlier technology when new ones are discovered or invented; culture grows by accretion, so that speech remains an essential and indispensable means of communication that supplements writing, printing, and electronic media as options for human communication. In this accretive process the development of new technologies alters our use of old media by changing the social value accorded to each medium and by fundamentally altering the context, the lifeworld, in which communication occurs. We will always have speeches, but mass-mediated oratory can never recapture the electric excitement of the crowd in the days before microphones and television. Similarly, writing will never be entirely supplanted by television; but the skills of print literacy may become increasingly those of a knowledge elite, necessary for the acquisition of wealth and social status although increasingly opaque to the operator of the cash register at the fast-food restaurant, who only knows how to charge customers for a meal by pushing buttons with pictures of a Big Mac, Coke, and fries.

The most significant issue for an inquiry into the implications of computer-mediated religion raised by Ong's theorizing is the potential comparison between the communication revolution that took place concurrently with the Reformation and our current transition into a digital age. Contemporary scholarship has exhaustively documented the crucial role that printing played in the Reformation, the most significant political and religious movement of post-medieval Western culture (see Eisenstein; Edwards); we may reasonably anticipate that the digital revolution will be accompanied by similarly massive upheavals in the social sphere in general and in religion in particular. In order to develop this comparison further, it will be useful to linger on an example that Ong uses as paradigmatic of the changes in Christian thought and communicative practice that accompanied the onset of print technology: the evolution of liturgy, the forms and ceremonies of Christian worship, during the Reformation era. Discussion of Protestant liturgical reform is germane to this argument for two reasons: first as an example of the way theories and practices of language and ritual may be profoundly altered by technological change; and second because this particular episode in the history of the Christian tradition illuminates the context of contemporary, mediated ritual practice. The fundamental problem of religious communication is how best to represent and mediate the sacred. By studying the Reformation battles and controversies over this question, over the nature and proper functions of word and image, we may find some historical roots of the ethics and the aesthetics of communication in the cultures influenced by Protestantism and thereby come to a deeper understanding of the significance of ritual in premodern, modern, and postmodern cultures.

Liturgy and Language in the Protestant Reformation

Consider the difference between Catholic and Protestant ritual in terms of Ong's sensorium. It is clear the religious aesthetic and sacramental theology of the Roman Catholic Church has always appealed to the aural and tactile imagination as well as the visual. In the Catholic Mass the spoken word retains the magical efficacy of language that Ong finds characteristic of an earlier stage of primary orality, and ritual action directs attention outward toward the exterior manifestation of the Word in the Eucharist. By contrast, the liturgical and cultural forms of Protestantism direct attention inward; the preaching of the Word, conceived and embodied textually rather than sacramentally, was meant to to induce an interior conviction of sin that was prerequisite to the experience of grace. Believing that the sole legitimate functions of language were education and exhortation, by which members of the congregation were to be taught the message of the Gospel and urged to improve their lives, the Protestant reformers set out to strip away the incantatory functions of language in worship. The most radical of reformers, such as Zwingli, stripped the churches bare of any ornamentation, banned the use of musical instruments, and banished altogether the whole panoply of ritual elements that had characterized the Latin Mass—vestments, stained glass, iconography of all kinds, incense. This had the deliberate effect of focusing attention upon the purely textual elements of the Christian message.

The differing notions of the symbolic function of language are most evident in the controversy over the nature of the communion ceremony—the fulcrum of the dispute between Protestant and Catholic theology. In the Catholic Mass, the communion comes to its symbolic climax in the "words of institution," the scriptural passage that is recited by the priest as he elevates the communion bread:

> On the day before he suffered death, he took bread into his. . . . hands, . . . and giving thanks to thee, he blessed it, broke it, and gave it to his disciples, saying: Take, all of you, and eat of this, FOR THIS IS MY BODY. (Thompson: 75)

What is important to stress here is the theory of language that underlies this ritual. For believers, the words of institution, "this is my body," authorized and commanded by Christ himself, were (and are) literally true: when performed by a duly ordained priest, they effected the miracle of transubstantiation by which the bread and wine served as vehicles of the Real Presence. In the terms of J.L. Austin (1970a), the founder of speech act theory, we can call this a "performative utterance," a speech act that effects what it describes. Like marriage vows and oaths of office, the words of institution belong to a class of communicative "acts in which saying the words does not merely describe an existing state of things, but rather creates a new relationship, social arrangement, or entitlement. In speech act terms, these are instances when saying is doing" (Danet). The formula used in Catholic theology to describe this mode of ritual action is to say that the sacrament succeeds *ex opere operato,* that is, that the words (when voiced by the duly ordained, in the right situation, with the right intention) are themselves efficacious as a vehicle of divine grace. Modern speech act theorists describe this efficacy in terms of the "illocutionary" force of the utterance (Austin 1970b).

In Catholic theology the visible elements of the sacrament are not signs of the thing, the spiritual reality of salvation through Christ's sacrifice; once transformed by the illocutionary force of the speech act, they *are* the thing, the bread and wine becoming the body and blood of God's saving Word through the power of the words of the liturgy, words that function as the bridge between the visible objects and the spiritual reality, uniting them in a single identity. Thus, the sacramental theory of language affirms the *essential* unity of signifier and signified. This theory is hierarchical; the ritual can only be enacted by a duly ordained priest. During the sixteenth century and up until the second Vatican council, the ritual was conducted in Latin, ensuring that the uneducated masses could only apprehend it on the formal and aesthetic levels; and the church hierarchy jealousy guarded their monopoly on scriptural interpretation.

When Luther and the printing press were able to break this monopoly by publishing the first German bible, interpretation become the prerogative of every believer, and the institutional authority of the church was weakened. Protestant liturgies further undercut the authority of the priesthood by divesting the liturgy of its mysterious elements. The liturgies devised by Calvin, Zwingli, and other reformers enacted a theory of language that differed radically from the Roman Catholic conception of the relationship of Word and sacrament; they reach their climax, their symbolic payoff, not in the communion, but in the sermon, a discourse which is delivered orally but which lacks the supernatural efficacy of the Catholic priest's speech over the eucharistic

elements. In contrast to the Catholic, the Protestant liturgy was enacted in the vernacular tongues; in its most austere forms, it eschewed ornament and visual representation and minimized all sensory input that might lead to idolatry; it focused on the sermon and the words of scripture to the exclusion of other messages; and it denied the performative character of liturgical speech-acts altogether, characterizing the ritual action of the priest as, in Calvin's words, "murmuring and gesticulating in the manner of sorcerers" (quoted in Thompson: 192).

To minimize the risk of idolatry, Calvin's communion liturgy placed, immediately prior to the distribution of communion elements, the minister's verbal directive to the congregation on how to interpret the sacrament:

> Let us not be fascinated by these earthly and corruptible elements which we see with our eyes and touch with our hands seeking Him there as though He were enclosed in the bread or wine. Then only shall our souls be disposed to be nourished and vivified by His substance when they are lifted up above all earthly things.... Therefore let us be content to have the bread and wine as signs and witnesses, seeking the truth spiritually where the Word of God promises that we shall find it. ("The Form of Church Prayers," 207)

The words of the minister were no longer a performative utterance; they simply directed the attention of the congregation. With the aesthetic and formal elements in the liturgy kept to an absolute minimum, this attention was less likely to rest upon external reality as apprehended through the senses and would presumably turn to an interior meditation on salvation characterized by a high degree of abstraction. Whereas the Catholic liturgy presented and represented God's Word in a variety of sensual, formal, and aesthetic embodiments, the Word in Protestant liturgy is dessicated, information-oriented, apprehended through scripture and sermon but most emphatically not in stained glass, statues, or the taste of bread upon the tongue.

The theology that followed from the devaluation of ritual language, gesture, and performance in favor of preaching thus changed the communion ceremony from its former status as an actual vehicle of God's presence and grace to a mere reminder or analogy. As Calvin wrote, "For while we refute transubstantiation by other valid arguments, we hold this one to be amply sufficient, that it destroys the analogy between the sign and the thing signified; for if there be not in the sacrament a visible and earthly sign corresponding to the spiritual gift, the nature of a sacrament is lost" (Calvin 1958: 467). In these statements of Calvin we can see the essential idea of language that lay behind the reform liturgies. Against the concept of identity created through sacramental language Calvin asserted the centrality of the sacrament solely as analogy; in his system words can only establish the relationship between the sign and the thing signified, a relationship that is analogical, not essential.

Consider the fact that these two conceptions of liturgy were a major cause of a controversy that divided Europe for centuries. From an Ongian perspective the most significant result of this controversy was that it led to the formation of two communicative cultures, the Catholic and the Protestant. Extending Ong's insight, I argue that the development of two competing cultures grounded in liturgical practice, supported by and elaborated in a whole literature of polemical debate and theorizing about the nature of symbolism and the interpretation and embodiment of the Word, was a significant part of the context for the formation of Enlightenment theories of language. If the religious rituals now visible on computer networks seem absurd, bizzare, and entirely without efficacy to those of us in the academy today, it may be because we have been so thoroughly imbued with Lockean, Humean, and Cartesian skepticism that the magical power of sacramental language is entirely foreign to us. As Jonathan Z. Smith notes, the absolute separation between signifier and signified, which was inaugurated by the liturgical reformers and which became a hallmark of Enlightenment thought, meant that "myth or ritual . . . was no longer literally *and* symbolically real and true. . . . The [subsequent] history of the imagination of the categories myth and ritual was sharply divergent. To say myth was false was to recognize it as having content; to declare ritual to be 'empty' was to deny the same" (101). Hence, we may measure the progress of the Enlightenment in terms of a gradual shrinking of the space in which the illocutionary force of ritual speech, supported by the social authority of the Church, held sway.

However, the old conception of the ritualistic power of symbolic action (a conception that, whether explicit or implicit, constitutes a theory of language) is not dead; it survives within the now limited domain of the Church and has a new home in the global communication network. Before turning to an example of the revival of ritual and performativity on computer networks, one more point regarding the influence of Catholic and Protestant communication theories seems appropriate. For those who wonder what this notion may have to do with today's world of microcomputers, consider the following application by the Italian scholar Umberto Eco:

> Insufficient consideration has been given to the new underground religious war which is modifying the modern world. . . . The fact is that the world is divided between users of the Macintosh computer and users of MS-DOS compatible computers. I am firmly of the opinion that the Macintosh is Catholic and that DOS is Protestant. Indeed, the Macintosh is counter-reformist and has been influenced by the 'ratio studiorum' of the Jesuits. It is cheerful, friendly, conciliatory, it tells the faithful how they must proceed step by step to reach—if not the Kingdom of Heaven—the moment in which their document is printed. It is catechistic: the essence of revelation is dealt with via simple formulae and sumptuous icons. Everyone has a right to salvation.
>
> DOS is Protestant, or even Calvinistic. It allows free interpretation of scripture, demands difficult personal decisions, imposes a subtle hermeneutics upon the user, and takes for granted the idea that not all can reach salvation. To make the system work you need to interpret the program yourself: a long way from the baroque community of revellers, the user is closed within the loneliness of his own inner torment.

Eco's point is a humorous one: but there is surely a significant underlying issue here. Though secular culture has long since denied or ignored the claims of Christian dogma, the old traditions are not so easily abandoned; they survive in the communicative cultures to which they gave birth, which may still fairly be labeled as "Catholic" and "Protestant" with regard to their aesthetic conventions and conceptions of language if not to the substantive content of their beliefs. Clearly, innovation is not accomplished only through newly invented forms but by bricolage, as fragments of the old systems are incorporated into the new cultural mosaic. If the past is any guide, the new media of communication will have cultural consequences that we can barely imagine, let alone predict; nevertheless, it is already possible to watch this process of transformation at work and to see how the old forms are taken up into the new. As the introduction of the printing press profoundly altered the symbolic world of Western cultures and forever changed the course of Christian history, so too religious discourse will have to reinvent itself to keep pace with modern technology. As one example of this reinvention, here is a recent text culled from a flood of offerings on the Internet, the "Cyberpunk's Prayer":

> Our Sysop,
>   Who art On-Line,
> High be thy clearance level.
> Thy System up,
> Thy Program executed
> Off-line as it is on-line.
> Give us this logon our database,
> And allow our rants,
>   As we allow those who flame against us.
> And do not access us to garbage,
>   But deliver us from outage.
> For thine is the System and the Software
> and the Password forever.

However ludicrous or parodic this prayer may seem, it was apparently intended by its author as an expression of sincere devotion. Consider the implications of this symbolic transformation in terms of the political and social impact of representations of deity: as male, as female, as patriarchal king, as benevolent earth mother—and now, as Sysop (Systems Operator). The divine plan is compared to a computer program ("thy will be done" = "thy program executed"); cyberspace itself is equated with heaven ("on earth as it is in heaven" = "off line as it is online"); the soul's nourishment is equated with information, the bread of the information age ("give us this logon our database"). Steering a course between those who might regard this poem as blasphemy and those who would dismiss it as inconsequential humor, let us take the "Cyberpunk's Prayer" as a sign of the process of cultural invention and adaptation that is currently underway and ask what this example portends for the future.

As ancient religious formulae are translated into contemporary idioms, their meaning will be profoundly altered along with the mode of their

reception. The old symbols will find new functional equivalents in the idioms of technological culture, and some of these will be unrecognizable to today's audiences. We must anticipate that the propositional content and presentational form of religion in the electronic communities of the future will differ as greatly from its contemporary incarnations as the teachings of Jesus differ from the dialectical theology of the medieval Scholastics or as the eucharistic ceremonies of the earliest Christians differ from the Latin High Mass. With the perspective afforded by an Ongian view of communication and culture, we can be sensitive to true novelty while at the same time retaining awareness of the continuity of tradition, of the manifold ways in which it adapts, mutates, and survives to prosper in a new communicative environment.

Religious Ritual on Computer Networks: Problems of Virtual Ethnography

In 1992 a student who knew of my interest in religious communication brought me a file of messages exchanged in a religion discussion group on the Prodigy computer network. I was intrigued enough to sign up for an email account through my university but went no further than exchanging electronic messages with colleagues. In the spring of 1993 I received a promotional package in the mail that included a free trial account with the Compuserve network. I took the bait and signed on, and spent months reading and occasionally posting to the various message boards in the Religion Forum. Most of the traffic that I observed was fairly conventional in nature: there were arguments about the meaning of scriptures, debates over homosexuality in the various denominations, and occasional requests for prayers from Forum participants. As my familiarity with the network grew, I began to discover groups meeting at preordained times in electronic "conference rooms" to engage in scripture study and prayer. A conference or chat room (as they are known on America OnLine) is a real-time connection in which everyone who enters the "room" may post a message that will be seen immediately by all who occupy that particular corner of cyberspace. What intrigued me about this type of connection to the network was that it allowed for group interaction of a sort not possible through basic email; people were not merely exchanging letters with each other but actually engaged in collective devotion, much as they would at church or in a Bible study group. For some regular participants this activity was a significant part of their spiritual life.

My curiosity was piqued. I explored the network further, looking for the ways in which the new medium was being used by less traditional religious groups, and found that groups stigmatized as "cults" were using the network to present a different face to the public. Practitioners of nontraditional religions can run a considerable risk by publicly declaring their allegiances in communities hostile to non-Christians; the network afforded an opportunity to meet with like-minded others and engage in religious activity without ever leaving one's home or alerting one's neighbors to one's nonconformity. After some months monitoring messages in the New Age section of the Religion Forum, I saw an announcement of an online full moon ritual to be held in a Compuserve conference room. The announcement was distributed by the leader of the ritual, a neopagan priestess who happens to be a registered nurse in Philadelphia, it included a brief statement that the ritual would feature a rite of initiation into the path of Goddess worship for those who desired.

I was fascinated by the idea that a virtual gathering could be an opportunity not just for religious discussion but for an actual rite of passage; unfortunately, I had other commitments for the time of the ritual and so was unable to observe. A few days afterward, the group leader posted a message indicating that a full transcript of the ritual was available for downloading from the Forum archives. Immediately, I went searching for the document and found not only the one text of the ritual I had missed but dozens of others that had taken place in Compuserve conference-rooms over an extended period of time. I downloaded them all and began to study them. From the transcripts it was evident that many of the people whose conversations I had been observing on the network shared a more intimate connection than I had realized. They constituted something close to an actual neopagan congregation, a community of people who gathered regularly to worship even though they had never seen each other face to face. Though I was convinced that I had stumbled upon something that was both novel and significant, I was

unsure how to study or write about the phenomenon; the conventional methods of academic research in religious ethnography seemed of little use in this case. One Lammas ritual that took place in a Compuserve New Age Forum conference room on July 25, 1990 typifies the geographic spread of these rituals and the consequent problems of studying them: participants entered in from New York, Los Angeles, Illinois, New Haven, Houston, Michigan, Louisiana, and Virginia. How is it possible to understand the religious practices of people one has not met and, even more strikingly, of a group whose participants have not even met each other?

Conventional ethnographic approaches assume that physical presence is prerequisite to study and cultural interaction; in short, that there is no substitute for fieldwork. As Barbara Myerhoff puts it, "Rituals are conspicuously physiological: witness their behavioral basis, the use of repetition and the involvement of the entire human sensorium through dramatic presentations employing costumes, masks, colors, textures, odors, foods, beverages, songs, dances, props, settings, and so forth" (199). If scholars maintain this understanding of ritual, they can only be led to the conclusion that rituals in cyberspace are simply "unreal," that their significance never transcends the virtual plane. However, one should be cautious of such an easy dismissal. Certainly, important elements of traditional ritual are lost without physical presence; but perhaps we should invert the question. Rather than assuming preemptively that the loss of physical presence produces a ritual that is unreal or "empty," we might ask what ritual *gains* in the virtual environment and what meanings the participants are able to derive from these practices, such that they will gather again and again to perform cyber-rituals together while paying a premium fee for their connect time. Further, some historical and contemporary parallels indicate that the validity of a ritual may not be so easily linked to physical presence or the mode of mediation.

Consider the following: the leader of the Roman Catholic Church celebrates a solemn pontifical mass which is broadcast on television and announces a plenary indulgence to the faithful who observe the live broadcast from around the world; or a couple decides to get married and arranges a legally valid wedding in which the participants are at remote locations and the vows are typed in via computer keyboards. These ritual events are not fanciful predictions of what is to come; they have already taken place. They are no more or less "unreal" than than the neopagan gatherings on Compuserve, insofar as the criterion is considered to be physical presence; but their validity, efficacy, and consequences (whether spiritual or legal) have the stamp of institutional approval. In fact, these are not the first instances of new technologies sparking a change in notions of ritual efficacy. In an essay entitled "Speech, Writing, and Performativity: An Evolutionary View of the History of Constituve Ritual," Brenda Danet brilliantly traces "the transfer of performativity from speech to writing," in periods when writing was in the process of becoming institutionalized, and applies the speech-act theories of Austin and Searle to documents such as Anglo-Saxon wills and modern wills on video, demonstrating yet again that technology can drive changes in our use of language and our concepts of symbolic action. If the creation of a written document can have the illocutionary force of a speech act, then it is not unreasonable to think that this force can be extended to cyber-communication; and, if considerable resources in software and system design have already been devoted to making commercial transactions possible on the Internet, who is to say that spiritual goods cannot be peddled there as well?

If the argument based on the "unreality" of virtual reality is set aside, discomforting questions still remain. Anyone who has studied ritual through conventional ethnographic participant-observation is likely to ask how ritual criticism (see Grimes) can be performed on a transcript. In response, I would argue that a departure from traditional ethnography is necessitated by the new technological environment in which these rituals occur. A transcript would certainly be insufficient evidence to support conclusions about a Catholic Mass or a Hopi kachina dance; lacking the dimensions of intonation, music, image, and gesture, the student of these rituals would clearly be unable to interpret them adequately. However, the rituals in this particular case never had these dimensions to begin with: they are thoroughly and completely textual. The study of cyber rituals must thus begin with the texts they generate. Ultimately, however, I do believe that academic study of these rituals will require an attempt to interview people in the off-line world to see how they interact with their computers in the material realm.

It may seem absurd to compare these rituals to the Catholic Mass or to Protestant worship services; but such objections are likely to rest more on the prestige and influence of established churches than on any objective scholarly considerations. If we recall that the neopagan movement is large and expanding, with regular gatherings in almost every state of the U.S. and all over Europe, some of which have brought suit in federal court against local ordinances which allegedly discriminate against their religious practices, and also that many, if not most, of the participants in these online rituals are active members of local groups which practice these rituals (or similar ones) outdoors in real time, we may be inclined to take them more seriously. My purpose in making this comparison is to conclude an earlier train of thought regarding the effect of communication technologies on the conceptions of symbolic action that are illustrated and exemplified in religious performances. Just as Protestant congregations and reformers, influenced by the culture of printing, reformed the liturgy in ways that privileged textuality over gesture and performance as the vehicle of symbolic meaning, so too modern religious practitioners rebel against current religious orthodoxy by devising new rituals that employ new technology to reassert the power of language as performative utterance.

A recent article in *Wired* magazine, a periodical that attempts to keep pace with the cutting edge of cyber-communication, dubs these ritual practitioners as "Technopagans" (a description that they seem to embrace willingly) and notes that "a startling number of Pagans work and play in technical fields, as sysops, computer programmers, and network engineers. . . . embody[ing] quite a contradiction: they are Dionysian nature worshipers who embrace the Apollonian artifice of logical machines" (Davis: 128). Refusing to accept any simple dichotomies of nature versus technology, these practitioners view the Internet as a theater of the imagination. The Technopagan community comes to life with the creation of performative rituals that create their virtual reality through text, their participants interacting with keyboards, screens, and modems. This is certainly odd for those who conceive ritual strictly in terms of situated *action*, as a drama involving chant, gesture, and props such as chalices, bread, wine, incense, etc.; yet in the online experience as revealed in archive files at least, such elements are replaced by textual simulations. The ritual objects of fire, bread, salt, and knife are embodied in the words: 'fire,' 'bread,' 'salt,' and 'knife.' As one Technopagan ritual leader puts it, "Both cyberspace and magical space are purely manifest in the imagination.... Both spaces are entirely constructed by your thoughts and beliefs" (Davis: 128).

Here is an example from an undated ritual transcript available in the archives of the Compuserve Religion Forum, Pagan/Occult section. In a neopagan parallel to the Christian eucharist, the group leader directs the assembly in the breaking of bread:

Take a moment to thank the Moon . . .
for all she/he means to you . . .
Connect deep within the heart of who she/he is—
honored by so many, many cultures.
Take now your bread, muffin, or grain. . . .
(if you don't have such in front of you,
virtual bread is okay)
Take it, and split it in half.
Hold one half in your hands . . .
Think of the intuitive healing that comes
through our
marking of time, one month to the next . . .
Think of the phases, the changes she/he takes
us through . . .
the mysteries.
This half of bread will be libated after
ritual outside.
visualize your thanks into it.
Place it aside.
Take up the remaining half.
See it, study it, sniff it, taste it.
Eat of it, and think of healing. (RITUAL.TXT)

Interestingly, the transcript is equivocal on the question of whether the bread needs to exist on the physical plane at all. It seems that some practitioners do enact the ritual at home in front of their computers, chanting at the direction of the online leader or high priestess, manipulating the ritual objects of bread, salt, candles, wands, with gestures that are learned off-line in "real time"; nevertheless, the ritual does not require the physical presence of the elements to be effective. Similarly, another ritual called for the placement of three candles in a triangular formation but added that "cyber-candles will do fine." In a final example participants in a May 1994 full

moon ritual kindled a cyber-flame in order to permanently dedicate an electronic conference room on Compuserve for the performance of neopagan worship. Observe how the introduction to the transcript, authored by the leader of this ritual, characterizes the action performed as using virtual fire to sacralize a portion of cyberspace:

A need for a place of healing, purification and inspiration was identified by several members of Section 15. To meet this need, we decided to call forth a Sacred Flame similar to those in many Holy Temples of the Past and the Present. This flame was to be raised in Conference Room 9, Earth Religions, of the New Age Forum on Compuserve. It was to remain as a site for workings of the Spirit and of Aid for future users of the room. It was to be maintained through the Love and Duty of those that would seek its Majesty and experience its Touch within them. Many were in attendance this night to do this Work. Many Magicks from many Paths converged within the flames. Some of these pathways led to other realms and other times. The Magick of the evening is still here in the pages of transcript that follow. The Flame that was raised still burns! The Circle lives in its people. It is the Spirit of our combined Will! (MYFM94.TRN)

The evidence of these transcripts indicates that the actual performance of ritual acts using objects in real space is possible but unnecessary: the textual reality of a candle as described on the screen is sufficient to ensure ritual efficacy, while the cyber-flame raised in the electronic conference room has no embodiment except in text. Signifier and signified are fused in the textual simulation of off-line sensory experiences.

A useful perspective on these activities may be gained from the work of one of our most noted theorists of ritual, Jonathan Z. Smith. In his book *To Take Place: Toward Theory in Ritual* Smith emphasizes the importance of geography and landscape in the history of religion and argues against the traditional view (as articulated by Eliade and others) that myth provides the script that is enacted in ritual. Smith claims that ritual cannot be understood as a mere dramatization of a mythic script; rather, it must be understood on its own terms, as a mode of enactment that is geographically situated in communal space and landscape. With this in mind, what can we say about rituals in cyberspace—a place that is no place, a place that transcends geography in the conventional sense? What is the landscape of this strange world, and how has religion sacralized this landscape?

Cyberspace is without geographic features in the ordinary sense. But there is a kind of geography here, a landscape composed of sites, nodes, systems, and channels between systems. The topography of this landscape is represented by a variety of graphic interfaces that help orient those who explore it; and, as in the "real" world, this landscape has memories attached to it. Electronic archives and libraries store documents and record transactions; threads of conversations persist in groups and in the minds of individual participants; new users are routinely referred to the FAQ (frequently asked questions list). Then, too, the lack of ordinary physical features seems to inspire an attempt to recreate these features textually. This quality of spatial imagination is highly evident in the rituals excerpted here.

> (Iuna) To all who have gathered, and to the
> Harvest King,
> (Iuna) I offer and dedicate the cyber Harvest Home,
> (Iuna) a Real place in the Virtual,
> (Iuna) Named Gallifrey (for the home of the Time
> Lords).
> (Iuna) The Harvest Home rests near the center of
> our touch,
> (Iuna) the place of CompuServe. . . .
> (Iuna) This is a magic place . . .
> (Iuna) and it will serve to link us,
> (Iuna) virtual to real,
> (Iuna) cyber to the plenty.

As Smith notes,

> Ritual is, above all, an assertion of difference. . . . [It] represents the creation of a controlled environment where the variables . . . of ordinary life may be displaced precisely because they are felt to be so overwhelmingly present and powerful. Ritual is a means of performing the way things ought to be in conscious tension with the way things are. (109)

This is made poignantly clear in an exclamation repeated throughout many of these rituals, a stock phrase in the neopagan lexicon; when participants pray for blessings or benefits, their utterances are punctuated and given force by the ritual declaration, "so mote [must] it be!" This is perhaps too easily explained with reference to Freud's theory of religion as wish fulfillment. The speech act most characteristic of this assertion of difference in these rituals is not the declaration of wishes but the ritual setting apart of space within the network.

> (Arianna) WE THE MEMBERS OF THIS
> FULL MOON CIRCLE
> CLAIM THIS SPACE.
> WE THE MEMBERS OF THIS
> FULL MOON CIRCLE
> CLAIM THIS SPACE.
> A space set apart.
> A world between worlds.
> Our special place to meet with the Goddess,
> For the purpose of spiritual growth,
> To promote and fellowship/sisterhood
> In the pagan community,
> and to witness the entrance of others
> into the Path of the Goddess of the Craft.
> (APRIL.TXT)

After the space is claimed, the angelic powers that inhabit the four directions of North, South, East, and West are invoked, and a ritual circle is cast. Within this circle a variety of other ritual actions are performed initiation, investiture, and so forth. But it is the initial declarative act of setting the space apart that sacralizes the acts within that space, which turns further uses of ordinary language into performative speech acts—for those who take the ritual seriously.

If this all seems absurd and unreal to readers, recall again the powerful performative language of the Catholic Mass—which in Western culture virtually invented "virtual reality," a reality supported by a panoply of sensory impressions but created wholly through language and symbolism. From the perspective of the social science of religion Technopagan rituals are no different in principle, and no less worthy of study, than the belief system that underlies the daily utterance of the ancient, fateful, and endlessly contested words, "This is My body," in churches throughout the world. Nevertheless, there is a certain absurdist quality to these rituals: an aura of theatrical performance that calls to mind adolescent games such as "Dungeons and Dragons." One notices, for example, the use of pastiche; ritual actors employ elements from many different sources—poems, literature, songs, and textual fragments—in an eclectic mix of numerous religious and aesthetic traditions. The aesthetic of pastiche makes for an astonishing variety of moods, interactions that fluctuate rapidly between reverence, pseudo-reverence, and irreverence. Some participants come prepared with a text file and paste in quotations at particular points in the ritual. Prominent is the use of parody and humor, as when one neopagan prankster concluded a Harvest ritual by virtually "singing" verses of a neopagan version an old Christian hymn:

(1-3, Willow) I would like to, while in this sacred space,
(1-3, Willow) thank the divine intervention of Aphrodite!
(1-3, Willow) She introduced Craig and I
(1-2, Shadow Hawk) Willow, do you know her verse in that great pagan classic,
(1-2, Shadow Hawk) Gimme that Old Time Religion?
(1-3, Willow) and, thankfully, my life will never be the same! (toast to Aprodite!)
(1-2, Shadow Hawk) (raising chalice to Aphrodite)
(1-3, Willow) Can you hum a few bars?
(1-2, Shadow Hawk) Hmmmmmmmmmm. . . .
(1-2, Shadow Hawk) We will worship Aphrodite,
(1-2, Shadow Hawk) Tho she seems a little flighty
(1-3, Willow) oh, no
(1-2, Shadow Hawk) Coming naked in her Nightie,
(1-2, Shadow Hawk) And that's Good enough for me! (grin)
(1-3, Willow) Oh, Gods!
(1-2, Shadow Hawk) Yes Goddess?
(1-1, Many Blue Sparks) Hee!
(1-10, Dave) Tis a nice ryme there Shadow Hawk.
(1-2, Shadow Hawk) (pouring more Wine for everyone)
(1-2, Shadow Hawk) Dave, there are about 200 or so verses…
(1-3, Willow) Hey, this may be a Spring ritual, but I'm engaged!
(1-2, Shadow Hawk) my favorite is the one that goes…
(1-2, Shadow Hawk) We will worship like the Druids
(1-2, Shadow Hawk) Drinking strange fermented fluids
(1-2, Shadow Hawk) Running Naked through the woods
(1-2, Shadow Hawk) and that's good enough for me!
(1-2, Shadow Hawk) (Gimme that old time religion. . . .) (g[rin]) (APRFMN.TXT)

But lest we think that the whole thing was an elaborate game, something to take up the time of people who enjoy role-playing, who might otherwise develop an affinity for Morris dancing and the Society for Creative Anachronism, consider that the occult and neopagan traditions that spawned or inspired these online rituals are, perhaps, second cousins (in their attitudes toward the power of ritual speech if not in the lineage of their belief) to such New Age groups as the Order of the Solar Temple, the previously obscure sect now notorious for its group murder/suicides in Switzerland, France, and Canada. This brings me to the final issue, the cognitive content of these rituals—which has implications for considering the efficacy of the speech acts, insofar as they fulfill or do not fulfill what John Searle calls the "sincerity condition." If we are to judge the illocutionary force of these verbal actions, the efficacy of the rituals for their participants, it appears that we must first understand the degree to which they actually exhibit sincere belief in the gods they invoke.

What is the actual cognitive status of belief in the Goddess or any pagan deity for those who participate in these rituals? When Technopagans invoke the angels of the four directions, when they declare the circle to be cast so that the Goddess may manifest herself—do they actually "believe" in these entities in the same sense that Catholics believe in the miracle of transubstantiation or in the Trinitarian formula of the Nicene creed? If we turn to the participants themselves for answers, we find that the question as posed is rejected altogether. By the testimony of some, at least, the cognitive content of Goddess belief, the "truth" of the myth in the conventional, empirical sense of that word, is irrelevant. What counts is the ritual act of invocation, which brings the deities into being or revivifies them. Some, at least, feel perfectly comfortable in viewing the Goddess and the pantheon of pagan deities as projections of a Jungian collective unconscious—but argue that this renders them no less worthy of worship. As Arianna, a leader of numerous online rituals, writes in a file available in the Compuserve archives:

What I'd like to say is that these deities are living and real. They are as real as anything that has been created. . . . Just as you created [the Goddess], men and women over the centuries have created their deities, and these are real and living. These deities may be seen as friends, as sisters, and brothers. They are alive, they may grant requests, if you so choose to call upon them. They are happy for all the love that you feel for them. . . . [A]ny deity that you choose will become strengthened by the power that you give it. And many still have power, throughout the centuries. The collective unconscious of mankind still recognizes their beauty. They are aspects of the unconscious, but they also live and love. (PAGAN.TXT)

The ritual is seen as primary; belief in the conventional sense of that term is almost beside the point. By participation in the ritual the actors invoke a goddess who may well be seen as a collective fiction, but who nevertheless provides some spiritual sustenance and comfort to her followers. For those who take the ritual practice seriously the Goddess becomes as real as any other collective fiction: certainly *more* real than the old man sitting on a cloud that many have lost the ability to believe in.

What lessons can be drawn from the ritual transcripts I have examined here? Though this question must await fuller treatment elsewhere, certain apects of computer-mediated neopagan religious practice can be noted that will be of interest to scholars and perhaps to religious practitioners. In almost all of these transcripts we witness an attempt to recreate or simulate real space in virtual space and to sanctify a portion of this space as a theatre in which spirit is manifested; an establishing of difference with the world outside as well as with other territories of cyberspace; and an assertion of the power of language to bring about wish fulfillment through the verbal act of declaring the wish within the ritual circle. To this extent, they appear as attempts to fulfill authentic spiritual needs now unmet by the major institutions of religious tradition. Yet there is an irreverence to these discourses that some will find distasteful: they are ludic and playful, they revel in pastiche and parody, and they make few (if any) cognitive demands upon the participants. This conjunction of reverence and irreverence seems to me to be in some way characteristic of the spiritual situation of postmodern culture, which can neither dismiss religion nor embrace it wholeheartedly, but which ultimately leads to its commodification along with every other product and project of the past that is not doomed to be discarded in the ash-heap of history.

What, after all, are we to make of a religious ritual that casts itself as a cybernetic reinvention of the ancient Samhain of pre-Christian Europe but includes an invocation of the oreishas, the deities of Afro-Cuban and Vodou spirituality (whose devotees have their own electronic forums and message boards)?

Such practices appear as the religious equivalent of the recent marketing phenomenon of "World Music," which gave us recordings of traditional Gaelic singing against a backdrop of African drums or the music of the medieval mystic Hildegard of Bingen backed up by a jazz combo. The postmodern sensibility of these audiences floats like a hummingbird over the flowers of the world's historical archive, extracting nectar from the offerings of folk culture and high culture alike without distinction, employing the language and the aesthetic conventions of a thousand traditions with allegiance to none. If one defining aspect of the postmodern era is that it is an age when *literally* nothing is sacred, then the options for traditional organized religious bodies in the world of cyber-religion would seem to be limited. They can be dismissed as irrelevant or simply ignored; or they can offer themselves up in the new spiritual marketplace of virtual culture as raw material for playful cyborgs (see Brasher, this issue; also O'Leary and Brasher) who cut-and-paste at will through the fragments of our traditions.

I will conclude by invoking again my earlier comparison regarding the similarity of these rituals to those practiced by other esoteric New Religious Movements such as the Order of the Solar Temple. We actually know very little about this particular group's beliefs and practices; there has been much speculation but little hard information reported. But let us suppose a degree of similarity, at least in regard to the belief in the power of ritualistic language. The meeting rooms of the Solar Temple used architecture along with powerful visual and spatial imagery to evoke certain states of acceptance in followers; we may easily imagine ceremonies taking place in these spaces that resemble those enacted by the online pagans. What the online ritual lacks, in and of itself, is precisely the quality of physical presence that enables ritual actors to become so deeply embedded in the belief system that they will end up in an underground chamber, clutched with each other in a death embrace. By way of illustration, there is an exchange in an online Harvest ritual where one participant is offered cybercakes and cyber-ale in the virtual feast that concludes the ceremony. She complains about her diet and is reminded that cyber-food has no calories. To put the point somewhat more brutally: unlike the flames of Waco, the ritual flames in these cyber-transactions cannot burn.

Rooted in textuality, ritual action in cyberspace is constantly faced with the evidence of its own quality as constructed, as arbitrary, and as artificial, a game played with no material stakes or consequences; but the efficacy of ritual is affirmed, time and time again, even in the face of a full, self-conscious awareness of its artificiality. As Ronald Grimes argues. "All ritual, whatever the idiom, is addressed to human participants and uses a technique which attempts to re-structure and integrate the minds and emotions of the actors" (196). If this is the true aim of all ritual, online as it is off-line, then I believe we can say that these cyber-rituals do have efficacy, that they do perform a function of restructuring and reintegrating the minds and emotions of their participants. Toward what end is this restructuring undertaken? And will its integrations be durable? These are questions that must await further investigation, while we all wait to see the nature of the beast now slouching down the information highway to be born.

In a sense the discourses presented here are already obsolete, in that they have been superseded by the superior integration of texts, graphics, video, and even sound afforded to users of the World Wide Web, the fastest growing segment of cyberspace. A clue to the future of religious experiments in cyberspace may be seen in a 1994 Samhain ritual that took place in real time on a Web page housed in San Francisco. The designers of the page used a program called Labyrinth to simulate an altar in three-dimensional space, upon which ritual participants placed offerings of graphic designs and images (see Davis: 133, 178). As we move from text-based transmissions into an era where the graphic user interface becomes the standard and new generations of programs such as Netscape are developed that allow the transmission of images and music along with words, we can predict that online religion will become more "Catholic" in Umberto Eco's sense, by which I mean

that iconography, image, music, and sound—if not taste and smell—will again find a place in ceremony. Surely computer rituals will be devised that exploit the new technologies to maximum symbolic effect. It does not seem too far-fetched to think of cyber-communication as coming to play a major role in the spiritual sustenance of postmodern humans. The possibilities are endless. Online confessions? Eucharistic rituals, more weddings, seders, witches' sabbats? There will be many such experiments.

The old rituals were enacted by social actors who had to deal with each other outside of the church, synagogue, and temple; by their very otherness they both constituted and affirmed the social hierarchies of their culture. In cyberspace we are seeing relationships develop that have no other embodiment but in textual interchange. The transition to online ritual thus allows, even encourages, the self itself to be seen as a textual construction. Ethos is transformed by its appearance in virtual reality, with the assumption of pseudonyms and the option of anonymity allowing a previously unknown freedom to construct an identity divorced from gender, age, or physical appearance (Turkle: 178–180). This results in new hierarchies that may mirror those of the world off-line or depart from them in as yet unknowable ways. It is too soon to tell what the fate of religious community in the digital age will be or, indeed, whether the idea of a "virtual community" will prove to be sustainable. What paradigms will win out in the religious wars of the future we cannot tell; whether this will mean a revival of the Earth religions, or reformulation of ancient beliefs and practices in a new guise, or both, or neither, is anyone's guess. It seems safe to predict, however, that we will continue to see old and new religions jostling for attention in the cultural marketplace and using available technology to reach new audiences. If current trends hold, computers and computer networks will play an increasingly significant role in the religions of the future.

57

Homer the Heretic and Charlie Church: Parody, Piety, and Pluralism in *The Simpsons*

Lisle Dalton, Eric Michael Mazur, and Monica Siems

Although some might argue that watching TV is a form of ritual activity, actual depictions of religion are conspicuously absent from most television programs. To the horror of some critics, and to the delight of millions of viewers around the world, a significant exception is the animated comedy series created by Matt Groening, The Simpsons. *Authors Dalton, Mazur, and Siems draw examples from throughout the hundreds of episodes that have aired since 1990 to make their case that religion is one of the most prominent themes in the show. Self-consciously utilizing stereotypes and irony,* The Simpsons *holds a comic mirror to religion in contemporary America. As the present authors put it, the characters are "us" but "not us," exaggerated and distorted images of ourselves as we struggle with diverse forms of personal and noninstitutional religiosity. Through it all, the authors suggest, the show posits an underlying human goodness, exposing but not debunking the myths that order our values.*

Most of the family shows are namby-pamby sentimentality or smarmy innuendo. We stay away from that.

—Matt Groening

The story goes like this: Marge and Homer take some time for themselves and leave Bart, Lisa, and Maggie with Grandpa. Agents from child welfare discover the children running amok and place them into foster care with the neighbors. The new foster father, Ned Flanders, faints upon hearing that the children

"Homer the Heretic and Charlie Church: Parody, Piety, and Pluralism in the Simpsons" by Lisle Dalton, Eric Michael Mazur and Monica Siems from GOD IN THE DETAILS: AMERICAN RELIGION IN POPULAR CULTURE edited by Eric Michael Mazur and Kate McCarthy, pp. 231–247. Reproduced by permission of Routledge/Taylor & Francis Group. Copyright © 2001.

have never been baptized, so he packs up the children and his own family and heads for the Springfield River. Homer, missing the point, panics because "in the eyes of God they'll be Flanderseses." At the river Homer pushes Bart out of "harm's way," and the baptismal water falls on his own head. When Bart asks him how he feels, Homer responds, in an uncharacteristically pious voice, "Oh, Bartholomew, I feel like St. Augustine of Hippo after his conversion by Ambrose of Milan." When Ned Flanders gasps, "Homer, what did you just say?" Homer replies nonchalantly, "I said shut your ugly face, Flanders!" The moment of spiritual inspiration has passed, and the children are back with their parents, unbaptized and safe ("Home Sweet Home-Diddily-Dum-Doodily").

The prominent role of religion and the attitude toward it are not unique to this episode. Once a week for nearly the past decade (and more in syndication) *The Simpsons* has proved itself unafraid to lampoon

Evangelicals, Hindus, Jews, and religion generally. The frequency of religious plots and subthemes would itself be enough to distinguish this show from other prime-time fare. Not since the Lutheran program *Davey and Goliath* has a cartoon addressed religion so forthrightly. But while that Sunday morning program carried moral lessons of faith, this Sunday evening program ridicules the pious, lampoons the religious, and questions traditional morality. Instead of sermonizing at the audience, this program speaks with them, and possibly for them as well.

This half-hour series emerged as one of the most popular shows of the 1990s, and it regularly addresses issues involving institutional religion—including representations of religious traditions, discussions of moral and religious themes, and portrayals of mythological figures—as well as that which is often labeled "spirituality." Regular characters include a Hindu convenience store manager, a Jewish entertainer, an Evangelical neighbor, and a Protestant minister. Evil, morality, sin, the soul, and other religious themes are openly discussed. In terms of the genres associated with the show—the situation comedy and the animated cartoon—*The Simpsons* represents quite a departure from traditional fare in which religion is rarely if ever addressed. The writers' treatment of religion might even be construed as a heresy of sorts. Yet it is often an insightful heresy, for although the program thrives on satire, caricature, and irony, it does so with a keen understanding of current trends in American religion. *The Simpsons* implicitly affirms an America in which institutional religion has lost its position of authority and where personal expressions of spirituality have come to dominate popular religious culture.

"Don't Have a Cow, Man!": Reactions to *The Simpsons*

The Simpsons were the brainchild of Matt Groening, who developed the characters in short cartoons on the *Tracey Ullman Show* in the late 1980s. When *The Simpsons* aired in January 1990, it was the first animated prime-time series on American television in more than two decades. An immediate success, within a year it was the highest rated show on its network and was often among the top ten shows on television. It occasionally outperformed *The Cosby Show*, a family-oriented situation comedy that dominated

the ratings in the late 1980s. Over time its weekly ratings have declined, but the program still consistently ranks as one of the network's top shows. Its success has continued in syndication, ranking first among reruns during the 1994–95 season (Freeman 1995, 14). The program has become so popular that it is able to attract popular cultural icons (including actors, comedians, musicians, athletes, and talk show hosts) as guest "voices."

The Simpsons has also been a merchandiser's dream. During its first season, more than a billion dollars' worth of licensed Simpsons merchandise was sold in the United States. In 1991, licensed manufacturers shipped up to a million T-shirts per week. In an example of a show's cultural impact, some school principals banned a shirt featuring Bart and the slogan "Underachiever and Proud of It" (Riddle 1994, A5), and unlicensed merchandise (including one with Bart depicted as an African American) is commonplace despite millions spent to enforce copyright (Lefton 1992, 16).

This popularity also brought in intense scrutiny from critics. Emerging amid the family values debates of early 1990s, *The Simpsons* has undergone close examination for its portrayal of family life. One famous jibe came from President George Bush in a 1992 speech before the National Religious Broadcasters Association, in which he called for "a nation closer to *The Waltons* than *The Simpsons*." Other critics have damned *The Simpsons* as a symptomatic expression of the contempt for traditional values that permeates American culture. In his critique of the entertainment industry, Michael Medved catalogs instances of religious characters portrayed as duplicitous, hypocritical, insincere, and even criminal (1992). He cites one scene from *The Simpsons* in which Bart utters an irreverent prayer ("Two Cars in Every Garage, Three Eyes on Every Fish") as proof of the industry's pattern of religious insensitivity. Another media critic, Josh Ozersky, places *The Simpsons* in a wider critique of "anti-families" that includes *Roseanne* and *Married . . . With Children,* noting that while "the playful suppression of unhappiness has always been one of TV's great strengths," this new breed of sitcom also deflects public concern away from social disintegration related to the decline of the family. As such, the irony and sarcastic humor of these shows—though he admits *The Simpsons* often tends toward "witty and valid social criticism"—serve to extend television's unhealthy influence over the American public's self-image. "TV," he laments, "has absorbed the American family's increasing sense of defeat and estrangement and presented it as an ironic in-joke." And while this mocking might temporarily placate the dysfunctional tendencies of our times, it does not "lift the spirits." Ozersky argues that the deployment of irony in the face of domestic discontents is an "assault on the family and on all human relationships" since it acts as the "antithesis of deep feeling," "discourages alarm at the decline of the family," and disparages the "earnest, often abject bonds of kin" that lie at the heart of family life. He urges readers to reject "the soullessness of TV's 'hip, bold,' anti-life world" (1991, 11–12, 14, 93).

Despite such condemnations, reactions to *The Simpsons* have not been entirely negative. Many writers (in secular and religious periodicals) praise the show's clever writing and, oddly enough—considering this is a cartoon—its realism. Danny Collum praises *The Simpsons* for "grasping the complexity and ambiguity of human life." He credits it for its insightful, even realistic portrayal of an American family that is frequently abrasive, argumentative, and beset by financial problems. Collum notes that the Simpsons are among the few TV families that go to church or consult a minister. And while he recognizes their religiosity tends toward "pretty lame K-mart evangelicalism," it merits consideration because it shows characters striving for a "moral anchor" and a "larger sense of meaning" in the midst of otherwise chaotic and aimless lives (1991, 38–39). Chiding religious groups and educators who have denounced the series as promoting bad behavior, Victoria Rebeck praises it as sharp satire that shows how parents are often ill equipped to cope with their children's (and their own) problems. For her, this comes as a welcome departure from the "pretentious misrepresentation of family life that one finds in the 'model family' shows" (1990, 622). Similarly, Frank McConnell notes that *The Simpsons* "deconstructs the myth of the happy family" and "leaves what is real and valuable about the myth unscathed. . . . They are caricatures not just of us, but of us in our national delusion that the life of the sitcom family is the way things are 'supposed' to be" (1990, 389). He praises the show's humanism and rapid-fire humor, which he considers "profoundly sane."

"Gabbin' About God": Scholarly Viewing of Religion and Television

That *The Simpsons* generates such divergent reactions from critics suggests that it has struck a sensitive nerve that lies close to the heart of the public debate over the portrayal of religious values in the media. In an ambitious 1994 study of religion on television, researchers conducted a five-week analysis of religious behaviors on prime-time shows. After cataloging the activities of 1,462 characters in one hundred episodes, the study found that religion was "a rather invisible institution" in prime time; fewer than 6 percent of the characters had an identifiable religious affiliation, and religiosity was rarely central to the plots or the characters. The report concluded that "television has fictionally 'delegitimized' religious institutions and traditions by symbolically eliminating them from our most pervasive form of popular culture" (Skill et al. 1994, 251–67, especially 265). The study may have been biased; other explanations for the "symbolic elimination" of religion in prime-time television range from skittishness about offending religious adherents to alleged irreligiosity within the entertainment industry. Nonetheless, as Medved claims, the result is programming that often seems an "affront [to] the religious sensibilities of ordinary Americans" (1992, 50).

On the other hand, other scholars argue that it is better to analyze television using broader conceptions of religion. For them, the very act of watching television serves as a religious event—a domestic ritual of devotion to stories that would function like religious narratives in other cultures and eras. Gregor Goethals, borrowing from sociologists Peter Berger and Thomas Luckmann, asserts that television provides a symbolic universe that serves as an overarching framework for ordering and interpreting experience (1981, 125; see also Greeley 1987). Hal Himmelstein analyzes television programming in terms of various persistent "myths," including "the sanctity of the ordinary American family," "the triumph of personal initiative over bureaucratic control," and "the celebration of celebrity." He further argues that these myths sustain the political and economic needs of various social institutions (1994, 3, 10).

These debates over religion on *The Simpsons* reflect what anthropologist Clifford Geertz called the "intrinsic double aspect" of cultural products that are both models *of* and models *for* reality. Does *The Simpsons* reflect our attitudes—particularly toward religion—or does it shape them? Does television act as mirror to show us ourselves as we really are, or as we ought to be? As the reactions to *The Simpsons* suggest, it is an important debate. Geertz argues that such cultural patterns "give meaning . . . to social and psychological reality both by shaping themselves to it and by shaping it to themselves" (1973, 93). The reaction to *The Simpsons,* mirroring broader debates about America's values and morality, suggests that the show serves as a model of contemporary belief and behavior in American life; the show is a microcosm of what Americans currently do and do not hold sacred. This picture of America delights some, and appalls others. And although *The Simpsons* targets many social institutions, myths, and presumptions, religion inspires some of the show's sharpest satire, and correspondingly some of its best insights into contemporary America.

"Home Sweet Home-Diddily-Dum-Doodily": Welcome to Springfield

It is the world of the Simpson family that feeds the recriminations and fears of those who despise it, while offering humor, irony, succor, and a subtle morality play for those who adore it. Through the television lens (or more appropriately, its mirror), viewers see the mundane lives of the Simpsons, and themselves in the reflection—an odd but often uncannily accurate portrait of Americana. The cast represents a cross section of ages, genders, races, and religions; it includes police officers, teachers, entertainers, clergy, bartenders, and janitors. The Simpson family includes Homer (a dim employee at a nuclear power plant), his wife Marge (a devoted but overworked housewife), and their children: Bart (a good-natured but mischievous boy), Lisa (a precocious, sensitive girl), and infant Maggie.

The fact that the characters are cartoons presents an interesting dynamic, separating the "reality" of our lives from the "pretend" world of the Simpsons. Even so, the family presents noble truths, painful realities, and ironic depths in a very "real" way, enabling viewers to identify with the sentiments and to

be altered by them. This two-way relationship invites viewers to enter the Everytown of Springfield, to visit the Simpsons' world and perhaps comprehend how it informs their own. While they rarely "mug" for the camera, the self-reflexive actions of the characters help by constantly acknowledging their television status. From the show's opening sequence that depicts the characters racing home to watch their own opening credits to the frequent subreferences to other television shows, networks, and personalities, viewers are reminded of television's importance in the lives of the Simpson family and—since we are watching them watch—our own. Indeed, as if to mock our own viewership, the Simpsons' television is often alluded to as the sixth (and most appreciated) member of the family. The Simpsons watch television and are conscious of its influence over their lives, while we watch them and ponder, fret, and complain about how they are reflecting and shaping our thoughts and attitudes.

In Springfield, representatives of religious communities are rendered as stereotypes, easily identifiable to viewers and easily objectionable to adherents. The only regularly appearing Jewish character, Herschel Schmuykl "Krusty the Klown" Krustofsky, is the star of Bart and Lisa's favorite television program. He is anything but devout. A gross caricature of a stereotypically secularized Jew corrupted by wealth and fame, Krusty is addicted to cigarettes, gambling, and pornography. He dislikes children, finances his lavish debt-ridden lifestyle by overmarketing his own image unabashedly, and fakes his own death to avoid paying taxes. In an episode that parodies *The Jazz Singer,* Krusty recites a Hebrew prayer while visiting the Simpsons and later admits that as a youth he disappointed his father by abandoning rabbinical studies to become a clown. The rest of the episode involves the attempts by Bart and Lisa to reconcile the estranged father and son. Using advice from various Jewish sources, they eventually succeed ("Like Father, Like Clown").

Another character, Apu Nehasapeemapetalan, is manager of the local "Kwik-E-Mart" and one of the few identifiable Hindus on network television. Apu practices vegetarianism, maintains an in-store shrine to the elephant-headed deity Ganesha (quite plausible insofar as Ganesha's connection to prosperity appeals to the ambitions of the Hindu diaspora), and marries according to Hindu ritual. In Springfield, however, Apu must endure the slights of his incredulous customers; Homer belittles Apu's diet, throws peanuts at the shrine, and suggests that Apu "must have been out taking a whiz when they were giving out gods" ("Homer the Heretic"). More problematic is the inference that South Asians manage all convenience stores; Homer joins Apu on a Himalayan pilgrimage to visit the high "guru" of Kwik-E-Marts, and during a visit to a seaside town, the Simpson family stops at a local convenience mart managed by another South Asian ("Homer and Apu"; "Summer of 4 ft. 2").

The subjects of the most mockery, however, are the Simpsons' evangelical Christian neighbors, the Flanders family. Exceedingly cheerful, Ned, his wife Maude, and their "goody-goody" children Rod and Todd provide the perfect foil to the Simpson family. They are polite, well-liked, righteous, generous, peaceful, and neighborly—all qualities the Simpsons seem to lack. They are also extraordinarily pious: spotting escaped zoo animals running through town, Ned exclaims that he has seen the elephants of the apocalypse. Maude reminds him that the Bible describes four horsemen, not elephants. "Gettin' closer," he replies ("Bart Gets an Elephant"). Bart uses a special microphone to fool Rod and Todd into thinking that God is communicating with them over the radio. On another occasion they bounce on a trampoline and exclaim, "Each bounce takes us closer to God," and "Catch me Lord, catch me," before crashing into each other ("Radio Bart"; "Homer Alone").

Stereotyping is not the only way institutional religion is lampooned; religious leadership is the butt of much of the program's humor. Though other religious figures appear on the program (most notably in an ecumenical radio program entitled "Gabbin' about God" with a minister, Krusty's father the rabbi, and a Catholic priest ["Like Father, Like Clown"]), there is no doubt that the Reverend Timothy Lovejoy represents all clergy—to their general misfortune. When ever-righteous Ned Flanders telephones Lovejoy upon learning that the Simpson children were never baptized, Lovejoy—clearly annoyed by Flanders's intrusion—suggests that Ned consider another religious tradition: "They're basically all the same," he notes before hanging up. When Marge asks if a particular activity is a sin, Lovejoy picks up the Bible and exclaims, "Have you read this thing lately, Marge? Everything's

a sin" ("Home Sweet Home-Diddily-Dum-Doodily"). He encourages Marge to seek a divorce during a weekend retreat she and Homer attend to fix their marriage ("War of the Simpsons"). And when a comet threatens to destroy Springfield—and immediately after Homer laments not being religious—Lovejoy is seen running down the street yelling, "It's all over, people, we don't have a prayer" ("Bart's Comet").

Lovejoy's anemic approach condemns all religious leadership and is part of a larger critique of religious traditions consistent with the other stereotypes and the actions of the regular characters. After eating potentially poisonous sushi, Homer prepares for death by spending his last moments listening to the Bible on tape. Unfortunately, the "begats" put him to sleep, causing him to miss the sunrise he had hoped to die watching ("One Fish, Two Fish, Blowfish, Blue Fish"). (He survives.) Bart responds to a request for grace with a somewhat irreverent prayer: "Dear God: We paid for all the stuff ourselves, so thanks for nothing" ("Two Cars").

The program also uses familiar supernatural religious figures for comic effects. Both Satan and God have appeared on the program, and their portrayals mix the sublime and demonic with the ridiculous, presenting them as much human as they are supernatural. Satan is a familiar visitor to Springfield; in various episodes he offers Homer a doughnut in exchange for his soul; holds appointments with Montgomery Burns, the devious owner of the local nuclear plant; and uses a personal computer to keeps tabs on lost souls. Satan manifests in different forms, and typical of the program's use of irony, he is portrayed in one episode by Ned Flanders ("Treehouse of Horror IV"). In contrast, God is a cross between Mel Brooks's "Two-thousand-year old man" character and Charlton Heston's aged Moses—a familiar stereotype with a humorous and not-too-blasphemous sting. As might be expected of an anthropomorphic God, however, certain divine attributes (omniscience, omnipresence) seem lacking; in a meeting with Homer, God inquires whether St. Louis still has a football team (at the time, it did not) and later excuses himself to appear on a tortilla in Mexico ("Homer the Heretic").

The depictions of God and Satan reinforce the morality play qualities of the Simpson characters. Homer, as Everyman, is a poorly educated working man. He is simple, well meaning, loving, and committed to his family, regardless of how much they annoy him. Marge, as Charity, is always doing for others, particularly her family, while neglecting herself. In the few cases where she is self-indulgent, she ends up plagued by guilt, and though tempted by vices, she always returns to care for her loved ones. The eldest child, Bart, as Temptation, is the animated Tom Sawyer. He is an irascible boy who never studies, serves detention, plays pranks, yet loves his sister, obeys his mother, and occasionally respects his father. The eldest daughter, Lisa, as Wisdom, is the smart student and teacher's pet, the child who dreams of Nobel prizes and presidential elections and who relies on her saxophone and the Blues to release her from her torment. The youngest child, Maggie, represents Hope, the embodiment of innocence and vulnerability.

Juxtaposed with the dubious portrayals of institutional religion are nuanced and intricate examples of admirable and noble behavior. Krusty, Apu, and Ned are volunteer fire fighters who help put out the burning Simpson home after Homer falls asleep on the couch smoking a cigar (and skipping church) ("Homer the Heretic"). Ned, despite Homer's frequent ribbing and abuse, adheres closely to the Christian ideals of turning the other cheek and practicing charity. He invites the Simpsons to his barbecues, shares football tickets with Homer, offers to donate organs (without solicitation), lets the town come into his family's bomb shelter to avoid a comet's destruction, and agrees to leave it and face near certain doom when it becomes too crowded ("Homer Loves Flanders"; "When Flanders Failed"; "Homer's Triple Bypass"; "Bart's Comet"). Even the Simpsons, "America's favorite dysfunctional family" (Rebeck 1990, 622) often overcome their John Bunyanesque characterizations. Marge and Homer reject opportunities to be unfaithful, attend a retreat to save their marriage, and drag the family to a seminar to improve their communication skills. Homer attempts to improve his relationship with his father, hunts down his half-brother, and tolerates his annoying sisters-in-law. Though constant rivals, Bart and Lisa share genuine affection and occasionally work together; when Lisa becomes the star goalie of Bart's rival ice hockey team, the two put down their sticks and exit the rink arm-in-arm rather than compete for their parents' love. Bart even solicits the

assistance of a Michael Jackson sound-alike to help write Lisa a birthday song ("Life on the Fast Lane"; "The Last Temptation of Homer"; "Colonel Homer"; "War of the Simpsons"; "Bart's Inner Child"; "One Fish, Two Fish"; "Grandpa vs. Sexual Inadequacy"; "Oh Brother, Where Art Thou?"; "Lisa on Ice"; "Stark Raving Dad").

The diverse attitudes toward religion come together in the episode titled "Homer the Heretic." Refusing to attend church, Homer embarks on a journey of personal spirituality, encounters Apu's Hinduism and Krusty's Judaism, and ultimately comes face to face with God. During a dream God grants Homer permission to miss church, and when he awakens he is a changed man: calm, peaceful, and able to commune directly with nature. The following week, while asleep on the couch, Homer sets the house alight, and the volunteer fire department (Krusty, Ned, and Apu, or as Reverend Lovejoy puts it, "the Jew, the Christian, and the miscellaneous") rushes to put it out. Homer questions the value of attending church, since the Flanderses' house is also on fire. "He's a regular Charlie Church," Homer notes, suggesting that religious faith did not protect the Flanderses' home. But just as Homer utters these words, a providential cloud forms over the Flanderses' home and rain extinguishes the blaze—but leaves the fire burning the Simpson home. Asked by Marge if he has learned anything, Homer notes that God is angry and vengeful. The Reverend Lovejoy replies that it is the charity of the pluralistic volunteer fire department and not God's anger that is the lesson to be learned. The house is saved, and so is Homer's faith—in humanity, if not in God.

And so, perhaps, is the viewers', if the focus shifts from the show's content to its context, to what is happening on *this* side of the glass. Reverend Lovejoy's sentiment—that "God was working in the hearts of your friends and neighbors when they came to your aid"—represents the sort of generic Christianity prevalent in today's mainline Protestant churches and in most television portrayals of religion. Against the backdrop of declining religious authority, increasing personal choice, and "flattening" of doctrines into more palatable themes, television presents revamped morality plays such as this in which personal piety, religious pluralism, and sincere goodness rate higher than denominational adherence and church attendance. The show's coda reinforces this point: having promised to be "front row center" in church the next Sunday, there is Homer, snoring through Lovejoy's sermon, dreaming of another tête-à-tête with God (in which God informs Homer not to be upset, since "nine out of ten religions fail in their first year").

"Send in the Clowns": Analyzing the Simpsons

It is helpful to take a step back and remember that this is (after all) a cartoon, written by comedy writers and drawn by comic artists. Several episodes feature gestures that highlight the characters' traditionally animated hands: three fingers and a thumb. Indeed, whatever "reality" is posited in the program is of the viewers' making. By working both sides of the reality mirror, the show engenders feelings of both identity and difference—the characters are both "us" and "not us." They are "us" in the sense that they are not ideal, but "not us" in the sense that—their cartoonishness aside—they fall far shorter of the mark than we think we do. The television mirror here is a funhouse one, which provides an exaggerated, distorted, yet still recognizable image of ourselves. Ozersky notes this and criticizes the show not only for failing to provide a positive model but for rewarding an attitude of superiority and ironic smugness in its viewers. Closer to the mark, however, might be Rebeck's observation that such critics "have missed the point. *The Simpsons* is satire," and as such its characters "are not telling people how to act" (1990, 622).

Interestingly, Rebeck illustrates her point with a religious-themed episode; she compares *The Simpsons'* detractors to a minor but recurring character in the show, the Sunday school teacher. Beleaguered by the children's questions about whether their pets will go to heaven—particularly Bart's inquiries about an amputee's leg and a robot with a human brain—she finally blurts out, "All these questions! Is a little blind faith too much to ask for?" ("The Telltale Head"). At best, some critics want proactive television that encourages viewers to maintain a level of "blind faith" in certain cherished ideals and values. At worst, they lambast *The Simpsons* because it fails to reinforce our society's "dominant ideology" with its cherished myths of eternal progress and traditional authority structures.

But exposing a myth to ridicule and debunking it are two different things. Recall that McConnell's highest praise for *The Simpsons* was that "it deconstructs the myth of the happy family wisely and miraculously leaves what is real and valuable about the myth unscathed" (1990, 390). Rebeck notes that the Simpsons are not characters to be emulated, but "if anything, they are giving people an outlet so they won't have to act out" (1990, 622). Herein lies another paradox; it is precisely *because* the program fails to offer us any sustained ideals of its own—least of all desirable ideals that challenge the majority— that it serves as a negative model for mainstream ideals of family and religion, if only by default, and offers instead a catharsis generated by a good laugh.

If many of television's early sitcoms were little more than thinly veiled presentations of the "American dream," *The Simpsons* and shows like it come much closer to actually representing "comedy" than most of its predecessors. Himmelstein notes that, to those having difficulty handling "the chaos of daily life," comedy represents "the logical order of the ideal" by revealing the "ludicrous and ridiculous aspects of our existence." It is most powerful, he concludes, "when it is possible for both the artist and the spectator to note the contradictions and value conflicts of society." Comedy shades into satire when it deals with what he calls "traditional and ever-present irritations which people know as evils but which they also find themselves powerless to eradicate" (1994, 77).

On *The Simpsons*, the disjunction between the way things are and the way they ought to be persists, and any bridge across that gap proves temporary and largely unrecognized by the supposedly victorious Simpsons themselves. At the end of an episode, the family often debates the "lesson" they've learned, with none of them seeming to get the point. Thus, if the inclusion of humor at the expense of institutional structures marks *The Simpsons* as satire, this recurring failure to offer true resolutions distinguishes it as irony. Defined by literary critic Alan Wilde, irony in our era is "a mode of consciousness, a perceptual response to a world without unity or cohesion" which nonetheless bears "the potential for affirmation" of both the world's absurdity and its "unfinished" nature (1981, 2, 6). Here it seems that the models "of" and "for" society coalesce. Rebeck notes, "The Simpsons show us . . . what it was about our upbringing that made us brats as kids and neurotic as adults" (1990, 622). They do not show us how to remedy those conditions, implying that they don't need fixing. In an imperfect world one fares best by behaving imperfectly.

Ozersky sees *The Simpsons* functioning this way, with profoundly negative implications for society. He argues that the show makes viewers "less inclined to object to the continuing presence of unsafe workplaces, vast corporations, the therapy racket, and all the other deserving targets of *The Simpsons'* harmless barbs" (1991, 92). But Ozersky fails to see another side to the "irony" coin. For segments of society who *cannot* object to those failings, *The Simpsons* reminds them that they are not *completely* powerless as long as they can laugh at the forces that oppress them. James Chesebro identifies irony as the "communication strategy" of the disenfranchised that reassures an audience because it presents characters who are "intellectually inferior and less able to control circumstances than is the audience" (Chesebro 1979; quoted in Himmelstein 1994, 79). In other words, the character's life is more absurd than the viewers'—a funhouse mirror. This is especially true in cases of what Chesebro calls "unknowing irony" in which the character's "ignorance and social powerlessness" are not feigned. Archie Bunker, the somewhat pitiable and perennially unredeemed bigot of *All in the Family,* is a perfect example of "unknowing irony" from the pre-*Simpsons* television era. In order for ironic programming to serve as a model "for" society, he had to remain unredeemed. Otherwise the show would have been something substantially different from what it was. As Himmelstein notes, self-knowledge and self-criticism in Archie would "sacrifice" the show's "unknowing irony" and turn it from "a biting artistic revelation of bigotry in a contemporary social milieu" to a "a popularized group-therapy session thrown in the audience's face" (1994, 125). And while *The Simpsons* contains far fewer "serious" moments than *All in the Family* did—Homer is clearly more absurd and less pitiable than Archie ever was—the two proceed in a decidedly "live and don't learn" manner.

Not surprisingly, Homer's lack of intellectual and moral progress is expressed most powerfully in the religious-themed episodes. The accidental baptism in the Springfield River mentioned earlier elicits in him only temporary piety. He becomes a messianic leader for the "Stonecutters" (a men's organization modeled on Freemasonry), but his attempts to get the members to dedicate themselves to charitable acts causes the group to disband ("Homer the Great"). In the "Homer the Heretic" episode, not even a face-to-face encounter with the Almighty can change Homer's character. At every turn the opportunity for redemption passes, and Homer is back where he started: marginal, powerless, and unenlightened. In all these episodes, it is not unbelief that is counseled, but rather belief in basic values (for example, charity, camaraderie, and support) in a different way—within the family rather than outside it. In the end, Homer realizes the folly of striving too hard to "belong," and instead ends most episodes proud and confident of who he is, warts and all. As Richard Corliss notes, "Homer isn't bright, but he loves his brood." He is also a faithful husband and father who "will do anything—go skateboarding off a cliff, defy his boss, buy Lisa a pony—if the tots scream loud enough and if Marge gives him a lecture" (1994, 77). In other words, Homer's progress (or lack thereof) in each episode reveals a character who can be counted on to do the right thing, if accidentally or begrudgingly. This conveys a sense of an underlying human goodness, however many layers of ineptitude one might have to penetrate to find it.

"All the World Loves a Clown": The Simpsons as Religious Archetypes

And thus we return to the notion of the Simpsons—especially Homer—as "us" and "not us." He has the same values and desires, but expresses them in a buffoonish style. This is the key to discerning the significance of *The Simpsons* not only as satire of religious phenomena, but also as a religious phenomenon in itself. The history of religions has many examples of clowns who convey messages to the faithful. Historian Don Handelman describes the linguistic connections between "buffoon" and "fool" and notes the "affinities" between the fool in medieval drama and the clown as religious performer. According to Handelman, "Clowns are ambiguous and ambivalent figures. . . . The clown in ritual is at once a character of solemnity and fun, of gravity and hilarity, of danger and absurdity, of wisdom and idiocy, and of the sacred and the profane" (1987).

A character such as Homer Simpson oscillates between knowing and not knowing, between knowing that he knows and not knowing that he knows. He approaches the divine but simultaneously defames it, and thus embodies the irony of a character who knows no real resolution.

In some religions, the identity and difference between clowns and their audiences is an immensely significant dialectic—that paradox of "us" but "not us." In the Hopi tradition, ritual clowns perform actions backward, upside down, or in an otherwise ridiculous fashion—for example, entering a plaza by climbing head-first down a ladder. They may engage in exaggerated simulated intercourse and perform other activities that violate Hopi social norms. Interpretations have stressed two aspects: entertainment value and the pedagogic value of illustrating the foolishness of misbehaving. In this sense, Hopi clowns foster a sense of superiority among the audience members who know more and are more sophisticated than the clowns. However, as Emory Sekaquaptewa notes, clowns, while parodies of the society, must be recognizable in order to have an effect. It may be a funhouse mirror, but it's still a mirror, and clowns show that the way *not* to behave is precisely the way we often behave in an imperfect world. As Sekaquaptewa explains, clowns show that people "have only their worldly ambition and aspirations by which to gain a spiritual world of eternity. . . . We cannot be perfect in this world after all and if we are reminded that we are clowns, maybe we can have, from time to time, introspection as a guide to lead us right" (1989, 151).

Thus sacred clowns, through their mockery of norms, serve to reinforce a tradition's values. They "contradict the laws of society to remind people of distinctions between the sacred and profane. They cross ordinary boundaries in order to define them" (Bastien 1987). *The Simpsons* represents both a model of and a model for contemporary American society, not only because it reveals contemporary attitudes about religious institutions, morality, and spirituality, but also because it functions in the time-honored way of religious satirists. As Joseph Bastien notes, "Traditionally, religions have employed humor and satire to bring people together and dissolve their differences. Clownish antics . . . [are] not intended to desecrate the sacred but to dispel some of the rigidity and pomposity of the church-goers" (1987). The targets of *The Simpsons'* ridicule are hardly malevolent forces but rather exponents of what Victoria Rebeck calls a "sincere but useless" form of religion, teaching us that the most ridiculous thing a person can do is take anything in life too seriously (1990, 622). "The laughter of fools," Bastien says, is "praise to a God who disdain[s] pride among his people" (1987). But surely such a God would permit us to be proud of ourselves for getting the joke.

Conclusion: "A Noble Spirit Embiggens the Smallest Man"

In a cartoon universe that thrives on irony, satire, and endless subversion there can be no heresy save an unreasonable dedication to convention. In Homer's world, and perhaps in our own, there is no longer a well-defined orthodoxy against which a meaningful heresy might be mounted. This does not diminish the fact that the Simpsons fulfill the important function of the sacred clowns—sustaining what is important by poking fun at religious conventions. What is important to believe and do, however, defies description. In keeping with the show's insight into the contemporary religious scene there is a persistent message of a loss of institutional authority (although institutional practice and loyalty linger) coupled with diverse forms of personal and noninstitutional religiosity. In this light the would-be "heretic" Homer fulfills the role of the American spiritual wanderer; though linked culturally (if unsteadily and unenthusiastically) to biblical tradition, he regularly engages a mosaic of other traditions, mythologies, and moral codes. In the face of these ever-shifting layers of meaning, he stumbles along, making the most of his limited understanding of their complexities. His comic antics remind us that the making of meaning (religious or otherwise) is ever an unfinished business and that humor and irony go a long way toward sweetening and sustaining the endeavor.

Suggested Readings

Coleman, Simon
  2000   *The Globalisation of Charismatic Christianity: Spreading the Gospel of Prosperity.* Cambridge: Cambridge University Press.

Coward, Harold, John R. Hinnell, and Raymond Brady Williams, eds.
  2000   *The South Asian Religious Diaspora in Britain, Canada, and the United States.* Albany: State University of New York Press.

Eickelman, Dale F., and Jon W. Anderson, eds.
  1999   *New Media in the Muslim World.* Bloomington: Indiana University Press.

Hefner, Robert
  1998   "Multiple Modernities: Christianity, Islam, and Hinduism in a Globalizing Age." *Annual Review of Anthropology* 27: 83–104.

Kinney, Jay
  1995   "Net Worth? Religion, Cyberspace, and the Future." *Futures* 27(7): 763–75.

Sylvan, Robin
  2002   *Traces of the Spirit: The Religious Dimensions of Popular Music.* Albany: State University of New York Press.

Veer, Peter van der, ed.
  1996   *Conversion to Modernities: The Globalization of Christianity.* New York: Routledge.

Glossary

acculturation: Culture change occurring under conditions of close contact between two societies. The weaker group tends to acquire cultural elements of the dominant group.

age-grade: An association that includes all the members of a group who are of a certain age and sex (for example, a warrior age-grade).

age-set: A group of individuals of the same sex and age who move through some or all of the stages of an age-grade together.

ancestor worship: A religious practice involving the worship of the spirits of dead family and lineage members.

animatism: The attribution of life to inanimate objects.

animism: The belief in the existence of spiritual beings (Tylor's minimal definition of religion).

anthropomorphism: The attribution of human physical characteristics to objects not human.

anthropophagy: The consumption of human flesh (cannibalism).

associations: Organizations whose membership is based on the pursuit of special interests.

Aum Shinrikyo: A Japanese religious movement, whose followers were accused of releasing nerve gas in a Tokyo subway station in 1995.

avoidance rules: Regulations that define or restrict social interaction between certain relatives.

berdache: A French term for North American Indian transvestites who assume the cultural roles of women.

binary opposition: Contrasting pairs of items or concepts, such as male/female, heaven/hell, black/white. According to Claude Lévi-Strauss and the structuralist school, a fundamental characteristic of human thought.

bokors: A Haitian term for Vodou sorcerers who administer so-called zombie powder to their intended victims.

cannibalism: See *anthropophagy*.

Cartesian: Ideas attributed to philosopher René Descartes; specifically, the notion that the human mind and body are two separate entities.

ceremony: A formal act or set of acts established by custom as proper to a special occasion, such as a religious rite.

chador: In Iran, a long, capelike form of women's dress that usually does not cover the face. Literally means "tent."

chaebol: In Korea, giant manufacturing companies that export internationally.

charisma: Personal leadership qualities that endow an individual with the ability to attract followers. Often this quality of leadership is attributed to divine intervention.

cicatrization: Ritual and cosmetic scarification.

clan: A unilineal descent group based on a fictive ancestor.

communitarianism: A secular or religious lifestyle in which groups share beliefs and material goods; these groups are ordinarily isolated from the general population.

convergent evolution: The biological process by which similar adaptations occur in species of different evolutionary lines.

cosmogony: Symbolic materials, such as myths, accounting for the origins of the universe.

cosmology: A theory or view of the nature of the universe, including humans' place in it.

couvade: Culturally prescribed behavior of a father during and after the birth of his child; for example, mimicking the mother's labor pains.

coven: An organization of witches with a membership traditionally set at thirteen.

creationism: The belief that the living world originated from a divine act of creation. In the United States, usually associated with acceptance of the biblical book of Genesis as literal truth, belief that the earth is relatively young, and belief that both the physical structures and the living species of the earth have not changed since creation.

cult: An imprecise term, generally used as a pejorative to describe an often loosely organized group possessing special religious beliefs and practices.

cultural relativism: The concept that any given culture must be evaluated in terms of its own belief system.

Cultural Revolution: The period of radical change in China, in 1966–76, instigated by Communist Party leaders as well as youth. Strict governmental policies attempted to intensify Chinese communism.

cultural universals: Aspects of culture believed to exist in all human societies.

culture: The integrated total of learned behavior that is characteristic of members of a society.

culture trait: A single unit of learned behavior or its product.

curse: An utterance calling upon supernatural forces to send evil or misfortune to a person.

dar al-Islam: Territory or land where Islamic law is practiced.

demon: A person, spirit, or thing regarded as evil.

descent: A recognized parent-child connection that defines relationships within larger family groups.

diaspora: The dispersion or scattering of a population. Today, peoples that have migrated in large numbers across the globe, but who retain some sense of community or common identity—for

example, the African diaspora, the South Asian diaspora, and, historically, the Jewish diaspora.

diffusion: A process in which cultural elements of one group pass to another.

divination: The process of contacting the supernatural to find an answer to a question regarding the cause of an event or to foretell the future.

ecosystem: Plants and animals connected to one another and their environment through a flow of energy and materials.

emic: Shared perceptions of phenomena and ideology by members of a society; insiders' views.

endocannibalism: The eating of the remains of kinsmen and/or members of one's own group.

ethnocentrism: A tendency to evaluate foreign beliefs and behaviors according to one's own cultural traditions.

ethnography: A detailed anthropological description of a culture.

ethnology: A comparison and analysis of the ethnographic data from various cultures.

ethnomedicine: Beliefs and practices relating to diseases of the indigenous peoples of traditional societies.

ethos: The characteristic and distinguishing attitudes of a people.

etic: An outside observer's viewpoint of a society's phenomena or ideology.

euhemerism: The belief that myths are inaccurate, primitive explanations of the natural world or distorted accounts of the historical past. Based on the name of the classical philosopher Euhemeros of Messene (330–260 BCE).

exogamy: A rule specifying marriage outside one's kin group or community.

exorcism: The driving away of evil spirits by ritual.

familiar: A spirit, demon, or animal that acts as an intimate servant.

fetish: An object that is worshipped because of its supernatural power.

folk medical syndrome: Illnesses that reflect a combination of emotional, cultural, and physical causes, usually associated with a particular culture or community.

folk model: A culturally based way of perceiving or understanding something, frequently in opposition to scientific or empirically based understandings.

folklore: The traditional beliefs, legends, myths, sayings, and customs of a people.

functionalism: An analytical approach that attempts to explain cultural traits in terms of the uses they serve within a society.

fundamentalism: A commitment to what are perceived as the original, core, and inerrant facets of a faith. May represent opposition to the status quo or to the current distribution of power within society or a religious group. In U.S. Protestantism, includes acceptance of the Bible as literal truth.

Ghost Dance: A nativistic movement among several tribes of North American Indians during the late nineteenth century.

ghosts: Spirits of the dead.

glossolalia: The verbalizing of utterances that depart from normal speech, such as the phenomenon of "speaking in tongues."

god: A supernatural being with great power over humans and nature.

gynophobia: An abnormal fear of women (also spelled *gynephobia*).

hajj: The Muslim pilgrimage to Mecca.

hajji: Honorific title for Muslims who have made the pilgrimage to Mecca.

hallucinogen: Any of a number of hallucination-producing substances, such as LSD, peyote, ebene, and marijuana.

harem: The interior, domestic space of a Muslim home that observes seclusion of women. Usually includes women related through the extended family.

hijab: An Arabic word meaning "covering," used widely by Muslims across the world to refer to modest women's dress, which might take a variety of forms. Often interpreted in the West as "the veil."

holistic: In anthropology, the approach that emphasizes the study of a cultural and bioecological system in its entirety.

idolatry: Excessive devotion to or reverence for a person or thing.

imam: In Arabic language, prayer leader.

incest taboo: The prohibition of sexual relations between close relatives as defined by society.

intercessory prayer: A request to a god, calling for aid to others.

invocation: The act of conjuring, or calling forth, good or evil spirits.

jihad: In Arabic language, lit. "struggle." Broadly conceived, this may be either internal or external struggle. May describe acts of war or resistance, though the word is not limited to this meaning.

Ka'ba: For Muslims, sacred shrine in Mecca.

kaiko: Part of the ritual cycle of the Tsembaga of New Guinea; a festival involving the sacrificial butchering of pigs, dancing, and the hosting of guests.

karma: The Buddhist idea, connected to the belief in reincarnation, that one's present status in life is determined by one's actions in past lives. Accumulating spiritual merit through one's own actions, or on behalf of others, can affect karma.

Lamarckian inheritance: The scientific principle, promoted by Jean Baptiste de Lamarck (1744–1829), that characteristics acquired by an individual during its lifetime could be passed on through heredity to that individual's offspring. A pre-Darwinian theory of evolution.

legend: A folk narrative that relates an important event popularly believed to have a historical basis although not verifiable.

Liberation Theology: A school of thought within Roman Catholicism, particularly in Latin America, that emphasizes social justice and the eradication of poverty.

liturgy: Public rituals and services of the Christian Church.

madrasa: In Arabic language, school.

mámas: Priests among the Kogi of Colombia.

magic: A ritual practice believed to compel the supernatural to act in a desired way.

magic, contagious: A belief that associated objects can exert an influence on each other—for example, a spell cast using the intended victim's property.

magic, imitative: A belief that imitating a desired result will cause it to occur.

magic, sympathetic: A belief that an object can influence others that have an identity with it—for example, a bow symbolizes the intended victim.

magisterium: From Latin *magister,* for "teacher"; in the Roman Catholic Church, the church's domain of teaching authority. Adopted by S. J. Gould to refer to the separate realms of religion and science.

mana: A sacred force inhabiting certain objects and people, giving them extraordinary power.

manioc: A nutritious, starchy, edible root grown in the tropics; also known as cassava.

mara'akáme: A religious leader or shaman among the Huichol.

mazeway: Anthony F. C. Wallace's term for an individual's cognitive map and positive and negative goals.

misogyny: The hatred of women.

monasticism: The institution or system of life associated with a monastery and its occupants.

monomyth: According to Joseph Campbell, the basic narrative that organizes all myths of the world.

monotheism: A belief that there is only one god.

moral injunction: A command, an order, or a prohibition regarding the right way to live.

mufti: Specialist in Islamic law, who is capable of making legal interpretations.

mysticism: A contemplative process whereby an individual seeks union with a spiritual being or force.

myth: A sacred narrative believed to be true by the people who tell it.

nationalism: The idea of, and advocacy of, independence and unity of a nation. Usually based on some aspect(s) of group identity, such as ethnicity, language, or shared history. May be combined with other words—for example, to distinguish nationalism based on religious ties (religious nationalism) or nationalism that ignores religious affiliations (secular nationalism).

necromancy: The ability to foretell the future by communicating with the dead.

neo-paganism: A range of contemporary nature-oriented religions that draw inspiration from folklore, mythology, academic sources, and popular culture. Includes contemporary witches and practitioners of Wicca.

neurosis: A mild psychological disorder.

New Age: A loosely used term describing a combination of spirituality and superstition, fad and farce, that supposedly helps believers gain knowledge of the unknown. Largely a North American phenomenon, the movement includes beliefs in psychic predictions, channeling, astrology, and the powers of crystals and pyramids.

novice: A person in training to become a priest.

oath: An appeal to a deity to witness the truth of what one says.

occult: Certain mystic arts or studies, such as magic, alchemy, and astrology.

orality: A term used by Walter J. Ong to refer to reliance on nonprint forms of communication technology.

ordeal: A ritual method to supernaturally determine guilt or innocence by subjecting the accused to a physical test.

organic unity: The idea that cultures are composed of integrated parts, balanced and functioning harmoniously.

orthodox: Being in line with the main teachings of a church or religious tradition; conforming to a standard doctrine.

otherworldly: Devoted to concerns beyond the present material world; in connection with spiritual concerns or the prospect of an afterlife.

pantheism: The belief that God is everything and everything is God; (also) the worship of all gods.

participant observation: An anthropological field technique in which the ethnographer is immersed in the day-to-day activities of the community being studied.

patrilineal: The rule of descent in which individuals are related through the father's line only.

Pentecostalism: A segment of Christianity that emphasizes involvement with the Holy Spirit (the third person of the holy trinity) through such experiences as divine healing, prophecy, and speaking in tongues.

petition prayer: A request to a god, calling for assistance or success for oneself.

peyote: A spineless cactus native to Mexico and Texas, scientific name *Lophophora williamsii;* sometimes referred to as peyotl (from Aztec or Nahuatl) or, mistakenly, as mescal. It is used ceremonially by indigenous peoples of Mexico, as well as the Native American Church, for its production of visual hallucinations.

peyote cult: A cult surrounding the ritual ingestion of peyote; commonly associated with certain Native American religious beliefs.

polygamy: Marriage to multiple partners.

polygyny: Marriage of one man to more than one woman.

polysemic: Having multiple meanings. A quality attributed to many symbols.

polytheism: See *pantheism.*

possession: A trance state in which malevolent or curative spirits enter a person's body.

primary source: Material coming from a source directly connected to a phenomenon. For example, texts authored by participants or newspaper stories published at the time of an event. Contrast to secondary sources, which are accounts, analyses, or interpretations written by later scholars or commentators.

primitive: A term used by anthropologists, especially in the past, to describe a culture lacking a written language; cultures also characterized by low-level technology, small numbers, few extra-societal contacts, and homogeneity (sometimes referred to as preliterate or nonliterate cultures).

profane: Not concerned with religion or the sacred; the ordinary.

prophet: A religious leader or teacher regarded as, or claiming to be, divinely inspired who speaks for a god.

propitiation: The act or acts of gaining the favor of spirits or deities.

psychosis: A psychological disorder sufficiently damaging that it may disrupt the work or activities of a person's life.

purdah: The seclusion of women as practiced by some Hindus and Muslims. From the Urdu language.

qadi: Judge in Islamic law or shari'a.

reciprocity: A system of repayment of goods, objects, actions, and sometimes money through which obligations are met and bonds created.

reincarnation: The belief that the soul reappears after death in another and different bodily form.

religion: A set of beliefs and practices pertaining to supernatural beings or forces.

revitalization movements: According to Anthony F. C. Wallace, a deliberate, organized, conscious effort by members of a society to construct a more satisfying culture.

rites of passage: Rituals associated with such critical changes in personal status as birth, puberty, marriage, and death.

ritual: A secular or sacred, formal, solemn act, observance, or procedure in accordance with prescribed rules or customs.

rumbim: A plant used ritually by the Tsembaga of New Guinea. Associated with a ritual period of obligations and prohibitions, at the termination of warfare.

sacred: Venerated objects and actions considered holy and entitled to reverence.

sacrifice: The ritualized offering of a person, a plant, or an animal as propitiation or in homage to the supernatural.

sect: A small religious group with distinctive beliefs and practices that set it apart from other similar groups in the society.

secular: Not sacred or religious.

shaman: A religious specialist and healer with powers derived directly from supernatural sources.

shari'a: The body of law and legal decisions associated with Islam.

shaykh: In Arabic language, respected elder, teacher, head of tribe, or head of religious order.

society: A group of people sharing a territory, language, and culture.

sorcery: The use of magical paraphernalia by an individual to harness supernatural powers ordinarily to achieve evil ends.

soul: The immortal or spiritual part of a person believed to separate from the physical body at death.

spontaneous memorials: Collections of mementoes taken by mourners either to the site of someone's death or to a place closely associated with the deceased. Most frequently associated with unanticipated, violent deaths.

structuralism: An anthropological approach to the understanding of the deep, subconscious, unobservable structure of human realities that is believed to determine observable behavior (a leading exponent: Claude Lévi-Strauss).

supernatural: A force or an existence that transcends the natural.

Sutras: The sacred texts or scriptures of Buddhism.

symbol: An object, a gesture, a word, or another representation to which an arbitrary shared meaning is given.

syncretism: A process of culture change in which the traits and elements of one culture are given new meanings or new functions when they are adapted by another culture—for example, the combining of Catholicism and African religion to form Vodou.

taboo: A sacred prohibition put upon certain people, things, or acts that makes them untouchable, unmentionable, and so on (also *tabu, tabou, tapu*).

talisman: A sacred object worn to ensure good luck or to ward off evil. Also known as an amulet or a charm.

teleology: The process of being directed by an end or shaped by a purpose, especially in nature.

theocracy: Rule by religious specialists.

theology: Religious knowledge or belief; the study of god or religion, from the perspective of believers.

totem: An animal, a plant, or an object considered related to a kin group and viewed as sacred.

trance: An altered state of consciousness induced by religious fervor, fasting, repetitive movements and rhythms, drugs, and so on.

transcendence: The condition of being separate from or beyond the material world.

'ulama: Muslim religious scholars.

'ummah: In Islam, the community of believers.

Vodou: A syncretic religion of Haiti that combines Catholicism and African religion; sometimes referred to as Tovodun or Vodun.

witchcraft: An evil power inherent in certain individuals that permits them, without the use of magical charms or other paraphernalia, to do harm or cause misfortune to others.

zombie: In Haiti, an individual believed to have been placed in a trancelike state through the administration of a psychotropic drug given secretly, thus bringing the victim under the control of another.

Bibliography

The following bibliography is a compilation of the lists of references or suggested readings that accompanied each article in its original publication. (In some cases, a list of references has been constructed from footnote citations in the original.) We have rendered the citations in as consistent a form as possible, but minor variations in form and content are inevitable because of the varied citation styles of the original publishers.

A few articles were not accompanied by references in their original publication and accordingly are not included here.

CHAPTER ONE
The Anthropological Study of Religion

Religion
Clifford Geertz

REFERENCES

Bettelheim, Bruno
    1954   *Symbolic Wounds: Puberty Rites and the Envious Male.* Glencoe, Ill.: Free Press.

Campbell, Joseph
    1949   *The Hero with a Thousand Faces.* New York: Pantheon.

Devereux, George
    1951   *Reality and Dream: Psychotherapy of a Plains Indian.* New York: International Universities Press.

Eliade, Mircea
    [1949] 1958   *Patterns in Comparative Religion.* New York: Sheed and Ward.

Erikson, Erik H.
    [1950] 1964   *Childhood and Society.* 2nd ed. New York: Norton.

Geertz, Clifford
    1966   "Religion as a Cultural System." In Michael Banton, ed., *Anthropological Approaches to the Study of Religion.* A.S.A. Monograph No. 3. London: Tavistock Publications Limited.

Hallowell, A. Irving
    1955   *Culture and Experience.* Philadelphia: University of Pennsylvania Press.

Kardiner, Abram
    1945   *The Psychological Frontiers of Society.* New York: Columbia University Press.

Kluckhohn, Clyde
    1944   *Navaho Witchcraft.* Harvard University. Peabody Museum of American Archaeology and Ethnology Papers, vol. 22, no. 2. Cambridge, Mass.: The Museum.

Lang, Andrew
    [1898] 1900   *The Making of Religion.* 2nd ed. New York: Longmans.

Lessa, William A., and Evon Z. Vogt, eds.
    1965   *Reader in Comparative Religion: An Anthropological Approach.* 2nd ed. New York: Harper.

Lévi-Strauss, Claude
    [1958] 1963   *Structural Anthropology.* New York: Basic Books.
    [1962] 1966   *The Savage Mind.* University of Chicago Press.

Radcliffe-Brown, A. R.
    [1952] 1961   *Structure and Function in Primitive Societies: Essays and Addresses.* Glencoe, Ill.: Free Press.

Róheim, Geza
    1950   *Psychoanalysis and Anthropology: Culture, Personality and the Unconscious.* New York: International Universities Press.

Spier, Leslie
    1921   *The Sun Dance of the Plains Indians: Its Development and Diffusion.* American Museum of Natural History Anthropological Papers, vol. 16, part 7. New York: The Museum.

Whiting, John, and Irvin L. Child
    1953   *Child Training and Personality: A Cross-Cultural Study.* New York: Yale University Press.

Religious Perspectives in Anthropology
Dorothy Lee

REFERENCES

Barton, R. F.
    1946   *The Religion of the Ifugao.* In American Anthropological Association *Memoirs,* no. 65.

Black Elk
    1932   *Black Elk Speaks. Being the Life Story of a Holy Man of the Oglala Sioux, as Told to John G. Neihardt (Flaming Rainbow).* New York: William Morrow.

Brown, Joseph Epes
    1953   *The Sacred Pipe: Black Elk's Account of the Seven Rites of the Oglala Sioux.* Norman: University of Oklahoma Press.

Firth, Raymond
    1940   *The Work of the Gods in Tikopia.* London: Lund, Humphries.
    1950   *Primitive Polynesian Economy.* New York: Humanities Press.

Henry, Jules
    1941   *Jungle People.* New York: J. J. Augustin.

Redfield, Robert, and W. Lloyd Warner
    1940   "Cultural Anthropology and Modern Agriculture." In *Farmers in a Changing World,* 1940 Yearbook of Agriculture. Washington, D.C.: United States Government Printing Office.

Thompson, Laura
    1946   *The Hopi Crisis: Report to Administrators.* (Mimeographed.)

Vanoverbergh, Morice
    1936   *The Isneg Life Cycle.* Publication of the Catholic Anthropological Conference, vol. 3, no. 2.

Anthropologists Versus Missionaries: The Influence of Presuppositions
Claude E. Stipe

REFERENCES

Bennett, John W.
    1946   "The Interpretation of Pueblo Culture: A Question of Values." *Southwestern Journal of Anthropology* 2: 361–74.

Boutilier, James A., Daniel T. Hughes, and Sharon W. Tiffany, eds.
    1978   *Mission, Church, and Sect in Oceania.* Ann Arbor: University of Michigan Press.

Burridge, Kenelm O. L.
    1978   "Introduction: Missionary Occasions." In J. A. Boutilier, D. T. Hughes, and S. Tiffany, eds., *Mission, Church, and Sect in Oceania,* pp. 1–30. Ann Arbor: University of Michigan Press.

Chagnon, Napoleon A.
    1967   "Yanomamö: The Fierce People." *Natural History* 78: 22–31.
    1974   *Studying the Yanomamö.* New York: Holt, Rinehart and Winston.

Codrington, R. H.
    1891   *The Melanesians: Studies in Their Anthropology and Folklore.* Oxford: Clarendon Press.

Colson, Elizabeth
    1976   "Culture and Progress." *American Anthropologist* 78: 261–71.

Ember, Carol R., and Melvin Ember
    1977   *Cultural Anthropology.* 2nd ed. Englewood Cliffs, N.J.: Prentice Hall.

Evans-Pritchard, E. E.
    1965   *Theories of Primitive Religion.* London: Oxford University Press.

1972 "Religion and the Anthropologists."
      Practical Anthropology 19: 193–206.
      (Originally published in *Blackfriars* 41
      [April 1960]: 104–18.)

Forman, Charles W.
1978 "Foreign Missionaries in the Pacific
      Islands During the 20th Century." In J. A.
      Boutilier, D. T. Hughes, and S. Tiffany,
      eds., *Mission, Church, and Sect in Oceania*,
      pp. 35–63. Ann Arbor: University of
      Michigan Press.

Fortune, Reo
1963 *Sorcerers of Dobu*. New York: Dutton.

Geertz, Clifford.
1966 "Religion as a Cultural System." In
      Michael Banton, ed., *Anthropological
      Approaches to the Study of Religion*,
      pp. 1–46. New York: Praeger.

Gluckman, Max
1962 "Les rites de passage." In Max
      Gluckman, ed., *Essays on the Ritual of
      Social Relations*, pp. 1–52. Manchester:
      University of Manchester Press.

Graburn, Nelson K. H.
1969 *Eskimos Without Igloos: Social and Economic
      Development in Sugluk*. New York: Little,
      Brown.

Hill, W. W.
1944 "The Navaho Indians and the Ghost
      Dance of 1890." *American Anthropologist*
      46: 523–27.

Hippler, Arthur E.
1974 "Some Alternative Viewpoints on the
      Negative Results of Euro-American
      Contact with Non-Western Groups."
      American Anthropologist 76: 334–37.

Hogbin, Ian
1964 *A Guadalcanal Society: The Koaka-Speakers*.
      New York: Holt, Rinehart and Winston.

Horton, Robin
1971 "African Conversion." *Africa* 41: 85–108.

Hughes, Daniel T.
1978 "Mutual Biases of Anthropologists and
      Missionaries." In J. A. Boutilier, D. T.
      Hughes, and S. Tiffany, eds., *Mission,
      Church, and Sect in Oceania*, pp. 65–82.
      Ann Arbor: University of Michigan Press.

Jocano, F. Landa
1969 *Growing Up in a Philippine Barrio*. New
      York: Holt, Rinehart and Winston.

Keesing, Roger M.
1976 *Cultural Anthropology: A Contemporary
      Perspective*. New York: Holt, Rinehart and
      Winston.

Kopytoff, Igor
1964 "Classifications of Religious Movements:
      Analytic and Synthetic." In June Helm,
      ed., *Symposium on New Approaches to the
      Study of Religion*, pp. 77–90. Seattle:
      University of Washington Press.

Latukefu, Sione
1978 "Conclusion: Retrospect and Prospect."
      In J. A. Boutilier, D. T. Hughes, and
      S. Tiffany, eds., *Mission, Church, and Sect
      in Oceania*, pp. 457–64. Ann Arbor:
      University of Michigan Press.

Lawrence, Peter
1964 *Road Belong Cargo: A Study of the Cargo
      Movement in the Southern Madang District
      of New Guinea*. Manchester: University of
      Manchester Press.

1970 "Daughter of Time." In T. G. Harding
      and B. J. Wallace, eds., *Cultures of the
      Pacific: Selected Readings*, pp. 267–84.
      New York: Free Press.

Leach, E. R.
1954 *Political Structures of Highland Burma: A
      Study of Kachin Social Structure*. London:
      G. Bell.

Lewis, Diane
1973 "Anthropology and Colonialism."
      Current Anthropology 14: 581–91.

Lowie, Robert H.
1963 "Religion in Human Life." *American
      Anthropologist* 65: 532–42.

Middleton, John
1970 *The Study of the Lugbara: Expectation
      and Paradox in Anthropological Research*.
      New York: Holt, Rinehart and
      Winston.

Miller, Elmer S.
1975 "Shamans, Power Symbols, and Change
      in Argentine Toba Culture." *American
      Ethnologist* 2: 477–96.

O'Brien, Denise, and Anton Ploeg
1964 "Acculturation Movements Among the Western Dani." *American Anthropologist* 66, no. 2, part 2: 281–92.

Osborne, Kenneth B.
1970 "A Christian Graveyard Cult in the New Guinea Highlands." *Practical Anthropology* 17: 10–15.

Peel, J. D. Y.
1968 *Aladura: A Religious Movement Among the Yoruba.* London: Oxford University Press.

Powdermaker, Hortense
1966 *Stranger and Friend: The Way of an Anthropologist.* New York: W. W. Norton.

Radcliffe-Brown, A. R.
1952 "Religion and Society." In A. R. Radcliffe-Brown, ed., *Structure and Function in Primitive Society,* pp. 153–77. New York: Free Press.

Ribeiro, René
1962 "Brazilian Messianic Movements." In S. L. Thrupp, ed., *Millennial Dreams in Action,* pp. 55–69. The Hague: Mouton.

Richards, Cara E.
1977 *People in Perspective: An Introduction to Cultural Anthropology.* 2nd ed. New York: Random House.

Richardson, Miles
1975 "Anthropologist—the Myth Teller." *American Ethnologist* 2: 517–33.

Salamone, Frank A.
1976 "Learning to Be a Christian: A Comparative Study." *Missiology* 4: 53–64.
1977 "Anthropologists and Missionaries: Competition or Reciprocity?" *Human Organization* 36: 407–12.
1979 "Epistemological Implications of Fieldwork and Their Consequences." *American Anthropologist* 81: 46–60.

Tiffany, Sharon W.
1978 "Introduction to Part 4: Indigenous Response." In J. A. Boutilier, D. T. Hughes, and S. Tiffany, eds., *Mission, Church, and Sect in Oceania,* pp. 301–5. Ann Arbor: University of Michigan Press.

Tonkinson, Robert
1974 *The Jigalong Mob: Aboriginal Victors of the Desert Crusade.* Menlo Park, Calif.: Cummings.

Turnbull, Colin
1961 *The Forest People: A Study of the Pygmies of the Congo.* Garden City, N.Y.: Doubleday.

Wallace, A. F. C.
1970 *The Death and Rebirth of the Seneca.* New York: Random House/Vintage Books.

CHAPTER TWO
Myth, Symbolism, and Taboo

The Study of Mythology
Scott Leonard and Michael McClure

REFERENCES

Boas, Franz
[1928] 1986 *Anthropology and Modern Life.* New York: Dover.

Bolen, Jean Shinoda
1985 *Goddesses in Every Woman.* New York: Harper and Row.

Campbell, Joseph
[1949] 1972 *The Hero with a Thousand Faces.* Princeton, N.J.: Princeton University Press.
1959 *The Masks of God.* Vol. 1: *Primitive Mythology.* New York: Viking.
1962 *The Masks of God.* Vol. 2: *Oriental Mythology.* New York: Viking.
1964 *The Masks of God.* Vol. 3: *Occidental Mythology.* New York: Viking.
1968 *The Masks of God.* Vol. 4: *Creative Mythology.* New York: Viking.
1972 *Myths to Live By.* New York: Viking.

Campbell, Joseph, with Bill Moyers
1985 *The Power of Myth.* New York: Doubleday.

Doniger, Wendy
1998 *The Implied Spider: Politics and Theology in Myth.* New York: Columbia University Press.

Doty, William G.
2000   *Mythography: The Study of Myths and Rituals.* 2nd ed. Tuscaloosa: University of Alabama Press.

Durkheim, Émile, and Marcell Mauss
1963   *Primitive Classification.* Trans. Rodney Needham. Chicago: University of Chicago Press.

Eliade, Mircea
1974   *Patterns in Comparative Religion.* New York: New American Library.
1975   *Myth and Reality.* New York: Harper and Row.
1975   *Myths, Dreams, and Mysteries.* New York: Harper and Row.
1983   *The Sacred and the Profane.* Magnolia, Mass.: Peter Smith.
1985   *Cosmos and History: The Myth of the Eternal Return.* New York: Garland.

Ellwood, Robert
1999   *The Politics of Myth: A Study of C. G. Jung, Mircea Eliade, and Joseph Campbell.* Issues in the Study of Religion series. Albany: State University of New York.

Fontenrose, Joseph
1971   *The Ritual Theory of Myth.* Berkeley: University of California Press.

Frazer, James George
1922   *The Golden Bough.* Abridged ed. London: Macmillan.

Freud, Sigmund
1900   *The Interpretation of Dreams.* London.
1918   *Totem and Taboo.* New York.
1953–66   *The Standard Edition of the Complete Psychological Works of Sigmund Freud.* London: Hogarth.

Jung, Carl Gustav
[1959] 1980   *The Archetypes and the Collective Unconscious.* Bollingen Series 20. Princeton, N.J.: Princeton University Press.
[1964] 1988   *Man and His Symbols.* New York: Doubleday.

Kirk, Geoffrey Stephen
1970   *Myth: Its Meaning and Functions in Ancient and Other Cultures.* Berkeley: University of California Press.

Lévi-Strauss, Claude
1979   *Myth and Meaning.* New York: Schocken/Pantheon.
[1981] 1990   *The Naked Man.* Trans. John and Doreen Weightman. Chicago: University of Chicago Press.
1990   *The Raw and the Cooked.* Trans. John and Doreen Weightman. Chicago: University of Chicago Press.

Lincoln, Bruce
1999   *Theorizing Myth: Narrative, Ideology, and Scholarship.* Chicago: University of Chicago Press.

Malinowski, Bronislaw
[1926] 1971   *Myth in Primitive Psychology.* Westport, Conn.: Negro Universities Press.

Propp, Vladimir
[1968] 1990   *Morphology of the Folktale.* Trans. Laurence Scott. Austin: University of Texas Press.

Scholes, Robert
1974   *Structuralism in Literature: An Introduction.* New Haven, Conn.: Yale University Press.

Segal, Robert A.
1996   *Theories of Myth: From Ancient Israel and Greece to Freud, Jung, Campbell, and Lévi-Strauss.* Philosophy, Religious Studies, and Myth Series, vol. 3. New York: Garland Press.

Taboo
Mary Douglas

REFERENCES

Douglas, Mary
1966   *Purity and Danger.* New York: Frederick A. Praeger.

Steiner, Franz
[1956] 1967   *Taboo.* London: Penguin.

CHAPTER THREE
Ritual

Betwixt and Between: The Liminal Period in *Rites de Passage*
Victor W. Turner

REFERENCES

Bettelheim, Bruno
    1954   *Symbolic Wounds, Puberty Rites and the Envious Male.* New York: Free Press.

Douglas, Mary
    1966   *Purity and Danger.* London: Routledge and Kegan Paul.

Elwin, Verrier
    1955   *The Religion of an Indian Tribe.* London: Geoffrey Cumberlege.

Harrison, Jane
    1903   *Prolegomena to the Study of Greek Religion.* London: Cambridge University Press.

Hocart, A. M.
    1952   *The Life-Giving Myth.* London: Methuen and Co.

James, William
    1918   *Principles of Psychology.* Vol. 1. New York: H. Holt.

Kuper, Hilda
    1947   *An African Aristocracy.* London: Oxford University Press.

McCulloch, J. A.
    1913   "Monsters," in *Hastings Encyclopaedia of Religion and Ethics.* Edinburgh: T. and T. Clark.

Richards, A.
    1956   *Chisungu.* London: Faber and Faber.

Turner, Victor
    1962   "Chihamba, the White Spirit." *Rhodes-Livingstone Papers,* no. 33. Manchester.

Warner, Lloyd
    1959   *The Living and the Dead: A Study of the Symbolic Life of Americans.* New Haven, Conn.: Yale University Press.

Female Circumcision in Egypt and Sudan: A Controversial Rite of Passage
Daniel Gordon

REFERENCES

Al-Hibri, Aziza, ed.
    1982   *Women and Islam.* New York: Pergamon Press.

Antoun, Richard
    1968   "On the Modesty of Women in Arab Muslim Villages: A Study in the Accommodation of Traditions." *American Anthropologist* 70: 671–97.

Beck, Luis, and Nikkie Keddie, eds.
    1980   *Women in the Muslim World.* Cambridge, Mass.: Harvard University Press.

Boddy, Janice
    1982   "Womb as Oasis: The Symbolic Context of Pharaonic Circumcision in Rural Northern Sudan." *American Ethnologist* 9: 682–98.

Dewhurst, Christopher, and Aida Michelson
    1964   "Infibulation Complicating Pregnancy." *British Medical Journal* 2: 1442.

El Dareer, Asma
    1982   *Women, Why Do You Weep?* London: Zed Press.

El Saadawi, Nawal
    1980   *The Hidden Face of Eve.* Boston: Beacon Press.

Hansen, Henry Harold
    1972/   "Clitoridectomy: Female Circumcision
    73   in Egypt." *Folk* 14–15: 15–26.

Hathout, H. M.
    1963   "Some Aspects of Female Circumcision." *Journal of Obstetrics and Gynecology of the British Empire* 70: 505–7.

Hosken, Fran P.
    1978   "Epidemiology of Female Genital Mutilation." *Tropical Doctor* 8: 150–56.
    1982   *The Hosken Report: Genital and Social Mutilation of Females.* Lexington, Mass.: Women's International News Network.

Huddleston, C. E.
1944 "Female Circumcision in the Sudan."
Lancet 1: 626.

Kennedy, J. G.
1970 "Circumcision and Excision in Egyptian
Nubia." *Man* 5: 175–91.

Koso-Thomas, Olayinka
1987 *The Circumcision of Women.* London: Zed
Books.

Mustafa, A. Z.
1966 "Female Circumcision and lnfibulation in
the Sudan." *Journal of Obstetrics and Gynecology of the British Commonwealth* 73: 302–6.

Oldfield, Hayes, Rose
1975 "Female Genital Mutilation, Fertility
Control, Women's Roles, and the
Patrilineage in Modern Sudan." *American
Ethnologist* 2: 617–33.

Rugh, Andrea
1984 *Family in Contemporary Egypt.* Syracuse:
Syracuse University Press.

Scotch, Norman
1963 "Sociocultural Factors in the Epidemiology of Zulu Hypertension." *American
Journal of Public Health* 53: 1205–13.

van Gennep, Arnold
[1908] 1960 *Rites of Passage.* Chicago:
University of Chicago Press.

Weingrod, Alex, ed.
1987 *Ethiopian Jews and Israel.* New Brunswick,
N.J.: Transaction Books.

Worsley, Alan
1938 "Infibulation and Female Circumcision."
*Journal of Obstetrics and Gynecology of the
British Empire* 45: 686–91.

Return to Wirikuta: Ritual Reversal and Symbolic Continuity on the Peyote Hunt of the Huichol Indians
Barbara G. Myerhoff

REFERENCES

Eliade, Mircea
1960 "The Yearning for Paradise in Primitive
Tradition." In H. A. Murray, ed., *Myth
and Mythmaking,* pp. 61–75. New York:
Braziller.
1962 *The Two and the One.* New York: Harper
Torchbooks.
1964 *Shamanism: Archaic Techniques of Ecstasy.*
Trans. W. R. Trask. Bollingen Series LXXVI.
New York: Pantheon.

Graves, Robert, and Raphael Patai
1966 *Hebrew Myths: The Book of Genesis.*
New York: McGraw-Hill.

Guillaumont, A., et al., trans.
1959 *The Gospel According to Thomas.* New York:
Harper.

Middleton, John
1960 *Lugbara Religion: Ritual and Authority
Among an East African People.* London:
Oxford University Press.
1974 *Peyote Hunt: The Sacred Journey of the
Huichol Indians.* Ithaca, N.Y.: Cornell
University Press.

Neumann, Erich
1954 *The Origins and History of Consciousness.*
New York: Bollingen.

Watts, Alan W.
1970 *The Two Hands of God: The Myths of
Polarity.* New York: Collier.

Ritual Regulation of Environmental Regulations Among a New Guinea People
Roy A. Rappaport

REFERENCES

Berg, C.
1948 "Protein Deficiency and Its Relation to
Nutritional Anemia, Hypoproteinemia,
Nutritional Edema, and Resistance to
Infection." In M. Sahyun, ed., *Protein and
Amino Acids in Nutrition,* pp. 290–317.
New York: Reinhold.

Burton, B. T., ed.
1959 *The Heinz Handbook of Nutrition.* New
York: McGraw-Hill.

Elman, R.
1951 *Surgical Care.* New York: Appleton-
Century-Crofts.

Food and Agriculture Organization of the United
  Nations.
  1964   "Protein: At the Heart of the World Food
          Problem." *World Food Problems* 5. Rome:
          FAO.

Homans, G. C.
  1941   "Anxiety and Ritual: The Theories
          of Malinowski and Radcliffe-Brown."
          American Anthropologist 43:
          164–72.

Houssay, B. A., et al.
  1955   *Human Physiology.* 2nd ed. New York:
          McGraw-Hill.

Large, A., and C. G. Johnston
  1948   "Proteins as Related to Burns." In M.
          Sahyun, ed., *Proteins and Amino Acids in
          Nutrition*, pp. 386–96. New York:
          Reinhold.

Lund, C. G., and S. M. Levenson
  1948   "Protein Nutrition in Surgical Patients."
          In M. Sahyun, ed., *Proteins and Amino
          Acids in Nutrition*, pp. 349–63. New York:
          Reinhold.

Moore, O. K.
  1957   "Divination—a New Perspective."
          American Anthropologist 59: 69–74.

National Research Council
  1963   *Evaluation of Protein Quality.* National
          Academy of Sciences—National Research
          Council Publication 1100. Washington,
          D.C.: NAS/NRC.

Vayda, A. P., A. Leeds, and D. B. Smith
  1961   "The Place of Pigs in Melanesian
          Subsistence." In V. E. Garfield, ed.,
          *Proceedings of the 1961 Annual Spring
          Meeting of the American Ethnological
          Society*, pp. 69–77. Seattle: University of
          Washington Press.

Wayne-Edwards, V. C.
  1962   *Animal Dispersion in Relation to Social
          Behaviour.* Edinburgh and London: Oliver
          & Boyd.

Zintel, Harold A.
  1964   "Nutrition in the Care of the Surgical
          Patient." In M. G. Wohl and R. S.

Goodhart, eds., *Modern Nutrition in
Health and Disease*, 3rd ed. pp. 1043–64.
Philadelphia: Lee & Febiger.

I Can Only Move My Feet Towards *mizuko kuyō*: Memorial Services for Dead Children in Japan
Elizabeth G. Harrison

REFERENCES

Harrison, Elizabeth G.
  1995   "Women's Responses to Child Loss in
          Japan: The Case of Mizuko Kuyō."
          Journal for Feminist Studies in Religion 11,
          no. 2 (Fall): 67–93.
  1996   "Mizuko Kuyō: The Reproduction of the
          Dead in Contemporary Japan." In P. F.
          Kornicki and I. J. McMullen, eds., *Religion
          in Japan: Arrows to Heaven and Earth*, pp.
          250–66. Cambridge: Cambridge
          University Press.

Hirochika, Nakamaki
  1986   "Continuity and Change: Funeral
          Customs in Modern Japan." *Japanese
          Journal of Religious Studies* 13(2–3):
          180, 188.

Hobsbawn, Eric, and Terence Ranger, eds.
  1984   *The Invention of Tradition.* Cambridge:
          Cambridge University Press.

Body Ritual Among the Nacirema
Horace Miner

REFERENCES

Linton, Ralph
  1936   *The Study of Man.* New York:
          D. Appleton-Century Co.

Malinowski, Bronislaw
  1948   *Magic, Science, and Religion.* Glencoe:
          Free Press.

Murdock, George P.
  1949   *Social Structure.* New York:
          Macmillan.

CHAPTER FOUR
Shamans, Priests, and Prophets
Religious Specialists
Victor W. Turner

REFERENCES

Buber, Martin
[1936] 1958 *I and Thou.* 2nd ed. New York: Scribner.

Callaway, Henry
1885 *The Religious System of the Amazulu.* Folklore Society Publication No. 15. London: Trubner.

Durkheim, Emile
[1893] 1960 *The Division of Labor in Society.* Glencoe, Ill.: Free Press.

Elwin, Verrier
1955 *The Religion of an Indian Tribe.* Bombay: Oxford University Press.

Evans-Pritchard, E. E.
[1949] 1954 *The Sanusi of Cyrenaica.* Oxford: Clarendon Press.
[1956] 1962 *Nuer Religion.* Oxford: Clarendon Press.

Firth, R. W.
1964a "Shaman." In Julius Gould and William L. Kolb, eds., *A Dictionary of the Social Sciences,* pp. 638–39. New York: Free Press.
1964b "Spirit Mediumship." In Julius Gould and W. L. Kolb, eds., *Dictionary of the Social Sciences,* p. 689. New York: Free Press.

Gelfand, Michael
1964 *Witch Doctor: Traditional Medicine Man of Rhodesia.* London: Harvill.

Herskovits, Melville J.
1938 *Dahomey: An Ancient West African Kingdom.* 2 vols. New York: Harvill.

Howells, William W.
1948 *The Heathens: Primitive Man and His Religions.* Garden City, N.Y.: Doubleday.

Knox, Ronald A.
1950 *Enthusiasm: A Chapter in the History of Religion; With Special Reference to the XVII and XVIII Centuries.* New York: Oxford University Press.

Lessa, William A., and Evon Z. Vogt, eds.
[1958] 1965 *Reader in Comparative Religion: An Anthropological Approach.* New York: Harper.

Lowie, Robert H.
1954 *Indians of the Plains.* American Museum of Natural History, Anthropological Handbook No. 1. New York: McGraw-Hill.

Nadel, Siegfried F.
1954 *Nupe Religion.* London: Routledge.

Parrinder, Edward G.
1954 *African Traditional Religion.* London: Hutchinson's University Library.

Parsons, Talcott
1963 "Introduction." In Max Weber, *The Sociology of Religion.* Boston: Beacon.

Piddington, Ralph
1950 *Introduction to Social Anthropology.* 2 vols. New York: Fredrick A. Praeger.

Richards, Audrey I.
[1940] 1961 "The Political System of the Bembe Tribe: Northeastern Rhodesia." In Meyer Fortes and E. E. Evans-Pritchard, eds., *African Political Systems.* New York: Oxford University Press.

Wach, Joachim
1958 *The Comparative Study of Religions.* New York: Columbia University Press.

Weber, Max
[1922] 1963 *The Sociology of Religion.* Boston: Beacon.

Worsley, P. M.
1957a "Millenarian Movements in Melanesia." *Rhodes-Livingstone Journal* 21: 18–31.
1957b *The Trumpet Shall Sound: A Study of "Cargo" Cults in Melanesia.* London: MacGibbon and Kee.

The Shaman: A Siberian Spiritualist
William Howells

REFERENCES

Bogoras, W.
1904– "The Chuckchee." In *Memoirs of the*
09   *American Museum of Natural History*, vol. 11.

Casanowicz, I. M.
1924   "Shamanism of the Natives of Siberia."
       In *Smithsonian Institution Annual Report.*

Czaplicka, M. A.
1914   *Aboriginal Siberia: A Study in Social
       Anthropology.*

Evans-Pritchard, E. E.
1937   *Witchcraft, Oracles and Magic Among the
       Azande.* Oxford: Clarendon Press.

Field, Margaret J.
1937   *Religion and Medicine of the Gã People.*

Handy, E. S. Craighill
1927   "Polynesian Religion." Bernice P. Bishop
       Museum *Bulletin*, no. 34. Honolulu.

Hoernle, Winifred
1937   In I. Schapera, ed., *The Bantu-Speaking
       Peoples of South Africa.*

Jochelson, W.
1908   "The Koryak." *Memoirs of the American
       Museum of Natural History*, vol. 10.
1926   "The Yukaghir and the Yukaghirized
       Tungus." In *Memoirs of the American
       Museum of Natural History*, vol. 13.

Training for the Priesthood Among the Kogi of Colombia
Gerardo Reichel-Dolmatoff

REFERENCES

Preuss, Konrad Theodor
1926– *Forschungsreise zu den Kágaba. Beobachtungen,*
1927   *Textaufnahmen und sprachliche Studien bei
       einem Indianerstamme in Kolumbien,
       Südamerika.* 2 vols. St. Gabriel-Mödling:
       Anthropos Verlag.

Reichel-Dolmatoff, Gerardo
1950   "Los Kogi: Una tribu indígena de la
       Sierra Nevada de Santa Marta,
       Colombia." Vol. 1. *Revista del Instituto
       Etnológico Nacional* (Bogota) 4: 1–320.
1951a *Datos histórico-culturales sobre las tribus de
       la antigua Governación de Santa Marta.*
       Bogota: Imprenta del Banco de la
       República.
1951b *Los Kogi: Una tribu indígena de la Sierra
       Nevada de Santa Marta, Colombia.* Vol. 2.
       Bogota: Editorial Iqueima.
1953   "Contactos y cambios culturales en la
       Sierra Nevada de Santa Marta." *Revista
       Colombiana de Antropología* (Bogota)
       1: 17–122.
1974   "Funerary Customs and Religious
       Symbolism Among the Kogi." In Patricia
       J. Lyon, ed., *Native South Americans—
       Ethnology of the Least Known Continent.*
       Boston/Toronto: Little, Brown.

CHAPTER FIVE
The Religious Use of Drugs

Ritual Enemas
Peter T. Furst and Michael D. Coe

REFERENCES

Benson, Elizabeth P.
1972   *The Maya World.* New York: Apollo.
1975   *Death and the Afterlife in Pre-Columbian
       America.* Washington, D.C.: Dumbarton
       Oaks.

Coe, Michael D.
1966   *The Maya.* New York: Frederick A.
       Praeger.
1975   *Classic Maya Pottery at Dumbarton Oaks.*
       Washington, D.C.: Dumbarton Oaks.

Furst, Peter T.
1972   *Flesh of the Gods: The Ritual Use of
       Hallucinogens.* New York: Frederick A.
       Praeger.
1976   *Hallucinogens and Culture.* Corte Madera,
       Calif.: Chandler & Sharp Publishers.
1977   "High States in Culture-Historical
       Perspective." In Norman E. Zinberg,
       ed., *Alternate States of Consciousness.*
       New York: Free Press.

Thompson, J. Eric
  1970   *Maya History and Religion.* Norman: University of Oklahoma Press.

The Sound of Rushing Water
Michael Harner

REFERENCES

Karsten, R.
  1935   "The Head-Hunters of Western Amazonas." In *Commentationes Humanarum Litteraru.* Finska Vetenskaps-Societeten 7(1). Helsingfors.

Stirling, M. W.
  1938   *Historical and Ethnographical Material on the Jivaro Indians.* U.S. Bureau of American Ethnology Bulletin 117. Washington, D.C.: Smithsonian Institution.

Up de Graff, F. W.
  1923   *Headhunters of the Amazon: Seven Years of Exploration and Adventure.* London: H. Jenkins.

Wilbert, Johannes
  1972   "Tobacco and Shamanistic Ecstasy Among the Warao Indians of Venezuela." In Peter J. Furst, ed., *Flesh of the Gods: The Ritual Use of Hallucinogens,* pp. 55–83. New York: Praeger.

Psychedelic Drugs and Religious Experience
Robert S. de Ropp

REFERENCES

Aaronson, Bernard, and Humphry Osmond, eds.
  1970   "Effects of Psychedelics on Religion and Religious Experience." In *Psychedelics.* New York.

Alpert, Richard
  1971   *Remember: Be Here Now.* San Cristobal, N.M.

Bloom, Richard et al.
  1964   *The Politics of Ecstasy.* New York.

de Ropp, Robert S., ed.
  1976   *Drugs and the Mind.* New York.

Ebib, David, ed.
  1961   *The Drug Experience.* New York.

Efron, Daniel H., ed.
  1967   *Ethnopharmocologic Search for Psychoactive Drugs.* Washington, D.C.

Huxley, Aldous
  1954   *The Doors of Perception.* New York.

James, William
  1902   *The Varieties of Religious Experience.*

LaBarre, Weston
  1964   *The Peyote Cult.* Hamden, Conn.

Ludlow, Hugh
  1970   *The Hasheesh Eater: Being Passages from the Life of a Pythagorean.* Upper Saddle River, N.J.

Masters, R. E. L., and Jean Houston
  1966   *The Varieties of Psychedelic Experience.* New York.

Myerhoff, Barbara G.
  1974   *Peyote Hunt: The Sacred Journey of the Huichol Indians.* Ithaca, N.Y.

Pavlovna, Valentina, and R. Gordon Wasson
  1957   *Mushrooms, Russia, and History.* New York.

Wasson, Gordon, R., et al.
  1975   *Maria Sabina and Her Mazatec Mushroom Velada.* New York.

Weil, Andrew
  1972   *The Natural Mind: A New Way of Looking at Drugs and Higher Consciousness.* Boston.

CHAPTER SIX
Ethnomedicine: Religion and Healing

Eyes of the *Ngangas:* Ethnomedicine and Power in Central African Republic
Arthur C. Lehmann

REFERENCES

Bahuchet, Serge
  1985   *Les Pygmées Aka et la Forêt Centrafricaine.* Paris: Bibliothèque de la Selaf.

Bibeau, Gilles
   1979   *De la maladie a la guerison. Essai d'analyse
           systematique de la medecine des Angbandi
           du Zaire.* Doctoral dissertation, Laval
           University.

Bichmann, Wolfgang
   1979   "Primary Health Care and Traditional
           Medicine—Considering the Background
           of Changing Health Care Concepts in
           Africa." *Social Science and Medicine* 13B:
           175–82.

Cavalli-Sforza, L. L.
   1971   "Pygmies: An Example of Hunters
           Gatherers, and Genetic Consequences
           for Man of Domestication of Plants and
           Animals." In J. de Grouchy, F. Ebling,
           and I. Henderson, eds., *Human Genetics:
           Proceedings of the Fourth International
           Congress of Human Genetics,* pp. 79–95.
           Amsterdam: Excerpta Medica.

Cavalli-Sforza, L. L., ed.
   1986   *African Pygmies.* New York: Academic
           Press.

Feierman, Steven
   1985   "Struggles for Control: The Social Roots
           of Health of Healing in Modern Africa."
           African Studies Review 28: 73–147.

Green, Edward
   1980   "Roles for African Traditional Healers in
           Mental Health Care." *Medical Anthropology*
           4(4): 490–522.

Hepburn, Sharon J.
   1988   "W. H. R. Rivers Prize Essay (1986):
           Western Minds, Foreign Bodies." *Medical
           Anthropology Quarterly* 2 (New Series):
           59–74.

Hewlett, Barry S.
   1986   "Causes of Death Among Aka Pygmies
           of the Central African Republic." In
           L. L. Cavalli-Sforza, ed., *African Pygmies,*
           pp. 45–63. New York: Academic
           Press.

Janzen, John M.
   1978   *The Quest for Therapy: Medical Pluralism in
           Lower Zaire.* Los Angeles: University of
           California Press.

Lewis, I. M.
   1986   *Religion in Context: Cults and Charisma.*
           Cambridge: Cambridge University Press.

Motte, Elisabeth
   1980   *Les plantes chez les Pygmées Aka et les
           Monzombode la Lobaye.* Paris: Bibliothèque
           de la Selaf.

Offiong, Daniel
   1983   "Witchcraft Among the Ibibio of Nigeria."
           African Studies Review 26(1): 107–24.

Turnbull, Colin
   1965   *Wayward Servants.* New York: Natural
           History Press.

Warren, Dennis M.
   1974   "Disease, Medicine, and Religion Among
           the Techinman-Bono of Ghana; A Study
           in Culture Change." Ph.D. dissertation,
           Indiana University.

Yoder, P. Stanley
   1982   "Issues in the Study of Ethnomedical
           Systems in Africa." In P. Stanley Yoder,
           ed., *African Health and Healing Systems:
           Proceedings of a Symposium,* p. 120. Los
           Angeles: Crossroads Press, University of
           California.

A School for Medicine Men
Robert Bergman

REFERENCES

Haile, B. O. F. M.
   1950   *Origin Legend of the Navaho Enemy Way.*
           Publications in Anthropology, no. 17.
           New Haven, Conn.: Yale University
           Press.

Kluckhohn, C.
   1956   "The Great Chants of the Navaho." In
           I. T. Sanders et al., eds., *Societies Around
           the World.* New York: Dryden Press.
   1967   *Navajo Witchcraft.* Boston: Beacon Press.

Kluckhohn, C., and D. Leighton
   1962   *The Navajo.* New York: Doubleday & Co.

Kluckhohn, C., and L. D. Wyman
   1940   *An Introduction to Navaho Chant Practice
           with an Account of the Behaviors Observed*

in Four Chants. American Anthropological Association, *Memoirs*, no. 53. Menasha, Wis.: American Anthropological Association.

Leighton, A. H., and D. Leighton
1941 "Elements of Psychotherapy in Navajo Religion." *Psychiatry* 4: 515–23.

Pfister, O.
1932 "Instinctive Psychoanalysis Among the Navajos." *Journal of Nervous and Mental Disease* 76: 234–54.

Reichard, G. A.
1938 *Navajo Religion*. New York: Bollingen Foundation.

Sandner, D.
1970 "Navajo Medicine Men." Paper read at the 123rd Annual Meeting of the American Psychiatric Association, San Francisco, May 11–15.

Mothering and the Practice of "Balm" in Jamaica

William Wedenoja

REFERENCES

Barry, H., M. K. Bacon, and I. L. Child
1957 "A Cross-Cultural Survey of Some Sex Differences in Socialization." *Journal of Abnormal and Social Psychology* 55: 327–32.

Frank, J. D.
[1961] 1974 *Persuasion and Healing: A Comparative Study of Psychotherapy*. Rev. ed. New York: Schocken.

Halifax, J.
1979 *Shamanic Voices*. New York: E. P. Dutton.

Jones, E., and C. L. Zoppel
1979 "Personality Differences Among Blacks in Jamaica and the United States." *Journal of Cross-Cultural Psychology* 10: 435–56.

Kakar, S.
1982 *Shamans, Mystics, and Doctors: A Psychological Inquiry into India and Its Healing Traditions*. Boston: Beacon Press.

Lambert, M. J., D. A. Shapiro, and A. E. Bergin
1986 "The Effectiveness of Psychotherapy." In S. L. Garfield and A. E. Bergin, eds., *Handbook of Psychotherapy and Behavior Change*. 3rd ed. New York: John Wiley.

Long, J. K.
1973 "Jamaican Medicine: Choices Between Folk Healing and Modern Medicine." Ph.D. dissertation, Department of Anthropology, University of North Carolina.

Martin, K., and B. Voorhies
1975 *Female of the Species*. New York: Columbia University Press.

Mitchell, G.
1981 *Human Sex Differences: A Primatologist's Perspective*. New York: Van Nostrand Reinhold.

Mitchell, M. F.
1980 "Class, Therapeutic Roles, and Self-Medication in Jamaica." Ph.D. dissertation, Medical Anthropology, University of California at Berkeley and San Francisco.

Mogul, K. M.
1982 "Overview: The Sex of the Therapist." *American Journal of Psychiatry* 139: 1–11.

Phillips, A. S.
1973 *Adolescence in Jamaica*. Kingston: Jamaica Publishing House.

Prince, Raymond
n.d. *Personal communication*.

Quinn, N.
1977 "Anthropological Studies on Women's Status." *Annual Review of Anthropology* 6: 181–225. Palo Alto, Calif.: Annual Reviews.

Rogers, C. R.
1957 "The Necessary and Sufficient Conditions of Therapeutic Personality Change." *Journal of Consulting Psychology* 21(2): 95–102.

Rossi, A. S.
1977 "A Biosocial Perspective on Parenting." *Daedalus* 106(2): 1–32.

Scheff, T. J.
  1975 "Labeling, Emotion, and Individual
        Change." In T. J. Scheff, ed., *Labeling
        Madness*, pp. 75–89. Englewood Cliffs,
        N.J.: Prentice Hall.
  1979 *Catharsis in Healing, Ritual, and Drama*.
        Berkeley: University of California Press.

Spiro, M. E.
  1978 *Burmese Supernaturalism*. Expanded ed.
        Philadelphia: Institute for the Study of
        Human Issues Press.
  1979 *Gender and Culture: Kibbutz Women
        Revisited*. New York: Schocken.

Torrey, E. F.
  1972 *The Mind Game*. New York: Bantam.

Wedenoja, W.
  1988 "The Origins of Revival, a Creole
        Religion in Jamaica." In G. Saunders, ed.,
        *Culture and Christianity: The Dialectics of
        Transformation*. Westport, Conn.:
        Greenwood.

Whiting, B. B., and J. M. Whiting
  1975 *Children of Six Cultures: A Psycho-Cultural
        Analysis*. Cambridge, Mass.: Harvard
        University Press.

Whyte, M. K.
  1978 *The Status of Women in Preindustrial
        Societies*. Princeton, N.J.: Princeton
        University Press.

Swallowing Frogs: Anger and Illness in Northeast Brazil

L. A. Rebhun

REFERENCES

Araujo, Tania Bacelar de
  1987 "Nordeste: Diferenciais demográficos
        regionais seus determinantes—Cademos
        de Estudos sociais." *Recife* 3(3): 167–92.

Averilll, James R.
  1982 *Anger and Agression: An Essay in Emotion*.
        New York: Springer.

Bernard, H. Russell
  1994 *Research Methods in Anthropology:
        Qualitative and Quantitative Approaches*.
        2nd ed. Thousand Oaks, Calif.: Sage.

Bolton, Ralph
  1981 "Susto, Hostility, and Hypoglycemia."
        Ethnology 19: 261–76.

Camino, Linda
  1989 "Nerves, Worriation, and Black Women:
        A Community Study in the American
        South." In D. L. Davis and S. Low, eds.,
        *Gender, Health, and Illness: The Case of
        Nerves*, pp. 295–314. New York:
        Hemisphere.

Clark, Margaret
  1978 "Three Cases of Folk Disorder Among
        Mexican-Americans: Implications for the
        Study of Culture Change." *Kroeber
        Anthropological Society Papers* 55/56
        (University of California, Berkeley).

Cosminsky, Sheila
  1967 "The Evil Eye in a Quiche Community."
        In C. Maloney, ed., *The Evil Eye*,
        pp. 163–74. New York: Columbia
        University Press.

Davis, Dona Lee
  1989 "The Variable Character of Nerves in a
        Newfoundland Fishing Village." *Medical
        Anthropology* 11: 63–78.

Davis, D., and N. O. Whitten
  1988 "Medical and Popular Traditions of
        Nerves." *Social Science and Medicine*
        26(12): 1209–21.

Duarte, Luiz Fernando D.
  1986 *Da vida nervosa nas clases trabalhadores
        urbanas*. Rio de Janeiro: Jorge Zahar
        Editor/CNPq.

Dunk, Pamela
  1989 "Greek Women and Broken Nerves in
        Montreal." *Medical Anthropology* 11:
        29–45.

Foster, George
  1965 "Peasant Society and the Image of
        Limited Good." *American Anthropologist*
        67: 293–315.
  1972 "The Anatomy of Envy: A Study in
        Symbolic Behavior." *Current Anthropology*
        13: 165–202.
  1976 "Disease Etiologies in Non-Western
        Medical Systems." *American
        Anthropologist* 78: 773–82.

Foster, George, and Barbara Anderson
1978   *Medical Anthropology.* New York:
        Wiley.

Foucault, Michel
1986   "Disciplinary Power and Subjection."
        In Steven Lukes, ed., *Power,* pp. 229–42.
        Oxford: Basil Blackwell.

Garrison, Vivian, and Conrad M. Arensberg
1976   "The Evil Eye: Envy or Risk of Seizure?
        Paranoia or Patronal Dependence?" In
        Clarence Maloney, ed., *The Evil Eye,*
        pp. 287–328. New York: Columbia
        University Press.

Gillen, J.
1945   *Mochel: A Peruvian Coastal Community.*
        Institute of Social Anthropology
        Publication 3. Washington, D.C.:
        Smithsonian Institution Press.
1948   "Magical Fright." *Psychiatry*
        11: 387–400.

Goebel, O.
1973   "El Susto: A Descriptive Analysis."
        International Journal of Social Psychiatry
        19: 38–43.

Guarnaccia, Peter J., Victor DeLaCancela, and
        Emilio Carrillo
1989   "The Multiple Meanings of Ataque
        de Nervios in the Latino
        Community." *Medical Anthropology*
        11: 47–62.

Herzfeld, Michael
1981   "Meaning and Morality: A Semiotic
        Approach to Evil Eye Accusations in a
        Greek Village." *American Ethnologist*
        8: 560–74.
1984   "The Horns of the Mediterraneanist
        Dilemma." *American Ethnologist*
        11: 439–54.
1986   "Closure as Cure: Tropes in the
        Exploration of Bodily and Social
        Disorder." *Current Anthropology*
        27(2): 107–20.

IGBE/UNICEF
1986   *Perfil estatistico de crianças e mäes no Brasil:
        Aspectos socio-economicos da mortalidade
        infantil em areas urbanas.* Rio de Janeiro:
        UNICEF.

Kiev, Ari
1968   *Curanderismo: Mexican American
        Folk Psychiatry.* New York: Free
        Press.
1972   *Transcultural Psychiatry.* New York:
        Free Press.

Krieger, Laurie
1989   "Nerves and Psychosomatic Illness: The
        Case of Um Ramadan." In D. L. Davis
        and S. M. Low, eds., *Gender, Health, and
        Illness: The Case of Nerves,* pp. 181–93.
        New York: Hemisphere.

Logan, M.
1979   "Variations Regarding Susto Causality
        Among the Cakchiquel of Guatemala."
        Culture, Medicine, and Psychiatry 3:
        153–66.

Low, Setha
1989   "Health, Culture, and the Nature of
        Nerves: A Critique." *Medical Anthropology*
        2: 91–95.

Madsen, William
1964   "Value Conflicts and Folk Psychiatry in
        South Texas." In Ari Kiev, ed., *Magic,
        Faith, and Healing,* pp. 420–40. New York:
        Free Press.

Migliore, Sam
1983   "Evil Eye or Delusions: On the
        Consistency of Folk Models." *Medical
        Anthropology Quarterly* 14(2): 4–9.

Nations, Marilyn
1982   "Illness of the Child: The Cultural
        Context of Childhood Diarrhea in
        Northeast Brazil." Ph.D. dissertation,
        Department of Anthropology,
        University of California,
        Berkeley.

Nations, Marilyn, and Mara Lucia Amaral
1991   "Flesh, Blood, Souls, and Households:
        Cultural Validity in Mortality Inquiry."
        Medical Anthropology Quarterly (n.s.) 5:
        204–20.

Nations, Marilyn, L. Camino, and F. Walker
1988   "'Nerves': Folk Idiom for Anxiety and
        Depression?" *Social Science and Medicine*
        26: 1245–59.

O'Nell, C. W.
1975   "An Investigation of Reported 'Fright' as a Factor in the Etiology of Sustos." *Ethos* 3: 41–63.

O'Nell, C. W., and A. Rubel
1976   "The Meaning of Sustos." *Actas del Congresso Internacional de Americanistas* 3: 343–49.

Perlman, Janice
1976   *The Myth of Marginality.* Berkeley: University of California Press.

Rebhun, L. A.
1993   "Nerves and Emotional Play in Northeast Brazil." *Medical Anthropology Quarterly* (n.s.) 7: 131–51.

Robben, Antonius C. M. G.
1988   "Conflicting Gender Conceptions in a Pluriform Fishing Economy: A Hermeneutic Perspective on Conjugal Relationships in Brazil." In J. Nadel-Klein and D. L. Davis, eds., *To Work and to Weep: Women in Fishing Economies,* pp. 106–29. St. Johns, Newfoundland: Institute of Social and Economic Research.

Roberts, J.
1976   "Belief in the Evil Eye in Western Perspective." In Clarence Maloney, ed., *The Evil Eye,* pp. 223–78. New York: Columbia University Press.

Rubel, A.
1964   "The Epidemiology of a Folk Illness: Susto in Hispanic America." *Ethnology* 3: 268–83.

Sarbin, Theodore R.
1986   "Emotion and Act: Roles and Rhetoric." In Rom Harré, ed., *The Social Construction of Emotions,* pp. 83–97. Oxford: Basil Blackwell.

Toussignant, M.
1979   "Espanto: A Dialogue with the Gods." *Culture, Medicine, and Psychiatry* 3: 347–61.

Uzzell, D.
1974   "Susto Revisited: Illness a Strategic Role." *American Ethnologist* 1: 369–78.

Should Academic Medical Centers Conduct Clinical Trials of the Efficacy of Intercessory Prayer?

Edward C. Halperin, MD

REFERENCES

Blazer, D.
1998   *Freud vs. Gods: How Psychiatry Lost Its Soul and Christianity Lost Its Mind.* Downers Grove, Ill.: Inter Varsity Press.

Byrd, R. C.
1988   "Positive Therapeutic Effects of Intercessory Prayer in a Coronary Care Unit Population." *Southern Medical Journal* 81: 826–29.

Byrd, R. C., and J. Sherrill
1995   "The Therapeutic Effects of Intercessory Prayer." *Journal of Christian Nursing* 12: 21–23.

Collipp, P. J.
1969   "The Efficacy of Prayer: A Triple-Blind Study." *Medical Times* 987: 201–4.

Cox, B. M.
1994   "Testing the Power of Prayer." *Science* 276: 1630–31.

Davis, T.
1994   "The Research Evidence on the Power of Prayer and Healing." *Canadian Journal of Cardiovascular Nursing* 5: 34–36.

Fish, S.
1995   "Can Research Prove That God Answers Prayers?" *Journal of Christian Nursing* 12: 24–46.

Hamm, R. M.
2000   "No Effect of Intercessory Prayer Has Been Proven." *Archives of Internal Medicine* 160: 1872–73.

Harris, E. S., J. Gowda, J. W. Kolb, et al.
1999   "A Randomized, Controlled Trial of the Effects of Remote, Intercessory Prayer on Outcomes in Patients Admitted to the Coronary Care Unit." *Archives of Internal Medicine* 159: 2273–78.

Joyce, C. R. B., and R. M. C. Whelldon
  1965   "The Efficacy of Prayer: A Double-Blind
          Clinical Trial." *Journal of Chronic Diseases*
          18: 367–77.

Kling, J.
  1997   "Testing the Power of Prayer." *Science*
          276: 1631.

Levitt, N.
  1999.   *Prometheus Bedeviled: Science and the
          Contradictions of Contemporary Culture.*
          New Brunswick, N.J.: Rutgers University
          Press.

Mayer, D.
  1997   "Testing the Power of Belief." *Science* 276:
          891.

O'Laire, S.
  1997   "An Experimental Study of the Effects of
          Distant, Intercessory Prayer on Self-
          Esteem, Anxiety, and Depression." *Alt.
          Ther. Health Med.* 3: 38–53.

Pande, D. N.
  2000   "Does Prayer Need Testing?" *Archives of
          Internal Medicine* 160: 1873–74.

Sicher, F., E. Targ, D. Moore II, and H. S. Smith
  1998   "A Randomized Double-Blind Study of
          the Effect of Distant Healing in a
          Population with Advanced AIDS: Report
          of a Small Scale Study." *Western Journal of
          Medicine* 169: 356–63.

Smith, J. G., and R. Fisher
  2000   "The Effect of Remote Intercessory
          Prayer on Clinical Outcomes." *Archives of
          Internal Medicine* 160: 1876.

Targ, E., and K. S. Thompson
  1997   "Can Prayer and Intentionality Be
          Researched? Should They Be?" *Alt. Ther.
          Health Med.* 3: 92–105.

Walker, S. R., J. S. Ronigan, W. R. Miller, S. Corner,
    and L. Kahlich
  1997   "Intercessory Prayer in the Treatment of
          Alcohol Abuse and Dependence: A Pilot
          Investigation." *Alt. Ther. Health Med.*
          79–86.

Waterhouse, W. C.
  2000   "Is It Prayer, or Is It Parity?" *Archives of
          Internal Medicine* 160: 1875.

CHAPTER SEVEN
Witchcraft, Sorcery, Divination, and Magic

An Anthropological Perspective on the Witchcraze

James L. Brain

REFERENCES

Bettlelheim, Bruno
  1977   *The Uses of Enchantment.* New York:
          Random House.

Brain, James L.
  1977a   "Handedness in Tanzania." *Anthropos*
          72: 180–92.
  1977b   "Sex, Incest and Death: Initiation Rites
          Reconsidered." *Current Anthropology*
          18(2): 371–84.

Bridges, E. L.
  1949   *The Uttermost Parts of the Earth.* New
          York: Dutton.

Browne, Thomas
  1964   *Religio Medici and Other Works.* In
          L. C. Martin, ed. Oxford: Clarendon
          Press.

Chapman, Anne
  1984   *Drama and Power in a Hunting Society.*
          Cambridge: Cambridge University
          Press.

Cohn, Norman
  1975   *Europe's Inner Demons: An Inquiry Inspired
          by the Great Witch-Hunt.* New York: Basic
          Books.

Darst, D. H.
  1979   "Witchcraft in Spain: The Testimony of
          Martin de Castenga's Treatise on
          Superstition and Witchcraft (1529)."
          *Proceedings of the American Philosophical
          Society* 123(5): 298–322.

Douglas, Mary
  1966   *Purity and Danger.* London: Routledge
          and Kegan Paul.

Driberg, J. H.
  1923   *The Lango.* London: T. Fisher Unwin.

Dykstra, B.
 1986 *Idols of Perversity.* New York: Oxford University Press.

Dyson-Hudson, N.
 1966 *Karimojong Politics.* Oxford: Clarendon Press.

Elkin, Adolphus Peter
 1938 *Australian Aborigines.* Sydney: Angus and Robertson.

Fortes, Meyer
 1953 "The Structure of Unilineal Descent Groups." *American Anthropologist* 55: 17–41.

Fox-Keller, E.
 1983 "Feminism and Science." In E. Abel and E. K. Abel, eds., *The Signs Reader.* Chicago: University of Chicago Press.

Ginzburg, Carlo
 1983 *The Night Battles: Witchcraft and Agrarian Cults in the Sixteenth and Seventeenth Centuries.* Baltimore: Johns Hopkins University Press.

Gluckman, Max
 1965 *Politics, Law and Ritual in Tribal Society.* Oxford: Blackwell.

Gulliver, P.
 1955 *The Family Herds.* London: Routledge and Kegan Paul.
 1963 *Social Control in an African Society.* Boston: Boston University Press.

Gulliver, P., and P. H. Gulliver
 1953 *The Central Nilo-Hamites.* London: International African Institute.

Huntingford, G. W. B.
 1953 *The Southern Nilo-Hamites.* London: International African Institute.

Jacobs, Alan
 1985 *Personal communication.*

Klaits, Joseph
 1985 *Servants of Satan.* Bloomington: Indiana University Press.

Kramer, Heinrich, and Jakob Sprenger
 1971 *Malleus Maleficarum.* Translated by Montague Summers. New York: Dover.

La Barre, Weston
 1984 *Muelos: A Stone Age Superstition.* New York: Columbia University Press.

Lamphere, L.
 1974 "Strategies, Cooperation and Conflict Among Women in Domestic Groups." In Michelle Z. Rosaldo and L. Lamphere, eds., *Women, Culture and Society,* pp. 97–112. Stanford, Calif.: Stanford University Press.

Langley, Michael
 1979 *The Nandi of Kenya.* New York: St. Martin's Press.

Lawrence, J. T. D.
 1957 *The Iteso.* London: Oxford University Press.

Leach, Edmund Ronald
 1970 *Claude Lévi-Strauss.* Harmondsworth, UK: Penguin Books.

Lee, Richard B.
 1972 "Work Effort, Group Structure and Land Use Among Contemporary Hunter-Gatherers." In B. Ucko and R. Trimingham, eds., *Man, Settlement and Urbanism.* London: George Duckworth and Company.
 1976 *Kalahari Hunter-Gatherers.* Cambridge: Harvard University Press.

Lewis, I. M.
 1965 "Shaikhs and Warriors in Somaliland." In J. L. Gibbs, ed., *Peoples of Africa.* New York: Holt, Rinehart and Winston.

Mair, L.
 1969 *Witchcraft.* New York: McGraw-Hill.

Marshall, L.
 1962 "!Kung Bushmen Religious Beliefs." *Africa* 32(3): 221–52.
 1976 *The !Kung of Nyae.* Cambridge, Mass.: Harvard University Press.

McCormack, C., and M. Strathern, eds.
 1980 *Nature, Culture and Gender.* Cambridge: Cambridge University Press.

Meggitt, M. J.
 1962 *Desert People.* Chicago: University of Chicago Press.

Middleton, John, and E. Winter, eds.
1963 *Witchcraft, Sorcery and Magic in East Africa.* London: Routledge and Kegan Paul.

Midelfort, H. C. Erik
1972 *Witch Hunting in Southwestern Germany.* Stanford, Calif.: Stanford University Press.

Mitchell, J. C.
1965 "The Meaning of Misfortune for Urban Africans." In M. Fortes and G. Dieterlen, eds., *African Systems of Thought.* London: Oxford University Press.

Murray, Margaret
1970 *The God of the Witches.* New York: Oxford University Press. (First published by Sampson, Low, and Matson, 1931.)

Nadel, Siegfried Frederick
1952 "Witchcraft in Four African Societies: An Essay in Comparison." *American Anthropologist* 54: 18–29.

Offiong, D. A.
1985 "Witchcraft Among the Ibibio." *African Studies Review* 21(1): 107–24.

Ortner, Sherry B.
1974 "Is Female to Nature as Man Is to Culture?" In Michelle Z. Rosaldo and L. Lamphere, eds., *Woman, Culture and Society,* pp. 67–87. Stanford, Calif.: Stanford University Press.

Peristiany, J. G.
1939 *The Social Institutions of the Kipsigis.* London: George Routledge.

Robertson, E.
n.d. *An Anchorhold of Her Own.* Knoxville: University of Tennessee Press.

Rosaldo, Michelle Z.
1974 "Introduction and Overview." In Michelle Z. Rosaldo and L. Lamphere, eds., *Woman, Culture and Society,* pp. 1–42. Stanford, Calif.: Stanford University Press.

Spencer, B., and J. Gillen
[1899] 1938 *The Native Tribes of Central Australia.* London: Macmillan.

1904 *The Northern Tribes of Central Australia.* London: Macmillan.

Stenning, D.
1959 *Savannah Nomads.* London: Oxford University Press.
1965 "The Pastoral Fulani of Northern Nigeria." In J. L. Gibbs, ed., *Peoples of Africa.* New York: Holt, Rinehart and Winston.

Thomas, Keith
1971 *Religion and the Decline of Magic.* New York: Charles Scribner's Sons.

Thomas, N. W.
1906 *The Natives of Australia.* London: Archibald Constable.

Trevor-Roper, H. R.
1969 *The European Witch-Craze of the Sixteenth and Seventeenth Centuries and Other Essays.* New York: Harper and Row.

Turnbull, C.
1961 *The Forest People.* New York: Simon and Schuster.
1968 "The Importance of Flux in Two Hunting Societies." In Richard B. Lee and I. DeVore, eds., *Man the Hunter,* pp. 132–37. Chicago: Aldine.

Wilson, M.
1951 "Witch Beliefs and Social Structure." *American Journal of Sociology* 56: 307–13.

Woodburn, J.
1968 "An Introduction to Hadza Ecology." In Richard B. Lee and I. DeVore, eds., *Man the Hunter,* pp. 49–55.
1979 "Minimal Politics: The Political Organization of the Hadza of North Tanzania." In W. A. Shack and P. S. Cohen, eds., *Leadership: A Comparative Perspective,* pp. 244–60. Oxford: Clarendon Press.
1982a "Egalitarian Societies." *Man* 17: 431–51.
1982b "Social Dimensions of Death in Four African Hunting and Gathering Societies." In Maurice Bloch and Jonathan Parry, eds., *Death and the Regeneration of Life,* pp. 187–210. Cambridge: Cambridge University Press.

Sorcery and Concepts of Deviance Among the Kabana, West New Britain
Naomi M. McPherson

REFERENCES

Becker, H.
1963   *Outsiders: Studies in the Sociology of Deviance.* New York: Free Press.

Counts, D. A., and D. R. Counts
1976– "The Good Death in Kalisi." *Omega* 7(4):
77   367–73.
1984   "People Who Act Like Dogs: Adultery and Deviance in a Melanesian Community." Paper read at the conference Deviance in a Cross-Cultural Context. University of Waterloo, Waterloo, Ontario, June.

Jorgensen, D.
1983– "The Clear and the Hidden: Person, Self,
84   and Suicide Among the Telefolmi of Papua New Guinea." *Omega* 14(2): 113–26.

Lawrence, P.
1984   *The Garia: An Ethnography of a Traditional Cosmic System in Papua New Guinea.* Carlton, Australia: Melbourne University Press.

Malinowski, B.
[1926] 1967   *Crime and Custom in Savage Society.* C. K. Ogden, ed. Totowa, N.J.: Littlefield Adams.

Scaletta, N.
1985   "Death by Sorcery: The Social Dynamics of Dying in Bariai, West New Britain." In D. A. Counts and D. R. Counts, eds. *Aging and Its Transformations: Moving Toward Death in Pacific Societies,* pp. 223–47. ASAO Monograph Series, no. 10. Lanham, Md.: University Press of America.

Vincent, Joan
1990   *Anthropology and Politica: Visions, Traditions, and Trends.* Tucson: University of Arizona Press.

Weiner, A.
1976   *Women of Value, Men of Renown: New Perspectives in Trobriand Exchange.* Austin: University of Texas Press.

Zelenietz, M.
1981   "One Step Too Far: Sorcery and Social Control in Kilenge, West New Britain." *Social Analysis* 8: 101–18.

The Goat and the Gazelle: Witchcraft
T. M. Luhrmann

REFERENCES

Adler, M.
1986   *Drawing Down the Moon.* Boston: Beacon Press.

Crowley, A.
[1929] 1976   *Magick in Theory and Practice.* New York: Dover.

Farrar, J., and S. Farrar
1981   *Eight Sabbats for Witches.* London: Robert Hale.
1984   *The Witches' Way.* London: Robert Hale.

Gardner, G. B.
[1954] 1982   *Witchcraft Today.* New York: Magickal Childe.

Le Roy Ladurie, E.
1987   *Jasmin's Witch.* Aldershot, UK: Scholar Press.

Starhawk
1979   *The Spiral Dance.* New York: Harper and Row.

Rational Mastery by Man of His Surroundings
Bronislaw Malinowski

REFERENCES

Boas, F.
1910   *The Mind of Primitive Man.*

Brinton, D. G.
1899   *Religions of Primitive Peoples.*

Codrington, R. H.
1891   *The Melanesians.*

Crawley, E.
  1902   *The Mystic Rose.*
  1905   *The Tree of Life.*

Durkheim, E.
  1912   *Les Formes elementaires de la Vie religieuse.*

Ehrenreich, P.
  1910   *Die Allgemeine Mythologie.*

Frazer, J. G.
  1910   *Totemism and Exogamy.* 4 vols.
  1911–   *The Golden Bough.* 3rd ed. 12 vols.
  14
  1913   *The Belief in Immortality and the Worship of the Dead.* 3 vols.
  1919   *Folklore in the Old Testament.* 3 vols.

Goldenweiser, A. A.
  1923   *Early Civilization.*

Harrison, J.
  1910–   *Themis.*
  12

Hastings, J.
  n.d.   *Encyclopedia of Religion and Ethics.*

Hobhouse, L. T.
  1915   *Morals in Evolution.* 2nd ed.

Hubert, H., and M. Mauss
  1909   *Melanges d'histoire des religions.*

King, I.
  1910   *The Development of Religion.*

Kroeber, A. L.
  1923   *Anthropology.*

Lang, A.
  1889   *The Making of Religion.*
  1901   *Magic and Religion.*

Lévy-Bruhl, M.
  1910   *Les Fonctions mentales dans les sociétés inférieures.*

Lowie, R. H.
  1920   *Primitive Society.*
  1925   *Primitive Religion.*

Malinowski, B.
  1915   *The Natives of Mailu.*
  1916   "Baloma." *Journal of the Royal Anthropological Institute.*
  1922   *Argonauts of the Western Pacific.*
  1923–   *Psyche.* Vols. III(2), IV(4), V(3).
  25

Marett, R. R.
  1909   *The Threshold of Religion.*

McLennan, J. F.
  1886   *Studies in Ancient History.*

Preuss, K. Th.
  1904   *Der Ursprung der Religion und Kunst.*

Schmidt, W.
  1912   *Der Ursprung der Gottesidee.*

Seligman, C. G.
  1910   *The Melanesians of British New Guinea.*

Smith, W. Robertson
  1889   *Lectures on the Religion of the Semites.*

Thurnwald, R.
  1912   *Forschungen auf den Solominseln und Bismarckarchipel.*
  1921   *Die Gemeinde der Banaro.*
  1922   "Psychologie des Primitiven Menschen." In G. Kafka, ed., *Handbuch der Vergl. Psychol.*

Tylor, E. B.
  1903   *Primitive Culture.* 4th ed. 2 vols.

Van Gennep, A.
  1909   *Les Rites de Passage.*

Westermarck, E.
  1905   *The Origin and Development of the Moral Ideas.* 2 vols.

Wundt, Wilh.
  1904   *Volkerpsychologie.*

Baseball Magic

George Gmelch

REFERENCES

Malinowski, B.
  1948   *Magic, Science and Religion and Other Essays.* Glencoe, Ill.: Free Press.

Mandel, Brett
  1997   *Minor Player, Major Dreams.* Lincoln: University of Nebraska Press.

Skinner, B. F.
  1938   *Behavior of Organisms: An Experimental Analysis.* New York: D. Appleton-Century.
  1953   *Science and Human Behavior.* New York: Macmillan.

Stouffer, Samuel
1965   *The American Soldier.* New York: Wiley.

Thrift, Syd, and Barry Shapiro
1990   *The Game According to Syd.* New York: Simon and Schuster.

Torrez, Danielle Gagnon
1983   *High Inside: Memoirs of a Baseball Wife.* New York: Putnam.

CHAPTER EIGHT
Ghosts, Souls, and Ancestors: Power of the Dead

A New Weapon Stirs Up Old Ghosts
William E. Mitchell

REFERENCES

Lawrence, P.
1967   *Road Belong Cargo.* Humanities Press.

Lawrence, P., and M. J. Meggitt, eds.
1965   *Gods, Ghosts and Men in Melanesia.* New York: Oxford University Press.

Vodou
Karen McCarthy Brown

REFERENCES

Brown, Karen McCarthy
2001   *Mama Lola: A Vodou Priestess in Brooklyn.* Updated edition. Berkeley: University of California Press.

Cosentino, Donald
1995   *The Sacred Arts of Haitian Vodou.* Los Angeles: UCLA Fowler Museum of Cultural History.

Courlander, Harold
1960   *The Drum and the Hoe: Life and Lore of the Haitian People.* Berkeley: University of California Press.

David, Wade
1985   *The Serpent and the Rainbow.* New York.
1988   Passage of Darkness. Chapel Hill: University of North Carolina Press.

Dayan, Joan
1998   *Haiti, History, and the Gods.* Berkeley: University of California Press.

Deren, Maya
1953   *Divine Horsemen: The Living Gods of Haiti.* New Paltz, N.Y. [Reprint 1983.]

Desmangles, Leslie G.
1993   *The Faces of the Gods: Vodou and Roman Catholicism in Haiti.* Chapel Hill: University of North Carolina Press.

Fick, Carolyn E.
1990   *The Making of Haiti: The San Domingue Revolution from Below.* Knoxville: University of Tennessee Press.

Greene, Anne
1993   *The Catholic Church in Haiti: Political and Social Change.* East Lansing: Michigan State University Press.

Herskovits, Melville J.
1937   *Life in a Haitian Village.* New York.

Larose, Serge
1977   "The Meaning of Africa in Haitian Vodu." In I. M. Lewis, ed., *Symbols and Sentiments: Cross-Cultural Studies in Symbolism.* New York.

Leyburn, James G.
1941   *The Haitian People.* New Haven, Conn. [Revised edition 1966.]

McAlister, Elizabeth
2002   Rara!: Vodou, Power, and Performance in Haiti and Its Diaspora. Berkeley: University of California Press.

Metraux, Alfred
1959   *Voodoo in Haiti.* New York.

Rey, Terry
1999   *Our Lady of Class Struggle: The Cult of the Virgin Mary in Haiti.* Trenton, N.J.: Africa World Press.

Thompson, Robert Farris
1981   *Flash of the Spirit: African and Afro-American Art and Philosophy.* New York.

Trouillot, Michel-Rolph
1996   *Silencing the Past: Power and the Production of History.* Boston, Mass.: Beacon Press.

The Cremated Catholic: The Ends of a Deceased Guatemalan
Stanley Brandes

REFERENCES

Anonymous
1996   "Families Win Awards from Crematorium." *San Francisco Chronicle,* July 24, A15.

Badone, Ellen, ed.
1990   *Religious Orthodoxy and Popular Faith in European Society.* Princeton, N.J.: Princeton University Press.

Brown, Peter
1981   *The Cult of the Saints: Its Rise and Function in Latin Christianity.* Chicago: University of Chicago Press.

Bynum, Carolyn Walker
1992   *Fragmentation and Redemption: Essays on Gender and the Human Body in Medieval Religion.* New York: Zone Books.

Fried, Rinat
1998   "Fees at Issue in $20M Cremate Case." *The Recorder,* October 16.

Hertz, Robert
1960   *Death and the Right Hand.* Glencoe, Ill.: Free Press.

Holding, Reynolds
1996   "16 Win Damages in Crematorium Suits." *San Francisco Chronicle,* July 10, A12.

Spontaneous Memorialization: Violent Death and Emerging Mourning Ritual
C. Allen Haney, Christina Leimer, and Juliann Lowery

REFERENCES

Bocock, R.
1974   *Ritual in Industrial Society: A Sociological Analysis of Ritualism in Modern England.* New York: Crane, Russak.

Bragg, R.
1994   "On Walls, Memories of the Slain Are Kept." *New York Times,* A1.

Campbell, Joseph, and Bill Moyers
1988   *The Power of Myth.* New York: Doubleday.

Collins, R.
1992   *Sociological Insight: An Introduction to Non-Obvious Sociology.* 2nd ed. New York: Oxford University Press.

Doka, K. J.
1989   "Disenfranchised Grief." In K. J. Doka, ed., *Disenfranchised Grief: Recognizing Hidden Sorrow.* Lexington, Mass.: Lexington Books.

Driver, T. F.
1991   *The Magic of Ritual: Our Need for Liberating Rites That Transform Our Lives and Our Communities.* San Francisco: HarperCollins.

Fulton, R.
1965   *Death and Identity.* New York: Wiley.

Gustaitis, R.
1996   "Pacific News Service." In G. E. Dickenson, M. R. Leming, and A. C. Mermann, eds., *Annual Editions: Dying, Death, and Bereavement,* p. 172.

Irion, P. E.
1990–   "Changing Patterns of Ritual Response to
91   Death." *Omega* 22(3): 159–72.

Littlewood, J.
1993   "The Denial of Death and Rites of Passage in Contemporary Societies." In *The Sociology of Death: Theory, Culture, Practice.* Cambridge, Mass.: Blackwell.

Lule, J.
1993   "News Strategies and the Death of Huey Newton." *Journalism Quarterly* 70(2): 287–99.

Mellor, P. A., and C. Shilling
1993   "Modernity, Self-Identity, and the Sequestration of Death." *Sociology* 27: 411–31.

Moller, D. W.
1996   *Confronting Death: Values, Institutions, and Human Mortality.* New York: Oxford University Press.

Patoski, J. N.
  1995   "The Queen Is Dead." *Texas Monthly,*
          May 23, p. 110.

Rando, T. A.
  1993   *Treatment of Complicated Mourning.*
          Champaign, Ill.: Research Press.

Simon, W. C., A. Haney, and R. J. Buenteo
  1993   "The Post-Modernization of Death and
          Dying." *Symbolic Interactions* 16(4):
          411–26.

Stein, M. A., and V. Basheda
  1989   "Huey Newton Is Killed." *Los Angeles
          Times,* August 23, pp. A1, A3.

CHAPTER NINE
Old and New Religions: The Changing Spiritual Landscape

The Revival of Monastic Life in Drepung Monastery
Melvyn C. Goldstein

REFERENCES

Anonymous
  1986   "The Education of a Monk." *Chö-Yang:
          The Voice of Tibetan Religion and Culture*
          1(1): 41–45.

Dawa, Norbu
  1985   "An Analysis of Sino-Tibetan
          Relationships, 1245–1911: Imperial
          Power, Non-Coercive Regime and
          Military Dependency." In B. N. Aziz and
          M. Kapstein, eds., *Soundings in Tibetan
          Civilization,* pp. 177–95.

Epstein, Israel
  1983   *Tibet Transformed.* Beijing: New World Press.

Goldstein, Melvyn C.
  1964   "A Study of the *Idab Idob.*" *Central Asiatic
          Journal* 9: 123–41.
  1989   *A History of Modern Tibet: The Demise of
          the Lamaist State.* Berkeley: University of
          California Press.
  1990a   "The Dragon and the Snowlion." In
          A. J. Kane, ed., *China Briefing,* pp. 129–68.
          Boulder, Colo.: Westview Press.
  1990b   "Religious Conflict in the Traditional
          Tibetan State." In L. Epstein and
          R. Sherburne, eds., *Reflections on Tibetan
          Culture: Essays in Memory of T. V. Wylie,*
          pp. 231–47.
  1995   "Tibet, China, and the United States:
          Reflections on the Tibet Question."
          Occasional paper of the Atlantic Council
          of the United States. Available on the
          World Wide Web at http://www.
          cwru.edu/orgs/tibet/.

McInnis, Donald E.
  1989   *Religion in China Today: Policy and Practice.*
          Maryknoll, N.Y.: Orbis Books.

Richardson, Hugh
  1984   *Tibet and Its History.* Boulder, Colo.:
          Shambala.

Schwartz, Ronald D.
  1994   *Circle of Protest: Political Ritual in the
          Tibetan Uprising.* New York: Columbia
          University Press.

Shakabpa, Tsepon W. D.
  1967   *Tibet: A Political History.* New Haven,
          Conn.: Yale University Press.

Tambiah, Stanley J.
  1976   *World Conqueror and World Renouncer.*
          Cambridge: Cambridge University
          Press.

Wang, Yao
  1994   "Hu Yaobang's Visit to Tibet, May 22–31,
          1980." In R. Barnett and S. Akiner, eds.,
          Resistance and Reform in Tibet, pp. 285–89.
          London: C. Hurst.

Pilgrimage and Its Influence on West African Islam
James Steel Thayer

REFERENCES

Birks, J. S.
  1978   *Across the Savannahs to Mecca: The
          Overland Pilgrimage Route from West
          Africa.* London: C. Hurst.

Boahen, A. Adu
  1963   "Trade in the Nineteenth Century."
          Journal of History 3(2): 349–59.

Cooley, John K.
1972   *Baal, Christ and Muhammad.* New York: Holt, Rinehart and Winston.

Eickelman, Dale F., and James Piscatori, eds.
1990   *Muslim Travellers: Pilgrimage, Migration and the Religious Imagination.* Berkeley: University of California Press.

Geertz, Clifford
1968   *Islam Observed: Religious Development in Morocco and Indonesia.* New Haven, Conn.: Yale University Press.

Hiskett, M.
1957   "Material Relating to the State of Learning Among the Fulani Before Their Jihad." *Bulletin of the School of Oriental and African Studies* 19(3): 550–78.
1977   "The Nineteenth Century Jihads in West Africa." In J. D. Fage and Roland Oliver, eds., *The Cambridge History of Africa,* vol. 5. Cambridge: Cambridge University Press.

Ismael, Tareq Y.
1971   *The U.A.R. in Africa: Egypt's Policy Under Nassar.* Evanston, Ill.: Northwestern University Press.

Kaba, Lansine
1974   *Wahhabiyya: Islamic Reform and Politics in West Africa.* Evanston, Ill.: Northwestern University Press.

Levtzion, Nehemia
1979   "Allah b. Yasin and the Almoravids." In J. R. Willis, ed., *Studies in West African History,* vol. 1. London: Cass.
1980   *Ancient Ghana and Mali.* New York: Homes and Meier.

Naqar, Umar al-
1972   *The Pilgrimage Tradition in West Africa: An Historical Study with Special Reference to the Nineteenth Century.* Khartoum, Sudan: Khartoum University Press.

Rahman, Fazlur
1966   *Islam.* Chicago: University of Chicago Press.

Rentz, G. S.
1969   "The Wahhabis." In A. J. Arberry, ed., *Religion in the Middle East,* vol. 2. Cambridge: Cambridge University Press.

Schimmel, Anne-Marie
n.d.   *Islam.* Unpublished manuscript.

Skinner, Elliott
1958   "Christianity and Islam Among the Mossi." *American Anthropologist* 60: 1102–19.

Trimingham, J. Spencer
1962   *A History of Islam in West Africa.* Oxford: Oxford University Press.
1964   *Islam in East Africa.* Oxford: Oxford University Press.

Wilks, Ivor
1968   "Transmission of Islamic Learning in the Western Sudan." In J. Goody, ed., *Literacy in Traditional Societies,* pp. 161–92. Cambridge: Cambridge University Press.

Works, J. A.
1976   *Pilgrims in a Strange Land: Hausa Communities in Chad.* New York: Columbia University Press.

Revitalization Movements
Anthony F. C. Wallace

REFERENCES

Burridge, K.
1960   *Mambu: A Melanesian Millennium.* New York: Humanities Press.

Gerlach, L. P.
1968   "Five Factors Crucial to the Growth and Spread of a Modern Religious Movement." *Journal for the Scientific Study of Religion* 7: 23–40.

Mead, M.
1956   *New Lives for Old.* New York: Morrow.

Wallace, A. F. C.
1956a   "Mazeway Resynthesis: A Bio-Cultural Theory of Religious Inspiration." *Transactions of the New York Academy of Sciences* 18: 626–38.
1956b   "Revitalization Movements." *American Anthropologist* 58: 264–81.
1970   *The Death and Rebirth of the Seneca.* New York: Knopf.

The Ghost Dance Religion
Alice Beck Kehoe

REFERENCES

Mooney, James
[1896] 1973 *The Ghost-Dance Religion and Wounded Knee.* New York: Dover Publications (Originally published as Part 2, *Fourteenth Annual Report 1892–93,* Bureau of Ethnology. Washington, D.C.: Government Printing Office.)

Cargo Cults
Peter M. Worsley

REFERENCES

Worsley, Peter
1957 *The Trumpet Shall Sound: A Study of "Cargo" Cults in Melanesia.* London: MacGibbon & Kee.

Adoring the Father: Religion and Charisma in an American Polygamous Community
William Jankowiak and Emilie Allen

REFERENCES

Bauer, Hans
1988 *Utopia in the Desert.* Albany: State University of New York Press.

Bradley, Martha
1993 *Kidnapped from That Land.* Provo: University of Utah Press.

Bohannon, Paul
1985 *All the Happy Families.* New York: McGraw-Hill.

Foster, Lawrence
1991 *Women, Family and Utopia.* Syracuse, N.Y.: Syracuse University Press.

Kilbride, Philip L.
1994 *Plural Marriages for Our Times: A Reinvented Option.* Westport, Conn.: Bergin and Garvey.

Musser, Joseph
1944 *Celestial or Plural Marriage.* Salt Lake City: Truth.

Quinn, Michael
1991 "Plural Marriage and Mormon Fundamentalism." In Martin Wilber, ed., *Fundamentalism,* pp. 240–86. Chicago: University of Chicago Press.

Ross, Marc H.
1993 *The Culture of Conflict.* New Haven, Conn.: Yale University Press.

Sered, Susan S.
1994 *Priestess, Mother, Sacred Sister: Religions Dominated by Women.* New York: Oxford University Press.

Shipps, Jan
1985 *Mormonism: The Story of a New Religious Tradition.* Urbana: University of Illinois Press.

van Wagoner, Richard S.
1986 *Mormon Polygamy: A History.* Salt Lake City: Signature Books.

Zablocki, Benjamin
1980 *Alienation and Charisma.* New York: Free Press.

Religious Dimensions of the UFO Abductee Experience
John Whitmore

REFERENCES

Bullard, Thomas E.
1987 *On Stolen Time.* Mount Ranier, Md.: Fund for UFO Research.

Conroy, Ed
1989 *Report on Communion.* New York: Avon Books.

Evans, Hillary
1985 *Visions, Apparitions, and Alien Visitors.* Wellingborough, UK: Aquarian Press.

Evans-Wentz, W. Y.
1966 *The Fairy-Faith in Celtic Countries.* New York: University Press.

Fiore, Edith
1989 *Encounters.* New York: Doubleday.

Fowler, Raymond
  1980   *The Andreasson Affair.* Englewood Cliffs, N.J.: Prentice Hall.
  1982   *The Andreasson Affair, Phase Two.* Englewood Cliffs, N.J.: Prentice Hall.
  1990   *The Watchers.* New York: Bantam Books.
Fuller, John G.
  1966   *The Interrupted Journey.* New York: Dial Press.
Halifax, J.
  1982   *Shaman: The Wounded Healer.* London: Thames and Hudson.
Hall, Richard
  1988   *Uninvited Guests.* Santa Fe, N.M.: Aurora Press.
Hamilton, William
  1991   *Cosmic Top Secret.* New Brunswick, N.J.: Inner Light.
Hopkins, Budd
  1981   *Missing Time.* New York: Richard Marek.
  1987   *Intruders.* New York: Random House.
Jacobs, David
  1992   *Secret Life.* New York: Simon and Schuster.
Jung, C. G.
  1958   *Flying Saucers.* Princeton, N.J.: Princeton University Press.
Keel, John
  1975   *The Mothman Prophecies.* New York: Saturday Review Press.
  1988   *Disneyland of the Gods.* New York: Amok Press.
Klass, Philip
  1988   *UFO Abductions: A Dangerous Game.* Buffalo, N.Y.: Prometheus Press.
Lewis, James
  1989   "Assessing the Impact of Indian Captivity on the Euro-American Mind: Some Critical Issues." *Connecticut Review* (Summer).
Persinger, Michael
  1989   "The 'Visitor' Experience and the Personality: The Temporal Lobe Factor." In D. Stillings, ed., *Cyberbiological Studies of the Imaginal Component in the UFO Contact Experience*, pp. 157–71. St. Paul: Archaeus Project.

Ring, Kenneth
  1992   *The Omega Project.* New York: William Morrow.
Rogo, D. Scott
  1990   *Beyond Reality.* Wellingborough, UK: Aquarian Press.
Silverman, J.
  1967   "Shamanism and Schizophrenia." *American Anthropologist* 69(2).
Strieber, Whitley
  1987   *Communion.* New York: Morrow/Beech Tree Books.
  1988   *Transformation.* New York: Morrow/Beech Tree Books.
Vallee, Jacques
  1969   *Passport to Magonia.* Chicago: Henry Regency.
  1988   *Dimensions.* Chicago: Contemporary Books.

CHAPTER TEN
Religion as Global Culture: Migration, Media, and Other Transnational Forces

The Veil in Their Minds and on Our Heads: Veiling Practices and Muslim Women
Homa Hoodfar

REFERENCES

Ahmed, Leila
  1982   "Feminism and Feminist Movement in the Middle East." *Women's Studies International Forum* 5(2): 153–68.
Alloula, Malek
  1986   *The Colonial Harem.* Minneapolis: University of Minnesota Press.
Atkinson, James
  1832   *Customs and Manners of Women of Persia and Their Domestic Superstitions.* New York: Burt Franklin.

Bedawi, Jamal A.
n.d.   *The Muslim Woman's Dress According to the Qur'an and the Sunnah.* London: Ta-Ha.

Eberhardt, Isabelle
1987   *The Passionate Nomad: The Diary of Isabelle Eberhardt.* Ed. and intro. by Rana Kabbani. London: Virago Press.

Esposito, John
1988   *Islam: The Straight Path.* New York: Oxford University Press.

Fernea, Elizabeth Warnock
1965   *Guests of the Sheikh.* New York: Doubleday.

Hoodfar, Homa
1989   "A Background to the Feminist Movement in Egypt." *Bulletin of Simone de Beauvoir Institute* 9(2): 18–23.
1991   "Return to the Veil: Personal Strategy and Public Participation in Egypt." In N. Redclift and M. T. Sinclair, eds., *Working Women: International Perspectives on Labour and Gender Ideology.* London: Routledge.
1992   "Feminist Anthropology and Critical Pedagogy: The Anthropology of Classrooms' Excluded Voices." *Canadian Journal of Education* 17(3): 303–20.

Jalabi, Afra
1992   "Veiled Oppression and Pointed Fingers." *McGill Daily,* September 28 (special issue on "Culture Fest").

Jayawardena, Kumari
1986   *Feminism and Nationalism in the Third World.* London: Zed Press.

Kabbani, Rana
1986   *Europe's Myths of the Orient.* Bloomington: Indiana University Press.

Kader, Soha Abdel
1988   *Egyptian Women in Changing Society 1899–1987.* Boulder, Colo.: Reinner.

Keddie, Nikki R., and Beth Baron
1991   *Women in Middle Eastern History: Shifting Boundaries in Sex and Gender.* New Haven, Conn.: Yale University Press.

Lazreg, M.
1988   "Feminism and Difference: The Perils of Writing as a Woman on Women in Algeria." *Feminist Studies* 14(1): 81–107.

Mabro, Judy
1982   *Veiled Half-Truths: Western Travellers' Perceptions of Middle Eastern Women.* London: I. B. Tauris.

MacLeod, Arlene Elowe
1991   *Accommodating Protests: Working Women and the New Veiling in Cairo.* New York: Columbia University Press.

Malcolm, John
1949   *Sketches of Persia from the Journals of a Traveler in the East.* London: J. Murray.

Mernissi, Fatima
1991   *The Veil and the Male Elite: A Feminist Interpretation of Women's Rights in Islam.* New York: Addison-Wesley.

Millet, Kate
1982   *Going to Iran.* New York: Coward, McCann and Geoghean.

Mir-Hosseini, Ziba
1992   *Marriage on Trial: A Study of Islamic Law.* London: I. B. Tauris.

Nader, Laura
1989   "Orientalism, Occidentalism and the Control of Women." *Cultural Dynamics* 2(3): 323–55.

Pastner, C. M.
1978   "Englishmen in Arabia: Encounters with Middle Eastern Women." *Signs* 4(2): 309–23.

Rugh, Andrea
1986   *Reveal and Conceal: Dress in Contemporary Egypt.* Syracuse, N.Y.: Syracuse University Press.

Said, Edward
1978   *Orientalism.* London: Routledge and Kegan Paul.
1993   *Culture and Imperialism.* New York: Knopf.

Suratgar, Olive Hepburn
1951   *I Sing in the Wilderness: An Intimate Account of Persia and Persians.* London: Edward Stanford.

Tabari, Azar, and Nahid Yeganeh
1982   *In the Shadows of Islam: The Women's Movement in Iran.* London: Zed Press.

Tillon, Germaine
  1983   *The Republic of Cousin: Women's Oppression in Mediterranean Society.* London: Al Saqi Books.

Wikan, Unni
  1982   *Behind the Veil in Arabia.* Chicago: University of Chicago Press.

South Korea: Modernization with a Vengeance, Evangelization with the Modern Edge

Steve Brouwer, Paul Gifford, and Susan D. Rose

REFERENCES

Barker, Eileen
  1991   "The Whole World in His Hands?" In R. Robertson and W. R. Garrett, eds., *Religion and the World Order.* New York: Paragon House.

Berger, Peter L., and Hsin-Huang Hsiao, eds.
  1987   *In Search of an East Asian Development Model.* New Brunswick, N.J.: Transaction Books.

Cho, Paul Yonggi
  1992   "Mobilizing the Laity for World Evangelism." *Church Growth* (Spring).

Christian Institute for the Study of Justice and Development
  1988   *Last Victory.* Seoul: Minjingsa.

Clark, Donald N.
  1988   *The Kwangju Uprising.* Boulder, Colo.: Westview Press.

Hadden, Jeffrey K.
  1978   *Televangelism.* New York: Knopf.
  1991   "The Globalization of Televangelism." In R. Robertson and W. R. Garrett, eds., *Religion and the World Order.* New York: Paragon House.

Hadden, Jeffrey K., and Anson Shupe
  1988   *Televangelism, Power, and Politics on God's Frontier.* New York: Henry Holt.

Harvey, Pharis
  1990   "No Justice for Workers in Korea." *Democratic Left,* September–October.

Kim, Kwang-il, and Mun, Sang-hee
  1971   *New Religions in Korea.* Korea Christian Academy, East Asia Christian Conference.

Kwak, Chun Hwan
  1980   *Outline of the Principle, Level 4.* New York: Unification Church.

Lee, Man Woo
  1990   *The Oddyssey of Korean Democracy.* New York: Praeger.

Marsden, George
  1991   *Understanding Evangelicalism and Fundamentalism.* Grand Rapids, Mich.: Eerdmans.

Martin, David
  1990   *Tongues of Fire: The Explosion of Protestantism in Latin America.* Oxford: Basil Blackwell.

Mickler, Michael L.
  1987   *The Unification Church in America: A Bibliography and Research Guide.* New York: Garland Press.

Rhee, Hang Yul
  1988   "The Economic Problems of the Korean Political Economy." In I. J. Kim and Y. W. Kihl, eds., *Political Change in South Korea.* New York: Paragon House.

Robertson, Roland, and JoAnn Chirico
  1985   "Humanity, Globalization, and Worldwide Religious Resurgence: A Theoretical Exploration." *Sociological Analysis* 46(3).

Rubenstein, Richard L.
  1987   "The Rational Society and the Future of Religion." In G. G. James, ed., *The Search for Faith and Justice in the Twentieth Century.* New York: Paragon House.

Song Kon-ho
  1985   "A History of the Christian Movement in Korea." *International Review of Missions* 74 (January).

Suh, David Kwang-sun
  1985   "American Missionaries and a Hundred Years of Korean Protestantism." *International Review of Missions* 74 (January).

Sunoo, Harold Hak-won
1970   *Korea: A History in Modern Times.* Seoul: Kunkuk University Press.

The Global Rise of Religious Nationalism
Mark Juergensmeyer

REFERENCES

Aho, James
1990   *The Politics of Righteousness: Idaho Christian Patriotism.* Seattle: University of Washington Press.

Asahara, Shoko
1995   *Disaster Approaches the Land of the Rising Sun: Shoko Asahara's Apocalyptic Predictions.* Tokyo: Aum.

Banisadr, Abolhassan
1981   *The Fundamental Principles and Precepts of Islamic Government.* Trans. Mohammad R. Ghanoonparvar. Lexington, Mass.: Mazda.

Chatterjee, Partha
1993   *The Nation and Its Fragments: Colonial and Postcolonial Histories.* Princeton, N.J.: Princeton University Press.

Habermas, Jürgen
1987   "Modernity: An Incomplete Project." In P. Rabinow and W. M. Sullivan, eds., *Interpretive Social Science: A Second Look.* Berkeley: University of California Press.

Juergensmeyer, Mark
1988   "The Logic of Religious Violence." In *Essay: Inside Terrorist Organizations.* London: Frank Cass.
1992   "Sacrifice and Cosmic War." In M. Juergensmeyer, ed., *Violence and the Sacred in the Modern World.* London: Frank Cass.

Khomeini, A., Imam
1985   *Islam and Revolution: Writings and Declarations.* Trans. Hamid Algar. London: Routledge and Kegan Paul.

Sells, Michael
1997   *The Bridge Betrayed: Religion and Genocide in Bosnia.* Berkeley: University of California Press.

Sprinzak, Ehud
1991   *The Ascendance of Israel's Radical Right.* New York: Oxford University Press.
1995   "Right-Wing Terrorism in a Comparative Perspective: The Case of Split Delegitimization." In Tore Bjongo, ed., *Terror from the Extreme Right.* London: Frank Cass.

Cyberspace as Sacred Space: Communicating Religion on Computer Networks
Stephen D. O'Leary

REFERENCES

Austin, J. L.
1970a   *How to Do Things with Words.* Oxford: Oxford University Press.
1970b   *Philosophical Papers.* Oxford: Oxford University Press.

Calvin, John
[1557] 1958   "Last Admonition to Joachim Westphal." Trans. Henry Beveridge. In *Tracts and Treatises on Doctrine and Worship of the Church.* Grand Rapids, Mich.: Eerdmans.
[1545] 1961   "The Form of Church Prayers and Hymns with the Manner of Administering the Sacraments and Consecrating Marriage According to the Custom of the Ancient Church." Trans. Bard Thompson. In B. Thompson, ed., *Liturgies of the Western Church.* Cleveland: Williams Collins.

Coate, John
1992   "Cyberspace Innkeeping: Building Online Community." Reproduced in CRTNET #905. (Communication Research and Theory Network, ed. Tom Benson. Back issues available from LISTSERV@PSUVM archives CRTNET.)

Danet, Brenda
    1996   "Speech, Writing, and Performativity: An Evolutionary View of the History of Constitutive Ritual." In G. Britt-Louise, P. Linnell, and B. Nordberg, eds., *The Construction of Professional Discourse.* London: Longmans.

Davis, Erik
    1995   "Technopagans: May the Astral Plane Be Reborn in Cyberspace." *Wired* 3(7): 126–33, 174–81.

Eco, Umberto
    1994   "Eco on Microcomputers." Available on the World Wide Web at http://www.well.com/user/cynsa/engine. html.

Edwards, Mark U.
    1994   *Printing, Propaganda, and Martin Luther.* Berkeley: University of California Press.

Eisenstein, Elisabeth
    1979   *The Printing Press as an Agent of Change: Communications and Cultural Transformation in Early-Modern Europe.* 2 vols. New York: Cambridge University Press.

Ellul, Jacques
    1985   *The Humiliation of the Word.* Grand Rapids, Mich.: Eerdmans.

Grimes, Ronald
    1990   *Ritual Criticism: Case Studies in Its Practice, Essays on Its Theory.* Columbia: University of South Carolina Press.

John Paul II
    1990   "The Gospel in the Computer Age." *L'Osservatore Romano,* January 29, p. 5. Published on the World Wide Web as "The Church Must Learn to Cope with Computer Culture" (http://listserv.american.edu/catholic/church/papal/jp.ii/computerculture.html).

Jones, Steven, ed.
    1994   *Cybersociety: Computer-Mediated Communication and Community.* Thousand Oaks, Calif.: Sage.

Kellner, Mark A.
    1996   *God on the Internet.* Foster City, Calif.: IDG Books Worldwide.

McLuhan, Marshall
    1964   *Understanding Media: The Extensions of Man.* 2nd ed. New York: New American Library.

McDonnell, Kilian
    1967   *John Calvin, the Church, and the Eucharist.* Princeton, N.J.: Princeton University Press.

Myerhoff, Barbara G.
    1977   "We Don't Wrap Herring in a Printed Page: Fusion, Fictions and Continuity in Secular Ritual." In S. F. Moore and B. Myerhoff, eds., *Secular Ritual.* Assen, Netherlands: Van Gorcum.

New Age Forum
    Documents available on Compuserve, New Age Forum Archive, Pagan/Occult section. Filenames: APRFMN.TXT, APRIL.TXT, PAGAN.TXT, MYFM94.TRN, RITUAL.TXT.

O'Leary, Stephen D., and Brenda Basher
    1996   "The Unknown God of the Internet: Religious Communication from the Ancient Agora to the Virtual Forum." In Charles Ess, ed., *Philosophical Approaches to Computer-Mediated Communication.* Albany: State University of New York Press.

Ong, Walter J.
    [1967] 1981   *The Presence of the Word: Some Prologomena for Cultural and Religious History.* Minneapolis: University of Minnesota Press.
    1982   *Orality and Literacy: The Technologizing of the Word.* London: Methuen.

Rheingold, Howard
    1993   *The Virtual Community: Homesteading on the Electronic Frontier.* Reading, Mass.: Addison-Wesley.

Smith, Jonathan Z.
    1987   *To Take Place: Toward Theory in Ritual.* Chicago: University of Chicago Press.

Taylor, Mark, and Esa Saarinen
    1994   *Media Philosophies.* London: Routledge.

Thompson, Bard
    1961   *Liturgies of the Western Church.* Cleveland: William Collins.

Turkle, Sherry
1995   *Life on the Screen: Identity in the Age of the Internet.* New York: Simon and Schuster.

Homer the Heretic and Charlie Church: Parody, Piety, and Pluralism in *The Simpsons*

Lisle Dalton, Eric Michael Mazur, and Monica Siems

REFERENCES

Bastien, Joseph
1987   "Humor and Satire." In Mircea Eliade, ed., *Encyclopedia of Religion.* New York: Macmillan.

Chesebro, James
1979   "Communication, Values, and Popular Television Series: A Four-Year Assessment." In H. Newcomb, ed., *Television: The Critical View.* 2nd ed. New York: Oxford University Press.

Collum, Danny Duncan
1991   " . . . Because He Made So Many of Them." *Sojourners* 20 (November): 38–39.

Corliss, Richard
1994   "Simpsons Forever!" *Time,* May 2, p. 77.

Freeman, Michael
1995   "The Official End (1994–95 Syndication Season Led by *The Simpsons*)." *Mediaweek,* September 18, p. 14.

Geertz, Clifford
1973   "Religion as a Cultural System." In *The Interpretation of Cultures*, pp. 87–125. San Francisco: Basic Books.

Goethals, Gregor
1981   *The TV Ritual.* Boston: Beacon Press.

Greeley, Andrew
1987   "Today's Morality Play: The Sitcom." *New York Times,* May 17, pp. 1, 40 (Arts and Leisure).

Handelman, Don
1987   "Clowns." In M. Eliade, ed., *Encyclopedia of Religion.* New York: Macmillan.

Himmelstein, Hal
1994   *Television Myth and the American Mind.* 2nd ed. Westport, Conn.: Praeger.

Lefton, Terry
1992   "Don't Tell Mom: Fox Looks to a Degenerate Clown and a Violent Cat-and-Mouse Duo to Revitalize *The Simpsons'* Merchandise Sales." *Brandweek,* August 10, pp. 16–17.

McConnell, Frank
1990   "'Real' Cartoon Characters: *The Simpsons.*" *Commonweal,* June 15, pp. 389–90.

Medved, Michael
1992   *Hollywood vs. America: Popular Culture and the War on Traditional Values.* New York: HarperCollins.

Olive, David
1992   *Political Babble: The 1,000 Dumbest Things Ever Said by Politicians.* New York: Wiley.

Ozersky, Josh
1991   "TV's Anti-Families: Married . . . with Malaise." *Tikkun* 6 (January–February): 11–14, 92–93.

"Prime-Time Religion."
1992   *Christianity Today,* March 9, p. 60.

Rebeck, Victoria
1990   "Recognizing Ourselves in *The Simpsons.*" *Christian Century,* June 27, p. 622.

Richmond, Ray, and Antonia Coffman, eds.
1997   *The Simpsons: A Complete Guide to Our Favorite Family.* New York: HarperCollins.

Riddle, Lyn
1994   "A Rascal Cartoon Character Sets Off a Controversy in South Carolina." *Los Angeles Times,* Mary 1, p. A5.

Rosenthal, Andrew
1992   "In a Speech, President Returns to Religious Themes." *New York Times,* January 18, p. A17.

Sekaquaptewa, Emory
1989   "One More Smile for a Hopi Clown." In D. M. Dooling and P. Jordan-Smith, eds., *I Become Part of It: Sacred Dimensions in Native American Life.* San Francisco: HarperSan Francisco.

Skill, Thomas, et al.
1994   "The Portrayal of Religion and
        Spirituality on Fictional Network
        Television." *Review of Religious Research*
        35 (March): 251–67.

Wilde, Alan
1981   *Horizon of Assent: Modernism,
        Postmodernism, and the Ironic Imagination.*
        Baltimore, Md.: Johns Hopkins
        University Press.

Index